first published in this edition 1995

© HarperCollins Publishers
& Shubun International Co., Ltd. 1995

latest reprint 1999

ISBN 0 00 470823-7

The Collins Gem website address is
www.**collins-gem**.com

---

original material by
CollinsBilingual

Japanese language edition
Richard Goris
Yukimi Okubo

---

*A catalogue record for this book is
available from the British Library*

All rights reserved

Typeset by Tosho Printing Co., Ltd.

*Printed and bound in Great Britain by
Caledonian International Book Manufacturing Ltd,
Glasgow, G64*

COLLINS SHUBUN

ENGLISH JAPANESE DICTIONARY

コリンズ 英和辞典
秀　文

Collins Gem

An imprint of HarperCollins*Publishers*
Shubun International Co.,Ltd.

ハーパーコリンズ／秀文インターナショナル

CONTENTS

INTRODUCTION

We are delighted you have decided to buy the Collins Shubun English-Japanese Dictionary and hope you will enjoy and benefit from using it at school, at home, on holiday or at work.

This introduction gives you a few tips on how to get the most out of your dictionary-not simply from its comprehensive wordlist but also from the information provided in each entry.

The Collins Shubun English-Japanese Dictionary begins by listing the abbreviations used in the text and follows with a guide to Japanese pronunciation and a chart of the two Japanese scripts "hiragana" and "katakana" together with the Roman letter transliteration used in this dictionary.

USING YOUR COLLINS SHUBUN DICTIONARY

A wealth of information is presented in the dictionary, using various typefaces, sizes of type, symbols, abbreviations and brackets. The conventions and symbols used are explained in the following sections.

Headwords

The words you look up in a dictionary -"headwords"- are listed alphabetically. They are printed in bold type for rapid identification. The headwords appearing at the top of each page indicate the first and last word dealt with on the page in question.

Information about the usage or form of certain headwords is given in brackets after the phonetic spelling. This usually appears in abbreviated form (e.g., (*fam*), (COMM).

Common expressions in which the headword appears are shown in bold italic type (e.g., **account...** *of no account*).

When such expressions are preceeded by a colon, it means that the headword is used mainly in that particular expression (e.g., **aback**... *adv: to be taken aback*).

Phonetic spellings

The phonetic spelling of each headword (indicating its pronunciation) is given in square brackets immediately after the headword (e.g., **able** [ei'bəl]). The phonetics show a standardized US English pronunciation in IPA (International Phonetic Alphabet) symbols. A list of these symbols is given on page (13).

Translations

Headword translations are given in ordinary type and, where more than one meaning or usage exists, these are separated by a semicolon. You will often find other words in brackets before the translations. These offer suggested contexts in which the headword might appear (e. g., **absentee** (from school, meeting etc) or provide synonyms (e. g. **able** (capable) or (skilled)). A white lozenge precedes a gloss giving information for the non-English native speaker.

"Keywords"

Special status is given to certain English words which are considered as "key" words in the language. They may, for example, occur very frequently or have several types of usage (e. g., **a, be**). A combination of lozenges and numbers helps you to distinguish different parts of speech and different meanings. Further helpful information is provided in brackets.

Grammatical Information

Parts of speech are given in abbreviated form in italics after the phonetic spellings of headwords (e. g., *vt*, *adv*, *conj*) and headwords with several parts of speech have a black lozenge before each new part of speech (e. g., **wash**).

使用上の注意

本辞典は英単語の意味を知りたい日本人だけでなく日本語を勉強している外国人も使えるよう、すべての訳語、補足説明などを日本文字とローマ字で併記した。ローマ字は原則としてヘボン式に従い、ローマ字・仮名対照表を (17)～(18) ページに示した。またローマ字には日本語のアクセントも加えた。右上がりのアクセント記号 (á) は声の上がりを、右下がりの記号 (à) は声の下がりを、記号のない場合は平坦に発音する事を示す。

見出し語は太字の立体活字で示した。つづりは米国の標準に従ったが、英国の標準がそれと異なる場合、アルファベット順にこれも示した。

> 例：**anaemia** [əniːˈmiːə] *etc (BRIT)* = **anaemia** *etc*

続いて発音を [ ] の中に国際音表文字で示した。発音記号表は (13) ページにある。

アクセントは ['] の記号でアクセントのある音節の後に示した。

> 例：**able** [ˈeibəl]

品詞は斜字の略語で示した。例：**able** [ˈeibəl] *adj*

品詞に続いて訳語を日本語とローマ字で示した。原則として1つの意味に対して1つだけ最も頻度の高い訳語を採用した。

> 例：**blockade**... 封鎖 fúsa

頻度が同じぐらいで複数の訳語がある場合、これを示すと共にコンマ (,) で分けた。

> 例：**blood**... 血 chi、血液 ketsúeki

訳語の前に丸括弧 ( ) の中でその見出し語についての情報を記した。

立体の大文字表記はその語が使われる「分野」などを示す。

> 例：**blood**... (BIO) 血 chi、血液 ketsúeki

すなわち、**blood** は「生物学」という分野の語である。

立体の小文字はその他の情報を示す。

> 例：**bleat**... *vi* (goat, sheep) 鳴く nakú

すなわち、**bleat** という動詞はヤギやヒツジについて使う語である。

> 例：**aperture**... (hole) 穴 anâ; (gap) すき間 sukíma; (PHOT) アパーチャ ápàcha

この例では類語を使って見出し語の意味をはっきりさせている。また、このように1つの見出し語に対して複数意味がある場合、セミコロン (;) で分ける。

見出し語の成句はその都度改行して太字の斜字で示した。

> 例：**bearing**...
> > *to take a bearing...*
> > *to find one's bearings...*

成句は主語＋動詞形式のものでも文頭の大文字と文尾のピリオドをつけずにあくまでも成句として扱った。ただし疑問を表す成句には？をつけた。

> 例：anyone...
>
> *anyone could do it*
>
> *can you see anyone?*

表示，標識，立て札などに使う成句は「...」で囲んだ。

> 例：entry...
>
> 「no entry」...

改行なしで品詞などに続くコロン（：）＋ 太斜字の成句は見出し語などがその成句以外には殆ど使われない事を示す。

> 例：aback [əbǽk] *adv*: *to be taken aback* 仰天する gyóten suru

丸括弧の中で *also*: に続く立体太字の語句はその意味では同意語である事を示す。

> 例：go about *vi* (*also*: go around: rumor) 流れる nagárerù

ここでは「噂が流れる」という意味では go about でも go around でも使える事を示している。

特殊記号：

◆：最初に示した品詞と品詞が異なったものにつけた。

> 例：abdicate... *vt* (responsibility, right) 放棄する ...
>
> **◆***vi* (monarch) 退位する ...

◇：補足説明を示す。

/：見出し語，成句の中で置き換えられる部分を示す。日本語訳やローマ字の中でこれを〔 〕で示した。

> 例：abide... *vt*: *I can't abide it/him* 私はそれ〔彼〕が大嫌いだ watáku-shi wá soré〔karè〕ga dáikirai da

KEYWORD: このタイトルは頻度の高い重要な語で特に徹底的に取り扱った見出し語（たとえば **be, can**）を示す。

Phonetic Symbols 発音記号表

[ɑː] father, hot, knowledge

[æ] at, have, cat

[ai] my, buy, like

[au] how, mouth

[e] men, says, friend

[ei] say, take, rain

[ɛr] air, care, where

[ə] above, payment, label

[ər] girl, learn, burn, worm

[i] sit, women, busy

[iː] see, bean, city

[ou] no, know, boat

[ɔi] boy, boil

[u] book, could, put

[uː] tool, soup, blue

[ɔː] law, walk, story

[ʌ] up, cut, above

[p] put, cup

[b] be, tab

[d] down, had

[t] too, hot

[k] come, back

[g] go, tag

[s] see, cups, force

[z] rose, buzz

[ʃ] she, sugar

[ʒ] vision, pleasure

[tʃ] church

[dʒ] jam, gem, judge

[f] farm, half, phone

[v] very, eve

[θ] thin, both

[ð] this, other

[l] little, ball

[r] rat, bread

[m] move, come

[n] no, run

[ŋ] sing, bank

[h] hat, reheat

[j] yes

[w] well, away

Table of Abbreviations 略語表

adj	adjective	形容詞
abbr	abbreviation	略語
adv	adverb	副詞
ADMIN	administration	管理
AGR	agriculture	農業
ANAT	anatomy	解剖学
ARCHIT	architecture	建築
AUT	automobiles	自動車関係
aux vb	auxiliary verb	助動詞
AVIAT	aviation	航空
BIO	biology	生物学
BOT	botany	植物学
BRIT	British English	英国つづり／用法
CHEM	chemistry	化学
COMM	commerce, finance, banking	商業, 金融関係
COMPUT	computing	コンピュータ関係
conj	conjunction	接続詞
cpd	compound	形容詞的名詞
CULIN	cookery	料理
def art	definite article	定冠詞
dimin	diminutive	指小辞
ECON	economics	経済学
ELEC	electricity, electronics	電気, 電子工学
excl	exclamation, interjection	感嘆詞
fam(!)	colloquial usage (! particularly offensive)	口語（！特に悪質なもの）
fig	figurative use	比喩
fus	(phrasal verb) where the particle cannot be separated from the main verb	vt fusを見よ
gen	in most or all senses; generally	たいがいの意味では, 一般に
GEO	geography, geology	地理学, 地質学
GEOM	geometry	幾何学
indef art	indefinite article	不定冠詞

inf(!)	colloquial usage (! particularly offensive)	口語（！特に悪質なもの）
infin	infinitive	不定詞
inv	invariable	変化しない
irreg	irregular	不規則な
LING	grammar, linguistics	文法，語学
lit	literal use	文字通りの意味
MATH	mathematics	数学
MED	medical term, medicine	医学
METEOR	the weather, meteorology	気象関係
MIL	military matters	軍事
MUS	music	音楽
n	noun	名詞
NAUT	sailing, navigation	海事
num	numeral adjective or noun	数詞
obj	(grammatical) object	目的語
pej	pejorative	蔑称
PHOT	photography	写真
PHYSIOL	physiology	生理学
pl	plural	複数
POL	politics	政治
pp	past participle	過去分詞形
prep	preposition	前置詞
pron	pronoun	代名詞
PSYCH	psychology, psychiatry	精神医学
pt	past tense	過去形
RAIL	railroad, railway	鉄道
REL	religion	宗教
SCOL	schooling, schools and universities	学校教育
sing	singular	単数
subj	(grammatical) subject	主語
superl	superlative	最上級
TECH	technical term, technology	技術(用語)，テクノロジー
TEL	telecommunications	電信電話
TV	television	テレビ
TYP	typography, printing	印刷

US	American English	米国つづり／用法
vb	verb	動詞
vi	verb or phrasal verb used intransitively	自動詞
vt	verb or phrasal verb used transitively	他動詞
vt fus	phrasal verb where the particle cannot be separated from main verb	パーチクルを動詞から分けられない句動詞
ZOOL	zoology	動物学
®	registered trademark	登録商標

THE ROMANIZATION AND PRONUNCIATION OF JAPANESE

There are several systems for writing Japanese in Roman characters, but the most understandable and least confusing to the speaker of English is the Hepburn ("hebon" in Japanese) system. The following table illustrates this system, with its "hiragana" and "katakana" equivalents, as it has been adopted in this dictionary.

a	i	u	e	o		ā	ī	ū	ē	ō
あ	い	う	え	お		―	―	うう	ええ	おお/おう
ア	イ	ウ	エ	オ		アー	イー	ウー	エー	オー

ka	ki	ku	ke	ko		kya	―	kyu	―	kyo
か	き	く	け	こ		きゃ	―	きゅ	―	きょ
カ	キ	ク	ケ	コ		キャ	―	キュ	―	キョ

ga	gi	gu	ge	go		gya	―	gyu	―	gyo
が	ぎ	ぐ	げ	ご		ぎゃ	―	ぎゅ	―	ぎょ
ガ	ギ	グ	ゲ	ゴ		ギャ	―	ギュ	―	ギョ

sa	shi	su	se	so		sha	shi	shu	she	sho
さ	し	す	せ	そ		しゃ	し	しゅ	しぇ	しょ
サ	シ	ス	セ	ソ		シャ	シ	シュ	シェ	ショ

za	ji	zu	ze	zo		ja	ji	ju	je	jo
ざ	じ	ず	ぜ	ぞ		じゃ	じ	じゅ	じぇ	じょ
ザ	ジ	ズ	ゼ	ゾ		ジャ	ジ	ジュ	ジェ	ジョ

ta	chi	tsu	te	to		cha	chi	chu	che	cho
た	ち	つ	て	と		ちゃ	ち	ちゅ	ちぇ	ちょ
タ	チ	ツ	テ	ト		チャ	チ	チュ	チェ	チョ

da	ji	zu	de	do		ja	ji	ju	je	jo
だ	ぢ	づ	で	ど		ぢゃ	ぢ	ぢゅ	ぢぇ	ぢょ
ダ	ヂ	ヅ	デ	ド		ヂャ	ヂ	ヂュ	ヂェ	ヂョ

na	ni	nu	ne	no	nya	—	nyu	—	nyo
な	に	ぬ	ね	の	にゃ	—	にゅ	—	にょ
ナ	ニ	ヌ	ネ	ノ	ニャ	—	ニュ	—	ニョ

ha	hi	fu	he	ho	hya	—	hyu	—	hyo
は	ひ	ふ	へ	ほ	ひゃ	—	ひゅ	—	ひょ
ハ	ヒ	フ	ヘ	ホ	ヒャ	—	ヒュ	—	ヒョ

ba	bi	bu	be	bo	bya	—	byu	—	byo
ば	び	ぶ	べ	ぼ	びゃ	—	びゅ	—	びょ
バ	ビ	ブ	ベ	ボ	ビャ	—	ビュ	—	ビョ

pa	pi	pu	pe	po	pya	—	pyu	—	pyo
ぱ	ぴ	ぷ	ぺ	ぽ	ぴゃ	—	ぴゅ	—	ぴょ
パ	ピ	プ	ペ	ポ	ピャ	—	ピュ	—	ピョ

ma	mi	mu	me	mo	mya	—	myu	—	myo
ま	み	む	め	も	みゃ	—	みゅ	—	みょ
マ	ミ	ム	メ	モ	ミャ	—	ミュ	—	ミョ

ya	—	yu	—	yo
や	—	ゆ	—	よ
ヤ	—	ユ	—	ヨ

ra	ri	ru	re	ro	rya	—	ryu	—	ryo
ら	り	る	れ	ろ	りゃ	—	りゅ	—	りょ
ラ	リ	ル	レ	ロ	リャ	—	リュ	—	リョ

wa	—	—	—	wo	n
わ	—	—	—	を	ん
ワ	—	—	—	ヲ	ン

Consonants:

Pronounce the consonants as you would in English. Exceptions are "w" in the objective particle "wo", "r", "g", and "f". In "wo" the "w" is normally not pronounced, but is written to distinguish it easily from other words that are pronounced "o". (Japanese word-processing software also usually requires that you type "wo" to get を or ヲ.)

"R" is pronounced with a very slight trill. Do not pronounce it as in the English word "rich"; you probably will not be understood. If you trill it as in Italian or Spanish, you can be understood, but you will sound foreign. The best strategy is to listen and imitate. Lacking access to native speakers, try pronouncing "r" as you would "d", but with the tongue farther forward, touching the upper teeth instead of the palate.

"G" is perfectly understandable pronounced as in English "get", "go" etc, and many Japanese always pronounce it in this way. Cultured people, however, prefer a softer, slightly nasal pronunciation, which they call a "half-voiced" or "nasal-voiced" "k". It is similar to the "ng" in "sing", but coming at the beginning of a syllable.

"F" also is quite understandable when given its usual English fricative value, with the lower lip touching the upper teeth. The Japanese, however, normally pronounce it by simply narrowing the gap between the lower lip and the teeth, without actually touching the lip to the teeth. Thus some individuals pronounce it much closer to "h" than to the English "f".

"N" at the end of a syllable or word is syllabic, that is, it is a syllable in its own right, with full syllabic length, as in English "butt*on*". In this dictionary when syllabic "n" is followed by a vowel or "y", a hyphen is inserted to indicate the proper pronunciation: e. g., 勧誘 かんゆう kan-yū, as opposed to 加入 かにゅう kanyū.

Before "p", "b", or "m", "n" naturally becomes an "m" sound; but in this dictionary, in keeping with the practice of other romanized dictionaries, the Japanese ん is consistently transliterated as "n", not "m": e. g., 文法 ぶんぽう bunpō, not bumpō.

Double consonants are pronounced in Japanese, as in US English "cattail". In "katakana" and "hiragana" they are indicated by a lowercase っ or ッ before the consonant to be doubled, and in this dictionary are printed as double consonants: かっぱ "kappa", いった "itta". The one exception is the combination っち, which we express as "tch": マッチ, "matchi".

A few Japanese exclamations are written with a lowercase っ at the end, indicating an articulated "t" sound at the end. These we have romanized with a quarter-sized "t": しっ "shi^t" (equivalent to the English "ssh !").

The sounds [ti:] and [di:] do not exist in Japanese. They are usually expressed as

ティ and ディ, which we romanize as "ti" and "di". Other sounds in loan words without Japanese equivalents are generally corrupted to some similar sound, e. g., "v" to "b".

Vowels:

The 5 Japanese vowels are the fundamental Latin vowels: [ɑ:], [i:], [u:], [e], and [o]. "U" is pronounced without rounding the lips, keeping them relaxed. A rounded "u" is understandable, but sounds outlandishly foreign. Again, listen and imitate.

The vowels can be long or short. Long vowels are pronounced the same as short vowels, but for double their length, with no break. Pay strict attention to this, for vowel length is essential to both meaning and comprehension. Using a short vowel for a long one, or vice versa, can produce a word of entirely different meaning from the one intended. In this dictionary, long vowels are marked with a macron: ā, ī, ū, ē, ō.

The syllable "-su" at the end of a word, especially in the verbal ending "-masu" frequently drops the "u", so that only the "s" is heard. This occurs more often in the east than in the west of the country. There are no hard and fast rules, so the student needs to rely on his experience from listening to spoken Japanese.

Japanese accents:

Japanese words do not have a strong tonic accent as in most European languages. Instead they are inflected, with the voice rising or falling gently on certain syllables, and remaining flat on others. Using the correct "accent" or inflection is necessary for intelligibility of speech, and often serves to distinguish between words of similar spelling. For example, depending on the "accent", "momo" can mean either "peach" or "thigh"; "kaki" can be either "persimmon" or "oyster"; "atsui" can be "hot" or "thick".

The Japanese accent is difficult to depict graphically with any accuracy, for there are no standard conventions. Many dictionaries simply ignore the problem, leaving the foreign student to his own devices. Language classes for foreigners both in Japan and abroad frequently do not teach accents explicitly, but rely on imitation of pronunciation by a native Japanese model.

We felt that the foreign student needed something to aid the memory in trying to pronounce words already learned in the past, as well as a guide to pronunciation of words being looked up in the dictionary. We settled on the acute accent (á) to indicate a rising inflection, and the grave accent (à) to indicate a falling inflection. No mark at all means that the voice is held flat on that syllable.

The one exception in this dictionary is when two "i"s occur together, as in the word for "good" いい ii. In most cases like this, the first "i" requires a rising inflection (í), and the second a falling inflection (ì). However, with standard typefaces this produces an unesthetic effect (íì). Therefore, we have omitted the accent mark of the second "i" in such cases: a rising inflection on the first of a "double i" combination indicates also a falling inflection on the second letter: íi = íì.

Doubtless the foreign student will be somewhat disconcerted to see such inflection marks on "n" in this dictionary. Remember that final "n" is always syllabic and may be pronounced by itself in Japanese. Thus, "n" can also have a rising or falling inflection, or be flat, as the case may be.

Accent differs markedly from region to region in Japan, particularly between the east and the west. The speech patterns of the Kanto region have generally been adopted as the standards for a "common" language, to be taught in the schools and used by television and radio announcers. Although the accents in this dictionary have followed the guidance of an expert in the field, we lay no claim to absolute accuracy. Our aim has been to guide the foreign student to a pronunciation that, if used, will be understandable in any part of the country, even when the listeners themselves follow a different standard of pronunciation.

English Irregular Verb Forms 不規則動詞表

present	pt	pp	present	pt	pp
arise	arose	arisen	dig	dug	dug
awake	awoke	awaked	do (3rd	did	done
be (am, is,	was,	been	person;		
are;	were		he/she/it/		
being)			does)		
bear	bore	born(e)	draw	drew	drawn
beat	beat	beaten	dream	dreamed,	dreamed,
become	became	become		dreamt	dreamt
begin	began	begun	drink	drank	drunk
behold	beheld	beheld	drive	drove	driven
bend	bent	bent	dwell	dwelt	dwelt
beset	beset	beset	eat	ate	eaten
bet	bet,	bet,	fall	fell	fallen
	betted	betted	feed	fed	fed
bid	bid,	bid,	feel	felt	felt
	bade	bidden	fight	fought	fought
bind	bound	bound	find	found	found
bite	bit	bitten	flee	fled	fled
bleed	bled	bled	fling	flung	flung
blow	blew	blown	fly (flies)	flew	flown
break	broke	broken	forbid	forbade	forbidden
breed	bred	bred	forecast	forecast	forecast
bring	brought	brought	forget	forgot	forgotten
build	built	built	forgive	forgave	forgiven
burn	burnt,	burnt,	forsake	forsook	forsaken
	burned	burned	freeze	froze	frozen
burst	burst	burst	get	got	got, (US)
buy	bought	bought			gotten
can	could	(been	give	gave	given
		able)	go (goes)	went	gone
cast	cast	cast	grind	ground	ground
catch	caught	caught	grow	grew	grown
choose	chose	chosen	hang	hung,	hung,
cling	clung	clung		hanged	hanged
come	came	come	have (has;	had	had
cost	cost	cost	having)		
creep	crept	crept	hear	heard	heard
cut	cut	cut	hide	hid	hidden
deal	dealt	dealt	hit	hit	hit

present	pt	pp	present	pt	pp
hold	held	held	sell	sold	sold
hurt	hurt	hurt	send	sent	sent
keep	kept	kept	set	set	set
kneel	knelt,	knelt,	shake	shook	shaken
	kneeled	kneeled	shall	should	—
know	knew	known	shear	sheared	shorn,
lay	laid	laid			sheared
lead	led	led	shed	shed	shed
lean	leant,	leant,	shine	shone	shone
	leaned	leaned	shoot	shot	shot
leap	leapt,	leapt,	show	showed	shown
	leaped	leaped	shrink	shrank	shrunk
learn	learnt,	learnt,	shut	shut	shut
	learned	learned	sing	sang	sung
leave	left	left	sink	sank	sunk
lend	lent	lent	sit	sat	sat
let	let	let	slay	slew	slain
lie (lying)	lay	lain	sleep	slept	slept
light	lit,	lit,	slide	slid	slid
	lighted	lighted	sling	slung	slung
lose	lost	lost	slit	slit	slit
make	made	made	smell	smelt,	smelt,
may	might	—			smelled	smelled
mean	meant	meant	sow	sowed	sown,
meet	met	met			sowed
mistake	mistook	mistaken	speak	spoke	spoken
mow	mowed	mown,	speed	sped,	sped,
		mowed		speeded	speeded
must	(had to)	(had to)	spell	spelt,	spelt,
pay	paid	paid		spelled	spelled
put	put	put	spend	spent	spent
quit	quit,	quit,	spill	spilt,	spilt,
	quitted	quitted		spilled	spilled
read	read	read	spin	spun	spun
rid	rid	rid	spit	spat	spat
ride	rode	ridden	split	split	split
ring	rang	rung	spoil	spoiled,	spoiled,
rise	rose	risen		spoilt	spoilt
run	ran	run	spread	spread	spread
saw	sawed	sawn	spring	sprang	sprung
say	said	said	stand	stood	stood
see	saw	seen	steal	stole	stolen
seek	sought	sought	stick	stuck	stuck

present	pt	pp	present	pt	pp
sting	stung	stung	**think**	thought	thought
stink	stank	stunk	**throw**	threw	thrown
stride	strode	stridden	**thrust**	thrust	thrust
strike	struck	struck,	**tread**	trod	trodden
		stricken	**wake**	woke,	woken,
strive	strove	striven		waked	waked
swear	swore	sworn	**wear**	wore	worn
sweep	swept	swept	**weave**	wove,	woven,
swell	swelled	swollen,		weaved	weaved
		swelled	**wed**	wedded,	wedded,
swim	swam	swum		wed	wed
swing	swung	swung	**weep**	wept	wept
take	took	taken	**win**	won	won
teach	taught	taught	**wind**	wound	wound
tear	tore	torn	**wring**	wrung	wrung
tell	told	told	**write**	wrote	written

A

A [ei] *n* (MUS: note) イ音 f-ðn; (: key) イ
調 íchó

KEYWORD

a [ei, a] *(before vowel or silent h: an)*
indef art 1 1つの hitótsu no, ある árù ◊
通常日本語では表現しない tsújō nihongo
de wa hyōgen shínai

a book/girl/mirror 本(少女, 鏡) hón
[shójo, kagámi]

an apple りんご ríngo

she's a doctor 彼女は医者です kánojo
wa ishá desu

2 (instead of the number "one") 1つの
hitótsu no

a loaf and 2 pints of milk, please パ
ン1本とミルク2パイント下さい pan íppoǹ-
to mírùku nipáìnto kudasái

a year ago 1年前 ichínen máè

a hundred/thousand/etc pounds
100(1000)ポンド hyakú(seǹ)póňdo

3 (in expressing ratios, prices etc) 1つ当
り... hitótsu átàri...

3 a day/week 1日(1週間)当り3つ ichí-
nichi(isshúkan)átàri mittsú

10 km an hour 時速10キロメーター jísòku jukkíromětà

£5 a person 1人当たり5ポンド hitóri
átàri gopóňdo

30p a kilo 1キロ30ペンス ichíkìro san-
júppeňsù

AA [eiei'] *n abbr* (= Alcoholics Anonymous) アルコール依存症自主治療協会 a-
rúkòru izohshō jishúchiryō kyōkai;
(BRIT: = Automobile Association) 英国
自動車連盟 efkoku jidósha reñmei

AAA [trip'əlei] *n abbr* (= American
Automobile Association) 米国自動車連盟
befkoku jidósha reñmei

aback [əbæk'] *adv*: *to be taken aback*
仰天する győten suru

abandon [əbæn'dən] *vt* (person) 見捨て
る misúterù; (car) 乗捨てる norísuterù;

(give up: search, idea, research) やめる
yaméru

◊*n* (wild behavior): *with abandon* 羽目
を外して hamé wo hazúshite

abashed [əbæʃt'] *adj* (person) 恥ずかしが
っている hazúkashigatté irú

abate [əbeit'] *vi* (lessen: storm, terror,
anger) 治まる osámarù

abattoir [æb'ətwɑːr'] *n* (BRIT) n と殺場
tosátsujō

abbey [æb'iː] *n* 修道院 shúdòin

abbot [æb'ət] *n* 修道院長 shúdòinchō

abbreviate [əbriː'vieit] *vt* (essay, word)
短縮する tañshuku suru

abbreviation [əbriːviˈei'ʃən] *n* (short
form) 短縮形 tañshukukei

abdicate [æb'dikeit] *vt* (responsibility,
right) 放棄する hőki suru

◊*vi* (monarch) 退位する táì-i suru

abdication [æbdikei'ʃən] *n* (of responsibility, right) 放棄 hőki; (by monarch) 退
位 táì-i

abdomen [æb'dəmən] *n* 腹部 fukúbù

abduct [æbdʌkt'] *vt* ら致する ráchi suru

aberration [æbəreiˈʃən] *n* (unusual behavior, event etc) 異状 ijō

abet [əbet'] *vt see* **aid**

abeyance [əbeiˈəns] *n*: *in abeyance*
(law) 無視されて múshì sarete; (matter)
保留されて horyú sarete

abhor [æbhɔːr'] *vt* (cruelty, violence etc)
ひどく嫌う hídòku kiráu

abide [əbaid'] *vt*: *I can't abide it/him*
私はそれ(彼)が大嫌いだ watákùshi wà
soré(karè)ga dáikirai da

abide by *vt fus* (law, decision) ...に従う
...ni shitágaù

ability [əbil'itiː] *n* (capacity) 能力 nőryo-
ku; (talent, skill) 才能 saínő

abject [æb'dʒekt] *adj* (poverty) 極度の
kyőkùdo no; (apology) 卑屈な hikútsu na

ablaze [əbleiz'] *adj* (building etc) 炎上し
ている eñjō shite iru

able [ei'bəl] *adj* (capable) 出来る dekírù;

able-bodied (skilled) 有能な yūnō na

to be able to do something …をする事が出来る …wo suru koto gā dékirū

able-bodied [eiʹbɑːdʹiːd] *adj* (person) がん健な ganken na

ably [eiʹbliː] *adv* (skilfully, well) 上手に jōzu ni

abnormal [æbnɔːrʹməl] *adj* (behavior, child, situation) 異常な ijō na

aboard [əbɔːrdʹ] *adv* (NAUT, AVIAT) …に乗って …ni notté

♦*prep* (NAUT, AVIAT) …に乗って …ni notté

abode [əboudʹ] *n* (LAW): *of no fixed abode* 住所不定の jūshofutéi no

abolish [əbɑːlʹiʃ] *vt* 廃止する haíshi suru

abolition [æbəliʹʃən] *n* 廃止 haíshi

abominable [əbɑːmʹinəbəl] *adj* (conditions) ひどい hídoi; (behavior) 忌わしい imáwashíi

aborigine [æbəridʹɕəniː] *n* 原住民 genjūmĭn

abort [əbɔːrtʹ] *vt* (MED: fetus) 流産する ryūzan suru; (plan, activity) 中止する chūshi suru

abortion [əbɔːrʹʃən] *n* (MED) 妊娠中絶 nińshinchűzetsu

to have an abortion 妊娠を中絶する nińshin wŏ chűzetsu suru

abortive [əbɔːrʹtiv] *adj* (attempt, action) 不成功の fuséikō no

abound [əbaundʹ] *vi* (exist in large numbers) …が多い …gā ōi

to abound in/with (possess in large numbers) …に富む …ni tŏmū

chī ni

to leave things lying about 物をあちこちに散らかしたままにする monŏ wo achíkochī ni chirakashita mamá ni sūrū

to run/walk etc about あちこち走り回る [歩き回る] achíkochī hashirimawárū (arukimawárū)

3: *to be about to do something* …するところである …suru tokoro dè árū

he was about to cry/leave/wash the dishes/go to bed 彼は泣き出す[帰る、皿を洗う、寝る]ところだった kárè wa nakidasu(kaeru, sara wo arau, neru) tokoro dattá

♦*prep* **1** (relating to) …について …ni tsúĭte, …に関して …ni kánshite

a book about London ロンドンについての本 róndōn ni tsúĭte no hon

what is it about? それは何についてですか sore wa nán ni tsúĭte desu ká

we talked about it 私たちはそれについて話し合った watakushitachĭ a sore ni tsúĭte hanashiáttá

what/how about having some coffee? コーヒーでも飲みましょうか kōhī de mŏ nomimashŏ kâ

2 (referring to place) …のあちこちに …no achíkochī ni

to walk about the town 町をあちこち歩き回る machí wo achíkochī arukimawárū

her clothes were scattered about the room 部屋のあちこちに彼女の服が散らかっていた heya no achíkochī ni kánojō no fukú gā chirakatte itá

about-face [əbautʹfeis] *n* (MIL) 回れ右 mawáremigĭ; (fig) *to do an about-face* 一変する ippén suru

about-turn [əbautʹtəːrn] *n* = **about-face**

above [əbʌvʹ] *adv* (higher up, overhead) 上の方に ué no hŏ ni; (greater, more) 以上 ijŏ ni

♦*prep* (higher than) …より上に …yórĭ ué ni; (greater than, more than: in number, amount etc) …以上 …ijŏ; (: in rank etc) 上である ué de arū

mentioned above 上記の jōki no

above all すべて第一に màzú daf-ichi ni

aboveboard [əbʌv'bourd] *adj* 公明正大 な kōmeiseidai na

abrasive [əbrei'siv] *adj* (substance) 研磨 の kênma no; (person, manner) とげとげ しい togétogeshiī

abreast [əbrest'] *adv* (people, vehicles) 横に並んで yokó ni narande

to keep abreast of (fig: news etc) ...に ついていく ...ni tsúīte ikú

abridge [əbridʒ'] *vt* (novel, play) 短縮す る tafishuku suru

abroad [əbrɔːd'] *adv* 海外に kâigai ni

abrupt [əbrʌpt'] *adj* (sudden: action, ending etc) 突然の totsúzen no; (curt: person, behavior) ぶっきらぼうな bukkírabô na

abruptly [əbrʌpt'li:] *adv* (leave, end) 突 然 totsúzen; (speak) ぶっきらぼうに bukkírabô ni

abscess [æb'ses] *n* のうよう nôyô

abscond [æbskɑːnd'] *vi* (thief): **to abscond with** ...を持ち逃げする ...wo mochínige suru; (prisoner): **to abscond (from)** (...から) 逃亡する ...(kara) tôbô suru

absence [æb'səns] *n* (of person: from home etc) 不在 fuzái; (: from school, meeting etc) 欠席 kekkén; (: from work) 欠勤 kekkín; (of thing) ない na nâi kotó

absent [æb'sənt] *adj* (person: from home etc) 不在 の fuzái no; (: from school, meeting etc) 欠席 の kessék no; (: from work) 欠勤 の kekkín no; (thing) ない na nâi

absentee [æbsənti:'] *n* (from school, meeting etc) 欠席者 kessékishà; (from work) 欠勤者 kekkínsha

absent-minded [æb'səntmain'did] *adj* 忘れっぽい wasúreppoī

absolute [æb'səlut] *adj* (complete) 全く の mattáku no; (monarch, rule, power) 専制的な sefiseiteki na; (principle, rule etc) 絶対的な zettáiteki na

absolutely [æbsəlut'li:] *adv* (totally) 全 く mattáku; (certainly) その通り sonô tôri

absolution [æbsəlu:'ʃən] *n* (REL) 罪の許

し tsúmí no yurúshì

absolve [æbzɑːlv'] *vt*: **to absolve someone (from blame, responsibility, sin)** ...の (...を) 許す ...no (...wð) yurúsū

absorb [æbsɔːrb'] *vt* 吸収する kyúshū suru; (assimilate: group, business) 併合す る hegô suru

to be absorbed in a book 本に夢中にな っている hôn ni muchû ni natté irú

absorbent cotton [æbsɔːr'bənt-] (US) 脱脂綿 dasshímēn

absorbing [æbsɔːr'biŋ] *adj* 夢中にさせる muchû ni saserû

absorption [æbsɔːrp'ʃən] *n* 吸収 kyúshū; (assimilation: of group, business etc) 併 合 hegô; (interest) 夢中になる事 muchû ni narú kotó

abstain [æbstein'] *vi*: **to abstain (from)** (eating, drinking) 控える hikáerù; (voting) 棄権する kíken suru

abstemious [æbsti:'mi:əs] *adj* (person) 節制する sesséi suru

abstention [æbsten'ʃən] *n* (refusal to vote) 棄権 kíken

abstinence [æb'stənəns] *n* 禁 欲 kíñ-yo-ku

abstract [æb'strækt] *adj* (idea, quality) 抽象的な chūshōteki na; (ART) 抽象派の chūshōha no; (LING): **abstract noun** 抽象名詞 chūshōmeishi

abstruse [æbstru:s'] *adj* 分かりにくい wakárinikuī

absurd [æbsəːrd'] *adj* ばかげた bakágetá

abundance [əbʌn'dəns] *n* 豊富さ hôfusa

abundant [əbʌn'dənt] *adj* 豊富な hôfu na

abuse [*n* əbju:s' *vb* əbju:z'] *n* (insults) のののしり nonóshiri; (ill-treatment) 虐待 gyakútai; (misuse: of power, drugs etc) 乱用 rañ-yō

♦*vt* (insult) ののしる nonóshirù; (ill-treat) 虐待する gyakútai suru; (misuse) 乱用する rañ-yō suru

abusive [əbju:'siv] *adj* (person) 口の悪い kuchî no warúi; (language) 侮辱的な bu-jókutei na

abysmal [əbiz'məl] *adj* (performance, failure) 最低の saftei no; (ignorance etc)

ひどい hidói

abyss [abis'] n 深えん shiń-en

AC [ei'si:] abbr = **alternating current**

academic [ækædem'ik] adj (person) インテリの ińteri no; (year, system, books, freedom etc) 教育関係の kyốikukańkei no; (pej: issue) 理論的な riróntekina na

♦n 学者 gakúsha

academy [əkæd'əmi:] n (learned body) アカデミー akádèmì; (school) 学院 gakú-in

academy of music 音楽学院 ofigakugakúin

accelerate [æksel'əreit] vt (process) 早める hayámeru

♦vi (AUT) 加速する kasóku suru

acceleration [ækseларei'ʃən] n (AUT) 加速 kasóku

accelerator [æksel'əreitəːr] n アクセル ákùseru

accent [æk'sent] n (pronunciation) なまり namári; (written mark) アクセント符号 akúsento fugố; (fig: emphasis, stress) 強調 kyốchò, アクセント akúsento

accept [æksept'] vt (gift, invitation) 受取る ukétoru; (fact, situation, risk) 認める mitómeru; (responsibility, blame) 負う oú

acceptable [æksep'təbəl] adj (offer, gift) 受入られる uké-irararerù; (risk etc) 許容できる kyoyố dekirù

acceptance [æksep'təns] n (of gift, offer etc) 受取る事 ukétoru koto; (of risk etc) 許容 kyoyố; (of responsibility etc) 負う事 oú koto

access [æk'ses] n (to building, room) 入る事 háìru kotó; (to information, papers) 利用する権利 riyố suru keńri

to have access to (child etc) ...への面会権がある ...no meńkaikeń ga árù

accessible [ækses'əbəl] adj (place) 行きやすい ikíyasuì; (person) 面会しやすい meńkai shiyasuì; (available: knowledge, art etc) 利用しやすい riyố shiyasuì

accessory [ækses'əːriː] n (dress, COMM, TECH, AUT) アクセサリー akúsesarí; (LAW): **accessory to** ...の共犯者 ...no kyốhańsha

accident [æk'sidənt] n (chance event) 偶然 gűzen; (mishap, disaster) 事故 jíkò

by accident (unintentionally) うっかり ukkári; (by chance) 偶然に gűzen ni

accidental [æksiden'təl] adj (death) 事故による jíkò ni yoru; (damage) 偶発的な gűhatsuteki na

accidentally [æksiden'təli:] adv (by accident) 偶然に gűzen ni

accident-prone [æk'sidəntproun'] adj 事故に会いがちな jíkò ni aigachi na

acclaim [əkleim'] n 賞賛 shōsan

♦vt: **to be acclaimed for one's achievements** 功績で有名である kốseki de yűmei de arú

acclimate [əklai'mit] (US) vt = **acclimatize**

acclimatize [əklai'mətaiz] vt: **to become acclimatized (to)** (...に) 慣れる (...ni) naréru

accolade [ækəleid'] n (fig) 賞賛 shōsan

accommodate [əkɑm'ədeit] vt (subj: person) 泊める toméru; (: car, hotel etc) 収容できる shūyố dekirù; (oblige, help) ...に親切にして上げる ...ni shińsetsu ni shite agérù

accommodating [əkɑm'ədeitiŋ] adj 親切な shińsetsu na

accommodation [əkɑːmədei'ʃən] n 宿泊設備 shukúhakusetsùbi

accommodations [əkɑːmədei'ʃənz] (US) npl 宿泊設備 shukúhakusetsùbi

accompaniment [əkʌm'pənimənt] n 伴奏 bańsố

accompany [əkʌm'pəni:] vt (escort, go along with) ...に付きそう ...ni tsukísoù; (MUS) ...の伴奏をする ...no bańsố wò suru

accomplice [əkɑm'plis] n 共犯者 kyốhańsha

accomplish [əkɑm'plij] vt (finish: task) 成遂げる nashítogerù; (achieve: goal) 達成する tasséi suru

accomplished [əkɑm'plijt] adj (person) 熟練の jukúren no; (performance) 優れた sugúretà

accomplishment [əkɑːm'plijmənt] n (completion, bringing about) 遂行 suíkò;

(skill: gen pl) 才能 sainō

accord [əkɔːrd'] n (treaty) 協定 kyōtei
♦vt 与える atáeru
of his own accord 自発的に jihátsuteki ni

accordance [əkɔːr'dəns] n: *in accordance with* (someone's wishes, the law etc) ...に従って ...ni shitágatte

according [əkɔːr'diŋ]: *according to* prep (person, account) ...によると ...ni yorú to

accordingly [əkɔːr'diŋli] adv (appropriately) それに応じて soré ni ōjite; (as a result) それで soré de

accordion [əkɔːr'diːən] n アコーデオン ākōdeon

accost [əkɔːst'] vt ...に近寄って話し掛ける ...ni chikáhikatte hanáshikakerù

account [əkaunt'] n (COMM: bill) 勘定書 kańjōgaki; (: monthly account) 計算書 keísansho; (in bank) 口座 kōza; (report) 報告 hōkoku
of no account 構わない kamáwanài
on account つけで tsuké de
on no account 何があっても... (すべき) でない nanî ga atte mo ...(subeki) de naî
on account of ...のために ...no tamé ni
to take into account, take account of ...を考慮に入れる ...wò kóryò ni irérù

accountable [əkaunt'əbəl] adj: *accountable (to)* (...に) 申開きする義務がある (...ni) mōshihiraki suru gimù ga árù

accountancy [əkaun'tənsi:] n 会計士の職 kaíkeìshi no shoku

accountant [əkaun'tənt] n 会計士 kaíkeìshi

account for vt fus (explain) 説明する setsúmeì suru; (represent) ...の割合を占める ...(no waríaì) wò shimérù

account number n (at bank etc) 口座番号 kōzabangō

accounts [əkaunts'] npl (COMM) 勘定 kańjō

accredited [əkred'itid] adj (agent etc) 資格のある shikáku no arù

accrued interest [əkruːd'-] n 累積利息

rufsekirísōku

accumulate [əkjuːm'jəleit] vt 貯める taméru
♦vi 貯まる tamáru

accuracy [æk'jɑːrəsi:] n 正確さ seíkakusa

accurate [æk'jɑːrit] adj 正確な seíkaku na

accurately [æk'jɑːritliː] adv (count, shoot, answer) 正確に seíkaku ni

accusation [ækjuːzei'ʃən] n 非難 hínàn

accuse [əkjuːz'] vt: *to accuse someone (of something)* (crime, incompetence) (...だと) ...を責める (...dá tò) ...wo semérù

accused [əkjuːzd'] n (LAW): *the accused* 容疑者 yōgishà

accustom [əkʌs'təm] vt 慣れさせる narésaserù

accustomed [əkʌs'təmd] adj (usual): *accustomed to* ...に慣れている ...ni narétè irú

ace [eis] n (CARDS, TENNIS) エース ēsu

ache [eik] n 痛み itámi
♦vi (be painful) 痛む itámù, ...が痛い ...gà itái
my head aches 頭が痛い atáma gà itáî

achieve [ətʃiːv'] vt (aim) 成し遂げる nashítogerù; (result) 上げる agérù; (victory, success) 獲得する kakútoku suru

achievement [ətʃiːv'mənt] n (completion) 完成 kańseì; (success, feat) 業績 gyōseki

acid [æs'id] adj (CHEM: soil etc) 酸性の sańsei no; (taste) 酸っぱい suppáì
♦n (CHEM) 酸 sań; (inf: LSD) LSD erúesudì

acid rain n 酸性雨 sańseiù

acknowledge [əknɑl'idʒ] vt (letter, parcel: also: **acknowledge receipt of**) 受け取った事を知らせる ukétotta koto wò shiráserù; (fact, situation, person) 認める mitómerù

acknowledgement [æknɑl'idʒmənt] n (of letter, parcel) 受領通知 juryōtsūchi

acne [æk'ni:] n にきび níkìbi

acorn [ei'kɔːrn] n ドングリ dóñguri

acoustic [əkuːsˈtik] *adj* (related to hearing) 聴覚の chōkaku no; (guitar etc) アコースティックの akōsútikku no

acoustics [əkuːsˈtiks] *n* (science) 音響学 oñkyōgaku

♦*npl* (of hall, room) 音響効果 oñkyōkōka

acquaint [əkweint'] *vt*: **to acquaint someone with something** (inform) ...に ...を知らせる ...ni ...wò shiráseru

to be acquainted with (person) ...と面識がある ...to meńshiki ga arù

acquaintance [əkweint'əns] *n* (person) 知合い shiríai; (with person, subject) 知識 chíshìki

acquiesce [ækwiːes'] *vi*: **to acquiesce (to)** (...) を承諾する (...wò) shōdaku suru

acquire [əkwaiˈəɹ] *vt* (obtain, buy) 手に入れる te ni iréru; (learn, develop: interest, skill) 取得する shutóku suru

acquisition [ækwizíʃən] *n* (obtaining etc) 入手 nyūshu; (development etc) 獲得 kakútoku; (thing acquired) 取得物 shutókubutsu

acquit [əkwitˈ] *vt* (free) 無罪とする múzài to suru

to acquit oneself well 見事な働きをする mígòto na határaki wo suru

acquittal [əkwitˈəl] *n* 無罪判決 múzài hañketsu

acre [ei'kəɹ] *n* エーカー ḗkā

acrid [æk'rid] *adj* (smell, taste, smoke) 刺激的な shigékiteki na

acrimonious [ækrəmou'niːəs] *adj* (remark, argument) 辛辣な shińratsu na

acrobat [æk'rəbæt] *n* アクロバット akúrobattò

acrobatic [ækrəbæt'ik] *adj* (person, movement, display) アクロバット的な akúrobatteki na

acronym [æk'rənim] *n* 頭字語 tōjigo

across [əkrɔːs'] *prep* (from one side to the other of) ...を渡って ...wo watátte; (on the other side of) ...の向こう側に ...no mukōgawa ni; (crosswise over) ...と交差して ...to kṓsa shite

♦*adv* (direction) 向こう側へ mukōgawa e; (measurement) 直径が...で chokkéi ga

... de

to run/swim across 走って〔泳いで〕渡る hashítte〔oyóide〕wataru

across from ...の向かいに ...no mukái ni

acrylic [əkril'ik] *adj* アクリルの ákùriru no

♦*n* アクリル akúriru

act [ækt] *n* (action) 行為 kṓi; (of play) 幕 makú; (in a show etc) 出し物 dashímono; (LAW) 法 hō

♦*vi* (do something, take action) 行動する kōdō suru; (behave) 振舞う furúmau; (have effect: drug, chemical) 作用する sāyō suru; (THEATER) 出演する shutsúen suru; (pretend) ...の振りをする ...no furí wò suru

♦*vt* (part) ...に扮する ...ni fuń suru

in the act of ...しているさなかに ...shite iru sanàka ni

to act as ...として勤める ...toshite tsutómerù

acting [æk'tiŋ] *adj* (manager, director etc) 代理の daíri no

♦*n* (activity) 演技 eñgi; (profession) 演劇 eñgeki

action [æk'ʃən] *n* (deed) 行為 kṓi; (motion) 動き ugóki; (MIL) 戦闘 señtō; (LAW) 訴訟 soshō

out of action (person) 活動不能で katsúdōfunō de; (thing) 作動不能で sadṓfunō de

to take action 行動を起こす kōdō wo okósù

action replay *n* (TV) 即時ビデオ再生 sokúji bideo saísei

activate [æk'təveit] *vt* (mechanism) 作動させる sadṓsaserù

active [æk'tiv] *adj* (person, life) 活動的な katsúdōteki na

active volcano 活火山 kakkázàn

actively [æk'tivli] *adv* (participate) 積極的に sekkyōkuteki ni; (discourage) 強く tsúyòku; (dislike) 非常に hijó ni

activist [æk'tivist] *n* 活動家 katsúdōka

activity [æktívˈətiː] *n* (being active) 活動 katsúdō; (action) 動き ugóki; (pastime, pursuit) 娯楽 goráku

actor [æk'təɹ] *n* 俳優 haíyū

actress [æk'tris] n 女優 joyū

actual [æk'tʃuːəl] adj 実際の jissai no

actually [æk'tʃuːali] adv (really) 本当 に hoñtō ni; (in fact) 実は jitsú wa

acumen [əkjuːˈmən] n 判断力 hañdañryoku

acupuncture [æk'jupəŋktʃər] n 針 hárí

acute [əkjuːt'] adj (illness) 急性の kyūsei no; (anxiety, pain) 激しい hagéshiī; (mind, person) 抜け目の無い nukéme no nai; (MATH): *acute angle* 鋭角 efkaku; (LING): *acute accent* 鋭アクセント efakúseňto

ad [æd] n abbr = **advertisement**

A.D. [eidi:'] adv abbr (= *Anno Domini*) 西暦...年 sefreki ...neñ

adamant [æd'əmənt] adj (person) 譲らない yuzúranai

Adam's apple [æd'əms-] n のど仏 nodóbotoke

adapt [ədæpt'] vt (alter, change) 適応させる tekíō saserú
♦vi: *to adapt (to)* (に) 適応する (...ni) tekíō suru

adaptable [ədæp'təbəl] adj (device, person) 適応性のある tekíōsei no arū

adapter [ədæp'tər] n (ELEC) アダプター adáputā

adaptor [ədæp'tər] n = **adapter**

add [æd] vt (to a collection etc) 加える kuwáerū; (comment etc) 付加える tsukékuwaerū; (figures: *also*: **add up**) 合計する gōkei suru
♦vi: *to add to* (increase) ...を増す masú

adder [æd'ər] n ヨーロッパクサリヘビ yóroppá kusáribeñ

addict [æd'ikt] n (to drugs etc) 中毒者 chúdokusha; (enthusiast) マニア mánia

addicted [ədik'tid] adj: *to be addicted to* (drink etc) ...中毒になっている ...chūdoku ni kakátte irú; (fig: football etc) ...マニアである ...mánia de arū

addiction [ədik'ʃən] n (to drugs etc) 中毒 chúdoku

addictive [ədik'tiv] adj (drug) 習慣性のある shúkansei no arū; (activity) 癖になる kusé ni narú

addition [ədiʃ'ən] n (adding up) 足し算 tashízañ; (thing added) 加えられた物 kuwáeraretá monó

in addition なお náō

in addition to ...の外に ...no hoká ni

additional [ədiʃ'ənəl] adj 追加の tsuíka no

additive [æd'ətiv] n 添加物 teñkabútsu

address [ədres'] n (postal address) 住所 júsho; (speech) 演説 eñzetsu
♦vt (letter, parcel) ...に宛名を書く ...ni aténa wo kákū; (speak to: person) ...に話し掛ける ...ni hanáshikakerū; (: audience) ...に演説する ...ni eñzetsu suru; (problem): *to address (oneself to) a problem* 問題に取組む mofidai ni torikumú

adept [ədept'] adj: *adept at* ...が上手な ...ga jōzu na

adequate [æd'əkwit] adj (enough: amount) 十分な júbuñ na; (satisfactory: performance, response) 満足な máñzoku na

adhere [ædhiːr'] vi: *to adhere to* (stick to) ...にくっつく ...ni kuttsúkú; (fig: abide by: rule, decision, treaty etc) ...を守る ...wo mamórú; (: hold to: opinion, belief etc) ...を固守する ...wo kóshū suru

adhesive [ædhiː'siv] n 粘着材 neñchakúzai

adhesive tape n (*US*: MED) ばん創こう bañsōkō; (*BRIT*) 粘着テープ neñchaku tépu

ad hoc [æd hɑːk'] adj (decision, committee) 特別な tokúbetsu na

adjacent [ədʒei'sənt] adj: *adjacent to* ...の隣の ...no tonári no

adjective [ædʒ'iktiv] n 形容詞 keíyōshi

adjoining [ədʒɔi'niŋ] adj (room etc) 隣の tonári no

adjourn [ədʒəːrn'] vt (trial) 休廷にする kyūtei ni suru; (meeting, discussion) 休会にする kyūkai ni suru
♦vi (trial) 休廷する kyūtei suru; (meeting) 休止する kyūshi suru

adjudicate [ədʒuː'dikeit] vt (contest) ...の審査員を勤める ...no shiñsa-iñ wo tsutómerū

adjust [ədʒʌst'] vt (change: approach etc) 調整する chōsei suru; (rearrange: clothing, machine etc) 調節する chōsetsu suru

♦vi: **to adjust (to)** 適応する tekíō suru

adjustable [ədʒʌst'əbəl] adj 調節できる chōsetsu dekirù

adjustment [ədʒʌst'mənt] n (PSYCH) 適応 tekíō; (to machine) 調節 chōsetsu; (of prices, wages) 調整 chōsei

ad-lib [ædlib'] vi アドリブで話す adóribu dè hanásù

ad lib [ædlib'] adv (speak) アドリブで adóribu de

administer [ædmin'istər] vt (country) 統治する tōchì suru; (department) 管理する kaǹri suru; (MED: drug) 投与する tōyo suru

  to administer justice 裁く sabákù

administration [ædminstrei'ʃən] n (management) 管理 kaǹri; (government) 政権 sefken

administrative [ædmin'istreitiv] adj (work, error etc) 管理的な kaǹriteki na

administrator [ædmin'istreitər] n 管理者 kaǹrishà

admiral [æd'mərəl] n 海軍大将 kaígun taíshō

Admiralty [æd'mərəlti:] (BRIT) n: **the Admiralty** (also: **Admiralty Board**) 海軍省 kaígunshō

admiration [ædmərei'ʃən] n 感心 kańshin

admire [ædmai'ər] vt (respect) ...に感心する ...ni kańshin suru; (appreciate) 観賞する kańshō suru

admirer [ædmai'ərər] n (suitor) 男友達 otókotomodachi; (fan) ファン fáǹ

admission [ædmiʃ'ən] n (admittance) 入場 nyújō; (entry fee) 入場料 nyújōryō; (confession) 自白 jiháku

admit [ædmit'] vt (confess) 自白する jiháku suru; (permit to enter) 入場させる nyújō saserù; (to club, organization) 入会させる nyúkai saserù; (to hospital) 入院させる nyúin saserù; (accept: defeat, responsibility etc) 認める mitómeru

admittance [ædmit'əns] n 入場 nyújō

admittedly [ædmit'idli:] adv 確かに...であるが táshìka ni ...de árù ga

admit to vt fus (murder etc) ...を自白する ...wo jiháku suru

admonish [ædmɑn'iʃ] vt (rebuke) たしなめる tashínamerù; (LAW) 忠告する chúkoku suru

ad nauseam [æd nɔː'zi:æm] adv (repeat, talk) いやというほど iyá to iú hodð

ado [əduː'] n: **without (any) more ado** さっさと sássàto

adolescence [ædəles'əns] n 10代 jūdai

adolescent [ædəles'ənt] adj 10代の jūdai no

♦n ティーンエージャー tíǹèjà

adopt [ədɑpt'] vt (child) 養子にする yōshi ni suru; (policy, attitude) とる tórù; (accent) まねる manérù

adopted [ədɑp'tid] adj (child) 養子の yōshi no

adoption [ədɑp'ʃən] n (of child) 養子縁組 yōshiéngùmi; (of policy etc) 採択 saítaku

adoptive [ədɑp'tiv] adj: **adoptive father/mother** 養父(母) yōfu(bo)

  adoptive country 第2の祖国 dáì ni no sókòku

adore [ədɔːr'] vt (person) 崇拝する sūhai suru

adorn [ədɔːrn'] vt (decorate) 飾る kazáru

adrenalin [ədren'əlin] n アドレナリン adórenarìn

Adriatic [eidriæt'ik] n: **the Adriatic (Sea)** アドリア海 adóriakài

adrift [ədrift'] adv (NAUT: loose) 漂流して hyōryū shite

adult [ədʌlt'] n (person) 大人 otóna; (animal, insect) 成体 seítai

♦adj (grown-up: person) 大人の otóna no; (: animal etc) 成体の seítai no; (for adults: literature, education) 成人向きの seíjinmuki no

adultery [ədʌl'təri:] n かん通 kaǹtsū

advance [ædvæns'] n (movement, progress) 進歩 shíǹpo; (money) 前借り maégari

♦adj (booking, notice, warning) 事前の jizèn no

♦*vt* (money) 前貸する maégashi suru

♦*vi* (move forward) 前進する zénshin suru; (make progress) 進歩する shínpo suru

to make advances (to someone) (gen) (...に) 言い寄る (...ni) ifyorù

in advance (book, prepare etc) 前もって maémottè

advanced [ædvænst'] *adj* (SCOL: studies) 高等の kôtô no; (country) 先進の senshin no; (child) ませた másèta

advancement [ædvæns'mənt] *n* (improvement) 進歩 shínpo; (in job, rank) 昇進 shôshin

advantage [ædvæn'tidʒ] *n* (supremacy) 有利な立場 yúri na táchìba; (benefit) 利点 ríten; (TENNIS) アドバンテージ adóbantèji

to take advantage of (person) ...に付込む ...ni tsukékomù; (opportunity) 利用する riyô suru

advantageous [ædventei'dʒəs] *adj*: *advantageous (to)* (...に) 有利な (...ni) yúri na

advent [æd'vent] *n* (appearance: of innovation) 出現 shutsúgen; (REL) *Advent* 待降節 taíkōsetsù

adventure [ædven'tʃər] *n* 冒険 bôken

adventurous [ædven'tʃərəs] *adj* (bold, outgoing) 大胆な daítañ na

adverb [æd'vəːrb] *n* 副詞 fukúshi

adversary [æd'vəːrseːri:] *n* (opponent, *also* MIL) 敵 teki

adverse [ædvəːrs'] *adj* (effect, weather, publicity etc) 悪い warúi

adversity [ædvəːr'siti:] *n* 逆境 gyakkyô

advert [æd'vəːrt] (BRIT) *n abbr* = **advertisement**

advertise [æd'vəːrtaiz] *vi* (COMM: in newspaper, on television etc) 広告する kôkoku suru

♦*vt* (product, event, job) ...を広告する ...wo kôkoku suru

to advertise for (staff, accommodation etc) ...を求める広告を出す ...wo motómerù kôkoku wo dasu

advertisement [ædvəːrtaiz'mənt] *n* 広告 kôkoku

advertiser [æd'vəːrtaizər] *n* (in newspaper, on television etc) 広告主 kôkokunùshi

advertising [æd'vəːrtaizin] *n* (advertisements) 広告 kôkoku; (industry) 広告業界 kôkokugyôkai

advice [ædvais'] *n* (counsel) 忠告 chúkoku; (notification) 知らせ shiráse

a piece of advice 一つの忠告 hítòtsu no chúkoku

to take legal advice 弁護士に相談する bengoshì ni sôdan suru

advisable [ædvai'zəbəl] *adj* 望ましい nozómashiì

advise [ædvaiz'] *vt* (give advice to: person, company etc) ...に忠告する ...ni chúkoku suru; (inform): *to advise someone of something* ...に...を知らせる ...ni ...wo shiráserù

to advise against something/doing something ...(するの) を避けた方がいいと忠告する (surú no) wo sakéta hôgà íì to chúkoku suru

advisedly [ædvai'zidli:] *adv* (deliberately) 意図的に itóteki ni

adviser [ædvai'zəːr] *n* (counsellor, consultant: to private person) 相談相手 sôdan aitè; (: to company etc) 顧問 kômon

advisor [ædvai'zəːr] *n* = **adviser**

advisory [ædvai'zəːri:] *adj* (role, capacity, body) 顧問の kômon no

advocate [vb æd'vəkit] *vt* (support, recommend) 主張する shuchô suru

♦*n* (LAW: barrister) 弁護士 bengoshì; (supporter): *advocate of* ...の主張者 ...no shuchôsha

Aegean [idʒi:'ən] *n*: *the Aegean (Sea)* エーゲ海 égekai

aerial [eːr'i:əl] *n* アンテナ afitena

♦*adj* (attack, photograph) 航空の kôkū no

aerobics [eːrou'biks] *n* エアロビクス éàrobikùsu

aerodynamic [eːroudainæm'ik] *adj* 空力的な kûrikiteki na

aeroplane [eːr'əplein] (BRIT) *n* 飛行機 hikôki

aerosol [eːr'əsɔ:l] *n* スプレー缶 supûrêkan

aerospace industry [ɛəˈɒspeis-] n 宇宙
開発業界 uchūkathatsugyōkai

aesthetic [iːsθetˈik] adj 美的な bíteki na

afar [əfɑːrˈ] adv **from afar** 遠くから tôku kará

affable [æfˈəbəl] adj (person) 愛想の良い
aísò no yoî; (behavior) 感じの良い kañji
no yoî

affair [əfɛrˈ] n (matter, business, question) 問題 mofídai; (romance: *also*: **love
affair**) 浮気 uwáki

affect [əfektˈ] vt (influence, concern:
person, object) ...に影響を与える ...ni eíkyō wo atáerù; (subj: disease: afflict) 冒
す okásù; (move deeply) 感動させる kañdō saserú

affected [əfekˈtid] adj (behavior, person) 気取った kidótta

affection [əfekˈʃən] n (fondness) 愛情 af-
jō

affectionate [əfekˈʃənit] adj (person,
kiss) 愛情深い aíjōbukaî; (animal) 人なつ
こい hitónatsukoî

affiliated [əfilˈieitid] adj (company,
body) 関連の kañren no

affinity [əfinˈatiː] n (bond, rapport): **to
have an affinity with/for** ...に魅力
を感じる ...ni miryóku wo kañjiru;
(resemblance): **to have an affinity
with** ...に似ている ...ni nité iru

affirmative [əfəːrˈmətiv] adj (answer,
nod etc) 肯定の kôtei no

affix [əfiksˈ] vt (stamp) はる harú

afflict [əfliktˈ] vt (subj: pain, sorrow,
misfortune) 苦しめる kurúshimerù

affluence [æfˈluːəns] n 裕福さ yûfukusa

affluent [æfˈluːənt] adj (wealthy: family,
background, surroundings) 裕福な yûfuku-
na

  the affluent society 豊かな社会 yútaka-
na na shákai

afford [əfɔːrdˈ] vt (have enough money
for) 買う余裕がある kaú yoyû ga arù;
(permit oneself: time, risk etc) 余裕が
あるsurú yoyû ga arù; (provide) 与え
る atáerù

affront [əfrʌntˈ] n (insult) 侮辱 bujóku

Afghanistan [æfgænˈistæn] n アフガニ
スタン afúganisùtan

afield [əfiːldˈ] adv **far afield** 遠くtôku

afloat [əflˈoutˈ] adv (floating) 浮んで ukáñ-
de

afoot [əfutˈ] adv: **there is something
afoot** 何か怪しい事が起っている nánika
ayáshii koto gà okóttè irú

afraid [əfreidˈ] adj (frightened) 怖がって
いる kowágattè irú

  to be afraid of (person, thing) ...を怖が
る ...wo kowágarù

  to be afraid to ...をするのを怖がる
...wo suru no wò kowágarù

  I am afraid that (apology) 申訳ないが
... môshiwakenai ga

  I am afraid so/not 残念ですがその通
りです (違います) zafíneñ desu ga sonó
tôri desu (chigáimasù)

afresh [əfreʃˈ] adv (begin, start) 新たに
árata ni

Africa [æfˈrikə] n アフリカ afúrika

African [æfˈrikən] adj アフリカの afúrika-
ka no

  ◆n アフリカ人 afúrikajìn

aft [æft] adv (to be) 後方に後方 kôhō ni; (to
go) 後方へ kôhō e

after [æfˈtəːr] prep (of time) ...の後に
...no átō ni; (of place) ...の後ろに ...no
ushíro ni; (of order) ...の次に ...no tsugí
ni

  ◆adv 後に átò ni

  ◆conj ...してから ...shité kara

  what/who are you after? 何(だれ)を
捜していますか nánì(dárè)wo sagáshitè
imásu ka

  after he left 彼が帰ってから kárè ga
kaétte kara

  after having done ...してから ...shité
kara

  to name someone after someone ...に
因んで...に名を付ける ...ni chfnañde ...ni
na wo tsukérù

  it's twenty after eight (US) 8時20分だ
hachíjì nijippùn da

  to ask after someone ...の事を尋ねる
...no kotó wò tazúnerù

  after all (in spite of everything) どうせ

dōse; (in spite of contrary expectations etc) 予想を裏切って yosō wō uragitté

after you! お先にどうぞ o-sáki ni dōzo

after-effects [æf'tərɪfekts] *npl* (of illness, radiation, drink etc) 結果 kekká

aftermath [æf'tərmæθ] *n* (period after) ...直後の期間 ...chókūgo no kikáñ; (aftereffects) 結果 kekká

afternoon [æftərnun'] *n* 午後 gógò

afters [æf'tərz] (*BRIT*: *inf*) *n* (dessert) デザート dézàto

after-sales service [æf'tərseilz-] (*BRIT*) *n* (for car, washing machine etc) アフターサービス afútāsābisu

after-shave (lotion) [æf'tərʃeɪv-] *n* アフターシェーブローション afútāshēbu-rōshon

afterthought [æf'tərθɔt] *n*: *as an afterthought* 後の思い付きで átò no omóitsuki de

afterwards [æf'tərwərdz] (*US also*: **afterward**) *adv* その後 sonó atò

again [əgen'] *adv* (once more) もう1度 mō ichido, 再び futátabi

not ... again もう...ない mō ... nai

to do something again ...をもう1度する ...wo mō ichido surū

again and again 何度も nańdo mo

against [əgenst'] *prep* (leaning on, touching) ...にもたれ掛って ...ni motárekakatté; (in opposition to, at odds with) ...に反対して ...ni hañtai shite; (compared to) ...に較べて ...ni kurábete

age [eidʒ] *n* (of person, object) 年齢 neñrei; (period in history) 時代 jidái

♦*vi* (person) 年を取る toshí wo torū

♦*vt* (subj: hairstyle, dress, make-up etc) ...を実際の年より...に見せる ...wo jissái no toshi yóri ni misérù

20 years of age 年齢二十 neñrei hatáchi

to come of age 成人する seíjin suru

it's been ages since ...は久し振りだ ...wa hisáshiburi da

aged[1] [ei'dʒd] *adj*: *aged 10* 10才の jússaì no

aged[2] [ei'dʒɪd] *npl*: *the aged* 老人 rōjin
◇総称 sōshō

age group *n* 年齢層 neñreisō

age limit *n* 年齢制限 neñreiselgen

agency [ei'dʒənsi] *n* (COMM) 代理店 daíriten; (government body) ...局 ...kyokú, ...庁 ...chō

agenda [ədʒen'də] *n* (of meeting) 議題 gídaì

agent [ei'dʒənt] *n* (representative: COMM, literary, theatrical etc) 代理人 daírinin, エージェント ējento; (spy) スパイ supát; (CHEM, *fig*) 薬剤 shíyàku

aggravate [æg'rəveit] *vt* (exacerbate: situation) 悪化させる akkā saserū; (annoy: person) 怒らせる okōraserū

aggregate [æg'rəgɪt] *n* (total) 合計 gō-kei

aggression [əgreʃ'ən] *n* (aggressive behavior) 攻撃 kōgeki

aggressive [əgres'iv] *adj* (belligerent, assertive) 攻撃的な kōgekiteki na

aggrieved [əgriːvd'] *adj* 不満を抱いた fumáñ wo idáìtà

aghast [əgæst'] *adj* あっけにとられた akké ni torárèta

agile [ædʒ'əl] *adj* (physically, mentally) 身軽な migáru na; (mentally) 機敏な ki-bín na

agitate [ædʒ'əteit] *vt* (person) 動揺させる dōyō saserū

♦*vi*: *to agitate for/against* ...の運動 [反対運動]をする ...no uñdō [hañtaiuñdō]wò suru

agitator [ædʒ'əteitər] *n* 扇動者 señdō-sha

AGM [eidʒiːem'] *n abbr* = **annual general meeting**

agnostic [ægnɑs'tik] *n* 不可知論者 fu-kāchirōñsha

ago [əgou'] *adv*: *2 days ago* 2日前 futsúkamaè

not long ago 少し前に sūkōshi máè ni

how long ago? どのぐらい前に? donó gural máè ni?

agog [əgɑg'] *adj* (excited, eager) わくわくしている wákūwaku shité irū

agonizing [æg'ənaizɪŋ] *adj* 苦しい kurú-shiī

agony [æg'əni] *n* (pain) 苦もん kumóñ

to be in agony 苦しむ kurushímù

agree [əgri:'] *vt* (price, date) 合意して決める gói shité kiméru

♦*vi* (have same opinion) ...と意見が合う ...to íkèn ga áù; (correspond) ...と一致する ...to itchí suru; (consent) 承諾する shódaku suru

to agree with someone (subj: person) ...と同意する ...to dóì suru; (: food) ...に合う ...ni áù

to agree (with) (statements etc) (...に) 同意する (...ni) dóì suru; (LING) (...と) 一致する (...to) itchí suru

to agree to something/to do something ...に[する事]に同意する ...ni [surú koto ni]dóì suru

to agree that (admit) ...だと認める ...dá tò mitómerù

agreeable [əgri:'əbəl] *adj* (sensation, person: pleasant) 気持ち良い kimóchi no yoì; (willing) 承知する shóchi suru

agreed [əgri:d'] *adj* (time, place, price) 同意で決めた dóì de kimetá

agreement [əgri:'mənt] *n* (concurrence, consent) 同意 dóì; (arrangement, contract) 契約 kefyaku

in agreement 同意して dóì shite

agricultural [ægrəkʌl'tʃərəl] *adj* (land, implement, show) 農業の nógyò no

agriculture [æg'rəkʌltʃər] *n* 農業 nógyò

aground [əgraund'] *adv*: *to run aground* (NAUT) 座礁する zashó suru

ahead [əhed'] *adv* (in front of: place, time) 前に máè ni; (into the future) 先に sakí

ahead of (in progress) ...より進んで ...yórì susúnde; (in ranking) ...の上に ...no ué ni; (in advance of: person, time, place) ...の前に ...no máè ni

ahead of time 早目に hayáme ni

go right/straight ahead (direction) 真っ直ぐに行って下さい mássùgu ni itté kudasai; (permission) どうぞ、どうぞ dózo, dózo

aid [eid] *n* (assistance: to person, country) 援助 éňjo; (device) ...を助けるもの

...wo tasúkerù monó

♦*vt* (help: person, country) 援助する éňjo suru

in aid of (BRIT) ...のために ...no támè ni

to aid and abet (LAW) ほう助する hójo suru ¶ *see also* **hearing**

aide [eid] *n* (person, *also* MIL) 側近 sokkfn

AIDS [eidz] *n abbr* (= *acquired immunodeficiency syndrome*) エイズ éfzu

ailing [ei'liŋ] *adj* (person) 病気の byókì no

ailment [eil'mənt] *n* 病気 byókì

aim [eim] *vt*: *to aim (at)* (gun, missile, camera, remark) (...に) 向ける (...ni) mukérù

♦*vi* (*also*: **take aim**) ねらう neráu

♦*n* (objective) 目的 mokúteki; (in shooting: skill) ねらい neráì

to aim at (with weapon; *also* objective) ねらう neráu

to aim a punch at げんこつで...を殴ろうとする gefíkotsu de ...wǒ nágurò to suru

to aim to do ...するつもりである ...surú tsumóri de arù

aimless [eim'lis] *adj* (person, activity) 当てのない até no naì

ain't [eint] (*inf*) = **am not; aren't; isn't**

air [e:r] *n* (atmosphere) 空気 kúki; (tune) メロディー mèrodi; (appearance) 態度 táìdo

♦*vt* (room) ...の空気を入れ替える ...no kúki wo irékaerù; (clothes) 干す hósù; (grievances, ideas) 打明ける uchfakeru

♦*cpd* (currents etc) 空気の kúki no; (attack) 空からの sorà kara no

to throw something into the air (ball etc) ...を投上げる ...wo nagéagerù

by air (travel) 飛行機で hfkòki de

on the air (RADIO, TV: programme, station) 放送中 hósòchuu

airbed [e:r'bed] (BRIT) *n* 空気布団 kúki-butòn

airborne [e:r'bɔ:rn] *adj* (airplane) 飛行中の hfkòchuu na

air-conditioned [e:r'kəndiʃənd] *adj* 空

調付きの kŭchôtsuki no

air conditioning [-kəndiʃ'əniŋ] n 空調 kŭchô

aircraft [er'kræft] n inv 航空機 kŭkŭki

aircraft carrier n 空母 kŭbo

airfield [er'fi:ld] n 飛行場 hikôjô

Air Force n 空軍 kŭgun

air freshener [-freʃ'ənər] n 消臭剤 shŏshŭzai

airgun [er'gʌn] n 空気銃 kŭkijŭ

air hostess (BRIT) n スチュワーデス suchûwâdesu

air letter (BRIT) n エアログラム eárogŭramu

airlift [er'lift] n エアリフト eárifûto

airline [er'lain] n エアライン eáraìn

airliner [er'lainər] n 旅客機 ryokyakŭki

airmail [er'meil] n: **by airmail** 航空便 で kŭkûbin de

airplane [er'plein] (US) n 飛行機 hikôki

airport [er'pɔrt] n 空港 kŭkô

air raid n 空襲 kŭshû

airsick [er'sik] adj: **to be airsick** 飛行機に酔う hikôki ni yô

airspace [er'speis] n 領空 ryôkû

air terminal n 空港ターミナルビル kŭkôtâminarubiru

airtight [er'tait] adj 気密の kimîtsu no

air-traffic controller [er'træfik-] n 管制官 kańseikan

airy [er'i:] adj (room, building) 風通しの良い kazétôshi no yoï; (casual: manner) 軽薄な keíhaku na

aisle [ail] n 通路 tsûro

ajar [ədʒɑr'] adj (door) 少し開いている sukôshi aite irû

akin [əkin'] adj: **akin to** (similar) ...の様な ...no yô na

alacrity [əlæk'riti:] n 敏速さ bińsokusa

alarm [əlɑrm'] n (anxiety) 心配 shińpai; (in shop, bank) 警報 keíhô
♦vt (person) 心配させる shińpai saserû

alarm call n (in hotel etc) モーニングコール môningukôru

alarm clock n 目覚し時計 mezámashidokêi

alas [əlæs'] excl 残念ながら zańnennagâ-

ra

Albania [ælbei'ni:ə] n アルバニア arúbania

albeit [ɔːlbiː'it] conj (although) ...では あるが ...de wa arû ga

album [æl'bəm] n (gen, also: LP) アルバム arúbamu

alcohol [æl'kəhɔl] n アルコール arúkôru

alcoholic [ælkəhɔl'ik] adj アルコールの入った arúkôru no haītta
♦n アルコール中毒者 arúkôru chûdokùsha

alcoholism [æl'kəhɔlizəm] n アルコール中毒 arúkôru chûdoku

alcove [æl'kouv] n アルコーブ arúkôbu

ale [eil] n (drink) エール êru

alert [ələrt'] adj 注意している chûi shité irû
♦n (alarm) 警報 keíhô
♦vt (guard, police etc) ...に知らせる ...ni shiráserû
to be on the alert (also MIL) 警戒している keíkai shite irû

algebra [æl'dʒəbrə] n 代数 daísû

Algeria [ældʒiː'riːə] n アルジェリア arújeria

algorithm [æl'gəriðəm] n アルゴリズム arúgorizûmu

alias [ei'li:əs] adv 別名は betsúmei wa
♦n (of criminal, writer etc) 偽名 giméi

alibi [æl'əbai] n (LAW: also gen) アリバイ arîbai

alien [eil'jən] n (foreigner) 外国人 gaíkokujîn; (extraterrestrial) 宇宙人 uchûjin
♦adj: **alien (to)** (...)の性に合わない (...no) shô ni awânai

alienate [eil'jəneit] vt (person) ...と仲がいがする ...to nakátagai suru

alight [əlait'] adj (burning) 燃えている moête iru; (eyes, expression) 輝いている kagáyaîte irû
♦vi (bird) とまる tomáru; (passenger) 降りる orírû

align [əlain'] vt (objects) 並べる narâberu

alike [əlaik'] adj 似ている nité irû
♦adv (similarly) 同様に dôyô ni;

(equally) ...に共に ...tomo ni

to look alike 似ている nité iru

alimony [ælˈəmouniː] *n* (payment) 離婚手当 rikónteàte

alive [əlaivˈ] *adj* (living) 生きている íkíte irú; (lively: person) 活発な kappátsu na; (place) 活気に満ちた kakkí ni michíta

alkali [ˈkælˌlai] *n* アルカリ arúkari

KEYWORD

all [ɔːl] *adj* 皆の mi(n)na no, 全ての subète no, 全部の zénbu nó, ...中 ...jū

all day/long 1日(1晩)中 ichinichi(hitoban)jū

all men are equal 全ての人間は平等である subète nó níngen wa byōdo de árù

all five came 5人とも来ました gonín tomo kimáshita

all the books/food 本(食べ物)は全部 hòn(tabémono) wa zénbu

all the time いつも ítsumo

he lived here all his life 彼は一生ここで暮らしました kàre wa isshō koko de kuráshimashìta

◆*pron* 1 皆 minà, 全て subète, 全部 zénbu

I ate it all, I ate all of it それを全部食べました soré wo zènbu tabémashìta

all of us/the boys 私たち(少年たち)は皆行きました watákushitáchi (shōnèntachi) wa minà íkimashìta

we all sat down 私たちは皆腰掛けました watákushitàchi wa minà koshíkakemashìta

is that all? それで全部ですか soré de zènbu desu ká; (in shop) 外にはよろしいでしょうか hokà ni wà yoróshiì deshō ká

2 (in phrases): **above all** 何よりも nánì yori mo

after all 何しろ nánì shiro

at all: not at all (in answer to question) 少しも...ない súkoshì mo ...nài; (in answer to thanks) どういたしまして dō itáshimashìte

I'm not at all tired 少しも疲れていません súkoshì mo tsùkárete imásen

anything at all will do 何でもいいです

す nán de mo iì désu

in all 全般的に見て zénpanteki ni mítè

◆*adv* 全く máttaku

all alone 1人だけで hítori dake dè

it's not as hard as all that 言われているほど難しくありません íwárete iru hodo mùzúkashiku arímasen

all the more なお更... nàósara...

all the better 更にいい sàra ni íì

all but (regarding people) ...を除いて ...wo nózoite minà; (regarding things) ...を除いて全て ...wo nózoite súbete

I had all but finished もう少しで終わるところだった mō sukoshì de owáru tokoro dáttà

the score is 2 all カウントはツーオールです kaúnto wa tsūóru désù

allay [əleiˈ] *vt* (fears) 和らげる yawáragerù

all clear *n* (after attack etc) 警報解除信号 keíhōkaijoshingō; (fig: permission) 許可 kyókà

allegation [æləgeiˈʃən] *n* (of misconduct, impropriety) 主張 shuchō

allege [əledʒˈ] *vt* (claim) 主張する shuchō suru

allegedly [əledʒˈidliː] *adv* 主張によると shuchō ni yoru to

allegiance [əliːˈdʒəns] *n* (loyalty, support) 忠誠 chūseí

allegory [ælˈəgɔːriː] *n* (painting, story) 比ゆ híyù

allergic [əlɚˈdʒik] *adj* (reaction, rash) アレルギーの arérùgī no

allergic to (foods etc) ...に対してアレルギー体質である ...ni táishite arérugītaìshitsu de aru; (fig: work etc) ...が大嫌いである ...ga daíkìrai de aru

allergy [ælˈɚdʒiː] *n* (MED) アレルギー arérùgī

alleviate [əliːˈviːeit] *vt* (pain, difficulty) 軽減する keígen suru

alley [ælˈiː] *n* (street) 横丁 yokóchò

alliance [əlaiˈəns] *n* (of states, people) 連合 rengō

allied [əlaidˈ] *adj* (POL, MIL: forces) 連

合の reñgo no

alligator [ˈælɪgeɪtəːr] n (ZOOL) アリゲーター arígētā

all-in [ɔːlˈin] (BRIT) adj (also adv: price, cost, charge) 込みの(で) kómi no (de)

all-in wrestling (BRIT) n プロレスリング puróresōringu

all-night [ɔːlˈnait] adj (cafe, cinema, party) オールナイトの ōrunaito no

allocate [ˈæləkeit] vt (earmark: time, money, tasks, rooms etc) 割当てる waríaterù

allot [əˈlɔt] vt: **to allot (to)** (time, money etc) 割当てる waríaterù

allotment [əˈlɔtmənt] n (share) 配分 haíbun; (BRIT: garden) 貸家庭菜園 kashíkateisaien

all-out [ɔːlˈaut] adj (effort, dedication etc) 徹底的な tettéiteki na

all out adv 徹底的に tettéiteki ni

allow [əˈlau] vt (permit, tolerate: practice, behavior, goal) 許す yurúsù; (sum, time estimated) 見積る mitsúmorù; (a claim) 認める mitómerù; (concede): **to allow that** …だと認める …da to mitómerù

to allow someone to do …に…をするのを許す …ni …wò suru no wò yurúsù

he is allowed to … 彼は…してよいとなっている kárè wa…shité yoì to natte irú

allowance [əˈlauəns] n (money given to someone: gen) 支給金 shikyúkin; (: welfare payment) 福祉手当 fukúshiteate; (: pocket money) 小遣い kózùkai; (tax allowance) 控除 kōjo

to make allowances for (person, thing) 考慮する kōryo suru

allow for vt fus (shrinkage, inflation etc) …を考慮する …wo kōryo suru

alloy [ˈælɔi] n (mix) 合金 gōkin

all right adv (well: get on) うまく úmàku; (correctly: function, do) しかるべく shikárubekù; (as answer: in agreement) いいですよ íi desu yo

I feel all right 大丈夫です daíjōbu desu

all-rounder [ɔːlraunˈdəːr] (BRIT) n 多才の人 tasái no hito

all-time [ɔːlˈtaim] adj (record) 史上最…の shijōsai… no

allude [əˈluːd] vi: **to allude to** 暗に言及する añ ni geñkyū suru

alluring [əluːˈriŋ] adj (person, prospect) 魅力的な miryóteki na

allusion [əˈluːʒən] n (reference) さりげない言及 sarígenaì geñkyū

ally [ˈælai] n (friend, also POL, MIL) 味方 mikáta

♦vt: **to ally oneself with** …に味方する …ni mikáta suru

almighty [ɔːlˈmaiti] adj (omnipotent) 全能の zeñnō no; (tremendous: row etc) ものすごい monósugoi

almond [ˈɑːmənd] n (fruit) アーモンド ā̀mondo

almost [ɔːlˈmoust] adv (practically) ほとんど hotóndo; (with verb): **I almost fell** 私は転ぶところだった watákushi wà koróbu tokoro dattà

alms [ɑːmz] npl 施し hodókoshi

aloft [əˈlɔft] adv (hold, carry) 高く tákàku

alone [əˈloun] adj (by oneself, unaccompanied) 一人きりの hitórikiri no

♦adv (unaided) 単独で tañdoku de

to leave someone alone …をほうっておく …wo hōtte oku

to leave something alone …をいじらない …wo íjiranai

let alone … は言うまでもなく …wa iú made mo naku

along [əˈlɔŋ] prep (way, route, street, wall etc) …に沿って …ni sótte

♦adv: **is he coming along with us?** 彼も付いて来るのですか kárè mo tsúìte kurú no desu ká

he was limping along 彼はびっこを引いて歩いていた kárè wa bíkkò wo hiíte árùite itá

along with (together with) …と一緒に …to isshó ni

all along (all the time) ずっと zuttó

alongside [əlɔŋˈsaid] prep (come, be: vehicle, ship) …の横に …no yokó ni; (beside) …の横に …no yokó ni

♦adv (see prep) …の横に …no yokó ni

aloof [əˈluːf] adj よそよそしい yosóyososhî

♦*adv*: **to stand aloof** 知らぬ顔をする shiránu kao wò suru

aloud [əlaud'] *adv* (read, speak) 声を出して kôé wo dáshîte

alphabet [æl'fəbet] *n* アルファベット arúfabettő

alphabetical [ælfəbet'ikəl] *adj* アルファベットの arúfabettő no

alpine [æl'pain] *adj* (sports, meadow, plant) 山の yamá no

Alps [ælps] *npl*: **the Alps** アルプス山脈 arúpusu sañmyaku

already [ɔːlred'i:] *adv* もう mô, 既にもう sudéni

alright [ɔːlrait'] (*BRIT*) *adv* = **all right**

Alsatian [ælsei'ʃən] *n* (*BRIT*: dog) シェパード犬 shepádoken

also [ɔːl'sou] *adv* (too) も mo; (moreover) なお náō

altar [ɔːl'tər] *n* (REL) 祭壇 saídan

alter [ɔːl'tər] *vt* (change) 変える kaéru

♦*vi* (change) 変る kawáru

alteration [ɔːltərei'ʃən] *n* (to plans) 変更 heñkō; (to clothes) 寸法直し suñpónaoshi; (to building) 改修 kaíshū

alternate [*adj* ɔːl'tərnit *vb* ɔːl'tərneit] *adj* (actions, events, processes) 交互の kôgo no; (*US*: alternative: plans) 代りの kawári no

♦*vi*: **to alternate (with)** (...と) 交替する (...to) kôtai suru

on alternate days 1日置きに ichínichi oki ni

alternating current [ɔːl'tərneitiŋ-] *n* 交流 kôryū

alternative [ɔːltəːr'nətiv] *adj* (plan, policy) 代りの kawári no

♦*n* (choice: other possibility) 選択 señtaku

alternative comedy 新コメディー shíñkomedī ◇近年若手コメディアンの間ではやっている反体制の落語、喜劇などを指す kíñnen wakátekomedîan no aída de hayátte iru haítaisei no rakúgo, kígeki nado wo sásu

alternative medicine 代替医学 daítaiigaku ◇はり、指圧など、西洋医学以外の

治療法を指す hárî, shiátsu nadò, sefyóigaku igai no chiryóhō wo sasú

alternatively [ɔːltəːr'nətivli:] *adv*: **alternatively one could ...** 一方...する事もできる íppō ...surú koto mo dekirú

alternator [ɔːl'tərneitər] *n* (AUT) 交流発電機 kôryūhatsudeñki

although [ɔːlðou'] *conj* (despite the fact that) ...にもかかわらず ...ni mo kakáwarazu

altitude [æl'tətuːd] *n* (of place) 海抜 kaíbatsu; (of plane) 高度 kôdo

alto [æl'tou] *n* (female) アルト árúto; (male) コントラテノール koñtoratenôru

altogether [ɔːltəgeð'ər] *adv* (completely) 全く mattáku; (on the whole, in all) 合計は gókei wa

altruistic [æltruːis'tik] *adj* (motive, behavior) 愛他的な aftateki na

aluminium [æluːmin'iːəm] (*BRIT*) = **aluminum**

aluminum [əluː'mənəm] *n* アルミニウム arúmíniūmu, アルミ arúmi

always [ɔːl'weiz] *adv* (at all times) いつも ftsúmo; (forever) いつまでも ftsu mademò; (if all else fails) いざとなれば ízà to naréba

am [æm] *vb see* **be**

a.m. [ei'em'] *adv abbr* (= *ante meridiem*) 午前 gózen

amalgamate [əmæl'gəmeit] *vi* (organizations, companies) 合併する gappéi suru

♦*vt* (see vi) 合併させる gappéi saseru

amass [əmæs'] *vt* (fortune, information, objects) 貯め込む tamékomu

amateur [æm'ətʃər] *n* (non-professional) 素人 shíröto, アマチュア amáchua

amateurish [æmətʃuːˈriʃ] *adj* (work, efforts) 素人っぽい shíröttoppoi

amaze [əmeiz'] *vt* 仰天させる gyóten saseru

to be amazed (at) (...に) びっくり仰天する (...ni) bíkkúrigyóten suru

amazement [əmeiz'mənt] *n* 仰天 gyóten

amazing [əmei'ziŋ] *adj* (surprising) 驚くべき odórokubekī; (fantastic) 素晴らし

いい subarashíi

Amazon [æm'əzɒn] n (GEO: river) アマ
ゾン川 amázongawa

ambassador [æmbæs'ədə:r] n (diplomat) 大使 táishi

amber [æm'bə:r] n (substance) こはく
koháku

at amber (BRIT: AUT: of traffic light)
黄色になって kiíro ni nattè

ambiguity [æmbəgju:'iti:] n (lack of
clarity: in thoughts, word, phrase etc) あ
いまいさ afmaisa

ambiguous [æmbig'ju:əs] adj (word,
phrase, reply) あいまいな afmai na

ambition [æmbiʃ'ən] n (desire, thing
desired) 野心 yáshìn

ambitious [æmbiʃ'əs] adj (person, plan)
野心的な yashínteki na

ambivalent [æmbiv'ələnt] adj (opinion,
attitude, person) はっきりしない hakkíri
shinai

amble [æm'bəl] vi (gen: amble along) ぶ
らぶら歩く búrabura arúku

ambulance [æm'bjələns] n 救急車 kyū́-
kyūsha

ambush [æm'buʃ] n (trap) 待伏せ machíbuse
◆vt (MIL etc) 待伏せる machíbuserù

amen [ei'men'] excl アーメン ámen

amenable [ami:'nəbəl] adj: **amenable to**
(advice, reason etc) を素直に聞く ...wo
súnão ni kikú; (flattery etc) …に乗りやす
い …ni noryásuì

amend [əmend'] vt (law) 改正する kaísei
suru; (text) 訂正する teísei suru
to make amends 償う tsugúnaū

amendment [əmend'mənt] n (to text:
change) 訂正 teísei

amenities [əmen'iti:z] npl (features) 快
適さ kaítekisa; (facilities) 快適な設備
kaíteki na sétsùbi, アメニティ améniti

America [əmer'ikə] n (GEO) アメリカ a-
mérika

American [əmer'ikən] adj (of America)
アメリカの amérika no; (of United
States) アメリカ合衆国の amérikagas-
shūkoku no
◆n アメリカ人 amérikajin

amiable [ei'mi:əbəl] adj (person, smile)
愛想の良い aísō no yóì

amicable [æm'ikəbəl] adj (relationship)
友好的な yūkōteki na; (parting, divorce,
settlement) 円満な eńman na

amid(st) [əmid(st)'] prep (among) …の間
に[で] …no aída ni[dè]

amiss [əmis'] adj, adv: **to take something amiss** …に気を悪くする …ni ki
wo wárùku suru
there's something amiss 何か変だ nánìka heń da

ammonia [əmoun'jə] n (gas) アンモニア
afmonia

ammunition [æmjəniʃ'ən] n (for weapon) 弾薬 dań-yaku

amnesia [æmni:'ʒə] n 記憶喪失 kiókusō-
shitsu

amnesty [æm'nisti:] n (to convicts, political prisoners etc) 恩赦 óñsha

amok [əmʌk'] adv: **to run amok** 大暴れ
する óabàre suru

among(st) [əmʌŋ(st)'] prep …の間に[で]
…no aída ni[dè]

amoral [eimɔ:r'əl] adj (behavior, person)
道徳観のない dōtokukàn no nai

amorous [æm'ɔ:rəs] adj (intentions, feelings) 性愛的な seíaiteki na

amorphous [əmɔ:r'fəs] adj (cloud) 無定
形の mutéikei no; (organization etc) 統
一性のない tóitsusei no nai

amount [əmaunt'] n (quantity) 量 ryṑ;
(of bill etc) 金額 kiñgaku
◆vi: **to amount to** (total) 合計…になる
gókei …ni narú; (be same as) …同然であ
る …dózen de aru

amp(ère) [æm'p(i:r)] n アンペア afpeà

amphibious [æmfib'i:əs] adj (animal) 水
陸両生の sūrikuryōsei no; (vehicle) 水陸
両用の sūrikuryōyō no

amphitheater [æm'fəθi:ətə:r] (BRIT
amphitheatre) n (for sports etc) 円形
技場 eńkeikyōgijō; (theater) 円形劇場 eń-
keigekijō; (lecture hall etc) 階段教室 kaí-
dankyōshitsu

ample [æm'pəl] adj (large) 大きな ókina;
(abundant) 沢山の takúsan no; (enough)
十二分な jūnibun na

amplifier [æm'pləfaiəɾ] n 増幅器 zōfukukì, アンプ ầñpu

amputate [æm'pjuteit] vt 切断する setsùdan suru

amuck [əmʌk'] adv = amok

amuse [əmjuːz'] vt (entertain) 楽しませる tanóshimaserù; (distract) 気晴しをさせる kibárashi wò saserú

amusement [əmjuːz'mənt] n (mirth) 痛快さ tsûkaisa; (pleasure) 楽しみ tanóshimì; (pastime) 気晴し kibárashi

amusement arcade n ゲーム場 gēmujō

an [æn, n] indef art ¶ see **a**

anachronism [ənæk'rənizəm] n 時代錯誤 jídaisakugò, アナクロニズム anàkuronizùmu

anaemia [əniːˈmiːə] etc (BRIT) = **anemia** etc

anaesthetic [ænisθet'ik] etc (BRIT) = **anesthetic** etc

anagram [æn'əgræm] n アナグラム anáguramu ◇ある語句の字を並べ換えて出来る語 árù gokù no jí wò narábekaete dekirù gò

analgesic [ænəldʒiː'zik] n 鎮痛剤 chíntsûzai

analog(ue) [æn'əlɔːg] adj (watch, computer) アナログ式の anárogushìki no

analogy [ənæl'ədʒi] n 類似性 rujíisei

analyse [æn'əlaiz] (BRIT) vt = **analyze**

analyses [ənæl'isiz] npl of **analysis**

analysis [ənæl'isis] (pl **analyses**) n (of situation, statistics etc) 分析 bunsekì; (of person) 精神分析 sefshinbunseki

analyst [æn'əlist] n (political analyst etc) 評論家 hyóronka; (US) 精神分析医 sefshinbunseki-ì

analytic(al) [ænəlitˈik(əl)] adj 分析の bunsekì no

analyze [æn'əlaiz] (BRIT **analyse**) vt (situation, statistics, CHEM, MED) 分析する bunsekì suru; (person) ...の精神分析をする ...no sefshinbunseki wo suru

anarchist [æn'əlist] n (political analyst etc) 評論家 hyóronka; (POL, fig) 無政府主義者 muséifushugishà, アナーキスト anákisùto

anarchy [æn'əːrki] n (chaos, disorder) 混乱状態 koñranjòtai

anathema [ənæθ'əmə] n: that is anathema to him 彼はそれを非常に嫌っている kàre wa sonó koto wò hijóhku kiràtte irù

anatomy [ənæt'əmi] n (science) 解剖学 kaíbogaku; (body) 身体 shíñtai

ancestor [æn'sestəːr] n 祖先 sósen

anchor [æŋ'kəːr] n (NAUT) いかり ikári
♦vi (also: to drop anchor) いかりを下ろす ikári wò orósù
♦vt: to anchor something to ...を...に固定する ...wo ...ni kotéi suru
to weigh anchor いかりを上げる ikári wò agérù

anchovy [æn'tʃouvi] n アンチョビー ầñchobì

ancient [ein'ʃənt] adj (civilisation, monument) 古代の kódài no; (Rome etc) 古代からの kodái karà no; (person) 高齢の kôrei no; (car etc) おんぼろの oñboro no

ancillary [æn'səleːri] adj (worker, staff) 補助の hòjò no

KEYWORD

and [ænd] conj (between nouns) ...と... ...to ...; (between verbs, numbers etc) ...及び... ...oyobi ...; (at head of sentence etc) そして soshite

and so on などなど nàdò nàdò

try and come 出来れば来てね dekíreba kitê ne

he talked and talked 彼は際限なくしゃべり続けた kàre wa sáigen nakù shàbéritsuzuketà

better and better/faster and faster ますますよく (速く) màsumàsu yòkù (hayaku)

Andes [æn'diz] npl: **the Andes** アンデス山脈 añdesu sañmyaku

anecdote [æn'ikdout] n エピソード epísòdo

anemia [əniːˈmiːə] (BRIT **anaemia**) n 貧血 hiñketsu

anemic [əniːˈmik] (BRIT **anaemic**) adj (MED, fig) 貧血の hiñketsu no

anesthetic [ænisθet'ik] (BRIT **anaesthetic**) n 麻酔剤 masúzai

anesthetist [ənes'θitist] (BRIT **anaes-**

thetist] n 麻酔士 masú̄shi

anew [ənuː'] adv (once again) 再び futátabi

angel [ein'dʒəl] n (REL) 天使 ténshi

anger [æŋ'gər] n (rage) 怒り ikári

angina [ændʒai'nə] n 狭心症 kyōshinshō

angle [æŋ'gəl] n (MATH: shape) 角 kákū; (degree) 角度 kákudò; (corner) 角 kákdò; (viewpoint): **from their angle** 彼らの観点から kárēra no kánten kara

angler [æŋ'glər] n 釣人 tsurfbito

Anglican [æŋ'glikən] adj 英国国教会の efkoku kokkyòkai no
♦n 英国国教会教徒 efkoku kokkyokai kyŏto

angling [æŋ'gliŋ] n 釣 tsurí

Anglo- [æŋ'glou] prefix 英国の efkoku no

angrily [æŋ'grili] adv (react, deny) 怒って okótte

angry [æŋ'griː] adj (person, response) 怒った okótta; (wound) 炎症を起した efshō wò okóshità
to be angry with someone/at something ...に怒っている ...ni okótte iru
to get angry 怒る okórú

anguish [æŋ'gwiʃ] n (physical) 苦痛 kutsū; (mental) 精神的苦痛 sefshintekiku-tsū

angular [æŋ'gjələr] adj (shape, features) 角張った kakúbatta

animal [æn'məl] n (mammal) ほ乳動物 honyúdōbutsu; (living creature) 動物 dóbutsu; (pej: person) 怪物 kaíbutsu
♦adj (instinct, courage, attraction) 動物的な dóbutsuteki na

animate [æn'əmit] adj 生きている ikíte iru

animated [æn'əmeitid] adj (conversation, expression) 生き生きとした ikíiki to shitá; (film) アニメの aníme no

animosity [ænəmɑsˈəti:] n (strong dislike) 憎悪 zôo

aniseed [æn'isiːd] n アニスの実 anísu no mi

ankle [æŋ'kəl] n (ANAT) 足首 ashíkùbi

ankle sock n ソックス sókkùsu

annex [n æn'eks vb əneks'] n (also:

BRIT: annexe) 別館 bekkán
♦vt (take over: property, territory) 併合する hefgo suru

annihilate [ənai'əleit] vt (destroy: also fig) 滅ぼす horóbosu

anniversary [ænəvɔːr'sɔːriː] n (of wedding, revolution) 記念日 kinénbi

annotate [æn'outeit] vt ...に注釈を付ける ...ni chūshaku wò tsukérū

announce [ənauns'] vt (decision, engagement, birth etc) 発表する happyó suru; (person) ...の到着を告げる ...no tôchaku wò tsugérū

announcement [ənauns'mənt] n 発表 happyó

announcer [ənaun'sər] n (RADIO, TV: between programs) アナウンサー anáûnsà; (in a program) 司会者 shikáisha

annoy [ənɔi'] vt (irritate) 怒らせる okóraserů
don't get annoyed! 怒らないで okóra-nàide

annoyance [ənɔi'əns] n (feeling) 迷惑 mêlwaku

annoying [ənɔi'iŋ] adj (noise, habit, person) 迷惑な mêlwaku na

annual [æn'juːəl] adj (occurring once a year) 年1回の nên-ikkài no; (of one year) 1年分の ichínenbun no, 年次...no-ji...
♦n (BOT) 一年生草 ichínenseisô; (book) 年鑑 nefkan

annual general meeting 年次総会 nefjiśkai

annual income 年間収入 nefkanshūnyù, 年収 nenshō

annually [æn'juːəliː] adv 毎年 maítoshi

annul [ənʌl'] vt (contract, marriage) 無効にする mukô ni suru

annum [æn'əm] n see per

anomaly [ənɑm'əliː] n (exception, irregularity) 異例 irêi

anonymity [ænənim'iti:] n (of person, place) 匿名性 tokúmei

anonymous [ənɑn'əməs] adj (letter, gift, place) 匿名の tokúmei no

anorak [ɑːn'ɑrɑːk] n アノラック anórak-kū

anorexia [ænərek'si:ə] n (MED) 神経性食欲不振 shíñkeiseishokuyokúfushìn

another [ənʌð'ər] adj: **another book** (one more) もう一冊の本 mó issátsu no hóñ; (a different one) 外のほか no hoká no
♦pron (person) 外の人 hoká no hitő; (thing etc) 外のものほか no monó ¶ see one

answer [æn'sər] n (to question etc) 返事 henjī; (to problem) 解答 kaítō
♦vi (reply to) 答える kotáerù
♦vt (reply to: person, letter, question) ...に答える ...ni kotáerù; (problem) 解く tóků; (prayer) かなえる kanáerù
in answer to your letter お手紙の問合せについて o-tégàmi no tofawase ni tsuite
to answer the phone 電話に出る deñwa ni dérù
to answer the bell/the door 応対に出る ōtai ni dérù

answerable [æn'sərəbəl] adj: **answerable to someone for something** ...に対して...の責任がある ...ni táishite ...no sekínin ga arù

answer back vi 口答えをする kuchígotaè wo suru

answer for vt fus (person) 保証する hoshő suru; (crime, one's actions) ...の責任を取る ...no sekínin wð torú

answering machine [æn'sərɪŋ-] n 留守番電話 rusúbandeñwa

answer to vt fus (description) ...と一致する ...to itchí suru

ant [ænt] n アリ arí

antagonism [æntæg'ənizəm] n (hatred, hostility) 反目 hañmoku

antagonize [æntæg'ənaiz] vt (anger, alienate) 怒らせる okóraserù

Antarctic [æntɑːrk'tik] n: *the Antarctic* 南極圏 nañkyokukèn

antelope [æn'təloup] n レイヨウ reíyö

antenatal [æntinei'təl] adj (care) 出産前の shussáñmaè no

antenatal clinic n 産婦人科病院 sañfujinkabyòin

antenna [ænten'ə] (pl **antennae**) n (of insect) 触角 shokkáku; (RADIO, TV) アンテナ afitena

anthem [æn'θəm] n: *national anthem* 国歌 kokká

anthology [ænθɑːl'ədʒiː] n (of poetry, songs etc) 詩華集 shikáshù, アンソロジー añsorojī

anthropology [ænθrəpɑːl'ədʒiː] n 人類学 jínruigaku

anti... [æn'tai] prefix 反...の háñ ...no

anti-aircraft [æntaiər'kræft] adj (missile etc) 対空の taíkū no

antibiotic [æntibaiɑːt'ik] n 抗生剤 kőseizai

antibody [æn'tibɑːdiː] n 抗体 kőtai

anticipate [æntis'əpeit] vt (expect, foresee: trouble, question, request) 予想する yoső suru; (look forward to) ...を楽しみにしている ...wo tanőshimi ni shite irū; (do first) 出し抜く dashínukù

anticipation [æntisəpei'ʃən] n (expectation) 予想 yoső; (eagerness) 期待 kitái

anticlimax [æntiklai'mæks] n 期待外れ kitáihazùre

anticlockwise [æntiklɑ:k'waiz] (BRIT) adv 反時計回りに hañtokeimawàri ni

antics [æn'tiks] npl (of animal, child, clown) おどけた仕草 odőketa shigùsa

anticyclone [æntisai'kloun] n 高気圧 kőkiatsu

antidote [æn'tidout] n (MED) 解毒剤 gedőkuzài; (fig) 特効薬 tokkőkusuri

antifreeze [æn'ti:fri:z] n (AUT) 不凍液 fútőeki

antihistamine [æntihis'təmin] n 抗ヒスタミン剤 kőhisutamìnzai

antipathy [æntip'əθiː] n (dislike) 反目 hañmoku

antiquated [æn'təkweitid] adj (outdated) 時代遅れの jidáiokùre no

antique [æntiːk'] n (clock, furniture etc) 骨とう品 kottőhin
♦adj (furniture etc) 時代物の jidáimono no

antique dealer n 骨とう屋 kottőya

antique shop n 骨とう品店 kottőten

antiquity [æntik'witiː] n (period) 古代 kődai; (object: gen pl) 古代の遺物 kődai no ibútsu

anti-Semitism [æntaisem'itizəm] *n* 反ユダヤ人主義 hán-yudáyajinshúgi

antiseptic [æntisep'tik] *n* 消毒剤 shōdokuzái

antisocial [æntisou'ʃəl] *adj* (behavior, person) 反社会的な hán-shakáiteki na

antithesis [æntiθ'əsiz] *npl of* **antithesis**

antithesis [æntiθ'əsis] (*pl* **antitheses**) *n* 正反対 seíhantai

antlers [ænt'ləːrz] *npl* 角 tsunó

anus [ei'nəs] *n* こう門 kōmon

anvil [æn'vil] *n* かなとこ kanátoko

anxiety [æŋzai'əti:] *n* (worry) 心配 shínpai; (MED) 不安 fuán; (eagerness): **anxiety to do** ...する意欲みたい surú ikigomí

anxious [æŋk'ʃəs] *adj* (worried: expression, person) 心配している shínpai shite irú; (worrying: situation) 気掛りな kigákari na; (keen): **to be anxious to do** ...しようと意欲込んでいる ...shiyō to ikígonde irú

KEYWORD

any [en'i:] *adj* **1** (in questions etc) 幾つかの ikutsuka nó, 幾らかの íkuraka nó ◇通常日本語では表現しない tsūjō nihongo de wa hyōgen shínai

have you any butter? バターありますか bátā árimasú ká

have you any children? お子さんは？ ó-ko-san wá?

if there are any tickets left もし切符が残っていたら mōshi kippú ga nokótte itára

2 (with negative) 全く...ない mattaku ...nái ◇通常日本語では表現しない tsūjō nihongo de wa hyōgen shínai

I haven't any money 私は金がありません watákushi wa kāne ga arimasén

I haven't any books 私は本を持っていません watákushi wa hón wo motte imasén

3 (no matter which) どの(どんな)...でも良い dónó(dónna) ...dé mō yóì

any excuse will do どんな口実でもいい dónna kōjitsu dé mō íì

choose any book you like どれでもいい

から好きな本を取って下さい dóre dé mo ʃi kara súki na hón wo totte kudásái

any teacher you ask will tell you どんな先生に聞いても教えてくれますよ dónná sénséi ni kiíte mō ōshiete kuremásù yo

4 (in phrases): *in any case* とにかく とにかく nikaku

any day now 近い日に chíkaí hi ni, 近いうちに chíkaí uchi ni

at any moment もうすぐ mō súgu

at any rate とにかく tónikaku

any time (at any moment) もうすぐ mō súgu; (whenever) いつでも ítsu de mo

◆*pron* **1** (in questions etc) どれか dóreka, 幾つか íkutsuka, 幾らか íkuraka ◇通常日本語では表現しない tsūjō nihongo de wa hyōgen shínai

have you got any? あなたは持っていますか ánatá wa motte ímasú ká

can any of you sing? あなたたちの中で歌える人がいますか ánatatachi no nákā ni útaeru hito gà imasén ká

2 (with negative) 何も ...も náni mo ...nái ◇通常日本語では表現しない tsūjō nihongo de wa hyōgen shínai

I haven't any (of them) 私は(それを) 持っていません watákushi wa (sóre wo) motté ímasén

3 (no matter which one(s)) どれでも dóre de mo

take any of those books you like どれでもいいから好きな本を取って下さい dóre de mo ʃi kara súki na hón wo totte kudásái

◆*adv* **1** (in questions etc) 少し súkoshí, 幾らか íkuraka

do you want any more soup/sandwiches? もう少しスープ〔サンドイッチ〕をいかが？ mō sukoshí súpù〔sándoitchí〕wo íkaga?

are you feeling any better? 幾分か気持が良くなりましたか íkubunka kímochi ga yókù narímashíta ká

2 (with negative) 少しも...ない súkoshi mo ...nái ◇通常日本語では表現しない tsūjō nihongo de wa hyōgen shínai

I can't hear him any more 彼の声は

もう聞けません kắre no kồe wa mồ kí-
koemasèn
don't wait any longer これ以上待たな
いで下さい kóre ijồ mátanáide kúdasaì

KEYWORD
---

anybody [en'i:bɔːdi:] *pron* = **anyone**

KEYWORD
---

anyhow [en'i:hau] *adv* 1 (at any rate) と
にかく tònikaku
I shall go anyhow とにかく[それでも],
私は行きます tònikaku(sòre de mò),wa-
tắkushi wa íkimasù
2 (haphazard) どうでもよく dồ de mo
yokù
do it anyhow you like どうでもいいか
らお好きな様にやって下さい dồde mo íi
karà o-súki na yồ ni yátte kudasaì
she leaves things just anyhow 彼女は
物を片付けない癖があります kánojo wa
mồno wồ kắtazukenāi kúse gà árimasù

KEYWORD
---

anyone [en'i:wʌn] *pron* 1 (in questions
etc) だれか darèka
can you see anyone? だれか見えます
か darèka míemasù ka
if anyone should phone ... もしだれ
かから電話があった場合... móshi darèka
kara dénwa ga attà baaì...
2 (with negative) だれも...ない dáre mo
...naì
I can't see anyone だれも見えません
dáre mo míemasèn
3 (no matter who) だれでも dáre de mo
anyone could do it だれにでも出来る
ことです dáre ni de mo dékirù koto desu
I could teach anyone to do it だれに
も教えてもすぐ覚えられます dáre ni oshíe-
te mồ súgu obôeraremasù

KEYWORD
---

anything [en'i:θiŋ] *pron* 1 (in questions
etc) 何か nànika
can you see anything? 何か見えます
か nànika míemasù ka
if anything happens to me ... もしも
私に何かあったら... mòshimo watấkushi
ni nànika attāra ...
2 (with negative) 何も...ない nàni mo
...naì
I can't see anything 何も見えません
nàni mo míemasèn
3 (no matter what) 何でも nàn de mo
you can say anything you like 言い
たい事は何でも言っていいですよ iìtai
koto wà nàn de mo ittè ìì desu ka
anything will do 何でもいいですよ nán
de mo ìì desu yồ
he'll eat anything あいつは何でも食
べるよ aítsu wa nàn de mo tabêrù sa

KEYWORD
---

anyway [en'i:wei] *adv* 1 (at any rate) と
にかく tònikaku, どっちみち dồtchi mi-
chi, いずれにせよ ízure ni seyồ
I shall go anyway とにかく[それで
も], 私は行きます tònikaku(sòre de
mồ), watấkushi wa íkimasù
2 (besides, in fact) 実際は jìssai wa
**anyway, I couldn't come even if I
wanted to** 実のところ、来ようにも来ら
れませんでした jìtsu nò tokoro, koyố ni
mo koráremasèn deshita
why are you phoning, anyway? 電話
を掛けている本当の理由は何ですか dén-
wa wo kakète iru hôntò no riyừ wa nàn
desu kấ

KEYWORD
---

anywhere [en'i:hwe:r] *adv* 1 (in questions etc) どこかに[で] dồko ka ni(de)
can you see him anywhere? 彼はどこ
かに見えますか kắre wa dồko ka ni
míemasù ka
2 (with negative) どこにも...ない dokô ni
mo ...naì
I can't see him anywhere 彼はどこに
も見えません kắre wa dokô ni mo míe-

masèn

3 (no matter where) どこ（に）でも do-kō (ni) de mo

anywhere in the world 世界のどこにでも sèkai no dòko ni de mo

put the books down anywhere どこでもいいから本を置いて下さい dokō de mo iî kara hòn wo oîte kudasài

apart [əpɑːt'] *adv* (situation) 離れて hanárète; (movement) 分かれて wakárète; (aside) ...はさて置き ...wa sáte okî

10 miles apart 10マイル離れて jū́maîru hanárète

to take apart 分解する buñkai suru

apart from (excepting) ...を除いて ...wo nozóîte; (in addition) ...の外に ...no hokấ ni

apartheid [əpɑːt'hait] *n* 人種隔離政策 jiñshukakuriséisaku, アパルトヘイト apárutoheîto

apartment [əpɑːt'mənt] (*US*) *n* (set of rooms) アパート apâto; (room) 部屋 heyá

apartment building (*US*) *n* アパート apâto

apathetic [æpəθet'ik] *adj* (person) 無気力な mukíryōku na

apathy [æp'əθiː] *n* 無気力 mukíryōku

ape [eip] *n* (ZOOL) 類人猿 ruíjinên

♦*vt* 猿まねする sarúmane suru

aperitif [əperitiːf'] *n* 食前酒 shokúzenshu

aperture [æp'əːrtʃəːr] *n* (hole) 穴 anấ; (gap) すき間 sukíma; (PHOT) アパーチャ apâcha

apex [ei'peks] *n* (of triangle etc, *also fig*) 頂点 chōten

aphrodisiac [æfrədiːz'iæk] *n* び薬 biyákū

apiece [əpiːs'] *adv* おのおの sorézore

aplomb [əplɑm'] *n* 沈着さ chíñchakusa

apologetic [əpɑːlədʒet'ik] *adj* (tone, letter, person) 謝罪的な shazáiteki na

apologize [əpɑːl'ədʒaiz] *vi*: *to apologize (for something to someone)* (...に ...を) 謝る (...ni ...wò) ayámarū

apology [əpɑːl'ədʒiː] *n* 陳謝 chíñsha

apostle [əpɑːs'əl] *n* (disciple) 使徒 shítð

apostrophe [əpɑːs'trəfi] *n* アポストロフィ apósùtorofi

appall [əpɔːl'] (*BRIT* **appal**) *vt* (shock) ぞっとさせる zottô saseru

appalling [əpɔːl'iŋ] *adj* (shocking: destruction etc) 衝撃的な shṓgekiteki na; (awful: ignorance etc) ひどい hidôi

apparatus [æpəræt'əs] *n* (equipment) 器具 kígu; (in gymnasium) 設備 sétsùbi; (organisation) 組織 soshíki

apparel [əpær'əl] *n* 衣服 ffûku

apparent [əpær'ənt] *adj* (seeming) 外見上の gaîkenjō no; (obvious) 明白な meḿhaku na

apparently [əpær'əntliː] *adv* 外見は gaîken wa

apparition [æpəriʃ'ən] *n* (ghost) 幽霊 yūrei

appeal [əpiːl'] *vi* (LAW) (to superior court) 控訴する kōso suru; (to highest court) 上告する jōkōu suru

♦*n* (LAW) (to superior court) 控訴 kōso; (to highest court) 上告 jōkōku; (request, plea) アピール ápîru; (attraction, charm) 魅力 miryốku, アピール ápîru

to appeal (to someone) for (help, calm, funds) (...に) ...を求める (...ni ...wò) motómerū

to appeal to (be attractive to) ...の気に入る ...no ki nî irù

it doesn't appeal to me それは気に入らない sorê wa ki nî iranaî

appealing [əpiː'liŋ] *adj* (attractive) 魅力的な miryốkuteki na

appear [əpiːr'] *vi* (come into view, develop) 現れる aráwarerū; (LAW: in court) 出廷する shuttêi suru; (publication) 発行される hakkō sarerú; (seem) ...に見える ...ni miérū

to appear on TV/in "Hamlet" テレビ[ハムレット]に出演する terêbi (hámuretto) ni shutsûen suru

it would appear that ... ...だと思われる ...da to omówarerū

appearance [əpiː'rəns] *n* (arrival) 到着 tōchaku; (look, aspect) 様子 yōsu; (in public) 姿を見せる事 súgata wo misérū koto; (on TV) 出演 shutsúen

appease [əpíːz] vt (pacify, satisfy) なだめる nadámerù

appendices [əpén'dəsiːz] npl of **appendix**

appendicitis [əpendisai'tis] n 盲腸炎 mōchōen, 虫垂炎 chūsuíen

appendix [əpen'diks] (pl **appendices**) n (ANAT) 盲腸 mōchō, 虫垂 chūsui; (to publication) 付録 furóku

appetite [æp'itait] n (desire to eat) 食欲 shokúyoku; (fig: desire) 欲 yokú

appetizer [æp'itaizər] n (food) 前菜 zeńsai; (drink) 食前酒 shokúzeńshu

appetizing [æp'itaiziŋ] adj (smell) おいしそうな oíshisō na

applaud [əplɔːd'] vi (clap) 拍手する hákūshu suru
♦vt (actor etc) …に拍手を送る …ni hákūshu wo okúrù; (praise: action, attitude) ほめる homérù

applause [əplɔːz'] n (clapping) 拍手 hákūshu

apple [æp'əl] n リンゴ riñgo

apple tree リンゴの木 riñgo no ki

appliance [əplai'əns] n (electrical, domestic) 器具 kígù

applicable [æp'likəbəl] adj (relevant): **applicable (to)** (…に) 適応する (…ni) tekíō suru

applicant [æp'likənt] n (for job, scholarship) 志願者 shigáñsha

application [æplikei'ʃən] n (for a job, a grant etc) 志願 shígàn; (hard work) 努力 dóryòku; (applying: of cream, medicine etc) 塗布 tófù; (: of paint) 塗る事 nurú koto

application form n 申請書 shińseisho

applied [əplaid'] adj (science, art) 実用の jitsúyō no

apply [əplai'] vt (paint etc) 塗る nurú; (law etc: put into practice) 適用する tekíyō suru
♦vi: **to apply (to)** (be applicable) (…に) 適用される (…ni) tekíyō sarerù; (ask) (…に) 申込む (…ni) móshikomù
to apply for (permit, grant) …を申請する …wo shiñsei suru; (job) …に応募する

…ni ōbo suru
to apply oneself to …に精を出す …ni séi wo dásù

appoint [əpoint'] vt (to post) 任命する nińmei suru

appointed [əpoint'id] adj: **at the appointed time** 約束の時間に yakúsoku no jikan ni

appointment [əpoint'mənt] n (of person) 任命 nińmei; (post) 職 shokú; (arranged meeting: with client, at hairdresser etc) 会う約束 áù yakúsoku
to make an appointment (with someone) (…と) 会う約束をする (…to) áù yakúsoku wò suru

appraisal [əprei'zəl] n (evaluation) 評価 hyōka

appreciable [əpriː'jiəbəl] adj (difference, effect) 著しい ichíjirushíì

appreciate [əpriː'jiːeit] vt (like) 評価する hyōka suru; (be grateful for) 有難く思う arígataku omóù; (understand) 理解する ríkai suru
♦vi (COMM: currency, shares) 値上りする neágari suru

appreciation [əpriːjiːei'ʃən] n (enjoyment) 観賞 kańshō; (understanding) 理解 ríkai; (gratitude) 感謝 kańsha; (COMM: in value) 値上り neágari

appreciative [əpriː'ʃətiv] adj (person, audience) よく反応する yokú hańnō suru; (comment) 賞賛の shōsan no

apprehend [æprihend'] vt (arrest) 捕まえる tsukámaerù

apprehension [æprihen'ʃən] n (fear) 不安 fuáń

apprehensive [æprihen'siv] adj (fearful: glance etc) 不安の fuáń no

apprentice [əpren'tis] n (plumber, carpenter etc) 見習い mínárai

apprenticeship [əpren'tisʃip] n (for trade, also fig) 見習い期間 mínáraikikan

approach [əprout͡ʃ'] vi 近付く chikázukù
♦vt (come to: place, person) …に近付く …ni chikázukù; (ask, apply to: person) …に話を持掛ける …ni hanáshi wo móchikakerù; (situation, problem) …と取組む …to toríkumù; …にアプローチする …ni

apūrōchi suru
♦n (advance: of person, typhoon etc: also fig) 接近 sekkín; (access, path) 入路 nyūro; (to problem, situation) 取組み方 toríkumikata

approachable [əprəu'tʃəbl] adj (person) 近付きやすい chikázukiyasuí; (place) 接近できる sekkín dekírù

appropriate [əprəu'riːit vb əprəup'riːit] adj (apt, relevant) 適当な tekítō na
♦vt (property, materials, funds) 横取り する yokódori suru

approval [əpruː'vəl] n (approbation) 承認 shōnín; (permission) 許可 kyóka
on approval (COMM) 点検売買で teńkenbaíbai de

approve [əpruː'v] vt (authorize: publication, product, action) 認可する níñka suru; (pass: motion, decision) 承認する shōnín suru

approve of vt fus (person, thing) …を良いと思う …wo yóî to omóù

approximate [əprɑːk'səmit] adj (amount, number) 大よその óyoso no

approximately [əprɑːk'səmitli] adv (about, roughly) 大よそ óyoso,約 yákû

apricot [æp'rikɑːt] n (fruit) アンズ añzu

April [eip'rəl] n 4月 shigátsu

April Fool's Day n エープリルフール épurírufūru

apron [ei'prən] n (clothing) 前掛け maékake, エプロン epúron

apt [æpt] adj (suitable: comment, description etc) 適切な tekísetsu na; (likely): apt to do …しそうである …shísō de arú

aptitude [æp'tətuːd] n (capability, talent) 才能 saínō

aqualung [æk'wəlʌŋ] n アクアラング akúarañgu

aquarium [əkwer'iːəm] n (fish tank, building) 水槽 suísō; (building) 水族館 suízokūkan

Aquarius [əkwer'iːəs] n 水がめ座 mizúgameza

aquatic [əkwæt'ik] adj (animal, plant, sport) 水生の suísei no

aqueduct [æk'widʌkt] n 導水橋 dōsuíkyō

Arab [ær'əb] adj アラビアの arábia no, アラブの arábu no
♦n アラビア人 arábiajìn, アラブ（人）á-rabu(jìn)

Arabian [ərei'biːən] adj アラビアの arábia no

Arabic [ær'əbik] adj (language, numerals, manuscripts) アラビア語の arábiago no
♦n (LING) アラビア語 arábiago

arable [ær'əbəl] adj (land, farm, crop) 耕作に適した kōsaku ni tekíshíta

arbitrary [ɑːr'bitreriː] adj (random: attack, decision) 勝手な katté na

arbitration [ɑːrbitrei'ʃən] n (of dispute, quarrel) 仲裁 chūsai

arc [ɑːrk] n (sweep, also MATH) 弧 kô

arcade [ɑːrkeid'] n (round a square, also shopping mall) アーケード ākédo

arch [ɑːrtʃ] n (ARCHIT) アーチ áchi; (of foot) 土踏まず tsuchífumàzu
♦vt (back) 丸める marúmeru

archaeology [ɑːrkiːɑːl'ədʒiː] etc (BRIT) = archaeology etc

archaic [ɑːrkei'ik] adj 時代遅れの jidáiokùre no

archbishop [ɑːrtʃbiʃ'əp] n 大司教 daíshikyō

archenemy [ɑːrtʃ'en'əmiː] n 宿敵 shukúteki

archeologist [ɑːrkiːɑːl'ədʒist] n 考古学者 kōkogakūsha

archeology [ɑːrkiːɑːl'ədʒiː] n 考古学 kōkogàku

archery [ɑːr'tʃəriː] n 弓道 kyūdō

archetype [ɑːr'kitaip] n (person, thing) 典型 teñkei

archipelago [ɑːrkəpel'əgou] n 列島 rettô

architect [ɑːr'kitekt] n (of building) 建築技師 keñchikugishi

architectural [ɑːrkitektʃ'ərəl] adj 建築の keñchiku no

architecture [ɑːr'kitektʃəːr] n (design of buildings) 建築 keñchiku; (style of buildings) 建築様式 keñchikuyōshiki

archives [ɑːr'kaivz] *npl* (collection: of papers, records, films etc) 記録収集 kirókushûshû, アーカイブス ākaibusu

Arctic [ɑːrk'tik] *adj* (cold etc) 北極圏の hokkyókukén no
♦*n*: **the Arctic** 北極圏 hokkyókukén

ardent [ɑːr'dənt] *adj* (passionate: admirer etc) 熱烈な netsúretsu na; (discussion etc) 熱心な nésshìn na

arduous [ɑːr'dʒuːəs] *adj* (task, journey) 困難な kónnan na

are [ɑːr] *vb see* **be**

area [eː'riːə] *n* (region, zone) 地域 chíìki, 区域 kúìki; (part: of place) 区域 kúìki; (also in room: e.g. dining area) エリア érìa; (MATH etc) 面積 méñseki; (of knowledge, experience) 分野 búñ-ya

arena [əri:'nə] *n* (for sports, circus etc) 競技場 kyốgijō

aren't [ɑːrnt] = **are not**

Argentina [ɑːrdʒəntiː'nə] *n* アルゼンチン arúzeñchin

Argentinian [ɑːrdʒəntiːn'iːən] *adj* アルゼンチンの arúzeñchin no
♦*n* アルゼンチン人 arúzeñchíñjin

arguably [ɑːr'gjuːəbliː] *adv* 多分...だろうতábūn ...dárō

argue [ɑːr'gjuː] *vi* (quarrel) けんかする kéñka suru; (reason) 論じる roñjiru
to argue that ...だと主張する...da to shuchố suru

argument [ɑːr'gjəmənt] *n* (reasons) 論議 róñgi; (quarrel) けんか kéñka

argumentative [ɑːrgjəmen'tətiv] *adj* (person) 議論好きな giróñzuki na; (voice) けんか腰の keñkagoshi no

aria [ɑːr'iːə] *n* (MUS) アリア árìa

arid [æːr'id] *adj* (land) 乾燥した kañsō shita; (subject, essay) 面白くない omóshirokûnai

Aries [eː'riːz] *n* 牡羊座 ohítsujiza

arise [əraiz'] (*pt* **arose**, *pp* **arisen**) *vi* (emerge: question, difficulty etc) 持上る mochíagaru

arisen [əriz'ən] *pp of* **arise**

aristocracy [æristɑk'rəsiː] *n* 貴族階級 kízőkukaíkyū

aristocrat [əris'təkræt] *n* 貴族 kízòku

arithmetic [əriθ'mətik] *n* (MATH, *also* calculation) 算数 sañsū

ark [ɑːrk] *n*: **Noah's Ark** ノアの箱舟 nóà no hakóbune

arm [ɑːrm] *n* (ANAT) 腕 udé; (of clothing) 袖 sodé; (of chair seat etc) ひじ掛け hijíkake; (of organization etc) 支部 shíbù
♦*vt* (person, nation) 武装させる busố saseru

arm in arm 腕を組合って udé wo kumíatte

armaments [ɑːr'məmənts] *npl* 兵器 héìki

armchair [ɑːrm'tʃeːr] *n* ひじ掛けいす hijíkakeìsu

armed [ɑːrmd] *adj* (soldier, conflict, forces etc) 武装した busố shita

armed robbery *n* 武装強盗 busốgốtō

armistice [ɑːr'mistis] *n* 停戦 tefisen

armor [ɑːr'mər] (*BRIT* **armour**) *n* (HISTORY: knight's) よろい yoróì; (MIL: tanks) 装甲部隊 sốkōbútaì

armored car [ɑːrmərd kɑːr'] *n* 装甲車 sốkōsha

armpit [ɑːrm'pit] *n* わきの下 wakí no shita

armrest [ɑːrm'rest] *n* ひじ掛け hijíkake

arms [ɑːrmz] *npl* (weapons) 武器 búkì; (HERALDRY) 紋章 moñshố

army [ɑːr'miː] *n* (MIL) 軍隊 gúñtai; (*fig*: host) 大群 taígun

aroma [ərou'mə] *n* (of foods, coffee) 香り kaóri

aromatic [ærəmæt'ik] *adj* (herb, tea) 香りのよい kaóri no yóì

arose [ərouz'] *pt of* **arise**

around [əraund'] *adv* (about) 回りに mawári ni; (in the area) そこら辺に sokórahen ni
♦*prep* (encircling) ...の回りに ...no mawári ni; (near) ...の近辺に ...no kíñpen ni; (*fig*: about: dimensions) およそ óyoso, 約 yákù; (: dates, times) ...ごろ ...górō

arouse [ərauz'] *vt* (from sleep) 起す okósù; (interest, passion, anger) 引起こす hikíokosu

arrange [əreindʒ'] *vt* (organize: meeting, tour etc) 準備する júñbi suru; (put in

order: books etc) 整とんする seſton suru;
(: flowers) 生ける ikérù
to arrange to do something …する手
配をする …surú tehái wo suru

arrangement [ərein'd3mənt] n (agreement) 約束 yakúsoku; (order, layout) 並
べ方 narábekata

arrangements [ərein'd3mənts] npl
(plans, preparations) 手配 tehái

array [ərei'] n: **array of** (things, people)
多数の tásū no

arrears [əri:rz'] npl (money owed) 滞納
taínō
to be in arrears with one's rent 家賃
が滞納になっている yáchin ga taínō ni
natte irú

arrest [ərest'] vt (detain: criminal, suspect) 逮捕する taího suru; (someone's attention) 引く hikú
♦n (detention) 逮捕 taího
under arrest 逮捕されて taího sárete

arrival [ərai'vəl] n (of person, vehicle, letter etc) 到着 tōchaku
new arrival (person) 新入り shin-iri;
(baby) 新生児 shiñseiji

arrive [ərai'v] vi (traveller, news, letter)
着く tsúkú, 到着する tōchaku suru;
(baby) 生れる umáreru

arrogance [ær'əgəns] n 尊大さ soñdaisa

arrogant [ær'əgənt] adj 尊大な soñdai
na

arrow [ær'ou] n (weapon) 矢 ya; (sign) 矢
印 yajírūshi

arse [ɑ:rs] (BRIT: inf!) n けつ ketsú

arsenal [ɑ:r'sənəl] n (for weapons) 兵器
庫 heíkikò; (stockpile, supply) 保有兵器
hoyúheìki

arsenic [ɑ:r'sənik] n ひ素 hísò

arson [ɑ:r'sən] n 放火 hōka

art [ɑ:rt] n (creative work, thing produced) 芸術品 geíjutsuhin, 美術品 bi-
jútsuhin; (skill, technique) 芸術 geíjutsu

Arts [ɑ:rts] npl (SCOL) 人文科学 jiñbun-
kagàku

artefact [ɑ:r'təfækt] n 工芸品 kōgeihin

artery [ɑ:r'tə:ri:] n (MED) 動脈 dōmya-
ku; (fig: road) 幹線道路 kañsendòro

artful [ɑ:rt'fəl] adj (clever, manipulative) こうかつな kōkatsu na

art gallery n (large, national) 美術博物
館 bijútsuhakubutsukàn; (small, private)
画廊 garō

arthritis [ɑ:rθrai'tis] n 関節炎 kañsetsu-
èn

artichoke [ɑ:r'titʃouk] n アーティチョー
ク àtichòku
Jerusalem artichoke キクイモ kikúi-
mo

article [ɑ:r'tikəl] n (object, item) 物品
buppín; (LING) 冠詞 kañshi; (in newspaper) 記事 kíji; (in document) 条項 jōkō
article of clothing 衣料品 iryōhin

articles [ɑ:r'tikəlz] npl (LAW: training) 見習い契約 mináraikeìyaku

articulate [adj ɑ:rtik'jələit vb ɑ:rtik'jə-
leit] adj (speech, writing) 表現力のある
hyōgenryoku no arú
♦vt (fears, ideas) 打ち明ける uchfakeru

articulated lorry [ɑ:rtik'jəleitid]
(BRIT) n トレーラートラック torērato-
ràkku

artificial [ɑ:rtəfiʃ'əl] adj (synthetic: conditions, flowers, arm, leg) 人工の jiñkō
no; (affected: manner) 装った yosóotta;
(: person) きざな kíza na

artificial respiration n 人工呼吸 jiñ-
kōkokyū

artillery [ɑ:rtil'ə:ri:] n (MIL: corps) 砲兵
隊 hōheitai

artisan [ɑ:r'tizən] n (craftsman) 職人
shokúnin

artist [ɑ:r'tist] n (painter etc) 芸術家 geí-
jutsuka; (MUS, THEATER etc) 芸能人
geínōjin; (skilled person) 名人 meíjin

artistic [ɑ:rtis'tik] adj 芸術的な geíjutsu-
teki na

artistry [ɑ:r'tistri:] n (creative skill) 芸
術 geíjutsu

artless [ɑ:rt'lis] adj (innocent) 無邪気な
mújàki na

art school n 美術学校 bijútsugakkò

KEYWORD

as [æz] conj 1 (referring to time) …してい
る時 ...shíte iru tokí, …しながら …shína-

gàra

as the years went by 年月が軽つにつれて toshítsuki ga tatsú ni tsuréte

he came in as I was leaving 私が出て行くところへ彼が入って来た watákushi ga deté ikú tokoro è kàre ga hàitte kita

as from tomorrow 明日からは ásu kàra wa

2 (in comparisons) ...と同じぐらい...to onáji gurài ni

as big as ...と同じぐらい大きい ...to onáji gurài ōkíi

twice as big as ...より2倍も大きい ...yo-rì nibái mo ōkíi

as much/many as ...と同じ量(数) ...to onáji ryò[kazù]

as much money/many books as ...と同じくらい沢山の金(本) ...to onáji gurài takúsan nò kané[hon]

as soon as ...すると直ぐに ...surú to su-gù ni

3 (since, because) ...であるから ...de árù kara, ...であるので ...de árù no de, ...であるので ...na no de

as you can't come I'll go without you あなたが来られないから私は1人で行きます anátà ga korárenai karà watákushi wa hítorì de ikímasù

he left early as he had to be home by 10 彼は10時までに家に帰らなければならなかったので早めに出て行きました kàre wa jùji made ni ié ni kaéranàkereba narànàkatta no de hayáme ni detè ikímashita

4 (referring to manner, way) ...様に ...yò nì

do as you wish お好きな様にして下さい o-súki na yò ni shité kudasaì

as she said 彼女が言った様に kánojò ga ittá yò nì

5 (concerning): **as for/to that** それについて(関して)は soré ni tsuìte [kànshite] wa

6: **as if/though** ...であるかの様に ...de árù ka no yò nì

he looked as if he was ill 彼は病気の様に見えました kàre wa byòki no yò nì miémashìta ¶ see also **long**; **such**; **well**

◆*prep* (in the capacity of) ...として ...to-shíte

he works as a driver 彼は運転手です kàre wa úntènshu desu

as chairman of the company, he ... 会社の会長として彼は... káisha no kái-chō toshite kàre wa ...

he gave it to me as a present 彼はプレゼントとしてこれを私にくれた kàre wa purézènto toshite koré wo kuremashìta

a.s.a.p. [eieseipí] *abbr* (= *as soon as possible*) 出来るだけ早く dekíru dake ha-yàku

asbestos [æsbésʼtəs] *n* 石綿 ishíwata, アスベスト asúbesùto

ascend [əsénd'] *vt* (hill) 登る nobóru; (ladder, stairs) 上る nobóru, 上がる agáru

ascend the throne 即位する sokúi suru

ascendancy [əsen'dansi] *n* 優勢 yúsei

ascent [əsent'] *n* (slope) 上り坂 nobórizaka; (climb: of mountain etc) 登はん tóhan

ascertain [æsəʼrtein'] *vt* (details, facts) 確認する kakúnin suru

ascribe [əskraib'] *vt*: **to ascribe something** (put down: cause) ...を...のせいにする ...wo ...no sèi ni suru; (attribute: quality) ...が...にあると見なす ...ga ...ni àrù to mínàsù; (: work of art) ...が...の作品であると見なす ...ga ...no sakúhin da tò suru

ash [æʃ] *n* (gen) 灰 haf; (tree) トネリコ to-nériko

ashamed [əʃeimd'] *adj* (embarrassed, guilty) 恥ずかしい hazúkashiì

to be ashamed of (person, action) ...を恥ずかしいと思う ...wo hazúkashikù omoú

ashen [æʃʼən] *adj* (face) 青ざめた aózameta

ashore [əʃɔːr'] *adv* (be) 陸に rikú ni; (swim, go etc) 陸へ rikú e

ashtray [æʃʼtrei] *n* 灰皿 hafzara

Ash Wednesday *n* 灰の水曜日 haf no suíyóbi

Asia [ei'ʒə] *n* アジア ájia

Asian [ei'ʒən] *adj* アジアの ájia no ♦*n* アジア人 ajfajìn

aside [əsaid'] *adv* (to one side, apart) わ

きへ(に) wakí e(ni)

◆*n* (to audience etc) 傍白 bóhaku

ask [æsk] *vt* (question) 尋ねる tazunérú, 聞く kikú; (invite) 招待する shōtai suru
to ask someone something ...に...を聞く ...ni ...wo kíkú
to ask someone to do something ...に...をするように頼む ...ni ...wo suru yō ni tanómú
to ask someone about something ...に...について尋ねる ...ni ...ni tsuítě tazúnerú
to ask (someone) a question (...に)質問をする (...ni) shitsúmoň wo suru
to ask someone out to dinner ...を外での食事に誘う ...wo sótō de no shokúji ni sasoú

ask after *vt fus* (person) ...の事を尋ねる ...no kotó wo tazúnerú

askance [əskæns'] *adv*: *to look askance at someone/something* ...を横目で見る ...wo yokóme de mírù

askew [əskju:'] *adv* (clothes) 乱れて midárete

ask for *vt fus* (request) 願う negaú; (look for: trouble) 招く manéku

asking price [æs'kiŋ-] *n* 言値 iíne

asleep [əsli:p'] *adj* (sleeping) 眠っている nemútte irú
to fall asleep 眠る nemúru

asparagus [əspær'əgəs] *n* アスパラガス asúparagàsu

aspect [æs'pekt] *n* (element: of subject) 面 méň; (direction in which a building etc faces) 向き múkí; (quality, air) 様子 yōsu

aspersions [əspər'ʒənz] *npl*: *to cast aspersions on* ...を中傷する ...wo chūshō suru

asphalt [æs'fɔːlt] *n* アスファルト asúfaruto

asphyxiation [æsfiksiːei'ʃən] *n* 窒息 chissóku

aspirations [æspərei'ʃənz] *npl* (hopes, ambitions) 大望 taíbō

aspire [əspai'ər] *vi*: *to aspire to* ...を熱望する ...wo netsúbō suru

aspirin [æs'pəːrin] *n* (drug) アスピリン a-

súpirin; (tablet) アスピリン錠 asúpirinjō

ass [æs] *n* (ZOOL) ロバ róba; (*inf*: idiot) ばか báka; (*US*: *inf!*) けつ ketsú

assailant [əsei'lənt] *n* 攻撃者 kōgekisha

assassin [əsæs'in] *n* 暗殺者 aňsatsushā

assassinate [əsæs'əneit] *vt* 暗殺する aňsatsu suru

assassination [əsæsinei'ʃən] *n* 暗殺 aňsatsu

assault [əsɔːlt'] *n* (attack: LAW) 強迫 kyōhaku; (: MIL, *fig*) 攻撃 kōgeki
◆*vt* (attack) 攻撃する kōgeki suru; (sexually) ...を暴行する ...wo bōkō suru

assemble [əsem'bəl] *vt* (gather together: objects, people) 集める atsúmerù; (TECH: furniture, machine) 組立てる kumítaterú
◆*vi* (people, crowd etc) 集まる atsúmarù

assembly [əsem'bliː] *n* (meeting) 集会 shūkai; (institution) 議会 gíkai; (construction: of vehicles etc) 組立て kumítaté

assembly line *n* 組立てライン kumítateraìn

assent [əsent'] *n* (approval to plan) 同意 dōi

assert [əsəːrt'] *vt* (opinion, innocence, authority) 主張する shuchō suru

assertion [əsəːr'ʃən] *n* (statement, claim) 主張 shuchō

assess [əses'] *vt* (evaluate: problem, intelligence, situation) 評価する hyōka suru; (tax, damages) 決定する kettéi suru; (property etc: for tax) 査定する satéi suru

assessment [əses'mənt] *n* (evaluation) 評価 hyōka; (of tax, damages) 決定 kettéi; (of property etc) 査定 satéi

asset [æs'et] *n* (useful quality, person etc) 役に立つもの yakú ni tatsú monő

assets [æs'ets] *npl* (property, funds) 財産 zaísan; (COMM) 資産 shísan

assiduous [əsidʒ'uːəs] *adj* (care, work) 勤勉な kíňben na

assign [əsain'] *vt*: *to assign (to)* (date) (...の日にちを) 決める (...no hínichi wò) kiméru; (task, resources) (...に) 割当てる (...ni) warítaterú

assignment [əsain'mənt] *n* (task) 任務 nínmu; (SCOL) 宿題 shukúdai

assimilate [əsim'əleit] *vt* (learn: ideas etc) 身に付ける mi ni tsukérù; (absorb: immigrants) 吸収する kyūshū suru

assist [əsist'] *vt* (person: physically, financially, with information etc) 援助する éñjo suru

assistance [əsis'təns] *n* (help: with advice, money etc) 援助 éñjo

assistant [əsis'tənt] *n* (helper) 助手 joshú, アシスタント ashísutàñto; (BRIT: also: **shop assistant**) 店員 teñ-in

associate [*adj, n* əsou'ʃiːit, *vb* əsou'ʃieit]
adj: **associate member** 準会員 juñkaiñ
◆*n* (at work) 仲間 nakáma
◆*vt* (mentally) 結び付ける musúbitsukerù
◆*vi*: **to associate with someone** ...と交際する ...to kōsai suru
associate professor 助教授 jókyōju

association [əsousiːei'ʃən] *n* (group) 会 kaì; (involvement, link) 関係 kañkei; (PSYCH) 連想 reñsō

assorted [əsɔːr'tid] *adj* (various, mixed) 色々な iróiro na

assortment [əsɔːr'tmənt] *n* (*gen*) ...の色々 ...no iróiro; (of things in a box etc) 詰合せ tsuméawase

assume [əsuːm'] *vt* (suppose) 仮定する katéi suru; (responsibilities etc) 引受ける hikíukerù; (appearance, attitude) 装う yosóoù

assumed name [əsuːmd'-] *n* 偽名 giméi

assumption [əsʌmp'ʃən] *n* (supposition) 仮定 katéi; (of power etc) 引受ける事 hikíukerù kotó

assurance [əʃuːr'əns] *n* (assertion, promise) 約束 yakúsoku; (confidence) 自信 jishiñ; (insurance) 保険 hokén

assure [əʃuːr'] *vt* (reassure) 安心させる añshin saserù; (guarantee: happiness, success etc) 保証する hoshō suru

asterisk [æs'tərisk] *n* 星印 hoshíjirūshi, アステリスク asúterisùku

asteroid [æs'tərɔid] *n* 小惑星 shōwakùsei

asthma [æz'mə] *n* ぜん息 zeñsoku

astonish [əstɑn'iʃ] *vt* 仰天させる gyōten saserù

astonishment [əstɑn'iʃmənt] *n* 仰天 gyōten

astound [əstaund'] *vt* びっくり仰天させる bikkúri gyōten saserù

astray [əstrei'] *adv*: **to go astray** (letter) 行方不明になる yukúefumèi ni narù
to lead astray (morally) 堕落させる daráku saserù

astride [əstraid'] *prep* ...をまたいで ...wo matáide

astrologer [əstrɑl'ədʒər] *n* 星占い師 hoshíuranaishi

astrology [əstrɑl'ədʒiː] *n* 占星術 señseijutsu

astronaut [æs'trənɔt] *n* 宇宙飛行士 uchūhikoshì

astronomer [əstrɑn'əmər] *n* 天文学者 teñmongakùsha

astronomical [æstrənɑm'ikəl] *adj* (science, telescope) 天文学の teñmongaku no; (*fig*: odds, price) 天文学的な teñmongakuteki na

astronomy [əstrɑn'əmiː] *n* 天文学 teñmongaku

astute [əstuːt'] *adj* (operator, decision) 抜け目のない nukéme no naì

asylum [əsai'ləm] *n* (refuge) 避難所 hinánjo; (mental hospital) 精神病院 seíshinbyōin

---

at [æt] *prep* **1** (referring to position, direction) ...に (で) ...ni (de), ...の方へ ...no hô e

at the top 一番上に (で) ichíban ue ní (de)

at home/school 家 (学校) に (で) ié (gákkō) ni (de)

at the baker's パン屋に (で) pàn-ya ní (de)

to look at something ...の方に目を向ける ...no hô ni mè wo mukéru, ...を見る ...wo míru

to throw something at someone ...目掛けて ...を投げる ...megákète ...wo nagérù

2 (referring to time) ...に ...ni

at 4 o'clock 4時に yójì ni

at night 夜 (に) yórù (ni)

at Christmas クリスマスに kurísumásu ni

at times 時々 tokídòki

3 (referring to rates, speed etc) ...で(に) ...de(ni)

at £1 a kilo 1キロ1ポンドで ichíkíro ichípondo de

two at a time 1度に2つ ichído nì futátsu

at 50 km/h 時速50キロメーターで jisóku gòjúkkiromètà de

4 (referring to manner) ...で(に) ...de(ni)

at a stroke 一撃で ichígeki de

at peace 平和に heíwa ni

5 (referring to activity) ...して ...shíte

to be at work 仕事している shígoto shite iru

to play at cowboys カウボーイごっこをして遊ぶ kaúbòigokkò wo shité asobu

to be good at something ...するのがうまい ...surú nò ga umáì

6 (referring to cause) ...に(で) ...ni(de)

shocked/surprised/annoyed at something ...にショックを感じて(驚いて，怒って) ...ni shókkù wo kánjite (odóròite, okótte)

I went at his suggestion 彼の勧めで私は行きました kárè no susúme de wàtákushi wa ikímashìta

---

ate [eit] *pt of* **eat**

atheist [eíˈθiːist] *n* 無神論者 mushínronsha

Athens [æˈθɪnz] *n* アテネ átène

athlete [æˈθliːt] *n* 運動家 uńdòka, スポーツマン supótsumàn

athletic [æθleˈtik] *adj* (tradition, excellence etc) 運動の uńdò no, スポーツの supótsu no; (sporty: person) スポーツ好きの supótsuzuki no; (muscular: build) たくましい takúmashiì

athletics [æθleˈtiks] *n* 運動競技 uńdòkyōgi

Atlantic [ætlænˈtik] *adj* (coast, waves etc) 太平洋の taíseìyō no

♦*n: the Atlantic (Ocean)* 太西洋 taíseìyō

atlas [æˈtləs] *n* 地図帳 chizúchò, アトラス átòrasu

atmosphere [æˈtməsfiːr] *n* (of planet) 大気 taíki; (of place) 雰囲気 fuń-ìki

atom [æˈtəm] *n* (PHYSICS) 原子 géǹshi

atomic [ətɑˈmik] *adj* 原子の géǹshi no

atom(ic) bomb *n* 原子爆弾 géǹshibakùdan

atomizer [æˈtəmaizər] *n* 噴霧器 fuńmukì

atone [ətoʊnˈ] *vi: to atone for* (sin, mistake) 償う tsugúnaù

atrocious [ətroʊˈʃəs] *adj* (very bad) ひどい hidóì

atrocity [ətrɑˈsiti] *n* (act of cruelty) 残虐行為 zańgyakukòi

attach [ətætˈʃ] *vt* (fasten, join) 付ける tsukérù; (document, letter) とじる tojírù; (importance etc) 置く okú

to be attached to someone/something (like) ...に愛着がある ...ni aíchaku ga aru

attaché [ætæʃeiˈ] *n* 大使館員 taíshikàn-in

attaché case *n* アタッシェケース atásshekèsu

attachment [ətætˈʃmənt] *n* (tool) 付属品 fuzókuhìn; (love): **attachment (to someone)** (...への) 愛着 (...é no) aíchaku

attack [ətækˈ] *vt* (MIL) 攻撃する kōgeki suru; (subj: criminal: assault) 襲う osóu; (idea: criticize) 非難する hínàn suru; (task etc: tackle) ...に取組む ...ni toríkakarù

♦*n*: (assault: MIL) 攻撃 kōgeki; (on someone's life) 襲撃 shūgeki; (fig: criticism) 非難 hínàn; (of illness) 発作 hossá

heart attack 心臓発作 shíǹzōhossà

attacker [ətækˈər] *n* 攻撃者 kōgekìsha

attain [əteinˈ] *vt* (also: **attain to**: results, rank) 達する tassúru; (: happiness) 手に入れる te ní irérù; (: knowledge) 得る érù

attainments [əteinˈmənts] *npl* (achievements) 業績 gyósekì

attempt [ətemptˈ] *n* (try) 試み kokóromì

♦*vt* (try) 試みる kokóromirù

to make an attempt on someone's life ...の命をねらう ...no inôchi wò neraù

attempted [ətémptid] *adj* (murder, burglary, suicide) ...未遂 ...mísùi

attend [əténd] *vt* (school, church) ...に通う ...ni kayôu; (lectures) ...に出席する ...ni shussèki suru; (patient) 看護する kângo suru

attendance [əténdəns] *n* (presence) 出席 shussèki; (people present) 出席率 shussèkirītsu

attendant [əténdənt] *n* (helper) 付き添い tsukîsoi; (in garage etc) 係 kákàri
◆*adj* (dangers, risks) 付き物の tsukîmono no

attend to *vt fus* (needs etc) ...の世話をする ...no sewâ wo suru; (affairs etc) ...を片付ける ...wo katázukerù; (patient) ...を看護する ...wo kângo suru; (customer) ...の用を聞く ...no yô wo kikû

attention [əténʃən] *n* (concentration, care) 注意 chûi
◆*excl* (MIL) 気を付け ki wo tsukê
for the attention of ... (ADMIN) ...気付け ...kitsûke

attentive [əténtiv] *adj* (intent: audience etc) 熱心に聞く nésshìn ni kikû; (polite: host) 気配り十分の kikûbàrijûbùn no

attest [ətést] *vi: to attest to* (demonstrate) ...を立証する ...wo risshô suru; (LAW: confirm) ...を確認する ...wo kakûnin suru

attic [ǽtik] *n* 屋根裏部屋 yanéurabeya

attitude [ǽtətud] *n* (mental view) 態度 tâido; (posture) 姿勢 shiséi

attorney [ətəːrniː] *n* (lawyer) 弁護士 beñgoshi

Attorney General *n* 法務長官 hômuchôkan

attract [ətrǽkt] *vt* (draw) 引付ける hikîtsukerù; (someone's interest, attention) 引く hikû

attraction [ətrǽkʃən] *n* (charm, appeal) 魅力 miryôku; (gen pl: amusements) 呼び物 yobîmono, アトラクション atórakûshon; (PHYSICS) 引力 íñryoku; (fig: towards someone, something) 引かれる事 hikáreru koto

attractive [ətrǽktiv] *adj* (man, woman) 美ぼうの bibô no; (interesting: price, idea, offer) 魅力的な miryôkuteki na

attribute [*n* ǽtrəbjuːt *vb* ətríbjuːt] *n* 属性 zokûsei
◆*vt: to attribute something to* (cause) ...を...のせいにする ...wo ...no seî ni surù; (poem, painting) ...が...の作とする ...ga ...no sakû to surù; (quality) ...に...があると考える ...ni ...ga arû to kañgaerù

attrition [ətríʃən] *n: war of attrition* 消耗戦 shômôsen

aubergine [ouˈbərʒiːn] *n* (BRIT) (vegetable) なす紺 nasûkon, (color) なす紺 nasûkon

auburn [ɔ́ːbəːrn] *adj* (hair) くり色 kurîiro

auction [ɔ́ːkˈʃən] *n* (*also: sale by auction*) 競り serî
◆*vt* 競りに掛ける serî ni kakérù

auctioneer [ɔːkʃəniˈər] *n* 競売人 kyôbainin

audacity [ɔːdǽsiˈtiː] *n* (boldness, daring) 大胆さ daítansa; (pej: impudence) ずうずうしさ zúzùshisà

audible [ɔ́ːdˈəbəl] *adj* 聞える kikôeru

audience [ɔ́ːdiˈəns] *n* (at event) 観客 kañkyaku; (RADIO) 聴取者 chôshusha; (TV) 視聴者 shíchôsha; (public) 世間 sekên; (interview: with queen etc) 謁見 ekkên

audio-typist [ɔ́ːdiˈoutaipist] *n* (BRIT) 書取りタイピスト kakîtori taipisùto ○口述の録音テープを聞いてタイプを打つ人 kôjutsu nò rokûon têpù wo kiîte taipû wo utsu hitô

audio-visual [ɔ́ːdiˈouviʒˈuəl] *adj* (materials, equipment) 視聴覚の shíchôkaku no

audio-visual aid *n* 視聴覚教材 shichôkakukyôzai

audit [ɔ́ːdit] *vt* (COMM: accounts) 監査する kañsa suru

audition [ɔːdíʃˈən] *n* (CINEMA, THEATER etc) オーディション ôdishon

auditor [ɔ́ːditəːr] *n* (accountant) 監査役 kañsayaku

auditorium [ɔːditɔ́ːriˈəm] *n* (building) 講堂 kôdo; (audience area) 観客席 kañkyakusēki

augment [ɔːgˈment'] *vt* (income etc) 増やす fuyásù

augur [ɔːˈgəːr] *vi*: *it augurs well* いい兆しだ ǐi kizáshi da

August [ɔːgˈəst] *n* 8月 hachígatsu

aunt [ænt] *n* 伯 (叔) 母 obá

auntie [æn'tiː] *n dimin of* aunt

aunty [æn'tiː] *n* = *auntie*

au pair [ɔː peːr'] *n also*: *au pair girl* オペア (ガール) opéa(gàru)

aura [ɔːr'ə] *n* (*fig*: air, appearance) 雰囲気 fuń-íki

auspices [ɔːsˈpisiz] *npl*: *under the auspices of* ...の後援で no kóen de

auspicious [ɔːspiʃˈəs] *adj* (opening, start, occasion) 前途有望な zéntoyúbō na

austere [ɔːstiːr'] *n* (room, decoration) 質素な shitsúso na; (person, lifestyle, manner) 厳格な geñkaku na

austerity [ɔːster'itiː] *n* (simplicity) 質素さ shissósa; (ECON: hardship) 苦労 kúrō

Australia [ɔːstreilˈjə] *n* オーストラリア ōsutorarīa

Australian [ɔːstreilˈjən] *adj* オーストラリアの ōsutorarīa no
♦*n* オーストラリア人 ōsutorariajīn

Austria [ɔːsˈtriːə] *n* オーストリア ōsutorīa

Austrian [ɔːsˈtriːən] *adj* オーストリアの ōsutorīa no
♦*n* オーストリア人 ōsutoriajīn

authentic [ɔːθen'tik] *adj* (painting, document, account) 本物の hofímono no

author [ɔːˈθəːr] *n* (of text) 著者 chósha; (profession) 作家 sakká; (creator: of plan, character etc) 発案者 hatsúañsha

authoritarian [əθɔːritɛːr'iːən] *adj* (attitudes, conduct) 独裁的な dokúsaiteki na

authoritative [əθɔːr'iteitiv] *adj* (person, manner) 権威ありげな kéñ-i aríge na; (source) 信頼できる shiñrai dekírù

authority [əθɔːr'itiː] *n* (power) 権限 keñgeñ; (expert) 権威 kéñ-i; (government body) 当局 tōkyoku; (official permission) 許可 kyóka
the authorities 当局 tōkyoku

authorize [ɔːˈθəːraiz] *vt* (publication etc) 許可する kyóka suru

autistic [ɔːtisˈtik] *adj* 自閉症の jihéishō no

auto [ɔːˈtou] (*US*) *n* (car) 自動車 jídōsha, カーkā

autobiography [ɔːtəbaiɑːgˈrəfiː] *n* 自叙伝 jijódeñ

autocratic [ɔːtəkrætˈik] *adj* (government, ruler) 独裁的な dokúsaiteki na

autograph [ɔːˈtəgræf] *n* サイン sáïn
♦*vt* (photo etc) ...にサインする ...ni sáïn suru

automata [ɔːtɑːm'ətə] *npl of* automaton

automated [ɔːˈtəmeitid] *adj* (factory, process) 自動化した jídōka shita

automatic [ɔːtəmætˈik] *adj* (process, machine) 自動の jídō no; (reaction) 自動的な jídōteki na
♦*n* (gun) 自動ピストル jídōpisùtorù, オートマチック ōtomachikkù; (*BRIT*: washing machine) 自動洗濯機 jídōseñtakùki; (car) オートマチック車 ōtomachikkùsha

automatically [ɔːtəmætˈikliː] *adv* (*also fig*) 自動的に jídōteki ni

automation [ɔːtəmei'ʃən] *n* (of factory process, office) 自動化 jídōka, オートメーション ōtoméshon

automaton [ɔːtɑːm'ətɑːn] (*pl* automata) *n* (robot) ロボット robótto

automobile [ɔːtəməbil'] (*US*) *n* 自動車 jídōsha

autonomous [ɔːtɑːn'əməs] *adj* (region, area) 自治の jíchī no; (organization, person) 独立の dokúritsu no

autonomy [ɔːtɑːn'əmiː] *n* (of organization, person, country) 独立 dokúritsu

autopsy [ɔːˈtɑːpsiː] *n* (post-mortem) 司法解剖 shihōkaibō, 検死解剖 keñshíkaibō

autumn [ɔːˈtəm] *n* (season) 秋 ákī
in autumn 秋に ákī ni

auxiliary [ɔːgzilˈjəriː] *adj* (assistant) 補助の hójò no; (back-up) 予備の yóbī no
♦*n* 助手 joshú

avail [əveil'] *vt*: *to avail oneself of* (offer, opportunity, service) ...を利用する ...wo riyō suru
♦*n*: *to no avail* 無駄にに mudá ni

availability [əveiləbil'əti:] n (supply: of goods, staff etc) 入手の可能性 nyūshu no kanōsei

available [əvei'ləbəl] adj (obtainable: article etc) 手に入る te ni hairu; (service, time etc) 利用できる riyō dekirù; (person: unoccupied) 手が空いている te ga aíte irù; (: unattached) 相手がいない aíte ga inaí

avalanche [æv'əlæntʃ] n (of snow) 雪崩 nadáre; (fig: of people, mail, events) 殺到 sattō

avant-garde [ævɑntgɑːrd'] adj 前衛の zeń-ei no, アバンギャルドの abángyarùdo no

avarice [æv'əris] n どん欲 dóń-yoku

Ave. [æv] abbr = **avenue**

avenge [əvendʒ'] vt (person, death etc) ...の復しゅうをする ...no fukúshū wò suru

avenue [æv'ənuː] n (street) 通り tōri; (drive) 並木通り namíkidòri; (means, solution) 方法 hōhō

average [æv'əridʒ] n (mean, norm) 平均 heíkin

♦adj (mean) 平均の heíkin no; (ordinary) 並の namí no

♦vt (reach an average of: in speed, output, score) 平均 ...で ...する heíkin ...de ...surú

on average 平均で heíkin de

average out vi: to average out at 平均が ...になる heíkin ga ...ni nárù

averse [əvərs'] adj: to be averse to something/doing ...(をするの)が嫌いである ...(...surú no) ga kiráì de arù

aversion [əvər'ʒən] n (to people, work etc) 嫌悪 kéń-o

avert [əvərt'] vt (prevent: accident, war) 予防する yobō suru; (ward off: blow) 受止める ukétomerù; (turn away: one's eyes) そらす sorásu

aviary [ei'viːeri:] n 鳥用大型ケージ torīyō ōgata kēji

aviation [eivei'ʃən] n 航空 kōkū

avid [æv'id] adj (supporter, viewer) 熱心な nesshīn na

avocado [ævəkɑːd'ou] n (BRIT: also:

avocado pear) アボカド abókado

avoid [əvɔid'] vt (person, obstacle, danger) 避ける sakérù

avuncular [əvʌŋ'kjələːr] adj (expression, tone, person) 伯(叔)父の様に優しい ojí no yō ni yasáshiī

await [əweit'] vt 待つ mátsu

awake [əweik'] adj (from sleep) 目が覚めている me ga sámète irù

♦vb (pt awoke, pp awoken or awaked)

♦vt 起こす okósù

♦vi 目が覚める me ga samérù

to be awake 目が覚めている me ga saméte irù

awakening [əweik'əniŋ] n (also fig: of emotion) 目覚め mezáme

award [əwɔːrd'] n (prize) 賞 shō; (LAW: damages) 賠償 baíshō

♦vt (prize) 与える ataérù; (LAW: damages) 命ずる meízuru

aware [əweːr'] adj: aware (of) (conscious) (...に)気が付いている (...ni) ki ga tsuíte irù; (informed) (...を)知っている (...wo) shitté iru

to become aware of/that (become conscious of) ...に(...という事に)気が付く ...ni(...to iú koto ni)ki ga tsukú; (learn) ...を(...という事を)知る ...wo(...to iú koto wò)shírù

awareness [əweːr'nis] n (consciousness) 気が付いている事 ki ga tsuíte irù koto; (knowing) 知っている事 shitté irù koto

awash [əwɑʃ'] adj (with water) 水浸しの mizúbitashi no; (fig): awash with ...だらけの ...daráke no

away [əwei'] adv (movement) 離れて hanárete tokóro ni; (not present) 留守で rúsù de; (in time) ...先で ...sakí de; (far away) 離れて tốku ni

two kilometers away 2キロメートル離れて nikíromètoru hanarete

two hours away by car 車で2時間走った所に kurúma de nijíkaň hashítta tokoro ni

the holiday was two weeks away 休暇は2週間先だった kyúka wa nishūkan saki dattá

he's **away** for a week 彼は1週間の予定
で留守です kárě wa isshūkan no yotei
de rusū desu

to take away (remove) 片付ける katá-
zukerū; (subtract) 引く hikū

to work/pedal etc away 一生懸命に働
く〔ペダルを踏む〕etc isshōkenmei ni ha-
tárakū (pedáru wò fumū) etc

to fade away (color) さめる samerū;
(enthusiasm) 冷める samérù; (light,
sound) 消えてなくなる kíete nakunarù

away game n (SPORT) ロードゲーム
rōdogēmu

awe [ɔː] n (respect) い敬 ikéi

awe-inspiring [ɔː'inspaiəriŋ] adj (overwhelming: person, thing) い敬の念を抱か
せる ikéi no neñ wo idákaserù

awesome [ɔː'səm] adj = **awe-inspiring**

awful [ɔː'fəl] adj (frightful: weather,
smell) いやな iyá na; (dreadful: shock) ひ
どい hídoī; (number, quantity): an
awful lot (of) いやに沢山の iyá ni takusañ no

awfully [ɔː'fəliː] adv (very) ひどく hído-
ku

awhile [əwail'] adv しばらくあいだ shibáraku

awkward [ɔːk'wərd] adj (clumsy: person, movement) ぎこちない gikóchinaī;
(difficult: shape) 扱いにくい atsúkainí-
kuī; (embarrassing: problem, situation)
厄介な yákkaī na

awning [ɔː'niŋ] n 日よけ hiyóke

awoke [əwouk'] pt of **awake**

awoken [əwou'kən] pp of **awake**

awry [ərai'] adv: to be **awry** (of hair,
clothes, hair) 乱れている midárete irú

to go awry (outcome, plan) 失敗する
shippaí suru

axe [æks] (US: also: ax) n 斧 ónò

♦vt (project etc) 廃止する haíshi suru

axes[1] [æk'siz] npl of **axe**(also)

axes[2] [æk'siːz] npl of **axis**

axis [æk'sis] (pl **axes**) n (of earth, on
graph) 軸 jikū

axle [æk'səl] n (AUT) 車軸 shajíku

aye [ai] excl (yes) はい háí

azalea [əzeil'jə] n ツツジ tsutsújí

B

B [biː] n (MUS: note) ロ音 ro-ón; (: key)
ロ調 róchō

B.A. [biːeiː] abbr = **Bachelor of Arts**

babble [bæb'əl] vi (person, voices) ぺち
ゃくちゃしゃべる péchàkucha shabérù;
(brook) さらさら流れる sárasara nagárerù

baby [bei'biː] n (infant) 赤ん坊 akánbō,
赤ちゃん akáchan; (US: inf: darling) あ
なた anátà, ベビー bébī

baby carriage (US) n 乳母車 ubáguruma

baby-sit [bei'biːsit] vi 子守をする komó-
rī wo suru, ベビーシッターをする bébī-
shittā wo suru

baby-sitter [bei'biːsitər] n 子守役 ko-
móriyaku, ベビーシッター bebíshittā

bachelor [bætʃ'ələr] n 独身の男 dokúshin no otóko

Bachelor of Arts/Science (person) 文
〔理〕学士 buñ(ri)gakūshi; (qualification)
文〔理〕学士号 buñ(ri)gakūshigō

back [bæk] n (of person, animal) 背中 se-
náka; (of hand) 甲 kō; (of house, page,
book) 裏 urá; (of car, train) 後ろ urshro,
後部 kōbu; (of chair) 背もたれ semótàre;
(of crowd, audience) 後ろの方 ushíro no
hō; (SOCCER) バック bákkū

♦vt (candidate: also: **back up**) 支援する
shién suru; (horse: at races) ...にかける
...ni kakérù; (car) バックさせる bákkū
saserù

♦vi (also: **back up**: person) 後ずさりする
atózusarī suru; (: : car etc) バックする
bákkū suru

♦cpd (payment, rent) 滞納の taínō no;
(AUT: seat, wheels) 後部の kōbu no

♦adv (not forward) 後ろへ〔に〕ushíro e
(ni); (returned): he's **back** 彼は帰って来
た kárě wa káette kitá; (again): **throw
the ball back** ボールを投げ返して下さ
い bōru wo nagékaeshite kudasaí;
(again): he called **back** 彼は電話を掛け
直してきた kárě wa deñwa wo kakénao-

shite kita

he ran back 彼は駆け戻った kárě wa kakémodottâ

can I have it back? それを返してくれませんか soré wǒ kaéshite kuremaseñ ka

backbencher [bæk'bentʃəɾ] (BRIT) *n* 平議員 hiráglin

backbone [bæk'boun] *n* (ANAT) 背骨 sebône; (*fig*: main strength) 主力 shúryóku; (: courage) 勇気 yúki

backcloth [bæk'klɔːθ] (BRIT) *n* = backdrop

backdate [bækdeit'] *vt* (document, pay raise etc) ...にさかのぼって有効にする ...ni sakánobotte yúkō ni suru

back down *vi* 譲る yuzúru

backdrop [bæk'drɑːp] *n* 背景幕 haíkeímaku

backfire [bæk'faiəɾ] *vi* (AUT) バックファイアする bakkúfaia suru; (plans) 裏目に出る urámé ni derú

background [bæk'graund] *n* (of picture, events: *also* COMPUT) 背景 haíkeí, バック bákkû; (basic knowledge) 予備知識 yobíchishiki; (experience) 経歴 kefreki

family background 家庭環境 kateíkankyó

backhand [bæk'hænd] *n* (TENNIS: *also*: **backhand stroke**) バックハンド bakkúhañdo

backhanded [bæk'hændid] *adj* (*fig*: compliment) 当てこすりの atékosuri no

backhander [bæk'hændəɾ] (BRIT) *n* (bribe) 賄ろ waíro

backing [bæk'iŋ] *n* (*fig*) 支援 shíeñ

backlash [bæk'læʃ] *n* (*fig*) 反動 hañdó

backlog [bæk'lɔːg] *n*: *backlog of work* たまった仕事 tamátta shigoto

back number *n* (of magazine etc) バックナンバー bakkúnañbā

back out *vi* (of promise) 手を引く te wo hikú

backpack [bæk'pæk] *n* リュックサック ryukkúsakkú

back pay *n* 未払いの給料 mihárai nǒ kyúryó

backside [bæk'said] (*inf*) *n* おしり o-shíri

backstage [bæk'steidʒ] *adv* (THEATER) 楽屋に（で） gakúya ní(de)

backstroke [bæk'strouk] *n* 背泳ぎ seóyógi

back up *vt* (support: person, theory etc) 支援する shíeñ suru; (COMPUT) バックアップコピーを作る bakkúappukopĭ wo tsukúrû

backup [bæk'ʌp] *adj* (train, plane) 予備の yóbĭ no; (COMPUT) バックアップ用の bakkúappu yôn no

◆*n* (support) 支援 shíeñ; (*also*: **backup file**) バックアップファイル bakkúappu faîru

backward [bæk'wəɾd] *adj* (movement) 後ろへの ushíro e no; (person, country) 遅れた okúreta

backwards [bæk'wəɾdz] *adv* (move, go) 後ろに（へ）ushíro ni (e); (read a list) 逆に gyakú nĭ; (fall) 仰向けに aómuke ni; (walk) 後ろ向きに ushíromuki ni

backwater [bæk'wɔːtəɾ] *n* (*fig*) 後進地 kóshiñchi

backyard [bæk'jɑːrd] *n* (of house) 裏庭 uráníwa

bacon [bei'kən] *n* ベーコン bēkon

bacteria [bæktiː'riːə] *npl* 細菌 saíkin

bad [bæd] *adj* (also: not good) 悪い warúi; (mistake, accident, injury) 大きな ôkina; (meat, food) 腐っている kusátte irú nattá

his bad leg 彼の悪い方の脚 kárě no wardí hǒ nǒ ashí

to go bad (food) 悪くなる warúku narû

bade [bæd] *pt* of **bid**

badge [bædʒ] *n* (of school etc) 記章 kishô; (of policeman) バッジ bájjî

badger [bædʒ'əɾ] *n* アナグマ anáguma

badly [bæd'liː] *adv* (work, dress etc) 下手に hetá ni; (reflect, think) 悪く warúku

badly wounded 重傷を負った jûshô wǒ ottá

he needs it badly 彼にはそれがとても必要だ kárě ni wa soré gǎ totémo hitsúyó dâ

to be badly off (for money) 生活が苦しい seíkatsu ga kurushíi

badminton [bæd'mintən] *n* バドミントン

ン badóminton

bad-tempered [bæd'tem'pərd] adj (person: by nature) 怒りっぽい okórippoí; (: on one occasion) 機嫌が悪い kigén gà warúì

baffle [bæf'əl] vt (puzzle) 困惑させる koñwaku saserú

bag [bæg] n (of paper, plastic) 袋 fukúro; (handbag) ハンドバッグ hañdobaggú; (satchel, case) かばん kabán

bags of (inf: lots of) 沢山の takúsan no

baggage [bæg'idʒ] n (luggage) 手荷物 tenímotsu

baggy [bæg'i:] adj だぶだぶの dabúdabu no

bagpipes [bæg'paips] npl バグパイプ bagúpaipu

Bahamas [bəhɑːm'əz] npl: *the Bahamas* バハマ諸島 bahámashotô

bail [beil] n (LAW: payment) 保釈金 hoshákukin; (: release) 保釈 hosháku
♦vt (prisoner: gen: grant bail to) 保釈する hosháku suru; (boat: also: bail out) ...から水をかい出す ...kará mizú wò kaídasù

on bail (prisoner) 保釈中 (の) hoshákuchû (no)

bailiff [bei'lif] n (LAW: US) 廷吏 teíri; (: BRIT) 執行吏 shíkkòri

bail out vt (prisoner) 保釈させる hosháku saserú ¶ see also bale

bait [beit] n (for fish, animal) えさ esá; (for criminal etc) おとり otóri
♦vt (hook, trap) ...にえさをつける ...ni esá wò tsukérù; (person: tease) からかう karákaú

bake [beik] vt (CULIN: cake, potatoes) オーブンで焼く ōbun de yakú; (TECH: clay etc) 焼く yakú
♦vi (cook) オーブンに入っている ōbun ni hâitte iru

baked beans [beikt-] npl ベークトビーンズ békutobìnzu

baker [bei'kər] n パン屋 pán-ya

bakery [bei'kə:ri] n (building) パン屋 pán-ya

baking [bei'kiŋ] n (act) オーブンで焼く事 ōbun de yakú koto; (batch) オーブン

で焼いたもの ōbun de yaíta mono

baking powder n ふくらし粉 fukúrakoshikô, ベーキングパウダー békingupaùdā

balance [bæl'əns] n (equilibrium) 均衡 kiñkô, バランス baránsu; (COMM: sum) 残高 záñdaka; (remainder) 残り nokóri; (scales) 天びん teñbin
♦vt (budget) ...の収入と支出を合わせる ...no shūnyū tò shíshutsu wò awáserù; (account) ...の決算をする ...no kessán wò suru; (make equal) 釣合を取る tsuríai wo torú

balance of trade 貿易収支 bóekishūshi

balance of payments 国際収支 kokúsaishūshi

balanced [bæl'ənst] adj (report) バランスの良い baránsu no yoì; (personality) 安定した añtei shita

a balanced diet 均衡食 kiñkô shòku

balance sheet n 貸借対照表 taíshakutaishôhyô, バランスシート barñsushìto

balcony [bæl'kəni:] n バルコニー barúkonì; (in theater) 天井さじき tefjôsajikì

bald [bɔːld] adj (head) はげた hágeta; (tire) 坊主になった bózu ni nattá

bale [beil] n (of paper, cotton, hay) こり kori

baleful [beil'fəl] adj (glance) 邪悪な jaáku na

bale out vi (of a plane) パラシュートで脱出する paráshùto de dasshútsū suru

ball [bɔːl] n (SPORT) 球 tamá, ボール bōru; (of wool, string) 玉 tamá; (dance) 舞踏会 butôkai

to play ball (co-operate) 協力する kyóryoku suru

ballad [bæl'əd] n (poem, song) バラード bárádo

ballast [bæl'əst] n (on ship, balloon) バラスト barásuto

ball bearings npl ボールベアリング bôrubearìngu

ballerina [bæl'əri:'nə] n バレリーナ barérìna

ballet [bælei'] n (art) バレエ barée; (an artistic work) バレエ曲 baréekyòku

ballet dancer n バレエダンサー barée-

ballistics [bəlis'tiks] n 弾道学 dańdōgaku

balloon [bəluːn'] n (child's) 風船 fúsen; (hot air balloon) 熱気球 netsúkikyū

ballot [bæl'ət] n (vote) 投票 tōhyō

ballot paper n 投票用紙 tōhyōyōshi

ballpoint (pen) [bɔːl'point] n ボールペン bōrupen

ballroom [bɔːl'ruːm] n 舞踏の間 butō no ma

balm [bɑːm] n バルサム bárūsamu

Baltic [bɔːl'tik] n: **the Baltic (Sea)** バルト海 barūtokái

balustrade [bæl'əstreid] n (on balcony, staircase) 手すり tesúri

bamboo [bæmbuː'] n (plant) 竹 takè; (material) 竹材 takúzai

ban [bæn] n (prohibition) 禁止 kińshi
♦vt (prohibit) 禁止する kińshi suru

banal [bənæl'] adj (remark, idea, situation) 陳腐な chíńpu na

banana [bənæn'ə] n バナナ bánàna

band [bænd] n (group) 一団 ichídan; (MUS: jazz, rock, military etc) バンド bańdo; (strip of cloth etc) バンド bańdo; (stripe) 帯状の物 obíjō no mono

bandage [bæn'didʒ] n 包帯 hōtai
♦vt ...に包帯を巻く ...ni hōtai wò makú

bandaid [bæn'deid'] ® (US) n バンドエイド bańdoeìdo ◊ばんそうこうの一種 bańsōkō no isshū

bandit [bæn'dit] n 盗賊 tōzoku

band together vi 団結する dańketsu suru

bandwagon [bænd'wægən] n: **to jump on the bandwagon** (fig) 便乗する bińjō suru

bandy [bæn'diː] vt (jokes, insults, ideas) やり取りする yarítòri surù

bandy-legged [bæn'diːlegid] adj がにまたの ganímata no

bang [bæŋ] n (of door) ばたんという音 bátàn to iú otò; (of gun, exhaust) ばんという音 páń to iú otò; (blow) 打撃 dagéki
♦excl ばたん páńpan
♦vt (door) ばたんと閉める batán to shimérù; (one's head etc) ぶつける butsúke-

ru
♦vi (door) ばたんと閉まる batán to shimárù; (fireworks) ばんばんと爆発する bánban to bakúhatsu surù

bangle [bæŋ'gəl] n (bracelet) 腕飾り udékazarì

bangs [bæŋz] (US) npl (fringe) 切下げ前髪 kirísagemaegamī

banish [bæn'iʃ] vt (exile: person) 追放する tsuíhō suru

banister(s) [bæn'istər(z)] n(pl) (on stairway) 手すり tesúri

bank [bæŋk] n (COMM: building, institution: also of blood etc) 銀行 gińkō, バンク báñku; (of river, lake) 岸 kishí; (of earth) 土手 doté
♦vi (AVIAT) 傾く katámukù

data bank n データバンク dētabáñku

bank account n 銀行口座 gińkōkòza

bank card n ギャランティーカード gyarántīkàdo ◊小切手を使う時に示すカード.カードのサインと小切手のサインが照合される kogíttè wo tsukáū tokí nì shimésu kàdo. kàdo no saín to kogíttè no saín ga shōgō sarerū

banker [bæŋ'kər] n 銀行家 gińkōka

banker's card (BRIT) n = **bank card**

Bank Holiday (BRIT) n 銀行定休日 gińkōteikyūbi

banking [bæŋ'kiŋ] n 銀行業 gińkōgyō

banknote [bæŋk'nout] n 紙幣 shíhèi

bank on vt fus ...を当てにする ...wo atéyòri ni suru

bank rate n 公定歩合 kōteibuai

bankrupt [bæŋk'rʌpt] adj (person, organization) 倒産した tōsan shita
to go bankrupt 倒産する tōsan suru
to be bankrupt 返済能力がない hensainōryoku ga naí

bankruptcy [bæŋk'rʌptsi:] n (COMM) 倒産 tōsan

bank statement n 勘定照合表 kańjōshōgōhyō

banner [bæn'ər] n (for decoration, advertising) 横断幕 ōdańmaku; (in demonstration) 手持ち横断幕 temóchi ōdańmaku

banns [bænz] npl: **the banns** 結婚予告

kekkon-yokóku

banquet [bǽŋkwit] n 宴会 eñkai

baptism [bǽptizəm] n (REL) 洗礼 señrei

baptize [bæptáiz'] vt ...に洗礼を施す ...ni
señrei wò hodókosū

bar [bɑːr] n (place: for drinking) バー bâ;
(counter) カウンター kaúntā; (rod: of
metal etc) 棒 bố; (slab: of soap) 1個 ikkó;
(fig: obstacle) 障害 shôgai; (prohibition)
禁止 kíñshi; (MUS) 小節 shôsetsu

♦vt (road) ふさぐ fuságu; (person) ...が
...するのを禁止する ...ga ...surú no wò
kíñshi suru; (activity) 禁止する kíñshi
suru

a bar of chocolate 板チョコ itachoko

the Bar (LAW: profession) 弁護士 beñgoshi ◇総称 sôshō

bar none 例外なく reigai nakú

barbaric [bɑːrbǽrik] adj (uncivilized,
cruel) 野蛮な yában na

barbarous [bɑːr'bərəs] adj (uncivilized,
cruel) 野蛮な yában na

barbecue [bɑːr'bəkjuː] n (grill) バーベキ
ューこんろ bắbekyūkoñro; (meal, party)
バーベキューパーティ bắbekyūpāti

barbed wire [bɑːrbd-] n 有刺鉄線 yúshi-
tessèn, バラ線 barásen

barber [bɑːr'bər] n 理髪師 ríhatsushì, 床
屋 tokóya

bar code n (on goods) バーコード bắkòdo

bare [beːr] adj (naked: body) 裸の hadáka no; (: tree) 葉の落ちた ha no óchìta;
(countryside) 木のない ki no nái; (minimum: necessities) ほんの hoñno

♦vt (one's body, teeth) むき出しにする
mukídashi ni suru

bareback [beːr'bæk] adv くらなしで ku-
ránashī de

barefaced [beːr'feist] adj (lie, cheek) 厚
かましい atsúkamashiī

barefoot [beːr'fut] adj 裸足の hadáshi
no

♦adv 裸足で hadáshi de

barely [beːr'liː] adv (scarcely) 辛うじて
károjite

bargain [bɑːr'gin] n (deal, agreement) 取
引 toríhìki; (good buy) 掘出し物 horída-

shimono, バーゲン bâgen

♦vi (negotiate): **to bargain (with
someone)** (...と) 交渉する (...to) kôshō
suru; (haggle) 駆引きする kakéhìki suru

into the bargain おまけに o-máke ni

bargain for vt fus: **he got more than
he bargained for** 彼はそんな結果を予
想していなかった kárè wa soñna kekká
wò yosô shite inakàtta

barge [bɑːrdʒ] n (boat) はしけ hashíke

barge in vi (enter) いきなり入り込む ikí-
nari hairikomù; (interrupt) 割込む waríi-
komù

bark [bɑːrk] n (of tree) 皮 kawá; (of dog)
ほえ声 hoégoe

♦vi (dog) ほえる hoérù

barley [bɑːr'liː] n 大麦 ômugi

barley sugar n 氷砂糖 kôrizatò

barmaid [bɑːr'meid] n 女性バーテン jo-
séibàten

barman [bɑːr'mən] (pl **barmen**) n バーテ
ン bâten

barn [bɑːrn] n 納屋 náya

barometer [bərɑːm'itər] n (for weather)
気圧計 kiátsukei

baron [bær'ən] n (nobleman) 男爵 dañ-
shaku; (of press, industry) 大立て者 ôdate-
temòno

baroness [bær'ənis] n 男爵夫人 dañshaku-
fujìn

barracks [bær'əks] npl (MIL) 兵舎 heísha

barrage [bərɑːʒ'] n (MIL) 弾幕 dañmaku;
(dam) ダム dámù; (fig: of criticism,
questions etc) 連発 reñpatsu

barrel [bær'əl] n (of wine, beer) たる tarú; (of oil) バレル bárèru; (of gun) 銃身
júshin

barren [bær'ən] adj (land) 不毛の fumô
no

barricade [bær'əkeid] n バリケード baríkèdo

♦vt (road, entrance) バリケードでふさぐ
baríkèdo de fuságu

to barricade oneself (in) (...に) ろう
城する (...ni) rôjō suru

barrier [bær'iər] n (at frontier,
entrance) 関門 kañmon; (fig: to prog-

ress, communication etc) 障害 shōgai

barring [bɑːrɪŋ] *prep* ...を除いて、...の nozōite

barrister [bær'istər] (BRIT) n 法廷弁護士 hōteibengōshì

barrow [bær'ou] n (wheelbarrow) 一輪車 ichírìnsha

bars [bɑːrz] npl (on window etc: grille) 格子 kōshi

behind bars (prisoner) 刑務所に[で] keímushò ni (de)

bartender [bɑːr'tendər] (US) n バーテン bāten

barter [bɑːr'tər] vt: *to barter something for something* ...を...と交換する ...wo ...to kōkan suru

base [beis] n (foot: of post, tree) 根元 nemóto; (foundation: of food) 主成分 shuséibun; (: of make-up) ファウンデーション faúndeshon; (center: for military, research) 基地 kichí; (: for individual, organization) 本拠地 hoñkyochí

◆vt: *to base something on* (opinion, belief) ...が...に基づく ...ga ...ni motózukù

◆adj (mind, thoughts) 卑しい iyáshiì

baseball [beis'bɔːl] n 野球 yakyū、ベースボール bēsubōru

basement [beis'mənt] n 地下室 chikáshìtsu

bases[1] [bei'siz] npl of **base**

bases[2] [bei'siz] npl of **basis**

bash [bæʃ] (inf) vt (beat) ぶん殴る bufnagurù

bashful [bæʃ'fəl] adj 内気な uchíkì na

basic [bei'sik] adj (fundamental: principles, problem, essentials) 基本的な kihónteki na; (starting: wage) 基本の kihón no; (elementary: knowledge) 初歩的な shohóteki na; (primitive: facilities) 最小限の saíshōgen no

basically [bei'sikli:] adv (fundamentally) 根本的に koñponteki ni; (in fact, put simply) はっきり言って hakkírì itté

basics [bei'siks] npl: *the basics* 基本 kihón

basil [bæz'əl] n メボウキ mébòki、バジル bájìru

basin [bei'sin] n (vessel) たらい taráì;

(also: **wash basin**) 洗面台 señmendai; (GEO: of river, lake) 流域 ryūìki

basis [bei'sis] (pl **bases**) n (starting point, foundation) 基礎 kisó

on a part-time/trial basis パートタイム〔見習い〕で pátotaimù(minarai)de

bask [bæsk] vi: *to bask in the sun* 日光浴をする nikkóyòku wo suru、日なたぼっこをする hinátabokkò wo suru

basket [bæs'kit] n (container) かご kagő、バスケット basúkettò

basketball [bæs'kitbɔːl] n バスケットボール basúkettobòru

bass [beis] n (part, instrument) バス bású; (singer) バス歌手 basúkashu

bassoon [bæsun'] n (MUS) バスーン básùn

bastard [bæs'tərd] n (offspring) 私生児 shiséiji; (inf!) くそ野郎 kusóyarò

bat [bæt] n (ZOOL) コウモリ kómòri; (for ball games) バット báttò; (BRIT: for table tennis) ラケット rakéttò

◆vt: *he didn't bat an eyelid* 彼は瞬き一つしなかった kárè wa mabátàki hitótsū shinákàtta

batch [bætʃ] n (of bread) 1かま分 hitōkamabùn; (of letters, papers) 1山 hitóyàma

bated [bei'tid] adj: *with bated breath* 息を殺して 1ki wo koróshite

bath [bæθ] n (bathtub) 風呂 fúrò、湯船 yúbùne; (act of bathing) 入浴 nyūyòku

◆vt (baby, patient) 風呂に入れる fúrò ni haíru

to have a bath 風呂に入る fúrò ni haíru

¶ see also **baths**

bathe [beið] vi (swim) 泳ぐ oyőgù、遊泳する yűei suru; (US: have a bath) 風呂に入る fúrò ni haíru

◆vt (wound) 洗う aráu

bather [bei'ðər] n 遊泳〔水泳〕する人 yűei(suíei) suru hito

bathing [bei'ðiŋ] n (taking a bath) 入浴 nyűyòku; (swimming) 遊泳 yűei、水泳 suíei

bathing cap n 水泳帽 suíeibò

bathing suit (BRIT **bathing costume**) n

n 水着 mizúgi

bathrobe [bæθ'roub] *n* バスローブ basúróbu

bathroom [bæθ'ru:m] *n* トイレ tóìre; (without toilet) 浴室 yokúshitsu

baths [bæðz] *npl* (also: **swimming baths**) 水泳プール suíeipúru

bath towel *n* バスタオル basútáoru

baton [bætən'] *n* (MUS) 指揮棒 shikíbō; (ATHLETICS) バトン batón; (policeman's) 警棒 keíbō

battalion [bətæl'jən] *n* 大隊 daítai

batter [bæt'ə:r] *vt* (child, wife) ...に暴力を振るう ...ni bōryokú wo furúù; (subj: wind, rain) ...に強く当たる ...ni tsúyòku atáru
♦*n* (CULIN) 生地 kíjì

battered [bæt'ə:rd] *adj* (hat, pan) 使い古した tsukáifurushíta

battery [bæt'ə:ri] *n* (of flashlight etc) 乾電池 kañdeñchì; (AUT) バッテリー battérī

battle [bæt'əl] *n* (MIL, *fig*) 戦い tatákai
♦*vi* 戦う tatákau

battlefield [bæt'əlfi:ld] *n* 戦場 señjō

battleship [bæt'əlʃip] *n* 戦艦 señkan

bawdy [bɔː'di:] *adj* (joke, song) わいせつな waísetsu na

bawl [bɔːl] *vi* (shout: adult) どなる donáru; (wail: child) 泣きわめく nakíwamekù

bay [bei] *n* (GEO) 湾 wáñ
to hold someone at bay ...を寄付けない ...wo yosétsukenaí

bay leaf *n* ゲッケイジュの葉 gekkéìju no ha, ローリエ rōrie, ベイリーフ befrīfu

bayonet [bei'ənet] *n* 銃剣 jūken

bay window *n* 張出し窓 harídashimadò

bazaar [bəzɑːr'] *n* (market) 市場 íchìba; (fete) バザー bazá

B. & B. [bi:' ænd bi:'] *n abbr* = **bed and breakfast**

BBC [bi:bi:si:'] *n abbr* (= *British Broadcasting Company*) 英国放送協会 eíkoku hōsō kyōkai

B.C. [bi:si:'] *adv abbr* (= *before Christ*) 紀元前 kigéñzen

be [bi:] (*pt* **was, were**, *pp* **been**) *aux vb* **1** (with present participle: forming continuous tenses) ...している ...shíte iru
what are you doing? 何をしていますか nánì wo shité imasù ká
it is raining 雨が降っています áme ga fúttè imasù
they're coming tomorrow 彼らは明日来る事になっています kárèra wa asú kurú koto ni náttè imásù
I've been waiting for you for hours 何時間もあなたを待っています nánjì kan mo anátà wo máttè imásù yo

2 (with *pp*: forming passives) ...される ...saréru
to be killed 殺される korósareru
the box had been opened 箱は開けられていた hakó wa ákéraretè ita
the thief was nowhere to be seen 泥棒はどこにも見当らなかった doróbō wa dókò ni mo míàtaranakàtta

3 (in tag questions) ...ね ...né, ...でしょう ...deshō
it was fun, wasn't it? 楽しかったね tanóshikàtta né
he's good-looking, isn't he? 彼は男前だね kárè wa otókomae da ne
she's back again, is she? 彼女はまた来たの kánòjo wa matá kita nò ka

4 (+ *to* + *infinitive*) ...すべきである ...subékî de aru
the house is to be sold 家は売る事になっている ié wà urú koto ni náttè iru
you're to be congratulated for all your work 立派な仕事を完成しておめでとう rippá na shigoto wo kansei shite ōmédetō
he's not to open it 彼はそれを開けてはならない kárè wa soré wo akete wa naránaî
♦*vb + complement* **1** (*gen*) ...である ...de árù
I'm English 私はイングランド人です watákushì wa íñgurandojîn desu
I'm tired/hot/cold 私は疲れた (暑い, 寒い) watákushì wa tsúkárèta (atsúì,

samūī

he's a doctor 彼は医者です kárè wa ishá desù

2 and 2 are 4 2足す2は4 ní tasù ní wa yón

she's tall/pretty 彼女は背が高い(きれいです) kánojò wa sé ga takái(kírèi desu)

be careful/quiet/good! 注意(静かに、行儀よく)して下さい chúī(shízùka ni, gyógi yokù)shité kudasaì

2 (of health): **how are you?** お元気ですか o-génkì desu ká

he's very ill 彼は重病です kárè wa jū-byō desù

I'm better now もう元気になりました mō génkì ni narímashìta

3 (of age): ...才です ...sai desu

how old are you? 何才ですか nánsai desu ka, (幼い) 幾つですか (ōsánai) íkùtsu desu ka

I'm sixteen (years old) 16才です 16-sai kusaì desu

4 (cost): **how much was the meal?** 食事はいくらでしたか shokújì wa ikùra deshìta ká

that'll be $5.75, please 5ドル75セント頂きます gódòru nanájūgòsentō itádakimasù

♦*vi* 1 (exist, occur etc) 存在する sónzai suru

the best singer that ever was 史上最高の歌手 shijō saikō no kashū

is there a God? 神は存在するか kámì wa sónzai suru ka

be that as it may それはそれとして soré wa sore toshite

so be it それでよい soré de yoì

2 (referring to place) ...にある(いる) ...ni árù(írù)

I won't be here tomorrow 明日はここに来ません私はもう来ない watakushi wa mō kìmasèn

Edinburgh is in Scotland エジンバラはスコットランドにある ejínbàra wa sukóttòrando ni árù

it's on the table テーブルの上にあります soré wa tébùru ni árímasù

we've been here for ages 私たちはずっ

と前からここにいます watakushitàchi wa zuttó maè kara kokó ni ímasù

3 (referring to movement) 行って来る itté kurù

where have you been? どこへ行っていましたか dókò e itté imashìta ka

I've been to the post office/to China 郵便局(中国)へ行って来ました yūbìn-kyoku(chūgōku)e itté kimashìta

I've been in the garden 庭にいました niwá ni imashìta

♦*impers vb* 1 (referring to time): **it's 5 o'clock** 5時です gójì desu

it's the 28th of April 4月28日です shigátsu nijūhachìnichi dèsu

2 (referring to distance): **it's 10 km to the village** 村まで10キロメーターです murá màde jukkírometā desu

3 (referring to the weather): **it's too hot** 暑過ぎる atsúsugirù

it's too cold 寒過ぎる samúsugirù

it's windy today 今日は風が強い kyō wà kazé ga tsuyoì

2 (emphatic): **it's only me/the postman** ご心配なく、私(郵便屋さん)です go-shínpai nakù, watákushi(yūbin-ya-san)desù

it was Maria who paid the bill 勘定を払ったのはマリアでした kánjō wo haráttà no wa márià deshìta

beach [biːtʃ] *n* 浜 hamá

♦*vt* (boat) 浜に引上げる hamá ni hikfagerù

beacon [biːkən] *n* (lighthouse) 燈台 tódai; (marker) 信号燈 shíngō

bead [biːd] *n* (glass, plastic etc) ビーズ bízu; (of sweat) 玉 tamá

beak [biːk] *n* (of bird) くちばし kuchíbashi

beaker [biːkəːr] *n* (cup) コップ koppú, グラス gúràsu

beam [biːm] *n* (ARCHIT) はり harí; (of light) 光線 kōsen

♦*vi* (smile) ほほえむ hohóemù

bean [biːn] *n* マメ mamé

runner bean サヤインゲン sayáingèn

broad bean ソラマメ sorámàme

coffee bean コーヒーマメ kôhīmāme

beansprouts [biːnˈsprauts] *npl* マメモヤシ mamémoyàshi

bear [beːr] *n* (ZOOL) クマ kumá
◆*vb* (*pt* **bore**, *pp* **borne**)
◆*vt* (carry, support: weight) 支える saséru; (: responsibility) おう oû; (: cost) 払う haráù; (tolerate: examination, scrutiny, person) ...に耐える ...ni taérù; (produce: children) 産む umú
◆*vi*: **to bear right/left** (AUT) 右(左)に曲る mígi(hidári)ni magárù
to bear fruit ...に実がなる ...ni mi ga narú

beard [biːrd] *n* ひげ higé

bearded [biːrdd] *adj* ひげのある higé no arû

bearer [beːrˈər] *n* (of letter, news) 運ぶ人 hakóbu hito; (of cheque) 持参人 jisánnin; (of title) 持っている人 môttê irû hito

bearing [beːrˈiŋ] *n* (air) 態度 tâîdo; (connection) 関係 kańkei
to take a bearing 方角を確かめる hôgaku wô tashîkamerù
to find one's bearings 自分の位置を確かめる jibûn no ichí wô tashîkamerù

bearings [beːrˈiŋz] *npl* (*also*: **ball bearings**) ボールベアリング bôrubeàringu

bear out *vt* (person) ...の言う事を保証する ...no iu koto wo hoshô suru; (suspicions etc) ...の事実を証明する ...ro jijîtsu wo shômei suru

bear up *vi* (person) しっかりする shikkârî suru

beast [biːst] *n* (animal) 野獣 yajû; (inf: person) いやなやつ iyâ na yatsú

beastly [biːstˈliː] *adj* (awful: weather, child, trick etc) ひどい hídoì

beat [biːt] *n* (of heart) 鼓動 kodô; (MUS) 拍子 hyôshi, ビート bîto; (of policeman) 巡回区域 juńkaikûîki
◆*vb* (*pt* **beat**, *pp* **beaten**)
◆*vt* (strike: wife, child) 殴る nagúrù; (eggs, cream) 泡立てる awádaterù, ホイップする hoíppû suru; (defeat: opponent) ...に勝つ ...ni kátsù; (: record) 破る yabúrù
◆*vi* (heart) 鼓動する kodô suru; (rain) た

たき付ける様に降る tatákitsukerù yô ni fúrù; (wind) たき付ける様に吹く tatákitsukerù yô ni fúkù; (drum) 鳴る narú
off the beaten track へんぴな所に héńpi na tokôro ni
to beat it (*inf*) ずらかる zurákarù

beating [biːtˈiŋ] *n* (punishment with whip etc) むち打ち muchfuchi; (violence) 激しい殴り mugéshiî nagúri

beat off *vt* (attack, attacker) 撃退する gekítai suru

beat up *vt* (person) 打ちのめす uchínomesù; (mixture) かき混ぜる kakú?sn; (eggs, cream) 泡立てる awádaterù, ホイップする hoíppû suru

beautiful [bjuːˈtəfəl] *adj* (woman, place) 美しい utsúkushiî; (day, weather) 素晴らしい subárashiî

beautifully [bjuːˈtəfəliː] *adv* (play music, sing, drive etc) 見事に mígôto ni

beauty [bjuːˈtiː] *n* (quality) 美しさ utsúkushîsâ; (beautiful woman) 美女 bî̀jo, 美人 bîjîn; (*fig*: attraction) 魅力 miryôku

beauty salon *n* 美容院 bîyôin

beauty spot *n* (BRIT: TOURISM) 景勝地 keíshôchî

beaver [biːˈvər] *n* (ZOOL) ビーバー bîbâ

became [bikeimˈ] *pt of* **become**

because [bikɔːzˈ] *conj* ...だから ...dâ kâ ra, ...であるので ...de árû nodé
because of ...のため、...の為に ...no tamê, ...no sef de

beck [bek] *n*: *to be at the beck and call of* ...の言いなりになっている ...no iínari ni nattê irú

beckon [bekˈən] *vt* (*also*: **beckon to**: person) ...に来いと合図する ...ni kôî to aîzu suru

become [bikʌmˈ] (*pt* **became**, *pp* **become**) *vi* ...になる ...ni nárù
to become fat 太る futôrù
to become thin やせる yasérù

becoming [bikʌmˈiŋ] *adj* (behavior) ふさわしい fusáwashiî; (clothes) 似合う niâû

bed [bed] *n* (piece of furniture) ベッド béddô; (of coal, clay) 層 sô; (bottom: of river, sea) 底 sokô; (of flowers) 花壇 kâdân *to go to bed* 寝る nerú

bed and breakfast *n* (place) 民宿 mín-shuku; (terms) 朝食付き宿泊 chōshokutsuki shukúhaku

bedclothes [bed'klouz] *npl* シーツと毛布 shītsu to mōfu

bedding [bed'iŋ] *n* 寝具 shíngu

bedlam [bed'lam] *n* 大騒ぎ ōsawági

bedraggled [bidrag'əld] *adj* (person, clothes, hair) びしょ濡れの bishónure no

bedridden [bed'ridən] *adj* 寝たきりの netákiri no

bedroom [bed'ru:m] *n* 寝室 shishitsu

bedside [bed'said] *n*: *at someone's bedside* ...の枕元に ...no makúramòto ni

bedsit(ter) [bed'sit(əxr)] (*BRIT*) *n* 寝室兼居間 shishitsu keñ imá

bedspread [bed'spred] *n* ベッドカバー beddōkabā

bedtime [bed'taim] *n* 寝る時刻 nerú jìkóku

bee [bi:] *n* ミツバチ mitsúbàchi

beech [bi:tʃ] *n* (tree) ブナ búnà; (wood) ブナ材 bunázai

beef [bi:f] *n* 牛肉 gyúnìku
roast beef ローストビーフ rōsutobìfu

beefburger [bi:f'bəxrgəxr] *n* ハンバーガー hañbāgā

Beefeater [bi:f'i:tər] *n* ロンドン塔の守衛 rofídontō nò shuéi

beehive [bi:'haiv] *n* ミツバチの巣箱 mitsúbàchi no súbàko

beeline [bi:'lain] *n*: *to make a beeline for* まっしぐらに...に向かう masshígura ni ...ni mukáu

been [bin] *pp* of **be**

beer [bi:r] *n* ビール bìru

beet [bi:t] *n* (vegetable) サトウダイコン satódàikon, ビート bìto; (*US: also:* red beet) ビーツ bītsu

beetle [bi:t'əl] *n* 甲虫 kóchū

beetroot [bi:t'ru:t] (*BRIT*) *n* ビーツ bītsu

before [bifəxr] *prep* (of time, space) ...の前に(で) ...no máe ni(de)
◆*conj* ...する前に ...surú maè ni
◆*adv* (time, space) 前に máe ni
before going 行く前に ikú maè ni

before she goes 彼女が行く前に kánòjo ga ikú maè ni

the week before (week past) 1週間前 isshúkan maè

I've never seen it before これまで私はそれを見た事はない koré madé watákushi wà soré wò mità koto wà nái

beforehand [bifəxr'hænd] *adv* あらかじめ arákajìme, 前もって maémotte

beg [beg] *vi* (as beggar) こじきをする kojíki wò suru
◆*vt* (*also:* beg for: food, money) こい求める koímotomerù; (: forgiveness, mercy etc) 願う negáù

to beg someone to do something ...に...してくれと頼む ...ni ...shité kurè to tanómù ¶ *see also* **pardon**

began [bigan'] *pt* of **begin**

beggar [beg'əxr] *n* こじき kojíki

begin [bigin'] (*pt* **began**, *pp* **begun**) *vt* 始める hajímeru
◆*vi* 始まる hajímaru

to begin doing/to do something ...し始める ...shi hajímeru

beginner [bigin'əxr] *n* 初心者 shoshínsha

beginning [bigin'iŋ] *n* 始め hajíme

begun [bigan'] *pp* of **begin**

behalf [bihæf'] *n*: *on behalf of* (as representative of) ...を代表して ...wo daíhyō shitè; (for benefit of) ...のために ...no tamé ni

on my/his behalf 私(彼)のために watákukushi[kárè]nò tamé ni

behave [biheiv'] *vi* (person) 振舞う furúmaù; (well: *also:* behave oneself) 行儀良くする gyōgi yokù suru

behavior [biheiv'jəxr] (*BRIT* **behaviour**) *n* 行動 kódō

behead [bihed'] *vt* ...の首を切る ...no kubí wò kírù

beheld [biheld'] *pt, pp* of **behold**

behind [bihaind'] *prep* (position: at the back of) ...の後ろに(で) ...no ushíro ni (de); (supporting) ...を支援して ...wo shién shite; (lower in rank, etc) ...に劣って ...ni otótte
◆*adv* (at/towards the back) 後ろに(の方へ) ushíro ni(nò hò e); (leave, stay) 後に

átò ni

◆n (buttocks) しり shirí

to be behind (schedule) 遅れている okúrete irú

behind the scenes (fig) 非公式に hikóshiki ni

behold [bihóuld'] (*pt, pp* **beheld**) *vt* 見る mírù

beige [beiʒ] *adj* ベージュ béju

Beijing [bei'dʒiŋ'] *n* 北京 pékìn

being [bi:'iŋ] *n* (creature) 生き物 ikímòno; (existence) 存在 sofizai

Beirut [beiruːt'] *n* ベイルート beírùto

belated [bilei'tid] *adj* (thanks, welcome) 遅ればせの okúrebase na

belch [beltʃ] *vi* げっぷをする geppú súrù

◆*vt* (*gen*: belch out: smoke etc) 噴出する fufíshutsu suru

belfry [bel'fri:] *n* 鐘楼 shórò

Belgian [bel'dʒən] *adj* ベルギーの berúgī no

◆*n* ベルギー人 berúgījin

Belgium [bel'dʒəm] *n* ベルギー berúgī

belie [bilai'] *vt* (contradict) 隠す kakúsù; (disprove) 反証する hańshō suru

belief [bili:f'] *n* (opinion) 信念 shíñnen; (trust, faith) 信仰 shíñkō

believe [bili:v'] *vt* 信じる shifjirù

◆*vi* 信じる shifjirù

to believe in (God, ghosts) ...の存在を信じる ...no sofzai wŏ shifjirù; (method) ...が良いと考える ...ga yőì to kafgaerù

believer [bili:v'əːr] *n* (in idea, activity) ...が良いと考える人 ...ga yőì to kafgaeru hito; (REL) 信者 shíñja

belittle [bilit'əl] *vt* 軽視する kefshì suru

bell [bel] *n* (of church) 鐘 kané; (small) 鈴 suzú; (on door, *also* electric) 呼び鈴 yobírin, ベル bérù

belligerent [bəlidʒ'ərənt] *adj* (person, attitude) けんか腰の keñkagoshi no

bellow [bel'ou] *vi* (bull) 大声で鳴く őgoè de nakú; (person) どなる donárù

bellows [bel'ouz] *npl* (for fire) ふいご fuígo

belly [bel'i:] *n* (ANAT: of person, animal) 腹 hará

belong [bilɔːŋ'] *vi: to belong to* (person) ...の物である ...no monó de arù; (club etc) ...に所属している ...ni shozóku shite irú

this book belongs here この本はここにしまうことになっている konó hoň wa kokó ni shimaú kotó ni natté irú

belongings [bilɔːŋ'iŋz] *npl* 持物 mochímòno

beloved [bilʌv'id] *adj* (person) 最愛の saf ai no; (place) 大好きな dáfsuki na; (thing) 愛用の aíyō no

below [bilou'] *prep* (beneath) ...の下に〔で〕...no shitá ni(de); (less than: level, rate) ...より低く ...yőrì hikúkù

◆*adv* (beneath) 下に shitá ni

see below (in letter etc) 下記参照 kakísañshō

belt [belt] *n* (of leather etc: *also* TECH) ベルト berúto; (*also*: belt of land) 地帯 chítaì

◆*vt* (thrash) 殴る nagúrù

beltway [belt'wei] (*US*) *n* (AUT: ring road) 環状道路 kañjōdòro

bemused [bimjuːzd'] *adj* (person, expression) ぼう然とした bőzen to shitá

bench [bentʃ] *n* (seat) ベンチ bénchì; (work bench) 作業台 sagyōdai; (BRIT: POL) 議員席 giñseki

the Bench (LAW: judges) 裁判官 safbankan ◇総称 sőshō

bend [bend] (*pt, pp* **bent**) *vt* (leg, arm, pipe) 曲げる magérù

◆*vi* (person) かがむ kagámu

◆*n* (BRIT: in road) カーブ kābu; (in pipe, river) 曲った所 magátta tokoro

bend down *vi* 身をかがめる mi wo kagámeru

bend over *vi* 身をかがめる mi wo kagámeru

beneath [bini:θ'] *prep* (position) ...の下に〔で〕...no shitá ni(de); (unworthy of) ...のこけんに関わる ...no kokén ni kakáwarù

◆*adv* 下に shitá ni

benefactor [ben'əfæktəːr] *n* (to person, institution) 恩人 oñjin

beneficial [benəfiʃ'əl] *adj* (effect, influence) 有益な yǔeki na

beneficial (to) (...に) 有益な (...ni) yǔeki na

benefit [ben'əfit] *n* (advantage) 利益 rǐeki; (money) 手当て téate
♦*vt* ...の利益になる ...no rǐeki ni narù
♦*vi*: **he'll benefit from it** それは彼のためになるだろう soré wà kárè no tamé ni narù darò"

Benelux [ben'əlʌks] *n* ベネルクス bénérukùsu

benevolent [bənev'ələnt] *adj* (person) 温和な ofiwa na; (organization) 慈善の jízén no

benign [binain'] *adj* (person, smile) 優しい yasáshii; (MED) 良性の ryósei no

bent [bent] *pt, pp* of **bend**
♦*n* 才能 saínó
♦*adj* (*inf*: corrupt) 不正な fuséi na
to be bent on doing ...しようと心掛けている ...shfyó to kokórogakete irù

bequest [bikwest'] *n* (to person, charity) 遺贈 izó

bereaved [biri:vd'] *n*: **the bereaved** 喪中の人々 mochǔ no hitóbìto

beret [bərei'] *n* ベレー帽 bérébó

Berlin [bə:rlin'] *n* ベルリン berúrin

berm [bə:rm] (*US*) *n* (AUT) 路肩 rokáta

Bermuda [bə:rmju:d'ə] *n* バーミューダ bámyùda

berry [be:r'i:] *n* ベリー berí の総称 sōshō

berserk [bə:rsə:rk'] *adj*: **to go berserk** (madman, crowd) 暴れ出す abáredasù

berth [bə:rθ] *n* (on ship or train) 寝台 shíndai; (for ship) バース bǎsu
♦*vi* (ship) 接岸する setsúgan suru

beseech [bisi:tʃ'] (*pt, pp* **besought**) *vt* (person, God) ...に嘆願する ...ni tañgan suru

beset [biset'] (*pt, pp* **beset**) *vt* (subj: fears, doubts, difficulties) 襲う osóu

beside [bisaid'] *prep* (next to) ...の横に 〔で〕...no yokó ni〔de〕
to be beside oneself (with anger) 逆上している gyakújó shite irù
that's beside the point それは問題外です soré wà mofídaigai desu

besides [bisaidz'] *adv* (in addition) それ

に; (moreover) その上 sonó ue; (in any case) とに角 toníkaku
♦*prep* (in addition to, as well as) ...の外に ...no hoká ni

besiege [bisi:dʒ'] *vt* (town) 包囲攻撃する hōíkōgeki suru; (*fig*: subj: journalists, fans) ...に押会せる ...ni oshíyoserù

besought [biso:t'] *pt, pp* of **beseech**

best [best] *adj* (quality, suitability, extent) 最も良い mottómo yoí
♦*adv* 最も良く mottómò yókù
the best part of (quantity) ...の大部分 ...no daíbubun
at best 良くても yókùte mo
to make the best of something ...を出来るだけ我慢する ...wo dekíru dake gamáñ suru
to do one's best 最善を尽す saízen wo tsukúsù, ベストを尽くす bésùto wo tsukúsù
to the best of my knowledge 私の知っている限りでは watákushi no shitté irú kagìri de wa
to the best of my ability 私に出来る限り watákushi ni dekírù kagíri

best man *n* 新郎付添い役 shífiró tsukísoìyaku

bestow [bistou'] *vt* (honor, title): **to bestow something on someone** ...に...を授ける ...ni ...wo sazúkerù

bestseller [best'selər] *n* (book) ベストセラー besútoserà

bet [bet] *n* (wager) かけ kaké
♦*vb* (*pt, pp* **bet** or **betted**)
♦*vt* (wager): **to bet someone something** ...と...をかける ...to ...wo kakérù
♦*vi* (wager) かける kakérù
to bet money on something ...に金をかける ...ni kané wò kakérù

betray [bitrei'] *vt* (friends, country, trust, confidence) 裏切る urágirù

betrayal [bitrei'əl] *n* (action) 裏切り urágiri

better [bet'ə:r] *adj* (quality, skill, sensation) より良い yorí yoì; (health) 良くなった yókù nattá
♦*adv* より良く yorí yókù
♦*vt* (score) ...より高い得点をする ...yorí

takáí tokúten wo suru; (record) 破る ya-búrù

♦n: to get the better of ...に勝つ ...ni kátsù

you had better do it あなたはそうした方が良い anáta wa sŏ shita hŏ ga yoí
he thought better of it 彼は考え直した kárè wa kańgaenaoshita

to get better (MED) 良くなる yókù naru, 回復する kaífuku suru

better off *adj* (wealthier) ...より金があ る ...yórì kané ga arù; (more comfortable etc) ...の力が良い ...no hŏ ga yoí

betting [bet'iŋ] *n* (gambling, odds) かけ事 kakégòto

betting shop (*BRIT*) *n* 私営馬券売り場 shiéibaken-urība

between [bitwin'] *prep* (all senses) ... の間に[で] ...no aída ni[de]
♦adv 間に aída ni

beverage [bev'əridʒ] *n* 飲み物 nomímòno, 飲料 inryō

beware [biwer'] *vi*: **to beware (of)** (dog, fire) ...に用心する ...(...wo) yōjin suru

「beware of the dog」猛犬注意 mŏken-chūi

bewildered [biwil'dəːrd] *adj* (stunned, confused) 当惑した tŏwaku shita

bewitching [biwitʃ'iŋ] *adj* (smile, person) うっとりさせる uttóri saseru

beyond [bianæd'] *prep* (in space) ...の向 こうに[で] ...no mukŏ ni[de]; (past: understanding) ...を越えて ...wo koéte; (after: date) ...以降に ...ikŏ ni; (above) ...以上に ...íjŏ ni
♦adv (in space, time) 先に sakí ni

beyond doubt 疑いもなく utágai mo nakù

beyond repair 修理不可能で shūri fukánò de

bias [bai'əs] *n* (prejudice) 偏見 heñken

bias(s)ed [bai'əst] *adj* (jury) 偏見 をもった heñken wo mottá; (judgement, reporting) 偏見に基づいた heñken ni motózuità

bib [bib] *n* (child's) よだれ掛け yodárekake

Bible [bai'bəl] *n* (REL) 聖書 seísho, バイブル baíburu

biblical [bib'likəl] *adj* 聖書の seísho no

bibliography [bibliɑg'rəfi:] *n* (in text) 文献目録 buñkenmokùroku

bicarbonate of soda [baikɑr'bənit-] *n* 重炭酸ソーダ jūtansansŏda, 重曹 jūsŏ

bicker [bik'əːr] *vi* (squabble) 口論する kŏron suru

bicycle [bai'sikəl] *n* 自転車 jitéñsha

bid [bid] *n* (at auction) 付値 tsukéne; (in tender) 入札 nyūsatsu; (attempt) 試み kokóromi
♦vb (*pt* **bade** *or* **bid**, *pp* **bidden** *or* **bid**)
♦vi (at auction) 競りに加わる serí ni kuwawarù
♦vt (offer) ...と値を付ける ...to né wò tsukérù

to bid someone good day (hello) ...に今 日はと言う ...ni konnichi wa to iu; (farewell) ...にさようならと言う ...ni sayŏnara to iu

bidder [bid'əːr] *n*: **the highest bidder** 最高入札者 saíkōnyūsatsùsha

bidding [bid'iŋ] *n* (at auction) 競り serí

bide [bid] *vt*: **to bide one's time** (for opportunity) 時期を持つ jíkí wo mátsù

bidet [bidei'] *n* ビデ bídè

bifocals [baifou'kəlz] *npl* 二重焦点眼鏡 nijūshŏtenmegane

big [big] *adj* (gen) 大きい ŏkii, 大きな ŏkina

big brother 兄 áni, 兄さん nísan
big sister 姉 ané, 姉さん nèsan

bigamy [big'əmi:] *n* 重婚 jūkon

big dipper [-dip'əːr] (*BRIT*) *n* (at fair) ジェットコースター jéttokōsutā

bigheaded [big'hedid] *adj* うぬぼれた u-núboreta

bigot [big'ət] *n* (on race, religion) 偏狭な 人 heñkyŏ na hito

bigoted [big'ətid] *adj* (on race, religion) 偏狭な heñkyŏ na

bigotry [big'ətri:] *n* 偏狭さ heñkyōsa

big top (at circus) 大テント ŏtento

bike [baik] *n* (bicycle) 自転車 jitéñsha

bikini [biki:'ni:] *n* ビキニ bíkini

bilateral [bailæt'əːrəl] *adj* (agreement)

双務的な sómuteki na

bile [bail] n (BIO) 胆汁 tańjū

bilingual [bailiŋ'gwəl] adj (dictionary) 二か国語の nikákokugo no; (secretary) 二か国語を話せる nikákokugo wò hanáserù

bill [bil] n (account) 勘定書 kańjōgakí; (invoice) 請求書 sefkyūshò; (POL) 法案 hoʻan; (US: banknote) 紙幣 shíhèi; (of bird) くちばし kuchíbashi; (THEATER: of show: on the bill) 番組 bańgumi
「*post no bills*」張紙厳禁 harígamigenkin

to fit/fill the bill (fig) 丁度いい chódo iì

billboard [bil'bɔːrd] n 広告板 kőkokuban

billet [bil'it] n (MIL) 軍人宿舎 guńjinshukūsha

billfold [bil'fould] (US) n 財布 saffu

billiards [bil'jɔːrdz] n ビリヤード birfyàdo

billion [bil'jən] n (BRIT) 兆 chō; (US) 10 億 jùoku

bin [bin] n (BRIT: for rubbish) ごみ入れ gomfire; (container) 貯蔵箱 chózòbako, 瓶 bín

binary [bai'nəːri] adj (MATH) 二進法の nishínhò no

bind [baind] (pt, pp **bound**) vt (tie, tie together) 縛る shibárù; (constrain) 束縛する sokúbaku suru; (book) 製本する seíhon suru
♦n (inf: nuisance) いやな事 iyá na koto

binding [bain'diŋ] adj (contract) 拘束力のある kōsokuryòku no aru

binge [bindʒ] (inf) n: *to go on a binge* (drink a lot) 酒盛りになる sakémori ni narù

bingo [biŋ'gou] n ビンゴ bíñgo

binoculars [bənɑːk'jələːrz] npl 双眼鏡 sōgankyō

biochemistry [baioukem'istri] n 生化学 seíkagaku

biography [baiɑːg'rəfi:] n 伝記 deńki

biological [baiəlɑːdʒ'ikəl] adj (science, warfare) 生物学の seíbutsugàku no; (washing powder) 酵素洗剤 kōsosèñzai

biology [baiɑːl'ədʒi:] n 生物学 seíbutsu-

gàku

birch [bəːrtʃ] n (tree) カバノキ kabá no ki; (wood) カバ材 kabázai

bird [bəːrd] n (ZOOL) 鳥 torf; (BRIT: inf: girl) 女の子 ofina no ko

bird's-eye view [bəːrdzaiz-] n (aerial view) 全景 zefkei; (overview) 概観 gaíkan

bird-watcher [bəːrdwɑːtʃəːr] n バード ウォッチャー bádowotchā

bird-watching [bəːrdwɑːtʃiŋ] n バード ウォッチング bádowotchìngu

Biro [bai'rou]® n ボールペン bőrupen

birth [bəːrθ] n (of baby, animal, also fig) 誕生 tańjō

to give birth to (BIO: subj: woman, animal) ...を生む ...wo umú

birth certificate n 出生証明書 shusshō (shusséi) shōmeisho

birth control n (policy) 産児制限 sańjiseìgen; (methods) 避妊 hinfn

birthday [bəːrθ'dei] n 誕生日 tańjōbi
♦cpd (cake, card, present etc) 誕生日の tańjōbi no ¶ see also **happy**

birthplace [bəːrθ'pleis] n (country, town etc) 出生地 shusshōchì (shusséichi), (: in more precise sense) 故郷 umárekokyò; (house place) 生家 seíka

birth rate n 出生率 shusshōritsu (shusséiritsu)

Biscay [bis'kei] n: *the Bay of Biscay* ビスケー湾 bisúkēwàn

biscuit [bis'kit] (BRIT) n ビスケット bisúkettò

bisect [baisekt'] vt (angle etc) 二等分する nitóbun suru

bishop [biʃ'əp] n (REL: Catholic etc) 司教 shíkyò; (: Protestant) 監督 kańtoku; (: Greek Orthodox) 主教 shúkyò; (CHESS) ビショップ bíshòppu

bit [bit] pt of **bite**
♦n (piece) 欠片ら kakéra; (COMPUT) ビット bíttò; (of horse) はみ hámì

a bit of 少しの sukóshì no, ちょっとの chottó no

a bit mad ちょっと頭がおかしい chóttó atáma ga okáshiì

a bit dangerous ちょっと危ない chóttó abúnaì

bit by bit 少しずつ sukóshi zutsù

bitch [bitʃ] *n* (dog) 雌犬 mesúinu; (*inf!*: woman) あま ámà

bite [bait] (*pt bit*, *pp bitten*) *vt* (subj: person) かむ kámù; (: dog etc) ...にかみ付く ...ni kamítsukù; (: insect etc) 刺す sásù
♦*vi* (dog etc) かみ付く kamítsukù; (insect etc) 刺す sásù
♦*n* (insect bite) 虫刺され mushísasàre; (mouthful) 一口 hitókuchi

to bite one's nails つめをかむ tsúme wo kámù

let's have a bite to eat (*inf*) 何か食べよう nánì ka tabéyò

bitten [bit'ən] *pp of* bite

bitter [bit'əːr] *adj* (person) 恨みを持った urámi wo mottá; (taste, experience, disappointment) 苦い nigái; (wind) 冷たい tsumétaì; (struggle) 激しい hagéshiì; (criticism) 辛らつな shiríratsu na
♦*n* (*BRIT*: beer) ビター苦ビ◇ホップの利いた苦いビール hoppú no kíita nigáì bíru

bitterness [bit'əːrnis] *n* (anger) 恨み urámi; (bitter taste) 苦み nigámi

bizarre [bizɑːr'] *adj* (conversation, contraption) 奇妙な kímyò na

blab [blæb] (*inf*) *vi* (to the press) しゃべる shabérù

black [blæk] *adj* (color) 黒い kuróì; (person) 黒人の kokújin no; (tea, coffee) ブラックの burákkù no
♦*n* (color) 黒 kúrò; (person): *Black* 黒人 kokújin
♦*vt* (*BRIT*: INDUSTRY) ボイコットする boíkottò suru

black humor ブラックユーモア burákkuyūmoa

to give someone a black eye ...を殴って目にあざを作る ...wo nagútte me ni azá wo tsukúrù

black and blue (bruised) あざだらけの azá daràke no

to be in the black (in credit) 黒字である kuróji de arù

blackberry [blæk'bəːriː] *n* ブラックベリー burákkuberì ◇キイチゴの一種 kíichigo no ísshù

blackbird [blæk'bəːrd] *n* (European bird) クロウタドリ kuróutadòri

blackboard [blæk'bɔːrd] *n* 黒板 kokúban

black coffee *n* ブラックコーヒー burákku kōhī

blackcurrant [blækkʌr'ənt] *n* クロスグリ kuró sugùri

blacken [blæk'ən] *vt* (*fig*: name, reputation) 汚す kegásù

black ice (*BRIT*) *n* (on road) 凍結路面 tóketsuromèn

blackleg [blæk'leg] (*BRIT*) *n* (INDUSTRY) スト破り sutóyabùri

blacklist [blæk'list] *n* ブラックリスト burákkurisùto

blackmail [blæk'meil] *n* ゆすり yusúri
♦*vt* ゆする yusúrù

black market *n* やみ市 yamíichi

blackout [blæk'aut] *n* (MIL) 灯火管制 tókakañsei; (power cut) 停電 teíden; (TV, RADIO) 放送 中止 hôsōchūshi; (faint) 一時的意識喪失 ichíjiteki íshikishitsu, ブラックアウト burákkuàto

Black Sea *n*: *the Black Sea* 黒海 kókkai

black sheep *n* (*fig*) 持て余し者 motéamashimòno

blacksmith [blæk'smiθ] *n* 鍛冶屋 kajíya

black spot (*BRIT*) *n* (AUT) 事故多発地点 jikótahàtsuchitèn; (for unemployment etc) ...が深刻になっている地域 ...ga shínkoku ni nattè irú chíiki

bladder [blæd'əːr] *n* (ANAT) ぼうこう bôkō

blade [bleid] *n* (of knife, sword) 刃 há; (of propeller) 羽根 hané

a blade of grass 草の葉 kusá no ha

blame [bleim] *n* (for error, crime) 責任 sekínìn
♦*vt*: *to blame someone for something* ...のせいにする ...wo ...no seí ni suru
to be to blame 責任が...にある sekínin ga ...ni arù

blameless [bleim'lis] *adj* (person) 潔白な keppáku na

bland [blænd] *adj* (taste, food) 味気ない ajíke naì

blank [blæŋk] *adj* (paper etc) 空白の kúhaku no; (look) ぼう然とした bőzen to shitá

♦ n (of memory) 空白 kúhaku; (in form) 空所 kúsho; (also: **blank cartridge**) 空包 kúhō

a blank sheet of paper 白紙 hakúshi

blank check n 金額未記入の小切手 kiñgakumikí-nyū no kogíttè

blanket [blæŋˈkit] n (of cloth) 毛布 mőfu; (of snow, fog etc) 一面の… ichímen no …

blare [blɛːr] vi (brass band, horns, radio) 鳴り響く naríhibikù

blasé [blɑːzei'] adj (reaction, tone) 無関心な mukáñshin na

blasphemy [blæsˈfəmiː] n (REL) 冒とく bőtoku

blast [blæst] n (of wind) 突風 toppú; (of explosive) 爆発 bakúhatsu

♦ vt (blow up) 爆破する bakúha suru

blast-off [blæstˈɔːf] n (SPACE) 発射 hasshá

blatant [blei'tənt] adj (discrimination, bias) 露骨な rokótsu na

blaze [bleiz] n (fire) 火事 kájì; (fig: of color, glory) きらめき kirámeki; (of publicity) 大騒ぎ ōsawägi

♦ vi (fire) 燃え盛る moésakerù; (guns) 続け様に発砲する tsuzúkezama ni happó suru; (fig: eyes) 怒りで燃える ikári de moérù

♦ vt: *to blaze a trail* (fig) 先べんを付ける señben wo tsúkerù

blazer [blei'zər] n (of school, team etc) ブレザー buréza

bleach [bliːtʃ] n (also: **household bleach**) 漂白剤 hyőhakuzài

♦ vt (fabric) 漂白する hyőhaku suru

bleached [bliːtʃt] adj (hair) 漂白した hyőhaku shitá

bleachers [bliː'tʃərz] (US) npl (SPORT) 外野席 gaíyaseki

bleak [bliːk] adj (countryside) もの寂しい monősabishii; (weather) 寒々とした sabűzabu to shitá; (prospect, situation) 暗い kurái; (smile) 悲しそうな kanáshisō na

bleary-eyed [bliː'riːaid] adj 目がしょぼしょぼしている me ga shobóshobo shité irú

bleat [bliːt] vi (goat, sheep) 鳴く nakú

bled [bled] pt, pp of **bleed**

bleed [bliːd] (pt, pp **bled**) vi (MED) 出血する shukkétsu suru

my nose is bleeding 鼻血が出ている hanáji ga déte irú

bleeper [bliː'pər] n (device) ポケットベル pokétto berú

blemish [blem'iʃ] n (on skin) 染み shimí; (on fruit) 傷 kizú; (on reputation) 汚点 otéñ

blend [blend] n (of tea, whisky) 混合物 koñgō, ブレンド buréndo

♦ vt 混ぜ合せる mazéawaserù, 混合する koñgō suru

♦ vi (colors etc: also: **blend in**) 溶け込む tokékomū

bless [bles] (pt, pp **blessed** or **blest**) vt (REL) 祝福する shukúfuku suru

bless you! (after sneeze) お大事に o-dáiji ni

blessing [bles'iŋ] n (approval) 承認 shőnin; (godsend) 恵み megúmi; (REL) 祝福 shukúfuku

blew [bluː] pt of **blow**

blight [blait] vt (hopes, life etc) 駄目にする damé ni suru

blimey [blai'miː] (BRIT: inf) excl おや oyá

blind [blaind] adj (MED) 盲目の mőmoku no; (pej) めくらの mekúra no; (euphemistically) 目の不自由な me no fujíyū na; (fig: **blind (to)** (…に) 見る目がない (…wo) mírù mé ga nái

♦ n (for window) ブラインド buráindo; (: also: **Venetian blind**) ベネシアンブラインド benéshian buráindo

♦ vt (MED) 失明させる shitsúmei sasérù; (dazzle) …の目をくらます …no me wo kurámasù; (deceive) だます damásù

the blind (blind people) 盲人 mőjin ◇総称 sőshō

blind alley n (fig) 行き詰り yukízumari

blind corner (BRIT) n 見通しの悪い曲り角 mitőshi no warúi magárikadō

blindfold [blaind'fould] n 目隠し mekákushi

◆*adj* 目隠しをした mekákūshi wo shitá
◆*adv* 目隠しをして mekákūshi wo shité
◆*vt* 目隠しする mekákūshi suru

blindly [blaind'li:] *adv* (without seeing) よく見ないで yókù mináide; (without thinking) めくら滅法に mekúrameppó ni

blindness [blaind'nis] *n* (MED) 盲目 mōmoku; (euphemistically) 目の障害 me no shōgai

blind spot *n* (AUT) 死角 shikáku; (*fig*: weak spot) 盲点 mōten

blink [bliŋk] *vi* (person, animal) 瞬く mabátakù; (light) 点滅する teñmetsu suru

blinkers [bliŋk'ə:rz] *npl* 馬の目隠し umá no mekákūshi

bliss [blis] *n* (complete happiness) 至福 shìfúkù

blister [blis'tə:r] *n* (on skin) 水膨れ mizúbukùre; (in paint, rubber) 気胞 kihō
◆*vi* (paint) 気胞ができる kihō ga dekirù

blithely [blaið'li:] *adv* (proceed, assume) 軽率に kefsotsu ni

blitz [blits] *n* (MIL) 空襲 kūshū

blizzard [bliz'ə:rd] *n* 吹雪 fubúkì, ブリザード burízàdo

bloated [blou'tid] *adj* (face, stomach: swollen) はれた haréta; (person: full) ぶくぶく食べた taráfūku tabèta

blob [bla:b] *n* (of glue, paint) 滴 shizúkù; (something indistinct) はっきり見えないもの hakkírì miénài monó

bloc [bla:k] *n* (POL) 連合 reñgō, ブロック burókků

block [bla:k] *n* (of buildings) 街区 gáìku, ブロック burókků; (of stone, wood) ブロック burókků; (in pipes) 障害物 shōgáìbutsu
◆*vt* (entrance, road) 塞ぐ fuságu; (progress) 邪魔する jamá suru

block of flats (BRIT) *n* マンション mañshon

mental block 精神的ブロック sefshinteki burokkū

blockade [bla:keid'] *n* 封鎖 fūsa

blockage [bla:k'idʒ] *n* 閉そく hefsoku

blockbuster [bla:k'bʌstə:r] *n* (film, book) センセーション sefséshon

block letters *npl* 活字体 katsújitai

bloke [blouk] (BRIT: *inf*) *n* 男 otóko, 野郎 yárō

blond(e) [bla:nd] *adj* (hair) 金髪の kiñpatsu no, ブロンドの buróñdo no
◆*n* (woman) 金髪の女性 kiñpatsu no josèi, ブロンド buróñdo

blood [blʌd] *n* (BIO) 血 chi, 血液 ketsúékì

blood donor *n* 献血者 kefketsūsha

blood group *n* 血液型 ketsúekigata

bloodhound [blʌd'haund] *n* ブラッドハウンド buráddohaùndo

blood poisoning [-pɔi'zəniŋ] *n* 敗血症 hafketsushō

blood pressure *n* 血圧 ketsúatsu

bloodshed [blʌd'ʃed] *n* 流血 ryūketsu

bloodshot [blʌd'ʃa:t] *adj* (eyes) 充血した júketsu shitá

bloodstream [blʌd'stri:m] *n* 血流 ketsúryū

blood test *n* 血液検査 ketsúekikeñsa

bloodthirsty [blʌd'θə:rsti:] *adj* (tyrant, regime) 血に飢えた chi ni úèta

blood vessel *n* 血管 kekkán

bloody [blʌd'i:] *adj* (battle) 血みどろの chimídoro no; (nose) 鼻血を出した hanáji wo dashìta; (BRIT: *inf!*): **this bloody ...** くそいまいましい ... kusóttare...

bloody strong/good (*inf!*) すごく強い (良い) sugóku tsuyóì(yoì)

bloody-minded [blʌd'maind'did] (BRIT: *inf*) *adj* 意地悪な ijíwàru na

bloom [blum] *n* (BOT: flower) 花 haná
◆*vi* (tree) ...の花が咲く ... no haná ga sakú; (flower) 咲く sakú

blossom [bla:s'əm] *n* (BOT) 花 haná
◆*vi* (BOT) 咲く haná ga sakú; (*fig*): **to blossom into** 成長して ...になる sefchōshite ...ni narú

blot [bla:t] *n* (on text) 染み shimí; (*fig*: on name etc) 傷 kizú
◆*vt* (with ink etc) 汚す yogósu

blotchy [bla:tʃ'i:] *adj* (complexion) 染みだらけの shimídarake no

blot out *vt* (view) 見えなくする miénàku suru; (memory) 消す kesú

blotting paper [bla:t'iŋ-] *n* 吸取り紙 sutórigàmi

blow [blou] n (punch etc: *also fig*) 打撃 dagéki; (with sword) 一撃 ichígeki
♦vb (pt blew, pp blown)
♦vi (wind) 吹く fukú; (person) 息を吹きける iki wo fukíkakerú
♦vt (subj: wind) 吹き飛ばす fukítobasú; (instrument, whistle) 吹く fukú; (fuse) 飛ばす tobásu

to blow one's nose 鼻をかむ haná wo kamú

blow away vt 吹飛ばす fukítobasú

blow down vt (tree) 吹倒す fukítaosú

blow-dry [blou'drai] n (hairstyle) ブロー仕上げ buróshiàge

blowlamp [blou'læmp] (BRIT) n = blowtorch

blow off vt (hat etc) 吹飛ばす fukítobasú

blow out vi (fire, flame) 吹消す fukíkesú

blow-out [blou'aut] n (of tire) パンク pañku

blow over vi (storm) 静まる shizúmarù; (crisis) 収まる osámarù

blowtorch [blou'tɔːrtʃ] n ブローランプ buróraňpu, トーチランプ tóchiraňpu

blow up vi (storm) 起きる okíru; (crisis) 起る okórù
♦vt (bridge: destroy) 爆破する bakúha suru; (tire: inflate) 膨らます fukúramasu; (PHOT: enlarge) 引延ばす hikínobasú

blue [blu:] adj (color) 青い aóì, ブルーの burú no; (depressed) 憂うつな yúutsu na

a blue film ポルノ映画 porúnoeîga

a blue joke わいせつなジョーク waísetsu na jòku

out of the blue (fig) 青天のへきれきの様に seîten no hekíreki no yó ni

bluebell [blu:'bel] n ツルボ tsurúbò

bluebottle [blu:'baːtəl] n (insect) アオバエ aóbae

blueprint [blu:'print] n (fig): a blueprint (for) ...(の) 計画 ...(no) keíkaku, ...(の) 青写真 ...(no) aójashìn

blues [bluz] npl: the blues (MUS) ブルース burúsu

bluff [blʌf] vi (pretend, threaten) はったりを掛ける hattári wo kakérù
♦n (pretense) はったり hattári

to call someone's bluff ...に挑戦する ...ni chósen suru

blunder [blʌn'dəːr] n (political) へま héma
♦vi (bungle something) へまをする héma wo suru

blunt [blʌnt] adj (pencil) 先が太い sakí ga futóì; (knife) 切れない kirénaì; (person, talk) 率直な sotchóku na

blur [bləːr] n (shape) かすんで見える物 kasúnde miérù monó
♦vt (vision) くらます kurámasu; (distinction) ぼかす bokásù

blurb [bləːrb] n (for book, concert etc) 宣伝文句 señdenmoňku

blurt out [bləːrt-] vt 言い抜けに言い出す dashínuke ni ídasù

blush [blʌʃ] vi (with shame, embarrassment) 赤面する sekímen suru
♦n 赤面 sekímen

blustering [blʌs'təːriŋ] adj (person) 威張り散らす ibárichirasù

blustery [blʌs'təːri] adj (weather) 風の強い kazé no tsuyóì

boar [bɔːr] n イノシシ inóshishì

board [bɔːrd] n (cardboard) ボール紙 bōrugami; (wooden) 板 itá; (on wall: notice board) 掲示板 keíjiban; (for chess etc) ...盤 ...bañ; (committee) 委員会 ifňkai; (in firm) 役員会 yakúiňkai; (NAUT, AVIAT): on board ...に乗る ...ni notte
♦vt (ship, train) ...に乗る ...ni norú

full/half board (BRIT) 3食(2食)付き sañshoku(nishóku)tsukí

board and lodging 賄い付き下宿 makánaitsuki geshùku

to go by the board (fig) 捨てられる sutérareru

boarder [bɔːr'dəːr] n (SCOL) 寄宿生 kishúkusêi

boarding card [bɔːr'diŋ-] n = boarding pass

boarding house n 下宿屋 geshúkuya

boarding pass n (AVIAT, NAUT) 搭乗券 tójōken

boarding school n 全寮制学校 zefiryōseigakkō

board room n 役員会議室 yakúinkaigíshìtsu

board up vt (door, window) ...に板を張る ...ni itá wo harú

boast [boust] vi to boast (about/of) (...を) 自慢する (...wo) jimán suru

boat [bout] n (small) ボート bōto; (ship) 船 fúne

boater [bou'tər] n (hat) かんかん帽 kańkańbō

boatswain [bou'sən] n 甲板長 kōhańchō, ボースン bōsun

bob [bɑːb] vi (boat, cork on water: also: bob up and down) 波に揺れる namí ni yuréru

bobby [bɑːbiː] (BRIT: inf) n (policeman) 警官 keíkan

bobsleigh [bɑːbslei] n ボブスレー bobúsurē

bob up vi (appear) 現れる aráwarerú

bode [boud] vi to bode well/ill (for) (...にとって) 良い (悪い) 前兆である (...ni totté) yoí[warúi] zeńchō de arú

bodily [bɑːd'əliː] adj (needs, functions) 身体の shíntai no
♦adv (lift, carry) 体ごと karádagoto

body [bɑːd'iː] n (ANAT: gen) 体 karáda, 身体 shíntai; (corpse) 死体 shitái; (object) 物体 búttai; (main part) 本体 hóntai; (of car) 車体 shatái, ボディー bódì; (fig: group) 団体 dańtai; (: organization) 組織 sóshìki; (quantity: of facts) 量 ryō; (of wine) こく kokú

body-building [bɑːd'iːbil'diŋ] n ボディービル bodíbìru

bodyguard [bɑːd'iːgɑːrd] n (of statesman, celebrity) 護衛 goéi, ボディーガード bodígādo

bodywork [bɑːd'iːwəːrk] n (AUT) 車体 shatái

bog [bɑːg] n (GEO) 沼沢地 shōtakúchì
♦vt to get bogged down 泥沼にはまり込む dorónuma ni hamárikomu

boggle [bɑːg'əl] vi the mind boggles 理解できない ríkai dekínài

bogus [bou'gəs] adj (claim, workman etc) 偽の nisé no

boil [boil] vt (water) 沸かす wakásu; (eggs, potatoes etc) ゆでる yudéru
♦vi (liquid) 沸く wakú; (fig: with anger) かんかんに怒る kańkan ni okóru; (: with heat) うだるような暑さになる udáru yō na atsúsa ni naru
♦n (MED) 出来物 dekímonò
to come to a (US)/the (BRIT) boil 沸き始める wakíhajimerù

boil down to vt fus (fig) 要するに...である yō surù ni ...de arù

boiled egg [boild-] n ゆで卵 yudétamàgo

boiled potatoes npl ゆでジャガイモ yudéjagáimo

boiler [boi'lər] n (device) ボイラー bóirā

boiler suit (BRIT) n つなぎの作業着 tsunági no sagyōgi

boiling point [boi'liŋ-] n (of liquid) 沸騰点 fúttōten

boil over vi (kettle, milk) 吹こぼれる fukíkoborerù

boisterous [bois'tərəs] adj (noisy, excitable: person, crowd) 騒がしい sozóshìi

bold [bould] adj (brave) 大胆な daítan na; (pej: cheeky) ずうずうしい zúzūshìi; (pattern) 際立った kiwádattà; (line) 太い futói; (color) 派手な hadé na

Bolivia [bouliv'iːə] n ボリビア boríbìa

bollard [bɑːl'əːrd] (BRIT) n (AUT) 標識柱 hyōshíkichù つ安全地帯などを示す ańzenchítài nadò wo shimésù

bolster [boul'stəːr] n (pillow) 長まくら nagámakùra

bolster up vt (case) 支持する shíjî suru

bolt [boult] n (lock) ラッチ rátchì; (with nut) ボルト bórùto
♦adv: bolt upright 背筋を伸ばして seśuji wo nobáshite
♦vt (door) ...のラッチを掛ける ...no ratchì wo kakérù; (also: bolt together) ボルトで止める borúto de toméru; (food) 丸のみする marúnomi suru
♦vi (run away: horse) 逃出す nigédasu

bomb [bɑːm] n (device) 爆弾 bakúdan
♦vt 爆撃する bakúgeki suru

bombard [bɑːmbɑːrd'] vt (MIL: with big guns etc) 砲撃する hōgeki suru; (: from planes) 爆撃する bakúgeki suru; (fig: with questions) ...に追撃する ...ni afbseru

bombardment [bɔmˈbɑːdmənt] n: **bombardment from guns** 砲撃 hōgeki **bombardment from planes** 爆撃 bakúgeki

bombastic [bɔmbæsˈtik] adj (person, language) もったい振った mottáibuttà

bomb disposal n: **bomb disposal unit** 爆弾処理班 bakúdanshorìhan

bomber [bɑːmˈəːr] n (AVIAT) 爆撃機 bakúgekikì

bombshell [bɑːmˈʃel] n (fig: revelation) 爆弾 bakúdan

bona fide [bouˈnafaid'] adj (traveler etc) 本物の hofímono no

bond [bɑːnd] n (of affection, also gen: link) きずな kizúna; (binding promise) 約束 yakúsoku; (FINANCE) 証券 shóken; (COMM): **in bond** (of goods) 保税倉庫で hozéisòko de

bondage [bɑːnˈdidʒ] n (slavery) 奴隷の身分 doréi no mìbun

bone [boun] n (ANAT, gen) 骨 honé
♦vt (meat, fish) 骨を抜く honé wò nukú

bone idle adj ぐうたらの gútara no

bonfire [bɑːnˈfaiəːr] n たき火 takíbi

bonnet [bɑːnˈit] n (hat: also BRIT: of car) ボンネット bofínettò

bonus [bouˈnəs] n (payment) ボーナス bônasu; (fig: additional benefit) おまけ o-máke

bony [bouˈniː] adj (MED: tissue) 骨の honé no; (arm, face) 骨張った honébattà; (meat, fish) 骨の多い honé no ōi

boo [buː] excl (to surprise someone) わっ wá; (to show dislike) ぶー bû
♦vt 野次る yajírū

booby trap [buːˈbiː-] n (MIL) 仕掛け爆弾 shikákebakùdan

book [buk] n (novel etc) 本 hóñ; (of stamps, tickets) 一つづり hitótsuzùri
♦vt (ticket, seat, room) 予約する yoyáku suru; (subj: traffic warden, policeman) ...に違反切符を書く ...ni ihánkippù wo kakú; (: referee) ...に勧告を与える ...ni kañkoku wo atáeru

bookcase [bukˈkeis] n 本棚 hóñdana

booking office [bukˈiŋ-] (BRIT) n (RAIL, THEATER) 切符売り場 kippú uríba

book-keeping [bukki-piŋ] n 簿記 bókì

booklet [bukˈlit] n 小冊子 shōsasshì, パンフレット pánfurettò

bookmaker [bukˈmeikəːr] n 馬券屋 bakén-ya

books [buks] npl (COMM: accounts) 帳簿 chōbo

bookseller [bukˈseləːr] n 本屋 hóñ-ya

bookshop [bukˈʃɑːp] n = **bookstore**

bookstore [bukˈstɔːr] n 本屋 hóñ-ya, 書店 shotén

boom [buːm] n (noise) とどろき todóroki; (in prices, population etc) ブーム bûmu
♦vi (guns, thunder) とどろく todórokù; (voice) とどろく様な声で言う todórokù yồ na koè de iú; (business) 繁盛する hañjō suru

boomerang [buːˈməraŋ] n ブーメラン bûmeran

boon [buːn] n (blessing, benefit) 有難い物 arígataì monó

boost [buːst] n (to confidence, sales etc) 増す事 masú kotó
♦vt (confidence, sales etc) 増す masú; (economy) 促進する sokúshin suru

booster [buːsˈtəːr] n (MED) ブースター bûsutā

boot [buːt] n (knee-length) 長靴 nagágutsu, ブーツ bûtsu; (also: **hiking/climbing boots**) 登山靴 tozáňgutsu; (also: **soccer boots**) サッカーシューズ sakkáshūzu; (BRIT: of car) トランク toráňku
♦vt (COMPUT) 起動する kidō suru
... **to boot** (in addition) おまけに o-máke ni

booth [buːð] n (at fair) 屋台 yátai; (telephone booth, voting booth) ボックス bokkúsu

booty [buːˈtiː] n 戦利品 sefírihin

booze [buːz] (inf) n 酒 saké

border [bɔːrˈdəːr] n (of a country) 国境 kokkyō; (also: **flower border**) ボーダー花壇 bōdákadàn; (band, edge: on cloth etc) へり herí
♦vt (road: subject: trees etc) ...に沿って

立っている ...ni sottē tattē irú; (another
country: also: **border on**) ...に隣接する
...ni rínsetsu suru

borderline [boːrdəːrlain] n (fig): **on the
borderline** 際どいところで kiwádoì to-
kóro de, ボーダーラインすれすれで bō-
dāraìn suresure de

borderline case n 決めにくいケース ki-
ménikuì kḗsu

border on vt fus (fig: insanity, brutality) ...に近い ...ni chikáì

Borders [boːrdəːrz] n: **the Borders** ボー
ダーズ州 bōdāzùshū ◊イングランド北部に
接するスコットランド南部の1州 íngurando
ni rínsetsu surú sukóttòrando nanbu
no isshū

bore [boːr] pt of **bear**
◊vt (hole) ...に穴を開ける ...ni aná wo
akérù; (oil well, tunnel) 掘る hórù; (person) 退屈させる tańkutsu sasérù
◊n (person) 詰まらない話で退屈させる人
tsumáranaì hanáshi de tańkutsu sasérù
hitő; (of gun) 口径 kōkei

to be bored 退屈する tańkutsu suru

boredom [boːrdəm] n (condition) 退屈
tańkutsu; (boring quality) 詰まらなさ
tsumáranasà

boring [boːriŋ] adj (tedious, unimagi-
native) 退屈な tańkutsu na

born [boːrn] adj: **to be born** 生れる umá-
rerù

I was born in 1960 私は1960年に生れ
ました watákushi wa sénkyûhyàkuroku-
jûnen ni umáremashìta

borne [boːrn] pp of **bear**

borough [bʌrˈə] n (POL) 区 kú

borrow [bʌrˈou] vt: **to borrow something** (from someone) ...を借りる ...wo
karírù

bosom [buzˈəm] n (ANAT) 胸 muné

bosom friend n 親友 shiń-yū

boss [bɔss] n (employer) 雇い主 yatóìnu-
shi; (supervisor, superior) 上司 jōshi, 親
方 óyakata, ボス bósù
◊vt (also: **boss around, boss about**) こき
使う kokítsukaù

bossy [bɔsˈiː] adj (overbearing) 威張り散
らす ibárichirasù

bosun [bouˈsən] n (NAUT) = **boatswain**

botany [bɑtˈəniː] n 植物学 shokúbutsu-
gàku

botch [bɑtʃ] vt (bungle: also: **botch up**)
不慣れで...をしくじる futégiwa de ...wo
shikújirì

both [bouθ] adj 両方の ryóhō no
◊pron (things, people) 両方 ryóhō
◊adv: **both A and B** AもBも A mo B
mo

both of us went, we both went 私たち
2人共行きました watákushitàchi futári-
tomo ikímashìta

bother [bɑðˈəːr] vt (worry) 心配させる
shifípai sasérù; (disturb) ...に迷惑を掛け
る ...ni méìwaku wo kakérù
◊vi (also: **bother oneself**) ...に気付かう
...ni kizúkaù
◊n (trouble) 迷惑 méìwaku; (nuisance)
いやな事 iyá na kotó

to bother doing わざわざ...する wáza-
waza ...surù

bottle [bɑtˈəl] n (container: for milk,
wine, perfume etc) 瓶 bíǹ, (of wine, whiskey etc) ボトル botórù; (amount
contained) 瓶一杯分 ippái sásèru; (baby's) ほ
乳瓶 hő-nyūbin
◊vt (beer, wine) 瓶に詰める bíǹ ni tsumérù

bottleneck [bɑtˈəlnek] n (AUT: also
fig: of supply) ネック nékkù

bottle-opener [bɑtˈəloupənəːr] n 栓抜
き seńnukì

bottle up vt (emotion) 抑える osáerù

bottom [bɑtˈəm] n (of container, sea
etc) 底 sokő; (buttocks) しり shirf; (of
page, list) 一番下 ichíbaǹ shitá no
tokóro; (of class) びり bírì
◊adj (lower: part) 下の方の 一番下 shitá no hő
no; (last: rung, position) 一番下の ichíbaǹ
shitá no

bottomless [bɑtˈəmlis] adj (funds,
store) 底なしの そうない saígeñ no naì

bough [bau] n 枝 edá

bought [bɔːt] pt, pp of **buy**

boulder [boulˈdəːr] n 大きな丸石 ōkìna
marúishi

bounce [bauns] vi (ball) 跳ね返る hanḗ-

kaéru; (check) 不渡りになる fuwátàri ni narú
♦vt (ball) 跳ねさせる hanésaserù
♦n (rebound) 跳ね返る事 hanékaerù kotó

bouncer [baun'sə:r] n (inf) (at dance, club) 用心棒 yójìnbō

bound [baund] pt, pp of **bind**
♦n (leap) 一飛び hitótòbi; (gen pl: limit) 限界 geńkai
♦vi (leap) 跳ぶ tobú
♦vt (border) …の境界になる …no kyókài ni narú
♦adj: **bound by** (law, regulation) …に拘束されている …ni kósòku sarête irú
to be bound to do something (obliged) やむを得ず…しなければならない yamú wo ezú …shínàkereba naranaí; (likely) 必ず…するだろう kanárazu …surú darò
bound for (NAUT, AUT, RAIL) …行きの …yukí no

out of bounds (fig: place) 立入禁止で tachíirikinshi de

boundary [baun'də:ri] n (border, limit) 境界 kyókài

boundless [baund'lis] adj (energy etc) 果てし無い hatéshinaì

bouquet [bu:kei'] n (of flowers) 花束 hanátaba, ブーケ búke

bourgeois [bur'ʒwɑ:] adj ブルジョア根性の buríjoakonjō no

bout [baut] n (of malaria etc) 発作 hossá; (of activity) 発作的にする事 hossáteki ni suru kotó; (BOXING etc) 試合 shiái

boutique [bu:ti:k'] n ブティック butíkku

bow¹ [bou] n (knot) チョウ結び chómusùbi; (weapon, MUS) 弓 yumí

bow² [bau] n (of the head) 会釈 éshàku; (of the head and body) お辞儀 ojígi; (NAUT: also: **bows**) 船首 seńshu, へ先 hesáki
♦vi (with head) 会釈する éshàku suru; (with head and body) お辞儀する ojígi suru; (yield): **to bow to/before** (reason, pressure) …に屈服する …ni kuppúku suru

bowels [bau'əlz] npl (ANAT) 腸 chō; (of the earth etc) 深い所 fukáì tokóro

bowl [boul] n (container) 鉢 hachí, ボール鉢; (contents) ボール一杯分 bōru ippái; (ball) 木球 mokkyū, ボール bōru
♦vi (CRICKET) 投球する tōkyū suru

bow-legged [bou'legid] adj がにまたの ganímata no

bowler [bou'lə:r] n (CRICKET) 投手 tōshu, ボーラー bōra; (BRIT: also: **bowler hat**) 山高帽 yamátakabò

bowling [bou'liŋ] n (game) ボーリング bōringu

bowling alley n (building) ボーリング場 bōringujō; (track) レーン reń

bowling green n ローンボーリング場 rōnbōringujō

bowls [boulz] n (game) ローンボーリング rōnbōringu

bow tie n チョウネクタイ chónekùtai

box [bɑ:ks] n (gen) 箱 hakó; (also: **cardboard box**) 段ボール箱 dańbōrubàko; (THEATER) ボックス bókkùsu
♦vt (put in a box) 箱に詰める hakó ni tsumérù
♦vi (SPORT) ボクシングする bókùshingu suru

boxer [bɑ:k'sə:r] n (person) ボクシング選手 bokúshingu seńshu, ボクサー bókùsā

boxing [bɑ:k'siŋ] n (SPORT) ボクシング bókùshingu

Boxing Day (BRIT) n ボクシングデー bokúshingudè

boxing gloves npl ボクシンググローブ bokúshinguguròbu

boxing ring n リング riñgu

box office n 切符売り場 kippú urìba

boxroom [bɑ:ks'ru:m] (BRIT) n 納戸 nańdo

boy [bɔi] n (young) 少年 shōnen, 男の子 otóko no kò; (older) 青年 seínen; (son) 息子 musúko

boycott [bɔi'kɑ:t] n ボイコット bofkottó
♦vt (person, product, place etc) ボイコットする bofkottó suru

boyfriend [bɔi'frend] n 男友達 otókotomòdachi, ボーイフレンド bōifurendo

boyish [bɔi'iʃ] adj (man) 若々しい wakáwakashiì; (looks, smile, woman) 少年の様な shōnen no yō na

B.R. [biːaːr] *n abbr* = **British Rail**

bra [brɑː] *n* ブラジャー burájà

brace [breis] *n* (on teeth) 固定器 kotéìki, ブレース burḗsu; (tool) 曲り柄ドリル magáriedorìru

♦*vt* (knees, shoulders) ...に力を入れる ...ni chikára wo iréru

to brace oneself (for weight) 構えて待つ kamáète matsù; (for shock) 心を静めて待つ kokóro wo shizúmetè matsu

bracelet [breis'lit] *n* 腕輪 udéwa, ブレスレット burésùretto

braces [brei'siz] (*BRIT*) *npl* ズボンつり zubóntsuri, サスペンダー sasúpeñdà

bracing [brei'siŋ] *adj* (air, breeze) さわやかな sawáyàka na

bracken [bræk'ən] *n* ワラビ warábi

bracket [bræk'it] *n* (TECH) 腕 udéganè; (group) グループ gúrùpu; (range) 層 sò; (*also*: **brace bracket**) 中括弧 chūkakkò, ブレース búrēsu; (*also*: **round bracket**) 小括弧 shōkakkò, 丸括弧 marúkakkò, パーレン pāren; (*also*: **square bracket**) かぎ括弧 kagíkakkò

♦*vt* (word, phrase) ...に括弧を付ける ...ni kakkò wo tsúkerù

brag [bræg] *vi* 自慢する jíman suru

braid [breid] *n* (trimming) モール mòru; (of hair) お下げ o-ságe

Braille [breil] *n* 点字 teñji

brain [brein] *n* (ANAT) 脳 nò; (*fig*) 頭脳 zúnò

brainchild [brein'tʃaild] *n* (project) 発案 hatsúañ; (invention) 発明 hatsúmei

brains [breinz] *npl* (CULIN) 脳みそ nōmisò; (intelligence) 頭脳 zúnò

brainwash [brein'wɑʃ] *vt* 洗脳する señnō suru

brainwave [brein'weiv] *n* 妙案 nóha

brainy [brei'niː] *adj* (child) 頭の良い atáma no yoí

braise [breiz] *vt* (CULIN) いためてから煮込む itámète kara nikómù

brake [breik] *n* (AUT) 制動装置 seídōsòchi, ブレーキ burḗki; (*fig*) 歯止め hadóme

♦*vi* ブレーキを掛ける burḗki wo kakérù

brake fluid *n* ブレーキ液 burḗkièki

brake light *n* ブレーキライト burḗkiraìto

bramble [bræm'bəl] *n* (bush) イバラ ibára

bran [bræn] *n* ふすま fusúma

branch [bræntʃ] *n* (of tree) 枝 edá; (COMM) 支店 shíteñ

branch out *vi* (*fig*): *to branch out into* ...に手を広げる ...ni te wo hirógeru

brand [brænd] *n* (trademark: *also*: **brand name**) 銘柄 meígara, ブランド burándo; (*fig*: type) 種類 shúrùi

♦*vt* (cattle) 焼印 yakíin

brandish [bræn'diʃ] *vt* (weapon) 振り回す furímawasù

brand-new [brænd'nuː'] *adj* 真新しい maátarashìi

brandy [bræn'diː] *n* ブランデー burándè

brash [bræʃ] *adj* (forward, cheeky) ずうずうしい zúzùshiì

brass [bræs] *n* (metal) 真ちゅう shiñchū

the brass (MUS) 金管楽器 kiñkangàkki

brass band *n* 吹奏楽団 sufsōgakùdan, ブラスバンド burásubañdo

brassiere [brəziːr'] *n* ブラジャー burájà

brat [bræt] (*pej*) *n* (child) がき gakí

bravado [brəvɑː'dou] *n* 空威張り karáibàri

brave [breiv] *adj* (attempt, smile, action) 勇敢な yūkan na

♦*vt* (face up to) ...に立ち向う ...ni tachímukaù

bravery [brei'vəriː] *n* 勇気 yūki

bravo [brɑː'vou] *excl* ブラボー burabò

brawl [brɔːl] *n* (in pub, street) けんか keñka

brawny [brɔː'niː] *adj* (arms etc) たくましい takúmashiì

bray [brei] *vi* (donkey) 鳴く nakú

brazen [brei'zən] *adj* (woman) ずうずうしい atsúkamashìi; (lie, accusation) 厚かましい atsúkamashìi

♦*vt*: *to brazen it out* 最後までしらばくれる saígo madè shirábakurerù

brazier [brei'ʒər] *n* (on building site etc) 野外用暖房や yagáiyō kañ-í-dañro

Brazil [brəzil'] *n* ブラジル burájiru

Brazilian [brəzil'iːən] *adj* ブラジルの bu-

rájiru no
♠ n ブラジル人 burájirujìn

breach [briːtʃ] vt (defence, wall) 突破す
る toppá suru
♠ n (gap) 突破口 toppákò; (breaking):
breach of contract 契約不履行 kefyaku-
kufirikò
breach of the peace 治安妨害 chiánbo̱-
gai

bread [bred] n (food) パン páñ

bread and butter n バターを塗ったパ
ン bátà wo nuttá páñ; (fig: source of
income) 金づる kanézuru

breadbox [bred̑bɑ̀ks] (BRIT **breadbin**)
n パン入れ páñ-irè

breadcrumbs [bred̑krʌmz] npl (gen) パ
ンくず páñkuzû; (CULIN) パン粉 páñko

breadline [bred̑lain] n: **on the breadline** 貧しい mazúshìi

breadth [bredθ] n (of cloth etc) 幅 habá;
(fig: of knowledge, subject) 広さ hírosa

breadwinner [bred̑wìnər] n (in family)
稼ぎ手 kaségite

break [breik] (pt **broke**, pp **broken**) vt
(cup, glass) 割る warú; (stick, leg, arm)
折る orú; (machine etc) 壊す kowásù;
(promise, law, record) 破る yabúrù;
(journey) 中断する chúdan suru
♠ vi (crockery) 割れる warérù; (stick,
arm, leg) 折れる orérù; (machine etc) 壊
れる kowárerù; (storm) 起る okórù;
(weather) 変る kawárù; (story, news) 報
道される hṑdō sarérù; (dawn): **dawn
breaks** 夜が明ける yó ga akérù
♠ n (gap) 破損した所 tsugéteta tokóro;
(fracture: gen) 破損 hasóñ; (: of limb) 骨
折 kossétsu; (pause for rest) 休息 kyūkè-
i; (at school) 休み時間 yasúmijìkan;
(chance) チャンス cháñsu
to break the news to someone ...に知
らせる ...ni shiráserù
to break even (COMM) 収支がとんとん
になる shūshi ga tofìton ni narù
to break free/loose (person, animal) 逃
出す nigédasu
to break open (door etc) ...を壊して開け
る ...wo kowáshite akérù
breakage [brei̯kìdʒ] n (act of breaking)

break down vt (figures, data) 分析する
buñseki suru
♠ vi (machine, car) 故障する koshō suru;
(person) 取り乱す torímidasù; (talks) 物別
れになる monówakare ni narù

breakdown [brei̯k̑daun] n (AUT) 故障
koshō; (in communications) 中断 chúdan;
(of marriage) 破たん hatán; (MED: also:
nervous breakdown) 神経衰弱 shiñkei-
suijaku; (of statistics) 分析 buñseki

breakdown van (BRIT) n レッカー車
rékkàsha

breakfast [brek̑fəst] n 朝ご飯 asá gohàn,
朝食 chōshoku

break in vt (horse etc) 慣らす narásù
♠ vi (burglar) 押入る oshírù; (interrupt)
割込む waríkomù

break-in [brei̯k̑in] n 押入り oshíri

breaking and entering [brei̯k̑iŋ
ænd entəriŋ] n (LAW) 不法侵入 fuhō-
shiñ-nyū

break into vt fus (house) ...に押入る
...ni oshírù

break off vi (branch) 折れる orérù;
(speaker) 話を中断する hanáshi wo chúdan suru

break out vi (begin: war) ぼっ発する
boppátsu suru; (: fight) 始まる hajímaru;
(escape: prisoner) 脱出する dasshútsu suru
to break out in spots/a rash にきび
(湿しん)になる níkibi(shisshìn) ni narù

breakthrough [brei̯k̑θruː] n (fig: in
technology etc) 躍進 yakúshin

break up vi (ship) 分解する buñkai suru;
(crowd, meeting) 解散する kaísan suru;
(marriage) 離婚に終る rikón ni owáru;
(SCOL) 終る owáru
♠ vt (rocks, biscuit etc) 割る warú; (fight
etc) やめさせる yamésaseru

breakwater [brei̯k̑wɔ̀tər] n 防波堤 bő-
hatei

breast [brest] n (of woman) 乳房 chíbu-
sa; (chest) 胸 muné; (of meat) 胸肉 muné-

nîkû

breast-feed [brest'fi:d] (pt, pp **breast-fed**) vt ...に母乳を飲ませる ...ni bonyū wo nomáserú
♦vi 子供に母乳を飲ませる kodómo ni bonyū wo nomáserú

breaststroke [brest'strouk] n 平泳ぎ hiráoyôgi

breath [breθ] n 息 íkî
out of breath 息を切らせて íkî wo kirásete

Breathalyser [breθ'əlaizəːr] ® n 酒気検査器 shukíkensakî

breathe [briːð] vt 呼吸する kokyú suru
♦vi 息をする kokyú suru

breathe in vt 吸込む suíkomū
♦vi 息を吸込む íkî wo suíkomū

breathe out vt 吐出す hakídasu
♦vi 息を吐く íkî wo haků

breather [briː'ðəːr] n (break) 休憩 kyúkei

breathing [briː'ðiŋ] n 呼吸 kokyú

breathless [breθ'lis] adj (from exertion) 息を切らせている íkî wo kirásete irú; (MED) 呼吸困難の kokyúkoñnan no

breathtaking [breθ'teikiŋ] adj (speed) 息が止る様な íkî ga tomáru yô na; (view) 息を飲むような íkî wo nomú yô na

bred [bred] pt, pp of **breed**

breed [briːd] (pt, pp **bred**) vt (animals) 繁殖させる hañshoku saséru; (plants) 栽培する saíbai suru
♦vi (ZOOL) 繁殖する hañshoku suru
♦n (ZOOL) 品種 hiñshu; (type, class) 種類 shúrui

breeding [briː'diŋ] n (upbringing) 育ち sodáchi

breeze [briːz] n そよ風 soyókaze

breezy [briː'zi:] adj (manner, tone) 快活な kaíkatsu na; (weather) 風の多い kazé no ôi

brevity [brev'iti:] n (shortness, conciseness) 簡潔さ kañketsusa

brew [bruː] vt (tea) 入れる iréru; (beer) 醸造する jôzô suru
♦vi (storm) 起ろうとしている okórô to shité irú; (fig: trouble, a crisis) 迫ってい

る semátte irú

brewery [bruː'əːri:] n 醸造所 jôzósho

bribe [braib] n 賄ろ waíro
♦vt (person, witness) 買収する baíshū suru

bribery [brai'bəːri:] n (with money, favors) 贈賄 zôwai

bric-a-brac [brik'əbræk] n 置物類 okímonorúi

brick [brik] n (for building) れんが réñga

bricklayer [brik'leiəːr] n れんが職人 reñgashokúnin

bridal [braid'əl] adj (gown) 花嫁の hanáyome no; (suite) 新婚者の shiñkoñsha no

bride [braid] n 花嫁 hanáyome, 新婦 shiñpu

bridegroom [braid'gruːm] n 花婿 hanámúko, 新郎 shiñrô

bridesmaid [braidz'meid] n 新婦付き添いの女性 shiñpuftsukísoi no joséi

bridge [bridʒ] n (TECH, ARCHIT) 橋 hashf; (NAUT) 船橋 señkyô, ブリッジ burijji; (CARDS, DENTISTRY) ブリッジ burijjî
♦vt (fig: gap, gulf) 乗越える norfkoerú
bridge of the nose 鼻柱 hanábashira

bridle [braid'əl] n くつわ kutsúwa

bridle path n 乗馬用の道 jôbayô no mi-chí

brief [briːf] adj (period of time, description, speech) 短い mijfkaí
♦n (LAW) 事件摘要書 jikéntekiyôsho; (gen: task) 任務 niñmu
♦vt (inform) ...に指示を与える ...ni shijf wo atáeru

briefcase [briːf'keis] n かばん kabáñ, ブリーフケース burifukêsu

briefing [briː'fiŋ] n (gen, PRESS) 説明 setsúmei

briefly [briː'li:] adv (smile, glance) ちらっと chiráttó; (explain, say) 短く mijfkakú

briefs [briːfs] npl (for men) パンツ páñtsu, ブリーフ burífu; (for women) パンティー pañtí, ショーツ shôtsu

brigade [brigeid'] n (MIL) 旅団 ryodán

brigadier [brigədi'əːr] n (MIL) 准将 juñshô

bright [brait] *adj* (*gen*) 明るい akáruí; (person, idea: clever) 利口な rikō na; (person: lively) 明朗な meírō na

brighten [brait'ən] (*also*: **brighten up**) *vt* (room) 明るくする akáruku suru; (event) 楽しくする tanóshiku suru
♦*vi* 明るくなる akáruku narú

brilliance [bril'jəns] *n* (of light) 明るさ akárusa; (of talent, skill) 素晴らしさ subárashisa

brilliant [bril'jənt] *adj* (person, idea) 天才的な teñsaiteki na; (smile, career) 輝かしい kagáyakashii; (sunshine, light) 輝く kagáyakú; (*BRIT*: *inf*: holiday etc) 素晴らしい subárashii

brim [brim] *n* (of cup etc) 縁 fuchí; (of hat) つば tsúba

brine [brain] *n* (CULIN) 塩水 shiómizu

bring [briŋ] (*pt*, *pp* **brought**) *vt* (thing) 持って来る motté kurú; (person) 連れて来る tsuréte kurú; (*fig*: satisfaction) もたらす motárasu; (trouble) 起す okósu

bring about *vt* (cause) 起こす okósu

bring back *vt* (restore: hanging etc) 引き戻させる fukkí saséru; (return: thing/person) 持って〔連れて〕帰る motté〔tsuréte〕kaerú

bring down *vt* (government) 倒す taósu; (MIL: plane) 撃墜する gekítsui suru; (price) 下げる sagérù

bring forward *vt* (meeting) 繰り上げる kuríagerù; (proposal) 提案する teían suru

bring off *vt* (task, plan) ...に成功する ...ni seíkō suru

bring out *vt* (gun) 取り出す torídasu; (meaning) 明らかにする akfráka ni suru; (publish, produce: book) 出版する shuppán suru; (: album) 発表する happyō suru

bring round *vt* (unconscious person) 正気付かせる shōkizukaserù

bring up *vt* (carry up) 上に持って来る〔行く〕ué ni motté kurú〔ikú〕; (educate: person) 育てる sodáteru; (question, subject) 持出す mochídasu; (vomit: food) 吐く hákù

brink [briŋk] *n* (of disaster, war etc) 瀬戸際 setógiwa

brisk [brisk] *adj* (tone, person) きびきびした kíbíkibi shitá; (pace) 早い hayáí; (trade) 盛んな sakán na

bristle [bris'əl] *n* (animal hair, hair of beard) 剛毛 gōmō; (of brush) 毛 ke
♦*vi* (in anger) 怒る okóru

Britain [brit'ən] *n* (*also*: **Great Britain**) 英国 eíkoku, イギリス igírisu ◇イングランド, スコットランド, ウェールズを含む íñgurañdo, sukóttorañdo, uēruzu wo fukúmù

British [brit'iʃ] *adj* 英国の eíkoku no, イギリスの igírisu no
♦*npl*: **the British** 英国人 eíkokujìn, イギリス人 igírisùjin

British Isles *npl*: **the British Isles** イギリス諸島 igírisu shotō

British Rail *n* 英国国有鉄道 eíkoku kokúyū tetsúdō

Briton [brit'ən] *n* 英国人 eíkokujìn, イギリス人 igírisùjin

brittle [brit'əl] *adj* (fragile: glass etc) 割れやすい waréyasuì; (: bones etc) もろい moróì

broach [broutʃ] *vt* (subject) 持出す mochídasu

broad [brɔːd] *adj* (street, shoulders, smile, range) 広い hirói; (general: outlines, distinction etc) 大まかな ōmaka na; (accent) 強い tsuyóì

in broad daylight 真っ昼間に mappírūma ni

broadcast [brɔːd'kæst] *n* (TV, RADIO) 放送 hōsō
♦*vt* (*pt*, *pp* **broadcast**)
♦*vt* (TV, RADIO) 放送する hōsō suru; (TV) 放映する hōei suru
♦*vi* (TV, RADIO) 放送する hōsō suru

broaden [brɔːd'ən] *vt* (scope, appeal) 広くする hírỏku suru, 広げる hirógeru
♦*vi* (river) 広くなる hírỏku narú, 広がる hírógaru

to broaden one's mind 心を広くする kokóro wo hírỏku suru

broadly [brɔːd'liː] *adv* (in general terms) 大まかに ōmaka ni

broad-minded [brɔːd'main'did] *adj* 心の広い kokóro no hirói

broccoli [brɑ:kˈɔli:] n (BOT, CULIN) ブロッコリー burókkórī

brochure [brouʃˈuːr] n (booklet) 小冊子 shōsasshī, パンフレット pánfuretto

broil [brɔil] vt (CULIN) じか火で焼く jikábi de yakú

♦**broke** [brouk] pt of **break**

♦**adj** (inf: person, company) 無一文になった mushímon ni nattá

broken [brouˈkən] pp of **break**

♦**adj** (window, cup etc) 割れた waréta; (machine: also: **broken down**) 壊れた kowáréta

a broken leg 脚の骨折 ashí no kossétsú
in broken English/Japanese 片言の英語(日本語)で katákoto no eígo[nihóngo]de

broken-hearted [brouˈkənhɑːrˈtid] adj 悲嘆に暮れた hitán ni kuréta

broker [brouˈkəːr] n (COMM: in shares) 証券ブローカー shōken burōkā; (: insurance broker) 保険代理人 hoken dairinin

brolly [brɑlˈiː] (BRIT: inf) n 傘 kása

bronchitis [brɑŋkaiˈtis] n 気管支炎 kíkánshíen

bronze [brɑnz] n (metal) 青銅 seídō, ブロンズ burónzu; (sculpture) 銅像 dōzō

brooch [broutʃ] n ブローチ burōchi

brood [bruːd] n (of birds) 一腹のひな hitóhara no hiná
♦vi (person) くよくよする kuyókuyo suru

brook [bruk] n 小川 ogáwa

broom [bruːm] n (for cleaning) ほうき hōki; (BOT) エニシダ eníshida

broomstick [bruːmˈstik] n ほうきの柄 hōki no e

Bros. abbr (= brothers) 兄弟 kyōdai

broth [brɔːθ] n (CULIN) スープ sūpu

brothel [brɑθˈəl] n 売春宿 baíshun-yadó

brother [brʌðˈəːr] n (also: **older brother**) 兄 anî, 兄さん niîsan; (also: **younger brother**) 弟 otôtô; (REL) 修道士 shūdōshi

brother-in-law [brʌðˈəːrinlɔː] (pl **brothers-in-law**) n (older) 義理の兄 giri no anî; (younger) 義理の弟 girî no otôtô

brought [brɔːt] pt, pp of **bring**

brow [brau] n (forehead) 額 hitái; (rare: gen: eyebrow) まゆ mayû; (of hill) 頂上 chōjō

brown [braun] adj (color) 褐色の kasshóku no, 茶色の chaîro no; (tanned) 日焼けした hiyáke shita
♦n (color) 褐色 kasshóku, 茶色 chaîro
♦vt (CULIN) ...に焼き目を付ける ...ni yakíme wo tsukérú

brown bread n 黒パン kurópan

brownie [brauˈniː] n (Brownie guide) ブラウニー burániī ◊ガールスカウトの幼年団員 gárusukaúto no yōnendań-in; (US: cake) チョコレートクッキーの一種 chokórētokukkī no isshú

brown paper n クラフト紙 kuráfutoshî

brown sugar n 赤砂糖 akázátō

browse [brauz] vi (through book) 拾い読みする hiróiyomi suru; (in shop) 商品を見て回る shōhin wo mité mawáru

bruise [bruːz] n (on face etc) 打撲傷 dabóku shō, あざ azá
♦vt (person) ...に打撲傷を与える ...ni dabókushō wo atáeru

brunch [brʌntʃ] n ブランチ buráńchi

brunette [bruːnetˈ] n (woman) ブルネット burúnettō

brunt [brʌnt] n: **to bear the brunt of** (attack, criticism) ...の矢面に立つ ...no yaómóte ni tatsú

brush [brʌʃ] n (for cleaning, shaving etc) ブラシ buráshi; (for painting) 刷毛 haké; (artist's) 筆 fudé, 絵筆 efūde; (quarrel) 小競り合い kozérìai
♦vt (sweep etc) ...にブラシを掛ける ...ni búráshi wo kakérú; (clean: teeth etc) 磨く migáku; (groom) ブラシでとかす búráshi de tokású; (also: **brush against**: person, object) ...に軽く触れる ...ni fúréru

brush aside vt (emotion, criticism) 無視する mushí suru

brush up vt (subject, language) 復習する fukúshū suru

brushwood [brʌʃˈwud] n (sticks) しば shibá

brusque [brʌsk] adj (person, manner) 無愛想な buáîsô na; (apology) ぶっきらぼうな bukkírabô na

Brussels [brʌs'əlz] n ブリュッセル bu-rýússèru

Brussels sprout n メキャベツ mekýábètsu

brutal [bru:t'əl] adj (person, actions) 残忍な zañnin na; (honesty, frankness) 厳しい程の kíbíshìì hodó no

brutality [bru:tæl'iti:] n 残忍さ zañnín-sa

brute [bru:t] n (person) 人でなし hitódenashi, けだもの kedámono; (animal) 獣 kemóno

♦adj: **by brute force** 暴力で bóryoku de

B.Sc. [bi:ssi:'] n abbr = **Bachelor of Science**

bubble [bʌb'əl] n (in liquid, soap) 泡 awá; (of soap etc) シャボン玉 shabóndama

♦vi (liquid) 沸く wakú; (: sparkle) 泡立つ awádatsù

bubble bath n 泡風呂 awáburo

bubble gum n 風船ガム fúsengamù

buck [bʌk] n (rabbit) 雄ウサギ osúsàgi; (deer) 雄ジカ ojíka; (US: inf: dollar) ドル dórù

♦vi (horse) 乗手を振り落そうとする no-ríte wo furótosò to surú

to pass the buck (to someone) (...に) 責任をなすり付ける (...ni) sekínin wo na-súritsukerù

bucket [bʌk'it] n (pail) バケツ bakétsu; (contents) バケツ一杯 bakétsu ippái

buckle [bʌk'əl] n (on shoe, belt) バックル bakkúru

♦vt (shoe, belt) ...のバックルを締める ...no bakkúru wo shimérù

♦vi (wheel) ゆがむ yugámu; (bridge, support) 崩れる kuzúrerù

buck up vi (cheer up) 元気を出す génki wo dasú

bud [bʌd] n (of tree, plant, flower) 芽 me

♦vi 芽を出す me wo dasú

Buddhism [buː'dizəm] n (REL) 仏教 bukkyō

budding [bʌd'iŋ] adj (actor, entrepreneur) 有望な yūbō na

buddy [bʌd'i:] n (US) (friend) 相棒 aíbò

budge [bʌdʒ] vt (object) ちょっと動かす chóttò ugókasù; (fig: person) 譲歩させる

jōho saséru

♦vi (object, person) ちょっと動く chóttò ugókù; (fig: person) 譲歩する jōho suru

budgerigar [bʌdʒ'əːrigɑːr] n セキセイインコ sekíseiìnko

budget [bʌdʒ'it] n (person's, government's) 予算 yosán, 予算案 yosán-an

♦vi: *to budget for something* ...を予算案に入れる ...wo yosán-an ni irérù

I'm on a tight budget 台所が苦しい daídokoro ga kúrushìì

budgie [bʌdʒ'i:] n = **budgerigar**

buff [bʌf] adj (color: envelope) 薄茶色 u-sóchairo

♦n (inf: enthusiast) マニア mánìa

buffalo [bʌf'əlou] (pl **buffalo** or **buffaloes**) n (BRIT) スイギュウ suígyū; (US: bison) バイソン báìson

buffer [bʌf'əːr] n (COMPUT) バッファ báffà; (RAIL) 緩衝器 kañshōki

buffet[1] [bufei'] (BRIT) n (in station) ビュッフェ byúffè; (food) 立食 risshóku

buffet[2] [bʌf't] vt (subj: wind, sea) もみ揺さぶる momíyusaburù

buffet car (BRIT) n (RAIL) ビュッフェ車 byúffēshà

bug [bʌg] n (esp US: insect) 虫 mushí; (COMPUT: of program) バグ bágù; (fig: germ) 風邪 kazé; (hidden microphone) 盗聴器 tochoki

♦vt (inf: annoy) 怒らせる okóraserù; (room, telephone etc) ...に盗聴器を付ける ...ni tochoki wo tsukérù

buggy [bʌg'i:] n (baby buggy) 乳母車 u-bágurùma

bugle [bju:'gəl] n (MUS) らっぱ rappá

build [bild] n (of person) 体格 taíkaku

♦vb (pt, pp **built**)

♦vt (house etc) 建てる tatérù, 建築する kenchiku suru; (machine, cage etc) 作る tsukúrù

builder [bil'dəːr] n (contractor) 建築業者 kenchikugyōsha

building [bil'diŋ] n (industry, construction) 建築業 kenchikugyō; (structure) 建物 tatémono, ビル birú

building society (BRIT) n 住宅金融組合 jūtakukin-yūkumíai

build up vt (forces, production) 増やす fuyásu; (morale) 高める takámeru; (stocks) 蓄積する chikúseki suru
shitá oóshi

built [bilt] pt, pp of **build**

built-in ♦adj: **built-in** (oven, wardrobes etc) 作り付けの tsukúritsuke no

built-up area [bilt̩ʌp-] n 市街化区域 shigáikakuíki

bulb [bʌlb] n (BOT) 球根 kyúkon; (ELEC) 電球 deñkyū

Bulgaria [bʌlgér'iːə] n ブルガリア burúgaria

Bulgarian [bʌlgér'iːən] adj ブルガリアの burúgaria no
♦n ブルガリア人 burúgariajiñ

bulge [bʌldʒ] n (bump) 膨らみ fukúrami
♦vi (pocket, file, cheeks etc) 膨らむ fukúramu

bulk [bʌlk] n (mass: of thing) 巨大な姿 kyodái na sugáta; (: of person) 巨体 kyotái
in bulk (COMM) 大口で óguchi de
the bulk of (most of) ...の大半 ...no taíhan

bulky [bʌl'kiː] adj (parcel) かさばった kasábatta; (equipment) 大きくて扱いにくい ōkikute atsúkainikuí

bull [bul] n (ZOOL) 雄牛 oóshi; (male elephant/whale) 雄 osú

bulldog [bul'dɔːg] n ブルドッグ burúdoggu

bulldozer [bul'douzəːr] n ブルドーザー burúdōza

bullet [bul'it] n 弾丸 dañgan

bulletin [bul'ətin] n (TV etc: news update) 速報 sokúhō; (journal) 会報 kaíhō, 紀要 kiyō

bulletproof [bul'itpruːf] adj (glass, vest, car) 防弾の bōdan no

bullfight [bul'fait] n 闘牛 tógyū

bullfighter [bul'faitəːr] n 闘牛士 tógyūshi

bullfighting [bul'faitiŋ] n 闘牛 tógyū

bullhorn [bul'hɔːrn] (US) n ハンドマイク hañdomaíku

bullion [bul'jən] n (gold, silver) 地金 jigáne

bullock [bul'ək] n 去勢した雄牛 kyoséi

bullring [bul'riŋ] n 闘牛場 tógyūjō

bull's-eye [bulz'ai] n (on a target) 的の中心 matố no chūshin

bully [bul'iː] n 弱い者いじめ yowáimono-ijíme
♦vt いじめる ijímeru

bum [bʌm] n (inf) n (backside) しり shirí; (esp US: tramp) ルンペン ruñpen; (: good-for-nothing) ろくでなし rokúdenashi

bumblebee [bʌm'bəlbiː] n クマンバチ kumáñbachi

bump [bʌmp] n (in car: minor accident) 衝突 shōtotsu; (jolt) 衝撃 shōgeki; (swelling: on head) こぶ kobú; (on road) 段差 dañsa
♦vt (strike) ...にぶつかる ...ni butsúkaru

bumper [bʌm'pəːr] n (AUT) バンパー bañpā
♦adj: **bumper crop/harvest** 豊作 hōsaku

bumper cars npl (in amusement park) バンパーカー bañpākā

bump into vt fus (strike: obstacle) ...にぶつかる ...ni butsúkaru; (inf: meet: person) ...に出くわす ...ni dekúwasu

bumptious [bʌmp'ʃəs] adj (person) うぬぼれた unúboreta

bumpy [bʌm'piː] adj (road) 凸凹な dekóboko na

bun [bʌn] n (CULIN) ロールパン rōrupan, パン菓子 (of hair) まげ magé, シニョン shíñyon

bunch [bʌntʃ] n (of flowers, keys) 束 tabà; (of bananas) 房 fusá; (of people) グループ gúrūpu

bunches [bʌntʃ'iz] npl (in hair) 左右のポニーテール sáyū no poníteru

bundle [bʌn'dəl] n (parcel: of clothes, samples etc) 包み tsutsúmi; (of sticks, papers) 束 tabà
♦vt (also: **bundle up**) 厚着させる atsúgi saséru; (put): **to bundle something/someone into** ...にほうり込む ...ni hốri (oshí) komú

bungalow [bʌŋ'gəlou] n バンガロー bañgarō

bungle [bʌŋ'gəl] *vt* (job, assassination) ...にしくじる...ni shikújirù

bunion [bʌn'jən] *n* (MED) けん膜りゅう kefímakuryū, バニオン bánîon

bunk [bʌŋk] *n* (bed) 作り付けベッド tsukúritsukebeddò

bunk beds *npl* 二段ベッド nídánbeddò

bunker [bʌŋ'kəːr] *n* (also: **coal bunker**) 石炭庫 sekítanko, (MIL) えんぺいごう efípelgō; (GOLF) バンカー bańka

bunny [bʌn'iː] *n* (also: **bunny rabbit**) ウサちゃん usáchan

bunting [bʌn'tiŋ] *n* (flags) 飾り小旗 kazárikobàta

buoy [buː'iː] *n* (NAUT) ブイ búi

buoyant [bɔi'ənt] *adj* (ship) 浮力のある fúryòku no arù; (economy, market) 活気のある kakkí no arù; (fig: person, nature) 朗らかな hogáràka na

buoy up *vt* (fig) 元気づける geńkizukerù

burden [bəːr'dən] *n* (responsibility, worry) 負担 fután; (load) 荷物 nímòtsu
♦*vt* (trouble): **to burden someone with** (oppress) ...を打明けて...に心配を背負わせる ...wo uchfakete ...ni shifípai wo kakérù

bureau [bjur'ou] (*pl* **bureaux** *or* **bureaus**) *n* (BRIT: writing desk) 書き物机 kakímonozukùe ふたが書く面になるのを指す futá ga kakú meñ ni narú tsukúe wo sasù; (US: chest of drawers) 整理だんす sefrídañsu; (office: government, travel, information) 局 kyókù, 課 ka

bureaucracy [bjurɑːk'rɑsiː] *n* (POL, COMM) 官僚制 kafíryōsei

bureaucrat [bjur'əkræt] *n* (administrator) 官僚 kafíryō; (*pej*: pen-pusher) 小役人 koyákùnin

bureaux [bjur'ouz] *npl of* **bureau**

burglar [bəːr'glər] *n* 押込み強盗 oshíkomigòtō

burglar alarm *n* 盗難警報機 tónankeihōki

burglary [bəːr'glɑːriː] *n* (crime) 住居侵入罪 júkyòshifínyūzai

burial [beːr'iəl] *n* 埋葬 maísō

burly [bəːr'liː] *adj* (figure, workman etc) ごつい gotsúi

Burma [bəːr'mɑ] *n* ビルマ bírùma

burn [bəːrn] (*pt, pp* **burned** *or* **burnt**) *vt* (papers, fuel etc) 燃やす moyásu; (toast, food etc) 焦がす kogásu; (house etc: arson) ...に放火する ...ni hōka suru
♦*vi* (house, wood etc) 燃える moéru; (cakes etc) 焦げる kogérù; (sting) ひりひりする hfríhiri suru
♦*n* やけど yakédo

burn down *vt* 全焼させる zeńshō saséru

burner [bəːr'nəːr] *n* (on cooker, heater) 火口 hfgòchi, バーナー bānā

burning [bəːr'niŋ] *adj* (house etc) 燃えている moéte irù; (sand) 焼ける様に熱い yakéru yō ni atsúi; (desert) しゃく熱の shakúnetsu no; (ambition) 熱烈な netsúretsu na

burnt [bəːrnt] *pt, pp of* **burn**

burrow [bəːr'ou] *n* (of rabbit etc) 巣穴 suána
♦*vi* (dig) 掘る hórù; (rummage) あさる asáru

bursary [bəːr'sɑːriː] *n* (BRIT) (SCOL) 奨学金 shōgakukin

burst [bəːrst] (*pt, pp* **burst**) *vt* (bag, balloon, pipe etc) 破裂させる harétsu sasérù; (subj: river: banks etc) 決壊させる kekkái saséru
♦*vi* (pipe, tire) 破裂する harétsu suru
♦*n* (also: **burst pipe**) 破裂した水道管 harétsu shita suídōkan

a burst of energy/speed/enthusiasm 突発的なエネルギー[スピード, 熱心さ] toppátsuteki na enérugī[supīdo, nesshíñsa]

a burst of gunfire 連射 reńsha

to burst into flames 急に燃え出す kyú ni moédasù

to burst into tears 急に泣き出す kyú ni nakídasù

to burst out laughing 急に笑い出す kyú ni waráidasù

to be bursting with (subj: room, container) はち切れんばかりに...で一杯になっている hachíkirenbakari ni ...de ippái ni natté irù; (: person: emotion) ...で胸が一杯になっている ...de muné ga ippái ni natté irù

burst into *vt fus* (room etc) ...に飛込む

...ni tobíkomù

bury [beːriʼ] *vt* (*gen*) 埋める uméru; (at funeral) 埋葬する maísō suru

bus [bʌs] *n* (vehicle) バス básù

bush [buʃ] *n* (in garden) 低木 teíbokù; (scrubland) 未開地 mikáĩchi, ブッシュ bússhù

to beat about the bush 遠回しに言う tōmawàshi ni iú

bushy [buʃiʼ] *adj* (tail, hair, eyebrows) ふさふさした fúsàfusa shitá

busily [biʼziliʼ] *adv* (actively) 忙しく isó-gashikú

business [biʼznis] *n* (matter, question) 問題 moñdaí; (trading) 商売 shōbai; (firm) 会社 kaísha; (occupation) 仕事 shígòto

to be away on business 出張して留守である shutchō shite rusù de arù

it's my business to ... ...するのは私の務めです ...surú no wa watákushi no tsutóme desù

it's none of my business 私の知った事じゃない watákushi no shitá kotó ja naî

he means business 彼は本気らしい karè wa hoñki rashìî

businesslike [biʼznislaik] *adj* てきぱきした tekípaki shitá

businessman [biʼznismæn] (*pl* **businessmen**) *n* 実業家 jitsúgyòka

business trip *n* 出張 shutchō

businesswoman [biʼzniswumən] (*pl* **businesswomen**) *n* 女性実業家 joséijitsugyōka

busker [bʌʼskəːr] (*BRIT*) *n* 大道芸人 daídōgeìnin

bus-stop [bʌʼstɑːp] *n* バス停留所 básùteíryūjo

bust [bʌst] *n* (ANAT) 乳房 chíbùsa, 胸 muné; (measurement) バスト básùto; (sculpture) 胸像 kyōzō

♦*adj* (*inf*: broken) 壊れた kowáretà

to go bust (company etc) つぶれる tsubúreru

bustle [bʌʼsəl] *n* (activity) 雑踏 zattō

♦*vi* (person) 忙しく飛回る isógashikù tobímawarù

bustling [bʌʼsliŋ] *adj* (town, place) にぎ

やかな nígiyàka na

busy [biʼziʼ] *adj* (person) 忙しい isógashiî; (shop, street) にぎやかな nígíyàka na; (TEL: line) 話し中の hanáshichū no

♦*vt: to busy oneself with* 忙しそうに...する isógashisō ni ...surú

busybody [biʼziːbɑːdiʼ] *n* でしゃばり屋 deshábariya

busy signal (*US*) *n* (TEL) 話中音 wáchūon

KEYWORD

but [bat] *conj* 1 (yet) ...であるが ...de arù ga, ...であるけれども ...de arù keredomo, しかし shikáshi

he's not very bright, but he's hard-working 頭はあまり良くないが、よく働きます kárè wa amári átàma wa yókùnaî ga, yókù határakimasù

I'm tired but Paul isn't 私は疲れていますが、ポールは疲れていません watákushi wa tsukárete imasu ga, pōrù wa tsukárete imasèn

the trip was enjoyable but tiring 旅行は楽しかったけれど、疲れました ryokō wa tanóshikàtta keredomo, tsukáremashìta

2 (however) ...であるが ...de arù ga, ...であるけれども ...de arù keredomo, しかし shikáshi

I'd love to come, but I'm busy 行きたいが、今忙しいんです ikítaì ga, îmà isógashiîn desu

she wanted to go, but first she had to finish her homework 彼女は行きたかったけれど、先に宿題を済ます必要がありました kánojò wa ikítakàtta keredomo, sakí ni shukúdai wo sumásù hitsúyō ga arímashìta

I'm sorry, but I don't agree 済みませんが、私は同意できません sumímasèn ga, watákushi wa dōi dekimasèn

3 (showing disagreement, surprise etc) しかし shikáshi

but that's far too expensive! しかしそれは高過ぎますよ shikáshi soré wa tákàsugimasù yo

but that's fantastic! しかし素晴らし

いじゃありませんか shikáshi subárashii ja arimasén ka

♦prep (apart from, except) ...を除いて ...wo nozóite, ...以外に ...ígai ni

he was nothing but trouble 彼は厄介な問題ばかり起こしていました yákkai na mōndai bakári okóshite imáshita

we've had nothing but trouble 厄介な問題ばかり起こっています yákkai na mōndai bakári okótte imásu

no one but him can do it 彼を除けば出来る人はいません kárè wo nozókèba dekírù hitó wa imásèn

who but a lunatic would do such a thing? 気違いを除けばそんな事をする人はいないでしょう kichígai wo nozókèba sónna koto wo suru hito wa ináì deshò

but for you あなたがいなかったら anátà ga inákàttara

but for your help あなたが助けてくれなかったら anátà ga tasúkète kurénakàttara

I'll do anything but that それ以外な何でもします igái nara nán de mo shimasù

♦adv (just, only) ただ tádà, ...だけ ...daké, ...しか...ないい ...shika ...náì

she's but a child 彼女はほんの子供です kánojò wa hōn no kódòmo desù

had I but known 私がそれを知っていえいたら watákushi ga sórè wo shitte saè itárà

I can but try やってみるしかありません yátte mirù shika arímasèn

all but finished もう少しで出来上りです mō sukóshì de dekíagari desù

---

butcher [butʃˈəːr] *n* (tradesman) 肉屋 nikúyà

♦vt (cattle etc for meat) と殺する tosátsu suru; (prisoners etc) 虐殺する gyakúsatsu suru

butcher's (shop) [butʃˈəːrz-] *n* 精肉店 seínikuten, 肉屋 nikúyà

butler [bʌtˈləːr] *n* 執事 shítsùji

butt [bʌt] *n* (large barrel) たる tarú; (of

---

pistol) 握り nigíri; (of rifle) 床尾 shóbi; (of cigarette) 吸い殻 suígara; (*fig*: target of teasing, criticism etc) 的 matő

♦vt (subj: goat, person) 頭で突く atáma de tsukú

butter [bʌtˈəːr] *n* (CULIN) バター bátā

♦vt (bread) ...にバターを塗る ...ni bátā wo nurú

buttercup [bʌtˈəːrkʌp] *n* キンポウゲ kínpòge

butterfly [bʌtˈəːrflai] *n* (insect) チョウチョウ chőchò; (SWIMMING: *also*: **butterfly stroke**) バタフライ bátàfurai

butt in *vi* (interrupt) ...に割込む ...ni warikomù

buttocks [bʌtˈəks] *npl* (ANAT) しり shirí

button [bʌtˈən] *n* (on clothes) ボタン botán; (on machine) 押しボタン oshíbotàn; (*US*: badge) バッジ bájjì

♦vt (*also*: **button up**) ...のボタンをはめる ...no botán wo hamérù

♦vi ボタンで止まる botán de tomáru

buttress [bʌtˈris] *n* (ARCHIT) 控え壁 hikáekàbe

buxom [bʌkˈsəm] *adj* (woman) 胸の豊かな muné no yútàka na

buy [bai] (*pt, pp* **bought**) *vt* 買う kaú

♦*n* (purchase) 買物 kaímono

to buy someone something/something for someone ...に...を買って上げる ...ni ...wo katté agérù

to buy something from someone ...から...を買う ...kará ...wo kaú

to buy someone a drink ...に酒をおごる ...ni saké wo ogóru

buyer [baiˈəːr] *n* (purchaser) 買手 kaíte; (COMM) 仕入係 shiíregakàri, バイヤー báiyà

buzz [bʌz] *n* (noise: of insect) ぶんぶんという音 bunbun to iú otő; (: of machine etc) うなり unári; (*inf*: phone call): *to give someone a buzz* ...に電話を掛ける ...ni deñwa wo kakérù

♦vi (insect) ぶんぶん羽音を立てる buñbun haóto wo taterù; (saw) うなる unáru

buzzer [bʌzˈəːr] *n* (ELEC) ブザー bûzā

buzz word (*inf*) *n* 流行語 ryūkogo

KEYWORD

by [bai] *prep* **1** (referring to cause, agent) ...に（よって） ...ni (yotte)

killed by lightning 雷に打たれて死んだ kamínari ni ûtárête shínda

surrounded by a fence 塀に囲まれた heí ni kakomareta

a painting by Picasso ピカソの絵画 píkasô no káiga

it's by Shakespeare シェイクスピアの作品です shéikusupia no sakúhin desù

2 (referring to method, manner, means) ...で ...de

by bus/car/train バス［車, 列車］で básu[kuŕuma, ŕéssha]de

to pay by check 小切手で払う kogítte de haráù

by moonlight/candlelight 月明り［ろうそくの灯］で tsukíakàri/[rósoku no akári]de

by saving hard, he ... 一生懸命に金を貯めて彼は... isshôkênmei ni kané wo tameté karè wa...

3 (via, through) ...を通って ...wo tôttê, ...経由で ...kéіyu de

we came by Dover ドーバー経由で来ました dôbâkéiyu de kimáshita

he came in by the back door 彼は裏口から入って来た káre wa uráguchi kara hairimashîta

4 (close to) ...のそばに［で］ ...no sôbà ni [de], ...の近くに［で］ ...no chikáku ni [de]

the house by the river 川のそばにある家 kawá no sobá ni áru íe

a holiday by the sea 海辺の休暇 umíbe no kyûka

she sat by his bed 彼女は彼のベッドのそばに座っていました kánojo wa kárè no béddo no soba ni suwátte imashita

5 (past) ...を通り過ぎて ...wo tôrisugíte

she rushed by me 彼女は足早に私の前を通り過ぎた kánojo wa ashîbaya ni watákushi no maè wo tôrisugíta

I go by the post office every day 私、毎日郵便局の前を通ります watákushi wa maínichi yûbínkyoku no maè wo

tôrimasû

6 (not later than) ...までに ...máde ni

by 4 o'clock 4時までに yójì made ni

by this time tomorrow 明日の今のこの時間までに myônichí no konô jíkan madè ni

by the time I got here it was too late 私がここに着いた時にはもう手遅れでした watákushi ga kôkô ni tsúita koro ni wâ mô teókùre deshita

7 (during): *by daylight* 日中に nitchû ni

8 (amount) ...につき ...nî

by the kilo/meter キロ［メーター］単位で kiró[mêtà]tán-i de

paid by the hour 時給をもらって jikyû wo moratte

one by one (people) 1人ずつ hítórìzutsū; (animals) 1匹ずつ ippíkìzutsū; (things) 1つずつ hitótsuzutsū

little by little 少しずつ sukóshìzutsū

9 (MATH, measure): *to divide by 3* 3で割る sán de waru

to multiply by 3 3を掛ける sán wo kakerû

a room 3 meters by 4 3メーター掛ける4メーターの部屋 sánmèta kakerû yónmètā no heyá

it's broader by a meter 1メーターも広くなっている ichímètā mô hiróku nátte iru

10 (according to) ...に従って ...nî shitâ-gatte

to play by the rules ルールを守る rûrû wo mamórů

it's all right by me 私は構いませんよ watákushi wa kamáimasên yó

11: *(all) by oneself etc* 一人だけで hitórì daké de

he did it (all) by himself 彼は彼1人だけの力でやりました káre wa kárè hitóri dake nô chikára de yarímashita

he was standing (all) by himself in the corner 彼は1人ぽつんと隅に立っていました kárè wa hitóribotchî de súmi ni tátté imashîta

12: *by the way* ところで tokóro dè

by the way, did you know Claire was back? ところで、クレアが帰って来たのをご存知？ tokóro dè ne, kûrea

ga kǎette kita no wo go-zònji?
this wasn't my idea by the way しかしね、これを提案したのは私じゃないからね shikǎshi nê, koré wo teian shita nò wa watǎkushi ja nái kara nê

♦*adv* 1 *see* go; pass *etc*

2: **by and by** やがて yagáte
by and by they came to a fork in the road やがて道路はY字路になりました yagáte dòro ha wafjirò ni narímashǐta
they'll come back by and by そのうち帰って来ますよ sonó uchi kǎette kimásǔ yo
by and large (*on the whole*) 大体において dáitai ni óite, 往々にして òò ni shǐte
by and large I would agree with you 大体あなたと同じ意見です dáitai ni anáta to onáji ikèn desu
Britain has a poor image abroad, by and large 海外における英国のイメージは往々にして悪い kǎigai ni okéru éǐkoku no ímèji wa òò ni shǐte warúǐ

bye(-bye) [bai'bai'] *n excl* じゃあねじゃね, バイバイ bǎibai

by(e)-law [bai'lɔː] *n* 条例 jórei

by-election [bai'ilekʃən] (*BRIT*) *n* 補欠選挙 hokétsusenkyo

bygone [bai'gɔːn] *adj* (*age, days*) 昔の mukáshi no

♦*n: let bygones be bygones* 済んだ事を水に流す sûnda kotó wo mizú ni nagásǔ

bypass [bai'pæs] *n* (*AUT*) バイパス bǎipasu; (*MED: operation*) 冠状動脈バイパス kanjōdōmyakubaĭpasu
♦*vt* (*town*) ...にバイパスを設ける ...ni baĭpasu wo mōkéru

by-product [bai'prɑːdækt] *n* (*of industrial process*) 副産物 fukúsanbutsu; (*of situation*) 二次的結果 nijítekikèkka

bystander [bai'stændər] *n* (*at accident, crime*) 居合せた通行人 iáwasèta tsūkōnin

byte [bait] *n* (*COMPUT*) バイト báito

byword [bai'wɔːrd] *n: to be a byword for* ...の代名詞である ...no daímeishi de arú

by-your-leave [baijuːrliːv'] *n: without*

so much as a by-your-leave 自分勝手に jibúnkattě ni

C

C [siː] *n* (MUS: *note*) ハ音 há-ôn; (: *key*) ハ調 háchō

C. [siː] *abbr* = centigrade

C.A. [siːeiˈ] *abbr* = **chartered accountant**

cab [kæb] *n* (*taxi*) タクシー tákǔshī; (*of truck, tractor etc*) 運転台 uñtendai

cabaret [kæbərei'] *n* (*nightclub*) キャバレー kyábàrē; (*floor show*) フロアショー furóashō

cabbage [kæb'idʒ] *n* キャベツ kyábètsu

cabin [kæb'in] *n* (*on ship*) キャビン kyábìn; (*on plane*) 操縦室 sōjūshǐtsu; (*house*) 小屋 koyá

cabin cruiser *n* 大型モーターボート ò-gata mōtābòto, クルーザー kúrūza ◊ 居室、炊事場などのある物を指す kyóshǐtsu, sufjiba nádò no árǔ monó wo sásǔ

cabinet [kæb'ənit] *n* (*piece of furniture*) 戸棚 todána, キャビネット kyabínettò; (*also: display cabinet*) ガラス戸棚 garásu todána; (*POL*) 内閣 náǐkaku

cable [kei'bəl] *n* (*strong rope*) 綱 tsunǎ; (ELEC, TEL, TV) ケーブル kḗburu
♦*vt* (*message, money*) 電信で送る deñshin de okúru

cable-car [kei'bəlkɑːr] *n* ケーブルカー kḗburuka

cable television *n* 有線テレビ yúsenterèbi

cache [kæʃ] *n: a cache of drugs* 隠匿された麻薬 íntoku sareta mayáku
a weapons cache 隠匿武器 íntokubǔki

cackle [kæk'əl] *vi* (*person, witch*) 薄気味悪い声で笑う usúkimiwarui kǒe de waráu; (*hen*) ここここ鳴く kokoko ni nákǔ

cacti [kæk'tai] *npl of* **cactus**

cactus [kæk'təs] (*pl* **cacti**) *n* サボテン sabóten

caddie [kæd'iː] *n* (*GOLF*) キャディー kyádǐ

caddy [kæd'iː] *n* = **caddie**

cadet [kədet'] *n* (MIL) 士官候補生 shikánkōhoseì; (POLICE) 警察学校の生徒 kefsatsugakkō no seìto

cadge [kæʤ] (*inf*) *vt* (lift, cigarette etc) ねだる nedárù

Caesarean [sizer'i:ən] (*BRIT*) = **Cesarean**

café [kæfei] *n* (snack bar) 喫茶店 kíssaten

cafeteria [kæfiti:'ri:ə] *n* (in school, factory, station) 食堂 shokúdō

caffein(e) [kæf'in] *n* カフェイン kaféìn

cage [keidʒ] *n* (of animal) おりorí; (also: bird cage) 鳥かご toríkago, ケージ kéjì; (of lift) ケージ kéjì

cagey [kei'dʒi:] (*inf*) *adj* 用心深い yōjinbukaì

cagoule [kəgu:l'] (*BRIT*) *n* カグール kágūru ◇薄手の雨ガッパ usúde no amágappa

Cairo [kai'rou] *n* カイロ káìro

cajole [kədʒoul'] *vt* 丸め込む marúmekomù

cake [keik] *n* (CULIN: large) デコレーションケーキ dekórēshonkēkì; (: small) 洋菓子 yōgashì

a cake of soap 石けん1個 sekkén íkkò

caked [keikt] *adj*: **caked with** (blood, mud etc) …の塊で覆われた …no katámari de ōwareta

calamity [kəlæm'iti:] *n* (disaster) 災難 safnaǹ

calcium [kæl'si:əm] *n* (in teeth, bones etc) カルシウム karúshìumu

calculate [kæl'kjəleit] *vt* (work out: cost, distance, numbers etc) 計算する kefsan surù; (: effect, risk, impact etc) 予測する yosókù surù

calculating [kæl'kjəleitiŋ] *adj* (scheming) ずる賢い zurúgashikoì

calculation [kælkjəlei'ʃən] *n* (MATH) 計算 kefsan; (estimate) 予測 yosókù

calculator [kæl'kjəleitər] *n* 電卓 defntakù

calculus [kæl'kjələs] *n* (MATH) 微積分学 bisékibungakù

calendar [kæl'əndər] *n* (of year) カレンダー kárendà; (timetable, schedule) 予定表 yotéìhyō

calendar month/year *n* 暦月〔年〕 rekígetsu(nen)

calf [kæf] (*pl* **calves**) *n* (of cow) 子ウシ koúshì; (of elephant, seal etc) …の子 …no ko; (*also:* **calfskin**) 子牛革 koúshigawa, カーフスキン kāfusukìn; (ANAT) ふくらはぎ fukúrahàgi

caliber [kæl'əbər] (*BRIT* **calibre**) *n* (of person) 能力 nōryokù; (of skill) 程度 téìdo; (of gun) 口径 kōkeì

call [kɔ:l] *vt* (christen, name) 名付ける nazúkerù; (label) …を … と呼ぶ …wo … to yobú; (TEL) …に電話を掛ける …ni defwa wo kakérù; (summon: doctor etc) 呼ぶ yobú; (: witness etc) 召喚する shōkan surù; (arrange: meeting) 召集する shōshū surù

◆*vi* (shout) 大声で言う ōgoè de iú; (telephone) 電話を掛ける defwa wo kakérù; (visit: *also*: **call in, call round**) 立寄る tachíyorù

◆*n* (shout) 呼声 yobígoè; (TEL) 電話 defwa; (of bird) 鳴声 nakígoè

: to be called … …と呼ばれる …to yobárerù, …という …to iú

on call (nurse, doctor etc) 待機して taíki shité

call back *vi* (return) また寄る matá yorù; (TEL) 電話を掛け直す defwa wo kakénaosù

callbox [kɔ:l'bɑ:ks] (*BRIT*) *n* 電話ボックス defwabokkùsu

caller [kɔ:l'ər] *n* (visitor) 訪問客 hōmonkyakù; (TEL) 電話を掛ける人 defwa wo kakéte kurú hitò

call for *vt fus* (demand) 要求する yōkyū surù; (fetch) 迎えに行く mukáe ni ikú

call girl *n* (prostitute) コールガール kōrugāru

call-in [kɔ:l'in] (*US*) *n* (phone-in) ◇視聴者が電話で参加する番組 shíchōsha ga defwa de safka suru baṅgumi

calling [kɔ:l'iŋ] *n* (occupation) 職業 shōkūgyō; (*also:* **religious calling**) 神のお召し kámì no o-meshí

calling card (*US*) *n* 名刺 meíshi

call off *vt* (cancel) 中止する chūshi surù

call on vt fus (visit) 訪ねる tazúnerú, 訪問する hómon suru; (appeal to) ...に ...を求める ...ni ...wo motómerú

callous [kæl'əs] adj (heartless) 冷淡な reftañ na

call out vt (name etc) 大声で言う ógoè de iú; (summon for help etc) 呼び出す yobídasu
♦vi (shout) 大声で言う ógoè de iú

call up vt (MIL) 召集する shóshù suru; (TEL) ...に電話をかける ...ni deñwa wo kakérù

calm [kɑːm] adj (unworried) 落着いている ochítsuite irú; (peaceful) 静かな shízûka na; (weather, sea) 穏やかな odáyàka na
♦n (quiet, peacefulness) 静けさ shizúkesà
♦vt (person, child) 落着かせる ochítsukaserù; (fears, grief etc) 鎮める shizúmerù

calm down vi (person) 落着く ochítsukú
♦vt (person) 落着かせる ochítsukaserù

Calor gas [kæ'lɔːr-]® n 携帯用燃料ガスボンベの商品名 keftaiyō neñryō gasu bonbe no shōhinmei

calorie [kæl'əriː] n カロリー kárðri

calves [kævz] npl of **calf**

camber [kæm'bəːr] n (of road) 真ん中が高くなっている事 mañnaka ga takakù nattê irú kotð

Cambodia [kæmbou'diːə] n カンボジア kañbòjìa

came [keim] pt of **come**

camel [kæm'əl] n (ZOOL) ラクダ rakúda

cameo [kæm'iːou] n (jewellery) カメオ kámèo

camera [kæm'əːrə] n (PHOT) 写真機 shashínki, カメラ kámèra; (CINEMA) 映画カメラ eíga kámèra; (also: TV camera) テレビカメラ terébi kamèra
in camera (LAW) 非公開で híkòkai de

cameraman [kæm'əːræn] (pl cameramen) n (CINEMA, TV) カメラマン kaméramàn

camouflage [kæm'əflɑːʒ] n (MIL) カムフラージュ kamúfurāju; (ZOOL) 隠ぺいの的手段 iñpeitekigìtày
♦vt (conceal: also MIL) 隠す kakúsù

camp [kæmp] n (encampment) キャンプ場 kyañpujō; (MIL: barracks) 基地 kichí; (for prisoners) 収容所 shúyōjo; (faction) 陣営 jiñ-ei
♦vi (in tent) キャンプする kyañpu suru
♦adj (effeminate) 女々しい meméshì

campaign [kæmpein'] n (MIL) 作戦 sakúsen; (POL etc) 運動 uñdō, キャンペーン kyañpèn
♦vi (objectors, pressure group etc) 運動をする uñdō wo suru

camp bed (BRIT) n 折畳みベッド orítatami beddō

camper [kæm'pəːr] n (person) キャンパー kyañpà; (vehicle) キャンピングカー kyañpingukà

camping [kæm'piŋ] n 野営 yaéi, キャンピング kyañpîngu
to go camping キャンピングに行く kyañpîngu ni iku

campsite [kæmp'sait] n キャンプ場 kyañpujō

campus [kæm'pəs] n (SCOL) キャンパス kyañpasu

can¹ [kæn] n (container: for foods, drinks, oil etc) 缶 kañ
♦vt (foods) 缶詰にする kañzume ni suru

KEYWORD

can² [kæn] (negative **cannot, can't** conditional and pt **could**) aux vb 1 (be able to) 出来る dekírù

you can do it if you try 努力すれば出来ますよ dóryðku surébà dekímasù yo

I'll help you all I can できるだけ力になりましょう dekírù dake chíkàra nī narímashð

she couldn't sleep that night その晩彼女は眠れませんでした sonð ban kanðjo wa nemúremasèn deshita

I can't go on any longer 私はもうこれ以上やっていけません watákushi wa mð koré ijð yattè ikemasèn

I can't see you あなたの姿が見えません anátà no súgàta ga miémasèn

can you hear me? 私の声が聞えますか watákushi no koè ga kikðemasù ka

I can see you tomorrow, if you're

free 明日でよかったらお会いできますよ asú dè yókàttara o-ái dekimasù yó

2 (know how to) ...の仕方が分かる ...no shikáta ga wakarù, ...ができる ...ga dekírù

I can swim/play tennis/drive 私は水泳(テニス, 運転)ができます watákushi wa sûfèi(ténisù, únten)ga dekímasu

can you speak French? あなたはフランス語ができますか anátà wa furánsugo ga dekímasù ká

3 (may) ...してもいいですか ...shité mò íi desu ká

can I use your phone? 電話をお借りしてもいいですか dénwa wo ò-kári shite mò íi desu ká

could I have a word with you? ちょっと話しがあるんですか chóttò hanáshi gà árùn desu ká

you can smoke if you like タバコを吸いたければ遠慮なくどうぞ tabáko wo suitákereba énryo nakú dôzò

can I help you with that? 手を貸しましょうか té wò kashímashô ka

4 (expressing disbelief, puzzlement): **it can't be true!** そんでしょう嘘 deshò **what CAN he want?** あいつは何をねらっているだろうね áìtsu wa nánì wo neráttte iru dàrō né

5 (expressing possibility, suggestion, etc) ...かも知れない ...ká mò shirenai **he could be in the library** 彼は図書室にいるかも知れません kárè wa ttoshóshìtsu ni irú ka mo shiremasén **she could have been delayed** 彼女は何かの原因で出発が遅れたかも知れません kánòjo wa nánìka no gén-in de shuppátsu ga ôkúreta ka mo shíremasén

Canada [kænədə] *n* カナダ kánàda

Canadian [kəneidiːən] *adj* カナダの kánàda no
♦*n* カナダ人 kanádajìn

canal [kənæl] *n* (for ships, barges, irrigation) 運河 úñga; (ANAT) 管 káñ

canary [kəneəriː] *n* カナリア kanáriya

cancel [kænsəl] *vt* (meeting) 中止する chûshi suru; (appointment, reservation,

contract, order) 取消す toríkesu, キャンセルする kyáñseru suru; (cross out: words, figures) 線を引いて消す sén wo hiíte kesú

the flight was canceled その便は欠航になった sonó bìñ wa kekkó ni nattà **the train was canceled** その列車は運休になった sonó ressha wa uñkyú ni nattá

cancellation [kænsəleiʃən] *n* (of meeting) 中止 chûshi; (of appointment, reservation, contract, order) 取消し toríkeshi, キャンセル kyáñseru; (of flight) 欠航 kekkó; (of train) 運休 uñkyú

cancer [kænsər] *n* (MED) がん gáñ **Cancer** (ASTROLOGY) かに座 kaníza

candid [kændid] *adj* (expression, comment) 率直な sotchóku na

candidate [kændideit] *n* (for job) 候補者 kôhoshà; (in exam) 受験者 jukéñsha; (POL) 立候補者 rikkóhoshà

candle [kændəl] *n* ろうそく rôsokù

candlelight [kændlait] *n*: **by candlelight** ろうそくの明りで akári de

candlestick [kændstik] *n* (*also*: **candle holder**: plain) ろうそく立て rôsokutàte; (: bigger, ornate) しょく台 shokúdai

candor [kændər] (*BRIT* **candour**) *n* (frankness) 率直さ sotchókusà

candy [kændiː] *n* (*also*: **sugar-candy**) 氷砂糖 kôrizatô; (*US*: sweet) あめ amé

candy-floss [kændiːflɔːs] (*BRIT*) *n* 綿あめ watá-àme, 綿菓子 watágashì

cane [kein] *n* (BOT) 茎 kukí ◇竹などの様に中が空洞になっている植物を指す také nadò no yò ni naká ga kûdō ni natté irú shokûbùtsu wo sasù; (for furniture) 藤 tò; (stick) 棒 bô; (for walking) 杖 tsúè, ステッキ sutékkì
♦*vt* (*BRIT*: SCOL) むちで打つ muchfutsû

canister [kænistər] *n* (container: for tea, sugar etc) 容器 yôkì ◇茶筒の様な物を指す chazútsu no yò na monô wo sasù; (pressurized container) スプレー缶 supúrēkàñ; (of gas, chemicals etc) ボンベ bóñbe

cannabis [ˈkænəbis] n マリファナ marífāna

canned [kænd] adj (fruit, vegetables etc) 缶詰の kanzúme no

cannibal [ˈkænibəl] n (person) 人食い人間 hitókuì nìngen; (animal) 共食いする動物 tomógui surù dôbutsu

cannon [ˈkænən] (pl **cannon** or **cannons**) n (artillery piece) 大砲 taíhō

cannot [ˈkænɑt] = **can not**

canny [ˈkæniː] adj (quick-witted) 抜け目ない nukémenaì

canoe [kəˈnuː] n (boat) カヌー kánū

canon [ˈkænən] n (clergyman) 司教座聖堂参事会員 shikyôzaséidò sañjikàiin; (rule, principle) 規準 kijún

canonize [ˈkænənaiz] vt (REL) 聖人の列に加える seíjin no retsû ni kuwáerù

can opener n 缶切 kañkiri

canopy [ˈkænəpiː] n (above bed, throne etc) 天がい teñgai

can't [kænt] = **can not**

cantankerous [kænˈtæŋkərəs] adj (fault-finding, complaining) つむじ曲りの tsumújimagàri no

canteen [kænˈtiːn] n (in workplace, school etc) 食堂 shokúdō; (also: **mobile canteen**) 移動食堂 idóshokudō; (BRIT: of cutlery) 収納箱 shúnōbako ナイフ、フォークなどを仕舞う箱 naífu, fôku nadò wo shimáu hakò

canter [ˈkæntər] vi (horse) キャンターで走る kyañtā de hashirù

canvas [ˈkænvəs] n (fabric) キャンバス kyáñbasu; (painting) 油絵 abúraè; (NAUT) 帆布 hò帆、総布 sôshò

canvass [ˈkænvəs] vi (POL): **to canvass for** ...のために選挙運動をする ...no tamè ni seňkyoundô wo surù
♦vt (investigate: opinions, views) 調査する chôsa surù

canyon [ˈkænjən] n 峡谷 kyôkoku

cap [kæp] n (hat) 帽子 bôshi ♦主に つばのある物を指す物 ní tsubá no arù monó wo sásù; (of pen) キャップ kyáppù; (of bottle) ふた futá; (contraceptive) ペッサリー pèssarī; (for toy gun) 紙雷管 kamfraíkan

♦vt (outdo) しのぐ shinógù

capability [keipəbilˈətiː] n (competence) 能力 nôryoku

capable [ˈkeipəbəl] adj (person, object): **capable of doing** ...ができる ...ga dekíru; (able: person) 有能な yūnō na

capacity [kəpæsˈitiː] n (of container, ship etc) 容積 yôseki; (of stadium etc) 収容力 shūyôryòku; (capability) 能力 nôryoku; (position, role) 資格 shikáku; (of factory) 生産能力 seísannôryòku

cape [keip] n (GEO) 岬 misáki; (short cloak) ケープ kêpu

caper [ˈkeipər] n (CULIN: gen: **capers**) ケーパー kêpā; (prank) いたずら itázura

capital [ˈkæpitəl] n (also: **capital city**) 首都 shûtò; (money) 資本金 shihóñkin; (also: **capital letter**) 大文字 ômoji

capital gains tax n 資本利得税 shihóñritokuzèi

capitalism [ˈkæpitəlizəm] n 資本主義 shihóñshugì

capitalist [ˈkæpitəlist] adj 資本主義の shihóñshugì no
♦n 資本主義者 shihóñshugishà

capitalize [ˈkæpitəlaiz]: **capitalize on** vt fus (situation, fears etc) 利用する riyô suru

capital punishment n 死刑 shikéi

capitulate [kəpitˈjuleit] vi (give in) 降参する kôsan suru

capricious [kəpriˈʃəs] adj (fickle: person) 気まぐれの kimágure no

Capricorn [ˈkæprikɔːrn] n (ASTROLOGY) やぎ座 yagíza

capsize [ˈkæpsaiz] vt (boat, ship) 転覆させる teñpuku sasérù
♦vi (boat, ship) 転覆する teñpuku suru

capsule [ˈkæpsəl] n (MED) カプセル kápùseru; (spacecraft) 宇宙カプセル uchûkapùseru

captain [ˈkæptin] n (of ship) 船長 señchō; (of plane) 機長 kíchō; (of team) 主将 shushô; (in army) 大尉 taíì; (in navy) 大佐 taísa; (US: in air force) 大尉 taíì; (BRIT: SCOL) 主席の生徒 shuséki no seíto

caption [ˈkæpʃən] n (to picture) 説明文

setsúmeíbun

captivate [kǽp'təveit] vt (fascinate) 魅了する miryŏ suru

captive [kǽp'tiv] adj (person) とりこの toríko no; (animal) 飼育下の shiíkukà no
♦n (person) とりこ toríko; (animal) 飼育下の動物 shiíkukà no dṓbutsu

captivity [kæptív'əti:] n 監禁状態 kaṅkinjótai

capture [kǽp'tʃər] vt (animal, person) 捕まえる tsukámaerù; (town, country) 占領する seńryŏ suru; (attention) 捕える toráerù; (COMPUT) 収納する shúnṓ suru
♦n (seizure: of animal) 捕獲 hokáku; (: of person: by police) 逮捕 táiho; (: of town, country: by enemy) 占領 seńryŏ; (COMPUT) 収納 shúnṓ

car [kɑːr] n (AUT) 自動車 jídṓsha, カー kúrúma; (: US: carriage) 客車 kyakúsha; (RAIL: BRIT: dining car, buffet car) 特殊車両 tokúshusharyŏ

carafe [kəræf'] n 水差し mizúsashì

caramel [kær'əməl] n (CULIN: sweet) キャラメル kyarámeru; (: burnt sugar) カラメル karámeru

carat [kær'ət] n (of diamond, gold) カラット karáttò

caravan [kær'əvæn] n (BRIT: vehicle) キャンピングカー kyańpiṅgukà; (in desert) 隊商 taíshŏ, キャラバン kyáraban

caravan site (BRIT) n オートキャンプ場 ŏtokyanpujŏ

carbohydrate [kɑːrbouhai'dreit] n (CHEM, food) 炭水化物 tańsuikabútsu

carbon [kɑːr'bən] n 炭素 táñso

carbon copy n カーボンコピー kâbon kopí

carbon dioxide [-daiɑːk'said] n 二酸化炭素 nisáñkatañso

carbon monoxide [-mənɑːk'said] n 一酸化炭素 issáñkatañso

carbon paper n カーボン紙 kâbonshi

carburetor [kɑːr'bəreitər] (BRIT **carburettor**) n (AUT) キャブレター kyábùretà

carcass [kɑːr'kəs] n (of animal) 死体 shitái

card [kɑːrd] n (cardboard) ボール紙 bŏrugami; (greetings card, index card etc) カード kầdo; (playing card) トランプのカード toráñpu no kầdo; (visiting card) 名刺 meíshi

cardboard [kɑːrd'bɔːrd] n ボール紙 bŏrugami

card game n トランプゲーム toráñpugēmu

cardiac [kɑːr'diːæk] adj (arrest, failure) 心臓の shíñzŏ no

cardigan [kɑːr'digən] n カーディガン kầdigàn

cardinal [kɑːr'dənəl] adj (chief: principle) 重要な jŭyŏ na
♦n (REL) 枢機卿けい sūkikèi
of cardinal importance 極めて重要で kiwámète jŭyŏ de

cardinal number 基数 kísŭ

card index n カード式索引 kầdoshiki sakúiṅ

care [keːr] n (attention) 注意 chǘi; (worry) 心配 shiñpai, (charge) 管理 káñri
♦vi: **to care about** (person, animal etc) …を気に掛ける …wo kí nì kakérù; …を愛する …wo aí surù; (thing, idea etc) …に関心を持つ …ni kańshin wo motsù
care of (on mail) …方 …gatá
in someone's care …の管理に任せる(られ)て …no kañri ni makáse(rare)tè
to take care (to do) …するよう心掛ける …wo suru yố kokórogakerù
to take care of (patient, child etc) …の世話をする …no sewá wo suru; (problem, situation) …の始末を付ける …no shimátsu wo tsukerù
I don't care 私は構いません watákushi wa kamáimasèn
I couldn't care less 私はちっとも気にしない watákushi wa chittő mő ki ni shináì

career [kəriːr'] n (job, profession) 職業 shokúgyŏ; (life: in school, work etc) キャリア kyaría
♦vi (also: **career along**: car, horse) 猛スピードで走る mŏspĩdo de hashírù

career woman (pl **career women**) n キャリアウーマン kyaríaûman

care for vt fus (look after) ...の世話をする...no sewá wo surú; (like) ...が好きである...ga sukí de arú, ...を愛している...wo aí shité irú

carefree [ker'fri:] adj (person, attitude) 気苦労のない kigúrō no naí

careful [ker'fəl] adj (cautious) 注意深い chūíbukaí; (thorough) 徹底的な tettéteki na

(be) careful! 気を付けてね ki wo tsukétte ne

carefully [ker'fəli:] adv (cautiously) 注意深く chūíbukakú; (methodically) 念入りに neń-iri ni

careless [ker'lis] adj (negligent) 不注意な fuchūi na; (heedless) 軽率な kefsotsu na

carelessness [ker'lisnis] n (negligence) 不注意 fuchūi; (lack of concern) 無とん着 mutońchaku

caress [kəres'] n (stroke) 愛ぶ aíbu
♦vt (person, animal) 愛ぶする aíbu suru

caretaker [ker'teikər] n (of flats etc) 管理人 kańrinin

car-ferry [kɑːr'feri:] n カーフェリー kāferī

cargo [kɑːr'gou] (pl cargoes) n (of ship, plane) 積荷 tsumíni, 貨物 kámotsu

car hire (BRIT) n レンタカーサービス reńtakā sābisu

Caribbean [kærəbi:'ən] n: **the Caribbean (Sea)** カリブ海 karíbukaí

caricature [kær'əkətʃər] n (drawing) 風刺漫画 fūshímañga, カリカチュア karíkachùa; (description) 風刺文 fūshíbūn; (exaggerated account) 真実のわい曲 shiñjitsu no waikyoku

caring [ker'iŋ] adj (person, society, behavior) 愛情深い aíjōbukai; (organization) 健康管理の keńkōkañri no

carnage [kɑːr'nidʒ] n (MIL) 虐殺 gyakúsatsu

carnal [kɑːr'nəl] adj (desires, feelings) 肉体的な nikútaiteki na

carnation [kɑːrnei'ʃən] n カーネーション kānéshon

carnival [kɑːr'nəvəl] n (festival) 謝肉祭 shańnikusai, カーニバル kānibaru; (US:

funfair) カーニバル kānibaru

carnivorous [kɑːrniv'ərəs] adj (animal, plant) 肉食の nikúshoku no

carol [kær'əl] n: **(Christmas) carol** クリスマスキャロル kurísumasu kyàroru

carp [kɑːrp] n (fish) コイ koí

car park (BRIT) n 駐車場 chūshajō

carp at vt fus (criticize) とがめ立てする togámedate suru

carpenter [kɑːr'pəntər] n 大工 daíku

carpentry [kɑːr'pəntri:] n 大工仕事 daíkushigoto

carpet [kɑːr'pit] n (in room etc) じゅうたん jūtan, カーペット kāpéttò; (fig: of pine needles, snow etc) じゅうたんの様な...jūtan no yō na...
♦vt (room, stairs etc) ...にじゅうたんを敷く ...ni jūtan wo shikú

carpet slippers npl スリッパ sūríppa

carpet sweeper [-swi:'pər] n じゅうたん掃除機 jūtan sōjiki

carriage [kær'idʒ] n (BRIT: RAIL) 客車 kyakúsha; (also: horse-drawn carriage) 馬車 bashá; (of goods) 運搬 uńpan; (transport costs) 運送料 uńsōryō

carriage return (on typewriter etc) 復帰キー fukkí kī

carriageway [kær'idʒwei] n (BRIT: part of road) 車線 shaséñ ◊自動車道の上りまたは下り半分を指す jidōshadō no nobóri mata wa kudári hañbuñ wo shisú

carrier [kær'iər] n (transporter, transport company) 運送会社 uńsōgaisha; (MED) 保菌者 hokíñsha, キャリア kyárìa

carrier bag (BRIT) n 買い物袋 kaímonobukûro, ショッピングバッグ shoppíngubaggù

carrot [kær'ət] n (BOT, CULIN) ニンジン niñjin

carry [kær'i:] vt (take) 携帯する keítai suru; (transport) 運ぶ hakóbu; (involve: responsibilities etc) 伴う tomónaú; (MED: disease, virus) 保有する hoyú suru
♦vi (sound) 通る tōru

to get carried away (fig: by enthusiasm, idea) 有頂天になる muchū ni narú

carrycot [kær'i:kɑt] (BRIT) n 携帯ベビ

一ベッド kéitai bebíbèddò

carry on *vi* (continue) 続ける tsuzúkeru
♦*vt* (continue) 続ける tsuzúkeru

carry-on [kær':x:n] (*inf*) *n* (fuss) 大騒ぎ ōsawàkgi

carry out *vt* (orders) 実行する jikkō suru; (investigation) 行う okónau

cart [kɑːrt] *n* (for grain, silage, hay etc) 荷車 nígŭruma; (also: **horsedrawn cart**) 馬車 bāsha; (also: **handcart**) 手押し車 teóshigurùma
♦*vt* (*inf*: people) 否応なしに連れて行く iyáō nashi ni tsurete ikú; (objects) 引きずる hikízuru

cartilage [kɑːr'təlidʒ] *n* (ANAT) 軟骨 nafíkotsu

carton [kɑːr'tən] *n* (large box) ボール箱 bōrubako; (container: of yogurt, milk etc) 容器 yōki; (of cigarettes) カートン kāton

cartoon [kɑːrtuːn'] *n* (drawing) 漫画 mañga; (*BRIT*: comic strip) 漫画 mañga ◇四こま漫画などを指す yofíkoma mañga nadò wo sasù; (CINEMA) アニメ映画 aníme-eìga

cartridge [kɑːr'tridʒ] *n* (for gun) 薬莢 dañ-yakutò, 実弾 jitsūdan; (of record-player) カートリッジ kátoríjji; (of pen) インクカートリッジ íñku kátoríjji

carve [kɑːrv] *vt* (meat) 切分ける kiráwakerù, スライスする suráisu surù; (wood, stone) 彫刻する chōkoku suru; (initials, design) 刻む kizámu

carve up *vt* (land, property) 切分ける ki-ríwakerù

carving [kɑːr'viŋ] *n* (object made from wood, stone etc) 彫物 horímonò; (: art) 彫刻 chōkoku

carving knife *n* カービングナイフ kā-bìngunaìfu

car wash *n* 洗車場 señshajò, カーウォッシュ kāuosshù

cascade [kæskeid'] *n* (waterfall) 小さい滝 chíísaì takí
♦*vi* (water) 滝になって流れ落ちる takí ni natté nagáreochìrù; (hair, people, things) 滝の様に落ちる takí no yō ni o-

chírù

case [keis] *n* (situation, instance) 場合 baái; (MED) 症例 shōrei; (LAW) 事件 jíkèn; (container: for spectacles etc) ケース kèsu; (box: of whisky etc) 箱 hakó, ケース kèsu; (*BRIT*: also: **suitcase**) スーツケース sútsukèsu

in case (of) (fire, emergency) ...の場合 ...no baái ni

in any case とにかく toníkaku

just in case 万一に備えて máñ-ichi ni sonáete

cash [kæʃ] *n* (money) 現金 geñkin
♦*vt* (check etc) 換金する kañkin suru

to pay (in) cash 現金で払う geñkin de haráu

cash on delivery 着払い chakúbaraì

cash-book [kæʃ'buk] *n* 出納簿 suítōbo

cash card (*BRIT*) *n* (for cash dispenser) キャッシュカード kyasshúkàdo

cash desk (*BRIT*) *n* 勘定カウンター kañjōkaùñtā

cash dispenser *n* 現金自動支払い機 geñkin jidōshiharaìki, カード機 kādoki

cashew [kæʃ'uː] *n* (also: **cashew nut**) カシューナッツ kashūnattsù

cash flow *n* 資金繰り shikíñguri

cashier [kæʃiər] *n* (in bank) 出納係 suí-tōgakàri; (in shop, restaurant) レジ係 re-jígakàri

cashmere [kæʒ'miːr] *n* (wool, jersey) カシミア kashímia

cash register *n* レジスター réjìsutā

casing [kei'siŋ] *n* (covering) 被覆 hífùku

casino [kəsiː'nou] *n* カジノ kájìno

cask [kæsk] *n* (of wine, beer) たる樽 tarú

casket [kæs'kit] *n* (for jewelery) 宝石箱 hōsekibakò; (*US*: coffin) 棺 kañ

casserole [kæs'aroul] *n* (: of lamb, chicken etc) キャセロール kyasèròru; (pot, container) キャセロールなべ kyasé-rórunabè

cassette [kəset'] *n* (tape) カセットテープ kasétto tèpu

cassette player *n* カセットプレーヤー kasétto purèyā

cassette recorder *n* カセットレコーダー kasétto rekòdā

cast [kæst] (pt, pp **cast**) vt (throw: light, shadow) 映す utsúsù; (: object, net) 投げる nagérù; (: fishing-line) キャストする kyásùto surú; (: aspersions, doubts) 投掛ける nagékakerù; (glance, eyes) 向ける mukérù; (THEATER) ...に...の役を振当てる ...ni ...no yakú wo furíaterù; (make: statue) 鋳込む ikómù

♦n (THEATER) キャスト kyásùto; (also: **plaster cast**) ギブス gíbùsu

to cast a spell on (subject: witch etc) ...に魔法を掛ける ...ni mahō wo kakérù

to cast one's vote 投票する tōhyō surú

castaway [kæs'tʌwei] n 難破した人 naħpa shita hitó

caste [kæst] n (social class) カースト kásùto; (also: **caste system**) 階級制 kaíkyūsei, カースト制 kásùtosei

caster [kæs'tʌr] n (wheel) キャスター kyásùta

caster sugar (BRIT) n 粉砂糖 konázatō

casting vote [kæs'tiŋ-] (BRIT) n 決定票 kettéihyō, キャスティングボート kyásùtingubōto

cast iron [kæst'ai'ʌrn] n 鋳鉄 chútetsu

castle [kæs'ʌl] n (building) 城 shiró; (CHESS) 城将 jōshō

cast off vi (NAUT) 綱を解く tsuná wo tokú; (KNITTING) 編み終える amíoerù

cast on vi (KNITTING) 編み始める amíhajimerù

castor [kæs'tʌr] n (BRIT) = **caster**

castor oil n ひまし油 himáshiyu

castrate [kæs'treit] vt (bull, man) 去勢する kyoséi suru

casual [kæʒ'uːal] adj (by chance) 偶然の gūzen no; (irregular: work etc) 臨時の rinji no; (unconcerned) さりげない sarígenaì; (informal: clothes) 普段用の fudán-yō no

casually [kæʒ'uːali] adv (in a relaxed way) さりげなく sarígenakù; (dress) 普段着で fudángi de

casualty [kæʒ'uːalti] n (: of war, accident: someone injured 負傷者 fushósha; (: someone killed) 死者 shishá; (: of situation, event: victim) 犠牲者 giséisha;

(MED: also: **casualty department**) 救急病棟 kyūkyūbyōtō

cat [kæt] n (pet) ネコ nékò; (wild animal) ネコ科の動物 nekóka no dōbutsu

catalogue [kæt'ʌlɔːg] (US also: **catalog**) n (COMM: for mail order) カタログ katárogu; (of exhibition, library) 目録 mokúroku

♦vt (books, collection, events) ...の目録を作る ...no mokúroku wo tsukurù

catalyst [kæt'ʌlist] n (CHEM, fig) 触媒 shokúbai

catapult [kæt'ʌpalt] (BRIT) n (slingshot) ぱちんこ pachínko

cataract [kæt'ʌrækt] n (MED) 白内障 hakúnaishō

catarrh [kʌtɑːr'] n カタル kátàru

catastrophe [kʌtæs'trʌfi:] n (disaster) 災害 saígai

catastrophic [kætʌstrɑːf'ik] adj (disastrous) 破局的な hakyókuteki na

catch [kætʃ] (pt, pp **caught**) vt (animal) 捕る tórù, 捕まえる tsukámaeru; (fish: with net) 捕る tórù; (: with line) 釣る tsurú; (ball) 捕る tórù; (bus, train etc) ...に乗る norú; (arrest: thief etc) 逮捕する taího suru; (surprise: person) びっくりさせる bikkúri saséru; (attract: attention) 引く hikú; (hear: comment, whisper etc) 聞く kikú; (MED: illness) ...に掛る ...ni kakarù; (person: also: **catch up with/to**) ...に追い付く ...ni oítsukù

♦vi (fire) 付く tsukú; (become trapped: in branches, door etc) 引っ掛る hikkákaru

♦n (of fish etc) 獲物 emóno; (of ball) 捕球 hokyū; (hidden problem) 裏 ura, 穴 otóshiàna; (of lock) 留め金 tomégane; (game) キャッチボール kyátchibōru

to catch one's breath (rest) 息をつく íkì wo tsukú, 一休みする hitóyasumi suru

to catch fire 燃え出す moédasù

to catch sight of 見付ける mitsúkeru

catching [kætʃ'iŋ] adj (infectious) 移る utsurú

catchment area [kætʃ'mʌnt-] (BRIT) n (of school) 学区 gákkù; (of hospital) 通院

圏 tsúïnken

catch on vi (understand) 分かる wakarù; (grow popular) 流行る ryūkô suru

catch phrase n キャッチフレーズ kyátchifurēzu

catch up vi (fig: with person, on work) 追付く oítsukù
♦vt (person) ...に追い付く ...ni oítsukù

catchy [kætʃi] adj (tune) 覚え易い obôeyasuî

catechism [kætəkizəm] n (REL) 公教要理 kôkyôyóri

categoric(al) [kætəgɔːrik(ə)l] adj (certain, absolute) 絶対的な zettáiteki na

category [kætəgɔːri:] n (set, class) 範ちゅう hañchū

cater [keitəːr] vi: **to cater for** (BRIT: person, group) ...向きである ...múkî de arû; (needs) ...を満たす ...wo mitasù; (COMM: weddings etc) ...の料理を仕出しする ...no ryôri wo shídashi suru

caterer [keitəːrər] n 仕出し屋 shídashiya

catering [keitəːriŋ] n (trade, business) 仕出し shídashi

caterpillar [kætəːrpilər] n (with hair) 毛虫 kemúshi; (without hair) 芋虫 imómushi

caterpillar track n キャタピラ kyatápirà

cathedral [kəθi:drəl] n 大聖堂 daíseidô

catholic [kæθəlik] adj (tastes, interests) 広い hiroî

Catholic [kæθəlik] adj (REL) カトリック教の katórikkukyô no
♦n (REL) カトリック教徒 katórikkukyōto

cat's-eye [kætsai] (BRIT) n (AUT) 反射ざよう hañshabyô ◇夜間の目印として道路の中央またはわきに埋込むガラスなどの反射器 yakán no mejírushi toshitè dôro no chûô mata wa wakî ni umékomù gárasu nadð no hañshakî

cattle [kætl] npl ウシ ushî ◇総称 sôshô

catty [kæti:] adj (comment, woman) 意地悪な íjîwarû na

caucus [kɔ:kəs] n (POL: group) 実力者会議 jitsúryokusha kaîgi; (: US) 党部会 tô-

bukâi

caught [kɔːt] pt, pp of **catch**

cauliflower [kɔːləflauəːr] n カリフラワー ― karîfurawâ

cause [kɔːz] n (of outcome, effect) 原因 geñ-in; (reason) 理由 riyû; (aim, principle: also POL) 目的 mokúteki
♦vt (produce, lead to: outcome, effect) 引起こす hikíokosû

caustic [kɔːstik] adj (CHEM) 腐食性の fushókusei no; (fig: remark) 辛らつな shifíratsu na

caution [kɔːʃən] n (prudence) 慎重さ shiñchōsa; (warning) 警告 kefkoku, 注意 chûi
♦vt (warn: also POLICE) 警告する kefkoku suru

cautious [kɔːʃəs] adj (careful, wary) 注意深い chúîbukaî

cautiously [kɔːʃəsli:] adv 注意深く chúîbukakù

cavalier [kævəliəːr] adj (attitude, fashion) ...に対して無礼な ...ni táî shite ibárikusattà

cavalry [kævəlri:] n (MIL: mechanized) 装甲部隊 sôkôbutâi; (: mounted) 騎兵隊 kihéitai

cave [keiv] n (in cliff, hill) 洞穴 horá-ana

cave in vi (roof etc) 陥没する kañbotsu suru, 崩れる kuzúrerù

caveman [keivmən] (pl **cavemen**) n 穴居人 kékkyôjin

cavern [kævəːrn] n どうくつ dôkutsu

caviar(e) [kæviɑːr] n キャビア kyábîa

cavity [kæviti:] n (in wall) 空どう kúdô; (ANAT) 腔 kô; (in tooth) 虫歯の穴 mushíba no anâ

cavort [kəvɔːrt] vi (romp) はしゃぎ回る hashá#imawaru

CB [si:bi:] n abbr (= Citizens' Band (Radio)) 市民バンド shimfnbañdo, シチズンバンド shichfzunbañdo

CBI [si:bi:ai] n abbr (= Confederation of British Industry) 英国産業連盟 eßkokusafigyôreñmei

cc [si:si:] abbr = cubic centimeter(s) 立方センチメートル rippócheñchîmêtoru, cc shíshî; = **carbon copy**

cease [si:s] vt (end, stop) 終える oêru
♦vi (end, stop) 終る owâru, 止る tomáru

ceasefire [siːsˈfaiəʳ] *n* (MIL) 停戦 teÎsen

ceaseless [siːsˈlis] *adj* (chatter, traffic) 絶間ない taÎma naì

cedar [siːˈdəʳ] *n* (tree) ヒマラヤスギ himárayasugí; (wood) シーダー材 shídaŕzai

cede [siːd] *vt* (land, rights etc) 譲る yuzúru

ceiling [siːˈliŋ] *n* (in room) 天井 teÎjō; (upper limit: on wages, prices etc) 天井 teÎjō, 上限 jōgen

celebrate [selˈəbreit] *vt* (gen) 祝う iwáù; (REL: mass) 挙げる agérù
◆*vi* お祝いする o-íwai suru

celebrated [selˈəbreitid] *adj* (author, hero) 有名な yūmeì na

celebration [seləbreiˈʃən] *n* (party, festival) お祝い o-íwai

celebrity [səlebˈriti] *n* (famous person) 有名人 yūmeíjin

celery [selˈəri] *n* セロリ séròri

celestial [səlesˈtʃəl] *adj* (heavenly) 天上的な teÎjōteki na

celibacy [selˈəbəsi] *n* 禁欲生活 kiÎ-yoku seíkatsu

cell [sel] *n* (in prison: *gen*) 監房 kaÎbō; (：solitary) 独房 dokúbō; (in monastery) 個室 koshítsu; (BIO, *also* of revolutionaries) 細胞 saíbō; (ELEC) 電池 deÎchi

cellar [selˈəʳ] *n* (basement) 地下室 chikáshitsu; (*also*: **wine cellar**) ワイン貯蔵室 waín chozōshitsu

cello [tʃelˈou] *n* (MUS) チェロ chérò

cellophane [selˈəfein] *n* セロハン séròhan

cellular [selˈjuləʳ] *adj* (BIO: structure, tissue) 細胞の saíbō no; (fabrics) 保温効果の高い hoóṇkōka no takaì, 防寒の dōkan no

cellulose [selˈjəlous] *n* (tissue) 繊維素 seíishò

Celt [selt, kelt] *n* ケルト人 kerútòjin

Celtic [selˈtik, kelˈtik] *adj* ケルト人の kerútòjin no; (language etc) ケルトの kerútò no

cement [siment] *n* (powder) セメント mento; (concrete) コンクリート koÎkuríto

cement mixer *n* セメントミキサー seménto mikísà

cemetery [semˈiteːri] *n* 墓地 bóchì

cenotaph [senˈətæf] *n* (monument) 戦没者記念碑 seÎbotsusha kineñhì

censor [senˈsəʳ] *n* (POL, CINEMA etc) 検閲官 keÎ-etsòkan
◆*vt* (book, play, news etc) 検閲する keÎetsu suru

censorship [senˈsəʳʃip] *n* (of book, play, news etc) 検閲 keÎ-etsu

censure [senˈʃəʳ] *vt* (reprove) とがめる togámerù

census [senˈsəs] *n* (of population) 国勢調査 kokúzeichòsa

cent [sent] *n* (US: *also*: **one-cent coin**) 1セント玉 isséntodamá; *also see* **per**

centenary [sentaneːri] *n* (of birth etc) 100周年 hyakúshūnen

center [senˈtəʳ] (*BRIT* **centre**) *n* (of circle, room, line) 中心 chūshin; (of town) 中心部 chūshiñbu, 繁華街 haÎkagai; (of attention, interest) 的 matò; (heart: of action, belief etc) 核心 kakúshin; (building: health center, community center) センター seÎtā; (POL) 中道 chūdō
◆*vt* (weight) …の中心に置く …no chūshin ni okú; (sights) …にぴったり合わせる …ni pittari awaserù; (SOCCER: ball) グランド中央へ飛ばす gurándo chūō e tobású; (TYP: on page) 中央に合わせる chūō ni awáserù

center forward *n* (SPORT) センターフォワード seÎtāfowádò

center half *n* (SPORT) センターハーフ seÎtāháfu

centigrade [senˈtigreid] *adj* 摂氏 sesshí

centimeter [senˈtəmiːtəʳ] (*BRIT* **centimetre**) *n* センチメートル seÎchimètoru

centipede [senˈtəpid] *n* ムカデ mukáde

central [senˈtrəl] *adj* (in the center) 中心点の chūshiñten no; (near the center) 中心の chūshin no; (committee, government) 中央の chūō no; (idea, figure) 中心の chūshin no

Central America *n* 中米 chūbei

central heating *n* セントラルヒーティング seÎtoraruhítìngu

centralize [sen'trəlaiz] vt (decision-making, authority) 中央に集中させる chūō ni shúchū saséru

central reservation (BRIT) n (AUT: of road) 中央分離帯 chūōbunritai

centre [sen'tər] (etc BRIT) = **center** etc

century [sen'tʃəri] n 世紀 séìki
20th century 20世紀 nijússeìki

ceramic [səræm'ik] adj (art, tiles) セラミックの serámikku no

ceramics [səræm'iks] npl (objects) 焼物 yakímono

cereal [si:r'i:əl] n (plant, crop) 穀物 kókùmotsu; (food) シリアル shírìarù

cerebral [ser'əbrəl] adj (MED: of the brain) 脳の nō no; (intellectual) 知的な chíteki na

ceremony [ser'əmouni:] n (event) 式 shikí; (ritual) 儀式 gíshìki; (behavior) 形式 keíshìki
to stand on ceremony 礼儀にこだわる reígi ni kodáwarù

certain [sɔːr'tən] adj (sure: person) 確信している kakúshin shité irù; (: fact) 確実な kakújitsu na; (person): a certain Mr Smith スミスと呼ばれる男 sumísù to yobareru otòko; (particular): certain days/places ある日(場所) árù hi (bashó); (some): a certain coldness/pleasure ある程度の冷たさ(喜び) árù teido no tsumétasa (yorókobi)
for certain 確実に kakújitsu ni

certainly [sɔːr'tənli:] adv (undoubtedly) 間違いなく machígai nakù; (of course) もちろん mochíron

certainty [sɔːr'tənti:] n (assurance) 確実性 kakújitsusei; (inevitability) 必然性 hitsúzensei

certificate [sɔːrtif'əkit] n (of birth, marriage etc) 証明書 shōmeisho; (diploma) 資格証明書 shikákushomeisho

certified mail [sɔːr'təfaid-] (US) n 配達証明付き郵便 haítatsushōmei tsukí kaíftome yúbin

certified public accountant (US) n 公認会計士 kōnin kaìkeishi

certify [sɔːr'təfai] vt (fact) 証明する shō-

mei suru; (award a diploma to) ...に資格を与える ...ni shikáku wo atáeru; (declare insane) 精神異常と認定する seíshinijō to niñtei suru

cervical [sɔːr'vikəl] adj (smear, cancer) 子宮けいの shikyūkeìbu no

cervix [sɔːr'viks] n (ANAT) 子宮けい部 shikyūkeìbu

Cesarean [size:r'i:ən] (BRIT **Caesarean**) adj: **Cesarean (section)** 帝王切開 teíōsekkaì

cesspit [ses'pit] n (sewage tank) 汚水だめ osúidame

cf. abbr = **compare**

ch. abbr = **chapter**

chafe [tʃeif] vt (rub: skin) 擦る súrù

chagrin [ʃəgrin'] n (annoyance) 悔しさ kuyáshisa; (disappointment) 落胆 rakútan

chain [tʃein] n (for anchor, prisoner, dog etc) 鎖 kusári; (on bicycle) チェーン chèn; (jewelery) 首飾り kubíkazàri; (of shops, hotels) チェーン chèn; (of events, ideas) 連鎖 reñsa
◆vt (also: **chain up**: prisoner, dog) 鎖につなぐ kusári ni tsunágu
an island chain/a chain of islands 列島 rettō
a mountain chain/a chain of mountains 山脈 sañmyaku

chain reaction n 連鎖反応 reñsahañnō

chain-smoke [tʃein'smouk] vi 立続けにタバコを吸う tatétsuzuke ni tabáko wo suú

chain store n チェーンストア chéñsutoà

chair [tʃe:r] n (seat) いす isú; (armchair) 安楽いす afirakuisù; (of university) 講座 kōza; (of meeting) 座長 zachō; (of committee) 委員長 iíñchō
◆vt (meeting) 座長を務める zachō wo tsutómerù

chairlift [tʃe:r'lift] n リフト rífùto

chairman [tʃe:r'mən] (pl **chairmen**) n (of committee) 委員長 iíñchō; (BRIT: of company) 社長 shachō

chalet [ʃælei'] n 山小屋 yamágoya

chalice [tʃæl'is] n (REL) 聖さん杯 seísañhai

chalk 80 chant

chalk [tʃɔːk] n (GEO) 白亜 hákùa; (for writing) 白墨 hakúboku, チョーク chóku

challenge [tʃǽlindʒ] n (of new job, unknown, new venture etc) 挑戦 chósen; (to authority, received ideas etc) 反抗 hańkò; (dare) 挑戦 chósen
♦vt (SPORT) ...に試合を申込む ...ni shiái wo móshikomù; (rival, competitor) 挑戦 する chósen suru; (authority, right, idea etc) ...に反抗する ...ni hańkò suru

to challenge someone to do something ...に...をやれるものならやってみ ろと挑戦する ...ni ...wo yaréru monó nara yatté miro to chósen suru

challenging [tʃǽlindʒiŋ] adj (career, task) やりがいを感じさせる yarígai wo kañjì saséru; (tone, look etc) 挑発的な chóhatsuteki na

chamber [tʃéimbər] n (room) 部屋 heyá; (POL: house) 院 ín; (BRIT: LAW: gen pl) 弁護士事務所 beñgoshi jimúshìtsu; (: of judge) 判事室 hañjishìtsu
chamber of commerce 商工会議所 shó- kōkaigisho

chambermaid [tʃéimbəːrmeid] n (in hotel) メード mèdo

chamber music n 室内音楽 shitsúnai oñgaku

chamois [ʃæmiː] n (ZOOL) シャモア shá- mòa; (cloth) セーム革 sèmugawa

champagne [ʃæmpéin] n シャンペン shañpeñ

champion [tʃǽmpiən] n (of league, con- test, fight) 優勝者 yúshòsha, チャンピオ ン chañpion; (of cause, principle, person) 擁護者 yógosha

championship [tʃǽmpiənʃip] n (con- test) 選手権決定戦 seńshuken kettéisen; (title) 選手権 seńshuken

chance [tʃæns] n (likelihood, possibility) 可能性 kanósei; (opportunity) 機会 kikái, チャンス cháñsu; (risk) 危険 kikén, か け kaké
♦vt (risk): *to chance it* 危険を冒すki- kén wo okasù, 冒険をする bóken wo su- ru
♦adj 偶然の gúzen no
to take a chance 危険を冒す kikén wo

okasù, 冒険をする bóken wo suru
by chance 偶然に gúzen ni

chancellor [tʃǽnsələr] n (head of gov- ernment) 首相 shushō

Chancellor of the Exchequer (BRIT) n 大蔵大臣 ókuradaijin

chandelier [ʃændəlíər] n シャンデリア shañderìa

change [tʃeindʒ] vt (alter, transform) 変 える kaéru; (wheel, bulb etc) 取替える toríkaerù; (clothes) 着替える kigáerù; (job, address) 変える kaéru; (baby, dia- per) 替える kaéru; (exchange: money) 両 替する ryógae suru
♦vi (alter) 変る kawáru; (change one's clothes) 着替える kigáerù; (change trains, buses) 乗換える noríkaerù; (traf- fic lights) 変る kawáru; (be trans- formed): *to change into ...*に変る ...ni ka- wáru, ...になる ...ni narú
♦n (alteration) 変化 héñka; (difference) 違い chigái; (also: *change of clothes*) 着 替え kigáe; (of government, climate, job) 変化 héñka; (coins) 小銭 kozéni; (money returned) お釣 o-tsúri
to change one's mind 気が変る ki gá kawárù
for a change たまには tamá ni wa

changeable [tʃéindʒəbəl] adj 変りやすい kawáriyasuì

change machine n 両替機 ryógaekì

changeover [tʃéindʒóuvər] n (to new system) 切替え kiríkae

changing [tʃéindʒiŋ] adj (world, nature) 変る kawáru

changing room (BRIT) n 更衣室 kói- shìtsu

channel [tʃǽnəl] n (TV) チャンネル cháñ- neru; (in sea, river etc) 水路 súiro; (groove) 溝 mizó; (fig: means) 手続 tetsú- zùki, ルート rùto
♦vt (money, resources) 流す nagásù
the (English) Channel イギリス海峡 igírisu kaíkyò
the Channel Islands チャネル諸島 chanèru shotō

chant [tʃænt] n (of crowd, fans etc) 掛声 kakégoè; (REL: song) 詠唱歌 eíshòka

♦vt (word, name, slogan) 唱える tonáerù

chaos [kei´as] n (disorder) 混乱 koñran

chaotic [keia´tik] adj (mess, jumble) 混乱した koñran shitá

chap [tʃæp] n (BRIT: inf) (man) やつ yátsù

chapel [tʃæp´əl] n (in church) 礼拝堂 refhaidò; (in hospital, prison, school etc) チャペル chápèru; (BRIT: non-conformist chapel) 教会堂 kyókaidò

chaperone [ʃæp´əroun] n (for woman) 付添い tsukísòi, シャペロン shapéroñ

♦vt (woman, child) ...に付添う ...ni tsukísòu

chaplain [tʃæp´lin] n (REL, MIL, SCOL) 付属牧師 fuzókubokùshi

chapped [tʃæpt] adj (skin, lips) あかぎれした akágire shitá

chapter [tʃæp´tər] n (of book) 章 shó; (of life, history) 時期 jíkì

char [tʃɑr] vt (burn) 黒焦げにする kurókoge ni suru

♦n (BRIT) = charwoman

character [kær´iktər] n (nature) 性質 seíshitsu; (moral strength) 気骨 kikótsu; (personality) 人格 jiñkaku; (in novel, film) 人物 jiñbutsu; (letter) 文字 mójì

characteristic [kæriktəris´tik] adj (typical) 特徴的な tokúchòteki na

♦n (trait, feature) 特徴 tokúchò

characterize [kær´iktəraiz] vt (typify) ...の特徴である ...no tokúchò de arù; (describe the character of) ...の特徴を描写する ...no tokúchò wo byósha suru

charade [ʃəreid´] n (sham, pretence) 装い yosóoi

charcoal [tʃɑr´koul] n (fuel) 炭 sumí, 木炭 mokútàn; (for drawing) 木炭 mokútàn

charge [tʃɑrdʒ] n (fee) 料金 ryókin; (LAW: accusation) 容疑 yógi; (responsibility) 責任 sekínin

♦vt (for goods, services) ...の料金を取る ...no ryókin wo torù; (LAW: accuse: to charge someone (with) ...の罪に問う kisó suru; (battery) 充電 する júden suru; (MIL: enemy) ...に突撃する ...ni totsúgeki suru

♦vi (animal) 掛って来る〔行く〕kakátte kurù〔ikù〕; (MIL) 突撃する totsúgeki suru

to take charge of (child) ...の面倒を見る ...no meñdò wo mirù; (company) ...の指揮を取る ...no shikí wo torù

to be in charge of (person, machine) ...の責任を持っている ...no sekínin wo motté irù; (business) ...の責任者である ...no sekíniñsha de arù

how much do you charge? 料金はいくらですか ryókin wa ikùra desù ka

to charge an expense (up) to someone's account ...の勘定に付ける ...no kañjò ni tsukerù

charge card n (for particular shop or organization) クレジットカード kuréjittokàdo ◆特定の店でしか使えない種々ま tokútei na no mise de shika tsukáenai monò wo sásù

charges [tʃɑr´dʒiz] npl (bank charges, telephone charges etc) 料金 ryókin

to reverse the charges (TEL) 先方払いする señpóbarai ni surù

charisma [kəriz´mə] n カリスマ性 karísumaseì

charitable [tʃær´itəbəl] adj (organization) 慈善の jízèn no

charity [tʃær´iti:] n (organization) 慈善事業 jízénjigyò; (kindness) 親切さ shiñsetsusa; (generosity) 寛大さ kañdaisa; (money, gifts) 施し hodókoshi

charlady [tʃɑr´leidi:] (BRIT) n = charwoman

charlatan [ʃɑr´lətən] n (偽者 nisémono

charm [tʃɑrm] n (attractiveness) 魅力 miryóku; (to bring good luck) お守 o-mámori; (on bracelet etc) 飾り kazári

♦vt (please, delight) うっとりさせる uttóri sasèru

charming [tʃɑr´miŋ] adj (person, place) 魅力的な miryókuteki na

chart [tʃɑrt] n (graph) グラフ gúràfu; (diagram) 図 zu; (map) 海図 kázu

♦vt (course) 地図に書く chízu ni kakù; (progress) 図に書く zú ni kakú

charter [tʃɑr´tər] vt (plane, ship etc) チャーターする chátà suru

♦n (document, constitution) 憲章 keñ

shō; (of university, company) 免許 mén-kyo

chartered accountant [tʃɑːˈtəːd-] (BRIT) n 公認会計士 kónin kaikeíshi

charter flight n チャーターフライト chátáfuraíto

charts [tʃɑːrts] npl (hit parade): **the charts** ヒットチャート hittócháto

charwoman [tʃɑːrˈwʊmən] (pl **char-women**) n 掃除婦 sójifu

chase [tʃeis] vt (pursue) 追跡する oíkake-rù; (also: **chase away**) 追払う oíharaù
♦n (pursuit) 追跡 tsuíseki

chasm [kæzˈəm] n (GEO) 深い割れ目 fúkāi waréme

chassis [ʃæsˈiː] n (AUT) シャシ shashí

chastity [tʃæsˈtiti] n (REL) 純潔 junke-tsu

chat [tʃæt] vi (also: **have a chat**) おしゃべりする o-sháberí surū
♦n (conversation) おしゃべり o-sháberí

chat show (BRIT) n トーク番組 tōku bañgumi

chatter [tʃætˈəːr] vi (person) しゃべりまくる shabérimakurù; (animal) きゃっきゃっと鳴く kyákkyattó nakú; (teeth) がちがち鳴る gachígachi narú
♦n (of people) しゃべり声 shabérígoè; (of birds) さえずり saézuri; (of animals) きゃっきゃっという鳴き声 kyákkyattó iú nakígoè

chatterbox [tʃætˈəːrbɑːks] (inf) n おしゃべり野郎 o-sháberizukài

chatty [tʃætˈiː] adj (style, letter) 親しみやすい shitáshimíyasuì; (person) おしゃべりな o-sháberí na

chauffeur [ʃouˈvəːr] n お抱え運転手 o-kákae-unteñshu

chauvinist [ʃouˈvənist] n (male chauvinist) 男性優越主義者 dañseiyúetsushugíshà; (nationalist) 熱狂的な愛国主義者 nek-kyótekiáikokushugíshà

cheap [tʃiːp] adj (inexpensive) 安い yasúì; (poor quality) 安っぽい yasúppoì; (behavior, joke) 下卑な gebíta na
♦adv: **to buy/sell something cheap** 安く買う(売る) yasúkù kaú (urú)

cheaper [tʃiːˈpəːr] adj (less expensive)

っと安い móttò yasuí

cheaply [tʃiːpˈliː] adv (inexpensively) 安く yasúkù

cheat [tʃiːt] vi (in exam) カンニングする kañningu suru; (at cards) いかさまをする ikásama wo suru
♦vt: **to cheat someone (out of something)** ...から ...を だまし取る ...kara ...wo damáshitorù
♦n (person) いかさま師 ikásamàshi

check [tʃek] vt (examine: bill, progress) 調べる shiráberù; (verify: facts) 確認する kakúnin suru; (halt: enemy, disease) 食止める kuítomerù; (restrain: impulse, person) 抑える osáerù
♦n (inspection) 検査 keñsa; (curb) 抑制 yokúsei; (US: bill) 勘定書 kañjógaki; (BANKING) 小切手 kogítte; (pattern: gen pl) 市松模様 ichímatsumoyó
♦adj (pattern, cloth) 市松模様の ichíma-tsumoyó no

checkbook [tʃekˈbuk] (US) n 小切手帳 kogíttechō

checkerboard [tʃekˈəːrbɔːrd] n チェッカー盤 chekkában

checkered [tʃekˈəːrd] (BRIT **chequered**) adj (fig: career, history) 起伏の多い kifúku no ói

checkers [tʃekˈəːrz] (US) npl (game) チェッカー chékkā

check in vi (at hotel, airport) チェックインする chekkúin surù
♦vt (luggage) 預ける azúkerù

check-in (desk) [tʃekˈin-] n フロント furónto

checking account [tʃekˈiŋ-] (US) n (current account) 当座預金 tōzayokìn

checkmate [tʃekˈmeit] n (CHESS) 王手 ōte

check out vi (of hotel) チェックアウトする chekkúaùto surù

checkout [tʃekˈaut] n (in shop) 勘定カウンター kañjó kauñtā

checkpoint [tʃekˈpoint] n (on border) 検問所 keñmonjo

checkroom [tʃekˈruːm] (US) n (left-luggage office) 手荷物一時預り所 tenímòtsu ichíjìazúkarijo

check up vi: **to check up on something/someone** ...を調べておく ...wo shirábeté okú

checkup [tʃek'ʌp] n (MED) 健康診断 kefikōshíhdàn

cheek [tʃiːk] n (ANAT) ほお hő; (impudence) ずうずうしさ zúzúshisà; (nerve) 度胸 dokyō

cheekbone [tʃiːk'boun] n ほお骨 hőbone

cheeky [tʃiː'kiː] adj (impudent) ずうずうしい zúzúshiì

cheep [tʃiːp] vi (bird) ぴよぴよ鳴く piyópiyo nakú

cheer [tʃiːr] vt (team, speaker) 声援する sefien suru; (gladden) 喜ばす yorōkobasù
♦vi (shout) 声援する sefien suru
♦n (shout) 声援する sefien

cheerful [tʃiːr'fəl] adj (wave, smile, person) 朗らかな hogaráka na

cheerio [tʃiː'riːou] (BRIT) excl じゃあねjã ne

cheers [tʃiːrz] npl (of crowd etc) 声援 sefien, かっさい kassái
cheers! (toast) 乾杯 kañpai

cheer up vi (person) 元気を出す gefiki wo dasú
♦vt (person) 元気づける gefikizukerù

cheese [tʃiːz] n チーズ chiizu

cheeseboard [tʃiːz'bourd] n チーズボード chizubòdo 〇チーズを盛り合せる板または皿 chízu wo morîawaserù ità mata wa sará

cheetah [tʃiː'tə] n チーター chiità

chef [ʃef] n (in restaurant, hotel) コック kókku

chemical [kem'ikəl] adj (fertilizer, warfare) 化学の kágàku no
♦n 化学薬品 kagékuyakùhin

chemist [kem'ist] n (BRIT: pharmacist) 薬剤師 yakúzaìshi; (scientist) 化学者 kagákùsha

chemistry [kem'istriː] n 化学 kágàku

chemist's (shop) [kem'ists-] (BRIT) n 薬局 yakkyókù

cheque [tʃek] (BRIT: BANKING) n = check

chequebook [tʃek'buk] (BRIT) n = checkbook

cheque card (BRIT) n (to guarantee cheque) 小切手カード kogítte kàdo

chequered [tʃek'ərd] (BRIT) adj = checkered

cherish [tʃer'iʃ] vt (person) 大事にする daíji ni suru; (memory, dream) 心に抱く kokórò ni idakù

cherry [tʃer'iː] n (fruit) サクランボウ sakúranbò; (also: cherry tree) サクラ sakúra

chess [tʃes] n チェス chésù

chessboard [tʃes'bourd] n チェス盤 chésùban

chest [tʃest] n (ANAT) 胸 muné; (box) ひつ hitsú
chest of drawers 整理だんす sefridahsu

chestnut [tʃes'nʌt] n クリ kurí; (also: chestnut tree) クリの木 kurí no ki

chew [tʃuː] vt (food) かむ kámù

chewing gum [tʃuː'iŋ-] n チューインガム chúingamù

chic [ʃiːk] adj (dress, hat etc) スマートな sumáto no; (person, place) 粋な ikí na

chick [tʃik] n (bird) ひな hìnà; (inf: girl) べっぴん beppìn

chicken [tʃik'ən] n (bird) ニワトリ niwátori; (meat) 鶏肉 keíniku; (inf: coward) 弱虫 yowamushì

chicken out (inf) vi お気付いて...から手を引く okízukezùte ...kara te wo hikú

chickenpox [tʃik'ənpæks] n 水ぼうそう mizúbōsō

chicory [tʃik'əriː] n チコリ chíkðri

chief [tʃiːf] n (of tribe) しゅう長 shúchò; (of organization, department) ...長 ...chô
♦adj (principal) 主な ômò na

chief executive n 社長 shachő

chiefly [tʃiːf'liː] adv (principally) 主に ô-mò ni

chiffon [ʃifɑːn] n (fabric) シフォン shíffon

chilblain [tʃil'blein] n 霜焼け shimóyàke

child [tʃaild] (pl **children**) n 子供 kodómo
do you have any children? お子さんは？ o-kô-san wa?

childbirth [tʃaild'bəːrθ] n お産 osán

childhood [tʃaild'hud] n 子供時分 kodómojibun

childish [tʃaɪl'dɪʃ] adj (games, attitude, person) 子供っぽい kodómoppoì

childlike [tʃaɪld'laɪk] adj 無邪気な mújaki na

child minder (BRIT) n 保母 hóbò

children [tʃɪl'drən] npl of **child**

Chile [tʃɪl'iː] n チリ chírì

Chilean [tʃɪl'eiən] adj チリの chírì no
♦n チリ人 chírìjìn

chill [tʃɪl] n (coldness: in air, water etc) 冷え hié; (MED: illness) 風邪 kazé
♦vt (cool: food, drinks) 冷す hiyasū; (person: make cold): **to be chilled** 体が冷え
る karáda ga hierū

chilli [tʃɪl'iː] n チリ chírì

chilly [tʃɪl'iː] adj (weather) 肌寒い hadásamuì; (person) 寒気がする samúke ga suru; (response, look) 冷たい tsumétai

chime [tʃaɪm] n (of bell, clock) チャイム cháìmu
♦vi チャイムが鳴る chaímu ga narū

chimney [tʃɪm'niː] n (of house, factory) 煙突 eñtotsu

chimney sweep n 煙突掃除夫 eñtotsu sōjìfu

chimpanzee [tʃɪmpænziː'] n チンパンジー chíñpañjì

chin [tʃɪn] n あご agó

China [tʃaɪ'nə] n 中国 chúgokù

china [tʃaɪ'nə] n (clay) 陶土 tōdò; (crockery) 瀬戸物 setómonò

Chinese [tʃaɪniːz'] adj 中国の chúgokù no; (LING) 中国語の chúgokugo no
♦n inv (person) 中国人 chúgokujìn; (LING) 中国語 chúgokugo

chink [tʃɪŋk] n (crack: in door, wall etc) 透き間 sukíma; (clink: of bottles etc) かちん kachín

chip [tʃɪp] n (BRIT: gen pl: CULIN) フライドポテト furáidopotèto; (US: also: **potato chip**) ポテトチップス potétochippùsu; (of wood, glass, stone) 欠けら kakéra; (COMPUT) チップ chíppù
♦vt: **to be chipped** (cup, plate) 縁が欠けている fuchí ga kakéte irú

chip in (inf) vi (contribute) 寄付する kifú surū; (interrupt) 口を挟む kuchí wo

hasámù

chiropodist [kirɑːp'ədist] (BRIT) n 足治療師 ashí chiryòshi

chirp [tʃərp] vi (bird) ちゅうちゅう鳴く chūchū nakú

chisel [tʃiz'əl] n (for wood) のみ nómì; (for stone) たがね tagáne

chit [tʃit] n (note) メモ mémò; (receipt) 領収書 ryōshūsho

chitchat [tʃit'tʃæt] n 世間話 sekénbanàshi

chivalrous [ʃiv'əlrəs] adj 親切な shíísetsu na

chivalry [ʃiv'əlriː] n (behavior) 親切さ shíísetsusa; (medieval system) 騎士道 kishídò

chives [tʃaivz] npl (herb) チャイブ cháìbu

chlorine [klɔːr'iːn] n (CHEM) 塩素 eñso

chock-a-block [tʃɑːk'əblɑːk'] adj 一杯で íppai de

chock-full [tʃɑːk'ful'] adj = **chock-a-block**

chocolate [tʃɔːk'əlit] n (bar, sweet, cake) チョコレート chokórèto; (drink) ココア kókòa

choice [tʃɔis] n (selection) 選んだ物 eránda monò; (option) 選択 señtaku; (preference) 好み konómi
♦adj (fine: cut of meat, fruit etc) 一級のikkyú no

choir [kwaiˈəːr] n (of singers) 聖歌隊 seíkatai; (area of church) 聖歌隊席 seíkataiðsèki

choirboy [kwaiˈəːrˌbɔi] n 少年聖歌隊員 shōnen seíkataiìn

choke [tʃouk] vi (on food, drink etc) ...がのどに詰る ...ga nodò ni tsumarū; (with smoke, dust, anger etc) むせる musérù
♦vt (strangle) ...の首を締める ...no kubì wo shimerū; (block): **to be choked (with)** (...で) 詰っている (...de) tsumatte irú

cholera [kɑːl'əːrə] n コレラ kórèra

cholesterol [kələs'tɑːrəl] n (fat) コレステロール korésutèrōru

choose [tʃuːz] (pt **chose**, pp **chosen**) vt (select)

ぶ erábu

to choose to do...をする事に決める
...wo suru kotó ni kiméru

choosy [tʃuːziː] *adj* (difficult to please)
えり好みする erígonómi suru

chop [tʃɔp] *vt* (wood) 割る warú;
(CULIN: *also*: **chop up**: vegetables, fruit,
meat) 刻む kizámu

♦*n* (CULIN) チョップ chóppù, チャップ
cháppu

chopper [tʃɔpər] *n* (helicopter) ヘリコ
プター heríkoputā

choppy [tʃɔpiː] *adj* (sea) しけの shiké no

chops [tʃɔps] *npl* (jaws) あご agó

chopsticks [tʃɔpstiks] *npl* はし háshì

choral [kɔːrəl] *adj* (MUS) 合唱の gasshō
no

chord [kɔːrd] *n* (MUS) 和音 wáòn

chore [tʃɔːr] *n* (domestic task) 家事 kájì;
(routine task) 毎日の雑用 maínichi no
zatsúyō

choreographer [kɔːriːɔːgrəfər] *n* 振付
師 furítsukeshī

chortle [tʃɔːrtəl] *vi* 楽しそうに笑う tanóshisō ni waraú

chorus [kɔːrəs] *n* (MUS: group) 合唱団
gasshōdan, コーラス kōrasu; (: song) 合唱
gasshō; (: refrain) リフレーン rifúrēn; (of
musical play) コーラス kōrasu

chose [tʃouz] *pt of* **choose**

chosen [tʃouzən] *pp of* **choose**

Christ [kraist] *n* キリスト kirísuto

christen [krisən] *vt* (REL: baby) ...に洗
礼を施す ...ni seírei wo hodókosù; (nickname) ...を...と呼ぶ ...wo ...to yobú

Christian [kristʃən] *adj* キリスト教の
kirísutokyō no

♦*n* キリスト教徒 kirísutokyōto

Christianity [kristʃiænitiː] *n* キリスト
教 kirísutokyō

Christian name *n* ファーストネーム fá-
sutonēmu

Christmas [krisməs] *n* (REL: festival)
クリスマス kurísumasu; (period) クリス
マスの季節 kurísumasu no kisetsú

Merry Christmas! メリークリスマス!
merí kurisumasu!

Christmas card *n* クリスマスカード
kurísumasu kādo

Christmas Day *n* クリスマス kurísumasu

Christmas Eve *n* クリスマスイブ kurf-
sumasu ibū

Christmas tree *n* クリスマスツリー kurísumasu tsurī

chrome [kroum] *n* クロームめっき kurō-
mumekkī

chromium [kroumiːəm] *n* = **chrome**

chromosome [krouməsoum] *n* 染色体
seńshokutai

chronic [krɑnik] *adj* (continual: ill-
health, illness etc) 慢性の mañsei no;
(: drunkenness etc) 常習的な jōshūteki
na; (severe: shortage, lack etc) ひどい
hídoī

chronicle [krɑnikəl] *n* (of events) 記録
kiróku 3年代順または日付順の記録を指
す neńdaijun mata wa hízúkejun no
kiróku wo sasú

chronological [krɑnəlɑdʒikəl] *adj*
(order) 日付順の hízúkejun no

chrysanthemum [krisænθəməm] *n* キ
ク kikú

chubby [tʃʌbiː] *adj* (cheeks, child) ぽっ
ちゃりした potchári shitá

chuck [tʃʌk] (*inf*) *vt* (throw: stone, ball
etc) 投げる nagerù; (BRIT: *also*: **chuck
up**) やめる yaméru

chuckle [tʃʌkəl] *vi* くすくす笑う kúsùkusu waraú

chuck out *vt* (person) 追い出す oídasù;
(rubbish etc) 捨てる sutéru

chug [tʃʌg] *vi* (machine, car engine etc)
ぽっぽっと音を立てる póppòtto otó wo
taterù; (car, boat: *also*: **chug along**) ぽっ
ぽっと音を立てて行く póppòtto otó wo
tatéte ikú

chum [tʃʌm] *n* (friend) 友達 tomódachi

chunk [tʃʌŋk] *n* (of stone, meat) 塊 katámari

church [tʃəːrtʃ] *n* (building) 教会 kyōkai;
(denomination) 教派 kyōha, ...教 ...kyō

churchyard [tʃəːrtʃjɑːrd] *n* 教会墓地
kyōkaibochī

churlish [tʃəːrliʃ] *adj* (silence, behavior)
無礼な buréi na

churn [tʃəːrn] n (for butter) かく乳器 kakúnyúki; (BRIT: also: **milk churn**) 大型ミルク缶 ōgata mirukukan

churn out vt (mass-produce: objects, books etc) 大量に作る taíryō ni tsukurù

chute [ʃuːt] n (also: **rubbish chute**) ごみ捨て場 gomísuteba; (for coal, parcels etc) シュート shúto

chutney [tʃʌt'niː] n チャツネ chátsune

CIA [siːaieiˈ] (US) n abbr (= Central Intelligence Agency) 中央情報局 chūōjōhōkyoku

CID [siːaidiːˈ] (BRIT) n abbr (= Criminal Investigation Department) 刑事部 keíjibu

cider [saiˈdəːr] n リンゴ酒 ríñgoshū

cigar [sigɑːrˈ] n 葉巻 hamáki

cigarette [sigəretˈ] n (紙巻) タバコ (kamímaki) tábako

cigarette case n シガレットケース shigárettokēsu

cigarette end n 吸殻 suígara

Cinderella [sindərelˈə] n シンデレラ shíndererā

cinders [sin'dəːrz] npl (of fire) 燃え殻 moégara

cine-camera [sin'iːkæməːrə] (BRIT) n 映画カメラ eíga kamèra

cine-film [sin'iːfilm] (BRIT) n 映画用フィルム eígayō firùmu

cinema [sin'əmə] n (THEATER) 映画館 eígakàn; (film-making) 映画界 eígakài

cinnamon [sin'əmən] n (CULIN) ニッケイ nikkéi, シナモン shinámoñ

cipher [saiˈfəːr] n (code) 暗号 añgṓ

circle [səːrˈkəl] n (shape) 円 éñ; (of friends) 仲間 nakáma; (in cinema, theater) 二階席 nikáiseki

♦vi (bird, plane) 旋回する señkai suru

♦vt (move round) 回る mawárù; (surround) 囲む kakómù

circuit [səːrˈkit] n (ELEC) 回路 káiro; (tour) 1周 isshū; (track) サーキット sākitto; (lap) 1周 isshū, ラップ ráppù

circuitous [səːrkjuˈitəs] adj (route, journey) 遠回りの tōmawàri no

circular [səːrˈkjələːr] adj (plate, pond etc) 丸い marúi

♦n (letter) 回状 kaíjō

circulate [səːrˈkjəleit] vi (traffic) 流れる nagárerù; (blood) 循環する juñkan suru; (news, rumour, report) 出回る demáwaru; (person: at party etc) 動き回る ugókimawarù

♦vt (report) 回す mawásu

circulation [səːrkjəleiˈʃən] n (of report, book etc) 回される事 mawásarerù kotó; (of traffic) 流れ nagáre; (of air, water, also MED: of blood) 循環 juñkan; (of newspaper) 発行部数 hakkṓbusū

circumcise [səːrˈkəmsaiz] vt (MED) …の包皮を切除する …no hṓhi wo setsūjo surù; (REL) …に割礼を行う …ni katsúrei wo okónau

circumference [səːrkʌmˈfərəns] n (edge) 周囲 shūi; (distance) 周囲の長さ shūi no nagàsa

circumflex [səːrˈkʌmfleks] n (also: **circumflex accent**) 曲折アクセント kyokúsetsu akùsento

circumspect [səːrˈkʌmspekt] adj (cautious, careful) 慎重な shiñchō na

circumstances [səːrˈkʌmstænsiz] npl (of accident, death) 状況 jōkyō; (conditions, state of affairs) 状態 jōtai; (also: **financial circumstances**) 経済状態 kefzaíjōtai

circumvent [səːrkəmventˈ] vt (regulation) …に触れない様にする …ni furénai yṑ ni surù; (difficulty) 回避する kaíhi suru

circus [səːrˈkəs] n (show) サーカス sākasu; (performers) サーカス団 sākasudaǹ

CIS [siːaieiˈs] n abbr = **Commonwealth of Independent States**

cistern [sisˈtəːrn] n (water tank) 貯水タンク chosúitaǹku; (of toilet) 水槽 suísō

cite [sait] vt (quote: example, author etc) 引用する in-yṓ suru; (LAW) 召喚する shṓkan suru

citizen [sit'əzən] n (gen) 住民 jūmin; (of a country) 国民 kokúmin, 市民 shímin; (of a city) 市民 shímin; (of other political divisions) …民 …min

citizenship [sit'əzənʃip] n (of a country) 市民権 shimíǹken

citrus fruit [sit'rəs fruːt] n カンキツ類 kañkitsurði

city [sit'iː] n 都市 toshí
the City (FINANCE) シティー shití ◇ ロンドンの金融業の中心地 rondon no kíñyügyō no chúshíñchi

civic [siv'ik] adj (leader, duties, pride) 公民の kômiñ no; (authorities) 自治体の jíchítai no

civic centre (BRIT) n 自治体中心部 jíchítaichúshíñbu

civil [siv'əl] adj (gen) 市民の shímíñ no, 公民の kômiñ no; (authorities) 行政の gyōsei no; (polite) 礼儀正しい reígitada-shíi

civil defense n 民間防衛 míñkañbōei

civil disobedience n 市民的不服従 shimíñtekifufukújū

civil engineer n 土木技師 dobókugishì

civilian [sivil'jən] adj (attitudes, casualties, life) 民間の míñkan no
♦n 民間人 míñkañjin

civilization [sivəlæzei'ʃən] n (a society) 文明社会 buñmeishakài; (social organization) 文化 búñka

civilized [siv'əlaizd] adj (society) 文明の buñmeiteki na; (person) 洗練された se-ñreñ saréta

civil law n 民法 míñpō

civil rights npl 公民権 kōmiñken

civil servant n 公務員 kōmuiñ

Civil Service n 文官職 buñkañshoku

civil war n 内乱 naíran

clad [klæd] adj: **clad (in)** ...を着た ...wo kítá

claim [kleim] vt (expenses) 請求する seí-kyū suru; (inheritance) 要求する yōkyū suru; (rights) 主張する shuchō suru; (assert): **to claim that/to be** ...である と主張する ...de arū to shuchō suru
♦vi (for insurance) 請求する seíkyū suru
♦n (assertion) 主張 shuchō; (for pension, wage rise, compensation) 請求 seíkyū; (to inheritance, land) 権利 kéñri
to claim responsibility (for) (...の) 犯行声明を出す (...no) hañkōseimeí wo dasū
to claim credit (for) (...の) 自分の業績

であると主張する (...ga) jíbun no gyṓseki de arū to shuchō suru

claimant [klei'mənt] n (ADMIN) 要求者 yōkyūsha; (LAW) 原告 geñkoku

clairvoyant [klerːvɔi'ənt] n (psychic) 霊媒 reíbai

clam [klæm] n (ZOOL, CULIN) ハマグリ hamagúri ◇英語では食用二枚貝の総称として使われる eígo de wa shokúyöninmai-gai no sōshō toshité tsukáwarerù

clamber [klæm'bəːr] vi (aboard vehicle) 乗る norú; (up hill etc) 登る nobóru ◇手足を使って物に乗ったり登ったりすると いう含みがある teáshi wo tsukátte mo-nó ni nottári nobóttari suru to iú fukūmi ga arū

clammy [klæm'iː] adj (hands, face etc) 冷たくてべとべとしている tsumétakūte betóbeto shité irū

clamor [klæm'əːr] (BRIT **clamour**) vi: **to clamor for** (change, war etc) ...をや かましく要求する ...wo yakámashikū yō-kyū suru

clamp [klæmp] n (device) 留金 toméga-ne, クランプ kuráñpu
♦vt (two things together) クランプで留 める kuráñpu de toméru; (put: one thing on another) 固定する koteí suru, 締めつ ける shimétsukerù

clamp down on vt fus (violence, speculation etc) 取り締まる toríshimarù

clan [klæn] n (family) 一族 ichízoku

clandestine [klændes'tin] adj (activity, broadcast) 秘密の himítsu no

clang [klæŋ] vi (bell, metal object) かん と鳴る kań to narú

clap [klæp] vi (audience, spectators) 拍手 する hákushu surū

clapping [klæp'iŋ] n (applause) 拍手 há-kushu

claret [klær'it] n クラレット kurárettò ◇ボルドー産の赤ワイン bórudōsan no akáŵaiñ

clarify [klær'əfai] vt (argument, point) はっきりさせる hakkíri saséru

clarinet [klærənet'] n (MUS: instrument) クラリネット kurárinettō

clarity [klær'itiː] n (of explanation, thought) 明りょうさ meíryōsa

clash [klæʃ] *n* (of opponents) 衝突 shōtotsu; (of beliefs, ideas, views) 衝突 shōtotsu, 対立 tairitsu; (of colors) 不調和 fuchōwa; (of styles) つり合わない事 tsurfawanai kotò; (of two events, appointments) かち合い kachfai; (noise) ぶつかる音 butsukarù otó
♦*vi* (fight: rival gangs etc) 衝突する shōtotsu suru; (disagree: political opponents, personalities) 角突合う tsunótsukaì wo surù; (beliefs, ideas, views) 相容れない afirénai; (colors, styles) 合わない awánai; (two events, appointments) かち合う kachfau; (make noise: weapons, cymbals etc) 音を立ててぶつかり合う otó wo tatéte butsukariaù

clasp [klæsp] *n* (hold: with hands) 握る事 nigirù kotò, 握り nigírì; (: with arms) 抱締めること dakfshimerù kotò, 抱擁 hōyō; (of necklace, bag) 留金 toménganè, クラスプ kúrasupù
♦*vt* (hold) 握る nigírù; (embrace) 抱締める dakfshimerù

class [klæs] *n* (SCOL: pupils) 学級 gakkyū, クラス kurásù; (: lesson) 授業 jugyō; (of society) 階級 kaíkyū; (type, group) 種類 shurùi
♦*vt* (categorize) 分類する bunfruì surù

classic [klæs'ik] *adj* (example, illustration) 典型的な teñkeiteki na; (film, work etc) 傑作の kessáku no; (style, dress) 古典的な kotenteki na
♦*n* (film, novel etc) 傑作 kessáku

classical [klæs'ikal] *adj* (traditional) 伝統的な deñtōteki na; (MUS) クラシックの kuráshikkù no; (Greek, Roman) 古代の kódài no

classification [klæsəfəkei'ʃən] *n* (process) 分類する事 bunfruì surù kotò; (category, system) 分類 buñruì

classified [klæs'əfaid] *adj* (information) 秘密の himítsu no

classified advertisement *n* 分類広告 buñruikōkoku

classify [klæs'əfai] *vt* (books, fossils etc) 分類する bunfruì surù

classmate [klæs'meit] *n* 同級生 dōkyūsei, クラスメート kurásumēto

classroom [klæs'ruːm] *n* 教室 kyōshitsu

clatter [klæt'əːr] *n* (of dishes, pots etc) がちゃがちゃ gáchagacha; (of hooves) かたかた kátakata
♦*vi* (dishes, pots etc) がちゃがちゃいう gáchagacha iú; (hooves) かたかた鳴る kátakata narù

clause [klɔːz] *n* (LAW) 条項 jōkō; (LING) 文節 buñsetsu

claustrophobia [klɔːstrəfou'biːə] *n* (PSYCH) 閉所恐怖症 heſshokyōfushō

claw [klɔː] *n* (of animal, bird) つめ tsumé; (of lobster) はさみ hasámi

claw at *fus* (curtains, door etc) 引っかく hikkáku

clay [klei] *n* 粘土 neñdo

clean [kliːn] *adj* (person, animal) きれい好きな kiréizuki na; (place, surface, clothes etc) 清潔な seſketsu na; (fight) 反則のない hañsoku no naì; (record, reputation) 無傷の mūkizu no; (joke, story) きれいな gehñ de naì; (MED: fracture) 単純な tañjun na
♦*vt* (car, hands, face etc) 洗う aráu; (room, house) 掃除する sōji suru

clean-cut [kliːn'kʌt] *adj* (person) 品の良い hiñ no yoí

cleaner [kliː'nəːr] *n* (person) 掃除係 sōjigakàri; (substance) 洗剤 señzai

cleaner's [kliː'nəːrz] *n* (*also:* **dry cleaner's**) クリーニング店 kurínínguten

cleaning [kliː'niŋ] *n* (of room, house) 掃除 sōji

cleanliness [klen'liːnis] *n* 清潔 seſketsu

clean out *vt* (cupboard, drawer) 中身を出してきれいにする nakámi wo dashìte kiréi ni surù

cleanse [klenz] *vt* (purify) 清める kiyómerù; (face, cut) 洗う aráu

cleanser [klen'zəːr] *n* (for face) 洗顔料 señgañryō

clean-shaven [kliːn'ʃei'vən] *adj* ひげのない higé no naì

cleansing department [klen'ziŋ-] (BRIT) *n* 清掃局 seſsōkyoku

clean up *vt* (mess) 片付ける katázukerù; (child) 身ぎれいにする migírei ni surù

clear [kliːr] *adj* (easy to understand:

report, argument) 分かりやすい wakáriyasuì; (easy to see, hear) はっきりした hakkírì shitá; (obvious: choice, commitment) 明らかな akíràka na; (glass, plastic) 透明な tômei na; (water, eyes) 澄んだ súnda; (road, way, floor etc) 障害のない shôgai no naì; (conscience) やましい所のない yamashíì tokóro no naì; (skin) 健康そうな kenkôsō na; (sky) 晴れた haréta

♦vt (space, room) 開ける akéru; (LAW: suspect) 容疑を晴す yôgi wo harasù; (fence, wall) 飛越える tobíkoerù; (check) 払う haraù

♦vi (weather, sky) 晴れる harerù; (fog, smoke) 消える kierú

♦adv: clear of (trouble) ...を避けて ...wo sakéte; (ground) ...から離れて ...kara hanárete

to clear the table 食卓を片付ける shokútaku wo katázukerù

clearance [kli:'rəns] n (removal: of trees, slums) 取払う事 toríharaù kotó; (permission) 許可 kyókà

clear-cut [kli:'ərkʌt'] adj (decision, issue) 明白な meíhaku na

clearing [kli:'riŋ] n (in woods) 開けた所 hirákèta tokóro

clearing bank (BRIT) n 手形交換組合銀行 tegátakōkankumiai gíñkō (ロンドンの中央手形交換所を通じて他の銀行との取引を行う rôñdon no chūō tegata kōkanjo no chūō ni giñkō to no torîhiki wò okónaù gíñkō)

clearly [kli:'ərli:] adv (distinctly, coherently) はっきりと hakkírì to; (evidently) 明らかに akíràka ni

clear up vt (room, mess) 片付ける katázukerù; (mystery, problem) 解決する kaíketsu suru

clearway [kli:'ərwei] (BRIT) n 駐停車禁止道路 chūteíshakiñshidôro

cleaver [kli:'vər] n 骨割包丁 honéwaribôchō (肉などに似た物で、肉のブロックをたたき切ったり骨を割ったりするのに使う natá ní nitá monò de, nikú no burokkû wò tatákikittàri honé wo wattári surú no ni tsukaù

clef [klef] n (MUS) 音部記号 oñbukigô

cleft [kleft] n (in rock) 割れ目 waréme

clemency [klem'ənsi:] n 恩情 oñjô

clench [klentʃ] vt (fist) 握り締める nigírishimerù; (teeth) 食いしばる kuíshibarù

clergy [klər'dʒi] n 聖職者 seíshokùsha ◇総称 sôshō

clergyman [klər'dʒi:mən] n (pl clergymen) n (Protestant) 牧師 bókùshi; (Catholic) 神父 shíñpu

clerical [kler'ikəl] adj (worker, job) 事務の jímu no; (REL) 聖職者の seíshokùsha no

clerk [klərk] n (BRIT: office worker) 事務員 jímuiñ; (US: sales person) 店員 teñíñ

clever [klev'ər] adj (intelligent) 利口な rikô na; (deft, crafty) こうかつな kôkatsu na; (device, arrangement) 良く工夫した yókù kufû shitá

cliché [kli:ʃei'] n 決り文句 kimárimoñku

click [klik] vt (tongue) 鳴らす narásu; (heels) 打鳴らす uchínarasu

♦vi (device, switch etc) かちっと鳴る kachíttò narú

client [klai'ənt] n (of bank, company) 客 kyakú; (of lawyer) 依頼人 iráinìn

cliff [klif] n (GEO) 断崖 dañgai

climate [klai'mit] n (weather) 気候 kikô; (of opinion etc) 雰囲気 fuñ-íkì

climax [klai'mæks] n (of battle, career) 頂点 chôteñ; (of film, book) クライマックス kuráimakkùsu; (sexual) オルガズム orúgazùmu

climb [klaim] vi (sun, plant) 上がる agáru; (plant) 伸び上がる hafugárù; (plane) 上昇する jôshō suru; (prices, shares) 上昇する jôshō suru; (move with effort): to climb over a wall 塀を乗り越える heí wo noríkoerú

♦vt (stairs, ladder) 上がる agáru, 登る nobóru; (hill) 登る noboru; (tree) ...に登る ...ni noború

♦n (of hill, cliff etc) 登る事 nobóru kotó; (of prices etc) 上昇 jôshō

to climb into a car 車に乗り込む kurúma ni noríkomu

climb-down [klaim'daun] n (retraction)

撤回 tekkái

climber [klai'mər] *n* (mountaineer) 登山者 tozanshá; (plant) つる性植物 tsuruséishokubùtsu

climbing [klai'miŋ] *n* (mountaineering) 山登り yamánobòri, 登山 tózàn

clinch [klintʃ] *vt* (deal) まとめる matómeru; (argument) ...に決着を付ける ...ni ketcháku wo tsukerú

cling [kliŋ] (*pt, pp* clung) *vi*: **to cling to** (mother, support) ...にしがみつく ...ni shigámitsukù; (idea, belief) 固執する koshú suru; (subj: clothes, dress) ...にぴったりくっつく ...ni pittári kuttsukù

clinic [klin'ik] *n* (MED: center) 診療所 shińryòjo

clinical [klin'ikəl] *adj* (MED: tests) 臨床の riñshò no; (: teaching) 臨床の riñshò no; (*fig*: thinking, attitude) 冷淡な reítàn na; (: building, room) 潤いのない uróoi no naî

clink [kliŋk] *vi* (glasses, cutlery) ちんと鳴る chíñ to narú

clip [klip] *n* (*also*: **paper clip**) クリップ kuríppù; (*also*: **hair clip**) 髪留 kamídome; (TV, CINEMA) 断片 dañpen
♦*vt* (fasten) 留める toméru; (cut) はさみで切る hasámi de kíru

clippers [klip'ərz] *npl* (for gardening) せん定ばさみ señteibasamì; (*also*: **nail clippers**) つめ切り tsumékirì

clipping [klip'iŋ] *n* (from newspaper) 切抜き kirínukì

clique [kli:k] *n* 徒党 totó

cloak [klouk] *n* (cape) マント máñto
♦*vt* (*fig*: in mist, secrecy) 隠す kakúsù

cloakroom [klouk'ru:m] *n* (for coats etc) クローク kurókù; (BRIT: WC) お手洗 o-téaraì

clock [kla:k] *n* 時計 tokéi

clock in *vi* (for work) 出勤する shukkíñ suru

clock off *vi* (from work) 退社する taísha suru

clock on *vi* = **clock in**

clock out *vi* = **clock off**

clockwise [kla:k'waiz] *adv* 時計回りに tokéimawàri ni

clockwork [kla:k'wə:rk] *n* 時計仕掛 tokéijikàke no
♦*adj* (model, toy) 時計仕掛の tokéijikàke no

clog [kla:g] *n* (leather) 木底の靴 kizóko no kutsú; (*also*: **wooden clog**) 木靴 kígutsu
♦*vt* (drain, nose) ふさぐ fuságu
♦*vi* (*also*: **clog up**: sink) 詰る tsumárù

cloister [klois'tə:r] *n* 回廊 kaírò

clone [kloun] *n* (of animal, plant) クローン kuróñ

close¹ [klous] *adj* (near) 近くの chikákù no; (friend) 親しい shitáshiì; (relative) 近縁の kiń-en no; (contact) 密な mítsù na; (link, ties) 密接な mìssétsu na; (examination, check) 注意深い chūbukaì; (contest) 互角の gokàku no; (weather) 重苦しい omókuroshìì
♦*adv* (near) 近くに chikákù ni
close to ...の近くに ...no chikákù ni
close at hand, close by 近くの chikákù no
♦*adv* 近くに chikákù ni
to have a close shave (*fig*) 間一髪で助かる kań-ippátsu de tasukaru

close² [klouz] *vt* (shut: door, window) 閉める shimérù; (finalize: sale) 取決める toríkimerù; (end: case, speech) 終える oéru
♦*vi* (shop etc) 閉店する heíten suru; (door, lid) 閉る shimárù; (end) 終る owárù

closed [klouzd] *adj* (door, window, shop etc) 閉っている shimátte irú

close down *vi* (factory) 廃業する haígyo suru; (magazine) 廃刊する haíkan suru

closed shop *n* (*fig*) クローズドショップ kurózudo shoppù ◆特定の労働組合員だけしか雇わない事業所 tokútei no ródokumiaiìn dake shika yatówanaì jigyósho

close-knit [klous'nit'] *adj* (family, community) 堅く結ばれた katáku musúbareta

closely [klous'li:] *adv* (examine, watch) 注意深く chūbukaỳku; (connected) 密接に mìssétsu ni; (related) 近縁に kiń-en ni natté; (resemble) そっくり sokkúrì

closet [klɔz'it] *n* (cupboard) たんす tań-su

close-up [klous'ʌp] *n* (PHOT) クローズアップ kurōzuappū

closure [klou'ʒəːr] *n* (of factory) 閉鎖 heísa; (of magazine) 廃刊 haíkan

clot [klɑt] *n* (*gen*: blood clot) 血の塊 chi no katamari; (*inf*: idiot) ばか bákà
♦*vi* (blood) 固まる katamaru, 凝固する gyōko suru

cloth [klɔθ] *n* (material) 布 nunó; (rag) ふきん fukíñ

clothe [klouð] *vt* (dress) ...に服を着せる ...ni fukú wo kiséru

clothes [klouz] *npl* 服 fukú

clothes brush *n* 洋服ブラシ yōfukuburāshi

clothes line *n* 物干綱 monóhoshizùna

clothes pin (*BRIT* **clothes peg**) *n* 洗濯ばさみ sefitakubasàmi

clothing [klou'ðiŋ] *n* = **clothes**

cloud [klaud] *n* (in sky) 雲 kúmò
a cloud of smoke/dust もうもうとした煙 (ほこり) mōmō to shita kemúri (hokori)

cloudburst [klaud'bəːrst] *n* 集中豪雨 shūchuūgōu

cloudy [klau'diː] *adj* (sky) 曇った kumóttà; (liquid) 濁った nigóttà

clout [klaut] *vt* (hit, strike) 殴る nagúrù

clove [klouv] *n* (spice) チョウジ chōji, クローブ kurōbu
clove of garlic ニンニクの一粒 nifíniku no hitótsubu

clover [klou'vəːr] *n* クローバー kurōbā

clown [klaun] *n* (in circus) ピエロ pfèro
♦*vi* (also: **clown about, clown around**) おどける odókeru

cloying [klɔi'iŋ] *adj* (taste, smell) むかつかせる mukátsukaseru

club [klʌb] *n* (society, place) クラブ kúràbu; (weapon) こん棒 kofíbō; (also: **golf club**) ゴルフクラブ gorúfukuràbu
♦*vt* (hit) 殴る nagúrù
♦*vi*: **to club together** (*BRIT*: for gift, card) 金を出し合う kané wo dashíaù

club car (*US*) *n* (RAIL) ラウンジカー ra-únjikā ^休憩用客車 kyūkeiyō kyakúsha

clubhouse [klʌb'haus] *n* (of sports club) クラブハウス kurábuhaùsu; スポーツクラブのメンバーが集まる部屋, 建物など supốtsukuràbu no meñba ga atsúmarù heyá, tatémono nadð

clubs [klʌbz] *npl* (CARDS) クラブ kúràbu

cluck [klʌk] *vi* (hen) こっこっと鳴く kókkòtto nakú

clue [kluː] *n* (pointer, lead) 手掛かり tegákari; (in crossword) かぎ kagí
I haven't a clue さっぱり分らない sáppàri wakáranaì

clump [klʌmp] *n* (*gen*) 塊 katámari; (of buildings etc) 一塊 hitókatamari
a clump of trees 木立 kódachi

clumsy [klʌm'ziː] *adj* (person, movement) 不器用な búkìyo na; (object) 扱いにくい atsúkainikuì; (effort, attempt) 下手な hetá na

clung [klʌŋ] *pt, pp* of **cling**

cluster [klʌs'təːr] *n* (of people, stars, flowers etc) 塊 katámari
♦*vi* 固まる katámaru, 群がる murágarù

clutch [klʌtʃ] *n* (grip, grasp) つかむ事 tsukamú kotó; (AUT) クラッチ kurátchi
♦*vt* (purse, hand, stick) しっかり持つ shíkkàri motsū

clutter [klʌt'əːr] *vt* (room, table) 散らかす chirákasu

cm *abbr* = **centimeter**

CND [siːendi'] *n abbr* (= *Campaign for Nuclear Disarmament*) 核廃絶運動 kakúhaizetsu uñdō

Co. *abbr* = **county; company**

c/o *abbr* = **care of**

coach [koutʃ] *n* (bus) バス básù; (*also*: **horse-drawn coach**) 馬車 bâsha; (of train) 客車 kyakúsha; (SPORT: trainer) コーチ kōchi; (tutor) 個人教師 kojínkyōshi
♦*vt* (sportsman/woman) コーチする kōchi suru; (student) ...に個人指導をする ...ni kojínshidō wo surū

coach trip *n* バス旅行 basúryokõ

coagulate [kouæg'jəleit] *vi* (blood, paint etc) 凝固する gyōko surū

coal [koul] *n* (substance) 石炭 sekítañ,

(also: lump of coal) 石炭1個 sekítan ik-kò

coal face n 石炭切り場 sekítankiríba

coalfield [koul'fi:ld] n 炭田 tañden

coalition [kouəli'ʃən] n (POL: also: **coalition government**) 連合政権 reñgôseikèn; (of pressure groups etc) 連盟 reñmei

coalman [koul'mən] (pl **coalmen**) n 石炭屋 sekítañya

coal merchant n = **coalman**

coalmine [koul'main] n 炭坑 tañkô

coarse [kɔːrs] adj (texture: rough) 荒い aráì; (person: vulgar) 下品な gehín na

coast [koust] n 海岸 kaígan

◆vi (car, bicycle etc) 惰力走行する daryôkusôkô suru

coastal [kous'təl] adj (cities, waters) 海岸沿いの kaíganzòi no

coastguard [koust'gɑːrd] n (officer) 沿岸警備隊員 eñgankeibitáiin; (service) 沿岸警備隊 eñgankeibitai

coastline [koust'lain] n 海岸線 kaígansen

coat [kout] n (overcoat) コート kôto; (of animal) 毛 ke; (of paint) 塗り nurí

◆vt: **coated with** ...で覆われた ...de ôwareta

coat hanger n ハンガー háñgâ

coating [kou'tiŋ] n (of dust, mud etc) 覆う物 ôù monó; (of chocolate, plastic etc) 被覆 hífuku

coat of arms n 紋章 mōñ

coax [kouks] vt (person: persuade) 説得する settóku suru

cob [kɑːb] n see **corn**

cobbler [kɑːb'lər] n (maker/repairer of shoes) 靴屋 kutsúyà

cobbles [kɑːb'əlz] npl 敷石 shikíishi

cobblestones [kɑːb'əlstounz] npl = **cobbles**

cobweb [kɑːb'web] n クモの巣 kúmô no su

cocaine [koukein'] n コカイン kókàin

cock [kɑːk] n (rooster) おん鳥 oñdori; (male bird) 鳥の雄 torí no osú

◆vt (gun) ...の撃鉄を起す ...no gekítetsu wo okosù

cockerel [kɑːk'ərəl] n 雄のひな鳥 osú no hiñádori

cock-eyed [kɑːk'aid] adj (fig: idea, method) ばかな bákà na

cockle [kɑːk'əl] n ホタテガイ hotátègai

cockney [kɑːk'ni:] n ロンドンのEast End地区生れの人 róñdon no East End chíkù umáre no hitó

cockpit [kɑːk'pit] n (in aircraft) 操縦室 sôjùshitsu, コックピット kokkúpittò; (in racing car) 運転席 uñteñseki, コックピット kokkúpittò

cockroach [kɑːk'rout] n ゴキブリ gokíburi

cocktail [kɑːk'teil] n (drink) カクテル kákùteru; (mixture: fruit cocktail, prawn cocktail etc) ...カクテル ...kakúteru

cocktail cabinet n ホームバー hômubâ

cocktail party n カクテルパーティ kakúterupâti

cocoa [kou'kou] n (powder, drink) ココア kókòa

coconut [kou'kənʌt] n (fruit) ヤシの実 yáshì no mi; (flesh) ココナッツ kokónattsu

cocoon [kəkuːn'] n (of butterfly) 繭 máyù

cod [kɑːd] n タラ tárà

C.O.D. [siːouːdiː'] abbr (= cash or also (US) collect on delivery) 着払い chakúbarài

code [koud] n (of practice, behavior) 規定 kitéi; (cipher) 暗号 añgô; (dialling code, post code) 番号 bañgô

cod-liver oil [kɑːd'livər-] n 肝油 kañ-yu

coercion [kouəːr'ʃən] n (pressure) 強制 kyôsei

coffee [kɔːf'iː] n (drink, powder) コーヒー kôhî; (cup of coffee) コーヒー一杯 kôhî ippai

coffee bar (BRIT) n 喫茶店 kíssàten

coffee bean n コーヒー豆 kôhîmame

coffee break n コーヒーブレーク kôhîburêku

coffeepot [kɔːf'iːpɑːt] n コーヒーポット kôhîpottò

coffee table n コーヒーテーブル kôhî

tēburu

coffin [kɔ:f'in] n ひつぎ hitsúgi

cog [kɑɡ] n (TECH: wheel) 歯車 hágùruma; (: tooth) 歯車の歯 hágùruma no há

cogent [kou'dʒənt] adj (argument etc) 説得力ある settókuryòku aru

cognac [koun'jæk] n コニャック kónyàkku

coherent [kouhi:'rənt] adj (answer, theory, speech) 筋の通った sujī no tòtta; (person) 筋の通った事を言う sujī no tòtta kotó wo iú

cohesion [kouhi:'ʒən] n (political, ideological etc) 団結 dañketsu

coil [kɔil] n (of rope, wire) 一巻 hitòmaki; (ELEC) コイル kóìru; (contraceptive) 避妊リング hinínrìngu

◆vt (rope) 巻く makú

coin [kɔin] n (money) 硬貨 kōka, コイン kóìn

◆vt (word, slogan) 造る tsukúru

coinage [kɔi'nidʒ] n (coins) 硬貨 kóka

coin-box [kɔin'bɑ:ks] n (BRIT) n コイン電話 koíndeñwa ◊公衆電話でカードだけしか使えない物に対比して言う kóshudeñwa de kádo dake shiká tsukáenai monó ni tashí shité iú

coincide [kouinsaid'] vi (events) 同時に起る dōji ni okòru; (ideas, views) 一致する itchí suru

coincidence [kouin'sidəns] n 偶然の一致 gūzen no itchí

Coke [kouk] ® n (drink) コカコーラ kokákòra

coke [kouk] n (coal) コークス kôkusu

colander [kɑl'əndər] n 水切り mizúkiri ◊穴の大きい物を出すボウル型で穴のない物を出すボウル型で穴の非破壊的水切り物 bóruguta de aná no hikákuteki chíkirí monó wo sasú

cold [kould] adj (water, food) 冷たい tsumétai; (weather, room) 寒い samúì; (person, attitude: unemotional) 冷たい tsumétai, 冷淡な reftañ na

◆n (weather) 寒さ samúsa, (MED) 風邪 kazé

it's cold 寒い samui

to be cold (person, object) 冷たい tsumétai

to catch (a) cold 風邪を引く kazé wo hiku

in cold blood (kill etc) 冷酷に reñkoku ni

coldly [kould'li:] adv (speak, behave) 冷たく tsumétaku, 冷淡に reñtañ ni

cold-shoulder [kould'jouldər] vt 冷たくあしらう tsumétaku ashíraù

cold sore n 口角炎 kōkakuèn

coleslaw [koul'slɔ:] n コールスロー kōrusurò

colic [kɑl'ik] n (MED) 腹痛 fukútsū

collaborate [kəlæb'əreit] vi (on book, research) 協力する kyódò suru; (with enemy) 協力する kyóryoku suru

collaboration [kəlæbərei'ʃən] n 協力 kyóryoku

collage [kəlɑ:ʒ'] n コラージュ kôràju

collapse [kəlæps'] vi (building, system, resistance) 崩れる kuzúrerù, 崩壊する hôkai suru; (government) 倒れる taórerù; (MED: person) 倒れる taórerù; (table) 壊れる kowárerù, つぶれる tsubúrerù; (company) つぶれる tsubúrerù, 破産する hasán suru

◆n (of building, system, government, resistance) 崩壊 hôkai; (MED: of person) 倒れる事 taórerù kotò; (of table) 壊れる〔つぶれる〕事 kowárerù(tsubúrerù)kotò; (of company) 破産 hasán

collapsible [kəlæps'əbəl] adj (seat, bed, bicycle) 折畳みの orítatami no

collar [kɑl'ər] n (of coat, shirt) 襟 erí, カラー kárà; (of dog, cat) 首輪 kubíwa, カラー kárà

collarbone [kɑl'ərboun] n (ANAT) 鎖骨 sakótsu

collateral [kəlæt'ərəl] n (COMM) 担保 tâñpo

colleague [kɑl'i:g] n 同僚 dôryō

collect [kəlekt'] vt (gather: wood, litter etc) 集める atsúmerù; (as a hobby) 収集する shūshú suru; (BRIT: call and pick up: person) 迎えに行く mukáe ni ikú; (: object) 取りに行く torí ni ikú; (for charity, in church) 募金する bokín suru; (debts, taxes etc) 集金する shúkin suru; (mail) 取集する shushū suru

♦vi (crowd) 集る atsúmarù

to call collect (US: TEL) コレクトコールする korékutokòru suru

collection [kəlek'ʃən] n (of art, stamps etc) コレクション kórèkushon; (of poems, stories etc) ...集 ...shū; (from place, person) 受取る事 ukétoru kotó; (for charity) 募金 bokín; (of mail) 取集 shushū

collective [kəlek'tiv] adj (farm, decision) 共同の kyódō no

collector [kəlek'tə:r] n (of art, stamps etc) 収集家 shūshūka; (of taxes etc) 集金人 shūkínnin

college [kɑːl'idʒ] n (SCOL: of university) 学寮 gakúryō; (: of agriculture, technology) 大学 daígaku

collide [kəlaid'] vi (cars, people) ぶつかる butsúkarù, 衝突する shótotsu suru

collie [kɑːl'i:] n コリー犬 koríken

colliery [kɑːl'jə:ri:] (BRIT) n 炭坑 tañkō

collision [kəliʒ'ən] n (of vehicles) 衝突 shótotsu

colloquial [kəlou'kwi:əl] adj (LING: informal) 口語の kōgo no

collusion [kəlu:'ʒən] n (collaboration) 結託 kettáku

colon [kou'lən] n (punctuation mark) コロン kóròn; (ANAT) 大腸 daíchō

colonel [kə:r'nəl] n 大佐 taísa

colonial [kəlou'ni:əl] adj 植民地の shokúmiñchi no

colonize [kɑːl'ənaiz] vt (country, territory) 植民地にする shokúmiñchi ni surù

colony [kɑːl'əni:] n (subject territory) 植民地 shokúmiñchi; (of people) ...人街 ...jíngai; (of animals) 個体群 kotáigùn

color [kʌl'ə:r] (BRIT **colour**) n (gen) 色 iro

♦vt (paint) ...に色を塗る ...ni iró wo nurú; (dye) 染める soméru; (fig: account) ...に色を付ける ...ni iró wo tsukerù; (judgment) ゆがめる yugámerù

♦vi (blush) 赤面する sekímen suru

in color 天然色で teńnenshoku de, カラーで kárā de

color bar n 人種差別 jiñshusabètsu ◇有色人種、特に黒人に対する差別を指す

yūshokujiñshu, tokù ni kokújin ni taí suru sabètsu wo sasú

color-blind [kʌl'ə:rblaind] adj 色盲の shikímō no

colored [kʌl'ə:rd] adj (person) 有色の yūshoku no; (illustration) カラーの kárā no

color film n カラーフィルム karáfirùmu

colorful [kʌl'ə:rfəl] adj (cloth) 色鮮やかな iró azáyaka na; (account, story) 華やかな hanáyaka na; (personality) 華々しい hanábōshii

color in vt (drawing) ...に色を塗る ...ni iró wo nurú

coloring [kʌl'ə:riŋ] n (complexion) 肌の色合い hadà no iróai; (also: **food coloring**) 着色料 chakúshokùryō

colors [kʌl'ə:rz] npl (of party, club etc) 色 iró

color scheme n 配色計画 haíshokukèkaku

color television n カラーテレビ karáterèbi

colossal [kəlɑːs'əl] adj 巨大な kyodái na

colour [kʌl'ə:r] etc (BRIT) n = **color** etc

colt [koult] n 子ウマ koúma

column [kɑːl'əm] n (ARCHIT) 円柱 eñchū; (of smoke) 柱 hashíra; (of people) 縦隊 jútai; (gossip column, sports column) コラム kórāmu

columnist [kɑːl'əmist] n コラムニスト korámunisùto

coma [kou'mə] n (MED) こん睡状態 końsuijōtai

comb [koum] n くし kushí

♦vt (hair) ...をくしでとかす kushí de tokasù; (fig: area) 捜索する sōsaku suru

combat [n kɑːm'bæt vb kəmbæt'] n (MIL: fighting) 戦闘 seńtō; (fight, battle) 戦い tatákai

♦vt (oppose) 反抗する hańkō suru

combination [kɑːmbənei'ʃən] n (mixture) 組合せ kumíawase; (for lock, safe etc) 組合せ番号 kumíawasebañgō

combine [vb kəmbain'] vt:

to combine something with something ...を...と組合せる ...wo ...to kumía-

waserù; (qualities) 兼ね備える kanèsonae-
rù; (two activities) 兼合する kenínin suru
♦*vi* (people, groups) 合併する gappéi suru
♦*n* (ECON) 連合 reñgō
combine (harvester) [kʌmˈbain(hɑrˈ-
vestəːr)] *n* コンバイン kóñbain
combustion [kəmbʌsˈtʃən] *n* (act, process) 燃焼 neñshō

KEYWORD

come [kʌm] (*pt* **came**, *pp* **come**) *vi* 1
(movement towards) 来る kúrù
come here! ここにおいて kokó ni oide
I've only come for an hour 1時間しか
いられません ichíjikan shika iráremasèn
come with me ついて来て下さい tsúite
kite kudasai
are you coming to my party? 私のパ
ーティに来てくれますわ watákushino no
pátì ni kité kúremasu né
to come running 走って来る hashíttè
kúrù
2 (arrive) 着く tsúkù, 到着する tōchaku
suru, 来る kúrù
he's just come from Aberdeen 彼はア
バーディーンから来たばかりです kárè
wa abádìn kara kitá bakàri desu
he's come here to work 彼はここには
働きに来ました kárè wa kokó ni wà
határaki ni kimashìta
they came to a river 彼らは川に着きま
した kárèra wa kawá ni tsukímashìta
to come home 家に戻って来る ié ni
modótte kuru
3 (reach): *to come to ...*に届く ...ni todókù, ...になる ...ni nárù
the bill came to £40 勘定は計40ポン
ドだった kañjō wa kéì yóñjuppóndo datta
her hair came to her waist 彼女の髪
の毛は腰まで届いていた kánojo no kamí
no kè wa koshí madè todóite ita
to come to power 政権を握る séìken
wo nigíru
to come to a decision 結論に達する
ketsúron ni tassúru
4 (occur): *an idea came to me* いい考え

が浮かびました íi kángaè ga ukábimasù-
shìta
5 (be, become) なる nárù
to come loose/undone etc 外れる hazúreru
I've come to like him 彼が好きになり
ました kárè wa sukí ni narímashìta

---

come about *vi* 起る okórù
come across *vt fus* (person, thing) ...に
出会う ...ni deáù
come away *vi* (leave) 帰る kaéru, 出て
来る détè kure; (become detached) 外れ
る hazúreru
come back *vi* (return) 帰って来る káètte
kuru
comeback [kʌmˈbæk] *n* (of film star
etc) 返り咲き kaérizaki, カムバック ka-
múbakkù
come by *vt fus* (acquire) 手に入れる té
nì iréru
comedian [kəmiːˈdiːən] *n* (THEATER,
TV) コメディアン kómèdian
comedienne [kəmidiˈɛn] *n* 女性コメデ
ィアン joséi komèdian
come down *vi* (price) 下がる sagárù;
(tree) 倒れる taórerù; (building) 崩れ落ち
る kuzúreochirù
comedy [kʌmˈidi] *n* (play, film) 喜劇 kí-
gèki, コメディー kómèdì; (humor) 喜劇
性 kigékisei, ユーモア yúmoa
come forward *vi* (volunteer) 進んで...す
る susúnde ...suru
come from *vt fus* (place, source etc)
...から来る ...kara kúrù
come in *vi* (visitor) 入る háìru; (on deal
etc) 加わる kuwáwarù; (be involved) 関
係する káñkei suru
come in for *vt fus* (criticism etc) 受け
る ukérù
come into *vt fus* (money) 相続する sō-
zoku suru; (be involved) ...に関係する
...ni káñkei suru
to come into fashion 流行する ryūkō
suru
come off *vi* (button) 外れる hazúrerù;
(attempt) 成功する seíkō suru
come on *vi* (pupil, work, project) 進歩す

る shinpo suru; (lights, electricity) つく
tsukú

come on! さあさあ sāsā

come out vi (fact) 発覚する hakkaku suru; (book) 出版される shuppan sareru;
(stain) 取れる torérù, 落ちる ochírù;
(sun) 出る dérù

come round vi (after faint, operation)
正気に返る shóki ni kaérù, 目が覚める
mé gà samérù, 気が付く ki gà tsukú

comet [kɑmˈit] n すい星 suísei

come to vi (regain consciousness) 正気に
戻る shóki ni modorù, 目が覚める mé
gà samérù

come up vi (sun) 出る dérù; (problem) 起
る okórù, 出る dérù; (event) 起る okórù;
(in conversation) 出る dérù

come up against vt fus (resistance,
difficulties) ぶつかる butsúkarù

come upon vt fus (find) 見付ける mitsúkerù

comeuppance [kʌmˈʌpˈəns] n: **to get
one's comeuppance** 当然の罰を受ける
tōzen no batsù wo ukerù

come up with vt fus (idea) 持ち出す mochídasù; (money) 出す dásù

comfort [kʌmˈfərt] n (well-being: physical, material) 安楽 ánraku; (relief) 慰め
nagúsame

♦vt (console) 慰める nagúsamerù

comfortable [kʌmˈfərtəbəl] adj (person: physically) 楽な rákù na; (: financially) 暮しに困らない kuráshi ni komá-
ranai; (furniture) 座り心地の良い suwá-
rigokochi no yoì; (room) 居心地の良い
igókochi no yoì; (patient) 苦痛のない kutsū no naì; (easy: walk, climb etc) 楽な
rákù na

comfortably [kʌmˈfərtəbli:] adv (sit,
live etc) 楽に rákù ni

comforts [kʌmˈfərts] npl (of home etc)
生活を楽にする せ設 seikatsu wo rakú ni
suru monó

comfort station (US) n お手洗 o-téarai

comic [kɑmˈik] adj (also: **comical**) こっ
けいな kokkei na

♦n (comedian) コメディアン kómèdian;
(BRIT: magazine) 漫画(雑誌) man-

ga(zasshi)

comic strip n 連続漫画 reñzokumañga

coming [kʌmˈiŋ] n (arrival) 到着 tóchaku

♦adj (event, attraction) 次の tsugí no, こ
れからの koré kara no

coming(s) and going(s) n(pl) 行き来
yukíki, 往来 ōrai

comma [kɑmˈə] n コンマ kónma

command [kəmænd'] n (order) 命令 mei-
rei; (control, charge) 指揮権 shikíken; (MIL:
authority) 司令部 shiréibu; (mastery: of
subject) マスターしていること masùtā
shité irú kotó

♦vt (give orders to): **to command
someone to do something** …に…をする
様に命令する …ni …wo suru yōni meírei
suru; (troops) …の司令官である …no shiréikan de arù

commandeer [kɑmˈəndiːr'] vt (requisition) 徴発する chóhatsu suru; (fig) 勝手
に取って使う katté ni tottè tsukáù

commander [kəmænd'ər] n (MIL) 司令
官 shiréikan

commandment [kəmænd'mənt] n (REL)
戒律 kaíritsu

commando [kəmænd'ou] n (group) コマ
ンド部隊 komándobútai; (soldier) コマン
ド隊員 komándotaiin

commemorate [kəmem'əreit] vt (with
statue, monument, celebration, holiday)
記念する kinén suru

commence [kəmens'] vt (begin, start) 始
める hajímeru

♦vi 始まる hajímaru

commend [kəmend'] vt (praise) ほめる
homérù; (recommend) ゆだねる yudánerù

commensurate [kəmen'sərit] adj: **commensurate with** …に相応した …ni sōō
shitá

comment [kɑmˈent] n (remark: written
or spoken) コメント kómento

♦vi: **to comment (on)** (…について) コ
メントする (…ni tsuíte) kómento surù

no comment ノーコメント nókomento

commentary [kɑmˈənteriː] n (TV,
RADIO) 実況放送 jikkyóhōsō; (book,

article) 注解 chûkai

commentator [kɑːm'ənteitər] n (TV, RADIO) 解説者 kaísetsùsha

commerce [kɑːm'əːrs] n 商業 shôgyō

commercial [kəməːr'ʃəl] adj (organization, activity) 商業の shôgyō no; (success, failure) 商業上の shôgyōjō no
♦n (TV, RADIO: advertisement) コマーシャル kômâsharu, CM shiému

commercialized [kəməːr'ʃəlaizd] (pej) adj (place, event etc) 営利本意の efrihon-i no

commercial radio/television n 民間ラジオ(テレビ)放送 miñkan rajio(terebi) hôsō, 民放 miñpō

commiserate [kəmiz'əreit] vi: **to commiserate with** ...をいたわる ...wo itáwarù

commission [kəmiʃ'ən] n (order for work: esp of artist) 依頼 iráì; (COMM) 歩合 buái, コミッション kômîsshon; (committee) 委員会 iîñkai
♦vt (work of art) 依頼する iráì suru
out of commission (not working) 故障して koshô shité

commissionaire [kəmiʃəneːr'] (BRIT) n ドアマン dôaman

commissioner [kəmiʃ'ənəːr] n (POLICE) 長官 chôkan

commit [kəmit'] vt (crime, murder etc) 犯す okásu; (money, resources) 充当する jûtō suru; (to someone's care) 任せる makáserù
to commit oneself (to do) (...する事を) 約束する (...surú kotð wo) yakúsoku suru
to commit suicide 自殺する jisátsu suru

commitment [kəmit'mənt] n (to ideology, system) 献身 keñshin; (obligation) 責任 sekínin; (undertaking) 約束 yakúsoku

committee [kəmit'iː] n (of organization, club etc) 委員会 iîñkai

commodity [kəmɑːd'itiː] n (saleable item) 商品 shôhin

common [kɑːm'ən] adj (shared by all: knowledge, property, good) 共同の kyôdo no; (usual, ordinary: event, object, experience etc) 普通の futsū no; (vulgar: person, manners) 下品な gehíñ na
♦n (area) 共有地 kyôyùchi
in common 共通で kyôtsū de

commoner [kɑːm'ənəːr] n 庶民 shomín

common law n コモン・ロー kómòn rô ◊成文化されてない慣習に基づく英米の一般法を指す seíbunka sarète naí kañshū ni motózukù eíbei no ippáñhō wo sasù

commonly [kɑːm'ənliː] adv (usually) 通常 tsūjō

Common Market n ヨーロッパ共同市場 yôroppa kyôdōshijō

commonplace [kɑːm'ənpleis] adj 平凡な heñbon na

common room n (SCOL) 談話室 dañwashìtsu

Commons [kɑːm'ənz] npl: **the Commons** (BRIT) 下院 ká-in

common sense n 常識 jôshiki, コモンセンス kómònsensu

Commonwealth [kɑːm'ənwelθ] n (British Commonwealth): **the Commonwealth** イギリス連邦 igírisureñpō
the Commonwealth of Independent States 独立国家共同体 dokúritsu kòkka kyôdōtai

commotion [kəmou'ʃən] n (uproar) 騒ぎ sáwàgi

communal [kəmju:'nəl] adj (shared) 共同の kyôdō no

commune [n kɑːm'ju:n vb kəmju:n'] n (group) コミューン komyûn
♦vi: **to commune with** (nature, God) ...に親しむ ...ni shitáshimù

communicate [kəmju:'nikeit] vt (idea, decision, feeling) 伝える tsutáerù
♦vi: **to communicate (with)** ...と通信する ...to tsūshin suru

communication [kəmju:nikeiʃ'ən] n (process) 通信 tsūshin; (letter, call) 連絡 refíraku

communication cord (BRIT) n (on train) 非常通報装置 hijôtsūhòsōchi

communion [kəmju:n'jən] n (also: **Holy Communion**) 聖体拝領 seítaihaìryō

communiqué [kəmjuːnikeiʹ] n (POL, PRESS) コミュニケ kómyùnike

communism [kámʹjənizəm] n 共産主義 kyósanshùgi

communist [kámʹjənist] adj 共産主義の kyósanshùgi no
♦n 共産主義者 kyósanshugìshà

community [kəmjuːʹniti:] n (group of people) 共同体 kyódótài; (within larger group) 社会 shákai

community center n 公民館 kóminkan

community chest n (US) 共同募金 kyódóbòkin

community home (BRIT) n 養育施設 yóikushisètsu

commutation ticket [kɑːmjəteiʹʃən-] (US) n 定期券 teíkikèn

commute [kəmjuːtʹ] vi (to work) 通う kayóu
♦vt (LAW: sentence) 減刑する gefíkei suru

commuter [kəmjuːtʹər] n 通勤者 tsúkìnsha

compact [kəmpæktʹ] adj (taking up little space) 小型の kogáta no
♦n (also: powder compact) コンパクト kófipakuto

compact disk n コンパクトディスク kófipakuto disùku

companion [kəmpænʹjən] n 相手 afte

companionship [kəmpænʹjənʃip] n つきあい tsukfai

company [kámʹpəni:] n (COMM) 会社 kaísha; (THEATER) 劇団 gekídan; (companionship) 付合い tsukfai
to keep someone company …の相手になる …no afte ni narú

company secretary (BRIT) n 総務部長 sómubùchó

comparable [kámʹpərəbəl] adj (size, style, extent) 匹敵する hittéki suru

comparative [kəmpærʹətiv] adj (peace, stranger, safety) 比較的 hikákuteki; (study) 比較の hikáku no

comparatively [kəmpærʹətivli:] adv (relatively) 比較的に hikákuteki ni

compare [kəmpeirʹ] vt: to compare someone/something with/to (set side by side) …を…と比較する …wo …to hikáku suru; (liken) …を…に例える …wo …ni tatóerù
♦vi: to compare (with) (…に) 匹敵する (…ni) hittéki suru

comparison [kəmpærʹisən] n (setting side by side) 比較 hikáku; (likening) 例え tatóe
in comparison (with) …と比較して …to hikáku shité

compartment [kəmpɑːrtʹmənt] n (RAIL) 客室 kyakúshitsu, コンパートメント kofípátomènto; (section: of wallet, fridge etc) 区画 kukáku

compass [kámʹpəs] n (instrument: NAUT, GEO) 羅針盤 rashífiban, コンパス kófipasu

compasses [kámʹpəsiz] npl (MATH) コンパス kófipasu

compassion [kəmpæʃʹən] n (pity, sympathy) 同情 dójò

compassionate [kəmpæʃʹənit] adj (person, look) 情け深い nasákebukaì

compatible [kəmpætʹəbəl] adj (people) 気が合う ki ga aù; (ideas etc) 両立できる ryóritsu dekfrù; (COMPUT) 互換性のある gokánsei no arù

compel [kəmpelʹ] vt (of force) 強制する kyósei suru

compelling [kəmpelʹiŋ] adj (fig: argument, reason) …に止まれない yamú ni yamárenù

compensate [kámʹpənseit] vt (employee, victim) …に補償する …ni hoshó suru
♦vi: to compensate for (loss, disappointment, change etc) …を埋め合せる …wo uméawaserù

compensation [kɑːmpənseiʹʃən] n (to employee, victim) 補償 hoshó; (for loss, disappointment, change etc) 埋め合せ uméawase

compère [kámʹpeːr] (BRIT) n (TV, RADIO) 司会者 shíkàisha

compete [kəmpiːtʹ] vi (companies, rivals): to compete (with) (…と) 競り合う (…to) serfaù; (in contest, game) 参加する safíka suru

competence [kámʹpitəns] n (of worker

etc) 能力 nṓryoku

competent [kɑm'pitənt] *adj* 有能な yū́nō na

competition [kɑmpitiʃ'ən] *n* (between firms, rivals) 競争 kyṓsō; (contest) コンクール kofíkūru; (ECON) ライバル商品 raíbaru shṓhin

competitive [kɑmpet'ətiv] *adj* (industry, society) 競争の激しい kyṓsō no hagéshiì; (person) 競争心の強い kyṓsōshin no tsuyṓi; (price, product) 競争できる kyṓsō dekírù

competitive sports 競技 kyṓgi

competitor [kɑmpet'itər] *n* (rival) 競争相手 kyṓsōaìte; (participant) 参加者 sañkashà

compile [kɑmpail'] *vt* (book, film, report) 編集する heńshū suru

complacency [kɑmplei'sənsi:] *n* (smugness) 自己満足 jikōmañzoku

complacent [kɑmplei'sənt] *adj* (smug) 自己満足にふける jikōmañzoku ni fukérù

complain [kɑmplein'] *vi* (grumble) 不平不満を言う fuhéifùman wo iú; (protest: to authorities, shop etc) 訴える uttáerù

to complain of (pain) を訴える ...wo uttáerù

complaint [kɑmpleint'] *n* (objection) 訴え uttáe; (criticism) 非難 hínàn; (MED: illness) 病気 byṓki

complement [*n* kɑm'pləmənt *vb* kɑm'pləmənt] *n* (supplement) 補う物 ogínaù monó; (esp ship's crew) 人員 jíñ-in

♦*vt* (enhance) 引立たせる hikítatàserù

complementary [kɑmpləmen'tæri:] *adj* (mutually supportive) 補足し合う hosóku shiaù

complete [kɑmplit'] *adj* (total, whole) 完全な kañzen na; (finished: building, task) 完成した kańsei shitá

♦*vt* (finish: building, task) 完成する kańsei suru; (: set, group etc) そろえる soróerù; (fill in: a form) ...に記入する ...ni kinyū́ suru

completely [kɑmpli:t'li:] *adv* (totally) 全く mattáku, 完全に kańzen ni

completion [kɑmpli:'ʃən] *n* (of building)

完成 kańsei; (of contract) 履行 rikṓ

complex [*adj* kɑmpleks', *n* kɑm'pleks] *adj* (structure, problem, decision) 複雑な fukúzatsu na

♦*n* (group: of buildings) 団地 dańchi; (PSYCH) コンプレックス koñpurekkùsu

complexion [kɑmplek'ʃən] *n* (of face) 顔の肌 kaó no hadà

complexity [kɑmplek'siti:] *n* (of problem, law) 複雑さ fukúzatsusa

compliance [kɑmplai'əns] *n* (submission) 服従 fukújū; (agreement) 同意 dṓi

in compliance with ...に従って ...ni shitágatte

complicate [kɑm'pləkeit] *vt* (matters, situation) 複雑にする fukúzatsu ni suru

complicated [kɑm'pləkeitid] *adj* (explanation, system) 複雑な fukúzatsu na

complication [kɑmpləkei'ʃən] *n* (problem) 問題 mońdai; (MED) 合併症 gappéishō

complicity [kɑmplis'əti:] *n* (in crime) 共犯 kyṓhan

compliment [*n* kɑm'pləmənt *vb* kɑm'pləmənt] *n* (expression of admiration) ほめ言葉 homékotòba

♦*vt* (express admiration for) ほめる homéru

to pay someone a compliment ...をほめる ...wo homéru

complimentary [kɑmpləmen'tæri:] *adj* (remark) 賛辞の sañji no; (ticket, copy of book etc) 無料の muryṓ no

compliments [kɑm'pləmənts] *npl* (regards) 挨拶 aísatsu

comply [kɑmplai'] *vi*: *to comply with* (law, ruling) ...に従う ...ni shitágaù

component [kəmpou'nənt] *adj* (parts, elements) 構成している kṓsei shité irù

♦*n* (part) 部分 búbùn

compose [kəmpouz'] *vt* (form): *to be composed of* ...から出来ている ...kará dekíte irù; (write: music, poem, letter) 書く kákù

to compose oneself 心を落着かせる kokórò wo ochítsukaserù

composed [kəmpouzd'] *adj* (calm) 落着いている ochítsuite irù

composer [kəmpou'zə:r] n (MUS) 作曲家 sakkyokuka

composition [kɔːmpəzi'ʃən] n (of substance, group etc) 構成 kōsei; (essay) 作文 sakubun; (MUS) 作曲 sakkyōku

compost [kɑːm'poust] n たい肥 taīhi

composure [kəmpou'ʒə:r] n (of person) 落着き ochítsuki

compound [kɑːm'paund] n (CHEM) 化合物 kágōbutsu; (enclosure) 囲い地 kakóichi; (LING) 複合語 fukúgōgo
◆adj (fracture) 複雑な fukúzatsu na
compound interest 複利 fukúri

comprehend [kɑːmprihend'] vt (understand) 理解する rikái suru

comprehension [kɑːmprihen'ʃən] n (understanding) 理解 rikái

comprehensive [kɑːmprihen'siv] adj (description, review, list) 包括的な hōkatsuteki na; (INSURANCE) 総合的な sōgōteki na

comprehensive (school) (BRIT) n 総合中等学校 sōgōchūtōgakkō あらゆる能力の子供に適した課程のある中等学校 aráyurū nōryoku no ko dómo ni tekí shita katéi no aru chūtōgakkō

compress [vb kəmpres' n kɑːm'pres] vt (air, cotton, paper etc) 圧縮する asshúku suru; (text, information) 要約する yōyaku suru
◆n (MED) 湿布 shippú

comprise [kəmpraiz'] vt (also: **be comprised of**) ...からなる ...kará narū; (constitute) 構成する kōsei suru

compromise [kɑːm'prəmaiz] n 妥協 dakyō
◆vt (beliefs, principles) 傷つける kizú tsukerū
◆vi (make concessions) 妥協する dakyō suru

compulsion [kəmpʌl'ʃən] n (desire, impulse) 強迫観念 kyōhakukanñen; (force) 強制 kyōsei

compulsive [kəmpʌl'siv] adj (liar, gambler etc) 病的な byōteki na; (viewing, reading) 止められない yamérarenai

compulsory [kəmpʌl'sɔːriː] adj (attendance, retirement) 強制的な kyōseiteki

na

computer [kəmpjuː'təːr] n コンピュータ koñpyūta

computerize [kəmpjuː'təraiz] vt (system, filing, accounts etc) コンピュータ化する koñpyūtaka surū; (information) コンピュータに覚えさせる koñpyūta ni obóesaserū

computer programmer n プログラマ ー puróguramā

computer programming n プログラミング puróguramiñgu

computer science n コンピュータ科学 koñpyūta kagáku

computing [kəmpjuː'tiŋ] n (activity, science) コンピュータ利用 koñpyūta riyō

comrade [kɑːm'ræd] n (POL, MIL) 同志 dōshi; (friend) 友人 yūjin

comradeship [kɑːm'rædʃip] n 友情 yūjō

con [kɑːn] vt (deceive) だます damásū; (cheat) ぺてんに掛ける petén ni kakérū
◆n (trick) いかさま ikásama

concave [kɑːnkeiv'] adj 凹面の ốmen no

conceal [kənsiːl'] vt (hide: weapon, entrance) 隠す kakúsū; (keep back: information) 秘密にする himítsu ni surū

concede [kənsiːd'] vt (admit: error, point, defeat) 認める mitómeru

conceit [kənsiːt'] n (arrogance) うぬぼれ unúbore

conceited [kənsiː'tid] adj (vain) うぬぼれた unúboreta

conceivable [kənsiː'vəbəl] adj (reason, possibility) 考えられる kañgaerarerū

conceive [kənsiːv'] vt (child) はらむ harámū; (plan, policy) 考え出す kañgaedasū
◆vi (BIO) 妊娠する niñshin suru

concentrate [kɑːn'səntreit] vi (on problem, activity etc) 専念する señnen suru; (in one area, space) 集中する shūchū suru
◆vt (energies, attention) 集中させる shūchū saserū

concentration [kɑːnsəntrei'ʃən] n (on problem, activity etc) 専念 señnen; (in one area, space) 集中 shūchū; (attention) 注意 chūi; (CHEM) 濃縮 nōshuku

concentration camp n 強制収容所 kyōseishūyōjo

concept [kɑːnsept] n (idea, principle) 概念 gāinen

conception [kənsep'ʃən] n (idea) 概念 gāinen; (of child) 妊娠 nińshin

concern [kənsəːrn'] n (affair) 責任 sekínin; (anxiety, worry) 心配 shińpai; (COMM: firm) 企業 kigyō
◆vt (worry) 心配させる shińpai saséru; (involve, relate to) …に関係がある …ni kańkē ga arù

to be concerned (about) (person, situation etc) (…について) 心配する (…ni tsuíte) shińpai suru

concerning [kənsəːr'niŋ] prep (regarding) …について …ni tsuíte

concert [kɑːnsəːrt] n (MUS) 演奏会 eńsōkai, コンサート końsāto

concerted [kənsəːr'tid] adj (effort etc) 共同の kyōdō no

concert hall n コンサートホール końsātohōru

concertina [kɑːnsəːrtiː'nə] n (MUS: instrument) コンサーティーナ końsātīna ◇六角形の小型コンサーティーナ rokkákkēi no kogáta akōdion

concerto [kəntʃer'tou] n 協奏曲 kyōsōkyoku, コンチェルト kóńcheruto

concession [kənseʃ'ən] n (compromise) 譲歩 jōho; (COMM: right) 特権 tokkén

tax concession 減税 geńzei

conciliatory [kənsil'iːətɔːri] adj (gesture, tone) 懐柔的な kaíjūteki na

concise [kənsais'] adj (description, text) 簡潔な kańketsu na

conclude [kənkluːd'] vt (finish: speech, chapter) 終える oéru; (treaty) 締結する teíketsu suru; (deal etc) まとめる matómeru; (decide) (…だと) 結論する (…da to) ketsúron suru

conclusion [kənkluː'ʒən] n (of speech, chapter) 終り owári; (of treaty) 締結 teíketsu; (of deal etc) まとめる matómeru kotó; (decision) 結論 ketsúron

conclusive [kənkluː'siv] adj (evidence, defeat) 決定的な kettéiteki na

concoct [kɑnkɑːkt'] vt (excuse) でっち上

げる detchíageru; (plot) 企てる kuwádateru; (meal, sauce) 工夫して作る kufū shité tsukúru

concoction [kɑnkɑːk'ʃən] n (mixture) 調合物 chōgōbutsu

concourse [kɑːnkɔːrs] n (hall) 中央ホール chūōhōru, コンコース końkōsu

concrete [kɑːnkriːt] n コンクリート końkurīto
◆adj (block, floor) コンクリートの końkurīto no; (proposal, idea) 具体的な gutáiteki na

concur [kankəːr'] vi (agree) 同意する dōi suru

concurrently [kankəːr'əntli] adv (happen, run) 同時に dōji ni

concussion [kənkʌʃ'ən] n (MED) 脳震とう nōshintō

condemn [kəndem'] vt (denounce: action, report etc) 非難する hínan suru; (sentence: prisoner) …に…刑を宣告する …ni…kēi wo seńkoku suru; (declare unsafe: building) 使用に耐えない物と決定する shiyō ni taénai monó to kettéi suru

condemnation [kɑːndemnei'ʃən] n (criticism) 非難 hínan

condensation [kɑːndensei'ʃən] n (on walls, windows) 結露 ketsúro

condense [kəndens'] vi (vapor) 液化する ekíka suru
◆vt (report, book) 要約する yōyaku suru

condensed milk n 練乳 reńnyū

condescending [kɑːndisen'diŋ] adj (reply, attitude) 恩着せがましい ofíkisegamashíi

condition [kəndiʃ'ən] n (state: gen) 状態 jōtai; (MED: of illness) 病状 byōjō; (requirement) 条件 jōken; (MED: illness) 病気 byōki
◆vt (person) 慣れさせる narésaseru

on condition that …という条件で …to iū jōken de

conditional [kəndiʃ'ənəl] adj 条件付きの jōkentsuki na

conditioner [kəndiʃ'ənər] n (also: **hair conditioner**) ヘアコンディショナー heákondishōnā; (for fabrics) 柔軟剤 jūnanzai

conditions [kəndíʃənz] *npl* (circumstances) 状況 jōkyō

condolences [kəndou'lənsiz] *npl* お悔みo-kúyami

condom [kɑn'dəm] *n* コンドーム kóñdomu, スキン sukíñ

condominium [kɑndəmín'i:əm] (*US*) *n* 分譲マンション buñjómañshon

condone [kəndoun'] *vt* (misbehavior, crime) 容認する yóniñ suru

conducive [kəndu:'siv] *adj*: **conducive to** (rest, study) ...を助ける ...wo tasúkerù

conduct [*n* kɑn'dʌkt *vb* kəndʌkt'] *n* (of person) 振舞 furúmai

♦*vt* (survey, research etc) 行う okónaù; (orchestra, choir etc) 指揮する shikí suru; (heat, electricity) 伝導する deñdō suru

    to **conduct oneself** (behave) 振舞う furúmaù

conducted tour [kəndʌk'tid-] *n* ガイド付き見物 gaídotsuki keñbutsu

conductor [kəndʌk'tə:r] *n* (of orchestra) 指揮者 shikíshà; (*BRIT*: on bus, *US*: on train) 車掌 shashō; (ELEC) 伝導体 deñdōtai

conductress [kəndʌk'tris] *n* (on bus) 女性車掌 joséishashò, バスガール basúgāru

cone [koun] *n* (shape) 円すい形 eñsuikei; (on road) カラーコーン karákōn, セーフティコーン séfutikōn; (BOT) 松かさ matsúkasà; (ice cream cornet) コーン状 kōñjō

confectioner [kənfek'ʃənə:r] *n* (person) 菓子職人 kashíshokùnin

confectioner's [kənfek'ʃənə:rz] (*shop*) [kənfek'ʃənə:rz-] *n* (sweet shop) 菓子屋 kashíyà

confectionery [kənfek'ʃənə:ri:] *n* (sweets, candies) 菓子類 kashírui

confederation [kənfedərei'ʃən] *n* (POL, COMM) 連合 reñgō

confer [kənfə:r'] *vt*: **to confer something (on someone)** (honor, degree, advantage) (...に) ...を与える (...ni) ...wo atáeru

♦*vi* (panel, team) 協議する kyōgi suru

conference [kɑn'fə:rəns] *n* (meeting) 会議 káigi

confess [kənfes'] *vt* (sin, guilt, crime) 白状する hakújō suru; (weakness, ignorance) 認める mitómeru

♦*vi* (admit) 認める mitómeru

confession [kənfeʃ'ən] *n* (admission) 白状 hakújō; (REL) ざんげ záñge

confetti [kənfet'i:] *n* コンフェティ kóñfeti ◇紙吹雪き用に細かく切った色紙 kamífubuki yō ni komákaku kittá irógami

confide [kənfaid'] *vi*: **to confide in** ...に打明ける ...ni uchiákerù

confidence [kɑn'fidəns] *n* (faith) 信用 shiń-yō; (*also*: **self-confidence**) 自信 jishíñ; (secret) 秘密 himítsu

    in confidence (speak, write) 内緒で naíshode

confidence trick *n* いかさま ikásama

confident [kɑn'fidənt] *adj* (self-assured) 自信のある jishíñ no arù; (positive) 確信している kakúshin shité irù

confidential [kɑnfiden'ʃəl] *adj* (report, information) 秘密の himítsu no; (tone) 意味しげな shitáshige na

confine [kənfain'] *vt* (limit) 限定する geñtei suru; (shut up) 閉じ込める tojíkomerù

confined [kənfaind'] *adj* (space) 限られた kagírareta

confinement [kənfain'mənt] *n* (imprisonment) 監禁 kañkin

confines [kɑn'fainz] *npl* (of area) 境 sakái

confirm [kənfə:rm'] *vt* (belief, statement) 裏付ける urázukerù; (appointment, date) 確認する kakúnin suru

confirmation [kɑnfə:rmei'ʃən] *n* (of belief, statement) 裏付け urázuke; (of appointment, date) 確認 kakúnin; (REL) 堅信礼 kefishiñrei

confirmed [kənfə:rmd'] *adj* (bachelor, teetotaller) 常習的な jōshūteki na

confiscate [kɑn'fiskeit] *vt* (impound, seize) 没収する bosshū suru

conflict [*n* kɑn'flikt *vb* kənflikt'] *n* (disagreement) 論争 rońsō; (difference: of interests, loyalties etc) 対立 taíritsu; (fighting) 戦闘 señtō

♦*vi* (opinions) 対立する taíritsu suru; (research etc) 矛盾する mujúñ suru

conflicting [kənflik'tiŋ] *adj* (reports) 矛盾する mujún suru; (interests etc) 対立する tafritsu suru

conform [kənfɔːrm'] *vi* (comply) 従う shitágaû

to conform to (law, wish, ideal) ...に従う ...ni shitágaû

confound [kanfaund'] *vt* (confuse) 当惑させる tôwaku saséru

confront [kənfrʌnt'] *vt* (problems, task) ...と取組む ...to torfkumu; (enemy, danger) ...に立向かう ...ni tachímukaû

confrontation [kɑnfrəntei'ʃən] *n* (dispute, conflict) 衝突 shôtotsu

confuse [kənfjuːz'] *vt* (perplex: person) 当惑させる tôwaku saséru; (mix up: two things, people etc) 混同する kofidô suru; (complicate: situation, plans) 混乱させる kofran saséru

confused [kənfjuːzd'] *adj* (bewildered) 当惑した tôwaku shitá; (disordered) 混乱した kofran shitá

confusing [kənfjuː'ziŋ] *adj* (plot, instructions) 分かりにくい wakárinikuî

confusion [kanfjuː'ʒən] *n* (perplexity) 当惑 tôwaku; (mix-up) 混同 kofidô; (disorder) 混乱 kofran

congeal [kəndʒiːl'] *vi* (blood, sauce) 凝結する gyôketsu suru

congenial [kəndʒiːn'jəl] *adj* (person) 気の合った ki no attá; (atmosphere etc) 楽しい tanóshiî

congenital [kəndʒen'itəl] *adj* (MED: defect, illness) 先天性の seftensei no

congested [kəndʒes'tid] *adj* (with blood) うっ血した ukkétsu shitá; (: with mucus: nose) 詰まった tsumátta; (road) 渋滞した jûtai shitá; (area) 人口密集の jifikômisshû no

congestion [kəndʒes'tʃən] *n* (MED: with blood) うっ血 ukkétsu; (: with mucus) 鼻詰まり hanázumari; (of road) 渋滞 jûtai; (of area) 人口密集 jifikômisshû

conglomerate [kənglɑm'əːrit] *n* (COMM) 複合企業 fukúgôkigyô, コングロマリット kofguromarītto

conglomeration [kənglɑməːrei'ʃən] *n* (group, gathering) 寄せ集め yoséatsume

congratulate [kəngrætʃ'uleit] *vt* (parents, bridegroom etc) ...にお祝いを言う ...ni o-íwai wo iû

congratulations [kəngrætʃulei'ʃənz] *npl* 祝賀 shukúgi

congratulations! おめでとうございます omédetô gozáimasu

congregate [kɑŋ'grəgeit] *vi* (people) 集る atsúmarû; (animals) 群がる murágarû

congregation [kɑŋgrəgei'ʃən] *n* (of a church) 会衆 kaíshû

congress [kɑŋ'gris] *n* (conference) 大会 taíkai; (US: **Congress**) 議会 gikai

congressman [kɑŋ'grismən] (US: *pl* **congressmen**) *n* 下院議員 ka-íngíin

conical [kɑn'ikəl] *adj* (shape) 円すい形の efsuikei no

conifer [kou'nifəːr] *n* 針葉樹 shiñ-yôju

conjecture [kəndʒek'tʃəːr] *n* (speculation) 憶測 okúsoku

conjugal [kɑn'dʒəgəl] *adj* 夫婦間の fûfúkàn no

conjugate [kɑn'dʒəgeit] *vt* (LING) ...の活用形を挙げる ...no katsúyôkei wo agéru

conjunction [kəndʒʌŋk'ʃən] *n* (LING) 接続詞 setsúzokushî

conjunctivitis [kəndʒʌŋktəvai'tis] *n* (MED) 結膜炎 ketsúmakuèn

conjure [kɑn'dʒəːr] *vi* (magician) 奇術をする kijútsu wo suru

conjurer [kɑn'dʒəːrəːr] *n* (magician) 奇術師 kijútsushî, マジシャン majíshan

conjure up *vt* (ghost, spirit) 呼び出す yobídasû; (memories) 思い起す omóiokosû

conk out [kɑŋk-] (*inf*) *vi* (machine, engine) 故障する koshô suru

con man [kɑn'mən] (*pl* **con men**) *n* ぺてん師 peténshi

connect [kənekt'] *vt* (join, also TEL) つなぐ tsunágû; (ELEC) 接続する setsúzoku suru; (fig: associate) 関係付ける kañkeízukeru

♦*vi*: **to connect with** (train, plane etc) ...に連絡する ...ni refíraku suru

to be connected with (associated) 関係付ける kañkeízukeru

connection [kənek'ʃən] n (joint, link) つ
なぎ tsunági; (train, plane etc) 連絡 reñraku; (tel:
association) 関係 kañkei

connive [kənaiv'] vi: **to connive at**
(misbehavior) ...を容認する ...wo yónin
suru

connoisseur [kɑːnɪsəːr'] n (of food,
wine, art etc) 通 tsū

connotation [kɑːnəteiʃən] n (implication) 含み fukúmi

conquer [kɑːŋ'kər] vt (MIL: country,
enemy) 征服する seífuku suru; (fear,
feelings) 克服する kokúfuku suru

conqueror [kɑːŋ'kərər] n (MIL) 征服者
seífukushà

conquest [kɑːn'kwest] n (MIL) 征服 seífuku; (prize) 勝得る物 kachíeta monó;
(mastery: of space etc) 征服 seífuku

cons [kɑːnz] npl see **convenience**; **pro**

conscience [kɑːn'ʃəns] n (sense of right
and wrong) 良心 ryōshin

conscientious [kɑːnʃiːen'ʃəs] adj
(worker) 良心的な ryōshinteki na

conscious [kɑːn'ʃəs] adj (aware): **conscious (of)** ...に 気が付いている
(...ni) ki ga tsuíte irù; (deliberate) 意識
的な ishíkiteki na; (awake) 目が覚めてい
る me ga saméte irù

consciousness [kɑːn'ʃəsnis] n (awareness, mentality: also MED) 意識 ishíki

conscript [kɑːn'skript] n (MIL) 徴集兵
chōshūhei

conscription [kənskrip'ʃən] n (MIL) 徴
兵 chōhei

consecrate [kɑːn'səkreit] vt (building,
place) 奉献する hōken suru

consecutive [kənsek'jətiv] adj (days,
wins) 連続の reñzoku no

consensus [kənsen'səs] n 合意 gōi

consent [kənsent'] n (permission) 許可
kyóka

◆vi: **to consent to** ...に同意する ...ni dōi
suru

consequence [kɑːn'səkwens] n (result)
結果 kekká; (significance) 重要さ júyōsa

consequently [kɑːn'səkwentli:] adv (as
a result, so) 従って shitágatte

conservation [kɑːnsərveiʃən] n (of the
environment) 保護 hogo, 保全 hozéñ; (of
energy) 節約 setsúyaku; (of paintings,
books) 保全 hozéñ

conservative [kənsəːr'vətiv] adj (traditional, conventional: person, attitudes)
保守的な hoshúteki na; (cautious: estimate etc) 控え目の hikáeme no; (BRIT:
POL): **Conservative** 保守党の hoshútō
no

◆n (BRIT: POL): **Conservative** 保守党
員 hoshútōin

conservatory [kənsəːr'vətɔːriː] n
(greenhouse) 温室 ofishitsu; (MUS) 音楽
学校 oñgaku gakkō

conserve [vb kənsəːrv' n kɑːn'səːrv] vt
(preserve) 保護する hógō suru; (supplies,
energy) 節約する setsúyaku suru

◆n (jam) ジャム jámù

consider [kənsid'əːr] vt (believe) ...だと
思う ...da to omóù; (study) 熟考する jukkō suru; (take into account) 考慮に入れる
...wo kōryo ni irérù

to consider doing something ...しよう
かと考える ...shiyō ka to kángaerù

considerable [kənsid'əːrəbl] adj
(amount, expense, difference etc) かなり
の kanári no

considerably [kənsid'əːrəbliː] adv (improve, deteriorate) かなり kanári

considerate [kənsid'əːrit] adj (person)
思いやりのある omóiyari no arù

consideration [kənsidəːrei'ʃən] n (delib-
eration) 熟考 jukkō; (factor) 考慮すべき
点 kōryo subéki téñ; (thoughtfulness) 思
いやり omóiyarí

considering [kənsid'əːriŋ] prep (bearing
in mind) ...を考慮すると ...wo kōryo sur̀u
to

consign [kənsain'] vt (something unwanted): **to consign to** (place) ...にしま
っておく ...ni shimátte okù; (person): **to
consign** (someone's care etc) ...に委
ねる ...ni yudánerù; (poverty etc) ...に追
込む ...ni ofkomù

consignment [kənsain'mənt] n (COMM)
輸送貨物 yusōkamòtsu

consist [kənsist'] vi: **to consist of** (comprise) ...から成る ...kará narù

consistency [kənsis'tənsi:] n (of actions, policies etc) 一貫性 ikkánsei; (of yoghurt, cream etc) 固さ katása

consistent [kənsis'tənt] adj (person) 変らない kawáranaì; (argument, idea) 一貫性のある ikkánsei no arù

consolation [kɑːnsəlei'ʃən] n (comfort) 慰め nagúsame

console [vb kɑnsoul' n kɑːn'soul] vt (comfort) 慰める nagúsameru ♦n (panel) コンソール konsóru

consolidate [kənsɑl'ideit] vt (position, power) 強化する kyóka suru

consommé [kɑːnsəmei'] n (CULIN) コンソメ konsome

consonant [kɑːn'sənənt] n (LING) 子音 shíìn

consortium [kənsɔːr'ʃiːəm] n (COMM) 協会 kyókai

conspicuous [kənspik'juːəs] adj (noticeable: person, feature) 目立つ medátsu

conspiracy [kənspir'əsiː] n (plot) 陰謀 ínbo

conspire [kənspai'əːr] vi (criminals, revolutionaries etc) 共謀する kyóbō suru; (events) 相重なる aíkasanarù

constable [kɑːn'stəbəl] n (BRIT) 巡査 júnsa

chief constable (BRIT) 警察本部長 keísatsu hoñbuchō

constabulary [kənstæb'jələːriː] n (BRIT) 警察 keísatsu ◇一地区の警察隊を指す ichíchiku no keísatsutai wo sasú

constant [kɑːn'stənt] adj (continuous: criticism, pain) 絶えない taénaì; (fixed: temperature, level) 一定の ittéi no

constantly [kɑːn'stəntliː] adv (continually) 絶間なく taémannàku

constellation [kɑːnstəlei'ʃən] n (ASTRONOMY) 星座 seíza

consternation [kɑːnstəːrnei'ʃən] n (dismay) ろうばい róbai

constipated [kɑːn'stəpeitid] adj (MED) 便秘している beñpi shité irù

constipation [kɑːnstəpei'ʃən] n (MED) 便秘 beñpi

constituency [kənstitʃ'uːənsiː] n (POL: area) 選挙区 señkyokù; (: electors) 選挙民 señkyomìn

constituent [kənstitʃ'uːənt] n (POL) 有権者 yúkeñsha; (component) 部分 búbùn

constitute [kɑːn'stitut] vt (represent: challenge, emergency) ...である ...de árù; (make up: whole) 構成する kósei suru

constitution [kɑːnstitu:'ʃən] n (of country) 憲法 keñpō; (of club etc) 会則 kaísoku; (health) 体質 taíshitsu; (make-up: of committee etc) 構成 kóséi

constitutional [kɑːnstitu:'ʃənəl] adj (government, reform etc) 憲法の keñpō no

constraint [kənstreint'] n (restriction) 制限 seígen; (compulsion) 強制 kyósei

construct [kənstrʌkt'] vt (building) 建てる tatérù; (bridge, road etc) 建設する keísetsu suru; (machine) 作る tsukúrù

construction [kənstrʌk'ʃən] n (of building etc) 建築 keñchiku; (of bridge, road etc) 建設 keñsetsu; (of machine) 製作 seísaku; (structure) 構造物 kózobùtsu

constructive [kənstrʌk'tiv] adj (remark, criticism) 建設的な keísetsuteki na

construe [kənstru:'] vt (statement, event) 解釈する kaíshaku suru

consul [kɑːn'səl] n (領事 ryóji

consulate [kɑːn'səlit] n (領事館 ryójikàn

consult [kənsʌlt'] vt (doctor, lawyer, friend) ...に相談する ...ni sódan suru; (reference book) 調べる shiráberù

consultant [kənsʌl'tənt] n (MED) 顧問医 komón-i; (other specialist) 顧問 kómòn, コンサルタント konsárutànto

consultation [kɑːnsəltei'ʃən] n (MED) 診察 shifisatsu; (discussion) 協議 kyógi

consulting room [kənsʌl'tiŋ-] n (BRIT) 診察室 shiñsatsushìtsu

consume [kənsuːm'] vt (food 食べる tabérù; (drink) 飲む nómù; (fuel, energy, time etc) 消費する shóhi suru

consumer [kənsuː'məːr] n (COMM) 消費者 shóhishà

consumer goods npl 消費財 shóhizài

consumerism [kənsuː'məːrizəm] n 消費者運動 shóhishaûndō

consumer society n 消費社会 shóhisha-kái

consummate [kɑn'səmeit] vt (ambition etc) 全うする mattó suru

to consummate a marriage 床入りする tokó-iri suru

consumption [kɑnsʌmp'ʃən] n (of food) 食べる事 tabérù kotó; (of drink) 飲む事 nómù kotó; (of fuel, energy, time etc) 消費 shóhi; (amount consumed) 消費量 shóhiryō; (buying) 消費 shóhi

cont. abbr (= continued) 続く tsuzúku

contact [kɑn'tækt] n (communication) 連絡 refiraku; (touch) 接触 sesshóku; (person) 連絡相手 refirakuáite
♦vt (by phone, letter) ...に連絡する ...ni refiraku suru

contact lenses npl コンタクトレンズ kofitakurénzu

contagious [kɑntei'dʒəs] adj (MED: disease) 伝染性の defisensei no; (fig: laughter, enthusiasm) 移りやすい utsúriyasuī

contain [kɑntein'] vt (hold: objects) ...に...が入っている ...ni ...ga hafitte irú; (have: component, ingredient etc) ...に...が含まれている ...ni ...ga fukúmarete irú; (subj: piece of writing, report etc) ...に...が書いてある ...ni ...ga káite árù; (curb: growth, spread, feeling) 抑える osáerù

to contain oneself 自制する jiséi suru

container [kɑntei'nəːr] n (box, jar etc) 入れ物 irémono; (COMM: for shipping etc) コンテナ kófitena

contaminate [kɑntæm'əneit] vt (water, food, soil etc) 汚染する osén suru

contamination [kɑntæmənei'ʃən] n (of water, food, soil etc) 汚染 osén

cont'd abbr (= continued) 続く tsuzúku

contemplate [kɑn'templeit] vt (idea, subject, course of action) じっくり考える jikkúrì kafigaerù; (person, painting etc) 眺める nagámerù

contemporary [kɑntem'pəreːriː] adj (present-day) 現代の gefidai no; (belonging to same time) 同時代の dójidài no
♦n (person) 同時代の人 dójidai no hitó

contempt [kɑntempt'] n (scorn) 軽べつ kefbetsu

contempt of court (LAW) 法廷侮辱罪 hóteibujokuzai

contemptible [kɑntemp'təbəl] adj (conduct) 卑劣な hirétsu na

contemptuous [kɑntemp'tʃuːəs] adj (attitude) 軽べつ的な kefbetsuteki na

contend [kɑntend'] vt (assert): *to contend that* ...だと主張する ...da to shuchó suru
♦vi (struggle): *to contend with* (problem, difficulty) ...と戦う ...to tatákaù; (compete): *to contend for* (power etc) ...を争う ...wo arásoù

contender [kɑntend'əːr] n (in competition) 競争者 kyósòsha; (POL) 候補者 kóhosha; (SPORT) 選手 séñshu

content [adj. kɑntent', n kɑn'tent] adj (happy and satisfied) 満足して mafizoku shite
♦vt (satisfy) 満足させる mafizoku saséru
♦n (of speech, novel) 内容 naíyō; (fat content, moisture content etc) 含有量 gafi-yúryō

contented [kɑntent'id] adj (happy and satisfied) 満足して mafizoku shité

contention [kɑnten'ʃən] n (assertion) 主張 shuchó; (disagreement, argument) 論争 rofisó

contentment [kɑntent'mənt] n (happiness, satisfaction) 満足 mafizoku

contents [kɑn'tents] npl (of bottle, packet) 中身 nakámi; (of book) 内容 naíyō

(table of) contents 目次 mokúji

contest [n kɑn'test vb kɑntest'] n (competition) コンテスト kófitesuto, コンクール kófikūru; (struggle: for control, power etc) 争い arásoi
♦vt (election, competition) ...で競う ...de kisóù; (statement, decision: also LAW) ...に対して異議を申立てる ...ni taíshite igí wo móshitaterù

contestant [kɑntes'tənt] n (in quiz, competition) 参加者 sañkasha; (in fight) 競争者 kyósòsha

context [kɑn'tekst] n (circumstances: of events, ideas etc) 背景 haíkei; (of word, phrase) 文脈 bufimyaku

continent [kɒn'tɪnənt] n (land mass) 大陸 tairiku

the Continent (BRIT) ヨーロッパ大陸 yōroppa tairiku

continental [kɒntɪnen'təl] adj 大陸の tairiku no

continental quilt (BRIT) n 掛布団 kakébuton

contingency [kɒntin'dʒənsi:] n 有事 yūji

contingent [kɒntin'dʒənt] n (group of people: also MIL) 一団 ichidan

continual [kɒntin'ju:əl] adj (movement, process, rain etc) 絶間ない taémanai

continually [kɒntin'ju:əli:] adv 絶間なく taémanaku

continuation [kɒntinju:ei'ʃən] n 継続 keízoku

continue [kɒntin'ju:] vi 続く tsuzukū
♦vt 続ける tsuzukerù

continuity [kɑntənu:'iti:] n (in policy, management etc) 連続性 reñzokusei; (TV, CINEMA) 撮影台本 satsúeidaihon, コンテ kóñte

continuous [kɒntin'ju:əs] adj (process, growth etc) 絶間ない taémanai; (line) 途切れのない togíre no nai; (LING) 進行形の shiñkōkei no

continuous stationery n 連続用紙 reñzokuyōshi

contort [kɒntɔ:rt'] vt (body) ねじる nejírù; (face) しかめる shikámerù

contortion [kɒntɔ:r'ʃən] n (of body) ねじ nejíre; (of face) こわばり kowábari

contour [kɑn'tu:r] n (on map: also: **contour line**) 等高線 tōkōsen; (shape, outline: gen pl) 輪郭 riñkaku

contraband [kɒn'trəbænd] n 密輸品 mitsúyuhin

contraception [kɒntrəsep'ʃən] n 避妊 hinín

contraceptive [kɒntrəsep'tiv] adj (method, technique) 避妊の hinín no
♦n (device) 避妊用具 hinín yōgu; (pill etc) 避妊薬 hiníñyaku

contract [n kɒn'trækt vb kɒntrækt'] n (LAW, COMM) 契約 keíyaku
♦vi (become smaller) 収縮する shúshuku suru; (COMM): *to contract to do something* ...をする契約をする ...wo suru keíyaku wo suru
♦vt (illness) ...に掛かる ...ni kakárù

contraction [kɒntræk'ʃən] n (of metal, muscle) 収縮 shúshuku; (of word, phrase) 短縮形 tañshukukei

contractor [kɒn'træktər] n (COMM) 請負人 ukéoinìn

contradict [kɒntrədikt'] vt (person) ...の言う事を否定する ...no iù kotó wo hitéi suru; (statement etc) 否定する hitéi suru

contradiction [kɒntrədik'ʃən] n (inconsistency) 矛盾 mujún

contradictory [kɒntrədik'tə:ri:] adj (ideas, statements) 矛盾する mujún suru

contraption [kɒntræp'ʃən] n (pej) (device, machine) 珍妙な機械 chiñmyō na kikái

contrary[1] [kɑn'tre:ri:] adj (opposite, different) 反対の hañtai no
♦n (opposite) 反対 hañtai
on the contrary それどころか sorédokoro ka
unless you hear to the contrary そうではないと聞かされない限り sō de wa nai to kikásarenai kagíri

contrary[2] [kɒntre:r'i:] adj (perverse) つむじ曲りな tsumújimagari na, へそ曲りな hesómagari na

contrast [n kɑn'træst vb kɒntræst'] n (difference) 相違 sōi, コントラスト kóñtorasùto
♦vt (techniques, texts etc) 対照する taíshō suru
*in contrast to ...*と違って ...to chigátte

contrasting [kɒntræs'tiŋ] adj (colors, attitudes) 対照的な taíshōteki na

contravene [kɒntrəvi:n'] vt (law) ...に違反する ...ni ihán suru

contribute [kɒntrib'ju:t] vi (give) 寄付する kifú suru
♦vt: *to contribute an article to* (commissioned) ...に記事を寄稿する ...ni kíji wo kikō suru; (unsolicited) ...に記事を投稿する ...ni kíji wo tōkō suru; *to contribute $10* 10ドルを寄付する júdoru wo kifú suru

to contribute to (charity) ...に寄付する ...ni kifú suru; (newspaper: commissioned) ...に寄稿する ...ni kikō suru; (unsolicited) ...に投稿する ...ni tōkō suru; (discussion) 意見を言う ikén wo iú; (problem etc) ...を悪くする ...wo warúku surú

contribution [kɑntrəbjuːˈʃən] *n* (donation) 寄付 kifú; (BRIT: for social security) 掛金 kakékin; (to debate, campaign) 貢献 kōken; (to journal: commissioned) 寄稿 kikō; (: unsolicited) 投稿 tōkō

contributor [kɑntribˈjətəːr] *n* (to appeal) 寄付者 kifúsha; (to newspaper) 投稿者(寄稿者) tōkōsha (kikōsha)

contrive [kɑntraivˈ] *vi*: *to contrive to do* 努力して...に成功する doryóku shité ...ni sefkō suru

control [kɑntroulˈ] *vt* (country, organization) 支配する shihái suru; (machinery, process) 制御する sefgyo suru; (wages, prices) 規制する kiséi suru; (temper) 自制する jiséi suru; (disease) 抑制する yokúsei suru

◆*n* (of country, organization) 支配 shihái; (of oneself, emotions) 自制心 jiséishin

to be in control of (situation) ...を掌握している ...wo shóaku shité irú; (car etc) ...を思いのままに動かしている ...wo omói no mamá ni ugókashite irú

under control (crowd) 指示に従って shijí ni shitágatte; (situation) 収拾が付いて shūshū ga tsuíte; (dog) 言う事を聞いて kíku kotó wo kiíte

out of control (crowd) 制止が利かなくなって sefshi ga kikánakú natté; (situation) 手に負えなくなって te ni oénakú natté; (dog) 言う事を聞かなくなって iú kotó wo kikánakú natté

control panel *n* 制御盤 sefgyoban

control room *n* 制御室 sefgyoshitsu

controls [kɑntroulzˈ] *npl* (of vehicle) ハンドル.ハンドウ.ブレーキ, クラッチなど全ての運転制御装置 hándoru.búrēki, kurátchi nadò subéte no uftenseigyochochi wo fukúmō; (on radio, television etc) コントロール盤 kofntorōruban◆全てのス

イッチ, 調節用つまみ, ボタンなどを含む subéte no suftchi, chōsetsu yō tsumami, botán nadò wo fukúmō; (governmental) 規制 kiséi

control tower *n* (AVIAT) 管制塔 kafseitō

controversial [kɑntravəːrˈʃəl] *adj* (topic, person) 論争の的になっている rofsō no matō ni natté iru

controversy [kɑnˈtrəvəːrsiː] *n* 論争 rofsō

conurbation [kɑnəːrbeiˈʃən] *n* 大都市圏 daítoshiken

convalesce [kɑnvəlesˈ] *vi* (MED) 回復する kaffuku suru

convalescence [kɑnvəlesˈəns] *n* (MED) 回復期 kaffukukí

convector [kɑnvekˈtəːr] *n* (heater) 対流式暖房器 taíryūshikidanbōki, コンベクター kofnbekútā

convene [kɑnviːnˈ] *vt* (meeting, conference) 召集する shōshū suru

◆*vi* (parliament, inquiry) 開会する kaffai suru

convenience [kɑnviːnˈjəns] *n* (easiness: of using something, doing something) 便利 bénri; (suitability: of date, meeting, house etc) 好都合 kōtsugō; (advantage, help) 便宜 béngi

at your convenience ご都合の良い時に go-tsúgō no yoì tokí ni

all modern conveniences, (BRIT) *all mod cons* 近代設備完備 kindaísetsubíkanbi◇不動産の広告などに使われる語句 fudōsan no kōkoku nadò ni tsukáwarerú gokù

convenient [kɑnviːnˈjənt] *adj* (handy) 便利な bénri na; (suitable) 都合の良い tsugō no yoì

convent [kɑnˈvent] *n* (REL) 女子修道院 joshîshūdōin

convention [kɑnvenˈʃən] *n* (custom) 慣例 kafrei; (conference) 大会 taíkai; (agreement) 協定 kyótei

conventional [kɑnvenˈʃənəl] *adj* (person) 型にはまった katá ni hamátta; (method) 伝統的な defntōteki na

converge [kɑnvəːrdʒˈ] *vi* (roads) 合流す

る gōryū suru; (people): *to converge on* (place, person) ...に集まる ...ni atsúmarú

conversant [kən'vɜː'sənt] *adj*: *to be conversant with* (problem, requirements) ...に通じている ...ni tsūjite irú

conversation [kɑnvə'seiʃən] *n* (talk) 会話 kaíwa

conversational [kɑnvə'seiʃənəl] *adj* (tone, language, skills) 会話的な kaíwatekí na

converse [*n* kɑn'vɜːs *vb* kənvɜːrs'] *n* (of statement) 逆 gyakú
♦*vi* (talk): *to converse (with someone)* (...と) 話をする ...to hanáshi wo suru

conversely [kənvɜːrs'liː] *adv* 逆に gyakú ni

conversion [kənvɜːr'ʒən] *n* (of weights, substances etc) 変換 heñkan; (REL) 改宗 kaíshū

convert [*vb* kənvɜːrt' *n* kɑːn'vɜːrt] *n* (change): *to convert something into/to* ...を...に変換する ...wo ...ni heñkan suru; (person: REL) 改宗させる kaíshū saséru; (: POL) 党籍を変えさせる tóseki wo kaésaserú
♦*n* (REL) 改宗者 kaíshūsha; (POL) 党籍を変える人 tóseki wo kaéru hitó

convertible [kənvɜːr'təbəl] *n* (AUT) コンバーチブル koñbáchibùru; (car) 畳み込み式屋根を持つ乗用車 tatámikomishikí yané wo mótsù jōyōsha

convex [kɑːnveks'] *adj* 凸面の totsúmen no

convey [kənvei'] *vt* (information, idea, thanks) 伝える tsutáerú; (cargo, traveler) 運ぶ hakóbu

conveyor belt [kənvei'ɜːr-] *n* ベルトコンベヤー berútokonbeyā

convict [*vb* kənvikt' *n* kɑːn'vikt] *vt* (of a crime) ...に有罪の判決を下す ...ni yūzai no hañketsu wo kudásù
♦*n* (person) 囚人 shūjin

conviction [kənvik'ʃən] *n* (belief) 信念 shíñnen; (certainty) 確信 kakúshin; (LAW) 有罪判決 yūzaihañketsu

convince [kənvins'] *vt* (assure) 分からせる wakáraserú; (persuade) 納得させる

nattóku saseru

convinced [kənvinst'] *adj*: *convinced of/that* ...を(だと)確信している ...wo (dáto) kakúshin shité irú

convincing [kənvin'siŋ] *adj* (case, argument) 納得のいく nattóku no ikú

convoluted [kɑːn'vəluːtid] *adj* (statement, argument) 込入った komfitta

convoy [kɑːn'voi] *n* (of trucks) 護衛付き輸送車隊 goéitsuki yusóshatai; (of ships) 護衛付き輸送船団 goéitsukiyusóseñdan

convulse [kənvʌls'] *vt*: *to be convulsed with laughter* 笑いこける waráikoke-rú
to be convulsed with pain もだえる modáerú

convulsion [kənvʌl'ʃən] *n* (MED) けいれん keñren

coo [kuː] *vi* (dove, pigeon) くーくー鳴く kūkū nakú; (person) 優しい声で言う yasáshii koè de iú

cook [kuk] *vt* (food, meal) 料理する ryōri suru
♦*vi* (person) 料理する ryōri suru; (meat, pie etc) 焼ける yakéru
♦*n* 料理人 ryōrinin, コック kokkú

cookbook [kuk'buk] *n* 料理の本 ryōri no hoñ

cooker [kuk'ɜːr] *n* (stove) レンジ réñji

cookery [kuk'ɜːriː] *n* 料理する事 ryōri suru kotó

cookery book (*BRIT*) *n* = cookbook

cookie [kuk'iː] (*US*) *n* ビスケット bisúkettò, クッキー kúkkī

cooking [kuk'iŋ] *n* (activity) 料理する事 ryōri suru kotó; (food) 料理 ryōri

cool [kuːl] *adj* (temperature, clothes) 涼しい suzúshii; (drink) 冷たい tsumétai; (person: calm) 落着いている ochítsuite irú; (: unfriendly) そっけない sokkénal
♦*vt* (make colder: tea) 冷ます samásù; (: room) 冷す hiyásù
♦*vi* (become colder: water) 冷たくなる tsumétaku narú; (: air) 涼しくなる suzúshiku narú

coolness [kuːl'nis] *n* (of temperature, clothing) 涼しさ suzúshisa; (of drink) 冷たさ tsumétasà; (calm) 落着き ochítsuki;

coop [kuːp] n 小屋 koya; (*also*: **rabbit coop**) ウサギ小屋 usá|gigoya; (*also*: **hen coop**) ニワトリ小屋 niwátorigoya
♦vt: **to coop up** (*fig*: imprison) 閉込める tojíkomerù

cooperate [kouɑːpˈəreit] vi (collaborate) 協力する kyōdō suru; (assist) 協力する kyōryoku suru

cooperation [kouɑːpəreiˈʃən] n (collaboration) 協力 kyōryoku; (assistance) 協力 kyōryoku

cooperative [kouɑːpˈrətiv] adj (farm, business) 協同組合の kyōdōkúmiai no; (person) 協力的な kyōryokuteki na
♦n (factory, business) 協同組合 kyōdōkúmiai

coordinate [vb kouɔːrˈdəneit n kouɔːrˈdənit] vt (activity, attack) 指揮する shikí suru; (movements) 調整する chōsei suru
♦n (MATH) 座標 zahyō

coordinates [kouɔːrˈdənits] npl (clothes) コーディネートされた服 kōdínēto saréta fukú

coordination [kouɔːrˈdəneiˈʃən] n (of services) 指揮 shikí; (of one's movements) 調整 chōsei

co-ownership [kououˈnəːrʃip] n 協同所有 kyōdōshoyū

cop [kɑːp] (inf) n (policeman/woman) 警官 keíkan

cope [koup] vi: **to cope with** (problem, situation etc) ...に対応する ...ni taíō suru

copious [kouˈpiəs] adj (helpings) たっぷりの táppúri no
copious amounts of 多量の taryō no

copper [kɑːpˈəːr] n (metal) 銅 dō; (inf: policeman/woman) 警官 keíkan

coppers [kɑːpˈəːrz] npl (small change, coins) 小銭 kozéni

coppice [kɑːpˈis] n 木立 kodáchi

copse [kɑːps] n = **coppice**

copulate [kɑːpˈjəleit] vi (people) 性交する seíkō suru; (animals) 交尾する kōbi suru

copy [kɑːpˈi] n (duplicate) 複写 fukúsha, コピー kópī; (of book) 1冊 issátsu; (of

record) 1枚 ichímai; (of newspaper) 1部 ichíbu
♦vt (person, idea etc) まねる manérù; (something written) 複写する fukúsha suru, コピーする kópī suru

copyright [kɑːpˈirait] n 著作権 chosákukèn

coral [kɔːrˈəl] n (substance) さんご sángo
coral reef n さんご礁 sangoshō

cord [kɔːrd] n (string) ひも himó; (ELEC) コード kōdo; (fabric) コールテン kōruten

cordial [kɔːrˈdʒəl] adj (person, welcome) 暖かい atátakaì; (relationship) 親密な shínmitsu na
♦n (BRIT: drink) フルーツシロップ furútsu shiróppù

cordon [kɔːrˈdən] n (MIL, POLICE) 非常線 hijōsen

cordon off vt 非常線を張って...への立入りを禁止する hijōsen wo hatté ...no tachíiri wo kiñshi suru

corduroy [kɔːrˈdərɔi] n コールテン kōruten

core [kɔːr] n (of fruit) しん shiñ; (of organization, system, building) 中心部 chūshínbu; (heart: of problem) 核心 kakúshin
♦vt (an apple, pear etc) ...のしんをくりぬく ...no shiñ wo kurínukù

coriander [kɔːriˈændəːr] n (spice) コリアンダー korfañda

cork [kɔːrk] n (stopper) 栓 señ; (bark) コルク kóruku

corkscrew [kɔːrkˈskruː] n 栓抜き señnuki

corn [kɔːrn] n (US: maize) トウモロコシ tōmórokoshi; (BRIT: cereal crop) 穀物 kokúmòtsu; (on foot) 魚の目 uó no me
corn on the cob 軸付きトウモロコシ jikútsuki tōmórokoshi

cornea [kɔːrˈniə] n (of eye) 角膜 kakúmaku

corned beef [kɔːrnd-] n コーンビーフ kōñbīfu

corner [kɔːrˈnəːr] n (outside) 角 kádò; (inside) 隅 súmì; (in road) 角 kádò; (SOCCER) コーナーキック kōnākikkù; (BOXING) コーナー kōnā
♦vt (trap) 追詰める oítsumerù; (袋のネズ

ミにする fukúro no nezumi ni suru;
(COMM: market) 独占する dokúsen suru

♦*vi* (in car) コーナリングする kônaríngu
surú

cornerstone [kɔːrˈnəːrstoun] *n* (*fig*) 土台
dodái

cornet [kɔːrˈnet] *n* (MUS) コルネット
korúnettò; (BRIT: of ice-cream) アイス
クリームコーン aísukurîmukôn

cornflakes [kɔːrnˈfleiks] *npl* コーンフレ
ーク kônfurêku

cornflour [kɔːrnˈflauəːr] (BRIT) *n* =
cornstarch

cornstarch [kɔːrnˈstɑːrtʃ] (US) *n* コーン
スターチ kônsutâchi

Cornwall [kourn'wəl] *n* コーンウォール
kôn-uôru

corny [kɔːrˈniː] (*inf*) *adj* (joke) さえない
saénai

corollary [kɔːrˈəleːri] *n* (of fact, idea) 当
然の結果 tôzen no kekká

coronary [kɔːrˈəneːri] *n* (*also:* **coronary
thrombosis**) 肝動脈血栓症 kańdômyaku-
kessénshō

coronation [kɔːrəneiˈʃən] *n* たい冠式 taí-
kañshiki

coroner [kɔːrˈənəːr] *n* (LAW) 検死官 keń-
shikàn

coronet [kɔːrˈənit] *n* コロネット korō-
nettò ◊貴族などがかぶる小さな冠 kizó-
ku nadò ga kabúrù chîsana kañmuri

corporal [kɔːrˈpəːrəl] *n* (MIL) ご長 gô-
chō

♦*adj*: **corporal punishment** 体罰 taíba-
tsu

corporate [kɔːrˈpərit] *adj* (action,
effort, ownership) 共同の kyôdō no;
(finance, image) 企業の kigyō no

corporation [kɔːrpəreiˈʃən] *n* (COMM)
企業 kigyō; (of town) 行政部 gyōseíbu

corps [kɔːr] *pl* **corps** [kɔːrz] *n* (MIL)
兵団 heídan; (of diplomats, journalists)
...団 ...dan

corpse [kɔːrps] *n* 遺体 itái

corpuscle [kɔːrˈpəsəl] *n* (BIO) 血球 kek-
kyū

corral [kəræl'] *n* (for cattle, horses) 囲い

kakói

correct [kərekt'] *adj* (right) 正しい tadáshiî; (proper) 礼儀正しい reígitadashiî

♦*vt* (mistake, fault) 直す naósù; (exam)
採点する saíten suru

correction [kərekˈʃən] *n* (act of correct-
ing) 直す事 naósù kotó; (instance) 直し
naóshi

correlation [kɔːrəleiˈʃən] *n* (link) 相互関
係 sôgokañkei

correspond [kɔːrəspɑːnd'] *vi* (write): **to
correspond (with)** (...と) 手紙のやり
取りをする (...to) tegámi no yarítòri
wo surù; (be equivalent): **to correspond
(to)** (...に) 相当する (...ni) sôtō suru;
(be in accordance): **to correspond
(with)** (...と) 一致する (...to) itchí
suru

correspondence [kɔːrəspɑːnˈdəns] *n*
(letters) 手紙 tegámi; (communication
by letters) 文通 buńtsū; (relationship) 一
致 itchí

correspondence course *n* (SCOL) 通
信講座 tsūshiñkōza

correspondent [kɔːrəspɑːnˈdənt] *n*
(journalist) 特派員 tokúhaìn

corridor [kɔːrˈidəːr] *n* (in house, building
etc) 廊下 rôka; (in train) 通路 tsûro

corroborate [kərɑːbˈəreit] *vt* (facts,
story) 裏付ける urázukerù

corrode [kərould'] *vt* (metal) 浸食する
shíshshoku suru

♦*vi* (metal) 腐食する fushóku suru

corrosion [kərouˈʒən] *n* 腐食 fushóku

corrugated [kɔːrˈəgeitid] *adj* (roof,
cardboard) 波型の namígata no

corrugated iron *n* なまこ板 namákoi-
tà

corrupt [kərʌpt'] *adj* (person) 腐敗した
fuháñ shità; (COMPUT: data) 化けたba-
kétà, 壊れた kowáretà

♦*vt* (person) 買収する baíshū suru;
(COMPUT: data) 化けさせる bakésase-
rù

corruption [kərʌpˈʃən] *n* (of person) 汚
職 oshóku; (COMPUT: of data) 化ける事
bakérù kotó

corset [kɔːrˈsit] *n* (undergarment: *also*

MED] コルセット kórùsetto

Corsica [kɔːrˈsikə] *n* コルシカ島 korùshikatò

cosh [kɔːʃ] (BRIT) *n* (cudgel) こん棒 kónbò

cosmetic [kɑːzmetˈik] *n* (beauty product) 化粧品 keshóhin
♦*adj* (fig: measure, improvement) 表面的な hyōmenteki na

cosmic [kɑːzˈmik] *adj* 宇宙の uchū no

cosmonaut [kɑːzˈmənɔːt] *n* 宇宙飛行士 uchūhikòshi

cosmopolitan [kɑːzməpɑːlˈitən] *adj* (place, person) 国際的な kokùsaiteki na

cosmos [kɑːzˈməs] *n* 宇宙 uchū

cosset [kɑːsˈit] *vt* (person) 甘やかす amáyakasù

cost [kɔːst] *n* (price) 値段 nedán; (expenditure) 費用 hiyṓ
♦*vt* (*pt*, *pp* cost) (be priced at) ...の値段である ...no nedán de arù; (find out cost of: project, purchase etc: *pt*, *pp* costed) ...の費用を見積る ...no hiyṓ wo mitsúmorù

how much does it cost? いくらですか ikúra desu ka

to cost someone time/effort ...に時間 (労力)を要する ...ni jíkan (rōryoku) wo yō surù

it cost him his life そのために彼は命をなくした sono tamé ni kárè wa ínòchi wo nákù shità

at all costs 何があっても nánì ga atté mò

co-star [kouˈstɑːr] *n* (TV, CINEMA) 共演者 kyōensha

cost-effective [kɔːstifekˈtiv] *adj* 費用効果比の高い hiyṓkōkahi no takáì

costly [kɔːstˈliː] *adj* (high-priced) 値段の高い nedán no takáì; (involving much expenditure) 費用の掛かる hiyṓ no kakárù

cost-of-living [kɔːstəvlívˈiŋ] *adj* (allowance, index) 生計費の sefkèihi no

cost price (BRIT) *n* 原価 génka

costs [kɔːsts] *npl* (COMM: overheads) 経費 kéihi; (LAW) 訴訟費用 soshóhiyò

costume [kɑːsˈtuːm] *n* (outfit, style of dress) 衣装 íshò; (BRIT: *also*: swimming costume) 水着 mizúgì

costume jewelry *n* 模造宝石類 mozṓhōsekirùi

cosy [kouˈziː] (BRIT) *adj* = **cozy**

cot [kɑːt] *n* (BRIT: child's) ベビーベッド bebíbeddò; (US: campbed) キャンプベッド kyáñpubeddò

cottage [kɑːtˈidʒ] *n* (house) 小さな家 chíisa na ie, コッテージ kottḗji

cottage cheese *n* カッテージチーズ kattḗji chízù

cotton [kɑːtˈən] *n* (fabric) 木綿 mómèn, コットン kóttòn; (BRIT: thread) 縫い糸 nuí-itò

cotton batting [-bætˈiŋ] *n* (US) 脱脂綿 dasshḗmen

cotton candy (US) *n* (candy floss) 綿菓子 watágashì, 綿あめ watá-àme

cotton on to (*inf*) *vt fus* ...に気が付く ...ni kí ga tsúkù

cotton wool (BRIT) *n* = **cotton batting**

couch [kautʃ] *n* (sofa) ソファー sófà; (doctor's) 診察台 shifsatsudai

couchette [kuːʃetˈ] *n* (on train, boat) 寝台 shindai の昼間壁に畳み掛けるか普通の座席に使う物を指す hirúma kabé ni tatámikakerù ka futsū no zaséki ni tsukáù monó wo sasù

cough [kɔːf] *vi* (person) せきをする sekí wo surù
♦*n* (noise) せき sekí; (illness) せきの多い病気 sekí no ōi byóki

cough drop *n* せき止めドロップ sekídome dóròppu

couldn't [kudˈənt] = **could not**

council [kaunˈsəl] *n* (committee, board) 評議会 hyōgikài

city/town council 市(町)議会 shi(chō) gíkài

council estate (BRIT) *n* 公営住宅団地 kōeijū̀takudañchi

council house (BRIT) *n* 公営住宅 kōeijū̀taku

councillor [kaunˈsələr] *n* 議員 gíìn

counsel [kaunˈsəl] *n* (advice) 助言 jogén; (lawyer) 弁護士 béngoshi

counsel(l)or (lawyer) 弁護人 béñgonin
♦vt (advise) ...に助言する ...ni jogén suru
counsel(l)or [kaun'sələr] n (advisor) カ ウンセラー káunserā; (US: lawyer) 弁護 人 béñgonin

count [kaunt] vt (add up: numbers, money, things, people) 数える kazóerū; (include) 入れる iréru, 含む fukúmū
♦vi (enumerate) 数える kazóerū; (be considered) ...と見なされる ...to mináseraru; (be valid) 効果をもつ kōka wo mótsū
♦n (of things, people, votes) 数 kázu; (level: of pollen, alcohol etc) 値 atái, 数 値 súchi; (nobleman) 伯爵 hakúshaku

countdown [kaunt'daun] n (to launch) 秒読み byőyomi

countenance [kaun'tənəns] n (face) 顔 kaó
♦vt (tolerate) 容認する yőnin suru

counter [kaun'tər] n (in shop, café, bank etc) カウンター káuntā; (in game) こま komá
♦vt (oppose) ...に対抗する ...ni taíkō suru
♦adv: **counter to** ...に反して ...ni hañ shite

counteract [kauntərækt'] vt (effect, tendency) 打消す uchíkesu

counter-espionage [kauntəres'piənɑːʒ] n 対抗的スパイ活動 taíkōteki supáikatsudō

counterfeit [kaun'tərfit] n (forgery) 偽物 nisémono
♦vt (forge) 偽造する giző suru
♦adj (coin etc) 偽物の nisémono no

counterfoil [kaun'tərfoil] n (of check, money order) 控え hikáe

countermand [kauntərmænd'] vt (order) 取消す toríkesu

counterpart [kaun'tərpɑːrt] n: **counterpart of** (person) ...に相当する人 ...ni sőtō suru hitő; (thing) ...に相当するもの ...ni sőtō suru mono

counterproductive [kauntərprədʌk'tiv] adj (measure, policy etc) 逆効果的な gyakúkōkateki na

countersign [kaun'tərsain] vt (document) ...に副署する ...ni fukúsho suru

countess [kaun'tis] n 伯爵夫人 hakúshakufújin

countless [kaunt'lis] adj (innumerable) 無数の músū no

count on vt fus (expect) ...の積りでいる ...no tsumóri de irú; (depend on) ...を頼り にする ...wo táyőri ni suru

country [kʌn'triː] n (state, nation) 国 kuní; (native land) 母国 bókōku; (rural area) 田舎 ináka; (region) 地域 chíiki

country dancing (BRIT) n 英国郷土舞 踊 eíkokukyődobuyő

country house n 田舎の大邸宅 ináka no daíteitaku

countryman [kʌn'triːmən] (pl countrymen) n (compatriot) 同国人 dőkokujín; (country dweller) 田舎者 inákamóno

countryside [kʌn'triːsaid] n 田舎 ináka

county [kaun'tiː] n (POL, ADMIN) 郡 gún

coup [kuː] (pl coups) n (MIL, POL: also: **coup d'état**) クーデター kūdetā; (achievement) 大成功 daíseikō

coupé [kuːpei'] n (AUT) クーペ kūpe

couple [kʌp'əl] n (also: **married couple**) 夫婦 fúfu; (cohabiting etc) カップル káppuru; (of things) 一対 ittsúi
a couple of (two people) 2人の futári no; (two things) 2つの futátsu no; (a few people) 数人の súnin no; (a few things) 幾 つかの ikútsuka no

coupon [kuː'pɑn] n (voucher) クーポン券 kūpoñken; (detachable form) クーポン kūpon

courage [kəːr'idʒ] n (bravery) 勇気 yūki

courageous [kərei'dʒəs] adj (person, attempt) 勇敢な yūkan na

courgette [kurʒet'] (BRIT) n ズッキー ニ zúkkíni

courier [kəːr'iːər] n (messenger) メッセ ンジャー méssenjā; (for tourists) 添乗員 teñjőin

course [kɔːrs] n (SCOL) 課程 katéi; (process: of life, events, time etc) 過程 katéi; (of treatment) クール kūru; (direction: of argument, action) 方針 hőshin; (of ship) 針路 shíñro; (part of meal) 一品 ippín, コース kōsu; (for golf) コース kōsu

the course of a river 川筋 kawásuji
of course (naturally) もちろん mochíròn, 当然 tṓzen; (certainly) いいとも íì to mo

court [kɔːrt] *n* (royal) 宮殿 kyūden; (LAW) 法廷 hốtei; (for tennis, badminton etc) コート kṓto

♦*vt* (woman) 妻にしようとして...と交際する tsumá ni shiyṓ to shité ...to kṓsai suru

to take someone to court (LAW) ...を相手取って訴訟を起す ...wo aítedottè soshṓ wo okósù

courteous [kɔːrˈtiːəs] *adj* (person, conduct) 丁寧な teínei na

courtesan [kɔːrˈtizən] *n* 宮廷しょう婦 kyūteishōfu

courtesy [kɔːrˈtisi] *n* (politeness) 礼儀正しさ reígitadashìsa

(by) courtesy of (thanks to) ...のお陰で ...no okáge de

court-house [kɔːrtˈhaus] (*US*) *n* 裁判所 saíbansho

courtier [kɔːrˈtiːər] *n* 廷臣 teíshin

court-martial [kɔːrtˈmɑːrʃəl] (*pl* **courts-martial**) *vt* (MIL) 軍法会議 guńpōkaĩgi

courtroom [kɔːrtˈruːm] *n* 法廷 hṓtei

courtyard [kɔːrtˈjɑːrd] *n* (of castle, house) 中庭 nakániwa

cousin [kʌzˈin] *n* (relative) 親せき shiñsekì

first cousin いとこ itókò

second cousin はとこ hatókò, またいとこ mata-itoko

cove [kouv] *n* (bay) 入江 iríe

covenant [kʌvˈənənt] *n* (promise) 契約 kefyaku

cover [kʌvˈər] *vt* (hide: face, surface, ground): *to cover (with)* ...で覆う ...de ṓu; (hide: feelings, mistake): *to cover (with)* ...で隠す ...de kakúsù; (shield: book, table etc): *to cover (with)* ...に (...を) 掛ける ...ni (...wo) kakérù; (with lid): *to cover (with)* ...にふたをする ...ni futá wo suru; (travel: distance) 行く ikú; (protect: *also* INSURANCE) カバーする kábā suru; (discuss: topic, subject: *also* PRESS) 取上げる toríageru; (include) 含

む fukúmù

♦*n* (for furniture) 覆い ối; (lid) ふた futá; (on bed) 上掛 uwágake; (of book, magazine) 表紙 hyṓshi; (shelter: for hiding) 隠れ場所 kakúrebasho; (: from rain) 雨宿りの場所 amáyàdori no bashò; (INSURANCE) 保険 hokén; (of spy) 架空の身分 kakū no míbùn

to take cover (shelter: from rain) 雨宿りをする amáyàdori wo suru; (: from gunfire etc) 隠れる kakúrerù

under cover (indoors) 屋根の下で (に) yané no shitá de (ni)

under cover of darkness やみに紛れて yamí ni magíretè

under separate cover (COMM) 別便で betsúbin de

coverage [kʌvˈəridʒ] *n* (TV, PRESS) 報道 hṓdō

cover charge *n* (in restaurant) サービス料 sábisuryō

covering [kʌvˈəriŋ] *n* (layer) 覆い ối; (of snow, dust etc) 覆う物 ốu monò

covering letter (*US also*: **cover letter**) *n* 添状 soéjō

cover note (*BRIT*) *n* (INSURANCE) 仮保険証 karíhokeñshō

covert [kouˈvɜːrt] *adj* (glance, threat) 隠れた kakúretà

cover up *vi*: *to cover up for someone* ...をかばう ...wo kabáù

cover-up [kʌvˈərʌp] *n* もみ消し momíkeshi

covet [kʌvˈit] *vt* (desire) 欲しがる hoshígarù

cow [kau] *n* (animal) 雌ウシ meúshi; (*inf*!: woman) あま amá

♦*vt* (oppress): *to be cowed* おびえる obíerù

coward [kauˈərd] *n* おく病者 okúbyōmono

cowardice [kauˈərdis] *n* おく病 okúbyō

cowardly [kauˈərdli] *adj* おく病な okúbyō na

cowboy [kauˈbɔi] *n* (in US) カウボーイ kaúbòi

cower [kauˈər] *vi* い縮する ishúku suru

coxswain [kɑːkˈsin] *n* (ROWING: abbr:

cox) コックス kókkùsu

coy [koi] *adj* (demure, shy) はにかんでいる せる hanīkànde miserù

coyote [kai'out'i] *n* コヨーテ kóyòte

cozy [kai'out'i] (*BRIT* **cosy**) *adj* (room, house) こじんまりした kojínmàri shita; (person) 心地よい kokóchi yoī

CPA [si:pi:ei'] (*US*) *abbr* = **certified public accountant**

crab [kræb] *n* カニ kanī

crab apple *n* ヒメリンゴ himéringo

crack [kræk] *n* (noise: of gun) パン pán; (: of thunder) ばりばり bāribari; (: of twig) ぽっきり pokkìri; (: of whip) パン ban; (gap) 割れ目 waréme; (in bone, dish, glass, wall) ひび hibī

♦*vt* (whip, twig) 鳴らす narásù; (bone, dish, glass, wall) ひびを入れる hibí wo iréru; (nut) 割る warú; (solve: problem) 解決する kaíketsu suru; (: code) 解く tó-kù; (joke) 飛ばす tobásu

♦*adj* (expert) 優秀な yūshū na

crack down on *vt fus* (crime, expenditure etc) 取り締まる toríshimarù

cracker [kræk'ɔːr] *n* (biscuit, Christmas cracker) クラッカー kurákkà

crackle [kræk'əl] *vi* (fire) ぱちぱちと音 を立てる páchipachi to otó wo tatérù; (twig) ぽきぽきと音を立てる pókìpoki to otó wo tatérù

crack up *vi* (PSYCH) 頭がおかしくなる atáma ga okáshikù narú

cradle [krei'dəl] *n* (baby's) 揺りかご yurí-kago

craft [kræft] *n* (skill) 芸術 geíjutsu; (trade) 職業 shokúgyò; (boat: *pl inv*) 船 fúne; (plane: *pl inv*) 飛行機 hikōki

craftsman [kræfts'mən] (*pl* **craftsmen**) *n* (artisan) 職人 shokúnin

craftsmanship [kræfts'mənʃip] *n* (quality) 芸術 geíjutsu

crafty [kræf'ti:] *adj* (sneaky) 腹黒い ha-rágurò, こうかつな kókatsu na

crag [kræg] *n* 険しい岩山 kewáshiì iwá-yama

cram [kræm] *vt* (fill): **to cram something with ...** を一杯にする ...wo ...de ippái ni surù; (put): **to cram some-thing into ...** を...に詰め込む ...wo ...ni tsu-mékomù

♦*vi*: **to cram for exams** 一夜漬の試験 勉強をする ichíyazuke no shikénbenkyò wo suru

cramp [kræmp] *n* (MED) けいれん keíren

cramped [kræmpt] *adj* (accommodation) 窮屈な kyúkutsu na

crampon [kræm'pɑːn] *n* (CLIMBING) アイゼン áìzen

cranberry [kræn'beri:] *n* (berry) コケモ モ kokémòmo, クランベリー kuránberì

crane [krein] *n* (machine) クレーン kúrèn; (bird) ツル tsúrù

crank [kræŋk] *n* (person) 変人 heńjin; (handle) クランク kuráňku

crankshaft [kræŋk'ʃæft] *n* (AUT) クラ ンクシャフト kuráňkushafùto

cranny [kræn'i:] *n* see **nook**

crash [kræʃ] *n* (noise) 大音響 daíoňkyò ♦ 物が落ちる、ぶつかるなどの大きな音を 指す monó ga ochírù, butsúkarù nádò no ōkina otó wo sásù; (of car, train etc) 衝突 shōtotsu; (of plane) 墜落 tsuíraku; (COMM: of stock-market) 暴落 bóraku; (COMM: of business etc) 倒産 tōsaǹ

♦*vt* (car etc) 衝突させる shōtotsu sasérù; (plane) 墜落させる tsuíraku sasérù

♦*vi* (car etc) 衝突する shōtotsu suru; (plane) 墜落する tsuíraku suru; (COMM: market) 暴落する bóraku suru; (COMM: firm) 倒産する tōsaǹ suru

crash course *n* 速成コース sokúseikòsu

crash helmet *n* ヘルメット herúmettò

crash landing *n* (AVIAT) 不時着陸 fu-jíchakùriku

crass [kræs] *adj* (behavior, comment, person) 驚呆な rokótsu na

crate [kreit] *n* (box) 箱 hakó; (for bottles) ケース kèsu

crater [krei'tɔːr] *n* (of volcano) 噴火口 fuńkakò; (on moon etc) クレーター kurè-tā

bomb crater 爆弾孔 bakúdaňkò

cravat [krəvæt'] *n* アスコットタイ asú-kottotaì

crave [kreiv] *vt, vi*: **to crave for ...** を強 く欲しがる ...wo tsuyókù hoshígarù

crawl [krɔːl] vi (person) 四つんばいには う yotsúnbai ni háù; (insect) はう háù; (vehicle) のろのろと進む nórònoro to susúmù

♦n (SWIMMING) クロール kúròru

crayfish [krei'fiʃ] n inv (freshwater) ザリガニ zarígàni; (saltwater) エビガニ ebígàni

crayon [krei'ɑn] n クレヨン kuréyòn

craze [kreiz] n (fashion) 大流行 dáíryùkò

crazy [krei'zi:] adj (insane) 正気で ない shóki de náî; (inf: keen): **crazy about someone/something** ...が大好きである ...ga dafsukí de arù

crazy paving (BRIT) n 不ぞろい舗装 fuzóroi hosô 不ぞろいの敷石からなる 舗装 fuzóroi no shikíishi kara narù hosô

creak [kri:k] vi (floorboard, door etc) きしむ kishímù

cream [kri:m] n (of milk) (生)クリーム (namá)kúrìmu; (also: **artificial cream**) 人造クリーム jinžôkùrìmu; (cosmetic) 化 粧クリーム keshôkùrìmu; (élite) 名士た ち meíshì tachì

♦adj (color) クリーム色の kúrìmuírò no

cream cake n クリームケーキ kurímu-kèki

cream cheese n クリームチーズ kurí-muchìzu

creamy [kri:'mi:] adj (color) クリーム色 の kurímuírò no; (taste) 生クリームたっ ぷりの namákùrìmu táppùri no

crease [kri:s] n (fold) 折り目 oríme; (wrinkle) しわ shiwá; (in trousers) 折り目 oríme

♦vt (wrinkle) しわくちゃにする shiwá-kucha ni suru

♦vi (wrinkle) しわくちゃになる shíwakucha ni naru

create [kri:eit'] vt (cause to happen, exist) 引き起こす hikífokosù; (produce, design) 作る tsukúrù

creation [kri:ei'ʃən] n (causing to happen, exist) 引き起こす hikífokosù koto; (production, design) 作る事 tsukúrù kotó; (REL) 天地創造 teñchísozô

creative [kri:ei'tiv] adj (artistic) 芸術的 な geśjutsuteki na; (inventive) 創造性の ある sôzosei no árù

creator [kri:ei'tə:r] n (maker, inventor) 作る人 tsukúrù hitô

creature [kri:'tʃər] n (living animal) 動 物 dôbutsu; (person) 人 hitô

crèche [kreʃ] n 託児所 takújìsho

credence [kri:d'əns] n: **to lend credence to** (prove) ...を信じさせる ...wo shiñjí saseru

to give credence to (prove) ...を信じさ せる ...wo shiñjí saserù; (believe) 信じる shiñjirù

credentials [kriden'ʃəlz] npl (references) 資格 shikáku; (identity papers) 身 分証明証 mibúnshòmeishô

credibility [kredəbil'əti:] n (of person, fact) 信頼性 shiñ'raisei

credible [kred'əbəl] adj (believable) 信じ られる shiñjiraréru; (trustworthy) 信用 できる shiñ-yô dekírù

credit [kred'it] n (COMM: loan) 信用 shiñ-yô; (recognition) 名誉 mêiyo

♦vt (COMM) ...の入金にする ...no nyûkin ni suru; (believe: also: **give credit to**) 信 じる shiñjirù

to be in credit (person, bank account) 黒字になっている kurójì ni natté irù

to credit someone with (fig) ...に...の美 徳があると思う ...ni...no bitóku ga arù to omóù

credit card n クレジットカード kuréjit-tokàdo

creditor [kred'itə:r] n (COMM) 債権者 saíkeñsha

credits [kred'its] npl (CINEMA) クレジ ット kuréjitto

creed [kri:d] n (REL) 信条 shiñjô

creek [kri:k] n (US: stream) 小川 ogáwa; (BRIT: inlet) 入江 iríe

creep [kri:p] (pt, pp **crept**) vi (person, animal) 忍び足で歩く shinóbiàshi de arúkù

creeper [kri:'pə:r] n (plant) つる tsurú

creepy [kri:'pi:] adj (frightening: story, experience) 薄気味の悪い usúkimiwarùi

cremate [kri:'meit] vt (corpse) 火葬にす る kasô ni suru

cremation [krimei'ʃən] n 火葬 kasô

crematoria [kri:mətɔ:r'i:ə] npl of crematorium

crematorium [kri:mətɔːr'i:əm] *n* (*pl* **crematoria**) 火葬場 kasôba

crêpe [kreip] *n* (fabric) クレープ kúrēpu; (rubber) クレープゴム kurépugomù ◊ 靴底に使う表面がしわ状のゴム kutsűzoko ni tsukáū hyőmen ga shiwájō no gômù

crêpe bandage (*BRIT*) *n* 伸縮性包帯 shíñshukuseihôtai

crept [krept] *pt, pp of* **creep**

crescent [kres'ənt] *n* (in shape) 三日月形 mikázukigata; (street) ...通り ...dōri ◊ 特にカーブになっている通りの名前に使うtôkñ ni kâbu ni natté irú tôri no namáe ni tsukáū

cress [kres] *n* (BOT, CULIN) クレソン kúreson

crest [krest] *n* (of hill) 頂上 chôjō; (of bird) とさか tosáka; (coat of arms) 紋章 mōñ

crestfallen [krest'fɔ:lən] *adj* しょんぼりした shoñbori shitá

Crete [kri:t] *n* クレタ島 kurétatō

crevice [krev'is] *n* (gap, crack) 割れ目 waréme

crew [kru:] *n* (NAUT) 乗組員 noríkumiìn; (AVIAT) 乗員 jôin; (TV, CINEMA) カメラ班 kaméraháñ ◊ 3つの意味とも総称として使う mittsú no imî to mo sôshō toshité tsukáū

crew-cut [kru:'kʌt] *n* 角刈り kakúgari

crew-neck [kru:'nek] *n* (of jersey) 丸首 marúkubi

crib [krib] *n* (cot) ベビーベッド bebíbeddò
◆*vt* (*inf*: copy: during exam etc) カンニングする kañníñgu suru; (: from writings etc of others) 盗用する tôyō suru

crick [krik] *n*: **to have a crick in one's neck** 首が痛い kubí ga itái

cricket [krik'it] *n* (game) クリケット kuríkettò; (insect) コオロギ kôrogi

crime [kraim] *n no pl*: illegal activities) 犯罪 hañzai; (illegal action) 犯罪(行為) hañzai(kôi); (*fig*) 罪 tsumì

criminal [krim'ənəl] *n* 犯罪者 hañzaisha
◆*adj* (illegal) 違法の ihô no; (morally wrong) 罪悪の zaíaku no

crimson [krim'zən] *adj* 紅色の beníiro no

cringe [krindʒ] *vi* (in fear, embarrassment) 縮こまる chijíkomarù

crinkle [kriŋ'kəl] *vt* (crease, fold) しわくちゃにする shiwákucha ni suru

cripple [krip'əl] *n* (MED) 身障者 shiñshôsha
◆*vt* (person) 不具にする fúgũ ni suru

crises [krai'si:z] *npl of* **crisis**

crisis [krai'sis] (*pl* **crises**) *n* 危機 kíkì

crisp [krisp] *adj* (vegetables) ぱりぱりした páríparì shitá; (bacon) からりと焼いた kárárì shitá; (weather) からっとした karáttò shitá; (manner, tone, reply) 無愛想な buáĩso na

crisps [krisps] (*BRIT*) *npl* ポテトチップス potétochippù

criss-cross [kris'krɔs] *adj* (pattern, design) 十字模様の jūjímoyō no

criteria [kraiti'ri:ə] *npl of* **criterion**

criterion [kraitir'i:ən] (*pl* **criteria**) *n* (standard) 規準 kijún

critic [krit'ik] *n* (of system, policy etc) 反対者 hañtaisha; (reviewer) 評論家 hyôronka

critical [krit'ikəl] *adj* (time, situation) 重大な jūdai na; (opinion, analysis) 批評的な hihyôteki na; (person: fault-finding) 粗探し好きな arásagashízūkì na; (illness) 危険な kikén na

critically [krit'ikli:] *adv* (speak, look etc) 批判的に híhánteki ni
critically ill 重症で jûshō de

criticism [krit'isizəm] *n* (disapproval, complaint) 非難 hínan; (of book, play etc) 批評 hihyô

criticize [krit'əsaiz] *vt* (find fault with) 非難する hínan suru

croak [krouk] *vi* (frog) げろげろ鳴く gérõgero nakù; (bird etc) かーかー鳴く kākā nakù; (person) がらがら声で言う garágaragoe de iu

crochet [krouʃei'] *n* かぎ針編み kagíbariami

crockery [krɑːk'əri:] *n* (dishes) 皿類 sarárùi

crocodile [krɑːk'ədail] *n* ワニ wánì

crocus [krou'kəs] n クロッカス kurókkàsu

croft [krɔft] (BRIT) n (small farm) 小農場 shónōjō

crony [krou'ni:] (inf: pej) n 仲間 nakáma

crook [kruk] n (criminal) 悪党 akútō; (also: shepherd's crook) 羊飼の杖 hitsújikai no tsúe ◊片端の曲った物を指す katáhashi no magátta monó wo sásù

crooked [kruk'id] adj (bent, twisted) 曲った magátta; (dishonest) 不正の fuséi no

crop [krɑp] n (of fruit, cereals, vegetables) 作物 sakúmòtsu; (harvest) 収穫 shūkaku; (riding crop) むち múchí ◊乗馬用の物を指す jóbayō no monó wo sásù
♦vt (hair) 刈込む karíkomù

crop up vi (problem, topic) 持ち上る mochíagarù

croquet [kroukei'] n クロッケー kurókkē ◊複雑なゲートボールに似た球技 fukúzatsu na gétobōru ni nitá kyúgi

croquette [krouket'] n (CULIN) コロッケ kórōkke

cross [krɔs] n (shape) 十字 jūji; (REL) 十字架 jūjika; (mark) ばつ(印) bátsù(jírùshi); (hybrid) 合の子 aínoko
♦vt (street, room etc) 横断する ōdan suru; (arms, legs) 組む kúmù; (animal, plant) 交雑する kózatsu suru
♦adj (angry) 怒 feminine...下線...

to cross a check 線引小切手にする senbiki kogítte ni surù

crossbar [krɔs'bɑr] n (SPORT) ゴールの横棒 gōru no yokóbō

cross country (race) n クロスカントリーレース kurósukantorīrèsu

cross-examine [krɔs'igzæm'in] vt (LAW) 反対尋問する hañtaijiñmon suru

cross-eyed [krɔs'aid] adj 寄り目の yoríme no

crossfire [krɔs'faiər] n 十字射撃 jūjishagèki

crossing [krɔs'iŋ] n (sea passage) 船旅 funátabi; (also: pedestrian crossing) 横断歩道 ōdanhodō

crossing guard (US) n 交通指導員 kótsūshidōīn ◊交通事故を防ぐために横断

歩道に立って学童などの横断を助ける係員 kótsūjiko wo fuségù tamé ni ōdanhodō ni tatté gakúdō nádò no ōdan wo tasúkerù kakáriīn

cross out vt (delete) 線を引いて消す séñ wo hiíte kesú

cross over vi (move across) 横断する ōdan suru

cross-purposes [krɔs'pər'pəsiz] npl:
to be at cross-purposes 話が食違っている hanáshi ga kuíchigatte irú

cross-reference [krɔs'ref'ərəns] n 相互参照 sōgosañshō

crossroads [krɔs'roudz] n 交差点 kōsatèn

cross section n (of an object) 断面 dañmeñ; (sketch) 断面図 dañmeñzu
cross section of the population 国民を代表する人々 kokúmin wo daíhyō suru hitóbitò

crosswalk [krɔs'wɔk] (US) n 横断歩道 ōdanhodō

crosswind [krɔs'wind] n 横風 yokókaze

crossword [krɔs'wərd] n クロスワードパズル kurósuwādopazùru

crotch [krɑtʃ] n (ANAT, of garment) また matá

crotchet [krɑtʃ'it] n (MUS) 四分音符 shíbuoñpu

crotchety [krɑtʃ'əti:] adj (person) 気難しい kimúzukashiī

crouch [krautʃ] vi (person, animal) うずくまる uzúkumarù

croupier [kru:p'iər] n (in casino) とばく台の元締 tobákudai no motójime, ディーラー dīrā

crow [krou] n (bird) カラス káràsu; (of cock) 鳴き声 nakígoè
♦vi (cock) 鳴く nakú

crowbar [krou'bɑr] n バール bāru

crowd [kraud] n: crowd of people 群衆 guñshū
♦vt (fill: room, stadium etc) ...にぎっしり入る ...ni gísshiri haírù
♦vi (gather): to crowd round ...の回りに群がる ...no mawári ni murágarù; (cram): to crowd in ...の中へ詰めかける ...no nákà e tsumékakerù

a crowd of fans 大勢のファン ōzei nò fáñ

crowded [krau'did] *adj* (full) 込み入った komfimita; (densely populated) 人口密度の高い jiñkōmitsùdo no takái

crown [kraun] *n* (gen) 冠 kafimuri; (of monarch) 王冠 ōkan; (monarchy): **the Crown** 国王 kokṓō; (of head, hill) てっぺん téppeñ; (of tooth) 歯冠 shikáñ
♦*vt* (monarch) 王位に就かせる ői ni tsukáserū; (fig: career, evening) ...に有終の美を飾る ...ni yūshū no bí wo kazárū

crown jewels *npl* 王位の象徴 no shṓchō ◇王冠, しゃくなど国家的儀式で王または女王が王位の象徴として用いられる物を指す ōkan, shákū nádð kokkáteki gishíki de ð matá wa jōō ga ði no shṓchō toshité mochíirú monō wo sásű

crown prince *n* 皇太子 kōtaīshi

crow's feet *n* 目じりの小じわ mejíri no kojíwa, カラスの足跡 kárāsu no ashfátð

crucial [kru:'ʃəl] *adj* (decision, vote) 重大な jūdai na

crucifix [kru'səfiks] *n* 十字架像 jūjikazṓ

crucifixion [kru:səfik'ʃən] *n* (REL) キリストのはりつけ kirísuto no harítsuke

crude [kru:d] *adj* (materials) 原...; (fig: basic) 原始的な gefishiteki na; (: vulgar) 骨薄な shimótsu na
crude (oil) *n* 原油 geñ-yu

cruel [kru:'əl] *adj* (person, action) 残酷な zafikoku na; (situation) 悲惨な hisán na

cruelty [kru'əlti:] *n* (of person, action) 残酷さ zafikoku sa; (of situation) 悲惨さ hisánsa

cruise [kru:z] *n* (on ship) 船旅 funátabi
♦*vi* (ship) 巡航する juñkṓ suru; (car) 楽に走行する rákū ni sṓkō suru

cruiser [kru:'zə:r] *n* (motorboat) 大型モーターボート ōgata mṓtābòto, クルーザー kurūza; (warship) 巡洋艦 juñ-yōkan

crumb [krʌm] *n* (of bread, cake) くず kúzú

crumble [krʌm'bəl] *vt* (bread, biscuit etc) 崩す kuzúsū
♦*vi* 崩れる kuzúrerū

crumbly [krʌm'bli:] *adj* (bread, biscuits etc) 崩れやすい kuzúreyasùi, ぼろぼろした pórðporo shitá

crumpet [krʌm'pit] *n* クランペット kuránpettò ◇マフィンの一種 mafíñ no isshù

crumple [krʌm'pəl] *vt* (paper, clothes) しわくちゃにする shiwákucha ni suru

crunch [krʌntʃ] *vt* (food etc) かみ砕く kamíkudakù; (underfoot) 踏み砕く fumfkudakù
♦*n* (fig: moment of truth) いざという時 izá to iū tokí

crunchy [krʌn'tʃi:] *adj* (food) ぱりぱりした parípari shitá

crusade [kru:seid'] *n* (campaign) 運動 uñdṓ

crush [krʌʃ] *n* (crowd) 人込み hitógomi; (love): **to have a crush on someone** ...にのぼせる ...ni nobóserū; (drink): **lemon crush** レモンスカッシュ remóñsukasshū
♦*vt* (press, squeeze) 押しつぶす oshítsubusū; (crumple: paper, clothes) しわくちゃにする shiwákucha ni suru; (defeat: army, opposition) 圧倒する attṓ suru; (devastate: hopes) 台無しにする daínashi ni suru; (: person) 落胆させる rakútan saserū

crust [krʌst] *n* (of bread, pastry) 皮 kawá; (of snow, ice) アイスバーン aísubāñ; (of the earth) 地殻 chikáku

crutch [krʌtʃ] *n* (support, stick) 松葉づえ matsúbazùe

crux [krʌks] *n* (of problem, matter) 核心 kakúshin

cry [krai] *vi* (weep) 泣く nakú; (shout: *also*: **cry out**) 叫ぶ sakébu
♦*n* (shriek) 悲鳴 himéi; (shout) 叫び声 sakébigoè; (of bird, animal) 鳴き声 nakígoè

cry off *vi* (change one's mind, cancel) 手を引くte wo hikú

crypt [kript] *n* 地下室 chikáshitsu ◇特に納骨堂などに使われる教会の地下室を指す tókū ni nṓkotsudō nadð ni tsukáwarerû kyṓkai no chikáshitsu wo sásū

cryptic [krip'tik] *adj* (remark, clue) なぞめいた nazómeità

crystal [kris'təl] n (mineral) 結晶 kesshō; (in jewelery) 水晶 suíshō; (glass) クリスタル kurísūtaru

crystal-clear [kris'təlkli:'ər] adj (transparent) よく澄んだ yōkù súñda; (fig: easy to understand) 明白な meíhaku na

crystallize [kris'təlaiz] vt (opinion, thoughts) まとめる matómeru
♦vi (sugar etc) 結晶する kesshō suru

cub [kʌb] n (of lion, wolf etc) ...の子 ...no ko; (also: **cub scout**) カブスカウト kabúsukaùto

Cuba [kju:'bə] n キューバ kyūba

Cuban [kju:'bən] adj キューバの kyūba no
♦n キューバ人 kyūbajìn

cubbyhole [kʌb'ihoul] n 小さな納戸 chíísa na naǹdo

cube [kju:b] n (shape) 立方体 rippótai; (MATH: of number) ...の3乗 ...no sañjō
♦vt (MATH) 3乗する sañjō suru

cube root n (MATH) 立方根 rippókon

cubic [kju:'bik] adj (volume) 立方の rippó no

cubic capacity n 体積 táiseki

cubicle [kju:'bikəl] n (at pool) 更衣室 kōíshitsu ◇小さい個室について言う chíísai koshítsu ni tsuíte iú; (in hospital) カーテンで仕切った小さなスペース kāten de shikítta ichíbyōshòbun no supésu

cuckoo [ku'ku:] n カッコウ kákkō

cuckoo clock n はと時計 hatódokèi

cucumber [kju:'kʌmbər] n キューリ kyūri

cuddle [kʌd'əl] vt (baby, person) 抱締める dakíshimerù
♦vi (lovers) 抱合う dakíaù

cue [kju:] n (snooker cue) キュー kyū; (THEATER etc) 合図 aízu, キュー kyū

cuff [kʌf] n (of sleeve) カフス káfusu; (US: of trousers) 折返し oríkaeshi; (blow) 平手打ち hiráteuchi
off the cuff (impromptu) 即座に (の) sókùza ni (no)

cufflinks [kʌf'liŋks] npl カフスボタン kafúsubotàn

cuisine [kwizi:n'] n (of country, region) 料理 ryōri

cul-de-sac [kʌl'dəsæk'] n (road) 行き止り yukídomari

culinary [kju:'ləne:ri:] adj 料理の ryōri no

cull [kʌl] vt (story, idea) えり抜く erínukù
♦n (of animals) 間引き mabíki

culminate [kʌl'məneit] vi: **to culminate in** (gen) 遂に...となる tsuí ni ...to narù; (unpleasant outcome) 挙句の果てに...となってしまう agéku no hatè ni ...to natté shimaù

culmination [kʌlmənei'ʃən] n (of career, process etc) 頂点 chōten

culottes [kju:lots'] npl キュロット kyúrottò

culpable [kʌl'pəbəl] adj (blameworthy) とがむべき togámubekì

culprit [kʌl'prit] n (of crime) 犯人 hañnin

cult [kʌlt] n (REL: worship) 崇拝 sūhai; (: sect, group) 宗派 shūha; (fashion) 流行 ryūkō

cultivate [kʌl'təveit] vt (land) 耕す tagáyasù; (crop) 栽培する saíbai suru; (person) 近付きになろうとする chikázuki ni narò to suru

cultivation [kʌltəvei'ʃən] n (AGR) 耕作 kōsaku

cultural [kʌl'tʃə:rəl] adj (traditions etc) 文化文明の buñkabuñmei no; (activities etc) 芸術の geíjutsu no

culture [kʌl'tʃə:r] n (of a country, civilization) 文明 buñmei, 文化 buñka; (the arts) 芸術 geíjutsu; (BIO) 培養 baíyō

cultured [kʌl'tʃə:rd] adj (individual) 教養のある kyōyō no arù

cumbersome [kʌm'bə:rsəm] adj (object) 扱いにくい atsúkainikuì ◇大きく張る物, 重い物, 大きくて不格好な物などについて言う kasábarí monò, omóì monò, ōkikùte bukákkō na monò nadò ni tsuíte iù; (process) 面倒な meńdō na

cumulative [kju:m'jələtiv] adj (effect, result) 累積する rufséki suru

cunning [kʌn'iŋ] n (craftiness) こうかつ さ kōkatsusa
♦adj (crafty) こうかつな kōkatsu na

cup [kʌp] n (for drinking) カップ káppù

(as prize) 賞杯 shōhai, カップ kappù; (of bra) カップ kappù

cupboard [kʌbˈəːrd] *n* 戸棚 todáma

Cupid [kjuːˈpid] *n* キューピッド kyūpiddo

cup-tie [kʌpˈtai] (*BRIT*) *n* (SOCCER) トーナメント tōnamento

curate [kjuˈrit] *n* 助任牧師 jonínbokúshi

curator [kjureiˈtəːr] *n* (of museum, gallery) キューレーター kyūrētā ◇学芸員の管理職に相当する人を指す gakúgeiin no kańrishoku ni sōtō suru hitó wo sásù

curb [kəːrb] *nt* (powers, expenditure: restrain) 制限する seígen suru; (person) 抑える osáerù

◆*n* (restraint) 抑制 yokúsei; (*US*: kerb) 縁石 fuchíishi

curdle [kəːrˈdəl] *vi* (milk) 凝結する gyōketsu suru

cure [kjuːr] *vt* (illness, patient) 治す naósù; (CULIN) 保存食にする hozónshoku ni suru

◆*n* (MED) 治療法 chiryōhō; (solution) 解決 kaíketsu

curfew [kəːrˈfjuː] *n* (MIL, POL) 夜間外出禁止令 yakán gaíshutsu kińshirei

curio [kjuːˈriːou] *n* 骨とう品 kottōhin

curiosity [kjuːriːɑːsˈəti:] *n* (of person) 好奇心 kōkishin; (object) 珍しい物 mezúrashiì monó

curious [kjuːˈriːəs] *adj* (person: interested) 好奇心がある kōkishin ga arù; (: nosy) せん索好きな seńsakuzúki na; (thing: strange, unusual) 変った kawátta

curl [kəːrl] *n* (of hair) カール kāru

◆*vt* (hair) カールする kāru suru

◆*vi* (hair) カールになっている kāru ni natté irù

curler [kəːrˈləːr] *n* (for hair) カーラー kārā

curl up *vi* (person, animal) 縮こまる chijfkomarù

curly [kəːrˈliː] *adj* 巻毛の makíge no

currant [kəːrˈtən] *n* (dried fruit) レーズン rēzun ◇小型の無核レブドウから作った物を指す kogáta no tanénashibùdo kara tsukútta monó wo sásù; (bush, fruit: blackcurrant, redcurrant) スグリ

currency [kəːrˈənsiː] *n* (system) 通貨 tsūka; (money) 貨幣 káhèi

to gain currency (fig) 通用する様になる tsūyō suru yō ni narú

current [kəːrˈənt] *n* (of air, water) 流れ nagáre; (ELEC) 電流 deńryū

◆*adj* (present) 現在の geńzai no; (accepted) 通用している tsūyō shité irù

current account (*BRIT*) *n* 当座預金 tōzayokìn

current affairs *npl* 時事 jiji

currently [kəːrˈəntliː] *adv* 現在は geńzai wa

curricula [kərikˈjələ] *npl of* curriculum

curriculum [kərikˈjələm] (*pl* curriculums *or* curricula) *n* (SCOL) 指導要領 shidōyōryō

curriculum vitae [-viːˈtai] *n* 履歴書 riŕekisho

curry [kəːrˈiː] *n* (dish) カレー karē

◆*vt*: *to curry favor with* ...にへつらう ...ni hetsurau

curry powder *n* カレー粉 karéko

curse [kəːrs] *vi* (swear) 悪態をつく akútai wo tsukù

◆*vt* (swear at) ののしる nonóshirù; (bemoan) のろう noróu

◆*n* (spell) 呪い norói; (swearword) 悪態 akútai; (problem, scourge) 災の元 wazáwai no motó

cursor [kəːrˈsəːr] *n* (COMPUT) カーソル kásoru

cursory [kəːrˈsəːriː] *adj* (glance, examination) 何気ない nanígenài

curt [kəːrt] *adj* (reply, tone) 無愛想な buáiso na

curtail [kəːrteilˈ] *vt* (freedom, rights) 制限する seígen suru; (visit etc) 短くする mijíkaku suru; (expenses etc) 減らす herásu

curtain [kəːrˈtən] *n* (at window) カーテン kāten; (THEATER) 幕 makú

curts(e)y [kəːrtˈsiː] *vi* (woman, girl) ひざを曲げて御辞儀をする hizá wo mageté ojígi wo suru

curve [kəːrv] *n* (bend: in line etc) 曲線 kyokúsen; (: in road) カーブ kābu

♦vi 曲る magárū

cushion [kuʃən] n (on sofa, chair) クッション kusshón, 座布団 zabúton; (also: **air cushion**) エアクッション eákusshòn ◇ホバークラフトなどを支える空気の事 hóbàkurafùto nádò wo sasáeru kūki no kotó

♦vt (collision, fall) ...の衝撃を和らげる ...no shōgeki wo yawáragerù (shock, effect) 和らげる yawáragerù

custard [kʌstə:rd] n カスタード kasútàdo

custodian [kʌstou'diːən] n (of building, collection) 管理人 kańrinin

custody [kʌs'tədiː] n (LAW: of child) 親権 shińken
  to take into custody (suspect) 逮捕する taího suru

custom [kʌs'təm] n (tradition) 伝統 deńtō; (convention) 慣習 kańshū; (habit) 習慣 shūkan; (COMM) ひいき hīki

customary [kʌs'təmeriː] adj (behavior, method, time) いつもの itsúmo no, 相変らずの aíkawarazu no

customer [kʌs'təmə:r] n (of shop, business etc) 客 kyakú

customized [kʌs'təmaizd] adj (car etc) 改造した kaízō shitá

custom-made [kʌs'təmmeid'] adj (shirt, car etc) あつらえた atsúraè no, オーダーメードの ōdāmèdo no

customs [kʌs'təmz] npl (at border, airport etc) 税関 zeíkan

customs duty n 関税 kańzei

customs officer n 税関吏 zeíkanri

cut [kʌt] (pt, pp cut) vt (bread, meat, hand etc) 切る kírū; (shorten: grass, hair) 刈る karú; (: text, program) 短くする mijíkakù suru; (reduce: prices, spending, supply) 減らす herásū

♦vi (knife, scissors) 切れる kirérù
♦n (in skin) 切り傷 kiríkìzu; (in salary) 減給 geńkyū; (in spending etc) 削減 sakúgen; (of meat) ブロック burókkū; (of garment) カット káttò

  to cut a tooth 歯が生える há ga haérù

cutback [kʌt'bæk] n 削減 sakúgen

cut down vt (tree) 切り倒す kirítaosù;

(consumption) 減らす herásū

cute [kjuːt] adj (US: pretty) かわいい kawáìi; (sweet) 気障な chínpu na

cuticle [kjuː'tikəl] n (of nail) 甘皮 amákawa

cutlery [kʌt'lə:riː] n ナイフとフォークとスプーン náìfu to fốku to súpùn ◇総称 sōshō

cutlet [kʌt'lit] n (piece of meat) カツレツ katsúretsu; (vegetable cutlet, nut cutlet) コロッケ korókkè

cut off vt (limb) 切断する setsúdan suru; (piece) 切る kírū, 切り分ける kiríwakerù; (person, village) 孤立させる korítsu saséru; (supply) 遮断する shádan suru; (TEL) 切る kírū

cut out vt (shape, article from newspaper) 切り抜く kirínukù; (stop: an activity etc) やめる yaméru; (remove) 切除する setsújo suru

cutout [kʌt'aut] n (switch) 非常遮断装置 hijōshadansōchi, 安全器 ańzeńki; (shape) 切抜き kirínukì

cut-rate [kʌt'reit] (BRIT **cut-price**) adj 安売りの yasúuri no

cutthroat [kʌt'θrout] n (murderer) 人殺し hitógoroshi
♦adj (business, competition) 殺人的な satsújinteki na

cutting [kʌt'iŋ] adj (remark) 辛らつな shiŕatsu na
♦n (from newspaper) 切抜き kirínukì; (from plant) 根木 hógi, さし穂 sashího

cut up vt (paper, meat) 刻む kizámu

CV [siː'viː'] n abbr = **curriculum vitae**

cwt abbr = **hundredweight(s)**

cyanide [sai'ənaid] n 青酸化物 seísanka-bùtsu

cyclamen [sik'ləmən] n シクラメン shikúramèn

cycle [sai'kəl] n (bicycle) 自転車 jitéňsha; (series: of events, seasons etc) 周期 shūki; (: TECH) サイクル sáìkuru; (: of songs etc) 一連 ichíren
♦vi (on bicycle) 自転車で行く jitéňsha de ikú

cycling [saik'liŋ] n サイクリング sáìkuringu

cyclist [saik'list] *n* サイクリスト sáɪkurisuto

cyclone [saik'loun] *n* (storm) サイクロン sáɪkuron

cygnet [sig'nit] *n* 若いハクチョウ wakáɪ hakúchō

cylinder [sil'indər] *n* (shape) 円柱 eñchū; (of gas) ボンベ bónbe; (in engine, machine etc) 気筒 kitō, シリンダー shíríndā

cylinder-head gasket [sil'indər:hed-] *n* (AUT) シリンダーヘッドのパッキング shiríndáheddō no pakkíngu

cymbals [sim'bəlz] *npl* (MUS) シンバル shíñbaru

cynic [sin'ik] *n* 皮肉屋 hiníkuya, シニック shínkku

cynical [sin'ikəl] *adj* (attitude, view) 皮肉な hiníku na, シニカルな shínikaru na

cynicism [sin'əsizəm] *n* シニカルな態度 shíníkaru na táïdo

cypress [sai'pris] *n* (tree) イトスギ itósugi

Cypriot [sip'ri:ət] *adj* キプロスの kípúrosu no
♦*n* キプロス人 kipúrosujin

Cyprus [saip'rəs] *n* キプロス kípúrosu

cyst [sist] *n* (MED) のうしゅ nóshu

cystitis [sistai'tis] *n* (MED) ぼうこう炎 bōkōen

czar [zɑːr] *n* = tsar

Czech [tʃek] *adj* チェコスロバキアの chékosuróbakla no
♦*n* (person) チェコスロバキア人 chékosuróbaklajìn; (language) チェコスロバキア語 chékosuróbakiago

Czechoslovak [tʃekəslou'væk] *adj, n* = Czechoslovakian

Czechoslovakia [tʃekəsləva:k'i:ə] *n* チェコスロバキア chékosuróbakla

Czechoslovakian [tʃekəsləva:k'iən] *adj* チェコスロバキアの chékosuróbakla no
♦*n* (person) チェコスロバキア人 chékosuróbaklajìn

D

D [di:] *n* (MUS: note) ニ音 níon; (: key) ニ

調 níchō

dab [dæb] *vt* (eyes, wound) 軽くふく karúku fukú; (paint, cream) 軽く塗る karúku nurú

dabble [dæb'əl] *vi*: **to dabble in** (politics, antiques etc) 趣味でやる shúmì de yarú

dad [dæd] (*inf*) *n* 父ちゃん tóchan

daddy [dæd'i:] (*inf*) *n* = **dad**

daffodil [dæf'ədil] *n* スイセン suísen

daft [dæft] *adj* (silly) ばかな bákà na

dagger [dæg'əːr] *n* 短刀 tántō

daily [dei'li:] *adj* (dose, wages, routine etc) 毎日の maínichi no
♦*n* (*also*: **daily paper**) 日刊新聞 nikkan-shínbun
♦*adv* (pay, see) 毎日 maínichi

dainty [dein'ti:] *adj* (petite) 繊細な sensai na

dairy [der'i:] *n* (BRIT: shop) 牛乳店 gyūnyūten; (on farm) 牛乳 小屋 gyūnyūgoya ◊酪農場で牛乳を置いたり加工したりする小屋 rakúnōjō dè gyūnyū wò oítarì kakó shitarì suru koyá

dairy farm *n* 酪農場 rakúnōjō

dairy products *npl* 乳製品 nyúseíhin

dairy store (*US*) *n* 牛乳店 gyúnyúten

dais [dei'is] *n* 演壇 éndan

daisy [dei'zi:] *n* デイジー deíjī

daisy wheel *n* (on printer) デイジーホイール detjíhoírù

dale [deil] *n* (valley) 谷 taní

dam [dæm] *n* (on river) ダム dámù
♦*vt* (river, stream) ...にダムを造る ...ni dámù wo tsukúrù

damage [dæm'idʒ] *n* (harm: *also fig*) 害 gaí; (dents etc) 損傷 soñshō
♦*vt* (harm: reputation etc) 傷付ける kizutsukérù; (spoil, break: toy, machine etc) 壊す kowásù

damages [dæm'idʒiz] *npl* (LAW) 損害賠償 sóngaibaíshō

damn [dæm] *vt* (curse at) ...に悪態を浴びせる ...ni akútaì wo ábíserù; (condemn) 非難する hínàn suru
♦*n* (*inf*): **I don't give a damn** おれの知った事じゃない oré no shíttá koto ja naí

◆*adj* (*inf: also*: **damned**) くそったれの kusóttare no, 畜生の chikúshō no
damn (it)! 畜生 chikúshō

damning [dæm'iŋ] *adj* (evidence) 動かぬ ugókanu

damp [dæmp] *adj* (building, wall) 湿っぽい shiméppoi; (cloth) 湿った shimétta
◆*n* (in air, in walls) 湿り気 shimérike
◆*vt* (*also*: **dampen**: cloth, hand) 湿らす shimérasu; (: enthusiasm etc) ...に水を差す ...ni mizú wo sasù

damson [dæm'zən] *n* (fruit) ダムソンス モモ damúsonsumòmo

dance [dæns] *n* (movements, MUS, dancing) 踊り odóri, ダンス dánsu; (social event) 舞踏会 butókai, ダンスパーティ dánsupàti
◆*vi* (person) 踊る odóru

dance hall *n* ダンスホール dánsuhòru

dancer [dæn'sə:r] *n* (for pleasure) 踊る人 odóru hito; (professional) ダンサー dánsā

dancing [dæn'siŋ] *n* (skill, performance) 踊り odóri, ダンス dánsu

dandelion [dæn'dəlaiən] *n* タンポポ tánpopo

dandruff [dæn'drəf] *n* ふけ fuké

Dane [dein] *n* デンマーク人 dénmakujìn

danger [dein'dʒə:r] *n* (hazard, risk) 危険 kikén; (possibility): **there is a danger of** ...の危険がある ...no kikén ga arù
「**danger!**」 (on sign) 危険 kikén
in danger 危険にさらされて kikén ni sárasarete
to be in danger of (risk, be close to) ...される危険がある ...saréru kikén ga arù

dangerous [dein'dʒə:rəs] *adj* 危険な kikén na

dangle [dæŋ'gəl] *vt* (keys, toy) ぶら下げる burásageru; (arms, legs) ぶらぶらさせる buráburasaséru
◆*vi* (earrings, keys) ぶら下がる burásagaru

Danish [dei'niʃ] *adj* デンマークの dénmaku no; (LING) デンマーク語の dénmakugo no
◆*n* (LING) デンマーク語 dénmakugo

dapper [dæp'ə:r] *adj* (man, appearance) きびきびした kíbìkibi shitá

dare [der] *vt*: **to dare someone to do** 出来るものならしてみろと...にけし掛ける dekírù monó nara shité mirò to ...ni keshíkakerù
◆*vi*: **to dare (to) do something** 敢えて ...する åete ...surú
I dare say (I suppose) 多分 tábùn

daredevil [der'devəl] *n* 無謀な人 mubó na hito

daring [der'iŋ] *adj* (escape, person, dress, film, raid, speech) 大胆な daítan na
◆*n* 大胆さ daítansa

dark [dɑrk] *adj* (room, night) 暗い kurái; (hair) 黒っぽい kuróppoì; (complexion) 浅黒い aságuroì; (color: blue, green etc) 濃い kói
◆*n*: **in the dark** やみの中で[に] yamf no nakà de(ni)
to be in the dark (*fig*) ...について何も知らない ...ni tsúite nanf mo shíranai
after dark 暗くなってから kuráku natté karà

darken [dɑr'kən] *vt* (color) 濃くする kókù suru
◆*vi* (sky, room) 暗くなる kuráku narù

dark glasses *npl* サングラス sánguràsu

darkness [dɑrk'nis] *n* (of room, night) 暗やみ kuráyami

darkroom [dɑrk'rum] *n* (PHOT) 暗室 ánshitsu

darling [dɑr'liŋ] *adj* (child, spouse) 愛する af surù
◆*n* (dear) あなた anátà; (favorite) ひいきの人 hfki no hitó

darn [dɑrn] *vt* (sock, jersey) 繕う tsukúroù

dart [dɑrt] *n* (in game) 投げ矢 nagéya, ダート dàto; (in sewing) ダーツ dátsu
◆*vi* 素早く走る subáyakù hashírù
to dart away/along 素早く走っていく subáyakù hashíttè ikú

dartboard [dɑrt'bɔrd] *n* ダーツの的 dátsu no matö

darts [dɑrts] *n* (game) ダーツ dátsu

dash [dæʃ] n (small quantity) 少々 shṓshṓ; (sign) ダッシュ dásshū
♦vt (throw) 投げ付ける nagétsukerù; (hopes) くじく kujíkù
♦vi 素早く行く subáyakù ikú

dash away vi 走って行く hashítte ikú

dashboard [dæʃbɔːrd] n (AUT) ダッシュボード dasshūbōdò

dashing [dæʃiŋ] adj さっそうとした sássō to shita

dash off vi = dash away

data [deita] npl (ADMIN, COMPUT) 情報 jōhō, データ dḗta

database [deitabeis] n データベース dḗtabēsu

data processing n 情報処理 jōhōshorī

date [deit] n (day) 日にち hiníchi; (with boy/girlfriend) デート dḗto; (fruit) ナツメヤシの実 natsúmeyashì no mí
♦vt (event) ...の年代を決める ...no néndai wo kiméru; (letter) ...に日付を書く ...ni hizúke wo kakù; (person) ...とデートをする ...to dḗto wo suru

date of birth 生年月日 seínengappì

to date (until now) 今まで imá madè

dated [deitid] adj (expression, style) 時代遅れの jidáiokùre no

daub [dɔːb] vt (mud, paint) 塗付ける nurítsukerù

daughter [dɔːtəːr] n 娘 musúme

daughter-in-law [dɔːtəːrinlɔː] (pl daughters-in-law) n 嫁 yomé

daunting [dɔːntiŋ] adj (task, prospect) しりごみさせる様な shirígomì saséru yō na, ひるませる様な hirúmaserù yō na

dawdle [dɔːdəl] vi (go slow) ぐずぐずする gúzùguzu suru

dawn [dɔːn] n (of day) 夜明け yoáke; (of period, situation) 始まり hajímari
♦vi (day) 夜が明ける yó ga akérù; (fig):
it dawned on him that ... 彼は...だと気が付いた kárè wa ...dá to ki gá tsuìta

day [dei] n (period) 日 hi, 1日 ichínichi; (daylight) 昼間 hirúma; (heyday) 全盛期 zenséiki

the day before 前の日 maé no hi, 前日 zénjitsu

the day after 翌日 yokújitsu

the day after tomorrow 明後日 asátte

the day before yesterday 一昨日 otótoi

the following day 次の日 tsugí nò hi, 翌日 yokújitsu

by day 昼間に hirúma nì

daybreak [deibreik] n 明け方 akégata, 夜明け yoáke

daydream [deidriːm] vi 空想にふける kusō ni fukérù

daylight [deilait] n (sunlight) 日光 nfkkō; (daytime) 昼間 hirúma, 日中 nftchū

daytime [deitaim] n 昼間 hirúma

day-to-day [deitədei] adj (life, organization) 日常の nichíjō no

daze [deiz] vt (stun) ぼう然とさせる bōzen to sáseru
♦n: in a daze (confused, upset) ぼう然として bōzen to shite

dazzle [dæzəl] vt (bewitch) 感嘆させる kántan sasérù; (blind) ...の目をくらます ...no mé wò kurámasu

DC [diːsiː] n abbr (= direct current) 直流 chokúryū

D-day [diːdei] n 予定日 yotéibi

dead [ded] adj (not alive: person, animal) 死んだ shínda; (flowers) 枯れた karéta; (numb) しびれた shibíreta; (telephone) 通じない tsūjinai; (battery) 上がった agátta
♦adv (completely) 全く máttakù; (directly, exactly) 丁度 chōdo
♦npl: the dead 死者 shíshà

to shoot someone dead 射殺す uchíkorosù

dead tired へとへとに疲れた hétoheto nì tsūkáreta

to stop dead 突然止る totsúzen tomáru

deaden [dedən] vt (blow, pain) 和らげる yawáragerù; (sound) 鈍くする nibúkù suru

dead end n (street) 行き止り ikídomari

dead heat n (SPORT) 同着 dṓchaku

deadline [dedlain] n (PRESS etc) 締切り shimékìri

deadlock [dedlɑːk] n (POL, MIL) 行き詰

り ikizumari

dead loss (inf) n: to be a dead loss (person) 役立たず yakúdatàzu

deadly [ded'li:] adj (lethal: poison) 致命的な chiméiteki na; (devastating: accuracy) 恐ろしい osóroshiì; (: insult) 痛烈な tsúretsu na

deadpan [ded'pæn] adj (look, tone) 無表情の muhyójòō no

Dead Sea n: the Dead Sea 死海 shikái

deaf [def] adj (totally) 耳の聞えない mimí no kikóenai

deafen [def'ən] vt ...の耳を聞えなくする ...no mimí wo kikóenaku sùrū

deafness [def'nis] n 難聴 nánchō

deal [di:l] n (agreement) 取引 toríhikì
♦vt (pt, pp **dealt**) (card) 配る kubárū
a great deal (of) 沢山（の）takúsan (nò)

dealer [di:'lər] n (COMM) 販売業者 hánbaigyōsha, ディーラー dírā

deal in vt fus 取扱う torfatsukau

dealings [di:'lipz] npl (business) 取引 toríhikì; (relations) 関係 kañkei

dealt [delt] pt, pp of **deal**

dean [di:n] n (REL) 主任司祭 shunfnshísài; (SCOL) 学部長 gakúbuchō

dear [di:r] adj (person) 愛しい itóshiì; (expensive) 高価な kóka na
♦n: my dear あなた anátà, お前 omáe
♦excl: dear me! おや おや 驚きを表す odóroki wo aráwasū
Dear Sir/Madam (in letter) 拝啓 hái kei
Dear Mr/Mrs X 親愛なる...さん shín-ai narù ...sàn

dearly [di:r'li:] adv (love) 深く fukákù
to pay dearly for one's carelessness 自らの不注意が高くつく mízukara no fuchúi ga tákàku tsukú

death [deθ] n (BIO) 死 shí, 死亡 shibō; (fig) 死 shí

death certificate n 死亡証明書 shibō-shōmeisho

deathly [deθ'li:] adj (color) 死人の様な shinfn no yō na; (silence) 不気味な bukími na

death penalty n 死刑 shikéi

death rate n 死亡率 shibōrītsu

death toll n 死者の数 shíshà no kázù

debacle [dəbɑk'əl] n 大失敗 daíshíppai

debar [dibɑr'] vt: to debar someone from doing ...が...をするのを禁止する ...ga ...wo sùrū nò wo kínshi suru

debase [dibeis'] vt (value, quality) 下げる sagérù

debatable [dibei'təbəl] adj (decision, assertion) 疑問のある gimón no arù

debate [dibeit'] n (discussion, also POL) 討論 tōrōn
♦vt 討論する tōgì suru

debauchery [debɔːʃʲəriː] n (drunkenness, promiscuity) 放とう hōtō

debilitating [dibil'əteitiŋ] adj (illness etc) 衰弱させる suíjaku sàséru

debit [deb'it] n (COMM) 支払額 shihárai-gàku
♦vt: to debit a sum to someone/to someone's account の...の口座から落す ...no kōza kara òtòsù ¶ see direct

debris [dabri:'] n (rubble) がれき garéki

debt [det] n 借金 shákkin
to be in debt 借金がある shákkin ga arù

debtor [det'ər] n 負債者 fusáishà

debunk [dibʌŋk'] vt (myths, ideas) ...の正体をあばく ...no shōtai wo abákù

début [deibju:'] n (THEATER, SPORT) デビュー débyū

decade [dek'eid] n 10年間 jūnènkan

decadence [dek'ədəns] n (moral, spiritual) 堕落 daráku

decaffeinated [dikæf'əneitid] adj カフェインを取除いた kaféin wo torínozoita

decanter [dikæn'tər] n (for wine, whiskey) デカンター dekántā

decay [dikei'] n (of meat, fish etc) 腐敗 fuhái; (of building) 老朽 rōkyū; (of tooth) カリエス kárìesu
♦vi (rot: body, leaves etc) 腐敗する fuhái suru; (teeth) 虫歯になる mushíba ni narù

deceased [disi:st'] n: the deceased 故人

kójìn

deceit [disi:t'] *n* (duplicity) 偽り itsuwari

deceitful [disi:t'fəl] *adj* 不正な fusei na

deceive [disi:v'] *vt* (fool) だます damásu

December [disem'bə:r] *n* 12月 júがtsu

decency [di:'sənsi:] *n* (propriety) 上品さ jóhìnsa; (kindness) 親切さ shìnsetsusa

decent [di:'sənt] *adj* (proper) 上品な jóhìn na; (kind) 親切な shìnsetsu na

deception [disep'ʃən] *n* ごまかし gomákashi

deceptive [disep'tiv] *adj* (appearance) 見掛けによらない mikáke ni yòrànai

decibel [des'əbəl] *n* デシベル déshìberu

decide [disaid'] *vt* (person: persuade) 納得させる nattóku sàséru; (question, argument: settle) 解決する káìketsu suru
♦*vi* 決める kiméru
to decide to do/that ...する[...だ]と決める ...súrú [...da] to kíméru
to decide on something (choose something) ...を選ぶ ...wo erábu

decided [disai'did] *adj* (resolute) 決意の固い kétsùi no katáì; (clear, definite) はっきりした hakkírì shita

decidedly [disai'didli:] *adv* (distinctly) はっきりと hakkírì to; (emphatically: act, reply) きぜんと kizén to

deciduous [disidʒ'u:əs] *adj* (tree, bush) 落葉の rakúyò no

decimal [des'əmal] *adj* (system, currency) 十進法 jísshínhò
♦*n* (fraction) 小数 shósù

decimal point *n* 小数点 shósùten

decimate [des'əmeit] *vt* (population) 多数の...を死なせる tasú nò ...wo shináseru

decipher [disai'fə:r] *vt* (message, writing) 解読する kaídoku sùrú

decision [disiʒ'ən] *n* (choice) 決定した事 kettéi shita koto; (act of choosing) 決定 kettéi; (decisiveness) 決断力 ketsùdánryòku

decisive [disai'siv] *adj* (action, intervention) 決定的な kettéiteki na; (person) 決断力のある ketsùdánryòku no árù

deck [dek] *n* (NAUT) 甲板 kánpàn, デッキ dekkí; (of bus) 階 kaí; (record deck)

デッキ dékkí; (of cards) 一組 hitôkumi

deckchair [dek'tʃe:r] *n* デッキチェア dekkíchèa

declaration [deklərei'ʃən] *n* (statement) 断言 dángen; (public announcement) 布告 fúkòku

declare [dikle:r'] *vt* (truth, intention, result) 発表する happyó suru; (reveal: income, goods at customs etc) 申告する shínkoku suru

decline [diklain'] *n: decline in/of* (drop, lowering) ...の下落 ...no gèràku; (lessening) ...の減少 ...no génshò
♦*vt* (turn down: invitation) 辞退する jítài suru
♦*vi* (strength, old person) 弱る yowárù; (business) 不振になる fushín ni narù

decode [di:koud'] *vt* (message) 解読する kaídoku suru

decompose [di:kəmpouz'] *vi* (organic matter, corpse) 腐敗する fuhái suru

décor [deikour'] *n* (of house, room) 装飾 shóshoku; (THEATER) 舞台装置 butáisòchi

decorate [dek'əreit] *vt* (adorn): *to decorate (with)* (...で) 飾る (...de) kazáru; (paint and paper) ...の室内を改装する ...no shitsúnài wo kaísò suru

decoration [dekərei'ʃən] *n* (on tree, dress etc) 飾り kazári; (act) 飾る事 kazáru koto; (medal) 勲章 kunshó

decorative [dek'ə:rətiv] *adj* 装飾の shóshoku no

decorator [dek'ə:reitə:r] *n* (BRIT: painter) ペンキ屋 pénkiya

decorum [dikɔ:r'əm] *n* (propriety) 上品さ jóhìnsa

decoy [di:'kɔi] *n* (person, object) おとり otóri

decrease [*n* di:'kri:s *vb* dikri:s'] *n* (reduction, drop): *decrease (in)* 減少 génshò
♦*vt* (reduce, lessen) 減らす herásu
♦*vi* (drop, fall) 減る herú

decree [dikri:'] *n* (ADMIN, LAW) 命令 meírei

decree nisi [-nai'sai] *n* 離婚の仮判決 ríkòn no kàríhànketsu

decrepit [dɪkrepˈɪt] *adj* (run-down: shack) おんぼろの ónboro no; (person) よぼよぼの yòbòyobo no

dedicate [dedˈɪkeɪt] *vt* (time, effort etc): **to dedicate to** ...に捧げる ...ni saságeru

dedication [dedɪkeɪˈʃən] *n* (devotion) 献身 kénshin; (in book, on radio) 献辞 kénji

deduce [dɪdjuːsˈ] *vt* 推測する suísoku suru

deduct [dɪdʌktˈ] *vt* (subtract) 差引く sashíhikú

deduction [dɪdʌkˈʃən] *n* (act of deducing) 推測 suísoku; (act of deducting) 差引 sashíhiki; (amount) 差引く分 sashíhikú bùn

deed [diːd] *n* (feat) 行為 kóì; (LAW: document) 証書 shósho

deem [diːm] *vt* (judge, consider) ...だと判断する ...dá to hándàn suru

deep [diːp] *adj* (hole, water) 深い fukáì; (in measurements) 奥行の okúyuki no; (voice) 太い futóì; (color) 濃い kóì

♦*adv*: **the spectators stood 20 deep** 観衆は20列に並んで立っていた kánshū wa nijúretsu ni naránde tátte ita

a deep breath 深呼吸 shínkokyū

to be 4 meters deep 深さは4メータである fukása wa yón mēta de árù

deepen [diːˈpən] *vt* (hole, canal etc) 深くする fukáku suru

♦*vi* (crisis, mystery) 深まる fukámarù

deep-freeze [diːpˈfriːzˈ] *n* 冷凍庫 réitōko, フリーザー furíza

deep-fry [diːpˈfraiˈ] *vt* 揚げる agéru

deeply [diːˈpliː] *adv* (breathe) 深く fukákù; (interested, moved, grateful) 非常に hijō ni

deep-sea diving [diːpˈsiːˈ-] *n* 深海ダイビング shínkaidàibingu

deep-seated [diːpˈsiːˈtid] *adj* (beliefs, fears, dislike etc) 根の深い né nò fukáì

deer [diːr] *n inv* (ZOOL) シカ shiká

deerskin [diːrˈskin] *n* シカ皮 shikágawa

deface [difeisˈ] *vt* (wall, notice) 汚す yogósu

defamation [defəmeiˈʃən] *n* (LAW) 名誉

毀損 mêiyokisón

default [difɔːltˈ] *n* (COMPUT) デフォルト値 défôrutone

by default (win) 不戦勝で fusénshō de

defeat [difiːtˈ] *n* (of enemy) 敗北 háiboku; (failure) 失敗 shippái

♦*vt* (enemy, opposition) 破る yabúrù

defeatist [difiːˈtist] *adj* 敗北主義の háibokushugí no

♦*n* 敗北主義者 háibokushugísha

defect [*n* diːˈfekt *vb* difektˈ] *n* (flaw, imperfection: in machine etc) 欠陥 kekkán; (: in person, character etc) 欠点 kettén

♦*vi*: **to defect to the enemy** 敵側に亡命する tekígawa ni bômei suru

defective [difektˈiv] *adj* (goods) 欠陥のある kekkán no arù

defence [difensˈ] (*BRIT*) *n* = defense

defend [difendˈ] *vt* (protect, champion) 守る mamórù; (justify) 釈明する shákúmei suru; (LAW) 弁護する bèngo suru; (SPORT: goal) 守る mamórù; (: record, title) 防衛する bóei suru

defendant [difenˈdant] *n* (LAW: in criminal case) 被告人 híkòkunin; (: in civil case) 被告 híkòku

defender [difenˈdər] *n* (*also fig*, SPORT) 防衛者 bóeisha

defense [difensˈ] (*BRIT* **defence**) *n* (protection, assistance) 防衛 bóei; (justification) 釈明 shákúmei

defenseless [difensˈlis] *adj* (helpless) 無防備の mùbóbi no

defensive [difenˈsiv] *adj* (weapons, measures) 防衛の bóei no; (behavior, manner) 釈明的な shákúmeiteki na

♦*n*: **on the defensive** 守勢に立って shusei ni tátte

defer [difərˈ] *vt* (postpone) 延期する énki suru

deference [defˈərəns] *n* (consideration) 丁重さ tèíchōsa

defiance [difaiˈəns] *n* (challenge, rebellion) 反抗 hánkō

in defiance of (despite: the rules, someone's orders etc) ...を無視して ...wo múshi shite

defiant [difaiˈənt] *adj* (challenging,

rebellious: tone, reply, person) 反抗的な hánkóteki na

deficiency [difíʃ'ənsi] n (lack) 欠如 kétsùjo; (defect) 欠点 kettèn

deficient [difíʃ'ənt] adj (inadequate): **deficient in** ...が不足している ...ga fùsòku shité iru; (defective) 欠点の多い kettèn no ōí

deficit [def'isit] n (COMM) 赤字 akáji

defile [difail'] vt (memory, statue etc) 汚す kegásu

define [difain'] vt (limits, boundaries) 明らかにする akírака ni suru; (expression, word) 定義する tēgì suru

definite [def'ənit] adj (fixed) 決まった kimáttà; (clear, obvious) 明白な méīhaku na; (certain) 確実な kakújitsu na
he was definite about it 彼はその事をはっきり言った kárè wa sonó koto wo hakkírì ittá

definitely [def'ənitli] adv (positively, certainly) 確実に kakújitsu ni

definition [defəníʃ'ən] n (of word) 定義 tēgì; (clearness of photograph etc) 鮮明さ sènmeisa

definitive [difin'ətiv] adj (account, version) 決定的な kettéiteki na

deflate [dəfleit'] vt (tire, balloon) ...の空気を抜く ...no kúkī wo nukú

deflect [diflekt'] vt (fend off: attention, criticism) 回避する kaíhi suru; (divert: shot, light) 横へそらす yokó e sōrásù

deform [difɔːrm'] vt (distort) 変形させる hénkei sáséru

deformed [difɔːrmd'] adj 変形した hénkei shita

deformity [difɔːr'miti:] n (of body) 奇形 kikéi

deft [deft] adj (movement, hands) 器用な kíyō na

defunct [difʌŋkt'] adj (industry, organization) 現存しない génzon shínaî

defuse [di:fjuːz'] vt (bomb) ...の信管を外す ...no shínkan wo házùsu; (fig: crisis, tension) 緩和する kánwa suru

defy [difai'] vt (resist) ...に抵抗する ...ni tēkō suru; (challenge) 挑発する chōhatsu suru; (fig: description, explanation) ...の仕様がない ...no shiyō ga naí

degenerate [vb didʒen'əreit adj didʒen'ərit] vi (condition, health) 悪化する akká suru
♦adj (depraved) 堕落した dáràku shita

degrading [digrei'diŋ] adj (conduct, activity) 恥ずべき házùbeki; (task etc) 誇りを傷つけられる様な hokórì wo kizútsukerárèrú yō na

degree [digri:'] n (extent) 度合 doái; (of temperature, angle, latitude) 度 do; (SCOL) 学位 gákùi
a degree in science 科学の学位 sūgaku no gákùi
by degrees (gradually) 徐々に jójò ni
to some degree ある程度 arú teìdo

dehydrated [di:haidreitid] adj (MED) 脱水状態の dassúijótai no; (milk) エバミルク ébámirúku

de-ice [di:ais'] vt (windshield) ...の霜取りをする ...no shimótori wo suru

deign [dein] vi: **to deign to do** ...をしてくれてやる ...wo shité kurete yaru

deity [di:'iti:] n 神様 kámì

dejected [didʒek'tid] adj (depressed) がっかりした gakkárishitá

delay [dilei'] vt (hold up) 遅らせる okúraseru
♦vi (linger) 待つ mátsù; (hesitate) ためらう tamérau
♦n (waiting period) 待つべき期間 mátsùbeki kìkan; (postponement) 延期 énki
to be delayed (person, flight, departure etc) 遅れる okúreru
without delay 直ちに tádàchi ni

delectable [dilek'təbəl] adj (person) 美しい útsùkushiî; (food) おいしい ōíshiî

delegate [n del'əgit vb del'əgeit] n 代表 daíhyo
♦vt (person) 任命する nínmei suru; (task) 任せる mákàseru

delegation [deləgei'ʃən] n (group) 代表団

dāthyōdan; (by manager, leader) 任命 nínmei

delete [dilí:t'] vt (cross out, *also* COMPUT) 消す kèsú, 削除する sákùjo suru

deliberate [adj dilíb'ərit vb dilíb'əreit] *adj* (intentional) 故意の kóī no; (slow) 落着いた óchítsuita
♦vi (consider) 熟考する jukkő suru

deliberately [dilíb'əritli:] *adv* (on purpose) 故意に kóī ni, わざと wázā to

delicacy [del'əkasi:] *n* (of movement) しとやかさ shítòyakasā; (of material) 繊細さ sénsaisa; (of problem etc) 微妙さ bìmyōsa; (choice food) 珍味 chínmi

delicate [del'əkit] *adj* (movement) しとやかな shítòyaka na; (taste, smell, color) 淡い awáĭ; (material) 繊細な sénsai na; (approach, problem) 微妙な bìmyō na; (health) 弱い yowáĭ

delicatessen [deləkətes'ən] *n* 総菜屋 sőzaiya, デリカテッセン dérìkatessèn

delicious [dilíʃ'əs] *adj* (food) おいしい ôĭshiĭ; (smell) おいしそうな óĭshisō na; (feeling) 心地好い kókòchiyoĭ; (person) 魅力的な míryòkuteki na

delight [dilait'] *n* 喜び yòrókobi
♦vt (please) 喜ばす yòrókobasu
to take (a) delight in ... するのが大好きである ...surú nō ga dáĭsuki de aru

delighted [dilai'tid] *adj*: **delighted (at/with)** (...で) 喜んでいる (...de) yòrókonde iru
delighted to do 喜んで...する yòrókònde ...suru

delightful [dilait'fəl] *adj* (evening, house, person etc) 楽しい tánòshiĭ

delinquency [dilíŋ'kwənsi:] *n* 非行 hikő

delinquent [dilíŋ'kwint] *adj* (boy/girl) 非行の hikő no
♦n (youth) 非行少年 (少女) hikőshōnen (shőjo)

delirious [dilir'i:əs] *adj*: **to be delirious** (with fever) うわ言を言う úwagotō wo iu; (with excitement) 夢中になっている mùchū ni nattè irú

deliver [dilív'ə:r] *vt* (distribute) 配達する hāftatsu suru; (hand over) 引き渡す hīkí-

watasù; (message) 届ける tòdókerù; (MED) 出産を助ける ...no shùssàn wo tàsúkerù

to deliver a speech 演説をする énzetsu wo sùrú

delivery [dilív'ə:ri:] *n* (distribution) 配達 hāftatsu; (of speaker) 演説振り énzetsuburi; (MED) 出産 shùssàn
to take delivery of ... を受取る ...wo ùkétorù

delta [del'tə] *n* (of river) デルタ地帯 dé-rùtachítai

delude [dilu:d'] *vt* (deceive) だます damásù

deluge [del'juːdʒ] *n* (also: **deluge of rain**) 大雨 ōamè; (fig: of petitions, requests) 殺到 sàttő

delusion [dilu:'ʒən] *n* (false belief) 錯覚 sàkkáku

de luxe [dəlʌks'] *adj* (car, holiday) 豪華な gőka na

delve [delv] *vi*: **to delve into** (subject) ...を探求する ...wo tánkyù suru; (cupboard, handbag) ...の中を捜す ...no nākà wo sagásu

demand [dimænd'] *vt* 要求する yőkyù suru
♦n 要求 yőkyù; (ECON) 需要 juyő
to be in demand ...の需要がある ...no jùyő ga arú
on demand (available, payable) 請求次第 séikyùshidai

demanding [dimænd'iŋ] *adj* (boss, child) 気難しい kìmúzukashiĭ; (work) きつい kìtsúĭ

demarcation [di:mɑːrkei'ʒən] *n* (of areas) 境 sàkáĭ; (of tasks) 区分 kùbún

demean [dimi:n'] *vt*: **to demean oneself** 軽べつを招く事をする kèĭbetsu wo mànékù kotő wo suru

demeanor [dimi:'nəːr] (*BRIT* **demeanour**) *n* 振舞 fùrúmai

demented [dimen'tid] *adj* 気の狂った kĭ nő kurúttà

demise [dimaiz'] *n* (end) 消滅 shőmetsu; (death) 死亡 shĭbő

demister [dimis'tə:r] (*BRIT*) *n* (AUT) 需取り装置 shĭmótorisōchi

demo [dem'ou] (*BRIT*: *inf*) *n abbr* = **demonstration**

democracy [dimɔk'rəsi:] *n* (POL: system) 民主主義 mínshushugí; (country) 民主主義国 mínshushugíkoku

democrat [dem'əkræt] *n* (*gen*) 民主主義者 mínshushugishá; (*US*) 民主党員 mínshutōin

democratic [deməkræt'ik] *adj* (*gen*) 民主的な mínshuteki na; (*US*) 民主党の mínshutō no

demolish [dimɑl'iʃ] *vt* (building) 取壊す toríkowasú; (*fig*: argument) 論破する rónpa suru

demolition [deməliʃ'ən] *n* (of building) 取壊し toríkowashi; (of argument) 論破 rónpa

demon [di:'mən] *n* (evil spirit) 悪魔 ákùma

demonstrate [dem'ənstreit] *vt* (prove: theory) 立証する rísshō suru; (show: skill, appliance) 見せる misérù
♦*vi* (POL) デモをする hímà wo suru

demonstration [demənstrei'ʃən] *n* (POL) デモ démò; (proof) 立証 risshō; (exhibition) 実演 jitsúen

demonstrator [dem'ənstreitər] *n* (POL) デモの参加者 démò no sánkasha; (COMM) 実演をする店員 jitsúen wo surú tén-in

demoralize [dimɔr'əlaiz] *vt* (dishearten) がっかりさせる gakkárì saserú

demote [dimout'] *vt* (*also* MIL) 降格する kōkaku surú

demure [dimjur'] *adj* (smile, dress, little girl) しとやかな shitóyàka ná

den [den] *n* (of animal) 巣穴 súàna; (of thieves) 隠れ家 kákuregá, アジト ájìto; (room) 書斎 shōsái

denatured alcohol [di:nei'tʃərd] (*US*) *n* 変性アルコール hénseiarúkōru

denial [dinai'əl] *n* (refutation) 否定 hítéi; (refusal) 拒否 kyóhi

denim [den'əm] *n* (fabric) デニム dénìmu

denims [den'əmz] *npl* ジーパン jípan, ジーンズ jínzu

Denmark [den'mɑrk] *n* デンマーク dénmāku

denomination [dinɑːmənei'ʃən] *n* (of money) 額面 gakúmen; (REL) 宗派 shū́ha

denominator [dinɑːm'əneitər] *n* (MATH) 分母 búnbo

denote [dinout'] *vt* (indicate, represent) 示す shimésù

denounce [dinauns'] *vt* (person, action) 非難する hínàn suru

dense [dens] *adj* (crowd) 密集した mísshū shita; (smoke, fog etc) 濃い kói; (foliage) 密生した mísséi shita; (*inf*: person) 鈍い níbuì

densely [dens'li:] *adv*: **densely populated** 人口密度の高い jínkōmitsúdo no takái

density [den'siti:] *n* (of population: *also* PHYSICS) 密度 mítsùdo

single / double-density disk (COMPUT) 単(倍)密度ディスク tán(bái)mítsùdo disuku ◇日本語では廃語 nihón go de wa hagó

dent [dent] *n* (in metal or wood) へこみ hékòmi
♦*vt also*: **make a dent in** へこませる hékòmaseru

dental [den'təl] *adj* (treatment, hygiene etc) 歯科の shíkà no

dental surgeon *n* 歯医者 hāísha

dentist [den'tist] *n* 歯医者 hāísha

dentistry [den'tistri:] *n* 歯科医学 shíkáigàku

dentures [den'tʃərz] *npl* 入れ歯 iréba

denunciation [dinʌnsiːei'ʃən] *n* (condemnation) 非難 hínàn

deny [dinai'] *vt* (charge, allegation, involvement) 否定する hítéi suru; (refuse: permission, chance) 拒否する kyóhi suru

deodorant [di:ou'dərənt] *n* 防臭剤 bōshūzài

depart [dipɑrt'] *vi* (visitor) 帰る kaérù; (plane) 出発する shuppátsu suru; (bus, train) 発車する hasshá suru
to depart from (*fig*: stray from) ...を離れる ...wo hanárerù

department [dipɑrt'mənt] *n* (COMM) 部 bú; (SCOL) 講座 kōza; (POL) 省 shō

department store n (COMM) デパート dèpáto

departure [dipɑːˈrtʃəːr] n (of visitor) 帰る事 káeru koto; (of plane) 出発 shuppátsu; (of bus, train) 発車 hasshá; (of employee, colleague) 退職 táishoku

a new departure (in or from policy etc) 新方針 shfnhōshìn

departure lounge n (at airport) 出発ロビー shuppátsurobì

depend [dipénd] vi: *to depend on* (be supported by) ...に頼っている ...ni táyotè irú; (rely on, trust) 信用する shfnyō suru

it depends 時と場合によりけりだ tòkí tò baái ni yòrfkeri dà

depending on the result ... 結果次第で...kèkka shídài dé

dependable [dipénəbəl] adj (person) 頼りになる táyòri ni nárù; (watch, car etc) 信頼性の高い shfnraisei no tàkáì

dependant [dipéndənt] n 扶養家族 fuyókazòku

dependence [dipéndəns] n (on drugs, systems, partner) 依存 izón

dependent [dipéndənt] adj: *to be dependent on* (person, decision) ...に頼っている ...ni táyotè iru

♦n = dependant

depict [dipíkt] vt (in picture) 描く egákù; (describe) 描写する byósha suru

depleted [diplíːtid] adj (stocks, reserves) 減少した génshō shita

deplorable [diplɔːˈrəbəl] adj (conditions) 悲惨な hisán na; (lack of concern) 嘆かわしい nàgékawashìì

deplore [diplɔːˈr] vt (condemn) 非難する hfnán suru

deploy [diplɔiˈ] vt (troops, resources) 配置する háichi suru

depopulation [dipɑːpjəleiˈʃən] n 人口減少 jfnkōgénshò

deport [dipɔːrtˈ] vt (criminal, illegal immigrant) 強制送還する kyóseisōkàn suru

deportment [dipɔːrtˈmənt] n (behavior, way of walking etc) 身のこなし mínò kònáshì

depose [dipouzˈ] vt (ruler) 退位させる táìsáseru

deposit [dipɑːzˈit] n (money: in account) 預金 yòkín; (: down payment) 手付金 tètsúkekin; (on bottle etc) 保証金 hòshókin; (CHEM) 沈殿物 chfndénbùtsu; (of ore) 鉱床 kóshò; (of oil) 石油埋蔵量 sèkíyumáizōryò

♦vt (money) 預金する yòkín suru; (case, bag) 預ける azúkerù

deposit account n 普通預金口座 fútsúyokinkòza

depot [díːˈpou] n (storehouse) 倉庫 sókò; (for vehicles) 車庫 shákò; (US: station) 駅 ékì

depraved [dipreivdˈ] adj (conduct, person) 邪悪な jàáku na

depreciate [dipríːˈʃieit] vi (currency, property, value etc) 値下がりする nésagari suru

depreciation [dipriːʃieiˈʃən] n 値下がり nèságari

depress [dipresˈ] vt (PSYCH) 憂うつにさせる yúutsu ni sáseru; (price, wages) 下落させる gèráku saseru; (press down: switch, button etc) 押える osáerù; (: accelerator) 踏む fùmú

depressed [diprestˈ] adj (person) 憂うつな yúutsu na; (price, industry) 下落した gèráku shita

depressing [dipresˈiŋ] adj (outlook, time) 憂うつな yúutsu na

depression [dipreʃˈən] n (PSYCH) 憂うつ病 yúutsubyò; (ECON) 不況 fúkyò; (of weather) 低気圧 tèfkiàtsù; (hollow) くぼみ kúbòmi

deprivation [depraveiˈʃən] n (poverty) 貧乏 bínbò

deprive [dipraivˈ] vt: *to deprive someone of* (liberty, life) ...から奪う ...kárà ubáù

deprived [dipraivdˈ] adj (person) 貧しい màzúshìì

depth [depθ] n (of hole, water) 深さ fùkásà; (of cupboard etc) 奥行 ókúyuki; (of emotion, feeling) 強さ tsúyòsa; (of knowledge) 豊富さ hófusa

in the depths of despair 絶望のどん底に zètsúbō no dònzòko ni

out of one's depth (in water) 背が立た

ない sé gà tatánái; (fig) 力が及ばない chìkára gà òyóbanai

deputation [depʲəˈteɪʲən] n (delegation) 代表団 dáíhyōdàn

deputize [ˈdepʲəˌtaɪz] vi: **to deputize for someone** (stand in) ...の代りにする ...no kàwári ni ...sūrū

deputy [ˈdepʲəˌti] adj: **deputy head** (BRIT: SCOL: primary/secondary) 副校長 fúkūkòchō

◆n (assistant) 代理 dáìri; (POL) (下院) 議員 (kàin)gíin; (: also: **deputy sheriff**) 保安官代理 hóánkàndáìri

derail [diˈreɪl] vt: **to be derailed** 脱線する dàssén suru

derailment [diˈreɪlmənt] n 脱線 dàssén

deranged [diˈreɪndʒd] adj (person) 精神病の sèíshìnbyō no

derby [ˈdɑːrbi:] (US) n (bowler hat) 山高帽 yámátàkabō

derelict [ˈderˈəlɪkt] adj (building) 廃虚になった hàíkyo ni nátta

deride [diˈraɪd] vt (mock, ridicule) ばかにする bàká ni suru

derisory [diˈraɪsəri] adj (sum) 笑うべき wáráubèkì; (laughter, person) ばかにするような bàká ni suru

derivative [diˈrɪvˈətɪv] n (CHEM) 派生物 hàséíbutsù; (LING) 派生語 hàséígo

derive [diˈraɪv] vt (pleasure, benefit) 受ける ukérù

◆vi: **to derive from** (originate in) ...に由来する ...ni yūrài suru

dermatitis [ˌdɜːrmətaɪˈtis] n 皮膚炎 hìfúèn

derogatory [diˈrɑːgˈəˌtɔːri] adj (remark) 中傷的な chūshōteki na

derv [dɜːrv] (BRIT) n 軽油 kéìyu

descend [disˈendʲ] vt (stairs, hill) 降りる òrìrù

◆vi (go down) 降りる òrìrù

to descend from ...から降りる ...kára orírù

to descend to (lying, begging etc) ...するまでに成り下がる ...surú madè ni nárìsagarù

descendant [disˈendˈəntʲ] n 子孫 shìsón

descent [disˈentʲ] n (of stairs, hill, by per-

son etc) 降りる事 òrìrù koto; (AVIAT) 降下 kōkà; (origin) 家系 kàkéi

describe [diskraɪb] vt (event, place, person, shape) 描写する byóshā suru

description [diskríp'ʃən] n (account) 描写 byósha; (sort) 種類 shúrùi

descriptive [diskríp'tiv] adj (writing, painting) 写実的な shájítsuteki na

desecrate [ˈdesˈəkreɪt] vt (altar, cemetery) 汚す kegásu

desert [n dezˈərt vb dizərt'] n (GEO) 砂漠 sàbáku; (fig: wilderness) 殺風景な所 sàppúkèi na tòkòro

◆vt (place, post) 放置して逃亡する hóchi shite tóbō sùrù; (partner, family) 見捨てる mìsúteru

◆vi (MIL) 脱走する dàssó suru

deserter [dizərˈtər] n (MIL) 脱走兵 dassóhei

desertion [dizər'ʃən] n (MIL) 脱走 dassó; (LAW) 遺棄 íkì

desert island n 熱帯の無人島 nèttái no mùjíntō

deserts [dizərts'] npl: **to get one's just deserts** 天罰を受ける tènbatsu wo ukérù

deserve [dizərv'] vt (merit, warrant) ...に値する ...ni àtái suru

deserving [dizər'viŋ] adj (person) 援助に値する énjò ni àtái suru; (action, cause) 立派な rìppá na

design [dizaín'] n (art, process) 意匠 íshō; (sketch) スケッチ sùkétchì; (layout, shape) デザイン dèzáin; (pattern) 模様 mòyò; (intention) 意図 ítò

◆vt (house, kitchen, product etc) 設計する sèkkéi suru; (test etc) ...の案を作る ...no àn wo tsùkúrù

designate [vb dezˈigneit adj dezˈignit] vt (nominate) 任命する nínmei suru

◆adj (chairman etc) 任命された nínmei sáréta

designer [dizaí'nər] n (ART) デザイナー dèzáinā; (TECH) 設計者 sèkkéisha; (also: **fashion designer**) ファッションデザイナー fásshöndèzáìnā

desirable [dizaí'ərəbəl] adj (proper) 望ましい nòzómashìi; (attractive) 魅力的な

mǐryókuteki na

desire [dizai'əɾ] n (urge) 望み nózomi; (also: **sexual desire**) 性欲 séiyoku
♦vt (want) 欲しがる hòshígarū; (lust after) …とセックスをしたがる …to sékkùsu wo shitágarū

desk [desk] n (in office, for pupil) 机 tsukúe, デスク désùku; (in hotel) フロント fúrônto; (at airport) カウンター káùnta; (BRIT: in shop, restaurant) 勘定カウンター kánjōkàunta

desolate [des'əlit] adj (place) 物寂しい mònòsabishíi; (person) 惨めな mijíme na

desolation [desəlei'ʃən] n (of place) 物寂しさ mònòsabishísà; (of person) 惨めさ mijímesà

despair [dispeːr'] n (hopelessness) 絶望 zètsúbō
♦vi: **to despair of** (give up on) …をあきらめる …wo ākíramerū

despatch [dispætʃ'] n, vt = **dispatch**

desperate [des'pəːrit] adj (scream, shout) 恐怖の kyófū no; (situation, shortage) 絶望的な zètsúbōteki na; (fugitive) 必死の hísshí no
to be desperate for something/to do 必死の思いで…を欲しがって [したがって] いる hísshí no òmói dé …wó hòshígatté [shitágatté] irú

desperately [des'pəːritli:] adv (in despair, frantically: struggle, shout etc) 必死になって hísshí ni nátte; (very) とても tòtémo

desperation [despəːrei'ʃən] n (recklessness) 必死の思い hísshí no òmói
in (sheer) desperation 必死の思いで hísshí no òmói dé, 死に物狂いで shinímonogurùi de

despicable [des'pikəbəl] adj (action, person) 卑劣な hírétsu na

despise [dispaiz'] vt 軽べつする kéïbetsu suru

despite [dispait'] prep (in spite of) …にもかかわらず …nf mò kakáwarāzu

despondent [dispan'dənt] adj (downcast) 意気消沈している íkìshōchin shíté iru

despot [des'pət] n 暴君 bókùn

dessert [dizəɾt'] n (CULIN) デザート dézàtō

dessertspoon [dizəɾt'spuːn] n (object) 小さじ kòsàji; (quantity) 小さじ一杯 kòsàji íppai

destination [destənei'ʃən] n (of traveler) 目的地 mòkútekīchi; (of mail) 宛先 átésaki

destined [des'tind] adj: **to be destined to do/for** …する[される]事になっている …sùrú (sareru)kotó nì nátté irū

destiny [des'təni] n (fate) 運命 únmei

destitute [des'titut] adj (person) 一文無しの íchímòn nàshi nó

destroy [distrɔi'] vt (demolish, wreck, also fig) 破壊する hàkái suru; (animal) 安楽死させる ánrakūshi sáserū

destroyer [distrɔi'əɾ] n (NAUT) 駆逐艦 kúchíkukan

destruction [distrʌk'ʃən] n (act, state) 破壊 hàkái

destructive [distrʌk'tiv] adj (capacity, force) 破壊的な hàkáiteki na; (child) 暴れん坊の abáreřbō no; (not constructive: criticism etc) 建設的でない kénsetsuteki de náî

detach [ditætʃ'] vt (remove, unclip, unstick) 外す hàzúsu

detachable [ditætʃ'əbəl] adj (removable) 外せる hàzúseru

detached [ditætʃt'] adj (attitude, person) 無とん着な mútònchaku ná
a detached house 一軒家 íkkén-ya

detachment [ditætʃ'mənt] n (aloofness) 無関心 mùkánshin; (MIL: detail) 分遣隊 bùnkéntaî

detail [diteil'] n (fact, feature) 詳細 shósai; (no pl: in picture, one's work etc) 細かい事 kómàkái kotó; (trifle) ささいな事 sásàì na kotó
♦vt (list) 詳しく話す kùwáshìku hanásù
in detail 細かく kómàkakū

detailed [diteild'] adj (account, description) 細かい kómàkakū

detain [ditein'] vt (keep, delay) 引留める hìkítomerū; (in captivity) 監禁する kánkin súrū; (in hospital) 入院させる nyúîn saserū

detect [ditekt'] *vt* (sense) ...に感づく ...ni kánzukù; (MED) 発見する hakkén suru; (MIL, POLICE, RADAR, TECH) 関知する kánchi suru

detection [ditek'ʃən] *n* (discovery) 発見 hakkén

detective [ditek'tiv] *n* (POLICE) 刑事 kéiji

private detective 私立探偵 shíritsutàntei

detective story *n* 探偵小説 tánteishōsetsu

detector [ditek'tə:r] *n* (TECH) 探知機 tánchiki

détente [deita:nt'] *n* (POL) 緊張緩和 kínchōkànwa, デタント détantò

detention [diten'tʃən] *n* (arrest) 監禁 kánkin; (SCOL) 居残り inókori

deter [ditə:r'] *vt* (discourage, dissuade) 阻止させる sóshì suru

detergent [ditə:r'dʒənt] *n* 洗剤 sénzai

deteriorate [diti:ri:əreit] *vi* (health, sight, weather) 悪くなる warúku narù; (situation) 悪化する ákka suru

deterioration [diti:ri:əreiʃən] *n* 悪化 ákka

determination [ditə:rmənei'ʃən] *n* (resolve) 決意 kétsùi; (establishment) 決定 kettéi

determine [ditə:r'min] *vt* (facts) 確認する kakúnin suru; (limits etc) 決める kiméru

determined [ditə:r'mind] *adj* (person) 意志の強い íshì no tsuyóì

determined to do どうしても...すると決心している ...súrù tò kesshín shité iru

deterrent [ditə:r'ənt] *n* (MIL, LAW) 抑止力 yókùshi suru mónò

detest [ditest'] *vt* 嫌う kiráu

detonate [det'əneit] *vi* 爆発する bakúhatsu suru

◆*vt* 爆発させる bakúhatsu sáseru

detour [di:'tu:r] *n* (from route) 回り道 mawárimichì; (US: AUT: diversion) う回路 úkairo

detract [ditrækt'] *vi: to detract from* (effect, achievement) ...を損なう ...wo sō-

kónaù

detriment [det'rəmənt] *n: to the detriment of* ...に損害を与えて ...ni sóngai wo atáete

detrimental [detrəmen'tal] *adj: detrimental to* 損害になる sóngai ni narú

devaluation [di:væljuei'ʃən] *n* (ECON) 平価切下げ héikakirīsage

devalue [di:væl'ju:] *vt* (work, person) 見くびる mikúbirù; (currency) ...の平価を切り下げる ...no héìka wo kirísageru

devastate [dev'əsteit] *vt* (destroy) さんざん荒らす sánzan árasù; (fig: shock): *to be devastated by* ...に大きなショックを受ける ...ni ōkina shokkù wo ukérù

devastating [dev'əsteitiŋ] *adj* (weapon, storm etc) 破壊力の大きい hakáiryoku no ōkii; (announcement, news, effect) 衝撃的な shōgekiteki na, ショッキングな shokkíngu na

develop [divel'əp] *vt* (business, land, idea, resource) 開発する kaíhatsu suru; (PHOT) 現像する génzō suru; (disease) ...にかかる ...ni kakárù; (fault, engine trouble) ...が発生する ...ga hasséi suru

◆*vi* (advance) 発展する hattén suru; (evolve: situation, design) 発生する hasséi suru; (appear: facts, symptoms) 現れる árawarerù

developer [divel'əpə:r] *n* (*also*: **property developer**) 開発業者 kaíhatsugyōsha

developing country [divel'əpiŋ-] *n* 発展途上国 hatténtojōkoku

development [divel'əpmənt] *n* (advance) 発展 hattén; (of affair, case) 新事実 shínjijitsù; (of land) 開発 kaíhatsu

deviate [di:'vieit] *vi: to deviate (from)* (...から) それる (...kára) sorérù

deviation [di:vi:ei'ʃən] *n* 脱線 dássen

device [divais'] *n* (apparatus) 仕掛け shíkake

devil [dev'əl] *n* (REL, fig) 悪魔 ákuma

devilish [dev'əliʃ] *adj* (idea, action) 悪魔的な ákumateki na

devious [di:'vi:əs] *adj* (person) 腹黒い haráguroì

devise [divaiz'] *vt* (plan, scheme, machine) 発案する hatsúan suru

devoid [dɪvɔ'ɪd] *adj*: **devoid of** (lacking) ...が全くない ...ga màttáku naì

devolution [devəlu:'ʃən] *n* (POL) 権限委譲 kéngénìjō

devote [dɪvout'] *vt*: **to devote something to** (dedicate) ...に...をつぎ込む ...ní ...wo tsùgíkomù

devoted [dɪvout'ɪd] *adj* (loyal: service, friendship) 忠実な chújitsu na; (: admirer, partner) 熱心な nésshìn na
to be devoted to someone ...を熱愛している ...wo nètsúai shìté irú
the book is devoted to politics その本は政治の専門書である sónō hòn wa séìji no sénmonsho dè árù

devotee [devouti:'] *n* (fan) ファン fàn, (REL) 信徒 shíntò

devotion [dɪvou'ʃən] *n* (affection) 愛情 aíjō; (dedication: to duty etc) 忠義 chúsei; (REL) 信心 shínjìn

devour [dɪvau'əːr] *vt* (meal, animal) むさぼり食う mùsáborikùū

devout [dɪvaut'] *adj* (REL) 信心深い shínjìnbùkaì

dew [du:] *n* (on grass) 露 tsúyù

dexterity [dekstəːr'ɪti:] *n* (manual, mental) 器用さ kíyōsà

diabetes [daiəbi:'tis] *n* 糖尿病 tónyōbyò

diabetic [daiəbet'ik] *adj n* 糖尿病の tónyōbyò no
♦*n* 糖尿病患者 tónyōbyōkànja

diabolical [daiəbɑl'ikəl] *adj* (behavior) 悪魔的な ákùmateki na; (weather) ひどい hídoì

diagnose [daiəgnous'] *vt* (illness, problem) 診断する shíndàn sùrù

diagnoses [daiəgnou'si:z] *npl of* **diagnosis**

diagnosis [daiəgnou'sis] (*pl* **diagnoses**) *n* 診断 shíndàn

diagonal [daiæg'ənəl] *adj* (line) 斜めの nánáme nó
♦*n* 対角線 taíkakùsèn

diagram [dai'əgræm] *n* 図 zu

dial [dail] *n* (of phone, radio etc) ダイヤル dáiyaru; (on instrument, clock etc) 文字盤 mòjíban
♦*vt* (number) ダイヤルする dáíyaru sùrù

dial code (*BRIT* **dialling code**) *n* 市外番号 shígàibàngō

dialect [dai'əlekt] *n* 方言 hògén

dialogue [dai'əlɔ:g] (*US also*: **dialog**) *n* (communication) 対話 taíwa; (conversation) 会話 kaíwa

dial tone (*BRIT* **dialling tone**) *n* 発信音 hàsshín-òn, ダイヤルトーン dáíyarutòn

diameter [daiæm'itəːr] *n* 直径 chòkkéi

diamond [dai'mənd] *n* (gem) ダイヤモンド dáíyamòndo, ダイヤ dáíya; (shape) ひし形 híshígata

diamonds [dai'məndz] *npl* (CARDS) ダイヤ dáíya

diaper [dai'pəːr] (*US*) *n* おむつ òmútsu

diaphragm [dai'əfræm] *n* (ANAT) 横隔膜 òkakumàkú; (contraceptive) ペッサリー péssarì

diarrhea [daiəri:'ə] (*BRIT* **diarrhoea**) *n* げり gèrí

diary [dai'əːri:] *n* (engagements book) 手帳 tèchō; (daily account) 日記 nìkkí

dice [dais] *n inv* (in game) さいころ saíkorò
♦*vt* (CULIN) 角切りにする kàkúgiri ni sùrù

dichotomy [daikɑt'əmi:] *n* 二分化 nìbúnka

Dictaphone [dik'təfoun]® *n* ディクタフォーン díkùtafòn 〇一種の録音機の商品名 ísshù no ròkúonkì no shōhinmeí

dictate [dik'teit] *vt* (letter) 書取らせる kàkítorasèrù; (conditions) 指図する sáshìzu sùrù

dictation [diktei'ʃən] *n* (of letter: *also* SCOL) 書取り kàkítori; (of orders) 指図 sáshìzu

dictator [dik'teitəːr] *n* (POL, MIL, *fig*) 独裁者 dòkúsaìsha

dictatorship [dikteit'əːrʃip] *n* 独裁政権 dòkúsaìséìken

diction [dik'ʃən] *n* (in speech, song) 発音 hàtsúon

dictionary [dik'ʃəneːri:] *n* (monolingual, bilingual etc) 辞書 jíshò, 字引 jìbíkì

did [did] *pt of* **do**

didactic [daidæk'tik] *adj* (teaching, film) 教育的な kyōikuteki na

didn't [dɪd'ənt] = **did not**

die [dai] vi (person, animal) 死ぬ shīnu; (plant) 枯れる karéru; (fig: cease) やむ yámū; (: fade) 次第に消える shídái ni kiéru

to be dying for something/to do something 死ぬ程...が欲しい (...をしたい) shīnu hodo ...ga hōshíī (...wo shitáī)

die away vi (sound, light) 次第に消える shídái ni kiéru

die down vi (wind) 弱まる yowámarū; (fire) 小さくなる chīisakū nárū; (excitement, noise) 静まる shízumarū

diehard [dai'hɑːrd] n 頑固な保守派 gánkona na hōshúha

die out vi (activity) 消えて無くなる kiéte nakū narū; (animal, bird) 絶滅する zétsúmetsu sūrū

diesel [diːˈzəl] n (vehicle) ディーゼル車 díːzeruzha; (also: **diesel oil**) 軽油 keíyu

diesel engine n ディーゼルエンジン díːzeruénjin

diet [dai'ət] n (food intake) 食べ物 tabémōnō; (restricted food: MED, when slimming) 減食 génshoku, (ダイエット daíetto)

◆vi (also: **be on a diet**) 減食する génshoku sūrū, ダイエットする daíetto sūrū

differ [dif'əːr] vi (be different): **to differ (from)** (...と) 違う (...to) chīgáu; (disagree): **to differ (about)** (...について) 意見が違う (...ni tsúite) íkēn ga chīgáu

difference [dif'əːrəns] n (dissimilarity) 違い chīgái; (disagreement) 意見の相違 íkēn no sōi

different [dif'əːrənt] adj 別の bétsu no

differentiate [difəren'tʃiːeit] vi: **to differentiate (between)** (...を) 区別する (...wo) kúbētsu sūrū

differently [dif'əːrəntli] adv 違う風に chīgáu fū ni

difficult [dif'əkʌlt] adj (task, problem) 難しい mūzūkashíī; (person) 気難しい kīmūzukashíī

difficulty [dif'əkʌlti] n 困難 kónnān; (problem) 問題 móndai

diffident [dif'ídənt] adj (hesitant, self-effacing) 気の小さい kī nō chíísai

diffuse [adj difjuːs' vb difjuːz'] adj (idea,

sense) 不鮮明な fūsénmei na

◆vt (information) 広める hīrómerū

diffuse light 反射光 hánshakō

dig [dig] (pt, pp **dug**) vt (hole, garden) 掘る hórū

◆n (prod) 小突く事 kozúkū kotó; (archeological) 発掘現場 hakkútsugénba; (remark) 当てこすり átékosuri

digest [did'ʒest] vt (food: also fig: facts) 消化する shōka suru

◆n (book) 要約 yōyaku, ダイジェスト版 dáíjesutoban

digestion [didʒes'tʃən] n (process) 消化 shōka; (system) 消化器系 shōkakikei

digestive [didʒes'tiv] adj (juices, system) 消化の shōka no

dig into vt (savings) 掘り出す hōrídasū

to dig one's nails into 引っかく hīkkákū

digit [didʒ'it] n (number) 数字 sūji; (finger) 指 yúbi

digital [didʒ'itəl] adj (clock, watch) デジタルの dejítaru nó

digital computer n デジタルコンピュータ dejítarukónpyútà

dignified [dig'nəfaid] adj (person, manner) 品のある hīn no arū

dignity [dig'niti] n (poise, self-esteem) 気品 kīhín

digress [digres'] vi: **to digress (from)** (topic, subject) (...から) それる (...kára) sórérù

digs [digz] (BRIT: inf) npl 下宿 geshúku

dig up vt (plant) 掘り起す hōríokosū; (information) 探り出す sagúridasū

dike [daik] n = **dyke**

dilapidated [diləp'ədeitid] adj (building) 老朽した rōkyū shitá

dilate [daileit'] vi (eyes) 見張る mīháru

dilemma [dilem'ə] n (political, moral) 板挟み itábasamí, ジレンマ jírénma

diligent [dil'idʒənt] adj (worker, research) 勤勉な kínben na

dilute [diluːt'] vt (liquid) 薄める usúmeru, 希釈する kisháku sūrū

dim [dim] adj (light, room) 薄暗い ūsúguraì; (outline, figure) ぼやけた boyáketa; (inf: person) 頭の悪い átàma

dime [daɪm] *n* (*US*) ю 10セント玉 jússéntodámà

dimension [dimen'ʃən] *n* (aspect) 面 mèn; (measurement) 寸法 súnpō; (*also pl*: scale, size) 大きさ ōkisa

diminish [dimin'iʃ] *vi* (size, effect) 小さくなる chíisakú nárū

diminutive [dimin'jətiv] *adj* (tiny) 小型 の kōgáta no
♦*n* (LING) 指小辞 shìshóshì

dimmers [dim'ərz] (*US*) *npl* (AUT: dipped headlights) 下向きのヘッドライト shítāmuki no hèddóraltō; (: parking lights) 車幅灯 shafūkutō

dimple [dim'pəl] *n* (on cheek, chin) えくぼ ékùbo

din [dɪn] *n* (row, racket) 騒音 sóon

dine [daɪn] *vi* 食事する shokúji suru

diner [daɪn'ər] *n* (person) レストランの客 résutoran no kyakú; (*US*: restaurant) 簡易食堂 kañ-ishokúdō

dinghy [diŋ'iː] *n* ボート bōto
rubber dinghy ゴムボート gomúbōto

dingy [din'dʒiː] *adj* (streets, room) 薄暗い usúgurai; (clothes, curtains etc) 薄汚い usúgitanaī

dining car [daɪn'iŋ-] *n* (RAIL) 食堂車 shokúdōsha

dining room [daɪn'iŋ-] *n* (in house, hotel) 食堂 shokúdō

dinner [din'ər] *n* (evening meal) 夕食 yūshoku; (lunch) 昼食 chūshoku; (banquet) 宴会 efkai

dinner jacket *n* タキシード takíshìdo

dinner party *n* 宴会 efkai

dinner time *n* (midday) 昼食時間 chūshokukudōki; (evening) 夕食時 yūshokujikan

dinosaur [daɪ'nəsɔːr] *n* 恐竜 kyōryū

dint [dɪnt] *n*: *by dint of* ...によって ...ni yottē

diocese [daɪ'əsiːs] *n* 司教区 shíkyōkū

dip [dɪp] *n* (slope) 下り坂 kudárizaka; (in sea) 一泳ぎ hitóoyògi; (CULIN) ディップ díppù
♦*vt* (in water etc) ...に浸す ...ni hitásū; (ladle etc) 入れる irérū; (*BRIT*: AUT: lights) 下向きにする shítāmuki ni surú
♦*vi* (ground, road) 下り坂になる kudárizaka ni narū

diphthong [dif'θɔːŋ] *n* 二重母音 nijūbóin

diploma [diplou'mə] *n* 卒業証書 sotsúgyōshōsho

diplomacy [diplou'məsiː] *n* (POL) 外交 gaíkō; (gen) 如才なさ josáinasā

diplomat [dip'ləmæt] *n* (POL) 外交官 gaíkōkan

diplomatic [dipləmæt'ik] *adj* (mission, corps) 外交の gaíkō no; (person, answer, behavior) 如才ない josáinai

dipstick [dip'stik] *n* (AUT) 油量計 yuryōkēi, オイルゲージ oírugēji

dipswitch [dip'switʃ] (*BRIT*) *n* (AUT) ヘッドライト切替えスイッチ heddóraīto kirfkaesuītchi

dire [daɪ'ər] *adj* (consequences, effects) 恐ろしい osóroshīi

direct [direkt'] *adj* (route) 直行の chokkō no; (sunlight, light) 直射の chokúsha no; (control, payment) 直接の chokúsetsu no; (challenge) あからさまな akárasāma na; (person) 率直な sotchóku na
♦*vt* (address: letter) 宛てる atérū; (aim: attention, remark) 向ける mukérū; (manage: company, project etc) 管理する káñri suru; (play, film, programme) 監督する kañtoku suru; (order): *to direct someone to do something* ...に ...する様に命令する ...ni ...surú yō ni mefrei suru
♦*adv* (go, write) 直接 chokúsetsu
can you direct me to ...? ...に行くにはどう行けばいいんですか ...ni ikú ni wa dō ikeba iñ desu ká

direct debit (*BRIT*) *n* 自動振替 jidófurikae

direction [direk'ʃən] *n* (way) 方向 hōkō; (TV, RADIO, CINEMA) 演出 efshutsu
sense of direction 方向感覚 hōkōkankaku

directions [direk'ʃənz] *npl* (instructions) 指示 shíji
directions for use 取扱い説明 toríatsu-

kaisetsúmei

directly [dirékt'li:] *adv* (in a straight line) 真っ直ぐに massúgù ni; (at once) 直ぐに súgù ni

director [direk'tə:r] *n* (COMM) 取締役 toríshimariyàku; (of project) 責任者 sekíninìsha; (TV, RADIO, CINEMA) 監督 kañtoku

directory [direk'tə:ri:] *n* (TEL) 電話帳 defiwachò; (COMPUT) ディレクトリー dirékutorì; (COMM) 名簿 meíbo

dirt [də:rt] *n* (stains, dust) 汚れ yogóre; (earth) 土 tsuchí

dirt-cheap [də:rt'tʃi:p'] *adj* べら安のberáyàsu no

dirty [də:r'ti:] *adj* (clothes, face) 汚い kitánai, 汚れた yogóretà; (joke) わいせつな waísetsu na

dirty trick *n*: **to play a dirty trick on someone** ...に卑劣なまねをする ...ni hirétsu na manè wo suru

disability [disəbil'əti:] *n* (*also*: **physical disability**) 身体障害 shińtaishògai; (*also*: **mental disability**) 精神障害 seíshinshōgai

disabled [disei'bəld] *adj* (physically) 身体障害のある shińtaishògai no aru; (mentally) 精神障害のある seíshinshògai no árù

♦*npl*: **the disabled** 身体傷害者 shińtaishōgaishà ◇総称 sốshō

disadvantage [disədvæn'tidʒ] *n* (drawback) 不利な点 fúrì na teñ; (detriment) 不利な立場 fúrì na tachìba

disaffection [disəfek'ʃən] *n* (with leadership etc) 不満 fumán

disagree [disəgri:'] *vi* (differ) 一致しない itchí shinaì; (be against, think otherwise): **to disagree (with)** (...と) 意見が合わない (...to) ìkén ga awanaì

disagreeable [disəgri:'əbəl] *adj* (encounter, person, experience) 嫌な iyá na

disagreement [disəgri:'mənt] *n* (lack of consensus) 不一致 fuítchì; (argument) けんか keñka

disallow [disəlau'] *vt* (LAW: appeal) 却下する kyákkà suru

disappear [disəpi:r'] *vi* (person, object, vehicle: from sight) 消える kiérù, 見えなくなる miénaku narù; (: deliberately) 姿を消す súgàta wo kesú; (custom etc) 消えてなくなる kiéte naku narù

disappearance [disəpi:r'əns] *n* (from sight) 消える事 kiérù kotŏ; (deliberate) 失そう shissŏ; (of custom etc) なくなる事 nakú naru kotŏ

disappoint [disəpoint'] *vt* (person) がっかりさせる gakkárì saserù

disappointed [disəpoin'tid] *adj* がっかりしている gakkárì shité irù

disappointing [disəpoin'tiŋ] *adj* (outcome, result, book etc) 期待外れの kitáihazure no

disappointment [disəpoint'mənt] *n* (emotion) 落胆 rakútañ; (cause) 期待外れ kitáihazure

disapproval [disəpru:'vəl] *n* 非難 hínàn

disapprove [disəpru:v'] *vi*: **to disapprove (of)** (person, thing) (...を) 非難の目で見る (...wo) hínàn no mè de mírù

disarm [disɑ:rm'] *vt* (MIL) 武装解除する busŏkaijo suru

disarmament [disɑ:r'məmənt] *n* (MIL, POL) 軍備縮小 guñbishukushŏ

disarming [disɑ:rm'iŋ] *adj* (smile, friendliness) 心を和ませるような kokóro wo nagōmaseru yŏ na

disarray [disərei'] *n*: **in disarray** (army, organization) 混乱して kofiran shitè; (hair, clothes) 乱れて midárettè

disaster [dizæs'tə:r] *n* (*also*: **natural disaster**) 天災 teñsai; (AVIAT etc) 災害 saígai; (fig: mess) 大失敗 daíshippài

disastrous [dizæs'trəs] *adj* (mistake, effect, results) 悲惨な hisán na

disband [disbænd'] *vt* (regiment, group) 解散する kaísan suru

♦*vi* (regiment, group) 解散する kaísan suru

disbelief [disbili:f'] *n* 信じられない事 shiñjirarenai kotŏ

disc [disk] *n* (ANAT) つい間板 tsufikan-bañ; (record) レコード rekŏdŏ; (COMPUT) = **disk**

discard [dɪskɑːd] vt (old things: also fig) 捨てる sutérù

discern [dɪsəːn] vt (see) 見分ける miwákerù; (identify) 理解する rīkái suru

discerning [dɪsəːnɪŋ] adj (judgement, look, listeners etc) 理解のある rīkái no árù

discharge [vb dɪstʃɑːdʒ] n dɪstʃɑːdʒ] vt (duties) 履行する rīkṓ suru; (waste) 排出する hāshutsu suru; (patient) 退院させる taīn saserù; (employee) 解雇する káīko suru; (soldier) 除隊にする jotái ni suru; (defendant) 釈放する shakúhō suru
◆n (CHEM, ELEC) 放電 hṓden; (of waste) 排出 haíshutsu; (of employee) 解雇 káīko; (of soldier) 除隊 jotái; (of defendant) 釈放 shakúhō

disciple [dɪsaɪpəl] n (REL: also fig: follower) 弟子 deshí

discipline [dɪsəplɪn] n (control) 規律 kirítsu; (self-control) 自制 jiséi; (branch of knowledge) 分野 búń-ya
◆vt (train) 訓練する kuńren suru; (punish) 罰する bassúrù

disc jockey [dɪskʹ-] n ディスクジョッキー disúkujokkí

disclaim [dɪskleɪm] vt (knowledge, responsibility) 否定する hitéi suru

disclose [dɪsklouz] vt (interest, involvement) 打明ける uchíakerù

disclosure [dɪsklouʒəːr] n (revelation) 打明け話 uchíakebanáshi

disco [dɪskou] n abbr (event) ディスコダンス disúkodańsu; (place) = **discotheque**

discolored [dɪskʌlʹəːrd] (BRIT **discoloured**) adj (teeth, pots) 変色した heńshoku shitá

discomfort [dɪskʌmʹfəːrt] n (unease) 不安 fuáñ; (physical) 不快 fukái

disconcert [dɪskənsəːrt] vt どぎまぎさせる dógìmagi saserù

disconnect [dɪskənekt] vt (pipe, tap) 外す hazúsu; (ELEC) 切断する setsúdan suru; (TEL) 切る kírù

discontent [dɪskəntent] n 不満 fumáñ

discontented [dɪskəntentʹid] adj 不満の fumáñ no

discontinue [dɪskəntɪnʹjuː] vt (visits) やめる yamérù; (payments) 止める tomérù

discontinued (COMM) 生産中止 sefsańchūshi

discord [dɪskɔːrd] n (quarrelling) 不和 fúwa; (MUS) 不協和音 fukyṓwàon

discordant [dɪskɔːrʹdənt] adj (fig) 不協和音の fukyṓwàon no

discotheque [dɪskʹoutek] n (place) ディスコ dísùko

discount [n dɪskaunt- vb diskaunt] n (for students, employees etc) 割引 waríbiki
◆vt (COMM) 割引く warfbikù; (idea, fact) 無視する múshì suru

discourage [dɪskəːʹridʒ] vt (dishearten) 落胆させる rakútan saserù; (advise against): **to discourage something** ...を阻止する ...wo sóshì suru
to discourage someone from doing ...するのを...に断念させようとする ...surú wo ...ni dańnen saseyṓ to suru

discouraging [dɪskəːʹridʒɪ ŋ] adj (remark, response) がっかりさせる様な gakkárì saserù yṓ na

discourteous [dɪskəːrʹtiːəs] adj 失礼な shitsúrei na

discover [dɪskʌvʹəːr] vt 発見する hakkén suru
to discover that (find out) ...だと発見する ...dá tò hakkén suru

discovery [dɪskʌvʹəːri] n 発見 hakkén

discredit [dɪskredʹit] vt (person, group) ...の信用を傷付ける ...no shiń-yō wò kizútsukerù; (claim, idea) ...に疑問を投げ掛ける ...ni gimóñ wò nagékakerù

discreet [dɪskriːt] adj (tactful, careful) 慎重な shifchṓ na; (unremarkable) 目立たない medátanaì

discrepancy [dɪskrepʹənsiː] n (difference) 不一致 futcchí

discretion [dɪskreʹʃən] n (tact) 慎重さ shifchṓsa
at the discretion of ...の判断次第で ...no hańdan shidái de

discriminate [dɪskrimʹəneit] vi: **to discriminate between** ...と...を区別する ...to ...wo kúbètsu suru

to discriminate against ...を差別する
...wo sábètsu suru

discriminating [diskrim'əneitiŋ] *adj* (public, audience) 理解のある rīkái no árù

discrimination [diskrimənei'ʃən] *n* (bias) 差別 sábètsu; (discernment) 理解 rīkái

discuss [diskʌs'] *vt* (talk over) 話し合う hanáshiaù; (analyze) 取上げる torfagerù

discussion [diskʌʃ'ən] *n* (talk) 話し合い hanáshiai; (debate) 討論 tōrōn

disdain [disdein'] *n* 軽べつ keíhetsu

disease [dizi:z'] *n* (MED, *fig*) 病気 byōki

disembark [disembɑːrk'] *vt* (goods) 陸揚げする rikűagè suru; (passengers: from boat) 上陸させる jōriku saserù; (: from plane, bus) 降ろす orósù
♦*vi* (passengers: from boat) 上陸する jōriku suru; (: from plane, bus) 降りる orírù

disenchanted [disentʃæn'tid] *adj*: *disenchanted (with)* (...の) 魅力を感じなくなった (...no) miryóku wò kañjinaku nattà

disengage [disengeidʒ'] *vt* (AUT: clutch) 切る kírù

disentangle [disentæŋ'gəl] *vt* ほどく hodókù

disfigure [disfig'jər] *vt* (person) ...の美ぼうを損なう ...no bibő wò sokónaù; (object, place) 汚す yogósù

disgrace [disgreis'] *n* (shame, dishonor) 恥 hají; (cause of shame, scandal) 恥ずべき事 hazúbeki kotő
♦*vt* (one's family, country) ...の恥になる ...no hají ni narù; (one's name) 汚す kegásù

disgraceful [disgreis'fəl] *adj* (behavior, condition, state) 恥ずべき hazúbeki na

disgruntled [disgrʌn'təld] *adj* (supporter, voter) 不満の fumán no

disguise [disgaiz'] *n* (make-up, costume) 変装の道具 heñsō no dőgu; (art) 変装 heñsō
♦*vt* (person, object): *to disguise (as)* (...に) 見せ掛ける (...ni) misékakerù
in disguise 変装して heñsō shitè

disgust [disgʌst'] *n* (aversion, distaste) 嫌悪 kén-o
♦*vt* うんざりさせる uñzari saserù

disgusting [disgʌs'tiŋ] *adj* (revolting: food etc) むかつかせる mukátsukaserù; (unacceptable: behavior etc) いやな iyá nà

dish [diʃ] *n* (piece of crockery) 皿 sará; (food) 料理 ryőri
to do/wash the dishes 皿洗いをする saráarai wo suru

dishcloth [diʃ'klɔːθ] *n* (for washing) 皿洗いの布きれ saráarai no nukíñ

dishearten [dishɑːr'tən] *vt* がっかりさせる gakkárì saserù

disheveled [diʃev'əld] (*BRIT* **dishevelled**) *adj* (hair, clothes) 乱れた midáreta

dishonest [disɑːn'ist] *adj* (person, means) 不正な fuséi na

dishonesty [disɑːn'isti] *n* 不正 fuséi

dishonor [disɑːn'ər] (*BRIT* **dishonour**) *n* 不名誉 fumêlyo

dishonorable [disɑːn'ərəbəl] *adj* 不名誉な fumêlyo na

dish out *vt* (distribute) 配る kubárù

dishtowel [diʃ'tauəl] *n* 皿ふきん sarábu-kiñ

dish up *vt* (food) 皿に盛る sará ni morù

dishwasher [diʃ'wɑʃər] *n* (machine) 皿洗い機 saráaraikì

disillusion [disilu:'ʒən] *vt* ...の迷いを覚ます ...no mayői wo samásù

disincentive [disinsen'tiv] *n* (to work, investment) 阻害要因 sogáiyòin

disinfect [disinfekt'] *vt* 消毒する shōdoku suru

disinfectant [disinfek'tənt] *n* 消毒剤 shōdokuzaî

disintegrate [disin'təgreit] *vi* (object) 分解する buñkai suru

disinterested [disin'tristid] *adj* (impartial: advice, help) 私欲のない shiyóku no nai

disjointed [disdʒɔin'tid] *adj* (thoughts, words) まとまりのない matómari no nai

disk [disk] *n* (COMPUT) ディスク dísùku

disk drive *n* ディスクドライブ disúkudoraibu

diskette [disket'] n = disk

dislike [dislaik'] n (feeling) 嫌悪 kén-o; (gen pl: object of dislike) 嫌いな物 kirái na monò

♦vt 嫌う kiráù

dislocate [dis'loukeit'] vt (joint) 脱きゅうさせる dakkyū saserù

dislodge [dislɑːdʒ'] vt (boulder etc) 取除く torínozokù

disloyal [dislɔi'əl] adj (to country, family) 裏切り者の urágirimono no

dismal [diz'məl] adj (depressing: weather, song, person, mood) 陰欝な ínki na; (very bad: prospects, failure) 最低の saítei no

dismantle [dismæn'təl] vt (machine) 分解する buñkai suru

dismay [dismei'] n 困惑 kofiwaku

♦vt 困惑させる kofiwaku saserù

dismiss [dismis'] vt (worker) 解雇する káiko suru; (pupils, soldiers) 解散させる kaísan saseru; (LAW: case) 却下する kyákka suru; (possibility, idea) 考えない様にする kañgaenai yō ni suru

dismissal [dismis'əl] n (sacking) 解雇 káiko

dismount [dismaunt'] vi (from horse, bicycle) 降りる orírù

disobedience [disəbi:'di:əns] n 不服従 fufúkujū

disobedient [disəbi:'di:ənt] adj (child, dog) 言う事を聞かない iú koto wo kikánaì

disobey [disəbei'] vt (person, order) 違反する ihán suru

disorder [disɔːr'dər] n (untidiness) 乱雑さ rañzatsu; (rioting) 騒動 sōdō; (MED) 障害 shōgai

disorderly [disɔːr'dərli:] adj (untidy: room etc) 整理されていない sefri sarete inai; (meeting) 混乱の koñran no; (behavior) 治安を乱す chián wo midásù

disorganized [disɔːr'gənaizd] adj (person, event) 支離滅裂な shírimetsúretsu na

disorientated [disɔː'ri:inteitid] adj (person: after journey, deep sleep) 頭が混乱

している atáma gà koñran shite irù

disown [disoun'] vt (action) …との関係を否定する …tó nò kañkei wò hitéi suru; (child) 勘当する kañdō suru

disparaging [dispær'idʒiŋ] adj (remarks) 中傷的な chūshōteki na

disparate [dis'pərit] adj (levels, groups) 異なった kotónattà

disparity [dispær'iti:] n 差異 saí

dispassionate [dispæʃ'ənit] adj (approach, reaction) 客観的な kyakkánteki na

dispatch [dispætʃ'] vt (send: message, goods, mail) 送る okúrù; (: messenger) 派遣する hakén suru

♦n (sending) 送付 sófu; (PRESS, MIL) 派遣 hakén

dispel [dispel'] vt (myths, fears) 払いのける haráinokerù

dispense [dispens'] vt (medicines) 調剤する chōzai suru

dispenser [dispen'sər] n (machine) 自動販売機 jidōhanbaikì

dispense with vt fus (do without) …なしで済ませる …náshi de sumáserù

dispensing chemist [dispens'iŋ-](BRIT) n (shop) 薬屋 kusúriya

dispersal [dispər'səl] n (of objects, crowd) 分散 buñsan

disperse [dispərs'] vt (objects, crowd etc) 散らす chirásù

♦vi (crowd) 散って行く chitté ikù

dispirited [dispir'itid] adj 意気消沈したfkíshōchin shita

displace [displeis'] vt (shift) 押し出す o-shídasù

displaced person [displeist'-] n (POL) 難民 nañmin

display [displei'] n (in shop) 陳列 chíretsu; (exhibition) 展示 tenji; (of feeling) 表現 hyőgen; (COMPUT, TECH) ディスプレー display、モニター mónitā

♦vt (show) 展示する tenji suru; (ostentatiously) 見せびらかす misébirakasù

displease [displiːz'] vt (offend, annoy) 怒らせる okóraserù

displeased [displiːzd'] adj: **displeased with** (unhappy, disappointed) …にがっか

りしている ...ni gakkári shité irù

displeasure [displeʒ'ɔːr] *n* 怒り ikári

disposable [dispou'zəbəl] *adj* (lighter, bottle) 使い捨ての tsukáisute no; (income) 自由に使える jiyú ni tsukáerù

disposable nappy (*BRIT*) *n* 紙 おむつ kamfomutsù

disposal [dispou'zəl] *n* (of goods for sale) 陳列 chifiretsu; (of property) 売却 bafkyaku; (of rubbish) 処分 shóbun

at one's disposal ...の自由になる ...no jiyú ní narù

dispose [dispouz'] *vi*: *to dispose of* (get rid of: body, unwanted goods) 始末する shímatsu suru; (deal with: problem, argument) 片付ける katázukerù

disposed [dispouzd'] *adj*: *disposed to do* (inclined, willing) ...する気がある ...surú ki gà árù

to be well disposed towards someone ...に好意を寄せている ...ni kōi wo yoséte irù

disposition [dispəziʃ'ən] *n* (nature) 性質 sefshitsu; (inclination) 傾向 kefkō

disproportionate [disprəpɔːr'ʃənit] *adj* (amount, effect) 過剰な kajō na

disprove [dispruːv'] *vt* (belief, assertion) 反証する hafishō suru

dispute [dispjuːt'] *n* (domestic) けんか kefka; (*also:* **industrial dispute**) 争議 sōgi; (POL) 論議 rófigi

♦*vt* (fact, statement) 反ばくする hafibaku suru; (ownership etc) 争う arásoù

territorial dispute 領土紛争 ryódofunsō

border dispute 国境紛争 kokkyófunsō

disqualify [diskwɔːl'əfai] *vt* (SPORT) ...の資格を取り上げる ...no shikáku wò torfagerù

to disqualify someone for something/from doing something ...から ...の...する)資格を取り上げる ...kárà ...no (...surú) shikáku wò torfagerù

disquiet [diskwai't] *n* (anxiety) 不安 fuán

disregard [disrigɑːrd'] *vt* (ignore, pay no attention to) 無視する múshī suru

disrepair [disripeːr'] *n*: *to fall into*

disrepair (machine, building) ひどく痛んでしまう hídòku itánde shimaù

disreputable [disrep'jətəbəl] *adj* (person, behavior) いかがわしい ikágawashii

disrespectful [disrispekt'fəl] *adj* (person, conduct) 無礼な búrèi na

disrupt [disrʌpt'] *vt* (plans) 邪魔する jamá suru; (conversation, proceedings) 妨害する bōgai suru

disruption [disrʌp'ʃən] *n* (interruption) 中断 chúdan; (disturbance) 妨害 bōgai

dissatisfaction [dissætisfæk'ʃən] *n* 不満 fumán

dissatisfied [dissæt'isfaid] *adj* 不満な fumán na

dissect [disekt'] *vt* (dead person, animal) 解剖する kafbō suru

disseminate [disem'əneit] *vt* 普及させる fukyú saserù

dissent [disent'] *n* (disagreement, protest) 反対 hafitai

dissertation [disərtei'ʃən] *n* (*also* SCOL) 論文 rofibun

disservice [dissɑːr'vis] *n*: *to do someone a disservice* (person: harm) ...に迷惑を掛ける ...ni mélwaku wo kakérù

dissident [dis'idənt] *adj* (faction, voice) 反対の hafitai no

♦*n* (POL, REL) 反対分子 hafitaibuñshi

dissimilar [disim'ilər] *adj* 異なる kotónarù

dissipate [dis'əpeit] *vt* (heat) 放散する hōsan suru; (clouds) 散らす chírásù; (money, effort) 使い果す tsukáihatasù

dissociate [disou'ʃieit] *vt* ...との関係を否定する ...tó nò kańkei wò hitéi suru

to dissociate oneself from ...との関係を否定する ...tó nò kańkei wò hitéi suru

dissolute [dis'əluːt] *adj* (individual, behavior) 道楽ざんまいの dōrakuzáñmai no

dissolution [disəluː'ʃən] *n* (of organization, POL) 解散 kańsan; (of marriage) 解消 kańshō

dissolve [dizɑːlv'] *vt* (in liquid) 溶かす tokásù; (organization, POL) 解散させる kańsan saserù; (marriage) 解消する kafshō suru

♦*vi* (material) 溶ける tokérù

to dissolve in(to) tears 泣き崩れる nakí-kuzurérù

dissuade [diswéid'] *vt*: *to dissuade someone (from)* (...を) 思い止まる様...を説得する (...wo) omóitodomaru yō ...wo settóku suru

distance [dis'təns] *n* (gap: in space) 距離 kyóri; (: in time) 隔たり hedátari

in the distance ずっと向うに zúttò mukó ni

distant [dis'tənt] *adj* (place, time, relative) 遠い tōì; (manner) よそよそしい yosóyososhii

distaste [disteist'] *n* (dislike) 嫌悪 kén-o

distasteful [disteist'fəl] *adj* (offensive) いやな iyá na

distended [distend'id] *adj* (stomach) 膨らんだ fukúrañda

distill [distil'] (*BRIT* **distil**) *vt* (water, whiskey) 蒸留する jóryū suru

distillery [distil'əːri] *n* 醸造所 jōzōjò

distinct [distiŋkt'] *adj* (different) 別個の békkò no; (clear) はっきりした hakkírì shita; (unmistakable) 明白な meíhaku na

as distinct from (in contrast to) ...ではなくて ...dé wà nákùte

distinction [distiŋk'ʃən] *n* (difference) 区別 kubétsu; (honor) 名誉 meíyo; (in exam) 優等の成績 yūtò no seíseki

distinctive [distiŋk'tiv] *adj* 独特な dokútoku na

distinguish [distiŋ'gwiʃ] *vt* (differentiate) 区別する kubétsu suru; (identify: details etc: by sight) 見分ける miwákerù; (: : by sound) 聞分ける kikíwakerù

to distinguish oneself (in battle etc) 見事な活躍をする mígòto na katsúyaku wo surù

distinguished [distiŋ'gwiʃt] *adj* (eminent) 有名な yūmei na; (in appearance) 気品のある kihín no arù

distinguishing [distiŋ'gwiʃiŋ] *adj* (feature) 特徴的な tokúchōteki na

distort [distɔːrt'] *vt* (argument) 曲げる magérù; (sound) ひずませる hizúmaserù; (shape, image) ゆがめる yugámerù

distortion [distɔːr'ʃən] *n* (of argument

etc) わい曲 waíkyoku; (of sound, image, shape etc) ひずみ hizúmi

distract [distrækt'] *vt* (sb's attention) 散らす chirásù; (person) ...の気を散らす...no ki wo chirásù

distracted [distræk'tid] *adj* (dreaming) ぼんやりした boñ-yari shita; (anxious) 気が動転している ki ga dóten shite irù

distraction [distræk'ʃən] *n* (inattention) 気を散らす事(物) ki wo chirásù kotó (monó); (confusion) 困惑 koñwaku; (amusement) 気晴らし kibárashi

distraught [distrɔːt'] *adj* (with pain, worry) 気が動転している ki ga dóten shite irù

distress [distres'] *n* (anguish) 苦痛 kutsū

♦*vt* (cause anguish) 苦しめる kurúshimerù

distressing [distres'iŋ] *adj* (experience, time) 苦しい kurúshii

distress signal *n* (AVIAT, NAUT) 遭難信号 sōnanshiñgō

distribute [distrib'jut] *vt* (hand out: leaflets, prizes etc) 配る kubárù; (share out: profits) 分ける wakérù; (spread out: weight) 分布する buñpu suru

distribution [distribju'ʃən] *n* (of goods) 流通 ryūtsū; (of profits etc) 分配 buñpai

distributor [distrib'jətəːr] *n* (COMM) 流通業者 ryūtsūgyōsha; (AUT, TECH) ディストリビュータ disútoribyūta

district [dis'trikt] *n* (of country) 地方 chihō; (of town, ADMIN) 地区 chikù

district attorney (*US*) *n* 地方検事 chíhōkeñji

district nurse (*BRIT*) *n* 保健婦 hokénfu

distrust [distrʌst'] *n* 不信感 fushíñkan

♦*vt* 信用しない shiñ-yō shinaí

disturb [distəːrb'] *vt* (interrupt) 邪魔する jamá suru; (bother) 心配させる shiñpai saserù; (disorganize) 乱す midásù

disturbance [distəːr'bəns] *n* (upheaval) 邪魔 jamá; (political etc) 騒動 sōdō; (violent event) 動乱 dóran; (of mind) 心配 shiñpai

disturbed [distəːrbd'] *adj* (person: worried, upset) 不安な fuán na; (childhood)

乱れた midáretà
emotionally disturbed 情緒障害の jóchoshōgai no

disturbing [distə:'riŋ] *adj* (experience, moment) 動転させる dōten saserú

disuse [disju:s'] *n*: **to fall into disuse** (be abandoned: methods, laws etc) 廃れる sutáreru

disused [disju:zd'] *adj* (building, airfield) 使われていない tsukáwarete inái

ditch [ditʃ] *n* (at roadside) どぶ dobú; (*also: irrigation ditch*) 用水路 yōsuirò
♦*vt* (*inf:* person) ...と縁を切る ...to én wo kírù; (: plan, car etc) 捨てる sutérù

dither [dið'əːr] (*pej*) *vi* (hesitate) ためらう taméraù

ditto [dit'ou] *adv* 同じく onájìku

divan [divæn'] *n* (*also*: **divan bed**) ソファベッド sofábeddò

dive [daiv] (*pt* **dived** *also US* **dove**, *pp* **dived**) *n* (from board) 飛込み tobíkomi; (underwater) 潜水 sensui, ダイビング dáibingu; (*of submarine*) 潜水 sensui
♦*vi* (swimmer: into water) 飛込む tobíkomù; (under water) 潜水する sensui suru, ダイビングする dáibingu suru; (fish) 潜る mogúrù, (bird) 急降下する kyúkōka suru; (submarine) 潜水する sensui suru
to dive into (bag, drawer etc) ...に手を突っ込む ...ni té wo tsukkómù; (shop, car etc) ...に飛込む ...ni tobíkomù

diver [dai'vəːr] *n* (person) ダイバー dáibā

diverge [divəːrdʒ'] *vi* (paths, interests) 分かれる wakárerù

diverse [divəːrs'] *adj* 様々な samázàma na

diversify [divəːr'safai] *vi* (COMM) 多様化する tayōka suru

diversion [divəːr'ʒən] *n* (BRIT: AUT) う回路 ukáirò; (distraction) 気分転換 kibúntenkan; (*of funds*) 流用 ryūyō

diversity [divəːr'siti:] *n* (range, variety) 多様性 tayōsei

divert [divəːrt'] *vt* (funds) 流用する ryūyō suru; (someone's attention) 反らす sorásù; (re-route) う回させる ukái saserù

divide [divaid'] *vt* (separate) 分ける wakérù; (MATH) 割る warù; (share out) 分

ける wakérù, 分配する buñpai suru
♦*vi* (cells etc) 分裂する buñretsu suru; (road) 分岐する búnki suru; (people, groups) 分裂する buñretsu suru
8 divided by 4 is 2 8割る4は2 hachí warù yón wa ní

divided highway [divaid'id-] (*US*) *n* 中央分離帯のある道路 chūōbuñritai no árù dōrò

dividend [div'idend] *n* (COMM) 配当金 haftōkin; (*fig*): **to pay dividends** 利益になる ríeki ni nárù

divine [divain'] *adj* (REL) 神の kámì no; (*fig*: person, thing) 素晴らしい subárashiì

diving [daiv'iŋ] *n* (underwater) 飛込み tobíkomi; (SPORT) 潜水 sensui, ダイビング dáibingu

diving board *n* 飛込み台 tobíkomidài

divinity [divin'əti:] *n* (nature) 神性 shíñsei; (god) 神 kámì; (subject) 神学 shiñgaku

division [diviʒ'ən] *n* (of cells etc) 分裂 buñretsu; (MATH) 割算 warízan; (sharing out) 分配 buñpai; (disagreement) 分裂 buñretsu; (COMM) 部門 búmon; (MIL) 師団 shídan; (especially SOCCER) 部 búrui

divorce [divɔːrs'] *n* 離婚 ríkòn
♦*vt* (spouse) ...と離婚する ...to ríkòn suru; (dissociate) 別々に扱う betsúbetsu ni atsúkaù

divorcé [divɔːrsi:'] *n* 離婚男性 rikóndañsei

divorced [divɔːrst'] *adj* 離婚した ríkònshita

divorcée [divɔːrsi:'] *n* 離婚女性 rikóñjosei

divulge [divʌldʒ'] *vt* (information, secret) 漏らす morásù

D.I.Y. [di:aiwai'] (*BRIT*) *n abbr* = **do-it-yourself**

dizzy [diz'i:] *adj*: **a dizzy spell/turn** めまい memái
to feel dizzy めまいがする memái ga suru

DJ [di:'dʒei] *n abbr* (= **disk jockey**) ディスクジョッキー disúkujokkī

KEYWORD

do [duː] (*pt* **did**, *pp* **done**) *aux vb* **1** (in negative constructions): *I don't understand* 分かりません wakárimasèn

she doesn't want it 彼女はそれを欲しがっていません kánojo wa soré wo hoshígattè imásèn

he didn't seem to care 彼はどうでもいい様でした kárè wa dó de mo íī yō dèshita

2 (to form questions): *didn't you know?* 知りませんでしたか shirímasèn deshita ká

why didn't you come? どうして来てくれなかったのですか dōshite kité kurénakàtta no desu ká

what do you think? どう思いますか dō omóimasù ká

3 (for emphasis, in polite expressions): *people do make mistakes sometimes* だれだって間違いをしますよ dáre datte machígaì wo shimasù yo

she does seem rather late 彼女は本当に遅い様ですね iébà kánojo wa hontō ni osói yò desu né

do sit down/help yourself どうぞお掛け[お召し上がり]下さい dózò o-kàke [o-méshiagari]kudasaí

do take care! くれぐれもお気をつけて kurégurè mo o-kí wo tsuketè

oh do shut up! いい加減に黙ってくれませんか ifkagen ni dámàtte kurémasèn ká

4 (used to avoid repeating vb): *she swims better than I do* 彼女は私より泳ぎがうまい kánojo wa watákushi yori oyógi ga umáī

do you agree? - yes, I do/no, I don't 賛成しますか — はい、します[いいえ、しません] sánsei shimasù ka - háī, shimásù[ífe, shimásèn]

she lives in Glasgow - so do I 彼女はグラスゴーに住んでいます — 私もそうです kánojo wa gurásugō ni súndè imásù - watákushi mo sō dèsu

he didn't like it and neither did we 彼はそれを気に入らなかったし、私たち

もそうでした kárè wa soré wo kí nì iranakàtta shí, watákushitàchi mó sō dèshita

who made this mess? - I did だれだ、ここを汚したのは — 私です watákushi desù, kokó wo yógoshità nò wa - watákushi desù

he asked me to help him and I did 助けてくれと彼に頼まれたのでそうしました tasúkète kure to kárè ni tanómarèta no de sō shimashìta

2 (in question tags): *you like him, don't you?* あなたは彼を好きでしょう? anátà wa kárè wo sukí dèshō?

he laughed, didn't he? 彼は笑ったでしょう? kárè wa warátta deshō?

I don't know him, do I? 私の知らない人でしょう? watákushi no shírànai hito dèshō?

♦*vt* **1** (*gen*: carry out, perform etc) する súrù, やる yárù

what are you doing tonight? 今夜のご予定は? kòn-ya no gò-yótei wá?

have you done your homework? 宿題をしましたか shùkúdai wo shimáshità ká

I've got nothing to do 何もする事があありません nàní mo súrù koto gà arimasèn

what can I do for you? どんなご用でしょうか dònna go-yō dèshō ka

to do the cooking/washing-up 料理[皿洗い]をする ryōri(saráaraī) wo súrù

to do one's teeth/hair/nails 歯を磨く[髪をとかす、つめにマニキュアをする] há wò migàku[kámí wò tokásù, tsúmé ni mánìkyua wo súrù]

we're doing "Othello" at school (studying it) 学校で今オセロを勉強しています gakkō de ímà ósèro wo bénkyō shite imasù; (performing it) 学校で今オセロを上演しています gakkō de ímà ósèro wo jōen shite imásù

2 (AUT etc) 進む hashírù

the car was doing 100 車は時速100マイルを出していた kurúma wa jísòku hyàkúmaìru wo dáshite ità

we've done 200 km already 私たちはもう200キロメーター走ってきました tákushitàchi wa mõ nihyàkukiromèta hashítte kimáshita

he can do 100 mph in that car あの車で彼は時速100マイルが出せます anó kuruma de karè wa jísoku hyakúmaìru dasémasù

♦ *vi* 1 (act, behave) する sùrú

do as I do 私のする通りにしなさい watákushi no sùrú tòrí ni shinásaì

do as I tell you 私の言う通りにしなさい watákushi no iu tòrí ni shinásaì

you did well to come so quickly すぐに来てくれて良かったよ súgù ni kité kúrete yókàtta yó

2 (get on, fare): **he's doing well/badly at school** 彼は学校の成績がいい(良くない) kárè wa gakkō no seiseki ga íì (yokúnaì)

the firm is doing well 会社は繁盛しています kaísha wa hànjō shité imasù

how do you do? 初めまして hajímemashìte

3 (suit) 適当である tekítō de arú

will it do? 役に立ちますかyakú ni tachímasù ká

will this dress do for the party? パーティにはこのドレスでいいかしら páàtì ni wa konó dóresu de íì kashira

4 (be sufficient) 十分である jūbùn de árù

will £ 10 do? 10ポンドで間に合いますか jūppòndo de ma ní aimasù ká

that'll do 十分です jūbùn desu

that'll do! (in annoyance) いい加減にしなさい íikagen ni shinásaì

to make do (with) ...で間に合せる (...dé) ma ní awaserú

you'll have to make do with $15 15ドルで間に合せなさい jūgódòru de ma ní awasenasaì

♦ *n* (*inf*: party etc) パーティ páàtì

we're having a little do on Saturday 土曜日にちょっとしたパーティをしようと思っています dòyóbi ni chótto shita páàtì wo shiyō tò omóttè imasù

it was rather a do なかなかいいパーティだった nakánaka iì páàtì datta

do away with *vt fus* (kill) 殺す korósu; (abolish: law etc) なくす nakúsu

docile [dəʊˈsaɪl] *adj* (person) 素直な sùnáo na; (beast) 大人しい otónashiì

dock [dɒk] *n* (NAUT) 岸壁 ganpeki; (LAW) 被告席 hikókuseki
♦ *vi* (NAUT) 接岸する setsúgan suru; (SPACE) ドッキングする dokkíngu suru

docker [dɒkˈəːr] *n* 港湾労働者 kówanrōdōsha

docks [dɒks] *npl* (NAUT) 係船きょ keísen kyo

dockyard [dɒkˈjɑːrd] *n* 造船所 zōsenjo

doctor [dɒkˈtəːr] *n* (MED) 医者 ishá; (PhD etc) 博士 hákàse
♦ *vt* (drink etc) ...に薬物をこっそり混ぜる ...ni yakúbùtsu ni kossórí mazérù

Doctor of Philosophy *n* 博士号 hakásegō

doctrine [dɒkˈtrin] *n* (REL) 教義 kyōgi; (POL) 信条 shíñjō

document [dɒkˈjəmənt] *n* 書類 shorúi

documentary [dɒkjəmenˈtəːriː] *adj* (evidence) 書類による shorúi ni yorù
♦ *n* (TV, CINEMA) ドキュメンタリー dokyúmeñtarī

documentation [dɒkjəmənteiˈʃən] *n* (papers) 書類 shorúi

dodge [dɒdʒ] *n* (trick) 策略 sakúryaku
♦ *vt* (question) はぐらかす hagúrakasù; (tax) ごまかす gomákasù; (blow, ball) 身を交して避ける mí wò kawáshite sakérù

dodgems [dɒdʒˈəmz] *npl* (*BRIT*) ドジェム dojému ◊遊園地の乗り物の一種: 相手にぶっつかったりして遊ぶ小型電気自動車 yùéñchi no norímono no isshù: afte nì buttsúketàri shité asobù kogáta denki jidōsha

doe [dəʊ] *n* (deer) 雌ジカ mesújikà; (rabbit) 雌ウサギ mesúusàgi

does [dʌz] *vb* see do

doesn't [dʌzˈnt] = does not

dog [dɔːg] *n* (ZOOL) イヌ inú
♦ *vt* (subj: person) ...の後を付ける ...no átò wo tsukérù; (: bad luck) ...に付きまとう ...ni tsukímatoù

dog collar *n* (of dog) 首輪 kubiwa, カラー kárà; (REL) ローマンカラー rōmankarà

dog-eared [dɔːgˈiːrd] *adj* (book, paper)

手擦れした tezúre shitá

dogged [dɔg'id] *adj* (determination, spirit) 根気強い koñkizuyoi

dogma [dɔːg'mə] *n* (REL) 教理 kyóri; (POL) 信条 shiñjó

dogmatic [dɔːgmæt'ik] *adj* (attitude, assertion) 独断的の dokúdanteki na

dogsbody [dɔːgz'bɑːdiː] (*BRIT: inf*) *n* 下っ端 shitáppa

doings [duː'iŋz] *npl* (activities) 行動 kódó

do-it-yourself [duː'itjurself'] *n* 日曜大工 nichíyódaíku

doldrums [doul'drəmz] *npl*: **to be in the doldrums** (person) ふさぎ込んでいる fuságikonde irú; (business) 沈滞して いる chiñtai shite irú

dole [doul] (*BRIT*) *n* (payment) 失業手当 shitsúgyóteáte
on the dole 失業手当を受けて shitsúgyóteáte wo úkete

doleful [doul'fəl] *adj* (voice, expression) 悲しげな kanáshíge na

dole out *vt* (food, money) 配る kubárú

doll [dɑːl] *n* (toy, US: *inf*: woman) 美人 bijín

dollar [dɑːl' əːr] (*US etc*) *n* ドル dórū

dolled up [dɑːld'ʌp''] (*inf*) *adj* めかめ いして o-mékashi shita

dolphin [dɑːl'fin] *n* イルカ irúka

domain [doumein'] *n* (sphere) 分野 búñ-ya; (empire) 縄張 nawábari

dome [doum] *n* (ARCHIT) 円がい eñgai, ドーム dómu

domestic [dəmes'tik] *adj* (of country: trade, situation) 国内の kokúnai no; (of home: tasks, appliances) 家庭の katéi no
domestic animal 家畜 kachíku

domesticated [dəmes'tikeitid] *adj* (animal) 家畜化の kachíkuka no; (husband) 家庭的の katéiteki na

dominant [dɑːm'ənənt] *adj* (share, part, role) 主な ómo na; (partner) 支配的な shihâiteki na

dominate [dɑːm'əneit] *vt* (discussion) ...の主な話題になる ...no ómo na wadái ni narú; (people) 支配する shihâi suru; (place) ...の上にそびえ立つ ...no ué ni so-

bíetatsú

domineering [dɑːmíːníːr'iŋ] *adj* (over-bearing) 横暴な óbó na

dominion [dəmin'jən] *n* (authority) 支配権 shihâiken; (territory) 領土 ryódó

domino [dɑːm'anou] (*pl* **dominoes**) *n* (block) ドミノ dómino

dominoes [dɑːm'anouz] (*game*) ドミノ 遊び dómínoasóbi

don [dɑːn] (*BRIT*) *n* (SCOL) 大学教官 da-ígakukyókan

donate [dou'neit] *vt* 寄付する kifú suru

donation [douneí'ʃən] *n* 寄付 kifú

done [dʌn] *pp* of **do**

donkey [dɑːŋ'kiː] *n* (ZOOL) ロバ róba

donor [dou'nəːr] *n* (MED: of blood, heart etc) 提供者 teîkyósha; (to charity) 寄贈者 kizóshá

don't [dount] = **do not**

doodle [duːd'əl] *vi* 落書する rakúgaki su-ru

doom [duːm] *n* (fate) 悲運 hiún
♦*vt*: **to be doomed to failure** 失敗するに決っている shippái suru ní kimátte irú

doomsday [duːmz'dei] *n* 世の終りの対 no owári

door [dɔːr] *n* 戸 to, 扉 tobíra, ドア dóa

doorbell [dɔːr'bel] *n* 呼び鈴 yobírin

door handle *n* (gen) 取っ手 totté; (of car) ドアハンドル doáhañdoru

doorman [dɔːr'mæn] (*pl* **doormen**) *n* (in hotel) ドアマン doámañ

doormat [dɔːr'mæt] *n* (mat) 靴ふき ku-tsúfúki, マット mátto

doorstep [dɔːr'step] *n* 玄関階段 geñkan-kaídan

door-to-door [dɔːr'tədɔːr'] *adj* (selling, salesman) 訪問販売の hómonhañbai no

doorway [dɔːr'wei] *n* 戸口 tógúchi

dope [doup] *n* (*inf*: illegal drug) 麻薬 mayáku; (: person) ばか báka
♦*vt* (horse, person) ...に麻薬を与える ...ni mayáku wo atáerú

dopey [dou'piː] (*inf*) *adj* (groggy) ふらふらになっている furáfura ní natté irú; (stupid) ばかな bákà na

dormant [dɔːr'mənt] *adj* (plant) 休眠中の kyúminchu no

a dormant volcano 休火山 kyūkazán

dormice [dɔːr'mais] *npl of* **dormouse**

dormitory [dɔːr'mitɔːri] *n* (room) 共同 寝室 kyódōshinshitsu; (*US*: building) 寮 ryó

dormouse [dɔːr'maus] (*pl* **dormice**) *n* ヤマネ yamáne

DOS [dous] *n abbr* (COMPUT) (= *disk operating system*) ディスク・オペレーティング・システム disúku operétingu shisutému

dosage [dou'sidʒ] *n* 投薬量 tóyakuryō

dose [dous] *n* (of medicine) 一回量 ikkáiryō

doss house [dɑːs-] (*BRIT*) *n* 安宿 yasúyado, どや doyá

dossier [dɑːs'iːei] *n* (POLICE etc) 調書一 式 chōsho isshíki

dot [dɑːt] *n* (small round mark) 点 teñ; (speck, spot) 染み shimí
♦*vt*: **dotted with** ...が点々とある ...ga teñteñ tó árù
on the dot (punctually) きっかり kikkárì

dote [dout]: **to dote on** *vt fus* (child, pet, lover) でき愛する dekíai suru

dot-matrix printer [dɑːtmeit'riks-] *n* (COMPUT) ドットプリンタ dottópurìnta

dotted line [dɑːt'id-] *n* 点線 teñsen

double [dʌb'əl] *adj* (share, size) 倍の bai no; (chin etc) 二重の nijū no; (yolk) 二つある futátsu arū
♦*adv* (twice): **to cost double** 費用は二倍 掛かる hiyō wa nibái kakarū
♦*n* (twin) そっくりな人 sokkúrì na hitó
♦*vt* (offer) 二倍にする nibái ni surù; (fold in two: paper, blanket) 二つに折る futátsu nī órù
♦*vi* (population, size) 二倍になる nibái ni narù
on the double, (*BRIT*) **at the double** 駆け足で kakéàshi de

double bass *n* コントラバス koñtorabasù

double bed *n* ダブルベッド dabúrubeddò

double bend (*BRIT*) *n* S-カーブ esúkābu

double-breasted [dʌb'əlbres'tid] *adj* (jacket, coat) ダブルの dabúru no

doublecross [dʌb'əlkrɔːs] *vt* (trick, betray) 裏切る urágirù

doubledecker [dʌb'əldek'əːr] *n* (*also:* **doubledecker bus**) 二階建てバス nikáidatebasù

double glazing [-glei'ziŋ] (*BRIT*) *n* 二 重ガラス nijūgarasu

double room *n* ダブル部屋 dabúrubeya

doubles [dʌb'əlz] *n* (TENNIS) ダブルス dábūrusu

doubly [dʌb'li:] *adv* (especially) 更に更に sárà ni

doubt [daut] *n* (uncertainty) 疑問 gimón
♦*vt* (disbelieve) 信じない shifjinaī; (mistrust, suspect) 怪しいと思う shifi-yō shinaī
to doubt that ... ...だとは思わない ...dá tò wa omówanaī

doubtful [daut'fəl] *adj* (fact, provenance) 疑わしい utágawashiī; (person) 疑っている utágatte irū

doubtless [daut'lis] *adv* (probably, almost certainly) きっと ...だろう kíttò ...daró

dough [dou] *n* (CULIN) 生地 kíjì

doughnut [dou'nʌt] *n* ドーナッツ dónattsu

do up *vt* (laces) 結ぶ musúbu; (buttons) かける kakérù; (dress) しめる shimérù; (renovate: room, house) 改装する kaísō suru

douse [daus] *vt* (drench) ...に水を掛ける ...ni mizú wò kakérù; (extinguish) 消す kesú

dove [dʌv] *n* (bird) ハト hátò

Dover [dou'vəːr] *n* ドーバー dóbā

dovetail [dʌv'teil] *vi* (*fig*) 合う áù

dowdy [dau'di:] *adj* (clothes, person) 野 暮な yábò na

do with *vt fus* (need) いる írù; (want) どう しい hōshíi; (be connected) ...と関係がある ...to káñkei ga arù
I could do with a drink 一杯飲みたい ìppai nomítaî
I could do with some help だれかに手 伝ってもらいたい daréka ni tetsúdattè

moráitaĩ

what has it got to do with you? あなたとはどういう関係ですか anátà tò wa dō ĩu kánkei desù ka

I won't have anything to do with it その件にはかかわりたくない sonó kèn ni wa kakáwaritakùnaĩ

it has to do with money 金銭関係の事です kínsen kánkei no kotó desù

do without vi なしで済ます náshĩ de sumásù

♦vt fus …なしで間に合せる …náshĩ de ma nĩ awáserù

if you're late for lunch then you'll do without 昼食の時間に遅れたら何もなしだからretárā nanf mo nashĩ da kara nē

I can do without a car 私には車はいりません watákushi ni wà kurúma wa irímasèn

we'll have to do without a holiday this year 私たちは今年休暇を取るのは無理な様です watákushitàchi wa kotóshi kyúka wo torù no wa múrì na yō desū

down [daun] n (feathers) 羽毛 úmõ

♦adv (downwards) 下へ shitá e; (on the ground) 下に shitá ni

♦prep (towards lower level) …の下へ …no shitá e; (movement along) …に沿って …ni sótte

♦vt (inf: drink) 飲む nómù

down with X! 打倒X! datố X!

down-and-out [daun'anaut] n 浮浪者 furốshà, ルンペン rúñpen

down-at-heel [daunæthi:l'] adj (shoes etc) 使い古した tsukáifurushità; (appearance, person) 見すぼらしい misúborashìĩ

downcast [daun'kæst] adj がっかりした gakkárĩ shita

downfall [daun'fɔ:l] n 失脚 shikkyáku

downhearted [daun'ha:r'tid] adj 落胆した rakútan shita

downhill [daun'hil] adv: **to go downhill** (road, person, car) 坂を下る saká wò kudárù; (fig: person, business) 下り坂になる kudárizaka ni narù

down payment n (first payment of series) 頭金 atámakin; (deposit) 手付金 tetsúkekin

downpour [daun'pɔ:r] n 土砂降り doshábùri

downright [daun'rait] adj (lie, liar etc) 全くの mattáku no; (refusal) きっぱりした kippári shita

a downright lie 真っ赤なうそ makká no úsò

downstairs [daun'ste:rz'] adv (below) 下の階に(で) shitá nò kái ni(de); (downwards: go, run etc) 下の階へ shitá nò kái e

downstream [daun'stri:m] adv (be) 川下に kawáshimo ni; (go) 川下へ kawáshimo e

down-to-earth [dauntuᵊr'θ'] adj (person, solution) 現実的な geñjitsuteki na

downtown [daun'taun] adv (be) 繁華街に(で, へ) hañkagai ni(de, e)

down under adv (Australia etc) オーストラリア〔ニュージーランド〕に(で) ósutorarĩa〔nyújìrañdo〕ni (de)

downward [daun'wa:rd] adv 下へ shitá e

♦adj 下への shitá e nò

downwards [daun'wᵊrdz] adv 下へ shitá e

dowry [dau'ri:] n (bride's) 持参金 jisáñkin

doz. abbr = **dozen**

doze [douz] vi 居眠りする inémurì suru

dozen [dʌz'an] n 1ダース ichĩ dásu

a dozen books 本12冊 hoñ jûni sátsu

dozens of 幾つもの fkûtsu mo no

doze off vi (nod off) まどろむ madóromù

Dr. abbr = **doctor** (in street names) = **drive**

drab [dræb] adj (weather, building, clothes) 陰気な íñki nà

draft [dræft] n (first version) 草案 sốan; (POL: of bill) 原案 geñ'an; (US: call-up) 徴兵 chốhei; (of an: BRIT: **draught**) すきま風 sukímakaze; (NAUT: BRIT: **draught**) 喫水 kissúi

♦vt (plan) 立案する ritsúan suru; (write roughly) …の下書きをする …no shitágaki wo surù

draft beer 生ビール namábìru

draftsman [dræfts'mən] (pl **draftsmen**: BRIT **draughtsman**) n 製図工 sefzukō

drag [dræg] vt (bundle, person) 引きずる hikízurū; (river) さらう saráu
♦vi (time, a concert etc) 長く感じられる nágāku kañjirarerū
♦n (inf: bore) 退屈な人 taíkutsu na hitó; (women's clothing): **in drag** 女装して joáō shite

drag on vi (case, concert etc) だらだらと長引く darádara to nagábikū

dragon [dræg'ən] n 竜 ryū

dragonfly [dræg'ɔnflai] n トンボ tôñbo

drain [drein] n (in street) 排水口 haísuikō; (on resources, source of loss) 負担 fután
♦vt (land, marshes, pond) 干拓する kañtaku suru; (vegetables) ...の水切りをする ...no mizúkiri wō suru
♦vi (liquid) 流れる nagárerū

drainage [drein'idʒ] n (system) 排水 haísui; (process) 水はけ mizúhake

drainboard [drein'bɔːrd] (BRIT **draining board**) n 水切り板 mizúkiriban

drainpipe [drein'paip] n 排水管 haísuikan

drama [drɑm'ə] n (art) 演劇文学 geкíbuñgaku; (play) 劇 gekí, ドラマ dóráma; (excitement) ドラマ dóráma

dramatic [drəmæt'ik] adj (marked, sudden) 劇的な gekíteki na; (theatrical) 演劇の eñgeki no

dramatist [dræm'ətist] n 劇作家 gekísakka

dramatize [dræm'ətaiz] vt (events) 劇的に描写する gekíteki ni byōsha suru; (adapt: for TV, cinema) 脚色する kyakúshoku suru

drank [dræŋk] pt of **drink**

drape [dreip] vt (cloth, flag) 掛けるkakérū

drapes [dreips] (US) npl (curtains) カーテン kâten

drastic [dræs'tik] adj (measure) 思い切った omóikittá; (change) 抜本的な bappónteki na

draught [dræft] (BRIT) = **draft**

draughtboard [dræft'bɔːrd] (BRIT) = **checkerboard**

draughts [dræfts] (BRIT) = **checkers**

draughtsman [dræfts'mən] (BRIT) = **draftsman**

draw [drɔː] (pt **drew**, pp **drawn**) vt (ART, TECH) 描く kákū; (pull: cart) 引く hikú; (: curtain) 引く hikú, 閉じる tojírū, 開ける shimérū; (take out: gun, tooth) 抜く nukú; (attract: admiration, attention) 引く hikú, 引付ける hikítsukerū; (money) 引出す hikídasū; (wages) もらう moráū
♦vi (SPORT) 引分けになる hikíwake ni narū
♦n (SPORT) 引分け hikíwake; (lottery) 抽選 chūsen

to draw near (approach: person, event) 近付く chikázukū

drawback [drɔː'bæk] n 欠点 kettéñ

drawbridge [drɔː'bridʒ] n 跳ね橋 hanébashi

drawer [drɔː'ər] n (of desk etc) 引出し hikídashi

drawing [drɔː'iŋ] n (picture) 図 zu, スケッチ sukétchi; (skill, discipline) 製図 sefzu

drawing board n 製図板 sefzuban

drawing pin (BRIT) n 画びょう gábyō

drawing room n 居間 imá

drawl [drɔːl] n のろい話振り norói hanáshibūri

drawn [drɔːn] pp of **draw**

draw out vi (lengthen) 引延ばす hikínobasū
♦vt (money: from bank) 引出す hikídasū, 下ろす orósū

draw up vi (stop) 止まる tomárū
♦vt (document) 作成する sakúsei suru; (chair etc) 引寄せる hikítsukerū

dread [dred] n (great fear, anxiety) 恐怖 kyōfu
♦vt (fear) 恐れる osórerū

dreadful [dred'fəl] adj (weather, day, person etc) いやな iyá ná

dream [driːm] n (PSYCH, fantasy, ambition) 夢 yumé
♦vb (pt, pp **dreamed** or **dreamt**)

◆vt 夢に見る yumé ni mirù
◆vi 夢を見る yumé wo mirù

dreamer [dri:'mə:r] n 夢を見る人　yumé wo mirù hitò; (fig) 非現実的な人 higeñjitsuteki na hitò

dreamt [dremt] pt, pp of **dream**

dreamy [dri:'mi:] adj (expression, person) うっとりした uttórì shita; (music) 静かな shízùka na

dreary [dri:'ri:] adj (weather, talk, time) 陰気な iñki na

dredge [dredʒ] vt (river, harbor) しゅんせつする shufisetsu suru

dregs [dregz] npl (of drink) かす kásù, おり orí; (of humanity) くず kúzù

drench [drentʃ] vt (soak) びしょ濡れにする bishónure ni suru

dress [dres] n (frock) ドレス dórèsu; (no pl: clothing) 服装 fukúsō
◆vt (child) ...に服を着せる ...ni fukú wò kisérù; (wound) ...の手当をする ...no téàte wo suru
◆vi 服を着る fukú wò kirú
to get dressed 服を着る fukú wò kirú

dress circle (BRIT) n (THEATER) 2階席 nikáiseki

dresser [dres'ə:r] n (BRIT: cupboard) 食器戸棚 shokkítodàna; (US: chest of drawers) 整理だんす séridañsu

dressing [dres'iŋ] n (MED) 包帯 hōtai; (CULIN: for salad) ドレッシング dorésshiñgu

dressing gown (BRIT) n ガウン gáùn

dressing room n (THEATER) 楽屋 gakúya; (SPORT) 更衣室 kōíshitsu

dressing table n 鏡台 kyōdai

dressmaker [dres'meikə:r] n 洋裁師 yōsaishī, ドレスメーカー dorésumèkā

dress rehearsal n (THEATER) ドレスリハーサル dorésurihāsaru ◆衣装を着けて本番並に行う舞台げいこ íshō wo tsukéte hoñbannami ni okónaū butáigeīko

dress up vi (wear best clothes) 盛装する seísō suru; (in costume) 仮装する kasō suru

dressy [dres'i:] (inf) adj (smart: clothes) スマートな sumátò na

drew [dru:] pt of **draw**

dribble [drib'əl] vi (baby) よだれを垂らす yodáre wo tarásu
◆vt (ball) ドリブルする dórìburu suru

dried [draid] adj (fruit) 干した hóshìta, 干し... hoshí...; (eggs, milk) 粉末の fuñmatsu no

drier [drai'ə:r] n = **dryer**

drift [drift] n (of current etc) 方向 hōkō; (of snow) 吹きだまり fukídamarī; (meaning) 言わんとする事 iwán tò suru kotð, 意味 ímì
◆vi (boat) 漂流する hyōryū suru; (sand, snow) 吹寄せられる fukíyoseraserú

driftwood [drift'wud] n 流木 ryūboku

drill [dril] n (also: **drill bit**) ドリル先 dorírusaki, ドリル dórìru; (machine: for DIY, dentistry, mining etc) ドリル dórìru; (MIL) 教練 kyōren
◆vt (troops) 教練する kyōren suru
◆vi (for oil) ボーリングする bōríñgu suru

to drill a hole in something ドリルで...に穴を開ける dórìru de ...ni aná wò akérù

drink [driŋk] n (gen) 飲物 nomímono, ドリンク doríñku; (alcoholic drink) 酒 saké; (sip) 一口 hitókuchi
◆vb (pt **drank**, pp **drunk**)
◆vt 飲む nómù
◆vi 飲む nómù
to have a drink 1杯飲む íppaì nómù
a drink of water 水1杯 mizú íppaì

drinker [driŋk'ə:r] n (of alcohol) 酒飲み sakénomī

drinking water [driŋ'kiŋ-] n 飲料水 iñryōsui

drip [drip] n (dripping, noise) 滴り shitátari; (one drip) 滴 shizúku; (MED) 点滴 teñteki
◆vi (water, rain) 滴る shitátarù; (tap) ...から水が垂れる ...kara mizú gà tarérù

drip-dry [drip'drai] adj (shirt) ドリップドライの doríppudoraì no

dripping [drip'iŋ] n (CULIN) 肉汁 nikújū

drive [draiv] n (journey) ドライブ doráibu; (also: **driveway**) 車道 shadō ◆私有地内を通って公道とを結ぶ私道

指す shiyúchinaî wo tôtté kôdô tò íé nadô wo tsunágû shidô wo sásù; (energy) 精力 séîryoku; (campaign) 運動 uídô; (COMPUT: also: **disk drive**) ディスクドライブ dísûkudoraîbu

♦vb (pt **drove**, pp **driven**)

♦vt (car) 運転する uíten suru; (push: also TECH: motor etc) 動かす ugokásù; (nail): **to drive something into** ...を...に 打込む ...wo ...ni uchíkomù

♦vi (AUT: at controls) 運転する uíten suru; (travel) 車で行く kurúma de ikú

left-/right-hand drive 左(右)ハンドル hidári(migî)haôdoru

to drive someone mad ...をいらいらさせる ...wo îraîra saséru

drivel [driv'əl] (inf) n 与太話 yótàbanàshi

driven [driv'ən] pp of **drive**

driver [drai'vər] n (of own car) 運転者 uítensha; ドライバー doráîbà; (chauffeur) お抱え運転手o-kákae untensha; (of taxi, bus) 運転手 uítensha; (RAIL) 運転士 uítenshi

driver's license (US) n 運転免許証 uítenmenkyoshô

driveway [draiv'wei] n 車道 shadô ◇ 私有地内を通って公道と家などをつなぐ私道を指す shiyúchinaî wo tôtté kôdô tò íé nadô wo tsunágû shidô wo sásù

driving [drai'viŋ] n 運転 uíten

driving instructor n 運転指導者 uíntenshidôsha

driving lesson n 運転教習 uítenkyôshû

driving licence (BRIT) n 運転免許証 uítenmenkyoshô

driving mirror n バックミラー bakkúmirâ

driving school n 自動車教習所 jidôshakyôshûjo

driving test n 運転免許試験 uítenmenkyoshiken

drizzle [driz'əl] n 霧雨 kirísame

drone [droun] n (noise) ぶーんという音 bûń to iû otò; (male bee) 雄バチ osúbàchi

drool [dru:l] vi (dog etc) よだれを垂らす yodáre wo tarásù

droop [dru:p] vi (flower) しおれる shiôre-

rù; (of person: shoulders) 肩を落す kátà wo otósù; (: head) うつむく utsúmukù

drop [dra:p] n (of water) 滴水 shízûku; (lessening) 減少 geńshô; (fall) 落差 rákûsa

♦vt (allow to fall: object) 落す otósù; (voice) 潜める hisómerù; (eyes) 落す otósù; (reduce: price) 下げる sagérù; (set down from car) 降ろす orósù; (omit: name from list etc) 削除する sakújo suru

♦vi (object) 落ちる ochírù; (wind) 弱まる yowámarù

drop off vi (go to sleep) 眠る nemúru
♦vt (passenger) 降ろす orósù

drop out vi (withdraw) 脱退する dattái suru

drop-out [dra:p'aut] n (from society) 社会からの脱落者 shákaî kara no dasúrakusha; (SCOL) 学校からの中退者 gakkô kara nô chútaisha

dropper [dra:p'ər] n スポイト supóîto

droppings [dra:p'iŋz] npl (of bird, mouse) ふん fuń

drops [dra:ps] npl (MED: for eyes) 点眼剤 teńganzaî; (: for ears) 点耳薬 teńjiyáku

drought [draut] n かんばつ kañbatsu

drove [drouv] pt of **drive**

drown [draun] vt (kill: person, animal) 水死させる suíshi saserù; (fig: voice, noise) 聞えなくする kikóenakù suru, 消す kesú

♦vi (person, animal) おぼれ死ぬ obóreshinû

drowsy [drau'zi:] adj (sleepy) 眠い nemúi

drudgery [drʌdʒ'ə:ri:] n (uninteresting work) 骨折り仕事 honéorishigòto

drug [drʌg] n (MED) 薬剤 yakúzai, 薬 kusúri; (narcotic) 麻薬 mayáku

♦vt (sedate: person, animal) 薬で眠らせる kusúri dè nemúraserù

to be on drugs 麻薬を打って(飲んで)いる mayáku wò utté (nôñde)irù

hard/soft drugs 中毒性の強い(弱い) 麻薬 chúdokusei nò tsuyóî (yowáî) mayáku

drug addict n 麻薬常習者 mayákujoshûsha

druggist [drʌg'ist] (US) n (person) 薬剤
師 yakúzaishì, (store) 薬屋 kusúriya

drugstore [drʌg'stɔːr] (US) n ドラッグ
ストア dorággusutòa

drum [drʌm] n (MUS) 太鼓 taíko, ドラム
dóràmu; (for oil, petrol) ドラム缶 doràmu-
kukàn

drummer [drʌm'əːr] n ドラマー doráma

drums [drʌmz] npl ドラム dóràmu

drunk [drʌŋk] pp of **drink**
♦adj (with alcohol) 酔っ払った yoppárattà
♦n (also: **drunkard**) 酔っ払い yoppárai

drunken [drʌŋ'kən] adj (laughter, party)
酔っ払いの yoppárai no; (person) 酔っ払
った yoppárattà

dry [drai] adj (ground, climate, weather,
skin) 乾いた kawáita, 乾燥した kañsō
shita; (day) 雨の降らない àmè no furánaì;
(lake, riverbed) 干上がった higágattà;
(humor) 皮肉っぽい hiníkuppoì; (wine)
辛口の karákuchi no
♦vt (ground, clothes etc) 乾かす kawá-
kasù; (tears) ふく fukú
♦vi (paint etc) 乾く kawákù

dry-cleaner's [drai'kliː'nəːrz] n ドライ
クリーニング屋 doráikurīninguya

dry-cleaning [drai'kliː'niŋ] n ドライク
リーニング doráikurīningu

dryer [drai'əːr] n (also: **hair dryer**) ヘア
ドライヤー heádoraiyà, (for laundry) 乾
燥機 kañsōki; (US: spin-drier) 脱水機
dassúiki

dryness [drai'nis] n (of ground, climate,
weather, skin) 乾燥 kañsō

dry rot n 乾腐病 kañpubyò

dry up vi (river, well) 干上がる hiágarù

DSS [diː'eses'] (BRIT) n abbr (= Department of Social Security) の社会保障省 sha-
káihoshōshō

dual [duː'əl] adj 二重の nijū no

dual carriageway (BRIT) n 中央分離
帯のある道路 chūōburitai no árù dórò

dual nationality n 二重国籍 nijúkoku-
sèki

dual-purpose [duː'əlpəːr'pəs] adj 二重目
的の nijúmokutèki no

dubbed [dʌbd] adj (CINEMA) 吹き替え

の fukíkae no

dubious [duː'biːəs] adj (claim, reputation, company) いかがわしい ikágawa-
shìì; (person) 疑っている utágatte irù

Dublin [dʌb'lin] n ダブリン dábùrin

duchess [dʌtʃ'is] n 公爵夫人 kóshakufujìn

duck [dʌk] n (ZOOL, CULIN: domestic
bird) アヒル ahíru; (wild bird) カモ kámò
♦vi (also: **duck down**) かがむ kagámù

duckling [dʌk'liŋ] n (ZOOL, CULIN:
domestic bird) アヒルの子 ahíru no kò;
(: wild bird) カモの子 kámò no ko

duct [dʌkt] n (ELEC, TECH) ダクト dá-
kùto; (ANAT) 管 kàn

dud [dʌd] n (bomb, shell etc) 不発弾 fuhá-
tsudàn; (object, tool etc) 欠陥品 kekkáñ-
hin
♦adj: **dud cheque** (BRIT) 不渡り小切手
fuwátarikogìtte

due [duː] adj (expected: meeting, publication, arrival) 予定した yotéi shita; (owed:
money) 払われるべき haráwarerubekì;
(proper: attention, consideration) 当然の
tōzen no
♦n: **to give someone his (or her) due**
...に当然の物を与える ...ni tōzen no monò wo atáerù
♦adv: **due north** 真北に ma-kíta ni
in due course (when the time is right)
時が来たら tokí ga kitárà; (eventually)
やがて yagáte

due to (owing to) ...が原因で ...ga geñ-in
de
to be due to do ...する事になっている
...surú koto ni natté irù

duel [duː'əl] n (also: **fig**) 決闘 kettō

dues [duːz] npl (for club, union) 会費 kái-
hi; (in harbor) 入港料 nyūkōryò

duet [duː'et'] n (MUS) 二重唱 nijūshō, デ
ュエット dúètto

duffel bag [dʌf'əl-] n 合切袋 gassáibukùro

duffel coat [dʌf'əl-] n ダッフルコート
daffúrukòto ◇丈夫なフード付き防寒コ
ート jōbu nà fūdotsuki bōkan kōto

dug [dʌg] pt, pp of **dig**

duke [duːk] n 公爵 kóshaku

dull [dʌl] adj (weak: light) 暗い kuráì;

(intelligence, wit) 鈍い nibúi; (boring: event) 退屈な taíkutsu na; (sound, pain) 鈍い nibúi; (gloomy: weather, day) 陰気な ínki na

♦vt (pain, grief) 和らげる yawárageru; (mind, senses) 鈍くする nibúku suru

duly [du:'li:] adv (properly) 正しく seftō ni; (on time) 予定通りに yotéidōri ni

dumb [dʌm] adj (mute, silent) 話せない hanásenai; (pej: stupid) ばかな báka na

dumbfounded [dʌmfaund'id] adj あ然とした azén tō shita

dummy [dʌm'i:] n (tailor's model) 人台 jindai; (TECH, COMM: mock-up) 模型 mokéi; (BRIT: for baby) おしゃぶり o-shábùri

♦adj (bullet) 模擬の mógi no; (firm) ダミーの dámì no

dump [dʌmp] n (also: **rubbish dump**) ごみ捨て場 gomísuteba; (inf: place) いやな場所 iyá na basho

♦vt (put down) 落す otósu; (get rid of) 捨てる sutéru; (COMPUT: data) 打ち出す uchídasù, ダンプする dáñpu suru

dumpling [dʌmp'liŋ] n (CULIN: with meat etc) 団子 dañgo

dumpy [dʌmp'i:] adj (person) ずんぐりした zuñgurì shita

dunce [dʌns] n (SCOL) 劣等生 rettósei

dune [du:n] n (in desert, on beach) 砂丘 sakyū

dung [dʌŋ] n (AGR, ZOOL) ふん fúñ

dungarees [dʌŋgəri:z'] npl オーバーオール ōbāòru

dungeon [dʌn'dʒən] n 地下ろう chikárō

duo [du:'ou] n (gen, MUS) ペア péà

dupe [du:p] n (victim) かも kámð

♦vt (trick) だます damásu

duplex [du:'pleks] (US) n (house) 2世帯用住宅 nisétaiyōjūtaku; (apartment) 複層式アパート fukúsōshikiapāto

duplicate [n du:'plikit vb du:'plikeit] n (of document, key etc) 複製 fukúsei

♦vt (copy) 複製する fukúsei suru; (photocopy) ...のコピーを取る ...no kópī wo tóru, ...を コピーする ...wo kópī suru; (repeat) 再現する saígen suru

in duplicate 2部で nibú de

duplicity [du:plis'əti:] n (deceit) いかさま ikásama

durable [du:r'əbəl] adj (goods, materials) 丈夫な jóbu na

duration [durei'ʃən] n (of process, event) 継続期間 keízokukikàn

duress [dures'] n: **under duress** (moral, physical) 強迫 kyóhaku

during [du:'riŋ] prep ...の間に ...no aída ni

dusk [dʌsk] n 夕暮 yūgure

dust [dʌst] n ほこり hokóri

♦vt (furniture) ...のほこりを拭く ...no hokóri wo fukú; (cake etc): **to dust with** ...に...を振掛ける ...ni ...wo furíkakerù

dustbin [dʌst'bin] (BRIT) n ごみ箱 gomíbako

duster [dʌs'tə:r] n (cloth) 雑きん zókin

dustman [dʌst'mæn] (BRIT pl **dustmen**) n ごみ収集人 gomíshūshùnin

dusty [dʌs'ti:] adj (road) ほこりっぽい hokóríppoì; (furniture) ほこりだらけの hokóridaràke no

Dutch [dʌtʃ] adj オランダの oráñda no; (LING) オランダ語の oráñdago no

♦n (LING) オランダ語 oráñdago

♦npl: **the Dutch** オランダ人 oráñdajin

to go Dutch (inf) 割勘にする waríkan ni suru

Dutchman/woman [dʌtʃ'mən/wumən] (pl **Dutchmen/Dutchwomen**) n オランダ人男性(女性) oráñdajin dañsei (joséi)

dutiful [du:'tifəl] adj (son, daughter) 従順な jújun na

duty [du:'ti:] n (responsibility) 義務 gímù; (tax) 税金 zeíkin

on/off duty (policeman, nurse) 当番(非番)で tóban(híban)de

duty-free [du:'ti:fri:'] adj (drink, cigarettes) 免税の meñzei no

duvet [du:'vei] (BRIT) n 掛布団 kakébutòn

dwarf [dwɔ:rf] (pl **dwarves**) n (person) 小人 kobíto; (animal, plant) わい小種 wafshōshu

♦vt 小さく見せる chíisaku misérù

dwarves [dwɔ:rvz] npl of **dwarf**

dwell [dwel] (pt, pp **dwelt**) vi (reside,

stay) 住む súmù

dwelling [dwel'iŋ] n (house) 住居 júkyò

dwell on vt fus (brood on) 長々と考える nagánaga to kañgaerù

dwelt [dwelt] pt, pp of **dwell**

dwindle [dwin'dəl] vi (interest, attendance) 減る hérù

dye [dai] n (for hair, cloth) 染料 señryò
◆vt 染める somérù

dying [dai'iŋ] adj (person, animal) 死に掛っている shiñkakatte irù

dyke [daik] (BRIT) n (wall) 堤防 teíbò

dynamic [dainæm'ik] adj (leader, force) 力強い chikárazuyoì

dynamite [dai'nəmait] n ダイナマイト daínamaîto

dynamo [dai'nəmou] n (ELEC) 発電機 hatsúdeñki, ダイナモ daínamo

dynasty [dai'nəsti:] n (family, period) 王朝 ōchō

dyslexia [dislek'si:ə] n 読書障害 dokúshoshogai

E

E [i:] n (MUS: note) ホ音 hō-oñ, (: key) ホ調 hōchō

each [i:tʃ] adj (thing, person, idea etc) それぞれの sorézòre no
◆pron (each one) それぞれ sorézòre

each other 互いを(に) tagái wò (nì)
they hate each other 彼らは互いに憎み合っている kárèra wa tagái nì nikúmiatte irù

they have 2 books each 彼らはそれぞれ2冊の本を持っている kárèra wa soréezòre nísàtsu no hóñ wo mottè irù

eager [i:'gər] adj (keen) 熱心な nesshín na

to be eager to do something 一生懸命に...しょうとしている isshôkeñmei ni ... wo shitágattè irù

to be eager for とても...をほしがっている tótemo ...wo hoshígattè irù

eagle [i:'gəl] n ワシ washí

ear [i:r] n (ANAT) 耳 mimí; (of corn) 穂 hó

earache [i:r'eik] n 耳の痛み mimí nò itámi

eardrum [i:r'dram] n 鼓膜 komáku

earl [ərl] (BRIT) n 伯爵 hakúshaku

earlier [ər'li:r] adj (date, time, edition etc) 前の mâe no
◆adv (leave, go etc) もっと早く móttð háyàku

early [ər'li:] adv (in day, month etc) 早く háyàku; (ahead of time) 早めに hayáme ni
◆adj (near the beginning: work, hours) 早期の sốchò no; (Christians, settlers) 初期の shồkì no; (sooner than expected: departure) 早めの hayáme no; (quick: reply) 早期の sốkì no

an early death 早死に hayájinì

to have an early night 早めに寝る hayáme nì nérù

in the early/early in the spring 春先に harúsaki ni

in the early/early in the 19th century 19世紀の初めに júkyúseíki no hajíme ni

early retirement n 早めの引退 hayáme nò íñtai

earmark [i:r'mɑrk] vt: **to earmark (for)** (...に) 当てる (...ni) atérù

earn [ərn] vt (salary etc) 稼ぐ kaségù; (COMM: interest) 生む umú; (praise) 受ける ukérù

earnest [ər'nist] adj (wish, desire) 心からの kokórò kara no; (person, manner) 真剣な shiñken na

in earnest 真剣に shiñken ni

earnings [ər'niŋz] npl (personal) 収入 shúnyù; (of company etc) 収益 shồeki

earphones [i:r'founz] npl イヤホーン iyáhòn

earring [i:r'riŋ] n イヤリング iyáriñgu

earshot [i:r'ʃɑt] n: **within earshot** 聞える範囲に kikóerù hâñ-i ni

earth [ərθ] n (planet) 地球 chíkyù; (land surface) 地面 jímèn; (soil) 土 tsuchí; (BRIT: ELEC) アース ásu
◆vt (BRIT: ELEC) アースに落す ásu ni otósu

earthenware [ər'θənwer] n 土器 dókì

earthquake [əːrˈθˈkweik] *n* 地震 jishín

earthy [əːrˈθiː] *adj* (*fig*: humor: vulgar) 下品な gehín na

ease [iːz] *n* (easiness) 容易さ yốisa; (comfort) 楽な rakú
♦*vt* (lessen: problem, pain) 和らげる yawárageru; (: tension) 緩和する kańwa suru

to ease something in/out ゆっくりと ...を入れる[出す] yukkúri to ...wo irérù [dásù]

at ease! (MIL) 休め! yasúme!

easel [iːˈzəl] *n* 画架 gáka, イーゼル ízeru

ease off *vi* (lessen: wind) 弱まる yowámaru; (: rain) 小降りになる kobúri ni narù; (slow down) スピードを落す supído wo otósù

ease up *vi* = **ease off**

easily [iːˈzili] *adv* (with ease) 容易に yối ni; (in comfort) 楽に rakú ni

east [iːst] *n* (direction) 東 higáshi; (of country, town) 東部 tốbu
♦*adj* (region) 東の higáshi no; (wind) 東からの higáshi karà no
♦*adv* 東に[へ] higáshi ni [e]

the East (Orient) 東洋 tốyō; (POL) 東欧 tốō, 東ヨーロッパ higáshi yōróppa

Easter [iːsˈtəːr] *n* 復活祭 fukkátsusài, イースター ísutā

Easter egg *n* イースターエッグ ísutāeggù ◇復活祭の飾り、プレゼントなどに使う色や模様を施したゆで卵 fukkátsusài no kazári, purézènto nádò ni tsukáu irò ya moyố wo nuttá yudétamàgo

easterly [iːsˈtəːrli] *adj* (to the east: direction, point) 東への higáshi e nò; (from the east: wind) 東からの higáshi karà nò

eastern [iːsˈtəːrn] *adj* (GEO) 東の higáshi no; (oriental) 東洋の tốyō no; (communist) 東欧の tốō no, 東ヨーロッパの higáshi yōróppa no

East Germany *n* 東ドイツ higáshi dóïtsu

eastward(s) [iːstˈwəːrd(z)] *adv* 東へ higáshi e

easy [iːˈziː] *adj* (simple) 簡単な kańtan na; (relaxed) 寛いだ kutsúroìda; (com-

fortable) 楽な rakú na; (victim) だまされやすい damásareyasuì; (prey) 捕まりやすい tsukámariyasuì
♦*adv*: *to take it/things easy* (go slowly) 気楽にやる kiráku ni yarù; (not worry) 心配しない shiñpai shinaì; (rest) 休む yasúmù

easy chair *n* 安楽いす añrakuisù

easy-going [iːˈziːgouˈiŋ] *adj* 穏やかな o-dáyàka na

eat [iːt] (*pt* **ate**, *pp* **eaten**) *vt* (breakfast, lunch, food etc) 食べる tabérù
♦*vi* 食べる tabérù

eat away *vt fus* = **eat into**

eat into *vt fus* (metal) 腐食する fushóku suru; (savings) ...に食込む ...ni kufkomù

eau de Cologne [ouˈ də kəlouˈ] *n* オーデコロン ốdekoròn

eaves [iːvz] *npl* (of house) 軒 nokí

eavesdrop [iːvzˈdrɑːp] *vi*: *to eavesdrop (on)* (person, conversation) (...を) 盗み聞きする (...wo) nusúmigiki suru

ebb [eb] *n* (of sea, tide) 引く事 hikú kotò
♦*vi* (tide, sea) 引く hikú; (*fig*: also: **ebb away**: strength, feeling) 段々なくなる dañdan nakúnaru

ebony [ebˈəniː] *n* (wood) 黒たん kokútan

EC [iːˈsiː] *n abbr* (= *European Community*) 欧州共同体 ốshū kyốdōtai

eccentric [iksenˈtrik] *adj* (choice, views) 風変りな fúgawàri na
♦*n* (person) 変り者 kawárimono

ecclesiastical [ikliːziːæsˈtikəl] *adj* 教会の kyốkai no

echo [ekˈou] (*pl* **echoes**) *n* (of noise) こだま kodáma, 反響 hańkyō
♦*vt* (repeat) 繰返す kurfkaesù
♦*vi* (sound) 反響する hańkyō suru; (place) ...で鳴り響く ...de narfhibikù

echoes [ekˈouz] *npl* (of) see **echo**

éclair [iklerˈ] *n* (cake) エクレア ékurea

eclipse [iklipsˈ] *n* (*also*: **eclipse of the sun**) 日食 nisshóku; (*also*: **eclipse of the moon**) 月食 gesshóku

ecology [ikɑːˈlədʒiː] *n* (environment) 環境 kañkyō, エコロジー ekốrojì; (SCOL) 生態学 seítaigaku

economic [iːkənɑːmˈik] *adj* (system, history) 経済の kefzai no; (*BRIT*: profitable: business etc) もうかる mókarū

economical [iːkəˈnɔmɪkəl] *adj* (system, car, machine) 経済的な kefzaiteki na; (person) 倹約な keñ-yaku na

economics [iːkəˈnɔmɪks] *n* (SCOL) 経済学 kefzaigāku
♦*npl* (of project, situation) 経済問題 kefzaimoñdai

economist [iˈkɔnəmist] *n* 経済学者 kefzaigakūsha

economize [iˈkɔnəmaiz] *vi* (make savings) 節約する setsúyaku suru

economy [iˈkɔnəmi] *n* (of country) 経済 kefzai; (financial prudence) 節約 setsúyaku

economy class *n* (AVIAT) エコノミークラス ekónomīkūrasu

economy size *n* (COMM) お買い得サイズ o-káidoku saîzu

ecstasy [ˈekstəsi] *n* (rapture) 狂喜 kyóki, エクスタシー ekúsutashī

ecstatic [ekˈstætik] *adj* (welcome, reaction) 熱烈な netsúretsu na; (person) 無我夢中になった múgamuchū ni nattá

ecumenical [ekjuˈmenikəl] *adj* 超宗派の chōshūha no

eczema [ˈeksmə] *n* (MED) 湿しん shisshín

edge [edʒ] *n* (border: of lake, table, chair etc) 縁 fuchí; (of knife etc) 刃 há
♦*vt* (trim) 縁取りする fuchídori suru
on edge (*fig*) = edgy
to edge away from じりじり...から離れる jírijiri ...kara hanárerū

edgeways [ˈedʒˈweiz] *adv*: **he couldn't get a word in edgeways** 何一つ発言出来なかった nanihitōtsu hatsúgen dekinakattá

edgy [ˈedʒiː] *adj* (nervous, agitated) いらいらした íraira shita

edible [ˈedəbl] *adj* (mushroom, plant etc) 食用の shokúyō no

edict [ˈiːdikt] *n* (order) 政令 sefrei

edifice [ˈedəfis] *n* (building, structure) 大建造物 daíkenzōbūtsu

Edinburgh [ˈedʲnbərə] *n* エジンバラ ejínbara

edit [ˈedit] *vt* (text, report) 校正する kōsei suru; (book, film, newspaper etc) 編集する hefishū suru

edition [idiˈʃən] *n* (of book) 版 háñ; (of newspaper, magazine) 号 gō; (TV, RADIO) 回 kái

editor [ˈeditər] *n* (of newspaper) 編集局長 hefishūkyokúchō, デスク désūku; (of magazine) 編集長 hefishūchō; (of column: foreign/political editor) 編集主任 hefishūshunin; (of book) 編集者 hefishūsha

editorial [editɔːˈriəl] *adj* (staff, policy, control) 編集の hefishū no
♦*n* (of newspaper) 社説 shasétsu

educate [ˈedʒukeit] *vt* (teach) 教育する kyóiku suru; (instruct) ...に教える ...ni oshíerū

education [edʒuˈkeiʃən] *n* (schooling, teaching) 教育 kyóiku; (knowledge, culture) 教養 kyóyō

educational [edʒuˈkeiʃənəl] *adj* (institution, policy etc) 教育の kyóiku no; (experience, toy etc) 教育的な kyóikuteki na

EEC [iːiːsiː] *n abbr* (= *European Economic Community*) 欧州経済共同体 ō-shūkeizaikyódōtai

eel [iːl] *n* ウナギ unági

eerie [ˈiːri] *adj* (strange, mysterious) 不気味な bukími na

effect [iˈfekt] *n* (result, consequence) 結果 kekká; (impression: of speech, picture etc) 効果 kōka
♦*vt* (repairs) 行う okónau; (savings etc) ...に成功する ...ni seíkō suru
to take effect (law) 実施される jisshí sarerū; (drug) 効き始める kikíhajimerū
in effect 実は jítsu wa, 事実上 jíjitsujō

effective [iˈfektiv] *adj* (successful) 効果的な kōkateki na; (actual: leader, command) 実際の jissái no

effectively [iˈfektivliː] *adv* (successfully) 効果的に kōkateki ni; (in reality) 実際には jissái ni wa

effectiveness [iˈfektivnis] *n* (success) 有効性 yūkōsei

effeminate [iˈfemɪnit] *adj* (boy, man) 女々しい meméshiī

effervescent [efərvesˈənt] *adj* (drink) 炭酸ガス入りの tansangasuirˈ no

efficacy [efˈikəsi:] *n* (effectiveness) 有効性 yūkˈosei

efficiency [ifiʃˈənsi:] *n* (of person, organization) 能率 nˈoritsu; (of machine) 効率 kˈoritsu

efficient [ifiʃˈənt] *adj* (person, organization) 能率的な nˈoritsuteki na; (machine) 効率の良い kˈoritsu no yoˈi

effigy [efˈidʒi:] *n* (image) 像 zō

effort [efˈərt] *n* (endeavor) 努力 dˈoryoku; (determined attempt) 試み kokˈoromi, 企て kuwˈadate; (physical/mental exertion) 苦労 kurˈō

effortless [efˈərtlis] *adj* (achievement) 楽な rakˈu nà; (style) ごく自然な gokˈu shizen na

effrontery [ifrʌnˈtæri:] *n* (cheek, nerve) ずうずうしさ zūzūshisà

effusive [ifjuːˈsiv] *adj* (handshake, welcome) 熱烈な netsˈuretsu na

e.g. [iːdʒiː] *adv abbr* (= *exempli gratia*) 例えば tatˈoeba

egg [eg] *n* 卵 tamˈagó
hard-boiled/soft-boiled egg 堅ゆで(半熟)卵 katˈayude(hanjˈuku)tamˈagó

eggcup [egˈkʌp] *n* エッグカップ eggˈukappú

egg on *vt* (in fight etc) そそのかす sosˈonokasu

eggplant [egˈplænt] (*esp US*) *n* (aubergine) ナス nasˈu

eggshell [egˈʃel] *n* 卵の殻 tamˈagó no karˈá

ego [iːˈgou] *n* (self-esteem) 自尊心 jisonˈshin

egotism [iːˈgətizəm] *n* 利己主義 rikˈoshugí

egotist [iːˈgətist] *n* 利己主義者 rikˈoshugishà, エゴイスト egˈoisuto

Egypt [iːˈdʒipt] *n* エジプト ejˈiputo

Egyptian [idʒipˈʃən] *adj* エジプトの ejˈiputo no
♦*n* エジプト人 ejˈiputojìn

eiderdown [aiˈdərdaun] *n* (quilt) 羽布団 hanebˈutòn

eight [eit] *num* 八 (の) hachˈi(no), 八つ

(の) yattsˈu no

eighteen [eiˈtiːn] *num* 十八 (の) jūhˈachi (no)

eighth [eitθ] *num* 第八の dˈaihachi no

eighty [eiˈti:] *num* 八十 (の) hachˈijū(no)

Eire [eˈrə] *n* アイルランド aˈiruraǹdo

either [iːˈðər] *adj* (one or other) どちらかの dˈochiraka no; (both, each) 両方の ryˈohō no
♦*pron*: **either (of them)** どちらも…よ dˈochìra mo …nai
♦*adv* …も…ない …nìo …nài
♦*conj*: **either yes or no** はいかいいえかhˈai ka ifè kà
on either side 両側に ryˈogawa ni
I don't like either どちらも好きじゃない dˈochìra mo sukˈi ja naì
no, I don't either いいえ、私もしないifè, watˈakushi mò shinˈai

eject [idʒekˈt] *vt* (object) 放出する hˈoshutsu suru; (tenant) 立ちのかせる tachˈinokaserù; (gatecrasher etc) 追出す oˈidasù

eke [iːk]: **to eke out** *vt* (make last) 間に合せる mà nf awˈaserù

elaborate [*n* ilæbˈərit *vb* ilæbˈəreit] *adj* (complex: network, plan, ritual) 複雑な fukˈuzatsu na
♦*vt* (expand) 拡張する kakˈuchō surù; (refine) 洗練する sefˈren suru
♦*vi*: **to elaborate (on)** (idea, plan etc) (…を) 詳しく説明する (…wo) kuwˈashikù setsˈumei suru

elapse [ilæpˈs] *vi* (time) 過ぎる sugˈirù

elastic [ilæsˈtik] *n* (material) ゴムひも gomˈuhimo
♦*adj* (stretchy) 弾力性のある danˈryoku sei no arˈu; (adaptable) 融通の利く yūzˈu no kikˈu

elastic band (*BRIT*) *n* 輪ゴム wagˈomu

elated [ileiˈtid] *adj*: **to be elated** 大喜びになっている ˈoyorˈokobi ni natté irù

elation [ileiˈʃən] *n* (happiness, excitement) 大喜び ˈoyorˈokobi

elbow [elˈbou] *n* (ANAT: *also* of sleeve) ひじ hijˈí

elder [elˈdər] *adj* (brother, sister etc) 年上の toshˈue no

♦n (tree) ニワトコ niwátoko; (older person: *gen pl*) 年上の人々 toshíue no hito-bíto

elderly [el'də:rli:] *adj* (old) 年寄の toshíyorī no

♦npl: the elderly 老人 rōjin

eldest [el'dist] *adj* 最年長の saínenchō no

♦n 最年長の人 saínenchō no hitó

the eldest child/son/daughter 長子 〔長男, 長女〕 chōshí(chōnàn, chōjò)

elect [ilekt'] *vt* (government, representative, spokesman etc) 選出する seshútsu suru

♦adj: the president elect 次期大統領 jíkídaftōryō ♦当選したものだが, まだ就任していない人について言う tōsen shita mono nò, mádà shúnin shite inaì hitó nì tsúíte iú

to elect to do (choose) ...する事にする ...surú kotò ni suru

election [ilek'ʃən] *n* (voting) 選挙 sénkyo; (installation) 当選 tōsen

electioneering [ilekʃəni:'riŋ] *n* (campaigning) 選挙運動 senkyoundō

elector [ilek'tə:r] *n* (voter) 有権者 yúkensha

electoral [ilek'tə:rəl] *adj* (register, roll) 有権者の yúkensha no

electorate [ilek'tə:rit] *n* (of constituency, country) 有権者 yúkensha ◇総称 sōshō

electric [ilek'trik] *adj* (machine, current, power) 電気の dénki no

electrical [ilek'trikəl] *adj* (appliance, system, energy) 電気の dénki no

electric blanket *n* 電気毛布 deńkimōfu

electric chair (US) *n* 電気いす deńkiisū

electric fire (*BRIT*) *n* 電気ヒーター deńkihītā

electrician [ilektriʃ'ən] *n* 電気屋 deńkiyà

electricity [ilektris'əti;] *n* 電気 dénki

electrify [ilek'trəfai] *vt* (fence) 帯電させる taíden saserù; (rail network) 電化する deńka suru; (audience) ぎょっとさせる gyóttó saserù

electrocute [ilek'trəkju:t] *vt* 感電死させる kańdeńshi saserù

electrode [ilek'troud] *n* 電極 deńkyoku

electron [ilek'trɑːn] *n* (PHYSICS) 電子 denshi

electronic [ilektrɑːn'ik] *adj* (device, equipment) 電子の deńshi no

electronic mail *n* 電子郵便 deńshiyūbin

electronics [ilektrɑːn'iks] *n* (industry, technology) 電子工学 deńshikōgaku

elegance [el'əgəns] *n* (of person, building) 優雅さ yūgàsa, エレガンス êregànsu; (of idea, plan) 見事さ migotosà

elegant [el'əgənt] *adj* (person, building) 優雅な yūga na; (idea, plan) 洗練された seńren saretà

element [el'əmənt] *n* (part of whole, job, process) 要素 yōso; (CHEM) 元素 geńso; (of heater, kettle etc) ヒーター素子 hītāsoshi

elementary [elimen'tə:ri:] *adj* (basic) 基本的な kihónteki na; (primitive) 原始的な geńshiteki na; (school, education) 初等の shotō no

elephant [el'əfənt] *n* ゾウ zō

elevation [eləvei'ʃən] *n* (raising, promotion) 向上 kōjō; (height) 海抜 kaíbatsu

elevator [el'əveitə:r] *n* (*US*: lift) エレベーター erébètā

eleven [ilev'ən] *num* 十一 (の) júichi no

elevenses [ilev'ənziz] (*BRIT*) *npl* (coffee-break) 午前のおやつ gózèn no o-yátsu

eleventh [ilev'ənθ] *num* 第十一の dáíjūichi no

elf [elf] (*pl* **elves**) *n* 小妖精 shōyōsei

elicit [ilis'it] *vt: to elicit (from)** (information, response, reaction) (...から) ...を引出す (...karà) ...wò hikídasù

eligible [el'idʒəbəl] *adj* (qualified, suitable) 資格のある shikáku no arù; (man, woman) 好ましい結婚相手である konómashiì kekkón aìte de árù

to be eligible for something (qualified, suitable) ...する資格がある ...suru shikáku ga arù

eliminate [ilim'əneit] *vt* (eradicate: poverty, smoking) 無くす nakúsù; (candidate, team, contestant) 除外する jogái suru

elimination [əlimənei'ʃən] *n* (eradication) 根絶 konzetsu; (of candidate, team etc) 除外する jogái

élite [ɪlit'] *n* エリート erítò

elm [elm] *n* (tree) ニレ niré; (wood) ニレ 材 nirézai

elocution [eləkju:'ʃən] *n* 話術 wájùtsu

elongated [ilɔːŋ'geitid] *adj* (body, shadow) 細長い hosónagaì

elope [iloup'] *vi* 駆落ちする kakéochi suru

elopement [iloup'mənt] *n* 駆落ち kakéochi

eloquence [el'akwəns] *n* (of person, description, speech) 雄弁 yúben

eloquent [el'akwənt] *adj* (person, description, speech) 雄弁な yúben na

else [els] *adv* (other) 外に hoká nì

something else 外の物 hoká nò monð

somewhere else 外の場所 hoká ni ba-shð

everywhere else 外はどこも hoká wà dókò mo

where else? 外にどこ? hoká nì dókò?

there was little else to do 外にする事 はなかった hoká nì suru kotò wa nákàt-ta

nobody else spoke 外にだれもしゃべら なかった hoká nì daré mò shabéranakàtta

elsewhere [els'we:r] *adv* (be) 外の所に hoká nò tokorð ni; (go) 外の所へ hoká no tokorð e

elucidate [ilu:'sideit] *vt* (argument, point) 解明する kaímei suru

elude [iluːd'] *vt* (subj: fact, idea: not realized) 気付かれない kizúkarenaì; (: : not remembered) 思い出せない omóídasenaì; (: not understood) 理解されない rikáì sarénai; (captor) ...から逃げる ...kara ni-gérù; (capture) 免れる manúgarerù

elusive [ilu:'siv] *adj* (person, animal) 見付けにくい mitsúkenikuì; (quality) 分か りにくい wakárinikuì

elves [elvz] *npl* of elf

emaciated [imei'ʃieitid] *adj* (person, animal) 衰弱した suíjaku shita

emanate [em'əneit] *vi: to emanate from* (idea, feeling) ...から放たれる ...ka-

ra hanatárerù; (sound) ...から聞こえる ...kara kikóerù; (light) ...から放射される ...kara hōsha sarerù

emancipate [imæn'səpeit] *vt* (poor, slave, women) 解放する kaíhō suru

emancipation [imænsəpei'ʃən] *n* (of poor, slaves, women) 解放 kaíhō

embankment [embæŋk'mənt] *n* (of road, railway) 土手 doté; (of river) 堤防 teibō

embargo [embɑːr'gou] (*pl* **embargoes**) *n* (POL, COMM) 通商停止 tsúshōteishi

embark [embɑːrk'] *vi* (NAUT): *to embark on* (...に) 乗船する (...ni) jōsen suru

♦*vt* (passengers, cargo) 乗せる nosérù

to embark on (journey) ...に出発する ...ni shuppátsu suru; (task, course of action) ...に乗出す ...ni noridàsu

embarkation [embɑːrkei'ʃən] *n* (of people) 乗船 jōsen; (of cargo) 船積み funázumi

embarrass [embær'əs] *vt* (emotionally) 恥をかかせる hají wò kakáserù; (politician, government) 困らせる komáraserù

embarrassed [embær'əst] *adj* (laugh, silence) 極り悪そうな kimáriwarusō na

embarrassing [embær'əsin] *adj* (statement, situation, moment) 恥ずかしい ha-zúkashiî

embarrassment [embær'əsmənt] *n* (shame) 恥 hají; (embarrassing problem) 厄介な問題 yákkaì na mofidai

embassy [em'bəsi:] *n* (diplomats) 使節団 shisétsudàn; (building) 大使館 taíshikàn

embedded [embed'id] *adj* (object) 埋め込 まれた umékomaretà

embellish [embel'iʃ] *vt* (place, dress) 飾 る kazárù; (account) 潤色する jufishoku suru

embers [em'bə:rz] *npl: the embers (of the fire)* 残り火 nokóribì

embezzle [embez'əl] *vt* (LAW) 横領する ōryō suru

embezzlement [embez'əlmənt] *n* 横領 ōryō

embitter [embit'əːr] *vt* (fig: sour) 世の中 を憎ませる yo nō nàka wo nikúmaserù

emblem [em'bləm] n (design) 標章 hyṓshō、マーク mấku; (symbol) 象徴 shṓchō

embody [embɔd'i:] vt (idea, principle) 現す aráwasù; (features: include, contain) 含む fukúmù

embossed [embɔst'] adj (design, word) 浮き出しの ukídashi no

embrace [embreis'] vt (hug) 抱く dakú; (include) 含む fukúmù
◆vi (hug) 抱合う dakíaù
◆n (hug) 抱擁 hōyō

embroider [embrɔi'də:r] vt (cloth) 刺しゅうする shishū suru

embroidery [embrɔi'də:ri:] n 刺しゅう shishū

embryo [em'bri:ou] n (BIO) はい haí

emerald [em'ə:rald] n エメラルド émérarùdo

emerge [imə:rdʒ'] vi: **to emerge (from)** (...から) 出て来る (...kara) détè kurú; (fact: from situation etc) (...で) 明らかになる (...de) akíràka ni narú; (new idea, industry, society) 現れる aráwarerù

to emerge from sleep 目が覚める mé gà samérù

to emerge from prison 釈放される shakúhō sarerù

emergency [imə:r'dʒənsi:] n (crisis) 非常時 hijṓjì

in an emergency 緊急の場合 kiñkyū no baái

state of emergency 緊急事態 kiñkyūjìtai

emergency cord (US) n 非常の際に引くコード hijō no saí ni hikú kōdo

emergency exit n 非常口 hijṓgùchi

emergency landing n (AVIAT) 不時着 陸 fujíchakurìku

emergency services npl (fire, police, ambulance) 非常時のサービス機関 hijōji no sábisukìkan

emergent [imə:r'dʒənt] adj (nation) 最近 独立した saíkin dokúritsu shità; (group) 最近創立された saíkin sṓritsu sareta

emery board n [em'ə:ri:-] n つめやすり tsumêyasùri ◇ボール紙製の物を指す bṓrugamisei no monò wo sásù

emigrant [em'əgrənt] n (from native country) 移住者 ijū́shà

emigrate [em'əgreit] vi (from native country) 移住する ijū́ suru

emigration [eməgrei'ʃən] n 移住 ijū́

eminent [em'ənənt] adj (scientist, writer) 著名な choméi na

emission [imiʃ'ən] n (of gas) 放出 hṓshutsu; (of radiation) 放射 hṓsha

emit [imit'] vt (smoke, smell, sound) 出す dásù; (light, heat) 放射する hṓsha suru

emotion [imou'ʃən] n 感情 kañjō

emotional [imou'ʃənəl] adj (needs, exhaustion, person, issue etc) 感情的な kañjōteki na; (scene etc) 感動的な kañdōteki na

emotive [imou'tiv] adj (subject, language) 感情に訴える kañjō ni uttáerù

emperor [em'pə:rə:r] n (gen) 皇帝 kōtei; (of Japan) 天皇 teñnō

emphases [em'fəsiz] npl of **emphasis**

emphasis [em'fəsis] (pl **emphases**) n (importance) 重点 jūten; (stress) 強調 kyṓchō

emphasize [em'fəsaiz] vt (word, point) 強調する kyṓchō suru; (feature) 浮彫にする ukíbori ni surù

emphatic [æmfæt'ik] adj (statement, denial, manner, person) 断固とした dáñko to shita

emphatically [æmfæt'ikli:] adv (forcefully) 断固として dáñko to shité; (certainly) 絶対に zéttái ni

empire [em'paiə:r] n (also fig) 帝国 tefkoku

empirical [empir'ikəl] adj (knowledge, study) 経験的な keśkeñteki na

employ [emplɔi'] vt (workforce, person) 雇う yatóù; (tool, weapon) 使用する shiyō suru

employee [emplɔi:'] n 雇用人 koyṓnìn

employer [emplɔi'ə:r] n 雇い主 yatóìnùshi

employment [emplɔi'mənt] n (work) 就職 shū́shoku

employment agency n 就職あっ旋会社 shūshokuassegaìsha

empower [empau'ə:r] vt: **to empower**

someone to do something (LAW, ADMIN) ...に ...する権限を与える ...ni ...suru keńgen wo atáerù

empress [em'pris] *n* (woman emperor) 女帝 jotéi; (wife of emperor) 皇后 kõgō

emptiness [emp'ti:nis] *n* (of area, region etc) 何もない事 nanî mo naî kotò; (of life etc) むなしさ munáshìsa

empty [emp'ti:] *adj* (container) 空の kará no, 空っぽの karáppò no; (place, street) だれもいない daré mo inâî; (house, room, space) 空きの akî no
♦*vt* 空にする karâ ni suru
♦*vi* (house, container) 空になる karâ ni nárù; (liquid) 注ぐ sosógù

an empty threat こけおどし kokéodòshi

an empty promise 空約束 karáyakùsoku

empty-handed [empti:hæn'did] *adj* 手ぶらの tebúra no

emulate [em'jəleit] *vt* (hero, idol) まねる manérù

emulsion [imʌl'ʃən] *n* (liquid) 乳剤 nyúzai; (*also:* **emulsion paint**) 水溶ペンキ suíyōpeñki

enable [enei'bəl] *vt*: ***to enable someone to do*** (permit, allow) ...が ...する事を許可する ...ga ...surú kotò wo kyőka suru; (make possible) ...が ...する事を可能にする ...ga ...surú kotò wo kanő ni surú

enact [enækt'] *vt* (law) 制定する seftei suru; (play, role) 上演する jően suru

enamel [inæm'əl] *n* (for decoration) エナメル enâmerù; (*also:* **enamel paint**) エナメルペイント enâmerupeiǹto; (of tooth) エナメル質 enâmerushìtsu

enamored [enæm'əːrd] *adj*: ***to be enamored of*** (person, pastime, idea, belief) ...に惚れる ...ni horérù

encased [enkeist'] *adj*: ***encased in*** (plaster, shell) ...に覆われた ...ni őwareta

enchant [ent'ʃænt'] *vt* (delight) 魅了する miryő suru

enchanted [entʃæn'tid] *adj* (castle, island) 魔法の mahő no

enchanting [entʃæn'tiŋ] *adj* (appearance, behavior, person) 魅力的な miryő-

kuteki na

encircle [ensɑːr'kəl] *vt* (place, prisoner) 囲む kakómù

encl. *abbr* (= *enclosed*) 同封の dőfū no

enclave [en'kleiv] *n* 飛び地 tobíchi

enclose [enklouz'] *vt* (land, space) 囲む kakómù; (object) 閉じ込める tojíkomerù; (letter etc): ***to enclose (with)*** (...に) 同封する (...ni) dőfū suru

please find enclosed ... を同封します ...wo dőfū shimasù

enclosure [enklou'ʒəːr] *n* (area of land) 囲い kakői

encompass [enkʌm'pəs] *vt* (include: subject, measure) 含む fukûmù

encore [ɑːŋˈkɔːr] *excl* アンコール añkóru
♦*n* (THEATER) アンコール añkóru

encounter [enkaun'təːr] *n* (with person etc) 出会い deáì; (with problem etc) 直面 chokúmen
♦*vt* (person) ...に出会う ...ni deáù; (new experience, problem) 直面する chokúmen suru

encourage [enkəːr'idʒ] *vt* (person): ***to encourage someone to (to do something)*** (...する事を) ...に勧める ...surú kotő wo) ...ni susúmerù; (activity, attitude) 激励する gekírei suru; (growth, industry) 刺激する shigéki suru

encouragement [enkəːr'idʒmənt] *n* (to do something) 勧め susúme; (of activity, attitude) 激励 gekírei; (of growth, industry) 刺激 shigéki

encroach [enkrout'] *vi*: ***to encroach (up)on*** (rights) ...を侵す ...wo okású; (property) ...に侵入する ...ni shifnyū suru; (time) ...の邪魔をする ...no jamá wo surú

encrusted [enkrʌs'tid] *adj*: ***encrusted with*** (gems) ...をちりばめられた ...wo chirfbamerareta; (snow, dirt) ...に覆われた ...ni őwareta

encumber [enkʌm'bəːr] *vt*: ***to be encumbered with*** (suitcase, baggage etc) ...が邪魔になっている ...ga jamá ni natté irù; (debts) ...を背負っている ...wo seőtte irù

encyclop(a)edia [ensaikləpi:'di:ə] *n* 百

科辞典 hyakkájiten

end [end] n (of period, event, book etc) 終り owári; (of table, street, line, rope) 端 hashí; (of town) 外れ hazúre; (of pointed object) 先 sakí; (aim) 目的 mokúteki
♦vt (finish) 終える oérù; (stop: activity, protest etc)
JPN や止める yamérù
♦vi (situation, activity, period etc) 終る owárù

in the end 仕舞いには shimái ni wà
on end (object) 縦になって tátè ni natté
to stand on end (hair) よだつ yodátsu̇
for hours on end ぶっ続けで何時間も buttsúzuke de nánjikàn mo

endanger [endein'dʒəːr] vt (lives, prospects) 危険にさらす kikén ni sarásù

endearing [endiːr'iŋ] adj (personality, conduct) 愛敬のある aíkyo no arù

endeavor [endev'əːr] (BRIT **endeavour**) n (attempt) 試み kokóromi; (effort) 努力 dóryōku
♦vi: *to endeavor to do* (attempt) ...しようとする ...shiyō tò surù; (strive) ...しようと努力する ...shiyō tò dóryòku suru

endemic [endem'ik] adj (poverty, disease) 地方特有の chihótokuyū no

ending [en'diŋ] n (of book, film, play etc) 結末 ketsúmatsu; (LING) 語尾 góbi

endive [en'daiv] n (curly) エンダイブ endaíbu; (smooth: chicory) チコリ chíkòri

endless [end'lis] adj (argument, search) 果てし無い hateshínaí; (forest, beach) 延々と続く en-en tò tsuzúkù

endorse [endɔːrs'] vt (check) ...に裏書きする ...ni urágaki suru; (approve: proposal, plan, candidate) 推薦する suísen suru

endorsement [endɔːrs'mənt] n (approval) 推 薦 suísen; (BRIT: on driving licence) 違反記録 ihánkirðku

endow [endau'] vt (provide with money) ...に金を寄付する ...ni kané wò kifú suru
to be endowed with (talent, quality) ...の持主である ...no mochínùshi de árù

end up vi: *to end up in* (place) ...に行ってしまう ...ni itté shimaù; (condition)

...になってしまう ...ni natté shimaù

endurance [endur'əns] n (stamina) 耐久力 taíkyūryòku; (patience) 忍耐強さ níntaizuyōsa

endure [endur'] vt (bear: pain, suffering) 耐える taérù
♦vi (last: friendship, love etc) 長続きする nagátsuzùki suru

an enduring work of art 不朽の名作 fukyū no meísaku

enemy [en'əmiː] adj (forces, strategy) 敵の tekí no
♦n 敵 tekí

energetic [enərdʒet'ik] adj (person, activity) 精力的な seíryokuteki na

energy [en'əːrdʒiː] n (strength, drive) 精力 seíryoku; (power: nuclear energy etc) エネルギー enérùgī

enforce [enfɔːrs'] vt (LAW) 実施する jísshi suru

engage [engeidʒ'] vt (attention, interest) 引く hikú; (employ: consultant, lawyer) 雇う yatóù; (AUT: clutch) つなぐ tsunágù
♦vt (TECH) 掛る kakárù

to engage in (commerce, study, research etc) ...に従事する ...ni júji suru
to engage someone in conversation ...に話し掛ける ...ni hanáshikakerù

engaged [engeidʒd'] adj (betrothed) 婚約している koń-yaku shite irú; (BRIT: busy, in use) 使用中 shiyóchū
to get engaged 婚約する koń-yaku suru

engaged tone (BRIT) n (TEL) 話し中の信号音 hanáshichū no shíñgōn

engagement [engeidʒ'mənt] n (appointment) 約束 yakúsoku; (booking: for musician, comedian etc) 仕事 shigóto; (to marry) 婚約 koń-yaku

engagement ring n 婚約指輪 koń-yakuyubiwa, エンゲージリング eñgéjiriñgu

engaging [engei'dʒiŋ] adj (personality, trait) 愛敬のある aíkyo no arù

engender [endʒen'dəːr] vt (feeling, sense) 起す okósù

engine [en'dʒən] n (AUT) エンジン éñjin; (RAIL) 機関車 kikáñsha

engine driver n (RAIL) 運転手 uńteńshu

engineer [endʒəníːr] n (designer) 技師 gíshì; (BRIT: for repairs) 修理工 shúrìkò; (US: RAIL) 運転手 uńteńshu; (on ship) 機関士 kìkańshi

engineering [endʒəníːriŋ] n (science) 工学 kōgaku; (design, construction: of roads, bridges) 建設 keńsetsu; (: of cars, ships, machines) 製造 seízō

England [íŋ'glənd] n イングランド íngurando

English [íŋ'glìʃ] adj イングランドの íngurando no; (LING) 英語の efgo no
◆n (LING) 英語 efgo
◆npl: **the English** イングランド人 íngurandojin ◇総称 sōshō

English Channel n: **the English Channel** イギリス海峡 igírisukaîkyō

Englishman/woman [íŋ'glìʃmən/wumən] (pl Englishmen/women) n イングランド人男性(女性) íngurandojin dańsei(jōsei)

engraving [engreí'viŋ] n (picture, print) 版画 hańga

engrossed [engroust'] adj: **engrossed in** (book, program) ...に夢中になった ...ni muchū ni nattà

engulf [engʌlf'] vt (subj: fire) 巻込む makfkomù; (water) 飲込む nomfkomù; (: panic, fear) 襲う osoù

enhance [enhæns'] vt (enjoyment, reputation) 高める takámerù; (beauty) 増す masù

enigma [enig'mə] n (mystery) なぞ nazó

enigmatic [enigmæt'ik] adj (smile) なぞめいた nazómeita; (person) 得体の知れない etái no shirenaî

enjoy [endʒoí'] vt (like) ...が好きである ...ga sukí de arù; (take pleasure in) 楽しむ tanóshimù; (have benefit of: health, fortune, success) ...に恵まれる ...ni megúmarerù

to enjoy oneself 楽しむ tanóshimù

enjoyable [endʒoí'əbəl] adj (pleasant, fun) 楽しい tanóshiî

enjoyment [endʒoí'mənt] n (feeling of pleasure) 楽しさ tanóshìsa; (activity) 楽

しみ tanóshimî

enlarge [enlɑːrdʒ'] vt (size, scope) 拡大する kakúdai suru; (PHOT) 引伸ばす hikínobasù
◆vi: **to enlarge on** (subject) 詳しく話す kuwáshìku hanásù

enlargement [enlɑːrdʒ'mənt] n (PHOT) 引伸ばし hikínobashi

enlighten [enlaít'ən] vt (inform) ...に教える ...ni oshíerù

enlightened [enlaít'ənd] adj (person, policy, system) 聡明な sōmei na

enlightenment [enlaít'ənmənt] n: **the Enlightenment** (HISTORY) 啓もう運動 keímoundō

enlist [enlist'] vt (soldier) 入隊させる nyútai saserù; (person) ...の助けを借りる ...no tasúke wò karírù; (support, help) 頼む tanómù
◆vi: **to enlist in** (army, navy etc) ...に入隊する ...ni nyútai suru

enmity [en'miti] n (hostility) 恨み urámi

enormity [inɔːr'miti] n (of problem, danger) 物すごさ monósugòsa

enormous [inɔːr'məs] adj (size, amount) 巨大な kyodái na; (delight, pleasure, success etc) 大きな ōkina

enough [inʌf'] adj (time, books, people etc) 十分な jūbún na
◆pron 十分 jūbún
◆adv: **big enough** 十分に大きい jūbún ni ōkîi

he has not worked enough 彼の努力が足りない kárè no dóryòku ga tarínaî

have you got enough? 足りましたか tarímashìta kấ

have enough to eat 食べ物が足りる tabémonò ga tarírù

enough! もういい! mố iî!

that's enough, thanks もう沢山です。有難う。mố takusañ desu. arígatò.

I've had enough of him 彼にはもううんざりだ kárè ni wa mố uñzari dá

... which, funnily/oddly enough ... おかしいけれども、それは ... okáshii kerèdomo, soré wa

enquire [enkwaí'əːr] vt, vi = inquire

enrage [enreídʒ'] vt (anger, madden) 激

怒させる gékìdo saserù

enrich [enritʃ'] *vt* (at morally, spiritually) 豊かにする yútàka ni suru; (financially) 金持ちにする kanémochi ni suru

enroll [enroul'] (*BRIT*: **enrol**) *vt* (at school, university) 入学させる nyúgaku saserù; (on course) 登録する tóroku suru; (in club etc) 入会させる nyúkai saserù

♦*vi* (at school, university) 入学する nyúgaku suru; (on course) 登録する tóroku saữ sañkatsetsuzùki wo surù; (in club etc) 入会する nyúkai suru

enrollment [enroul'mənt] (*BRIT*: **enrolment**) *n* (registration) 登録 tóroku

en route [en rut'] *adv* (on the way) 途中で tochū de

ensue [ensu'] *vi* (follow) …の結果として起る …no kekkà toshitè okórù

ensure [enʃur'] *vt* (result, safety) 確実にする kakújitsu ni surù

entail [enteil'] *vt* (involve) 要する yó suru

entangled [entæn'gəld] *adj*: **to become entangled (in)** (in net, rope etc) …に絡まる …ni karámarù

enter [en'tər] *vt* (room, club) …に入る …ni háìru; (race, competition) …に出場する …ni sañka suru, …ni shutsújo suru; (someone for a competition) …に…の参加を申込む …ni …no sañka wo móshikomù; (write down) 記入する kinyú suru; (COMPUT: data) 入力する nyúryòku suru

♦*vi* (come or go in) 入る háìru

♦*vt fus* (race, competition, examination) …に参加を申込む …ni sañka wo móshikomù

enter for *vt fus* (race, competition, examination) …に参加を申込む …ni sañka wo móshikomù

enter into *vt fus* (discussion, correspondence, negotiations) 始める hajímerù; (agreement) 結ぶ musúbù

enterprise [en'tərpraiz] *n* (company, business) 企業 kigyō; (undertaking) 企画 kikàku; (initiative) 進取の気 shíñshu no ki

free enterprise 自由企業 jiyúkigyō
private enterprise (private company) 民間企業 miñkankigyō, 私企業 shikígyō

enterprising [en'tərpraiziŋ] *adj* (adventurous) 進取の気に富んだ shíñshu no ki ni tóñda

entertain [entərtein'] *vt* (amuse) 楽しませる tanóshimaserù; (invite; guest) 接待する séttai suru; (idea, plan) 考える kañgaerù

entertainer [entərtein'ər] *n* (TV etc) 芸能人 geínōjiñ

entertaining [entərtei'niŋ] *adj* 面白い omóshiroì

entertainment [entərtein'mənt] *n* (amusement) 娯楽 goráku; (show) 余興 yokyō

enthralled [enθrɔːld'] *adj* (engrossed, captivated) 魅せられた misérareta

enthusiasm [enθu'ziæzəm] *n* (eagerness) 熱心さ nesshíñsa

enthusiast [enθu'ziæst] *n* (fan) マニア mánia

enthusiastic [enθuːziæs'tik] *adj* (excited, eager) 熱心な nesshíñ na
to be enthusiastic about …に夢中になっている …ni muchū ni natté irù

entice [entais'] *vt* (lure, tempt) 誘惑する yūwaku suru

entire [entai'ər] *adj* (whole) 全体の zeñtai no

entirely [entai'əːliː] *adv* (completely) 全く mattáku

entirety [entai'əːrtiː] *n*: **in its entirety** 全体に zeñtai ni

entitle [entait'əl] *vt*: **to entitle someone to something** …に…に対する権利を与える …ni …ni tafsúru keñri wò atáerù

entitled [entait'əld] *adj* (book, film etc) …という題の …to iū dai no
to be entitled to do (be allowed) …する権利がある …suru keñri ga árù

entity [en'titiː] *n* 物 monó

entourage [antuːraːʒ'] *n* (of celebrity, politician) 取巻き連 torímakireñ

entrails [en'treilz] *npl* (ANAT, ZOOL) 内臓 naízō

entrance [n en'trəns *vb* entræns'] *n* (way in) 入口 iríguchi; (arrival) 登場 tōjō

♦*vt* (enchant) 魅惑する miwàku suru

to gain entrance to (university, profession etc) ...に入る ...ni háiru

entrance examination n 入学試験 nyúgakushikèn, 入試 nyúshi

entrance fee n 入場料 nyújōryō

entrance ramp (US) n (AUT) 入口ランプ iríguchiránpu

entrant [en'trənt] n (in race, competition etc) 参加者 sańkashà; (BRIT: in exam) 受験者 jukénsha

entreat [entrit'] vt (implore) 嘆願する tańgan suru

entrenched [entrentʃ'] adj (position, power) 固められた katámerareta; (ideas) 定着した teńchakushtá

entrepreneur [ɑntrəprənər'] n (COMM) 企業家 kigyóka

entrust [entrʌst'] vt: **to entrust something to someone** ...を...に預ける ...wo ...ni azúkerù

entry [en'tri:] n (way in) 入口 iríguchi; (in competition) 参加者 sańkashà; (in register, account book) 記入 kinyū; (in reference book) 記事 kíjì; (arrival) 登場 tōjō; (to country) 入国 nyūkoku
「**no entry**」(for entry etc) 立入禁止 tachíirikiñshi; (AUT) 進入禁止 shifnyúkiñshi

entry form n (for club etc) 入会申込書 nyūkaimōshikomishō; (for competition etc) 参加申込書 sańkamōshikomishō

entry phone n 玄関のインターホン géñkan no iñtāhon

enumerate [inu:'məreit] vt (list) 列挙する rékkyo suru

enunciate [inʌn'si:eit] vt (word) はっきりと発音する hakkfri to hatsúon suru; (principle, plan etc) 明確に説明する meīkaku ni setsúmei suru

envelop [envel'əp] vt (cover, enclose) 包い包む őitsutsumù

envelope [en'vəloup] n 封筒 fūtō

envious [en'vi:əs] adj (person, look) うらやましい uráyamashī

environment [envai'rənmənt] n (surroundings) 環境 kańkyō; (natural world): **the environment** 環境 kańkyō

environmental [envairənmen'təl] adj 環境の kańkyō no

envisage [enviz'idʒ] vt (foresee) 予想する yosō suru

envoy [en'voi] n (diplomat) 特使 tókùshi

envy [en'vi:] n (jealousy) せん望 señbō
♦vt うらやましく思う uráyamashíku omóù
to envy someone something ...の...をうらやましく思う ...no ...wo uráyamashíku omóù

enzyme [en'zaim] n (BIO, MED) 酵素 kōso

ephemeral [ifem'ərəl] adj (fashion, fame) つかの間の tsuká no mà no

epic [ep'ik] n (poem) 叙事詩 jojíshì; (book, film) 大作 taisaku
♦adj (journey) 歴史的な rekíshiteki na

epidemic [epidem'ik] n (of disease) 流行病 ryūkōbyō

epilepsy [ep'əlepsi:] n (MED) てんかん teñkan

epileptic [epəlep'tik] adj てんかんのteñkan no
♦n てんかん患者 teñkankañja

episode [ep'isoud] n (period, event) 事件 jíkèn; (TV, RADIO: installment) 1回 ikkái

epistle [ipis'əl] n (letter: also REL) 書簡 shokán

epitaph [ep'itæf] n 墓碑銘 bohímei

epithet [ep'iθet] n 形容詞句 keíyōgòkù

epitome [ipit'əmi:] n (model, archetype) 典型 teñkei

epitomize [ipit'əmaiz] vt (characterize, typify) ...の典型である ...no teñkei de árù

epoch [ep'ək] n (age, era) 時代 jidái

equable [ek'wəbəl] adj (climate) 安定した añteishita; (temper, reply) 落着いた ochítsuità

equal [i:'kwəl] adj (size, number, amount) 等しい hitóshiī; (intensity, quality) 同様な dōyō na; (treatment, rights, opportunities) 平等な byódō na
♦n (peer) 同輩 dōhai
♦vt (number) イコール ikóru; (quality) ...と同様である ...to dōyō de árù
to be equal to (task) ...を十分出来る ...wo jūbuñ dekíru

equality [ikwɑl'iti:] n 平等 byódō

equalize [i:'kwəlaiz] vi (SPORT) 同点に

する dóten ni surú

equally [i:'kwəli:] *adv* (share, divide etc) 平等に byōdō ni; (good, brilliant, bad etc) 同様に dōyō ni

equanimity [i:kwanim'iti:] *n* (calm) 平静さ hefseisá

equate [ikweit'] *vt*: *to equate something with* ...を...と同等視する ...wo ...to dōtōshī surú

equation [ikwei'ʒən] *n* (MATH) 方程式 hōteishíki

equator [ikwei'təːr] *n* 赤道 sekídō

equestrian [ikwes'tri:ən] *adj* 乗馬の jṓba no

equilibrium [i:kwəlib'ri:əm] *n* (balance) 均衡 kíñkō; (composure) 平静さ hefseisá

equinox [i:'kwanɑːks] *n*: *spring/autumn equinox* 春(秋)分の日 shúñ(shū)bun no hí

equip [ikwip'] *vt* (person, army, car etc) ...に...を装備させる ...ni ...wo sóbi saserú; (room) ...に...を備え付ける ...ni ...wo sónaetsukerú

to be well equipped 装備が十分である sóbi gā júbuñ de árù

to be equipped with ...を装備している ...wo sóbi shite irú

equipment [ikwip'mənt] *n* (tools, machinery) 装備 sóbi

equitable [ek'witəbəl] *adj* (settlement, agreement) 公正な kōsei na

equities [ek'witi:z] (*BRIT*) *npl* (COMM) 普通株 futsúkabu

equivalent [ikwiv'ələnt] *adj*: *equivalent (to)* (...に) 相当する (...ni) sōtō suru
   ♦*n* (equal) 相当の物 sōtō no monó

equivocal [ikwiv'əkəl] *adj* (ambiguous) あいまいな aímai na; (open to suspicion) いかがわしい ikágawashiī

era [i:'rə] *n* (age, period) 時代 jidái

eradicate [iræd'ikeit] *vt* (disease, problem) 根絶する koñzetsu suru

erase [ireis'] *vt* (tape, writing) 消す kesú

eraser [irei'səːr] *n* (for pencil etc) 消しゴム keshígomu; (*US*: for blackboard etc) 黒板消し kokúbañkeshi

erect [irekt'] *adj* (posture) 直立の chokúritsu no; (tail, ears) ぴんと立てた piñ tò

tatétā
   ♦*vt* (build) 建てる tatérù; (assemble) 組立てる kumítaterù

erection [irek'ʃən] *n* (of building) 建築 keñchiku; (of statue) 建立 koñryū́; (of tent) 張る事 harú kotò; (of machinery etc) 組立て kumítate; (PHYSIOL) ぼっ起 bokkí

ermine [əːr'min] *n* (fur) アーミン ámiñ

erode [iroud'] *vt* (soil, rock) 侵食する shiñshoku suru; (metal) 腐食する fushóku suru; (confidence, power) 揺るがす yurúgasù

erosion [irou'ʒən] *n* (of soil, rock) 侵食 shiñshoku; (of metal) 腐食 fushóku; (of confidence, power) 揺るがされる事 yurúgasarerù kotó

erotic [irɑt'ik] *adj* (activities) 性的な seíteki na; (dreams, books, films) 扇情的な señjōteki na, エロチックな eróchikkù na

eroticism [irɑt'isizəm] *n* 好色 kōshoku, エロチシズム eróchishizùmu

err [əːr] *vi* (formal: make a mistake) 過ちを犯す ayámachi wò wókà sù

errand [er'ənd] *n* お使い o-tsúkai

erratic [iræt'ik] *adj* (behavior) 突飛な toppí na; (attempts, noise) 不規則な fukísoku na

erroneous [irou'ni:əs] *adj* (belief, opinion) 間違った machígattà

error [er'əːr] *n* (mistake) 間違い machígaì, エラー érà

erudite [er'judait] *adj* (person) 博学な hakúgaku na

erupt [irʌpt'] *vi* (volcano) 噴火する fuñka suru; (war, crisis) 突っ発する boppátsu suru

eruption [irʌp'ʃən] *n* (of volcano) 噴火 fuñka; (of fighting) ぼっ発 boppátsu

escalate [es'kəleit] *vi* (conflict, crisis) 拡大する kakúdai suru, エスカレートする esúkarēto suru

escalator [es'kəleitəːr] *n* エスカレーター esúkarēta

escapade [es'kəpeid] *n* (adventure) 冒険 bóken

escape [eskeip'] *n* (from prison) 脱走 dassṓ; (from person) 逃げる事 nigéru kotò; (of gas) 漏れる事 moréru kotò

♦*vi* (get away) 逃げる nigérù; (from jail) 脱走する dassṓ suru; (leak) 漏れる morérù

♦*vt* (consequences, responsibility etc) 回避する kaíhi suru; (elude): **his name escapes me** 彼の名前を思い出せない kárè no namáe wò omóidasenaì

to escape from (place) ...から脱出する ...kara dasshútsu suru; (person) ...から逃げる ...kara nigérù

escapism [eskeiˈpizəm] *n* 現実逃避 geñjitsutṓhi

escort [*n* esˈkɔːt *vb* eskɔːtˈ] *n* (MIL, POLICE) 護衛 goéi; (companion) 同伴者 dṓhañsha

♦*vt* (person) ...に同伴する ...ni dṓhan suru

Eskimo [esˈkəmou] *n* エスキモー人 esúkimōjìn

esoteric [esəteˈrik] *adj* 難解な nañkai na

especially [espeˈʃəli] *adv* (above all, particularly) 特に tókù ni

espionage [esˈpiːənɑːʒ] *n* (POL, MIL, COMM) スパイ行為 supáikōi

esplanade [esˈpləneid] *n* (by sea) 海岸の遊歩道 kaígan nò yū́hodō

espouse [espauzˈ] *vt* (policy) 採用する saíyō suru; (idea) 信奉する shiñpō suru

Esq. *n abbr* = **Esquire**

Esquire [esˈkwaiər] *n*: **J. Brown, Esquire** J.ブラウン様 jē buráùn samá

essay [esˈei] *n* (SCOL) 小論文 shōrónbuñ; (LITERATURE) 随筆 zuíhitsu, エッセー éssē

essence [esˈəns] *n* (soul, spirit) 本質 hoñshitsu; (CULIN) エキス ékìsu, エッセンス éssènsu

essential [əsenˈtʃəl] *adj* (necessary, vital) 不可欠な fukáketsu na; (basic) 根本的な koñpoñteki na

♦*n* (necessity) 不可欠な事柄 fukáketsu nà kotógarà

essentially [əsenˈtʃəli] *adv* (basically) 根本的に koñpoñteki ni

establish [əstæbˈliʃ] *vt* (organization, firm) 創立する sṓritsu suru; (facts,

proof) 確認する kakúnin suru; (relations, contact) 樹立する jurítsu suru; (reputation) 作り上げる tsukúriagerù

established [əstæbˈliʃt] *adj* (business) 定評のある teíhyō no arù; (custom, practice) 定着した teíchaku shitá

establishment [əstæbˈliʃmənt] *n* (of organization etc) 創立 sṓritsu; (of facts etc) 確認 kakúnin; (of relations etc) 樹立 jurítsu; (of reputation) 作り上げる事 tsukúriagerù kotò; (shop etc) 店 misé; (business, firm) 会社 kaísha; (institution) 施設 shísètsu

the Establishment 体制 taísei

estate [esteitˈ] *n* (land) 屋敷 yashíki; (BRIT: *also*: **housing estate**) 住宅団地 jū́takudañchi; (LAW) 財産 zaísan

estate agent (BRIT) *n* 不動産屋 fudṓsan-yà

estate car (BRIT) *n* ステーションワゴン sutḗshoñwagòn

esteem [əstiːmˈ] *n*: **to hold someone in high esteem** (admire, respect) ...を尊敬する ...wo soñkei suru

esthetic [esθetˈik] (US) *adj* = **aesthetic**

estimate [*n* esˈtəmit *vb* esˈtəmeit] *n* (calculation) 概算 gaísan; (assessment) 推定 suítei; (COMM: builder's etc) 見積 mitsúmori

♦*vt* (reckon, calculate) 推定する suítei suru

estimation [estəmeiˈʃən] *n* (opinion) 意見 íkèn; (calculation) 推定 suítei

estranged [estreindʒdˈ] *adj* (from spouse) ...と別居している ...to bekkyó shite irù; (from family, friends) ...と仲たがいしている ...to nakátagai shite irù

estuary [esˈtʃuːeriː] *n* 河口 kakṓ

etc *abbr* (= *et cetera*) など nádò

etching [etʃˈiŋ] *n* 版画 hañga, エッチング etchíngu

eternal [itəːrˈnəl] *adj* (everlasting, unceasing) 永遠の eíen no; (unchanging: truth, value) 不変の fuhéñteki na

eternity [itəːrˈnitiː] *n* (REL) 永遠 eíen

ether [iːˈθəːr] *n* (CHEM) エーテル éteru

ethical [eθˈikəl] *adj* (question, problem) 道徳的な dṓtokuteki na

ethics [eθ'iks] *n* (science) 倫理学 rińrigaku

♦*npl* (morality) 道徳 dṓtoku

Ethiopia [i:θi:òu'pi:ə] *n* エチオピア echíopìa

ethnic [eθ'nik] *adj* (population, music, culture etc) 民族の mińzoku no

ethos [i:'θɑːs] *n* 気風 kifū

etiquette [et'əkit] *n* (manners, conduct) 礼儀作法 reígisahō, エチケット échìketto

eucalyptus [ju:kəlip'təs] *n* (tree) ユーカリ yūkari

euphemism [ju:'fəmizəm] *n* えん曲表現 eńkyokuhyōgen

euphoria [ju:fɔːr'i:ə] *n* (elation) 幸福感 kófukukàn

Eurocheque [ju:'routʃek] *n* ユーロチェック yūrochekkù ◊ヨーロッパ諸国で通用する小切手 yōroppa shokòku de tsúyō surù kogítte

Europe [ju:'rəp] *n* 欧州 ṓshū, ヨーロッパ yóroppà

European [ju:rəpi:'ən] *adj* 欧州 の ṓshū no, ヨーロッパの yōrappā no

♦*n* ヨーロッパ人 yōroppájìn

euthanasia [ju:θənei'ʒə] *n* 安楽死 ańrakushì

evacuate [ivæk'ju:eit] *vt* (people) 避難させる hínàn sasérù; (place) ...から避難させる ...kara hínàn sasérù

evacuation [ivækju:ei'ʃən] *n* 避難 hínàn

evade [iveid'] *vt* (tax, duty) 脱税する datsúzei suru; (question) 言逃れる ifnogarerù; (responsibility) 回避する kấihi suru; (person) 避ける sakérù

evaluate [ivæl'ju:eit] *vt* (importance, achievement, situation etc) 評価する hyṓka suru

evaporate [ivæp'əreit] *vi* (liquid) 蒸発する jṓhatsu su; (feeling, attitude) 消えてなくなる kiéte nakunárù

evaporated milk [ivæp'əreitid-] *n* エバミルク ebámìrùku

evasion [ivei'ʒən] *n* (of responsibility, situation etc) 回避 kấihi

tax evasion 脱税 datsúzei

evasive [ivei'siv] *adj* (reply, action) 回避

的な kaíhitekì na

eve [iːv] *n*: on the eve of ...の前夜に ...no zéñ-ya ni

even [iː'vən] *adj* (level) 平らな taíra na; (smooth) 滑らかな naméraka na; (equal) 五分五分の gobúgobu no

♦*adv* (showing surprise) ...さえ ...sáè; (introducing a comparison) 更に sárà ni

an even number 偶数 gū̀sū

even if 例え...だとしても tatóe ...dá tò shité mò

even though 例え...だとしても tatóe ...dá tò shité mò

even more なおさら naósara

even so それにしても soré ni shite mò

not even ...さえ...ない ...sáè mo ...naí

even he was there 彼さえもいた kárè sáè mo itá

even on Sundays 日曜日にも nichíyòbi ni mo

to get even with someone ...に復しゅうする ...ni fukúshū suru

evening [iːv'niŋ] *n* (early) 夕方 yūgata; (late) 夜 yórù; (whole period, event) ...の夕べ ...no yūbe

in the evening 夕方に yūgata ni

evening class *n* 夜間学級 yakáñgakkyú

evening dress *n* (no pl: formal clothes) 夜会服 yakáifuku; (woman's) イブニングドレス ibúniñgu dorèsu

even out *vi* (ground) 平らになる taíra ni narú; (prices etc) 安定する antei suru

event [ivent'] *n* (occurrence) 事件 jíkeñ; (SPORT) イベント ibéñto

in the event of ...の場合 ...no baái

eventful [ivent'fəl] *adj* (day) 忙しい isógashiì; (life, game) 波乱の多い háràn no ōì

eventual [iven'tʃu:əl] *adj* (outcome, goal) ゆくゆくの yukúyuku no

eventuality [iventʃu:æl'iti:] *n* (possibility) 可能性 kanósei

eventually [iven'tʃu:əli:] *adv* (finally) 結局 kekkyóku; (in time) やがて yagáte

ever [ev'əːr] *adv* (always) 常 に tsúnè ni; (at any time) いつか ítsùka; (in question): *why ever not?* どうしてまたしないのか dṓshite matá shinaí no ká *the best ever* 絶対に一番良い物 zettái ni ichíban yoi monó

have you ever seen it? それを見た事がありますか soré wò mítá kotó gà arímasù ká

better than ever なお一層良くなった nâò issô yokú náttà

ever since adv それ以来 soré irái

♦*conj* ...して以来 ...shité irái

evergreen [ev'ərgrin] n (tree, bush) 常緑樹 jóryokujù

everlasting [evər'læs'tiŋ] adj (love, life etc) 永遠の efen no

every [ev'ri:] adj 1 (each) すべての subéte no, 皆の miná nò

every one of them (persons) 彼らは〔皆〕karéra wa (wo)miná; (objects) それらは〔皆〕soréra wa(wo)miná

I interviewed every applicant 私は応募者全員に面接しました watákushi wa ōboshà zén-in ni mènsetsu shimashíta

every shop in the town was closed 町の店が閉っていました machíjū no misé gà shimátte imáshìta

2 (all possible) 可能な限りすべての kanô na kagírì subéte no

I gave you every assistance 私はできる限りあなたを助けました watákushi wa kanô na kagírì anátà wo tasúkemashìta

I have every confidence in him 私は完全に彼を信用しています watákushi wa kánzen ni karè wo shín-yoshite imasú

we wish you every success ご成功を祈りますgo-séikō wo inórimasù

he's every bit as clever as his brother 才能に関しては彼に少しも引けを取りません saínō ni kàn shite wa karè wa karè no ánī ni sukóshi mo hike wo tòrímasèn

3 (showing recurrence) 毎... mâi...

every day/week 毎日〔週〕máìnichi〔shū〕

every Sunday 毎日曜日 máìnichiyòbì

every other car (had been broken

into) 車は2台に1台ドアが壊されていた kuróma wa nidáì ni ichídaì doa ga kowásaréte ita

she visits me every other/third day 彼女は1日〔2日〕置きに面会に来ています kánojo wa ichínichi(futsúka)oki nì ménkai ni kite kùrémasù

every now and then 時々 tokídoki

everybody [ev'ri:bɑːdi:] pron (gen) だれも dáré mo; (form of address) 皆さん minásàn

everyday [ev'ri:dei] adj (daily) 毎日の máìnichi no; (usual, common) 平凡な hefbon na

everyone [ev'ri:wʌn] pron = **everybody**

everything [ev'ri:θiŋ] pron 何もかも nánì mo ká mò

everywhere [ev'ri:hwɛər] adv (all over) いたる所に itárù tokoro ni; (wherever) どこにでも dókò ni de mo

evict [ivikt'] vt (squatter, tenant) 立ちのかせる tachínokaserù

eviction [ivik'ʃən] n (from house, land) 立ちのかせる事 tachínokaseru kotò

evidence [ev'idəns] n (proof) 証拠 shôko; (of witness) 証言 shôgen; (sign, indication) 印 shírushì

to give evidence 証言する shôgen surú

evident [ev'idənt] adj (obvious) 明らかな akfràka na

evidently [ev'idəntli:] adv (obviously) 明らかに akfràka ni; (apparently) ...らしい ...rashíì

evil [i:'vəl] adj (person, system, influence) 悪い warúì

♦n (wickedness, sin) 罪悪 zaíaku; (unpleasant situation or activity) 悪事 ákù

evocative [ivɑk'ətiv] adj (description, music) 想像を刺激する sôzō wò shigéki surú

evoke [ivouk'] vt (feeling, memory, response) 呼び起す yobíokosù

evolution [evəlu:'ʃən] n (BIO: process) 進化 shínka; (also: **theory of evolution**) 進化論 shínkaròn; (development) 発展 hàttén

evolve [ivɑːlv'] vt (scheme, style) 練上げ

る neriágerù
♦*vi* (animal, plant etc) 進化する shínka suru; (plan, idea, style etc) 展開する teñkai suru

ewe [ju:] *n* 雌ヒツジ mesúhitsùji

ex- [eks] *prefix* 元... mótò...

exacerbate [igzæs'ərbeit] *vt* (crisis, problem) 悪化させる akká saserù

exact [igzækt'] *adj* (correct: time, amount, word etc) 正確な sefkaku na; (person, worker) 綿密な kichómen na
♦*vt*: **to exact something (from)** (obedience, payment etc) (...に) ...を強要する (...ni) ...wo kyóyò suru

exacting [igzæk'tiŋ] *adj* (task, conditions) 難しい muzúkashiì; (person, master etc) 厳しい kibíshiì

exactly [igzækt'li:] *adv* (precisely) 正確に sefkaku ni, 丁度 chódo; (indicating emphasis) 正に mása ni; (indicating agreement) その通り sonó tòri

exaggerate [igzædʒ'əreit] *vt* (difference, situation, story etc) 大げさに言う ōgesa nī iú
♦*vi* 大げさな事を言う ōgesa na kotò wo iú

exaggeration [igzædʒəreiʃən] *n* 大げさ ōgesa

exalted [igzɔːl'tid] *adj* (prominent) 著名 な choméi na

exam [igzæm'] *n abbr* (SCOL) = **examination**

examination [igzæməneiʃən] *n* (of object, accounts etc) 検査 kéñsa; (of idea, plan etc) 検討 keñtō; (SCOL) 試験 shíkeñ; (MED) 診察 shiñsatsu

examine [igzæm'in] *vt* (inspect: object, idea, plan, accounts etc) 調べる shirábe-rù; (SCOL: candidate) 試験する shíkeñ suru; (MED: patient) 診察する shiñsatsu suru

examiner [igzæm'inɔːr] *n* (SCOL) 試験 官 shikéñkan

example [igzæm'pəl] *n* (typical illustration) 例 réi; (model: of good behavior etc) 手本 tehóñ
for example 例えば tatóèba

exasperate [igzæs'pəreit] *vt* (annoy, frustrate) 怒らせる okóraserù

exasperating [igzæs'pəreitiŋ] *adj* いらいらさせる fráira saserù

exasperation [igzæspəreiʃən] *n* いらだ ち irádachi

excavate [eks'kəveit] *vt* (site) 発掘する hakkútsu suru

excavation [eks'kəveiʃən] *n* (act) 発掘 hakkútsu; (site) 発掘現場 hakkútsugeñ-ba

exceed [iksi:d'] *vt* (number, amount, budget) 越える koérù; (speed limit etc) 越す kosú; (powers, hopes) 上回る uwá-mawarù

exceedingly [iksi:'diŋli:] *adv* (enormously) 極めて kiwámète

excel [iksel'] *vi*: **to excel (in/at)** (sports, business etc) (...に) 優れる (...ni) sugúrerù

excellence [ek'sələns] *n* 優れる事 sugú-reru kotó

Excellency [ek'selənsi:] *n*: **His Excellency** 閣下 kákka

excellent [ek'sələnt] *adj* (idea, work etc) 優秀な yúshū na

except [iksept'] *prep* (apart from: *also*: **except for, excepting**) ...を除いて ...wo nozóite
♦*vt*: **to except someone (from)** (attack, criticism etc) (...から) ...を除く (...kara) ...wo nozókù
except if/when ...する場合を除いて ...suru baái wo nozóite
except that がしかし... ga shikáshì

exception [iksep'ʃən] *n* (special case) 例外 refgai
to take exception to ...が気に食わない ...ga kí nì kuwanaí

exceptional [iksep'ʃənəl] *adj* (person, talent) 優れた sugúreta; (circumstances) 例外的な refgaiteki na

excerpt [ek'sə:rpt] *n* (from text, film) 抜粋 bassúi

excess [ek'ses] *n* (surfeit) 過剰 kajó

excess baggage *n* 超過手荷物 chōkate-nimótsu

excesses [ekses'iz] *npl* (of cruelty, stupidity etc) 極端な行為 kyokútan na kōi

excess fare (*BRIT*) *n* (RAIL) 乗越し運賃 noríkoshi uñchin

excessive [iks's'iv] *adj* (amount, extent) 過剰の kajó no

exchange [ikst∫éindʒ] *n* (of presents, prisoners etc) 交換 kókan; (conversation) 口論 kóron; (*also*: **telephone exchange**) 電話局 deñwakyóku

◆*vt*: *to exchange (for)* (goods etc) (...と) 交換する (...to) kókan suru

exchange rate *n* 為替相場 kawásesòba

Exchequer [eks't∫ékər] (*BRIT*) *n*: *the Exchequer* 大蔵省 ókurashō

excise [ék'saiz] *n* (tax) 消費税 shóhizèi

excite [iksáit] *vt* (stimulate) 興奮させる kófun saserù; (arouse) 性的に刺激する séfteki ni shigéki suru

to get excited 興奮する kófun suru

excitement [iksáit'mənt] *n* (agitation) 興奮 kófun; (exhilaration) 喜び yorókobī

exciting [iksái'tiŋ] *adj* (time, event, place) 興奮の kófun no, エキサイティングな ekfsaitíñgu na

exclaim [ikskléim'] *vi* (cry out) 叫ぶ sakébū

exclamation [ekskləméi∫'ən] *n* (cry) 叫び sakébi

exclamation mark *n* 感嘆符 kañtañfu

exclude [iksklúːd'] *vt* (fact, possibility, person) 除外する jogái suru

exclusion [iksklúː'ʒən] *n* 除外 jogái

exclusive [iksklúː'siv] *adj* (club, district) 高級な kókyū na; (use, story, interview) 独占の dokúsen no

exclusive of tax 税別の zefbetsu no

exclusively [iksklúː'sivli] *adv* (only, entirely) 独占的に dokúsenteki ni

excommunicate [ekskəmjuː'nəkeit] *vt* (REL) 破門する hamón suru

excrement [eks'krəmənt] *n* ふん furí

excruciating [ikskruː'ʃieitiŋ] *adj* (pain, agony, embarrassment etc) 極度の kyókùdo no, 耐えがたい taégatai; (noise) 耳をつんざくような mimf wò tsuñzaku yỏ na

excursion [ikskəːr'ʒən] *n* (tourist excursion, shopping excursion) ツアー tsúã

excuse [*n* ekskjuːs'- *vb* ekskjuːz'] *n* (justi-

fication) 言訳 iífwake

◆*vt* (justify: personal fault, mistake) ...の言訳をする ...no iífwake wo surù; (forgive: someone else's mistake) 許す yurúsù

to excuse someone from doing something ...する義務を...に免除する ...suru gímù wo ...ni méñjo suru

excuse me! (attracting attention) 済みません(が) sumímaseñ (ga)...; (as apology) 済みません sumímaseñ

if you will excuse me ... ちょっと失礼します chóttò shitsúrei shimasù

ex-directory [eksdirek'təːri] (*BRIT*) *adj* 電話帳に載っていない deñwachō ni notté inaí

execute [ek'səkjuːt] *vt* (person) 死刑にする shikéi ni surù; (plan, order) 実行する jikkó suru; (maneuver, movement) する surú

execution [eksəkjuː'ʃən] *n* (of person) 死刑 shikéi; (of plan, order, maneuver etc) 実行 jikkó

executioner [eksəkjuː'ʃənəːr] *n* 死刑執行人 shikéishikkóñin

executive [igzek'jətiv] *n* (person: of company) 重役 jūyaku; (committee: of organization, political party etc) 執行委員会 shikkóiìnkai

◆*adj* (board, role) 幹部の káñbu no

executor [igzek'jətəːr] *n* (LAW) 執行人 shikkóñin

exemplary [igzem'plɑːri] *adj* (conduct) 模範的な mohánteki na; (punishment) 見せしめの misésime no

exemplify [igzem'pləfai] *vt* (typify) ...の典型である ...no teñkei de arù; (illustrate) ...の例を挙げる ...no reí wò agérù

exempt [igzempt'] *adj*: *exempt from* (duty, obligation) ...を免除された ...ni méñjo saréta

◆*vt*: *to exempt someone from* (duty, obligation) ...の...を免除する ...no ...wo méñjo suru

exemption [igzemp'ʃən] *n* 免除 méñjo

exercise [ek'sərsaiz] *n* (*no pl*: keep-fit) 運動 uñdō; (energetic movement) 体操 tafsō; (SCOL) 練習問題 refshūmoñdai;

(MUS) 練習曲 reñshûkyoku; (MIL) 軍事演習 guñjieñshû; (of authority etc) 行使 kôshî

♦vt (right) 行使する kôshî suru; (mind) 働かせる határakaserü; ...に運動をさせる ...ni uñdô wò saserü;

♦vi (also: to take exercise) 運動する uñdô suru

to exercise patience 我慢する gámaṇ suru

exercise book n (SCOL) ノート nôto

exert [igzэ́:rt] vt (influence) 及ぼす oyóbosù; (authority) 行使する kôshî suru

to exert oneself 努力する dóryòku suru

exertion [igzэ́:rʃən] n 努力 dóryòku

exhale [eksheíl] vt (air, smoke) 吐き出す hakídasù

♦vi (breathe out) 息を吐く íkì wo hakú

exhaust [igzэ́:st] n (AUT: also: exhaust pipe) 排気管 hafkíkaṇ; (: fumes) 排気ガス hafkígasù

♦vt (person) へとへとに疲れさせる hetóhetò ni tsukáresaserù; (money, resources etc) 使い果す tsukáihatasù; (topic) ...について語り尽す ...ni tsûſte katáritsukusù

exhausted [igzэ́:stid] adj (person) へとへとに疲れた hetóhetò ni tsukáretà

exhaustion [igzэ́:stʃən] n (tiredness) 極度の疲労 kyôkùdo no hirô

nervous exhaustion 神経衰弱 shiñkeisuijàku

exhaustive [igzэ́:stiv] adj (search, study) 徹底的な tettéiteki na

exhibit [igzíbit] n (ART) 展示品 teñjihìn; (LAW) 証拠品 shôkohìn

♦vt (quality, ability, emotion) 見せる misérù; (paintings) 展示する teñji suru

exhibition [eksəbíʃən] n (of paintings etc) 展示会 teñjikài; (of ill-temper etc) 極端な態度 kyokútaṇ na táido; (of talent etc) 素晴らしい例 subárashiì reí

exhibitionist [eksəbíʃənist] n (show-off) 取巧り屋 kidóriya

exhilarating [igzíl'əreitiŋ] adj (experience, news) 喜ばしい yorókobashiì

exhort [igzэ́:rt] vt 訓戒する kuñkai suru

exile [eg'zail] n (condition, state) 亡命 bômei; (person) 亡命者 bômeìsha

♦vt 追放する tsuíhô suru

exist [igzíst] vi (be present) 存在する sofzai suru; (live) 生活する sefkatsu suru

existence [igzís'təns] n (reality) 存在 sofzai; (life) 生活 sefkatsu

existing [igzís'tiŋ] adj (present) 現存の geñzon no, geñson no

exit [eg'zit] n (from room, building, motorway etc) 出口 dégùchi; (departure) 出ていく事 détè ikú kotò

♦vi (THEATER) 退場する taíjô suru; (COMPUT) プログラムを終了する purógurầmu wo shûryô suru

exit ramp (US) n (AUT) 出口ランプ degúchìrañpu

exodus [ek'sədəs] n 大脱出 daídasshùtsu

exonerate [igzɑn'əreit] vt: to exonerate someone from something (blame, guilt etc) ...について...の容疑を晴らす ...ni tsûſte ...no yôgì wo harásù

exorbitant [igzɔ́:r'bətənt] adj (prices, rents) 法外な hôgai na

exorcize [ek'sɔ:rsaiz] vt (spirit) 追い払う oíharaù; (person, place) ...から悪霊を追い払う ...kara ákùma wo oíharaù

exotic [igzɑt'ik] adj (food, place) 異国的な ikókuteki na, エキゾチックな ekízochikkù na

expand [ikspǽnd] vt (business etc) 拡張する kakúchô suru; (staff, numbers etc) 増やす fuyásù

♦vi (population etc) 増える fuérù; (business etc) 大きくなる ôkìku nárù; (gas, metal) 膨脹する bôchô suru

expanse [ikspǽns] n (of sea, sky etc) 広がり hirógarì

expansion [ikspǽn'tʃən] n (of business, population, economy etc) 増大 zôdai

expatriate [ikspei'triit] n 国外在住者 kokúgai zaijùsha

expect [ikspekt'] vt (anticipate) 予想する yosô suru; (await) 待つ mátsù; (require) 要求する yôkyû suru; (suppose) ...だと思う ...dá tò omóù

♦vi: to be expecting (be pregnant) 妊娠している niñshin shite irù

expectancy [ikspek'tənsi:] n (anticipation) 期待 kitái
life expectancy 寿命 jumyō

expectant mother [ikspek'tənt-] n 妊婦 nínpu

expectation [ikspektei'ʃən] n (hope, belief) 期待 kitái

expedience [ikspi:'di:əns] n (convenience) 便宜 béngi, 都合 tsugō

expediency [ikspi:'di:ənsi:] n = **expedience**

expedient [ikspi:'di:ənt] adj (useful, convenient) 都合の良い tsugō no yoí
♦n (measure) 便法 benpo

expedition [ikspədiʃ'ən] n (for exploration) 探検旅行 tañkenryokō; (for shopping etc) ツアー tsūā

expel [ikspel'] vt (person: from school) 退学させる taígaku saserú; (: from organization, place) 追出す oídasū; (gas, liquid) 排出する haíshutsu suru

expend [ikspend'] vt (money, time, energy) 費やす tsuíyasū

expendable [ikspen'dəbəl] adj (person, thing) 消耗品的な shōmōhinteki na

expenditure [ikspen'ditʃər] n (of money, energy, time) 消費 shōhi

expense [ikspens'] n (cost) 費用 híyō; (expenditure) 出費 shuppí
at the expense of ...を犠牲にして ...wo giséi ni shité

expense account n 交際費 kōsaíhi

expenses [ikspen'siz] npl (traveling expenses, hotel expenses etc) 経費 keíhi

expensive [ikspen'siv] adj (article) 高い takái; (mistake, tastes) 高く付く tákāku tsukú

experience [ikspi:r'i:əns] n 経験 keíken
♦vt (situation, feeling etc) 経験する keíken suru

experienced [ikspi:r'i:ənst] adj (in job) 熟練した jukúren shitá

experiment [ikspe:r'əmənt] n (trial: also SCIENCE) 実験 jikkén
♦vi: **to experiment (with/on)** (...を使って) 実験する (...wo tsukátté) jikkén suru

experimental [ikspe:rəmen'təl] adj 実験

的な jikkénteki na

expert [ek'spə:rt] adj (opinion, help) 専門家の seńmonka no; (driver etc) 熟練した jukúren shitá
♦n (specialist) 専門家 seńmonka, エキスパート ekísupāto

expertise [ekspə:rti:z'] n (know-how) 技術 gíjutsu, ノーハウ nōhaù

expire [ikspai'ə:r] vi (passport, licence etc) 切れる kirérù

expiry [ikspai'ə:ri:] n (of passport, lease etc) 満期 máñki

explain [iksplein'] vt 説明する setsúmei suru

explanation [eksplənei'ʃən] n 説明 setsúmei

explanatory [eksplæn'ətɔ:ri:] adj (statement, comment) 説明の setsúmei no

explicit [iksplis'it] adj (clear) 明白な meíhaku na; (frank) 隠し立てしない kakúshidate shinaí

explode [iksploud'] vi (bomb) 爆発する bakúhatsu suru; (population) 爆発的に増える bakúhatsuteki ní fuérù; (person: with rage etc) 激怒する gékīdo suru

exploit [n eks'plɔit vb iksplɔit'] n (deed, feat) 手柄 tegára
♦vt (workers) 搾取する sákūshu suru; (person, idea) 私利私欲に利用する shírī-shíyóku ni riyō suru; (opportunity, resources) 利用する riyō suru

exploitation [eksplɔitei'ʃən] n (of workers) 搾取 sákūshu; (of person, idea, resources, opportunity etc) 利用 riyō

exploration [eksplərei'ʃən] n (of place, space) 探検 tañken; (with hands etc) 探る事 sagúru kotó; (of idea, suggestion) 検討 keñtō

exploratory [eksplɔ:r'ətɔ:ri:] adj (expedition) 探検の tañken no; (talks, operation) 予備的な yobíteki na

explore [eksplɔ:r'] vt (place, space) 探検する tañken suru; (with hands etc) 探る sagúrù; (idea, suggestion) 検討する keñtō suru

explorer [eksplɔ:r'ə:r] n (of place, country etc) 探検家 tañkenka

explosion [iksplou'ʒən] n (of bomb) 爆発

bakúhatsu;(increase: of population etc) 爆発的 bakúhatsuteki;(outburst: of rage, laughter etc) 激怒 gékidō

explosive [iksplou'siv] *adj* (device, effect) 爆発の bakúhatsu no;(situation, temper) 爆発的な bakúhatsuteki na
♦*n* (substance) 爆薬 bakúyaku; (device) 爆弾 bakúdan

exponent [ekspou'nent] *n* (of idea, theory) 擁護者 yōgoshà;(of skill, activity) 達人 tatsújin

export [*vb* ekspɔ:rt' *n* eks'pɔ:rt] *vt* (goods) 輸出する yushútsu suru
♦*n* (process) 輸出 yushútsu; (product) 輸出品 yushútsuhìn
♦*cpd* (duty, permit) 輸出... yushútsu...

exporter [ekspɔ:r'tər] *n* 輸出業者 yushútsugyōsha

expose [ikspouz'] *vt* (reveal: object) むき出しにする mukídashi ni surù;(unmask: person) ...の悪事を暴く ...no ákùji wo abákù

exposed [ikspouzd'] *adj* (house, place etc) 雨風にさらされた ámekaze ni sarásaretà

exposure [ikspou'ʒər] *n* (to heat, cold, radiation) さらされる事 sarásareru kotò; (publicity) 報道 hódō;(of person) 暴露 bákùro; (PHOT) 露出 roshútsu
to die from exposure (MED) 低体温症で死ぬ teítaioñshō de shínù

exposure meter *n* (PHOT) 露出計 roshútsukei

expound [ikspaund'] *vt* (theory, opinion) 説明する setsúmei suru

express [ikspres'] *adj* (clear: command, intention etc) 明白な meíhaku na; (BRIT: letter etc) 速達の sokútatsu no
♦*n* (train, bus, coach) 急行 kyúkō
♦*vt* (idea, view) 言い表わす iíarawasù;(emotion, quantity) 表現する hyőgen suru

expression [ikspreʃ'ən] *n* (word, phrase) 言方 iíkata; (of idea, emotion) 表現 hyőgen;(on face) 表情 hyőjō; (of actor, singer etc: feeling) 表現力 hyőgenryoku

expressive [ikspres'iv] *adj* (glance: expressing) 意味ありげな ímìarige na; (ability) 表現の hyőgen no

expressly [ikspres'li:] *adv* (clearly, intentionally) はっきりと hakkírì to

expressway [ikspres'wei] (*US*) *n* (urban motorway) 高速道路 kōsokudōro

expulsion [ikspʌl'ʃən] *n* (SCOL) 退学処分 taígakushobùn;(from organization etc) 追放 tsuíhō;(of gas, liquid etc) 排出 haíshutsu

expurgate [eks'pərgeit] *vt* (text, recording) 検閲する keñ-etsu suru

exquisite [ekskwiz'it] *adj* (perfect: face, lace, workmanship, taste) 見事な mígòto na

extend [ikstend'] *vt* (visit) 延ばす nobásù; (street) 延長する eñchō suru; (building) 増築する zōchiku suru;(arm, hand) 伸ばす nobásù
♦*vi* (land) 広がる hirógarù;(road) 延びる nobírù;(period) 続く tsuzúkù
to extend an offer of help 援助を申し込む éñjo wo mōshíderù
to extend an invitation to ...を招待する ...wo shōtai suru

extension [iksten'tʃən] *n* (of building) 増築 zōchiku;(of time) 延長 eñchō;(of campaign, rights) 拡大 kakúdai;(ELEC) 延長コード eñchōkōdo;(TEL: in private house, office) 内線 naísen

extensive [iksten'siv] *adj* (area) 広い hiróì;(effect, damage) 甚大な jiñdai na;(coverage, discussion) 広範囲の kōhañ-i no

extensively [iksten'sivli:] *adv*: *he's traveled extensively* 彼は広く旅行している kárè wa híròku ryokō shite irù

extent [ikstent'] *n* (size: of area, land etc) 広さ hírosa; (: of problem etc) 大きさ ōkìsa
to some extent ある程度 árù teído
to the extent of ...まで...で ...máde mo
to such an extent that ...という程...to iú hodò
to what extent? どのぐらい? donó gural?

extenuating [iksten'ʒu:eitiŋ] *adj*:
extenuating circumstances 酌量すべき情状 shakúryō subèki jōjō

exterior [ikstɪə'riːər] *adj* (external) 外部
の gáîbu no
♦*n* (outside) 外部 gáîbu; (appearance) 外
見 gaîken

exterminate [ikstəː'mæneit] *vt* (animals) 撲滅する bokúmetsu suru; (people)
根絶する koñzetsu suru

external [ikstəː'nəl] *adj* (walls etc) 外部
の gáîbu no; (examiner, influence) 外部の
búgai no
external evidence 外的証拠 gaîtekishō-
ko
「*for external use*」外用薬 gaîyōyaku

extinct [ikstiŋkt'] *adj* (animal, plant) 絶
滅した zetsúmetsu shità
an extinct volcano 死火山 shikázan

extinction [ikstiŋk'ʃən] *n* (of species) 絶
滅 zetsúmetsu

extinguish [ikstiŋ'gwiʃ] *vt* (fire, light) 消
す kesú

extinguisher [ikstiŋ'gwiʃəːr] *n* 消 火 器
shōkakī

extort [ikstɔːrt'] *vt* (money) ゆすり取る
yusúritorù; (confession) 強要する kyōyō
suru

extortion [ikstɔːr'ʃən] *n* (of money etc)
ゆすり yusúri; (confession) 強要 kyōyō

extortionate [ikstɔːr'ʃənit] *adj* (price,
demands) 法外な hōgai na

extra [eks'trə] *adj* (thing, person,
amount) 余分の yobún no
♦*adv* (in addition) 特別に tokúbetsu ni
♦*n* (luxury) 特別の物 tokúbetsu no monò, 余分の物 yobún no monò; (surcharge)
追加料金 tsuíkaryōkin; (CINEMA,
THEATER) エキストラ ekísutòra

extra– [eks'trə] *prefix* 特別に ... tokúbetsu ni ...

extract [*vt* ikstrækt' *n* eks'trækt] *vt*
(take out: object) 取出す torídasù;
(: tooth) 抜く nukú, 抜歯する basshí suru;
(mineral: from ground) 採掘する saïkutsu
suru, 抽出する chūshutsu suru;
(money) 強要して取る kyōyō shité torù;
(promise) 無理強いする murījii suru
♦*n* (of novel, recording) 抜粋 bassúi;
(malt extract, vanilla extract etc) エキ
ス ékìsu, エッセンス éssènsu

extracurricular [ekstrəkərik'jələːr] *adj*
(activities) 課外の kagái no

extradite [eks'trədait] *vt* (from country)
引渡す hikíwatasù; (: to country) の引渡
しを受ける ...no hikíwatashi wò ukérù

extradition [ekstrədiʃ'ən] *n* 外国への犯
人引渡し gaîkoku e no hañnin hikíwatashi

extramarital [ekstrəmæːr'itəl] *adj*
(affair, relationship) 婚外の koñgai no,
不倫の furín no

extramural [ekstrəmjuːr'əl] *adj* (lectures, activities) 学外の gakúgai no

extraordinary [ikstrɔːr'dəneːriː] *adj*
(person) 抜きんでた nukíndetà; (conduct,
situation) 異常な ijō na; (meeting) 臨時の
rîñji no

extravagance [ikstræv'əgəns] *n* (no pl:
spending) 浪費 rōhi; (example of spending) 浪費など zeftaku

extravagant [ikstræv'əgənt] *adj* (lavish: person) 気前の良い kimáe no yoì;
(: gift) ぜいたくな zeîtaku na; (: wasteful:
person) 金遣いの荒い kanézukāi no araì;
(: machine) 不経済な fukéizai na

extreme [ikstriːm'] *adj* (cold, poverty
etc) 非常な hijō na; (opinions, methods
etc) 極端な kyokútan na; (point, edge) 末
端の mattán no
♦*n* (of behavior) 極端 kyokútan

extremely [ikstriːm'liː] *adv* 非常に hijō
ni

extremity [ikstrem'itiː] *n* (edge, end) 端
hashí; (of situation) 極端 kyokútan

extricate [eks'trikeit] *vt*: *to extricate
someone/something (from)* (trap, situation) (...から) ...を救い出す (...kara)
...wo sukúidasù

extrovert [eks'trouvəːrt] *n* 外向的な人
gaîkōteki na hitó

exuberant [igzuː'bəːrənt] *adj* (person
etc) 元気一杯の geñkiippài no; (imagination etc) 豊かな yútàka na

exude [igzuːd'] *vt* (liquid) にじみ出させる
nijímidasaserù; (smell) 放つ hanátsu
to exude confidence 自信満々である
jishín mañman dè árù
to exude enthusiasm 意気込む ikígo-

mù

exult [igzʌlt'] vi (rejoice) 喜び勇む yorókobíisamù

eye [ai] n (ANAT) 目 mé
♦vt (look at, watch) 見詰める mitsúmerù
the eye of a needle 針の目 hárì no mé
to keep an eye on ...を見張る ...wo mihárù

eyeball [ai'bɔːl] n 眼球 gañkyū

eyebath [ai'bæθ] n 洗眼カップ señgankappū

eyebrow [ai'brau] n 眉毛 máyùge

eyebrow pencil n アイブローペンシル aíburòpeñshiru

eyedrops [ai'drɑːps] npl 点眼薬 teñgańyaku

eyelash [ai'læʃ] n まつげ mátsùge

eyelid [ai'lid] n まぶた mábùta

eyeliner [ai'lainər] n アイライナー aíraìnā

eye-opener [ai'oupənər] n (revelation) 驚くべき新事実 odórokubèki shíñjijìtsu

eyeshadow [ai'ʃædou] n アイシャドー afshadò

eyesight [ai'sait] n 視力 shíryòku

eyesore [ai'sɔːr] n (building) 目障り mezáwàri

eye witness n (to crime, accident) 目撃者 mokúgekìshà

F

F [ef] n (MUS: note) へ音 hé-òn; (: key) へ調 héchò

F. abbr (= Fahrenheit) 華氏 kàshì

fable [fei'bəl] n (story) ぐう話 gūwa

fabric [fæb'rik] n (cloth) 生地 kíjì

fabrication [fæbrikei'ʃən] n (lie) うそ núsò; (making) 製造 sefzò

fabulous [fæb'jələs] adj (inf: super) 素晴らしい subárashiì; (extraordinary) 途方もない tohô mo naì; (mythical) 伝説的な defisetsuteki na

facade [fəsɑːd'] n (of building) 正面 shômen; (fig: pretence) 見せ掛け mísèkake

face [feis] n (ANAT) 顔 kaó; (expression) 表情 hyójò; (of clock) 文字盤 mojí-

ban; (of cliff) 面 méñ; (of building) 正面 shômen
♦vt (particular direction) ...に向かう ...ni mukáù; (facts, unpleasant situation) 直視する chókushi suru

face down (person) 下向きになって shitámuki ni natté; (card) 伏せてあって fuséte attè

to lose face 面目を失う meñboku wo ushínaù

to make/pull a face 顔をしかめる kaó wo shikámerù

in the face of (difficulties etc) ...にめげず ...ni megézù

on the face of it (superficially) 表面は hyômen wa

face to face (with person, problem) 面と向かって meñ to mukatté

face cloth (BRIT) n フェースタオル fésutaòru

face cream n フェースクリーム fésukurìmu

face lift n (of person) 顔のしわ取り手術 kaó no shiwátori shujùtsu; (of building etc) 改造 kafzò

face powder n フェースパウダー fésupaùdā

face-saving [feis'seiviŋ] adj (compromise, gesture) 面子を立てる méñtsu wo tatérù

facet [fæs'it] n (of question, personality) 側面 sokúmen; (of gem) 切子面 kírfkomèn

facetious [fəsiː'ʃəs] adj (comment, remark) ふざけた fuzáketà

face up to vt fus (obligations, difficulty) ...に立ち向かう ...ni tachímukaù

face value n (of coin, stamp) 額面 gakúmen
to take something at face value (fig) そのまま信用する sonó mama shiñ-yò suru

facial [fei'ʃəl] adj (hair, expression) 顔の kaó no

facile [fæs'əl] adj (comment, reaction) 軽々しい karúgarushiî

facilitate [fəsil'əteit] vt 助ける tasúkerù

facilities [fəsil'ətiːz] npl (buildings,

equipment) 設備 setsúbi

credit facilities 分割払い取扱い buñkatsubarái torfatsukai

facing [feiˈsiŋ] *prep* ...の向い側の ...no mukáigawa no

facsimile [fæksimˈəli] *n* (exact replica) 複製 fukúsei; (also: **facsimile machine**) ファックス fákkùsu; (transmitted document) ファックス fákkùsu

fact [fækt] *n* (true piece of information) 事実 jijítsu; (truth) 真実 shiñjítsu

in fact 実は jijítsu wa

faction [fækˈʃən] *n* (group: also REL, POL) 派 há

factor [fækˈtəːr] *n* (of problem, decision etc) 要素 yóso

factory [fækˈtəːri] *n* (building) 工場 kójō

factual [fækˈtʃuəl] *adj* (analysis, information) 事実の jijítsu no

faculty [fækˈəlti] *n* (sense, ability) 能力 nóryoku; (of university) 学部 gakúbu; (US: teaching staff) 教職員 kyōshokuin
◇総称 sōshō

fad [fæd] *n* (craze) 一時的流行 ichíjitekiryúkō

fade [feid] *vi* (color) あせる asérù; (light, sound) 次第に消える shidái ni kiérù; (flower) しぼむ shibómù; (hope, memory, smile) 消える kiérù

fag [fæg] (BRIT: inf) *n* (cigarette) もく mokú

fail [feil] *vt* (exam) 落第する rakúdai surù; (candidate) 落第させる rakúdai saserù; (subj: leader) ...の期待を裏切る ...no kitái wo urágirù; (: courage, memory) なくなる nakúnarù
◇*vi* (candidate, attempt etc) 失敗する shippái surù; (brakes) 故障する koshō suru; (eyesight, health) 衰える otóroerù; (light) 暗くなる kuráku narù

to fail to do something (be unable) ...する事が出来ない ...surú koto gà dekínài; (neglect) ...する事を怠る ...surú koto wò okótarù

without fail 必ず kanárazu

failing [feiˈliŋ] *n* (weakness) 欠点 kettéñ
◇*prep* ...がなければ ...ga nakéreba

failure [feiˈljəːr] *n* (lack of success) 失敗 shippái; (person) 駄目な人間 daméniñgen; (mechanical etc) 故障 koshō

faint [feint] *adj* (recollection, mark etc) かすかな kásùka na
◇*n* (MED) 気絶 kizétsu
◇*vi* (MED) 気絶する kizétsu suru

to feel faint 目まいがする memái ga suru

fair [feːr] *adj* (reasonable, right) 公平な kóhei na; (quite large) かなり大きい kánàri na; (quite good) 悪くない warúkunài; (skin) 白い shiróì; (hair) 金色の kiñ-iro no; (weather) 晴れの haré no
◇*adv* (play) 正々堂々と seíseidōdō to
◇*n* (also: **trade fair**) トレードフェアー torédofeā; (BRIT: funfair) 移動遊園地 idōyúenchì

fairly [feːrˈli] *adv* (justly) 公平に kóhei ni; (quite) かなり kánàri

fairness [feːrˈnis] *n* (justice, impartiality) 公平さ kóheisa

fair play *n* 公平さ kóheisa

fairy [feriˈ] *n* (sprite) 妖精 yósei

fairy tale *n* おとぎ話 otógibanàshi

faith [feiθ] *n* (trust) 信用 shiñ-yō; (religion) 宗教 shūkyō; (religious belief) 信仰 shiñkō

faithful [feiθˈfəl] *adj* 忠実な chújitsu na

faithfully [feiθˈfəli] *adv* 忠実に chújitsu ni

yours faithfully (BRIT: in letters) 敬具 kéìgu

fake [feik] *n* (painting etc) 偽物 nísèmono; (person) ぺてん師 petéñshi
◇*adj* (phoney) いんちきな íñchiki no
◇*vt* (painting etc) 偽造する gizō suru; (illness, emotion) ...だと見せ掛ける ...da to misékakerù

falcon [fælˈkən] *n* ハヤブサ hayábusa

fall [fɔːl] *n* (of person, object: from height) 転落 teñraku; (of person, horse: from standing position) 転倒 teñtō; (of price, temperature, dollar) 下がる事 sagáru koto; (of government, leader, country) 倒れる事 taóreru kotò; (US: autumn) 秋 ákì
◇*vi* (*pt* **fell**, *pp* **fallen**) (person, object: from height) 落ちる ochírù; (person,

horse: from standing position) 転ぶ koróbù; (snow, rain) 降る fúrù; (price, temperature, dollar) 下がる sagárù; (government, leader, country) 倒れる taórerù; (night, darkness) (...に) なる (...ni) nárù

snowfall 降雪 kósetsu

rainfall 降雨 kóu

the fall of darkness 暗くなる事 kuráku naru kotó

the fall of night 夜になる事 yórù ni náru kotó

to fall flat (on one's face) うつぶせに倒れる utsúbuse ni taórerù; (plan) 失敗する shippái suru; (joke) 受けない ukénai

fallacy [fæl'əsi:] *n* (misconception) 誤信 goshín

fall back *vt fus* (retreat) 後ずさりする atózusarì suru; (MIL) 後退する kótaisuru

fall back on *vt fus* (remedy etc) ...に頼る ...ni táyorù

fall behind *vi* 遅れる okúrerù

fall down *vi* (person) 転ぶ koróbù; (building) 崩壊する hókai suru

fallen [fɔːl'ən] *pp of* **fall**

fall for *vt fus* (trick) ...にだまされる ...ni damásarerù; (person) ...にほれる ...ni horérù

fallible [fæl'əbəl] *adj* (person, memory) 間違いをしがちな machígaì wo shigáchìna

fall in *vi* (roof) 落ち込む ochíkomù; (MIL) 整列する sefretsu suru

fall off *vi* (person, object) 落ちる ochírù; (takings, attendance) 減る herú

fall out *vi* (hair, teeth) 抜ける nukérù; (friends etc) けんかする kénka suru

fallout [fɔːl'aut] *n* (radiation) 放射性降下物 hóshaseiràkkabutsu, 死の灰 shí no hai

fallout shelter *n* 放射性落下物特避所 hóshaseiràkkabutsu taíhìjo

fallow [fæl'ou] *adj* (land, field) 休閑中の kyúkañchū no

falls [fɔːlz] *npl* (waterfall) 滝 takí

false [fɔːls] *adj* (untrue: statement, accusation) うその usó no; (wrong: impres-

sion, imprisonment) 間違った machígattà; (insincere: person, smile) 不誠実な fuséijitsu na

false alarm *n* 誤った ayámattà keñkóku

false pretenses *npl: under false pretenses* うその申立てで usó no móshitate de

false teeth *npl* 入れ歯 iréba

falter [fɔːl'tɑːr] *vi* (engine) 止りそうになる tomárisò ni nárù; (person: hesitate) ためらう tamérau; (: stagger) よろめく yorómekù

fame [feim] *n* 名声 meísei

familiar [fəmil'jɑːr] *adj* (well-known: face, voice) おなじみの onájimi no; (intimate: behavior, tone) 親しい shitáshiì

to be familiar with (subject) よく知っている yókù shitté iru

familiarize [fəmil'jɑːraiz] *vt: to familiarize oneself with* ...になじむ ...ni najímu

family [fæm'li:] *n* (relations) 家族 kázðku; (children) 子供 kodómo ◇総称 sóshò

family business *n* 家族経営の商売 kazóku keíei no shóbai

family doctor *n* 町医者 machí-ìsha

famine [fæm'in] *n* 飢饉 kígà

famished [fæm'iʃt] *adj* (hungry) 腹がぺこぺこの harága pekópeko no

famous [fei'məs] *adj* 有名な yúmei na

famously [fei'məsli:] *adv* (get on) 素晴らしく subárashiku

fan [fæn] *n* (person) ファン fáñ; (folding) 扇子 séñsu; (ELEC) 扇風機 señpúki

◆*vt* (face, person) あおぐ aógù; (fire, quarrel) あおる aórù

fanatic [fənæt'ik] *n* (extremist) 熱狂する nekkyósha; (enthusiast) マニア máñia

fan belt *n* (AUT) ファンベルト fañberúto

fanciful [fæn'sifəl] *adj* (notion, idea) 非現実的な hígeñjitsuteki na; (design, name) 凝った kóttà

fancy [fæn'si:] *n* (whim) 気まぐれ kímàgure; (imagination) 想像 sózò; (fantasy) 夢 yumé

◆*adj* (clothes, hat, food) 凝った kóttà,

(hotel etc) 高級の kốkyū no
♦vt (feel like, want) ほしいなと思う hoshī na to omóu; (imagine) 想像する sōzō suru; (think) ...だと思う ...da to omóu
to take a fancy to ... ...を気に入る ...wo kí ní irú
he fancies her (inf) 彼は彼女が好きだ kárè wa kanójò ga sukí dà

fancy dress n 仮装の衣装 kasố nì ishố
fancy-dress ball n 仮装舞踏会 kasôbutôkai

fanfare [fæn'fer] n ファンファーレ fanfáre

fang [tæŋ] n (tooth) きば kibá

fan out vi 扇形に広がる ốgigata nì hirogarū

fantastic [fæntæs'tik] adj (enormous) 途方もない tohômonai; (strange, incredible) 信じられない shinjirarenái; (wonderful) 素晴らしい subá rashiī

fantasy [fæn'təsi:] n (dream) 夢 yumế; (unreality, imagination) 空想 kūsố

far [fɑːr] adj (distant) 遠い tối
♦adv (a long way) 遠く tốku; (much) はるかに hárùka ni
far away/off 遠く tốku
far better ...の方がはるかにいい ...no hố ga hárùka ni ii
far from 決して...でない kesshíte ...denái 強い否定を表す tsuyói hitéi wo arấwasū
by far はるかに hárùka ni
go as far as the farm 農場まで行って下さい nốjō madè itté kudasaì
as far as I know 私の知る限り watákushi nò shirú kagirì
how far? (distance) どれぐらいの距離 doré gurai no kyòri; (referring to activity, situation) どれ程 doré hodò

faraway [fɑːr'əwei] adj (place) 遠くの tốku no; (look) 夢見る様な yumémiru yố na; (thought) 現実離れの genjitsubanare no

farce [fɑːrs] n (THEATER) 笑劇 shốgeki, ファース fấsū; (fig) 茶番劇 chabángeki

farcical [fɑːr'sikəl] adj (situation) ばかげた bakágeta

fare [feːr] n (on trains, buses) 料金 ryōkin; (also: **taxi fare**) タクシー代 takúshīdai; (food) 食べ物 tabémòno
half/full fare 半(全)額 hañ(zeñ)gaku

Far East n: **the Far East** 極東 kyokutố

farewell [feːr'wel] excl さようなら sayônarā
♦n 別れ wakáre

farm [fɑːrm] n 農場 nốjō
♦vt (land) 耕す tagáyasū

farmer [fɑːr'mər] n 農場主 nốjōshū

farmhand [fɑːrm'hænd] n 作男 sakúotòko

farmhouse [fɑːrm'haus] n 農家 nốka

farming [fɑːr'miŋ] n (agriculture) 農業 nôgyố; (of crops) 耕作 kốsaku; (of animals) 飼育 shíìku

farmland [fɑːrm'lænd] n 農地 nốchi

farm worker n = **farmhand**

farmyard [fɑːrm'jɑːrd] n 農家の庭 nốka nò niwa

far-reaching [fɑːr'riː'tʃiŋ] adj (reform, effect) 広範囲の kốhàn-i no

fart [fɑːrt] (inf!) vi おならをする onára wo surū

farther [fɑːr'ðəːr] compar of **far**

farthest [fɑːr'ðist] superl of **far**

fascinate [fæs'əneit] vt (intrigue, interest) うっとりさせる uttóri saserū

fascinating [fæs'əneitiŋ] adj (story, person) 魅惑的な miwákuteki na

fascination [fæsənei'ʃən] n 魅惑 miwáku

fascism [fæʃ'izəm] n (POL) ファシズム fashízùmu

fashion [fæʃ'ən] n (trend: in clothes, thought, custom etc) 流行 ryūkố, ファッション fásshòn; (also: **fashion industry**) ファッション業界 fasshòn gyốkai; (manner) やり方 yarîkata
♦vt (make) 作る tsukúrù
in fashion 流行して ryūkố shite
out of fashion 廃れて sutárete

fashionable [fæʃ'ənəbəl] adj (clothes, club, activity) 流行の ryūkố no

fashion show n ファッションショー fasshòn shố

fast [fæst] adj (runner, car, progress) 速い hayái; (clock): **to be fast** 進んでいる susúnde irú; (dye, color) あせない asénai
♦adv (run, act, think) 速く hayákù; (stuck, held) 固く katákù
♦n (REL etc) 断食 danjíki
♦vi (REL etc) 断食する danjíki suru
fast asleep ぐっすり眠っている gussúrì nemútte irú

fasten [fæs'ən] vt (tie, join) 縛る shibárù; (buttons, belt etc) 締める shimérù
♦vi 締まる shimárù

fastener [fæs'ənər] n (button, clasp, pin etc) ファスナー fásùnā

fastening [fæs'ənɪŋ] n = fastener

fast food n (hamburger etc) ファーストフード fásùtofùdo

fastidious [fæstɪd'iːəs] adj (fussy) やかましい yakámashii

fat [fæt] adj (person, animal) 太った futóttà; (book, profit) 厚い atsúi; (wallet) 金がたんまり入った kané gà tánmarì hafttá; (profit) 大きな ókina
♦n (on person, animal: also CHEM) 脂肪 shibó; (on meat) 脂身 abúramí; (for cooking) ラード rádo

fatal [feit'əl] adj (mistake) 重大な júdai na; (injury, illness) 致命的な chiméiteki na

fatalistic [feitəlɪs'tik] adj (person, attitude) 宿命論的な shukúmeironteki na

fatality [feitæl'iti:] n (road death etc) 死亡事故 shibójikò

fatally [feit'əli:] adv (mistaken) 重大に júdai ni; (injured etc) 致命的に chiméiteki ni

fate [feit] n (destiny) 運命 úñmei; (of person) 安否 áñpi

fateful [feit'fəl] adj (moment, decision) 決定的な kettéiteki na

father [fɑː'ðər] n 父 chichí, 父親 chichíoya, おやじ o-tósàn

father-in-law [fɑː'ðərɪnlɔ:] n しゅうと shúto

fatherly [fɑː'ðərli:] adj (advice, help) 父親の様な chichíoya no yó na

fathom [fæð'əm] n (NAUT) 尋 hiró ◇水深の単位、約1.83メーター sufshìn no táñ-i,

yákù 1.83métà
♦vt (understand: mystery, reason) 理解する rikái suru

fatigue [fætiːg'] n (tiredness) 疲労 hiró
metal fatigue 金属疲労 kíñzokuhiró

fatten [fæt'ən] vt (animal) 太らせる futóraserù
♦vi 太る futórù

fatty [fæt'iː] adj (food) 脂肪の多い shibó no ói
♦n (inf: person) でぶ débù

fatuous [fætʃ'uːəs] adj (idea, remark) ばかな bákà na

faucet [fɔː'sit] n (US) (tap) 蛇口 jagúchi

fault [fɔːlt] n (blame) 責任 sekíniñ; (defect: in person) 欠点 ketteñ; (: in machine) 欠陥 kekkáñ; (GEO: crack) 断層 dañsó; (TENNIS) フォールト fórùto
♦vt (criticize) 非難する hínàn suru
it's my fault 私が悪かった watákushi gà warúkattà
to find fault with ...を非難する ...wo hínàn suru
at fault ...のせいで ...no séï de

faulty [fɔːl'tiː] adj (machine) 欠陥のある kekkán no arù

fauna [fɔːn'ə] n 動物相 dóbutsusó

faux pas [fou'pɑː'] n inv 非礼 hiréi

favor [fei'vər] (BRIT favour) n (approval) 賛成 sańsei; (help) 助け tasúke
♦vt (prefer: solution etc) ...の方に賛成する ...no hó ñ nì sańsei surù; (: pupil etc) ひいきする hfíki suru; (assist: team, horse) ...に味方する ...ni mikáta suru
to do someone a favor ...の頼みを聞く ...no táñomi wo kfkù
to find favor with ...の気に入る ...no kí nì irú
in favor of ...に賛成して ...ni sańsei shite

favorable [fei'vərəbəl] adj (gen) 有利な yúri na; (reaction) 好意的な kóiteki na; (impression) 良い yói; (comparison) 賛賞する shósantekì na; (conditions) 好適な kóteki na

favorite [fei'vərit] adj (child, author etc) 一番好きな ichíban suki na
♦n (of teacher, parent) お気に入り o-kf-

niiri; (in race) 本命 hofimei

favoritism [fei'vəritizəm] *n* えこひいき ekohiïki

favour [fei'vər] *etc* = **favor** *etc*

fawn [fɔːn] *n* (young deer) 子ジカ kojíka
♦*adj* (also: **fawn-colored**) 薄茶色 usúcha-iro
♦*vi*: **to fawn (up)on** ...にへつらう ...ni hetsúraú

fax [fæks] *n* (machine, document) ファックス fákkùsu
♦*vt* (transmit document) ファックスで送る fákkùsu de okúrù

FBI [efbiːai'] (*US*) *n abbr* (= *Federal Bureau of Investigation*) 連邦捜査局 refípōsakyòku

fear [fiːr] *n* (being scared) 恐怖 kyófu; (worry) 心配 shifípaī
♦*vt* (be scared of) 恐れる osórerù; (be worried about) 心配する shifípaī suru
for fear of (in case) ...を恐れて ...wo osóretè

fearful [fiːr'fəl] *adj* (person) 怖がっている kowágattè irù; (risk, noise) 恐ろしい osóroshiî

fearless [fiːr'lis] *adj* (unafraid) 勇敢な yúkan na

feasible [fiː'zəbəl] *adj* (proposal, idea) 可能な kanó na

feast [fiːst] *n* (banquet) 宴会 efíkai; (delicious meal) ごちそう gochísō; (REL: *also:* **feast day**) 祝日 shukújitsu
♦*vi* (take part in a feast) ごちそうを食べる gochísō wò tabérù

feat [fiːt] *n* (of daring, skill) 目覚しい行為 mezámashiī kói

feather [feð'ər] *n* (of bird) 羽根 hané

feature [fiː'tʃər] *n* (characteristic) 特徴 tokúchō; (of landscape) 目立つ点 medátsu tèn; (PRESS) 特別記事 tokúbetsukiji; (TV) 特別番組 tokúbetsu bañgumi
♦*vt* (subj: film) 主役とする shuyáku to surú
♦*vi*: **to feature in** (situation, film etc) ...で主演する ...de shuén suru

feature film *n* 長編映画 chôhen eiga

features [fiː'tʃərz] *npl* (of face) 顔立ち kaódachi

fed [fed] *pt, pp of* **feed**

federal [fed'ərəl] *adj* (system, powers) 連邦の refípō no

federation [fedəreiʃən] *n* (association) 連盟 refímei

fed up [fed ʌp'] *adj*: **to be fed up** うんざりしている ufízarī shite iru

fee [fiː] *n* (payment) 料金 ryōkin; (of doctor, lawyer) 報酬 hōshū; (for examination, registration) 料金 tesúryō
school fees 授業料 jugyōryō

feeble [fiː'bəl] *adj* (weak) 弱い yowáí; (ineffectual: attempt, joke) 効果的でない kókateki de nái

feed [fiːd] *n* (of baby) ベビーフード bebífūdo; (of animal) えさ esá; (on printer) 給紙装置 kyúshisōchi
♦*vt* (*pt, pp* **fed**) (person) ...に食べさせる ...ni tabésaserù; (baby) ...に授乳する ...ni junyú suru; (horse etc) ...にえさをやる ...ni esá wò yarú; (machine) ...に供給する ...ni kyókyū suru; (data, information): **to feed into** ...に入力する ...ni nyúryoku suru

feedback [fiːd'bæk] *n* (response) フィードバック fídobàkku

feeding bottle [fiː'diŋ-] (*BRIT*) *n* ほ乳瓶 honyúbin

feed on *vt fus* (*gen*) ...を食べる ...wo tabérù, ...を常食とする ...wo jōshoku to surú; (*fig*) ...にはぐくまれる ...ni hagúkumarerù

feel [fiːl] *n* (sensation, touch) 感触 kañshoku; (impression) 印象 ifíshō
♦*vt* (*pt, pp* **felt**) (touch) ...に触る ...ni sawárù; (experience: desire, anger) 覚える obóerù; (: cold, pain) 感じる kafíjirù; (think, believe) ...だと思う ...da to omóù
to feel hungry おなかがすく onáka gà sukú

to feel cold 寒がる samúgarù

to feel lonely 寂しがる sabíshigarù

to feel better 気分がよくなる kíbun ga yóku narù

I don't feel well 気分が悪い kíbun ga warúī

it feels soft 柔らかい感じだ yawárakai

kaṅji da

to feel like (want) ...が欲しい ...ga hoshī

feel about/around vi ...を手探りで探す ...wo teságuri de sagasù

feeler [fiː'lər] n (of insect) 触角 shokkáku

to put out a feeler/feelers (fig) 打診する dashín suru

feeling [fiː'liŋ] n (emotion) 感情 kaṅjō; (physical sensation) 感触 kaṅshoku; (impression) 印象 iṅshō

feet [fiːt] npl of **foot**

feign [fein] vt (injury, interest) 見せ掛ける misékakerù

feline [fiː'lain] adj (cat-like) ネコの様な nékò no yṓ na

fell [fel] pt of **fall**

♦vt (tree) 倒す taósù

fellow [fel'ou] n (man) 男 otóko; (comrade) 仲間 nakáma; (of learned society) 会員 kaín

fellow citizen n 同郷の市民 dṓkyō no shímìn

fellow countryman (pl **countrymen**) n 同国人 dṓkokujìn

fellow men npl 外の人間 hoká no niṅgen

fellowship [fel'ouʃip] n (comradeship) 友情 yūjō; (society) 会 káì; (SCOL) 大学特別研究員 daígaku tokubetsu kenkyūin

felony [fel'æni:] n 重罪 jūzai

felt [felt] pt, pp of **feel**

♦n (fabric) フェルト férùto

felt-tip pen [felt'tip'-] n サインペン saíñpen

female [fiː'meil] n (ZOOL) 雌 mesù; (pej: woman) 女 oñna

♦adj (BIO) 雌の mesú no; (sex, character, child) 女の oñna no, 女性の joséi no; (vote etc) 女性たちの joséitachì no

feminine [fem'ænin] adj (clothes, behavior) 女性らしい joséi rashíì; (LING) 女性の joséi no

feminist [fem'ænist] n 男女同権論者 dañjodōkenrōnsha, フェミニスト fémìnisuto

fence [fens] n (barrier) 塀 hef

♦vt (also: **fence in**: land) 塀で囲む hef de kakómù

fencing [fen'siŋ] n (SPORT) フェンシング feṅshingu

fend [fend] vi: **to fend for oneself** 自力でやっていく jíriki dè yatté ikù

fender [fen'dər] n (of fireplace) 火格子 higóshi; (on boat) 防げん物 bōgeṅbutsu; (US: of car) フェンダー féñdā

fend off vt (attack etc) 受流す ukénagasù

ferment [vb fərment' n fəːr'ment] vi (beer, dough etc) 発酵する hakkṓ suru

♦n (fig: unrest) 動乱 dṓran

fern [fəːrn] n シダ shídà

ferocious [fərou'ʃəs] adj (animal, behavior) どう猛な dṓmō na; (competition) 激しい hagéshiì

ferocity [fərɑs'iti:] n (of animal, behavior) どう猛さ dṓmōsa; (of competition) 激しさ hagéshisa

ferret [fer'it] n フェレット férètto

ferret out vt (information) 捜し出す sagáshidasù

ferry [fer'i:] n (also: **ferry boat**) フェリー férī, フェリーボート feríbōto

♦vt (transport: by sea, air, road) 輸送する yusṓ suru

fertile [fəːr'təl] adj (land, soil) 肥よくな hiyóku na; (imagination) 豊かな yútàka na; (woman) 妊娠可能な niñshinkanō na

fertility [fəːrtil'əti:] n (of land) 肥よくさ hiyókusa; (of imagination) 独創性 dokúsōsei; (of woman) 繁殖力 hañshokuryòku

fertilize [fəːr'təlaiz] vt (land) ...に肥料をやる ...ni hiryṓ wò yarù; (BIO) 受精させる juséi saserù

fertilizer [fəːr'təlaizəːr] n (for plants, land) 肥料 hiryṓ

fervent [fəːr'vənt] adj (admirer, belief) 熱心な nesshín na

fervor [fəːr'vəːr] n 熱心さ nesshíñsa

fester [fes'təːr] vi (wound) 化のうする kanṓ suru

festival [fes'təvəl] n (REL) 祝日 shukújitsu; (ART, MUS) フェスティバル fésùtibaru

festive [fes'tiv] *adj* (mood, atmosphere) お祭気分の o-mátsurikibùn no
the festive season (BRIT: Christmas) クリスマスの季節 kurísùmasu no kisétsu

festivities [festiv'itiz] *npl* (celebrations) お祝い o-fwai

festoon [festun'] *vt*: *to festoon with* ...で飾る ...de kazárù

fetch [fetʃ] *vt* (bring) 持って来る motté kurù; (sell for) ...の値で売れる ...no ne de urérù

fetching [fetʃ'iŋ] *adj* (woman, dress) 魅惑的な miwákuteki na

fête [feit] *n* (at church, school) バザー bazá

fetish [fet'iʃ] *n* (obsession) 強迫観念 kyóhakukañnen

fetus [fi:'təs] (BRIT **foetus**) *n* (BIO) 胎児 táñji

feud [fju:d] *n* (quarrel) 争い arásoi

feudal [fju:d'əl] *adj* (system, society) 封建的な hőkenteki na

fever [fi:'vəːr] *n* (MED) 熱 netsú

feverish [fi:'vəriʃ] *adj* (MED) 熱がある netsú ga arù; (emotion) 激しい hagéshiì; (activity) 慌ただしい awátadashiì

few [fju:] *adj* (not many) 少数の shốsù no; (some): *a few* 幾つかの íkùtsuka no
♦*pron* (not many) 少数 shōsù; (some): *a few* 幾つかの íkùtsuka

fewer [fju:'əːr] *adj compar of* **few**

fewest [fju:'ist] *adj superl of* **few**

fiancé [fi:ɑːnsei'] *n* 婚約者 koñ-yakushà, フィアンセ fìañse ◇男性 dañsei

fiancée [fi:ɑːnsei'] *n* 婚約者 koñ-yakushà, フィアンセ fìañse ◇女性 jòséi

fiasco [fiːæs'kou] *n* (disaster) 失敗 shippái

fib [fib] *n* (lie) うそ úsò

fiber [fai'bəːr] (BRIT **fibre**) *n* (thread, roughage) 繊維 señ-i; (cloth) 生地 kíjì; (ANAT: tissue) 神経繊維 shiñkeiseñ-i

fiber-glass [fai'bəːrglæs] *n* ファイバーグラス faíbàgurasu

fickle [fik'əl] *adj* (person) 移り気な utsúrigi na; (weather) 変りやすい kawáriyasuì

fiction [fik'ʃən] *n* (LITERATURE) フィクション fíkùshon; (invention) 作り事 tsukúrigoto; (lie) うそ úsò

fictional [fik'ʃənəl] *adj* (character, event) 架空の kakū no

fictitious [fiktiʃ'əs] *adj* (false, invented) 架空の kakū no

fiddle [fid'əl] *n* (MUS) バイオリン baíorin; (*inf*: fraud, swindle) 詐欺 sági
♦*vt* (BRIT: accounts) ごまかす gomákasù

fiddle with *vt fus* (glasses etc) いじくる ijíkurù

fidelity [fidel'iti:] *n* (faithfulness) 忠誠 chúsei

fidget [fidʒ'it] *vi* (nervously) そわそわする sōwàsowa suru; (in boredom) もぞもぞする mózòmozo suru

field [fi:ld] *n* (on farm) 畑 hatáke; (SPORT: ground) グランド gurándo; (*fig*: subject, area of interest) 分野 bún-ya; (range: of vision) 視界 shfyà; (: of magnet: *also* ELEC) 磁場 jíbà

field marshal *n* (MIL) 元帥 geñsui

fieldwork [fi:ld'wəːrk] *n* (research) 現地調査 genchichōsa, 実地調査 jitchíchōsa, フィールドワーク fírudowāku

fiend [fi:nd] *n* (monster) 怪物 kaíbutsu

fiendish [fi:n'diʃ] *adj* (person, problem) 怪物の様な kaíbutsu no yố na; (problem) ものすごく難しい monósugokù muzúkashiì

fierce [fi:rs] *adj* (animal, person) どう猛な dốmô na; (fighting) 激しい hagéshiì; (loyalty) 揺るぎない yurúginaì; (heat) 猛烈な mōretsu na; (heat) うだる様な udáru yố na

fiery [fai'əːri:] *adj* (burning) 燃え盛る moésakarù; (temperament) 激しい hagéshiì

fifteen [fif'ti:n'] *num* 十五（の）jùgo (no)

fifth [fifθ] *num* 第五（の）dáigo (no)

fifty [fif'ti:] *num* 五十（の）gojù (no)

fifty-fifty [fif'ti:fif'ti:] *adj* (deal, split) 五分五分の gobúgobu na
♦*adv* 五分五分に gobúgobu ni

fig [fig] *n* (fruit) イチジク ichíjiku

fight [fait] n 戦い tatákai
♦vb (pt, pp **fought**)
♦vt (person, enemy, cancer etc: also
MIL) ...と戦う ...to tatákaù; (election)
...に出馬する ...ni shutsúba suru; (emotion) 抑える osáerù
♦vi (people: also MIL) 戦う tatákaù

fighter [fai'tər] n (combatant) 戦う人
tatákaù hitò; (plane) 戦闘機 seńtōkì

fighting [fai'tiŋ] n (battle) 戦い tatákai;
(brawl) けんか kéñka

figment [fig'mənt] n: **a figment of the
imagination** 気のせい ki nó séi

figurative [fig'jərativ] adj (expression,
style) 比喩的な hiyúteki na

figure [fig'jər] n (DRAWING, GEOM)
図 zu; (number, statistic etc) 数字 sújì;
(body, shape, outline) 形 katáchì; (person, personality) 人物 hitő
♦vt (think: esp US) ...(だと) 思う (...da
to) omőù
♦vi (appear) 現れる míerù

figurehead [fig'jərhed] n (NAUT) 船首
像 señshuző; (pej: leader) 名ばかりのリー
ダー na bákarì no rídā

figure of speech n 比喩 hiyú

figure out vt (work out) 理解する ríkai
suru

filament [fil'əmənt] n (ELEC) フィラメ
ント fíràmento

filch [filtʃ] (inf) vt (steal) くすねる kusúnerù

file [fail] n (dossier) 資料 shiryő; (folder)
書類ばさみ shorúibàsami; (COMPUT)
ファイル fáiru; (row) 列 rétsù; (tool) やす
り yasúrì
♦vt (papers) 保管する hokán suru;
(LAW: claim) 提出する teíshutsu suru;
(wood, metal, fingernails) ...にやすりを
掛ける ...ni yasúrì wo kakérù

file in/out n 1列で入る(出る) ichíretsu
de haírù(dé rù)

filing cabinet [fai'liŋ-] n ファイルキャ
ビネット fáiru kyabínètto

fill [fil] vt (container, space): **to fill
(with)** ...で一杯にする(...de) ippái
ni suru; (vacancy) 補充する hojű suru;
(need) 満たす mitásù

♦n: **to eat one's fill** たらふく食べる
taráfuku taberù

fillet [filei'] n (of meat, fish) ヒレ hiré

fillet steak n ヒレステーキ hirésutèki

fill in vt (hole) うめる umérù; (time) つぶ
す tsubúsù; (form) ...に書き入れる ...ni ka-
kíírerù

filling [fil'iŋ] n (for tooth) 充てん jüten;
(CULIN) 中身 nakámi
♦vt (scene) 撮影する satsúei suru
♦vi 撮影する satsúei suru

filling station n ガソリンスタ
ンド gasőrinsutando

fill up vt (container, space) 一杯にする
ippái ni surù
♦vi (AUT) 満タンにする mañtan ni surù

film [film] n (CINEMA, TV) 映画 éiga;
(PHOT) フィルム fírùmu; (of powder,
liquid etc) 膜 makú
♦vt (scene) 撮影する satsúei suru
♦vi 撮影する satsúei suru

film star n 映画スター eíga sutā

film strip n (slide) フィルムスライド fí-
rùmusuraido

filter [fil'tər] n (device) ろ過装置 rokáa-
sőchi, フィルター fírùta; (PHOT) フィル
ター fírùta
♦vt (liquid) ろ過する rokáa suru

filter lane (BRIT) n (AUT) 右(左)折車
線 u(sa)setsu shasèn

filter-tipped [fil'tərtipt] adj フィルター
付きの fírùtatsuki no

filth [filθ] n (dirt) 汚物 obútsu

filthy [fil'θi:] adj (object, person) 不潔な
fukétsu na; (language) みだらな mídàra
na

fin [fin] n (of fish) ひれ hiré

final [fai'nəl] adj (last) 最後の saígo no;
(ultimate) 究極の kyűkyoku no; (definitive: answer, decision) 最終的な saíshūteki na
♦n (SPORT) 決勝戦 kesshősen

finale [finæl'i:] n フィナーレ fínàre

finalist [fai'nəlist] n (SPORT) 決勝戦出
場選手 kesshősen shutsujő señshu

finalize [fai'nəlaiz] vt (arrangements,
plans) 最終的に決定する saíshūteki ni
kettéi suru

finally [fai'nəli:] adv (eventually) ようや
く yőyaku; (lastly) 最後に saígo ni

finals [fai'nəlz] *npl* (SCOL) 卒業試験 sotsúgyōshikén

finance [*n* fai'næns *vb* finæns'] *n* (money, backing) 融資 yūshi; (money management) 財政 zaísei
♦*vt* (back, fund) 融資する yūshí suru

finances [finæn'siz] *npl* (personal finances) 財政 zaísei

financial [finæn'tʃəl] *adj* (difficulties, year, venture) 経済的な kefzaiteki na

financial year *n* 会計年度 kaíkeinéñdo

financier [finænsir'] *n* (backer, funder) 出資者 shusshsha

find [faind] (*pt, pp* **found**) *vt* (person, object, answer) 見付ける mitsúkerù; (discover) 発見する hakkén suru; (think) ...だと思う ...da to omóu
♦*n* (discovery) 発見 hakkén

to find someone guilty (LAW) ...に有罪判決を下す ...ni yūzaihañketsu wo kudásù

findings [fain'diŋz] *npl* (LAW, of report) 調査の結果 chōsa no kekká

find out *vt* (fact, truth) 知る shírù; (person) ...の悪事を知る ...no akúji wo shírù
to find out about (subject) 調べる shiráberù; (by chance) 知る shírù

fine [fain] *adj* (excellent: quality, performance etc) 見事な mígòto na; (thin: hair, thread) 細い hosóî; (not coarse: sand, powder etc) 細かい komákaì; (subtle: detail, adjustment etc) 細かい komákaì
♦*adv* (well) うまく úmaku
♦*n* (LAW) 罰金 bakkín
♦*vt* (LAW) ...に罰金を払わせる ...ni bakkín wò haráwaserù

to be fine (person) 元気である geñki de árù; (weather) 良い天気である yóì téñki de árù

fine arts *npl* 美術 bíjùtsu

finery [fai'nə:ri] *n* (dress) 晴着 harégi; (jewelery) 取って置きの装身具 tottéoki nô sōshíñgu

finesse [fines'] *n* 手腕 shúwàn

finger [fiŋ'gə:r] *n* (ANAT) 指 yubí
♦*vt* (touch) ...に指で触る ...ni yubí de sawárù

little/index finger 小〔人差し〕指 ko

〔hitósashi〕yúbi

fingernail [fiŋ'gə:rneil] *n* つめ tsume

fingerprint [fiŋ'gə:rprint] *n* (mark) 指紋 shímoñ

fingertip [fiŋ'gə:rtip] *n* 指先 yubísaki

finicky [fin'iki:] *adj* (fussy) 気難しい kimúzukashiî

finish [fin'iʃ] *n* (end) 終り owárî; (SPORT) ゴール gōru; (polish etc) 仕上り shiágari
♦*vt* (work, eating, book etc) 終える oérù
♦*vi* (person, course, event) 終る owárù
to finish doing something ...し終える ...shi óerù
to finish third (in race etc) 3着になる sañchaku ni naru

finishing line [fin'iʃiŋ-] *n* ゴールライン gōrurain

finishing school [fin'iʃiŋ-] *n* 花嫁学校 hanáyomegakkō

finish off *vt* (complete) 仕上げる shiágerù; (kill) 止めを刺す todóme wo sasù

finish up *vt* (food, drink) 平らげる taíragerù
♦*vi* (end up) 最後に...に行ってしまう saígo ni ...ni itté shimaù

finite [fai'nait] *adj* (time, space) 一定の ittéi no; (verb) 定形の teíkei no

Finland [fin'lənd] *n* フィンランド fíñrando

Finn [fin] *n* フィンランド人 fíñrandojiñ

Finnish [fin'iʃ] *adj* フィンランドの fíñrando no; (LING) フィンランド語の fíñrando-go no
♦*n* (LING) フィンランド語 fíñrandogo

fiord [fjourd] *n* = **fjord**

fir [fə:r] *n* モミ mómì

fire [faiə:r] *n* (flames) 火 hí; (in hearth) たき火 takíbi; (accidental) 火事 kaji; (gas fire, electric fire) ヒーター hītā
♦*vt* (shoot: gun etc) うつ útsù; (: arrow) 射る írù; (stimulate: imagination, enthusiasm) 刺激する shigéki suru; (*inf*: dismiss: employee) 首にする kubí ni suru
♦*vi* (shoot) 発砲する happō suru
on fire 燃えて móete

fire alarm *n* 火災警報装置 kasáikeihōsōchi

firearm [faiə:r'ɑ:rm] *n* 銃砲 jūhō ◇ 特に

ピストルを指す tōkū ni písutoru wò sásu

fire brigade *n* 消防隊 shōbōtai

fire department (*US*) *n* = **fire brigade**

fire engine *n* 消防自動車 shōbōjídōsha

fire escape *n* 非常階段 hijōkáidan

fire extinguisher *n* 消化器 shōkakí

fireman [faiər'mən] (*pl* **firemen**) *n* 消防士 shōbōshi

fireplace [faiər'pleis] *n* 暖炉 dánro

fireside [faiər'said] *n* 暖炉のそば dánro no sóba

fire station *n* 消防署 shōbōsho

firewood [faiər'wud] *n* まき makí

fireworks [faiər'wərks] *npl* 花火 hánabi

firing squad [faiər'iŋ-] *n* 銃殺隊 jūsatsutai

firm [fərm] *adj* (mattress, ground) 固い katái; (grasp, push, tug) 強い tsuyóī; (decision) 断固とした dánko to shita; (faith) 固い katái; (measures) 強固な kyōko na; (look, voice) しっかりした shikkárī shita

　◆*n* (company) 会社 kaísha

firmly [fərm'li:] *adv* (grasp, pull, tug) 強く tsuyóku; (decide) 断固として dánko to shite; (look, speak) しっかりと shikkárī to

first [fərst] *adj* (before all others) 第一の dáīchi no, 最初の saísho no

　◆*adv* (before all others) 一番に ichíban ni, 一番最初に saísho ni; (when listing reasons etc) 第一に dáīchi ni

　◆*n* (person: in race) 1着 itcháku; (AUT) ローギヤ rōgiya; (BRIT SCOL: degree) 1級優等卒業学位証 ikkyū yūtō sotsugyō gakui 《英国では優等卒業学位は成績の高い順に1級、2級、3級に分けられる efkoku de wá yūtō sotsugyō gakui wa seíseki no takái jūn ni ikkyū, nikyū, sankyū nī wakérarerú

at first 最初は saísho wa

first of all まず第一に mázu dáīchi ni

first aid *n* 応急手当 ōkyūteáte

first-aid kit *n* 救急箱 kyūkyúbako

first-class [fərst'klæs'] *adj* (excellent: mind, worker) 優れた sugúretà; (car-

riage, ticket, post) 1等の ittō no

first-hand [fərst'hænd'] *adj* (account, story) 直接の chokúsetsu no

first lady (*US*) *n* 大統領夫人 daítōryōfujín

firstly [fərst'li:] *adv* 第一に dáīchi ni

first name *n* 名 na, ファーストネーム fāsutonēmu

first-rate [fərst'reit'] *adj* (player, actor etc) 優れた sugúretà

fiscal [fis'kəl] *adj* (year) 会計の kaíkei no; (policies) 財政の zaísei no

fish [fiʃ] *n inv* 魚 sakána

　◆*vt* (river, area) …で釣をする …de tsurí wo surú

　◆*vi* (commercially) 漁をする ryō wo surú; (as sport, hobby) 釣をする tsurí wo surú

to go fishing 釣りに行く tsurí ni ikú

fisherman [fiʃ'ərmən] (*pl* **fishermen**) *n* 漁師 ryōshi

fish farm *n* 養魚場 yṓgyojō

fish fingers (*BRIT*) *npl* = **fish sticks**

fishing boat [fiʃ'iŋ-] *n* 漁船 gyosén

fishing line *n* 釣糸 tsurfitō

fishing rod *n* 釣ざお tsurízao

fishmonger's (shop) [fiʃ'mʌŋgərz-] *n* 魚屋 sakánaya

fish sticks (*US*) *npl* フィッシュスティック físshūsutikkù 《細長く切った魚に小麦粉をまぶして揚げた物 hosónagaku kittá sakána ni pánko wo mabúshite agéta monó

fishy [fiʃ'i:] (*inf*) *adj* (tale, story) 怪しい ayáshiī

fission [fiʃ'ən] *n* 分裂 bunretsu

fissure [fiʃ'ər] *n* 亀裂 kiretsu

fist [fist] *n* こぶし kóbushi, げんこつ genkotsu

fit [fit] *adj* (suitable) 適当な tekítō na; (healthy) 健康な kenkō na

　◆*vt* (subj: clothes, shoes) …にぴったり合う …ni pittárī au; (put in) …に入れる …ni irérū; (attach, equip) …に取付ける …ni torítsukerú; (suit) …に合う …ni áū

　◆*vi* (clothes etc) ぴったり合う pittárī áū; (parts) 合う áū; (in space, gap) ぴったりはいる pittárī haírū

♦*n* (MED) 発作 hossā; (of coughing, giggles) 発作的に...する事 hossāteki ni ...suru kotó

fit to (ready) ...出来る状態にある ...dekirū jōtai ni arū

fit for (suitable for) ...に適当である ...ni tekítō de arū

a fit of anger かんしゃく kańshaku

this dress is a good fit このドレスはぴったりした体に合う konó doresu wa pittárì karáda ni áù

by fits and starts 動いたり止ったりして ugóitarì tomáttarì shité

fitful [fit'fəl] *adj* (sleep) 途切れ途切れの togíretogìre no

fit in *vi* (person) 溶込む tokékomù

fitment [fit'mənt] *n* (in room, cabin) 取付け家具 torítsukekagù ◇つり戸棚など壁などに固定した家具を指す tsurítodāna nádò kabé nadò ni kotéi shitá kagù wo sásù

fitness [fit'nis] *n* (MED) 健康 keńkō

fitted carpet [fit'id-] *n* 敷込みじゅうたん shikíkomijūtan

fitted kitchen [fit'id-] *n* システムキッチン shisútemu kitchín

fitter [fit'əːr] *n* (of machinery, equipment) 整備工 seíbikō

fitting [fit'iŋ] *adj* (compliment, thanks) 適切な tekísetsu na
♦*n* (of dress) 試着 shicháku; (of piece of equipment) 取付け torítsuke

fitting room *n* (in shop) 試着室 shichákushìtsu

fittings [fit'iŋz] *npl* (in building) 設備 sétsubi

five [faiv] *num* 五 (の) gó (no), 五つ (の) itsútsù (no)

fiver [fai'vəːr] *n* (*inf*: BRIT: 5 pounds) 5ポンド札 gópondo satsù; (US: 5 dollars) 5ドル札 gódoru satsù

fix [fiks] *vt* (attach) 取付ける torítsukerū; (sort out, arrange) 手配する tehái suru; (mend) 直す naósù; (prepare: meal, drink) 作る tsukúrù
♦*n*: *to be in a fix* 困っている komátte irū

fixed [fikst] *adj* (price, amount etc) 一定の ittéi no

a fixed idea 固定観念 kotéikañnen

a fixed smile 作り笑い tsukúriwarài

fixture [fiks'tʃəːr] *n* (bath, sink, cupboard etc) 設備 sétsubi; (SPORT) 試合の予定 shiái no yotéi

fix up *vt* (meeting) 手配する tehái suru

to fix someone up with something ...のために...を手に入れる ...no tamé ni ...wo té ni irerū

fizzle out [fiz'əl-] *vi* (event) しりすぼみに終ってしまう shirísubomì ni owátte shimaù; (interest) 次第に消えてしまう shidáì ni kiéte shimaù

fizzy [fiz'i:] *adj* (drink) 炭酸入りの tańsan-irì no

fjord [fjourd] *n* フィヨルド fíyorudo

flabbergasted [flæb'əːrgæstid] *adj* (dumbfounded, surprised) あっけにとられた akké ni torareta

flabby [flæb'i:] *adj* (fat) 締まりのない shimári no nái

flag [flæg] *n* (of country, organization) 旗 hatá; (for signalling) 手旗 tebáta; (*also*: **flagstone**) 敷石 shikíishi
♦*vi* (person, spirits) 弱る yowárù

to flag someone down (taxi, car etc) 手を振って...を止める té wo futté ...wo toméru

flagpole [flæg'poul] *n* 旗ざお hatázao

flagrant [fleig'rənt] *adj* (violation, injustice) 甚だしい hanáhadashìi

flagship [flæg'ʃip] *n* (of fleet) 旗艦 kíkan; (*fig*) 看板施設 kańbanshisètsu

flair [fleːr] *n* (talent) 才能 saínō; (style) 粋なセンス ikí na sensu

flak [flæk] *n* (MIL) 対空砲火 taíkūhōka; (*inf*: criticism) 非難 hínan

flake [fleik] *n* (of rust, paint) はげ落ちた欠けら hagéochità kákera; (of snow, soap powder) 一片 íppen
♦*vi* (*also*: **flake off**: paint, enamel) はげ落ちる hagéochirù

flamboyant [flæmboi'ənt] *adj* (dress, design) けばけばしい kebákebashìi; (person) 派手な hadé na

flame [fleim] *n* (of fire) 炎 honó-ò

flamingo [fləmiŋ'gou] *n* プラミンゴ fu-rámīngo

flammable [flæm'əbəl] *adj* (gas, fabric) 燃えやすい moéyasuí

flan [flæn] *n* (BRIT) フラン fúràn ◇菓子の一種 kashí no isshū

flank [flæŋk] *n* (of animal) わき腹 wakíbāra; (of army) 側面 sokúmèn
◇*vt* ...のわきをはさむ(いる) ...no wakí ni arú (iru)

flannel [flæn'əl] *n* (fabric) フランネル furánneru; (BRIT: also: **face flannel**) フェースタオル fēsutaoru

flannels [flæn'əlz] *npl* フランネルズボン furánneruzubòn

flap [flæp] *n* (of pocket, envelope, jacket) ふた futá
◇*vt* (arms, wings) ばたばたさせる bátàbata saserú
◇*vi* (sail, flag) はためく hátamekú; (*inf: also:* **be in a flap**) 興奮している kófun shité irú

flare [fler'] *n* (signal) 発煙筒 hatsúèntō; (in skirt etc) フレア furéa

flare up *vi* (fire) 燃え上る moéagarù; (*fig:* person) 怒る okórù; (: fighting) ぼっ発する boppátsu suru

flash [flæʃ] *n* (of light) 閃光 seńkō; (also: **news flash**) ニュースフラッシュ nyúsufuràsshu; (PHOT) フラッシュ furásshù
◇*vt* (light, headlights) 点滅させる teńmetsu saserú; (send: news, message) 速報する sokúhō suru; (: look, smile) 見せる misérù
◇*vi* (lightning, light) 光る hikárù; (light on ambulance etc) 点滅する teńmetsu suru

in a flash 一瞬にして isshún ni shite

to flash by/past (person) 走って通り過ぎる hashíttè tōrisugirú

flashback [flæʃ'bæk] *n* (CINEMA) フラッシュバック furásshubakkù

flashbulb [flæʃ'bʌlb] *n* フラッシュバルブ furásshubarùbu

flashcube [flæʃ'kjub] *n* フラッシュキューブ furásshukyùbu

flashlight [flæʃ'lait] *n* 懐中電灯 kaíchūdentō

flashy [flæʃ'i:] (*pej*) *adj* 派手な hadé na

flask [flæsk] *n* (bottle) 瓶 bíñ; (also: **vacuum flask**) 魔法瓶 máhōbin, ポット póttò

flat [flæt] *n* (ground, surface) 平な tañra na; (tire) パンクした páñku shita; (battery) 上がった agáttà; (beer) 気が抜けた ki ga núketa; (refusal, denial) きっぱりした kippárì shita; (MUS: note) フラットの furáttò no; (: voice) そっけない sokkénāi; (rate, fee) 均一の kiń-itsu no
◇*n* (BRIT: apartment) アパート apáto; (AUT) パンク páñku; (MUS) フラット furáttò

to work flat out 力一杯働く chikára ippái hataraku

flatly [flæt'li:] *adv* (refuse, deny) きっぱりと kippárì to

flatten [flæt'ən] *vt* (also: **flatten out**) 平にする tañra ni surù; (building, city) 取壊す toríkowasù

flatter [flæt'ə:r] *vt* (praise, compliment) ...にお世辞を言う ...ni oséji wò iú

flattering [flæt'ə:riŋ] *adj* (comment) うれしい uréshiī; (dress) よく似合う yókù niáù

flattery [flæt'ə:ri:] *n* お世辞 oséji

flaunt [flɔ:nt] *vt* (wealth, possessions) 見せびらかす misébirakasù

flavor [flei'və:r] (BRIT **flavour**) *n* (of food, drink) 味 ajī; (of ice-cream etc) 種類 shúrùi
◇*vt* ...に味を付ける ...ni ajī wo tsukerú
strawberry-flavored イチゴ味の ichígoajì no

flavoring [flei'və:riŋ] *n* 調味料 chōmiryō

flaw [flɔ:] *n* (in argument, policy) 不備な点 fúbì na teñ; (in character) 欠点 ketteñ; (in cloth, glass) 傷 kizú

flawless [flɔ:'lis] *adj* 完璧な kañpeki na

flax [flæks] *n* 亜麻 amá

flaxen [flæk'sən] *adj* (hair) ブロンドの buróñdo no

flea [fli:] *n* (human, animal) ノミ nomí

fleck [flek] *n* (mark) 細かい斑点 komákaì hañten

fled [fled] *pt, pp of* flee

flee [fli:] (*pt, pp* **fled**) *vt* (danger, famine, country) 逃れる nogarérù, ...から逃げる ...kara nigérù
♦*vi* (refugees, escapees) 逃げる nigérù

fleece [fli:s] *n* (sheep's wool) 羊毛一頭分 yōmóittōbùn; (sheep's coat) ヒツジの毛 hitsúji no ke
♦*vt* (*inf*: cheat) ...から大金をだまし取る ...kara taíkìn wò damáshitorù

fleet [fli:t] *n* (of ships: for war) 艦隊 kańtai; (: for fishing etc) 船団 seńdan; (of trucks, cars) 車両団 sharyōdan

fleeting [fli:'tiŋ] *adj* (glimpse) ちらっと見える chiráttò miérù; (visit) 短い mijíkaì; (happiness) つかの間の tsuká no mà no

Flemish [flem'iʃ] *adj* フランダースの furándasu no; (LING) フランダース語の furándasugo no
♦*n* (LING) フランダース語 furándasugo

flesh [fleʃ] *n* (ANAT) 肉 nikú; (skin) 肌 hadá; (of fruit) 果肉 kańnìku

flesh wound *n* 軽傷 keíshō

flew [flu:] *pt of* **fly**

flex [fleks] *n* (of appliance) コード kódo
♦*vt* (leg, muscles) 曲げたり伸したりする magétarì nobáshitarì suru

flexibility [fleksəbil'əti:] *n* (of material) しなやかさ shináyakasà; (of response, policy) 柔軟性 jūnansei

flexible [flek'səbəl] *adj* (material) 曲げやすい magéyasuì; (response, policy) 柔軟な jūnan na

flick [flik] *n* (of hand, whip etc) 一振り hitófurì
♦*vt* (with finger, hand) はじき飛ばす hajíkitobasù; (towel, whip) びしっと鳴らす pishíttò narú; (switch: on) 入れる iréru; (: off) 切る kírù

flicker [flik'ər] *n* (light) ちらちらする chíràchira suru; (flame) ゆらゆらする yúràyura suru; (eyelids) まばたく mabátakù

flick through *vt fus* (book) ぱらぱらと ...のページをめくる páràpara to ...no pējì wo mekúru

flier [flai'ər] *n* (pilot) パイロット pařróttò

flight [flait] *n* (action: of birds, plane) 飛行 hikō; (AVIAT: journey) 飛行機旅行 hikōkiryokō; (escape) 逃走 tōhi; (*also*: flight of steps/stairs) 階段 kaídan

flight attendant (*US*) *n* 乗客係 jōkyakukakàri

flight deck *n* (AVIAT) 操縦室 sōjūshitsu; (NAUT) 空母の飛行甲板 kūbo no hikōkañpan

flimsy [flim'zi:] *adj* (shoes) こわれやすい kowáreyasuì; (clothes) 薄い usúì; (building) もろい moróì; (excuse) 見え透いた miésuità

flinch [flintʃ] *vi* (in pain, shock) 身震いする mibúruì suru
to flinch from (crime, unpleasant duty) ...するのをしり込みする ...surú no wò shirígomi suru

fling [fliŋ] (*pt, pp* **flung**) *vt* (throw) 投げる nagérù

flint [flint] *n* (stone) 火打石 hiúchiishì; (in lighter) 石 ishí

flip [flip] *vt* (switch) はじく hajíkù; (coin) トスする tósù suru

flippant [flip'ənt] *adj* (attitude, answer) 軽率な keísotsu na

flipper [flip'ər] *n* (of seal etc) ひれ足 hiréashì; (for swimming) フリッパー furíppà

flirt [flərt] *vi* (with person) いちゃつく ichátsukù
♦*n* 浮気者 uwákimonò

flit [flit] *vi* (birds, insects) ひょいと飛ぶ hyoí tò tobú

float [flout] *n* (for swimming, fishing) 浮き ukí; (vehicle in parade) 山車 dashí; (money) つり用の小銭 tsuríyō no kozéni
♦*vi* 浮く ukú

flock [flɑːk] *n* 群れ muré; (REL) 会衆 kaíshū
♦*vi*: **to flock to** (place, event) ぞくぞく集まる zókùzoku atsúmarù

flog [flɑːg] *vt* (whip) むち打つ múchìutsu

flood [flʌd] *n* (of water) 洪水 kōzui; (of letters, imports etc) 大量 taíryō
♦*vt* (subj: water) 水浸しにする mizúbitashi ni suru; (: people) ...に殺到する ...ni sattō suru

♦vi (place) 水浸しになる mizúbitàshi ni nárù; (people): **to flood into** ...に殺到する ...ni sattō suru

flooding [flʌd'iŋ] n 洪水 kōzui

floodlight [flʌd'lait] n 照明灯 shōmeitō

floor [flɔːr] n (of room) 床 yuká; (storey) 階 kái; (of sea, valley) 底 soko

♦vt (subj: blow) 打ちのめす uchínomesù; (: question) 仰天させる gyōten saserú

ground floor 1階 ikkai

first floor (US) 1階 ikkai (BRIT) 2階 nikái

floorboard [flɔːr'bɔːrd] n 床板 yuká-ita

floor show n フロアショー furóashō

flop [flɑp] n (failure) 失敗 shippái

♦vi (fail) 失敗する shippái suru; (fall: into chair, onto floor etc) どたっと座り込む dotáttò suwárikomù

floppy [flɑp'i:] adj ふにゃふにゃした fúnyàfunya shita

floppy (disk) n (COMPUT) フロッピー（ディスク）furóppi(dìsùku)

flora [flɔːr'ə] n 植物相 shokúbutsusō

floral [flɔːr'əl] adj (dress, wallpaper) 花柄の hanágara no

florid [flɔːr'id] adj (style) ごてごてした gótègote shitá; (complexion) 赤らんだ akáranda

florist [flɔːr'ist] n 花屋 hanáya

florist's (shop) n 花屋 hanáya

flounce [flauns] n (frill) 縁飾り fuchíkazarí

flounce out vi 怒って飛び出す okótte tobídasù

flounder [flaun'dəːr] vi (swimmer) もがく mogákù; (fig: speaker) まごつく magótsukù; (economy) 停滞する teítai suru

♦n (ZOOL) ヒラメ hiráme

flour [flau'əːr] n (gen) 粉 koná; (also: wheat flour) 小麦粉 komúgiko

flourish [flɔːr'iʃ] vi (business) 繁栄する hañ-ei suru; (plant) 生い茂る oíshigerù

♦n (bold gesture): **with a flourish** 大げさな身振りで ōgesa na mibúri de

flourishing [flɔːr'iʃiŋ] adj (company) 繁栄する hañ-ei suru; (trade) 盛んな sakán na

flout [flaut] vt (law, rules) 犯す okásù

flow [flou] n 流れ nagáre

♦vi 流れる nagárerù

flow chart n 流れ図 nagárezù, フローチャート furōchāto

flower [flau'əːr] n 花 haná

♦vi (plant, tree) 咲く sakú

flower bed n 花壇 kádàn

flowerpot [flau'əːrpɑt] n 植木鉢 uékibàchi

flowery [flau'əːri:] adj (perfume) 花の様な haná no yō na; (pattern) 花柄の hanágara no; (speech) 仰々しい gyōgyōshī

flown [floun] pp of **fly**

flu [fluː] n (MED) 流感 ryūkan

fluctuate [flʌk'tʃueit] vi (price, rate, temperature) 変動する heñdō suru

fluctuation [flʌktʃuei'ʃən] n: **fluctuation (in)** (...の) 変動 (...no) heñdō

fluent [fluː'ənt] adj (linguist) 語学たん能な gakúgakutànnō na; (speech, writing etc) 滑らかな naméràka na

he speaks fluent French, he's fluent in French 彼はフランス語が堪能だ kárè wa furánsugo ga tańnō da

fluently [fluː'əntli:] adv (speak, read, write) 流ちょうに ryūchō ni

fluff [flʌf] n (on jacket, carpet) 毛羽 kebá; (fur: of kitten etc) 綿毛 watáge

fluffy [flʌf'i:] adj (jacket, toy etc) ふわふわした fúwàfuwa shitá

fluid [fluː'id] adj (movement) しなやかなshináyàka na; (situation, arrangement) 流動的な ryūdōteki na

♦n (liquid) 液 ékì

fluke [fluːk] n (inf) まぐれ magúre

flung [flʌŋ] pt, pp of **fling**

fluorescent [fluəres'ənt] adj (dial, paint, light etc) 蛍光の keíkō no

fluoride [fluː'əːraid] n フッ化物 fukkábùtsu

flurry [fləːr'iː] n: **a snow flurry** にわか雪 niwákayùki

flurry of activity 慌ただしい動き awátadashiì ugóki

flush [flʌʃ] n (on face) ほてり hotéri; (fig: of youth, beauty etc) 輝かしさ kagáyakashisà

♦vt (drains, pipe) 水を流して洗う mizú

wǒ nagashite araú

♦vi (become red) 赤くなる akáku narú

♦adj: flush with (level) ...と同じ高さの
...to onáji takasà no

to flush the toilet トイレの水を流す
tôîre no mizú wo nagasú

flushed [flʌʃt] adj 赤らめた akárameta

flush out vt (game, birds) 茂みから追出
す shigémì kàra oídasù

flustered [flʌ́stərd] adj (nervous, confused) まごついた magótsuità

flute [fluːt] n フルート furúto

flutter [flʌ́tər] n (of wings) 羽ばたき
hàbátakì; (of panic, excitement, nerves)
うろたえ urótae

♦vi (bird) 羽ばたきする habátaki suru

flux [flʌks] n: in a state of flux 流動の
状態で ryūdōtekíjōtai de

fly [flai] n (insect) ハエ haé; (on trousers:
also: flies) ズボンの前 zubón no maé

♦vb (pt flew, pp flown)

♦vt (plane) 操縦する sōjū suru; (passengers, cargo) 空輸する kúyū suru; (distances) 飛ぶ tobú

♦vi (bird, insect, plane) 飛ぶ tobú; (passengers) 飛行機で行く hikōki de ikú;
(escape) 逃げる nigérù; (flag) 掲げられる
kakágerarerù

fly away vi (bird, insect) 飛んで行く toñde
ikú

flying [flaíiŋ] n (activity) 飛行機旅行 hikōkiryokō; (action) 飛行 hikō

♦adj: a flying visit ほんの短い訪問 hoñno míjìkaì hōmon

with flying colors 大成功で daíseikō de

flying saucer n 空飛ぶ円盤 sórà tobú
eñban

flying start n: to get off to a flying
start 好調な滑りだしをする kóchō na
suberídashi wo suru

fly off vi = fly away

flyover [flaíouvər] (BRIT) n (overpass)
陸橋 rikkyó

flysheet [flaíʃiːt] n (for tent) 入口の垂れ
布 iríguchi nò tarénuno

foal [foul] n 子ウマ koúma

foam [foum] n (of surf, water, beer) 泡
awā; (also: foam rubber) フォームラバー
fómurabā

♦vi (liquid) 泡立つ awádatsu

to foam at the mouth (person, animal)
泡をふく awá wo fukú

fob [fɑb] vt: to fob someone off ...をだ
ます ...wo damásu

focal point [fouʹkəl-] n (of room, activity etc) 中心 chúshin

focus [fouʹkəs] (pl focuses) n (PHOT) 焦
点 shōten; (of attention, storm etc) 中心
chúshin

♦vt (field glasses etc) ...の焦点を合せる
...no shōten wo awáserù

♦vi: to focus (on) (with camera)
(...に) カメラを合せる (...ni) kámèra wò
awáserù; (person) (...に) 注意を向ける
(...ni) chūi wo mukérù

in/out of focus 焦点が合っている(い
ない) shōten ga attè irú (inái)

fodder [fɑ́dər] n (food) 飼葉 kaíba

foe [fou] n (rival, enemy) 敵 tekí

foetus [fíːtəs] n (BRIT) = fetus

fog [fɔg] n 霧 kirí

foggy [fɔ́gíː] adj: it's foggy 霧が出てい
る kirí ga detè irú

fog light (BRIT fog lamp) n (AUT) フ
ォッグライト fóggùraito

foil [fɔil] vt (attack, plot) くじく kujíkù

♦n (metal foil, kitchen foil) ホイル hōí-
ru; (complement) 引立てる物 hikítaterù
monó; (FENCING) フルーレ furúrè

fold [fould] n (bend, crease) 折目 oríme;
(of skin etc) しわ shiwá; (in cloth, curtain etc) ひだ hidá; (AGR) 羊の囲い
hitsújì nò kakóì; (fig) 仲間 nakáma

♦vt (clothes, paper) 畳む tatámù; (arms)
組む kúmù

folder [fouʹldər] n (for papers) 書類挟み
n shorúibasàmi

folding [fouʹldiŋ] adj (chair, bed) 折畳み
式の orítatamishìki no

fold up vi (map, bed, table) 折畳める orí-
tatamerù; (business) つぶれる tsubúrerù

♦vt (map, clothes etc) 畳む tatámù

foliage [fouʹliːidʒ] n (leaves) 葉 há ◇総称
sōshō

folk [fouk] npl (people) 人々 hitobito

♦adj (art, music) 民族の mínzoku no

folks (parents) 両親 ryōshin

folklore [fouk'lɔːr] n 民間伝承 mínkandénshō

folk song n 民謡 mín'yō

follow [fɑːl'ou] **vt** (person) ...について行く ...ni tsúite ikú; (suspect) 尾行する bikō suru; (event) ...に注目する ...ni chūmoku suru; (story) 注意して追う chūi shite ōú; (leader, example, advice, instructions) ...に従う ...ni shitágaú; (route, path) たどる tadóru

♦vi (person, period of time) 後に来る（いく）átò ni kúru(ikú); (result) ...という結果になる ...to iú kekkà ni nárù

to follow suit (fig) (...と) 同じ事をする (...to) onáji kotò wo suru

follower [fɑːl'ouəːr] n (of person) 支持者 shijíshà; (of belief) 信奉者 shínpōsha

following [fɑːl'ouiŋ] **adj** 次の tsugí no

♦n (of party, religion, group etc) 支持者 shijíshà ◇総称 sōshō

follow up **vt** (letter, offer) ...に答える ...ni kotáerù; (case) 追及する tsuíkyū suru

folly [fɑːl'iː] n (foolishness) ばかな事 báka na kotó

fond [fɑːnd] **adj** (memory) 楽しい tanóshiì; (smile, look) 愛情に満ちた ajō ni michìta; (hopes, dreams) 愚かな órōka na

to be fond of ...が好きである ...ga sukí de arù

fondle [fɑːn'dəl] **vt** 愛ぶする aíbú suru

font [fɑːnt] n (in church) 洗礼盤 senréìban; (TYP) フォント fóntò

food [fuːd] n 食べ物 tabémonð

food mixer n ミキサー mīkísà

food poisoning [-poi'zəniŋ] n 食中毒 shokúchūdoku

food processor [-prɑːs'esəːr] n ミキサー mīkísà ◇食べ物を混ぜたりひいたりおろしたりするための家庭電気製品 tabemono wo mazetari hiitari oroshitari suru tame no katei denki seihin

foodstuffs [fuːd'stʌfs] **npl** 食料 shokúryō

fool [fuːl] n (idiot) ばか bákà; (CULIN

フール fūru ◇果物及びムースの一種 kudámono-iri mūsu no isshú

♦vt (deceive) だます damásù

♦vi (also: **fool around**: be silly) ふざける fuzákerù

foolhardy [fuːl'hɑːrdiː] **adj** (conduct) 無謀な mubō na

foolish [fuː'liʃ] **adj** (stupid) ばかな bákà na; (rash) 無茶な muchá na

foolproof [fuːl'pruːf] **adj** (plan etc) 絶対確実な zettáikakùjitsu na

foot [fut] (pl **feet**) n (of person, animal) 足 ashí; (of bed, cliff) ふもと fumótò; (measure) フィート fītò

♦vt (bill) 支払う shiháraù

on foot 徒歩で tóhò de

footage [fut'idʒ] n (CINEMA) 場面 bámèn

football [fut'bɔːl] n (ball: round) サッカーボール sakkáboru; (: oval) フットボール futtóboru; (sport: BRIT) サッカー sakkā; (: US) フットボール futtóbōru

football player (BRIT: also: **footballer**) サッカー選手 sakkā senshu; (US) フットボール選手 futtóbōru senshu

footbrake [fut'breik] n 足ブレーキ ashí burèki

footbridge [fut'bridʒ] n 橋 hashí ◇歩行者しか渡れない狭い物を指す hokóshà shika watárenaì semái monó wo sasù

foothills [fut'hilz] **npl** 山ろくの丘陵地帯 safíroku no kyūryōchítai

foothold [fut'hould] n 足場 ashíba

footing [fut'iŋ] n (fig: position) 立場 tachíba

to lose one's footing 足を踏み外す ashí wo fumíhazusù

footlights [fut'laits] **npl** (THEATER) フットライト futtóraìto

footman [fut'mən] (pl **footmen**) n (servant) 下男 genán

footnote [fut'nout] n 脚注 kyakúchū

footpath [fut'pæθ] n 遊歩道 yūhodō

footprint [fut'print] n (of person, animal) 足跡 ashíato

footstep [fut'step] n (sound) 足音 ashíoto; (footprint) 足跡 ashíato

footwear [fut'weːr] n (shoes, sandals

etc)履物 hakímono

KEYWORD

for [fɔːr] *prep* **1** (indicating destination, intention) ...行きの ...yuki no, ...に向かって ...ni mūkátte, ...のために(の) ...notaménī(no)

the train for London ロンドン行きの電車 róndonyuki no densha

he left for Rome 彼はローマへ出発しました kárè wa rômà e shúppatsu shimashīta

he went for the paper 彼は新聞を取りに行きました kárè wa shínbun wo torī ni ikímashīta

is this for me? これは私に? korě wa wátákushi ni?

there's a letter for you あなた宛の手紙が来ています ánàta ate no tegami ga kítě ímasu

it's time for lunch 昼食の時間です chûshoku no jikan desù

2 (indicating purpose) ...のために(の) ...no tamé ní(no)

what's it for? それは何のためですか sorě wa nàn no tamé desù ká

give it to me - what for? それをよこせ-何で? sorě wo yòkósé - nàndé?

clothes for children 子供服 kodőmofuku

to pray for peace 平和を祈る héiwa wo inorū

3 (on behalf of, representing) ...の代理として ...no daíri toshite

the MP for Hove ホーブ選出の議員 hôbùsénshutsu no gíin

he works for the government/a local firm 彼は政府(地元の会社)に雇われています kárè wa séìfu(jimôto no kaísha)ni yatówárète imásù

I'll ask him for you あなたに代って私が彼に聞きましょう wátákushi ga kárè ni kikímashő

G for George Gはジョージの G G wà jôjì no G

4 (because of) ...の理由で ...no ríyù de, ...のために ...no tamé no

for this reason このため kónò tame

for fear of being criticized 批判を恐れて híhàn wo ósórète

the town is famous for its canals 町は運河で有名です machí wà úngà de yûmei desù

5 (with regard to) ...にしては ...ni shité wà

it's cold for July 7月にしては寒い shíchígatsu ni shité wà samúi

he's mature for his age 彼はませている kárè wa másète irú

a gift for languages 語学の才能 gógàku no saínő

for everyone who voted yes, 50 voted no 賛成1人に対して反対50だった sánsei íchí nì tái shite hántaíhyő gojû dàtta

6 (in exchange for) ...と交換して ...to kőkan shite

I sold it for $5 5ドルでそれを売りました gódőru de soré wo úrímashíta

to pay $2.50 for a ticket 切符を2ドル50セントで買う kíppù wo nídőru gojússéntő de kaú

7 (in favor of) ...に賛成して ...ni sánsei shite

are you for or against us? あなたは我々に賛成なのか反対なのかはっきり言いなさい ánàta wa waréwarè ni sánsei na nő ka hántai na nő ka hakkírí sínasaí

I'm all for it 私は無条件で賛成です wátákushi wa mújőkèn de sánsei desù

vote for X Xに投票する ékkùsu ni tőhyő suru

8 (referring to distance) *there are roadworks for 5 km* 5キロもの区間が工事中です gőkíro mo no kúkàn ga kőjíchů desù

we walked for miles 何マイルも歩きました nánmaîru mo arúkímashīta

9 (referring to time) ...の間 ...no aída

he was away for 2 years 彼は2年間家を離れていました kárè wa nínéhkan iế wő haăreте imáshīta

she will be away for a month 彼女は1か月間出掛ける事になっています kánòjo wa ikkágetsukàn dekákeru kotô ni natté imásù *it hasn't rained for 3 weeks* 雨は3週間も降っていません áme wa sańshúkan mo futté imaseń

I have known her for years 何年も前から彼女とは知り合いです nánnen mo máe kara kánòjo to wa shírìai desù

can you do it for tomorrow? 明日までに出来ますか asú madè ni dekímasù ká

10 (with infinitive clause): *it is not for me to decide* 私が決める事ではありません watákushi gà kiméru kotò de wa arímaseń

it would be best for you to leave あなたは帰った方がいい anátà wa káètta hō ga íì

there is still time for you to do it あなたはまだまだそれをする時間がありますが anátà wa mádàmada soré wo surú jikaṅ ga arímasù

for this to be possible ... これが可能になるのには... koré gà kanō ni narú no ni wa...

11 (in spite of) ...nf mó kakáwarazú

for all his complaints, he is very fond of her 彼は色々と文句を言うが、結局彼女を愛しています kárè wa iróiro tò móńku wo iú gà, kekkyóku kanòjo wo áì shite imásù

for all he said he would write, in the end he didn't 手紙を書く書くと言っていましたけれども、結局書いてはくれませんでした tegámi wò kákù kákù to itté imashìta keredomo, kekkyóku kaité kurémaseǹ deshìta

♦*conj* (since, as: rather formal) なぜならば...だから názènaraba ...dá kàra

she was very angry, for he was late again 彼女はかんかんになっていました、というのは彼はまたも遅刻したからです kánòjo wa kańkaṅ ni natté imashìta, to iú no wà kárè wa matá mò chíkòku shita kara desù

forage [fɔːˈridʒ] *vi* (search: for food, interesting objects etc) ...をあさる ...wo asárù

foray [fɔːˈrei] *n* (raid) 侵略 shińryaku

forbad(e) [fɔːrˈbæd] *pt of* forbid

forbid [fɔːrˈbid] (*pt* forbad(e), *pp* forbidden) *vt* (sale, marriage, event etc) 禁じる kińzurú

to forbid someone to do something ...に...するのを禁ずる ...ni ...surú no wò kińzurú

forbidden [fɔːrˈbidⁿ] *pp of* forbid

forbidding [fɔːrˈbidˈiŋ] *adj* (look, prospect) 怖い kowáì

force [fɔːrs] *n* (violence) 暴力 bōryoku; (PHYSICS, also strength) 力 chikára

♦*vt* (compel) 強制する kyōsei suru; (push) 強く押す tsúyòku osú; (break open: lock, door) こじ開ける kojíakerù

in force (in large numbers) 大勢で ōzei de; (LAW) 有効で yūkō de

to force oneself to do 無理して...する múrì shite ...suru

forced [fɔːrst] *adj* (labor) 強制的な kyōseiteki na; (smile) 作りの tsukúri no

forced landing (AVIAT) 不時着 fujíchaku

force-feed [fɔːrsˈfiːd] *vt* (animal, prisoner) ...に強制給餌をする ...ni kyōseikyúji wo suru

forceful [fɔːrsˈfəl] *adj* (person) 力強いchikárazuyoì; (attack) 強烈な kyōretsu na; (point) 説得力のある settókuryoku no arù

forceps [fɔːrˈsəps] *npl* ピンセット pińsettò

forces [fɔːrsˈiz] (*BRIT*) *npl: the Forces* (MIL) 軍隊 guńtai

forcibly [fɔːrˈsəbliː] *adv* (remove) 力ずくで chikárazukù de; (express) 力強く chikárazuyokú

ford [fɔːrd] *n* (in river) 浅瀬 asáse ♦*n* (船を使わないで)川を渡れる場所を指す場所 wo tsukáwanaìde kawá wò watáreru bashò wo sásù

fore [fɔːr] *n: to come to the fore* 前面に出て来る zeńmen ni dete kurù

forearm [fɔːrˈɑːrm] *n* 前腕 máeude

foreboding [fɔːrˈbouˈdiŋ] *n* (of disaster) 不吉な予感 fukítsu na yokáṅ

forecast [fɔːrˈkæst] *n* (of profits, prices,

weather) 予報 yohō

♦vt (pt, pp forecast) (predict) 予報する yohō suru

forecourt [fɔːrˈkɔːrt] n (of garage) 前庭 maéniwa

forefathers [fɔːrˈfɑːðərz] npl (ancestors) 先祖 seńzo

forefinger [fɔːrˈfɪŋgər] n 人差指 hitósashiyùbi

forefront [fɔːrˈfrʌnt] n: **in the forefront of** (industry, movement) ...の最前線で ...no saízeńsen de

forego [fɔːrˈgou] (pt **forewent** pp **foregone**) vt (give up) やめる yaméru; (go without) ...なしで我慢する ...náshi de gámàn suru

foregone [fɔːrˈgɔːn] adj: **it's a foregone conclusion** 結果は決まっている kekká wa kimattè irú

foreground [fɔːrˈgraund] n (of painting) 前景 zeńkei

forehead [fɔːrˈhed] n 額 hitái

foreign [fɔːrˈin] adj (country) 外国の gaíkoku no; (trade) 対外の taígai no; (object, matter) 異質の ishítsu no

foreigner [fɔːrˈənər] n 外国人 gaíkokujin

foreign exchange n 外国為替 gaíkokukawàse; (currency) 外貨 gaíka

Foreign Office (BRIT) n 外務省 gaímushō

Foreign Secretary (BRIT) n 外務大臣 gaímudaìjin

foreleg [fɔːrˈleg] n (of animal) 前足 maéàshi

foreman [fɔːrˈmən] (pl **foremen**) n (in factory, on building site etc) 現場監督 geńbakańtoku

foremost [fɔːrˈmoust] adj (most important) 最も大事な mottómò daíji na

♦adv: **first and foremost** 先ず第一に mázù daíichi ni

forensic [fərenˈsik] adj (medicine, test) 法医学的な hōigakuteki na

forerunner [fɔːrˈrʌnər] n 先駆者 seńkushā

foresee [fɔːrsiːˈ] (pt **foresaw** pp **foreseen**) vt (problem, development) 予想する

yosō suru

foreseeable [fɔːrsiːˈəbəl] adj (problem, development) 予想出来る yosō dekirù

foreshadow [fɔːrʃædˈou] vt (event) ...の前兆となる ...no zeńchō to narù

foresight [fɔːrˈsait] n 先見の明 seńken nò meí

forest [fɔːrˈist] n 森 morí

forestall [fɔːrstɔːlˈ] vt (person) 出し抜く dashínuku; (discussion) 防ぐ fuségù

forestry [fɔːrˈistri] n 林業 riñgyō

foretaste [fɔːrˈteist] n 前兆 zeńchō

foretell [fɔːrtelˈ] (pt, pp **foretold**) vt (predict) 予言する yogén suru

forever [fɔːrevˈər] adv (for good) 永遠に efen ni; (continually) いつも ítsùmo

forewent [fɔːrwentˈ] pt of **forego**

foreword [fɔːrˈwəːrd] n (in book) 前書 maégaki

forfeit [fɔːrˈfit] vt (lose: right, friendship etc) 失う ushínaù

forgave [fərgeivˈ] pt of **forgive**

forge [fɔːrdʒ] n (smithy) 鍛冶屋 kajíyà

♦vt (signature, money) 偽造する gizō suru; (wrought iron) 鍛えて作る kitáeté tsukúrù

forge ahead vi (country, person) 前進する zeńshin suru

forger [fɔːrˈdʒər] n 偽造者 gizōshà

forgery [fɔːrˈdʒəːri] n (crime) 偽造 gizō; (object) 偽物 nisémono

forget [fərgetˈ] (pt **forgot**, pp **forgotten**) vt (fact, face, skill, appointment) 忘れる wasúrerù; (leave behind: object) 置忘れる okíwasurerù; (put out of mind: quarrel, person) 考えない事にする kañgaenài kotó ni surù

♦vi (fail to remember) 忘れる wasúrerù

forgetful [fərgetˈfəl] adj (person) 忘れっぽい wasúreppoì

forget-me-not [fərgetˈmiːnɑːt] n ワスレナグサ wasúrenagùsa

forgive [fərgivˈ] (pt **forgave**, pp **forgiven**) vt (pardon) 許す yurúsù

to forgive someone for something (excuse) ...の...を許す ...no ...wo yurúsù

forgiveness [fərgivˈnis] n 許し yurúshi

forgo [fɔːrgouˈ] vt = **forego**

forgot [fəˈɡɒt] *pt of* forget

forgotten [fəˈɡɒt(ə)n] *pp of* forget

fork [fɔːk] *n* (for eating) フォーク fôku; (for gardening) ホーク hôku; (in road, river, railway) 分岐点 bunkíten
♦ *vi* (road) 分岐する buñki suru

fork-lift truck [fɔːkˈlift-] *n* フォークリフトトラック fôkurifûto

fork out (*inf*) *vt* (pay) 払う haráu

forlorn [fɔːrˈlɔːrn] *adj* (person, place) わびしい wabíshii; (attempt) 絶望的な zetsúbôteki na; (hope) 空しい munáshii

form [fɔːrm] *n* (type) 種類 shúrui; (shape) 形 katáchi; (SCOL) 学年 gakúnen; (questionnaire) 用紙 yôshi
♦ *vt* (make: shape, queue, object, habit) 作る tsukúrù; (make up: organization, group) 構成する kôsei suru; (idea) まとめる matómerù

in top form 調子が最高で chôshi ga saíkô de

formal [fɔːrˈmæl] *adj* (offer, statement, occasion) 正式な sefshiki na; (person, behavior) 堅苦しい katágurushii; (clothes) 正装の sefsô no; (garden) 伝統的な deftôteki na 極めて幾何学的な配置の庭園について言う kiwámete kikágakuteki na hachi nò teien ni tsuite iú; (education) 正規の sefki no

formalities [fɔːrˈmælˈitiz] *npl* (procedures) 手続き tetsúzúki

formality [fɔːrˈmælˈiti] *n* (procedure) 形式 kefshiki

formally [fɔːrˈmæli] *adv* (make offer etc) 正式に sefshiki ni; (act) 堅苦しく katágurushikù; (dress): **to dress formally** 正装する sefsô suru

format [fɔːrˈmæt] *n* (form, style) 形式 kefshiki
♦ *vt* (COMPUT: disk) 初期化する shokíka suru, フォーマットする fômatto suru

formation [fɔːrmeíˈʃən] *n* (creation: of organization, business) 創立 sôritsu; (: of theory) 発展 hatter; (pattern) 隊列 heftai; (of rocks, clouds) 構造 kôzô

formative [fɔːrˈmætiv] *adj* (years, influence) 形成的な kefseiteki na

former [fɔːrˈmər] *adj* (one-time) かつて

の kátsute no; (earlier) 前の mâe no: **the former ... the latter ...** 前者... zeñsha... kôshà...

formerly [fɔːrˈmərli] *adv* (previously) 前は mâe wa

formidable [fɔːrˈmidəbəl] *adj* (task, opponent) 手ごわい tegówai

formula [fɔːrˈmjələ] (*pl* **formulae** *or* **formulas**) *n* (MATH, CHEM) 公式 kôshiki; (plan) 方式 hôshiki

formulate [fɔːrˈmjəleit] *vt* (plan, strategy) 練る nérù; (opinion) 表現する hyôgen suru

forsake [fɔːrseík] (*pt* **forsook**, *pp* **forsaken**) *vt* (abandon: person) 見捨てる misúterù; (: belief) 捨てる sutérù

forsook [fɔːrˈsuk] *pt of* forsake

fort [fɔːrt] *n* (MIL) とりで toríde

forte [fɔːrˈtei] *n* (strength) 得意 tokúi

forth [fɔːrθ] *adv* (out) 外へ sôtò e
back and forth 行ったり来たりして ittári kitári shité
and so forth など nádò

forthcoming [fɔːrˈθʌmiŋ] *adj* (event) 今度の koñdò no; (help, evidence) 手に入る té ni hairù; (person) 率直な sotchóku na

forthright [fɔːrˈθrait] *adj* (condemnation, opposition) はっきりとした hakkíri to shita

forthwith [fɔːrθwíθ] *adv* 直ちに tádachi ni

fortify [fɔːrˈtəfai] *vt* (city) ...の防備を固める ...no bôbi wo katámerù; (person) 力付ける chikárazukerù

fortitude [fɔːrˈtətuːd] *n* 堅忍 kefnin

fortnight [fɔːrˈtnait] *n* (two weeks) 2週間 nishúkan

fortnightly [fɔːrˈtnaitli-] *adj* (payment, visit, magazine) 2週間置きの nishúkan-oki no
♦ *adv* (pay, meet, appear) 2週間置きに nishúkan-oki ni

fortress [fɔːrˈtris] *n* 要塞 yôsai

fortuitous [fɔːrˈtuːitəs] *adj* (discovery, result) 偶然の gûzen no

fortunate [fɔːrˈtʃənit] *adj* (person) 運のいい ûñ no f(; (event) 幸運な kôun na *it is fortunate that ...* 幸いに... safwai ni ..

fortunately [fɔːr'tʃənitli] *adv* (happily, luckily) 幸いに safwai ni

fortune [fɔːr'tʃən] *n* (luck) 運 úñ; (wealth) 財産 zaísan

fortune-teller [fɔːr'tʃəntelər] *n* 易者 e-kísha

forty [fɔːr'tiː] *num* 40 (の) yóñjū (no)

forum [fɔːr'əm] *n* フォーラム fōramu

forward [fɔːr'wərd] *adj* (in position) 前方の zeñpō no; (in movement) 前方への zeñpō e no; (in time) 将来のための shōrai nð tame no; (not shy) 出過ぎた desúgità

◆*n* (SPORT) フォワード fowádo

◆*vt* (letter, parcel, goods) 転送する teñsō suru; (career, plans) 前進させる zeñshin saserū

to move forward (progress) 進歩する shiñpo suru

forward(s) [fɔːr'wərd(z)] *adv* 前へ máe e

fossil [fɑs'əl] *n* 化石 kaséki

foster [fɔs'tər] *vt* (child) 里親として育てる satóoya toshitè sodáterū; (idea, activity) 助成する joséi suru

foster child *n* 里子 satógo

fought [fɔːt] *pt, pp of* **fight**

foul [faul] *adj* (state, taste, smell, weather) 悪い warúi; (language) 汚い kitánai; (temper) ひどい hidói

◆*n* (SPORT) 反則 hañsoku, ファウル fáūru

◆*vt* (dirty) 汚す yogósù

foul play *n* (LAW) 殺人 satsújin

found [faund] *pt, pp of* **find**

◆*vt* (establish: business, theater) 設立する setsúritsu suru

foundation [faundei'ʃən] *n* (act) 設立 setsúritsu; (base) 土台 dodái; (organization) 財団 zaídan; (*also:* **foundation cream**) ファンデーション fañdēshon

foundations [faundei'ʃənz] *npl* (of building) 土台 dodái

founder [faun'dər] *n* (of firm, college) 設立者 setsúritsushà

◆*vi* (ship) 沈没する chíñbotsu suru

foundry [faun'driː] *n* 鋳造工場 chūzōkō-

jō

fountain [faun'tən] *n* 噴水 fuñsui

fountain pen *n* 万年筆 mañneñhitsu

four [fɔːr] *num* 4 (の) yóñ (no), 四つ (の) yotsu (no)

on all fours 四つんばいになって yotsúñbai ni nattè

four-poster [fɔːr'pous'tər] *n* (*also:* **four-poster bed**) 天蓋付きベット teñgaitsukibetto

foursome [fɔːr'səm] *n* 4人組 yoñniñgumi

fourteen [fɔːr'tiːn'] *num* 14 (の) jūyon (no)

fourth [fɔːrθ] *num* 第4 (の) daíyon (no)

fowl [faul] *n* 家きん kakíñ

fox [fɑks] *n* キツネ kitsúne

◆*vt* (baffle) 困らす komárasu

foyer [fɔi'ər] *n* (of hotel, theater) ロビー róbī

fraction [fræk'ʃən] *n* (portion) 一部 ichíbù; (MATH) 分数 buñsū

fracture [fræk'tʃər] *n* (of bone) 骨折 kossétsu

◆*vt* (bone) 折る orú

fragile [frædʒ'əl] *adj* (breakable) 壊れやすい kowáreyasuī

fragment [fræg'mənt] *n* (small piece) 破片 hahéñ

fragrance [freig'rəns] *n* (scent) 香り kaóri

fragrant [freig'rənt] *adj* 香り高い kaórìtakaì

frail [freil] *adj* (person, invalid) か弱い kayówaì; (structure) 壊れやすい kowáreyasuì

frame [freim] *n* (of building, structure) 骨組 honégumi; (of human, animal) 体格 taíkaku; (of door, window) 枠 wakú; (of picture) 額縁 gakúbuchi; (of spectacles: *also:* **frames**) フレーム fúrēmu

◆*vt* (picture) 額縁に入れる gakúbuchi ni irerú

frame of mind *n* 気分 kibúñ

framework [freim'wəːrk] *n* (structure) 骨組 honégumi

France [fræns] *n* フランス furáñsu

franchise [fræn'tʃaiz] *n* (POL) 参政権 sañseìken; (COMM) フランチャイズ furánchaìzu

frank [fræŋk] *adj* (discussion, look) 率直な sotchóku na, フランクな furáŋku na
♦*vt* (letter) ...に料金別納の判を押す ...ni ryókinbetsunō no hán wo osú

frankly [fræŋk'li:] *adv* (honestly) 正直に shójiki ni; (candidly) 率直に sotchóku ni

frankness [fræŋk'nis] *n* (honesty) 正直さ shójikisà; (candidness) 率直さ sotchókusa

frantic [fræn'tik] *adj* (distraught) 狂乱した kyóran shita; (hectic) てんてこ舞いの teñtekomái no

fraternal [frətɑr'nəl] *adj* (greetings, relations) 兄弟の様な kyódai no yố na

fraternity [frətɑr'niti:] *n* (feeling) 友愛 yū́ai; (group of people) 仲間 nakáma

fraternize [fræt'ɔːrnaiz] *vi* 付き合う tsukíaù

fraud [frɔːd] *n* (crime) 詐欺 sagí; (person) ペてん師 petéñshi

fraudulent [frɔː'dʒələnt] *adj* (scheme, claim) 不正な fuséi na

fraught [frɔːt] *adj*: **fraught with** (danger, problems) ...をはらんだ ...wo haráñda

fray [frei] *n* (battle, fight) 戦い tatákai
♦*vi* (cloth, rope) 擦切れる surúkirerù; (rope end) ほつれる hotsúrerù
tempers were frayed 皆短気になっていた miná táñki ni nátte ità

freak [friːk] *n* (person: in attitude, behavior) 変人 heñjin; (: in appearance) 奇形 kikéi
♦*adj* (event, accident) まぐれの mágure no

freckle [frek'əl] *n* そばかす sobákasù

free [friː] *adj* (person, press, movement) 自由な jíyū̀ na; (not occupied: time) 暇な hímà na; (: seat) 空いている aíte irū; (costing nothing: meal, pen etc) 無料の muryó no
♦*vt* (prisoner etc) 解放する kaíhō suru; (jammed object) 動ける様にする ugókeru yố ni suru
free (of charge) 無料で muryó de
for free = free of charge

freedom [friː'dəm] *n* (liberty) 自由 jíyū̀

free-for-all [friː'fɔːrɔl'] *n* 乱闘 rañtō

free gift *n* 景品 keíhin

freehold [friː'hould] *n* (of property) 自由保有権 jiyū́hoyū́ken

free kick *n* (SPORT) フリーキック furíkikkù

freelance [friː'læns] *adj* (journalist, photographer, work) フリーランサーの furíraṅsà no

freely [friː'li:] *adv* (without restriction, limits) 自由に jíyū̀ ni; (liberally) 気ままにkimáma ni

Freemason [friː'meisən] *n* フリーメーソン furímèson

Freepost [friː'poust] *n* (ⓇBRIT) (postal service) 料金受取人払い ryókin uketorininbarai

free-range [friː'reindʒ] *adj* 放し飼いのhanáshigai no ◆特にニワトリやその卵について言う tókù ni niwátori ya sonó tamagó ni tsúite iú

free trade *n* 自由貿易 jiyū́bōeki

freeway [friː'wei] *n* (US) 高速道路 kốsokudòro

free will *n* 自由意志 jiyū́ishì
of one's own free will 自発的に jihátsuteki ni

freeze [friːz] (*pt* **froze**, *pp* **frozen**) *vi* (weather) 氷点下になる hyóteñka ni nárù; (liquid, pipe) 凍る kốrù; (person: with cold) 冷える hiérù; (: stop moving) 立ちすくむ tachísukumù
♦*vt* (water, lake) 凍らせる kốraserù; (food) 冷凍にする reítō ni surú; (prices, salaries) 凍結する tốketsu surú
♦*n* (weather) 氷点下の天気 hyóteñka no téñki; (on arms, wages) 凍結 tốketsu

freeze-dried [friːz'draid'] *adj* 凍結乾燥の tốketsukańsō no

freezer [friː'zəːr] *n* フリーザー furízā̀

freezing [friː'ziŋ] *adj* (wind, weather, water) 凍える様な kốru yố na
3 degrees below freezing 氷点下3度 hyóteñka sáñdo

freezing point *n* 氷点 hyốten

freight [freit] *n* (goods) 貨物 kámòtsu; (money charged) 運送料 uñsōryồ

freight train *n* (US) (goods train) 貨物

列車 kamótsuresshà

French [frentʃ] *adj* フランスの furánsu no; (LING) フランス語の furánsugo no
♦n (LING) フランス語 furánsugo
♦npl: the French (people) フランス人 furánsujìn

French bean *n* サヤインゲン sayá-ìŋgen

French fried potatoes *npl* フレンチフライ（ポテト）furénchifurái(pótèto)

French fries [-fraiz] (*US*) *npl* = **French fried potatoes**

Frenchman/woman [frentʃmən /wumən] (*pl* **Frenchmen/women**) *n* フランス人男性(女性) furánsujin dañsei (jòsei)

French window *n* フランス窓 furánsu madò

frenetic [frənet'ik] *adj* (activity, behavior) 熱狂的な nekkyóteki na

frenzy [fren'zi:] *n* (of violence) 逆上 gyakújò; (of joy, excitement) 狂乱 kyōran

frequency [fri:'kwənsi:] *n* (of event) 頻度 híndo; (RADIO) 周波数 shūhasū

frequent [*adj* fri:'kwint *vb* frikwent'] *adj* (intervals, visitors) 頻繁な híñpan na
♦vt (pub, restaurant) ...によく行く ...ni yókū ikú

frequently [fri:'kwintli:] *adv* (often) しばしば shìbashìba

fresco [fres'kou] *n* フレスコ画 furésukoga

fresh [freʃ] *adj* (food, vegetables, bread, air etc) 新鮮な shìñsen na; (memories, footprint) 最近の saíkin no; (instructions) 新たな árata na; (paint) 塗立ての nurítate no; (new: approach, start) 新しい atárashiì; (cheeky: person) 生意気な namáiki na

freshen [freʃ'ən] *vi* (wind) 強くなる tsuyókù narù; (air) 涼しくなる suzúshikù narù

freshen up *vi* (person) 化粧直しをする keshónaòshi wo suru

fresher [freʃ'əːr] (*BRIT: inf*) *n* = **freshman**

freshly [freʃ'li:] *adv* (made, cooked, painted) ...されたばかりで ...saréta bakàri de

freshman [freʃ'mən] (*pl* **freshmen**) *n* (*US*: SCOL) 1年生 ichínensei ◊大学生や高校生について言う dafgakūsei ya kōkōsei ni tsuitè iú

freshness [freʃ'nis] *n* 新鮮さ shìñsensà

freshwater [freʃ'wɔːtəːr] *adj* (lake, fish) 淡水の tańsui no

fret [fret] *vi* (worry) 心配する shiñpai suru

friar [frai'əːr] *n* (REL) 修道士 shūdòshi

friction [frik'ʃən] *n* (resistance, rubbing) 摩擦 masátsu; (between people) 不仲 fúnàka

Friday [frai'dei] *n* 金曜日 kiñ-yóbi

fridge [fridʒ] (*BRIT*) *n* 冷蔵庫 refzóko

fried [fraid] *adj* (steak, eggs, fish etc) 焼いた yaítà; (chopped onions etc) いためた itámetà; (in deep fat) 揚げた agétà, フライした furái shita

friend [frend] *n* 友達 tomódachi

friendly [frend'li:] *adj* (person, smile) 愛想のいい aísō no iì; (government) 友好的な yūkóteki na; (place, restaurant) 居心地の良い igókochi no yoì; (game, match) 親善の shiñzen no

friendship [frend'ʃip] *n* 友情 yūjō

frieze [fri:z] *n* フリーズ fúrìzu ◊壁の一番高い所に付ける細長い飾り、彫刻などを指す kabé no ichíban takaì tokórò ni tsukérù hosónagaì kazárì, chōkoku nadò wo sásù

frigate [frig'it] *n* フリゲート艦 furígètokan

fright [frait] *n* (terror) 恐怖 kyốfu; (scare) 驚き odórokì
to take fright 驚く odórokù

frighten [frait'ən] *vt* 驚かす odórokasu

frightened [frait'ənd] *adj* (afraid) 怖がった kowágatta; (worried, nervous) 不安に駆られた fúàn ni karáreta

frightening [frait'niŋ] *adj* (experience, prospect) 恐ろしい osóroshiì

frightful [frait'fəl] *adj* (dreadful) 恐ろしい osóroshiì

frightfully [frait'fəli:] *adv* 恐ろしく osóroshikù

frigid [fridʒ'id] *adj* (woman) 不感症の fukáñshō no

frill [frɪl] n (of dress, shirt) フリル fúríru

fringe [frɪndʒ] n (BRIT: of hair) 前髪 maégami; (decoration: on shawl, lampshade etc) 縁飾り fuchíkazàri; (edge: of forest etc) へり herí

fringe benefits npl 付加給付 fukákyùfu

frisk [frɪsk] vt (suspect) ボディーチェックする bodíchekkù suru

frisky [frɪs'ki:] adj (animal, youngster) はつらつとした hatsúratsu to shità

fritter [frɪt'əːr] n (CULIN) フリッター furítta

fritter away vt (time, money) 浪費する rṓhi suru

frivolous [frɪv'ələs] adj (conduct, person) 軽率な kefsotsu na; (object, activity) 下らない kudáranaí

frizzy [frɪz'i:] adj (hair) 縮れた chijíretà

fro [frou] see to

frock [frɑːk] n (dress) ドレス dórèsu

frog [frɑːg] n カエル kaérù

frogman [frɑːg'mæn] (pl frogmen) n ダイバー dáibà

frolic [frɑːl'ik] vi (animals, children) 遊び回る asóbimawarù

KEYWORD

from [frʌm] prep **1** (indicating starting place) ...から ...kára

where are you come from?, where are you from? (asking place of birth) ご出身はどちらですか go-shússhìn wa dóchìra désù ká

from London to Glasgow ロンドンからグラスゴーへ róhdon kara gurásugồ e

to escape from something/someone ...から逃げる ...kára nigérù

2 (indicating origin etc) ...から ...kára

a letter/telephone call from my sister 妹からの手紙(電話) ímòto kará no tegámi(déñwa)

tell him from me that ... 私からの伝言で彼に...と言って下さい watákushi karà no deñgon dè kárè ni ...to itté kudasaí

a quotation from Dickens ディケンズからの引用 díkềnzu kara no iñyō

to drink from the bottle 瓶から飲む bíñ kara nómù

3 (indicating time) ...から ...kára

from one o'clock to/until/till two 1時から2時まで ichíji karà níji madè

from January (on) 1月から(先) ichígatsu karà (sakí)

4 (indicating distance) ...から ...kárà

the hotel is 1 km from the beach ホテルは浜辺から1キロ離れています hótèru wa hamàbé karà ichíkìro hanárète imàsù

we're still a long way from home まだまだ家から遠い mádamada iè madè tṓi

5 (indicating price, number etc) ...から ...kára, ...ないし... ...náishi

prices range from $10 to $50 値段は10ドルから50ドルで nedáň wa júdồru naîshi gojúdồru désù

there were from 20 to 30 people there 20ないし30人いました níjù naîshi sañjùnîn imáshita

the interest rate was increased from 9% to 10% 公定歩合は9パーセントから10パーセントに引き上げられました kṓteibùai wa kyū́pāséňto kara juppáséňto ni hikságeraremashìta

6 (indicating difference) ...と ...tò

he can't tell red from green 彼は赤と緑の区別ができない kárè wa ákà to mídòri no kúbètsu ga dekímaseñ

to be different from someone/something ...と違っている ...tò chigátte irù

7 (because of, on the basis of) ...から ...kárà, ...によって ...ni yotté

from what he says 彼の言う事による と kárè no iú kotò ni yorú to

from what I understand 私が理解した ところでは watákushi gà ríkai shita tokóro dè wa

to act from conviction 確信に基づいて行動する kakúshiñ ni motozúìte kṓdo suru

weak from hunger 飢えでぐったりになって ué dè guttári ni nàttè

---

front [frʌnt] n (of house, dress) 前面 zeñ-

meñ; (of coach, train, car) 最前部 saízeñbu; (promenade: also: **sea front**) 海岸沿いの遊歩道 kaígañzoi no yūhodō; (MIL) 戦線 señseñ; (METEOROLOGY) 前線 zeñseñ; (fig: appearances) 外見 gaíkeñ
♦adj (gen) 前の máe no, 一番前の ichíbañmáe no; (gate) 正面の shōmeñ no
in front (of) (...の) 前に (...no) máe ni
front tooth n 前歯 máeba

frontage [frʌn'tidʒ] n (of building) 正面 shōmeñ

frontal [frʌn'təl] adj 真っ向からの makkṓ kara no

front door n 正面玄関 shōmeñgéñkan

frontier [frʌntiːr'] n (between countries) 国境 kokkyṓ

front page n (of newspaper) 第一面 daíichímeñ

front room (BRIT) n 居間 imá

front-wheel drive [frʌnt'wiːl-] n (AUT) 前輪駆動 zeñríñkūdō

frost [frɔːst] n (weather) 霜が降りる事 shimó ga oríru koto; (also: **hoarfrost**) 霜 shimó

frostbite [frɔːst'bait] n 霜焼け shimóyake

frosted [frɔːs'tid] adj (glass) 曇った kumóri no

frosty [frɔːs'tiː] adj (weather, night) 寒い samúi ◊ 気温が氷点下であるが雪が降っていない状態について言う事 kíoñ ga hyṓteñka de arú ga yukí ga futte inái jōtai ni tsuíte iú; (welcome, look) 冷たい tsumétaí

froth [frɔːθ] n (on liquid) 泡 awá

frown [fraun] vi 顔をしかめる kấo wo shikámerù

froze [frouz] pt of **freeze**

frozen [frou'zən] pp of **freeze**

frugal [fruː'gəl] adj (person) 倹約的な keñ-yakuteki na; (meal) つましい tsumáshiì

fruit [fruːt] n inv (AGR, BOT) 果物 kudámoño; (fig: results) 成果 seíka

fruiterer [fruː'tərəːr] (BRIT) n 果物屋 kudámonoya

fruiterer's (shop) [fruːt'əːrəːrz-] (BRIT) n 果物屋 kudámonoya

fruitful [fruːt'fəl] adj (meeting, discussion) 有益な yū̃eki na

fruition [fruːiʃ'ən] n: **to come to fruition** 実る minórù

fruit juice n 果汁 kajū́, フルーツジュース furū́tsujū̀su

fruit machine (BRIT) n スロットマシン suróttomashin

fruit salad n フルーツサラダ furū́tsusaràda

frustrate [frʌs'treit] vt (upset) ...に 不満を起させる ...ni yokkyū́fumàn wo okósaserù; (block) 邪魔させる zasétsu saserō

frustration [frʌstreiʃ'ən] n (irritation) 欲求不満 yokkyū́fumàn; (disappointment) がっかり gakkári

fry [frai] (pt, pp **fried**) vt (CULIN: steak, eggs etc) 焼く yákū; (: chopped onions etc) いためる itámerù; (: in deep fat) 揚げる agérù ¶ see also **small fry**

frying pan [frai'iŋ-] n フライパン furáipàn

ft. abbr = **foot; feet**

fuddy-duddy [fʌd'iːdʌdiː] (pej) n 古臭い人 furúkusaì hitó

fudge [fʌdʒ] n (CULIN) ファッジ fájjì

fuel [fjuː'əl] n 燃料 neñryō

fuel oil n 重油 jū́yu

fuel tank n 燃料タンク neñryōtañku

fugitive [fjuː'dʒətiv] n (runaway, escapee) 逃亡者 tṓbōsha

fulfil [fulfil'] vt (function) 果す hatásù; (condition) 満たす mitásù; (request, wish, desire) かなえる kanáerù; (order) 実行する jikkṓ suru

fulfilment [fulfil'mənt] n (satisfaction) 満足 mañzoku; (of promise, desire) 実現 jitsúgen

full [ful] adj (container, cup, car, cinema) 一杯の ippái no; (maximum: use, volume) 最大限の saídaigèn no; (complete: details, information) 全ての súbete no; (price) 割引なしの warībikinàshi no; (skirt) ゆったりした yuttári shitá
♦adv: **to know full well that** ...という事を重々承知している ...to iú kotò wo jūjū́ shōchi shite irù

I'm full (up) 満腹だ maṅpuku da
a full two hours 2時間も nijíkan mo
at full speed 全速力で zeṅsokuryòku de
in full (reproduce, quote, pay) 完全に kaṅzen ni

full employment *n* 100パーセントの就業率 hyakú pāseṅto no shúgyòritsu

full-length [ful'leŋkθ'] *adj* (film, novel etc) 長編の chôhen no; (coat) 長い nágài; (portrait) 全身の zeṅshin no

full moon *n* 満月 maṅgetsu

full-scale [ful'skeil'] *adj* (attack, war) 全面的な zeṅmenteki na; (model) 実物大の jitsùbutsudài no

full stop *n* 終止符 shùshifù, ピリオド pírìodo

full-time [ful'taim] *adj* (work, study) 全時間制の zeṅjikañsei no
♦*adv* 全時間で zeṅjikàn de

fully [ful'i:] *adv* (completely) 完全に kaṅzen ni; (at least) *fully as big as* 少なくとも...と同じぐらいの大きさの sukùnàkutomo ...to onaji gurai no ôkìsa no

fully-fledged [ful'i:fledʒd'] *adj* (teacher, barrister) 一人前の ichíninmaè no

fulsome [ful'səm] (*pej*) *adj* (praise, compliments) 大げさな ôgesa na

fumble [fʌm'bəl] *vi*: *to fumble with* (key, catch) ...でもたもたする ...de mótàmota suru

fume [fjum] *vi* (rage) かんかんに怒る kaṅkan ni okórù
fumes of fire, fuel, car) ガス gásù

fun [fʌn] *n* (amusement) 楽しみ tanóshimì
to have fun 楽しむ tanóshimù
for fun 冗談として jôdan toshite
to make fun of (ridicule, mock) ばかにする bákà ni suru

function [fʌŋk'ʃən] *n* (role) 役割 yakúwari, 機能 kínò; (product) ...による物 ...ni yórù monò; (social occasion) 行事 gyôji
♦*vi* (operate) 作動する sadô suru

functional [fʌŋk'ʃənəl] *adj* (operational) 作動できる sadô dekirù; (practical) 機能的な kínòteki na

fund [fʌnd] *n* (of money) 基金 kikín;

(source, store) 貯蓄 chochíku

fundamental [fʌndəmen'tal] *adj* (principle, change, mistake) 基本的な kíhònteki na

fundamentalist [fʌndəmen'təlist] *n* 原理主義者 geñrishugìsha

funds [fʌndz] *npl* (money) 資金 shikín

funeral [fju:'nəːrəl] *n* 葬式 sôshiki

funeral parlor *n* 葬儀屋 sôgiyà

funeral service *n* 葬式 sôshiki

funfair [fʌn'fe:r] (*BRIT*) *n* 移動遊園地 idôyùeñchi

fungi [fʌn'dʒai] *npl* of **fungus**

fungus [fʌŋ'gəs] (*pl* **fungi**) *n* (plant) キノコ kínòko; (mold) かび kabí

funnel [fʌn'əl] *n* (for pouring) じょうご jôgo; (of ship) 煙突 eṅtotsu

funny [fʌn'i:] *adj* (amusing) こっけいな kokkéi na; (strange) 変な heṅ na

fur [fəːr] *n* (on animal) 毛皮 kegáwa; (animal skin for clothing etc) 毛皮 kegáwa; (*BRIT*: in kettle etc) 湯あか yuáka

fur coat *n* 毛皮コート kegáwakòto

furious [fjuːr'iːəs] *adj* 猛烈な môretsu na

furlong [fəːr'lɔːŋ] *n* (HORSE-RACING) ハロン hárðn 〈距離の単位で、約201メーター kyôrì no táñ-i de, yakú 201 mèta〉

furlough [fəːr'lou] *n* (MIL: leave) 休暇 kyûka

furnace [fəːr'nis] *n* (in foundry) 炉 ro; (in power plant) ボイラー bóirā

furnish [fəːr'niʃ] *vt* (room, building) ...に家具調度を置く ...ni kagúchðdo wo sonáerù; (supply) ...に供給する ...ni kyôkyū suru

furnishings [fəːr'niʃiŋz] *npl* 家具と設備 kágù to setsúbì

furniture [fəːr'nitʃəːr] *n* 家具 kágù
piece of furniture 家具一点 kágù itteñ

furrow [fəːr'ou] *n* (in field) 溝 mizô; (in skin) しわ shiwá

furry [fəːr'i:] *adj* 毛で覆われた ke de ôwareta

further [fəːr'ðəːr] *adj* (additional) その上の sonô ue no, 追加の tsuñka no
♦*adv* (farther) もっと遠くに móttò tôku ni; (more) それ以上に soré ijô ni; (moreover) 更に sárà ni, なお nâô

♦vt (career, project) 促進する sokúshin suru

further education (BRIT) n 成人教育 seíjin kyóiku

furthermore [fəːˈðəːmɔːr] adv (moreover) 更に sárà ni, なお nao

furthest [ˈfəːrðist] superl of **far**

furtive [ˈfəːrtiv] adj (glance, movement) こっそりとする kossórì to surù

fury [ˈfjuri] n (anger, rage) 憤慨 fuñgai

fuse [fjuːz] n (ELEC: in plug, circuit) ヒューズ hyúzu; (for bomb etc) 導火線 dókasèn

♦vt (metal) 融合させる yúgō saserù; (fig: ideas, systems) 混合する koñgō suru

♦vi (metal: also fig) 融合する yúgō suru
to fuse the lights (BRIT: ELEC) ヒューズを飛ばす hyúzu wo tobásù

fuse box (ELEC) ヒューズ箱 hyúzubàko

fuselage [ˈfjuːsəlɑːʒ] n (AVIAT) 胴体 dótai

fusion [ˈfjuːʒən] n (of ideas, qualities) 混合 koñgō; (also: **nuclear fusion**) 核融合 kakúyūgō

fuss [fʌs] n (anxiety, excitement) 大騒ぎ ōsawàgi; (complaining, trouble) 不平 fuhéi
to make a fuss 大騒ぎをする ōsawàgi wo suru
to make a fuss of someone …をちやほやする …wo chíyahoya suru

fussy [ˈfʌsiː] adj (person) 小うるさい koúrusaì; (clothes, room etc) 凝った kottà

futile [ˈfjuːtail] adj (attempt, comment, existence) 無駄な mudá na

future [ˈfjuːtʃər] adj (date, generations) 未来の mírài no; (president, spouse) 将来の shórai no
♦n (time to come) 未来 mírài; (prospects) 将来 shórai; (LING) 未来形 mírài-kei
in future 将来に shórai ni

fuze [fjuːz] (US) = **fuse**

fuzzy [ˈfʌziː] adj (PHOT) ぼやけた boyáketa; (hair) 縮れた chijíretà

G

G [dʒiː] n (MUS: note) ト音 to-óñ; (: key) ト調 tóchō

g. abbr = **gram(s)**

gabble [ˈgæbəl] vi ぺちゃくちゃしゃべる péchàkucha shábèru

gable [ˈgeibəl] n (of building) 切妻 kirízuma

gadget [ˈgædʒit] n 装置 sóchi

Gaelic [ˈgeilik] adj ゲール語の gérugo no
♦n (LING) ゲール語 gérugo

gaffe [gæf] n (in words) 失言 shitsúgen; (in actions) 失態 shittái

gag [gæg] n (on mouth) 猿ぐつわ sarúgutsuwa; (joke) ギャグ gyágù
♦vt (prisoner) …に猿ぐつわをはめる …ni sarúgutsuwa wo hamérù

gaiety [ˈgeiəti] n お祭り騒ぎ o-mátsuri sawàgi

gaily [ˈgeili] adv (talk, dance, laugh) 楽しそうに tanóshisō ni; (colored) 華やかに hanáyaka ni

gain [gein] n (increase) 増加 zōka; (improvement) 進歩 shíñpo; (profit) 利益 rīeki
♦vt (speed, weight, confidence) 増す masú
♦vi (benefit): **to gain from something** …から利益を得る …kara rīeki wo érù; (clock, watch) 進む susúmu
to gain on someone …に迫る …ni semárù
to gain 3lbs (in weight) (体重が) 3 ポンド増える (taíjū ga) sañpoñdo fuérù

gait [geit] n 歩調 hochō

gal. abbr = **gallon**

gala [ˈgeilə] n (festival) 祝祭 shukúsai

galaxy [ˈgæləksi] n (SPACE) 星雲 sefun

gale [geil] n (wind) 強風 kyōfū

gallant [ˈgælənt] adj (brave) 勇敢な yúkan na; (polite) 紳士的な shiñshiteki na

gallantry [ˈgæləntri] n (bravery) 勇気 yūki; (politeness) 礼儀正しさ reígitadashisa

gall bladder [gɔːl-] n 胆のう tañnō

gallery [gæl'əri:] n (also: **art gallery**; public) 美術博物館 bijutsu hakubutsukan; (: private) 画廊 garṓ; (in hall, church, theater) 二階席 nikáiseki

galley [gæl'i:] n (ship's kitchen) 調理室 chṓrishitsu

gallon [gæl'ən] n (= 8 pints; BRIT = 4.5 l; US = 3.8 l) ガロン garón

gallop [gæl'əp] n ギャロップ gyárōppu
♦vi (horse) ギャロップで走る gyárōppu de hashírù

gallows [gæl'ouz] n 絞首台 kṓshudai

gallstone [gɔːl'stoun] n (MED) 胆石 tanseki

galore [gəlɔːr'] adj どっさり dossárì

galvanize [gæl'vənaiz] vt (audience) ぎょっとさせる gyóttò saserú; (support) 求める motómerù

gambit [gæm'bit] n (fig): (opening) **gambit** 皮切り kawákiri

gamble [gæm'bəl] n (risk) かけ kaké
♦vt (money) かける kakérù
♦vi (take a risk) 冒険をする bṓken wo surú; (bet) じけちをする bakúchi wo surú, ギャンブルをする gyánburu wo suru
to gamble on something (horses, race, success etc) ...にかける ...ni kakérù

gambler [gæm'blə:r] n (punter) ばくち打ち bakúchiuchi

gambling [gæm'bliŋ] n (betting) ばくち bakúchi, ギャンブル gyánburu

game [geim] n (activity, sport) 遊び asóbi; (match) 試合 shiái; (part of match: esp TENNIS: also: **board game**) ゲーム gēmu; (strategy, scheme) 策略 sakúryaku; (HUNTING) 猟鳥獣 ryóchōjū; (CULIN) 猟鳥獣の肉 ryóchōjū no niku
♦adj (willing): **game (for)** (...をする) 気がある (...wo suru) kí ga arú
big game 大型鳥獣 ṓgataryōjū

gamekeeper [geim'ki:pə:r] n 猟番 ryōban

gammon [gæm'ən] n (bacon) ベーコン bēkon; (ham) スモークハム sumókuhamù

gamut [gæm'ət] n (range) 範囲 haṅ-i

gang [gæŋ] n (of criminals, hooligans) 一味 ichími; (of friends, colleagues) 仲間 nakama; (of workmen) 班 hán

gangrene [gæŋ'gri:n] n (MED) えそ ésò

gangster [gæŋ'stə:r] n (criminal) 暴力団 員 bōryokudań-in, ギャング gyáng

gang up vi: **to gang up on someone** 寄ってたかって...をやっつける yotté takatté ...wo yattsukerù

gangway [gæŋ'wei] n (from ship) タラップ taráppu; (BRIT: in cinema, bus, plane etc) 通路 tsūro

gaol [dʒeil] n, vt = **jail**

gap [gæp] n (space) すき間 sukíma, ギャップ gyappu; (: in time) 空白 kūhaku; (difference) **gap (between)** (...の)断絶 (...no) daṅzetsu

gape [geip] vi (person) ぽかんと口を開けて見詰める pokáñ to kuchi wo akéte mitsúmerù; (shirt, hole) 大きく開いている ōkiku aíte irú

gaping [gei'piŋ] adj (shirt, hole) 大きく開いた ōkiku aíta

garage [gərɑːʒ'] n (of private house) 車庫 sháko; (for car repairs) 自動車修理工場 jidōshashūrikōjō

garbage [gɑːr'bidʒ] n (US: rubbish) ごみ gomí; (inf: nonsense) でたらめ detárame

garbage can (US) n ごみ容器 gomíyōki

garbled [gɑːr'bəld] adj (account, message) 間違った machígattà

garden [gɑːr'dən] n (private) 庭 niwá

gardener [gɑːrd'nə:r] n 庭師 niwáshi

gardening [gɑːr'dəniŋ] n 園芸 eṅgei

gardens [gɑːr'dənz] npl (public park) 公園 kōen

gargle [gɑːr'gəl] vi うがいをする ugái suru

garish [geir'iʃ] adj けばけばしい kebákebashìi

garland [gɑːr'lənd] n (also: **garland of flowers**) 花輪 hanáwa

garlic [gɑːr'lik] n (BOT, CULIN) ニンニク nifniku

garment [gɑːr'mənt] n (dress) 衣服 ffúku

garnish [gɑːr'niʃ] vt (food) 飾る kazárù

garrison [gær'isən] n (MIL) 守備隊 shubítai

garrulous [gær'ələs] adj (talkative) 口数の多い kuchíkazu no ói

garter [gɑːr'tə:r] n (for sock etc) 靴下止

め kutsúshitadome, ガーター gâta; (US: suspender) ガーターベルト gâtáberùto

gas [gæs] n (CHEM) 気体 kitái; (fuel) ガス gásù; (US: gasoline) ガソリン gasórin
♦vt (kill) ガスで殺す gásù de korósù

gas cooker (BRIT) n ガスレンジ gasúrenji

gas cylinder n ガスボンベ gasúbonbe

gas fire (BRIT) n ガスストーブ gasúsutōbu

gash [gæʃ] n (wound) 切り傷 kirſkfzu; (tear) 裂け目 sakéme
♦vt (wound) 傷を負わせる kizú wò owáserù

gasket [gæs'kit] n (AUT) ガスケット gasúkettò

gas mask n ガスマスク gasúmasùku

gas meter n ガスメーター gasúmētà

gasoline [gæsəlin'] (US) n ガソリン gasórin

gasp [gæsp] n (breath) 息切れ ikígire; (of shock, horror) はっとする事 háttð suru kotð
♦vi (pant) あえぐ aégù

gasp out vt (say) あえぎながら言う aéginagàra iú

gas station (US) n ガソリンスタンド gasórinsutando

gassy [gæs'i:] adj (beer etc) 炭酸ガスの入った tafsangasð no hattta

gastric [gæs'trik] adj 胃の í no

gastroenteritis [gæstrouentarai'tis] n 胃腸炎 ichōen

gate [geit] n (of garden, field, grounds) 門 món; (at airport) ゲート gēto

gatecrash [geit'kræʃ] (BRIT) vt ...に押し掛ける ...ni oshíkakerù

gateway [geit'wei] n (entrance: also fig) 入口 iríguchi

gather [gæð'ə:r] vt (flowers, fruit) 摘む tsúmù; (pick up) 拾う hiróù; (assemble, collect: objects, information) 集める atsúmerù; (understand) 推測する suísoku suru; (SEWING) ...にギャザーを寄せる ...ni gyázā wo yoséru
♦vi (assemble) 集まる atsúmarù

to gather speed スピードを上げる supído wo agerù

gathering [gæð'ə:riŋ] n 集まり atsúmari

gauche [gouʃ] adj (adolescent, youth) ぎごちない gigóchinài

gaudy [gɔ:'di:] adj 派手な hadé na

gauge [geidʒ] n (instrument) 計器 kefki
♦vt (amount, quantity) 計る hakárù; (fig: feelings, character etc) 判断する handan suru

gaunt [gɔːnt] adj (haggard) やせこけた yasékoketà; (bare, stark) 荒涼とした kôryō to shita

gauntlet [gɔːnt'lit] n (glove) 長手袋 nagátebukûro; (fig): **to run the gauntlet** 方々からやられる hôbō kara yarárerù

to throw down the gauntlet 挑戦する chôsen suru

gauze [gɔːz] n (fabric: also MED) ガーゼ gāze

gave [geiv] pt of **give**

gay [gei] adj (homosexual) 同性愛の dôseiai no, ホモの hômo no; (cheerful) 陽気な yôki na; (color, music, dress etc) 華やかな hanáyàka na

gaze [geiz] n (look, stare) 視線 shisén
♦vi: **to gaze at something** ...をじっと見る ...wo jíttð mírù

gazelle [gəzel'] n ガゼル gázèru

gazetteer [gæzitir'] n (index) 地名辞典 chiméijiten

gazumping [gəzʌm'piŋ] (BRIT) n (of house buyer) 詐欺 ságí

GB [dʒi:bi:'] abbr = **Great Britain**

GCE [dʒi:si:i:'] (BRIT) n abbr (= General Certificate of Education) 普通教育証書 futsúkyoikushōsho ◇16才の時に受けるOレベルと大学入学前に受けるAレベルの2種類がある jūrokúsai no tokí ní ukérù O rébèru to dafgaku nyūgaku máè ni ukérù A rébèru no nishúrui ga arù

GCSE [dʒi:si:si:'] (BRIT) n abbr (= General Certificate of Secondary Education) ◇1988年からGCEのOレベルはGCSEに置換られた sefikyūyakuhachijúhachi nèn ní GCE no O rébèru wa GCSE ni okíkaerareta

gear [gir] n (equipment) 道具 dôgu; (TECH) 歯車 hagúruma; (AUT) ギヤ gíyá

◆ *vt (fig:* adapt): *to gear something to* ...に...を適応させる ..ni ..wo tekíō saserú

high *(US)* or **top** *(BRIT)* / **low gear** ハイ（ロー）ギヤ haí[róō]giyá

in gear ギヤを入れて giyá wo írete

gear box *n* ギヤボックス giyábokkūsu

gear shift *(BRIT* **gear lever)** *n* シフトレバー shífutorebā

geese [giːs] *npl of* **goose**

gel [dʒel] *n* (for hair) ジェル jérù; (CHEM) ゲル gérù

gelatin(e) [dʒeĺətin] *n* (CULIN) ゼラチン zeráchiñ

gelignite [dʒeĺignait] *n* (explosive) ゼリグナイト zerígunaito

gem [dʒem] *n* (stone) 宝石 hóseki

Gemini [dʒeḿənai] *n* (ASTROLOGY) 双子座 futágoza

gender [dʒeńdəːr] *n* (sex: *also* LING) 性 sef

gene [dʒiːn] *n* (BIO) 遺伝子 idéñshi

general [dʒeńərəl] *n* (MIL) 大将 taíshō
◆ *adj* (overall, non-specific, miscellaneous) 一般の ippán no, 一般的な ippánteki na; (widespread: movement, interest) 全面的な zeñmenteki na

in general 一般に ippán ni

general delivery *(US)* n (poste restante) 局留 kyokúdōme

general election *n* 総選挙 sōseñkyo

generalization [dʒenərəlezeíʃən] *n* 一般化 ippánka

generally [dʒeńərəliː] *adv* (in general) 一般に ippán ni; (usually) 普通は futsū wa

general practitioner *n* 一般開業医 ippán kaigyōi

generate [dʒeńəreit] *vt* (power, energy) 発生させる hassef saserú; (jobs, profits) 生み出す umídasu

to generate electricity 発電する hatsúden suru

generation [dʒenəreíʃən] *n* (period of time) 世代 sedái; (of people, plants) 同じ世代の人々 onáji sedái no hitobito; (of heat, steam, gas etc) 発生 hassef; (of

electricity) 発電 hatsúden

generator [dʒeńəːreitəːr] *n* (ELEC) 発電機 hatsúdeñki

generosity [dʒenərɑ:sə'ti:] *n* 寛大さ kañdaisa

generous [dʒeńərəs] *adj* (person, measure, remuneration etc) 寛大な kañdai na

genetics [dʒəneĺiks] *n* (science) 遺伝学 idéñgaku

Geneva [dʒəni:ˈvə] *n* ジュネーブ júnēbu

genial [dʒi:ˈni:əl] *adj* (host, smile) 愛想の良い人 aísō no yoí

genitals [dʒeńitəlz] *npl* (ANAT) 性器 sefki

genius [dʒi:ˈni:əs] *n* (ability, skill, person) 天才 teñsaí

genocide [dʒeńəsaid] *n* 民族虐殺 mínzokugyakusatsu, ジェノサイド jénōsaido

gent [dʒent] *n abbr* = **gentleman**

genteel [dʒenti:ĺ] *adj* (person, family) 家柄の良い iégara no yoí

gentle [dʒeńtəl] *adj* (person) 優しい yasáshii; (animal) 大人しい otónashii; (movement, shake) 穏やかな odáyaka na, 静かな shizúka na; (slope, curve) 緩やかな yurúyaka na

a gentle breeze そよ風 soyókaze

gentleman [dʒeńtəlmən] *(pl* **gentlemen)** *n* (man) 男の方 otóko no katá; (referring to social position: *also* wellmannered man) 紳士 shíñshi, ジェントルマン jéñtoruman

gentleness [dʒeńtəlnis] *n* (of person) 優しさ yasáshisà; (of animal) 大人しさ otónashisà; (of movement, breeze, shake) 穏やかさ odáyakasa, 静かさ shizúkasa; (of slope, curve) 緩やかさ yurúyakasa

gently [dʒeńtli:] *adv* (subj: person) 優しく yasáshikù; (: animal) 大人しく otónashikù; (: breeze etc) 静かに shizúkāni (: slope, curve) 緩やかに yurúyakāni

gentry [dʒeńtri:] *n* 紳士階級 shíñshikaíkyū

gents [dʒents] *(BRIT)* n (men's toilet) 男性トイレ dañseítoirè

genuine [dʒeńju:in] *adj* (real) 本物の hoñmonō no; (person) 誠実な sefjitsu na

geographic(al) [dʒiːəgrǽf'ik(əl)] *adj* 地理の chírí no

geography [dʒiːáːgʹrəfiː] *n* (of town, country etc: *also* SCOL) 地理 chírí

geological [dʒiːəláːdʒˈikəl] *adj* (of area, rock etc) 地質学の chishítsugaku no

geologist [dʒiːáːlədʒist] *n* 地質学者 chishítsugakusha

geology [dʒiːáːlədʒiː] *n* (of area, rock etc) 地質 chíshitsu; (SCOL) 地質学 chishítsugaku

geometric(al) [dʒiːəmét'rik(əl)] *adj* (problem, design) 幾何学的な kikágakuteki na

geometry [dʒiːáːm'ətriː] *n* (MATH) 幾何学 kikágaku

geranium [dʒərei'niːəm] *n* ゼラニウム zeránìumu

geriatric [dʒeriːǽt'rik] *adj* (of old people) 老人の rójìn no

germ [dʒəːrm] *n* ばい菌 baíkìn

German [dʒəːr'mən] *adj* (of Germany) ドイツの dóìtsu no; (LING) ドイツ語の dóìtsugo no
◆*n* ドイツ人 doítsujin; (LING) ドイツ語 doítsugo

German measles *n* (rubella) 風しん fúːshin

Germany [dʒəːr'məniː] *n* ドイツ dóìtsu

germination [dʒəːrmənei'ʃən] *n* (of seed) 発芽 hatsúga

gesticulate [dʒestik'jəleit] *vi* (with arms, hands) 手振りをする tebúrì wo suru

gesture [dʒes'tʃəːr] *n* (movement) 手振り tebúrì; (symbol, token) ジェスチャー jésùchā

KEYWORD

get [get] (*pt, pp* **got**, (*US) pp* **gotten**) *vi* 1 (become, be) ...になる ...ni nárù

to get old (thing) 古くなる fúrùku naru; (person) 年を取る toshí wo toru

to get cold 寒くなる samúku naru

to get annoyed/bored/tired 怒る(退屈する, 疲れる) okórù(taíkutsu surù, tsukárerù)

to get drunk 酔っ払う yopparau

to get dirty 汚れる yogórerù

to get killed 殺される korósarerù

to get married 結婚する kekkón surù

when do I get paid? 金はいつ払ってくれますか kané wa ìtsu harátte kuremasù ká

it's getting late 遅くなってきました osóku natté kimáshìta

2 (go): *to get to/from* ...へ[から]行く ...é(kará)ikú

to get home 家に帰る ié ni kaerù

how did you get here? あなたはどうやってここへ来ましたか anátà wa dó yattè kokó e kimáshìtà ká

3 (begin): *to get to know someone* ...と親しくなる ...tò shitáshìku naru

I'm getting to like him 彼を好きになってきました kárè wo sukí ni nattè kimáshìta

let's get going/started さあ、行きましょう sā, ikímashō

◆*modal aux vb: you've got to do it* あなたはどうしてもそれをしなければなりません anátà wa dōshitè mò soré wò shinákereba narimasèn

I've got to tell the police 警察に知らせなければなりません keísatsu ni shirásenakèreba narimasèn

◆*vt* 1 *to get something done* (do) ...を済ます ...wò sumásù; (have done) ...をしてもらう ...wò shité moraù

to get the washing/dishes done 洗濯 (皿洗い)を済ます sefitaku(saráaraì) wo sumásù

to get one's hair cut 散髪してもらう sanpatsu shite moraù

to get the car going/to go 車のエンジンをかける kurúma no efjìn wo kakérù

to get someone to do something ...に ...をさせる ...ní ...wò sasérù

to get something ready ...を用意する ...wò yōi suru

to get someone ready ...に用意をさせる ...ní yōi wo sasérù

to get someone drunk/into trouble ...を酔っ払わせる(困らせる) ...wò yoppárawaserù(komáraserù)

2 (obtain: money) 手に入れる té ni irerù

(: permission, results) 得る érů; (find: job, flat) 見付ける mitsúkerů; (fetch: person, doctor) 呼んで来る yónde kurú; (: object) 持って来る motté kurú

to get something for someone ...のために...を持って来る ...no tamé nǐ ...wð motté kurú

he got a job in London 彼はロンドンに仕事を見付けました kárě wa rṓndon ni shigóto wð mitsúkemashīta

get me Mr Jones, please (TEL) ジョーンズさんをお願いしたいんですが jṓnzu san wo o-négai shitainⁿ desⁿ

I think you should get the doctor 医者を呼んだ方がいいと思います ishá wð yónda hṓ ga fi to omóimasⁿ

can I get you a drink? 何か飲みませんか nánika nomftmaseⁿ ka

3 (receive: present, letter) 受ける ukérů; (acquire: reputation, prize) 得る érů; 獲得する kakútoku suru

what did you get for your birth-day? お誕生日に何をもらいましたか o-tánjōbi ni nánⁿ wo moráimashīta ká

he got a prize for French 彼はフランス語の成績で賞をもらいました kárě wa furánsugð no seíseki dè shṓ wð moráimashīta

how much did you get for the paint-ing? 絵画はいくらで売れましたか kálga wa íkura de urémashīta ká

4 (catch) つかむ tsukámů; (hit: target etc) ...に当る ...ni atáru

to get someone by the arm/throat ...の腕〔のど〕をつかむ ...no udé〔nódð〕wð tsukámů

get him! やつを捕まえろ yátsů wo tsukámaerŏ

the bullet got him in the leg 弾丸は彼の脚に当った dangan wà kárě no ashí ni atátta

5 (take, move) 連れて〔持って〕いく tsuréte〔motté〕ikú, 移動する idṓ suru

to get something to someone ...に...を持って行く ...nǐ ...wð motté ikú

do you think we'll get it through the door? それは戸口から入ると思いますか soré wà tǒguchi kara háiru to omó-

imasⁿ ká

I'll get you there somehow 何とかしてあなたを連れて行きます náⁿ to ka shite anáta wo tsuréte ikimasⁿ

we must get him to (US the) hospital どうしても彼を病院に連れて行かなくちゃ dṓshite mo kárě wo byṓin ni tsuréte ikanakūcha

6 (catch, take: plane, bus etc) 乗る norú

where do I get the train - Birming-ham? 汽車にどこで乗ればいいんですか - バーミンガムですか defsha wà dőko de noréba íin desⁿ ká - bámingamu desu ká

7 (understand) 理解する ríkai suru; (hear) 聞き取る kikftorù

I've got it 分かった wakátta

I don't get your meaning あなたが言おうとしている事が分かりません anáta ga iṓ to shite iru kotð ga wakárimaseⁿ

I'm sorry, I didn't get your name 済みませんが、お名前を聞き取れませんでした sumſmaseⁿ ga, o-námae wð kikſtoremaseⁿ deshīta

8 (have, possess): **to have got** 持つ mótsⁿ

how many have you got? いくつ持っていますか íkutsu motté imasⁿ ká

get about vi 動き回る ugókimawarù; (news) 広まる hirómarù

get along vi (agree) 仲良くする nákāyoku suru; (depart) 帰る káěru; (manage) = **get by**

get at vt fus (attack, criticize) 批判する hihán suru; (reach) ...に手が届く ...ni té gà todókù

get away vi (leave) 帰る káěru; (escape) 逃げる nigérù

get away with vt fus ...をうまくやりおおせる ...wð úmaku yaríōseru

get back vi (return) 帰る káěru
◆vt 取る tórù

get by vi (pass) 通る tṓrù; (manage) やって行く yatté ikú

get down vi 降りる orírù
◆vt 降りる orírù
◆vt 降ろす orósù; (depress: person) がっかりさせる gakkárĭ saseru

get down to vt fus (work) ...に取り掛かる ...ni toríkakarù

get in vi 入る haírù; (train) 乗る norú; (arrive home) 帰って来る kaétte kurù

get into vt fus ...に入る ...ni haírù; (vehicle) ...に乗る ...ni norú; (clothes) 着る kirú

to get into bed ベッドに入る béddò ni haírù

to get into a rage かんかんに怒る kañkan ni okórù

get off vi (from train etc) 降りる orírù; (depart: person, car) 出発する shuppátsu suru; (escape punishment) 逃れる nogárerù

♦vt (remove: clothes) 脱ぐ núgù; (: stain) 消す kesú, 落す otósù; (send off) 送る okúrù

♦vt fus (train, bus) 降りる orírù

get on vi (at exam etc): *how are you getting on?* 万事うまくいっていますか bánji úmàku ittè imasù ká; (agree): *to get on (with)* (...と) 気が合う (...tò) ki gá aù

♦vt fus ...に乗る ...ni norú

get out vi 出る dérù; (of vehicle) 降りる orírù

♦vt 取り出す torídasù

get out of vt fus ...から出る ...kara dérù; (vehicle) ...から降りる ...kara orírù; (bed) ...から起きる ...kara okírù; (duty etc) 避ける sakérù, 逃れる nogárerù

get over vt fus (illness) ...が直る ...ga naórù

get round vt fus (problem, difficulty) 避ける sakérù; (law, rule) ...に触れないようにする ...ni furénai yò ni suru; (fig: person) 言いくるめる iíkurumerù

get through vi (TEL) 電話が通じる deñwa gà tsújirù

get through to vt fus (TEL) ...に電話が通じる ...ni deñwa gà tsújirù

get together vi (people) 集まる atsúmarù

♦vt 集める atsúmerù

get up vi (rise) 起きる okírù

♦vt fus 起す okósù

get up to vt fus (reach) ...に 着く ...ni

tsukú; (*BRIT*: prank etc) 仕出かす shidékasù

geyser [gai'zə:r] n (GEO) 間欠温泉 kañketsu oñsen; (*BRIT*: water heater) 湯沸かし器 yuwákashikì

Ghana [gɑːn'ə] n ガーナ gằna

ghastly [gæst'liː] adj (horrible: person, behavior, situation) いやな iyá na, ひどい hídòi; (: building, appearance) 見た目の悪い usúkimiwaruì, (pale: complexion) 青白い aójirol

gherkin [gəːr'kin] n キュウリのピクルス kyūri no píkùrusu

ghetto [get'ou] n (ethnic area) ゲットー géttò

ghost [goust] n (spirit) 幽霊 yūrei, お化け o-bákè

giant [dʒai'ənt] n (in myths, children's stories) 巨人 kyojîn, ジャイアント jáìanto; (fig: large company) 大企業 daîkigyō

♦adj (enormous) 巨大な kyodài na

gibberish [dʒib'əːriʃ] n (nonsense) でたらめ detárame

gibe [dʒaib] n = **jibe**

giblets [dʒib'lits] npl 鳥の内臓 torí nò naîzō

Gibraltar [dʒibrɔːl'təːr] n ジブラルタル jíbùraruta

giddy [gid'iː] adj (dizzy) めまいがする memái gà suru

gift [gift] n (present) 贈り物 okúrimonò, プレゼント purézènto, ギフト gífùto; (ability) 才能 saínō

gifted [gif'tid] adj (actor, sportsman, child) 才能ある saínō árù

gift token n ギフト券 gifútòken

gift voucher n = **gift token**

gigantic [dʒaigæn'tik] adj 巨大な kyodài na

giggle [gig'əl] n くすくす笑う kusúkùsu waráù

gill [dʒil] n (= 0.25 pints; *BRIT* = 0.15 l; *US* = 0.12 l) ギル gírù

gills [gilz] npl (of fish) えら erá

gilt [gilt] adj (of frame, jewelery) 金めっきした kiñmekkī shita

♦n 金めっき kiñmekkì

gilt-edged [gilt'edʒd] adj (stocks, securities) 優良な yūryō na

gimmick [gim'ik] n (sales, electoral) 仕掛け shikáke

gin [dʒin] n ジン jín

ginger [dʒin'dʒəːr] n (spice) ショウガ shōga

ginger ale n ジンジャーエール jíñjaēru

ginger beer n ジンジャービール jíñjabīru

gingerbread [dʒin'dʒəːrbred] n (cake) ジンジャーブレッドケーキ jíñjaburedkēki; (biscuit) ジンジャーブレッドクッキー jíñjaburedokukkī

gingerly [dʒin'dʒəːrli:] adv (tentatively) 慎重に shíñchō ni

gipsy [dʒip'si:] n = gypsy

giraffe [dʒəræf'] n キリン kírin

girder [gəːr'dəːr] n 鉄骨 tekkótsu

girdle [gəːr'dəl] n (corset) ガードル gādoru

girl [gəːrl] n (child) 女の子 ofína nò ko, 少女 shōjo; (young unmarried woman) 若い女性 wakái josèi, ガール gāru; (daughter) 娘 musúme

an English girl 若いイングランド人女性 wakái íñgurandòjìn josèi

girlfriend [gəːrl'frend] n (of girl) 女友達 ofína tomodachì; (of boy) ガールフレンド gārufureñdo

girlish [gəːr'liʃ] adj 少女の様な shōjo nó yō na

giro [dʒai'rou] n (also: **bank giro**) 銀行振替 giñkōfurikaekawāse; (also: **post office giro**) 郵便振替為替 yūbinfurikaekawāse; (BRIT: welfare check) 生活保護の小切手 sefkatsuhogò no kogítte

girth [gəːrθ] n (circumference) 周囲 shūi; (of horse) 腹帯 harádoi

gist [dʒist] n (of speech, program) 骨子 kósshi

KEYWORD

give [giv] (pt **gave**, pp **given**) vt 1 (hand over): *to give someone something, give something to someone* ...に...を与える ...ni ...wò atáerù, ...に...を渡す ...ni ...wò watásu

I gave David the book, I gave the

book to David 私は本をデービッドに渡しました watákushi wà hóñ wò débiddo ni watáshimashìta

give him your key あなたのかぎを彼に渡しなさい anátà no kagí wò kárè ni watáshinasaì

he gave her a present 彼は彼女にプレゼントをあげた kárè wa kánòjo ni purézeñto wo agétà

give it to him, give him it それを彼に渡しなさい soré wò kárè ni watáshinasaì

I'll give you £5 for it それを5ポンドで私に売ってくれませんか soré wò gopóñdo de watákushi nì utté kuremaseñ ká

2 (used with noun to replace a verb): *to give a sigh* ため息をつく taméikì wo tsuku

to give a cry/shout 叫ぶ sakébù

to give a push 押す osú

to give a groan うめむ umékù

to give a shrug 肩をすくめる kátà wo sukúmerù

to give a speech/a lecture 演説〔講演〕をする eñzetsu〔kōen〕wo suru

to give three cheers 万歳三唱をする bañzaisañshō wo suru

3 (tell, deliver: news, advice, message etc) 伝える tsutáerù, 言う iú, 与える atáerù

did you give him the message/the news? 彼にメッセージ〔ニュース〕を伝えましたか kárè ni mésseji〔nyūsu〕wo tsutáemashìta ká

let me give you some advice ちょっと忠告をあげよう chóttò chūkoku wo ageyō

he gave me his new address over the phone 彼は電話に新しい住所を教えてくれました kárè wa deñwa dè atárashiì jūsho wo oshíete kuremashìta

to give the right/wrong answer 正しい〔間違った〕答えを言う tadáshiì〔machígatta〕kotáe wo iú

4 (supply, provide: opportunity, surprise, job etc) 与える atáerù, 提供する tefkyō suru; (bestow: title) 授与する júyò suru;

(: honor, right) 与える ataérù

I give him the chance to deny it それを否定するチャンスを彼に与えました soré wò hitéi suru chañsu ni kárè ni atáemashìta

the sun gives warmth and light 太陽は熱と光を我々に与えてくれる táiyò wa netsú tò hikari wò waréware nì atáete kurerù

what gives you the right to do that? 何の権利でそんな事をするのか nàn no kéñri de sofina kotò wo suru nò ka

that's given me an idea あれでいい考えを思い付いたんですが aré de ii kotò wo omóitsuitan desù ga

5 (dedicate: time) 当てる ateru; (: one's life) 捧げる saságerù, (: attention) 払う haraù

you'll need to give me more time もっと時間を下さい móttò jikàn wo kudasai

she gave it all her attention 彼女はそれに専念した kánòjo wa soré nì sefinen shità

6 (organize): *to give a party/dinner etc* パーティ (晩さん会) を開催する pátì (bañsañkai) wo kaisai suru

♦vi 1 (also: **give way**: break, collapse) 崩れる kuzúrerù

his legs gave beneath him 彼は突然立てなくなった kárè wa tótsùzen taténakunatta

the roof/floor gave as I stepped on it 私が踏んだとたん屋根 [床] が抜け落ちた watákushi ga fundá totań yáné [yuká] ga nukéochita

2 (stretch: fabric) 伸びる nobírù

give away vt (money) ただにやる hitó nì yarú; (opportunity) 失う ushínaù; (secret, information) 漏らす morásù; (bride) 新郎に渡す shifiró nì watásù

give back vt 返す káèsu

give in vi 降参する kōsan suru
♦vt (essay etc) 提出する teíshutsu suru

give off vt (heat) 放つ hanátsù; (smoke) 出す dásù

give out vt (distribute: prizes, books,

---

drinks etc) 配る kubárù; (make known: news etc) 知らせる shiráserù

give up vi (surrender) 降参する kōsan suru
♦vt (renounce: job, habit) やめる yaméru; (: boyfriend) ...との交際をやめる ...to no kōsai wò yamérù; (abandon: idea, hope) 捨てる sutérù

to give up smoking タバコをやめる tabáko wò yamérù

to give oneself up 自首する jishú suru

give way vi (yield) 譲る yuzúru; (break, collapse: floor, ladder etc) 崩れる kuzúrerù, 壊れる kowárerù; (: rope) 切れる kiréru; (BRIT: AUT) 道を譲る michí wò yuzúru

glacier [glei'ʒər] n 氷河 hyōga

glad [glæd] adj (happy, pleased) うれしい uréshii

gladly [glæd'li:] adv (willingly) 喜んで yorókoñde

glamorous [glæm'ərəs] adj 魅惑的な miwákuteki na

glamour [glæm'ər] n 魅惑 miwáku

glance [glæns] n (look) ちらっと見る事 chiráttò mírù koto
♦vi: *to glance at ...*をちらっと見る ...wo chiráttò mírù

glance off vt fus ...に当って跳ね返る ...ni attáte hanékaerù

glancing [glæns'iŋ] adj (blow) かすめる kasúmerù

gland [glænd] n せん señ

glare [gler'] n (of anger) にらみ nirámi; (of light) まぶしい mabúshisà; (of publicity) 脚光 kyakkō
♦vi (light) まぶしく光る mabúshikù hikárù

to glare at (glower) ...をにらみ付ける ...wo nirámitsukerù

glaring [gler'iŋ] adj (mistake) 明白な meíhaku na

glass [glæs] n (substance) ガラス garásu; (container) コップ koppú, グラス gúrasu; (contents) コップ一杯 koppú ippái

glasses [glæs'iz] npl 眼鏡 mégàne

glasshouse [glæs'haus] n 温室 oñshitsu

glassware [glæs'wer] n グラス類 gurásurui

glassy [glæs'i:] *adj* (eyes) うつろな utsuro na

glaze [gleiz] *vt* (door, window) ...にガラスをはめる ...ni garásu wò hamérù; (pottery) ...にうわぐすりを掛ける ...ni uwágusùri wo kakérù

♦*n* (on pottery) うわぐすり uwágusùri

glazed [gleizd] *adj* (eyes) うつろな utsuro na; (pottery, tiles) うわぐすりを掛けた uwágusùri wo kakéta

glazier [glei'ʒəːr] *n* ガラス屋 garásuyà

gleam [gli:m] *vi* (shine: light, eyes, polished surface) 光る hikárù

glean [gli:n] *vt* (information) かき集める kakíatsumerù

glee [gli:] *n* (joy) 喜び yorókobi

glen [glen] *n* 谷間 tańíai

glib [glib] *adj* (person) 口達者な kuchídasshà na; (promise, response) 上辺だけの uwábe dake no

glide [glaid] *vi* (snake, dancer, boat etc) 滑る様に動く subérù yō ni ugókù; (AVIAT, birds) 滑空する kañkū suru

glider [glai'dəːr] *n* (AVIAT) グライダー guráidà

gliding [glai'diŋ] *n* (AVIAT) 滑空 kańkū

glimmer [glim'əːr] *n*: **a glimmer of light** かすかな光 kásùka na hikári

a glimmer of interest かすかな表情 kásùka na hyōjō

a glimmer of hope かすかな希望 kásùka na kibō

glimpse [glimps] *n* (of person, place, object) ...がちらっと見える事 ...ga chíráttò mièrú koto

♦*vt* ...がちらっと見える ...ga chíráttò miérù

glint [glint] *vi* (flash: light, eyes, shiny surface) ぴかっと光る pikáttò hikárù

glisten [glis'ən] *vi* (with sweat, rain etc) ぎらぎらする gíràgira suru

glitter [glit'əːr] *vi* (sparkle: light, eyes, shiny surface) 輝く kagáyakù

gloat [glout] *vi*: **to gloat (over)** (exult) ...しくそえむ ...ni hokúsoemu

global [glou'bəl] *adj* (worldwide) 世界的な sekáiteki na

globe [gloub] *n* (world) 地球 chikyū; (model) 地球儀 chikyūgì; (shape) 球 kyū

gloom [glu:m] *n* (dark) 暗やみ kuráyami; (sadness) 失望 shitsúbō

gloomy [glu:'mi:] *adj* (dark) 薄暗い usúgurai; (sad) 失望した shitsúbō shità

glorious [glɔːr'i:əs] *adj* (sunshine, flowers, weather) 素晴らしい subárashiì; (victory, future) 栄光の eíkō no

glory [glɔːr'i:] *n* (prestige) 栄光 eíkō; (splendor) 華々しさ hanábanashisà

gloss [glɔs] *n* (shine) つや tsuyá; (also: **gloss paint**) つや出しペイント tsuyádashipeìnto

glossary [glɔs'əːri:] *n* 用語集 yōgoshū

gloss over *vt fus* (error) 言繕う iítsukuroù; (problem) 言いくるめる iíkurumerù

glossy [glɔs'i:] *adj* (hair) つやつやした tsuyátsuya shità; (photograph) つや出しの tsuyádashi no; (magazine) アート紙の átoshi no

glove [glʌv] *n* (gen) 手袋 tebúkùro; (in baseball) グローブ gūròbu, グラブ gùràbu

glove compartment *n* (AUT) グローブボックス gurōbubokkùsu

glow [glou] *vi* (embers) 赤く燃える akákù moérù; (stars) 光る hikárù; (face, eyes) 輝く kagáyakù

glower [glau'əːr] *vi*: **to glower at** ...をにらみ付ける ...wo nirámitsukerù

glucose [glu:'kous] *n* ブドウ糖 budótō, グルコース gurúkōsu

glue [glu:] *n* (adhesive) 接着剤 setchákuzài

♦*vt* 接着する setchákù suru

glum [glʌm] *adj* (miserable) ふさぎ込んだ fuságikonda

glut [glʌt] *n* (of oil, goods etc) 生産過剰 seísankajō

glutton [glʌt'ən] *n* 大食らい ōgurai

a glutton for work 仕事の鬼 shigóto nò oní

gluttony [glʌt'əni:] *n* 暴食 bōshoku

glycerin(e) [glis'əːrin] *n* グリセリン guríserìn

gnarled [nɑːrld] *adj* (tree, hand) 節くれだった fushíkuredattà

gnat [næt] n ブヨ búyò

gnaw [nɔː] vt (bone) かじる kajírù

gnome [noum] n 地の小鬼 chí no kóòni

KEYWORD
---

go [gou] (pt **went**, pp **gone**) vi 1 (travel, move) 行く ikú

she went into the kitchen 彼女は台所に行った kánojo wa daídokoro ni ittá

shall we go by car or train? 車で行きましょうか、それとも電車で行きましょうか kurúma de ikímashō ka, soréto-mò defísha de ikímashō ka

a car went by 車が通り過ぎた kurúma ga tōri sugítà

to go round the back 裏へ回る urá e mawáru

to go by the shop 店の前を通る misé no maè wo tōrù

he has gone to Aberdeen 彼はアバディーンへ行きました kárè wa abádìn e ikímashīta

2 (depart) 出発する shuppátsu suru, たつ tátsù, 帰る káèru, 行ってしまう itté shimaù

"I must go," *she said* 「帰ります」と彼女は言った "kaérimasù" to kánojo wa ittá

our plane went at 6 pm 我々の飛行機は午後6時に出発しました waréware no hikōki wa yúgata rokújī ni shuppátsu shimashīta

they came at 8 and went at 9 彼らは8時に来て9時に帰った kárèra wa hachíjì ni kíté kújì ni kaérimashīta

3 (attend) 通う kayóu

she went to university in Aberdeen 彼女はアバディーンの大学に通った kánojo wa abádìn no daígaku ni kayóttà

she goes to her dancing class on Tuesdays 彼女はダンス教室に毎週火曜日です kánojo wa dańsukyōshitsu ni kayóu no wà kayōbi desu

he goes to the local church 彼は地元の教会に通っています kárè wa jimóto no kyōkai ni kayótte imasù

4 (take part in an activity) …に行く ...ni ikú, …する ...surù

to go for a walk 散歩に行く sańpo ni ikú, 散歩する sańpo suru

to go dancing ダンスに行く dáńsu ni ikú

5 (work) 作動する sadō suru

the clock stopped going 時計が止りました tokéi ga tomárimashita

is your watch going? あなたの時計は動いていますか anátà no tokéi wa ugóite imasù ká

the bell went just then 丁度その時ベルが鳴りました chódo sono tokí bérù ga narímashīta

the tape recorder was still going テープレコーダーはまだ回っていました tépurekōdà wa mádà mawátte imashīta

6 (become) …に…なる ...ni ...ni nárù

to go pale 青白くなる aójiroku narù

to go moldy かびる kabíru

7 (be sold) …で売れる ...de urérù

to go for $10 10ドルで売れる jūdòru de urérù

8 (fit, suit) 合う áù

to go with …に合う ...ni áù

that tie doesn't go with that shirt そのネクタイはシャツと合いません sonó nékùtai wa shátsù to aímasén

9 (be about to, intend to): *he's going to do it* 彼は今それをやる所です kárè wa ímà soré wò yarú tokoro desu

we're going to leave in an hour 1時間したら出発します ichíjìkan shitará shuppátsu shimasù

are you going to come? あなたも一緒に来ますか anátà mo isshó ni kimásù ká

10 (time) 経つ tátsù

time went very slowly/quickly 時間が経つのがとても遅く（早く）感じられました jikán ga tatsù no ga totémò osóku (háyàku) kanjíraremashīta

11 (event, activity) 行く ikú

how did it go? うまく行きましたか úmàku ikímashīta ká

12 (be given) 与えられる atáerarerù

the job is to go to someone else その ポストは他の人のところへいきました sonó pósùto wa hoká no hito no tokoró e ikímashīta

13 (break etc: glass etc) 割れる warérù;

(: stick, leg, pencil etc) 折れる orérù; (: thread, rope, chain etc) 切れる kirérù

the fuse went ヒューズが切れた (飛んだ) hyúzù ga kiréta (tóñda)

the leg of the chair went いすの脚が折れた isú no ashí ga órèta

14 (be placed) ...にしまう事になっている ...ni shimáu kotò ni nátte irù

where does this cup go? このカップはどこにしまうのですか konó kappù wa dókò ni shimáù no desu ká

the milk goes in the fridge ミルクは冷蔵庫にしまう事になっています mírùku wa refzókò ni shimáu kotò ni nátte imasù

♦*n* (*pl* **goes**) 1 (try): *to have a go (at)* (...を) やってみる (...wo) yatté mirù

2 (turn) 番 báñ

whose go is it? だれの番ですか dáre no báñ desu ká

3 (move): *to be on the go* 忙しくする isógashiku surù

go about *vi* (*also*: **go around**: rumor) 流れる nagárerù

♦*vt fus*: *how do I go about this?* どういう風にやればいいんですか dó iu fú ni yaréba íi desu ká

goad [goud] *vt* 刺激する shigéki suru

go ahead *vi* (make progress) 進歩する shíñpo suru; (get going) 取り掛る toríkakarù

go-ahead [gou'əhed] *adj* (person, firm) 進取の気に富んだ shíñshu no ki ni tóñda

♦*n* (for project) 許可 kyóka, ゴーサイン gósaìn

goal [goul] *n* (SPORT) ゴール góru; (aim) 目標 mokúhyò

goalkeeper [goul'ki:pər] *n* ゴールキーパー górukipà

go along *vi* ついて行く tsúite ikú

♦*vt fus* ...を行く ...wò ikú

to go along with (agree with: plan, idea, policy) ...に賛成する ...ni sañsei surù

goalpost [goul'poust] *n* ゴールポスト górusupòto

goat [gout] *n* ヤギ yágì

go away *vi* (leave) どこかへ行く dókò ka e ikú

go back *vi* (return) 帰る káèru; (go again) また行く máta ikú

go back on *vt fus* (promise) 破る yabúrù

gobble [gɑːbəl] *vt* (*also*: **gobble down**, **gobble up**) むさぼり食う musáborikuù

go-between [gou'bitwiːn] *n* 仲介者 chúkaisha

go by *vi* (years, time) 経つ tátsù

♦*vt fus* (book, rule) ...に従う ...ni shitágaù

God [gɑːd] *n* (REL) 神 kámì

god [gɑːd] *n* (MYTHOLOGY, *fig*) 神 kámì

godchild [gɑːd'tʃaild] *n* 名付け子 nazúkegò

goddaughter [gɑːd'dɔːtər] *n* 名付け娘 nazúkemusùme

goddess [gɑːd'is] *n* (MYTHOLOGY, REL, *fig*) 女神 megámi

godfather [gɑːd'fɑːðər] *n* 名付け親 nazúkeoyà, 代父 dáìfu, 教父 kyófù

godforsaken [gɑːd'fɑːrsei'kən] *adj* (place, spot) 荒れ果てた aréhatetà

godmother [gɑːd'mʌðər] *n* 名付け親 nazúkeoyà, 代母 daíbo, 教母 kyóbò

go down *vi* (descend) 降りる orírù; (ship) 沈む shizúmù, 沈没する chíñbotsu suru; (sun) 沈む shizúmu

♦*vt fus* (stairs, ladder) ...を降りる ...wo orírù

godsend [gɑːd'send] *n* (blessing) 天の恵み teñ nó megúmì

godson [gɑːd'sʌn] *n* 名付け息子 nazúkemusùko

go for *vt fus* (fetch) 取りに行く tórì ni ikú; (like) 好きである ...ga sukí de arù, ...を気に入る ...wò ki ní nf irù

goggles [gɑːg'əlz] *npl* (for skiing, motorcycling) ゴーグル góguru

go in *vi* (enter) 入る háìru

go in for *vt fus* (competition) ...に参加する ...ni sañka suru; (like) ...が好きである ...ga sukí de arù, ...を気に入る ...wò ki nf irù

going [gou'iŋ] *n* (conditions) 状況 jókyò

♦*adj*: *the going rate* 相場 sôba

go into *vt fus* (enter) ...に入る ...ni háiru; (investigate) 調べる shiráberu; (embark on) ...に従事する ...ni jûjî suru

gold [gould] *n* (metal) 金 kíñ

♦*adj* (jewelery, watch, tooth etc) 金の kíñ no

gold reserves 金の正貨準備 kíñ no sefka juñbî

golden [gouˈdən] *adj* (made of gold) 金の金 no; (gold in color) 金色の kíñ-iro no

goldfish [gouldˈfiʃ] *n* 金魚 kíñgyo

goldmine [gouldˈmain] *n* 金山 kíñzan; (*fig*) ドル箱 dorúbako

gold-plated [gouldpleiˈtid] *adj* 金めっきの kíñmékki no

goldsmith [gouldˈsmiθ] *n* 金細工師 kíñzaikushî

golf [gɑlf] *n* ゴルフ górufu

golf ball *n* (for game) ゴルフボール gorúfubōru; (on typewriter) 電動タイプライターのボール deñdôtaipuraîta no bôru

golf club *n* (organization, stick) ゴルフクラブ gorúfukurâbu

golf course *n* ゴルフコース gorúfukôsu

golfer [gɑlˈfəːr] *n* ゴルファー górùfâ

gondola [gɑnˈdələ] *n* (boat) ゴンドラ goñdora

gone [gɔːn] *pp* of **go**

gong [gɔːŋ] *n* どら dorá, ゴング góñgu

good [gud] *adj* (pleasant, satisfactory etc) 良い yoì; (high quality) 高級な kôkyū na; (tasty) おいしい ofshiî; (kind) 親切な shifisetsu na; (well-behaved: child) 行儀の良い gyôgi no yoî; (morally correct) 正しい tadâshii; (useful) 役立つ...ni yakú dats̱ù

♦*n* (virtue, morality) 善 zéñ; (benefit) 利益 rîeki

good! よろしい! yoróshiî!

to be good at ...が上手である ...ga jôzu de árù

to be good for (useful) ...に使える ...ni tsukáeru

it's good for you あなたのためにいい anáta no tamé ni íi

would you be good enough to ...? 済みませんが...して下さいませんか sumí-

maseñ ga ...shite kudásaimaseñ ká

a good deal (of) 沢山 (の) takúsan (no)

a good many 沢山の takúsan no

to make good (damage, loss) 弁償する beñshô suru

it's no good complaining 不平を言ってもしようがない fuhéi wo ittê mo shiyô ga náì

for good (forever) 永久に efkyû ni

good morning! お早うございます o-háyō gozaimasû

good afternoon! 今日は koñnichi wa

good evening! 今晩は koñban wa

good night! お休みなさい o-yásumi nasaî

goodbye [gudbaiˈ] *excl* さようなら sayônara

to say goodbye 別れる wakárerù

Good Friday *n* (REL) 聖金曜日 sefkiñyôbi

good-looking [gudˈlukˈiŋ] *adj* (woman) 美人の bijíñ no; (man) ハンサムな háñsamu na

good-natured [gudˈneiˈtʃəːrd] *adj* (person, pet) 気立ての良い kidáte no yoî

goodness [gudˈnis] *n* (of person) 優しさ yasáshîsà

for goodness sake! 後生だから goshô da kara

goodness gracious! あらまあ! ará mâ

goods [gudz] *npl* (COMM) 商品 shôhin

goods train (BRIT) *n* 貨物列車 kamótsuresshâ

goodwill [gudˈwil] *n* (of person) 善意 zéñi

go off *vi* (leave) どこかへ行く dókò ka é ikû; (food) 悪くなる warûku naru; (bomb) 爆発する bakúhatsu suru; (gun) 暴発する bakúhatsu suru; (event): *to go off well* うまくいく úmàku ikù

♦*vt fus* (person, place, food etc) 嫌いになる kiráì ni narû

go on *vi* (continue) 続く tsuzúku; (happen) 起る okôru

to go on doing something ...をし続ける ...wò shitsúzukerû

goose [guːs] (*pl* **geese**) *n* ガチョウ gachô

gooseberry [guːsˈbeːriː] *n* (tree, fruit) ス

グリ súguri

to play gooseberry (BRIT) アベックの邪魔をする abékkò no jamá wo surú

gooseflesh [guːsˈfleʃ] n 鳥肌 toríhada

goose pimples npl = **gooseflesh**

go out vi (leave: room, building) 出る dérù; (for entertainment): **are you going out tonight?** 今夜どこかへ出掛けますか kón-ya dókòka e dekakemasū ká; (couple): **they went out for 3 years** 彼らは3年交際した kárèra wa sañnen kōsai shita; (fire, light) 消える kiérù

go over vi (ship) 転覆する teñpuku surú
♦vt fus (check) 調べる shirábérù

gore [gɔːr] vt (subj: bull, buffalo) 角で刺す tsunó dè sásù
♦n (blood) 血のり chinóri

gorge [gɔːrdʒ] n (valley) 峡谷 kyōkoku
♦vt: **to gorge oneself (on)** (...を) たらふく食う (...wo) taráfùku kúù

gorgeous [gɔːrdʒəs] adj (necklace, dress etc) 豪華な gōka na; (weather) 素晴らしい subárashìi; (person) 美しい utsúkushìi

gorilla [gərílˈə] n ゴリラ górìra

gorse [gɔːrs] n ハリエニシダ harfenishìda

gory [gɔːrˈiː] adj (details, situation) 血みどろの chimídoro no

go-slow [gouˈslouˈ] (BRIT) n 遅法闘争 juñpōtōsō

gospel [gɑsˈpəl] n (REL) 福音 fukúìn

gossip [gɑsˈəp] n (rumors) うわさ話 uwásabanashī, ゴシップ goshíppù; (chat) 雑談 zatsúdan; (person) おしゃべり osháberi, ゴシップ屋 goshíppuya
♦vi (chat) 雑談する zatsúdan suru

got [gɑt] pt, pp of **get**

go through vt fus (town etc) ...を通る ...wò tōrù; (search through: files, papers) ...を一つ一つ調べる ...wò hitótsu hitótsu shirábérù; (examine: list, book, story) 調べる shirábérù

gotten [gɑtˈən] (US) pp of **get**

go up vi (ascend) 登る nobórù; (price, level) 上がる agárù

gout [gaut] n 痛風 tsūfū

govern [gʌvˈərn] vt (country) 統治する tōchi suru; (event, conduct) 支配する shi-

hái suru

governess [gʌvˈərnis] n (children's) 女性家庭教師 joséikateikyōshī

government [gʌvˈərnmənt] n (act of governing) 政治 seíji; (governing body) 政府 seífu; (BRIT: ministers) 内閣 naíkaku

governor [gʌvˈərnər] n (of state) 知事 chíji; (of colony) 総督 sōtoku; (of bank, school, hospital) 理事 ríji; (BRIT: of prison) 所長 shochō

go without vt fus (food, treats) ...無しで済ます ...náshī de sumásù

gown [gaun] n (dress: also of teacher) ガウン gáùn; (BRIT: of judge) 法服 hōfuku

GP [dʒiːpiː'] n abbr = **general practitioner**

grab [græb] vt (seize) つかむ tsukámù
♦vi: **to grab at** ...をつかもうとする ...wo tsukámō to suru

grace [greis] n (REL) 恩恵 oñkei; (gracefulness) しとやかさ shitóyakasà
♦vt (honor) ...に栄誉を与える ...ni éìyo wo atáerù; (adorn) 飾る kazárù

5 days' grace 5日間の猶予 itsúkakañ no yúyo

graceful [greisˈfəl] adj (animal, athlete) しなやかな shináyàka na; (style, shape) 優雅な yūga na

gracious [greiˈʃəs] adj (person) 親切な shifsetsu na

grade [greid] n (COMM: quality) 品質 hiñshitsu; (in hierarchy) 階級 kaíkyū; (SCOL: mark) 成績 seíseki; (US: school class) 学年 gakúnen
♦vt (rank, class) 格付けする kakúzuke suru; (exam papers etc) 採点する saíten suru

grade crossing (US) n 踏切 fumíkirì

grade school (US) n 小学校 shōgakkō

gradient [greiˈdiːənt] n (of road, slope) こう配 kōbai

gradual [grædʒˈuːəl] adj (change, evolution) 少しずつの sukóshìzutsu no

gradually [grædʒˈuːəli:] adv 徐々に jójò ni

graduate [n grædʒˈuːit vb grædʒˈuːeit] n (also: **university graduate**) 大学の卒

学生 daígaku nð sotsúgyòsei; (US: also: high school graduate) 高校の卒業生 kôkô nð sotsúgyòsei

♦vi 卒業する sotsúgyô suru

graduation [grædʒuei'ʃən] n (also: graduation ceremony) 卒業式 sotsúgyò-shiki

graffiti [grəfiːt'iː] npl 落書き rakúgaki

graft [græft] n (AGR) 接ぎ木 tsugíki; (MED) 移植 ishóku; (BRIT: inf: hard work) 苦労 kúrð; (bribery) 汚職 oshóku

♦vt (AGR) 接木する tsugíki suru; (MED) 移植する ishóku suru

grain [grein] n (of rice, wheat, sand, salt) 粒 tsúbù; (no pl: cereals) 穀物 kokúmòtsu; (of wood) 木目 mokúme

gram [græm] n グラム gúràmu

grammar [græm'əːr] n (LING) 文法 buñpō; (book) 文法書 buñpōsho

grammar school [BRIT] n 公立高等学校 kôritsukòtōgakkō ◇大学進学教育をする公立高校 daígakushingakukyòiku o suru kôritsukôkō; (US) 小学校 shôgakkō

grammatical [grəmæt'ikəl] adj (LING) 文法の buñpō no

gramme [græm] n = gram

gramophone [græm'əfoun] n 蓄音機 chikúoñki

grand [grænd] adj (splendid, impressive) 壮大な sôdai na; (inf: wonderful) 素晴らしい subárashiì; (also humorous: gesture etc) 大げさな ôgesa na

grandchildren [grænt'tʃil'drən] npl 孫 mágð

granddad [græn'dæd] n (inf) おじいちゃん ojíichan

granddaughter [græn'dɔːtəːr] n 孫娘 magómusume

grandeur [græn'dʒəːr] n (of scenery etc) 壮大さ sôdaisa

grandfather [græn'fɑːðəːr] n 祖父 sófù

grandiose [græn'diːous] adj (scheme, building) 壮大な sôdai na; (pej) 大げさな ôgesa na

grandma [græm'ɑ] n (inf) おばあちゃん obáachan

grandmother [græn'mʌðəːr] n 祖 母 só-

bð

grandpa [græn'pɑ] n (inf) = granddad

grandparents [græn'peːrənts] npl 祖 父 母 sófùbo

grand piano n グランドピアノ gurándopiàno

grandson [græn'sʌn] n 孫息子 magómusùko

grandstand [græn'stænd] n (SPORT) 観覧席 kañrañseki, スタンド sutáñdo

granite [græn'it] n 御影石 mikágeìshi

granny [græn'iː] n (inf) おばあちゃん o-báàchan

grant [grænt] vt (money) 与える atáerù; (request etc) かなえる kanáerù; (visa) 交付する kôfu suru; (admit) 認める mitómerù

♦n (SCOL) 助成金 joséìkin; (ADMIN: subsidy) 交付金 kôfùkin

to take ... for granted ...を軽く見る ...wo karúkù mírù

granulated sugar [græn'jəleitid-] n グラニュー糖 gurányùtō

granule [græn'juːl] n (of coffee, salt) 粒 tsúbù

grape [greip] n ブドウ budô

grapefruit [greip'fruːt] (pl grapefruit or grapefruits) n グレープフルーツ gu-rêpufurùtsu

graph [græf] n (diagram) グラフ gúràfu

graphic [græf'ik] adj (account, description) 写実的な shajítsuteki na; (art, design) グラフィックの guráfikkù no

graphics [græf'iks] n (art, process) グラフィックス guráfikkùsu

♦npl (drawings) グラフィックス guráfikkùsu

grapple [græp'əl] vi: to grapple with someone ...ともみ合う ...to momíaù

to grapple with something (problem etc) ...と取組む ...to toríkumù

grasp [græsp] vt (hold, seize) 握る nigírù; (understand) 理解する rikái suru

♦n (grip) 握り nigírì; (understanding) 理解 rikái

grasping [græs'piŋ] adj (money-grabbing) 欲深い yokúfukaì

grass [græs] n (BOT) 草 kusá; (lawn) 芝生 shibáfu

grasshopper [græs'hɑːpər] n バッタ báttá

grass-roots [græs'ruːts] adj (level, opinion) 一般人の ippáñjin no

grate [greit] n (for fire) 火格子 higóshi
♦vi (metal, chalk): **to grate (on)** (...に すれて) きしる ...ni suréte) kishírû
♦vt (CULIN) すりおろす surforosû

grateful [greit'fəl] adj (...to) 感謝の kâñsha no; (person) 有難く思っている arígatakû omótte irû

grater [grei'tər] n (CULIN) 卸し金 oróshigàne

gratifying [græt'əfaiiŋ] adj (pleasing, satisfying) 満足な mañzoku na

grating [grei'tiŋ] n (iron bars) 鉄格子 tetsúgóshi
♦adj (noise) きしる kishírû

gratitude [græt'ətuːd] n 感謝 kâñsha

gratuity [grətuː'iti:] n (tip) 心付け kokórozûke, チップ chíppû

grave [greiv] n (tomb) 墓 haká
♦adj (decision, mistake) 重大な jûdai na; (expression, person) 重々しい omóomoshiî

gravel [græv'əl] n 砂利 jarí

gravestone [greiv'stoun] n 墓石 hakáishi

graveyard [greiv'jɑːrd] n 墓場 hakába, 墓地 bóchi

gravity [græv'əti] n (PHYSICS) 引力 íñryoku; (seriousness) 重大さ jûdaisa

gravy [grei'vi:] n (juice of meat) 肉汁 nikújû; (sauce) グレービーソース gurébīsōsu

gray [grei] adj = **grey**

graze [greiz] vi (animal) 草を食う kusá wo kûû
♦vt (touch lightly) かすめる kasúmerù; (scrape) こする kosúrû
♦n (MED) かすり傷 kasúrikîzu

grease [griːs] n (lubricant) グリース gurísù; (fat) 脂肪 shibô
♦vt ...にグリースを差す ...ni gurísù wo sásù

greaseproof paper [griːs'pruːf-] (BRIT)

n パラフィン紙 paráfiñshi

greasy [griː'si:] adj (food) 脂っこい abúrakkoì; (tools) 油で汚れた abúra dè yogóretà; (skin, hair) 脂ぎった abúragittà

great [greit] adj (large: area, amount) 大きい ôkiì; (intense: heat, pain) 強い tsuyôì; (important, famous: city, man) 有名な yûmei na; (inf: terrific) 素晴らしい subárashiî

Great Britain n 英国 efkoku, イギリス igírisu

great-grandfather [greit'græn'fɑːðər] n そう祖父 sôsofù

great-grandmother [greit'græn'mʌðər] n そう祖母 sôsobò

greatly [greit'li:] adv とても totémo

greatness [greit'nis] n (importance) 偉大さ idáisa

Greece [griːs] n ギリシア gírìshia

greed [griːd] n (also: **greediness**) どん欲 dóñ-yoku

greedy [griː'di:] adj どん欲な dóñ-yoku na

Greek [griːk] adj ギリシアの gírìshia no; (LING) ギリシア語の gírìshiago no
♦n (person) ギリシア人 gírìshiajìn; (LING) ギリシア語 gírìshiago

green [griːn] adj (color) 緑 (色) の mídòri(iro) no; (inexperienced) 未熟な mijúku na; (POL) 環境保護の kañkyóhogò no
♦n (color) 緑 (色) mídòri(iro); (stretch of grass) 芝生 shibáfu; (on golf course) グリーン gurín

green belt n (round town) 緑地帯 ryokúchitaì, グリーンベルト gurímberùto

green card n (BRIT: AUT) グリーンカード gurínkàdo ◆海外自動車保険証 kafgai jidósha hokeñshò; (US: ADMIN) グリーンカード gurínkàdo ◆外国人入国就労許可書 gaskokujìn nyúkoku shúrò kyokásho

greenery [griː'nəːriː] n 緑 mídòri ◆主に人為的に植えた樹木などを指す ômò ni jiñ-íteki ni uéta júmòku nádà wo sásù

greengrocer [griːn'grousər] (BRIT) n 八百屋 yaóya

greenhouse [griːn'haus] n 温室 oñshitsu

greenish [griː'niʃ] adj 緑がかった midórigakattá

Greenland [griːnˈlənd] n グリーンランド gurīnrándo

greens [griːnz] npl (vegetables) 葉物ha-móno, 葉菜 yōsai

greet [griːt] vt (welcome: person) …にあいさつする …ni áisatsu suru; (welcome a kańgei suru); (receive: news) 受けとめるuketómerù

greeting [griːtiŋ] n (welcome) あいさつ áisatsu, 歓迎 kańgei

greeting(s) card n グリーティングカード gurītiñgukádo

gregarious [grigˈɛːrˈiəs] adj (person) 社交的な shakóteki na

grenade [grineid] n (also: **hand grenade**) 手りゅう弾 shuryūdan, 手投げ弾 tenáge dan

grew [gruː] pt of **grow**

grey [grei] adj (color) 灰色 hafiro; (dismal) 暗い kurái

grey-haired [greiˈheːrd] adj 白髪頭のshirágaatáma no, 白髪の hakúhatsu no

greyhound [greiˈhaund] n グレーハウンドgurēhaundo

grid [grid] n (pattern) 基盤の目 góban no me; (ELEC: network) 送電網 sōdenmō

grief [griːf] n (distress, sorrow) 悲しみkanáshimì

grievance [griːvəns] n (complaint) 苦情kujō

grieve [griːv] vi (feel sad) 悲しむ kanáshimù
◆vt (cause sadness or distress to) 悲しませる kanáshimaserù
to grieve for (dead spouse etc) …を嘆く …wo nagékù

grievous [griːvəs] adj: **grievous bodily harm** (LAW) 重傷 jūshō

grill [gril] n (on cooker) グリル gurīru; (grilled food: also: **mixed grill**) グリル料理 gurírīryōri
◆vt (BRIT: food) グリルで焼く gurīru de yákū; (inf: question) 尋問する jińmon suru

grille [gril] n (screen: on window, counter etc) 鉄格子 tetsúgōshi; (AUT) ラジエーターグリル rajíētāgūriru

grim [grim] adj (unpleasant: situation)

厳しい kibíshiì; (unattractive: place) 陰気な fńki na; (serious, stern) 険しい ke-wáshiì

grimace [grimˈas] n (ugly expression) しかめっ面 shikámetsura
◆vi しかめっ面をする shikámetsura wo suru

grime [graim] n (dirt) あか aká

grin [grin] n (smile) にやにや笑い nfyáni-yawarai
◆vi にやにやと笑う nfyániya ni waráù

grind [graind] (pt, pp **ground**) vt (crush) もみつぶす mộtsubusù; (coffee, pepper etc: also US: meat) 挽く hikú; (make sharp: knife) 研ぐ tógù
◆n (work) 骨折れ仕事 honéoreshigòto

grip [grip] n (hold) 握り nigíri; (control, grasp) 支配 shihái; (of tire, shoe) グリップ guríppù; (handle) 取っ手 tótté; (hold-all) 旅行かばん ryokőkabàn
◆vt (object) つかむ tsukámů, 握る nigírů; (audience, attention) 引付ける hikítsuke-rù
to come to grips with (problem, difficulty) …と取組む …to toríkumù

gripping [gripˈiŋ] adj (story, film) 引付ける hikítsukerù

grisly [grizˈli] adj (death, murder) ひどい hídoì

gristle [grisˈəl] n (on meat) 軟骨 nańko-tsu

grit [grit] n (sand, stone) 砂利 jarí; (determination, courage) 根性 kofijō
◆vt (road) …に砂利を敷く …ni jarí wo shíkù
to grit one's teeth 歯を食いしばる há wò kuíshibarù

groan [groun] n (of person) うめき声 u-mékigòe
◆vi うめく umékù

grocer [grouˈsər] n 食料品商 shokúryō-hìńshō

groceries [grouˈsəriz] npl (provisions) 食料品 shokúryōhìn

grocer's (shop) [grouˈsərz-] n 食料品店 shokúryōhíntèn

groggy [grɑːgˈiː] adj ふらふらする fúra-fura suru, グロッキーの gurókkī no

groin [grɔin] n そけい部 sokébu

groom [grum] n (for horse) 馬丁 batéi; (also: **bridegroom**) 花婿 hanámukò

♦vt (horse) ...の手入れをする ...no teíre wò suru; (fig): **to groom someone for** (job) 仕込む shikómù

well-groomed (person) 身だしなみのいい midáshinami no fi

groove [gruv] n 溝 mizó

grope [group] vi (fumble): **to grope for** 手探りで探す teságuri de sagásù

gross [grous] adj (flagrant, injustice) 甚だしい hanáhadashìi; (vulgar: behavior, building) 下品な gehín na; (COMM: income, weight) 全体の zeítai no

grossly [grous'liː] adv (greatly) 甚だしく hanáhadashikù

grotesque [groutesk'] adj (exaggerated, ugly) 醜悪な shūaku na, グロテスクな gurótesùku na

grotto [grɑt'ou] n (cave) 小さな洞穴 chíisana horáana

grotty [grɑt'iː] adj (BRIT inf) (dreadful) ひどい hídòi

ground [graund] n pt, pp of **grind**

♦n (earth, soil) 土 tsuchí; (land) 地面 jímèn; (SPORT) グランド gurándo; (US: also: **ground wire**) アース線 ásùsen; (reason: gen pl) 根拠 koñkyo

♦vt (plane) 飛べない状態にする tobénai yò ni suru; (US: ELEC) ...のアースを取付ける ...no ásu wò tsuítsukerù

on the ground 地面に(で) jímèn ni (de)

to the ground 地面へ jímèn e

to gain/lose ground 前進(後退)する zeńshin (kōtai)surù

ground cloth (US) n = **groundsheet**

grounding [graun'diŋ] n (in education) 基礎 kisó

groundless [graund'lis] adj (fears, suspicions) 根拠のない koñkyo no nâi

grounds [graundz] npl (of coffee etc) かす kásù; (gardens etc) 敷地 shikíchi

groundsheet [graund'ʃiːt] n グラウンドシート gurâundoshîto

ground staff n (AVIAT) 整備員 seíbiìn

◇総称 sōshō

ground swell n (of opinion) 盛り上がり moríagari

groundwork [graund'wəːrk] n (preparation) 準備 júnbi

group [gruːp] n (of people) 集団 shūdan, グループ gurūpu; (of trees etc) 一群れ hitómùre; (of cars etc) 一団 ichídan; (also: **pop group**) グループ gurūpu; (COMM) グループ gurūpu

♦vt (also: **group together**: people, things etc) 一緒にする isshô ni suru, グループする gurūpu ni suru

♦vi (also: **group together**) 群がる murágarù, グループになる gurūpu ni naru

grouse [graus] n inv (bird) ライチョウ ráichō

♦vi (complain) 不平を言う fuhéi wò iú

grove [grouv] n 木立 kodáchi

grovel [grʌv'əl] vi (fig): **to grovel (before)** (boss etc) (...に) ぺこぺこする (...ni) pékòpeko suru

grow [grou] (pt **grew**, pp **grown**) vi (plant, tree) 生える haérù; (person, animal) 成長する seíchō suru; (increase) 増える fuérù; (become) なる nárù; (develop): **to grow (out of/from)** (...から) 発生する (...kara) hasséi suru

♦vt (roses, vegetables) 栽培する saíbai suru; (beard) 生やす hayásù

grower [grou'əːr] n (BOT, AGR) 栽培者 saíbaishà

growing [grou'iŋ] adj (fear, awareness, number) 増大する zōdai suru

growl [graul] vi (dog, person) うなる unárù

grown [groun] pp of **grow**

grown-up [groun'ʌp'] n (adult) 大人 otóna

growth [grouθ] n (development, increase: of economy, industry) 成長 seíchō; (what has grown: of weeds, beard etc) 生えた物 haéta monò; (growing: of child, animal etc) 発育 hatsúiku; (MED) しゅよう shuyō

grow up vi (child) 育つ sodátsu

grub [grʌb] n (larva) 幼虫 yōchū; (inf: food) 飯 meshí

grubby [grʌb'i:] *adj* (dirty) 汚い kitánaì

grudge [grʌdʒ] *n* (grievance) 恨み urámì

♦*vt:* **to grudge someone something** (be unwilling to give) ...に...を出し惜しみする ...ni ...wo dashíoshimi suru; (envy) ...の...をねたむ ...no ...wo netámù

to bear someone a grudge ...に恨みがある ...ni urámì ga arù

gruelling [gru:'əliŋ] *adj* (trip, journey, encounter) きつい kitsuì

gruesome [gru:'səm] *adj* (tale, scene) むごたらしい mugótarashiì

gruff [grʌf] *adj* (voice, manner) ぶっきらぼうな bukkírabò na

grumble [grʌm'bəl] *vi* (complain) 不平を言う fuhéi wò iú

grumpy [grʌm'pi:] *adj* (bad-tempered) 機嫌が悪い kigén ga waruì

grunt [grʌnt] *vi* (pig) ぶーぶー言う bûbū iú; (person) うなる unárù

G-string [dʒi:'striŋ] *n* (garment) バタフライ bătáfurai

guarantee [gærənti:'] *n* (assurance) 保証 hoshó; (COMM: warranty) 保証書 hoshóshò

♦*vt* 保証する hoshó suru

guard [gɑ:rd] *n* (one person) 警備員 kefbìn, ガードマン gādoman; (squad) 護衛隊 goéitai; (BRIT: RAIL) 車掌 shashó; (on machine) 安全カバー afizénkabà; (also: **fireguard**) 安全柵 afizénkòshi

♦*vt* (protect: place, person, secret etc) ...を守る ...wo mamórù

to guard (against) ...から守る (...kara) mamórù; (prisoner) 見張るを見張る mihárù

to be on one's guard 警戒する kefkai suru

guard against *vt fus* (prevent: disease, damage etc) 防ぐ fuségù

guarded [gɑ:r'did] *adj* (statement, reply) 慎重な shifchō na

guardian [gɑ:r'di:ən] *n* (LAW: of minor) 保護者 hógòsha; (defender) 監視人 kańshinìn

guard's van (BRIT) *n* (RAIL) 乗務員車 jómuìnsha

guerrilla [gəril'ə] *n* ゲリラ gérìra

guess [ges] *vt, vi* (estimate: number, dis-

tance etc) 推定する suítei suru; (correct answer) 当てる atétè mírù; (US: think) ...だと思う ...da to omóù

♦*n* (attempt at correct answer) 推定 suítei

to take/have a guess 推定する suítei suru, 当ててみる atétè mírù

guesswork [ges'wə:rk] *n* (speculation) 当て推量 atézuryò

guest [gest] *n* (visitor) 客 kyákù; (in hotel) 泊り客 tomárikyakù

guest-house [gest'haus] *n* 民宿 mífshuku

guest room *n* 客間 kyakúma

guffaw [gʌfɔ:'] *vi* げらげら笑う bakáwaraì

guidance [gaid'əns] *n* (advice) 指導 shidó

guide [gaid] *n* (person: museum guide, tour guide, mountain guide) 案内人 annáinìn, ガイド gáìdo; (book) ガイドブック gaídobukkù; (BRIT: also: **girl guide**) ガールスカウト gärusukaùto

♦*vt* (round city, museum etc) 案内する annái suru; (lead) 導く michíbikù; (direct) ...に道を教える ...ni michí wò oshíerù

guidebook [gaid'buk] *n* ガイドブック gaídobukkù

guide dog *n* 盲導犬 mōdōkèn

guidelines [gaid'lainz] *npl* (advice) 指針 shishín, ガイドライン gaídorain

guild [gild] *n* (association) 組合 kumíai, ギルド gírùdo

guile [gail] *n* (cunning) 悪意 akúì

guillotine [gil'əti:n] *n* (for execution) 断頭台 dafítōdai, ギロチン giróchìn; (for paper) 裁断機 saídafki

guilt [gilt] *n* (remorse) 罪の意識 tsumí nò ishìki; (culpability) 有罪 yúzai

guilty [gil'ti:] *adj* (person) 有罪の yúzai no; (expression) 後ろめたそうな ushírometasō na; (secret) やましい yamáshiì

guinea [gin'i:] (BRIT) *n* (old money) ギニー gínì

guinea pig *n* (animal) モルモット morúmottò; (fig: person) 実験台 jikkéndai

guise [gaiz] *n:* **in/under the guise of** ...の装いで ...no yosóoì de

guitar [gɪtɑːʳ] n ギター gítā

gulf [gʌlf] n (GEO) 湾 wáñ; (abyss: also fig: difference) 隔たり hedátarī

gull [gʌl] n カモメ kamóme

gullet [gʌl'it] n 食道 shokúdō

gullible [gʌl'əbəl] adj (naive, trusting) だまされやすい damásareyāsui

gully [gʌl'i:] n (ravine) 峡谷 kyókoku

gulp [gʌlp] vi (swallow) 息を飲み込む iki wo nomíkomù

♦vt (also: **gulp down**: drink) がぶがぶ飲み込む gábùgabu nomíkomù; (: food) 急いで食べる isóide tabérū

gum [gʌm] n (ANAT) 歯茎 hágùki; (glue) アラビア糊 arábia nòri; (sweet: also: **gumdrop**) ガムドロップ gamúdoroppù; (also: **chewing-gum**) チューインガム chúīngaguma, ガム gámù

♦vt (stick): **to gum (together)** 張り合わせる harîawaserū

gumboots [gʌm'bu:ts] (BRIT) npl ゴム靴 gomúgutsu

gumption [gʌmp'ʃən] n (sense, wit) 度胸 dokýō

gun [gʌn] n (small: revolver, pistol) けん銃 keñjū, ピストル pisútoru, がん銃; (medium-sized: rifle) 銃 jū, ライフル raffūru; (: also: **airgun**) 空気銃 kūkijū; (large: cannon) 大砲 taíhō

gunboat [gʌn'bout] n 砲艦 hōkan

gunfire [gʌn'faiəʳ] n 砲撃 hōgeki

gunman [gʌn'man] (pl **gunmen**) n (criminal) ガンマン gáñman

gunpoint [gʌn'point] n: **at gunpoint** (pointing a gun) ピストルを突付けて pisútoru wo tsukítsukete; (threatened with a gun) ピストルを突付けられて pisútoru wo tsukítsukerarete

gunpowder [gʌn'paudəʳ] n 火薬 kayákù

gunshot [gʌn'ʃɑːt] n (act) 発砲 happō; (sound) 銃声 jūsei

gurgle [gəːr'gəl] vi (baby) のどを鳴らす nodó wo narásu; (water) ごぼごぼ流れる góbògobo nagárerū

guru [guːruː] n (REL: also fig) 教師 kyōshi

gush [gʌʃ] vi (blood, tears, oil) どっと流れ出る dōttð nagárederù; (person) 大げさに言う ōgesa ni iu

gusset [gʌs'it] n (SEWING) まち máchi

gust [gʌst] n (also: **gust of wind**) 突風 toppū; (of smoke) 渦巻 uzúmaki

gusto [gʌs'tou] n (enthusiasm) 楽しみ tanóshimi

gut [gʌt] n (ANAT: intestine) 腸 chō

guts [gʌts] npl (ANAT: of person, animal) 内臓 naízō; (inf: courage) 勇気 yūki, ガッツ gáttsù

gutter [gʌt'əʳ] n (in street) どぶ dobu; (of roof) 雨どい amádòi

guttural [gʌt'əːrəl] adj (accent, sound) のどに絡まった様な nódò ni karámatta yō na

guy [gai] n (inf: man) 野郎 yarō, やつ yátsù; (also: **guyrope**) 支綱 shiséñ; (figure) ガイフォークスの人形 gaífòkusu no niñgyō

guzzle [gʌz'əl] vt (drink) がぶがぶ飲む gábùgabu nómù; (food) がつがつ食う gátsùgatsu kúù

gym [dʒim] n (building, room: also: **gymnasium**) 体育館 taíikukàn; (activity: also: **gymnastics**) 体操 taísō

gymnast [dʒim'næst] n 体操選手 taísōsenshu

gymnastics [dʒimnæs'tiks] n 体操 taísō

gym shoes npl 運動靴, uñdōgùtsu, スニーカー súnīkā

gym slip (BRIT) n (tunic) スモックsmókkù 女の無しの上っ張りでかつて女子学童の制服として使われた物. sodénashi no uwáppari de katsúté joshí gakúdō no seffuku toshite tsukáwareta monó

gynecologist [gainəkɑːl'ədʒist] (US) n 婦人科医 fujíñka-i

gynecologist [gainəkɑːl'ədʒist] (BRIT) **gynaecologist** n 婦人科医 fujíñka-i

gypsy [dʒip'si:] n ジプシー jípùshī

gyrate [dʒai'reit] vi (revolve) 回転する kaíten suru

H

haberdashery [hæb'əːrdæʃəːri:] n (US) 紳士服店 shíñshifukutèn; (BRIT) 小間物店 kómamonotèn

habit [hæb'it] *n* (custom, practice) 習慣 shūkan; (addiction) 中毒 chūdoku; (REL: costume) 修道服 shūdōfuku

habitable [hæb'itəbəl] *adj* 住める sumérù

habitat [hæb'itæt] *n* 生息地 sefsokuchī

habitual [həbit'uəl] *adj* (action) 習慣的 な shūkanteki na; (drinker, liar) 常習的 の jōshūteki na

hack [hæk] *vt* (cut, slice) ぶった切る buttágirū

♦*n* (pej: writer) 三文文士 safimonbunshi

hacker [hæk'əːr] *n* (COMPUT) コンピュータ破り cofipyūtayaburi, ハッカー hakkā

hackneyed [hæk'niːd] *adj* 陳腐な chīnpu na

had [hæd] *pt, pp* of **have**

haddock [hæd'ək] (*pl* **haddock** or **haddocks**) *n* タラ tárà

hadn't [hæd'ənt] = **had not**

haemorrhage [hem'əːridʒ] (*BRIT*) *n* = **hemorrhage**

haemorrhoids [hem'əːroidz] (*BRIT*) *npl* = **hemorrhoids**

haggard [hæg'əːrd] *adj* (face, look) やつれた yatsúretà

haggle [hæg'əl] *vi* (bargain) 値切る negírù

Hague [heig] *n*: **The Hague** ハーグ hāgù

hail [heil] *n* (frozen rain) ひょう hyō; (of objects, criticism etc) 降り注ぐ物 furísogu monó

♦*vt* (call: person) 呼ぶ yobú; (flag down: taxi) 呼止める yobítomerù; (acclaim: person, event etc) ほめる homérù

♦*vi* (weather) ひょうが降る hyō ga fúrù

hailstone [heil'stoun] *n* ひょうの粒 hyō no tsubú

hair [heːr] *n* (of animal: also gen) 毛 ke; (of person's head) 髪の毛 kamí no kè

to do one's hair 髪をとかす kamí wò tokásu

hairbrush [heːr'brʌʃ] *n* ヘアブラシ heáburashì

haircut [heːr'kʌt] *n* (action) 散髪 safipatsu; (style) 髪型 kamígata, ヘアスタイル heásutaìru

hairdo [heːr'duː] *n* 髪型 kamígata, ヘアスタイル heásutaìru

hairdresser [heːr'dresəːr] *n* 美容師 biyōshī

hairdresser's [heːr'dresəːrz] *n* (shop) 美容院 biyōin

hair dryer *n* ヘアドライヤー heádoraìyā

hairgrip [heːr'grip] *n* 髪止め kamídome

hairnet [heːr'net] *n* ヘアネット heánettò

hairpin [heːr'pin] *n* ヘアピン heápìn

hairpin curve (*BRIT* **hairpin bend**) *n* ヘアピンカーブ heápìnkābu

hair-raising [heːr'reiziŋ] *adj* (experience, tale) ぞっとする様な zóttò suru yō na

hair remover [-rimuː'vəːr] *n* (cream) 脱毛クリーム datsúmōkurīmu

hair spray *n* ヘアスプレー heásupurè

hairstyle [heːr'stail] *n* 髪型 kamígata, ヘアスタイル heásutaìru

hairy [heːr'iː] *adj* (person, animal) 毛深い kebúkaì; (inf: situation) 恐ろしい osóroshiì

hake [heik] (*pl inv* or **hakes**) *n* タラ tárà

half [hæf] (*pl* **halves**) *n* (of amount, object) 半分 hanbun; (of beer etc) 半パイント hafipaìnto; (RAIL, bus) 半額 hafigaku

♦*adj* (bottle, fare, pay etc) 半分の hanbun no

♦*adv* (empty, closed, open, asleep) 半ば nakába

two and a half 2と2分の1 nf to nibún no ichi

two and a half years/kilos/hours 2年（キロ，時間）半 ninén (kíro, jíkan) hàn

half a dozen 半ダース hafidāsu

half a pound 半ポンド hafipòndo

to cut something in half ...を半分に切る ...wo hanbun ni kírù

half-baked [hæf'beikt'] *adj* (idea, scheme) ばかげた bakágetà

half-caste [hæf'kæst] *n* 混血児 kofiketsujī, ハーフ hāfu

half-hearted [hæf'hɑːr'tid] *adj* (attempt) いい加減な iíkagen na

half-hour [hæf'au'ər] *n* 半時間 hañjikàn

half-mast [hæf'mæst']: *a flag at half-mast* 半旗 háñki

halfpenny [hei'pəni:] *n* (BRIT) 半ペニー hañpenī

half-price [hæf'prais'] *adj* 半額の hañgaku no
♦*adv* 半額で hañgaku de

half term (BRIT) *n* (SCOL) 中間休暇 chūkankyùka

half-time [hæf'taim'] *n* (SPORT) ハーフタイム hāfutaimù

halfway [hæf'wei'] *adv* (between two points in place, time) 中途で chúto de

halibut [hæl'əbət] *n inv* オヒョウ ohyồ

hall [hɔːl] *n* (entrance way) 玄関ホール gefikanhòru; (for concerts, meetings etc) 調堂 kṓdō, ホール hồru

hall of residence (BRIT) *n* 学生寮 gakúseiryô

hallmark [hɔːl'mɑːrk] *n* (on metal) 太鼓判 tañkoban; (of writer, artist etc) 特徴 tokúchō

hallo [həlou'] *excl* = **hello**

Hallowe'en [hæləwiːn'] *n* ハロウィーン haróuin

hallucination [həluːsənei'ʃən] *n* 幻覚 gefkaku

hallway [hɔːl'wei] *n* (entrance hall) 玄関ホール gefkanhòru

halo [hei'lou] *n* (of saint) 後光 gokô

halt [hɔːlt] *n* (stop) 止まる事 tomáru kotò
♦*vt* (progress, activity, growth etc) 止める tomérù
♦*vi* (stop) 止まる tomárù

halve [hæv] *vt* (reduce) 半分に減らす hañbuñ ni heràsù; (divide) 半分に切る hañbuñ ni kírù

halves [hævz] *pl of* **half**

ham [hæm] *n* (meat) ハム hámù

hamburger [hæm'bɑːrgər] *n* ハンバーガー hañbāgâ

hamlet [hæm'lit] *n* (village) 小さな村 chísana murá

hammer [hæm'əːr] *n* (tool) 金づち kanáḍzuchī, とんかち toñkáchi
♦*vt* (nail) たたく tatákù
♦*vi* (on door, table etc) たたく tatákù

to hammer an idea into someone ...に ある考えを叩き込ませる ...ni árù kañgáekata wo tátakikomù

to hammer a message across ある考えを繰返し強調する aru kañgáe wo kuríkaeshī kyōchō suru

hammock [hæm'ək] *n* (on ship, in garden) ハンモック hañmokkù

hamper [hæm'pəːr] *vt* (person, movement, effort) 邪魔する jamá suru
♦*n* (basket) ふた付きバスケット futátsukibasukettò

hamster [hæm'stəːr] *n* ハムスター hámùsutā

hand [hænd] *n* (ANAT) 手 tê; (of clock) 針 hárì; (handwriting) 筆跡 hisséki; (worker) 使用人 shíyōnin; (of cards) 持札 mochífuda
♦*vt* (pass, give) 渡す watásù

to give/lend someone a hand ...の手伝いをする ...no tetsúdaī wo suru

at hand 手元に temótò ni

in hand (time) 空いていて aíte itè; (job, situation) 当面の tômen no

on hand (person, services etc) 利用できる ríyò dekirù

to hand (information etc) 手元に temótò ni

on the one hand ..., on the other hand ... 一方では...他方では... ippồ de wa..., tahồ de wa...

handbag [hænd'bæg] *n* ハンドバッグ hañdobaggù

handbook [hænd'buk] *n* (manual) ハンドブック hañdobukkù

handbrake [hænd'breik] *n* (AUT) サイドブレーキ saídoburêki

handcuffs [hænd'kʌfs] *npl* (POLICE) 手錠 tejô

handful [hænd'ful] *n* (of soil, stones) 握り hitónigirì

a handful of people 数人 súnin

handicap [hæn'di:kæp] *n* (disability) 障害 shồgai; (disadvantage) 不利 fúrì; (SPORT) ハンデ háñde
♦*vt* (hamper) 不利にする fúrì ni suru

mentally/physically handicapped 精神的(身体)障害のある sefshinteki (shíñtai) shōgai no árú

handicraft [hǽndi:kræft] *n* (activity) 手芸 shúgèi; (object) 手芸品 shugéihìn

hand in *vt* (essay, work) 提出する teíshutsu suru

handiwork [hǽndi:wə:rk] *n* やった事 yattá kotò

handkerchief [hǽŋkɔːrtʃif] *n* ハンカチ hafikachi

handle [hǽndəl] *n* (of door, window, drawer etc) 取っ手 totté; (of cup, knife, brush etc) 柄 e; (for winding) ハンドル hafidòru

♦*vt* (touch: object, ornament etc) いじる ijírū; (deal with: problem, responsibility etc) 処理する shórì suru; (treat: people) 扱う atsúkaū

「*handle with care*」取扱い注意 toriatsukai chûi

to fly off the handle 怒る okórù

handlebar(s) [hǽndəlbaːr(z)] *n(pl)* ハンドル hafidòru

hand luggage *n* 手荷物 tenímòtsu

handmade [hǽnd'meid'] *adj* (clothes, jewellery, pottery etc) 手作りの tezúkùri no

hand out *vt* (object, information) 配る kubárù; (punishment) 与える atáerù

handout [hǽnd'aut] *n* (money, clothing, food) 施し物 hodókoshimono; (publicity leaflet) パンフレット páñfurettò; (summary: of lecture) 講義の要約 kôeñ nò yōyaku

hand over *vt* (thing) 引渡す hikíwatasù; (responsibility) 譲る yuzúrù

handrail [hǽnd'reil] *n* (on stair, ledge) 手すり tesúri

handshake [hǽnd'ʃeik] *n* 握手 ákùshu

handsome [hǽnsəm] *adj* (man) 男前の otőkomàe no, ハンサムな háñsamu na; (woman) りっとした kiríttò shita; (building) 立派な rippá na; (fig: profit, return) 相当な sōtō na

handwriting [hǽnd'raitiŋ] *n* (style) 筆跡 hisséki

handy [hǽndi:] *adj* (useful) 便利な bénrì na; (skilful) 手先の器用な tesáki nò kíyò na; (close at hand) 手元にある temótò ní

árù

handyman [hǽndi:mæn] (*pl* **handymen**) *n* (at home) 手先の器用な人 tesáki nò kíyò na hitó; (in hotel etc) 用務員 yōmuin

hang [hæŋ] (*pt, pp* **hung**) *vt* (painting, coat etc) 掛ける kakérù; (criminal: *pt, pp* hanged) 絞首刑にする kōshukei ni surù

♦*vi* (painting, coat, drapery etc) 掛っている kakátte irù; (hair etc) 垂れ下がる tarésagarù

to get the hang of something (*inf*) ...のこつが分かる ...no kótsù ga wakárù

hang about *vi* (loiter) ぶらつく burátsukù

hangar [hǽŋ'ər] *n* (AVIAT) 格納庫 kakúnòko

hang around *vi* = **hang about**

hanger [hǽŋ'ər] *n* (for clothes) 洋服掛け yōfukukàke, ハンガー háñgā

hanger-on [hǽŋ'ərɑːn'] *n* (parasite) 取巻き torímaki

hang-gliding [hǽŋ'glaidiŋ] *n* (SPORT) ハンググライダー hafíguguraídā

hang on *vi* (wait) 待つ mátsù

hangover [hǽŋ'ouvər] *n* (after drinking) 二日酔い futsúkayoì

hang up *vi* (TEL) 電話を切る defíwa wò kírù

♦*vt* (coat, painting etc) 掛ける kakérù

hang-up [hǽŋ'ʌp] *n* (inhibition) ノイローゼ noíròze

hanker [hǽŋ'kər] *vi: to hanker after* (desire, long for) 渇望する katsúbò suru

hankie [hǽŋ'ki:] *n abbr* = **handkerchief**

hanky [hǽŋ'ki:] *n abbr* = **handkerchief**

haphazard [hǽphæz'ɑːrd] *adj* (system, arrangement) いい加減な ífkagen na

happen [hǽp'ən] *vi* (event etc: occur) 起る okórù; (chance): *to happen to do something* 偶然に ... する gűzen ni ...surù *as it happens* 実は jitsú wà

happening [hǽp'əniŋ] *n* (incident) 出来事 dekígotò

happily [hǽp'ili:] *adv* (luckily) 幸い saíwai; (cheerfully) 楽しそうに tanőshisò ni

happiness [hæp'i:nis] n (contentment) 幸せ shíawase

happy [hæp'i:] adj (pleased) うれしい uréshii; (cheerful) 楽しい tanóshii
to be happy (with) (content) (...に) 満足する (...ni) mańzoku suru
to be happy to do (willing) 喜んで...する yorókonde ...surú
happy birthday! 誕生日おめでとう! tańjōbi omédetō!

happy-go-lucky [hæp'i:goulʌk'i:] adj (person) のんきな nónki na

harangue [həræŋ'] n (to audience, class) ...に向かって熱弁を振るう ...ni mukátte netsúben wo furúū

harass [hæræs'] vt (annoy, pester) ...にいやがらせをする ...ni iyágarase wo surú

harassment [hæræs'mənt] n (hounding) 鎌がらせ iyágarase

harbor [hɑːr'bər] (BRIT **harbour**) n (NAUT) 港 mináto
♦vt (hope, fear etc) 心に抱く kokórō ni idáku; (criminal, fugitive) かくまう kakúmau

hard [hɑːrd] adj (surface, object) 堅い katái; (question, problem) 難しい muzúkashii; (work) 骨の折れる honé no oréru; (life) 苦しい kurúshii; (person) 非情な hijō na; (facts, evidence) 確実な kakújitsu na
♦adv (work, think, try) 一生懸命に isshókenmei ni
to look hard at ...を見詰める ...wo mitsúmeru
no hard feelings! 悪く思わないから warúkū omówanai kará
to be hard of hearing 耳が遠い mimí ga tōi
to be hard done by 不当な扱いを受けた futó na atsukái wo ukéta

hardback [hɑːrd'bæk] n (book) ハードカバー hádokabā

hard cash n 現金 geñkin

hard disk n (COMPUT) ハードディスク hádodisùku

harden [hɑːr'dən] vt (wax, glue, steel) 固める katámeru; (attitude, person) かたくなにする katákūna ni suru

hard-headed [hɑːrd'hed'id] adj (businessman) 現実的な geñjitsuteki na

hard labor n (punishment) 懲役 chōeki

hardly [hɑːrd'li:] adv (scarcely) ほとんど...ない hotóndo ...nái; (no sooner) ...するや否や...surú ya ináya
hardly ever ほとんど...しない hotóndo ...shínái

hardship [hɑːrd'ʃip] n (difficulty) 困難 kofínañ

hard up (inf) adj (broke) 金がない kané ga nái, 懐が寂しい futókoro ga sabíshii

hardware [hɑːrd'wer] n (ironmongery) 金物 kanámono; (COMPUT) ハードウェア hádoueā; (MIL) 兵器 hēiki

hardware shop n 金物屋 kanámonoya

hard-wearing [hɑːrd'wer'iŋ] adj (clothes, shoes) 丈夫な jōbu na

hard-working [hɑːrd'wər'kiŋ] adj (employee, student) 勤勉な kiñben na

hardy [hɑːr'di:] adj (plants, animals, people) 丈夫な jōbu na

hare [her] n ノウサギ noúsagi

hare-brained [her'breind] adj (scheme, idea) ばかげた bakágetà

harem [her'əm] n (of wives) ハーレム hấremu

harm [hɑːrm] n (injury) 害 gái; (damage) 損害 sofígai, ダメージ daméjì
♦vt (person) ...に危害を加える ...ni kígai wo kuwáerù; (thing) 損傷する sofíshō suru
out of harm's way 安全な場所に añzen na bashō ni

harmful [hɑːrm'fəl] adj (effect, toxin, influence etc) 有害な yúgai na

harmless [hɑːrm'lis] adj (animal, person) 無害な mugái na; (joke, pleasure, activity) たわいのない tawai no nai

harmonica [hɑːrmɑːn'ikə] n ハーモニカ hấmonika

harmonious [hɑːrmou'ni:əs] adj (discussion, relationship) 友好的な yūkōteki na; (layout, pattern) 調和の取れた chōwa no toréta; (sound, tune) 調子の良い chōshi no yoî

harmonize [hɑːrˈmənaiz] *vi* (MUS) ハーモニーを付ける hàmonî wo tsukérù; (colors, ideas): *to harmonize (with)* (...と)調和する (...to) chôwa suru

harmony [hɑːrˈməni] *n* (accord) 調和 chôwa; (MUS) ハーモニー hâmonî

harness [hɑːrˈnis] *n* (for horse) 馬具 bágù; (for child, dog) 胴輪 dôwa, ハーネス hânesū; (safety harness) 安全ハーネス ańzenhânesu

♦*vt* (resources, energy etc) 利用する riyô suru; (horse) ...に馬具をつける ...ni bágù wo tsukérù; (dog) ...にハーネスを付ける ...ni hânesū wo tsukérù

harp [hɑːrp] *n* (MUS) たて琴 tátégòto, ハープ hâpu

♦*vi: to harp on about* (pej) ...の事をどくどくと話し続ける ...no kotó wo kúdòkudo to hanáshitsuzukérù

harpoon [hɑːrˈpuːn] *n* もり môrî

harrowing [hærˈouiŋ] *adj* (experience, film) 戦慄つの sefrìtsu no

harsh [hɑːrʃ] *adj* (sound) 耳障りな mimízawàri na; (light) どぎつい dogîtsui; (judge, criticism) か酷な kakôku na; (life, winter) 厳しい kibîshiî

harvest [hɑːrˈvist] *n* (harvest time) 収穫期 shûkakukî; (of barley, fruit etc) 収穫 shûkaku

♦*vt* (barley, fruit etc) 収穫する shûkaku suru

has [hæz] *vb see* **have**

hash [hæʃ] *n* (CULIN) ハッシュ hásshù; (fig: mess) めちゃめちゃな有様 mechámecha na arisama

hashish [hæʃˈiʃ] *n* ハシシ hâshishi

hasn't [hæzˈənt] = **has not**

hassle [hæsˈəl] (*inf*) *n* (bother) 面倒 meńdò

haste [heist] *n* (hurry) 急ぎ isógi

hasten [heisˈən] *vt* (decision, downfall) 早める hayámerù

♦*vi* (hurry): *to hasten to do something* 急いで...する isôide ...surù

hastily [heisˈtili] *adv* (hurriedly) 慌ただしく awátadashikù; (rashly) 軽はずみに karúhazūmi ni

hasty [heisˈtiː] *adj* (hurried) 慌ただしい awátadashiî; (rash) 軽はずみの karúhazūmi no

hat [hæt] *n* (headgear) 帽子 bôshi

hatch [hætʃ] *n* (NAUT: *also*: **hatchway**) 倉口 sôkò, ハッチ hátchì; (*also*: **service hatch**) サービス口 sâbisugðchi, ハッチ hátchì

♦*vi* (bird) 卵からかえる tamágò kara kaérù, (egg) かえる kaérù, ふ化する fuká suru

hatchback [hætʃˈbæk] *n* (AUT) ハッチバック hatchíbakkù

hatchet [hætʃˈit] *n* (axe) おの ônò

hate [heit] *vt* (wish ill to: person) 憎む nikúmù; (dislike strongly: person, thing, situation) 嫌う kiráù

♦*n* (illwill) 増悪 zôō; (strong dislike) 嫌悪 kén̄o

hateful [heitˈfəl] *adj* ひどい hidôi

hatred [heitˈrid] *n* (illwill) 増悪 zôō; (strong dislike) 嫌悪 kén̄o

haughty [hɔːˈtiː] *adj* (air, attitude) 尊大な soń̄daì na

haul [hɔːl] *vt* (pull) 引っ張る hippáru

♦*n* (of stolen goods etc) 獲物 emôno; (*also*: a haul of fish) 漁獲 gyokáku

haulage [hɔːˈlidʒ] *n* (business, costs) 運送 uñsô

hauler [hɔːlˈər] (BRIT **haulier**) *n* 運送屋 uñsôya

haunch [hɔːntʃ] *n* (ANAT) 腰 koshî; (of meat) 腰肉 koshíniku

haunt [hɔːnt] *vt* (subj: ghost) (place) ...に出る ...ni dérù; (: person) ...に付きまとう ...ni tsukímatou; (: problem, memory etc) 悩ます nayámasù

♦*n* (of crooks, childhood etc) 行き付けの場所 ikítsuke nð bashò

haunted house お化け屋敷 obákeyashìki

KEYWORD

have [hæv] (*pt, pp* **had**) *aux vb* **1** (*gen*)
to have arrived/gone/eaten/slept 着いた(行った、食べた、眠った)tsúìta(ítta, tábèta, nemútta)

he has been kind/promoted 彼は親切

だった〔昇格した〕kárè wa shínsetsu dátta(shōkaku shita)

has he told you? 彼はあなたにそれを話しましたか kárè wa anátà ni soré wò hanáshimashìta ká

having finished/when he had finished, **he left** 仕事が済むと彼は帰った shigóto ga sumù to kárè wa kâètta

2 (in tag questions): **you've done it, haven't you?** あなたはその仕事をしたんでしょう anátà wa sonó shigòto wo yattán deshô

he hasn't done it, has he? 彼は仕事をやらなかったんでしょう kárè wa shigóto wo yaránakàttan deshô

3 (in short answers and questions): **you've made a mistake - no I haven't!** あなたは間違いをしましたー違いますよ〔そうですね〕anátà wa machígaì wo shimáshìta - chigáimasù yó〔sō desu né〕

we haven't paid - yes we have! 私たちはまだお金を払っていません払いましたよ watákushitàchi wa mádà kané wo haráttè imasén - haráimashìta yó

I've been there before, have you? 私は前にあそこへ行った事がありますが、あなたは? watákushi wà maè ni asóko è ittá kotò ga arímasù ga, anátà wà?

◆**modal aux vb** (be obliged): **to have (got) to do something** …をしなければならない …wò shinákereba naranaî

she has (got) to do it 彼女はどうしてもそれをしなければなりません kánòjo wa dôshitè mo soré wò shinákereba narimasèn

I have (got) to finish this work 私はこの仕事を済まさなければなりません watákushi wà konó shigòto wo sumásanakereba narimasèn

you haven't to tell her 彼女に言わなくてもいい〔言ってはならない〕kánòjo ni iwánakute mò íi〔itté wa naranaî〕

I haven't just/I don't have to wear glasses 私は眼鏡を掛けなくてもいい watákushi wà mègàne wò kakénakute mo ìi

this has to be a mistake これは何かの

間違いに違いない koré wa nánìka no machígaì ni chigáì naî

◆**vt 1** (possess) 持っている mótte iru, …がある …gá arù

he has (got) blue eyes/dark hair 彼は目が青い(髪が黒い)kárè wa mé gà aóî(kamí gà kuróî)

do you have/have you got a car/ phone? あなたは車〔電話〕を持っていますか anátà wa kurúma(defiwa)wò mótte imasù ká

I have (got) an idea いい考えがありますげ kángaè ga arímasû

have you any more money? もっとお金がありませんか móttò o-káne ga arímasên ká

2 (take: food) 食べる tabérù; (: drink) 飲む nómû

to have breakfast/lunch/dinner 朝食(昼食、夕食)を食べる chôshoku(chûshoku, yūshoku)wò tabérù

to have a drink 何かを飲む nánìka wo nómû

to have a cigarette タバコを吸う tabáko wo suù

3 (receive, obtain etc) 受ける ukérù, 手に入れる té ni irérù

may I have your address? ご住所を教えて頂けますか go-júsho wò oshíete itadakemasû ká

you can have it for $5 5ドルでそれを譲ります góddòru de soré wò yuzúrimasù

I must have it by tomorrow どうしても明日までにそれをもらいたいのです dôshite mò ashíta madè ni soré wò morátiai no desù

to have a baby 子供を産む kodómo wo umù

4 (maintain, allow) 主張する shuchô suru, 許す yurúsù

he will have it that he 彼は自分が正しいと主張している kárè wa jibún gà tadáshiî to shuchô shite irù

I won't have it/this nonsense! それ〔こんなばかげた事〕は許せません soré〔koñna bakageta kotò〕wa yurúsemasèn

we can't have that そんな事は許せません soñna kotò wa yurúsemasèn

5: *to have something done* ...をさせる
...wo saserù, ...をしてもらう、...wò shité
mòrau

to have one's hair cut 散髪をしてもら
う sañpatsu wò shité morau

to have a house built 家を建てる ié wò
taterù

to have someone do something ...に
...させる ...nf ...wò saserù

*he soon had them all laughing/
working* まもなく彼は皆を笑わせて[働
かせて]いた ma mó naku kàrè wa miná
wò warawasete[hatarakasete]ità

6 (experience, suffer) 経験する kefken
suru

to have a cold 風邪を引いている kazé
wò hífte irú

to have (the) flu 感冒にかかっている
kañbō nì kakátte irú

*she had her bag stolen/her arm
broken* 彼女はハンドバッグを盗まれた
[腕を折った] kánòjo wa hañdobaggù wo
nusúmareta[udé wo ottá]

to have an operation 手術を受ける
shújùtsu wo ukérù

7 (+ noun: take, hold etc) ...する ...su
ru

to have a swim/walk/bath/rest 泳ぐ
[散歩する、風呂に入る、ひと休みする]
oyógù[sañpo suru, fúrò nì hàfru, hitóyà-
sumi suru]

let's have a look ちょっと見てみましょ
う mítè mimashō

to have a meeting/party 会議(パーテ
ィ)を開く kàfgì(pàtì)wo hiràkú

let me have a try 私に試させて下さい
watàkushi nì tamésasete kudasái

8 (*inf:* dupe) だます damásu

he's been had 彼はだまされた kàrè wa
damásareta

---

haven [hei'vən] *n* (harbor) 港 mináto;
(safe place) 避難所 hináñjo

haven't [hæv'ənt] = **have not**

have on *vt: to have it out with
someone* (settle a problem etc) ...と決着
をつける ...tò ketcháku wo tsukérù

haversack [hæv'ərsæk] *n* (of hiker, soldier) リュックサック ryukkúsakkù

---

havoc [hæv'ək] *n* (chaos) 混乱 koñran

Hawaii [hawai'ji:] *n* ハワイ háwai

hawk [hɔ:k] *n* タカ taká

hay [hei] *n* 干草 hoshíkusa

hay fever *n* 花粉症 kafúñshō

haystack [hei'stæk] *n* 干草の山 hoshíkusa no yama

haywire [hei'waiə:r] (*inf*) *adj: to go
haywire* (machine etc) 故障する koshō
suru; (plans etc) とんざする tóñza suru

hazard [hæz'ə:rd] *n* (danger) 危険 kikén
♦*vt* (risk: guess, bet etc) やってみる yatté mirù

hazardous [hæz'ə:rdəs] *adj* (dangerous)
危険な kikén na

hazard (warning) lights *npl* (AUT)
非常点滅灯 hijōteñmetsutō

haze [heiz] *n* (of heat, smoke, dust) かす
み kasúmi

hazelnut [hei'zəlnʌt] *n* ヘーゼルナッツ
hēzerunattsù

hazy [hei'zi:] *adj* (sky, view) かすんだ ka-
súnda; (idea, memory) ぼんやりとした
boñ-yarí to shita

he [hi:] *pron* 彼は(が) kàrè wa (ga)

he who ...する人は ...surú hitò wa

head [hed] *n* (ANAT, mind) 頭 atáma;
(of table) 上席 jóseki; (of queue) 先頭 señtō; (of company, organization) 最高責任
者 safkōsekíninsha; (of school) 校長 kōchō

♦*vt* (list, queue) ...の先頭にある(いる)
...no señtō ni arú (irú); (group, company) 取仕切る toríshikirù

heads (or tails) 表か(裏か) òmote
kà (urá kà)

head first (fall) 頭から massákasama
ni; (rush) 向こう見ずに mukō mìzu ni

head over heels (in love) ぞっこん zok-
kón

to head a ball ボールをヘディングで飛
ばす bōru wo hedíñgu de tobásu

headache [hed'eik] *n* 頭痛 zutsū

headdress [hed'dres] *n* (BRIT) *n* (of
bride) ヘッドドレス heddódoresù

head for *vt fus* (place) ...に向かう ...ni
mukáù; (disaster) ...を招く ...wo manékù

heading [hed'iŋ] *n* (of chapter, article)

表題 hyódai, タイトル táitoru

headlamp [hed'læm] (*BRIT*) *n* = headlight

headland [hed'lænd] *n* 岬 misáki

headlight [hed'lait] *n* ヘッドライト heddóraito

headline [hed'lain] *n* (PRESS, TV) 見出し midáshi

headlong [hed'lɔːŋ] *adv* (fall) 真っ逆様に massákasama ni; (rush) 向こう見ずに mukó mizu ni

headmaster [hed'mæs'tər] *n* 校長 kóchō ◊男性の場合 dańsei nò báai

headmistress [hed'mis'tris] *n* 校長 kóchō ◊女性の場合 joséi nò báai

head office *n* (of company etc) 本社 hóňsha

head-on [hed'ɑn'] *adj* (collision, confrontation) 正面の shómen no

headphones [hed'founz] *npl* ヘッドホン heddóhòn

headquarters [hed'kwɔrtərz] *npl* (of company, organization) 本部 hóňbu; (MIL) 司令部 shiréfbu

headrest [hed'rest] *n* (AUT) ヘッドレスト heddórèsuto

headroom [hed'rum] *n* (in car) 天井の高さ teñjō no takàsa; (under bridge) 通行可能な高さ tsūkōkanō na takàsa

headscarf [hed'skɑrf] *n* スカーフ sukáfù

headstrong [hed'strɔŋ] *adj* (determined) 強情な gójō na

head waiter *n* (in restaurant) 給仕頭 kyúgigashira

headway [hed'wei] *n*: **to make headway** 進歩する shíňpo suru

headwind [hed'wind] *n* 向かい風 mukáikaze

heady [hed'iː] *adj* (experience, time) 陶酔の tōsui no; (drink, atmosphere) 酔わせる yowáserù

heal [hiːl] *vt* (injury, patient) 治す naósù
◊*vi* (injury, damage) 治る naórù

health [helθ] *n* (condition: *also* MED) 健康状態 keńkōjōtai; (good health) 健康 keńkō

health food *n* 健康食品 keńkōshokùhin

Health Service (*BRIT*) *n*: **the Health Service** 公共衛生機構 kókyōeiseikikō

healthy [hel'θiː] *adj* (person, appetite etc) 健康な keńkō na; (air, walk) 健康に良い keńkō ni yoì; (economy) 健全な keńzen na; (profit etc) 大いなる ôi naru

heap [hip] *n* (pile: of clothes, papers, sand etc) 山 yamá
◊*vt* (stones, sand etc): **to heap (up)** 積み上げる tsumíagerù

to heap something with (plate) ...に...を山盛りする ...ni ...wo yamámori suru; (sink, table etc) ...に...を山積みする ...ni ...wo yamázumi suru

to heap something on (food) ...に山盛りする ...wo ...ni yamámori suru; (books etc) ...に...を山積みする ...wo ...ni yamázumi suru

heaps of (*inf*: time, money, work etc) 一杯の ippái no

hear [hiːr] (*pt, pp* **heard**) *vt* (sound, voice etc) ...を聞く ...wo kikú, ...が聞える ...ga kikóeru; (news, information) ...を聞く ...wo kikú, ...で聞いて知る ...de kifte shirú; (LAW: case) 審理する shíňri suru

to hear about (event, person) ...の事を聞く ...no kotó wo kikú

to hear from someone ...から連絡を受ける ...kara reńraku wo ukérù

heard [həːrd] *pt, pp of* **hear**

hearing [hiː'riŋ] *n* (sense) 聴覚 chōkaku; (of facts, witnesses etc) 聴聞会 chōmoñkai

hearing aid *n* 補聴器 hochōki

hearsay [hiːr'sei] *n* (rumor) うわさ uwása

hearse [həːrs] *n* 霊きゅう車 reíkyūsha

heart [hɑrt] *n* (ANAT) 心臓 shiňzō; (*fig*: emotions, character) 心 kokórò; (of problem) 核心 kakúshin; (of city) 中心部 chūshiňbu; (of lettuce) しん shíň; (shape) ハート形 hátogata

to lose heart (courage) 落胆する rakútan suru

to take heart (courage) 勇気を出す yúki wo dásù

at heart (basically) 根は... né wà ...

by heart (learn, know) 暗記で ańki de

heart attack n (MED) 心臓発作 shinzṓhossa

heartbeat [hɑːtˈbiːt] n 心拍 shíńpaku

heartbreaking [hɑːtˈbreikiŋ] adj (news, story) 悲痛な hitsū́ na

heartbroken [hɑːtˈbroukən] adj: to be heartbroken 悲嘆に暮れている hitán ni kurete irú

heartburn [hɑːtˈbəːn] n (indigestion) 胸焼け munéyake

heart failure n (MED) 心不全 shinfū́zen

heartfelt [hɑːtˈfelt] adj (prayer, wish) 心からの kokóró kara no

hearth [hɑːθ] n (fireplace) 炉床 roshṓ

heartland [hɑːtˈlænd] n (of country, region) 中心地 chūshíńchi

heartless [hɑːtˈlis] adj (person, attitude) 非情な hijō na

hearts [hɑːts] npl (CARDS) ハート hā́to

hearty [hɑːtˈiː] adj (person) 明朗な mefrō na; (laugh) 大きな ōkina; (appetite) お う盛な ōsei na; (welcome) 熱烈な netsū́retsu na; (dislike) 絶対的な zettáiteki na; (support) 心からの kokóró kara no

heat [hiːt] n (warmth) 暑さ átsusa; (temperature) 温度 ốndo; (excitement) 熱気 nekkí; (SPORT: also: **qualifying heat**) 予選 yosén
♦vt (water) 沸かす wákasù; (food) ...に火 を通す ...ni hí wo tốsu; (room, house) 暖 める atátamerù

heated [hiːˈtid] adj (pool) 温水の ốnsui no; (room etc) 暖房した dańbō shita; (argument) 激しい hagéshiì

heater [hiːˈtəːr] n ヒーター hítà

heath [hiːθ] (BRIT) n 荒野 aréno

heathen [hiːˈðən] n (REL) 異教徒 ikyṓto

heather [heðˈəːr] n エリカ erfka, ヒース hísù

heating [hiːˈtiŋ] n (system, equipment) 暖房 dáńbō

heatstroke [hiːtˈstrouk] n (MED) 熱射病 nesshábyō

heat up vi (water, room) 暖まる atátamarù
♦vt (food, water, room) 暖める atátamerù

heatwave [hiːtˈweiv] n 熱波 néppa

heave [hiːv] vt (pull) 強く引く tsúyòku hikú; (push) 強く押す tsúyòku osú; (lift) 強 いと持上げる gút to mochíagerù
♦vi (vomit) 吐く hákù; (feel sick) むかむ く mukátsukù
♦n (of chest) あえぎ áegi; (of stomach) むかつき mukátsuki
to heave a sigh ため息をつく taméikí wo tsukú
his chest was heaving 彼はあえいでい た kárè wa aéide itá

heaven [hevˈən] n (REL) 天国 téńgoku

heavenly [hevˈənli] adj (REL) 天からの téñ kara no; (fig: day, place) 素晴らしい subárashiì

heavily [hevˈili] adv (land, fall) どしんと dóshìn to; (drink, smoke) 大量に taíryō ni; (sleep) ぐっすりと gussúrī to; (sigh) 深く fukákù; (depend, rely) すっかり sukkárī

heavy [hevˈiː] adj (person, load, responsibility) 重い omóì; (clothes) 厚い atsúì; (rain, snow) 激しい hagéshiì; (of person: build, frame) がっしりした gasshírì shitá; (blow) 強い tsúyòi; (breathing) 荒い aráì; (sleep) 深い fukáì; (schedule, week) 過密な kamítsu na; (work) きつい kitsúì; (weather) 蒸し暑い mushíatsuì; (food, meal) もたれる motárerù

a heavy drinker 飲兵衛 nóńbē
a heavy smoker ヘビースモーカー hebísumōkā

heavy goods vehicle (BRIT) n 大型ト ラック ōgatatórakku

heavyweight [hevˈiweit] n (SPORT) ヘ ビー級選手 hebíkyūsénshu

Hebrew [hiːˈbruː] adj ヘブライの hebúrài no; (LING) ヘブライ語の hebúraigo no
♦n (LING) ヘブライ語 hebúraigo

Hebrides [hebˈridiːz] npl: the Hebrides ヘブリディーズ諸島 hebúrídizushotṓ

heckle [hekˈəl] vt (speaker, performer) 野次る yajírù

hectic [hekˈtik] adj (event, week) やたら に忙しい yatára ni isógashiì

he'd [hiːd] = he would; he had

hedge [hedʒ] n (in garden, on roadside)

生け垣 ikégāki
♦vi (stall) あいまいな態度を取る aímai na táìdo wo tórù

to hedge one's bets (fig) 失敗に備える shippaí nl sonaérù

hedgehog [hedʒˈhɔːg] *n* ハリネズミ harínezùmi

heed [hiːd] *vt* (*also*: **take heed of**: advice, warning) 聞き入れる kikíírerù

heedless [hiːdˈlis] *adj*: **heedless (of)** (...を) 無視して (...wo) múshì shité

heel [hiːl] *n* (of foot, shoe) かかと kakáto
♦vt: *to heel shoes* 靴のかかとを修理する kutsú nð kakáto wo shúrì suru

hefty [hefˈtiː] *adj* (person) がっしりした gasshfrí shita; (parcel etc) 大きくて重い ōkikute omói; (profit) 相当な sōtō na

heifer [hefˈəːr] *n* 若い雌ウシ wakáì mēúshì ◇まだ子を生んだ事のない物を指す mádà kò wo ufída kotò no nái monó wo sásù

height [hait] *n* (of tree, building, mountain) 高さ tákàsa; (of person) 身長 shifchō; (of plane) 高度 kōdo; (high ground) 高地 kōchi; (*fig*: of powers) 絶頂期 zetchōkì; (: of season) 真っ盛り massákìchū; (: of luxury, stupidity) 極み kiwámi

heighten [haitˈən] *vt* (fears, uncertainty) 高める takámerù

heir [eːr] *n* (to throne) 継承者 kefshōshà; (to fortune) 相続人 sōzokunín

heiress [eːˈris] *n* 大遺産の相続人 daísan no sōzokunín ◇女性について言う joseí ni tsuité iú

heirloom [eːrˈluːm] *n* 家宝 kahō

held [held] *pt, pp* of **hold**

helicopter [helˈəkɑːptəːr] *n* (AVIAT) ヘリコプター herfkoputā

heliport [helˈəpɔːrt] *n* (AVIAT) ヘリポート herfpòto

helium [hiːˈliːəm] *n* ヘリウム herfumu

he'll [hiːl] = **he will, he shall**

hell [hel] *n* (life, situation: *also* REL) 地獄 jigóku
hell! (*inf*) 畜生！ chikúshò!, くそ！ kusó!

hellish [helˈiʃ] (*inf*) *adj* (traffic, weather, life etc) 地獄の様な jigóku no yō na

hello [heloʊˈ] *excl* (as greeting) やあ yáà, 今日は kofnichi wa; (to attract attention) おい ól; (on telephone) もしもし móshìmoshi; (expressing surprise) おや oyá

helm [helm] *n* (NAUT: stick) かじ棒 kajíbò, チラー chírā; (: wheel) だ輪 darín

helmet [helˈmit] *n* (gen) ヘルメット herúmettò

help [help] *n* (assistance, aid) 助け tasúke, 手伝い tetsúdaì; (charwoman) お手伝いさん o-tétsùdaisan
♦vt (person) 助ける tasúkerù, 手伝う tetsúdau; (situation) ...に役に立つ ...ni yakú ni tatsú

help! 助けてくれ！ tasúketè kuré!

help yourself (to) ご自由に取って下さい (...wo) jiyū ni tottè kudásaì

he can't help it 彼はそうせざるを得ない kárè wa sõ sezarù wo ēnái

helper [helˈpəːr] *n* (assistant) 助手 joshú, アシスタント ashfsùtanto

helpful [helpˈfəl] *adj* (person, advice, suggestion etc) 役に立つ yakú ni tatsú

helping [helˈpiŋ] *n* (of food) 一盛り hitómòri

a second helping お代わり o-káwarì

helpless [helpˈlis] *adj* (incapable) 何もできない nanî mo dekínaì; (defenceless) 無防備の mubōbi na

hem [hem] *n* (of skirt, dress) すそ susó
♦vt (skirt, dress etc) ...のすそを縫いをする ...no susónuì wo suru

hem in *vt* 取囲む torfkakomù

hemisphere [hemˈisfiːr] *n* 半球 hañkyū

hemorrhage [hemˈəːridʒ] (BRIT **haemorrhage**) *n* 出血 shukkétsu

hemorrhoids [hemˈəːrɔidz] (BRIT **haemorrhoids**) *npl* じ痔 ji

hen [hen] *n* (female chicken) メンドリ mefdori; (female bird) 雌の鳥 mesú no torí

hence [hens] *adv* (therefore) 従って shitágattè

2 years hence 今から2年先 ímà kara nífnen sakí

henceforth [hensˈfɔːrθ] *adv* (from now on) 今後 kōñgo; (from that time on) その

後 sonó go

henchman [hentʃˈmən] (*pej*: *pl* henchmen) *n* (of gangster, tyrant) 手下 teshíta, 子分 kóbun

henpecked [hen'pekt] *adj* (husband) 妻のしりに敷かれた tsúma no shirí ni shikaretá

hepatitis [hepətaiˈtis] *n* (MED) 肝炎 kánen

her [həːr] *pron* (direct) 彼女を kánojo wo; (indirect) 彼女に kánojo ni
◆*adj* 彼女の kánojo no ¶ *see also* me; my

herald [her'əld] *n* (forerunner) 兆し kizáshi
◆*vt* (event, action) 予告する yokóku suru

heraldry [her'əldri:] *n* (study) 紋章学 mońshōgàku; (coat of arms) 紋章 mońshō ◆総称 sóshō

herb [əːrb] *n* (gen) ハーブ hấbu; (BOT, MED) 薬草 yakúsō; (CULIN) 香草 kósō

herd [həːrd] *n* (of cattle, goats, zebra etc) 群れ muré

here [hiːr] *adv* (this place): she left here yesterday 彼女は昨日ここを出ました kanójo wa kinō kokó wo demáshità; (beside me): I have it here ここに持っています kokó ni mótte imásù; (at this point): here he stopped reading ... その時彼は読むのをやめて... sonó tokí kárè wa yomú no wo yamête ...
here! (I'm present) はい！ hái!; (take this) はいどうぞ hái dôzo
here is/are はい、...です hái, ...désù
here she is! 彼女はここにいました！ kanójo wa kokó ni imáshità!

hereafter [hiəræf'təːr] *adv* (in the future) 今後 kóngo

hereby [hiːrbai'] *adv* (in letter) これをもって koré wo mótte

hereditary [hæred'iteːriː] *adj* (disease) 先天的な señtenteki na; (title) 世襲の seshū no

heredity [hæred'itiː] *n* (BIO) 遺伝 idén

heresy [her'isiː] *n* (opposing belief: also REL) 異端 itáń

heretic [her'itik] *n* 異端者 itáñsha

heritage [her'itidʒ] *n* (of country,

nation) 遺産 isán

hermetically [həːrmet'ikliː] *adv*: hermetically sealed 密閉した mippéi shita

hermit [həːr'mit] *n* 隠とん者 ińtoǹsha

hernia [həːr'niːə] *n* (MED) 脱腸 datchō

hero [hiː'rou] (*pl* heroes) *n* (in book, film) 主人公 shujíñkō, ヒーロー hĩrō◆男性を指す dansei wo sasu; (of battle, struggle) 英雄 efyū; (idol) アイドル áidoru

heroic [hirou'ik] *adj* (struggle, sacrifice, person) 英雄的な efyūteki na

heroin [her'ouin] *n* ヘロイン heróiǹ

heroine [her'ouin] *n* (in book, film) 女主人公 oñnashujíñkò, ヒロイン hiróiǹ; (of battle, struggle) 英雄的な女性 efyūtekijòsei; (idol) アイドル áidoru

heroism [her'ouizəm] *n* (bravery, courage) 勇敢さ yūkansa

heron [her'ən] *n* アオサギ aósagi

herring [her'iŋ] *n* (fish) ニシン níshiǹ

hers [həːrz] *pron* 彼女の物 kánojo no monó ¶ *see also* mine

herself [həːrself'] *pron* 彼女自身 kánojojishìn ¶ *see also* oneself

he's [hiːz] = he is; he has

hesitant [hez'ətənt] *adj* (smile, reaction) ためらいがちな taméraigachi na

hesitate [hez'əteit] *vi* (because of doubt) ためらう taméraù; (be unwilling) 後込みする shirígomi suru

hesitation [hezətei'ʃən] *n* (pause) ためらい tamérai; (unwillingness) 後込み shirígomi

heterosexual [hetərəsek'ʃuːəl] *adj* (person, relationship) 異性愛の iséiai no

hew [hjuː] *vt* (stone, wood) 刻む kizámu

hexagonal [heksæg'ənəl] *adj* (shape, object) 六角形の rokkákukèi no

heyday [hei'dei] *n*: the heyday of ...の全盛時代 ...no zeńseijidài

HGV [eitʃgiːviː'] (BRIT) *n abbr* = heavy goods vehicle

hi [hai] *excl* (as greeting) あ、やぁ、らぁ a yả, yả; (to attract attention) おい 01

hiatus [haiei'təs] *n* (gap: in manuscript etc) 脱落箇所 datsúrakukashð; (pause)

中断 chūdan

hibernate [haɪˈbɜːneɪt] *vi* (animal) 冬眠する tōmin suru

hiccough [ˈhɪkʌp] *vi* しゃっくりする shákkūri suru

hiccoughs [ˈhɪkʌps] *npl* しゃっくり shákkūri

hiccup [ˈhɪkʌp] *vi* = hiccough

hiccups [ˈhɪkʌps] *npl* = hiccoughs

hid [hɪd] *pt of* hide

hidden [ˈhɪdən] *pp of* hide

hide [haɪd] *n* (skin) 皮 kawá
♦*vb* (*pt* hid, *pp* hidden)
♦*vt* (person, object, feeling, information) 隠す kakúsù; (obscure: sun, view) 覆い隠す ōikakusù
♦*vi*: **to hide (from someone)** (...に見つからない様に) 隠れる (...ni mitsúkaranai yō ni) kakúrerù

hide-and-seek [haɪdˈənsiːk] *n* (game) 隠れん坊 kakúrenbō

hideaway [ˈhaɪdəweɪ] *n* (retreat) 隠れ家 kakúregà

hideous [ˈhɪdiːəs] *adj* (painting, face) 醜い minkkuì

hiding [ˈhaɪdɪŋ] *n* (beating) むち打ち muchúchi
to be in hiding (concealed) 隠れている kakúrete irù

hierarchy [ˈhaɪərɑːrkiː] *n* (system of ranks) 階級制 kaftkyūseì; (people in power) 幹部 kánbu の総称 sōshò

hi-fi [ˈhaɪfaɪ] *n* ステレオ sutéreo
♦*adj* (equipment, system) ステレオの sutéreo no

high [haɪ] *adj* (gen) 高い takáì; (speed) 速い hayáì; (wind) 強い tsuyóì; (quality) 上等な jōtō na; (principles) 崇高な sūkō na
♦*adv* (climb, aim etc) 高く takáku
it is 20 m high その高さは20メーターです sonó takása wa nijū mētá desu
high in the air 空高く sōratakaku

highbrow [ˈhaɪbraʊ] *adj* (intellectual) 知的な chitéki na

highchair [ˈhaɪtʃɛr] *n* (for baby) ベビーチェア bebíchèa

higher education [ˈhaɪər-] *n* 高等教育 kōtōkyōìku

high-handed [haɪˈhænˈdɪd] *adj* (decision, rejection) 横暴な ōbō na

high-heeled [haɪˈhiːld] *adj* (shoe) ハイヒールの haífhìru no

high jump *n* (SPORT) 走り高飛び hashíritakatobi

highlands [ˈhaɪləndz] *npl*: **the Highlands** スコットランド高地地方 sukóttorandò kōchìchihō

highlight [ˈhaɪlaɪt] *n* (fig: of event) 山場 yamába, ハイライト haíraìto; (of news etc) 要点 yōten, ハイライト haíraìto; (in hair) 光る部分 hikárù bùbùn, ハイライト haíraìto
♦*vt* (problem, need) ...に焦点を合せる ...ni shōten wo awáserù

highly [ˈhaɪliː] *adv* (critical, confidential) 非常に hijō ni; (a lot): **to speak highly of** ...をほめる ...wo homérù
to think highly of ...を高く評価する ...wo tákàku hyōka suru

highly paid 高給取りの kōkyūtòri no

highly strung (BRIT) *adj* = **high-strung**

highness [ˈhaɪnɪs] *n*: **Her (or His) Highness** 陛下 héìka

high-pitched [haɪˈpɪtʃt] *adj* (voice, tone, whine) 調子の高い chōshi no takáì

high-rise block [ˈhaɪraɪz-] *n* 摩天楼 maténrò

high school *n* (US: for 14-18 year-olds) 高等学校 kōtōgakkō, ハイスクール haísukūru; (BRIT: for 11-18 year-olds) 総合中学学校 sōgochūtōgakkō

high season (BRIT) *n* 最盛期 saíseiki, シーズン shízun

high street (BRIT) *n* 本通り hondōri

high-strung [haɪˈstrʌŋ] (US) *adj* 神経質な shiñkeishitsu na

highway [ˈhaɪweɪ] *n* 幹線道路 kañsendōro, ハイウェー haíuè

Highway Code (BRIT) *n* 道路交通法 dōrokōtsūhō

hijack [ˈhaɪdʒæk] *vt* (plane, bus) 乗っ取る nottórù, ハイジャックする haíjakkù suru

hijacker [ˈhaɪdʒækər] *n* 乗っ取り犯 nottórìhàn

hike [haik] *vi* (go walking) ハイキングする hafkingu suru

♦*n* (walk) ハイキング háfkingu

hiker [hai'kər] *n* ハイカー haíkā

hilarious [hiler'i:əs] *adj* (account, adventure) こっけいな kokkéi na

hill [hil] *n* (small) 丘 oká; (fairly high) 山 yamá; (slope) 坂 saká

hillside [hil'said] *n* 丘の斜面 oká no shamèn

hilly [hil'i:] *adj* 丘の多い oká no ōì
a hilly area 丘陵地帯 kyūryōchítài

hilt [hilt] *n* (of sword, knife) 柄 e
to the hilt (*fig*: support) とことんまで tokóton made

him [him] *pron* (direct) 彼を kárè wo; (indirect) 彼に kárè ni *see also* **me**

himself [himself'] *pron* 彼自身 káréjishin *see also* **oneself**

hind [haind] *adj* (legs, quarters) 後ろの ushíro no

hinder [hin'də:r] *vt* (progress, movement) 妨げる samátageru

hindrance [hin'drəns] *n* 邪魔 jamá

hindsight [haind'sait] *n*: *with hindsight* 後になってみると átò ni nátte mírù う

Hindu [hin'du:] *adj* ヒンズーの híñzū no

hinge [hindʒ] *n* (on door) ちょうつがい chōtsugai

♦*vi* (*fig*): *to hinge on* ...による ...ni yorú

hint [hint] *n* (suggestion) 暗示 añji, ヒント híñto; (advice) 勧め susúme, 提言 tefgen; (sign, glimmer) 兆し kizáshi

♦*vt*: *to hint that* (suggest) ...だとほのめかす ...da to honómekasū

♦*vi*: *to hint at* (suggest) ほのめかす honómekasū

hip [hip] *n* (ANAT) 腰 koshí, ヒップ híppù

hippopotamus [hipəpɑ:t'əməs] (*pl* **hippopotamuses** *or* **hippopotami**) *n* カバ kábà

hire [haiə:r] *vt* (*BRIT*: car, equipment, hall) 賃借りする chíñgari suru; (worker) 雇う yatóu

♦*n* (*BRIT*: of car, hall etc) 賃借り chíñgari

for hire (taxi, boat) 賃貸し用の chíñga-shiyō no

hire purchase (*BRIT*) *n* 分割払い購入 buñkatsubaraikōnyū

his [hiz] *pron* 彼の物 kárè no monó

♦*adj* 彼の kárè no *see also* **my**; **mine**

hiss [his] *vi* (snake, gas, roasting meat) しゅーっと言う shūtto iú; (person, audience) しーっと野次る shītto yajírù

historian [histɔ:r'i:ən] *n* 歴史学者 rekíshigakushā

historic(al) [histɔ:r'ik(əl)] *adj* (event, person) 歴史上の rekíshijō no, 歴史的な rekíshiteki na; (novel, film) 歴史に基づく rekíshi ni motózukū

history [his'tə:ri:] *n* (of town, country, person: *also* SCOL) 歴史 rekíshi

hit [hit] (*pt, pp* **hit**) *vt* (strike: person, thing) 打つ utsū, たたく tatákū; (reach: target) ...に当る ...ni atárù; (collide with: car) ...にぶつかる ...ni butsúkarū; (affect: person, services, event etc) ...に打撃を与える ...ni dagéki wo atáerū

♦*n* (knock) 打撃 dagéki; (success: play, film, song) 大当り ōatàri, ヒット hítto

to hit it off with someone ...と意気投合する ...to íkitōgō suru

hit-and-run driver [hit'ænrʌn'-] *n* ひき逃げ運転者 hikínige unteñsha

hitch [hitʃ] *vt* (fasten) つなぐ tsunágù; *also*: **hitch up**: trousers, skirt) 引上げる hikíagerù

♦*n* (difficulty) 問題 mońdai

to hitch a lift ヒッチハイクをする hitchíhaīku wo suru

hitch-hike [hitʃ'haik] *vi* ヒッチハイクをする hitchíhaīku wo suru

hitch-hiker [hitʃ'haikə:r] *n* ヒッチハイクをする人 hitchíhaīku wo suru hitó

hi-tech [hai'tek'] *adj* ハイテクの hafteku no

hitherto [hið'ə:rtu:] *adv* (until now) 今まで ímà madé

hive [haiv] *n* (of bees) ミツバチの巣箱 mitsúbachi no súbàko

hive off (*inf*) *vt* (company) ...の一部を放す ...no ichíbu wo kírhanasù

HMS [eitʃemes'] *abbr* (= *Her/His Majesty's Ship*) 軍艦...号 gunkan ...gō♢英国海軍の軍艦の名前の前に付ける eikokukaigun no gunkan no namāe no māe ni tsukerū

hoard [hɔːrd] *n* (of food etc) 買いだめ kafdame; (of money, treasure) 蓄え takúwaè
♦*vt* (food etc) 買いだめする kaídamesuru

hoarding [hɔːr'diŋ] *n* (*BRIT*) (for posters) 掲示板 keíjiban

hoarfrost [hɔːr'frɔːst] *n* (on ground) 霜 shimó

hoarse [hɔːrs] *adj* (voice) しわがれた shiwágaretà

hoax [houks] *n* (trick) いんちき ínchiki, いかさま ikásama

hob [hɑb] *n* (of cooker, stove) レンジの上部 renji no jōbu

hobble [hɑb'əl] *vi* (limp) びっこを引く bíkko wo hikú

hobby [hɑb'iː] *n* (pastime) 趣味 shúmì

hobby-horse [hɑb'ihɔːrs] *n* (*fig:* favorite topic) 十八番の話題 oháko no wadái

hobo [hou'bou] *n* (*US*) (tramp) ルンペン rūnpen

hockey [hɑːk'iː] *n* (game) ホッケー hókkè

hoe [hou] *n* (tool) くわ kuwá, ホー hồ

hog [hɑːg] *n* (pig) ブタ būtá♢去勢した雄ブタを指す kyoséishita osubutá wo sasu
♦*vt* (*fig:* road, telephone etc) 独り占めにする hitórijime ni suru
to go the whole hog とことんまでやる tokótoñ made yarú

hoist [hɔist] *n* (apparatus) 起重機 kijūkī, クレーン kurễn
♦*vt* (heavy object) 引上げる hikíagerù; (flag) 掲げる kakágerù; (sail) 張る harú

hold [hould] (*pt*, *pp* **held**) *vt* (bag, umbrella, someone's hand) 持つ mótsù; (contain: subj: room, box etc) ...が入っている ...ga hāītte irù; (have: power, qualification, opinion) ...を持っている ...wo mōtté irù, ...がある ...ga árù; (meeting) 開く hiråkù; (detain: prisoner, hostage) 監禁する kañkin suru; (consider): *to hold someone responsible/liable etc* ...の責任を見なす ...no sekínin tò minásù; (keep in certain position): *to hold one's head up* 頭を上げる atáma wò agerù
♦*vi* (withstand pressure) 持ちこたえる mochíkotaeru; (be valid) 当てはまる atéhamarù
♦*n* (grasp) 握り nigírì; (of ship) 船倉 señsō; (of plane) 貨物室 kamótsushītsu; (control): *to have a hold over* ...の急所を握っている ...no kyūsho wò nigétte irù
to hold a conversation with ...と話し合う ...to hanáshiaù

hold the line! (TEL) 少々お待ち下さい shōshō o-máchī kudasai

hold on! ちょっと待って chótto mátte
to hold one's own (*fig*) 引けを取らない hiké wò toránai, 負けない makénaì

to catch/get a) hold of ...に捕まる ...ni tsukámarù

holdall [hould'ɔːl] (*BRIT*) *n* 合切袋 gassáibukùro

hold back *vt* (person, thing) 制止する seíshi suru; (thing, emotion) 押さえる osáerù; (secret, information) 隠す kakúsù

hold down *vt* (person) 押さえつける osáetsukerù; (job) ...についている ...ni tsuíte iru

holder [houl'dəːr] *n* (container) 入れ物 irémono, ケース kềsu, ホールダー hồrudà; (of ticket, record, title) 保持者 hojísha; (of office) 在職者 zaíshokusha

holding [houl'diŋ] *n* (share) 持株 mochíkabu; (small farm) 小作農地 kosákunồchi

hold off *vt* (enemy) ...に持ちこたえる ...ni mochíkotaerù

hold on *vi* (hang on) 捕まる tsukámarù; (wait) 待つ mátsù

hold on to *vt fus* (for support) ...に捕まる ...ni tsukámarù; (keep) 預かる azúkarù

hold out *vt* (hand) 差伸べる sashínoberù; (hope, prospect) 持たせる motáserù
♦*vi* (resist) 抵抗する teskō suru

hold up *vt* (raise) 上げる agérù; (support) 支える sasáerù; (delay) 遅らせる o-kúraserù; (rob: person, bank) 武器を突付けて...から金を奪う búkì wo tsukétsuk*té ...kara kané wò ubáù

hold-up [hould'ʌp] *n* (robbery) 強盗 gótō; (delay) 遅れ okúre; (BRIT: in traffic) 渋滞 jútai

hole [houl] *n* 穴 aná
◆*vt* (ship, building etc) ...に穴を開ける ...ni aná wò akéru

holiday [hɑ:l'idei] *n* (BRIT: vacation) 休暇 kyúka; (day off) 休養の日 kyúka no hi; (public holiday) 祝日 shúkujitsu
on holiday 休暇中 kyúkachū

holiday camp (BRIT) *n* (also: holiday centre) 休暇村 kyúkamura

holiday-maker [hɑ:l'ideimeikəːr] (BRIT) *n* 行楽客 kōrakukyaku

holiday resort *n* 行楽地 kōrakuchi, リゾート rizótò

holiness [hou'li:nis] *n* (of shrine, person) 神聖さ shinséisa

Holland [hɑ:l'ənd] *n* オランダ oráṅda

hollow [hɑːl'ou] *adj* (container) 空っぽの karáppo no; (log, tree) うろある uró no arú; (cheeks, eyes) ぼんだ kubōńda; (laugh) わざとらしい wazátorashiì; (claim) 根拠のない końkyo no naí; (sound) うつろな utsúro na
◆*n* (in ground) くぼみ kubómi
◆*vt*: *to hollow out* (excavate) がらんどうにする garańdō ni surù

holly [hɑːl'i:] *n* (tree, leaves) ヒイラギ híiragi

holocaust [hɑːl'əkɔːst] *n* 大虐殺 dáigyakúsatsu

hologram [hou'ləgræm] *n* ホログラム horóguramu

holster [houl'stəːr] *n* (for pistol) ホルスター horúsutā

holy [hou'li:] *adj* (picture, place, person) 神聖な shiṅséi na
holy water 聖水 seísui

homage [hɑːm'idʒ] *n* (honor, respect) 敬意 kéìi
to pay homage to (hero, idol) ...に敬意を表す ...ni kéìi wo aráwasù

home [houm] *n* (house) 家 ié, 住い sumái;

(area, country) 故郷 kokyō; (institution) 収容施設 shúyōshisetsu
◆*cpd* (domestic) 家庭の katéi no; (ECON, POL) 国内の kokúnai no; (SPORT: team, game) 地元の jimóto no
◆*adv* (go, come, travel etc) 家に ié ni
at home (in house) 家に(で) ié ni (de); (in country) 本国に(で) hóṅgoku ni (de); (in situation) ...に慣れて ...ni tsúkarete
make yourself at home どうぞお楽にどぞ o-ráku no

to drive something home (nail etc) ...を打込む ...wo uchíkomù; (fig: point etc) ...を強調する ...wo kyóchō suru

home address *n* 自宅の住所 jitáku no júsho

home computer *n* パーソナルコンピュータ pásonarukonpyúta, パソコン pasókon

homeland [houm'lænd] *n* 母国 bókòku

homeless [houm'lis] *adj* (family, refugee) 家のない ié no naí

homely [houm'li:] *adj* (simple, plain) 素朴な sobóku na; (US: not attractive: person) 不器量な bukíryō na

home-made [houm'meid'] *adj* (bread, bomb) 手製の teséi no, 自家製の jikásei no

Home Office (BRIT) *n* 内務省 naímushō

homeopathy [houmi:ɑ:p'əθi:] (BRIT **homoeopathy**) *n* (MED) ホメオパシー homéopashii

home rule *n* (POL) 自治権 jichíken

Home Secretary (BRIT) *n* 内務大臣 naímudaijin

homesick [houm'sik] *adj* ホームシックの hómushikkú no

hometown [houm'taun'] *n* 故郷 kokyō

homeward [houm'wəːrd] *adj* (journey) 家に帰る ié ni kaérù

homework [houm'wəːrk] *n* (SCOL) 宿題 shukúdai

homicide [hɑːm'isaid] (US) *n* 殺人 satsújin

homeopathy [houmi:ɑ:p'əθi:] (BRIT) *n* = homeopathy

homogeneous [houmədʒi:'ni:əs] *adj*

(group, class) 均質の kínshitsu no

homosexual [houməsɛk'ʃuəl] adj (person, relationship: gen) 同性愛の dôseiai no; (man) ホモの hômo no; (woman) レズの rézu no
♦n (man) 同性愛者 dôseiaishà, ホモ hômò; (woman) 同性愛者 dôseiaishà, レズ rézu

honest [ɑn'ist] adj (truthful, trustworthy) 正直な shôjiki na; (sincere) 率直な sotchoku na

honestly [ɑn'istli] adv (truthfully) 正直に shôjiki ni; (sincerely, frankly) 率直に sotchoku ni

honesty [ɑn'isti:] n (truthfulness) 正直 shôjiki, (sincerity, frankness) 率直さ sotchókusa

honey [hʌn'i:] n (food) はちみつ hachímitsu

honeycomb [hʌn'i:koum] n (of bees) ミツバチの巣 mitsúbachi no su

honeymoon [hʌn'i:mun] n (holiday, trip) 新婚旅行 shínkonryokô, ハネムーン hanémûn

honeysuckle [hʌn'i:sʌkəl] n (BOT) スイカズラ suíkazùra

honk [hɑŋk] vi (AUT: horn) 鳴らす narásu

honorary [ɑn'ɔreri:] adj (unpaid: job, secretary) 無給の mukyû no; (title, degree) 名誉の méiyo no

honor [ɑn'ər] (BRIT **honour**) vt (hero, author) ほめたたえる hométataerù; (commitment, promise) 守る mamórù
♦n (pride, self-respect) 名誉 méiyo; (tribute, distinction) 光栄 kôei

honorable [ɑn'ərabəl] adj (person, action, defeat) 名誉ある méiyo aru

honors degree [ɑn'ərz-] n (SCOL) 専門学士号 seńmongakushigô

hood [hud] n (of coat, cooker etc) フードfûdo; (US: AUT: engine cover) ボンネット bofinéttò; (BRIT: AUT: folding roof) 折畳み式ルーフ orítatamishiki tóppu

hoodlum [hud'ləm] n (thug) ごろつき gorótsukì, 暴力団員 bôryokudan-ìn

hoodwink [hud'wiŋk] vt (con, fool) だます damásu

hoof [huf] (pl **hooves**) n ひずめ hizúme

hook [huk] n (for coats, curtains etc) かぎ kagí, フック fúkkù; (on dress) ホックhókkù; (also: **fishing hook**) 釣針 tsurfbàri
♦vt (fasten) 留める tomérù; (fish) 釣る tsurú

hooligan [hu:'ligən] n ちんぴら chíñpira

hoop [hu:p] n (ring) 輪 wá

hooray [hərei'] excl = **hurrah, hurray**

hoot [hut] vi (AUT: horn) クラクションを鳴らす kurákûshon wo narásù; (siren) 鳴る narú; (owl) ほーほーと鳴く hôhô to nakú

hooter [hu:'tər] n (BRIT: AUT) クラクション kurákûshon, ホーン hôn; (NAUT, factory) 警報機 keíhôkì

hoover [hu:'vər] ®(BRIT) n (vacuum cleaner) (真空) 掃除機 (shíñkû)sôjikì
♦vt (carpet) ...に掃除機を掛ける ...ni sôjikî wo kakérù

hooves [huvz] npl of **hoof**

hop [hɑp] vi (on one foot) 片足で跳ぶ katáashi de tobú; (bird) ぴょんぴょん跳ぶ pyóñpyon tobú

hope [houp] vt: to hope that/to do ...だと[する事を]望む ...da to [surú kotð wo]nozómù
♦vi 希望する kibô suru
♦n (desire) 望み nozómi; (expectation) 期待 kitái; (aspiration) 希望 kibô
I hope so/not そう[そうでない]といいがsô da [de nái]to íi desu

hopeful [houp'fəl] adj (person) 楽観的なrakkáñteki na; (situation) 見込みのあるmikómi no arù

hopefully [houp'fəli:] adv (expectantly) 期待して kitái shite; (one hopes) うまくいけば úmàku ikéba

hopeless [houp'lis] adj (grief, situation, future) 絶望的な zetsúbôteki na; (person: useless) 無能な munôna

hops [hɑps] npl (BOT) ホップ hóppu

horde [hɔrd] n (of critics, people) 大群 taígun

horizon [hərai'zən] n (skyline) 水平線 suíheìsen

horizontal [hɔrizɑn'təl] adj 水平の suíhei no

hormone [hɔːˈmoun] n (BIO) ホルモン hórumon

horn [hɔːrn] n (of animal) 角 tsunó; (material) 角質 kakúshitsu; (MUS: also: **French horn**) ホルン hórun; (AUT) クラクション kuràkùshon, ホーン hōn

hornet [hɔːrˈnit] n (insect) スズメバチ suzúmebàchi

horny [hɔːrˈniː] (inf) adj (aroused) セックスをしたがっている sékkùsu wo shitágatte irù

horoscope [hɔːrˈəskoup] n (ASTROLOGY) 星占い hoshíuranaì

horrendous [hɔːrenˈdəs] adj (crime) 恐ろしい osóroshiì; (error) ショッキングな shókkìngu na

horrible [hɔːrˈəbəl] adj (unpleasant: color, food, mess) ひどい hidőì; (terrifying: scream, dream) 恐ろしい osóroshiì

horrid [hɔːrˈid] adj (person, place, thing) いやな iyá na

horrify [hɔːrˈəfai] vt (appall) ぞっとさせる zóttő saserù

horror [hɔːrˈər] n (alarm) 恐怖 kyōfù; (abhorrence) 憎悪 zőo; (of battle, warfare) むごたらしさ mugótarashisà

horror film n ホラー映画 horáèiga

hors d'oeuvre [ɔːr ˈdəːrv] n (CULIN: gen) 前菜 zefisaì; (: Western food) オードブル ōdobùru

horse [hɔːrs] n 馬 umá

horseback [hɔːrsˈbæk] n: **on horseback** adj 乗馬の jōba no

◆adv 馬に乗って umá ni nottè

horse chestnut n (tree) トチノキ tochínò kì; (nut) とちの実 tochí no mì

horseman/woman [hɔːrsˈmən/wumən] (pl **horsemen/women**) n (rider) 馬の乗り手 umá no norîte

horsepower [hɔːrsˈpauər] n (of engine, car etc) 馬力 bárìki

horse-racing [hɔːrsˈreisiŋ] n (SPORT) 競馬 keíba

horseradish [hɔːrsˈrædiʃ] n (BOT, CULIN) ワサビダイコン wasábidaìkon, セイヨウワサビ seíyōwasàbi

horseshoe [hɔːrsˈʃuː] n てい鉄 teítetsu

horticulture [hɔːrˈtəkʌltʃər] n 園芸 eńgei

hose [houz] n ホース hōsu

hosiery [houˈʒəriː] n (in shop) 靴下類 kutsúshitaruì

hospice [hɑːsˈpis] n (for the dying) ホスピス hōsúpisu

hospitable [hɑːspitˈəbəl] adj (person) 持て成しの良い moténashi no yoì; (behavior) 手厚い teátsuì

hospital [hɑːsˈpitəl] n 病院 byōin

hospitality [hɑːspitæˈliti] n (of host, welcome) 親切な持て成し shinsetsu na moténashi

host [houst] n (at party, dinner etc) 主人 shújìn, ホスト hósùto; (TV, RADIO) 司会者 shikáisha; (REL) 御聖体 go-séìtai; (large number): **a host of** 多数の tasū no

hostage [hɑːsˈtidʒ] n (prisoner) 人質 hitőjichi

hostel [hɑːsˈtəl] n (for homeless etc) 収容所 shūyōjo; (also: **youth hostel**) ユースホステル yūsuhosùteru

hostess [houˈstis] n (at party, dinner etc) 女主人 ofinashujìn, ホステス hósùtesu; (BRIT: air hostess) スチュワーデス suchūwàdesu; (TV, RADIO) (女性) 司会者 (joséi)shikàisha

hostile [hɑːsˈtəl] adj (person, attitude: aggressive) 敵対する tekítai suru, (person, attitude) 敵意のある tékì-i no árù; (: unwelcoming): **hostile to** ...に対して排他的な ...ni táishite haítateki na; (conditions, environment) 劣悪な rakúaku na

hostilities [hɑːstilˈətiːz] npl (fighting) 戦闘 sentō

hostility [hɑːstilˈətiː] n (antagonism) 敵対 tekítai, 敵意 tékì-i; (lack of welcome) 排他的態度 haítatekitàido; (of conditions, environment) か酷さ kakókusa

hot [hɑːt] adj (moderately hot) 暖かい atátakaì; (very hot) 熱い atsúì; (weather, room etc) 暑い atsúì; (spicy: food) 辛い karáì; (fierce: temper, contest, argument) 激しい hageshìì

it is hot (weather) 暑い atsúì; (object) 熱い atsúì

I **am hot** (person) 私は暑い watakushi wa atsúi

he is hot 彼は暑がっている kárè wa atsúgatte irú

hotbed [hɔːtˈbed] *n* (fig) 温床 onshō

hot dog *n* (snack) ホットドッグ hottódoggù

hotel [houteɪ] *n* ホテル hóteru

hotelier [ɔːtˈeljei] *n* (owner) ホテルの経営者 hóteru no kefeísha; (manager) ホテルの支配人 hóteru no shíhàinin

hotheaded [hɑːtˈhedid] *adj* (impetuous) 気の早い kí no hayaí

hothouse [hɑːtˈhaus] *n* (BOT) 温室 onshítsu

hot line *n* (POL) ホットライン hottóraìn

hotly [hɑːtˈliː] *adv* (speak, contest, deny) 激しく hagéshìku

hotplate [hɑːtˈpleit] *n* (on cooker) ホットプレート hottópurèto

hot-water bottle [hɑːtwɔːtˈəːr-] *n* 湯たんぽ yutánpo

hound [haund] *vt* (harass, persecute) 迫害する hakúgai suru

◆*n* (dog) 猟犬 ryókèn, ハウンド haúndo

hour [auˈəːr] *n* (sixty minutes) 1時間 ichí jikan; (time) 時間 jikán

hourly [auəˈrliː] *adj* (service, rate) 1時間当りの ichí jikan atàri no

house [*n* haus *vb* hauz] *n* (home) 家 ié, うち uchí; (household) 家族 kazóku; (company) 会社 kaísha; (POL) 議院 gíìn; (THEATER) 客席 kyakúseki; (dynasty) ...家 ...ké

◆*vt* (person) ...に住宅を与える ...ni jútaku wò atáerù; (collection) 収容する shūyō suru

on the house (fig) サービスで sābisu de

house arrest *n* (POL, MIL) 軟禁 nañkin

houseboat [hausˈbout] *n* 屋形船 yakátabùne, ハウスボート haúsubòto の住宅用の船を指す jútakuyō no funè wo sásu

housebound [hausˈbaund] *adj* (invalid) 家から出られない ié kara derárenaì

housebreaking [hausˈbreikiŋ] *n* 家宅侵入 kátakushiñnyū

housecoat [hausˈkout] *n* 部屋着 heyági

household [hausˈhould] *n* (inhabitants)

家族 kazóku; (home) 家 ié

housekeeper [hausˈkiːpər] *n* (servant) 家政婦 kaséifu

housekeeping [hausˈkiːpiŋ] *n* (work) 家事 kájì; (money) 家計費 kakéihi

house-warming party [hausˈwɔːrmiŋ-] *n* 新居祝いのパーティ shíñkyo-iwaì no pàti

housewife [hausˈwaif] (*pl* **housewives**) *n* 主婦 shúfu

housework [hausˈwəːrk] *n* (chores) 家事 kájì

housing [hauˈziŋ] *n* (homes) 住宅 jútaku; (provision) 住宅供給 jútakukyōkyū

housing development *n* 住宅団地 jútakudañchi

housing estate (BRIT) *n* 住宅団地 jútakudañchi

hovel [hʌvˈəl] *n* (shack) あばら屋 abárayà

hover [hʌvˈəːr] *vi* (bird, insect) 空中に止る kūchū ni tomarù

hovercraft [hʌvˈəːrkræft] *n* (vehicle) ホバークラフト hobākurafùto

how [hau] *adv* **1** (in what way) どう dò, どの様に donō yò ni, どうやって dō yatté

how did you do it? どうやってそれができたんですか yatté soré gà dekítan desù ká

I **know how you did it** あなたがどの様にしてそれができたか私には分かっています anátà ga donō yò ni shite soré gà dekíta kà watákushi nì wa wakátte imasù

to know how to do something ...の仕方を知っている ...no shikáta wò shitté irú

how is school? 学校はどうですか gakkō wa dò desu ká

how was the film? 映画はどうでしたか eíga wa dò deshìta ká

how are you? お元気ですか o-géñki desu ká

2 (to what degree) どのくらい donō kuraì

how much milk? どのくらいのミルク

donó kurai nò mírúku

how many people? 何人の人々 náñnin no hitóbito

how much does it cost? 値段はいくらですか nedán wà íkúra desu ká

how long have you been here? いつからここにいますか ítsù kara kokó ní imásù ká

how old are you? お幾つですか o-íkùtsu desu ká

how tall is he? 彼の身長はどれくらいですか kárè no shíñchō wà doré gùrai desu ká

how lovely/awful! なんて美しい〔ひどい〕 náñte utsúkushíî〔hidóì〕

---

howl [haul] *vt* (animal) 遠ぼえする tôboe suru; (baby, person) 大声で泣く ôgoè de nakú; (wind) うなる unárù

H.P. [eitʃpiː] *abbr* = **hire purchase**

h.p. *abbr* = **horsepower**

HQ [eitʃkjuː] *abbr* = **headquarters**

hub [hʌb] *n* (of wheel) ハブ hábū; (*fig*: centre) 中心 chūshin

hubbub [hʌbʌb] *n* (din, commotion) どよめき doyómeki

hubcap [hʌbkæp] *n* (AUT) ホイールキャップ hoírukyappū

huddle [hʌdʹəl] *vi*: *to huddle together* (for heat, comfort) 体を寄せ合う karáda wò yoséaū

hue [hjuː] *n* (color) 色 iró; (shade of color) 色合い iróai

hue and cry *n* (outcry) 騒ぎ sáwàgi

huff [hʌf] *n*: *in a huff* (offended) 怒って okótte

hug [hʌg] *vt* (person, thing) 抱締める dakíshimerù

huge [hjuːdʒ] *adj* (enormous) ばく大な bakúdai na

hulk [hʌlk] *n* (ship) 廃船 haísen; (person) 図体ばかり大きい人 zútai bakari ôkii hitó, うどの大木 udo no taiboku; (building etc) ばかでかい物 bakádekai monð

hull [hʌl] *n* (of ship) 船体 seńtai, ハル haru

hullo [həlouʹ] *excl* = **hello**

hum [hʌm] *vt* (tune, song) ハミングで歌

う hamíngu de utau

♦*vi* (person) ハミングする hamíngu suru; (machine) ぶーんと鳴る buń to narú; (insect) ぶんぶんいう buńbun iu

human [hjuːmən] *adj* (existence, body) 人の hitó no, 人間の niñgen no; (weakness, emotion) 人間的な niñgenteki na

♦*n* (person) 人間 hitó, 人間 niñgen

humane [hjuːmeinʹ] *adj* (treatment, slaughter) 苦痛を与えない kutsú wò atáenai

humanitarian [hjuːmæniterʹiːən] *adj* (aid, principles) 人道的な jińdōteki na

humanity [hjuːmænʹitiː] *n* (mankind) 人類 jińrui, 人間 niñgen; (human nature) 人間性 niñgensei; (humaneness, kindness) 思いやり omóiyari

humble [hʌmʹbəl] *adj* (modest) 謙虚な kéñkyo na; (lowly: background) 身分の低い物 mibún no hikúi

♦*vt* (humiliate, crush) …の高慢な鼻を折る …no kôman na haná wò órū

humbug [hʌmʹbʌg] *n* (of statement, writing) でたらめ detárame; (*BRIT*: sweet) はっか飴 hakká-ame

humdrum [hʌmʹdrʌm] *adj* (dull, boring) 退屈な taíkutsu na

humid [hjuːʹmid] *adj* (atmosphere, climate) 湿度の高い shitsúdò no takái

humidity [hjuːmidʹətiː] *n* 湿度 shitsúdò

humiliate [hjuːmilʹiːeit] *vt* (rival, person) …の高慢な鼻を折る …no kôman na haná wò órū

humiliation [hjuːmiliːeiʹʃən] *n* (embarrassment) 恥 hajī; (situation, experience) 恥辱 chijóku

humility [hjuːmilʹətiː] *n* (modesty) 謙虚 na kefisoń

humor [hjuːʹmər] (*BRIT* **humour**) *n* (comedy, mood) ユーモア yūmoa

♦*vt* (child, person) …の機嫌を取る …no kigén wo tórù

humorous [hjuːʹmərəs] *adj* (remark, book) おどけた odóketa; (person) ユーモアのある yūmoa no árū

hump [hʌmp] *n* (in ground) 小山 koyáma; (of camel: also deformity) こぶ kobú

humpbacked [hʌmpʹbækt] *adj*: **hump-**

backed bridge 反り橋 soríhàshi

hunch [hʌntʃ] *n* (premonition) 直感 chokkán

hunchback [hʌntʃ'bæk] *n* せむしの人 se-múshi nò hitó べっ背 bésshò

hunched [hʌntʃt] *adj* (bent, stooped: shoulders) 曲げた magéta; (: person) 肩を落とした kátà wo otóshìtà

hundred [hʌn'drid] *num* 百 (の) hyakú (no); (before *n*): *a/one hundred books* 100冊の本 hyakúsàtsu nò hón: *a/one hundred people* 100人の人 hyakúnìn nò hitó: *a/one hundred dollars* 100ドル hyakú dòru

hundreds of 何百もの nañbyaku mo no

hundredweight [hʌn'dridweit] *n* (US = 45.3 kg, 100 lb; BRIT = 50.8 kg, 112 lb)

hung [hʌŋ] *pt, pp of* **hang**

Hungarian [hʌŋgær'i:ən] *adj* ハンガリーの hañgarì no; (LING) ハンガリー語の hañgarìgo no

♦*n* (person) ハンガリー人 hañgarìjìn; (LING) ハンガリー語 hañgarìgo

Hungary [hʌŋ'gə:ri:] *n* ハンガリー hañgarì

hunger [hʌŋ'gə:r] *n* (lack of food) 空腹 kúfuku; (starvation) 飢餓 kígà

♦*vi*: *to hunger for* (desire) ...に飢える ...ni uérù

hunger strike *n* ハンガーストライキ hañgásutoràiki, ハンスト hañsuto

hungry [hʌŋ'gri:] *adj* (person, animal) 空腹な kúfuku na; (keen, avid): *hungry for* ...に飢えた ...ni uétà

to be hungry おなかがすいた onáka ga suítà

hunk [hʌŋk] *n* (of bread etc) 塊 katámarì

hunt [hʌnt] *vt* (for food: subj: animal) 捜し求める sagáshimotomerù, あさる asárù; (SPORT) 狩る kárù, ...の狩りをする ...no kárì wo surù; (criminal, fugitive) 捜す sagásù, 捜索する sōsaku suru

♦*vi* (search): *to hunt (for)* (...を) 捜す (...wo) sagásù; (SPORT) ...の狩りをする (...no) kárì wo surù

♦*n* (search: also SPORT) 狩り kárì; (search) 捜す事 sagásù kotò; (for crimi-

nal) 捜索 sōsaku

hunter [hʌn'tə:r] *n* (sportsman) ハンター hāntà

hunting [hʌn'tiŋ] *n* (for food: *also* SPORT) 狩り kárì

hurdle [hə:r'dəl] *n* (difficulty) 障害 shōgai; (SPORT) ハードル hādoru

hurl [hə:rl] *vt* (object) 投げる nagérù; (insult, abuse) 浴びせ掛ける abísekakerù

hurrah [hərɑ:'] *n* (as cheer) 歓声 kañsei

hurray [hərei'] *n* = **hurrah**

hurricane [hə:r'əkein] *n* (storm) ハリケーン haríkèn

hurried [hə:r'i:d] *adj* (hasty, rushed) 大急ぎの ōisògi no

hurriedly [hə:r'i:dli:] *adv* 大急ぎで ōisògi de

hurry [hə:r'i:] *n* (haste, rush) 急ぎ isógi

♦*vi* (*also*: **hurry up**): hasten, rush) 急ぐ isógù

♦*vt* (*also*: **hurry up**: person) 急がせる isógaserù; (: work) 急いでする isóide surù

to be in a hurry 急いでいる isóide irù

hurt [hə:rt] (*pt, pp* **hurt**) *vt* (cause pain to) 痛める itámerù; (injure, *fig*) 傷付ける kizútsukerù

♦*vi* (be painful) 痛む itámù

it hurts! 痛い！ itái!

hurtful [hə:rt'fəl] *adj* (remark) 傷付ける様な kizútsukerù yō na

hurtle [hə:r'təl] *vi*: *to hurtle past* (train, car) 猛スピードで通り過ぎる mōsupído de tōrisugirù

to hurtle down (rocks) 落ちる ochírù

husband [hʌz'bənd] *n* 夫 ottó

hush [hʌʃ] *n* (silence) 沈黙 chiñmoku; (stillness) 静けさ shizúkesà

♦*vt* (silence) 黙らせる damáraserù

hush! 静かに shízùka ni!

hush up *vt* (scandal etc) もみ消す momíkesù

husk [hʌsk] *n* (of wheat, rice) 殻 kará; (of maize) 皮 kawá

husky [hʌs'ki:] *adj* (voice) しわがれた shiwágaretà, ハスキーな hásukì na

♦*n* (dog) ハスキー hásukì

hustle [hʌs'əl] *vt* (hurry) 急がせる isógaserù

♦n: hustle and bustle 雑踏 zattò

hut [hʌt] n (house) 小屋 koyá; (shed) 物置 monó-oki

hutch [hʌtʃ] n (also: **rabbit hutch**) ウサギ小屋 uságigoya

hyacinth [ˈhaiəsinθ] n ヒヤシンス hiyáshìsu

hybrid [ˈhaibrid] n (plant, animal) 交雑種 kòzatsushů, ハイブリッド haíburiddò; (mixture) 混成物 kòseíbùtsu

hydrant [ˈhaidrənt] n (also: **fire hydrant**) 消火栓 shòkasen

hydraulic [haiˈdrɔːlik] adj (pressure, system) 油圧の yuátsu no

hydroelectric [haidrouilekˈtrik] adj (energy, complex) 水力発電の suíryokuhatsůden no

hydrofoil [ˈhaidrəfɔil] n (boat) 水中翼船 suíchùyokůsen

hydrogen [ˈhaidrədʒən] n (CHEM) 水素 súìso

hyena [haiˈiːnə] n ハイエナ hafena

hygiene [ˈhaidʒiːn] n (cleanliness) 衛生 efsei

hygienic [haidʒiˈenik] adj 衛生的な efseiteki na

hymn [him] n 賛美歌 sañbika

hype [haip] (inf) n 派手な口上 urfkomíkòjò

hypermarket [ˈhaipɑːrmɑːrkit] (BRIT) n 大型スーパー ògatasùpå

hyphen [ˈhaifən] n (dash) ハイフン haífun

hypnosis [hipnoˈsis] n 催眠 saímin

hypnotic [hipˈnɑtik] adj (trance) 催眠術の saímiñjutsu no; (rhythms) 催眠的な saímiñteki na

hypnotism [ˈhipˈnɑtizəm] n 催眠術 saímiñjutsu

hypnotist [ˈhipˈnɑtist] n (person) 催眠術師 saímiñjutsushì

hypnotize [ˈhipˈnɑtaiz] vt (MED etc) ...に催眠術を掛ける ...ni saímiñjutsu wo kakérù; (fig: mesmerise) 魅惑する miwáku suru

hypochondriac [haipəkɑnˈdriæːk] n 心気症患者 shíñkishòkañja

hypocrisy [hipɑkˈrəsi] n (falseness, in-

sincerity) 偽善 gízen

hypocrite [ˈhipəkrit] n (phoney) 偽善者 gízéñsha

hypocritical [hipəkritˈikəl] adj (person) 偽善の gízen no; (behavior) 偽善者的な gízéñshateki no

hypothermia [haipəθəˈrmiːə] n (MED) 低体温症 teitaioñshò

hypothesis [haipɑˈθəsis] (pl **hypotheses**) n (theory) 仮説 kasétsu

hypothetic(al) [haipəθetˈik(əl)] adj (question, situation) 仮定の katéi no

hysteria [histiˈriːə] n (panic; also MED) ヒステリー hísúteri

hysterical [histeˈriːkəl] adj (person, rage) ヒステリックな hísúterikkù na; (situation: funny) 笑いがとられない様な waráigà tomáranai yō na

     hysterical laughter ばか笑い bakáwarai

hysterics [histeˈriks] npl (anger, panic) ヒステリー hísúteri; (laughter) 大笑い ōwarai

I

I [ai] pron 私は(が) watákushi wa (ga)

ice [ais] n (frozen water) 氷 kòri; (also: **ice cream**) アイスクリーム aísukurïmu

♦vt (cake) ...にアイシングを掛ける ...ni aíshingu wo kakérù

♦vi (also: **ice over, ice up**: road, window etc) 氷に覆われる kòri nì ōwarerù

iceberg [ˈaisbəːrg] n 氷山 hyòzan

icebox [ˈaisbɑks] n (US: fridge) 冷蔵庫 refzòko; (BRIT: compartment) 冷凍室 reftòshitsu; (insulated box) クーラー kùrà

ice cream n アイスクリーム aísukurïmu

ice cube n 角氷 kakúgòri

iced [aist] adj (cake) ...にアイシングを掛けた aíshingu wo kákéta; (beer) 冷した hiyáshìta

     iced tea アイスティー aísutì

ice hockey n (SPORT) アイスホッケー aísuhokkë

Iceland [ˈaisˈlənd] n アイスランド aísurañdo

ice lolly [-lɔːˈliː] (BRIT) n アイスキャンディー aísukyàndī

ice rink n スケートリンク sukéetorìnku

ice-skating [aisˈskeitiŋ] n アイススケート aísusukèto

icicle [aiˈsikəl] n (on gutter, ledge etc) つらら tsurára

icing [aiˈsiŋ] n (CULIN) 砂糖衣 satógoròmo, アイシング áishingu

icing sugar (BRIT) n 粉砂糖 konázatō

icon [aiˈkɑn] n (REL) 聖像画 seízōga, イコン íkòn

icy [aiˈsiː] adj (air, water, temperature) 冷たい tsumétaì; (road) 氷に覆われた kōˈri ni ówareta

I'd [aid] = I would; I had

idea [aiˈdiːə] n (scheme, notion) 考え kañgaè; (opinion) 意見 íkèn; (objective) つもり tsumóri

ideal [aiˈdiːəl] n (principle) 理想 risō; (epitome) 模範 mohán
♦adj (perfect) 理想的な risôteki na

idealist [aiˈdiːəlist] n 理想主義者 risōshugìsha

identical [aiˈdentikəl] adj 同一の dōitsu no

identification [aidentəfəkeiˈʃən] n (process) 識別 shikíbetsu; (of person, dead body) 身元の確認 mímoto nò kakúnin
(means of) identification 身分証明書 mibúnshōmeìsho

identify [aiˈdentəfai] vt (recognize) 見分ける miwákerù; (distinguish) 識別する shikíbetsu suru; (associate): to identify someone/something (with) ...を(...と) 関連付ける ...wo (...to) kañrenzukerù

Identikit [aiˈdentəkit] ® n: Identikit (picture) モンタージュ写真 moñtājushashìn

identity [aiˈdentiti] n (of person, suspect etc) 身元 mímòto; (of group, culture, nation etc) 特性 tokúsei

identity card n 身分証明書 mibúnshōmeìsho

ideology [aidiːɑˈlɔdʒiː] n (beliefs) 思想 shisō, イデオロギー idéorogī

idiom [idiˈəm] n (style) 作風 sakúfū; (phrase) 熟語 jukúgo, イディオム ídìomu

idiomatic [idiəmætˈik] adj 熟語的な jukúgoteki na

idiosyncrasy [idiəsiŋˈkrəsi] n (foible) 特異性 tokúisei

idiot [idˈiːət] n (fool) ばか báka

idiotic [idiːɑtˈik] adj (stupid) ばかな báka na

idle [aiˈdəl] adj (inactive) 暇な himá na; (lazy) 怠惰な taída na; (unemployed) 失業中の shitsúgyōchū no; (machinery) 動いていない ugóite inái; (factory) 休業中の kyúgyōchū no; (question, conversation) 無意味な mujmi na; (pleasure) むなしい munáshiī
♦vi (machine, engine) 空回りする káramawàri suru, アイドリングする áídoriñgu suru

idle away vt: to idle away the time のらくらする nóràkura suru

idol [aiˈdəl] n (hero) アイドル áidoru; (REL) 偶像 gūzō

idolize [aiˈdəlaiz] vt ...に心酔する ...ni shíñsui suru

idyllic [aidiˈlik] adj のどかな nódòka na

i.e. [aiiˈ] abbr (= id est: that is) 即ち sunáwàchi

─────────────
KEYWORD
─────────────

if [if] conj 1 (conditional use: given that, providing that etc) (もし)...すれば(する ならば) (móshi) ...suréba (surú naraba)
I'll go if you come with me あなたが一緒に来れば、私は行ってもいいです anátà ga isshó ni kuréba watákushi wà itté mó īi desu
I'd be pleased if you could do it あなたがそれをやって下さればうれしいですが anátà ga soré wò yatté kudasaréba watákushi wà tasúkarimasù ga
if anyone comes in だれかが入って来れば dárèka ga háitte kùreba
if necessary 必要であれば hitsúyo de aréba
if I were you 私があなただったら watákushi gà anátà dáttàra

2 (whenever) ...の時 ...no tokí

if we are in Scotland, we always go to see her スコットランドにいる時たちは必ず彼女に会いに行きますsukóttorañdo ni irú tokí watákushitachi wa kanárazu kánojo ni áí ni ikímasu

3 (although): *(even) if* たとえ...でも tatóe ...dé mò

I am determined to finish it, (even) if it takes all week たとえ今週いっぱいかかっても私はこの仕事を片付けたいtatóe koñshū ippái kakátte mò watákushi wa konó shigoto wò katázukétai

I like it, (even) if you don't あなたがいやでも、私はこれが好きですanáta ga iyá de mò, watákushi wa koré ga sukí desu

4 (whether) ...かどうか ...ka dò ka

I don't know if he is here 彼がここにいるかどうか私には分かりません kárè ga kokó ni irú ka dòka watákushi ni wa wakárimaseñ

ask him if he can come 来られるかどうか彼に聞いて下さい koráreru ka dò ka kárè ni kííte kudasái

5: *if so/not* そうであれば(なければ) sò de arèba(nakerèba)

if only ...であったらなあ ...dè áttara nà

if only I could 私に、それだできたらなあ watákushi nì soré gà dékítara nà

¶ *see also* **as**

igloo [ig'lu:] *n* イグルー ígùrū

ignite [ignaít'] *vt* (set fire to) ...に火をつける ...ni hí wò tsukérò
♦*vi* 燃出す moédasù

ignition [igniʃ'ən] *n* (AUT: process) 点火 tefíka; (: mechanism) 点火装置 tefíkasòchi

to switch on/off the ignition エンジンスイッチを入れる(切る) efíjinsuitchi wo irérò(kírù)

ignition key *n* (AUT) カーキー kākì

ignorance [ig'nɔrəns] *n* (lack of knowledge) 無知 múchì

ignorant [ig'nɔrənt] *adj* (uninformed, unaware) 無学な múgàku na, 無知な múchì na

to be ignorant of (subject, events) ...を知らない ...wo shiránaí

ignore [ignɔr'] *vt* (person, advice, event, fact) 無視する mushí suru

I'll [ail] = I will; I shall

ill [il] *adj* (sick) 病気の byókì no; (harmful: effects) 悪い warúì
♦*n* (evil) 悪 ákù; (trouble) 凶悪 kyóchò
♦*adv*: *to speak ill of someone* ...の悪口を言う ...no warúgùchi wo iú

to think ill (of someone) (...を) 悪く思う (...wo) warúkù omóú

to be taken ill 病気になる byókì ni narú, 倒れる taóreru

ill-advised [il'ædvaizd'] *adj* (decision) 軽率な keísotsu na; (person) 無分別な mu, fuñbetsu na

ill-at-ease [il'ətiːz'] *adj* (awkward, uncomfortable) 落着かない ochítsukanaí

illegal [ili:'gəl] *adj* (not legal: action, organization, immigrant etc) 不法のfuhó no

illegible [iledʒ'əbəl] *adj* (writing) 読めない yoménaí

illegitimate [ilidʒit'əmit] *adj*: *an illegitimate child* 私生児 shiséíji

ill-fated [il'fei'tid] *adj* (doomed) 不運な fúùn na

ill feeling *n* (animosity, bitterness) 恨み urámi

illicit [ilis'it] *adj* (unlawful: sale, association, substance) 不法の fuhó no

illiterate [ilit'ərit] *adj* (person) 文盲の mofímò no; (letter) 無学な múgàku na

ill-mannered [il'mæn'ərd] *adj* (rude: child etc) 行儀の悪い gyógi no warúì

illness [il'nis] *n* 病気 byókì

illogical [iladʒ'ikəl] *adj* (fear, reaction, argument) 不合理な fugóri na

ill-treat [il'trit] *vt* (child, pet, prisoner) 虐待する gyakútai suru

illuminate [iluː'məneit] *vt* (light up: room, street) 明るくする akárukù suru; (decorate with lights: building, monument etc) ライトアップする raítoapùru suru; (shine light on) 照らす terásù

illumination [iluːmænei'ʃən] *n* (lighting) 照明 shómeí

illuminations [ɪlumɪˈəneɪʃ(ə)nz] *npl* (decorative lights) 電飾 deñshoku, イルミネーション irúminéshon

illusion [ɪluˈʒən] *n* (false idea, belief) 錯覚 sakkáku; (trick) いんちき ínchiki, トリック torîkkū

illusory [ɪluˈsɔːriː] *adj* (hopes, prospects) 錯覚の sakkáku no

illustrate [ilˈəstreɪt] *vt* (point) 例を挙げて説明する rei wò agětē setsúmei suru; (book) ...に挿絵を入れる ...ni sashíē wo irérù; (talk) ...にスライド（など）を使う ...ni surâido (nádð) wo tsukáù

illustration [iləstreiˈʃən] *n* (act of illustrating) 図解 zukái; (example) 例 ref; (in book) 挿絵 sashíē

illustrious [ilˈʌstriːəs] *adj* (career) 輝かしい kagáyakashiî; (predecessor) 著名な chómei na

ill will *n* (hostility) 恨み urámi

I'm [aim] = **I am**

image [imˈidʒ] *n* (picture) 像 zõ; (public face) イメージ ímējî; (reflection) 姿 sugáta

imagery [imˈidʒri:] *n* (in writing, painting etc) 比喩 hîyǔ

imaginary [imædʒəneriː] *adj* (being, danger) 想像上の sőzōjō no

imagination [imædʒəneɪˈʃən] *n* (part of the mind) 想像 sôzō; (inventiveness) 想像力 sôzōryoku

imaginative [imædʒˈənətɪv] *adj* (person) 想像力に富んだ sôzōryoku ni tofdâ; (solution) 奇抜な kibátsu na

imagine [imædʒˈin] *vt* (visualise) 想像する sôzō suru; (dream) ...だと錯覚する ...da to sakkáku suru; (suppose) ...だと思う ...da to omóù

imbalance [imbælˈəns] *n* (inequality) 不均等 fukhñtō, アンバランス ánbaransu

imbecile [imˈbəsil] *n* (idiot) ばか bâka

imbue [imbjuˈ] *vt*: **to imbue someone/something with** ...に を吹き込む ...wo fukíkomù

imitate [imˈəteit] *vt* (copy) まねる manérù; (mimic) ...の物まねをする ...no monómane wð suru

imitation [iməteiˈʃən] *n* (act of copying)

まね manê; (act of mimicking) 物まね monómane; (copy) 偽物 nisémono

immaculate [imækˈjəlit] *adj* (room) 汚れ一つない yogôre hitotsū nâî; (appearance) 清潔な sefketsu na; (piece of work) 完璧な kañpeki na; (REL) 原罪のない geñzai nò nâî

immaterial [imatíˈriəl] *adj* (unimportant) どうでもいい dô dê mo fi

immature [imatúrˈ] *adj* (fruit, cheese) 熟していない jukú shite inaí; (organism) 未成熟の miséijuku no; (person) 未熟な mijûku na

immediate [imiˈdiːət] *adj* (reaction, answer) 即時の sokûji no; (pressing: need) 緊迫した kiñpaku shita; (nearest: neighborhood, family) 最も近い mottô-mð chikáî

immediately [imiˈdiːtli:] *adv* (at once) 直ぐに súgū ni, 直ちに tádachi ni; (directly) 真っ直ぐに massûgū ni
immediately next to ...の直ぐ隣に ...no súgū tonárî ni

immense [imensˈ] *adj* (huge: size) 巨大な kyodái na; (: progress, importance) 大変な taíhen na

immerse [iməːsˈ] *vt* (submerge) 浸す hitásù
to be immersed in (*fig*: work, study etc) ...に熱中している ...ni netchû shite irû
to be immersed in thought 考え込んでいる kañgaekoñde irú

immersion heater [iməːrˈʒən-] (*BRIT*) *n* 投込式湯沸かし器 tônyushiki yuwakashikî

immigrant [imˈəgrənt] *n* 移民 imín

immigration [imagreiˈʃən] *n* (process) 移住 íjû; (control: at airport etc) 入国管理局 nyûkoku kañrikyokū

imminent [imˈənənt] *adj* (arrival, departure) 差迫った sashísematta

immobile [imouˈbail] *adj* (motionless) 動かない ugókanâî

immobilize [imouˈbailz] *vt* (person, machine) 動けなくする ugôkenákù suru

immoral [imɔːrˈəl] *adj* (person, behavior, idea etc) 不道徳な fudôtoku na

immorality [iməræl'iti:] n 不道 徳 fudō-toku

immortal [imɔːr'təl] adj (living for ever: god) 永遠に生きる efen nī ikirū; (unforgettable: poetry, fame) 不滅の fumétsu no

immortalize [imɔːr'təlaiz] vt (hero, event) ...に不朽の名声を与える ...ni fukyū no melsei wo atéerū

immune [imjuːn'] adj: **immune (to)** (disease) (...に) 免疫がある (...ni) meň-eki ga arū; (flattery) (...が) ...に通じない (...ga) ...ni tsūjinai; (criticism, attack) ...に (...の) しようがない ...ni (...no) shiyō ga nai

immunity [imjuː'niti:] n (to disease etc) 免疫 meň-eki; (from prosecution, taxation etc) 免除 meňjo

diplomatic immunity 外交特権 gaíkoutokkén

immunize [im'jənaiz] vt (MED: gen) ...に免疫性を与える ...ni meň-ekisei wo atáerū; (with injection) ...に予防注射をする ...ni yobōchūsha wo suru

imp [imp] n (small devil) 小鬼 ko-óni; (child) いたずらっ子 itázurakkŏ

impact [im'pækt] n (of bullet, crash) 衝撃 shōgeki, インパクト íňpakuto; (of law, measure) 影響 eíkyō

impair [impeːr'] vt (vision, judgement) 損なう sokónaū

impale [impeil'] vt くし刺しにする kushî-zashi ni suru

impart [impɑːrt'] vt (make known: information) 与える atáerū; (bestow: flavor) 添える soérū

impartial [impɑːr'ʃəl] adj (judge, observer) 公平な kōhei na

impassable [impæs'əbəl] adj (river) 渡れない watárenai; (road, route etc) 通行不可能な tsūkófukanō na

impasse [im'pæs] n (in war, negotiations) 行き詰り ikízumari

impassive [impæs'iv] adj (face, expression) 無表情な muhyōjō na

impatience [impei'ʃəns] n (annoyance due to waiting) いらだった気持 irádatta kimochi; (eagerness) 意欲 íyoku

impatient [impei'ʃənt] adj (annoyed by waiting) じれった い jiréttai; (irritable) 短気な táňki na; (eager, in a hurry): **impatient to ...** ...に従っている ...shitagatte irū

to get/grow impatient もどかしがる modókashigarū

impeccable [impek'əbəl] adj (perfect: manners, dress) 申分のない mōshibun no nái

impede [impiːd'] vt (progress, development etc) 妨げる samátagerū

impediment [imped'əmənt] n (to growth, movement) 障害 shōgai; (also: **speech impediment**) 言語障害 geňgoshōgai

impending [impen'diŋ] adj (arrival, catastrophe) 差迫る sashísemarū

impenetrable [impen'itrəbəl] adj (wall, jungle) 通れない tōrenai; (fig: law, text) 難解な naňkai na

imperative [imper'ətiv] adj (need) 緊急 の kiňkyū no; (tone) 命令的な mefreiteki na

♦n (LING) 命令形 mefreikei

imperceptible [impərsep'təbəl] adj (change, movement) 気付かれない kizúkarenai

imperfect [impəːr'fikt] adj (goods, system etc) 不完全な fukáňzen na

♦n (LING: also: **imperfect tense**) 過去進行形 kakóshinkōkei

imperfection [impərfek'ʃən] n (failing, blemish) 欠点 kettéň

imperial [impiː'riəl] adj (history, power) 帝国の teíkoku no; (BRIT: measure) ヤードポンド法の yādopondohō no

imperialism [impiː'iːalizəm] n 帝国主義 teíkokushūgi

impersonal [impəːr'sənəl] adj (place, organization) 人間味のない niňgenmi no nái

impersonate [impəːr'səneit] vt (another person, police officer etc) ...の名をかたる ...no nā wo katárū, ...に成り済ます ...ni narísumasū; (THEATER) ...にふんする ...ni fuň surū

impertinent [impəː'tənənt] adj (pupil, question) 生意気な namáiki na

impervious [impəː'viːəs] adj (fig): **impervious to** (criticism etc) ...に影響されない ...ni eſkyō sarenái

impetuous [impet'uːəs] adj (impulsive) 無鉄砲な mutéppō na

impetus [im'pitəs] n (momentum: of flight, runner) 惰性 daséi; (fig: driving force) 原動力 geñdōryoku

impinge [impindʒ']: **to impinge on** vt fus (person) ...の行動を制限する ...no kōdō wò seīgen suru; (rights) 侵害する shiñgai suru

implacable [implæk'əbəl] adj (hatred, anger etc) なだめがたい nadámegatái; (opposition) 執念深い shúnenbúkai

implement [n im'pləmənt vb im'pləment] n (tool: for farming, gardening, cooking etc) 道具 dōgu
♦vt (plan, regulation) 実行する jikkō suru

implicate [im'plikeit] vt (in crime, error) ...のかかわり合いを立証する ...no kakáwariaí wo risshō suru

implication [implikei'ʃən] n (inference) 含み fukúmi; (involvement) 係り合い kakáwariaí

implicit [implis'it] adj (inferred: threat, meaning etc) 暗黙の añmoku no; (unquestioning: belief, trust) 盲目的な mōmokuteki na

implore [imploːr'] vt (beg) ...に嘆願する ...ni tañgan suru

imply [implai'] vt (hint) ...の意味を含む ...no ímī wo fukúmù; (mean) ...を意味する ...wo ímī suru

impolite [impəlait'] adj (rude, offensive) 失礼な shitsúrei na

import [vb impoːrt' n im'poːrt] vt (goods etc) 輸入する yunyū suru
♦n (COMM: article) 輸入品 yunyūhin; (: importation) 輸入 yunyū

importance [impoːr'təns] n (significance) 重大さ jūdaisa; (of person) 有力 yūryoku

important [impoːr'tənt] adj (significant: decision, difference etc) 重要な jūyō na, 重大な jūdai na; (influential: person) 偉い erái
it's not important 大した事じゃない taíshita kotò ja náī

importer [impoːr'tər] n (COMM) 輸入業者 yunyūgyōsha

impose [impouz'] vt (sanctions, restrictions, discipline etc) 負わせる owáserù
♦vi: *to impose on someone* ...に付込む ...ni tsukékomù, ...に迷惑を掛ける ...ni mélwaku wo kakérù

imposing [impouz'iŋ] adj (building, person, manner) 貫ろくある kañroku arù

imposition [impəziʃ'ən] n (of tax etc) 賦課 fukà
to be an imposition on (person) ...に付込む ...ni tsukékomù, ...に迷惑を掛ける ...ni mélwaku wo kakérù

impossible [impaːs'əbəl] adj (task, demand etc) 不可能な fukánō na; (situation) 厄介な yakkáî na; (person) どうしようもない dō shiyō mo nai

impostor [impaːs'tər] n 偽者 nisémono

impotence [im'pətəns] n (lack of power) 無力 múryòku; (MED) 性交不能 seíkōfúnō

impotent [im'pətənt] adj (powerless) 無力な múryòku na; (MED) 性交不能の seíkōfúnō no

impound [impaund'] vt (belongings, passports) 没収する bosshū suru

impoverished [impaːv'ərisht] adj (country, person etc) 貧しくなった mazáshiku nattá

impracticable [impræk'tikəbəl] adj (idea, solution) 実行不可能な jikkófukanō na

impractical [impræk'tikəl] adj (plan) 実用的でない jitsúyōteki na; (person) 不器用な bukíyō na

imprecise [imprisais'] adj (inexact) 不正確な fuséikaku na

impregnable [impreg'nəbəl] adj (castle, fortress) 難攻不落の nañkófuràku no

impregnate [impreg'neit] vt (saturate) ...に染込ませる ...ni shimíkomaserù

impresario [imprəsaːri'ou] n (THEA-

TER) 興業師 kógyóshì

impress [impres'] vt (person) ...に印象を与える ...ni ínshō wò atáerù; (mark) ...に押付ける ...ni oshítsukerù

to impress something on someone ...に...を強く言い聞かす ...ni ...wo tsuyóku ífkikasù

impression [impreʃ'ən] n (of place, situation, person) 印象 ínshō; (of stamp, seal) 判 hán, 刻印 kokúín; (idea) 思い込み omóikomi; (effect) 効果 kōka; (mark) 跡 átò; (imitation) 物まね monómane

to be under the impression that ...だと思い込んでいる ...da to omóikonde irú

impressionable [impreʃ'ənəbəl] adj (child, person) 感じやすい kañjiyasuí

impressionist [impreʃ'ənist] n (entertainer) 物真似師 mónomanéshì; (ART): **Impressionist** 印象派画家 ínshōhagaka

impressive [impres'iv] adj (reputation, collection) 印象的な ínshōteki na

imprint [im'print] n (outline: of hand etc) 跡 ato; (PUBLISHING) 奥付 okúzuke

imprison [impriz'ən] vt (criminal) 拘置する kốchi suru, 刑務所に入れる keímushò ni irérù

imprisonment [impriz'ənmənt] n 拘置 kốchi

improbable [imprɑːb'əbəl] adj (unlikely: outcome) ありそうもない arísō mò náì; (: explanation, story) 本当らしくない hoñtōrashikú náì

impromptu [imprɑːmp'tuː] adj (celebration, party) 即席の sokúseki no

improper [imprɑːp'əːr] adj (unsuitable: conduct, procedure) 不適切な futékisetsu na; (dishonest: activities) 不正な fuséi na

improve [impruːv'] vt (make better: character, housing, result) 改善する kaízen suru

♦vi (get better: weather, pupil, patient, health etc) 良くなる yókù naru

improvement [impruːv'mənt] n (making better) 改善 kaízen; (getting better) 良くなる事 yókù naru kotó; improve-

ment (in) (making better) (...を) 改善する事 (...wo) kaízen surù kotó; (getting better) (...が) 良くなる事 (...ga) yókù naru kotó

improvise [im'prəvaiz] vt (meal, bed etc) 有り合せの物で作る aríawase no mono dè tsukúrù

♦vi (THEATER, MUS) 即興的にしゃべる (演奏する) kyókkyóteki nì shabérù (eñsō suru), アドリブする adóribu suru

imprudent [impruːd'ənt] adj (unwise) 賢明でない keñmei de naí

impudent [im'pjədənt] adj (child, comment, remark) 生意気な namáiki na

impulse [im'pʌls] n (urge: gen) 衝動 shốdō; (: to do wrong) 出来心 dekígokoro; (ELEC) 衝撃 shōgeki, インパルス ñparusu

to act on impulse 衝動的に行動する shốdōteki ni kódō suru

impulsive [impʌl'siv] adj (purchase, gesture, person) 衝動的な shốdōteki na

impunity [impjuː'niti] n: **with impunity** 罰せられずに bassérarezù ni

impure [impjuːr'] adj (adulterated) 不純な fujún na; (sinful) みだらな mídàra na

impurity [impjuːr'iti] n (foreign substance) 不純物 fujúnbutsu

KEYWORD

in [in] prep **1** (indicating place, position) ...に(で) ...nì(dè)

in the house/garden 家(庭)に(で) ié (niwá) nì(dè)

in the box/fridge/drawer 箱(冷蔵庫, 引き出し)に(で) hakó(reízòko, hikídashì) nì(dè)

I have it in my hand 手に持っています té nì mótté imasu

to spend a day in town/the country 町(田舎)で1日を過ごす machí(ináka) dè ichínichi wò sugósù

in school 学校に(で) gakkō nì(dè)

in here/there ここ(あそこ)に(で) kokó(asóko) nì(dè)

2 (with place names: of town, region, country) ...に(で) ...nì(dè)

in London ロンドンに(で) róñdon ni

(de)

in *England / Japan / Canada / the United States* 英国(日本, カナダ, アメリカ)に(で) efkoku(nippón, kánada, amérīka) ni(de)

in *Burgundy* バーガンディーに(で) bágandī ni(de)

3 (indicating time: during) ...に ...nī(na-tsū)ni

in *spring/summer* 春(夏)に hárū(na-tsū)ni

in *1998* 1998年に sefikyūhyakukyūjūhachi nēn ni

in *May* 5月に gógatsu ni

I'll see you in July 7月に会いましょう shichígatsu ni aímashō

in the afternoon 午後に gógo ni

at 4 o'clock in the afternoon 午後4時に gógo yójī ni

4 (indicating time: in the space of) ...で ...dè

I did it in 3 hours/days 3時間(3日)でやりました safíjikàn(mikká)de yarímashīta

I'll see you in 2 weeks/2 weeks' time 2週間したあとに会いましょう ni-shūkàn shitara matá aimashō

5 (indicating manner etc) ...で ...dè

in a loud/soft voice 大きな(小さな)声で ōkīna(chísana)kòè de

in pencil/ink 鉛筆(インク)で efípitsu (fìnku)de

in English/French 英語(フランス語)で efgo(furánsugo)de

the boy in the blue shirt 青いシャツの少年 aói shátsū no shōnen

6 (indicating circumstances): **in the sun** 直射日光に当って chokúshanikkô ni átattè, 日なたに hináta ni

in the rain 雨の中 ámē no nākà

in the shade 日陰で hikáge de

a change in policy 政策の変更 sefsaku nò hefikō

a rise in prices 物価の上昇 bûkkà no jōshō

7 (indicating mood, state): **in tears** 泣いて nafte

in anger 怒って okóttè

in despair 失望して shitsúbō shitè

in good condition 無事に bujī ni

to live in luxury ぜいたくに暮す zeftaku ni kurāsu

8 (with ratios, numbers): *1 in 10 households have a second car* 10世帯中1世帯は車を2台持っている jussètaichū issétai wà kurúma wò nídài mótte irû

1 household in 10 has a second car 10世帯中1世帯は車を2台持っている jussètaichū issétai wà kurúma wò nídài mótte irû

6 months in the year 1年の内6か月 ichínen no uchí rokkágetsu

they lined up in twos 彼ら は2人ずつ並んだ kárèra wa futárìzutsu narátda

9 (referring to people, works): *the disease is common in children* この病気は子供によく見られる konó byōkì wa kodómo nì yōkù mírárerû

in the works of Dickens ディケンズの作品の中に dfkènzu no sakúhin no naká ni

she has it in her to succeed 彼女には成功する素質がある kánòjo ni wa sefkō suru soshítsū ga árù

they have a good leader in him 彼らにとって彼は素晴らしいリーダーです kárèra ni tóttè kárè wa subárashiî rídà desu

10 (indicating profession etc): **to be in teaching** 教員である kyōîn de árû

to be in publishing 出版関係の仕事をしている shuppánkafikei no shigóto wò shitè irû

to be in the army 軍人である gufíjîn de árû

11 (after superlative): *the best pupil in the class* クラスで最優秀の生徒 kúràsu de safyūshū no seîto

the biggest/smallest in Europe ヨーロッパ中で最も大きな(小さな)物 yōroppajū de mottômo ōkīna(chísana)monó

12 (with present participle): *in saying this* こう言って kō ittè

in doing things the way she did, she alienated everyone 彼女のやり方は皆の反感を買った kánòjo no yaríkata wà miná no hafikan wo káttà

♦*adv*: **to be in** (person: at home) 在宅である zaftaku de árù; (: at work) 出社して irû

いる shusshá shite irú; (train, plane) 到着
している tốchaku shite irú; (ship) 入港し
ている nyūkō shite irú; (in fashion) 流行
している ryūkō shite irú

he'll be in later today 彼は2-3時間したら
出社すると思います nisánjikan shitará
shusshá suru tó omóimasù

miniskirts are in again this year 今
年ミニスカートが再び流行しています
kotóshi minísukàto ga futátabí ryūkō
shite imasú

to ask someone in ... を家に上がらせる
...wò ié nì agáraserù

to run/limp etc **in** 走って(びっこを引
いて)入って来る hashíttè(bíkkò wo híf-
tè)háttte kuru

♦n: **the ins and outs** (of proposal,
situation etc) 詳細 shôsaí

**he explained all the ins and outs of
the deal to me** 彼は私に取引の詳細を
説明してくれました kárè wa watákushi
nì toríhiki no shôsai wo setsúmei shite
kuremashìta

in. abbr = **inch**

inability [inəbil'əti:] n (incapacity): **inability (to do)** (...する事が) できない
事 (...surú kotò ga) dekínai kotó

inaccessible [inækses'əbəl] adj (place)
入りにくい hafrinikúi, 近付きにくい chi-
kázukinikúi; (fig: text, music) 難解な nań-
kai na

inaccurate [inæk'jə:rit] adj (account,
answer, person) 不正確な fuséikaku na

inactivity [inæktiv'iti:] n (idleness) 活動
しない事 katsúdôshinai kotó

inadequate [inæd'əkwit] adj (income,
amount, reply) 不十分な fujúbùn na;
(person) 無能な munō na

inadvertently [inədvə:r'təntli:] adv (unintentionally) うっかり ukkárì

inadvisable [inədvai'zəbəl] adj 得策でな
い tokúsaku de naí

inane [inein'] adj (smile, remark) 愚かな
óròka na

inanimate [inæn'əmit] adj 生命のない
seímei no naí

inappropriate [inəprou'pri:it] adj (un-

suitable) 不適切な futékisetsu na; (improper: word, expression) 非難すべき hinánsubeki

inarticulate [inɑ:rtik'jəlit] adj (person)
口下手な kuchíbeta no; (speech) 分かり
にくい wakárinikúi

inasmuch [inəzmʌtʃ'-] adv (in that)
...という点で ...to iú tén de; (insofar as)
できる限り dekíru kagíri

inaudible [inɔː'dəbəl] adj (voice, aside)
聞ami取れない kikítorenaí

inaugural [inɔː'gjə:rəl] adj (speech) 就任
の shūnin no; (meeting) 発会の hakkái no

inaugurate [inɔː'gjə:reit] vt (president,
official) ...の就任式を行う ...no shúnin-
ñchiki wo okónàu; (system, measure) 始
める hajímeru; (organization) 発足させ
る hossóku saserú

inauguration [inɔːgjəːrei'ʃən] n (of president, official) 就任式 shūninshiki; (of
system, measure) 開始 kaíshi; (of organization) 発足 hossóku

in-between [in'bitwin'] adj (intermediate) 中間的な chūkanteki na

inborn [in'bɔ:rn] adj (quality) 生れ付きの
umáretsuki no

inbred [in'bred] adj (quality) 生まれつき
の umáretsuki no; (family) 近親交配の
kińshinkôhai no

Inc. abbr = **incorporated**

incalculable [inkæl'kjələbəl] adj (effect,
loss) 途方もない tohô mo naí

incapable [inkei'pəbəl] adj (helpless) 無
能な munō na; (unable to): **to be incapable of something/doing something** ...が (する事が) できない ...ga (surú
kotò ga) dekínaí

incapacitate [inkəpæs'əteit] vt 不具に
する fúgù ni suru

incapacity [inkəpæs'iti:] n (weakness)
弱さ yówàsa; (inability) 無能 hi munō

incarcerate [inkɑːr'sərit] vt 拘置する
kôchi suru, 刑務所に入れる keímushò ni
irérù

incarnation [inkɑːrnei'ʃən] n (of beauty)
化身 keshín; (of evil) 権化 gónge; (REL)
神が人間の姿を取る事 kámì ga ningén

no sugata wo tōru koto

incendiary [insen'di:əri:] *adj* (device) 放火の hōka no

an incendiary bomb 焼い弾 shōidan

incense [*n* in'sens *vb* insens'] *n* (perfume: *also* REL) 香 kō

♦*vt* (anger) 怒らせる okóraserū

incentive [insen'tiv] *n* (inducement) 動機 dōki, 刺激 shigéki

incessant [inses'ənt] *adj* (bickering, criticism) 引っ切り無しの hikkíri nashí no

incessantly [inses'əntli:] *adv* 引っ切り無しに hikkíri nashí ni

incest [in'sest] *n* 近親相かん kiñshinsōkan

inch [intʃ] *n* (measurement) インチ íñchi

to be within an inch of doing 危うく ...するところである ayáuku ...surú tokoró de árū

he didn't give an inch (fig: back down, yield) 一寸も譲ろうとしなかった issúñ mo yuzúrō to shinákatta

inch forward *vi* 一寸刻みに進む issúñkizami ni susúmù

incidence [in'sidəns] *n* (of crime, disease) 発生率 hasséiritsu

incident [in'sidənt] *n* (event) 事件 jíkeñ

incidental [insiden'təl] *adj* (additional, supplementary) 付随的な fuzúiteki na

incidental to ...に対して二次的な ...ni táishite nijíteki na

incidentally [insiden'təli:] *adv* (by the way) ところで tokóro dè

incinerator [insin'əreitə:r] *n* (for waste, refuse) 焼却炉 shōkyakurō

incipient [insip'i:ənt] *adj* (baldness, madness) 初期の shókī no

incision [insiʒ'ən] *n* (cut: *also* MED) 切開 sékkái

incisive [insai'siv] *adj* (comment, criticism) 痛烈な tsúretsu na

incite [insait'] *vt* (rioters, violence) 扇動する señdō suru; (hatred) あおりたてる aóritatèru

inclination [inklənei'ʃən] *n* (tendency) 傾向 keíkō; (disposition, desire) 望み nozómi

incline [in'klain] *n* (slope) 坂 saká

♦*vt* (bend: head) 下げる sagérù

♦*vi* (surface) 傾斜する keísha suru

to be inclined to (tend) ...する傾向がある ...suru keíkō ga arù

include [inklud'] *vt* (incorporate: in plan, team etc) 入れる irérù; (: in price) 含む fukúmù

including [inklud'iŋ] *prep* ...を含めて ...wo fukúmetè

inclusion [inklu:'ʒən] *n* (incorporation: in plan etc) 入れる事 irérù kotó; (: in price) 含む事 fukúmù kotó

inclusive [inklu:'siv] *adj* (price, terms) 含んでいる fukúñde irù

inclusive of ...を含めて ...wo fukúmetè

incognito [inkɑːgniː'tou] *adv* (travel) 御忍びで o-shínobi de

incoherent [inkouhiːr'ənt] *adj* (argument, speech, person) 分かりにくい wakárinikuí

income [in'kʌm] *n* 収入 shūnyū

income tax *n* 所得税 shotókuzeí

incoming [in'kʌmiŋ] *adj* (flight, passenger) 到着の tōchaku no; (call, mail) 着信の chakúshin no; (government, official) 新任の shifnin no; (wave) 寄せて来る yoséte kurú

the incoming tide 上げ潮 agéshio

incomparable [inkɑm'pɑːrəbəl] *adj* (genius, efficiency etc) 類のない ruí no naí

incompatible [inkəmpæt'əbəl] *adj* (lifestyles, systems, aims) 相容れない aíirenai

incompetence [inkɑm'pitəns] *n* 無能 munō

incompetent [inkɑm'pitənt] *adj* (person) 無能な munō na; (job) 下手な hetá na

incomplete [inkəmpliːt'] *adj* (unfinished: book, painting etc) 未完成の mikánseí no; (partial: success, achievement) 部分的な bubúnteki na

incomprehensible [inkɑmprihen'səbəl] *adj* (conduct) 不可解な fukákai na; (language) 分からない wakáranaì

inconceivable [inkɑnsiː'vəbəl] *adj* (unthinkable) 考えられない kañgaerarenaì

incongruous [inkɔːŋ'gruːəs] adj (strange: situation, figure) 変った kawátta; (inappropriate: remark, act) 不適当な futékitō na

inconsiderate [inkənsíd'ərit] adj (person, action) 心ない kokóronaî

inconsistency [inkənsís'tənsi:] n (of behavior, person etc) 一貫しない事 ikkán shinai koto; (in work) むら murá; (in statement, action) 矛盾 mujún

inconsistent [inkənsís'tənt] adj (behavior, person) 変りやすい kawáriyasuî; (work) むらの多い murá no ōi; (statement, action) 矛盾した mujún shita

inconsistent with (beliefs, values) …と矛盾する …to mujún suru

inconspicuous [inkənspík'juːəs] adj (person, color, building etc) 目立たない medátanaî

incontinent [inkɑn'tənənt] adj (MED) 失禁の shikkín no

inconvenience [inkənviːn'jəns] n (problem) 問題 mońdai; (trouble) 迷惑 mewáku

♦vt …に迷惑を掛ける …ni meîwaku wò kakérù

inconvenient [inkənviːn'jənt] adj (time, place, house) 不便な fubén na; (visitor, incident etc) 厄介な yakkái na

incorporate [inkɔr'pəreit] vt (make part of) 取入れる toríireru; (contain) 含む fukúmù

incorporated company [inkɔr'pəreitid-] (US) n (abbr Inc.) 会社 kaísha

incorrect [inkərekt'] adj (information, answer, attitude etc) 間違った machígattâ

incorrigible [inkɔr'idʒəbəl] adj (liar, crook) 救い様のない sukúiyô no naî

incorruptible [inkərʌp'təbəl] adj (not open to bribes) 買収のできない baíshū no dekínaî

increase [n in'kriːs vb inkriːs'] n (rise): **increase (in/of)** (…の) 増加 (…no) zōka

♦vi (: price, level, productivity etc) 増す masú

♦vt (make greater: price, knowledge etc) 増す masú

increasing [inkríːsiŋ] adj (number, use) 増加する zōka suru

increasingly [inkríːsiŋliː] adv (more clearly, more often) ますます masúmasu

incredible [inkred'əbəl] adj (unbelievable) 信じられない shinjirarenaî; (enormous) ばく大な bakúdai na

incredulous [inkred'ʒələs] adj (tone, expression) 半信半疑の hańshinhangi no

increment [in'krəmənt] n (in salary) 定期昇給 teíkishōkyū

incriminate [inkrim'əneit] vt (LAW) …の罪を立証する …no tsúmi wo risshō suru

incubation [inkjəbei'ʃən] n (of eggs) ふ卵 furán; (of illness) 潜伏期間 seńpukukikān

incubator [in'kjəbeitər] n (for babies) 保育器 hoíkukî

incumbent [inkʌm'bənt] n (official: POL, REL) 現役 gén-eki

♦adj: **it is incumbent on him to …** …するのが彼の義務である …surú no ga kárè no gímu de árù

incur [inkər'] vt (expenses) …が掛る …ga kakárù; (loss) 受ける ukérù; (debt) こしらえる koshíraerù; (disapproval, anger) 被る kómurù

incurable [inkjur'əbəl] adj (disease) 不治の fújî no

incursion [inkər'ʒən] n (MIL: invasion) 侵入 shíńnyū

indebted [indet'id] adj: **to be indebted to someone** (grateful) …に感謝している …ni kańsha shité irû

indecent [indiː'sənt] adj (film, book) みだらな mídâra na

indecent assault (BRIT) n 強制わいせつ罪 kyōsei waisetsuzai

indecent exposure n 公然わいせつ罪 kōzen waisetsuzai

indecisive [indisai'siv] adj (person) 決断力のない ketsúdanryoku no naî

indeed [indiːd'] adv (certainly) 確かに tášhîka ni, 本当に hońtō ni; (in fact) 実は jitsú wà; (furthermore) なお nâō

yes indeed! 確かにそうだ! táshika ni sō
dà!

indefinite [indefˈənit] *adj* (answer, view)
不明確な fuméikaku na; (period, num-
ber) 不定の futéi no

indefinitely [indefˈənitliː] *adv* (continue,
wait) いつまでも itsú made mo

indelible [indelˈəbəl] *adj* (mark, stain,
ink) 消せない kesénai

indelible pen 油性フェルトペン yuséi
ferútopen

indemnity [indemˈnitiː] *n* (insurance) 賠
償保険 baíshōhokèn; (compensation) 賠
償 baíshō

independence [indipenˈdəns] *n* (of country, person, nation) 独立 dokúritsu; (of
thinking etc) 自主性 jishúsei

independent [indipenˈdənt] *adj* (country, business etc) 独立した dokúritsu shita; (person, thought) 自主的な jishúteki
na; (school) 私立の shíritsu no; (broadcasting company) 民間の mínkan no;
(inquiry) 独自の dokúji no

indestructible [indistrʌkˈtəbəl] *adj* 破壊
できない hakái dekinái

indeterminate [inditərˈmənit] *adj*
(number, nature) 不明の fuméi no

index [inˈdeks] (*pl* **indexes**) *n* (in book)
索引 sakúin, インデックス ifidekkùsu; (in
library etc) 蔵書目録 zōshomokùroku; (*pl*:
indices: ratio) 率 rítsù, 指数 shísū;
(: sign) 印 shírushi

index card *n* インデックスカード ifidek-
kusukádo

indexed [inˈdekst] (*BRIT* price-linked)
adj (income, payment) スライド制の suráidosei no

index finger *n* 人差指 hitósashiyùbi

India [inˈdiːə] *n* インド ífido

Indian [inˈdiːən] *adj n* インドの ífido no

Red Indian アメリカインディアンa-
mérika ifdian

Indian Ocean *n: the Indian Ocean* イ
ンド洋 ífidoyò

indicate [inˈdikeit] *vt* (show) 示す shimésù; (point to) 指す sásù; (mention) 示唆す
る shísa suru

indication [indikeiˈʃən] *n* (sign) しるし
shirúshi

indicative [indikˈətiv] *adj*: *indicative
of* ...のしるしである ...no shirúshi de aru
♦ *n* (LING) 直説法 chokúsetsuhō

indicator [inˈdikeitər] *n* (marker, signal) しるし shirúshi; (AUT) 方向指示器
hōkōshijīki, ウインカー uífikā

indices [inˈdisiːz] *npl of* **index**

indictment [indaitˈmənt] *n* (denunciation) 避難 hínan; (charge) 起訴 kisó

indifference [indifˈrəns] *n* (lack of
interest) 無関心 mukánshin

indifferent [indifˈrənt] *adj* (uninter-
ested: attitude) 無関心な mukánshin na;
(mediocre: quality) 平凡な heíbon na

indigenous [indidʒˈənəs] *adj* (wildlife) 固
有の koyū no

the indigenous population 原住民 geñ-
jūmin

indigestion [indidʒesˈtʃən] *n* 消化不良
shōkafuryō

indignant [indigˈnənt] *adj*: *to be indignant at something/with someone*
(angry) ...に怒っている ...ni okótte irù

indignation [indigneiˈʃən] *n* (outrage,
resentment) 立腹 rippúku

indignity [indigˈnitiː] *n* (humiliation) 侮
辱 bujóku

indigo [inˈdigou] *n* (color) あい色 aíiro

indirect [indirektˈ] *adj* (way, route) 遠回
しの tōmawáshi no; (answer, effect) 間
接的な kañsetsuteki na

indirectly [indirektˈliː] *adv* (responsible)
間接的に kañsetsuteki ni

indiscreet [indiskriːtˈ] *adj* (person,
behavior, comment) 軽率な kesótsu na

indiscriminate [indiskrimˈənit] *adj*
(bombing) 無差別の musábetsu no;
(taste) はっきりしない hakkírì shinái

indispensable [indispenˈsəbəl] *adj* (tool,
worker) 掛替えのない kakégae no naì

indisposed [indispouzdˈ] *adj* (unwell) 体
調の悪い taíchō no warúi

indisputable [indispjuːˈtəbəl] *adj* (undeniable) 否めない iṅámenai

indistinct [indistinktˈ] *adj* (image, memory) ぼんやりした boñ-yarì shita; (noise)
かすかな kásùka na

individual [ìndəvídʒ'u:əl] n (person: different from all others) 個人 kójìn, (: with adj) 人 hitó, 人物 jinbutsu
♦adj (personal) 個人の kojínkòjin no; (single) それぞれの sorézòre no; (particular: characteristic) 独特な dokútoku na

individualist [ìndəvídʒ'u:əlist] n 個人主義者 kojínshugìshà

individually [ìndəvídʒ'u:əli:] adv (singly: persons) 一人一人で hitóri hitórì de; (: things) 一つ一つで hitótsuhitotsù de

indivisible [ìndəvíz'əbəl] adj (matter, power) 分割できない bufkátsu dekínài

indoctrinate [ìndɑːk'trəneit] vt ...に ...を教え込む ...ni ...wo oshíekomù, 洗脳する séfnō suru

indoctrination [ìndɑːktrəneí'ʃən] n 教え込む事 oshíekomù kotó, 洗脳 séfnō

indolent [ín'dələnt] adj (lazy) 怠惰な táìda na

Indonesia [ìndəní:'ʒə] n インドネシア ìndoneshìa

indoor [ín'dɔːr] adj 屋内の okúnai no

indoors [ìndɔːrz'] adv (inside) 屋内で okúnai de

induce [ìndus'] vt (bring about) 引起こす hikíokosù; (persuade) 説得する settóku suru; (MED: birth) 誘発する yúhatsu suru

inducement [ìndus'mənt] n (incentive) 動機 dôki, 刺激 shigéki; (pej: bribe) 賄ろ wáìro

indulge [ìndʌldʒ'] vt (desire, whim) 満たす mitásù; (person, child) 気ままにさせる kimáma ni saserù
♦vi: to indulge in (vice, hobby) ...にふける ...ni fukéru

indulgence [ìndʌl'dʒəns] n (pleasure) 楽しみ tanóshimì; (leniency) 寛大さ kafídaisa

indulgent [ìndʌl'dʒənt] adj (parent, smile) 甘やかす amáyakasù

industrial [ìndʌs'tri:əl] adj (of production) 生産の... seísan no..., 産業の sañgyō no, 工業の kôgyō no

industrial action (BRIT) n 争議行為 sôgikôì

industrial estate (BRIT) n = **indus-trial park**

industrialist [ìndʌs'tri:əlist] n 実業家 jitsúgyōka

industrialize [ìndʌs'tri:əlaiz] vt (country, society) 工業化する kôgyōka suru

industrial park (US) n 工業団地 kôgyōdañchi

industrious [ìndʌs'tri:əs] adj (student, worker) 勤勉な kifíben na

industry [ín'dəstri:] n (manufacturing) 産業 sañgyō, 工業 kôgyō; (oil industry, textile industry etc) ...業界 ...gyókai; (diligence) 勤勉さ kifíbensa

inebriated [ìnib'rieitid] adj (drunk) 酔っ払った yoppáratta

inedible [ìned'əbəl] adj (disgusting) 食べられない tabérarenài; (poisonous) 食用に適さない shokúyō ni tekísanai

ineffective [ìnifek'tiv] adj (policy, government) 効果のない kôka no naì

ineffectual [ìnifek'tʃuəl] adj = **ineffective**

inefficiency [ìnifiʃ'ənsi:] n 非能率 hínôritsu

inefficient [ìnifiʃ'ənt] adj (person, machine, system) 能率の悪い nôritsu no warúì

inept [ìnept'] adj (politician, management) 無能な munô na

inequality [ìnikwɑːl'iti:] n (of system) 不平等 fubyôdô; (of amount, share) 不等 futô

inert [ìnəːrt'] adj (immobile) 動かない ugókanaì; (gas) 不活性の fukássei no

inertia [ìnəːr'ʃə] n (apathy) 物臭 monôgusa; (PHYSICS) 慣性 kañsei

inescapable [ìnəskei'pəbəl] adj (conclusion, impression) 避けられない sakérarenaì

inevitable [ìnev'itəbəl] adj (outcome, result) 避けられない sakérarenaì, 必然的の hitsúzentekì na

inevitably [ìnev'itəbli:] adv 必然的に hitsúzentekì ni

inexcusable [ìnikskju:'zəbəl] adj (behavior, error) 許されない yurúsarenaì

inexhaustible [ìnigzɔːs'təbəl] adj (wealth, resources) 無尽蔵の mujínzō no

inexorable [inek'sɔːrəbəl] adj (progress, decline) 止め様のない toméyō no naī

inexpensive [inikspen'siv] adj (cheap) 安い yasúī

inexperience [inikspiːr'iːəns] n (of person) 不慣れ fúnàre

inexperienced [inikspiːr'iːənst] adj (swimmer, worker) 不慣れの fúnàre no

inexplicable [ineks'plikəbəl] adj (decision, mistake) 不可解な fukákāi na

inextricably [ineks'trikəbliː] adv (entangled, linked) 分けられない様な wakérarenāi hodo

infallible [infæl'əbəl] adj (person, guide) 間違いのない machígaī no naī

infamous [in'fəməs] adj (crime, murderer) 悪名高い akúmeidakaī

infamy [in'fəmiː] n (notoriety) 悪評 akúhyō

infancy [in'fənsiː] n (of person) 幼年時代 yónenjidài

infant [in'fənt] n (baby) 赤ちゃん ákàchan; (young child) 幼児 yójī

infantile [in'fəntail] adj (disease) 幼児の yójī no; (foolish) 幼稚な yóchī na

infantry [in'fəntriː] n (MIL) 歩兵隊 hohéitai

infant school (BRIT) n 幼稚園 yóchien

infatuated [infætʃ'ueitid] adj: **to be infatuated with** ...にのぼせている ...ni nobósete irū

infatuation [infætʃ:ueiʃən] n (passion) ...にのぼせる事 ...ni nobóseru koto

infect [infekt'] vt (person, animal) ...に感染させる ...ni kańsen saserū; (food) 汚染する osén suru

infection [infek'ʃən] n (MED: disease) 感染 kańsen; (contagion) 伝染 defisen

infectious [infek'ʃəs] adj (person, animal) 伝染病にかかった defísenbyō ni kakáttà; (disease) 伝染性の defísensei no; (fig: enthusiasm, laughter) 移りやすい utsúriyasuī

infer [infəːr'] vt (deduce) 推定する suru; (imply) ...の意味を言う ...no imī wo fukúmù

inference [in'fəːrəns] n (deduction) 推定 suítei; (implication) 含み fukúmi

inferior [infiːr'iːəːr] adj (in rank) 下級の kakýū no; (in quality, quantity) 劣った otótta

◆n (subordinate) 下の者 shitá no monô; (junior) 年下の者 toshíshita no monô

inferiority [infiːr'iːɔːr'itiː] n (in rank) 下級 kakýū de arù kotô; (in quality) 品質の悪さ hifíshitsu no wárūsa

inferiority complex n (PSYCH) 劣等感 rettókan

infernal [infəːr'nəl] adj (racket, temper) ひどい hídoi

inferno [infəːr'nou] n (blaze) 大火事 ōkajī

infertile [infəːr'təl] adj (soil) 不毛の fumó no; (person, animal) 不妊の fumín no

infertility [infəːrtil'ətiː] n (of soil) 不毛 fumó; (of person, animal) 不妊症 funínshō

infested [infes'tid] adj: **infested with** (vermin, pests) ...がうじゃうじゃいる ...ga djàuja irū

infidelity [infidel'itiː] n (unfaithfulness) 浮気 uwáki

in-fighting [in'faitiŋ] n 内紛 naífun, 内ゲバ uchígeba

infiltrate [infil'treit] vt ...に潜入する ...ni seńnyū suru

infinite [in'fənit] adj (very great: variety, patience) ばく大な bakúdai na; (without limits: universe) 無限の mugén no

infinitive [infin'ətiv] n (LING) 不定詞 futéishi

infinity [infin'ətiː] n (infinite number) 無限大 mugéndai; (infinite point) 無限 mugén

infirm [infəːrm'] adj (weak) 虚弱な kyojáku na; (ill) 病弱な byójaku na

infirmary [infəːr'məriː] n (hospital) 病院 byóin

infirmity [infəːr'mitiː] n (weakness) 虚弱さ kyojákusa; (being ill) 病弱さ byójakusa; (specific illness) 病気 byóki

inflamed [infleimd'] adj (tongue, appendix) 炎症を起した efishō no okóshitā

inflammable [inflæm'əbəl] adj (fabric, chemical) 可燃性の kanénsei no, 燃えや

すい moéyasù

inflammation [infləmei´ʃən] *n* (of throat, appendix etc) 炎症 eńshō

inflatable [inflei´təbəl] *adj* (life jacket, dinghy, doll) 膨らますことのできる fukúramasu kotŏ no dekírù

inflate [infleit´] *vt* (tire, balloon) 膨らます fukúramasù; (price) つり上げる tsuríagerù

inflation [inflei´ʃən] *n* (ECON) インフレ íñfure

inflationary [inflei´ʃəne:ri:] *adj* (spiral) インフレを引起こす iñfure no; (demand) インフレを助長こす iñfure wo hikíokosù

inflexible [inflek´səbəl] *adj* (rule, timetable) 融通の利かない yūzū ga kikánai; (person) 譲らない yuzúranai

inflict [inflikt´] *vt*: **to inflict something on someone** (damage, suffering) ...に...を加える ...ni ...wo kuwáerù

influence [in´flu:əns] *n* (power) 実力 jitsúryoku; (effect) 影響 eíkyō
◊*vt* (person, situation, choice etc) 左右する sáyū suru
under the influence of alcohol 酒に酔って saké ni yottè

influential [influen´tʃəl] *adj* (politician, critic) 有力な yūryoku na

influenza [influen´zə] *n* (MED) 流感 ryúkan

influx [in´flʌks] *n* (of refugees, funds) 流入 ryúnyū

inform [infɔːrm´] *vt*: **to inform someone of something** (tell) ...に...を知らせる ...ni ...wo shiráserù
◊*vi*: **to inform on someone** (to police, authorities) ...を密告する ...wo mikkóku suru

informal [infɔːr´məl] *adj* (manner, discussion, party) 気楽な kutsúroidà; (clothes) 普段の fúdàn no; (unofficial visit, meeting) 非公式の hikóshiki no

informality [infɔːrmæl´iti:] *n* (of manner, party etc) 寛いだ雰囲気 kutsúroida fuñ-iki

informant [infɔːr´mənt] *n* (source) 情報提供者 jōhóteikyōsha, インフォーマント iñfōmañto

information [infərmei´ʃən] *n* 情報 jōhō
a piece of information 1つの情報 hitótsù no jōhō

information office *n* 案内所 añnaijo

informative [infɔːr´mətiv] *adj* (report, comment) 有益な yūekì na

informer [infɔːr´mər] *n* (*also:* **police informer**) 密告者 mikkókushà, スパイ supái

infra-red [in´frared] *adj* (rays, light) 赤外線の sekígaisen no

infrastructure [in´frəstrʌk´tʃər] *n* (of system etc) 下部構造 kabúkōzō, インフラストラクチャー iñfurasutorakúchā

infrequent [infri´kwint] *adj* (visits) 間遠な mádō na; (buses) 本数の少ない hoñsū nò sukúnai

infringe [infrindʒ´] *vt* (law) 破る yabúrù
◊*vi*: **to infringe on** (rights) ...を侵す ...wo okásù

infringement [infrindʒ´mənt] *n* (of law) 違反 ihán; (of rights) 侵害 shiñgai

infuriating [infjur´ieitiŋ] *adj* (habit, noise) いらいらさせる frāira saséru

ingenious [indʒin´jəs] *adj* (idea, solution) 巧妙な kōmyō na

ingenuity [indʒənu:´iti:] *n* (cleverness, skill) 才能 saínō

ingenuous [indʒen´ju:əs] *adj* (innocent, trusting) 無邪気な mújàki na

ingot [iŋ´gət] *n* (of gold, platinum) 延べ棒 nobébō, インゴット iñgótto

ingrained [ingreind´] *adj* (habit, belief) 根深い nebúkaī

ingratiate [ingrei´ʃi:eit] *vt*: **to ingratiate oneself with** ...に取入る ...ni torīrù

ingratitude [ingræt´ətu:d] *n* (of beneficiary, heir) 恩知らず oñshírazu

ingredient [ingri´di:ənt] *n* (of cake) 材料 zaíryō; (of situation) 要素 yōso

inhabit [inhæb´it] *vt* (town, country) ...に住む ...ni súmù

inhabitant [inhæb´ətənt] *n* (of town, street, house, country) 住民 júmin

inhale [inheil´] *vt* (breathe in: smoke, gas etc) 吸込む sukômù
◊*vi* (breathe in) 息を吸う íkì wo suu; (when smoking) 煙を吸込む kemúri wo

suíkomù

inherent [inhɛ:r'ent] *adj*: **inherent in** ...に固有の ...ni koyú no

inherit [inhɛr'it] *vt* (property, money) 相続する sôzoku suru; (characteristic) 遺伝で受継ぐ idén de ukétsugù

inheritance [inhɛr'itəns] *n* (property, money etc) 相続財産 sôzoku zaìsan; (characteristics etc) 遺伝 idén

inhibit [inhib'it] *vt* (growth: *also* PSYCH) 抑制 yokúsei

inhibited [inhib'itid] *adj* (PSYCH) 抑制の多い yokúsei no ôi

inhibition [inibíʃ'ən] *n* 抑制 yokúsei

inhospitable [inhɑ:spit'əbəl] *adj* (person) もてなしの悪い moténashi no waruì; (place, climate) 住みにくい sumínikuì

inhuman [inhju:'mən] *adj* (behavior) 残忍な zanínin na; (appearance) 非人間的な hinîngenteki na

inimitable [inim'itəbəl] *adj* (tone, style) まねのできない manê no dekinâi

iniquity [inik'witi:] *n* (wickedness) 悪名 akû; (injustice) 不正 fuséi

initial [iniʃ'əl] *adj* (stage, reaction) 最初の saísho no

♦*n* (letter) 頭文字 kashírafmojī

♦*vt* (document) ...に頭文字で署名する ...ni kashírafmojī de shomêi surû

initials [iniʃ'əlz] *npl* (of name) 頭文字 kashírafmojī; (as signature) 頭文字の署名 kashírafmojī no shomêi

initially [iniʃ'əli:] *adv* (at first) 最初は saísho wa; (first) まず最初に mázù saísho ni

initiate [iniʃ'i:it] *vt* (begin: talks, process) 始める hajimérù; (new member) 入会させる nyúkai saserù

to initiate someone into a secret ...に秘密を教える ...ni himîtsu wò oshíerù

to initiate proceedings against someone (LAW) ...を起訴する ...wo kisô suru

initiation [iniʃi:ei'ʃən] *n* (beginning) 開始 kaíshi; (into organization etc) 入会式 nyúkaishiki; (into secret etc) 伝授 dénju

initiative [iniʃ'i:ətiv] *n* (move) 企画 kikáku; (enterprise) 進取の気 shínshu no kî

to take the initiative 先手を打つ señte no utsu

wò útsù

inject [indʒekt'] *vt* (drugs, poison) 注射する chûsha suru; (patient): **to inject someone with something** ...に...を注射する ...wo chûsha suru; (funds) つぎ込む tsugíkomù

injection [indʒek'ʃən] *n* (of drugs, medicine) 注射 chûsha; (of funds) つぎ込む事 tsugíkomù kotó

injunction [indʒʌŋk'ʃən] *n* (LAW) 差止め命令 sashítomemeirei

injure [in'dʒər] *vt* (hurt: person, leg etc) 傷付ける kizútsukerù; (: feelings, reputation) 害する gaf surû

injured [in'dʒəːrd] *adj* (person, arm) 傷付いた kizútsuità; (feelings) 害された gaí saretà; (tone) 感情を害された kizú wò gaf sareta

injury [in'dʒəːri:] *n* (wound) 傷 kizú, けが kegá

injury time *n* (SPORT) 延長時間 eńchòjikàn ◇傷の手当てなどに使った分の延長時間 kizú no teâte nádò ni tsukátta buñ no eńchòjikàn

injustice [indʒʌs'tis] *n* (unfairness) 不公平 fukôhei

ink [iŋk] *n* (in pen, printing) インク íñku

inkling [iŋk'liŋ] *n* (idea, clue) 薄々と気付く事 usûusu tò kizûku kotó

inlaid [in'leid] *adj* (with gems, wood etc) ...をちばめた ...wo chiríbametà

inland [in'lænd] *adj* (port, sea, waterway) 内陸の naríku no

♦*adv* (travel) 内陸へ naríku e

Inland Revenue (BRIT) *n* 国税庁 kokúzeichò

in-laws [in'lɔːz] *npl* 義理の親せき girí nò shiñseki, 姻せき iñseki

inlet [in'let] *n* (GEO) 入江 iríe

inmate [in'meit] *n* (in prison) 受刑者 jukéisha; (in asylum) 入院患者 nyúinkañja

inn [in] *n* 旅館 ryokán

innate [ineit'] *adj* (skill, quality, characteristic) 生来の seírai no

inner [in'əːr] *adj* (office, courtyard) 内側の uchígawa no; (calm, feelings) 内心の naíshin no

inner city *n* インナーシティー iñnāshī-

ti ◇スラム化した都心部を指す súramu-
ka shita toshíñbu wo sásu

inner tube *n* (of tire) チューブ chûbu

inning [in'iŋ] *n* (BASEBALL) イニング
iníngu

innings [in'iŋz] *n* (CRICKET) イニング
iníngu

innocence [in'əsəns] *n* (LAW) 無罪 múzài; (naivety: of child, person) 純真さ juñ-
shinsa

innocent [in'əsənt] *adj* (not guilty: of crime etc) 無罪の múzài no, 潔白な keppáku na; (naive: child, person) 純真な juñ-
shíñ na; (not involved: victim) 罪のない
tsúmi no nái; (remark, question) 無邪気な
mújàki na

innocuous [inɑk'juəs] *adj* (harmless) 無
害の múgài no

innovation [inəvei'ʃən] *n* (change) 刷新
sasshíñ

innuendo [injuen'dou] *(pl* **innuendoes***)*
n (insinuation) 当てこすり atékosuri

innumerable [inu:'mərəbəl] *adj* (countless) 無数の musû no

inoculation [inɑkjəlei'ʃən] *n* (MED) 接
種 sesshú

inopportune [inɑːpərtu:n'] *adj* (event,
moment) 都合の悪い tsugô no wàrùi

inordinately [inɔːr'dənitli] *adv* (proud,
long, large etc) 極度に kyokúdò ni

in-patient [in'peiʃənt] *n* (in hospital) 入
院患者 nyûíñkanja

input [in'put] *n* (information) 情報 jôhô;
(resources etc) つぎ込む事 tsugíkomù
kotó; (COMPUT) 入力 nyúryoku, インプ
ット íñputtó

inquest [in'kwest] *n* (on someone's death) 検死誾問 keñshishíñmon

inquire [inkwaiər'] *vi* (ask) 尋ねる tazúnerù, 聞く事 kiku

♦*vt* (ask) ...に尋ねる ...ni tazúnerù, ...に
聞く ...ni kíkù

to inquire about (person, fact) ...につい
て問い合せする ...ni tsúite tofawase surú

inquire into *vt fus* (death, circumstances) 調べる shiráberù

inquiry [inkwaiə'ri:] *n* (question) 質問
shitsúmon; (investigation) 調査 chôsa

inquiry office (*BRIT*) *n* 案内所 afinaijo

inquisitive [inkwiz'ətiv] *adj* (curious) 詮
索好きな señsakuzuki na

inroads [in'roudz] *npl*: *to make inroads into* (savings, supplies) ...を消費
する ...wo shôhi suru

ins *abbr* = **inches**

insane [insein'] *adj* (foolish, crazy) 気遠
い染みた kichígaijimità; (MED) 狂気の
kyôki no

insanity [insæn'iti:] *n* (foolishness) 狂気
さた kyôki no satá; (MED) 狂気 kyôki

insatiable [insei'ʃəbəl] *adj* (greed, appetite) 飽く事のない akú kotò no nái

inscription [inskrip'ʃən] *n* (on gravestone, memorial etc) 碑文 hibún, (in
book) 献辞の言葉 keñtei no kotóba

inscrutable [inskru:'təbəl] *adj* (comment, expression) 不可解な fukákài na

insect [in'sekt] *n* 虫 mushi, 昆虫 koñchū

insecticide [insek'tisaid] *n* 殺虫剤 sat-
chúzài

insecure [insikjur'] *adj* (structure, lock,
door: weak) 弱い yówài; (: unsafe) 安全
でない añzen de nái; (person) 自信のない
jishíñ no nái

insecurity [insikjur'iti:] *n* (of structure,
lock etc: weakness) 弱さ yówàsa; (: lack
of safety) 安全でない añzen de nái
kotó; (of person) 自信欠如 jishíñketsujò

insemination [inseminei'ʃən] *n*: *artificial insemination* (AGR, MED) 人工授
精 jiñkôjùsei

insensible [insen'səbəl] *adj* (unconscious) 意識を失った íshìki wo ushínattà

insensitive [insen'sətiv] *adj* (uncaring,
indifferent) 思いやりのない omóiyarì no
nái

inseparable [insep'ərəbəl] *adj* (ideas,
elements) 分離できない buñri dekínài;
(friends) いつも一緒の ítsùmo isshó no

insert [insərt'] *vt* (between two things)
...の間に入れる ...no áìda ni irérù; (into
something) 差込む sashíkomù, 挿入する
sônyû suru

insertion [insər'ʃən] *n* (of needle, comment, peg etc) 差込む事 sashíkomù kotó,
挿入 sônyû

in-service [in'sɜːrvis] *adj* (training, course) 現職の geñshoku no

inshore [in'ʃɔːr] *adj* (fishing, waters) 近海の kíñkai no

◆*adv* (be) 岸の近くに kishí no chikákù ni; (move) 岸の近くへ kishí no chikákù e

inside [in'said'] *n* (interior) 内 nákà, 内側 uchigawa

◆*adj* (interior) 中(の)内(側)nákà (uchigawa) no

◆*adv* (go) 中(内側)へ nákà(uchigawa) e; (be) 中(内側)に nákà(uchigawa) ni

◆*prep* (of location) ...の中へ(に) ...no nákà e(ni); (of time): **inside 10 minutes** 10分以内に juppún inai ni

inside forward *n* (SPORT) インサイドフォワード íñsaidofowādo

inside information *n* 内部情報 naíbujōhò

inside lane *n* (AUT) 内側車線 uchígawashaseñ

inside out *adv* (be, turn) 裏返しに urágaeshi de; (know) すっかり sukkárì

insides [in'saidz] *npl* (*inf*: stomach) おなか onáka

insidious [insid'iːəs] *adj* (effect, power) 潜行的な señkōteki na

insight [in'sait] *n* (into situation, problem) 洞察 dōsatsu

insignia [insig'niːə] *npl* 記章 kishō

insignificant [insignif'ikənt] *adj* (extent, importance) ささいな sasái na

insincere [insinsiːr'] *adj* (smile, welcome) 偽りの itsúwarì no

insinuate [insin'jueit] *vt* (imply) 当てこする atékosurù

insipid [insip'id] *adj* (person, activity, color) 面白くない omóshirokunaì; (food, drink) 風味のない fûmi no naî

insist [insist'] *vi* (maintain) 主張する shuchō suru, 言い張る iíharù

to insist on (demand) …を要求する ...wo yōkyū suru

to insist that (demand) …する様要求する ...suru yō yōkyū suru; (claim) …だと言い張る ...da to iíharù

insistence [insis'təns] *n* (determination) 強要 kyōyō

insistent [insis'tənt] *adj* (determined: person) しつこい shitsúkoi; (continual: noise, action) 絶間ない taémanaī

insole [in'soul] *n* (of shoe) 敷皮 shikíkawa

insolence [in'sələns] *n* (rudeness) 横柄さ ōheisa

insolent [in'sələnt] *adj* (attitude, remark) 横柄な ōhei na

insoluble [insɑːl'jəbəl] *adj* (problem) 解決のできない kaíketsu nò dekínaī

insolvent [insɑːl'vənt] *adj* (bankrupt) 破産した hasáñ shita

insomnia [insɑːm'niːə] *n* 不眠症 fumíñshō

inspect [inspekt'] *vt* (examine: gen) 調べる shiráberù; (premises) 捜査する sōsa suru; (equipment) 点検する teñken suru; (troops) 査閲する saétsu suru; (BRIT: ticket) 改札する kaísatsu suru

inspection [inspek'ʃən] *n* (examination: gen) 検査 keñsa; (of premises) 捜査 sōsa; (of equipment) 点検 teñken; (of troops) 査閲 saétsu; (BRIT: of ticket) 改札 kaísatsu

inspector [inspek'tɜːr] *n* (ADMIN) 検査官 keñsakañ; (BRIT: on buses, trains) 車掌 shashō; (: POLICE) 警部 keibu

inspiration [inspəreiʃ'ən] *n* (encouragement) 発憤 happúñ; (influence source) 発憤させる happúñ saserū mono; (idea) 霊感 reíkan, インスピレーション íñspirēshòn

inspire [inspaiɜːr'] *vt* (workers, troops) 奮い立たせる furúitataserù; (confidence, hope etc) 持たせる motáserù

instability [instəbil'iːti] *n* (of place, person, situation) 不安定 fuáñtei

install [instɔːl'] *vt* (machine) 取付ける torítsukerù; (official) 就任させる shúnin saserū

installation [instəleiʃ'ən] *n* (of machine, equipment) 取付け torítsuke, 設置 sétchi; (plant: INDUSTRY) 工場施設 kōjōshisètsu, プラント puráñto; (: MIL) 基地 kichí

installment [instɔːl'mənt] (*BRIT* **instalment**) *n* (of payment, story, TV

serial etc) 1回分 ikkáibun
in installments (pay, receive) 分割払い
で bufikatsubarái de
instance [in'stəns] *n* (example) 例 réi
for instance 例えば tatóëba
in the first instance まず最初に mázu
safsho ni
instant [in'stənt] *n* (moment) 瞬間 shufi-
kan
♦*adj* (reaction, success) 瞬間的な shufi-
kanteki na; (coffee, food) 即席の sokúseki no, インスタントの fisutanto no
instantaneous [instəni:əs] *adj*
(immediate) 即時の sokúji no
instantly [in'stəntli:] *adv* (immediately)
即時に sokúji ni
instead [insted'] *adv* (in place of) (そ
の) 代りに (soñó) kawári ni
instead of ...の代りに ...no kawári ni
instep [in'step] *n* (of foot) 足の甲 ashí no
kō; (of shoe) 靴の甲 kutsū no kō
instigate [in'stəgeit] *vt* (rebellion etc) 起
させる okósaserù; (talks etc) 始めさせる
hajímesaserù
instil(l) [instil'] *vt*: *to instil something
into* (confidence, fear etc) ...を...に吹込
む ...wo ...ni fukíkomerù
instinct [in'stiŋkt] *n* 本能 hofinō
instinctive [instiŋk'tiv] *adj* (reaction,
feeling) 本能的な hofinōteki na
institute [in'stitu:t] *n* (for research,
teaching) 施設 shisétsu; (professional
body: of architects, planners etc) 協会
kyōkai
♦*vt* (system, rule, course of action) 設け
る mōkérù; (proceedings, inquiry) 始める
hajímerù
institution [institu:'ʃən] *n* (of system
etc) 開設 kaísetsu; (custom, tradition) 伝
統 deñtō; (organization: financial, religious, educational) 協会 kyōkai; (hospital, mental home) 施設 shisétsu
instruct [instrʌkt'] *vt*: *to instruct
someone in something* (teach) ...に...を
教える ...ni ...wo oshíerù
to instruct someone to do something
(order) ...する様に...に命令する ...surú yō
...ni mefrei suru

instruction [instrʌk'ʃən] *n* (teaching) 教
育 kyōiku
instructions [instrʌk'ʃənz] *npl* (orders)
命令 mefrei
instructions (for use) 取扱い説明 torí-
atsukai setsúmei
instructive [instrʌk'tiv] *adj* (lesson,
response) 有益な yū́eki na
instructor [instrʌk'tər] *n* (teacher) 先
生 sefisei; (for skiing, driving etc) 指導者
shidōsha
instrument [in'strəmənt] *n* (tool) 道具
dōgu; (measuring device etc) 計器 keíki;
(MUS) 楽器 gakki
instrumental [instrəmen'təl] *adj* (MUS)
器楽の kígaku no
to be instrumental in ...に大きな役割
を果す ...ni ōkina yakúwari wo hatasú
instrument panel *n* 計器盤 keíkiban
insubordination [insəbɔːrdənei'ʃən] *n*
(disobedience) 不服従 fufúkujū
insufferable [insʌf'ɜːrəbəl] *adj* (arrogance, laziness) 耐えがたい taégatal;
(person) 我慢のならない gámàn no nará-
nai
insufficient [insəfiʃ'ənt] *adj* (funds,
data, research) 不十分な fujūbùn na
insular [in'sələr] *adj* (outlook, person)
狭量な kyōryō na
insulate [in'səleit] *vt* (protect: person,
group) 孤立させる korítsu saserù;
(against cold: house, body) 断熱する dañnetsu suru; (against sound) 防音する bṓ-
òn suru; (against electricity) 絶縁する
zetsúen suru
insulating tape [in'səleitiŋ-] *n* (ELEC)
絶縁テープ zetsúeñteipu
insulation [insəlei'ʃən] *n* (of person,
group) 孤立させる事 korítsu saserù ko-
tó; (against cold) 断熱 dañnetsu; (against
electricity) 絶縁 zetsúenzai
insulin [in'səlin] *n* (MED) インシュリン iñ-
shurin
insult [*n* in'sʌlt *vb* insʌlt'] *n* (offence) 侮
辱 bujōku
♦*vt* (offend) 侮辱する bujōku suru
insulting [insʌl'tiŋ] *adj* (attitude, lan-

guage) 侮辱的な bujókútékí na

insuperable [insuˈpɔːrəbəl] *adj* (obstacle, problem) 乗越えられない norīkoearenaī

insurance [inˈʃuˈrəns] *n* (on property, car, life etc) 保険 hokén
fire/life insurance 火災〔生命〕保険 kasáī(seímeí)hokén

insurance agent *n* 保険代理店 hokéndairíten

insurance policy *n* 保険証書 hokénshósho

insure [inʃuːr] *vt* (life, property): *to insure (against)* ...に（...の）保険を掛ける ...ni (...no) hokén wò kakérù
to insure (oneself) against (disappointment, disaster) ...に備える ...ni sonáerù

insurrection [insərekˈʃən] *n* (uprising) 反乱, hañrañ

intact [inˈtækt] *adj* (whole) 元のままの mótō no mamá no; (unharmed) 無傷の múkīzu no

intake [inˈteik] *n* (gen) 取込み torīkomí; (of food etc) 摂取 sésshû; (of air) 吸入 kyúnyû; (BRIT: SCOL): *an intake of 200 a year* 毎年の新入生は200人, maítoshi nò shīńnyúseí wa nihyákuníñ

intangible [intænˈdʒəbəl] *adj* (quality, idea, benefit) ばく然とした bakúzen to shita

integral [inˈtəgrəl] *adj* (feature, element) 不可欠な fukákëtsu na

integrate [inˈtəgreit] *vt* (newcomer) 溶け込ませる tokékomaserù; (ideas, systems) 取入れる torīirerù
♦*vi* (groups, individuals) 溶け込む tokékomù

integrity [integˈriti:] *n* (morality: of person) 誠実さ seíjítsusa

intellect [inˈtəlekt] *n* (intelligence) 知性 chísei; (cleverness) 知恵 chié

intellectual [intəˈktʃuəl] *adj* (activity, interest, pursuit) 知的な chítékí na
♦*n* (intelligent person) 知識人 chíshíkíjìn, インテリ íntéri

intelligence [intelˈidʒəns] *n* (cleverness, thinking power) 知能 chínō; (MIL etc) 情

報 jóhō

intelligence service *n* 情報部 jóhōbu

intelligent [intelˈidʒənt] *adj* (person) 知能の高い chínō no takáī; (decision) 利口な rikó na; (machine) インテリジェントの íntéríjéñto no

intelligentsia [inteːlidʒénsiːə] *n* 知識階級 chíshíkíkaíkyû, インテリ階級 íntéríkaíkyû

intelligible [intelˈidʒəbəl] *adj* (clear, comprehensible) 分かりやすい wakáriyasuī

intend [inˈtend] *vt* (gift etc): *to intend something for* ...に上げようと思っている ...wo ...ni ageyō to omótte irú
to intend to do something (mean) ...する決心でいる ...suru kesshíñ de irú; (plan) ...するつもりである ...suru tsumórì de arú

intended [inˈtendid] *adj* (effect, insult) 意図した ítō shita; (journey) 計画した kefkaku shita; (victim) ねらった nerátta

intense [inˈtens] *adj* (heat, effort, anger, joy) 猛烈な mōretsu na; (person) 情熱の jónetsuteki na

intensely [inˈtensliː] *adv* (extremely) 激しく hagéshiků

intensify [inˈtensafai] *vt* (efforts, pressure) 増す másù

intensity [inˈtensiti:] *n* (of heat, anger, effort) 激しさ hagéshisa

intensive [inˈtensiv] *adj* (concentrated) 集中的な shúchûteki na

intensive care unit *n* (MED) 集中治療室 shúchûchiryôshitsu, ICU aíshíyû

intent [inˈtent] *n* (intention) 意図 ítō; (LAW) 犯意 háń-ì
♦*adj* (absorbed): *intent (on)* (...しようとして) 余念がない (...shíyô to shite) yonéñ ga naí; (attentive) 夢中な muchû na
to all intents and purposes 事実上 jíjítsujô
to be intent on doing something (determined) ...しようとして余念がない ...shíyô to shite yonéñ ga naí

intention [inˈtenˈtʃən] *n* (purpose) 目的 mokúteki; (plan) 意図 ítō

intentional [inten'tʃənəl] *adj* (deliberate) 意図的な ítóteki na

intentionally [inten'tʃənəli:] *adv* (deliberately) 意図的に ítóteki ni, わざと wáza to

intently [intent'li:] *adv* (listen, watch) 熱心に nesshín ni

inter [intə:r'] *vt* (bury) 埋葬する maísó suru

interact [intərækt'] *vi*: **to interact (with)** (people, things, ideas) (...と)相互に反応し合う (...)sōgo ni hafnó shiaú

interaction [intəræk'ʃən] *n* 相互反応 sōgohańnó

intercede [intərsi:d'] *vi*: **to intercede (with)** (...に) 取りなしをする (...ni) torínashi wo surú

intercept [in'tə:rsept'] *vt* (person, car) 途中で捕まえるtochū de tsukamaerú; (message) 傍受する bṓju suru

interchange [in'tə:rtʃeindʒ] *n* (exchange) 交換 kṓkan; (on motorway) インターチェンジ íntáchieñji

interchangeable [intə:rtʃein'dʒəbəl] *adj* (terms, ideas, things) 置換えられる okíkaerarerú

intercom [in'tə:rkɑm] *n* (in office etc) インターホーン íntáhon

intercourse [in'tə:rkɔ:rs] *n* (*also*: **sexual intercourse**) 性交 sefkó

interest [in'trist] *n* (in subject, idea, person etc) 興味 kyṓmi; (pastime, hobby) 趣味 shúmi; (advantage, profit) 利益 ríeki; (COMM: in company) 株 kábu; (: sum of money) 利息 rísoku
♦*vt* (subj: work, subject, idea etc) ...の興味をそそる ...no kyṓmi wo sosórú
to be interested in ...に興味がある ...ni kyṓmi ga árú

interesting [in'tristiŋ] *adj* (idea, place, person) 面白い omóshiroi

interest rate *n* 利率 ríritsu

interface [in'tə:rfeis] *n* (COMPUT) インターフェース íntáfēsu

interfere [intərfi:r'] *vi*: **to interfere in** (quarrel, other people's business) ...に干渉する ...ni kańshó suru
to interfere with (object) ...をいじる

...wo ijfrú; (plans, career, duty, decision) ...を邪魔する ...wo jamá suru

interference [intərfi:r'əns] *n* (in someone's affairs etc) 干渉 kańshó; (RADIO, TV) 混信 kofishin

interim [in'tə:rim] *adj* (agreement, government) 暫定的な zańteiteki na
♦*n*: **in the interim** (meanwhile) その間 sonó aídá

interior [inti:'ri:ə:r] *n* (of building, car, box etc) 内部 náfbu; (of country) 内陸 naírfku
♦*adj* (door, window, room etc) 内部の náfbu no; (minister, department) 内務の náfmu no

interior designer *n* インテリアデザイナー íntériadezaínā

interjection [intərdʒek'ʃən] *n* (interruption) 野次 yáji; (LING) 感嘆詞 kańtańshi

interlock [in'tə:rlɑk] *vi* かみ合う kamfaú

interloper [intərlou'pə:r] *n* (in town, meeting etc) ちん入者 chífnyūsha

interlude [in'tə:rlu:d] *n* (break) 小休止 kyūkei; (THEATER) 休憩時間 kyūkeijíkan

intermarry [intə:rmær'i:] *vi* 交婚する kṓkon suru

intermediary [intərmi:'di:eri:] *n* 仲介者 chūkaisha

intermediate [intərmi:'di:it] *adj* (stage, student) 中間の chūkan no

interminable [intə:r'mənəbəl] *adj* (process, delay) 果てし無い hatéshinai

intermission [intərmiʃ'ən] *n* (pause) 休止 kyūshi; (THEATER, CINEMA) 休憩時間 kyūkeijikan

intermittent [intərmit'ənt] *adj* (noise, publication etc) 断続的な dańzokuteki na

intern [in'tə:rn] *vt* (imprison) 拘置する kṓchi suru
♦*n* (*US*: houseman) 研修医 keńshūi

internal [intə:r'nəl] *adj* (layout, structure, memo etc) 内部の náfbu no; (pipes etc) 埋め込みの umékomi no; (bleeding, injury) 体内の táinai no; (security, politics) 国内の kokúnai no

internally [intəːrˈnəli] *adv*: 「*not to be taken internally*」内服外用薬 naífukugaíyōyaku

Internal Revenue Service (*US*) *n* 国税庁 kokúzeíchō

international [intəːrnǽʃanəl] *adj* (trade, agreement etc) 国際的な kokúsaiteki na, 国際... kokúsai...
◆*n* (*BRIT*: SPORT: match) 国際試合 kokúsaijíaì

interplay [inˈtəːrpleì] *n: interplay (of/between)* (...の) 相互反応 (...no) sốgohañnō

interpret [inˈtəːrprit] *vt* (explain, understand) 解釈する kaíshaku suru; (translate) 通訳する tsúyaku suru
◆*vi* (translate) 通訳する tsúyaku suru

interpretation [intəːrpritéiʃən] *n* (explanation) 解釈 kaíshaku; (translation) 通訳 tsúyaku

interpreter [inˈtəːrpritəːr] *n* (translator) 通訳 (者) tsúyaku(sha)

interrelated [intəːrilˈeitid] *adj* (causes, factors etc) 相互関係のある sốgokankeí no aru

interrogate [inˈterɑgeit] *vt* (question: witness, prisoner, suspect) 尋問する jiñmon suru

interrogation [interɑgeiˈʃən] *n* (of witness, prisoner etc) 尋問 jiñmon

interrogative [intərɑgˈətiv] *adj* (LING) 疑問の gímòn no

interrupt [intərˈʌptʼ] *vt* (speaker) ...の話に割り込む ...no hanáshi nì waríkomù; (activity) 邪魔する jamá suru
◆*vi* (during someone's conversation etc) 話に割り込む hanáshi ni waríkomù; (during activity) 邪魔する jamá suru

interruption [intərˈʌpʃən] *n* (act) 邪魔する事 jamá suru kotò; (instance) 邪魔 jamá

intersect [intəːrsékt] *vi* (roads) 交差する kốsa suru

intersection [intəːrsékʃən] *n* (of roads) 交差点 kốsaten

intersperse [intəːrspəːrs] *vt: to intersperse with* ...を所々に入れる ...wo tokórodokòro ni irérù

intertwine [intəːrtwaín] *vi* 絡み合う karámiaù

interval [inˈtəːrval] *n* (break, pause) 間隔 kañkaku; (*BRIT*: SCOL: *also* THEATER, SPORT) 休憩時間 kyūkeijíkan
at intervals (periodically) 時々 tokídoki

intervene [intəːrviːn] *vi* (person: in situation: interfere) 介入する kaínyū suru; (: : to help) 仲裁に入る chúsai ni haírù; (: in speech) 割込む waríkomù; (event) 間に起る aída ni okorù; (time) 経つ tátsù

intervention [intəːrvénʃən] *n* (interposn: interference) 介入 kaínyū; (help) 仲裁 chúsai

interview [inˈtəːrvjuː] *n* (for job etc) 面接 meñsetsu; (RADIO, TV etc) インタビュー íñtabyuū
◆*vt* (for job etc) ...と面接する ...to meñsetsu suru; (RADIO, TV etc) ...にインタビューする ...ni íñtabyū suru

interviewer [inˈtəːrvjuːəːr] *n* (of candidate, job applicant) 面接者 meñsetsushà; (RADIO, TV etc) インタビューア íñtabyūa

intestine [intésˈtin] *n* 腸 chố

intimacy [inˈtəməsi] *n* (closeness) 親しみ shitáshimi

intimate [*adj* inˈtəmit *vb* inˈtəmeit] *adj* (friendship, relationship) 親しい shitáshii; (detail) 知られざる shirárezarù; (restaurant, dinner, atmosphere) こじんまりした kojínmarì shita; (knowledge) 詳しい kuwáshiì
◆*vt* (announce) ほのめかす honómekasù

intimidate [intimˈideit] *vt* (frighten) 脅す odósu

intimidation [intimideiˈʃən] *n* 脅し odóshi

KEYWORD

into [inˈtuː] *prep* **1** (indicating motion or direction) ...の中に(へ) ...no nákà ni(e)
come into the house/garden 家に入って来て下さい ié(niwá)nì háìtte kité kudasaí
go into town 町に出掛ける machí ni dekakerù

he got into the car 彼は車に乗った
kárě wa kurúma ni nottá

throw it into the fire 火の中へ捨てて下さい hí no nakǎ e sutéte kudasaí

research into cancer がんの研究 gán no keñkyǔ

he worked late into the night 彼は夜遅くまで働いた kárě wa yórǔ osóku madě hataráreta

the car bumped into the wall 車は塀にぶつかった kurúma wǎ hef ni butsúkattá

she poured tea into the cup 彼女は紅茶をカップについだ kánǒjo wa kócha wǒ káppǔ ni tsuídá

2 (indicating change of condition, result; *she burst into tears* 彼女は涙を出した kánǒjo wa kyǔ ní nakídashita

he was shocked into silence 彼はショックで物も言えなかった kárě wa shókkǔ de monó mǒ iénakattá

it broke into pieces ばらばらに割れた barábara ni warétá

she translated into French 彼女はフランス語に訳した kánǒjo wa furánsugo ní yakúshita

they got into trouble 彼らは問題を起した kárěra wa mońdai wǒ okóshita

intolerable [intɒˈlərəbl] *adj* (extent, quality) 我慢できない gámǎn dekínai

intolerance [intɒˈlərɑnt] *n* (bigotry, prejudice) 偏狭さ heñkyǒsa

intolerant [intɒˈlərɑnt] *adj*: **intolerant (of)** (...に対して) 偏狭な (...ni táishite) heñkyǒ na

intonation [intouˈneiʃən] *n* (of voice, speech) 抑揚 yokǔyǒ, イントネーション íftoněshon

intoxicated [intɒˈkˈsikeitid] *adj* (drunk) 酔っ払った yoppáratta

intoxication [intɒˈksikeiˈʃən] *n* 泥酔 deísui

intractable [inˈtræktəbl] *adj* (child, problem) 手に負えない tě ni oénai

intransigent [inˈtrænˈsidʒənt] *adj* (attitude) 頑固な gañko na

intransitive [inˈtrænˈsətiv] *adj* (LING): **intransitive verb** 自動詞 jidǒshi

intravenous [intrəˈviːnəs] *adj* (injection, drip) 静脈内の jǒmyakunai no

in-tray [inˈtrei] *n* (in office) 着信のトレー chakúshin nǒ torě

intrepid [inˈtrepˈid] *adj* (adventurer, explorer) 勇敢な yǔkan na

intricate [inˈtrikit] *adj* (pattern, design) 複雑な fukúzatsu na

intrigue [intriːg] *n* (plotting) 策略 sakúryaku
◆*vt* (fascinate) ...の好奇心をそそる ...no kǒkishin wǒ sosórǔ

intriguing [intriːgin] *adj* (fascinating) 面白い omóshiroi

intrinsic [intrˈinˈsik] *adj* (quality, nature) 本質的な hoñshitsuteki na

introduce [intrəˈdjuːs] *vt* (new idea, measure etc) 導入する dǒnyǔ suru; (speaker, TV show etc) 紹介する shǒkai suru
to introduce someone (to someone) (...に) ...を紹介する (...ni) ...wo shǒkai suru
to introduce someone to (pastime, technique) ...に...を初めて経験させる ...ni ...wo hajímete keñken saserú

introduction [intrəˈdʌkˈʃən] *n* (of new idea, measure etc) 導入 dǒnyǔ; (of person) 紹介 shǒkai; (to new experience) 初めて経験させる事 hajímete keñken saserú kotǒ; (to book) 前書 maégaki

introductory [intrəˈdʌkˈtəːri] *adj* (lesson) 導入の dǒnyǔ no; (offer) 初回の shǒkai no

introspective [intrəspekˈtiv] *adj* (person, mood) 内省的な naíseiteki na

introvert [inˈtrəvəːrt] *n* 内向性の人 naíkǒsei no hitǒ
◆*adj* (also: **introverted**: behavior, child etc) 内向性の naíkǒsei no

intrude [intruːd] *vi* (person) 邪魔する jamá suru
to intrude on (conversation, grief, party etc) ...のところを邪魔する ...no tokǒro wǒ jamá suru

intruder [intruːˈdəːr] *n* (into home, camp) 侵入者 shiñnyǔsha

intrusion [intruːˈʒən] *n* (of person, outside influences) 邪魔 jamá

intuition [intjuːˈɪʃən] *n* (feeling, hunch) 直感 chokkan

intuitive [intuːˈətiv] *adj* (instinctive) 直感的な chokkánteki na

inundate [ˈɪnʌndeit] *vt* (with calls, letters etc): **to inundate with** (calls, letters etc) ...が殺到する ...ga sattō suru

invade [inveid'] *vt* (MIL) ...を侵略する ...wo shińryaku suru

invalid [*n* inˈvalid *adj* invæˈlid] *n* (MED: disabled person) 身障者 shińshōsha; (: sick and weak person) 病弱な人 byōjaku na hitò

♦*adj* (not valid) 無効の mukó no

invaluable [invælˈjuːəbəl] *adj* (person, thing) 貴重な kichō na

invariable [invɛˈriːəbəl] *adj* 変らない kawáranaì, 不変の fuhén no

invariably [invɛˈriːəbliː] *adv* 必ず kanárazů

invasion [inveiˈʒən] *n* (MIL) 侵略 shińryaku

invent [invent'] *vt* (machine, game, phrase etc) 発明する hatsúmei suru; (fabricate: lie, excuse) でっち上げる detchágerů

invention [invenˈʃən] *n* (machine, system) 発明品 hatsúmeihin; (untrue story) 作り話 tsukúribanashi; (act of inventing: machine, system) 発明 hatsúmei

inventor [inventˈəːr] *n* (of machines, systems) 発明家 hatsúmeika

inventory [inˈvəntɔːriː] *n* (of house, ship etc) 物品目録 buppíumokuroku

inverse [invəˈrs] *adj* (relationship) 逆の gyakú no

invert [inˈvəːrt] *vt* (turn upside down) 逆さにする sakása ni surů

invertebrate [invəˈrtəbrit] *n* 無せきつい動物 musékitsuidōbutsu

inverted commas [invəˈrtid-] (BRIT) *npl* 引用符 ińyōfù

invest [invest'] *vt* (money) 投資する tōshi suru; (fig: time, energy) つぎ込む tsugíkomù

♦*vi*: **invest in** (COMM) ...に投資する

...ni tōshi suru; (fig: something useful) 購入する kōnyū suru

investigate [invesˈtəgeit] *vt* (accident, crime, person) 取調べる toríshiraberù, 捜査する sōsa suru

investigation [invesˈtəgeiʃən] *n* 取調べ toríshirabe, 捜査 sōsa

investigator [invesˈtəgeitəːr] *n* (of events, situations, people) 捜査官 sōsakàn

investiture [invesˈtitʃəːr] *n* (of chancellor) 就任式 shūninshiki; (of prince) たい冠式 taíkanshiki

investment [investˈmənt] *n* (activity) 投資 tōshi; (amount of money) 投資額 tōshigàku

investor [invesˈtəːr] *n* (COMM) 投資者 tōshishà

inveterate [invetˈəːrit] *adj* (liar, cheat etc) 常習的な jōshūteki na

invidious [invidˈiːəs] *adj* (task, job: unpleasant) 憎まれ役の nikúmareyàku no; (comparison, decision: unfair) 不公平な fukōhei na

invigilator [invidʒˈəleitəːr] (BRIT) *n* (in exam) 試験監督 shikénkañtoku

invigorating [invigˈəːreitiŋ] *adj* (air, breeze etc) さわやかな sawáyàka na; (experience etc) 元気が出る様な geńki ga derù yṓ na

invincible [invinˈsəbəl] *adj* (army, team: unbeatable) 無敵の mútěki no

invisible [invizˈəbəl] *adj* 目に見えない mé ni mienài

invitation [invitei'ʃən] *n* (to party, meal, meeting etc) 招待 shōtai; (written card, paper) 招待状 shōtaijō

invite [invait'] *vt* (to party, meal, meeting etc) 招く manékù, 招待する shōtai suru; (encourage: discussion, criticism) 求める motómerù

to invite someone to do ...に...するよう求める ...ni ...surú yō motómerù

inviting [invai'tiŋ] *adj* (attractive, desirable) 魅力的な miryókuteki na

invoice [inˈvɔis] *n* (COMM) 請求書 sefkyūsho

♦*vt* ...に請求書を送る ...ni sefkyūsho wo

okúrù

invoke [invouk'] vt (law, principle) ...に
訴える ...ni uttáerù

involuntary [invɑːl'əntɛːri:] adj (action,
reflex etc) 反射的な hańshateki na

involve [invɑːlv'] vt (person, thing:
include, use) 伴う tomónaù, 必要とする
hitsuyō to surú; (: concern, affect) ...に関
係する ...ni kańkei surù

to involve someone (in something)
(...に) ...を巻込む (...ni) ...wo makíkomù

involved [invɑːlvd'] adj (complicated) 複
雑な fukúzatsu na

to be involved in (take part: in activity
etc) ...にかかわる ...ni kakáwarù; (be engrossed) ...に夢中になっている ...ni muchū ni nattë irú

involvement [invɑːlv'mənt] n (participation) 参加 sańka; (concern, enthusiasm) depth的かかわり合い kańjōteki na
kakáwariaĭ

inward [in'wərd] adj (thought, feeling)
内心の naíshin no; (movement) 中の方へ
の nákā no hố e

inward(s) [in'wərd(z)] adv (move, face)
中の方へ nákā no hố e

I/O [ai'ou'] abbr (COMPUT: = input/
output) 入出力 nyúshutsuryòku

iodine [ai'ədain] n (chemical element) ヨ
ウ素 yōso, ヨード yōdo; (disinfectant) ヨ
ードチンキ yōdochíñki

ion [ai'ən] n イオン ion

iota [aiou'tə] n: *not one/an iota* 少しも
...ない sukóshi̇́ mo ...naí

IOU [aiouju:'] n abbr (= I owe you) 借用
証 shakúyóshō

IQ [aikju:'] n abbr (= intelligence quotient) 知能指数 chinōshisū, IQ aikyū

IRA [aiɑːrei'] n abbr (= Irish Republican Army) アイルランド共和国軍 áiru-
rando kyōwakokúgun

Iran [iræn'] n イラン iráň

Iranian [irei'ni:ən] adj イランの iráň no
♦n イラン人 iráňjin

Iraq [iræk'] n イラク iráku

Iraqi [iræk'i:] adj イラクの iráku no
♦n イラク人 iráyjin

irascible [iræs'əbəl] adj 怒りっぽい okó-

rippoì

irate [aireit'] adj 怒っている okótte irú

Ireland [ai'ərlənd] n アイルランド áiru-
rándo

iris [ai'ris] (pl **irises**) n (ANAT) こう彩
kōsai; (BOT) アヤメ ayáme, アイリス áĭ-
risu

Irish [ai'riʃ] adj アイルランドの afrurán-
do no
♦npl: *the Irish* アイルランド人 áirurán-
dojîn ◇総称 sōshō

Irishman/woman [ai'riʃmən/wumən]
(pl **Irishmen/women**) n アイルランド人
男性〔女性〕afrurandojîn dańsei〔joséi〕

Irish Sea n: *the Irish Sea* アイリッシ
ュ海 afrisshúkài

irksome [ərk'səm] adj いらいらさせる i-
ráha saséru

iron [ai'ərn] n (metal) 鉄 tetsú; (for
clothes) アイロン afron
♦cpd (bar, railings) 鉄の tetsú no; (will,
discipline etc) 鉄の様な tetsú no yō na
♦vt (clothes) ...にアイロンを掛ける ...ni
afron wò kakérù

Iron Curtain n: *the Iron Curtain* 鉄
のカーテン tetsú no kâten

ironic(al) [airɑːn'ik(əl)] adj (remark,
gesture, situation) 皮肉な hínîku na

ironing [ai'ərniŋ] n (activity) アイロン
掛け afronkake; (clothes) アイロンを掛
ける べき衣類 afron wò kakérubki irûi

ironing board n アイロン台 afrondai

ironmonger [ai'ərnmʌŋgəːr] (BRIT) n
金物屋 kanámonoya ◇人を指す hitó wò
sásù

ironmonger's (shop)
[ai'ərnmʌŋgəːrz-] n 金 物 屋 kanámonoya ◇店を指す misé wò sásù

iron out vt (fig: problems) 打開する da-
kái suru

irony [ai'rəni:] n 皮肉 hínîku

irrational [iræʃ'ənəl] adj (feelings,
behavior) 不合理な fugóri na

irreconcilable [irek'ənsailəbəl] adj
(ideas, views) 両立しない ryōritsu shiná-
ĭ; (disagreement) 調和不可能な chōwafu-
kanō na

irrefutable [irifju:'təbəl] adj (fact) 否め

られない inámerarenaǐ; (argument) 反ばくできない hanbaku dekínaǐ

irregular [iregʲɔləʳ] adj (surface) 凸凹の dekóɪ̀̀oko no; (pattern, action, event etc) 不規則な fukísoku na; (not acceptable: behavior) 良くない yókunaǐ; (verb, noun, adjective) 不規則変化の fukísokuheñka no

irregularity [iregʲə'læriti] n (of surface) 凸凹 dekóboko; (of pattern, action etc) 不規則 fukísoku; (instance of behavior) 良くない行為 yókunai kôi

irrelevant [irél'əvənt] adj (fact, information) 関係のない kañkei no naǐ

irreparable [irép'əːrəbəl] adj (harm, damage etc) 取返しの付かない toríkaeshi no tsukánaǐ

irreplaceable [iripleɪ'səbəl] adj 掛替えのない kakégae no naǐ

irrepressible [iripres'əbəl] adj 陽気な yôki na

irresistible [irizis'təbəl] adj (force) 抵抗できない teḱkô dekínaǐ; (urge, desire) 抑えきれない osáekirenaǐ; (person, thing) とても魅惑的な totémo miwákuteki na

irresolute [irez'əluːt] adj 決断力のない ketsúdanryòku no naǐ

irrespective [irispek'tiv]: **irrespective of** prep ...と関係なく ...to kañkei nakú

irresponsible [irispɑn'səbəl] adj (person, action) 無責任な musékinin na

irreverent [irev'əːrənt] adj 不敬な fukéi na

irrevocable [irev'əkəbəl] adj (action, decision) 変更できない heñkô dekínaǐ

irrigate [ir'igeit] vt (AGR) かんがいする kañgai suru

irrigation [irigei'ʃən] n (AGR) かんがい kañgai

irritable [ir'itəbəl] adj 怒りっぽい okórippoǐ

irritate [ir'əteit] vt (annoy) いらいらさせる fráira saséru; (MED) 刺激する shígeki suru

irritating [ir'əteitiŋ] adj (person, sound etc) いらいらさせる fráira saséru

irritation [iritei'ʃən] n (feeling of annoyance) いら立ち irádachi; (MED) 刺激 shi-

géki; (annoying thing) いら立ちの元 irádachi no motô

IRS [aiɑːres'] (US) n abbr = **Internal Revenue Service**

is [iz] vb see **be**

Islam [iz'lɑm] n イスラム教 isúramukyô

Islamic [izlɑm'ic] adj イスラム教の isúramukyô no

island [ai'lənd] n (GEO) 島 shimá

islander [ai'ləndəːr] n 島の住民 shimá no jûmin

isle [ail] n (GEO) 島 shimá

isn't [iz'ənt] = **is not**

isolate [ai'səleit] vt (physically, socially: set apart) 孤立させる koŕitsu saseru; (substance) 分離する buńri suru; (sick person, animal) 隔離する kakúri suru

isolated [ai'səleitid] adj (place) へんぴな heñpi na; (person) 孤立した koŕitsu shita; (incident) 単独の tañdoku no

isolation [aisəlei'ʃən] n 孤立 koŕitsu

isotope [ai'sətoup] n (PHYSICS) 同位体 dôitai, アイソトープ aísotôpu

Israel [iz'reiəl] n イスラエル isúraèru

Israeli [izreɪ'liː] adj イスラエルの isúraèru no

♦n イスラエル人 isúraeruʲin

issue [iʃ'uː] n (problem, subject, most important part) 問題 mońdai; (of newspaper, magazine etc) 号 gô; (of book) 発行 hakkô; (of stamp) 発行部数 hakkôbùsû

♦vt (statement) 発表する happyô suru; (rations, equipment, documents) 配給する kañkyû suru

at issue 問題は(の) mońdai wa(no)
to take issue with someone (over) (...について) ...と争う(..ni tsúite) ...to arásoû

isthmus [is'məs] n (GEO) 半島 hañtô

KEYWORD

it [it] pron **1** (specific: subject) それは [が] soré wa(ga); (: direct object) それを soré wo; (: indirect object) それに soré nǐ 通常日本語では表現しない tsújô nihongo de wa hyôgen shínái

where's my book? - **it's on the table** 私の本は どこ?・テーブルにあります

watákushi no hóñ wa dókō desu ká - téburu ni arímasu

I can't find it 見当りません miátari-maseñ

give it to me それを私に渡して下さい soré wò watákushi nì watáshite kudasaí

about/from/in/of/to it について〔から, の中に, の, の方へ〕soré ni tsuíte〔kára, no nákà ni, nó, no hō è〕

I spoke to him about it その件について私は彼に話しました watákushi wà kárè ni hanáshimashìta

what did you learn from it? それからあなたは何を学びましたか sonó kotò kara anátà wa nánì wo manábimashìta ká

what role did you play in it? その件に関してこあなたはどんな投割をしましたか sonó keñ ni káñ shite anátà wa dońna yakúwari wo shimáshìta ká

I'm proud of it それを誇りに思っています soré wò hokóri nì omótte imasù

did you go to it? (party, concert etc) 行きましたか ikímashìta ká

2 (impersonal): **it's raining** 雨が降っている áme ga fútté irù

it's cold today 今日は寒い kyō wà samúi

it's Friday tomorrow 明日は金曜日です asú wà kiñ-yóbi desu

it's 6 o'clock/the 10th of August 6時〔8月10日〕です rokúji〔hachígàtsu tōkà〕desu

how far is it? - it's 10 miles/2 hours on the train そこまでどのくらいありますか-10マイルの〔列車で2時間で〕sokó madè donó gurai arimasù ká - jūmàru arimasù〔ressha de ní jìkan desu〕

who is it? - it's me どなたですか-私です dónàta desu ká - watákushi desù

Italian [ɪˈtæljən] adj イタリアの itária no; (LING) イタリア語の itáriago no
♦n (person) イタリア人 itáriajin; (LING) イタリア語 itáriago

italics [ɪˈtælɪks] npl (TYP) 斜体文字 shatáimòji, イタリック体 itárikkutai

Italy [ɪˈtəli] n イタリア itária

itch [ɪtʃ] n (irritation) かゆみ kayúmi
♦vi (person) かゆがる kayúgarù; (part of body) かゆい kayúi
to itch to do something ...をしたくてむずむずしている ...wo shítakutè múzumuzu shité irù

itchy [ɪtʃiː] adj (person) かゆがっている kayúgatte irù; (skin etc) かゆい kayúi

it'd [ɪtəd] = **it would; it had**

item [aɪˈtəm] n (one thing: of list, collection) 品目 hiñmoku; (on agenda) 項目 kómoku; (also: **news item**) 記事 kíjì

itemize [aɪˈtəmaiz] vt (list) 明細に書く mefsai ni kakù, リストアップする risútoappù surù

itinerant [aitinˈərənt] adj (laborer, salesman, preacher etc) 巡回する juñkai surù

itinerary [aitinˈərɛːriː] n 旅程 ryotéi

it'll [ɪtəl] = **it will; it shall**

its [ɪts] adj その〔あれの〕sonó〔aré〕no

it's [ɪts] = **it is; it has**

itself [ɪtsˈelf] pron それ〔あれ〕自身 soré〔aré〕jishiñ

ITV [aitʃviː] n abbr (BRIT: = Independent Television) 民間テレビ放送 miñkan terebi hōsō

IUD [aijuːdiː] n abbr (= intra-uterine device) 子宮内避妊具 shikyúnaihìniñgu, IUD aiyúdi

I've [aiv] = **I have**

ivory [aiˈvəri] n (substance) 象げ zóge; (color) アイボリー áibori

ivory tower n (fig) 象げの塔 zóge no tō

ivy [aiˈviː] n (BOT) キヅタ kízuta, アイビー áibi

J

jab [dʒæb] vt (poke: with elbow, stick) 突く tsukú
♦n (inf: injection) 注射 chúsha
to jab something into something ...を...に突っ込む ...wo...ni tsukkómù

jabber [dʒæbˈəːr] vi (also: **jabber away**) ぺちゃくぺちゃしゃべる péchàkucha shabérù

jack [dʒæk] *n* (AUT) ジャッキ jákkì; (CARDS) ジャック jákkù

jackal [dʒæk'əl] *n* ジャッカル jákkàru

jackdaw [dʒæk'dɔː] *n* コクマルガラス kokúmarugarāsu

jacket [dʒæk'it] *n* (garment) ジャケット jákètto; (of book) ジャケット jákètto, カバー kâbaā

potatoes in their jackets 皮ごと料理したジャガイモ kawágòto ryóri shita jagáimo

jack-knife [dʒæk'naif] *vi* (trailer truck) ジャックナイフ現象を起す jakkúnaifu genshō wo okósù ◊ (sharply) 鋭角に折り曲って動けなくなる efkaku ni orímagatte ugokenāku nárù

jack plug *n* (ELEC: for headphones etc) プラグ purágù

jackpot [dʒæk'pɑːt] *n* 大賞金 daíshōkin

to hit the jackpot 大賞金を当てる daíshōkin wo atérù, 大当りする óatàri suru

jack up *vt* (AUT) ジャッキで持上げる jákkì de mochíageru

jade [dʒeid] *n* (stone) ひすい hisúi

jaded [dʒei'did] *adj* (tired) 疲れ切った tsukárekittà; (fed-up) うんざりした uñzarìshita

jagged [dʒæg'id] *adj* (outline, edge) ぎざぎざの gízàgìza no

jail [dʒeil] *n* 刑務所 keímushò

◊ *vt* 刑務所に入れる keímushò ni irérù

jam [dʒæm] *n* (food) ジャム jámù; (also: **traffic jam**) 交通渋滞 kōtsūjūtai; (*inf*: difficulty) ピンチ píñchi

to be in a jam 困っている komátte irù

◊ *vt* (passage etc) ふさぐ fuságù; (mechanism, drawer etc) 動けなくする ugokenāku suru; (RADIO) 妨害する bōgai suru

◊ *vi* (mechanism, drawer etc) 動けなくなる ugokenāku nárù

to jam something into something (cram, stuff) ...に...を押込む ...ni...wo oshíkomù

Jamaica [dʒəmei'kə] *n* ジャマイカ jámàika

jangle [dʒæŋ'gəl] *vi* (keys, bracelets etc) じゃらじゃら鳴る járàjara nárù

janitor [dʒæn'itəːr] *n* (caretaker: of building) 管理人 kañrinin

January [dʒæn'juːweːriː] *n* 1月 ichígatsu

Japan [dʒəpæn'] *n* 日本 nihóñ(nippóñ)

Japanese [dʒæpəniːz'] *adj* 日本の nihóñ (nippóñ) no; (LING) 日本語の nihóñgo no

◊ *n inv* (person) 日本人 nihóñ(nippóñ)jìn; (LING) 日本語 nihóñgo

jar [dʒɑːr] *n* (container: glass with wide mouth) 瓶 bíñ; (: stone, earthenware) つぼ tsubó, かめ kamé

◊ *vi* (sound) 耳ざわりである mimízawàri de aru, きしむ kishírù; (colors) 釣合わない tsuríawanài

jargon [dʒɑːr'gən] *n* 専門用語 señmon-yōgo, 隠語 íñgo

jasmine [dʒæz'min] *n* ジャスミン jásùmin

jaundice [dʒɔːn'dis] *n* (MED) 黄だん ódan

jaundiced [dʒɔːn'dist] *adj* *to view with a jaundiced eye* 白い目で見る shiróì me de mírù

jaunt [dʒɔːnt] *n* (trip, excursion) 遠足 eñsoku

jaunty [dʒɔːn'tiː] *adj* (attitude, tone) 陽気な yóki na; (step) 軽やかな karóyàka na

javelin [dʒæv'lin] *n* (SPORT) やり投げ yarínage

jaw [dʒɔː] *n* (ANAT) あご agó

jay [dʒei] *n* カケス kakésu

jaywalker [dʒei'wɔːkəːr] *n* ◊ 交通規則を無視して道路を横断する人 kōtsūkisòku wo mushí shite dòro wo ōdan surù hitó

jazz [dʒæz] *n* (MUS) ジャズ jázù

jazz up *vt* (liven up: party) 活気付ける kakkízukerù; (: taste) ぴりっとさせる píríttò saserù; (: image) 派手にする hadé ni surù

jazzy [dʒæz'iː] *adj* (shirt, pattern) 派手な hadé na

jealous [dʒel'əs] *adj* (suspicious: husband etc) 嫉妬深い shittóbukài; (envious: person) うらやましい uráyamashìi, うらやましがっている uráyamashìgatte irù; (look etc) うらやましそうな uráyamashisòna

jealousy [dʒel'əsiː] *n* (resentment) ねたみ

み netámi; (envy) うらやむ事 uráyamù kotð

jeans [dʒi:nz] *npl* (trousers) ジーパン jíːpaǹ

jeep [dʒi:p] *n* (AUT, MIL) ジープ jíːpu

jeer [dʒi:r] *vi* (mock, scoff): **to jeer (at)** 野次る yajírù

jelly [dʒel'i:] *n* (CULIN) ゼリー zérì

jellyfish [dʒel'i:fiʃ] *n* クラゲ kuráge

jeopardize [dʒep'ə:rdaiz] *vt* 危険にさらす kikén ni sarásù

jeopardy [dʒep'ə:rdi:] *n*: **to be in jeopardy** 危険にさらされる kikén ni sarásarerù

jerk [dʒə:rk] *n* (jolt, wrench) 急な動き kyū na ugóki; (*inf*: idiot) 間抜け manúke
♦*vt* (*pull*) ぐいと引っ張る gút to hípparù
♦*vi* (vehicle, person, muscle) 急に動く kyū ni ugókù

jerkin [dʒə:r'kin] *n* チョッキ chokkí

jersey [dʒə:r'zi:] *n* (pullover) セーター sḕtā; (fabric) ジャージー jâjī

jest [dʒest] *n* 冗談 jṓdaǹ

Jesus [dʒi:'zəs] *n* イエス íesù

jet [dʒet] *n* (of gas, liquid) 噴射 funsha, ジェット jéttò; (AVIAT) ジェット機 jéttoki

jet-black [dʒet'blæk'] *adj* 真っ黒な makkúrð na

jet engine *n* ジェットエンジン jétto eñjin

jet lag *n* 時差ぼけ jísàbòke

jettison [dʒet'əsən] *vt* (fuel, cargo) 捨てる sutérù

jetty [dʒet'i:] *n* 波止場 hatóba

Jew [dʒu:] *n* ユダヤ人 yudáyajìn

jewel [dʒu:'əl] *n* (*also fig*) 宝石 hṓsekì; (in watch) 石 ishí

jeweler [dʒu:'ələ:r] (*BRIT* **jeweller**) *n* (dealer in jewelery) 宝石商 hōsekishō; (dealer in watches) 時計屋 tokéiya

jeweler's (shop) *n* (*jewelery shop*) 宝石店 hōsekiteǹ; (watch shop) 時計店 tokéiteǹ

jewelry [dʒu:'əlri:] (*BRIT* **jewellery**) *n* 装身具 sōshíngu

Jewess [dʒu:'is] *n* ユダヤ人女性 yudáyajìn jòsei

Jewish [dʒu:'iʃ] *adj* ユダヤ人の yudáyajìn no

jibe [dʒaib] *n* 野次 yájì

jiffy [dʒif'i:] (*inf*) *n*: **in a jiffy** 直ぐ súgù

jig [dʒig] *n* (dance) ジグ jígu 活発なダンス ugóki nð hayáī kappátsu na dáňsu

jigsaw [dʒig'sɔː] *n* (*also*: **jigsaw puzzle**) ジグソーパズル jígùsō-pazuru

jilt [dʒilt] *vt* (lover etc) 振る furú

jingle [dʒiŋ'gəl] *n* (for advert) コマーシャルソング komāsharu soǹgu
♦*vi* (bells, bracelets) ちりんちりんと鳴る chíríñchirin to narú

jinx [dʒiŋks] *n* ジンクス jíñkusu

jitters [dʒit'ə:rz] (*inf*) *npl*: **to get the jitters** びびる bibírù

job [dʒɑb] *n* (chore, task) 仕事 shigóto; (post, employment) 職 shokú
it's not my job (duty, function) それは私の仕事ではない soré wa watákushi nð shigóto de wa naí
it's a good job that ... (*BRIT*) ...して良かったね ...shite yókàtta né
just the job! (*BRIT*: *inf*) おあつらえ向きだ o-átsurae muki da, 丁度いい chōdo íi

job centre (*BRIT*) *n* 公共職業安定所 kōkyōshokugyō anteishò

jobless [dʒɑb'lis] *adj* (ECON) 失業の shitsúgyō no

jockey [dʒɑk'i:] *n* (SPORT) 騎手 kíshù
♦*vi*: **to jockey for position** (rivals, competitors) 画策する kakúsaku suru

jocular [dʒɑk'jələ:r] *adj* (person, remark) ひょうきんな hyốkìn na

jog [dʒɑg] *vt* (bump) 小突く kozúkù
♦*vi* (run) ジョギングする jógìngu suru
to jog someone's memory ...に...を思い起させる ...ni...wo omói okosaserù

jog along *vi* (person, vehicle) のんびりと進む noñbirí to susúmù

jogging [dʒɑg'iŋ] *n* ジョギング jógìngu

join [dʒɔin] *vt* (queue) ...に加わる ...ni kuwáwarð; (party) ...に参加する ...ni sañka suru; (club etc) ...に入会する ...ni nyúkai suru; (put together: things, places) つなぐ tsunágù; (meet: group of people) 一緒

になる isshó ni narú

♦vi (roads, rivers) 合流する gőryū suru

♦n つなぎ目 tsunagíme

joiner [dʒɔiˈnəːr] n (BRIT) n 建具屋 tatéguya

joinery [dʒɔiˈnəːriː] n 建具職 tatégushóku

join in vi 参加する sańka suru

♦vt fus (work, discussion etc) ...に参加す る ...ni sańka surù

joint [dʒɔint] n (TECH: in woodwork, pipe) 継ぎ目 tsugíme; (ANAT) 関節 kańsetsu; (of meat) ブロック肉 búròkku niku; (inf: nightclub, pub, cheap restaurant etc) 店 misé; (: of cannabis) マリファナタバコ maríf̄ana tabakô

♦adj (common) 共通の kyőtsū no; (combined) 共同の kyődō no

joint account n (at bank etc) 共同預金 口座 kyődō yokin kōza

join up vi (meet) 一緒になる isshó ni na-rú; (MIL) 入隊する nyútai suru

joist [dʒɔist] n はり harí

joke [dʒouk] n (gag) 冗談 jődaǹ; (also: practical joke) いたずら itázura

♦vi 冗談を言う jődaǹ wo iű

to play a joke on ...をからかう ...wo karákaù

joker [dʒouˈkəːr] n (inf) 冗談を言う人 jődaǹ wo iu hitő; (pej: person) 野郎 yárō; (cards) ジョーカー jőkā

jolly [dʒɑˈliː] adj (merry) 陽気な yőki na; (enjoyable) 楽しい tanóshiì

♦adv (BRIT: inf) とても totémo

jolt [dʒoult] n (physical) 衝撃 shőgeki; (emotional) ショック shókkù

♦vt (physically) ...に衝撃を与える ...ni shőgeki wo ataérù; (emotionally) ショックを与える shókkù wo ataérù

Jordan [dʒɔːrˈdən] n ヨルダン yórùdaṅ

jostle [dʒɑsˈəl] vt: _to be jostled by the crowd_ 人込みにもまれる hitőgomi ni momárerù

jot [dʒɑt] n: _not one jot_ 少しも...ない sukóshĭ mo...náì

jot down vt (telephone number etc) 書 留める kakítomerù

jotter [dʒɑtˈəːr] n (BRIT) n (notebook,

pad) ノート (ブック) nőto(búkkù), メモ memóchō

journal [dʒəːrˈnəl] n (magazine, periodical) 雑誌 zasshí; (diary) 日記 nikkí

journalese [dʒəːrnəlíːz] n (pej) 大衆新聞 調 taíshūshinbunchō

journalism [dʒəːrˈnəlizəm] n ジャーナリ ズム jánarizùmu

journalist [dʒəːrˈnəlist] n ジャーナリスト jánarisùto

journey [dʒəːrˈniː] n (trip, route) 旅行 ryokő; (distance covered) 道のり michínori

jovial [dʒouˈviːəl] adj (person, air) 陽気な yőki na

joy [dʒɔi] n (happiness, pleasure) 喜び yorőkobi

joyful [dʒɔiˈfəl] adj (news, event) うれしい uréshiĭ; (look) うれしそうな uréshisō na

joyride [dʒɔiˈraid] n (AUT: US) 無銭運転のドライブ mubőnunten no dorái̇bu; (: BRIT) 盗難車でのドライブ tőnansha de no dorái̇bu

joystick [dʒɔiˈstik] n (AVIAT) 操縦かん sőjūkan; (COMPUT) 操縦レバー・sőjū re-bā, ジョイスティック jősutikku

JP [dʒeiˈpiː] n abbr = **Justice of the Peace**

Jr abbr = **junior**

jubilant [dʒuːˈbələnt] adj 大喜びの őyorokobi no

jubilee [dʒuːˈbəliː] n (anniversary) ...周年 記念日 ...shūnen kinénbi

judge [dʒʌdʒ] n (LAW) 裁判官 saíbankan; (in competition) 審査員 shíñsa-in; (fig: expert) 通 tsū

♦vt (LAW) 裁く sabákù; (competition) 審査する shíñsa suru; (person, book etc) 評価する hyőka suru; (consider, estimate) 推定する suítei suru

judg(e)ment [dʒʌdʒˈmənt] n (LAW) 判決 hańketsu; (REL) 審判 shíñpan; (view, opinion) 意見 iken; (discernment) 判断力 hańdaǹryoku

judicial [dʒuːdíʃˈəl] adj (LAW) 司法の shíhő no

judiciary [dʒuːdíʃˈiːeːriː] n 司法部 shíhőbù

judicious [dʒuːˈdɪʃəs] *adj* (action, decision) 分別のある funbetsu no áru

judo [ˈdʒuːdou] *n* 柔道 jūdō

jug [dʒʌg] *n* 水差し mizúsashi

juggernaut [ˈdʒʌgəʌːnɔːt] (*BRIT*) *n* (huge truck) 大型トラック ōgata torakkù

juggle [ˈdʒʌgəl] *vi* ジャグ玉を使う shinádama wo surù ◊幾つもの玉などを投げ上げて受止める曲芸 fkútsu mo no tamá nado wo nagéagetè ukétomerù kyokúgei

juggler [ˈdʒʌgləʀ] *n* ジャグ玉をする曲芸師 shinádama wo suru kyokúgeishi

Jugoslav [juːˈgouslɑːv] *etc* = **Yugoslav** *etc*

juice [dʒuːs] *n* (of fruit, plant, meat) 汁 shiru; (beverage) ジュース jūsu

juicy [ˈdʒuːsi] *adj* (food) 汁の多い shíru no ôi; (*inf*: story, details) エッチな étchi na

jukebox [ˈdʒuːkbɑːks] *n* ジュークボックス júkùbokkusu

July [dʒuˈlaɪ] *n* 7月 shichí gatsu

jumble [ˈdʒʌmbəl] *n* (muddle) ごたまぜ gotámaze
◆*vt* (*also*: **jumble up**) ごたまぜにする gotámaze ni suru

jumble sale (*BRIT*) *n* 慈善バザー jizén bazā

jumbo (**jet**) [ˈdʒʌmbou] *n* ジャンボジェット機 jánbo jettóki

jump [dʒʌmp] *vi* (into air) 飛び上る tobíagarù; (with fear, surprise) ぎくっとする gíkùtto suru; (increase: price etc) 急上昇する kyújōshó suru; (: population etc) 急増する kyúzō suru
◆*vt* (fence) 飛び越える tobíkoeru
◆*n* (into air etc) 飛び上る事 tobíagarù kotô; (increase: in price etc) 急上昇 kyújōshô; (: in population etc) 急増 kyúzō

to jump the queue (*BRIT*) 列に割込む retsú ni warfkomù

jumper [ˈdʒʌmpəʀ] *n* (*BRIT*: pullover) セーター sētà; (*US*: dress) ジャンパースカート jánpàsukāto

jumper cables *npl* (*US*) ブースターケーブル bùsutākēburu ◊外のバッテリーから

電気を得るために用いるコード hokà nò bátterî kara dénki wo érù tamé nì mochfírù kōdo

jump leads (*BRIT*) [-liːdz] *npl* = **jumper cables**

jumpy [ˈdʒʌmpi] *adj* (nervous) びくびくしている bíkùbiku shité frù

Jun. *abbr* = **junior**

junction [ˈdʒʌŋkʃən] *n* (*BRIT*: of roads) 交差点 kōsaten; (*RAIL*) 連絡駅 refiraku-eki

juncture [ˈdʒʌŋktʃəʀ] *n*: **at this juncture** この時 konó tokî

June [dʒuːn] *n* 6月 rokúgatsu

jungle [ˈdʒʌŋgəl] *n* ジャングル jánguru; (*fig*) 弱肉強食の世界 jakúniku kyóshoku nð sékâi

junior [ˈdʒuːnjəʀ] *adj* (younger) 年下の toshíshita no; (subordinate) 下位の kái no; (*SPORT*) ジュニアの jùnia no
◆*n* (office junior) 後輩 kōhai; (young person) 若者 wakámono

he's my junior by 2 years 彼は私より2才年下です kárè wa watákushi yorí nísaî toshíshita desu

junior school (*BRIT*) *n* 小学校 shōgakkô

junk [dʒʌŋk] *n* (rubbish, cheap goods) がらくた garákuta; (ship) ジャンク jánku

junk food *n* ジャンクフード jánku fūdo ◊ポテトチップス、ファーストフードなど高カロリーだが低栄養のスナック食品 potétochippùsu, fâsuto fùdo nadò kôkarorī da ga teíeiyō no sunákku shokûhin

junkie [ˈdʒʌŋki] *n* (*inf*) ペイ中 peíchū

junk shop *n* 古物商 kobútsushō

Junr. *abbr* = **junior**

jurisdiction [dʒuːrisdíkʃən] *n* (*LAW*) 司法権 shihôken; (*ADMIN*) 支配権 shihâiken

juror [ˈdʒuːrəʀ] *n* (person on jury) 陪審員 baíshin-in

jury [ˈdʒuːri] *n* (group of jurors) 陪審員 baíshin-in

just [dʒʌst] *adj* (fair: decision) 公正な kôsei na; (: punishment) 適切な tekísetsu na

♦*adv* (exactly) 丁度 chōdo; (only) ただ tádà; (barely) ようやく yóyakù

he's just done it ついさっきそれをやったばかりだ tsuí sakkí sore wo yatta bákàri da

he's just left ついさっき出た〔帰った〕ばかりだ tsuí sakkí détá 〔káèttá〕 bákàri da

just right 丁度いい chōdo iĩ

just two o'clock 丁度2時 chōdo nîji

she's just as clever as you 彼女はあなたに負けないぐらい頭がいい kánòjo wa anátà ni makénai gùrài atáma ga iĩ

just as well that ... ...して良かった ...shîte yókàtta

just as he was leaving 丁度出掛けるところに chōdo dekákerù tokóro ni

just before 丁度前に chōdo máè ni

just enough 辛うじて間に合って kárōjite ma nî aitte

just here ぴったりここに pittárì kokó ni

he just missed わずかの差で外れた wázùka no sá de hazúreta

just listen ちょっと聞いて chottó kiíte

justice [dʒʌs'tis] *n* (LAW: system) 司法 shihō; (rightness of cause, complaint) 正当さ seítōsa; (fairness) 公正さ kōseisa; (US: judge) 裁判官 saíbankan

to do justice to (fig: task) ...をやりこなす ...wo yaríkonasù; (: meal) ...を平らげる ...wo tafragerù; (: person) ...を正当に扱う ...wo seítō ni atsúkaù

Justice of the Peace *n* 治安判事 chíàn hañji

justifiable [dʒʌs'tifaiəbəl] *adj* (claim, statement etc) もっともな móttòmo na

justification [dʒʌstəfəkei'ʃən] *n* (reason) 正当とする理由 seítō to suru riyū

justify [dʒʌs'təfai] *vt* (action, decision) 正当である事を証明する seítō de arù kotó wo shōmei suru; (text) 行の長さをそろえる gyō no nágàsa wo soróerù

justly [dʒʌst'li:] *adv* (with reason) 正当に seítō ni; (deservedly) 当然 tōzen

jut [dʒʌt] *vi* (also: **jut out**: protrude) 突出し tsukíderù

juvenile [dʒu:'vənəl] *adj* (court) 未成年の

misélnen no; (books) 少年少女向きの shōnen shōjo mukí no; (humor, mentality) 子供っぽい kodómoppoì

♦*n* (LAW, ADMIN) 未成年者 miséineñsha

juxtapose [dʒʌkstəpouz'] *vt* (things, ideas) 並べておく narábete okù

K

K [kei] *abbr* (= *one thousand*) 1000 séñ = **kilobyte**

kaleidoscope [kəlai'dəskoup] *n* 万華鏡 mañgekyō

Kampuchea [kæmpu:tʃi:'ə] *n* カンプチア kâñpuchia

kangaroo [kæŋgəru:'] *n* カンガルー kañgarū

karate [kəra:'ti:] *n* 空手 karáte

kebab [kəba:b'] *n* くし刺しの焼肉 kushísashi no yakíniku, シシカバブ shishíkababu

keel [ki:l] *n* 竜骨 ryūkotsu

on an even keel (fig) 安定して añtei shite

keen [ki:n] *adj* (eager) やりたがっている yarítagattè irú; (intense: interest, desire) 熱心な nesshíñ na; (acute: eye, intelligence) 鋭い surúdoì; (fierce: competition) 激しい hagéshiĩ; (sharp: edge) 鋭い surúdoì

to be keen to do/on doing something (eager, anxious) ...をやりたがっている ...wo yarítagattè irú

to be keen on something/someone ...に熱を上げている ...ni netsú wò agéte irú

keep [ki:p] (*pt, pp* **kept**) *vt* (retain: receipt etc) 保管する hokán suru; (: money etc) 自分の物にする jíbuñ no monó ni surú; (: job etc) なくさない様にする nakúsanai yō ni suru, 守る mamórù; (: preserve, store) 貯蔵する chozō suru; (maintain: house, garden etc) 管理する kâñri suru; (detain) 引留める hikítomerù; (run: shop etc) 経営する keíei suru; (chickens, bees etc) 飼育する shíiku suru; (accounts, diary etc) ...を付ける ...wo tsukerú; (support: family etc) 養う yashínaú; (fulfill: promise) 守る mamórù; (prevent): **to keep someone from doing something** ...が...をするのに阻止する ...ga ...wo dekínai yō ni soshí surú

♦*vi* (remain: in a certain state) ...ている (ある) ...de irú (árù); (: in a certain place) ずっと...にいる zuttó ...ni irú; (last: food) 保存がきく hozón ga kíkù

♦*n* (cost of food etc) 生活費 sefkatsuhí; (of castle) 本丸 hofmaru

to keep doing something ...をし続ける ...wo shitsúzukerú

to keep someone happy ...の期限をとる ...no kígen wo torú

to keep a place tidy ある場所をきちんとさせておく árù bashó wo kíchín to sasete okú

to keep something to oneself ...について黙っている ...ni tsúìte dámatte irú

to keep something (back) from someone ...の事を...に隠す ...no kotó wo ...ni kakúsù

to keep time (clock) 時間を正確に計る jíkàn wo seíkaku ni hakárù

for keeps (*inf*) 永久に eíkyù ni

keeper [ki:'pər] *n* (in zoo, park) 飼育係 shí-íkugakàri, キーパー kípā

keep-fit [ki:p'fit'] *n* (*BRIT*) 健康体操 kefkōtaìsō

keeping [ki:'piŋ] *n* (care) 保管 hokán

in keeping with ...に合って ...ni áttè, ...に従って ...ni shitagatte

keep on *vi* (continue) ...しつづける ...shitsúzukerú

to keep on (about something) (...を話題に) うるさくしゃべる (...wo wadái ni) urúsakū shabérù

keep out *vt* (intruder etc) 締出す shimédasù

「*keep out*」立入禁止 tachíiri kinshi

keepsake [ki:p'seik] *n* 形見 katámi

keep up *vt* (maintain: payments etc) 続ける tsuzúkerú; (: standards etc) 保持する hojí surú

♦*vi*: **to keep up (with)** (match: pace)

(...と)速度を合せる (...to) sókùdo wo awáserú; (: level) (...に) 遅れない様にする (...ni) okúrenai yō ni suru

keg [keg] *n* たる tarú

kennel [ken'əl] *n* イヌ小屋 inúgoya

kennels [ken'əlz] *npl* (establishment) イヌ屋 inúya

Kenya [ken'jə] *n* ケニア kénìa

Kenyan [ken'jən] *adj* ケニアの kénìa no

♦*n* ケニア人 keníajìn

kept [kept] *pt, pp of* **keep**

kerb [kə:rb] (*BRIT*) *n* = **curb**

kernel [kə:r'nəl] *n* (BOT: of nut) 実 mi; (*fig*: of idea) 核 kákù

kerosene [ker'əsin] *n* 灯油 tóyu

ketchup [ketʃ'əp] *n* ケチャップ kecháppù

kettle [ket'əl] *n* やかん yakán

kettle drum *n* ティンパニ tínpani

key [ki:] *n* (to lock etc) かぎ kagí; (MUS: scale) 調 chō; (of piano, computer, typewriter) キー kī

♦*adj* (issue etc) 重要な jūyō na

♦*vt* (*also*: **key in**: into computer etc) 打込む uchíkomù, 入力する nyūryoku suru

keyboard [ki:'bɔ:rd] *n* (of computer, typewriter) キーボード kíbòdo; (of piano) けん盤 kénban, キーボード kíbòdo

keyed up [ki:d-] *adj* (person) 興奮している kófun shite irù

keyhole [ki:'houl] *n* 鍵穴 kagíana

keynote [ki:'nout] *n* (MUS) 主音 shúòn; (of speech) 基調 kichō

key ring *n* キーホルダー kíhorùdā

kg *abbr* = **kilogram**

khaki [kæk'i:] *n* (color) カーキ色 kákì iro; (also: **khaki cloth**) カーキ色服地 kákì iro fukúji)

kibbutz [kibuts'] *n* キブツ kíbùtsu, キブヌ イスラエルの農業共同体 fsùraeru no nógyō kyódòtai

kick [kik] *vt* (person, table, ball) ける kérù; (*inf*: habit, addiction) やめる yamérù

♦*vi* ける kérù

♦*n* (from person, animal) けり kéri; (to ball) キック kíkkù; (thrill): **he does it for kicks** 彼はそんな事をやるのはスリ

ルのために kárè wa soñna kotŏ wo yárû no wa surírû no tamé dâ

kick off vi (FOOTBALL, SOCCER) 試合を開始する shiái wò kaíshi suru

kick-off [kik'ɔːf] n (FOOTBALL, SOCCER) 試合開始 shiái kaishí, キックオフ kíkkûofu

kid [kid] n (inf: child) がき gakí, じゃりjárí; (animal) 子 ヤギ koyágí; (also: **kid leather**) キッド革 kíddôgawa

♦vi (inf) 冗談を言う jódañ wo iû

kidnap [kid'næp] vt 誘拐する yûkai suru

kidnapper [kid'næpər] n 誘拐犯人 yúkai hañniñ

kidnapping [kid'næpiŋ] n 誘拐事件 yúkai jíkeñ

kidney [kid'niː] n (ANAT) じん臓 jiñzô; (CULIN) キドニー kídônî

kill [kil] vt (person, animal) 殺す korósû; (plant) 枯らす karásû; (murder) 殺す korosu, 殺害する satsúgai suru

♦n 殺し korôshi

to kill time 時間をつぶす jíkañ wo tsubúsû

killer [kil'əːr] n 殺し屋 koróshiya

killing [kil'iŋ] n (action) 殺す事 korósû kotŏ; (instance) 殺人事件 satsújiñ jíkeñ

to make a killing (inf) 大もうけする ŏmôke suru

killjoy [kil'dʒɔi] n 白けさせる人 shirákesaseru hitŏ

kiln [kiln] n 窯 kamá

kilo [kiː'lou] n キロ kírô

kilobyte [kil'əbait] n (COMPUT) キロバイト kíróbaîto

kilogram(me) [kil'əgræm] n キログラム kíróguràmu

kilometer [kil'əmiːtər] n (BRIT **kilometre**) n キロメーター kírómêtà

kilowatt [kil'əwɑːt] n キロワット kírówattô

kilt [kilt] n キルト kírûto

kimono [kimou'nou] n 着物 kimóno, 和服 wafúku

kin [kin] n see **kith; next-of-kin**

kind [kaind] adj 親切な shiñsetsu na

♦n (type, sort) 種類 shûrùi; (species) 種shú

to pay in kind 現物で支払う geñbutsu de shiháraû

a kind of ... …の一種 …no ísshu

to be two of a kind 似たり寄ったりする nitári yottárí suru, 似たもの同志である nitá mono dŏshi de árû

kindergarten [kin'dəːrgɑːrtən] n 幼稚園 yŏchieñ

kind-hearted [kaind'hɑːr'tid] adj 心の優しい kokórò no yasáshiî

kindle [kin'dəl] vt (light: fire) たく takû, つける tsukerù; (arouse: emotion) 起す okósû, そそる sosórû

kindly [kaind'liː] adj 親切な shiñsetsu na

♦adv (smile) 優しく yasáshikû; (behave) 親切に shiñsetsu ni

will you kindly ... …して下さいませんか …shîtê kudásaimaseñ ká

kindness [kaind'nis] n (personal quality) 親切 shiñsetsu; (helpful act) 親切な行為 shiñsetsu na kŏi

kindred [kin'drid] adj: **kindred spirit** 自分と気の合った人 jíbuñ to kî no attá hitŏ

kinetic [kinet'ik] adj 動的な dŏteki na

king [kiŋ] n (monarch) 国王 kokúô; (CARDS, CHESS) キング kíñgu

kingdom [kiŋ'dəm] n 王国 ŏkoku

kingfisher [kiŋ'saiz] n カワセミ kawásemi

king-size [kiŋ'saiz] adj 特大の tokúdai no

kinky [kiŋ'kiː] (pej) adj (person, behavior) へんてこな heñteko na, 妙な myŏ na; (sexually) 変態気味の heñtaigimi no

kiosk [kiːɑːsk'] n (shop) キオスク kíôsôku; (BRIT: TEL) 電話ボックス deñwa bokkûsu

kipper [kip'əːr] n 薫製ニシン kuñsei nishíñ

kiss [kis] n キス kísû

♦vt ...にキスする ...ni kísû suru

to kiss (each other) キスする kísû suru

kiss of life n 人工呼吸 kuchfukutsushi no jiñkôkokyû

kit [kit] n (clothes: sports kit etc) 運動服一式 uñdŏfuku isshíki; (equipment, set of tools: also MIL) 道具一式 dŏgu isshíki; (for assembly) キット kíttò

kitchen [kɪtʃʃən] *n* 台所 daídokoro, キッ チン kítchìn

kitchen sink *n* 台所の流し daídokoro no nagáshi

kite [kaɪt] *n* (toy) たこ takó

kith [kɪθ] *n*: **kith and kin** 親せき知人 shíñsekichijìn

kitten [kɪtʲən] *n*子ネコ konéko

kitty [kɪtʲiː] *n* (pool of money) お金の蓄 え o-káne no takúwae; (CARDS) 総掛金 sókakekìn

kleptomaniac [kleptəmeɪˈniːæk] *n* 盗 癖 のある人 tốheki no árù hitó

km *abbr* = kilometer

knack [næk] *n*: **to have the knack of doing something** ...するのが上手でも ある...を する のが じょうず jòzu

knapsack [næpˈsæk] *n* ナップサック nappúsakkù

knead [niːd] *vt* (dough, clay) 練る nérù

knee [niː] *n* ひざ hizá

kneecap [niːˈkæp] *n* ひざ頭 hizágashìra, ひざ小僧 hizákozò

kneel [niːl] (*pt, pp* **knelt**) *vi* (*also:* **kneel down**) ひざまずく hizámazukù

knelt [nelt] *pt, pp of* **kneel**

knew [nuː] *pt of* **know**

knickers [nɪkˈəːz] (*BRIT*) *npl* パンティ ー páñtì

knife [naɪf] (*pl* **knives**) *n* ナイフ náìfu

♦*vt* ナイフで刺す náìfu de sásù

knight [naɪt] *n* (HISTORY) 騎士 kishí; (*BRIT*) ナイト náìto; (CHESS) ナイト náìto

knighthood [naɪtˈhud] (*BRIT*) *n* (title): **to get a knighthood** ナイト爵位を与え られる naíto shakùi wo atáerarerù

knit [nɪt] *vt* (garment) 編む ámù

♦*vi* (with wool) 編物をする amímòno wo suru; (broken bones) 治る naórù

to knit one's brows まゆをひそめる máyù wo hisómerù

knitting [nɪtˈiŋ] *n* 編物 amímòno

knitting machine *n* 編機 amíkì

knitting needle *n* 編針 amíbò

knitwear [nɪtˈwè:r] *n* ニット・ウェア ー níttò ueà

knives [naɪvz] *npl of* **knife**

knob [nɑːb] *n* (handle: of door) 取っ手 tottè, つまみ tsumámi; (: of stick) 握り nigírì; (on radio, TV etc) つまみ tsumá-mi

knock [nɑːk] *vt* (strike) たたく tatákù; (*inf*: criticize) 批判する hiháñ suru

♦*vi* (at door etc): **to knock at/on** ...に ノックする nókkù suru

♦*n* (blow, bump) 打撃 dagéki; (on door) ノック nokkú

knock down *vt* (subj: person) 殴り倒す nagúritaosù; (: car) ひき倒す hikítaosù

knocker [nɑːkˈəːr] *n* (on door) ノッカー nokká

knock-kneed [nɑːkˈniːd] *adj* X脚の ekú-sukyakù no

knock off *vi* (*inf*: finish) 終りにする owári ni suru, やめる yaméru

♦*vt* (from price) 値引する nebíki suru; (*inf*: steal) くすねる kusúnerù

knock out *vt* (subj: drug etc) 気絶させる kizétsu saserù, 眠らせる nemúraserù; (BOXING etc, *also fig*) ノックアウトす る nokkúaùto suru; (defeat: in game, competition) ...に勝つ ...ni kátsù, 敗退さ せる haítai saserù

knockout [nɑːkˈaut] *n* (BOXING) ノッ クアウト nokkúaùto

♦*cpd* (competition etc) 決定的な kettéi-teki na

knock over *vt* (person, object) 倒す taó-sù

knot [nɑːt] *n* (in rope) 結び目 musúbime; (in wood) 節目 fushíme; (NAUT) ノット nóttò

♦*vt* 結ぶ musúbù

knotty [nɑːtˈiː] *adj* (*fig*: problem) 厄介な yakkái na

know [nou] (*pt* **knew**, *pp* **known**) *vt* (facts, dates etc) 知っている shitté irù; (language) できる dekírù; (be acquainted with: person, place, subject) 知っている shitté irù; (recognize: by sight) 見て分か る mítè wakárù; (: by sound) 聞いて分か る kiíte wakáru

to know how to swim 泳げる oyógerù

to know about/of something/some-

one ...の事を知っている ...no kotó wo shitté irú

know-all [nou'ɔ:l] n 知ったか振りの人 shittákaburi no hitó

know-how [nou'hau] n 技術知識 gijútsuchíshìki, ノウハウ nóūhaù

knowing [nou'iŋ] adj (look: of complicity) 意味ありげな imárige na

knowingly [nou'iŋli] adv (purposely) 故意に kóī ni; (smile, look) 意味ありげに ímárige ni

knowledge [nɑːl'idʒ] n (understanding, awareness) 認識 nínshìki; (learning, things learnt) 知識 chíshìki

knowledgeable [nɑːl'idʒəbəl] adj 知識のある chíshìki no árū

known [noun] pp of **know**

knuckle [nʌk'əl] n 指関節 yubí kañsetsu ◆特に指の付根の関節を指す tókū ni yubí no tsukéne no kañsetsu wo sásù

KO [kei'ou'] n abbr = **knockout**

Koran [kɔːræn'] n コーラン kōran

Korea [kɔːri:'ə] n 韓国 káňkoku, 朝鮮 chōsen

Korean [kɔːri:'ən] adj 韓国の káňkoku no, 朝鮮の chōsen no; (LING) 韓国語の kaňkokugo no, 朝鮮語の chōsengo no
◆n (person) 韓国人 kaňkokujìn, 朝鮮人 chōsenjìn; (LING) 韓国語 kaňkokugo, 朝鮮語 chōsengo

kosher [kou'ʃər] adj ユダヤ教の戒律に合った食物などについて言う yudáyakyō no kaíritsu ni attá shokúmòtsu nádō ni tsuíte iú

L

L (BRIT) abbr = **learner driver**

l. abbr = **liter**

lab [læb] n abbr = **laboratory**

label [lei'bəl] n (on suitcase, merchandise etc) ラベル rábèru
◆vt (thing) ...にラベルを付ける ...ni rábèru wo tsukérù

labor [lei'bər] (BRIT **labour**) n (hard work) 労働 ródō; (work force) 労働者 ródōsha; (work done by work

force) 労働 ródō; (MED): **to be in labor** 陣痛が始まっている jíňtsū ga hajímatte irú
◆vi: **to labor (at something)** (...に) 苦しむ (...ni) kushímù suru
◆vt: **to labor a point** ある事を余計に強調する árū kotó wo yokéi ni kyóchō suru

laboratory [læb'rətɔːri:] n (scientific: building, institution) 研究所 keñkyūjo; (: room) 実験室 jíkkeñshìtsu; (school) 理科教室 rikákyōshìtsu

labored [lei'bərd] adj (breathing: one's own) 苦しい kurúshiì; (: someone else's) 苦しそうな kurúshisō na

laborer [lei'bərər] n (industrial) 労働者 ródōsha
farm laborer 農場労務者 nójōrōmùsha

laborious [ləbɔːr'i:əs] adj 骨の折れる honé no orérù

labour [lei'bər] etc n = **labor** etc
Labour, the Labour Party (BRIT) 労働党 ródōtō

labyrinth [læb'ərinθ] n 迷路 méìro

lace [leis] n (fabric) レース rḗsù; (of shoe etc) ひも hímò
◆vt (shoe etc: also: **lace up**) ...のひもを結ぶ ...no hímò wo musúbù

lack [læk] n (absence) 欠如 kétsùjo
◆vt (money, confidence) ...が無い ...ga náì; (intelligence etc) ...に欠けている ...ni kakéte irú
through/for lack of ...が無いために ...ga náì tamé ni
to be lacking ...がない ...ga náì
to be lacking in (intelligence, generosity etc) ...を欠いている ...wo kaíte irú

lackadaisical [lækədei'zikəl] adj (lacking interest, enthusiasm) 気乗りしない kiñóri shinaì

laconic [ləkɑːn'ik] adj 言葉数の少ない kotóbakazð no sukúnaì

lacquer [læk'ər] n (paint) ラッカー rákkà; (also: **hair lacquer**) ヘアスプレー heá supurě

lad [læd] n (boy) 少年 shónen; (young man) 若者 wakámonð

ladder [læd'ər] n (metal, wood, rope) は

しご子 hashígo; (BRIT: in tights) 伝線 defíseñ

laden [leiˈdɔn] *adj*: **laden (with)** (ship, truck etc) (...を) たっぷり積んだ (...wo) tappúrí tsuñda; (person) (...を) 沢山抱えている (...wo) takúsañ kakáete irú

laden with fruit (tree) 実をたわわに付けている mi wo tawáwa ni tsukéte irú

ladle [leiˈdəl] *n* 玉じゃくし tamájakôshi

lady [leiˈdiː] *n* (woman) 女性 joséi; (: dignified, graceful etc) 婦女 shukójò, レディー rédī; (in address): **ladies and gentlemen** ... 紳士淑女の皆様 shíñshishukujô no mínásàma

young lady 若い女性 wakáì joséi

the ladies' (room) (woman's) 女性用トイレ joséiyôtoîre

ladybird [leiˈdiːbəːrd] *n* テントウムシ tefítômushi

ladybug [leiˈdebʌg] (*US*) *n* = **ladybird**

ladylike [leiˈdiːlaik] *adj* (behavior) レディーらしい rédīrashìi

ladyship [leiˈdiːʃip] *n*: **your ladyship** 奥様 ôkûsama

lag [læg] *n* (period of time) 遅れ okúre
♦*vi* (*also*: **lag behind**: person, thing) ...に遅れる ...ni okúrerû; (: trade, investment etc) ...の勢いが衰える ...no ikíoî ga otóroerù
♦*vt* (pipes etc) ...に断熱材を巻く ...ni dañnetsuzài wo makú

lager [lɑːˈgəːr] *n* ラガービール ragábiru

lagoon [ləguːn] *n* 潟 katá, ラグーン rágūn

laid [leid] *pt, pp* of **lay**

laid back (*inf*) *adj* のんびりした noñbiri shitá

laid up *adj*: **to be laid up (with)** (...で) 寝込んでいる (...de) nekônde irú

lain [lein] *pp* of **lie**

lair [leːr] *n* (ZOOL) 巣穴 suána

lake [leik] *n* 湖 mizú-umî

lamb [læm] *n* (animal) 子ヒツジ kohítsujî; (meat) ラム肉 ramú

lamb chop *n* ラムチャップ ramúchappù, ラムチョップ ramúchoppù

lambswool [læmzˈwul] *n* ラムウール ramúūru

lame [leim] *adj* (person, animal) びっこの bíkkô no; (excuse, argument, answer) 下手な hetá na

lament [ləmentˈ] *n* 嘆き nagéki
♦*vt* 嘆く nagéku

laminated [læmˈəneitid] *adj* (metal, wood, glass) 合板の gôhan no; (covering, surface) プラスチック張りの purásuchikkubari no

lamp [læmp] *n* (electric, gas, oil) 明り akári, ランプ rañpu

lamppost [læmpˈpoust] *n* 街灯 gaítō

lampshade [læmpˈʃeid] *n* ランプの傘 rañpu no kasá, シェード shêdo

lance [læns] *n* やり yarí
♦*vt* (MED) 切開する sekkáì suru

land [lænd] *n* (area of open ground) 土地 tochí; (property, estate) 土地 tochí, 所有地 shoyúchì; (as opposed to sea) 陸 rikú; (country, nation) 国 kuní
♦*vi* (from ship) 上陸する jôriku suru; (AVIAT) 着陸する chakúriku suru; (fig: fall) 落ちる ochíru
♦*vt* (passengers, goods) 降ろす orósù

to land someone with something (*inf*) ...に...を押付ける ...ni ...wo oshítsukerù

landing [lænˈdiŋ] *n* (of house) 踊り場 odóriba; (AVIAT) 着陸 chakúriku

landing gear *n* (AVIAT) 着陸装置 chakúrikusôchi

landing strip *n* 滑走路 kassôrò

landlady [lændˈleidi] *n* (of rented house, flat, room) 女大家 oñnaôya; (of pub) 女主人 oñnashujîn, おかみ okámi

landlocked [lændˈlɔkt] *adj* 陸地に囲まれた rikúchi ni kakómareta

landlord [lændˈlɔːrd] *n* (of rented house, flat, room) 大家 ôya; (of pub) 主人 shujîn

landmark [lændˈmɑːrk] *n* (building, hill etc) 目標 mokúhyô; (fig) 歴史的な事件 rekíshiteki na jíkèñ

landowner [lændˈounəːr] *n* 地主 jínûshi

landscape [lændˈskeip] *n* (view over land, buildings etc) 景色 késhìki; (ART) 風景画 fûkeiga

landscape gardener *n* 造園家 zôenka

landslide [lændˈslaid] *n* (GEO) 地滑り jisúberi; (fig: electoral) 圧勝 asshō

land up vi: **to land up in/at** 結局...に行くはめになる kekkyókú ...ni ikú hame ni narú

lane [lein] n (in country) 小道 komíchi; (AUT: of carriageway) 車線 shasén; (of race course, swimming pool) コース kōsu

language [lǽŋgwidʒ] n (national tongue) 国語 kokúgo; (ability to communicate verbally) 言語 géngo; (specialized terminology) 用語 yōgo; (style: of written piece, speech etc) 言葉遣 kotóbazukái; (SCOL) 語学 gógaku

bad language 下品な言葉 gehín na kotóba

he is studying languages 彼は外国語を勉強している kare wa gaikokugo no benkyō shite iru

language laboratory nラングージラボラトリー rañgéjiraborátòrī, エルエルérùeru

languid [lǽŋgwid] adj (person, movement) 元気のない géñki no naí

languish [lǽŋgwiʃ] vi 惨めに生きる míjìme ni ikírù

lank [lǽŋk] adj (hair) 長くて手入れしない nágàkutè tefre shinai

lanky [lǽŋki] adj ひょろっとした hyoróttò shita

lantern [lǽntərn] n カンテラ kañtera

lap [lǽp] n (of person) ひざの上 hizá no ué; (in race) 1周 fsshū, ラップ ráppù
♦vt (also: **lap up**): (drink) ぴちゃぴちゃ飲む pí chapichà nómu
♦vi (water) ひたひたと打寄せる hitáhità to uchíyoserù

lapel [ləpél] n 折えり orféri, ラペル rápèru

Lapland [lǽpˌlænd] n ラップランド ráppùrando

lapse [lǽps] n (bad behavior) 過失 kashítsu; (of memory) 喪失 sōshitsu; (of time) 経過 kékka
♦vi (law) 無効になる mukó ni narú; (contract, membership, passport) 切れる kirérù

a lapse of concentration 不注意 fu

chúi

to lapse into bad habits (of behavior) 堕落する daráku suru

lap up vt (fig: flattery etc) 真に受ける ma ni ukérù

larceny [lɑ́rsəni] n (LAW) 窃盗罪 settōzai

larch [lɑ́rtʃ] n (tree) カラマツ karámatsu

lard [lɑ́rd] n ラード rādo

larder [lɑ́rdər] n 食料貯蔵室 shokúryóchozòshitsu

large [lɑ́rdʒ] adj (big: house, person, amount) 大きい ōkii

at large (as a whole) 一般に ippán ni; (at liberty) 捕まらないで tsukámaranaide 1 see also **by**

largely [lɑ́rdʒli] adv (mostly) 大体 daítai; (mainly: introducing reason) 主に ómò ni

large-scale [lɑ́rdʒˈskeil] adj (action, event) 大規模の daíkibò no; (map, diagram) 大縮尺の daíshukushaku no

largesse [lɑrdʒés] n (generosity) 気前良さ kimáeyosà; (money etc) 贈り物 okúrimonò

lark [lɑ́rk] n (bird) ヒバリ hibári; (joke) 冗談 jōdañ

lark about vi ふざけ回る fuzákemawaru

larva [lɑ́rvə] (pl **larvae**) n 幼虫 yóchū

larvae [lɑ́rviː] npl of **larva**

laryngitis [lærəndʒaíˈtis] n こうとう炎 kōtōen

larynx [lǽriŋks] n (ANAT) こうとう kōtō

lascivious [ləsíviəs] adj (person, conduct) みだらな midárà na

laser [léiˈzər] n レーザー rēzà

laser printer n レーザープリンター rēzāpurintà

lash [lǽʃ] n (eyelash) まつげ mátsùge; (blow of whip) むち打ち muchfuchi
♦vt (whip) むち打つ muchfutsū; (subj: rain) 激しくたたく hageshiku tatákù; (: wind) 激しく揺さぶる hageshiku yusáburù; (tie): **to lash to/together** ...を...に (...と一緒に) 縛る ...wo ...ni (...to isshó ni)

shibáru

lash out *vi*: *to lash out (at someone)* (hit) (...に) 打ち掛かる (...ni) uchíkakarù
to lash out against someone (criticize) ...を激しく非難する ...wo hagéshiku hínán suru

lass [læs] *n* (*girl*) 少女 shōjo; (*young woman*) 若い女性 wakái joséi

lasso [læs'ou] *n* 投げ縄 nagénawa

last [læst] *adj* (*latest*: period of time, event, thing) 前の máe no; (*final*: bus, hope etc) 最後の sáigo no; (*end*: of series, row) 一番後の ichíban átò no; (*remaining*: traces, scraps etc) 残りの nokórí no
♦*adv* (*most recently*) 最近 saíkin; (*finally*) 最後に saígo ni
♦*vi* (*continue*) 続く tsuzúkù; (: *in good condition*) 保つ tamótsù; (*money, commodity*) ...に足りる ...ni tarírù
last week 先週 senshū
last night 昨晩 sakúban, 昨夜 sakúya
at last (*finally*) とうとう tótò
last but one 最後から2番目 sáigo kara nibánme

last-ditch [læst'ditʃ] *adj* (*attempt*) 絶体絶命の zettáizetsumei no

lasting [læs'tiŋ] *adj* (*friendship, solution*) 永続的な eízokuteki na

lastly [læst'li:] *adv* 最後に saígo ni

last-minute [læst'min'it] *adj* (*decision, appeal etc*) 土壇場の dotánba no

latch [lætʃ] *n* (*on door, gate*) 掛け金 kakégàne, ラッチ rátchi

late [leit] *adj* (*far on in time, process, work etc*) 遅い osóì; (*not on time*) 遅れた okúreta; (*former*) 前の máe no, 前... zén...
♦*adv* (*far on in time, process, work etc*) 遅く osóku; (*behind time, schedule*) 遅れて okúrete
of late (*recently*) 最近 saíkin
in late May 5月の終り頃 gógàtsu no owári gorò
the late Mr X (*deceased*) 故X さん ko ékusu san

latecomer [leit'kʌmər] *n* 遅れて来る人 okúrete kurú hitò

lately [leit'li:] *adv* 最近 saíkin

latent [lei'tənt] *adj* (*energy, skill, abil-*

---

ity) 表に出ない omóte ni dénài

later [lei'tər] *adj* (*time, date, meeting etc*) もっと後の móttò átò no; (*version etc*) もっと新しい móttò atárashiì
♦*adv* 後で átò de
later on 後で átò de

lateral [læt'ərəl] *adj* (*position*) 横の yokó no; (*direction*) 横への yokó e no

latest [lei'tist] *adj* (*train, flight etc*) 最後の sáigo no; (*novel, film, news etc*) 最新の saíshin no
at the latest 遅くとも osókùtomo

lathe [leið] *n* (*for wood, metal*) 旋盤 senban

lather [læð'ər] *n* 石けんの泡 sekkén nò awá
♦*vt* ...に石けんの泡を塗る ...ni sekkén nò awá wò nurú

Latin [læt'in] *n* (LING) ラテン語 raténgo
♦*adj* ラテン語の raténgo no

Latin America *n* ラテンアメリカ ratén-amèrika

Latin American *adj* ラテンアメリカの ratén-amèrika no
♦*n* ラテンアメリカ人 ratén-amerikajìn

latitude [læt'ətud] *n* (GEO) 緯度 ídò; (*fig*: *freedom*) 余裕 yoyú

latrine [lətrin'] *n* 便所 benjo

latter [læt'ər] *adj* (*of two*) 後者の kósha no; (*recent*) 後の saíkin no; (*later*) 後の方の átò no hó no
♦*n*: *the latter* (of two people, things, groups*) 後者 kósha

latterly [læt'ərli:] *adv* 最近 saíkin

lattice [læt'is] *n* (*pattern, structure*) 格子 kōshi

laudable [lɔ:'dəbəl] *adj* (conduct, motives etc) 感心な kańshin na

laugh [læf] *n* 笑い waráì
♦*vi* 笑う waráù
(to do something) for a laugh 冗談として (...をする) jōdàn toshìte (...wo suru)

laugh at *vt fus* ...をばかにする ...wo bakáni surù

laughable [læf'əbəl] *adj* (*attempt, quality etc*) ばかげた bakágeta

laughing stock [læf'iŋ stɒk] *n*: to be the laughing stock of ...の笑い者になる ...no waráimono ni narú

laugh off *vt* (criticism, problem) 無視する mushf suru

laughter [læf'tər] *n* 笑い声 waráigoè

launch [lɔːntʃ] *n* (of rocket, missile) 発射 hasshá; (of satellite) 打上げ uchfage; (COMM) 新発売 shínhatsubai; (motorboat) ランチ ránchi

♦*vt* (ship) 進水させる shifsui saséru; (rocket, missile) 発射する hasshá suru; (satellite) 打上げる uchfageru; (*fig*: start) 開始する kaíshi suru; (COMM) 発売する hatsúbai suru

launch into *vt fus* (speech, activity) 始める hajímerù

launch(ing) pad [lɔːn'tʃ(iŋ)-] *n* (for missile, rocket) 発射台 hasshádai

launder [lɔːn'dər] *vt* (clothes) 洗濯する sefítaku suru

launderette [lɔːndəret'] *n* コインランドリー kofnrándorì

Laundromat [lɔːn'drəmæt] (®) *US n* コインランドリー kofnrándorì

laundry [lɔːn'driː] *n* (dirty, clean) 洗濯物 sefítakumono; (business) 洗濯屋 sefítakuya ◇ドライクリーニングはしない dorái-kurìningu wa shínàī; (room) 洗濯場 sefítakuba

laureate [lɔːr'iːit] *adj see* **poet laureate**

laurel [lɔːr'əl] *n* (tree) ゲッケイジュ gekkéiju

lava [lɑː'və] *n* 溶岩 yógan

lavatory [læv'ətɔːriː] *n* お手洗い otéarài

lavender [læv'əndər] *n* (BOT) ラベンダー rabéndā

lavish [læv'iʃ] *adj* (amount) たっぷりの tappúrì no, 多量の taryó no; (person): *lavish with* ...を気前良く与える ...wo kimáeyokù atáerù

♦*vt*: to lavish something on someone ...に...を気前良く与える ...ni ...wo kimáeyokù atáerù

law [lɔː] *n* (system of rules: of society, government) 法 hó; (a rule) 法律 hóritsu; (of nature, science) 法則 hósoku; (lawyers) 弁護士 bengóshi no shokū;

law-abiding [lɔː'əbaidiŋ] *adj* 法律を遵守する hóritsu wò júnshu suru

law and order *n* 治安 chfān

law court *n* 法廷 hótei

lawful [lɔː'fəl] *adj* 合法の góhò no

lawless [lɔː'lis] *adj* (action) 不法の fuhó no

lawn [lɔːn] *n* 芝生 shibáfu

lawnmower [lɔːn'mouər] *n* 芝刈機 shibákarikì

lawn tennis *n* ローンテニス róntenisu

law school (US) *n* (SCOL) 法学部 hógakùbu

lawsuit [lɔː'suːt] *n* 訴訟 soshó

lawyer [lɔː'jər] *n* (gen) 弁護士 bengóshi; (solicitor) 事務弁護士 jimúbeñgoshi; (barrister) 法廷弁護士 hóteibèngoshi

lax [læks] *adj* (behavior, standards) いい加減な iíkagen na

laxative [læk'sətiv] *n* 下剤 gezái

lay[1] [lei] *pt of* **lie**

lay[2] [lei] *adj* (REL) 俗人の zokújin no; (not expert) 素人の shfróto no

lay[3] [lei] (*pt, pp* **laid**) *vt* (place) 置く okú; (table) ...に食器を並べる ...ni shokkf wo náraberù; (carpet etc) 敷く shikú; (cable, pipes etc) 埋設する maísetsu suru; (ZOOL: egg) 産む úmù

layabout [lei'əbaut] (*BRIT*: *inf*) *n* のらくら者 norákuramono

lay aside *vt* (put down) わきに置く wakí ni okú; (money) 貯蓄する chochfku suru; (belief, prejudice) 捨てる sutérù

lay by *vt* = **lay aside**

lay-by [lei'bai] (*BRIT*) *n* 待避所 taíhijo

lay down *vt* (object) 置く okú; (rules, laws etc) 設ける mókerù

to lay down the law (*pej*) 威張り散らす ibárichirasu

to lay down one's life (in war etc) 命を捨てる inóchi wo sutérù

layer [lei'ər] *n* 層 só

layman [lei'mən] (*pl* **laymen**) *n* (nonexpert) 素人 shfróto

lay off *vt* (workers) 一時解雇にする i-chfjikaíko ni suru, レイオフにする refo-

lay on *vt* (meal, entertainment etc) 提供する tekyō suru

lay out *vt* (spread out: things) 並べて置く narábete okù

layout [lei'aut] *n* (arrangement: of garden, building) 配置 haíchi; (: of piece of writing etc) レイアウト refaûto

laze [leiz] *vi* (*also:* **laze about**) ぶらぶらする búrabura suru

laziness [lei'zi:nis] *n* 怠惰 táida

lazy [lei'zi:] *adj* (person) 怠惰な táida na; (movement, action) のろい norói

lb *abbr* = **pound** (weight)

lead [li:d] *n* (front position: SPORT, *fig*) 先頭 señtō, (piece of information) 手掛り tegākàri; (in play, film) 主役 shuén; (for dog) 引綱 híkízuna, ひも hímò; (ELEC) リード線 rīdosen

♦*vb* (*pt, pp* **led**)

♦*vt* (walk etc in front) 先導する señdō suru; (guide): **to lead someone somewhere** ...を...に案内する ...wo ...ni afinai suru; (group of people, organization) ...のリーダーになる ...no rīdā ni nárū; (start, guide: activity) ...の指揮を取る ...no shíkí wo torù

♦*vi* (road, pipe, wire etc) ...に通じる ...ni tsújíru; (SPORT) 先頭に立つ señtō ni tatsù

in the lead (SPORT, *fig*) 先頭に立って señtō ni tatte

to lead the way (*also fig*) 先導する señdō suru

lead [led] *n* (metal) 鉛 namári; (in pencil) しん shíñ

lead away *vt* 連れ去る tsurésarù

lead back *vt* 連れ戻す tsurémodosù

leaden [led'ən] *adj* (sky, sea) 鉛色の namáriiro no

leader [li:'də:r] *n* (of group, organization) 指導者 shidōshà, リーダー rīdā; (SPORT) 先頭を走る選手 señtō wo hashírù señshū

leadership [li:'də:rʃip] *n* (group, individual) 指導権 shidōkèn; (position, quality) リーダーシップ rīdáshìppu

lead-free [ledfri:'] *adj* (petrol) 無鉛の muén no

leading [li:'diŋ] *adj* (most important: person, thing) 主要な shuyō na; (role) 主演の shuén no; (first, front) 先頭の señtō no

leading lady *n* (THEATER) 主演女優 shuénjoyū

leading light *n* (person) 主要人物 shuyójinbútsu

leading man (*pl* **leading men**) *n* (THEATER) 主演男優 shuéndań-yū

lead on *vt* (tease) からかう karákaù

lead singer *n* (in pop group) リードシンガー rīdoshiñgà, リードボーカリスト rīdobōkarìsuto

lead to *vt fus* ...の原因になる ...no gen-in ni narù

lead up to *vt fus* (events) ...の原因になる ...no gen-in ni narù; (in conversation) 話題を...に向ける wadái wo ...ni mukérù

leaf [li:f] (*pl* **leaves**) *n* (of tree, plant) 葉 ha

♦*vi:* **to leaf through** (book, magazine) ...にきっと目を通す ...ni sàtto me wò tósù

to turn over a new leaf 心を入れ換える kokórò wo irékaerù

leaflet [li:f'lit] *n* ビラ bírà, 散らし chiráshi

league [li:g] *n* (group of people, clubs, countries) 連盟 refimèi, リーグ rīgu

to be in league with someone ...と手を組んでいる ...to te wo kuñdé irù

leak [li:k] *n* (of liquid, gas) 漏れ moré; (hole: in roof, pipe etc) 穴 aná; (piece of information) 漏えい róei

♦*vi* (shoes, ship, pipe, roof) ...から...が漏れる ...kara ...ga moreru; (liquid, gas) 漏れる moréru

♦*vt* (information) 漏らす morásu

the news leaked out そのニュースが漏れた sonő nyūsu ga moréta

lean [li:n] *adj* (person) やせた yaséta; (meat) 赤身の akámi no

♦*vb* (*pt, pp* **leaned** *or* **leant**)

♦*vt:* **to lean something on something** ...を...にもたせかける ...wo ...ni motáse-kakerù

lean back vi 後ろへもたれる ushiro e motárerù

lean forward vi 前にかがむ máe ni kagámù

leaning [liːniŋ] n: **leaning (towards)** (tendency, bent) (...する) 傾向 (...surú) kefkô

lean out vi ...から体を乗出す ...kara karáda wò norídasù

lean over vi ...の上にかがむ ...no ué ni kagámù

leant [lent] pt, pp of **lean**

leap [liːp] n (jump) 跳躍 chôyaku; (in price, number etc) 急上昇 kyújōshō

♦vi (pt, pp **leaped** or **leapt**) (jump: high) 跳ね上がる (far) 跳躍する chôyaku suru; (price, number etc) 急上昇する kyújōshō suru

leapfrog [liːpˈfrɔːg] n 馬跳び umátobi

leapt [lept] pt, pp of **leap**

leap year n うるう年 urúdoshi

learn [ləːrn] (pt, pp **learned** or **learnt**) vt (facts, skill) 学ぶ manábù; (study, repeat: poem, play etc) 覚える obóerù; 暗記する añki suru

♦vi 習う naráù

to learn about something (hear, read) ...を知る ...wo shírù

to learn to do something ...の仕方を覚える ...no shikáta wo obóerù

learned [ləːrˈnid] adj (person) 学識のある gakúshiki no arù; (book, paper) 学術の gakújùtsu no

learner [ləːrˈnəːr] (BRIT) n (also: **learner driver**) 仮免許運転者 karímenkyo unténsha

learning [ləːrˈniŋ] n (knowledge) 学識 gakúshiki

learnt [ləːrnt] pt, pp of **learn**

lease [liːs] n (legal agreement, contract: to borrow something) 賃借契約 chíñshakukukeíyaku, リース rīsu; (: to lend something) 賃貸契約 chíñtaikeíyaku, リース rīsu

♦vt (borrow) 賃借する chíñshaku suru; (lend) 賃貸する chíñtai suru

leash [liːʃ] n (for dog) ひも himó

least [liːst] adj: **the least** (+noun: smallest) 最も小さい móttòmo chíísaì; (: smallest amount of) 最も少ない móttòmo sukúnaì

♦adv (+verb) 最も...しない móttòmo ...shináì; (+adjective): **the least** もっとも...でない móttòmo ...de náì

the least possible effort 最小限の努力 saíshōgen no dóryòku

at least 少なくとも sukúnakùtomo

you could at least have written 少なくとも手紙をくれたら良かったのに sukúnakùtomo tegámi wò kurétara yokáttà no ni

not in the least ちっとも...でない chíttòmo ...de náì

leather [leðˈəːr] n なめし革 naméshigàwa, 革 kawá

leave [liːv] (pt, pp **left**) vt (place: go away from) 行ってしまう itté shimaù, 帰る kaérù; (place, institution: permanently) 去る sárù, 辞める yamérù; (leave behind: person) 置き去りにする okízari ni surù, 見捨てる misúterù; (: thing: accidentally) 置忘れる okíwasurerù; (: deliberately) 置いて行く oíte ikù; (husband, wife) ...と別れる ...to wakárerù; (allow to remain: food, space, time etc) 残す nokósù

♦vi (go away) 去る sárù, 行ってしまう itté shimaù; (: permanently) 辞める yamérù; (bus, train) 出発する shuppátsu suru, 出る dérù

♦n 休暇 kyúka

to leave something to someone (money, property etc) ...に...を残して死ぬ ...ni ...wo nokóshite shinú; (responsibility etc) ...を任せる ...ni ...wo makáserù

to be left 残る nokórù

there's some milk left over ミルクは少し残っている mírùku wa sukóshì nokótte irù

on leave 休暇中で kyúkachū de

leave behind vt (person, object) 置いて

行く ofte ikú; (object: accidentally) 置忘れる okíwasurerù

leave of absence n 休暇 kyūka, 暇 himá

leave out vt 抜かす nukásù

leaves [li:vz] npl of **leaf**

Lebanon [leb'ənən] n レバノン rebánòn

lecherous [letʃ'ərəs] (pej) adj 助平な sukébè na

lecture [lek'tʃəːr] n (talk) 講演 kóèn; (SCOL) 講義 kógì

♦vi (talk) 講演する kóèn suru; (SCOL) 講義する kógì sūru

♦vt (scold): **to lecture someone on/about something** ...の事で...をしかる ...no kotó de ...wo shikárù

...no kotó de ...wo shikárù
to give a lecture on ...について講演する ...ni tsúite kóèn suru

lecturer [lek'tʃəːrər] (BRIT) n (at university) 講師 kóshì

led [led] pt, pp of **lead[1]**

ledge [ledʒ] n (of mountain) 岩棚 iwádana; (of window) 桟 sán; (on wall) 棚 taná

ledger [ledʒ'əːr] n (COMM) 台帳 dáìchō

lee [li:] n 風下 kazáshìmo

leech [li:tʃ] n ヒル hírù

leek [li:k] n リーキ ríkì, リーク ríkù

leer [li:r] vi: **to leer at someone** ..をいん乱な目で見る ...wo ifnran na me de mírù

leeway [li:'wei] n (fig): **to have some leeway** 余裕がある yoyǘ ga arù

left [left] pt, pp of **leave**

♦adj (direction, position) 左の hidári no

♦n (direction, side, position) 左 hidári

♦adv (turn, look etc) 左に(へ) hidári ni(e)

on the left 左に(で) hidári ni(de)

to the left 左に(へ) hidári ni(e)

the Left (POL) 左翼 sáyòku

left-handed [left'hæn'ded] adj 左利きの hidárikiki no, ぎっちょの gítchò no

left-hand side [left'hænd'-] n 左側 hidárigawa

left-luggage (office) [left'lʌg'idʒ-] (BRIT) n 手荷物預かり所 tenímotsu azúkarishò

leftovers [left'ouvəːrz] npl (of meal) 残り物 nokórimono

left-wing [left'win] adj (POL) 左翼の sáyòku no

leg [leg] n (gen) 脚 ashí; (CULIN: of lamb, pork, chicken) もも mómò; (part: of journey etc) 区切り kugíri

legacy [leg'əsi:] n (of will: also fig) 遺産 isán

legal [li:'gəl] adj (of law) 法律の hóritsu no; (action, situation) 法的な hóteki na

legal holiday (US) n 法定休日 hóteikyūjitsu

legality [ligæl'iti:] n 合法性 góhòsei

legalize [li:'gəlaiz] vt 合法化する góhòka suru

legally [li:'gəli:] adv (by law) 法的に hóteki ni

legal tender n (currency) 法定通貨 hóteitsǔka, 法貨 hóka

legend [ledʒ'ənd] n (story) 伝説 defsetsu; (fig: person) 伝説的人物 defsetsutekijinbutsu

legendary [ledʒ'ənderi:] adj (of legend) 伝説の defsetsu no; (very famous) 伝説的な defsetsuteki na

legible [ledʒ'əbəl] adj 読める yomérù

legion [li:'dʒən] n (MIL) 軍隊 guñtai

legislation [ledʒislei'ʃən] n 法律 hóritsu

legislative [ledʒ'isleitiv] adj 立法の rippō no

legislature [ledʒ'isleitʃəːr] n (POL) 議会 gíkai

legitimate [lidʒit'əmit] adj (reasonable) 正当な seftō na; (legal) 合法な góhō na

leg-room [leg'ruːm] n (in car, plane etc) 脚を伸ばせる空間 ashí wo nobáserù kūkan

leisure [li:'ʒəːr] n (period of time) 余暇 yoká, レジャー rejā

at leisure ゆっくり yukkúrì

leisure centre (BRIT) n レジャーセンター rejāsèntā ◇スポーツ施設, 図書室, 会議室, 喫茶店などを含んだ大衆向け娯楽施設 supótsushisetsù, toshóshìtsu, kafgishìtsu, kissátèn nádò wo fukúǹda buñkashisetsù

leisurely [li:'ʒəːrli:] adj (pace, walk) ゆっくりした yukkúrì shitá

lemon [lem'ən] n (fruit) レモン rémòn

lemonade [leməneid'] n (BRIT: fizzy drink) ラムネ rámùne; (with lemon juice) レモネード remónèdo

lemon tea n レモンティー remóñtì

lend [lend] (pt, pp **lent**) vt: to lend something to someone (money, thing) ...に...を貸す ...ni ...wo kásù

lending library [len'diŋ-] n 貸出し図書館 kashídashitoshokàn

length [leŋkθ] n (measurement) 長さ nagása; (distance): the length of ...の端から端まで ...no hashí kara hashí madè; (of swimming pool) プールの長さ pùrù no nagása; (piece: of wood, string, cloth etc) 1本 ippóñ; (amount of time) 時間 jikáñ

at length (at last) とうとう tòtò; (for a long time) 長い間 nagái aída

lengthen [leŋk'θən] vt 長くする nágàku suru

♦vi 長くなる nágàku naru

lengthways [leŋkθ'weiz] adv (slice, fold, lay) 縦に táte ni

lengthy [leŋk'θi:] adj (meeting, explanation, text) 長い nagái

lenient [li:'ni:ənt] adj (person, attitude) 寛大な kańdai na

lens [lenz] n (of spectacles, camera) レンズ réñzu; (telescope) 望遠鏡 bóeñkyo

Lent [lent] n 四旬節 shijúñsetsu

lent [lent] pt, pp of **lend**

lentil [len'təl] n ヒラマメ hirámame

Leo [li:'ou] n (ASTROLOGY) ヒョウ座 shíza

leopard [lep'ərd] n (ZOOL) ヒョウ hyo

leotard [li:'ətɑːrd] n レオタード reótàdo

leprosy [lep'rəsi:] n らい病 raíbyò, ハンセン病 hañseñbyò

lesbian [lez'bi:ən] n 女性同性愛者 joséidòseiaishà, レズビアン resúbìan

less [les] adj (in size, degree) ...より小さい ...yórì chiísài; (in amount, quality) ...より少ない ...yórì sukúnaì

♦pron ...より少ないもの ...yórì sukúnaì monó

♦adv ...より少なく ...yórì sukúnakù

♦prep: less tax/10% discount ...から税金(1割)引いて ...kara zeíkin(ichí-

wári)wo híte

less than half 半分以下 hañbùn ikà

less than ever 更に少なく sárà ni sukúnàku

less and less ますます少なく masúmàsu sukúnakù

the less he talks the better ... 彼はできるだけしゃべらない方がいい kárè wa dekíru dake shabéranai hò ga íi

lessen [les'ən] vi 少なくなる sukúnaku narù

♦vt 少なくする sukúnàku suru

lesser [les'ər] adj (smaller: in degree, importance, amount) 小さい(少ない)方の chíísài(sukúnaì)hò no

to a lesser extent それ程ではないが ...も soré hodò de wa naí ga ...mo

lesson [les'ən] n (class: history etc) 授業 jugyō; (: ballet etc) けいこ kéīko, レッスン réssùn; (example, warning) 見せしめ miséshime

to teach someone a lesson (fig) ...に思い知らせてやる ...ni omóishirasete yarù

lest [lest] conj ...しない様に ...shinái yò ni

let [let] (pt, pp **let**) vt (allow) 許す yurúsù; (BRIT: lease) 賃貸する chíñtai suru

to let someone do something ...に...するのを許す ...ni ...surú no wò yurúsù

to let someone know something ...に...を知らせる ...ni ...wo shiráserù

let's go 行きましょう ikímashò

let him come (permit) 彼が来るのを邪魔しないで下さい kárè ga kúrù no wo jamá shinàide kudásaì

「to let」貸し家 kashíyà

let down vt (tire etc) ...の空気を抜く ...no kùki wo nukù; (person) がっかりさせる gakkárì saséru

let go vi (stop holding: thing, person) 手を放す te wo hanásù

♦vt (release: person, animal) 放す hanásu

lethal [li:'θəl] adj (chemical, dose etc) 致命的な chímeíteki na

a lethal weapon 凶器 kyōki

lethargic [ləθɑːr'dʒik] adj 無気力の mukíryòku no

let in vt (water, air) ...が漏れる ...ga morérù; (person) 入らせる hafraserù

let off vt (culprit) 許す yurùsù; (firework, bomb) 爆発させる bakùhatsu saserù; (gun) 撃つ útsù

let on vi 漏らす moràsù

let out vt (person, dog) 外に出す sótò ni dásù; (breath) 吐く hákù; (water, air) 抜く nůkù; (sound) 出す dásù

letter [let'əːr] n (correspondence) 手紙 tegámì; (of alphabet) 文字 mójì

letter bomb n 手紙爆弾 tegámibakùdan

letterbox [let'əːrbɑːks] (BRIT) n (for receiving mail) 郵便受け yúbin-uke; (for sending mail) 郵便ポスト yúbinposùto, ポスト pósùto

lettering [let'əːriŋ] n 文字 mójì

lettuce [let'is] n レタス rétàsu

let up vi (cease) やむ yámù; (diminish) 緩む yurúmù

let-up [let'ʌp] n (of violence, noise etc) 減少 gefishô

leukaemia [luːkiː'miːə] (BRIT **leukemia**) n 白血病 hakkétsubyô

level [lev'əl] adj (flat) 平らな taíra na
♦adv: **to draw level with** (person, vehicle) ...に追い付く ...ni oítsukù
♦n (point on scale, height etc) 高さ tákàsa, レベル rébèru; (of lake, river) 水位 súì
♦vt (land: make flat) 平らにする taíra ni surù; (building, forest etc: destroy) 破壊する hakái suru
to be level with ...と同じぐらいである ...to onáji gurài de árù
"A" levels (BRIT) 学科の上級試験 gakká no jôkyû shikèn 大学入学資格を得るための試験 daígakunyûgaku shikakù wo érù tamé no shikèn
"O" levels (BRIT) 学科の普通級試験 gakká no futsúkyû shikèn 中等教育を5年受けた後に受ける試験 chûtôkyôiku wò gonén uketà nochi ni ukérù shikèn
on the level (fig: honest) 正直で shôjiki de

level crossing (BRIT) n 踏切 fumíkiri

level-headed [lev'əlhed'id] adj (calm) 分別のある fuñbetsu no árù

level off vi (prices etc) 横ばい状態になる yokóbaijôtai ni nárù

level out vi = **level off**

lever [lev'əːr] n (to operate machine) レバー rébâ; (bar) バール bârù; (fig) 人を動かす手段 hitó wò ugôkasu shûdañ, てこ tékò

leverage [lev'əːridʒ] n (using bar, lever) てこの作用 tékò no sáyô; (fig: influence) 影響力 eíkyôryòku

levity [lev'iti:] n (frivolity) 不真面目さ fumájimesa

levy [lev'iː] n (tax, charge) 税金 zefkin
♦vt 課する ka súrù

lewd [luːd] adj (look, remark etc) わいせつな waísetsu na

liabilities [laiəbil'ətiːz] npl (COMM) 債務 sáìmu

liability [laiəbil'əti:] n (person, thing) 負担 futáñ; (LAW: responsibility) 責任 sekínin

liable [lai'əbəl] adj (subject): **liable to** ...の前触れの適用される ...no bassòku ga tekýô sarerù; (responsible): **liable for** ...の責任を負うべきである ...no sekńin wò oúbekì de árù; (likely): **liable to do** ...しがちである ...shígachi de árù

liaise [liːeiz'] vi: **to liaise (with)** (...と) 連携する (...to) refkei suru

liaison [liːeiz'ɑːn] n (cooperation, coordination) 連携 refkei; (sexual relationship) 密通 mittsû

liar [lai'əːr] n うそつき usôtsùki

libel [lai'bəl] n 名誉毀損 meíyokisòn
♦vt 中傷する chûshô suru

liberal [lib'əːrəl] adj (tolerant) 開放的な kaíhôteki na; (large: offer, amount etc) 寛大な kañdai na

liberate [lib'əreit] vt 解放する kaíhô suru

liberation [libərei'ʃən] n 解放 kaíhô

liberty [lib'əːrti:] n (gen) 自由 jiyû; (criminal): **to be at liberty** 捕まらないでいる tsukámaranaìde 'írù, 逃走中である tôsôchû de arù
to be at liberty to do 自由に...できる jiyû ni ...dekíru
to take the liberty of doing something 勝手に...する katté ni ...surù

Libra [li:'brə] n (ASTROLOGY) 天びん座 teñbínza

librarian [laibrɛə'riːən] n (worker) 図書館員 toshókah-in; (qualified) 司書 shísho

library [lai'brɛriː] n (institution, SCOL: building) 図書館 toshókáň; (: room) 図書室 toshóshitsu; (private collection) 蔵書 zósho

libretto [libret'ou] n (OPERA) 脚本 kyakúhon

Libya [lib'iːə] n リビア ríbia

Libyan [lib'iːən] adj リビアの ríbia no
♦n リビア人 ribíajìn

lice [lais] npl of **louse**

licence [lai'səns] (US also: **license**) n (official document) 免許 méñkyo; (AUT) 運転免許証 uñteñmeñkyoshō

license [lai'səns] n (US) = **licence**
♦vt (person, organization, activity) 認可する níñka suru

licensed [lai'sənst] adj (driver, pilot etc) 免許を持った méñkyo wo mottá; (for alcohol) 酒類販売許可を持った sakérui-hanbaikyòka wo mottá

license plate (US) n ナンバープレート nañbápurèto

licentious [laisen'tʃəs] adj いん乱な íñran na

lichen [lai'kən] n 地衣 chíi

lick [lik] vt (stamp, fingers etc) なめる namérù; (inf: defeat) ...に楽勝する ...ni rakúshō suru
to lick one's lips (fig) 舌なめずりする shitánamezùri suru

licorice [laik'ris] (US) n カンゾウあめ kañzóame

lid [lid] n (of box, case, pan) ふた futá; (eyelid) まぶた mábùta

lie [lai] (pt **lay**, pp **lain**) vi (person) 横になる yókò ni narú; (be situated: place, object: also fig) ...にある ...ni árù; (be placed: in race, league etc) 第...位である dái ...í de arù; (tell lies: pt, pp **lied**) うそをつく usó wo tsukú
♦n (untrue statement) うそ usó
to lie low (fig) 人目を避ける hitóme wo sakéru

lie about/around vi (things) 散らばっ

ている chirábatte iru; (people) ごろりと寝ている goróri te neté iru

lie-down [lai'daun] (BRIT) n: *to have a lie-down* 昼寝する hirúne suru

lie-in [lai'in] (BRIT) n: *to have a lie-in* 寝坊する nebó suru

lieu [luː]: *in lieu of* prep ...の代りに ...no kawári ni

lieutenant [luːten'ənt] n (MIL) (also: **first lieutenant**) 中尉 chùi; (also: **second lieutenant**) 少尉 shói

life [laif] (pl **lives**) n (quality of being alive) 生命 seímeì; (live, living: sea bottom, etc) 生物 seíbùtsu; (state of being alive) 命 ínòchi; (lifespan) 一生 isshó; (events, experience, activities) 生活 seíkatsu
to come to life (fig: person, party etc) 活気付く kakkízukù

life assurance (BRIT) n = **life insurance**

lifebelt [laif'belt] n 救命具 kyúmeìgu

lifeboat [laif'bout] n (rescue launch) 巡視艇 juñshitèi; (on ship) 救命ボート kyúmeibòto

lifeguard [laif'gɑːrd] n (at beach, swimming pool) 看視員 kañshiìn

life imprisonment n 無期懲役 mukíchòeki

life insurance n 生命保険 seímeihokèn

life jacket n 救命胴衣 kyúmeidòi

lifeless [laif'lis] adj (dead: person, animal) 死んだ shíñda; (fig: person) 元気のない géñki no nái; (: party etc) 活気のない kakkí no nái

lifelike [laif'laik] adj (model, dummy, robot etc) 生きているような様な íkìte irú yòna; (realistic: painting, performance) 写実的な shajítsuteki na

lifeline [laif'lain] n (means of surviving) 命綱 ínòchizùna

lifelong [laif'lɔːŋ] adj (friend, ambition etc) 一生の isshó no

life preserver (US) n = **lifebelt**; **life jacket**

life sentence n 無期懲役 mukíchòeki

life-size(d) [laif'saiz(d)] adj (painting, model etc) 実物大の jitsúbutsudaì no

life-span [laif'spæn] n (of person, animal, plant: *also fig*) 寿命 jumyō

life style *n* 生き方 ikíkata, ライフスタイル raffusutáiru

life support system *n* (MED) 生命維持装置 seímeiijísochi

lifetime [laif'taim] *n* (of person) 生涯 shōgai; (of thing) 寿命 jumyō

lift [lift] *vt* (raise: thing, part of body) 上げる agérù; (end: ban, rule) 撤廃する teppái suru

♦*vi* (fog) 晴れる harérù

♦*n* (BRIT: machine) エレベーター erébētā

to give someone a lift (AUT) ...を車に乗せて上げる ...wo kurúma ni nosete agerù

lift-off [lift'ɔːf] *n* (of rocket) 離昇 rishō

ligament [lig'əmənt] *n* じん帯 jíntai

light [lait] *n* (brightness: from sun, moon, lamp, fire) 光 hikári; (ELEC) 電気 deńki; (AUT) ライト ráito; (for cigarette etc): *have you got a light?* 火をお持ちですか hì wó o-móchì desu ká

♦*vt* (*pt, pp* **lit**) (fire) たく takú; (candle, cigarette) ...に火を付ける ...ni hí wo tsukérù; (room): *to be lit by* ...で照明されている ...de shōmei sarete irù

♦*adj* (pale) 淡い awáì; (not heavy: object) 軽い karúì; (: rain) 細かい komákaì; (: traffic) 少ない sukúnaì; (not strenuous: work) 軽い karúì; (bright: building, room) 明るい akárùì; (graceful, gentle: movement, action) 軽やかな karóyàka na; (not serious: book, play, film, music) 肩の凝らない katá no korániì

to come to light 明るみに出る akárumi ni derù

in the light of (discussions, new evidence etc) ...を考慮して ...wo kōryo shite

light bulb *n* 電球 deńkyū

lighten [lait'ən] *vt* (make less heavy) 軽くする karúku surù

lighter [lait'əːr] *n* (*also:* **cigarette lighter**) ライター ráitā

light-headed [lait'hed'id] *adj* (dizzy) 頭がふらふらする atáma ga fúràfura suru; (excited) 浮わついた uwátsuita

light-hearted [lait'hɑːr'tid] *adj* (person)

陽気な yṓki na; (question, remark etc) 気楽な kiráku na

lighthouse [lait'haus] *n* 燈台 tōdai

lighting [lait'iŋ] *n* (system) 照明 shōmei

lightly [lait'liː] *adv* 軽く karúku; (thoughtlessly) 軽はずみに kefsotsu ni; (slightly) 少し sukóshì

to get off lightly 軽い罰だけで逃れるkarúi bátsu dáke de nogárerù

lightness [lait'nis] *n* (in weight) 軽さ karúsa

lightning [lait'niŋ] *n* (in sky) 稲妻 ináżuma

lightning conductor (*BRIT*) *n* = lightning rod

lightning rod (*US*) *n* 避雷針 hiráìshin

light pen *n* ライトペン ráitopen

lights [laits] *npl* (AUT: traffic lights) (交通)信号 (kōtsū)shíngō

light up *vi* (face) 輝く kagáyakù

♦*vt* (illuminate) 明るくする akáruku suru

lightweight [lait'weit] *adj* (suit) 薄い usúi

♦*n* (BOXING) ライト級のボクサー ráitokyū no bókùsā

light year *n* (PHYSICS) 光年 kōnen

like [laik] *vt* (find pleasing, attractive, acceptable: person, thing) ...が好きである ...ga sukí de arù

♦*prep* (similar to) ...の様な ...no yṓ na; (in comparisons) ...の様に ...no yṓ ni; (such as) 例えば...などの様な(に) tatóèba ...nádò no yṓ na(ni)

♦*adj* 似た nitá

♦*n: and the like* など nádò

his likes and dislikes 彼の好きな物と嫌いな物 kárè no sukí na monò to kiráì na monò

I would like, I'd like ...が欲しいのですが ...ga hoshíi no desu ga

would you like a coffee? コーヒーはいかがですか kōhī wa ikága desu ká

to be/look like someone/something ...に似ている ...ni nité irù

what does it look/taste/sound like? どんな格好(味、音)ですか dóñna kákkō [ajī, otō]dèsu ká *that's just like him* 彼らしいね karé rashíi né

do it like this やり方はこうです yari-kata wa kó desu

it is nothing like ... ...とは全く違います ...to wa mattáku chigaímasu

likeable [laiˈkəbəl] *adj* (person) 人好きのする hitózuki no suru

likelihood [laikˈliːhud] *n* 可能性 kanōsei

likely [laikˈliː] *adj* (probable) ありそうな aríso na

to be likely to do ... ...しそうである ...shi-só de arú

not likely! 何があっても...しない nání ga atté mo ...shínái, とんでもない tondemonái

likeness [laikˈnis] *n* (similarity) 似ている事 nité irú kotó

that's a good likeness (photo, portrait) 実物そっくりだ jitsúbùtsu sokkúri da

likewise [laikˈwaiz] *adv* (similarly) 同じく onájiku

to do likewise 同じ様にする onáji yô ni suru

liking [laiˈkiŋ] *n*: *to have a liking for* (person, thing) ...が好きである ...ga sukí de arú

to be to someone's liking ...の気に入っている ...no kí ni itte irú

lilac [laiˈlək] *n* (BOT: tree, flower) ライラック rafrakkù, リラ rírâ

lily [lilˈiː] *n* (plant, flower) ユリ yurí

lily of the valley *n* スズラン suzúrañ

limb [lim] *n* (ANAT) 手足 téashi, 肢 shí

limber up [limˈbəːr-] *vi* (SPORT) 準備運動をする junbíuñdō wo suru, ウオーミングアップする uómingúappù suru

limbo [limˈbou] *n*: *to be in limbo* (fig) 忘れ去られている wasúresararete irú

lime [laim] *n* (fruit) ライム ráîmu; (also: *lime tree*) ライムの木 ráîmu no ki; (also: *lime juice*) ライムジュース raímujùsu; (for soil) 石灰 sékkái; (rock) 石灰岩 sekkáígan

limelight [laimˈlait] *n*: *to be in the limelight* 注目を浴びている chúmoku wo abíte irú

limerick [limˈəːrik] *n* 五行わい歌 gogyówaîka

limestone [laimˈstoun] *n* 石灰岩 sekkáígan

limit [limˈit] *n* (greatest amount, extent, degree) 限界 geñkai; (restriction: of time, money etc) 制限 seígen; (of area) 境界 kyōkai

♦*vt* (production, expense etc) 制限する seígen suru

limitation [limitei'ʃən] *n* (control, restriction) 制限 seígen; (of person, thing) 限界 geñkai

limited [limˈitid] *adj* (small: choice, resources etc) 限られた kagírareta

to be limited to ...に限られる ...ni kagírarerú

limited (liability) company (BRIT) *n* 有限会社 yūgen gaîsha

limousine [limˈəzin] *n* リムジン rímùjin

limp [limp] *n*: *to have a limp* びっこを引く bíkkò wo hikú

♦*vi* (person, animal) びっこを引く bíkkò wo hikú

♦*adj* (person) ぐにゃぐにゃの gúnyàgunya no

limpet [limˈpit] *n* カサガイ kaságaî

line [lain] *n* (long thin mark) 線 séñ; (wrinkle: on face) しわ shiwá; (row: of people, things) 列 rétsú; (of writing, song) 行 gyō; (rope) 綱 tsunà, ロープ rôpu; (also: *fishing line*) 釣糸 tsurííto; (also: *power line*) 送電線 sōdensen; (also: *telephone line*) 電話線 deñwasen; (TEL) 回線 kaísen; (railway track) 線路 séñro; (bus, coach, train route) ...線 ...sen; (fig: attitude, policy) 方針 hōshin; (: business, work) 分野 búñ-ya; (COMM: of product(s)) シリーズ shírîzu

♦*vt* (road, room) ...に並ぶ ...ni narábù; (subj: person: container) ...の内側に...を張る ...no uchigawa ni ...wo hárù; (: clothing) ...に裏地を付ける ...ni uráji wo tsukérù

to line something with ...に...の裏を付ける ...ni ...no urá wo tsukérù

to line the streets 道路の両側に並ぶ dòro no ryógawa ni narábù

in line (in a row) 1列に ichíretsu ni

in line with (according to) ...に従って ...ni shitágatte

linear [lin'i:ər] *adj* (process, sequence) 一直線の itchókusen no; (shape, form) 線形の sefikei no

lined [laind] *adj* (face) しわのある shiwá no arú; (paper) 線を引いた séñ wo hiíta

linen [lin'ən] *n* (cloth) リンネル ríñneru, リネン ríñen; (tablecloths, sheets etc) リネン ríñen

liner [lai'nər] *n* (ship) 豪華客船 gókakyakúsen; (for bin) ごみ袋 gomfbúkuro

linesman [lainz'mən] (*pl* **linesmen**) *n* (SPORT) 線審 sénshin, ラインズマン raínzuman

line up *n* 列を作る rétsu wo tsukúru

♦*vt* (people) 1列に並ばせる ichíretsu ni narábaserù; (prepare: event, celebration) 手配する teháì suru

line-up [lain'ʌp] *n* (US: queue) 行列 gyóretsu; (SPORT) ラインアップ raín-appù

linger [liŋ'gər] *vi* (smell, tradition etc) 残る nokórù; (person) ぐずぐずする gúzùguzu suru

lingerie [lɑːn'dʒəreì] *n* 女性下着類 joséishitagírùi, ランジェリー ráñjerī

lingo [liŋ'gou] (*pl* **lingoes**: *inf*) *n* (language) 言葉 kotóba

linguist [liŋ'gwist] *n* (person who speaks several languages) 数カ国語を話せる人 sükakokúgo wo hanáserù hitó

linguistic [liŋgwis'tik] *adj* (studies, developments, ideas etc) 語学の gógaku no

linguistics [liŋgwis'tiks] *n* 語学 gógaku

lining [lai'niŋ] *n* (cloth) 裏地 uráji; (ANAT) 粘膜 néñmaku

link [liŋk] *n* (relationship) 関係 kañkei; (of a chain) 輪 wá

♦*vt* (join) つなぐ tsunágu; (associate): **to link with/to** ...と関連付ける ...to kañrenzukerù

links [liŋks] *npl* (GOLF) ゴルフ場 gorúfujò

link up *vt* (machines, systems) つなぐ tsunágu

♦*vi* 合流する góryù suru

lino [lai'nou] *n* = **linoleum**

linoleum [linou'liːəm] *n* リノリウム ríñoriumu

lion [lai'ən] *n* (ZOOL) ライオン raíon

lioness [lai'ənis] *n* 雌ライオン mesúraìon

lip [lip] *n* (ANAT) 唇 kuchíbiru

lip-read [lip'riːd] *vi* 読唇する dokúshin suru

lip salve *n* 唇の荒れ止め kuchíbiru no arédome

lip service *n*: **to pay lip service to something** (*pej*) 口先だけ ...に賛成する u-wábe dake ...ni sañsei suru

lipstick [lip'stik] *n* 口紅 kuchíbeni

liqueur [likəːr'] *n* リキュール ríkyùru

liquid [lik'wid] *adj* 液体の ekítai no

♦*n* 液体 ekí, 液体 ekítai

liquidate [lik'wideit] *vt* (opponents, rivals) 消す késù, 殺す korósù; (company) つぶす tsubúsù

liquidize [lik'widaiz] *vt* (CULIN) ミキサーに掛ける mfkìsā ni kakérù

liquidizer [lik'widaizər] *n* (BRIT) ミキサー mfkìsā

liquor [lik'ər] *n* 酒 saké

liquorice [lik'əːris] (BRIT) *n* = **licorice**

liquor store (US) *n* 酒屋 sakáya

Lisbon [liz'bən] *n* リスボン rísùbon

lisp [lisp] *n* 舌足らずの発音 shitátarázu no hatsúòn

♦*vi* 舌足らずに発音する shitátarázu ni hatsúòn suru

list [list] *n* (catalog: of things) 目録 mokúroku, リスト rísùto; (: of people) 名簿 mefbo, リスト rísùto

♦*vt* (mention) 並べてあげる narábete agerù; (put on list) ...のリストを作る ...no rísùto wo tsukúrù

listed building [lis'tid-] (BRIT) *n* 指定建造物 shitéìkenzòbutsu

listen [lis'ən] *vi* 聞く kikú

to listen to someone/something ...を [...の言う事を]聞く ...wo[...no iú kotò wo] kikú

listener [lis'ənər] *n* (person listening to speaker) 聞いている人 kiíte irú hitó; (RADIO) 聴取者 chóshushà

listless [list'lis] *adj* 物憂い monóuì

lit [lɪt] *pt, pp of* **light**

liter [liːtər] *n* (*US*) = **litre**

literacy [lɪtərəsi] *n* 識字 shíkíji

literal [lɪtərəl] *adj* (exact: sense, meaning) 厳密な gefimitsu na; (word for word: translation) 逐語的な chikúgoteki na

literally [lɪtərəli] *adv* (in fact) 本当に hontō ni; (really) 文字通りに mojídōri ni

literary [lɪtəreriː] *adj* 文学の buńgaku no

literate [lɪtərit] *adj* (able to read etc) 読み書きできる yomíkaki dekirū; (educated) 教養のある kyōyō no arū

literature [lɪtərətʃər] *n* (novels, plays, poetry) 文学 buńgaku; (printed information: scholarly) 文献 buńken; (: brochures etc) 印刷物 insatsubūtsu, カタログ katárogu

lithe [laɪð] *adj* (person, animal) しなやかな shináyaka na

litigation [lɪtəgeɪʃən] *n* 訴訟 soshō

litre [liːtər] (*BRIT*) *n* = **liter**

litter [lɪtər] *n* (rubbish) 散らかっているごみ chirábatte iru gomí; (young animals) 一腹 hitóhara

litter bin (*BRIT*) *n* ごみ入れ gomfire

littered [lɪtərd] *adj*: **littered with** (scattered) ...で散らかされた ...de chirákasareta

little [lɪtəl] *adj* (small: thing, person) 小さい chiísaì; (young: child) 幼い osánaì; (short: distance) 近い chikáì; (time, event) 短い mijíkaì

♦*adv* 少ししか...ない sukóshì shika ...naì

a little (amount) 少し sukóshì

a little bit 少し sukóshì

little brother/sister 弟[妹] otóto[i-móto]

little by little 少しずつ sukóshizùtsu

little finger *n* 小指 koyúbi

live [*vb* liv *adj* laiv] *vi* (reside: in house, town, country) 住む súmù; (lead one's life) 暮す kurásù; (be alive) 生きている íkíte irù

♦*adj* (animal, plant) 生きている íkíte irù; (TV, RADIO) 生の namá no, ライブの ráìbu no; (performance) 実演の jitsúen no; (ELEC) 電流が通じている defíryū ga tsújite irù, 生きている íkíte irù; (bullet, bomb, missile) 使用可能状態の shiyō-kanōjotai no, 実の jitsú no

to live with someone (cohabit) ...と同せいする ...to dōsei surù

live down *vt* (defeat, error, failure): *I'll never live it down* 一生の恥だ isshō no hájí da

livelihood [laɪvliːhuːd] *n* (income source) 生計 sefkei

lively [laɪvliː] *adj* (person) 活発な kappátsu na; (interesting: place etc) 活気に満ちた kakkf ni michítà; (: event) にぎやかな nigíyaka na; (: book) 面白い omóshirò; (enthusiastic: interest, admiration etc) 熱心な nesshín na

liven up [laɪvən-] *vt* (person) ...に元気を付ける ...ni géñki wo tsukérù; (discussion, evening etc) 面白くする omóshirokù suru

♦*vi* (person) 元気になる géñki ni nárù; (discussion, evening etc) 面白くなる omóshirokù nárù

live on *vt fus* (food) ...を食べて暮す ...wo tábète kurásù

liver [lɪvər] *n* (ANAT) 肝臓 kañzō; (CULIN) レバー rêbā

livery [lɪvəriː] *n* (of servant) お仕着せ o-shíkise

lives [laɪvz] *npl of* **life**

livestock [laɪvstɑːk] *n* (AGR) 家畜 kachíku

live together *vi* (cohabit) 同せいする dōsei surù

live up to *vt fus* (fulfil) 守る mamórù

livid [lɪvid] *adj* (color: of bruise) 青黒い aógurol; (: of angry face) どす黒い dosúgurol; (: of sky) 鉛色の namáriiro no; (furious) 激怒した gékìdo shitá

living [lɪviŋ] *adj* (alive: person, animal) 生きている íkíte irù

♦*n*: *to earn/make a living* 生計を立てて sefkei wo tatérù

living conditions *npl* 暮しの状況 kuráshi no jōkyō

living room *n* 居間 imá

living standards *npl* 生活水準 sefkatsusuijun

tsusuijûn

living wage n 生活賃金 sefkatsuchiǹgin

lizard [lɪzəd] n トカゲ tokáge

load [loud] n (thing carried: of person) 荷物 nímotsu; (: of animal) 荷 ní; (: of vehicle) 積荷 tsumíni; (weight) 負担 fután

♦vt (also: **load up**: vehicle, ship etc): to **load (with)** (...を) ...に積む (...wo) ...ni tsumú; (COMPUT: program) メモリーに読込む mémorí ni yomíkomù, ロードす る rôdo suru; (gun) ...に弾丸を込める ...ni dańgan wo komérù; (camera) ...にフィルムを入れる ...ni fírumu wo irérù; (tape recorder) ...にテープを入れる ...ni têpu wo irérù

a load of rubbish (inf) ごたらめ dotárame

loads of/a load of (fig) 沢山の takúsaǹ no

loaded [loudid] adj (vehicle): to be **loaded with** ...を積んでいる ...wo tsuǹde iru; (question) 誘導的な yûdôteki na; (inf: rich) 金持の kanémochi na

loaf [louf] (pl **loaves**) n 一かたまりのパン hitókatamari no pan

loan [loun] n (sum of money) 貸付金 kashítsukekin, ローン rôn

♦vt (money, thing) 貸す kasú

on loan (borrowed) 借りている karíte irú

loath [louθ] adj: to be **loath to do something** ...をしたくない ...wo shitákunai

loathe [louð] vt (person, activity) ...が大嫌いである ...ga dáskiraí de árù

loaves [louvz] npl of **loaf**

lobby [lɑb'i:] n (of building) ロビー robí; (POL: pressure group) 圧力団体 atsúryokudańtai

♦vt (POL) ...に圧力をかける ...ni atsúryoku wò kakérù

lobe [loub] n (also: **earlobe**) 耳たぶ mimítabù

lobster [lɑb'stər] n ロブスター róbùsutā

local [lou'kəl] adj (council, paper, police station) 地元の jimóto no

♦n (BRIT: pub) 地元のパブ jimóto no

pábù

local anesthetic n (MED) 局部麻酔 kyokúbumasùi

local authority n 地方自治体 chihójichítai

local call n (TEL) 市内通話 shináitsūwa

local government n 地方自治体 chihójichítai

locality [loukæl'iti:] n 場所 basho

locally [lou'kəli:] adv 地元で jimóto de

locals [lou'kəlz] npl: the **locals** (local inhabitants) 地元の住民 jimóto no jûmìn

locate [lou'keit] vt (find: person, thing) 見付ける mitsúkeru; (situate): to be **located in** ...にある (いる) ...ni árù(irù)

location [loukei'ʃən] n (particular place) 場所 básho

on location (CINEMA) ロケで roke de

loch [lɑk] n 湖 mizúumi

lock [lɑk] n (of door, drawer, suitcase) 錠 jô; (on canal) こう門 kômon; (also: **lock of hair**) 髪の一房 kamí no hitófùsa

♦vt (door, drawer, suitcase: with key) ...のかぎを掛ける ...no kagí wo kakérù

♦vi (door etc) かぎが掛る kagí ga kakárù; (wheels) 回らなくなる mawáranaku narú

locker [lɑk'ər] n (in school, railway station etc) ロッカー rókkà

locket [lɑk'it] n ロケット rokéttò

lock in vt 閉じ込める tojíkomerù

lock out vt (person) 閉出す shimédasu

locksmith [lɑk'smiθ] n 錠前師 jômaeshi

lock up vt (criminal) 刑務所に入れる kéimushò ni irérù; (mental patient) 施設に預ける shisétsu ni azúkerù; (house) ...のかぎを掛ける ...no kagí wo kakérù

♦vi ...のかぎをかける ...no kagí wo kakérù

lockup [lɑk'ʌp] n (jail) 刑務所 kéimushò

locomotive [loukəmou'tiv] n 機関車 kikánsha

locum tenens [lou'kəm ti:'nenz] (BRIT **locum**) n (MED) 代診 dafshin

locust [lou'kəst] n イナゴ inágo

lodge [lɑdʒ] n (small house) 守衛室 shuéishìtsu; (hunting lodge) 山小屋 yamágoya

lodger ♦ *vi* (person): *to lodge (with)* (...の家に)下宿する (...no ể ni) geshukú suru; (bullet, bone etc) ...に支える ...ni tsukaérù

♦ *vt* (complaint, protest etc) 提出する tefshútsu suru

lodger [lɑːdʒˈər] *n* 下宿人 geshúkunin

lodgings [lɑːdʒˈiŋz] *npl* 下宿 geshúku

loft [lɔːft] *n* (attic) 屋根裏部屋 yanéurabèya

lofty [lɔːftiː] *adj* (noble: ideal, aim) 高尚な kóshō na; (self-important: manner) 横柄な ốhei na

log [lɔːg] *n* (piece of wood) 丸太 marúta; (written account) 日誌 nisshí

♦ *vt* (event, fact) 記録する kiróku suru

logarithm [lɔːgˈəriðəm] *n* (MATH) 対数 taísū

logbook [lɔːgˈbuk] *n* (NAUT) 航海日誌 kōkainisshì; (AVIAT) 飛行日誌 hikōnisshì; (BRIT: of car) 登録帳 tōrokuchō

loggerheads [lɔːgˈərhedz] *npl*: *to be at loggerheads* 対立している tañritsu shite iru

logic [lɑːdʒˈik] *n* (method of reasoning) 論理学 roñrigaku; (process of reasoning) 論理 róñri

logical [lɑːdʒˈikəl] *adj* (argument, analysis) 論理的な roñriteki na; (conclusion, result) 当然な tốzen na; (course of action) 合理的な gōriteki na

logistics [loudʒisˈtiks] *n* (planning and organization) 仕事の計画と実行 shigoto nò kefkaku tồ jikkō

logo [lou'gou] *n* (of firm) シンボルマーク shíñborumāku, ロゴ rốgo

loin [lɔin] *n* (of meat) 腰肉 koshíniku

loiter [lɔi'tər] *vi* (linger) ぶらつく burátsuku

loll [lɑːl] *vi* (person: also: *loll about*) ごろ寝する goróne suru

lollipop [lɑːl'iːpɑːp] *n* 棒あめ bốame

lollipop lady (*BRIT*) *n* 緑のおばさん midóri no obasan ◇学童道路横断監視員 gakúdō dōrodan kañshìin

lollipop man (*BRIT*: *pl* **lollipop men**) *n* 緑のおばさんの仕事をする男性 midó-

ri no obasan no shigóto wồ suru dansei

London [lʌn'dən] *n* ロンドン róñdon

Londoner [lʌn'dənər] *n* ロンドンっ子 roñdonkko

lone [loun] *adj* (person) たったひとりの tattá hítori no; (thing) たったひとつの tattá hítotsu no

loneliness [loun'liːnis] *n* 孤独 kodóku

lonely [loun'liː] *adj* (person) 寂しい sabíshiì; (situation) 孤独な kodóku na; (place) 人気のない hitóke no naì

long [lɔːŋ] *adj* 長い nagáì

♦ *adv* 長く nágàku

♦ *vi*: *to long for something* ...を恋しがる ...wo koíshigarù

so/as long as ...さえすれば ...sáè suréba

don't be long! 早く帰って来て下さいね háyàku kaétte kite kudàsaì nè

how long is the street? この道の端から端までどのぐらいありますか koñố míchì no hashí kara hashí madè donố gurai arímasồ ká

how long is the lesson? レッスンの時間はどのぐらいですか ressuñ no jíkàn wa donố guraì desu ká

6 meters long 長さは6メーター nágàsa wa rokú mētā

6 months long 期間は6か月 kíkàn wa rokkágetsu

all night long 一晩中 hitóbañjū

he no longer comes 彼はもう来ない kárè wa mố kónaì

long before 随分前に zuttố máè ni

before long (+future, +past) まもなく mamốnàku

at long last やっと yattố

long-distance [lɔːŋ'disˈtəns] *adj* (travel, phone call) 長距離の chốkyori no

longevity [lɑːndʒevˈitiː] *n* 長生き nagáiki

long-haired [lɔːŋ'heːrd] *adj* (person) 長髪の chốhatsu no

longhand [lɔːŋ'hænd] *n* 普通の書き方 futsū no kakíkata

longing [lɔːŋ'iŋ] *n* あこがれ akógare

longitude [lɑːn'dʒətuːd] *n* 経度 keído

long jump *n* 走り幅跳び hashírihabàtobi

long-life [lɔŋ'laif] adj (batteries etc) 寿命の長い jumyō no nagái; (milk) ロングライフの rōŋguraīfu no

long-lost [lɔŋ'lɔːst] adj (relative, friend) 長年会わなかった naganen awánakàtta

long-playing record [lɔŋ'plei'iŋ-] n L Pレコード erúpírekōdo

long-range [lɔŋ'reindʒ] adj (plan, forecast) 長期の chōki no; (missile, rocket etc) 長距離の chōkyori no

long-sighted [lɔŋ'saitid] adj (MED) 遠視の efishi no

long-standing [lɔŋ'stæn'diŋ] adj 長年にわたる naganen ni watárù

long-suffering [lɔŋ'sʌf'əriŋ] adj (person) 忍耐強い nińtaizuyoi

long-term [lɔŋ'tə:rm] adj (project, solution etc) 長期の chōki no

long wave (RADIO) 長波 chōha

long-winded [lɔŋ'win'did] adj (speech, text) 長たらしい nagatarashii

loo [luː] (BRIT: inf) n トイレ tōïre

look [luk] vi (see) 見る mírù; (seem, appear) ...に見える ...ni mièrù; (building etc): **to look south/(out) onto the sea** 南/海に面している minámi/(úmī)ni mén shite irú

♦n (gen): **to have a look** 見る mírù; (glance: expressing disapproval etc) 目付き métsùki; (appearance, expression) 様子 yōsu

look (here)! (expressing annoyance etc) おい oí

look! (expressing surprise: male language) 見て kké mité kuré; (: female language) 見て mité

look after vt fus (care for) ...の面倒を見る ...no meñdō wo mírù; (deal with) 取扱う toríatsukaù

look at vt fus (see) ...を見る ...wo mírù; (read quickly) ...にさっと目を通す ...ni sattó me wo tốsù; (study: problem, subject etc) 調べる shiráberù

look back vi (remember) 振返ってみる furíkaette mirù

look down on vt fus (fig) 軽べつする kefbetsu suru

look for vt fus (person, thing) 捜す sagásu

look forward to vt fus ...を楽しみにする ...wo tanőshimi ni suru; (in letters): **we look forward to hearing from you** ご返事をお待ちしております go-héñji wo o-máchi shitè orímasù

look into vt fus (investigate) ...を調べる ...wo shiráberù

look on vi (watch) 傍観する bốkan suru

look out vi (beware): **to look out (for)** (...に) 注意する (...ni) chúï suru

lookout [luk'aut] n (tower etc) 看視所 kañshijo; (person) 見張り人 mihárinín

to be on the lookout for something ...を警戒する ...wo keíkai suru

look out for vt fus (seek) 捜す sagásu

look round vi 見回す mimáwasù

looks [luks] npl (good looks) 容ぼう yốbō

look through vt fus (examine) ...を調べる ...wo shiráberù

look to vt fus (rely on) ...を頼りにする ...wo tayóri ni surù

look up vi (with eyes) 見上げる miágerù; (situation) ...の見通しがよくなる ...no mitõshi ga yokú naru

♦vt (piece of information) 調べる shiráberù

look up to vt fus (hero, idol) ...を尊敬する ...wo sofikei suru

loom [luːm] vi (also: **loom up**: object, shape) ぼんやりと姿を現す boñ-yarī to sugáta wò aráwasù; (: event: approach) 迫っている semátte irú

♦n (for weaving) 機織機 hatáorikī

loony [luː'niː] (inf) adj 狂っている kurútte irú

♦n 気違い kichígaì

loop [luːp] n (in string, ribbon etc) 輪 wá

♦vt: **to loop something round something** ...を巻付ける ...wo makítsukerù

loophole [luːp'houl] n (fig) 抜け穴 nukéana

loose [luːs] adj (not firmly fixed) 緩い yurúì; (not close fitting: clothes etc) ゆったりした yuttárī shita; (not tied back: long hair) 縛ってない shibátte naì; (promiscuous: life, morals) ふしだらな fushídàra na

♦n: **to be on the loose** (prisoner, maniac) 逃亡中である tốbôchǜ de arù

loose change n 小銭 kozéni

loose chippings [-tʃip'inz] npl (on road) 砂利 jarí

loose end n: **to be at loose ends** (US) or **a loose end** (BRIT) 暇を持て余している hima wo motéamashite irù

loosely [luːs'liː] adv 緩く yúrûku

loosen [luː'sən] vt 緩める yurúmerù

loot [luːt] n (inf) 分捕り品 bundórihin
♦vt (steal from: shops, homes) 略奪する ryakúdatsu suru

lop off [lɑːp-] vt (branches etc) 切り落す kiríotosù

lopsided [lɑːp'said'id] adj (crooked) 偏った katáyottà

lord [lɔːrd] n (BRIT: peer) 貴族 kízòku
Lord Smith スミス卿 sumísukyô
the Lord (REL) 主 shū
my lord (to bishop, noble, judge) 閣下 kákkà
good Lord! えっ ett
the (House of) **Lords** (BRIT) 上院 jốin

lordship [lɔːrd'ʃip] n: **your Lordship** 閣下 kákkà

lore [lɔːr] n (of particular culture) 伝承 deñshô

lorry [lɔːr'iː] (BRIT) n トラック torákkù

lorry driver (BRIT) n トラック運転手 torákku unteñshu

lose [luːz] (pt, pp **lost**) vt (object) 紛失する fuñshitsu suru, なくす nakúsù; (job) 失う ushínaù; (weight) 減らす herásù; (friend, relative through death) 失う ushínaù, なくす nakúsù; (waste: time) 無駄にする mudá ni surù; (: opportunity) 逃す nogásù; (money) 損する sóñ suru
♦vi (competition, argument) ...に負ける ...ni makérù
to lose (time) (clock) 遅れる okúrerù

loser [luː'zər] n (in game, contest) 敗者 hāisha; (inf: failure: person, thing) 出来損ない dekísokonai

loss [lɔːs] n (act of losing something) 紛失 fuñshitsu; (occasion of losing some-

thing) 喪失 sốshitsu; (death) 死亡 shibố; (COMM): **to make a loss** 損する sốñ suru

heavy losses (MIL) 大きな損害 ốkina songai

to be at a loss 途方に暮れる tohố ni kurérù

lost [lɔːst] pt, pp of **lose**
♦adj (person, animal: in unknown place) 道に迷った michí ni mayőtta; (: missing) 行方不明の yukúe fumêi no; (object) なくした nakúshita

lost and found (US) n 遺失物 ishítsubùtsu

lost property (BRIT) n = **lost and found**

lot [lɑːt] n (set, group of things) ひと組 hitőkumi; (at auctions) ロット rốttò
the lot (everything) 全部 zéñbu
a lot (large number, amount) 沢山 takúsan
a lot of 沢山の takusan no
lots of (things, people) 沢山の takúsan no
I read a lot 私は沢山の本を読みます watákushi wa takúsan no hoñ wò yomímasù
to draw lots (for something) (...の為に) くじを引く (...no tamê ni) kújì wo hîkù

lotion [lou'ʃən] n (for skin, hair) ローション rôshon

lottery [lɑːt'əːriː] n (game) 宝くじ takárakùji

loud [laud] adj (noise, voice, laugh) 大きい ốkii; (support, condemnation) 強い tsuyôi; (clothes) 派手な hadé na
♦adv (speak etc) 大きな声で ốkina kôè de
out loud (read, laugh, pray etc) 声を出して kôè wo dâshìte

loudhailer [laud'heilər] (BRIT) n = **bullhorn**

loudly [laud'liː] adv 大きな声で ốkina kôè de

loudspeaker [laud'spiːkər] n 拡声器 kakúseîki, スピーカー sûpîkā

lounge [laundʒ] n (BRIT: in house) 居間

imá; (in hotel, at airport, station) ロビー
róbī; (BRIT: also: **lounge bar**) ラウンジ
バー raúnjibā

♦vi ぐったりもたれる guttárī motárerù

lounge about vi ぶらぶらする búrabura
suru

lounge around vi = lounge about

lounge suit (BRIT) n 背広 sebíro, スー
ツ sútsu

louse [laus] (pl **lice**) n (insect) シラミ shi-
rámi

lousy [lau'zi:] adj (inf: bad quality: show,
meal etc) 最低の saítei no; (: ill) 気持が悪
い kimóchi gà warúi

lout [laut] n ちんぴら chífipira

lovable [lʌv'əbəl] adj 愛らしい aírashii

love [lʌv] n (strong affection: romantic,
sexual) 恋愛 refi-ai; (sexual) 性愛 seíai;
(strong liking: for music, football, animals etc) 愛着 aíchaku, 好み konómi

♦vt (gen) 愛する ai surù; (thing, activity
etc) ...が大好きである ...ga daísukī de
arù

to love to do ...するのが大好きである
...surú nò ga daísukī de arù

to be in love with ...にほれている ...ni
horéte irù, ...が好きである ...ga sukí de
arù

to fall in love with ...と恋に落ちる ...to
kóī ni ochírù, ...が好きになる ...ga sukí ni
narù

to make love (have sex) 性交する sefkō
suru, セックスする sékkusu suru

15 love (TENNIS) 15対0 jūgo taí zéro,
フィフティーンラブ fíftītīn rabu

I love chocolate 私はチョコレートが大
好きです watákushi wà chokórēto ga
daísukī desù

love affair n 情事 jōji

love letter n ラブレター rábùreta

love life n 性生活 seíseikatsu

lovely [lʌv'li:] adj (beautiful) 美しい utsú-
kushī; (delightful) 楽しい tanóshiī

lover [lʌv'əːr] n (sexual partner) 愛人 aíjin; (person in love) 恋人 koíbito

a lover of art/music 美術(音楽)の愛

好者 bíjutsu(óñgaku)no aíkōsha

loving [lʌv'iŋ] adj (person) 愛情深い aíjō-
bukaì; (actions) 愛情のこもった aíjō no
komótta

low [lou] adj (gen) 低い hikuì; (income,
price etc) 安い yasúì; (quality) 粗悪な so-
áku na; (sound: deep) 低い hikuì; (: quiet)
低い hikuì

♦adv (sing) 低音で teíon de; (fly) 低く hikúkù

♦n (METEOROLOGY) 低気圧 teíkiatsu

to be low on (supplies etc) ...が少なくな
っている ...ga sukúnàku natté irù

to feel low (depressed) 元気がない géñki ga naì

low-alcohol [lou'ælˈkəhɔl] adj (wine,
beer) 度の低いの no lùkūl

low-cut [lou'kʌt] adj (dress) 襟ぐりの深
い eríguri no fukaì, ローカットの rōkat-
to no

lower [lou'əːr] adj (bottom, less important) 下の shitá no

♦vt (object, price etc) 下げる sagérù;
(voice) 低くする híkùku suru; (eyes) 下に
向ける shitá ni mukéru

low-fat [lou'fæt'] adj (milk) 低脂肪の
teíshibō no, ローファットの rōfattò no

lowlands [lou'ləndz] npl (GEO) 低地 teíí-
chi

lowly [lou'li:] adj (position, origin) 卑し
い iyáshiī

loyal [loi'əl] adj (friend, support etc) 忠実
な chújitsu na

loyalty [loi'əlti:] n 忠誠 chūsei

lozenge [lɑz'indʒ] n (MED) ドロップ dó-
rōppu

LP [el'pi:'] n abbr = **long-playing
record**

L-plates [el'pleits] (BRIT) npl 仮免許運
転中の表示プレート karímenkyo unten-
chū no hyójīpurēto

Ltd abbr (COMM) = **limited (liability)
company**

lubricate [lub'rikeit] vt (part of
machine, chain etc) ...に油を差す ...ni a-
búra o sásù

lucid [lu:'sid] adj (writing, speech) 分かり
やすい wakáriyasuì; (able to think clear-

ly) 正気な shōki na

luck [lʌk] n (also: **good luck**) 運 ún
bad luck 悪運 akúun

good luck! 成功を祈るよ sefkō wō inórù yo

bad/hard/tough luck! 残念だね zañneñ da né

luckily [lʌk'ili:] adv 幸いに saíwai ni

lucky [lʌk'i:] adj (person: fortunate) 運の良い úñ no yóì; (: at cards etc) ...に強い ...ni tsuyóì; (situation, event) まさの magúrè no; (object) 好運をもたらる kōun wo motárasù

lucrative [lu:'krətiv] adj もうかる mōkarù

ludicrous [lu:'dəkrəs] adj (feeling, situation, price etc) ばかばかしい bákabakashii

lug [lʌg] (inf) vt (heavy object, suitcase etc) 引きずる hikízurù

luggage [lʌg'idʒ] n 手荷物 tenímotsu

luggage rack n (on car) ルーフラック rūfurakku; (in train) 網棚 amidana

lukewarm [lu:k'wɔːrm'] adj (liquid) ぬるい nurúì; (person, reaction etc) 気乗りしない kinōri shinai

lull [lʌl] n (break: in conversation, fighting etc) 途切れる事 togírerù kotó
◆vt: *to lull someone to sleep* ゆすって ...を寝付ばせる yusútte ...wo netsúkaserù

to be lulled into a false sense of security 油断すう yudán suru

lullaby [lʌl'əbai] n 子守歌 komóriùta

lumbago [lʌmbei'gou] n (MED) 腰痛 yōtsú

lumber [lʌm'bɚr] n (wood) 材木 zaímoku; (BRIT: junk) 粗大ごみ sodáigomi

lumberjack [lʌm'bɚrdʒæk] n きこり kikóri

lumber with vt: *to be lumbered with something* ...を押付けられる ...wo oshítsukerarerù

luminous [lu:'minəs] adj (fabric, color, dial, instrument etc) 蛍光の kefkō no

lump [lʌmp] n (of clay, butter etc) 塊 katámari; (on body) しこり shikóri; (on head) こぶ kobú; (also: **sugar lump**) 角砂

糖 kakúzatō
◆vt: *to lump together* 一緒くたに扱う isshókuta ni atsúkaù

a lump sum 一時払い金額 ichíjibaraikiñgaku

lumpy [lʌm'pi:] adj (sauce) 塊のある katámaridaràke no; (bed) ごつごつの gotsúgotsuna

lunar [lu:'nɚr] adj (landscape, module, landing etc) 月の tsukí no

lunatic [lu:'nətik] adj (behavior) 気違い染みた kichígaijimità

lunch [lʌntʃ] n 昼食 chūshoku

luncheon [lʌn'tʃən] n (formal meal) 昼食会 chūshokukai

luncheon meat n ランチョンミート rañchonmīto

luncheon voucher (BRIT) n 昼食券 chūshokukèn

lunch time n 昼食時 chūshokudoki

lung [lʌŋ] n (ANAT) 肺 haí

lunge [lʌndʒ] vi (also: **lunge forward**) 突進する tosshíñ suru
to lunge at ...を目掛けて突っ掛る ...wo megákkete tsukkákarù

lurch [lɚrtʃ] vi (person) よろめく yorómekù; (vehicle) 揺れる yurérù
◆n (movement: of person) よろめき yorómeki; (: of vehicle) 揺れる事 yurérù kotó

to leave someone in the lurch 見捨てる misúterù

lure [lur] n (attraction) 魅惑 miwáku
◆vt (entice, tempt) 魅惑する miwáku suru

lurid [lu:'rid] adj (violent, sexually graphic: story etc) どぎつい dogítsuì; (pej: brightly colored: dress etc) けばけばしい kebákebashiì

lurk [lɚrk] vi (animal, person) 待ち伏せする machíbuse surù

luscious [lʌʃ'əs] adj (attractive: person, thing) 魅力的な miryókuteki na; (food) おいしそうな oíshisō na

lush [lʌʃ] adj (fields, gardens) 生茂った oíshigettà

lust [lʌst] (pej) n (sexual desire) 性欲 sefyoku; (desire for money, power etc) 欲望

yokūbō

lust after *vt fus* (desire: strongly) ...の欲に駆られる ...no yokū ni karárerŭ; (: sexually) ...とセックスをしたがる ...to sekkúsŭ wo shitágarŭ

luster [lʌs'tər] (BRIT **lustre**) *n* (shining: of metal, polished wood etc) つや tsuyá

lust for *vt fus* = **lust after**

lusty [lʌs'ti:] *adj* (healthy, energetic) 元気一杯の geńkiippai no

Luxembourg [lʌk'səmbɑːrg] *n* ルクセンブルク rukŭséhburuku

luxuriant [lugzuːr'iːənt] *adj* (plants, trees) 生茂った oíshigettá; (gardens) 植込みの生茂った uékomi no oíshigettá; (hair) 豊富な hốfu na

luxurious [lugzuːr'iːəs] *adj* (hotel, surroundings etc) 豪華な gốka na

luxury [lʌk'ʃəriː] *n* (great comfort) ぜいたく zeítaku; (expensive extra) ぜいたく品 zeítakŭhin; (infrequent pleasure) 得難い楽しみ egátaí tanóshimí
♦*cpd* (hotel, car etc) 豪華... gốka...

lying [laiʔiŋ] *n* うそをつく事 usó wo tsukū kotó
♦*adj* うそつきの usótsuki no

lynch [lintʃ] *vt* (prisoner, suspect) 勝手に絞り首にする katté ni shibárikŭbi ni suru

lyrical [lirʔikəl] *adj* (poem) 叙情の jojố no; (fig: praise, comment) 叙情的な jojốteki na

lyrics [lirʔiks] *npl* (of song) 歌詞 káshi

M

m. *abbr* = meter; mile; million

M.A. [emei'] *abbr* = Master of Arts

mac [mæk] (BRIT) *n* = mackintosh

macabre [makɑːʔbrə] *adj* 背筋の凍る様な sesŭji no kốru yố na

macaroni [mækərouʔniː] *n* マカロニ makároni

machine [məʃiːn'] *n* (piece of equipment) 機械 kikái; (fig: party machine, war machine etc) 組織 sốshiki
♦*vt* (TECH) 機械で作る kikái de tsukú-

rŭ; (dress etc) ミシンで作る míshīn de tsukúrŭ

machine gun *n* 機関銃 kikáñjū

machine language *n* (COMPUT) 機械語 kikáigo

machinery [məʃiːʔnəriː] *n* (equipment) 機械類 kikáirŭi; (fig: of government) 組織 sốshiki

macho [mɑːtʃou] *adj* (man, attitude) 男っぽい otókkoppoi

mackerel [mækʔərəl] *n inv* サバ sabá

mackintosh [mækʔintɑʃ] (BRIT) *n* レーンコート réhkōto

mad [mæd] *adj* (insane) 気の狂った ki no kurúttá; (foolish) ばかげた bakágetá; (angry) 怒っている okótte irú; (keen: to be mad about (person, football etc) ...に夢中になっている ...ni muchū ni nattế iru

madam [mædʔəm] *n* (form of address) 奥様 ốkŭsama

madden [mædʔən] *vt* 怒らせる okőraserŭ

made [meid] *pt, pp* of **make**

Madeira [mədiːʔrə] *n* (GEO) マデイラ madéira; (wine) マデイラ madéira

made-to-measure [meidʔtəmeʒʔər] (BRIT) *n* = **made-to-order**

made-to-order [meidʔtuːʔɔːrdər] (US) *adj* オーダーメードの ốdāmềdo no

madly [mædʔliː] *adv* (frantically) 死物狂いで shinímonogŭrŭi de
madly in love そっこんほれ込んで zokkốn horékoñde

madman [mædʔmæn] (*pl* **madmen**) *n* 気違い kichígai

madness [mædʔnis] *n* (insanity) 狂気 kyốki; (foolishness) 気違い沙汰 kichígaizata

Madrid [mədridʔ] *n* マドリード madốrīdo

Mafia [mɑːrʔfiːə] *n* マフィア mấfia

magazine [mægəziːnʔ] *n* (PRESS) 雑誌 zasshí; (RADIO, TV) 放送ジャーナル hốsō jānárŭ

maggot [mægʔət] *n* ウジムシ ujímŭshi

magic [mædʔʒik] *n* (supernatural power) 魔法 mahố; (conjuring) 手品 tejína, マジック májīkku

♦*adj* (powers, ritual) 魔法の mahō no

magical [mædʒ'ikal] *adj* (powers, ritual) 魔法の mahō no; (experience, evening) 夢の様な yumé no yō na

magician [mədʒiʃ'ən] *n* (wizard) 魔法使い mahôtsukaí; (conjurer) マジシャン májìshan

magistrate [mædʒ'istreit] *n* 軽犯罪判事 keíhanzai hañji

magnanimous [mægnæn'əməs] *adj* (person, gesture) 寛大な kañdai na

magnate [mæg'neit] *n* 大立者 ôdatemóno, ...王 ...ō

magnesium [mægni:'ziəm] *n* マグネシウム magúneshiùmu

magnet [mæg'nit] *n* 磁石 jíshàku

magnetic [mægnet'ik] *adj* (PHYSICS) 磁石の jíshàku no; (personality) 魅力的な miryōkuteki na

magnetic tape *n* 磁気テープ jikí tèpu

magnetism [mæg'nitizəm] *n* 磁気 jíkì

magnificent [mægnif'əsənt] *adj* 素晴らしい subárashiì

magnify [mæg'nəfai] *vt* (enlarge: object) 拡大する kakúdai suru; (increase: sound) 大きくする ōkiku suru

magnifying glass [mæg'nəfaiɪŋ-] *n* 拡大鏡 kakúdaikyō

magnitude [mæg'nətu:d] *n* (size) 大きさ ōkisa; (importance) 重要性 jûyōsei

magnolia [mægnoul'jə] *n* マグノリア magúnorìa ◊モクレン、コブシ、タイサンボクを含む植物の類 mokûren, kóbùshi, taísañboku wo fukúmù shokúbùtsu no ruí

magpie [mæg'pai] *n* カササギ kasásagì

mahogany [məhɑːɡ'əni:] *n* マホガニー mahógànī ◊マホガニー材 mahógànizai

maid [meid] *n* (servant) メイド meído

old maid *n* (pej: spinster) ハイミス haímìsu

maiden [meid'ən] *n* (literary: girl) 少女 shōjo

♦*adj* (aunt etc) 未婚の mikón no; (speech, voyage) 処女... shójò ...

maiden name *n* 旧姓 kyūsei ◊既婚女性について使う kikónjosei ni tsúìte tsukáù

mail [meil] *n* (postal service) 郵便 yūbin; (letters etc) 郵便物 yūbínbutsu

♦*vt* (post) 投かんする tôkan suru

mailbox [meil'bɑ:ks] (*US*) *n* ポスト pósùto

mailing list [mei'liŋ-] *n* 郵送先名簿 yūsōsaki mèìbo

mail-order [meil'ɔːrdəːr] *n* (system) 通信販売 tsúshinhañbai

maim [meim] *vt* 重傷を負わせる jûshō wo owáserù ◊その結果不具になる場合について言う時の結果 fúgù ni nárù baái ni tsúìte iú

main [mein] *adj* 主な ómò na, 主要な shuyō na, メーンの mēn no

♦*n* (pipe) 本管 hoñkan

in the main (in general) 概して gái shite

mainframe [mein'freim] *n* (COMPUT) メインフレーム meínfurèmu

mainland [mein'lənd] *n* 本土 hóndo

mainly [mein'li:] *adv* 主に ómò ni

main road *n* 幹線道路 kañsendôro

mains [meinz] *npl*: *the mains* (gas, water) 本管 hoñkan; (ELEC) 本線 hoñsen

mainstay [mein'stei] *n* (fig: prop) 大黒柱 daíkokubàshira

mainstream [mein'stri:m] *n* (fig) 主流 shuryū

maintain [meintein'] *vt* (preserve: contact, friendship, system) 続ける tsuzúkerù; (keep in good repair) 保守する hojî suru; (keep up: momentum, output) 維持する ijí suru; (provide for: dependant) 養う yashínaù; (look after: building) 管理する kâñri suru; (affirm: belief, opinion) 主張する shuchō suru

maintenance [mein'tənəns] *n* (of contact, friendship, system) 保持 hojî; (of momentum, output) 維持 ijî; (provision for dependent) 扶養 fuyô; (looking after: building) 管理 kâñri; (affirmation: of belief, opinion) 主張する shuchō suru koto; (*BRIT:* LAW: alimony) 離婚手当 rikônteate

maize [meiz] *n* トウモロコシ toûmorokoshi

majestic [mədʒes'tik] *adj* (splendid: scenery etc) 壮大な sodái na; (dignified)

堂々とした dōdō to shitá

majesty [mædʒ'isti] n (title: *Your Majesty* 陛下 héika; (sovereignty) 王位 ôi; (splendor) 威厳 igén

major [mei'dʒər] n (MIL) 少佐 shōsa
◆adj (important, significant: event, factor) 重要な jūyō na; (MUS: key) 長調の chōchō no

Majorca [mɑjɔr'kə] n マジョルカ majórūka

majority [mədʒɔr'iti:] n (larger group: of people, things) 過半数 kahánsū; (margin: of votes) 得票差 tokúhyōsa

make [meik] (pt, pp **made**) vt (produce, form: object, clothes, cake) 作る tsukúrū; (: noise) 立てる tatérū; (: speech, mistake) する surú; (: remark) 言う iú; (manufacture: goods) 作る tsukúrū, 製造する seízō suru; (cause to be): **to make someone sad** ...を悲しくさせる ...wo kanáshiku saséru; (force): **to make someone do something** ...に...をさせる ...ni ...wo saséru; (earn: money) もうける mōkérū; (equal): **2 and 2 make 4** 2足す2は4 tású 2 wá 4
◆n (brand): **it's a Japanese make** 日本製です nihónsei desu

to make the bed ベッドを整える béddò wo totónoerū

to make a fool of someone ...をばかにする ...wo bákà ni surú

to make a profit 利益を得る ríèki wo érū

to make a loss 損をする són wo suru

to make it (arrive on time) 間に合う ma ní aū; (achieve something) 成功する seíkō suru

what time do you make it? 今何時ですか imá nánji desu ká

to make do with ...で間に合せる ...de ma ní awaserū

make-believe [meik'bili:v] n (pretense) 見せ掛け misékake

make for vt fus (place) ...に向かう ...ni mukáū

make out vt (decipher) 解読する kaídoku suru; (understand) 分かる wakárū; (see) 見る mírù; (write: cheque) 書く kákù

maker [mei'kər] n (of program, etc) 制作者 seísakushā; (manufacturer) 製造者 seízōshà, メーカー mēka

makeshift [meik'ʃift] adj (temporary) 間に合せの ma ní awase no

make up vt (constitute) 構成する kōsei suru; (invent) でっち上げる detchágerù; (prepare) 用意する yōi suru; (: parcel) 包む tsutsúmū
◆vi (after quarrel) 仲直りする nakánaori suru; (with cosmetics) 化粧する keshō suru

make-up [meik'ʌp] n (cosmetics) メーキャップ mēkyappū

make up for vt fus (loss, disappointment) ...の埋め合せをする ...no umáwase wo suru

make-up remover n 化粧落し keshō otōshi

making [mei'kiŋ] n (fig): **a doctor etc in the making** 医者の卵 ishá no tamágo

to have the makings of ...の素質がある ...no soshítsu ga arú

malaise [mæleiz'] n 倦怠 keńtai

malaria [məler'i:ə] n マラリア marária

Malaya [məlei'jə] n マラヤ mārāya

Malaysia [məlei'ʒə] n マレーシア maréshìa

male [meil] n (BIOL: not female) 雄 osú
◆adj (animal) 雄の osú no; (human) 男の otőko no, 男性の dańsei no; (attitude etc) 男性的な dańseiteki na

malevolent [məlev'ələnt] adj (evil, harmful: person, intention) 悪魔の様な ákùma no yō na

malfunction [mælfʌŋk'ʃən] n (of computer, machine) 故障 koshō

malice [mæl'is] n (ill will) 悪意 ákùi; (rancor) 恨み urámi

malicious [məliʃ'əs] adj (spiteful: person, gossip) 悪意に満ちた ákùi ni michíta

malign [məlain'] vt (slander) 中傷する chūshō suru

malignant [məlig'nənt] adj (MED: tumor, growth) 悪性の akúsei no

mall [mɔl] n (also: **shopping mall**) ショ

ッピング・モール shoppíngu mòru

mallet [mǽl'it] *n* 木づち kízuchi

malnutrition [mælnutrí∫'ən] *n* 栄養失調 eíyōshìtchō

malpractice [mælpræk'tis] *n* (MED) 医療過誤 iryōkagò; (LAW) 不正行為 fuséikōi

malt [mɔːlt] *n* (grain) もやし moyáshi, モルト mórùto; (*also*: **malt whisky**) モルトウイスキー mórùto uísùkī

Malta [mɔːl'tə] *n* マルタ márùta

Maltese [mɔːltiːz'] *adj* マルタの márùta no

♦*n inv* マルタ人 marútajìn

maltreat [mæltriːt'] *vt* (treat badly, violently: child, animal) 虐待する gyakútai suru

mammal [mǽm'əl] *n* ほ乳類 honyúrùi

mammoth [mǽm'əθ] *n* (animal) マンモス máñmosu

♦*adj* (colossal, enormous: task) ばく大な bakúdai na

man [mæn] (*pl* **men**) *n* (adult male) 男 otóko, 男性 dañsei; (mankind) 人間 jíñrui

♦*vt* (NAUT: ship) 乗組ませる noríkumaserù; (MIL: gun, post) 配置につく haíchi ni tsúkù; (operate: machine) 操作する sōsa suru

an old man 老人 rōjìn

man and wife 夫婦 fúfu

manage [mǽn'idʒ] *vi* (succeed) うまくなんとかする úmàku nántoka suru; (get by financially) なんとかして暮す nántoka shite kurásù

♦*vt* (be in charge of: business, shop, organization) 管理する káñri suru; (control: ship) 操縦する sōjū suru; (: person) うまくあしらう úmàku atsúkaìwasù

manageable [mǽn'idʒəbəl] *adj* (task, number) 扱いやすい atsúkaiyasuì

management [mǽn'idʒmənt] *n* (of business etc: control, organization) 管理 káñri; (: persons) 経営陣 kaíeijìn

manager [mǽn'idʒəːr] *n* (of business etc) 支配人 shiháinin; (of pop star) マネージャー manéjà; (SPORT) 監督 kañtoku

manageress [mæn'idʒəris] *n* (of business etc) 女性支配人 joséishihaìnin; (of pop star) 女性マネージャー joséi manéjà; (SPORT) 女性監督 joséi kàñtoku

managerial [mænidʒíːriəl] *adj* (role, skills) 管理職の kañríshòku no

managing director [mǽn'idʒiŋ-] *n* 専務取締役 señmutoríshimariyàku

mandarin [mǽn'dərin] *n* (*also*: **mandarin orange**) みかん mikàn; (high-ranking bureaucrat) 高級官僚 kōkyū kañryō

mandate [mǽn'deit] *n* (authority) 権限 keñgen; (task) 任務 nímmu

mandatory [mǽn'dətɔːri] *adj* (obligatory) 義務的な gimúteki na

mane [mein] *n* (of horse, lion) たてがみ tatégami

maneuver [mənuːˈvəːr] (*US*) *vt* (move: car, bulky, object) 巧みに動かす tákùmi ni ugókasù; (manipulate: person, situation) 操る ayátsurù

♦*vi* (move: car, plane) 巧みに動く tákùmi ni ugókù; (MIL) 軍事演習を行う guñjieńshū wo okonau

♦*n* 巧みな動き tákùmi na ugóki

manfully [mǽn'fəli] *adv* (valiantly) 勇ましく isámashikù

mangle [mǽŋ'gəl] *vt* (crush, twist) めちゃくちゃにする mechákucha ni suru

mango [mǽŋ'gou] (*pl* **mangoes**) *n* マンゴー máñgō

mangy [mein'dʒiː] *adj* (animal) 汚らしい kitánarashìī

manhandle [mǽn'hændəl] *vt* (mistreat) 手荒に扱う teára ni atsúkaù

manhole [mǽn'houl] *n* マンホール mañhóru

manhood [mǽn'hud] *n* (age) 成人時代 seíjin jídai; (state) 成人である事 seíjin de arù kótó （男性のみについて言う dañsei nomì ni tsúkìte iù

man-hour [mǽn'auər] *n* (time) 人時 hitójì

manhunt [mǽn'hʌnt] *n* (POLICE) 人間狩り ningéngari

mania [mei'niːə] *n* (craze) ...狂 ...kyō; (illness) そう病 sōbyō

maniac [mei'niːæk] *n* (lunatic) 狂人 kyōjin; (*fig*) 無謀な人 mubō na hitó

manic [mæn'ik] *adj* (behavior, activity) 猛烈な mōretsu na

manic-depressive [mæn'ikdipres'iv] *n* そううつ病患者 sōutsubyō kañja

manicure [mæn'əkju:r] *n* マニキュア maníkyùa

manicure set *n* マニキュア・セット maníkyua settò

manifest [mæn'əfest] *vt* (show, display) 表す aráwasù

♦*adj* (evident, obvious) 明白な meíhaku na

manifestation [mænəfestéi'ʃən] *n* 現れ aráware

manifesto [mænəfes'tou] *n* 声明書 seímeisho

manipulate [mənip'əleit] *vt* (people) 操る ayátsurù; (system, situation) 操作する sōsa suru

mankind [mæn'kaind'] *n* (human beings) 人類 jíñrui

manly [mæn'li:] *adj* (masculine) 男らしい otókorashìi

man-made [mæn'meid] *adj* (environment, satellite etc) 人工の jíñkō no; (fiber, lake etc) 人造の jíñzō no

manner [mæn'ə:r] *n* (way) やり方 yaríkata; (behavior) 態度 táìdo; (type, sort):
all manner of things あらゆる物 aráyuru monò

mannerism [mæn'ərizəm] *n* 癖 kusé

manners [mæn'ə:rz] *npl* (conduct) 行儀 gyógì, マナー mánà
bad manners 行儀の悪い事 gyógi no warúî kotó

manoeuvre [mənu:'və:r] (*BRIT*) = maneuver

manor [mæn'ə:r] *n* (*also:* **manor house**) 屋敷 yashíki

manpower [mæn'pauə:r] *n* (workers) 人手 hitóde

mansion [mæn'tʃən] *n* 豪邸 gôtei

manslaughter [mæn'slɔ:tə:r] *n* (LAW) 殺意なき殺人 satsúinaki satsújiñ

mantelpiece [mæn'təlpi:s] *n* マントルピース mañtorupìsu

manual [mæn'ju:əl] *adj* (work, worker) 肉体の nikútai no; (controls) 手動の shu-

dō no
♦*n* (book) マニュアル mányùaru

manufacture [mænjəfæk'tʃə:r] *vt* (make, produce: goods) 製造する seízō suru
♦*n* (making) 製造 seízō

manufacturer [mænjəfæk'tʃərə:r] *n* 製造業者 seízōgyōsha, メーカー mēkā

manure [mənu:r'] *n* 肥やし koyáshi

manuscript [mæn'jəskript] *n* (of book, report) 原稿 geñkō; (old document) 写本 shahóñ

many [men'i:] *adj* (a lot of: people, things, ideas) 沢山の takúsañ no
a great many 非常に沢山の hijō ni takúsañ no
many a time 何回も nañkai mo

map [mæp] *n* (of town, country) 地図 chízu

maple [mei'pəl] *n* (tree) カエデ kaéde; (wood) カエデ材 kaédezài

map out *vt* (plan, task) 計画する keíkaku su suru

mar [mɑːr] *vt* (spoil: appearance) 損なう sokónaù; (: day, event) ぶち壊す buchí kowasù

marathon [mær'əθɑːn] *n* (race) マラソン maráson

marauder [mərɔːd'ə:r] *n* (robber, killer) 荒し回る無法者 satsújiñ, ryakúdatsu nado wo kurfkaeshinagara arashimawarù muhómòno

marble [mɑːr'bəl] *n* (stone) 大理石 daírisèki; (toy) ビー玉 bídama

March [mɑːrtʃ] *n* 3月 sañgatsu

march [mɑːrtʃ] *vi* (MIL: soldiers) 行進する kōshin suru; (*fig:* protesters) デモ行進をする demó kōshin wo suru; (walk briskly) 足音も高く歩く ashfoto mo takáku arúkù
♦*n* (MIL) 行進 kōshin; (demonstration) デモ行進 demó kōshin

mare [me:r] *n* 牝ウマ mesú uma

margarine [mɑːr'dʒəri:n] *n* マーガリン māgarin

margin [mɑːr'dʒin] *n* (difference: of

votes) 差 sa; (extra amount) 余裕 yoyū́; (COMM: profit) 利ざや rizáya, マージン májin; (space: on page) 余白 yohǎku; (edge of area, group) 外れ hazúre

marginal [maːrˈdʒinəl] *adj* (unimportant) 二次的な nijíteki na

marginal (seat) *n* (POL) 不安定な議席 fuántei na gisékí♢わずかな票の差で得たので、次の選挙で失う可能性のある議席 wǎzūka na hyő nó sá de etá node, tsugí nő senkyo de ushínaū kanôsei no arū giséki

marigold [mærˈigould] *n* マリーゴールド marígōrudo

marijuana [mærəwɑːˈnə] *n* マリファナ marffana

marina [məriˈnə] *n* (harbor) マリーナ marína

marinate [mærˈəneit] *vt* (CULIN) マリネにする marīne ni suru

marine [məriːnˈ] *adj* (life, plant, biology) 海の umí no; (engineer, engineering) 船舶の senpaku no
♦*n* (US: sailor) 海兵隊員 kaíheitàin; (BRIT: soldier) 海兵隊員 kaíheitàin

marital [mærˈitəl] *adj* (problem, relations) 夫婦の fúfu no
marital status n未婚、既婚、離婚を尋ねる時の言葉 mikón, kikón, ríkón wo tazúnerū tokí ni tsukaú kotóba

maritime [mærˈitaim] *adj* 海事の kǎiji no

marjoram [mɑːrˈdʒərəm] *n* マヨラナ mayónàra, マージョラム májōramu

mark [mɑːrk] *n* (symbol: cross, tick etc) 印 shirúshi; (stain) 染み shimí; (of shoes, fingers, tires: in snow, mud etc) 跡 átò; (sign: of friendship, respect etc) 印 shirúshi; (SCOL) 成績 sefseki; (level, point): *the halfway mark* 中間点の目印 chúkanten no mejírùshi; (currency) マルク márùku
♦*vt* (make a mark on: with pen etc) 印を書く shirúshi wo kákù; (: with shoes, tires etc) 跡を残す átò wo nokósù; (damage: furniture etc) 傷を付ける kizú wo tsukérù; (stain: clothes, carpet etc) 染みを付ける shimí wo tsukérù; (indicate:

place, time, price) 示す shimésù; (commemorate: event) 記念する kinén suru; (BRIT: SCOL) 成績をつける seíseki wð tsukérù

to mark time (MIL, *fig*) 足踏みする a-shífumi suru

marked [mɑːrkt] *adj* (obvious) 著しい i-chíjirushii

marker [mɑːrˈkər] *n* (sign) 目印 mejírùshi; (bookmark) しおり shióri

marker pen n サインペン saínpen

market [mɑːrˈkit] *n* (for fish, cattle, vegetables etc) 市場 íchìba, 市場 ichíba; (for names) 市場 íchìba, 市場 shijô; (COMM: business and trading activity) 市場 shijô; (: demand) 需要 juyô
♦*vt* (COMM: sell) 市場に出す shijô ni dásù

market garden (BRIT) *n* 野菜農園 yasáindèn♢主に市場向けの野菜や果物を栽培する小規模農場 ómð ni shijômuke no yasái ya kudámono wò saíbai surú shôkibo nôjô

marketing [mɑːrˈkitiŋ] *n* (COMM) 販売 hañbai

marketplace [mɑːrˈkitpleis] *n* (area, site: *also* COMM) 市場 íchìba

market research *n* 市場調査 shijôchôsa

marksman [mɑːrksˈmən] (*pl* **marksmen**) *n* 射撃の名手 shagéki no meíshū

marmalade [mɑːrˈməleid] *n* マーマレード mâmarèdo

maroon [məruːnˈ] *vt: to be marooned* (shipwrecked) 遭難で置去りになる sônan dè okízari ni narū; (*fig*: abandoned) 置去りにされる okízari ni sarérù
♦*adj* (color) クリ色 kuríiro

marquee [mɑːrkiːˈ] *n* (tent) テント marquee♢運動会、野外パーティなどで使う物を指す uñdôkai, yagái pâti nâdò de tsukáũ monó wo sásù

marquess [mɑːrˈkwis] *n* 侯爵 kôshaku

marquis [mɑːrˈkwis] *n* = **marquess**

marriage [mærˈidʒ] *n* (relationship, institution) 結婚 kekkón; (wedding) 結婚式 kekkôñshiki

marriage bureau *n* 結婚相談所 kekkónsōdanjo

marriage certificate *n* 結婚証明書 kekkónshōmeishō

married [mær'i:d] *adj* (man, woman) 既婚の kikón no; (life, love) 結婚の kekkón no

marrow [mær'ou] *n* (vegetable) セイヨウカボチャ sefyōkabōcha; (also: **bone marrow**) 骨髄 kotsúzui

marry [mær'i:] *vt* (man, woman) ...と結婚する ...to kekkón suru; (subj: father, priest etc) ...の結婚式を行う ...no kekkónshiki wo okónaū
♦*vi* (also: **get married**) 結婚する kekkón suru

Mars [mɑːrz] *n* (planet) 火星 kaséi

marsh [mɑːrʃ] *n* (bog) 湿原地 shitsúgeñchi; (also: **salt marsh**) 塩性沼沢地 eñsei shótakuchi

marshal [mɑːr'ʃəl] *n* (MIL: also: **field marshal**) 陸軍元帥 rikúgun geñsui; (official: at sports meeting etc) 役員 yakúiñ; (US: of police, fire department) 長官 chōkan
♦*vt* (organize: thoughts) 整理する sefri suru; (: support) 集める atsúmerū; (: soldiers) 整列させる sefretsu saserū

marshy [mɑːr'ʃi:] *adj* 沼沢の多い shótaku nō ōi

martial [mɑːr'ʃəl] *adj* (military) 軍の gúñ no

martial arts *npl* 武術 bújutsu

martial law *n* 戒厳令 kaígeñrei

martyr [mɑːr'tər] *n* (for beliefs) 殉教者 juñkyōsha

martyrdom [mɑːr'tərdəm] *n* 殉教 juñkyō

marvel [mɑːr'vəl] *n* (wonder) 驚異 kyōi
♦*vi*: **to marvel (at)** 驚嘆する kyōtan suru

marvelous [mɑːr'vələs] (*BRIT* **marvellous**) *adj* 素晴らしい subárashiī

Marxism [mɑːrk'sizəm] *n* マルクス主義 marúkushúgi

Marxist [mɑːrk'ksist] *adj* マルクス主義の marúkushúgi no
♦*n* マルクス主義者 marúkushúgìsha

marzipan [mɑːr'zəpæn] *n* マジパン mají-

pan

mascara [mæskær'ə] *n* マスカラ masúkara

mascot [mæs'kɔt] *n* マスコット masúkòtto

masculine [mæs'kjəlin] *adj* (male: characteristics, pride) 男性の dañsei no; (: atmosphere) 男性的な dañseiteki na; (woman) 男の様な otóko no yō na; (LING: noun, pronoun etc) 男性の dañsei no

mash [mæʃ] *vt* つぶす tsubúsu

mashed potatoes [mæʃt-] *npl* マッシュポテト masshú potèto

mask [mæsk] *n* (disguise) 覆面 fukúmen; (shield: gas mask, face mask) マスク másùku
♦*vt* (cover: face) 覆い隠す ōikakúsu; (hide: feelings) 隠す kakúsu

masochist [mæs'əkist] *n* マゾヒスト mazóhisùto

mason [mei'sən] *n* (also: **stone mason**) 石屋 ishíya; (also: **freemason**) フリーメーソン furíméson

masonic [məsɑːn'ik] *adj* (lodge, dinner) フリーメーソンの furíméson no

masonry [mei'sənri:] *n* (stonework) 石造部 sekízòbu ◊建物の石やれんがなどで造られた部分 tatémòno no ishí yà refiga nadò de tsukúrarèta bûbûn

masquerade [mæskəreid'] *vi*: **to masquerade as ...** を装う ...wo yosōoū

mass [mæs] *n* (large number: of papers, people etc) 多数 tasū; (large amount: of detail, hair etc) 大量 tafryō; (amount: of air, liquid, land) 集団 shūdan; (PHYSICS) 物質 butsúryō; (REL) ミサ聖祭 misá seisai
♦*cpd* (communication, unemployment etc) 大量の tafryō no
♦*vi* (troops, protesters) 集合する shúgo suru

massacre [mæs'əkər] *n* 大虐殺 daígyakùsatsu

massage [məsɑːʒ'] *n* マッサージ massáji
♦*vt* (rub) マッサージする massáji suru

masses [mæs'iz] *npl*: **the masses** (ordinary people) 大衆 taíshū

masses of (*inf*: food, money, people) 一杯の ippai no

masseur [mæˈsəːʳ] *n* マッサージ師 massájìshì

masseuse [mɑsuːsˈ] *n* マッサージ嬢 massájìjô

massive [mæsˈiv] *adj* (large and heavy: furniture, door, person) どっしりした dosshírì shita; (huge: support, changes, increase) 膨大な bôdai na

mass media [-miːˈdiːə] *npl* マスメディア masúmèdia

mass production [BRIT mass-production] *n* 大量生産 taíryōseisan, マスプロ masúpùro

mast [mæst] *n* (NAUT) マスト másùto; (RADIO etc) 放送アンテナ hōsō añtena

master [mæsˈtəːʳ] *n* (of servant, slave) 主人 shujín, (in secondary school) 先生 señsei; (title for boys): **Master X X**君 ékusu kùn

♦*vt* (control: situation) 掌握する shôaku suru; (: one's feelings etc) 抑える osáerù; (learn: skills, language) 修得する shútoku suru, マスターする masútā suru

to be master of the situation (*fig*) 事態を掌握している jítài wo shôaku shite irù

master key *n* マスターキー masútā kî

masterly [mæsˈtəːrliː] *adj* あっぱれな appáre na

mastermind [mæsˈtəːrmaind] *n* (of crime etc) 首謀者 shubôsha, 黒幕 kurómaku

♦*vt* 計画を練って実行させる keíkaku wò néttè jikkō saserù

Master of Arts/Science *n* (person) 文学 (理学) 修士 buñgaku (rigàku) shúshì; (qualification) 文学 (理学) 修士号 buñgaku (rigàku) shúshigô

masterpiece [mæsˈtəːrpiːs] *n* 傑作 kessáku

mastery [mæsˈtəːriː] *n* (of skill, language) 修得 shútoku

masturbate [mæsˈtəːrbeit] *vi* マスターベーションをする masútābèshon(onáni)wo suru

masturbation [mæstəːrbeiˈʃən] *n* マスタ

ーベーション masútābèshon, オナニー onánì

mat [mæt] *n* (on floor) マット máttò; (at door: *also*: **doormat**) ドアマット doámattò; (on table: *also*: **table mat**) テーブルマット tēburumattò

♦*adj* = **matt**

match [mætʃ] *n* (game: of football, tennis etc) 試合 shiái, マッチ mátchì; (for lighting fire, cigarette) マッチ mátchì; (equal) 力が同等な人 chíkàra ga dôtō na hitô

♦*vt* (go well with: subj: colors, clothes) ...に合う ...ni áù; (equal) ...と同等である ...to dôtō de arù; (correspond to) ...に合う ...ni áù; (pair: *also*: **match up**) ...と合せる ...to awáserù

...**to awaserù** ...と組ませる ...to kumáserù

♦*vi* (colors, materials) 合う áù

to be a good match (colors etc) よく合う yokú áù; (couple) 似合いの...である niáì no ...de arù

matchbox [mætʃˈbɑks] *n* マッチ箱 matchíbakò

matching [mætʃˈiŋ] *adj* (clothes etc) その...にそろいの sono ...ni soróì no

mate [meit] *n* (workmate) 仲間 nakáma; (*inf*: friend) 友達 tomódachi; (animal) 相手 aíte; (in merchant navy: first, second) ...等航海士 ...tô kokaishi

♦*vi* (animals) 交尾する kôbi suru

material [mətiːˈriəl] *n* (substance) 物質 busshítsu; (cloth) 生地 kijf; (information, data) 情報 jôhō

♦*adj* (possessions, existence) 物質的な busshftsuteki na

materialistic [mətiəˈrialistˈik] *adj* 唯物主義的な yuíbutsushugìteki na

materialize [mətiːˈriəlaiz] *vi* (happen) 起る okórù; (appear) 現れる aráwarerù

materials [mətiːˈriəlz] *npl* (equipment) 材料 zaíryô

maternal [mətəːrˈnəl] *adj* (feelings, role) 母性の boséi no

maternity [mətəːrˈnitiː] *n* 母性 boséi

maternity dress *n* マタニティドレス matánitidorèsu

maternity hospital *n* 産院 sań-in

math [mæθ] (*BRIT* **maths**) *n* 数学 sū́gaku

mathematical [mæθəmæt'ikəl] *adj* (formula) 数学の sū́gaku no; (mind) 数学的な sū́gakuteki na

mathematician [mæθəməti'ʃən] *n* 数学者 sū́gakusha

mathematics [mæθəmæt'iks] *n* 数学 sū́gaku

maths [mæθs] (*BRIT*) *n* = **math**

matinée [mætənei'] *n* マチネー machíne

mating call [mei'tiŋ-] *n* (of animals) 求愛の声 kyū́ai no kóè

matrices [meit'risiz] *npl of* **matrix**

matriculation [mətrikjəlei'ʃən] *n* (enrollment) 大学入学 daígakunyūgaku

matrimonial [mætrəmou'ni:əl] *adj* 結婚の kekkón no

matrimony [mæt'rəmouni:] *n* (marriage) 結婚 kekkón

matrix [mei'triks] (*pl* **matrices**) *n* (context, environment) 環境 kankyō

matron [mei'trən] *n* (in hospital) 婦長 fuchō; (in school) 養護員 yōgoin

matted [mæt'id] *adj* つや消しの tsuyákeshi

…われた motsúretá
…nt) 事件 jikén;
…) 問題 mon-
…shítsu; (text)
…i; (written
…印刷物 in-
…うみ umí
…etc) 大切

…… 構わない kamáwa-

…**s the matter?** どうしましたか dō shimashita ká

no matter what (whatever happens) 何があっても nánì ga atté mo

as a matter of course (automatically) 当然ながら tṓzen nagara

as a matter of fact 実は jitsú wa

matter-of-fact [mæt'ərʌvfækt'] *adj* 無味乾燥な mumíkañsō na

matters [mæt'ərz] *npl* (affairs) 物事 monógòto; (situation) 状況 jōkyō

mattress [mæt'ris] *n* マットレス mattórèsu

mature [mətu:r'] *adj* (person) 成熟した seíjuku shita; (cheese, wine etc) 熟成した jukúsei shita

♦*vi* (develop: child, style) 成長する seíchō suru; (grow up: person) 成熟する seíjuku suru; (ripen, age: cheese, wine etc) 熟成する jukúsei suru

maturity [mətu:'riti:] *n* (adulthood) 成熟 seíjuku; (wisdom) 分別 fúñbetsu

maul [mɔːl] *vt* ...に大けがをさせる ...ni ṓkega wo sasérù

mausoleum [mɔːsəli:'əm] *n* 納骨堂 nṓkotsudō

mauve [mouv] *adj* フジ色の fujíiro no

maverick [mæv'ərik] *n* 一匹オオカミ ippíki ókami

maxim [mæk'sim] *n* 格言 kakúgen

maximum [mæk'səməm] (*pl* **maxima**) *adj* (efficiency, speed, dose) 最大の saídai no

♦*n* 最大限 saídaigen

May [mei] *n* 5月 gógàtsu

may [mei] (*conditional*: **might**) *vi* (indicating possibility): **he may come** 彼は来るかも知れない kárè wa kurú ka mo shirénài; (be allowed to): **may I smoke?** タバコ吸ってもいいですか tabáko wo sutté mò íi desu ká; (wishes): **may God bless you!** 神の祝福をあなたに！ kamí nò shukúfuku wò anáta ni; **you may as well go** 行ってもいいかも知れない itté mò íi ka mo shirénài; (dismissive) 行った方がいいかも知れない itta hō ga íi ka mo shirénài

maybe [mei'bi:] *adv* 事によると kotó ni yorù to

May Day *n* メーデー mḗdē

mayhem [mei'hem] *n* 混乱 koñran

mayonnaise [meiəneiz'] *n* マヨネーズ mayónēzu

mayor [mei'əːr] *n* (of city, town) 市(町、村)長 shi (chō, son) chō

mayoress [mei'əːris] *n* (partner) 市(町、村)長夫人 shi (chō, son) chō fujìn

maze [meiz] *n* (labyrinth, puzzle) 迷路 meíro

M.D. [emdi:'] *abbr* = Doctor of Medicine

KEYWORD

me [mi:] *pron* **1** (direct) 私 wa watákushi
wo
can you hear me? 私の声が聞けますか
watakushi no koè ga kikóemasù ká
he heard me 彼は私の声を聞いた kárè
wa watákushi no koè wo kiftá
he heard ME! (not anyone else) 彼が聞
いたのは私の声だった kárè ga kiftá no
wa watákushi no koè dâttá
it's me 私です watákushi desu
2 (indirect) 私に watákushi nì
*he gave me the money, he gave the
money to me* 彼は私に金を渡した kárè
wa watákushi nì kanê wo watáshìta
give them to me それらを私に下さい
sorérà wo watákushi nì kudásaí
3 (after prep) 私 watákushi
the letter's for me 手紙
は私宛ての tegámi wà watákushi ate
dèsu
with me 私と一緒に watákushi tò isshó ni
nì
without me 私抜きに watákushi nukí
de

meadow [med'ou] *n* 草原 kusáhara
meager [mi:'gɔr] (BRIT **meagre**) *adj* 乏
しい tobóshiì
meal [mi:l] *n* (occasion, food) 食事 shokúji; (flour) 粉 koná
mealtime [mi:l'taim] *n* 食事時 shokúji-
dòki
mean [mi:n] *adj* (with money) けちな kechí na; (unkind: person, trick) 意地悪な
ijfwarù na; (shabby: street, lodgings) 見
すぼらしい misúborashiì; (average:
height, weight) 中位の chûgurai no
◆*vt* (pt, pp **meant**) (signify) 意味する fmí
suru; (refer to): *I thought you meant
her* あなたは彼女の事を言っていると私
は思った anátà wa kanójð no kotò wò
itté irù to watákushi wà omótta;
(intend): *to mean to do something* ...を
するつもりでいる ...wo suru tsumorí de
irú

◆*n* (average) 平均 heíkin
do you see it? 本当ですか honítð desù ká
what do you mean? それはどういう事
ですか soré wa dð íu kotð desu ká
to be meant for someone/something
...に当てた物である ...ni atéta monð de
árú

meander [mizæn'dɔr] *vi* (river) 曲がりく
ねって流れる magárikunettè nagárerù
meaning [mi:'niŋ] *n* (of word, gesture,
book) 意味 fmí; (purpose, value) 意義 fgí
meaningful [mi:'niŋfal] *adj* (result) 意味
のある fmí no árù; (explanation) 納得で
きる nattóku dekirù; (glance, remark) 意
味ありげな imfarige na; (relationship,
occasion) 意味深い imfbúkai
meaningless [mi:'niŋlis] *adj* 無意味な
muímì na
meanness [mi:n'nis] *n* (with money) けち
kechí; (unkindness) 意地悪 ijfwarù; (shab-
biness) 見すぼらしさ misúborashiì-
sà
means [mi:nz] *npl* (way) 方法 hóhð;
(money) 財産 zaísan
by means of ... を使って ...wo tsukátte
by all means! ぜひ ...
meant [ment] *pt, pp* of **mean**
meantime [mi:n'taim] *adv*
meantime その間に sonð aìda ni
meanwhile [mi:n'wail] *adv* ...
その間に sonð aìda ni
measles [mi:'zəlz] *n* はしか hashiká
measly [mi:z'li:] (inf) *adj* ちっぽ
chippókè na
measure [meʒ'ɔr] *vt* (size, weight,
tance) 計る hakárù
◆*vi* (room, person) ...だけの寸法があ
...dakê nð sunpð ga arù
(amount: of protection etc) ある程度
árù tefðð; (: of whisky etc) 定量 teíryð;
(ruler, also: **tape measure**) 巻尺 makíja-
ku, メジャー mejã; (action) 処置 shochí
measured [meʒ'ɔrd] *adj* 慎重な shíñchò
na
measurements [meʒ'ɔrmɔnts] *npl* (size)
寸法 sunpð
meat [mi:t] *n* 肉 nikú

cold meat コールドミート kórudomíto

meatball [miːˈbɔːl] n ミートボール mítobōru

meat pie n ミートパイ mítopai

Mecca [mekˈə] n (city) メッカ mékkà; (fig) あこがれの地 akógare nò chí

mechanic [məkænˈik] n 自動車整備士 jidōsha seíbishi

mechanical [məkænˈikəl] adj 機械仕掛の kikáijikakè no

mechanics [məkænˈiks] n (PHYSICS) 力学 rikígaku
♦npl (of reading, government etc) 機構 kikó

mechanism [mekˈənizəm] n (device) 装置 sóchì; (procedure) 方法 hṓhō; (automatic reaction) 反応 hańnō

mechanization [mekənizeiˈʃən] n 機械化 kikáika

medal [medˈəl] n (award) メダル médàru

medallion [mədælˈjən] n メダリオン medáriòn

medalist [medˈlist] (BRIT **medallist**) n (SPORT) メダリスト medárisùto

meddle [medˈəl] vi: **to meddle in** ...にちょっかいを出す ...ni chokkái wo dásù
to meddle with something ...をいじる ...wo ijírù

media [miːˈdiːə] npl マスメディア masúmedìa

mediaeval [miːdiːˈvəl] adj = medieval

median [miːˈdiːən] (US) n (also: **median strip**) 中央分離帯 chūō buńritai

mediate [miːˈdiːit] vi (arbitrate) 仲 裁 する chūsai suru

mediator [miːˈdiːeitər] n 仲裁者 chūsaìsha

Medicaid [medˈəkeid] (US) n メディケイド medíkeidò ◇低所得者への医療扶助 teíshotokùsha e no iryṓjo

medical [medˈikəl] adj (treatment, care) 医学的な igákutekì na
♦n (BRIT: examination) 健康診断 keńkōshiňdan

Medicare [medˈəkerː] (US) n メディケア medíkèa ◇高齢者への医療扶助 kṓreìsha e no iryṓjo

medicated [medˈikeitid] adj 薬用の ya-

kúyō no

medication [medikeiˈʃən] n (drugs etc) 薬 kusúri

medicinal [mədisˈənəl] adj 薬効のある yakkṓ no arù

medicine [medˈisin] n (science) 医学 ígaku; (drug) 薬 kusúri

medieval [miːdiːˈvəl] adj 中世の chūsei no

mediocre [miːˈdiːoukər] adj (play, artist) 凡末な sońmatsu na

mediocrity [miːdiːokˈritiː] n (poor quality) 凡末さ sońmatsùsa

meditate [medˈəteit] vi (think carefully) 熟考する jukkṓ suru; (REL) めい想する meísō suru

meditation [medɪteiˈʃən] n (thinking) 熟考 jukkṓ; (REL) めい想 meísō

Mediterranean [meditərei'niːən] adj 地中海の chichūkai no
the Mediterranean (Sea) 地中海 chichūkai

medium [miːˈdiːəm] adj (average: size, color) 中位の chūgurai no
♦n (pl **media**: means) 手段 shūdàn; (pl **mediums**: people) 霊媒 reíbai

medium wave n 中波 chūha

medley [medˈliː] n (mixture) ごったまぜ gottámazè; (MUS) メドレー médòrē

meek [miːk] adj 穏和な ońwa na

meet [miːt] (pt, pp **met**) vt (friend: accidentally) ...に 出会う ...ni deáù; (: by arrangement) ...に会う ...ni áù; (stranger: for the first time) ...と知合いになる ...to shíriai ni narù; (go and fetch: at station, airport) 出迎える demúkaerù; (opponent) ...と試合をする ...to shiái wo surù; (obligations) 果す hatásù; (problem, need) 解決する kaíketsu suru
♦vi (friends: accidentally) 出会う deáù; (: by arrangement) 会う áù; (strangers: for the first time) 知合いになる shíriai ni narù; (for talks, discussion) 会合する kaígō suru; (join: lines, roads) 合流する gōryū suru

meeting [miːˈtiŋ] n (assembly: of club, committee etc) 会合 kaígō; (: of people) 集会 shūkai; (encounter: with friend) 出

会い deaí; (COMM) 会議 káigi; (POL) 集会 shūkai

meet with vt fus (encounter: difficulty) 合う aú

to meet with success 成功する sefkō suru

megabyte [meg'əbait] n (COMPUT) メガバイト megabáito

megaphone [meg'əfoun] n メガホン megáhòn

melancholy [mel'ənka:li:] n (sadness) 憂うつ yūutsu, メランコリー meránkorī

♦adj (sad) 憂鬱な yūutsu na

mellow [mel'ou] adj (sound, light, color) 柔らかい yawárakaì; (wine) 芳じゅんな hōjun na

♦vi (person) 角が取れる kádò ga torérù

melodrama [mel'ədræmə] n メロドラマ meródðrama

melody [mel'ədi:] n 旋律 sefritsu, メロディー méròdi

melon [mel'ən] n メロン méròn

melt [melt] vi (metal, snow) 溶ける tokérù

♦vt (metal, snow, butter) 溶かす tokásù

melt down vt (metal) 溶かす tokásù

meltdown [melt'daun] n (in nuclear reactor) メルトダウン merútodàun

melting pot [melt'iŋ-] n (fig: mixture) るつぼ rútsùbo

member [mem'bær] n (of group, family) 一員 ichf-in; (of club) 会員 kafin, メンバー ménba; (ANAT) 体の一部 karáda no íchìbu

Member of Parliament (BRIT) 国会議員 kokkái gìn

Member of the European Parliament (BRIT) 欧州議会議員 ōshūgikai gìn

membership [mem'bærʃip] n (members) 会員一同 kafin ichidò; (state) 会員である事 kafin de arù kotó

membership card n 会員証 kafínshò

membrane [mem'brein] n 膜 makú

memento [məmen'tou] n 記念品 kinénhin

memo [mem'ou] n 覚書 obógegaki, メモ mémò

memoirs [mem'wɑ:rz] npl 回顧録 kaíko-

roku

memorable [mem'ə:rəbəl] adj 記念すべき kinénsubeki

memorandum [meməræn'dəm] (pl **memoranda**) n (official note) 覚書 obógegaki; (order to employees etc) 社内通達 shanái tsūtatsu

memorial [məmɔ:'ri:əl] n (statue, monument) 記念碑 kinénhi

♦adj (service) 追悼の tsuftō no; (prize) 記念の kinén no

memorize [mem'ə:raiz] vt (learn) 暗記する ańki suru

memory [mem'ə:ri:] n (ability to remember) 記憶 kióku; (things one remembers) 思い出 omóide; (instance) 思い出 omóide; (of dead person): *in memory of ...*を記念して ...wo kinén shite; (COMPUT) 記憶装置 kíókusòchi, メモリー mémòri

men [men] pl of **man**

menace [men'is] n (threat) 脅威 kyóì; (nuisance) 困り者 komárimono

♦vt (threaten) 脅かす odókasu; (endanger) 危険にさらす kikén ni saràsu

menacing [men'isiŋ] adj (person, gesture) 脅迫的な kyóhakuteki na

mend [mend] vt (repair) 修理する shúri suru; (darn: socks etc) 繕う tsukúroù, 修繕する shúzen suru

♦n: *to be on the mend* 回復に向かって いる kaffuku nì mukátte irù

to mend one's ways 心を入替える kokórò wo irékaerù

mending [men'diŋ] n (repairing) 修繕 shúzen; (clothes) 繕い物 tsukúroimòno

menial [mi:'ni:əl] adj (lowly: often pej) 卑しい iyáshiì

meningitis [menindʒai'tis] n 脳膜炎 nōmakuèn

menopause [men'əpɔ:z] n 更年期 kōnehki

menstruation [menstruei'ʃən] n 月経 gekkéi, 生理 sefri, メンス méñsu

mental [men'təl] adj (ability, effort) 精神的な sefshinteki na; (illness, health) 精神の sefshin no

mental arithmetic/calculation 暗算 ańzan

mentality [mentæl'iti:] n (attitude) 考え方 kañgaekàta

menthol [men'θɔ:l] n メントール meñtōru

mention [men'tʃən] n (reference) 言及 geñkyū
♦vt (speak of) ...に言及する ...ni geñkyū suru
don't mention it! どういたしまして dō itàshimashìté

mentor [men'tər] n 良き指導者 yokí shidōsha

menu [men'ju:] n (set menu) 献立 koñdate; (printed) 献立表 koñdatehyō, メニュー ményū; (COMPUT) メニュー ményū

MEP [emi:pi'] n abbr (BRIT) = Member of the European Parliament

mercenary [mɑr'sæneri:] adj 金銭ずくの kiñsenzuku no
♦n (soldier) よう兵 yōhei

merchandise [mɑr'tʃəndàis] n 商品 shōhin

merchant [mɑr'tʃənt] n (trader) 貿易商 bōekishō

merchant bank (BRIT) n マーチャントバンク māchantobàñku

merchant marine (BRIT **merchant navy**) n 商船 shōsen 〜一国の全商船を集合的に指す ikkóku no zeñshōsen wo shūgōteki ni sasú

merciful [mɑr'sifəl] adj (kind, forgiving) 情け深い nasàkebukai; (fortunate): **merciful release** 苦しみからの解放 kurúshimì kara no kaíhō←重病人などの死亡について言う jūbyōnin nado no shibō ni tsuité iú

merciless [mɑr'silis] adj (person, regime) 冷酷な reñkoku na

mercury [mɑr'kjə:ri:] n 水銀 suígin

mercy [mɑr'si:] n (clemency: also REL) 情け nasàke, 慈悲 jihí
at the mercy of ...のなすがままになって ...no nasú ga mamá ni natté

mere [mi:r] adj (emphasizing insignificance: child, trifle, amount) ほんの hoñ no; (emphasizing importance): **his mere presence irritates her** 彼がそこにいるだけで彼女は頭に来る kárè ga sokó ni

irú dakè de kánòjo wa atáma ni kurù

merely [mi:r'li:] adv ただ...だけ tádà ...dáke

merge [mɑrdʒ] vt (combine: companies, institutions etc) 合併させる gappéi saserù
♦vi (COMM) 合併する gappéi suru; (colors, sounds, shapes) 次第に溶け合う shídài ni tokéaù; (roads) 合流する gōryū suru

merger [mɑr'dʒər] n (COMM) 合併 gappéi

meringue [məræŋ'] n メレング meréngu

merit [me'rit] n (worth, value) 価値 kachí; (advantage) 長所 chōsho, 利点 ritén
♦vt ...に値する ...ni atái suru

mermaid [mɑr'meid] n 人魚 niñgyo

merry [me'ri:] adj (happy: laugh, person) 陽気な yōki na; (cheerful: music) 活気ある kakkí arù
Merry Christmas! メリークリスマス merí kurisùmasu

merry-go-round [me'ri:gouraund] n 回転木馬 kaíteñmokuba

mesh [meʃ] n (net) メッシュ mésshù

mesmerize [mez'mə:raiz] vt 魅惑する miwáku suru

mess [mes] n (muddle: in room) 散らかし っ放し chiràkashippanashi, めちゃくちゃ mechákucha; (: of situation) 混乱 koñran; (dirt) 汚れ yogóre; (MIL) 食堂 shokúdō

mess about/around (inf) vi (fool around) ぶらぶらする búràbura suru

mess about/around with vi fus (play around with) いじる ijírù

message [mes'idʒ] n (piece of information) 伝言 deñgon, メッセージ mésséji; (meaning: of play, book etc) 教訓 kyōkun

messenger [mes'indʒər] n 使者 shíshà, メッセンジャー mésséñja

Messrs. [mes'ərz] abbr (on letters) ◊Mr. の複数形 Mr. no fukúsūkei

mess up vt (spoil) 台無しにする daínashi ni suru; (dirty) 汚す yogósù

messy [mes'i:] adj (dirty) 汚れた yogóreta; (untidy) 散らかした chirákashita

met [met] pt, pp of **meet**

metabolism [mətǽb'əlizəm] n 新陳代謝 shińchintaísha

metal [met'əl] n 金属 kińzoku

metallic [mitǽl'ik] adj (made of metal) 金属の kińzoku no; (sound, color) 金属的な kińzokuteki na

metallurgy [met'ələːrdʒiː] n 金ヤ学 kińgaku

metamorphosis [metəmɔːr'fəsis] (pl **metamorphoses**) n 変態 heńtai

metaphor [met'əfɔːr] n 隠ゆ fń-yu, メタファー metáfā

mete [miːt] vt: **to mete out** (punishment, justice) 与える atáerú, 加える kuwáerú

meteor [miː'tiːour] n 流れ星 nagárebóshi

meteorite [miː'tiːərait] n いん石 ińseki

meteorology [miːtiːərɑːl'ədʒiː] n 気象学 kishōgaku

meter [miː'təːr] n (instrument: gas meter, electricity meter) ...計 ...kéi, メーター mētā; (also: **parking meter**) パーキングメーター pákingumētā; (US: unit) メートル métoru

method [meθ'əd] n (way) 方法 hōhō

methodical [məθɑːd'ikəl] adj (careful, thorough) 慎重な shińchō na

Methodist [meθ'ədist] n メソジスト教徒 mesójisuto kyótò

methodology [meθədɑːl'ədʒiː] n 方法論 hōhōròn

meths [meθs] (BRIT) n = **methylated spirit**

methylated spirit [meθ'əleitid-] (BRIT) n 変性アルコール heńsei arukōru

meticulous [mətik'jələs] adj 厳密な geńmitsu na

metre [miː'təːr] (BRIT) n (unit) = **meter**

metric [met'rik] adj メートル法の métoruhō no

metropolis [mitrɑːp'əlis] n 大都会 daítokai

metropolitan [metrəpɑːl'itən] adj 大都会の daítokai no

Metropolitan Police (BRIT) n: **the Metropolitan Police** ロンドン市警察 rońdon shikeísatsu

mettle [met'əl] n (spirit, courage): **to be on one's mettle** 張切っている haríkitte irù

mew [mjuː] vi (cat) にゃあと鳴く nyá tò nakú

mews [mjuːz] n (BRIT): **mews flat** アパート・アパートや昔の馬屋をアパートに改造した物を指す mukáshi nò umáya wò apáto ni kaízō shita monò wo sásù

Mexican [mek'səkən] adj メキシコの mekíshiko no
◆n メキシコ人 mekíshikojìn

Mexico [mek'səkou] n メキシコ mekíshiko

Mexico City n メキシコ市 mekíshikoshi

miaow [miːau'] vi (cat) にゃあと鳴く nyá tò nakú

mice [mais] pl of **mouse**

micro- [mai'krou] prefix 微小... bishō ...

microbe [mai'kroub] n 細菌 saíkin

microchip [mai'krətʃip] n マイクロチップ maíkurochippù

micro(computer) [maikrou(kəmpjuː'təːr)] n マイクロコンピュータ maíkurokompyùta, パソコン pasókòn

microcosm [mai'krəkɑːzəm] n 小宇宙 shōuchū, ミクロコスモス mikúrokosumòsu

microfilm [mai'krəfilm] n マイクロフィルム maíkurofirùmu

microphone [mai'krəfoun] n マイクロホン maíkurohòn

microprocessor [maikrouprɑːs'esəːr] n マイクロプロセッサー maíkuropurosessà

microscope [mai'krəskoup] n 顕微鏡 keńbikyò

microscopic [mai'krəskɑːp'ik] adj 微小の bishō no

microwave [mai'krouweiv] n (also: **microwave oven**) 電子レンジ deńshi reñji

mid [mid] adj: **in mid May** 5月半ばに gogátsu nakàba ni
in mid afternoon 昼下がりに hirúsagàri ni
in mid air 空中に kūchū ni

midday [mid'dei] n 正午 shōgo

middle [mid'əl] n (center) 真ん中 mańna-

irù

ka, 中央 chūō; (half-way point) 中間 chūkan; (waist) ウエスト uésŭto

♦adj (of place, position) 真ん中の mañnaka no; (average: quantity, size) 中位の chūgurai no

in the middle of the night 真夜中に mayónaka ni

middle-aged [mid'ǝleidʒd] adj 中年の chūnen no

Middle Ages npl: **the Middle Ages** 中世 chūséi

middle-class [mid'ǝlklæs] adj 中流の chūryū no

middle class(es) [mid'ǝlklæs(iz)] n(pl): **the middle class(es)** 中流階級 chūryū kaíkyū

Middle East n: **the Middle East** 中東 chūtō

middleman [mid'ǝlmæn] (pl **middlemen**) n 仲買人 nakágainin

middle name n ミドルネーム mídórunēmu

middle-of-the-road [mid'ǝlǝvðǝroud'] adj (politician, music) 中道の chūdō no

middleweight [mid'ǝlweit] n (BOXING) ミドル級の mídórukyū no

middling [mid'liŋ] adj 中位の chūgurai no

midge [midʒ] n ブヨ būyō ◇ブヨの様な小さい虫の総称 būyō no yō na chíísaí mushí no sōshō

midget [midʒ'it] n 小人 kobíto

Midlands [mid'lǝndz] (BRIT) npl: **the Midlands** イングランド中部地方 íngurañdo chūbu chihō

midnight [mid'nait] n 真夜中 mayónaka

midriff [mid'rif] n おなか onáka ◇ウエストから胸までの部分を指す uésŭto kara muné madé no bubún wo sásŭ

midst [midst] n: **in the midst of** (crowd, group) ...の中に〔で〕...no nákà ni (de); (situation, event) ...の真ん中に...no sanàka ni; (action) ...をしている所 ...wo shité iṛú tokóro

midsummer [mid'sʌm'ǝr] n 真夏 manátsu

midway [mid'wei] adj: **midway (between/through)** ...の途中で ...no to-

chū de

♦adv: **midway (between/through)** ...の途中に〔で〕...no tochū ni (de)

midweek [mid'wi:k] adv 週半ば shū nakabā

midwife [mid'waif] (pl **midwives**) n 助産婦 josáñpu

midwinter [mid'win'tǝr] n: **in midwinter** 真冬に mafúyu ni

might[1] [mait] see **may**

might[2] [mait] n (power) 力 chikára

mighty [mai'ti:] adj 強力な kyōryoku na

migraine [mai'grein] n 偏頭痛 heñzutsū

migrant [mai'grǝnt] adj: **migrant bird** 渡り鳥 watáridòri

  migrant worker 渡り季節労働者 watári kísetsu ródōshā

migrate [mai'greit] vi (bird etc) 移動する idō suru; (person) 移住する ijū suru

migration [maigrei'ʃǝn] n (bird etc) 移動 idō; (person) 移住 ijū

mike [maik] n abbr = **microphone**

Milan [milæn'] n ミラノ mirándo

mild [maild] adj (gentle: character) 大人しい otónashìī; (climate) 穏やかな odáyàka na; (slight: infection, illness) 軽い karúi; (: interest) 少しの sukóshì no; (taste) 甘口の amákuchi no

mildew [mil'du:] n かび kabí

mildly [maild'li:] adv (gently) 優しく yasáshìkù; (somewhat) 少し sukóshi

  to put it mildly 控え目に言って hikáeme ni ittě

mile [mail] n (unit) マイル maírù

mileage [mai'lidʒ] n (number of miles) マイル数 maírusū

mileometer [mailɑm'itǝr] (BRIT) n = **odometer**

milestone [mail'stoun] n (marker) 一里塚 ichíri zùka; (fig: important event) 画期的な出来事 kakkíteki na dekígòto

milieu [mi:lju:'] n 境遇 kañkyō

militant [mil'ǝtǝnt] adj 戦闘的な señtōteki na

military [mil'iteri:] adj 軍隊の guñtai no

militate [mil'ǝteit] vi: **to militate against** (prevent) 邪魔する jamá suru

militia [miliʃ'ǝ] n 民兵 míñpei

milk [milk] *n* (of any mammal) 乳 chichí; (of cow) 牛乳 gyūnyū, ミルク mírúku
♦*vt* (cow, goat) ...の乳を搾る ...no chichí wò shibórù; (*fig*: situation, person) 食い物にする kúimonó ni suru

milk chocolate *n* ミルクチョコレート mírúkuchokorēto

milkman [milk'mæn] (*pl* **milkmen**) *n* 牛乳配達人 gyūnyūhaítatsunín

milkshake [milk'ʃeik] *n* ミルクセーキ mírúkusēki

milky [mil'ki:] *adj* (color) 乳白色の nyūhakúshoku no; (drink) ミルク入りのmírúku iri no

Milky Way *n* 銀河 gíñga

mill [mil] *n* (windmill etc: for grain) 製粉機 seffunki; (*also*: **coffee mill**) コーヒーひき kṓhìhikí; (factory: steel mill, saw mill) 製...工場 seí...kṓjō
♦*vt* (grind: grain, flour) ひく hìkú
♦*vi* (*also*: **mill about**: people, crowd) 右往左往する uốsaō suru

woolen mill 織物工場 orímonokṓjo

miller [mil'ə:r] *n* 製粉業者 seffungyōsha

milligram(me) [mil'əgræm] *n* ミリグラム míríguràmu

millimeter [mil'əmi:tə:r] (*BRIT* **millimetre**) *n* ミリメートル mírímētoru

millinery [mil'əne:ri:] *n* 婦人帽子店 fujìnbōshiten

million [mil'jən] *n* 100万 hyakúmaǹ

a million times 何回も nañkai mo

millionaire [miljəneə'r] *n* 大富豪 daífugṓ

milometer [mai'loumi:tə:r] *n* = **mileometer**

mime [maim] *n* (action) パントマイム pañtomaìmu; (actor) パントマイム役者 pañtomaimu yakusha
♦*vt* (act) 身振り手振りでまねる mibúritebùri de manérù
♦*vi* (act out) パントマイムを演ずる pañtomaìmu wo eñzurū

mimic [mim'ik] *n* 物まね師 monómaneshì
♦*vt* (imitate) ...のまねをする ...no mané wo surū

min. *abbr* minute(s); minimum

minaret [minəret'] *n* ミナレット mína-

rètto ◊モスクのせん塔 mósuku no señtō

mince [mins] *vt* (meat) ひく hìkú
♦*vi* (in walking) 気取って歩く kidótte arukū
♦*n* (*BRIT*: CULIN) ひき肉 hikíniku

mincemeat [mins'mi:t] *n* (fruit) ミンスミート mínsumīto ◊ドライフルーツなどの細切り doráifurūtsu nadó no komágiri; (*US*: meat) ひき肉 hikíniku

mincemeat pie (*US*) *n* (sweet) ミンスミートパイ mínsumītopaì

mince pie (*BRIT*) *n* (sweet) = **mince-meat pie**

mincer [min'sə:r] *n* 肉ひき器 nikúhikìkì

mind [maind] *n* (thoughts) 考え kañgaé; (intellect) 頭脳 zunṓ; (opinion): *to my mind* 私の言うでは watákushi no iken dē wa; (sanity): *to be out of one's mind* 気が狂っている ki ga kurútte irù
♦*vt* (attend to, look after: shop, home etc) ...の番をする ...no bañ wo surū; (: children, pets etc) ...の面倒を見る ...no meñdō wò mírù; (be careful of) ...に注意する ...ni chū'i surū; (object to): *I don't mind the noise* その音を気にしません soñō otó wo kì ní shimáseñ

it is on my mind 気に掛けている kì ni kakátte irù

to keep/bear something in mind ...を気にする ...wo kì ni suru

to make up one's mind 決心する kesshín suru

I don't mind 構いませんよ kamáimaseñ yo

mind you, ... でもこれだけ言っておく ...de mo koré dakè itté okù ...

never mind! (it makes no odds) 気にしないで下さい ki ni shináide kudásaì; (don't worry) ほうっておきなさい hőtte oki nasaì, 心配しないで下さい shiñpai shinaíde kudásaì

「*mind the step*」階段に注意 kaídan ni chū'i

minder [main'də:r] *n* (childminder) ベビーシッター bebìshittā; (*BRIT inf*: bodyguard) ボディーガード bodígādo

mindful [maind'fəl] *adj*: *mindful of ...*を気に掛ける ...wo kì ni kakérù

mindless [maɪndlɪs] adj (violence) 愚 か な ôrôka na; (stupid: gurétsu na; (boring: job) 退屈な taīkutsu na

---
KEYWORD
---

mine[1] [main] pron 私の物 watákushi no monó

that book is mine その本は私のです sonó hoñ wa watákushi no désu

these cases are mine それらのケースは 私のです sorérá no kếsù wa watákushi no désu

this is mine これは私の物です koré wa watákushi no monó desu

yours is red, mine is green あなたの は赤いが、私のは緑色です anátà no wa akáì ga, watákushi no wa mídorì iró dèsu

a friend of mine 私のある友達 watákushi no árù tomódachì

mine[2] [main] n (gen) 鉱山 kôzan; (also: land mine) 地雷 jiráì; (bomb in water) 機雷 kíraì

♦vt (coal) 採掘する saíkutsu suru; (beach) 地雷を敷設する jiráì wo fusétsu suru; (harbor) 機雷を敷設する kíraì wo fusétsu suru

coal mine 炭坑 tañkō

gold mine 金鉱 kíñkō

minefield [maɪnfiːld] n (area: land) 地雷 原 jiráìgeñ; (: water) 機雷敷設水域 kíraì-fusétsu suíìki; (fig: situation) 危険をはら んだ事態 kíkeñ wo haráñda jítaì

miner [maɪnər] n (: 鉱山労働者 kôzanrōdōsha

mineral [mɪnərəl] adj (deposit, resources) 鉱物の kôbutsu no

♦n (in earth) 鉱物 kôbutsu; (in food) ミネ ラル mínèraru

minerals [mɪnərəlz] npl (BRIT) (soft drinks) 炭酸飲料水 tañsan-iñryōsuī

mineral water n ミネラルウォーター mínèraru suī

mingle [mɪŋgəl] vi: *to mingle with ...*と 交わる ...to majíwaru; 特にパーティーな どで多くの人に声を掛けて回るなどの意 味で使う tôku ni páti nádò de ôkù no

hitó ni kôè wo kakétè mawárù nádò no ímì de tsukáù

miniature [mɪnˈiːətʃər] adj (small, tiny) ミニチュアの miníchùa no

♦n ミニチュア miníchùa

minibus [mɪniːbʌs] n マイクロバス maí-kurobasu

minim [mɪnəm] n (MUS) 二分音符 níbun-oñpu

minimal [mɪnˈəməl] adj 最小限(度)の saí-shōgeñ(do) no

minimize [mɪnˈəmaɪz] vt (reduce: risks, disease) 最小限(度)に抑える saíshōgeñ (do) ni osáerù; (play down: role) 見くび る mikúbirù; (: weakness) 問題にしない mondái ni shínaì, 避けて通る sakête tôru

minimum [mɪnˈəməm] (pl minima) n 最 小限(度) saíshōgeñ(do)

♦adj 最小限(度)の saíshōgeñ(do) no

mining [maɪnɪŋ] n 鉱業 kôgyō

miniskirt [mɪniːskərt] n ミニスカート minísukàto

minister [mɪnˈistər] n (POL) 大臣 dáìjin; (REL) 牧師 bókùshi

♦vi: *to minister to* (people, needs) ...に 仕える ...ni tsukáerù

ministerial [ministiːˈriːəl] (BRIT) adj (POL) 大臣の dáìjin no

ministry [mɪnˈistriː] n (POL) ...省 ...shō; (REL) 聖職 seíshoku

mink [mɪŋk] n (fur) ミンクの毛皮 míñku no kegáwa; (animal) ミンク míñku

mink coat n ミンクのコート míñku no kôto

minnow [mɪnˈou] n 小魚 kozákàna

minor [maɪnər] adj (unimportant: repairs) ちょっとした chottó shitá; (: injuries) 軽い karúì; (: poet) 二流の ni-ryū no; (MUS) 短調の tanchō no

♦n (LAW) 未成年 misénen

minority [minɔːˈritiː] n (less than half: of group, society) 少数派 shōsūha

mint [mɪnt] n (plant) ハッカ hakká; (sweet) ハッカあめ hakká amè

♦vt (coins) 鋳造する chūzō suru

the (US) Mint (US), the (Royal) Mint (BRIT) 造幣局 zôheìkyoku

in mint condition 新品同様で shíñpindōyō de

minus [mai'nəs] *n* (*also*: **minus sign**) マイナス記号 mainasu kigō

◆*prep*: *12 minus 6 equals 6* 12引く6は 6 jūni hikū rokú wā rokú; (temperature): *minus 24* 零下24度 refka nijūyon do

minuscule [min'əskju:l] *adj* 微々たる bíbitaru

minute [min'it] *n* (unit) 分 fún; (*fig*: short time) ちょっと chottó

◆*adj* (search, detail) 細かい komákaī
at the last minute 土壇場に dotánba ni

minutes [min'its] *npl* (of meeting) 会議 録 kaígiroku

miracle [mir'əkəl] *n* (REL, *fig*) 奇跡 ki-séki

miraculous [miræk'jələs] *adj* 奇跡的な kisékiteki na

mirage [miroːʒ'] *n* しん気楼 shinkírō

mirror [mir'əːr] *n* (in bedroom, bathroom) 鏡 kagámī, ミラー mírā; (in car) バックミラー bakkúmirā

mirth [məːrθ] *n* (laughter) 笑い warái

misadventure [misædven'tʃəːr] *n* 災難 saínaā

misapprehension [misæprihen'tʃən] *n* 誤解 gokái

misappropriate [misəprou'priːeit] *vt* (funds, money) 横領する ōryō suru

misbehave [misbiheiv'] *vi* 行儀悪くする gyōgiwarukū suru

miscalculate [miskæl'kjəleit] *vt* 見込み 違いする mikómichigāi suru

miscarriage [miskær'idʒ] *n* (MED) 流産 ryūzan; (failure): *miscarriage of justice* 誤審 goshín

miscellaneous [misəlei'niːəs] *adj* (collection, group: of tools, people) 雑多な zattá na; (subjects, items) 種々の shujū no

mischance [mistʃæns'] *n* (misfortune) 不 運 fúūn

mischief [mis'tʃif] *n* (naughtiness: of child) いたずら itázura; (playfulness, fun) いたずら itázura; (maliciousness) 悪 さ wárūsa

mischievous [mis'tʃəvəs] *adj* (naughty, playful) いたずらな itázura na

misconception [miskənsep'tʃən] *n* 誤解 gokái

misconduct [miskɑːn'dʌkt] *n* (behavior) 非行 hikō
professional misconduct 背任 haínin, 職権乱用 shokkén ranyō

misdemeanor [misdimi'nəːr] (*BRIT* **misdemeanour**) *n* 軽犯罪 keíhanzai

miserable [miz'əːrəbəl] *adj* (unhappy: person, expression) 惨めな mijíme na, 不 幸な fukō na; (conditions) 哀 れな āware na; (unpleasant: weather, person) いやな iyá na; (contemptible: offer, donation) ちっぽけな chippóke na; (: failure) 惨 めな nasákenaī

miserly [mai'zəːrli] *adj* けちな kechí na

misery [miz'əːri] *n* (unhappiness) 惨めさ mijímesā, 不幸せ fushíawase; (wretchedness) 哀れな状態 āware na jōtai

misfire [misfaiːr'] *vi* (plan etc) 失敗する shippáī suru

misfit [mis'fit] *n* (person) 適応不能者 tekíōfunōsha

misfortune [misfɔːr'tʃən] *n* (bad luck) 不 運 fúūn

misgiving [misgiv'iŋ] *n* (apprehension) 心もとなさ kokóromotonasā, 疑念 ginén
to have misgivings about something ...を疑問に思う ...wo gimón ni omóū

misguided [misgai'did] *adj* (opinion, view) 心得違いの kokóroechigāi no

mishandle [mishæn'dəl] *vt* (mismanage: problem, situation) ...の処置を誤る ...no shōchī wo ayámarū

mishap [mis'hæp] *n* 事故 jíkō

misinform [misinfɔːrm'] *vt* ...にうそを伝 える ...ni úsō wo tsutáerū

misinterpret [misintəːr'prit] *vt* 誤解す る gokái suru

misjudge [misdʒʌdʒ'] *vt* ...の判断を誤る ...no hañdan wo ayámarū

mislay [mislei'] (*pt, pp* **mislaid**) *vt* (lose) なくす nakúsū, 置忘れる okíwasurerū

mislead [misliːd'] (*pt, pp* **misled**) *vt* ...を信じ込ませる ...wo shiñjikomaserū

misleading [misli'diŋ] *adj* (information)

mismanage [mɪsˈmænɪdʒ] vt (manage badly: business, institution) 下手な管理をする hétà na kánri wo suru; (: problem, situation) ...に対処しそこなう ...no shóchi wo ayámarù

misnomer [mɪsnouˈməːr] n (term) 誤った名称 ayámattà meíshō

misogynist [mɪsɑːdʒˈənist] n 女嫌いの人 onnágirai

misplace [mispleisˈ] vt (lose) なくす nakúsù, 置忘れる okíwasurerù

misprint [mɪsˈprint] n (in text) 誤植 goshóku

Miss [mis] n ...さん ...sán ◊ 未婚の女性に対する敬称 mikón no joséi ni taí surù keíshō

miss [mis] vt (train, bus etc) ...に乗遅れる ...ni nokúrerù; (fail to hit: target) ...に当て損なう ...ni atésokonaù; (fail to see): **you can't miss it** 見逃すことはないよ mínogasù kotó wa naí yo; (regret the absence of): **I miss you** 君が恋しい ...ga koíshiì, お前が懐かしい ...ga natsúkashiì; (chance, opportunity) 逃す nigásù, のがす nogásù; (class, meeting) ...に欠席する ...ni kesséki suru
◊vi (fail to hit) 当り損なう atárisokonaù, それる sorérù
◊n (failure to hit) 当て損ない atésokonaì, ミス mísù

misshapen [mɪsʃeíˈpən] adj 不格好な bukákkō na

missile [mɪsˈəl] n (weapon: MIL) ミサイル misáìru; (: object thrown) 飛道具 tobídōgu

missing [mɪsˈiŋ] adj (lost: person, pupil) 行方不明の yukúefumei no; (: object) なくなっている nakúnatte irù; (removed: tooth) 抜かれた hazúkaretà; (: wheel) 外された hazúsaretà; (MIL) 行方不明の yukúefumei no
to be missing 行方不明である yukúefuméi de aru

mission [mɪʃˈən] n (task) 任務 nínmu; (official representatives) 代表団 daíhyōdan; (MIL) 出撃 shutsúgeki ◊ 特に爆撃機について言う tokù ni bakúgekikì ni tsuíte iú; (REL: activity) 伝道 deńdō; (: building) 伝道所 deńdōjo

missionary [mɪʃˈəneːriː] n 伝道師 deńdōshi

miss out (BRIT) vt (leave out) 落す otósù

misspent [mɪsˈspent] adj: **his misspent youth** 浪費した彼の青春 rōhi shitá kárè no seíshun

mist [mɪst] n (light) もや móyà; (heavy) 濃霧 nōmu
◊vi (also: **mist over; mist up**) (eyes) 涙ぐむ namídagumù; (windows) 曇る kumórù

mistake [misteíkˈ] n (error) 間違い machígaì
◊vt (pt **mistook**, pp **mistaken**) (be wrong about) 間違える machígaerù
by mistake 間違って machígattè
to make a mistake 間違いをする machígaì wo suru
to mistake A for B AをBと間違える A wo B to machígaerù

mistaken [misteíˈkən] (pp of **mistake**) adj (idea, belief etc) 間違った machígattà
to be mistaken 間違っている machígattè irú

mister [mɪsˈtəːr] (inf) n ◊ 男性への呼び掛け dańsei e no yobíkake ◊ see **Mr.**

mistletoe [mɪsˈəltou] n ヤドリギ yadóriki

mistook [mistukˈ] pt of **mistake**

mistress [mistrisˈ] n (lover) 愛人 aíjin; (of house, servant) 主人 ofína shújin; (in primary, secondary schools) 先生 seńsei
to be mistress of the situation (fig) 事態を掌握している jitái wo shókaku shité irú

mistrust [mistrʌstˈ] vt 信用しない shiń-yō shináì

misty [mistˈiː] adj (day etc) もやった moyáttà; (glasses, windows) 曇った kumóttà

misunderstand [misʌndəːrstændˈ] (irreg) vt (fail to understand: person, book) 誤解する gokái suru
◊vi (fail to understand) 誤解する gokái suru

misunderstanding [misʌndəːrstænˈdiŋ]

n (failure to understand) 誤解 gokái; (disagreement) 口げんか kuchígeñka

misuse [misjùːs] *n* (of power) 乱用 rañyō; (of funds) 悪用 akúyō
♦*vt* (power) 乱用する rañ-yō suru; (funds) 悪用する akúyō suru

mitigate [mit'əgeit] *vt* 和らげる yawáragerù

mitt(en) [mit'(ən)] *n* ミトン mítton

mix [miks] *vt* (combine: liquids, ingredients, colors) 混ぜる mazérù; (cake, cement) こねる konérù; (drink, sauce) 作る tsukúrù
♦*vi* (people): **to mix (with)** ...と交わる ...to majíwarù ◇特にパーティなどで多くの人に声を掛けて回るなどの意味で使う tókù ni páti nádð de ðku no hitó nǐ kóè wo kakéte máwarù nádð no ími de tsukáù
♦*n* (combination) 混合物 koñgṓbùtsu; (powder) ミックス míkkùsu

mixed [mikst] *adj* (salad) コンビネーションの koñbíneshon no; (grill) 盛り合せのmoríawàse no; (feelings, reactions) 複雑な fukúzatsu na; (school, education etc) 共学の kyṓgakù no
a mixed marriage (religion) 異なった宗教の信徒間の結婚 kotónatta shūkyó no shinto kan no kekkon; (race) 異なった人間間の結婚 kotónatta jiñshu kan no kekkon

mixed-up [mikst'ʌp] *adj* (confused) 混乱している koñran shite irú

mixer [mik'səːr] *n* (for food) ミキサー mīkīsà; (person): **to be a good mixer** 付合い上手である tsukáaìjōzu de aru

mixture [miks'tʃəːr] *n* (combination) 混合物 koñgṓbùtsu; (MED: for cough etc) 飲薬 nomígusùri

mix up *vt* (confuse: people, things) 混同する koñdō suru

mix-up [miks'ʌp] *n* (confusion) 混乱 koñran

mm *abbr* = **millimeter**

moan [moun] *n* (cry) うめき umḗki
♦*vi* (inf: complain): **to moan (about)** (...について) 愚痴を言う (...ni tsúīte) guchí wo iù

moat [mout] *n* 堀 horí

mob [mɑːb] *n* (crowd) 群衆 guñshū
♦*vt* (person) ...の回りにわっと押し寄せる ...no mawárī nǐ wáttð oshíyoserù

mobile [mou'bəl] *adj* (able to move) 移動式の idṓshiki no
♦*n* (decoration) モビール mṓbìru

mobile home *n* モビールハウス mṓbìruhaùsu

mobility [moubil'əti:] *n* 移動性 idṓsei

mobilize [mou'bəlaiz] *vt* (friends, work force) 動員する dṓin suru; (MIL: country, army) 戦時態勢を取らせる sefiji taísei wo toráserù

moccasin [mɑːk'əsin] *n* モカシン mokáshin

mock [mɑːk] *vt* (ridicule) ばかにする bákà ni suru; (laugh at) あざ笑う azáwaraù
♦*adj* (fake) 見せ掛けの misékake no; (exam, battle) 模擬の mógì no

mockery [mɑːk'əːri:] *n* (derision) あざ笑い azáwarai
to make a mockery of ...をばかにする ...wo bákà ni suru

mock-up [mɑːk'ʌp] *n* (model) 模型 mokéi

mod [mɑːd kɑːnz] *adj see* **convenience**

mode [moud] *n* (form: of life) 様式 yóshiki; (: of transportation) 手段 shūdan

model [mɑːd'əl] *n* (representation: of boat, building etc) 模型 mokéi; (fashion model, artist's model) モデル mṓdèru; (example) 手本 tḗhon
♦*adj* (excellent) 模範的な mohánteki na
♦*vt* (clothes) ...のモデルをする ...no módèru wo suru; (with clay etc) ...の模型を作る ...no mokéi wo tsukúrù; (copy): **to model oneself on** ...の模範に習う ...no móhàn ni naráù
♦*vi* (for designer, photographer etc) モデルをする módèru wo suru

model railway *n* 模型鉄道 mokéi tetsudṓ

modem [mou'dem] *n* (COMPUT) モデム mṓdèmu

moderate [*adj* mɑːd'əːrit *vb* mɑːd'əːreit] *adj* (views, opinion) 穏健な oñken na; (amount) 中位の chūgurai no; (change)

ある程度の arú teído no
♦vi (storm, wind etc) 弱まる yawámarù
♦vt (tone, demands) 和らげる yawárage-rù

moderation [mɔdərei'ʃən] n 中庸 chúyō

modern [mɔd'ərn] adj 現代的な gendáiteki na, 近代的な kindáiteki na, モダンな modán na

modernize [mɔd'ərnaiz] vt 現代的にする gendáiteki ni suru

modest [mɔd'ist] adj (small: house, budget) 質素な shíssō na; (unassuming: person) 謙虚な kefíkyo na

modesty [mɔd'isti] n 慎み tsutsúshimi

modicum [mɔd'əkəm] n: *a modicum of* ちょっとだけの... chóttō dake no ...

modification [mɔdəfəkei'ʃən] n (alteration: of law) 改正 kaísei; (: of building) 改修 kaíshū; (: of car, engine etc) 改造 kaízō

modify [mɔd'əfai] vt (law) 改正する kaísei suru; (building, car, engine etc) 改造する kaízō suru

module [mɔdʒ'uːl] n (unit, component, SPACE) モジュール mojúrù

mogul [mou'gəl] n (fig) 大立者 ōdatemono

mohair [mou'her] n モヘア móheà

moist [mɔist] adj (slightly wet: earth, eyes, lips) 湿った shimétta

moisten [mɔis'ən] vt (lips, sponge) 湿らす shimérasù

moisture [mɔis'tʃər] n 湿り気 shimérike

moisturizer [mɔis'tʃəraizər] n (cream) モイスチャークリーム mofsuchua kurímu; (lotion) モイスチュアローション mofsuchua rōshon

molar [mou'lər] n きゅう歯 kyúshi

mold [mould] (BRIT **mould**) n (cast: for jelly, metal) 型紙 katá; (mildew) かび kabí
♦vt (shape: plastic, clay etc) ...で...の形を作る ...de ...no katáchi wō tsukúrù; (fig: influence: public opinion, character) 作り上げる tsukúriagerù

moldy [moul'di:] (BRIT **mouldy**) adj (bread, cheese) かびた kabíta; (smell) かび臭い kabíkusaì

mole [moul] n (spot) ほくろ hokúro; (ani-

mal) モグラ mogúra; (fig: spy) 秘密工作員 himítsukōsakuìn

molecule [mɔl'əkjuːl] n 分子 búnshi

molest [məlest'] vt (assault sexually) ...にいたずらをする ...ni itázura wo surù; (harass) いじめる ijímerù

mollycoddle [mɔl'i:kɔːdəl] vt (pamper) 甘やかす amáyakasù

molt [moult] (BRIT **moult**) vi (animal, bird) 換毛する kaímō suru

molten [moul'tən] adj (metal, rock) 溶解の yōkai no

mom [mɑm] (US: inf) n かあちゃん kā-chan, ママ mámà

moment [mou'mənt] n (period of time): *for a moment* ちょっと chóttō; (point in time): *at that moment* 」度その時 chốdō sonó tokì

at the moment 今の所 imá no tokòro

momentary [mou'mənteːriː] adj (brief: pause, glimpse) 瞬間的な shuñkanteki na

momentous [moumen'təs] adj (occasion, decision) 重大な jūdai na

momentum [moumen'təm] n (PHYSICS) 運動量 uñdōryō; (fig: of events, movement, change) 勢い ikíoì, 惰性 daséi

to gather momentum (lit, fig) 勢いが付く ikíoi ga tsúkù

mommy [mɑm'iː] (US) n ママ mámà ◊幼児語 yōjìyōgo

Monaco [mɑn'əkou] n モナコ mónàko

monarch [mɑn'ərk] n 君主 kúnshu

monarchy [mɑn'ərkiː] n (system) 王制 ōsei; (royal family) 王室 ōshitsu, 王族 ōzoku

monastery [mɑn'əsteːriː] n 修道院 shūdōin

Monday [mʌn'dei] n 月曜日 getsúyōbi

monetary [mɑn'iteriː] adj (system, policy, control) 金融の kiñ-yū no

money [mʌn'iː] n (coins and notes) 金 kané; (currency) 通貨 tsūka

to make money (earn) 金をもうける kané wo mōkerù

money order n 郵便為替 yūbínkawase

money-spinner [mʌn'iːspinər] n (BRIT:

inf] n (person, idea, business) ドル箱 do-rúbako

mongol [mɒŋ'gəl] adj モンゴルの môn-goru no
♦n (MED) ダウン症候群患者 daúnshōkō-gun kańja

mongrel [mʌŋ'grəl] n (dog) 雑種 zasshú

monitor [mɒn'itər] n (machine) モニタ
一装置 monítāsōchi; (screen: *also*: **tele-vision monitor**) ブラウン管 buráuńkan;
(of computer) モニター mónítā
♦vt (broadcasts) 傍受する bôju suru;
(heartbeat, pulse) モニターする mónítā
suru; (progress) 監視する kańshi suru

monk [mʌŋk] n 修道師 shúdōshi

monkey [mʌŋ'ki] n (animal) サル sarú

monkey nut (*BRIT*) n ピーナッツ pî-nattsu

monkey wrench n モンキーレンチ mof-kíreńchi

mono [mɑ:n'ou] adj (recording) モノラル
の môńdraru no

monochrome [mɑ:n'əkroum] adj (film,
photograph) 白黒の shírōkuro no, モノク
ロの monókūro no

monogram [mɑ:n'əgræm] n モノグラム
monógūramu

monologue [mɑ:n'ɔ:lɔ:g] n 会話の独白
kańwa no dokúhaku; (THEATER) 独白
dokúhaku, モノローグ monórōgu

monopolize [mənɑ:p'əlaiz] vt 独占する
dokúsen suru

monopoly [mənɑ:p'əli:] n (domination)
独占 dokúsen; (COMM) 専売 seńbai, モ
ノポリー monópórī

monosyllable [mɑ:n'əsiləbəl] n 単音節語
tań-onsetsugó

monotone [mɑ:n'ətoun] n: **to speak in
a monotone** 単調な声で話す tańchō na
kóè de hanásù

monotonous [mənɑ:t'ənəs] adj (life, job
etc) 退屈な taíkutsu na; (voice, tune) 単
調な tańchō na

monotony [mənɑ:t'əni:] n 退屈 taíkutsu

monsoon [mɑ:nsu:n'] n モンスーン môń-sūn

monster [mɑ:n'stər] n (animal, plant:
misshapen) 奇形 kikéi; (: enormous) 怪物

kańbútsu, お化け obákè; (imaginary
creature) 怪物 kańbútsu; (person: cruel,
evil) 怪物 kańbútsu

monstrosity [mɑ:nstrɑ:s'əti:] n (hideous
object, building) 見るに堪えない物 mí-rù ni taénaì shírőmòno

monstrous [mɑ:n'strəs] adj (huge) 巨大
な kyodái na; (ugly) 見るに堪えない mí-rù ni taénaì; (atrocious) 極悪な gokúaku
na

month [mʌnθ] n 月 tsukí

monthly [mʌnθ'li:] adj (ticket etc) 一カ
月の ikkágetsu no; (magazine) 月刊の
gekkán no; (payment etc) 毎月の maítsuki no; (meeting) 月例の getsúrei no
♦adv 毎月 maítsuki

monument [mɑ:n'jəmənt] n (memorial)
記念碑 kinéňhi; (historical building) 史的
記念物 shitékikineňhbutsu

monumental [mɑ:njəmen'təl] adj (large
and important: building, statue) 歴史的
な rekíshìteki na; (important: book,
piece of work) 画期的な kakkíteki na;
(terrific: storm, row) すごい sugóí, すさ
まじい susámajiì

moo [mu:] vi (cow) もーと鳴く mó tò na-kú

mood [mu:d] n (humor: of person) 機嫌
kigén; (: of crowd, group) 雰囲気 fuń-ikī,
ムード mûdo
to be in a good/bad mood (temper) 機
嫌がいい(悪い) kigén gà íi(warúi)

moody [mu:'di:] adj (variable) 気分屋の
muráki na; (sullen) 不機嫌な fukígeñ na

moon [mu:n] n 月 tsukí

moonlight [mu:n'lait] n 月光 gekkō

moonlighting [mu:n'laitiŋ] n (work) ア
ルバイト arúbaito ◊本職の外にする仕事
で, 特に規定, 規則違反の仕事を指す
hofshōku no hoká ni suru shigóto dè,
tókù ni kitéi, kisóku ihán no shigóto o
sásù

moonlit [mu:n'lit] adj: **a moonlit night**
月夜 tsukíyò

moor [mur] n (heath) 荒れ野 aréno
♦vt (ship) つなぐ tsunágù
♦vi 停泊する teńhaku suru

moorland [mur'lænd] n 荒れ野 aréno

moose [muːs] *n inv* アメリカヘラジカ a-mérikaheraJīka

mop [mɔp] *n* (for floor) モップ moppū; (for dishes) スポンジたわし supónjitawashī (短い柄の付いた皿洗い用を指す mijīkaī e no tsūtā saráaraī yō wo sásū ◆*vt* (floor) モップでふく moppū de fukū; (eyes, face) ふく fukū, ぬぐう nugúū

a mop of hair もじゃもじゃ頭 mojámoja atáma

mope [moup] *vi* ふさぎ込む fuságikomū

moped [mou'ped] *n* モペット mopéttō ◇ペダルで動かす事も出来る小型オートバイ pedárū de ugókasū kotó mo dekírū kogáta ōtobaī

mop up *vt* (liquid) ふく fukū

moral [mɔːr'əl] *adj* 倫理の rínri no, 倫理的 rínritekī na ◆*n* (of story etc) 教訓 kyōkun

moral support (encouragement) 精神的な支え seíshintekī sasáe

morale [mæræl'] *n* (of army, staff) 士気 shīkī

morality [mæræl'iti:] *n* (good behavior) 品行 hínkō; (system of morals: also correctness, acceptability) 倫理 rínri

morals [mɔːr'əlz] *npl* (principles, values) 倫理 rínri

morass [mɔːræs'] *n* (*lit, fig*) 泥沼 dorónuma

morbid [mɔːr'bid] *adj* (imagination, ideas) 陰気な fíki na

KEYWORD

more [mɔːr] *adj* **1** (greater in number etc) より多くの yorí ōku no

more people/work/letters than we expected 私たちが予定していたより多くの人々(仕事, 手紙) watákushitàchi ga yotéī shite ita yorí ōku no hítòbito (shigóto, tegámi)

I have more books/money than you 私はあなたより沢山の本(金)を持っています watákushi wà anátā yori takúsan nð hóñ(kané) wo mótte imasū

this store has more wine than beer この店はビールよりワインが沢山あります konó mise wà bírū yori wáīn ga takúsan arimasū

2 (additional) もっと móttō

do you want (some) more tea? もっと紅茶をいかがですか móttō kōcha wð ikága desū ká

is there any more wine? ワインはまだありますか wáīn wa mádā arimasū ká

I have no/I don't have any more money お金はもうありません o-káne wa mð arímasèñ

it'll take a few more weeks あと数週間掛かります áto sūshūkan kakárimasū

◆*pron* **1** (greater amount) もっと沢山 móttō takúsan

more than 10 10以上 jūijō ◇この成句の英語には「10」が含まれないが、日本語の場合「10」も含まれる konó seīku no eīgo nī wa「10」ga fukūmarénāī ga, nīhòngo no baaī「10」mo fukūmarerù. (Note: the English phrase indicates a quantity of 11 and above, but the Japanese indicates 10 and above.)

it cost more than we expected 予想以上に金が掛かりました yosó ijō nī kané gà kakárimashtā

2 (further or additional amount) もっと沢山 móttō takúsan

is there any more? まだありますか mádā arímasū ká

there's no more もうありません mð arímasèñ

a little more もう少し mð sukoshī

many/much more よりずっと沢山 yorí zuttō takúsan

◆*adv* ...よりもっと... ...yorí móttō...

more dangerous/difficult etc (than) ...より危ない(難しい)... yorí abúnaī(muzúkashiī)

more easily/economically/quickly (than) ...よりたやすく(経済的に, 早く)... yorí tayasukū(keizaiteki ni, hayákū)

more and more ますます masúmasū

more and more excited/friendly/expensive ますます興奮して(親しくなって, 高くなって) masúmasū kófun shité(shitáshiku nattè, tákàku natte)

he grew to like her more and more 彼はますます彼女が好きになった kárè wa masúmasū kánòjo ga sukí ní nattá

more or less 大体 dáitai, 大よそ óyoso

the job's more or less finished 仕事は大体できています shígoto wà daítai dékite imásu

it should cost £ 500, more or less 大よそ500ポンド掛りそうです óyoso go-hyáku¬póndo kakárisō desu

more than ever ますます masúmasu, より一層 yorí issó

more beautiful than ever ますます美しい masúmasu utsukushíi

more quickly than ever ますます早く masúmasu háyaku

he loved her more than ever 彼はより一層彼女を愛する様になった kárè wà yorí issó kánòjo wo ái suru yō ni nátta

moreover [mɔːrou'vər] adv なお náò

morgue [mɔːrg] n 死体保管所 shitáihokanjo, モルグ morúgù

moribund [mɔr'əbʌnd] adj (organization, industry) 斜陽の shayō no

Mormon [mɔːr'mən] n モルモン教徒 morúmon kyōto

morning [mɔːr'niŋ] n (period after daybreak) 朝 ásà; (from midnight to noon) 午前 gózèn

in the morning 朝に ásà ni, 午前中に gozénchū ni

7 o'clock in the morning 午前7時 gózèn shichíji

morning paper 朝刊 chōkan

morning sun 朝日 ásàhi

morning walk 朝の散歩 ásà no sáñpo

morning sickness n つわり tsuwári

Morocco [mərak'ou] n モロッコ morókkò

moron [mɔːr'ɑn] (inf) n ばか bákà

morose [mərous'] adj (miserable) 陰気な íñki na

morphine [mɔːr'fiːn] n モルヒネ morúhine

Morse [mɔːrs] n (also: **Morse code**) モールス信号 mórusu shíñgō

morsel [mɔːr'səl] n (of food) 一口 hitókùchi

mortal [mɔːr'təl] adj (man) いつか死ぬ定 tsuka shinú; (wound) 致命的な chiméite-

ki na; (danger) 命にかかわる ínòchi ni kakáwarù

mortal combat 死闘 shitō

mortal enemy 宿敵 shukúteki

mortal remains 遺骨 ikótsu

mortal sin 大罪 taízai

mortality [mɔːrtæl'iti] n いつか死ぬ事 tsuka shinú kotó; (number of deaths) 死亡率 shibōritsu

mortar [mɔːr'tər] n (cannon) 迫撃砲 ha-kúgekihō; (CONSTR) モルタル morúta-ru; (bowl) 乳鉢 nyūbachi

mortgage [mɔːr'gidʒ] n 住宅ローン jūtaku-rōn

◆vt (house, property) 抵当に入れて金を借りる teítō ni írète kané wo karírù

mortify [mɔːr'təfai] vt: **to be mortified** 恥を感じる hají wo kañjirù

mortuary [mɔːr'tʃuːeriː] n 霊安室 reíañshitsu

mosaic [mouzei'ik] n モザイク mozáìku

Moscow [mɑs'kau] n モスクワ mosúkùwa

Moslem [mɑz'ləm] adj, n = Muslim

mosque [mɑsk] n イスラム教寺院 isúra-mukyō jiìn, モスク mósùku

mosquito [məski'tou] (pl mosquitoes) n 蚊 ká

moss [mɔːs] n (plant) コケ kokè

KEYWORD

most [moust] adj 1 (almost all: people, things etc) ほとんどの hotóndo no

most people ほとんどの人 hotóndo no hitó

most men/dogs behave like that ほとんどの男性(イヌ)はそういう振舞をする hotóndo no dañsei(inú)wà sō iú furúmai wo surú

most houses here are privately owned ここのほとんどの家は個人所有の物です koko nò hotóndo no ié wà kojínshoyú no monó desù

2 (largest, greatest: interest, money etc) 最も沢山の mottómò tákùsan no

who has (the) most money? 最も多くの金を持っているのは誰でしょう mottómō ōku no kane wo motte iru no wa dare deshō

he derived the most pleasure from her visit 最も彼を喜ばせたのは彼女の訪問だった mottómò kárè wo yorókobaseta no wa kánòjo no hómon dattá

◆*pron* (greatest quantity, number) ほとんど hotóndo

most of it/them それ(それら)のほとんど sorè(sorèra) no hotóndo

most of the money/her friends 金(彼女の友達)のほとんど kané(kánòjo no tomódàchi) nò hotóndo

most of the time ほとんどの場合 hotóndo no baái

do the most you can できるだけの事をして下さい dekíru dakè no kotò wo shitè kudasaí

I saw the most 私が一番沢山見ました watákushi gà ichíban takùsan mimáshìta

to make the most of something …を最大限に利用する …wò saídaìgen ni riyō surù

at the (very) most 最大に見積っても saídaì nì mitsúmotte mó

◆*adv* (+ verb: spend, eat, work etc) 最も多く mottómò ōkù; (+ adjective: *the most intelligent/expensive* etc) 最も利口(高価)な mottómò rikō(kōka)nà; (+ adverb: carefully, easily etc) 最も意深く(たやすく) mottómò chūíbukakù(tayásukù); (very: polite, interesting etc) とても totémo

a most interesting book とても面白い本 totémo omoshirói hón

mostly [moust'li:] *adv* (chiefly) 主に ómò ni; (usually) 普段は fúdàn wa, 普通は futsū wa

MOT [emouti:'] *n abbr* = **Ministry of Transport**; *the MOT (test)* (*BRIT*) 車検 shakén

motel [moutel'] *n* モーテル mōteru

moth [mɔ:θ] *n* (insect) ガ gá; (clothes moth) イガ igá

mothball [mɔ:θ'bɔ:l] *n* 防虫剤 bōchūzài

mother [mʌð'ə:r] *n* 母 háhà, 母親 haháoya

ya, お母さん o-káasan

◆*adj:* **mother country** 母国 bókòku

◆*vt* (act as mother to) 母親として育てる haháoya toshitè sodáterù; (pamper, protect) 甘やかす amáyakasù

mother company 親会社 oyágaìsha

motherhood [mʌð'ə:rhud] *n* 母親である事 haháoya de arū kotó

mother-in-law [mʌð'ə:rinlɔ:] (*pl* **mothers-in-law**) *n* しゅうとめ shūto

motherly [mʌð'ə:rli:] *adj* 母の様な háhà no yō na

mother-of-pearl [mʌð'ə:rəvpə:rl'] *n* 真珠母 shifijibo

mother-to-be [mʌð'ə:rtəbi:'] (*pl* **mothers-to-be**) *n* 妊婦 nínpù

mother tongue *n* 母国語 bokókugò

motif [mouti:f'] *n* (design) 模様 moyō

motion [mou'ʃən] *n* (movement) 動き ugóki; (gesture) 合図 aízù; (at meeting) 動議 dōgi

◆*vt:* **to motion (to) someone to do something** …する様に…に合図をする …surū yō ni …ni aízù wo suru

motionless [mou'ʃənlis] *adj* 動かないugókanaì

motion picture *n* (film) 映画 eígà

motivated [mou'təveitid] *adj* (enthusiastic) 張切っている haríkìtte irù; (impelled): **motivated by** (envy, desire) …の動機で …no dōki de

motivation [moutəvei'ʃən] *n* (drive) 動機 dōki

motive [mou'tiv] *n* (aim, purpose) 目標 mokúhyò

motley [mɑːt'li:] *adj* 雑多る/奇妙な zattá dé kimyō na

motor [mou'tə:r] *n* (of machine) 原動機 gendóki, モーター mōtà; (of vehicle) エンジン éñjin; (*BRIT: inf*: vehicle) 車 kurúma

◆*cpd* (industry, trade) 自動車の jídòsha no

motorbike [mou'tə:rbaik] *n* オートバイ ōtòbai

motorboat [mou'tə:rbout] *n* モーターボート mōtàboto

motorcar [mou'tə:rkɑ:r] (*BRIT*) *n* 自動車

motorcycle [mou'tərsai'kəl] *n* オートバイ ôtôbai

motorcycle racing *n* オートバイレーシング ôtôbairêshingu

motorcyclist [mou'tərsaiklist] *n* オートバイのライダー ôtôbai no raídâ

motoring [mou'təriŋ] (*BRIT*) *n* 自動車運転 jidôsha uñten

motorist [mou'tərist] *n* 運転者 uñtensha

motor racing (*BRIT*) *n* カーレース kârêsu

motor vehicle *n* 自動車 jidôsha

motorway [mou'tərwei] (*BRIT*) *n* ハイウェー haîuê

mottled [mɑt'əld] *adj* ぶちの buchí no

motto [mɑt'ou] (*pl* **mottoes**) *n* 標語 hyôgo, モットー mottô

mould [mould] *n, vt* = **mold**

mouldy [moul'di:] (*BRIT*) *adj* = **moldy**

moult [moult] (*BRIT*) *vi* = **molt**

mound [maund] *n* (heap: of blankets, leaves, earth etc) 一山 hitóyàma

mount [maunt] *n* (mountain in proper names): *Mount Carmel* カルメル山 karúmeruzàn

♦*vt* (horse) ...に乗る ...ni norú; (exhibition, display) 開催する kaísai suru; (fix: jewel) 台座にはめる daíza ni hamérù; (: picture) 掛ける kakérù; (: staircase) 昇る noborù

♦*vi* (increase: inflation) 上昇する jôshô suru; (: tension) つのる tsunorú; (: problems) 増える fuérù

mountain [maun'tən] *n* (GEO) 山 yamá

♦*cpd* (road, stream) 山の yamá no

mountaineer [mauntəni'rl] *n* 登山家 tozánka

mountaineering [mauntəni'riŋ] *n* 登山 tózán

mountainous [maun'tənəs] *adj* (country, area) 山の多い yamá no ôi

mountain rescue team *n* 山岳救助隊 sañgaku kyûjotaì

mountainside [maun'tənsaid] *n* 山腹 sañpuku

mount up *vi* (bills, costs, savings) たまる tamáru

mourn [mɔrn] *vt* (death) 悲しむ kanáshimù

♦*vi: to mourn for* (someone) ...の死を悲しむ ...no shî wo kanáshimù

mourner [mɔr'nər] *n* 会葬者 kaísôsha

mournful [mɔrn'fəl] *adj* (sad) 悲しそうな kanáshisô na

mourning [mɔr'niŋ] *n* 喪 mo
in mourning 喪中で mochû de

mouse [maus] (*pl* **mice**) *n* (animal) ハツカネズミ hatsúkanezùmi; (COMPUT) マウス máusu

mousetrap [maus'træp] *n* ネズミ取り nezúmitòri

mousse [mus] *n* (CULIN) ムース mûsu; (*also*: **hair mousse**) ヘアムース heámûsu

moustache [məstæʃ] (*BRIT*) *n* = **mustache**

mousy [mau'si:] *adj* (hair) 薄汚い茶色の usugítanai cha-íro no

mouth [mauθ] (*pl* **mouths**) *n* (ANAT) 口 kuchî; (of cave, hole) 入口 iríguchi; (of river) 河口 kakô

mouthful [mauθ'ful] *n* (amount) 口一杯 kuchî ippaì

mouth organ *n* ハーモニカ hâmonika

mouthpiece [mauθ'pi:s] *n* (of musical instrument) 吹口 fukíguchì; (spokesman) スポークスマン supôkusumàn

mouthwash [mauθ'wɔʃ] *n* マウスウォッシュ máusuwosshù 口以外防止洗口液 kôshûbôshi senkôeki

mouth-watering [mauθ'wɔːtəriŋ] *adj* おいしそうな oíshisô na

movable [mu'vəbəl] *adj* 可動な kadô na

move [muːv] *n* (movement) 動き ugóki; (in game: change of position) 手 té; (: turn to play) 番 bâñ; (change of house) 引っ越し hikkóshi; (: of job) 転職 teñshoku

♦*vt* (change position of: furniture, car, curtains etc) 動かす ugókasù; (chessmen etc: in game) 動かす ugókasù; (emotionally) 感動させる kañdô saserù; (POL: resolution etc) 提議する teígi suru

♦*vi* (person, animal) 動く ugókù; (traffic) 流れる nagárerù; (*also*: **move house**)

に kańdóteki ni; (that moves) 動く ugó-
ku

mow [mou] (pt **mowed**, pp **mowed** or
mown) vt (grass, corn) 刈る karú

mow down vt (kill) なぎ払う様に殺す
nagiharaú yố ni korósù

mower [mou'əːr] n (also: **lawnmower**) 芝
刈機 shibákarikì

to get a move on 急ぐ isógù

to move someone to do something ...に
...をする気を起させる ...ni ...wo suru ki
wò okósaserù

moveable [muːˈvəbəl] adj = **movable**

move about/around vi (change position) そわそわする sówàsowa suru;
(travel) 頻繁に旅行する hińpan ni ryokó
suru; (change: residence) 頻繁に引っ越す
hińpan ni hikkósù; (: job) 頻繁に転職する
hińpan ni teńshoku suru

m.p.h. [empieitʃˈ] abbr (= **miles per
hour**) 時速...マイル jísoku ...maïru

Mr, Mr. [misˈtəːr] n: **Mr. Smith** スミス
さん sumísu sáñ 男性の敬称 dańsei no
kefshố

move along vi 立ち去る tachísarù
move along! 立ち止まるな tachídomarù
ná

move away vi (leave: town, area) よそ
へ引っ越す yosó e hikkósù

Mrs, Mrs. [misˈiz] n: **Mrs Smith** スミ
スさん sumísu sáñ 既婚女性の敬称 kí-
końjosei no kefshố

move back vi (return) 元の所へ引っ越す
mótò no tokóro e hikkósù

Ms, Ms. [miz] n: **Ms. Smith** スミスさん
sumísu sáñ 既婚・未婚を問わず女性の
敬称 kíkòn, míkòn wo towázù josei no
kefshố

move forward vi (advance) 前進する
zefshin suru

move in vi (to a house) 入居する nyúkyo
suru; (police, soldiers) 攻撃を加える kốgeki wò kuwaérù

M.Sc. [emessiːˈ] abbr = **Master of Science**

movement [muːvˈmənt] n (action: of
person, animal) 動き ugóki, 動作 dósa;
(: of traffic) 流れ nagáre; (gesture) 合図
aízu; (transportation: of goods etc) 運輸
uń-yu; (shift: in attitude, policy) 変化 heń-
ka; (group of people: esp REL, POL) 運
動 uńdô; (MUS) 楽章 gakúshô

much [mʌtʃ] adj (time, money, effort) 沢
山の takúsañ no, 多くの ókù no
we haven't got much time/money あ
まり多くの時間［金］はありません amári
ốku no jíkàn[kané]wà arímaseñ
much effort was expended on the
project その企画にかなりの努力を費や
した sonó kikàku ni ốkù no dóryòku wo
tsufyashîta

move on vi 立ち去る tachísarù
move on! 立ち止まるな tachídomarù ná

move out vi (of house) 引っ越す hikkósù

how much money/time do you need?
お金［時間］はどのぐらい必要ですか o-
káne[jikàn]wà donó gurai hitsúyò desú
kấ

move over vi (to make room) 横へどい
て場所を空ける yokó e dóîte bashó wò
akérù

move up vi (employee, deputy) 昇進する
shốshin suru; (pupil) 進級する shińkyu
suru

he's done so much work for the
charity その慈善事業のために彼は様々
な仕事をしてくれました sonó jizéñjigyô
no tamé ni kárè wa samázàma na shigô-
to wò shité kuremashìta

it's too much あんまりだ afmari da
it's not much 大した事じゃない táîshita
kotó jà nai

movie [muːviː] n 映画 efga
to go to the movies 映画を見に行く
efga wo mf ni ikù

to have too much money/free time 金

movie camera n 映画カメラ efga kamé-
ra

moving [muːvˈiŋ] adj (emotional) 感動的

(暇)が有り余る kané(himá)gà arfamarù
as much as ...と同じぐらい ...to onáji
gurái

*I have as much money/intelligence
as you* 私はあなたと同じぐらいの金(知
識)を持っています watákushi wà anáta
to onáji gurái no kané(chíshiki)wò
mótte imasu

♦*pron* 沢山のもの takúsan no monò

there isn't much to do あまりする事は
ありません amári suru kotò wa arímasen

*much has been gained from our
discussions* 我々の話し合いは多くの成
果を産みました waréwaré no hanáshiai
wà ókù no séfka wò umímashita

how much does it cost? - *too much*
値段はいくらですか - べらぼうな nedán
wà íkura desu ká - berábò na

how much is it? いくらですか íkura
desu ká

♦*adv* **1** (greatly, a great deal) とても
tétemo

thank you very much 大変有難うござ
います taíhen arígatò gozáimasù

much bigger (than) (...より) はるか
に大きい (...yori) haruka ni ókii

*we are very much looking forward
to your visit* あなたが来られるのを首
を長くして待っております anáta ga ko-
rárerú no wo kubí wò nágàku shite
mattè orímasù

*he is very much the gentleman/poli-
tician* 彼はれっきとした紳士(政治家)で
す kárè wa rekkí to shita shi(seíji-
ka)desu

however much he tries 彼はどんなに努
力しても kárè wa dónna ni doryókù
shite mò

as much as ...と同じぐらい沢山 ...to
onáji gurái takúsaǹ

I read as much as ever 私はいつもと
同じぐらい沢山の本を読んでいます wa-
tákushi wà ítsumo to onáji gurái takúsaǹ no hón wo yóǹde imásù

I read as much as possible/as I can
私はできるだけ沢山の本を読む事にして
います watákushi wà dekíru dakè takúsaǹ no hón wo yómù koto ni shité imasù

*he is as much a part of the commu-
nity as you* 彼はあなたと同様ここの社
会の一員です kárè wa anáta to dóyò
kokó no shakái no ichíin desù

2 (*by far*) ずっと zúttó

I'm much better now 私はずっと元気
になっています watákushi wà zúttó gé-
ǹki ni nátte imasù

much reduced in price ずっと安くなって
いる zúttó yasúku natte

*it's much the biggest publishing
company in Europe* あれは断然ヨーロ
ッパ最大の出版社です aré wa dańzen
yóroppasaidaì no shuppáǹsha desu

3 (*almost*) ほとんど hotóǹdo

*the view is much as it was 10 years
ago* 景色は10年前とほとんど変っていま
せん késhíki wa júnen maè to hotóǹdo
kawátte imaseǹ

the 2 books are much the same この
2冊の本はどちらも同じ様な物です sonó
nisàtsu no hóñ wa dóchira mo onáji yò
na monó desù

how are you feeling? - *much the
same* ご気分はいかがですか - 大して変り
ません go-kíbùn wa ikága dèsu ká -
taíshite kawárimaseǹ

muck [mʌk] *n* (dirt) 泥 doró; (excrement)
くそ kusó

muck about/around *vi* (*inf*: fool a-
bout) ぶらぶらする búrabura suru

muck up *vt* (*inf*: ruin) 台無しにする daínashi ni suru

mucus [mju:'kəs] *n* 粘液 néñ-eki

mud [mʌd] *n* 泥 doró

muddle [mʌd'əl] *n* (mess, mix-up) めちゃ
くちゃ mechákucha, 混乱 koñran

♦*vt* (*also*: **muddle up**) (confuse: person,
things) 混乱させる koñran saserú;
(: story, names) ごちゃごちゃにする ro-
chágocha ni suru

muddle through *vi* (get by) どうにかし
て片をつける dóu ni ka shite kirínukerù

muddy [mʌd'i] *adj* (floor, field) どろどろ
の doródoro no

mudguard [mʌd'gɑ:rd] *n* フェンダー féñdā

muesli [mjuːzˈliː] n ムースリ mūsuri ◇朝食用のナッツ、ドライフルーツ、穀物の混合 chōshoku yō no nāttsū, doráifurūtsu, kokúmotsu no kóñgō

muffin [mʌfˈin] n (US) マドレーヌ madórēnu; (BRIT) マフィン máfiñ

muffle [mʌfˈəl] vt (sound) 弱める yowámerù; (against cold) ...に防寒具を付ける ...ni bōkañgu wo tsukérù

muffled [mʌfˈəld] adj (sound) 弱い yowáì

muffler [mʌfˈlər] n (AUT) マフラー máfūrā

mug [mʌg] n (cup) マグ mágù; (inf: face) 面 tsurá; (: BRIT: fool) ばか bákà
♦vt (assault) 襲う osóù ◇特に強盗行為について言う tōkù ni gōtōkōi ni tsuitè iú

mugging [mʌgˈiŋ] n 強盗事件 gōtōjìken

muggy [mʌgˈiː] adj (weather, day) 蒸暑い mushíatsuì

mule [mjuːl] n ラバ rábà

mull [mʌl] vt: to mull over ...について考える ...ni tsúttе kañgaekomù

multi... [mʌlˈtiː] prefix 複数の... fukúsū no ...

multicolored [mʌltikʌlərd] (BRIT **multicoloured**) adj 多色の tashóku no

multilateral [mʌltilætˈərəl] adj (disarmament, talks) 多国間の takőkukan no

multi-level [mʌltiːlevˈəl] (US) adj = **multistory**

multinational [mʌltənæʃˈənəl] adj (company, business) 多国籍の takőkuseki no

multiple [mʌlˈtəpəl] adj (collision) 玉突きの tamátsuki no; (interests) 複数の fukúsū no
♦n (MATH) 倍数 baísū

multiple sclerosis [-sklirouˈsis] n 多発性硬化症 tahátsusei kōkashō

multiplication [mʌltəplikeiˈʃən] n (MATH) 掛算 kakézan; (increase) 増加 zōka

multiply [mʌlˈtəplai] vt (MATH): 4 multiplied by 2 is 8 4掛ける2は8 yốn kakérù ní wa hachí
♦vi (increase) 増える fuérù

multistory [mʌltiːstɔrˈiː] (BRIT **multistorey**) adj (building etc) 高層の kōsō no

multitude [mʌlˈtətuːd] n (crowd) 群衆 guñshū; (large number): a multitude of (reasons, ideas) 沢山の takúsaň no

mum [mʌm] n (inf) = mom
♦adj: to keep mum 黙っている damátte irù

mumble [mʌmˈbəl] vt (speak indistinctly) もぐもぐ言う mógumogu iú
♦vi ぶつぶつ言う bútsubutsu iú

mummy [mʌmˈiː] n (embalmed) ミイラ mfira; (BRIT: mother) = mommy

mumps [mʌmps] n おたふく風邪 otáfukukaze

munch [mʌntʃ] vt (chew) かむ kámù
♦vi かむ kámù

mundane [mʌndeinˈ] adj (task, life) 平凡な hefbon na

municipal [mjuːnisˈəpəl] adj 市の shí no

munitions [mjuːniʃˈənz] npl 兵器弾薬 heíkidañ-yaku

mural [mjuˈrəl] n 壁画 hekíga

murder [məːrˈdər] n (killing) 殺人 satsújin
♦vt (kill) 殺す korósù

murderer [məːrˈdərər] n 人殺し hitógoroshi

murderous [məːrˈdərəs] adj (person) 殺人も辞さない satsújin mo jisánaì; (attack) 殺しを目的とする koróshi wò mokúteki to surù

murky [məːrˈkiː] adj (street, night) 暗い kuráì; (water) 濁った nigótta

murmur [məːrˈmər] n: a murmur of voices かすかな人声 kásùkana hitógòe; (of wind, waves) さざめき sazámeki
♦vt (speak quietly) 声をひそめて言う kôè wo hisómetè iú
♦vi 声をひそめて話す kôè wo hisómetè hanású

muscle [mʌsˈəl] n (ANAT) 筋肉 kiňniku; (fig: strength) 力 chikára

muscle in vi 割込む warfkomù

muscular [mʌsˈkjələr] adj (pain) 筋肉の kiňniku no; (build) たくましい takúmashiì; (person) 強そうな tsuyósō na

muse [mju:z] vi (think) 考え込む kangaekomù

♦n (MYTHOLOGY) ミューズ myūzu ◊
人間の知的活動をつかさどるという女神 ningen no chitékikatsudō wo tsukásadorù to iú mégami

museum [mju:zi:'əm] n 博物館 hakubūtsukan

mushroom [mʌʃ'ru:m] n (fungus: edible, poisonous) キノコ kínòko

♦vi (fig: town, organization) 急速に成長 する kyūsoku ni seíchō suru

music [mju:'zik] n (sound, art) 音楽 ōngaku; (written music, score) 楽譜 gakúfu

musical [mju:'zikəl] adj (career, skills, person) 音楽の ōngaku no; (sound, tune) 音楽的な ongákuteki na

♦n (show, film) ミュージカル myūjikaru

musical instrument n 楽器 gakkí

music hall n (place) ボードビル劇場 bōdobiru gekíjō

musician [mju:ziʃ'ən] n ミュージシャン myūjishàn

musk [mʌsk] n じゃ香 jakō

Muslim [mʌz'lim] adj イスラム教の isúramukyō no

♦n イスラム教徒 isúramukyòto

muslin [mʌz'lin] n モスリン mósùrin

mussel [mʌs'əl] n ムールガイ mūrugai

must [mʌst] aux vb (necessity, obligation): I must do it 私はそれをしなければならない watákushi wa soré wo shínakereba naranài; (probability): he must be there by now もう彼はあそこに着いているでしょう mō kárè wa asóko ni tsúite irù deshō; (suggestion, invitation): you must come and see me soon ぜひ近いうちに来て下さい sonó uchi zéhì asóbi ni kite kudasaì; (indicating something unwelcome): why must he behave so badly? どうしてあの子はそんなに行儀悪いのだろう dōshīte mata ánò ko wa sofína ni gyógiwarukù suru no darō

♦n (necessity): it's a must 必需品だ hitsújuhin da

mustache [mʌstæʃ'] (US) n 鼻ひげ hanáhige

mustard [mʌs'tə:rd] n (Japanese) 辛子 karáshi, 和辛子 wagárashi; (Western) 辛子 karáshi, 洋辛子 yōgárashi, マスタード masútàdo

muster [mʌs'tə:r] vt (support) 求める motómerù; (energy, strength) 奮い起す furúiokosù; (MIL) 召集する shōshū suru

mustn't [mʌs'ənt] = must not

musty [mʌs'ti:] adj かび臭い kabíkusaì

mutation [mju:tei'ʃən] n (alteration) 変化 heñka

mute [mju:t] adj (silent) 無言の mugón no

muted [mju:'tid] adj (color) 地味な jimí na; (reaction) ひかえ目な hisómeta

mutilate [mju:'təleit] vt (person, thing) 傷付ける kizútsukerù ◊特に体の部分を 切断する場合に使う tōkū ni karáda no būbūn wo setsúdan suru baái ni tsukáù

mutiny [mju:'təni:] n (rebellion: of soldiers, sailors) 反乱 hañran

♦vi 反乱を起す hañran wo okósù

mutter [mʌt'ə:r] vt (speak quietly) つぶやく tsubúyakù

♦vi ぶつぶつ不平を言う bútsubutsu fuhéi wo iú

mutton [mʌt'ən] n (meat) マトン mátòn

mutual [mju:'tʃu:əl] adj (shared: benefit, interest) 共通の kyōtsū no; (reciprocal: feeling, attraction) 相互の sōgo no

mutually [mju:'tʃu:əli:] adv 相互に sōgo ni

muzzle [mʌz'əl] n (mouth: of dog) ふん fūñ, 鼻づら hanázura; (: of gun) 銃口 jūkō; (guard: for dog) 口輪 kuchíwa

♦vt (dog) ...に口輪をはめる ...ni kuchíwa wo hamérù

my [mai] adj 私の watákushi nò

this is my house/car/brother これは 私の家[車、兄]です koré wa watákushi nò ié[kurúma, ánì]desù

I've washed my hair/cut my finger 私は髪を洗いました[指を切りました] watákushi wa kamí wò aráimashìta (yubí wò kirímashìta)

is this my pen or yours? これは私の

ペンですか，それともあなたのですか koré wà watákushi nò péñ desu ká, sorétomò anátà no desu ká

Myanmar [mai'ænmɑːr] n ミャンマー myáñmàā

myopic [mai'ɒp'ik] adj 近眼の kíñgan no

myriad [mir'iːəd] n (of people, things) 無数 musū

myself [maiself'] pron 私自身 watákushi-jishíñ ¶ see also **oneself**

mysterious [mistiːr'iːəs] adj (strange) なぞの nazó no

mystery [mis'təriː] n (puzzle) なぞ nazó
shrouded in mystery (place) なぞに包まれた nazó nì tsutsúmàréta

mystic [mis'tik] n (person) 神秘主義者 shiñpishíkujisha

mystic(al) [mis'tik(əl)] adj 神秘的な shiñpiteki na

mystify [mis'təfai] vt (perplex) ...の理解を越える ...no rikái wò koérù

mystique [mistiːk'] n 神秘 shiñpi

myth [miθ] n (legend, story) 神話 shiñwa; (fallacy) 俗信 zokúshin

mythology [miθɑː'lədʒiː] n 神話集 shiñwàshū

N

n/a abbr (= not applicable) ◇申請用紙などで空欄にしてよい場合に書く shiñsei yōshi nádò de kúran ni shité oku baái ni kákù

nag [næg] vt (scold) がみがみ言う gámígami iú

nagging [næg'iŋ] adj (doubt) 晴れない harénaī; (pain) しつこい shitsúkoī

nail [neil] n (on fingers, toes) つめ tsumé; (metal) くぎ kugí
♦vt: to nail something to something ...を...にくぎで留める ...wo ...ni kugí de tomérù
to nail someone down to doing something 強制的に...に...をさせる kyőseiteki ni ...ni ...wò saserù

nailbrush [neil'brʌʃ] n つめブラシ tsu-

méburàshi

nailfile [neil'fail] n つめやすり tsuméyasùri

nail polish n マニキュア manīkyuà

nail polish remover n 除光液 jokóèki, マニキュア落し manīkyua otòshi

nail scissors npl つめ切りばさみ tsumékiribasàmi

nail varnish n = nail polish

naive [naiːv'] adj (person, ideas) 無邪気な mújàki na, ナイーブな naíbù na

naked [nei'kid] adj 裸の hadáka no

name [neim] n (of person, animal, place) 名前 namáe; (surname) 名字 myốjī, 姓 séī; (reputation) 評判 hyőban
♦vt (child) ...に名前を付ける ...ni namáe wò tsukérù; (identify: accomplice, criminal) 名指す namásàsu; (specify: price, date etc) 指定する shitéi suru
what's your name? お名前は何とおっしゃいますか o-námae wà náñto osshái-masù ká
by name 名指しで nazáshi dè
in the name of (fig) ...の名において ...no ná ni òlte
to give one's name and address (to police etc) 名前と住所を知らせる namáe tò jūshò wo shiráserù

nameless [neim'lis] adj (unknown) 無名の muméi no; (anonymous: witness, contributor) 匿名の tokúmei no

namely [neim'liː] adv 即ち sunáwàchi

namesake [neim'seik] n 同姓同名の人 dőseidőmei no hitó

nanny [næn'iː] n 乳母 o-ñbàgakàri

nap [næp] n (sleep) 昼寝 hirúne
to be caught napping (fig) 不意を突かれる fuī wò tsukárerù

napalm [nei'pɑːm] n ナパーム napámù

nape [neip] n: nape of the neck えり首 erīkùbi

napkin [næp'kin] n (also: table napkin) ナプキン nápùkin

nappy [næp'iː] n (BRIT) n おむつ o-mútsù

nappy rash (BRIT) n おむつかぶれ o-mútsukabùre

narcissus [nɑːrsis'əs] n (pl narcissi) n (BOT) スイセン suísen

narcotic [nɑːr'kɒ:t'ik] *adj* 麻酔性の masûisei no
◆*n* 麻薬 mayâku

narrative [nær'ətiv] *n* 物語 monôgatári

narrator [nær'eitər] *n* (in book) 語り手 katárite; (in film etc) ナレーター narétâ

narrow [nær'ou] *adj* (space, road etc) 狭い semâi; (fig: majority, advantage) ぎりぎりの girígirì no; (: ideas, attitude) 狭量な kyôryo na
◆*vi* (road) 狭くなる sêmàku naru; (gap, difference: diminish) 小さくなる chíisakù naru

to have a narrow escape 間一髪で逃れる kán-ìppátsu dè nogárerù

to narrow something down to (choice, possibility) …を…に絞る …wo …ni shibórù

narrowly [nær'ouli] *adv* (miss) 辛うじて karôjîte, 間一髪 kán-ìppátsu de

narrow-minded [nær'oumin'did] *adj* 狭量な kyôryo na

nasal [nei'zəl] *adj* (of the nose) 鼻の hanâ no; (voice, sound) 鼻にかかった hanâ ni kakátta

nasty [næs'ti] *adj* (unpleasant: remark, person) いやな iyá nà; (malicious) 腹黒い harâguroì; (rude) 無礼な búrèi na; (revolting: taste, smell) むかつかせる mukátsukaserù; (wound, disease etc) ひどい hidôi

nation [nei'ʃən] *n* (country) 国 kunî, 国家 kôkka; (people) 国民 kokúmin

national [næʃ'ənəl] *adj* 国の kunî no
◆*n*: *a foreign national* 外国人 gaíkokujìn

national dress *n* 民族衣装 mińzokuishô

National Health Service (*BRIT*) *n* 国民医療制度 kokúmin iryôseidò

National Insurance (*BRIT*) *n* 国民保険 kokúminhokèn

nationalism [næʃ'ənəlizəm] *n* 国家主義 kokkáshugì, 民族主義 mínzokushugì

nationalist [næʃ'ənəlist] *adj* 国家主義の kokkáshugì no, 民族主義の mínzokushugì no
◆*n* 国家主義者 kokkáshugìshà, 民族主義者 mínzokushugìshà

nationality [næʃənæl'əti:] *n* 国籍 kokúseki

nationalization [næʃnəlɑzei'ʃən] *n* 国有化 kokúyûka, 国営化 kokúeìka

nationalize [næʃ'nəlaiz] *vt* 国営にする kokúei ni surù

nationally [næʃ'nəli:] *adv* (nationwide) 全国的に zeńkokuteki ni; (as a nation) 国として kunî toshite

nationwide [nei'ʃənwaid'] *adj* (problem, campaign) 全国的な zeńkokuteki na
◆*adv* (campaign, search) 全国的に zeńkokuteki ni

native [nei'tiv] *n* (local inhabitant) 地元の人 jimôto no hitð; (of tribe etc) 原住民 geńjûmin
◆*adj* (indigenous) 地元の jimôto no, 地元の jimôto umâre no; (of one's birth) 生れの umâre no; (innate) 生れつきの umâretsuki no

a native of Russia ロシア生れの人 roshîa umare no hitð

a native speaker of French フランス語を母国語として使う人 furánsugo wð bokð kugo to suru hitð

native language *n* 母国語 bokðkugo

Nativity [nətiv'əti:] *n*: **the Nativity** キリストの降誕 kirísuto no kôtan

NATO [nei'tou] *n abbr* (= *North Atlantic Treaty Organization*) 北大西洋条約機構 kitátaiseiyô jôyaku kikô

natural [næt'ʃərəl] *adj* (gen) 自然の shizen no; (innate) 生れつきの umâretsuki no

natural gas *n* 天然ガス teñneṅgasu

naturalist [næt'ʃərəlist] *n* 博物学者 hakúbutsugakushà

naturalize [næt'ʃərəlaiz] *vt*: **to become naturalized** (person, plant) 帰化する kiká suru

naturally [næt'ʃərəli:] *adv* (gen) 自然に shizen ni; (of course) もちろん mochîron, 当然 tōzen

nature [nei'tʃər] *n* (also: **Nature**) 自然 shizen, 大自然 dafshizen; (character) 性質 seíshitsu; (type, sort) 種類 shurùi
by nature 生れつき umáretsuki

naught [nɔːt] *n* 零 rêi, ゼロ zérð

naughty [nɔːˈtiː] *adj* (child) 行儀の悪い gyōgi no warúi

nausea [nɔːˈziə] *n* 吐気 hakíke

nauseate [nɔːˈzieit] *vt* むかつかせる mukátsukaserù, 吐気を起こさせる hakíke wð okósaserù; (*fig*) いやな感じを与える iyá na kaṇji wo atáerù

nautical [nɔːˈtikəl] *adj* (uniform) 船員の seń-in no; (uniform, academy) 海軍の kaígun no

a **nautical mile** 海里 káɪri

naval [neivəl] *adj* (uniform, academy) 海軍の kaígun no

a **naval battle** 海戦 kaísen

naval forces 海軍力 kaígunryòku

naval officer *n* 海軍将校 kaígunshōkō

nave [neiv] *n* 外陣 gaíjin

navel [neivəl] *n* へそ hesó

navigate [nævˈəgeit] *vi* (NAUT, AVIAT) 航行する kōkō suru; (AUT) 道案内する michfaṇnai suru

navigation [nævəˈgeiʃən] *n* (action) 航行 kōkō; (science) 航海術 kōkaíjùtsu

navigator [nævˈəgeitər] *n* (NAUT) 航海長 kōkaíchō; (AVIAT) 航空士 kūkū-shi; (AUT) 道案内をする人 michfaṇnai wo suru hitò

navvy [nævˈiː] (*BRIT*) *n* 労働者 rōdōsha

navy [neiˈviː] *n* 海軍 kaígun

navy(-blue) *adj* 濃紺の nōkon no

Nazi [nɑːtˈsiː] *n* ナチ náchi

NB [ɛnˈbiː] *abbr* (= *nota bene*) 注 (の脚注などに使う略語 kyakúchū nadð ni tsukáù ryakúgo

near [niɾ] *adj* (place, time, relation) 近い chikáì

♦*adv* 近く chikáku

♦*prep* (also: **near to**: space, time) ...の近くに ...no chikákù ni

♦*vt* (place, event) ...に近づく ...ni chikázukù

nearby [niɾˈbai] *adj* 近くの chikákù no

♦*adv* 近くに chikákù ni

nearly [niɾˈliː] *adv* (not totally) ほとんど hotóndò; (on the point of) 危うく ayáukù

I **nearly fell** 危うく転ぶところだった ayáukù koróbu tokoro dattà

near miss *n* (narrow escape) ニアミス niámisù; (of planes) 異常接近 ijōsekkìn,

ニアミス niámisù; (of cars etc): *that was a near miss!* 危ないところだった abúnai tokoro dattà

nearside [niɾˈsaid] *n* (AUT: in Britain, Japan) 左側 hidárigawa; (: in US, Europe etc) 右側 migígawa

near-sighted [niɾˈsaitid] *adj* 近眼の kiń-gan no, 近視の kińshi no

neat [niːt] *adj* (place, person) きちんとした kichíñ to shita; (skillful: work, plan) 上手な jōzu na; (spirits) ストレートの sutórēto no

neatly [niːtˈliː] *adv* (tidily) きちんと kichíñ to; (skillfully) 上手に jōzu ni

necessarily [nesəserˈiliː] *adv* (inevitably) 必然的に hitsúzenteki ni

not necessarily (not automatically) ...必ずしも...でない kanárazushimo ...de náì

necessary [nesˈiseriː] *adj* (required: skill, quality, measure) 必要な hitsúyō na; (inevitable: result, effect) 必然の hitsúzen no

it is necessary to/that ...する必要がある ...suru hitsúyō ga arù

necessitate [nasesˈəteit] *vt* 必要とする hitsúyō to surù

necessities [nasesˈitiːz] *npl* (essentials) 必需品 hitsújuhin

necessity [nasesˈitiː] *n* (thing needed) 必需品 hitsújuhin; (compelling circumstances) 必然 hitsúzen

neck [nek] *n* (of person, animal, garment, bottle) 首 kubí

♦*vi* (*inf*) ペッティングする pettíñgu suru

neck and neck 接戦して sessén shite

necklace [nekˈlis] *n* ネックレス nékkùresu

neckline [nekˈlain] *n* ネックライン nekkúraìn

necktie [nekˈtai] (*US*) *n* ネクタイ nékùtai

née [nei] *adj*: *née Scott* 旧姓スコット kyūsei sukóttð

need [niːd] *n* (lack) 欠乏 ketsúbō; (necessity) 必要 hitsúyō; (thing needed) 必需品 hitsújuhin

♦*vt* (require) ...を必要とする ...wo hitsú-

I need to do it 私はそれをしなければならない watákushi wa soré wo shinákereba naranai, 私はそれをする必要があるwatákushi wa soré wo suru hitsuyō ga arū

you don't need to go 行かなくてもいい ikánakute mo iî

needle [niːdəl] *n* (gen) 針 hárî; (for knitting) 編棒 amíbō

♦*vt* (fig: inf) からかう karákaú

needless [niːdlis] *adj* (criticism, risk) 不必要な fuhítsuyō na

needless to say 言うまでもなく iú made mo nakū

needlework [niːdəlwərk] *n* (item(s) of needlework) 縫い物 nuímonò; (activity) 針仕事 harîshigòto

needn't [niːdənt] = **need not**

needy [niːdi] *adj* 貧しい mazúshiî

negation [nigéiʃən] *n* 否定 hitéi

negative [négətiv] *adj* (answer) 否定の hitéi no; (attitude) 否定的な hitéiteki na; (reaction) 消極的な shōkyokuteki na; (ELEC) 陰極の ínkyoku no, マイナスのmaínasu no

♦*n* (LING) 否定形 hitéikei, (PHOT) 陰画 íñga, ネガ négà

neglect [niglékt] *vt* (child) 放任する hōnin suru, ほったらかす hottárakasù; (one's duty) 怠る okótarū

♦*n* (of child) 放任 hōnin; (of area, house, garden) 怠る事 okótaru kotò; (of duty) 怠る事 okótaru kotò

negligee [néglizei] *n* (dressing gown) ネグリジェ négùrijè

negligence [néglidʒəns] *n* (carelessness) 不注意 fuchúi

negligible [néglidʒəbəl] *adj* (cost, difference) わずかな wázùka na

negotiable [nigóuʃəbəl] *adj* (check) 譲渡できる jōto dekirù

negotiate [nigóuʃièit] *vi*: *to negotiate (with)* (...と) 交渉する (...to) kōshō suru

♦*vt* (treaty, transaction) 協議して決める kyōgi shite kimerù; (obstacle) 乗越える noríkoerù; (bend in road) 注意して通る

negotiation [nigóuʃiéiʃən] *n* 交渉 kōshō

negotiator [nigóuʃièitər] *n* 交渉する人 kōshō suru hitò

Negress [níːgris] *n* 黒人女性 kokújinjosei

Negro [níːgrou] *adj* 黒人の kokújin no

♦*n* 黒人 kokújin

neigh [nei] *vi* いななく inánakù

neighbour [néibər] (BRIT **neighbour**) *n* (next door) 隣の人 tonári no hitò; (in vicinity) 近所の人 kínjo no hitò

neighbourhood [néibərhùd] *n* (place) 近所 kínjo, 界隈 kāiwai; (people) 近所の人々 kínjo no hitóbìto

neighboring [néibəriŋ] *adj* (town, state) 隣の tonári no

neighbourly [néibərli] *adj* (person, attitude) 親切な shínsetsu na

neighbour [néibər] *etc* (BRIT) = **neighbor** *etc*

neither [níːðər] *adj* どちらの...も...でない dóchira no ...mo ...de naì

neither story is true どちらの話も本当ではない dóchira no hanáshi mò honító de wa naì

♦*conj*: *I didn't move and neither did John* 私も動かなかったしジョンも動かなかった watákushi mò ugókanakatta shì, jóñ mo ugókanakattà

♦*pron* どちらも...でない dóchira mo ...de naì

neither is true どちらも本当でない dóchira mo honítō de naì

♦*adv*: *neither good nor bad* よくも悪くもない yókù mo warúkù mo naì

neon [níːɑn] *n* ネオン néòn; (also: **neon sign**) ネオンサイン neónsaìn

neon light [níːɑn-] *n* ネオン灯 neóntō

nephew [néfjuː] *n* おい oî

nerve [nəːrv] *n* (ANAT) 神経 shínkeì; (courage) 勇気 yūkî; (impudence) 厚かましさ atsúkamashisà, 図々しさ zūzūshisà

to have a fit of nerves 神経質になる shínkeìshitsu ni narù

nerve-racking [nəːrvrǽkiŋ] *adj* いらいらさせる îràira saserù

nervous [nɔːr'vəs] adj (ANAT) 神経の shíñkei no; (anxious) 神経質な shíñkeishitsu na; (timid: person) 気の小さい ki no chîisai; (: animal) おく病な okûbyô na

nervous breakdown n 神経衰弱 shíñkeisuijaku

nest [nest] n 巣 su

♦vi 巣を作る su wò tsukûrû

nest egg n (fig) へそくり hesôkuri

nestle [nes'əl] vi: to nestle in a valley/ the mountains (village etc) 谷間(山あい)に横たわる tanima(yamá-aí)ni yokôtawarù

net [net] n (gen) 網 amî; (fabric) レース rêsù; (TENNIS, VOLLEYBALL etc) ネット nettô; (fig) わな wánà

♦adj (COMM) 正味の shômi no

♦vt (fish, game) 網で取る amî de tôrù; (profit) 得る érù

netball [net'bɔːl] n ネットボール nettôbôru 《英国で行われるバスケットボールに似た球技 efkoku de okonawarerù basúkettobôru ni nîtà kyûgî》

net curtains npl レースのカーテン rêsù no kâtèn

Netherlands [neð'ərləndz] npl: the Netherlands オランダ oránda

nett [net] (BRIT) adj = net

netting [net'iŋ] n 網網 amî

nettle [net'əl] n イラクサ irákusa

network [net'wəːrk] n (of roads, veins, shops) ネットワーク nettôwâku; (TV, RADIO) 放送網 hôsômô, ネットワーク nettôwâku

neurotic [nuːrɑt'ik] adj 神経過敏な shíñkeikabûn na, ノイローゼの noîrôze no

♦n ノイローゼの人 noîrôze no hitô

neuter [nuː'tər] adj (LING) 中性の chûsei no

♦vt (cat etc) 去勢する kyósei suru

neutral [nuː'trəl] adj (person) 中立の chûritsu no; (color etc) 中間色の chûkañshoku no; (ELEC) 中性の chûsei no

♦n (AUT) ニュートラル nyûtôraru

neutrality [nuːtral'iti:] n 中立 chûritsu

neutralize [nuː'trəlaiz] vt (acid, poison etc) 中和する chûwa suru; (campaign, goodwill) 無駄にする daînashi ni surù

never [nev'əːr] adv どんな時でも…ない dôñna tokì de mo ...náì

I never went 行かなかった ikánakattà

never in my life …したことがない ...shítá kotò ga náì ¶ see also mind

never-ending [nev'əːren'diŋ] adj 終りのない owári no naî, 果てしない hatéshinaî

nevertheless [nevəːrðəles'] adv それにもかかわらず soré ni mô kakáwarazû, それでもやはり soré de mò yahârî

new [nuː] adj (brand new) 新しい atárashiî; (recent) 最近の saîkin no; (different) 今までになかった imá madê ni nákàttá; (inexperienced) 新入りの shíñ-iri no

newborn [nuː'bɔːrn] adj 生れたばかりの umáreta bakâri no

newcomer [nuː'kʌmər] n 新顔 shiñgao, 新入り shíñ-iri

new-fangled [nuː'fæŋ'gəld] (pej) adj 超モダンな chômodàn na

new-found [nuː'faund'] adj (enthusiasm, confidence) 新たに沸いた áràta ni wafta; (friend) 新しくできた atárashikû dékîta

newly [nuː'li:] adv 新しく atárashikû

newly-weds [nuː'li:wedz] npl 新婚者 shiñkoñsha

new moon n 新月 shíñgetsu

news [nuːz] n ニュース nyûsu

a piece of news ニュース項目 nyûsukômoku, ニュース nyûsu

the news (RADIO, TV) ニュース nyûsu

news agency n 通信社 tsûshiñsha

newsagent [nuːz'eidʒənt] (BRIT) n = newsdealer

newscaster [nuːz'kæstəːr] n ニュースキャスター nyûsukyasûtâ

newsdealer [nuːz'diːlər] (US) n (shop) 新聞販売店 shíñbuñhanbaiten; (person) 新聞販売業者 shíñbuñhanbaigyôsha

newsflash [nuːz'flæʃ] n ニュース速報 nyûsusokuhô

newsletter [nuːz'letər] n ニュースレター nyûsuretâ

newspaper [nuːz'peipəːr] n 新聞 shíñbun

newsprint [nuːz'print] n 新聞印刷用紙 shíñbun insatsuyôshi

newsreader [nuːz'riːdəːr] n = newscaster

newsreel [nuːzˈriːl] n ニュース映画 nyúsuelga

newsstand [nuːzˈstænd] n (in station etc) 新聞スタンド shífibun sutándo

newt [nuːt] n イモリ imóri

New Year n 新年 shſnnen

New Year's Day n 元旦 gafitan, 元日 gafijitsu

New Year's Eve n 大みそ日 ómisòka の

New York [-jɔːrk] n ニューヨーク nyúyòku

New Zealand [-ziːˈlənd] n ニュージーランド nyújïrándo

New Zealander [-ziːˈləndər] n ニュージーランド人 nyújïrandojìn

next [nekst] adj (in space) 隣の tonári no; (in time) 次の tsugí no
♦adv (place) 隣に tonári ni; (time) 次に tsugí ni, 今度 kóndo
the next day 日の tsugí no hî, 翌日 yokújitsu
next time 次回に jíkài ni, 今度 kóndo
next year 来年 raínen
next to ...の隣に ...no tonári ni
to cost next to nothing ただ同然である tádà dòzen de arù
to do next to nothing ほとんど何もしない hotóndo nanî mo shināì
next please! (at doctor's etc) 次の方 tsugí no katà

next door (location) 隣の家に ié ni
♦adj (neighbor, flat) 隣の家の tonári no

next-of-kin [nekstˈəvkin'] n 最も近い親せき mottómo chikáì shífisekì

NHS [eneitʃes'] n abbr = **National Health Service**

nib [nib] n ペン先 peñsákì

nibble [nib'əl] vt 少しずつかじる sukóshizutsu kajírù, ちびちび食べる chíbìchibi tabérù

Nicaragua [nikərəˈgwa] n ニカラグア nikáragua

nice [nais] adj (likeable) 感じのよい kañjì no yoî; (kind) 親切な shífisetsu na; (pleasant) 天気のよい tênkì no yoî; (attractive) 魅力的な miryókutekì na

nicely [nais'liː] adv (pleasantly) 気持よく kimóchi yokù; (kindly) 親切に shífisetsu

ni; (attractively) 魅力的に miryókutekì ni

niceties [nai'sətiːz] npl 細かい点 komákaì teñ

nick [nik] n (wound) 切傷 kiríkìzu; (cut, indentation) 刃の跡 há no atò
♦vt (BRIT inf: steal) かっ払う kappáraù
in the nick of time どい時に kiwádot tôkì ni, 危ういところで ayáuì tokoro dè

nickel [nik'əl] n (metal) ニッケル nikkéru; (US) 5セント玉 5 sénto dama

nickname [nik'neim] n あだ名 adána, 愛称 aíshò, ニックネーム nakkúnèmu
♦vt ...に...のあだ名をつける ...ni ...no adá na wò tsukérù

nicotine [nik'ətin] n ニコチン nikóchin

niece [niːs] n めい meí

Nigeria [naidʒiːˈriːə] n ナイジェリア nafjeria

Nigerian [naidʒiːˈriːən] adj ナイジェリアの nafjeria no
♦n ナイジェリア人 nafjeriajìn

nigger [nig'əːr] (inf!) n (highly offensive) 黒人坊 kurónbò

niggling [nig'liŋ] adj (trifling) つまらない tsumáranaì; (annoying) いらいらさせる írаìra sasérù

night [nait] n (period of darkness) 夜 yórù; (evening) 夕方 yúgata
the night before last おとといの夜 otótoì no yórù
at night 夜に yórù (ni)
by night 夜に yórù ni

nightcap [nait'kæp] n (drink) 寝酒 nezáke, ナイトキャップ naftokyappù

nightclub [nait'klʌb] n ナイトクラブ naftokurabù

nightdress [nait'dres] n 寝巻 nemáki ◊ 女性用のを指す joséiyò no wò sású

nightfall [nait'fɔːl] n 夕暮 yúgure

nightgown [nait'gaun] n = **nightdress**

nightie [nai'tiː] n = **nightdress**

nightingale [nait'əngeil] n ヨナキウグイス uïkiugùtsu, サヨナキドリ sayónakidòri, ナイチンゲール nafchingèru

nightlife [nait'laif] n 夜の生活 yórù no sefkatsu

nightly [nait'li:] *adj* 毎晩の mâïban no
◆*adv* 毎晩 mâïban

nightmare [nait'mer] *n* 悪夢 ákûmu

night porter *n* 夜間のフロント係 yakán furôntogakàri

night school *n* 夜間学校 yakángakkô

night shift *n* 夜間勤務 yakánkìnmu

night-time [nait'taim] *n* 夜 yórù

night watchman *n* 夜警 yakéì

nil [nil] *n* ゼロ zérò; (*BRIT: SPORT*) 零点 reîteñ, ゼロ zérò

Nile [nail] *n*: **the Nile** ナイル川 naîrugàwa

nimble [nim'bəl] *adj* (agile) 素早い subáyaì, 軽快な keîkai na; (skillful) 器用な kíyô na

nine [nain] *num* 9 (の) kyû (no), 九つ (の) kokónôtsu (no)

nineteen [nain'ti:n'] *num* 19 (の) jûku (no)

ninety [nain'ti:] *num* 90 (の) kyûjû (no)

ninth [nainθ] *adj* 第9の dáîku (no)

nip [nip] *vt* (pinch) つねる tsunérù; (bite) かむ kámù

nipple [nip'əl] *n* (*ANAT*) 乳首 chikûbì

nitrogen [nai'trədʒən] *n* 窒素 chîssò

KEYWORD

no [nou] (*pl* **noes**) *adv* (opposite of "yes") いいえ iîe

are you coming? - no (I'm not) 一緒に来ませんか-いいえ（行きません）isshô ni kimaseñ ká - iîe (ikímaseñ)

would you like some? - no thank you いりませんか-いいえ、結構です irímaseñ ká - iîe, kékkô desu

◆*adj* (not any) 何も...ない naní mò ...náï

I have no money/time/books 私には金（時間、本）がありません watákushi ni wà kané (jikan, hôñ) ga arimaseñ

no other man would have done it 他の人ならそれをしてくれなかったでしょう hoká no hitô nara daré mò soré wò shité kurenakatta deshô

「*no entry*」 立入禁止 tachíirikìnshi

「*no smoking*」 禁煙 kín-eñ

◆*n* 反対意見 hañtai ikèn, 反対票 hañtaihyô

there were 20 noes and one "don't know" 反対意見20に対し、「分からない」は1つだった hañtai ikèn nîjû ni tai shi, "wakáranaì" wa hitótsu dattà

nobility [noubil'əti:] *n* (dignity) 気高さ kedákasà; (social class) 貴族 kîzòku

noble [nou'bəl] *adj* (person, character: worthy) 気高い kedákaì; (title, family: of high social class) 貴族の kîzòku no

nobody [nou'bɑdi:] *pron* だれも ...ない daré mò ...náï

nocturnal [nɑktər'nəl] *adj* (tour, visit) 夜の yórù no, 夜間の yakân no; (animal) 夜行性の yakôsei no

nod [nɑd] *vi* (gesture) 会釈する áízu surû; (*also*: **nod in agreement**) うなずく unázukù; (doze) うとうとする útòuto suru

◆*vt*: **to nod one's head** うなずく unázukù

◆*n* うなずき unazuki

nod off *vi* 居眠りする inémuri suru

noise [nɔiz] *n* (sound) 音 otô; (din) 騒音 sôon

noisy [nɔi'zi:] *adj* (audience, child, machine) うるさい urúsaì

nomad [nou'mæd] *n* 遊牧民 yûbokumîn

nominal [nɑm'ənəl] *adj* (leader) 名目上の meîmokujô no; (rent, price) わずかな wázùka na

nominate [nɑm'əneit] *vt* (propose) 推薦する suîseñ suru; (appoint) 任命する nîmei suru

nomination [nɑmənei'ʃən] *n* (proposal) 推薦 suîseñ; (appointment) 任命 nîmei

nominee [nɑməni:'] *n* (proposed person) 推薦された人 suîseñ sareta hitô; (appointed person) 任命された人 nîmei sareta hitô

non... [nɑn] *prefix* 非... hî..., 無... mú..., 不... fû...

non-alcoholic [nɑnælkəhɔ:l'ik] *adj* アルコールを含まない arúkôru wò fukúmanaì

non-aligned [nɑnəlaind'] *adj* 非同盟の hídômei no

nonchalant [nɔnʃələɑnt'] *adj* 平然とした hefzen to shita

noncommittal [nɔnkəmɪt'əl] *adj* (person, answer) どっちつかずの dotchí tsukazú no

nondescript [nɔn'dɪskrɪpt] *adj* (person, clothes, color) 特徴のない tokúchō no naí

none [nʌn] *pron* (person) だれも …ない daré mò …naí; (thing) どれも…ない dóre mo …naí

none of you あなたたちの1人も…ない anátatàchi no hitóri mò …naí

I've none left 何も残っていません naní mò nokótte imasén

he's none the worse for it それでも彼は大丈夫です soré de mò kare wa daíjōbu desu

nonentity [nɔnen'titi:] *n* 取るに足らない人 tórù ni taránai hitó

nonetheless [nʌnðəlēs'] *adv* それにもかかわらず soré ni mò kakáwarazù, それでもやはり soré de mò yahári

non-existent [nɑnigzis'tənt] *adj* 存在しない soñzai shinaí

non-fiction [nɑnfik'ʃən] *n* ノンフィクション noñfikūshon

nonplussed [nɑnplʌst'] *adj* 困惑した koñwaku shita, 困った komáttà

nonsense [nɑn'sens] *n* でたらめ detáramè, ナンセンス náñsensu

nonsense! そんな事はない sofina koto wà naí, ナンセンス náñsensu

non-smoker [nɑnsmou'kəːr] *n* タバコを吸わない人 tabáko wò suwánai hitó, 非喫煙者 hfkitsueñsha

non-stick [nɑnstik'] *adj* (pan, surface) こげつかない kogétsukanaí

non-stop [nɑn'stɑp'] *adj* (conversation) 止らない tomáranaí; (flight, train) 直行の chokkō no, ノンストップの noñsutoppū no

♦*adv* 止らずに tomárazu ni

noodles [nu:'dlz] *n* ヌードル núdòru

nook [nuk] *n*: *every nook and cranny* 隅々 sumízùmi

noon [nu:n] *n* 正午 shṓgò

no one (*BRIT* **no-one**) *pron* = **nobody**

noose [nu:s] *n* (loop) 引結び hikímusùbi

hangman's noose 絞首刑用の縄 kōshukeiyō no nawá

nor [nɔːr] *conj* = **neither**

♦*adv* see **neither**

norm [nɔːrm] *n* (convention) 慣習 kañshū; (rule, requirement) ノルマ nórùma

normal [nɔːr'məl] *adj* (usual, ordinary): life, behavior, result) 普通の futsū no; (child: not abnormal) 異常でない ijō de naí, ノーマルな nṓmàru na

normally [nɔːr'məli:] *adv* 普通 は futsū wa, 普通に futsū ni

north [nɔːrθ] *n* 北 kitá

♦*adj* 北の kitá no

♦*adv* 北へ kitá e

North America *n* 北米 hokúbei

north-east [nɔːrθiːst'] *n* 北東 hokútō

northerly [nɔːr'ðərli:] *adj* (point) 北方の hoppō no; (direction) 北方への hoppō e nó

a northerly wind 北からの風 kitá kara nò kazé

northern [nɔːr'ðərn] *adj* 北の kitá no

the northern hemisphere 北半球 kitáhañkyū

Northern Ireland *n* 北アイルランド kitá airurando

North Pole *n* 北極 hokkyóku

North Sea *n* 北海 hokkái

northward(s) [nɔːrθ'wəːrd(z)] *adv* 北へ kitá e

north-west [nɔːrθwest'] *n* 北西 hokúsei

Norway [nɔːr'wei] *n* ノルウェー norúè

Norwegian [nɔːrwiː'dʒən] *adj* ノルウェーの norúè no; (LING) ノルウェー語の norúègo no

♦*n* (person) ノルウェー人 norúèjìn; (LING) ノルウェー語 norúègo

nose [nouz] *n* (ANAT, ZOOL) 鼻 haná; (sense of smell) きゅう覚 kyūkaku

♦*vi*: *nose about* を嗅する sefisaku suru

nosebleed [nouz'bliːd] *n* 鼻血 hanáji

nose-dive [nouz'daiv] *n* (of plane) 急降下 kyūkōka

nosey [nou'zi:] (*inf*) *adj* = **nosy**

nostalgia [nəstæl'dʒə] *n* 郷愁 kyōshū, ノ

スタルジア nosútarújia

nostalgic [nəstǽl'dʒik] *adj* (person, book, film) 懐かしい natsúkashiī

nostril [nɑːs'trəl] *n* (of person, animal) 鼻のあな haná no aná, 鼻孔 bikó

nosy [nou'ziː] (*inf*) *adj* せん索好きな señsakuzūki na

KEYWORD

not [nɑːt] *adv* ...でない ...de naí

he is not/isn't here 彼はいません kárē wa imáseñ

you must not/you mustn't do that それをしてはいけません soré wo shité wā ikémaseñ

it's too late, isn't it? 遅過ぎますよね osósugimasū yo né, 遅過ぎるでしょう osósugirū deshō

he asked me not to do it それをしないで下さいと彼に頼まれました soré wo shináide kudasaī to kárē ni tanómaremashīta

not that I don't like him/he isn't interesting 彼を嫌い(面白くない)というのではないが kárē wo kiráī(omóshirokūnai)tō iū no de wa naí gá

not yet まだ mádà

not now 今は駄目 ímà wa damé ¶ *see also* all; only

notably [nou'təbliː] *adv* (particularly) 特に tókū ni; (markedly) 著しく ichígirushikū

notary [nou'tɑːriː] *n* 公証人 kōshōnin

notch [nɑːtʃ] *n* (in wood, blade, saw) 刻み目 kizámime, ノッチ notchí

note [nout] *n* (record) 覚書 obógaki, ノート nŏto, メモ mémō; (letter) 短い手紙 mijíkai tegámi; (banknote) 紙幣 shíhēi, 札 satsú; (MUS) 音符 ofipu; (tone) 音 otó

◆*vt* (observe) ...に気が付く ...ni ki gá tsukū; (write down) 書留める kakftomerū

notebook [nout'buk] *n* 帳面 chŏmen, ノート nŏto

noted [nou'tid] *adj* (famous) 有名な yǔmei na

notepad [nout'pæd] *n* メモ用紙 memó-yōshi ¶ 綱などでつづった物を指す norí

nadð de tsuzútta mono wð sásù

notepaper [nout'peipɑːr] *n* 便せん biñsen

nothing [nʌθ'iŋ] *n* (not anything) 何も ...ない naní mð ...naī; (zero) ゼロ zěrð

he does nothing 彼は何もしない kárē wa naní mð shināī

nothing new/much/special 目新しい(大した、特別)ことはない meátarashiī(táishita, tokúbetsu nā)kotó wa naī

for nothing (free) 無料で muryó de, ただで tádà de; (in vain) 無駄に mudá ni

notice [nou'tis] *n* (announcement) 通知 tsǔchi; (warning) 通告 tsǔkoku; (dismissal) 解雇 kaíko; (resignation) 辞表 jihyó; (period of time) 予告 yokóku

◆*vt* (observe) ...に気が付く ...ni ki gá tsukū

to bring something to someone's notice (attention) ...を...に知らせる ...wo ...ni shiráserū

to take notice of ...に気が付く ...ni ki gá tsukū

at short notice 急に kyǔ ni

until further notice 追って通知があるまで otté tsǔchi ga arū madè

to hand in one's notice 辞表を出す jihyó wo dásù

noticeable [nou'tisəbəl] *adj* (mark, effect) はっきりした hakkíri shita

noticeboard [nou'tisbɔːrd] (*BRIT*) *n* 掲示板 keíjiban

notify [nou'təfai] *vt*: *to notify someone (of something)* (...を) ...に知らせる (...wo) ...ni shiráserū

notion [nou'ʃən] *n* (idea) 考え kañgaé, 概念 gáinen; (opinion) 意見 íken

notorious [noutɔːr'iːəs] *adj* (criminal, liar, place) 悪名高い akúmeítakaī

notwithstanding [nɑːtwiθstæn'diŋ] *adv* ...にもかかわらず ...nf mð kakáwarazū

◆*prep* ...にもかかわらず ...nf mð kakáwarazū

nougat [nuːˈgət] *n* ヌガー nǔgā ¶ クルミなどの入ったキャラメル風のお菓子 kurúmi nadð no hafttá kyarámerufù no okáshī

nought [nɔːt] n = **naught**

noun [naun] n 名詞 méìshi

nourish [ˈnʌrɪʃ] vt (feed) 養う yashínaù; (fig: foster) 心中にはぐくむ shínchū ni hagúkumù

nourishing [ˈnʌrɪʃɪŋ] adj (food) 栄養のある eíyō no arú

nourishment [ˈnʌrɪʃmənt] n (food) 栄養 eíyō

novel [ˈnɔvəl] n (小説 shōsetsu
♦adj (new, fresh: idea, approach) 目新しい meátarashiì, 新鮮な shínsen na

novelist [ˈnɔvəlist] n 小説家 shōsetsuka

novelty [ˈnɔvəlti] n (newness) 新鮮さ shínsensa; (object) 変ったもの kawátta monò

November [nouvˈembər] n 11月 jūíchigatsu

novice [ˈnɔvis] n (beginner) 初心者 shoshínsha; (REL) 修練者 shúrensha

now [nau] adv 今 imá
♦conj: **now (that)** ...であるから ...de arú kara
right now (immediately) 今すぐ imá súgù; (at the moment) 今の所 imá no tokoro
by now 今ごろはもう imágoro wà mô
just now 今の所 imá no tokoro
now and then, now and again 時々 tokídòki
from now on 今後 kóngo

nowadays [ˈnauədeiz] adv このごろ(は) konógoro (wa)

nowhere [ˈnouweər] adv どこにも...ない dóko ni mo...náì

nozzle [ˈnɔzəl] n (of hose, fire extinguisher etc) ノズル nózùru; (of vacuum cleaner) 吸口 suíkuchi

nuance [ˈnuːɑːns] n ニュアンス nyúànsu

nubile [ˈnuːbail] adj (woman) セクシーな sékùshī na

nuclear [ˈnuːkliər] adj (fission, weapons) 核... kákù...
the nuclear industry 原子力産業界 geńshiryoku sangyōkai
nuclear physics 原始物理学 geńshibutsurigàku, 核物理学 kakúbutsurigàku
nuclear power 原子力 geńshiryoku

nucleus [ˈnuːkliəs] n (pl **nuclei**) n (of atom, cell) 核 kákù; (of group) 中心 chúshin

nude [nuːd] adj 裸の hadáka no
♦n ヌード núdo
in the nude (naked) 裸で hadáka de

nudge [nʌdʒ] vt (person) 小突く kozúkù

nudist [ˈnuːdist] n 裸体主義者 ratáishugishà, ヌーディスト núdisùto

nudity [ˈnuːditi] n 裸 hadáka

nuisance [ˈnuːsəns] n (state of affairs) 厄介な事情 yákkai na jijò; (thing) 厄介な物 yákkai na monò; (person: irritating) 迷惑な人 meíwaku na hitò
what a nuisance! 困ったもんだ komátta moñ dá

null [nʌl] adj: **null and void** (contract, agreement) 無効な mukó na

numb [nʌm] adj: **numb (with)** (with cold etc) ...でしびれた ...de shibíretà; (fig: with fear etc) ...で気が動転した ...de ki ga dṓten shità

number [ˈnʌmbər] n (MATH) 数字 súji; (quantity) 数 kázù; (of house, bank account etc) 番号 bañgṓ
♦vt (pages etc) ...に番号を付ける ...ni bañgṓ wo tsukérù; (amount to) 総数は...である sṓsū wa ...de arú
to be numbered among ...の1人である ...no hitórí de árù
a number of (several) 数...の sū... no
they were ten in number (people) 彼ら は10人だった kárera wa júnin dattà; (things) 10個あった júkkò attà

number plate (BRIT) n (AUT) ナンバープレート nañbápurèto

numeral [ˈnuːmərəl] n 数詞 súshi

numerate [ˈnuːmərit] adj 数学ができる súgaku gà dekírù

numerical [nuːˈmerikal] adj (value) 数字で表した súji de aráwashità; (order) 数字の súji no

numerous [ˈnuːmərəs] adj (many, countless) 多くの ṓkù no, 多数の tasū no

nun [nʌn] n (Christian) 修道女 shūdṓjo; (Buddhist) 尼 amá

nurse [nəːrs] n (in hospital) 看護婦 kańgofù; (also: **nursemaid**) 保母 hobò

◆*vt* (patient) 看護する kángo suru; (baby) ...に乳を飲ませる ...ni chichí wò nomáserù

nursery [nəːrˈsəriː] *n* (institution) 保育園 hoíkuèn; (room) 育児室 ikújìshìtsu; (for plants: commercial establishment) 種苗園 shubyōen

nursery rhyme *n* 童謡 dóyō

nursery school *n* 保育園 hoíkuèn

nursery slope (*BRIT*) *n* (SKI) 初心者用ゲレンデ shoshínshayō gerènde

nursing [nəːrˈsiŋ] *n* (profession) 看護職 kángoshòku; (care) 看病 kánbyò

nursing home *n* (老人) 療養所 ryōyòjo; (for old people) 老人ホーム rōjínhòmu

nursing mother *n* 授乳している母親 junyū shite irù haháoya

nurture [nəːrˈtʃər] *vt* (child, plant) 育てる sodáterù

nut [nʌt] *n* (TECH) ナット náttò; (BOT) 木ノ実 kínòmi(kónòmi), ナッツ náttsù

nutcracker [nʌtˈkrækər] *npl* クルミ割り kurúmiwarì

nutmeg [nʌtˈmeg] *n* ニクズク nikúzòku, ナツメグ natsúmegù ◆香辛料の一種 kōshínryò no ísshù

nutrient [nuːˈtriənt] *n* 養分 yóbun

nutrition [nutriˈʃən] *n* (diet, nourishment) 栄養 eíyō; (proteins, vitamins etc) 養分 yóbun

nutritious [nutriˈʃəs] *adj* (food) 栄養価の高い eíyōka no takái

nuts [nʌts] (*inf*) *adj* 頭がおかしい atáma gà okáshii

nutshell [nʌtˈʃel] *n* クルミの殻 kurúmi no karà

in a nutshell (fig) 簡単に言えば kañtan nì iébà

nylon [naiˈlɑn] *n* ナイロン náiron

◆*adj* ナイロンの náiron no

O

oak [ouk] *n* オーク ōkù

◆*adj* (table) オークの ōkù no

O.A.P. [oueipiˈ] (*BRIT*) *n abbr* = old-age pensioner

oar [ɔːr] *n* かい kaî, オール ōrù

oasis [oueiˈsis] (*pl* **oases**) *n* (in desert) オアシス oáshìsu

oath [ouθ] *n* (promise) 誓い chikái; (swear word) 悪態 akútaî

under or *on* (*BRIT*) *oath* 宣誓して sefísei shìte

oatmeal [outˈmiːl] *n* オートミール ōtómìru

oats [outs] *n* カラスムギ karásumugì

obedience [oubiːˈdiːəns] *n* 服従 fukújū

obedient [oubiːˈdiːənt] *adj* (child, dog etc) 素直な sunáo na, よく言う事を聞く yokû iû koto wo kikû

obesity [oubiːˈsitiː] *n* 肥満 himán

obey [oubeiˈ] *vt* (instructions, person) ...に従う ...ni shitágau; (regulations) 守る mamóru

obituary [oubitʃˈuːeriː] *n* 死亡記事 shibōki

object [*n* ɑːbˈdʒikt *vt* əbdʒektˈ] *n* (thing) 物 monó; (aim, purpose) 目的 mokúteki; (of affection, desires) 対象 taishō; (LING) 目的語 mokútekìgo

◆*vi*: *to object to* ...に反対する ...ni hañtai suru

to object that ...だと言って反対する ...da to itté hañtai suru

expense is no object 費用にはこだわらない hiyō nì wa kodáwaranaî

I object! 反対です hañtai dèsu

I have no objection to ...に...に異議はありません ...ni igî wa arímasèn

objection [əbdʒekˈʃən] *n* 異議 igî

objectionable [əbdʒekˈʃənəbəl] *adj* (person, language, conduct) いやな iyá na

objective [əbdʒekˈtiv] *adj* (impartial: person, information) 客観的な kyakúkanteki na

◆*n* (aim, purpose) 目的 mokúteki

obligation [ɑːblageiˈʃən] *n* (duty, commitment) 義務 gimû

without obligation (COMM) 買う義務なしで kaú gimù nashi de

obligatory [əbligˈətɔːriː] *adj* 強制的な kyōseiteki na

oblige [əblaidʒˈ] *vt* (force): *to oblige someone to do something* 強制的に

...に..をさせる kyốseiteki ni ...ni ...wo saserú; (do a favor for) ...no tanómi wo kikú

to be obliged to someone for something (grateful) ...no 事で...に感謝している ...no kotó de ...ni kañsha shité irú

obliging [əblàiˈdʒiŋ] *adj* (helpful) 親切な shiñsetsu na

oblique [əbliːkˈ] *adj* (line) 斜めの nanáme no; (comment, reference) 間接的な kañsetsuteki na

obliterate [əblítˈəreit] *vt* 跡形もなくさせる atókata mo nakúsurú

oblivion [əblívˈiːən] *n* (unawareness) 無意識 mushíki; (being forgotten) 忘却 bốkyaku

oblivious [əblívˈiːəs] *adj*: **oblivious of/ to** ...を意識していない...wo ishíki shité inai

oblong [ɑːbˈlɔŋ] *adj* 長方形の chốhôkei no
♦*n* 長方形 chốhôkei

obnoxious [əbnɑːkˈʃəs] *adj* (unpleasant: behavior, person) 不愉快な fuyúkai na; (: smell) いやな iyá na

oboe [ouˈbou] *n* オーボエ ôboe

obscene [əbsiːnˈ] *adj* (gesture, remark, behavior) わいせつな waísetsu na

obscenity [əbsénˈitiː] *n* (of book, behavior etc) わいせつ waísetsu; (offensive word) 卑語 higð

obscure [əbskjuːrˈ] *adj* (little known: place, author etc) 無名の mumếi no; (difficult to understand) 難解な nañkai na
♦*vt* (obstruct: view, sun etc) 覆い隠す ôôikakúsu; (conceal: truth, meaning etc) 隠す kakúsu

obsequious [əbsiːˈkwiːəs] *adj* ぺこぺこする pekòpeko suru

observance [əbzəːrˈvəns] *n* (of law) 遵守 juñshu; (of custom) 守る事 mamórú koto

observant [əbzəːrˈvənt] *adj* (person) 観察力の優れた kañsatsuryòku no sugureta; (remark) 鋭い surúdoi

observation [ɑːbzəːrveiˈʃən] *n* (remark) 意見 ikên; (act of observing) 観察 kañsatsu; (MED) 監視 kañshi

observatory [əbzəːrˈvətɔːriː] *n* 観測所

kañsokujo

observe [əbzəːrvˈ] *vt* (watch) 観察する kañsatsu suru; (comment) 意見を述べる ikên wo noberú; (abide by: rule) 守る mamórú, 遵守する juñshu suru

observer [əbzəːrˈvəːr] *n* 観察者 kañsatsusha

obsess [əbsésˈ] *vt* ...に取付く ...ni torítsuku

obsession [əbséˈʃən] *n* 強迫観念 kyôhakukannen

obsessive [əbsésˈiv] *adj* (person, tendency, behavior) 取付かれたような mösô ni torítsukareta yô na

obsolescence [ɑːbsəlésˈəns] *n* 旧式化 kyûshikika

obsolete [ɑːbsəliːtˈ] *adj* (out of use: word etc) 廃れた sutáreta; (: machine etc) 旧式の kyûshiki no

obstacle [ɑːbˈstəkəl] *n* (obstruction) 障害物 shôgaibutsù; (fig: problem, difficulty) 障害 shôgai

obstacle race *n* 障害物競走 shôgaibutsukyôsò

obstetrics [əbstétˈriks] *n* 産科 sañka

obstinate [ɑːbˈstənit] *adj* (determined: person, resistance) 頑固な gañko na

obstruct [əbstrʌktˈ] *vt* (block) ふさぐ fuságu; (fig: hinder) 妨害する bôgai suru

obstruction [əbstrʌkˈʃən] *n* (action) 妨害 bôgai; (object) 障害物 shôgaibutsù

obtain [əbtéinˈ] *vt* (get) 手に入れる te ni irérù, 獲得する kakútoku suru; (achieve) 達成する tasséi suru

obtainable [əbtéinˈəbəl] *adj* (object) 入手できる nyûshu dekírù

obvious [ɑːbˈviːəs] *adj* (clear) 明かな akírāka na; (self-evident) 分かり切った wakárikitta

obviously [ɑːbˈviːəsliː] *adv* 明らかに akíráka ni

obviously not 明らかに...でない akírāka ni ...de nai

occasion [əkeiˈʒən] *n* (point in time) 時 tokî, 時点 jitén; (event, celebration etc) 行事 gyôji, イベント ibénto; (opportunity) 機会 kikái, チャンス chañsu

occasional [əkeiˈʒənəl] *adj* (infrequent)

時々の tokídokì no

occasionally [əkeiˈʒənəli] *adv* 時々 tokídokì ni

occult [əkʌltˈ] *n: the occult* 超自然 chōshizen, オカルト okáruto

occupant [ɑːkˈjəpənt] *n* (long-term: of house etc) 居住者 kyojūsha; (of office etc) テナント tenánto; (temporary: of car, room etc) 中にいる人 nakā ni iru hitó

occupation [ɑːkjəpeiˈʃən] *n* (job) 職業 shokūgyō; (pastime) 趣味 shumī; (of building, country etc) 占領 senryō

occupational hazard [ɑːkjəpeiˈʃənəl-] *n* 職業上の危険 shokūgyōjō no kiken

occupier [ɑːkˈjəpaiə] *n* 居住者 kyojūsha

occupy [ɑːkˈjəpai] *vt* (inhabit: house) ...に住む ...ni sumú; (take: seat, place etc) ...に居る ...ni irú; (take over: building, country etc) 占領する senryō suru; (take up: time) ...かける ...kakéru; (: attention) 奪う ubáu; (: space) 取る tóru

to occupy oneself in doing ...に専念する ...ni sénnen suru

occur [əkəːrˈ] *vi* (event: take place) 起る okórù; (phenomenon: exist) 存在する sofzai suru

to occur to someone ...の頭に浮ぶ ...no atáma ni ukábu

occurrence [əkəːrˈəns] *n* (event) 出来事 dekígoto; (existence) 存在 sofzai

ocean [ouˈʃən] *n* 海 úmi

Indian Ocean インド洋 índoyō ¶ *see also* Atlantic; Pacific

ocean-going [ouˈʃəngouiŋ] *adj* 外洋の gaíyō no

ocher [ouˈkəːr] (*BRIT*: **ochre**) *adj* (color) 黄土色の ódòiro no, オークルの ókūru no

o'clock [əklɑːkˈ] *adv: it is 5 o'clock* 5 時です gojī desu

OCR [ousiːɑːrˈ] *n abbr* (COMPUT: = *optical character recognition*) 光学読取り kōgakuyomítorì (: = *optical character reader*) 光学読取り装置 kōgakuyomisōchì

octagonal [ɑːktægˈənəl] *adj* 八角形の hákkakukèi no

octave [ɑːkˈtiv] *n* (MUS) オクターブ okútābù

October [ɑːktouˈbəːr] *n* 10月 jūgatsu

octopus [ɑːkˈtəpəs] *n* タコ takó

odd [ɑːd] *adj* (strange: person, behavior, expression) 変な heń na, 妙な myō na; (uneven: number) 奇数の kísū no; (not paired: sock, glove, shoe etc) 片方の kátahō no

60-odd 60幾つ rokújū ikutsu

at odd times 時々 tokídokì

to be the odd one out 例外である reígai de aru

oddity [ɑːdˈiti] *n* (person) 変り者 kawárimono; (thing) 変った物 kawatta mono

odd-job man [ɑːdʒɑːbˈ-] *n* 便利屋 beńriya

odd jobs *npl* 雑用 zatsúyō

oddly [ɑːdˈliː] *adv* (strangely: behave, dress) 変な風に heń na fū ni ¶ *see also* **enough**

oddments [ɑːdˈmənts] *npl* (COMM) 残り物 nokórimono

odds [ɑːdz] *npl* (in betting) 賭け率 kaké-rìtsu, オッズ ozzū

it makes no odds 構いません kamáimaseń

at odds 仲たがいして nakátagàishite

odds and ends *npl* 半端物 hańpamono

ode [oud] *n* しょう歌 shōka, オード ōdò

odious [ouˈdiəs] *adj* 不快な fukái na

odometer [oudɑːmˈitəːr] *n* 走行距離計 sōkōkyorikeì

odor [ouˈdəːr] (*BRIT*: **odour**) *n* (smell) におい niói; (: unpleasant) 悪臭 akúshū

KEYWORD

of [ʌv] *prep* 1 (gen) ...の ...nò

the history of France フランスの歴史 furánsu nò rekíshi

a friend of ours 私たちのある友達 watákushitàchi no árù tomódachi

a boy of 10 10才の少年 jússai no shōnen

that was kind of you ご親切にどうも go-shíhsetsu ni dōmo

a man of great ability 才能抜群の人 saínō batsugùn no hitó

the city of New York ニューヨーク市 nyúyōkushì

south of Glasgow グラスゴーの南 gurásugō no mínami

2 (expressing quantity, amount, dates etc): **a kilo of flour** 小麦粉1キロ komúgiko ichíkiro

how much of this do you need? これはどのぐらい要りますか koré wa donò gurai irimasù ká

there were 3 of them (people) 3人いました sańnin imáshìta; (objects) 3個ありました sáńko arímashìta

3 of us went 私たちの内から3人行きました watákushitàchi no uchí karà sáńnin ikimashita

the number of road accidents is increasing 交通事故の数が増えていますkōtsūjìkò no kázù ga fúète imásù

a cup of tea お茶1杯 o-chá ippài

a vase of flowers 花瓶に生けた花 kabin nì ikèta haná

the 5th of July 7月5日 shichígatsu itsúkà

the winter of 1987 1987年の冬 señkyūhyakuhachíjūnaneń no fuyú

3 (from, out of): **a bracelet of solid gold** 純金の腕輪 juńkin nò udéwa

a statue of marble 大理石の彫像 dafriséki no chōzō

made of wood 木製の mokúsei no

KEYWORD

off [ɔːf] *adv* 1 (referring to distance, time) 離れて hanárète

it's a long way off あれは遠いareわ tōi

the game is 3 days off 試合は3日先です shiái wà mikkà sakí desù

2 (departure) 出掛けて dekákète

to go off to Paris/Italy パリ〔イタリア〕へ出掛ける párì(itária) e dekákerù

I must be off そろそろ出掛けます sorósoro dekákemasù

3 (removal) 外して hazúshìte

to take off one's hat/coat/clothes 帽子〔コート, 服〕を脱ぐ bōshi(kōto, fu-

kú)wo núgù

the button came off ボタンが取れた botán gà tóreta

10% off (COMM) 10パーセント引き juppásentobiki

4 (not at work: on holiday) 休暇中で kyūkachū dè; (: due to sickness) 欠勤して kékkin shitè

I'm off on Fridays 私の休みは金曜日です watákushi nò yasúmi wa kiń-yōbi desu

he was off on Friday (on holiday) 金曜日には彼は休みでした kiń-yōbi ni wa kárè wa yasúmi deshìta; (sick etc) 金曜日には彼は欠勤しました kiń-yōbi ni wa kárè wa kékkin shimashìta

to have a day off (from work) 1日の休みを取る ichínichi nò yasúmi wò tórù

to be off sick 病欠する byōketsu suru

♦*adj* 1 (not turned on: machine, engine, water, gas etc) 止めてある tomête arù; (: tap) 締めてある shimête arù; (: light) 消してある keshíte arù

2 (cancelled: meeting, match, agreement) 取消された toríkesaretà

3 (BRIT: not fresh: milk, cheese, meat etc) 悪くなった wárùku natta

4: **on the off chance** (just in case) ...の場合に備えて ...no baái ni sonaete

to have an off day (not as good as usual) 厄日である yakúbi de arù

♦*prep* 1 (indicating motion, removal etc) ...から ...kárà

to fall off a cliff 崖から落ちる gake kara ochírù

the button came off my coat コートのボタンが取れた kōto no botán gà tóretà

to take a picture off the wall 壁に掛けてある絵を降ろす kabé nì kákète arù e wò orósù

2 (distant from) ...から離れて ...kárà hanárète

it's just off the M1 国道M1を降りて直ぐの所にあります kokúdō emúwań wo órìte súgu no tokórò ni arímasu

it's 5 km off the main road 幹線道路から5キロの所にあります kańsendōro

kara góktri no tokórò ni arímasù

an island off the coast 神óf no shimá

to be off work (no longer eat it) 肉をやめていた肉 wò yaméte irù; (no longer like it) 肉がいやになっている肉 gà kirái ni natté irù

offal [ɔːfˀəl] *n* (CULIN) もつ motsù

off-color [ɔːfˈkʌlˀər] (BRIT **off-colour**) *adj* (ill) 病気の byóki no

offend [əfénd] *vt* (upset: person) 怒らせる okóraserù

offender [əfénˈdər] *n* (criminal) 犯罪者 hañzáisha, 犯人 hañnin, ...犯 ...hañ

offense [əféns] (BRIT **offence**) *n* (crime) 犯罪 hañzaì

*to take offense at ...*に怒る ...ni okóru

offensive [əfénˈsiv] *adj* (remark, gesture, behavior) 侮辱的な bujókuteki na; (smell etc) いやな ìyá na; (weapon) 攻撃用の kốgekiyố no

♦*n* (MIL) 攻撃 kốgeki

offer [ɔːfˈər] *n* (proposal: to help etc) 申し出 móshide; (: to buy) 申込み móshikomi

♦*vt* (advice, help, information) ...する ...surù to móshideru; (opportunity, service, product) 提供する teíkyō suru

on offer (BRIT: COMM) 値下げ品で neságehin de

offering [ɔːfˈəriŋ] *n* (of a company: product) 売物 urímono; (REL) 供物 sonáemono

off-hand [ɔːfˈhænd] *adj* (behavior etc) いい加減な ìíkagen na

♦*adv* 直ちに sokúza ni

office [ɔːfˈis] *n* (place) 事務所 jimúshò, オフィス ofìsu; (room) 事務室 jimúshìtsu; (position) 職 shokú

doctor's office (US) 医院 ìn

to take office 職に就く shokú ni tsuku

office automation *n* オフィスオートメーション ofìsu ốtomēshòn

office building (BRIT **office block**) *n* オフィスビル ofìsubiru

office hours *npl* (COMM) 業務時間 gyốmujikan; (US: MED) 診察時間 shiñsatsujikan

officer [ɔːfˈisər] *n* (MIL etc) 将校 shốkō; (also: **police officer**) 警官 keíkan; (of organization) 役員 yakúin

office worker *n* 事務員 jimúin

official [əfìʃˀəl] *adj* (authorized) 公認の kốnin no; (visit, invitation, letter etc) 公式の kốshiki no

♦*n* (in government) 役人 yakúnin; (in trade union etc) 役員 yakúin

official residence 官邸 kañtei

officialdom [əfìʃˀəldəm] (pej) *n* 官僚の世界 kañryố no sekái

officiate [əfìʃˈiːit] *vi* 司会する shikái suru

officious [əfìʃˀəs] *adj* (person, behavior) 差出がましい sashídegamashíì

offing [ɔːfˈiŋ] *n*: *in the offing* (fig: imminent) 差迫って sashísematté

off-licence [ɔːfˈlaisəns] BRIT *n* (shop selling alcohol) 酒屋 sakáya

off-line [ɔːfˈlain] *adj* (COMPUT) オフラインの ofúrain no

♦*adv* オフラインで ofúrain de

off-peak [ɔːfˈpiːk] *adj* (heating) オフピークの ofúpīku no; (train, ticket) 混んでいない時の koñde inai tokí no

off-putting [ɔːfˈputˀiŋ] (BRIT) *adj* (person, remark etc) 気を悪くさせる kí wo warúku saseru

off-season [ɔːfˈsiːzən] *adj* (holiday, ticket) オフシーズンの ofúshīzun no

♦*adv* (travel, book etc) オフシーズンに ofúshīzun ni

offset [ɔːfsét] (*pt*, *pp* **offset**) *vt* (counteract) 補う oginaù

offshoot [ɔːfˈʃuːt] *n* (fig) 副産物 fukúsanbutsu

offshore [ɔːfˈʃɔːr] *adj* (breeze) 陸からの rikú kara no; (oilrig, fishing) 沖合の okíai no

offside [ɔːfˈsaid] *adj* (SPORT) オフサイドの ofúsaido no; (AUT: with right-hand drive) 右の migí no; (: with left-hand drive) 左の hidári no

offspring [ɔːfˈspriŋ] *n inv* 子孫 shisòn

offstage [ɔːfˈsteidʒ] *adv* 舞台裏に butáiura ni(de)

off-the-rack [ɔːf'ðəræk'] (BRIT **off-the-peg**) adj (clothing) 出来合いのdekí-ai no, 既製のkiséi no

off-white [ɔːf'wait'] adj (grayish white) 灰色がかった白のhaírogakatta shiró no; (yellowish white) 黄色がかった白のkiírogakatta shiró no

often [ɔːf'ən] adv (frequently) よく yokú, しょっちゅう shotchū, 度々 tabítabi
  how often do you go? どのくらい行きますか donó gurai ikímasu ká

ogle [ou'gəl] vt 色目で見る irốme de mirú

oh [ou] excl あっ át

oil [ɔil] n (gen) 油 abūra, オイル ofrū; (CULIN) サラダ油 sarádayu; (petroleum) 石油 sekíyu; (crude) 原油 geńyu; (for heating) 石油 sekíyu, 灯油 tốyu
  ♦vt (lubricate: engine, gun, machine) ...に油を差す ...ni abūra wo sasú

oilcan [ɔil'kæn] n 油差し abúrasashi

oilfield [ɔil'fiːld] n 油田 yudén

oil filter n (AUT) オイルフィルター oírufirutā

oil painting n 油絵 abūrae

oil refinery [-riːfai'əːriː] n 精油所 seíyujo

oil rig n 石油掘削装置 sekíyu kússakusốchi

oilskins [ɔil'skinz] npl 防水服 bốsuifuku

oil tanker n (ship) オイルタンカー oíru-tankaā; (truck) タンクローリー tañkurốrī

oil well n 油井 yuséi

oily [ɔi'liː] adj (rag) 油染みた abūrajimitá; (substance) 油の様な abūra no yố na; (food) 脂っこい aburákkoi

ointment [ɔint'mənt] n 軟こう nańkõ

O.K., okay [ouei'] (inf) excl (agreement: alright) よろしい yoróshii, オーケー ōkē; (: don't fuss) 分かったよ wakátta yo
  ♦adj (average: film, book, meal etc) まあまあの māma no
  ♦vt (approve) 承認する shōnin suru

old [ould] adj (aged: person) 年寄の toshíyori no; (: thing) 古い furúi; (former: school, home etc) 元の motō no, 前の maē no

how old are you? お幾つですか o-íkutsu desu ká

he's 10 years old 彼は10才です karè wa jussái desu

older brother (one's own) 兄 ani; (of person spoken to) お兄さん o-níisan; (of third party) 兄さん níisan

old age n 老齢 rōréi

old-age pensioner [ould'eidʒ-] (BRIT) n 年金で生活する老人 neñkin de seíkatsu surú rōjin, 年金暮しの人 neñkingurashi no hitó

old-fashioned [ould'fæʃ'ənd] adj (style, design) 時代遅れの jidáiokūre no, 古くさい furúkusai; (person, values) 保守的な hoshūteki na

olive [ɑl'iv] n (fruit) オリーブ oríbù; (also: **olive tree**) オリーブの木 oríbù no ki
  ♦adj (also: **olive-green**) オリーブ色の oríbùiro no

olive oil n オリーブ油 oríbùyu

Olympic [oulim'pik] adj 五輪の goríñ no, オリンピックの oríñpikkū no

Olympic Games npl: **the Olympic Games** 五輪 goríñ, オリンピック oríñpikkū
  the Olympics 五輪 goríñ, オリンピック oríñpikkū

omelet(te) [ɑm'lit] n オムレツ omúretsu

omen [ou'mən] n (sign) 兆し kizáshi, 前触れ maēbure

ominous [ɑm'ənəs] adj (worrying) 不気味な bukími na

omission [oumiʃ'ən] n 省略 shōryaku

omit [oumit'] vt (deliberately) 省略する shōryaku suru; (by mistake) うっかりして抜かす ukkárì shite nukásu

on [ɑn] prep 1 (indicating position) ...の(上)に(で) ...no ué ni (de)
  on the wall 壁に kabé ni
  it's on the table テーブルの(上)にあります tēbùru no ué ni arímasù
  on the left 左に hidári ni
  the house is on the main road 家は幹線道路に面しています ié wà kańsendōro ni

ni mén shite imásù

2 (indicating means, method, condition etc) ...で ...dè

on foot (go, be) 歩いて arúitè

on the train/plane (go) 電車(飛行機)で dénsha(hikóki)de; (be) 電車(飛行機)に乗って dénsha(hikóki)ni notté

on the telephone/radio/television 電話(ラジオ, テレビ)で dénwa(rájio, térèbi)de

she's on the telephone 彼女は電話に出ています(電話中です) kánojo wa dénwa ni détè imasu(deńwachū desù)

I heard it on the radio/saw him on television 私はラジオで聞きました(テレビで彼を見ました) watákushi wà rájio de kikimashìta(térèbi de kárè wo míta)

to be on drugs 麻薬をやっている mayáku wò yatté irù

to be on holiday 休暇中である kyúkachū de arù

to be away on business 商用で出掛ける shóyo dè dekákerè irù

3 (referring to time) ...に ...ni

on Fridays 金曜日に kiń-yòbi ni

on Fridays 金曜日に kiń-yòbi ni, 毎週金曜日に maíshū kiń-yòbi ni, 金曜日毎に kiń-yòbi gòtò ni

on June 20th 6月20日に rokúgatsu hatsùka ni

on Friday, June 20th 6月20日金曜日に rokúgatsu hatsùka kiń-yòbi ni

a week on Friday 来週の金曜日に raíshū nò kiń-yòbi ni

on arrival he went straight to his hotel 到着すると彼は真っ直ぐにホテルへ行きました tóchaku suru tò kárè wa massúgù ni hótèru e ikimashìta

on seeing this これを見ると koré wò mírù to

4 (about, concerning) ...について ...ni tsúite, ...に関して ...ni kán shite

information on train services 列車に関する情報 resshá ni kań surù jóhò

a book on physics 物理の本 bútsùri no hón

♦**adv 1** (referring to dress) 身につけて

mi ní tsukète

to have one's coat on コートを着ている kóto wo kité irù

what's she got on? 彼女は何を着ていますか kánojo wa nánì wo kité imasù ká

she put her boots/gloves/hat on 彼女はブーツを履いた(手袋をはめた, 帽子をかぶった) kánojo wa bútsu wo haíta (tebùkuro wo hámèta, bōshì wo kabúttà)

2 (referring to covering): **screw the lid on tightly** ふたをしっかり締めて下さい futá wò shikkárì shímète kudásaí

3 (further, continuously) 続けて tsuzúkète

to walk/drive/go on 歩き[車で走り, 行き]続ける arúki(kuruma dè hashíri, ikí)tsuzukèru

to read on 読み続ける yomítsuzukèru

♦**adj 1** (functioning, machine: machine) 動いている ugóite irù; (: radio, TV, light) ついている tsúite irù; (: water) 水が出ている mizú gà deté irù; (: brakes) かかっている kakátte irù; (: meeting) 続いている tsuzúite irù

is the meeting still on? (in progress) まだ会議中ですか mádà kaígichū desù ká; (not cancelled) 会議は予定通りにやるんですか kaígi wa yotéi dòri ni yarún desù ká

there's a good film on at the cinema 映画館で今いい映画をやっています efgakàn de ímà iì efga wò yatté imasù

2: that's not on! (inf: of behavior) それはいけません soré wà ikémasen

---

once [wʌns] *adv* (on one occasion) 一度 ichídò, 一回 ikkáì; (formerly) 前は maè wa, かつて katsùte

♦**conj** (immediately afterwards) ...した後 ...shitá ato, ...してから ...shité kara

once he had left/it was done 彼が出て(事が済んで)から karè ga deté(kotó ga súnde)kara

at once (immediately) 直ちに tadáchi ni, 直ぐに súgù ni; (simultaneously) 同時に dójì ni

once a week 週一回 shū ikkáì

once more もう一度 mó ichído

once and for all 断然 dánzen

once upon a time 昔々 mukáshii mukashi

oncoming [ɒnˈkʌmɪŋ] *adj* (approaching: traffic etc) 向ってくる mukátte kurù

KEYWORD

one [wʌn] *num* 一 (の) ichí (no)、1つ (の) hitótsù (no)

one hundred and fifty 150 hyakúgojù

I asked for two coffees, not one 注文 したのは1つじゃなくて2つのコーヒーで す chûmon shita no wa hitótsu jànakutè futátsu nò kôhî desu

one day there was a sudden knock at the door ある日突然だれかがドアを ノックした arù hi totsúzen dárèka ga dóà wo nòkkú shita

one by one 1つずつ hitótsu zùtsu

◆*adj* 1 (sole) ただ一つの tádà hitótsu no、 唯一の yúìtsu no

it's the one book which interests me 私が興味を感じる唯一の本です watákushi gà kyômì wo kañjiru yúìtsu no hôñ desu

that is my one worry 私が心配してい るのはそれだけです watákushi gà shíñpai shite irù nò wa soré dake dèsu

the one man who ... する唯一の人 ...suru yúìtsu no hitó

2 (same) 同じ onáji

they came in the one car 彼らは皆同 じ車で来ました kárèra wa mínà onáji kurùma de kimáshìta

they all belong to the one family 彼 らは皆身内です kárèra wa mínà míuchi desù

◆*pron* 1 物 monó

this one これ koré

that one それ soré、あれ aré

I've already got one/a red one 私は 既に1つ（赤いのを）持っています watákushi wa sùde ni hitótsu(akái no wo) mótte imasu

2: *one another* お互いに o-tágai nì

do you two ever see one another? お 二人は付合っていますか o-fútàri wa tsu-

kíatte imasu ká

the boys didn't dare look at one another 少年たちはあえて顔を合せる事 ができなかった shônentàchi wa aéte ka-ô wo awáseru kotò ga dekínakattà

3 (impersonal): *one never knows* どう なるか分かりませんね dô naru ka wakárimaseñ né

to cut one's finger 指を切る yubí wo kírù

one needs to eat 人は食べる必要がある hitó wa tabéru hitsúyð ga arù

one-day excursion [wʌndeɪ-] (*US*) *n* (day return) 日帰り往復乗券 higáeri ðfukuken

one-man [wʌnˈmæn] *adj* (business) 1人 だけの hitóri dake no、ワンマンの wañman no

one-man band *n* ワンマンバンド wañmanbando

one-off [wʌnˈɔːf] (*BRIT*: *inf*) *n* 一つだ けの物 hitótsù dake no mono

KEYWORD

oneself [wʌnˈself] *pron* (reflexive) 自分 自身を jibúñjishìn wo; (after prep) 自分 自身に jibúñjishìn ni; (alone: often *after* prep) 自分一人で jibún hitòri de; (emphatic) 自分で jibún dè

to hurt oneself けがする kegá surù

to keep something for oneself 自分の ために...を取って置く jibún no tamè ni ...wð tóttè oku

to talk to oneself 独り言を言う hitórigotò wo iú

one-sided [wʌnˈsaidid] *adj* (argument) 一方的な ippôteki na

one-to-one [wʌnˈtəwʌn] *adj* (relationship) 一対一の ittáiichi no

one-upmanship [wʌnˈʌpmənʃip] *n* 自分 の方が一枚上だと見せ付ける事 jibún no hô ga ichímai uè da to misétsukerù koto

one-way [wʌnˈwei] *adj* (street, traffic) 一方通行の ippótsükõ no

ongoing [ɒnˈgouiŋ] *adj* (project, situation etc) 進行中の shiñkõchü no

onion [ˈʌnjən] n タマネギ tamánegi

on-line [ˈɔnˈlain] adj (COMPUT) オンラインの ofraìn no
♦adj (COMPUT) オンラインで ofraìn de

onlooker [ˈɔnˈlukəːr] n 見物人 kefibutsuniǹ

only [ˈounliː] adv ...だけ ...dake
♦adj (sole, single) ただ一つ(一人)の tada hitótsu(hitóri) no
♦conj (but) しかし shikáshì
an only child 一人っ子 hitórikkò
not only ... but also ...ばかりでなく...も ...bakári de naku ...mo

onset [ˈɔnˌset] n (beginning: of war, winter, illness) 始まり hajímari, 始め hajíme

onshore [ˈɔnˈʃɔːr] adj (wind) 海からの umi kara no

onslaught [ˈɔnˌslɔt] n 攻撃 kốgeki

onto [ˈɔntuː] prep = on to

onus [ˈounəs] n 責任 sekíniǹ

onward(s) [ˈɔnwəːrd(z)] adv (forward: move, progress) 先へ saki e
from that time onward(s) それ以後 soré igo

onyx [ˈɔniks] n オニキス oníkisu

ooze [uːz] vi (mud, water, slime) にじみでる nijímideru

opal [ˈoupəl] n オパール opáru

opaque [oupeikˈ] adj (substance) 不透明な futốmei na

OPEC [ˈoupek] n abbr (= Organization of Petroleum-Exporting Countries) 石油輸出国機構 sekíyu yushutsukoku kikố

open [ˈoupən] adj (not shut: window, door, mouth etc) 開いた afta; (: shop, museum etc) 開いている efgyốchū no, 開いている afte iru; (unobstructed: road) 開通している kaítsū shite iru; (: view) 開けた hiráketa; (not enclosed: land) 囲いのない kakói no nai; (fig: frank: person, manner, face) 率直な sotchokú na; (unrestricted: meeting, debate, championship) 公開の kōkai no
♦vt 開ける akéru, 開く hiráku
♦vi (flower, eyes, door, shop) 開く akú, 開く hiráku; (book, debate etc: commence) 始まる hajímaru

in the open (air) 野外に yagái ni
an open car オープンカー ōpúnkā

opening [ˈoupəniŋ] adj (commencing: speech, remarks etc) 開会の kaíkai no, 冒頭の bốtō no
♦n (gap, hole) 穴 aná; (start: of play, book etc) 始め hajíme, 冒頭 bốtō; (opportunity) 機会 kikái, チャンス chañsu

openly [ˈoupənliː] adv (speak, act) 公然と kōzen to; (cry) 人目をはばからず hitóme wo habákarazu

open-minded [ˈoupənmaínˈdid] adj 偏見のない heñken no nai

open-necked [ˈoupənnektˈ] adj (shirt) 開かん kaíkin no

open on to vt fus (subj: room, door) ...に面している ...ni méñ shite iru

open-plan [ˈoupənplænˈ] adj 間仕切りのない majíkiri no nai

open up vt (building, room: unlock) 開ける akéru; (blocked road) ...の障害物を取り除く ...no shốgaìbutsu wo torínozokù
♦vi (COMM: shop, business) 開く akú

opera [ˈɑːpəːrə] n 歌劇 kagéki, オペラ opéra

opera singer n オペラ歌手 opérakashu

operate [ˈɑːpəreit] vt (machine) 操作する sốsa suru; (vehicle) 運転する uñten suru
♦vi (machine) 動く ugókù; (vehicle) 走る hashíru, 動く ugókù; (company, organization) 営業する efgyố suru
to operate on someone (for) (MED) ...に(...の) 手術する ...ni (...no) shujútsu suru

operatic [ɑːpərætˈik] adj 歌劇の kagéki no, オペラの opéra no

operating [ˈɑːpəːreitiŋ] adj: **operating table** 手術台 shujútsudai
operating theater 手術室 shujútsushìtsu

operation [ɑːpəreiˈʃən] n (of machine etc) 操作 sốsa; (of vehicle) 運転 uñten; (MIL, COMM etc) 作戦 sakúseǹ; (MED) 手術 shujútsu
to be in operation (law, regulation) 実施されている jisshí sarete iru
to have an operation (MED) 手術をする shujútsu wo suru

ける shujŭtsu wo ukérŭ

operational [ɑːpəreiˈʃənəl] *adj* (working: machine, vehicle etc) 使用可能な shíyṓkanṓ na

operative [ɑːpˈrətiv] *adj* (law, measure, system) 実施されている jisshí sarete iru

operator [ɑːpˈəreitər] *n* (TEL) 交換手 kṓkanshu, オペレーター opérḗtā; (of machine) 技師 gishí

ophthalmic [ɑːfˈθælˈmik] *adj* 眼科の gañka no

opinion [əpinˈjən] *n* (point of view, belief) 意見 ikén

in my opinion 私の意見では watákushi no ikén de wa

opinionated [əpinˈjəneitid] *adj* (*pej*) 独善的な dokúzenteki na

opinion poll *n* 世論調査 yorónchōsa

opium [ouˈpiːəm] *n* あへん ahén

opponent [əpouˈnənt] *n* (person not in favor) 反対者 hañtaisha; (MIL) 敵 tekí; (SPORT) 相手 aíte

opportunism [ɑːpərtuːˈnizəm] (*pej*) *n* 日和見主義 hiyórimishugî

opportunist [ɑːpərtuːˈnist] (*pej*) *n* 日和見主義者 hiyórimishugîsha

opportunity [ɑːpərtuːˈnitiː] *n* 機会 kíkai, チャンス chańsu

to take the opportunity of doing 折角の機会を利用して...する sekkakuwo kikái wo riyṓ shite ...suru

oppose [əpouzˈ] *vt* (object to: wish, opinion, plan) ...に反対する ...ni hañtai suru

to be opposed to something ...に反対である ...ni hañtai de aru

as opposed to ...ではなくて ...de wa na kutè

opposing [əpouzˈiŋ] *adj* (side, ideas) 反対の hañtai no; (team) 相手の aíte no

opposite [ɑːpˈəzit] *adj* (house) 向かい側の mukáigawa no; (end, direction, side) 反対の hañtai no; (point of view, effect) 逆の gyakú no

♦*adv* (live, stand, work, sit) 向い側に(で) mukáigawa ni(de)

♦*prep* (in front of) ...の向い側に(で) ni mukáigawa ni(de)

♦*n*: *the opposite* (say, think, do etc) 反対 hañtai

the opposite sex 異性 iséi

opposition [ɑːpəziˈʃən] *n* (resistance) 反対 hañtai; (those against) 反対勢力 hañtaiseiryokù; (POL) 野党 yatṓ

oppress [əpresˈ] *vt* 抑圧する yokúatsu suru

oppression [əpreʃˈən] *n* 抑圧 yokúatsu

oppressive [əpresˈiv] *adj* (political regime) 抑圧的な yokúatsuteki na; (weather, heat) 蒸し暑い mushfatsuî

opt [ɑːpt] *vi*: *to opt for* ...を選ぶ ...wo erábu

to opt to do ...する事にする ...surú koto ni suru

optical [ɑːpˈtikəl] *adj* (instrument, device etc) 光学の kṓgaku no

optical illusion *n* 目の錯覚 mé no sakkáku

optician [ɑːptiʃˈən] *n* 眼鏡屋 megáneya

optimism [ɑːpˈtəmizəm] *n* 楽観 rakkán, 楽天主義 rakútenshugî

optimist [ɑːpˈtəmist] *n* 楽天家 rakútenka

optimistic [ɑːptəmisˈtik] *adj* 楽観的な rakkánteki na

optimum [ɑːpˈtəməm] *adj* (conditions, number, size) 最良の saíryṓ no, 最善の saízen no

option [ɑːpˈʃən] *n* (choice) 選択 señtaku, オプション opúshon

optional [ɑːpˈʃənəl] *adj* (not obligatory) 自由選択の jiyṹsentakuno

opt out *vi*: *to opt out of* ...から手を引く ...kara te wò hiku

opulent [ɑːpˈjulənt] *adj* (very wealthy: person, society etc) 大金持の ṓganèmochi no

or [ɔːr] *conj* (linking alternatives: up or down, in or out etc) それとも soré tomò, または matá wa; (otherwise) でなけ ná i to, さもないと sa mò naí to; (with negative): *he hasn't seen or heard anything* 彼は何一つ見ても聞いても いない karè wa nanî hitótsu mitè mo kíîte mo inai

or else (otherwise) でないと de naî to

oracle [ɔr'əkəl] *n* 予言者 yogénsha

oral [ɔr'əl] *adj* (spoken: test, report) 口頭の kōtō no; (MED: vaccine, medicine) 経口の keíkō no
♦*n* (spoken examination) 口頭試問 kōtō-shimon

orange [ɔr'indʒ] *n* (fruit) オレンジ orénji
♦*adj* (color) だいだい色の daídaiiro no, オレンジ色の orénjiiro no

orator [ɔr'ətər] *n* 雄弁家 yūbenka

orbit [ɔr'bit] *n* (SPACE) 軌道 kidō
♦*vt* (circle: earth, moon etc) …の周囲を軌道を描いて回る …no shūī wo kidō wo egaíte mawáru

orchard [ɔr'tʃərd] *n* 果樹園 kajúen

orchestra [ɔr'kistrə] *n* (MUS) 楽団 gakúdan, オーケストラ ōkesutora; (*US*: THEATER: seating) 舞台前の特等席 butáimae no tokútōseki

orchestrate [ɔr'kistreit] *vt* (stage-manage) 指揮する shikí suru

orchid [ɔr'kid] *n* ラン ran

ordain [ɔrdein'] *vt* (REL) 聖職に任命する seíshoku ni nínmei suru

ordeal [ɔrdiːl'] *n* 試練 shíren

order [ɔr'dər] *n* (command) 命令 meírei; (COMM: from shop, company etc: also in restaurant) 注文 chūmon; (sequence) 順序 junjo; (good order) 秩序 chitsújo; (law and order) 治安 chían
♦*vt* (command) 命ずる meízuru; (COMM: from shop, company etc: also in restaurant) 注文する chūmon suru; (also: **put in order**) 整理する seíri suru

in order (permitted) 認可されて niñka sarete; (of document) 規定通りで kitéidōri de

in (working) order 整備されて seíbi sarete

in order to do/that …するために …surú tame ni

in order to (COMM) 発注してあって hatchū shite atte

out of order (not in correct order) 順番が乱れてて juñban ga midárete; (not working) 故障して koshō shite

to order someone to do something …に…する様に命令する …ni …suru yō ni meírei suru

order form *n* 注文用紙 chūmon yōshi

orderly [ɔr'dərli:] *n* (MIL) 当番兵 tōban-hei; (MED) 雑役夫 zatsúekifu
♦*adj* (well-organized: room) 整とんされた seíton sareta; (: person, system etc) 規則正しい kisókutadashii

ordinary [ɔr'dəneri:] *adj* (everyday, usual) 普通の futsū no; (*pej*: mediocre) 平凡な heíbon na

out of the ordinary (exceptional) 変ったkawátta

Ordnance Survey [ɔrd'nəns-] (*BRIT*) *n* 英国政府陸地測量局 eíkokuseífu ríkuchi sokuryōkyoku

ore [ɔːr] *n* 鉱石 kōseki

organ [ɔr'gən] *n* (ANAT: kidney, liver etc) 臓器 zōki; (MUS) オルガン orúgan

organic [ɔrgæn'ik] *adj* (food, farming etc) 有機の yūkī no

organism [ɔr'gənizəm] *n* 有機体 yūkītai, 生物 seíbutsu

organist [ɔr'gənist] *n* オルガン奏者 orúgansōsha, オルガニスト orúganisuto

organization [ɔrgənəzei'ʃən] *n* (business, club, society) 組織 soshíki, 機構 kikō, オーガニゼーション ōganízēshon

organize [ɔr'gənaiz] *vt* (arrange: activity, event) 企画する kikáku suru

organizer [ɔr'gənaizər] *n* (of conference, party etc) 主催者 shusáisha

orgasm [ɔr'gæzəm] *n* オルガズム orúgazumū

orgy [ɔr'dʒiː] *n* 乱交パーティ rañkōpāti

Orient [ɔr'i:ənt] *n*: *the Orient* 東洋 tōyō

oriental [ɔri:en'təl] *adj* 東洋の tōyō no

orientate [ɔr'i:enteit] *vt*: *to orientate oneself* (in place) 自分の居場所を確認する jibún no ibásho wo kakúnin suru; (in situation) 環境になれる kañkyō ni naréru

origin [ɔr'idʒin] *n* (beginning, source) 起源 kigén; (of person) 生れ umáre

original [əridʒ'ənəl] *adj* (first: idea, occupation) 最初の saísho no; (genuine: work of art, document etc) 本物の honmono no; (*fig*: imaginative: thinker, writer, artist) 独創的な dokúsōteki na

been mentioned: person, thing) 外の hoká no; (second of 2 things) もう一つの mō hitotsu no

♦*pron*: *the other (one)* 外の物 hoká no mono

♦*adv*: *other than* ...を除いて ...wo nozóite

others (other people) 他人 tanín

the other day (recently) 先日 senjitsu, この間 konó aida

otherwise [ʌðˈəːwaiz] *adv* (in a different way) 違ったやり方で chígatta yaríkata de; (apart from that) それを除けば soré wo nozókeba

♦*conj* (if not) そうでないと sō dé nai to

otter [ɑtˈəːr] *n* カワウソ kawáuso

ouch [autʃ] *excl* 痛い itái

ought [ɔːt] (*pt* *ought*) *aux vb*: *she ought to do it* 彼女はそれをやるべきです kanójo wa soré wo yarubekí desu

this ought to have been corrected これは直すべきだった koré wa naósubeki datta

he ought to win (probability) 彼は勝つはずです karé wa katsú hazu desu

ounce [auns] *n* (unit of weight) オンス ónsu

our [auˈəːr] *adj* 私たちの watákushitachi no ¶ *see also* **my**

ours [auˈəːrz] *pron* 私たちの物 watákushitachi no mono ¶ *see also* **mine**

ourselves [auəːrselvz'] *pron* 私たち自身 watákushitachi jishín ¶ *see also* **oneself**

oust [aust] *vt* (forcibly remove): government, MP etc) 追放する tsuíhō suru

KEYWORD

out [aut] *adv* 1 (not in) 外に(で、へ) sótō ni(de, e)

they're out in the garden 彼らは庭にいます kárēra wa niwá ni imásu

(to stand) out in the rain/snow 雨〔雪〕の降る中に立っている ámē〔yukí〕no fúrū nákā ni tátte irū

it's cold out here/out in the desert 外〔砂漠〕は寒い sótō(sabáku)wa samúi

out here/there ここ〔あそこ〕だ・ドに kokó(asóko)dà - sótō no hṓ nì

♦*n* (genuine work of art, document) 本物 hofmóno

originality [ɔridʒənælˈiti:] *n* (imagination: of artist, writer etc) 独創性 dokúsōsei

originally [ɔridʒˈənəli:] *adv* (at first) 最初は saísho wa, 当初 tṓsho

originate [ɔridʒˈəneit] *vi*: *to originate from* (person, idea, custom etc) ...から始まる ...kará hajímaru

to originate in ...で始まる ...dé hajímaru

Orkneys [ɔːrkˈniːz] *npl*: *the Orkneys* (*also*: *the Orkney Islands*) オークニー諸島 ōkúnīshotō

ornament [ɔːrˈnəmənt] *n* (*gen*) 飾り kazári, 装飾 sōshoku; (to be worn) 装身具 sōshíngu

ornamental [ɔːrnəmenˈtəl] *adj* (decorative: garden, pond) 装飾的な sōshokutekí na

ornate [ɔːrneit'] *adj* (highly decorative: design, style) 凝った kottá

ornithology [ɔːrnəθɑːˈlədʒi:] *n* 鳥類学 chōruigaku

orphan [ɔːrˈfən] *n* 孤児 kojí

orphanage [ɔːrˈfənidʒ] *n* 孤児院 kojíin

orthodox [ɔːrˈθədɑːks] *adj* (REL: *also fig*) 正統派の seftóha no

orthodoxy [ɔːrˈθədɑːksi:] *n* (traditional beliefs) 正統思想 seftō shísō

orthopedic [ɔːrθəpiːˈdik] (*BRIT* **orthopaedic**) *adj* 整形外科の seíkeigeka no

oscillate [ɑsˈəleit] *vi* (ELEC) 発振する hasshín suru; (PHYSICS) 振動する shindō suru; (*fig*: mood, person, ideas) 頻繁に変る hínpan ni kawáru

ostensibly [ɑstenˈsəbliː] *adv* 表面上 hyṓmenjō

ostentatious [ɑstenteiˈʃəs] *adj* (showy: building, car etc) 派手な hadé na; (: person) 見えっぱりの mieппari no

osteopath [ɑsˈtiːəpæθ] *n* 整骨療法医 seíkotsuryōhōi

ostracize [ɑsˈtrəsaiz] *vt* のけ者にする nokémono ni suru

ostrich [ɑsˈtritʃ] *n* ダチョウ dachō

other [ʌðˈəːr] *adj* (that which has not

to go/come etc out 出て行く〔来る〕déte iku(kuru)

(to speak) out loud 大きな声で言う ōkina koè de iú

2 (not at home, absent) 不在で fuzái de, 留守で rúsù de

Mr Green is out at the moment グリーンさんはただ今留守ですが gurín san wa tadáīma rūsù desu ga

to have a day/night out 1日〔1晩〕外出して遊ぶ ichínichí(hitóbàn)gaíshutsu shite asóbù

3 (indicating distance): *the boat was 10 km out* 船は10キロ沖にあった fúnè wa jukkíro okí ni attá

3 days out from Plymouth プリマスを出港して3日の所 purímasu wo shukkō shité mikka no tokoró

4 (SPORT) アウトで áùto de

the ball is/was out ボールはアウトだ〔出た〕bōru wa áùto da(déta)

out! (TENNIS etc) アウト áùto

♦*adj* **1**: *to be out* (person: unconscious) 気絶(失神)している kizétsu(shisshín) shite irú; (: SPORT) アウトである áùto de árù; (: out of fashion: style) 流行遅れである ryūkōokùre de árù, 廃れている sutárete irú; (: singer) 人気がなくなった nínki ga nakúnattá

2 (have appeared: flowers): *to be out* 咲いている saíte irú; (: news) 報道されている hōdō sarete irú; (: secret) ばれた báretà, 発覚した hakkáku shità

3 (extinguished: fire, light, gas) 消えた kiétà

before the week was out (finished) その週が終わらない内に sonó shū ga owáranai uchi nì

4: *to be out to do something* (intend) ...しようとしている ...shiyō to shité irú

to be out in one's calculations (wrong) 計算が間違っている kefsan gà machígatte irú

---

out-and-out [aut'ɔndaut] *adj* (liar, thief etc) 全くの mattáku no, 根っからの nekkára no

outback [aut'bæk] *n* (in Australia) 奥地 okúchi

outboard [aut'bɔːrd] *adj*: *outboard motor* アウトボードエンジン aùtobōdoenjin

outbreak [aut'breik] *n* (of war, disease, violence etc) ぼっ発 boppátsu

outburst [aut'bəːrst] *n* (sudden expression of anger etc) 爆発 bakúhatsu

outcast [aut'kæst] *n* 除け者 nokémono

outcome [aut'kʌm] *n* (result) 結果 kekká

outcrop [aut'krɑp] *n* (of rock) 露頭 rotō

outcry [aut'krai] *n* 反発 hanpatsu

outdated [autdei'tid] *adj* (old-fashioned) 時代遅れの jidáiokùre no

outdo [autduː'] (*pt* **outdid** *pp* **outdone**) *vt* しのぐ shinógu

outdoor [aut'dɔːr] *adj* (open-air: activities, games etc) 野外の yagái no, 屋外の okúgai no; (clothes) 野外用の yagáiyo no

outdoors [autdɔːrz'] *adv* (play, stay, sleep: in the open air) 野外に〔で〕yagái ni(de)

outer [aut'ɔːr] *adj* (exterior: door, wrapping, wall etc) 外側の sotógawa no

outer space *n* 宇宙空間 uchūkūkan

outfit [aut'fit] *n* (set of clothes) 衣装 ishō

outgoing [aut'gouiŋ] *adj* (extrovert) 外向性の gaíkōsei no; (retiring: president, mayor etc) 退職する taíjin surú

outgoings [aut'gouiŋz] *npl* (BRIT) 出費 shuppí

outgrow [autgrou'] (*pt* **outgrew** *pp* **outgrown**) *vt* (one's clothes) 大きくなって...が着られなくなる ōkiku natte ...ga kirárenaku naru

outhouse [aut'haus] *n* 納屋 nayà; (US) 屋外便所 okúgaibenjo

outing [aut'iŋ] *n* (excursion: family outing, school outing) 遠足 eńsoku

outlandish [autlæn'diʃ] *adj* (strange: looks, behavior, clothes) 奇妙な kimyō na

outlaw [aut'lɔː] *n* 無法者 muhōmono ♦*vt* (person, activity, organization) 禁止する kińshi surú

outlay [aut'lei] *n* (expenditure) 出費

shuppſ

outlet [aut'let] n (hole, pipe) 排水口 haisuikō; (US: ELEC) コンセント konsento; (COMM: also: **retail outlet**) 販売店 hanbaiten

outline [aut'lain] n (shape: of object, person etc) 輪郭 rinkaku, アウトライン autorain; (brief explanation: of plan) あらまし arámashi, アウトライン autorain; (rough sketch) 略図 ryakúzu

♦vt (fig: theory, plan etc) ...の あらましを説明する ...no arámashi wo setsúmei suru

outlive [autliv'] vt (survive: person) ...より 長生きする ...yorí nagá-ikí suru; (: war, era) を生き延びる ikínobiru

outlook [aut'luk] n (view, attitude) 見方 mikáta; (fig: prospects) 見通し mitōshi; (: for weather) 予報 yohō

outlying [aut'laiiŋ] adj (away from main cities: area, town etc) 中心部を離れた chūshinbu wo hanáreta

outmoded [autmou'did] adj (old-fashioned: custom, theory) 時代遅れの jidáiokúre no

outnumber [autnʌm'bə:r] vt ...より 多い ...yorí ōi

─────────────────────

KEYWORD

out [aut] prep 1 (outside, beyond) ...の 外へ 〈に、で〉...no sótó e〈ni, de〉

to go out of the house 家から外へ出る ié kará sótó e déru

to look out of the window 窓から外を見る mádò kara sótò wo mírù

to be out of danger (safe) 危険がなくなった kiken ga nakúnatta

2 (cause, motive) ...に 駆られて ...ni kárárete

out of curiosity/fear/greed 好奇心 〈恐怖、どん欲〉に駆られて kōkíshin 〈kyōfu, dóń-yoku〉ni karárete

3 (origin) ...から ...kara

to drink something out of a cup カップから...を飲む káppù kara ...wo nomú

to copy something out of a book 本から...を写す hóń kara ...wð utsúsù

4 (from among) ...の 中から ...no nákà

kara, ...の 内 ...no uchí

1 out of every 3 smokers 喫煙者3人に1人 kitsúeńsha sańnin ni hitórì

out of 100 cars sold, only one had any faults 売れた100台の車の内、1台だけに欠陥があった uréta hyakúdái no kurúma no uchí, íchídai dake ni kekkán ga atta

5 (without) ...が切れて ...ga kírète, ...がなくなって ...ga nakúnatte

to be out of milk/sugar/gas (US)/petrol (BRIT) etc ミルク〈砂糖、ガソリン〉が切れている mírùku〈sató, gasórin〉ga kírète iru

─────────────────────

out-of-date [autˈəvdeit'] adj (passport) 期限の切れた kigén no kíréta; (clothes etc) 時代遅れの jidáiokúre no

out-of-the-way [autˈəvðəwei'] adj (place) へんぴな heńpi na

outpatient [aut'peiʃənt] n (MED) 外来患者 gafraikanja

outpost [aut'poust] n (MIL, COMM) 前しょう zefíshō; (COMM) 前進基地 zefíshinkichi

output [aut'put] n (production: of factory, mine etc) 生産高 sefsańdaka; (: of writer) 作品数 sakúhinsū; (COMPUT) 出力 shutsúryoku, アウトプット aútopùtto

outrage [aut'reidʒ] n (action: scandalous) 不法行為 fuhōkóì; (: violent) 暴力行為 bōryokukóì; (anger) 激怒 gekído

♦vt (shock, anger) 激怒させる gekído saseru

outrageous [autrei'dʒəs] adj 非難すべき hinánsubeki

outright [adv autrait' adj aut'rait] adv (absolutely: win) 圧倒的に attóteki ni; (at once: kill) 即座に sokúza ni; (openly: ask, deny, refuse) はっきりと hakkíri to

♦adj (absolute: winner, victory) 圧倒的な attóteki na; (: open: refusal, denial, hostility) 明らかな meíhaku na

outset [aut'set] n (start) 始め hajíme

outside [aut'said'] n (exterior: of container, building) 外側 sotógawa

♦adj (exterior) 外側の sotógawa no

♦adv (away from the inside: to be, go,

wait) 外に〔で〕sotó ni〔de〕
♦*prep* (not inside) ...の外に〔で〕...no sotó ni〔de〕; (not included) ...の外に ...no hoká ni; (beyond) ...を越えて ...wo koéte
at the outside (*fig*) せいぜい seízei

outside lane *n* (AUT) 追越し車線 ofkoeshishaseñ

outside line *n* (TEL) 外線 gafseñ

outsider [autsai'dər] *n* (stranger) 部外者 bugáisha

outside-left/-right [aut'saidleft'/rait] *n* (SOCCER) レフト〔ライト〕ウイング refúto〔raíto〕uñgu

outsize [aut'saiz] *adj* (clothes) キングサイズの kíñgusaìzu no

outskirts [aut'skərts] *npl* (of city, town) 外れ hazúre

outspoken [aut'spou'kən] *adj* (statement, opponent, reply) 遠慮のない eñryo no nai

outstanding [autstæn'diŋ] *adj* (exceptional) 並外れた namíhazureta, 優れた sugúreta; (remaining: debt, work etc) 残っている nokótte iru

outstay [autstei'] *vt*: **to outstay one's welcome** 長居して嫌われる nagái shite kiráwareru

outstretched [autstret∫t'] *adj* (hand) 伸ばした nobáshìta; (arms) 広げた hirógetà

outstrip [autstrip'] *vt* (competitors, demand) 追抜く ofnuku

out-tray [aut'trei] *n* 送信のトレー sóshin no torē

outward [aut'wərd] *adj* (sign, appearance) 外部の gaíbu no; (journey) 行きの ikí no

outwardly [aut'wərdli:] *adv* 外部的に gaíbuteki ni

outweigh [autwei'] *vt* ...より重要である ...yorí jūyõ de aru

outwit [autwit'] *vt* ...の裏をかく ...no urá wo káku

oval [ou'vəl] *adj* (table, mirror, face) だ円形の daéñkei no
♦*n* だ円形 daéñkei

ovary [ou'vəri:] *n* 卵巣 rañsõ

ovation [ouvei'∫ən] *n* 大喝さい daíkassai

oven [ʌv'ən] *n* (CULIN) 天火 teñpi, オーブン ōbun; (TECH) 炉 ro

ovenproof [ʌv'ənpru:f] *adj* (dish etc) オーブン用の ōbun yõ no

<hr>

KEYWORD

over [ou'vər] *adv* 1 (across: walk, jump, fly etc) ...を越えて ...wò koéte
to cross over to the other side of the road 道路を横断する dõro wo ōdan suru
over here/there ここ〔あそこ〕に〔で〕kokó〔asóko〕nì〔de〕
to ask someone over (to one's house) ...を家に招く ...wò ié nì manékù
2 (indicating movement from upright: fall, knock, turn, bend etc) 下へ shità e, 地面へ jímèn e
3 (excessively: clever, rich, fat etc) 余り amári, 過度に kádò ni
she's not over intelligent, is she? 彼女はあまり頭が良くないね kánòjo wa atáma gà yókùnai nē
4 (remaining: money, food etc) 余って amáttè, 残って nokóttè
there are 3 over 3個が残っている sáñko ga nokótte irù
is there any cake (left) over? ケーキが残っていませんか kẽki ga nokótte imaseñ ká
5: **all over** (everywhere) 至る所に〔で〕itárù tokoro ni〔de〕, どこもかしこも dókò mo kashìkò mo
over and over (again) (repeatedly) 何度〔何回, 何返〕も nañdo〔nañkai, nañben〕mo
♦*adj* (finished): **to be over** (game, life, relationship etc) 終りである owári de aru
♦*prep* 1 (on top of) ...の上に〔で〕...no ué ni〔de〕; (above) ...の上方に〔で〕...no jōhō ni〔de〕
to spread a sheet over something ...の上にシーツを掛ける ...no ué nì shítsu wo kakérù
there's a canopy over the bed ベッドの上に天がいがある béddò no ué nì teñgai ga arù
2 (on the other side of) ...の向こうに

[で] ...no mukǒgawa nǐ(dè)
the pub over the road 道路の向こう側
にあるパブ dǒrò no mukǒgawa ni arù
pábù

he jumped over the wall 彼は塀を飛
越えた kárè wa heí wò tobíkoèta

3 (*more than*) 以上 ijò
over 200 people came 200人以上の人
が来ました nihyákunìn ǐjò no hitó ga
kimáshìta

over and above ...の外に ...no hōkà ni,
...に加えて ...ni kuwáetè

*this order is over and above what
we have already ordered* この注文は
これまでの注文への追加です konó chū-
mon wa koré madè no chūmón e no
tsuíka desù

4 (*during*) ...の間 ...no aída
over the last few years 過去数年の間
kákò sūnèn no aída

over the winter 冬の間 fuyú nò aída
let's discuss it over dinner 夕食をし
ながら話し合いましょう yūshoku wò
shínágàra hanáshiaimashò

overall [*adj, n* ouváːrɔːl *adv* ouvaːrɔːl']
adj (length, cost etc) 全体の zeńtai no;
(general: study, survey) 全面的な zeńmen-
teki na
♦*adv* (view, survey etc) 全面的に zeńmen-
teki ni; (measure, paint) 全体に zeńtai ni
♦*n* (BRIT: woman's, child's, painter's)
上っ張り uwáppari

overalls [ou'vəːrɔːlz] *npl* オーバーオール
ōbáōrù

overawe [ouvəːrɔː'] *vt* 威圧する iátsu suru

overbalance [ouvəːrbæl'əns] *vi* バラン
スを失う baránsu wo ushínau

overbearing [ouvəːrber'iŋ] *adj* (person,
behavior, manner) 横暴な ōbō na

overboard [ou'vəːrbɔːrd] *adv* (NAUT):
to fall overboard 船から水に落ちる fu-
nè kara mizú ni ochírù

overbook [ou'vəːrbuk] *vt* 予約を取り過
ぎる yoyáku wo torísugiru

overcast [ou'vəːrkæst] *adj* (day, sky) 曇
った kumótta

overcharge [ou'vəːrtʃɑːrdʒ] *vt* ...に不当
な金額を請求する ...ni futō na kíngaku
wo sefkyū suru

overcoat [ou'vəːrkout] *n* オーバーコー
ト ōbákōto, オーバー ōbā

overcome [ouvəːrkʌm'] (*pt* **overcame** *pp*
overcome) *vt* (defeat: opponent, enemy)
...に勝つ ...ni katsù; (*fig*: difficulty, problem) 克服する kokúfuku suru

overcrowded [ouvəːrkrau'did] *adj*
(room, prison) 超満員の chōman-in no;
(city) 過密な kamítsu na

overdo [ouvəːrduː'] (*pt* **overdid** *pp* **over-
done**) *vt* (exaggerate: concern, interest)
誇張する kochō suru; (overcook) 焼き過
ぎる yakísugiru
to overdo it (work etc) やり過ぎる yarí-
sugirù

overdose [ou'vəːrdous] *n* (MED: dangerous dose) 危険量 kikénryō; (: fatal dose)
致死量 chíshíryō

overdraft [ou'vəːrdræft] *n* 当座借越 tō-
zakaríkoshi

overdrawn [ouvəːrdrɔːn'] *adj* (account)
借越した karíkoshi shita

overdue [ouvəːrduː'] *adj* (late: person,
bus, train) 遅れている okúrete iru;
(change, reform etc) 待望の taíbō no

overestimate [ouvəːres'tæmeit] *vt* (cost,
importance, time) 高く見積りすぎる ta-
kàku mitsúmorisugirù; (person's ability,
skill etc) 買いかぶる kaíkaburu

overexcited [ouvəːriksaiʼtid] *adj* 過度に
興奮した kadò ni kōfun shita

overflow [vb ouvəːrflou' *n* ou'vəːrflou]
vi (river) はん濫する hafran suru; (sink,
vase etc) あふれる afúreru
♦*n* (*also*: **overflow pipe**) 放出パイプ hō-
shutsupaipu

overgrown [ouvəːrgroun'] *adj* (garden)
草がぼうぼうと生えた kusa ga bōbō to
haèta

overhaul [*vb* ouvəːrhɔːl' *n* ou'vəːrhɔːl]
vt (engine, equipment etc) 分解検査する
buńkaikensa suru, オーバーホールする
ōbáhōru suru
♦*n* オーバーホール ōbāhōru

overhead [*adv* ouvəːrhed' *adj*, *n*

ou'vəːrhed] adv (above) 頭上に[で] zujó
ni[de]; (in the sky) 上空に[で] jōkū ni
[de]
◆adj (lighting) 上からの ué kara no;
(cables, railway) 高架の kōka no
◆n (US) = **overheads**

overheads [ou'vəːrhedz] npl (expenses)
経費 keíhi

overhear [ouvəːrhiəːr] (pt, pp **over-
heard**) vt 耳にする mimf ni suru

overheat [ouvəːrhiːt] vi (engine) 過熱す
る kanétsu suru, オーバーヒートする ō-
bāhīto suru

overjoyed [ouvəːrdʒɔid] adj 大喜びした
ōyórokobi shita

overkill [ou'vəːrkil] n やり過ぎ yarísugi

overland [ou'vəːrlænd] adj (journey) 陸
路の rikúro no
◆adv (travel) 陸路で rikúro de

overlap [ouvəːrlæp] vi (edges) 部分的に
重なる bubúnteki ni kasánaru, オーバー
ラップする ōbārappu suru; (fig: ideas,
activities etc) 部分的に重複する bubúnteki ni chōfuku suru, オーバーラップす
る ōbārappu suru

overleaf [ouvəːrliːf] adv ページの裏に
pēji no urá ni

overload [ou'vəːrloud] vt (vehicle) ...に積
み過ぎる ...ni tsumísugirù; (ELEC) ...に負
荷を掛け過ぎる ...ni fuká wo kakésugi-
ru; (fig: with work, problems etc) ...に負
担を掛け過ぎる ...ni fután wo kakésugi-
ru

overlook [ouvəːrluk] vt (have view
over) 見下ろす miórosu; (miss: by mistake) 見落す miótosu; (excuse, forgive)
見逃す minógasu

overnight [adv ouvəːrnait] adj ou'vəːr-
nait] adv (during the whole night) 一晩中
hitóbanjū; (fig: suddenly) いつの間にか
itsú no ma ni ka
◆adj (bag, clothes) 1泊用の ippákuyō no
to stay overnight 一泊する ippáku suru

overpass [ou'vəːrpæs] n 陸橋 ríkkyō

overpower [ouvəːrpauːr] vt (person) 腕
力で抑え込む wañryoku de osékomù;
(subj: emotion, anger etc) 圧倒する attő

suru

overpowering [ouvəːrpauːəriŋ] adj
(heat, stench) 圧倒する様な attő suru yō
na

overrate [ouvəːreit] vt (person, film,
book) 高く評価し過ぎる takáku hyōka
shisúgirù

override [ouvəːraid] (pt **overrode** pp
overridden) vt (order) 無効にする mukó
ni suru; (objection) 無視する mushf suru

overriding [ouvəːraidiŋ] adj (importance) 最大の saídai no; (factor, consideration) 優先的な yūsénteki na

overrule [ouvəːruːl] vt (decision, claim,
person) 無効にする mukó ni suru; (per-
son) ...の提案を退ける ...no tefan wo shi-
rízokerù

overrun [ou'vəːrʌn] (pt **overran** pp
overrun) vt (country) 侵略する shifíryа-
ku suru; (time limit) 越える koérù

overseas [adv ouvəːrsiːz] adj ou'vəːr-
siːz] adv (live, travel, work: abroad) 海外
に[で] kaígai ni[de]
◆adj (market, trade) 海外の kaígai no;
(student, visitor) 外国人の gaíkokujìn no

overshadow [ouvəːrʃædou] vt (throw
shadow over: place, building etc) ...の上
にそびえる ...no ué ni sobíerù; (fig) ...の
影を薄くさせる ...no kagé wo usúku saseru

overshoot [ouvəːrʃuːt] (pt, pp **overshot**)
vt (subj: plane, train, car etc) ...に止らず
に行き過ぎる ...ni tomárazu ni ikísugirù

oversight [ou'vəːrsait] n 手落ち teóchi

oversleep [ouvəːrsliːp] (pt, pp **overslept**)
vi 寝過ごす nesúgosu, 寝坊する nebő su-
ru

overstate [ouvəːrsteit] vt (exaggerate:
case, problem, importance) 誇張する ko-
chő suru

overstep [ouvəːrstep] vt: **to overstep
the mark** (go too far) 行き過ぎをやる
ikísugi wo yaru

overt [ou'vəːrt] adj あからさまな akára-
sama na

overtake [ouvəːrteik] (pt **overtook** pp
overtaken) vt (AUT) 追越す ofkősu

overthrow [ouvəːrθrou] vt (government, leader) 倒す taósu

overtime [ou'vərtaim] n 残業 zańgyō

overtone [ou'vərtoun] n (fig) 含み fukúmi

overture [ou'vərtʃər] n (MUS) 序曲 jokyóku; (fig) 申出 mōshíde

overturn [ouvərtə:rn'] vt (car, chair) 引っ繰り返す hikkúrikaèsu; (fig: decision, plan, ruling) 覆す hirúgaèsu; (: government, system) 倒す taósu

♦vi (car, train, boat etc) 転覆する teńpuku suru

overweight [ouvərweit'] adj (person) 太り過ぎの futórisugì na

overwhelm [ouvərwelm'] vt 圧倒する attō suru

overwhelming [ouvərwel'miŋ] adj (victory, heat, feeling) 圧倒的な attōteki na

overwork [ou'vərwə:rk'] n 働き過ぎ határakisugĭ, 過労 karō

♦vi 働き過ぎる határakisugĭru

♦vt (person) こき使う kokítsukaù

overwrought [ou'vərɔːt'] adj 神経が高ぶった shińkei ga tákabuttà

owe [ou] vt: to owe someone something, to owe something to someone (money) ...に...を借りている ...ni ...wo karíte iru, ...に...を払う義務がある ...ni ...wo haráũ gĩmu ga aru; (fig: gratitude, respect, loyalty) ...にしなければならない ...ni ...shinákereba naranaĭ; (: life, talent, good looks etc) ...は...のおかげである ...wa ...no o-kágè de aru

owing to [ou'iŋ tu:] prep (because of) ...のために ...no tamé ni

owl [aul] n フクロウ fukúrō, ミミズク mimízuku

own [oun] vt (possess: house, land, etc) 所有する shoyū́ suru, 保有する hoyū́ suru

♦adj (house, work, style etc) 自分の jibúń no, 自分自身の jubúnjishṇ no

a room of my own 自分の部屋 jibúń no heyá

to get one's own back (take revenge) 復しゅうする fukúshū suru

on one's own (alone) 自分で jibúń de, 自分の力で jibúń no chikará de

owner [ou'nər] n (gen) 所有者 shoyū́sha, 持主 mochínushi, オーナー ōnā; (of shop)

主人 shujín, 経営者 kéiefsha; (of pet) 飼主 kaínushi

ownership [ou'nə:rʃip] n (possession) 所有権 shoyū́ken

own up vi (admit: guilt, error) ...を認める ...wo mitómeru

ox [ɑks] (pl **oxen**) n ウシ ushí の通常去勢した牡ウシを指す tsūjō kyoséi shita oùshi wo sasu

oxtail [ɑks'teil] n: **oxtail soup** オックステールスープ okkúsutèrusūpu

oxygen [ɑːk'sidʒən] n 酸素 saǹso

oxygen mask/tent n 酸素マスク(テント) saǹsomasukù(tento)

oyster [ois'tə:r] n カキ kaki

oz. abbr = **ounce(s)**

ozone [ou'zoun] n オゾン ozòn

ozone layer n オゾン層 ozòńsō

P

p [pi:] abbr = **penny**; **pence**

P.A. [pi:'ei] n abbr = **personal assistant**; **public address system**

p.a. abbr = **per annum**

pa [pɑː] (inf) n 父ちゃん tōchan, パパ pápá

pace [peis] n (step) 1歩 íppò; (distance) 歩幅 hobàba; (speed) 早さ háyàsa, 速度 sókùdo, ペース pèsu

♦vi: to pace up and down (walk around angrily or impatiently) うろうろする úrôuro suru

to keep pace with (person) ...と足並をそろえる ...to ashínami wò soróerù

pacemaker [peis'meikə:r] n (MED) ペースメーカー pḗsumèkā; (SPORT: also: **pacesetter**) ペースメーカー pḗsumèkā

Pacific [pəsif'ik] n: **the Pacific (Ocean)** 太平洋 taíheiyō

pacifist [pæs'əfist] n 平和主義者 hefwashugìsha

pacify [pæs'əfai] vt (soothe: person) なだめる nadámerù; (: fears) 鎮める shizúmerù

pack [pæk] n (packet) 包み tsutsúmi; (US: of cigarettes) 1箱 hitóhàko; (group:

of hounds) 群れ muré; (: of people) グループ gúrūpu; (back pack) リュックサック ryukkúsakkù; (of cards) 1組 hitókùmi

♦vt (fill: box, container, suitcase etc) ...に詰込む ...ni tsumékomù; (cram: people, objects): **to pack into** ...を...に詰込む ...wo ...ni tsumékomù

to pack (one's bags) 荷造りをする nizúkùri wo suru

to pack someone off ...を追出す ...wo oídasù

pack it in! (inf: stop it!) やめなさい! yaménasaì!

package [pæk'idʒ] n (parcel) 小包 kozútsumi; (also: **package deal**) 一括取引 ikkátsutoríhìki

package holiday n = **package tour**

package tour n パッケージツアー pakkéjitsuà, パックツアー pakkútsuà

packed lunch [pækt-] n 弁当 beńtō

packet [pæk'it] n (box) 1箱 hitóhàko; (bag) 1袋 hitófùkuro

packing [pæk'iŋ] n (act) 詰込む tsumékomù kotó; (external: paper, plastic etc) 包装 hōsō

packing case n 木箱 kíbàko

pact [pækt] n 協定 kyōtei

pad [pæd] n (block of paper) 一つづり hitótsùzuri; (to prevent friction, damage) こん包材 koñpózaì; (in shoulders of dress, jacket etc) パッド páddò; (inf: home) 住い sumái

♦vt (SEWING: cushion, soft toy etc) ...に詰物をする ...ni tsumémòno wo suru

padding [pæd'iŋ] n (material) 詰物 tsumémòno

paddle [pæd'əl] n (oar) かい kaí, パドル páddòru; (US: table tennis) ラケット rakéttò

♦vt (boat, canoe etc) こぐ kógù

♦vi (with feet) 水の中を歩く mizú no nakà wo arúkù

paddle steamer n (on river) 外輪船 gaírinsèn

paddling pool [pæd'liŋ-] (BRIT) n (children's) 子供用プール kodómoyō pūru

paddock [pæd'ək] n (for horse: small field) 放牧場 hóbokujò; (: at race course)

パドック pádòkku

paddy field [pæd'i-] n 水田 suíden, 田んぼ tañbo

padlock [pæd'lɑk] n (on door, bicycle etc) 錠(前) jṓmae

paediatrics [pi:di:æt'riks] (BRIT) n = **pediatrics**

pagan [pei'gən] adj (gods, festival, worship) 異教の ikyṓ no ◇キリスト教、ユダヤ教、イスラム教以外の宗教をさげすんで言う語 kirísutokyō, yudáyakyō, isúramukyō igài no shūkyō wo sagésuñde iú go

◆n (worshipper of pagan gods) 異教徒 ikyṓto

page [peidʒ] n (of book, magazine, newspaper) ページ pḗji; (also: **page boy**) 花嫁付添いの少年 hanáyòmetsukìsoi no shṓnen

♦vt (in hotel etc) ボーイ bōi

pageant [pædʒ'ənt] n (historical procession, show) ページェント pèjento

pageantry [pædʒ'əntri:] n 見世物 misémono

paid [peid] pt, pp of **pay**

◆adj (work) 有料の yūryō no; (staff, official) 有給の yūkyū no; (gunman, killer) 雇われた yatówareta

a paid holiday 有給休暇 yūkyūkyūka

to put paid to (BRIT: end, destroy) ...を台無しにする ...wo dafnashi ni surú

pail [peil] n (for milk, water etc) バケツ bakétsu

pain [pein] n (unpleasant physical sensation) 痛み itámi, 苦痛 kutsū; (fig: unhappiness) 苦しみ kurúshìmi, 心痛 shiñtsū

to be in pain (person, animal) 苦痛を感じている kutsū wo kañjite irù, 苦しんでいる kurúshìnde irù

to take pains to do something (make an effort) 苦心して...する kushín shite ...surù

pained [peind] adj (expression) 怒った okóttà

painful [pein'fəl] adj (back, wound, fracture etc) 痛い itái, 痛む itámù; (upsetting, unpleasant: sight etc) 痛ましい itámashii; (memory) 不快な fukái na; (decision) 苦しい kurúshiî; (laborious: task, progress etc) 骨の折れる honé no orerú

painfully [pein'fəli] *adv* (fig: very) 非常に hijō ni 程 itáihodo

painkiller [pein'kilər] *n* (aspirin, paracetamol etc) 鎮痛剤 chifitsúzaì

painless [pein'lis] *adj* (operation, childbirth) 無痛の mutsū no

painstaking [peinz'teikiŋ] *adj* (work) 骨の折れる honére no; (person) 動勉な kíñben na

paint [peint] *n* (decorator's: for walls, doors etc) 塗料 toryō, ペンキ peñkì, ペイント peínto; (artist's: oil paint, watercolor paint etc) 絵の具 e nó gu
♦*vt* (wall, door, house etc) ...にペンキを塗る ...ni peñki no nurú; (picture, portrait) 描く kákû

to paint the door blue ドアに水色のペンキを塗る dōā ni mizúiro no peñki wo nurú

paintbrush [peint'brʌʃ] *n* (decorator's) 刷毛 haké, ブラシ búrashì; (artist's) 絵筆 efúde

painter [pein'tər] *n* (artist) 画家 gáka; (decorator) ペンキ屋 peñkiya

painting [pein'tiŋ] *n* (activity: decorating) ペンキ塗り peñkinùri; (: art) 絵描き ekáki; (picture) 絵画 káigà

an oil painting 油絵 abúraè

paintwork [peint'wərk] *n* (painted parts) 塗装の部分 tosō no bubún

pair [per] *n* (of shoes, gloves etc) 対 tsúi

a pair of scissors はさみ hasámi

a pair of trousers ズボン zubóñ

pajamas [pədʒɑːm'əz] (*US*) *npl* パジャマ pájàma

Pakistan [pæk'istæn] *n* パキスタン pakísùtan

Pakistani [pæk'əstæn'iː] *adj* パキスタンの pakísùtan no
♦*n* パキスタン人 pakísutanjìn

pal [pæl] (*inf*) *n* (friend) 友達 tomódachì

palace [pæl'is] *n* (residence: of monarch) 宮殿 kyúdèn; (: of president etc) 官邸 kañtei; (: of Japanese emperor) 皇居 kōkyo, 御所 góshò

palatable [pæl'ətəbəl] *adj* (food, drink)

おいしい oíshiî

palate [pæl'it] *n* 口蓋 kógai

palatial [pəlei'ʃəl] *adj* (surroundings, residence) 豪華な gōka na

palaver [pəlæv'ɑːr] *n* (*US*) 話し合い hanáshiaì; (*BRIT*: *inf*: fuss) 大騒ぎ ōsàwàgì

pale [peil] *adj* (whitish: color) 白っぽい shiróppoì; (: face) 青白い aójiroì, 青ざめた aózametà; (: light) 薄暗い usúguraì
♦*n*: *beyond the pale* (unacceptable) 容認できない yōnin dekìnai

Palestine [pæl'istain] *n* パレスチナ parésùchina

Palestinian [pælistin'iːən] *adj* パレスチナの parésùchina no
♦*n* パレスチナ人 parésùchinajìn

palette [pæl'it] *n* (ART: paint mixing board) パレット parétto

palings [pei'liŋz] *npl* (fence) さく sakú

pall [pɔːl] *n*: *a pall of smoke* 一面の煙 ichímen no kemuri
♦*vi* ...が詰まらなくなる ...ga tsumáranakû naru, ...に飽きる ...ni akírù

pallet [pæl'it] *n* (for goods) パレット parétto

pallid [pæl'id] *adj* (person, complexion) 青白い aójiroì

pallor [pæl'ɔːr] *n* そう白 sōhaku

palm [pɑːm] *n* (*also*: **palm tree**) ヤシ yáshì; (of hand) 手のひら tenóhìra
♦*vt*: *to palm something off on someone* (*inf*) ...に...をつかませる ...ni ...wo tsukámaserù

Palm Sunday *n* 枝の主日 edá nò shujítsu

palpable [pæl'pəbəl] *adj* (obvious: lie, difference etc) 明白な meíhaku na

palpitations [pælpitei'ʃənz] *npl* (MED) 動き dōki

paltry [pɔːl'triː] *adj* (amount: tiny, insignificant) さいな sásài na

pamper [pæm'pər] *vt* (cosset: person, animal) 甘やかす amáyakasù

pamphlet [pæm'flit] *n* (political, literary etc) 小冊子 shōsasshì, パンフレット páñfuretto

pan [pæn] *n* (CULIN: *also*: **saucepan**) 片

手なべ katátenabè; (: *also*: **frying pan**) フライパン furáipan

panacea [pænəsí:ə] *n* 万能薬 bañnóyaku

panache [pənǽʃ] *n* 気取り kidóri

Panama [pǽnəmɑ:] *n* パナマ pánama

Panama Canal *n*: *the Panama Canal* パナマ運河 panáma uñga

pancake [pǽnkeik] *n* パンケーキ pañkéki, ホットケーキ hottōkéki

pancreas [pǽnkriəs] *n* すい臓 suízō

panda [pǽndə] *n* (ZOOL) ジャイアントパンダ jafantopáñda

panda car (BRIT) *n* (police car) パトカー patōkā

pandemonium [pændəmóu'niəm] *n* (noisy confusion) 大混乱, dafkoñran

pander [pǽndər] *vi*: *to pander to* (person, whim, desire etc) ...に迎合する ...ni geígō suru

pane [pein] *n* (of glass) 窓ガラス madōgarásu

panel [pǽn'əl] *n* (oblong piece: of wood, metal, glass etc) 羽目板 haméíta, パネル páneru; (group of judges, experts etc) ...の一団 ...no ichídan, パネル páneru

paneling [pǽn'əliŋ] (BRIT **panelling**) *n* 羽目板 haméíta ◇総称 sōshō

pang [pæŋ] *n*: *a pang of regret* 悔恨の情 kaíkon no jō

hunger pangs (physical pain) 激しい空腹感 hageshíí kūfukukan

panic [pǽn'ik] *n* (uncontrollable terror, anxiety) パニック páníkku
◆*vi* (person) うろたえる urótaerù; (crowd) パニック状態になる paníkkujōtai ni nárù

panicky [pǽn'iki] *adj* (person) うろたえる urótaerù

panic-stricken [pǽn'ikstrìkən] *adj* (person, face) パニックに陥った pánikku ni ochíttà

panorama [pænəræm'ə] *n* (view) 全景 zeñkei, パノラマ panórama

pansy [pæn'zi:] *n* (BOT) サンシキスミレ sañshikisumíre, パンジー pañjī; (*inf*: *pej*) 弱虫 yowámùshi

pant [pænt] *vi* (gasp: person, animal) あえぐ aégu

panther [pæn'θər] *n* ヒョウ hyō

panties [pæn'ti:z] *npl* パンティー pántī

pantomime [pæn'təmaim] (BRIT) *n* クリスマスミュージカル kurísumasu myū̀jikaru

pantry [pæn'tri:] *n* 食料室 shokúryōshìtsu, パントリー pañtorī

pants [pænts] *n* (BRIT: underwear: woman's) パンティー pántī; (: man's) パンツ pántsu; (US: trousers) ズボン zubón

panty hose *n* パンティーストッキング pañtísutokkiñgu

papal [pei'pəl] *adj* ローマ法王の rōmahṑō no

paper [pei'pər] *n* (gen) 紙 kamí; (*also*: **newspaper**) 新聞 shíñbun; (exam) 試験 shikén; (academic essay) 論文 roñbun, ペーパー pēpà; (*also*: **wallpaper**) 壁紙 kabégami

◆*adj* (made from paper: hat, plane etc) 紙の kamí no

◆*vt* (room: with wallpaper) ...に壁紙を張る ...ni kabégami wò hárù

paperback [pei'pərbæk] *n* ペーパーバック pēpàbàkku

paper bag *n* 紙袋 kamíbukùro

paper clip *n* クリップ kuríppu

paper hankie *n* ティッシュ tísshù

papers [pei'pərz] *npl* (documents) 書類 shorùi; (*also*: **identity papers**) 身分証明書 mibúnshōmeishò

paperweight [pei'pərweit] *n* 文鎮 buñchin

paperwork [pei'pərwərk] *n* (in office: dealing with letters, reports etc) 机上の事務 kijō no jimù, ペーパーワーク pēpàwàku

papier-mâché [pei'pərməʃei'] *n* 張り子 haríko

paprika [pəpri:'kə] *n* パプリカ papúrìka

par [pɑːr] *n* (equality of value) 同等 dōtō; (GOLF) 基準打数 kijúndasū̀, パー pā
to be on a par with (be equal with) ...と同等である ...to dōtō de arú

parable [pær'əbəl] *n* たとえ話 tatóebanàshi

parachute [pær'əʃut] *n* 落下傘 rakkásàn, パラシュート paráshùto

parade [pəreid'] n (public procession) パレード parêdo
♦vt (show off: wealth, knowledge etc) 見せびらかす misébirakasù
♦vi (MIL) 行進する kōshin suru

paradise [pær'ədais] n (REL: heaven, nirvana etc) 天国 têngoku, 極楽 gokûraku

paradox [pær'ədɑːks] n (thing, statement) 逆説 gyakúsetsu

paradoxically [pærədɑːk'sikli:] adv 逆説的に言えば gyakúsetsuteki nì iêba

paraffin [pær'əfin] (BRIT) n (also: paraffin oil) 灯油 tôyu

paragon [pær'əgɑn] n (of honesty, virtue etc) 模範 mohân, かがみ kagámi

paragraph [pær'əgræf] n 段落 dañrakù, パラグラフ parágùrafu

Paraguay [pær'əgwei] n パラグアイ parágùai

parallel [pær'əlel] adj (lines, walls, streets etc) 平行の hefkō no; (fig: similar) 似た nitá
♦n (line) 平行線 hefkōsen; (surface) 平行面 hefkōmen; (GEO) 緯度線 idôsen; (fig: similarity) 似た所 nitá tokoro

paralysis [pəræl'isis] n (MED) 麻 ひ máhi

paralyze [pær'əlaiz] vt (MED) 麻ひさせる máhì saséru; (fig: organization, production etc) 麻ひ状態にする mahîjōtai ni suru

parameters [pəræm'itəːrz] npl (fig) 限定要素 geñteiyōso

paramilitary [pær'əmil'iteːri:] adj (organization, operations) 準軍事的な juñgunjiteki na

paramount [pær'əmaunt] adj: of paramount importance 極めて重要な kiwámète jûyō na

paranoia [pærənɔi'ə] n 被害妄想 higáimōsō

paranoid [pær'ənɔid] adj (person, feeling) 被害妄想の higáimōsō no

parapet [pær'əpit] n 欄干 rañkan

paraphernalia [pærəfəːrneil'jə] n (gear) 道具 dôgu

paraphrase [pær'əfreiz] vt (poem, arti-

cle etc) やさしく言替える yasáshikù ifkaerù

paraplegic [pærəpliː'dʒik] n 下半身麻ひ患者 kahánshinmahi kañja

parasite [pær'əsait] n (insect: also fig: person) 寄生虫 kiséichū; (plant) 寄生植物 kiséishokubutsu

parasol [pær'əsɔːl] n 日傘 higasa, パラソル párasoru

paratrooper [pær'ətruːpəːr] n (MIL) 落下傘兵 rakkásanhei

parcel [pɑːr'səl] n (package) 小包 kozútsumi
♦vt (object, purchases: also: parcel up) 小包にする kozútsumi ni suru

parch [pɑːrtʃ] vt (land) 干上がらす hiágarasu; (crops) からからに枯らす karákara ni karaû

parched [pɑːrtʃt] adj (person) のどがからからの nôdo ga karákara no

parchment [pɑːrtʃ'mənt] n (animal skin) 羊皮紙 yôhishi; (thick paper) 硫酸紙 ryûsanshi

pardon [pɑːr'dən] n (LAW) 敦免 shamén
♦vt (forgive: person, sin, error etc) 許す yurúsù

pardon me!, I beg your pardon! (I'm sorry) 済みません sumímaseñ, 失礼しました shitsúrei shimashîta, ご免なさい gomén nasaî

(I beg your) pardon?, pardon me? (what did you say?) もう一度言って下さい もう ichido ittê kudásai

parent [peːr'ənt] n (mother or father) 親 oyá; (mother) 母親 hahâoya; (father) 父親 chichîoya

parental [pəren'təl] adj (love, control, guidance etc) 親の oyá no

parenthesis [pəren'θəsis] (pl parentheses) n 括弧 kákkò

parents [peːr'ənts] npl (mother and father) 両親 ryôshin

Paris [pær'is] n パリ párî

parish [pær'iʃ] n (REL) 教区 kyôkù; (BRIT: civil) 行政教区 gyôseikyōku

Parisian [pəriʒ'ən] adj パリの párî no
♦n パリっ子 parîkko

parity [pær'itiː] n (equality: of pay, conditions etc) 平等 byódō

park [pɑːrk] *n* (public) 公園 kṓen
♦*vt* (AUT) 駐車させる chūsha saseru
♦*vi* (AUT) 駐車する chūsha suru

parka [pɑːrkə] *n* パーカ pā́ka, アノラック anórakkù

parking [pɑːrkiŋ] *n* 駐車 chū́sha
「no parking, 駐車禁止 chūshakinshi

parking lot (US) *n* 駐車場 chūshajō

parking meter *n* パーキングメーター pākingumḕtā

parking ticket *n* (fine) 駐車違反切符 chūshaihan kippú

parlance [pɑːrləns] *n* 用語 yṓgo

parliament [pɑːrləmənt] (BRIT) *n* (institution) 議会 gíkai

parliamentary [pɑːrləménːtəriː] *adj* (business, behavior etc) 議会の gíkai no

parlor [pɑːrlər] (BRIT **parlour**) *n* (in house) 居間 imá, 応接間 ōsetsuma

parochial [pəroukíːəl] (pej) *adj* (person, attitude) 偏狭な heñkyō na

parody [pǽrədiː] *n* (THEATER, LITERATURE, MUS) パロディー páròdī

parole [pəroul] *n*: **on parole** (LAW) 仮釈放で karíshakuhō de

paroxysm [pǽrəksizm] *n* (of rage, jealousy, laughter) 爆発 bakúhatsu

parquet [pɑːrkéi] *n*: **parquet floor(ing)** 寄せ木張りの床 yoségibari nò yuká

parrot [pǽrət] *n* オウム ómu

parry [pǽriː] *vt* (blow) かわす kawásu

parsimonious [pɑːrsəmouníːəs] *adj* けちな kechí na

parsley [pɑːrsliː] *n* パセリ pásèri

parsnip [pɑːrsnip] *n* 白にんじん shironinjin, パースニップ pā́sunippù

parson [pɑːrsən] *n* (REL) 牧師 bókùshi

part [pɑːrt] *n* (section, division) 部分 búbun; (of machine, vehicle) 部品 buhín; (THEATER, CINEMA etc: role) 役 yakú; (PRESS, RADIO, TV: of serial) 第 ...部 dái...bù; (US: in hair) 分け目 wakéme
♦*adv* = **partly**
♦*vt* (separate: people, objects, hair) 分ける wakéru

♦*vi* (people: leave each other) 別れる wákarerù; (crowd) 道を開ける michí wo akerú

to take part in (participate in) ...に参加する ...ni sañka suru

to take something in good part ...を怒らない ...wo okóranaì

to take someone's part (support) ...の肩を持つ ...no kátà wo mótsù

for my part 私としては watákushi toshite wà

for the most part (usually, generally) ほとんどは hotóndo wa

part exchange *n* (BRIT: COMM) 下取りで shitádòri de

partial [pɑːrʃəl] *adj* (not complete: victory, support, solution) 部分的な bubúnteki na

to be partial to (like: person, food, drink etc) ...が大好きである ...ga daísukì de arù

participant [pɑːrtísəpənt] *n* (in competition, debate, campaign etc) 参加者 sañkashà

participate [pɑːrtísəpeit] *vi*: **to participate in** (competition, debate, campaign etc) ...に参加する ...ni sañka suru

participation [pɑːrtisəpéiʃən] *n* (in competition, debate, campaign etc) 参加 sañka

participle [pɑːrtisipəl] *n* (LING) 分詞 búñshi

particle [pɑːrtikəl] *n* (tiny piece: gen) 粒子 ryū́shi; (: of dust) 一片 ippéñ; (of metal) 砕片 saíhen; (of food) 粒 tsúbù

particular [pərtíkjələr] *adj* (distinct from others: person, time, place etc) 特定の tokútei no; (special) 特別な tokúbetsu na; (fussy, demanding) やかましい yakámashiī

in particular 特に tókù ni

particularly [pərtíkjələːliː] *adv* 特に tókù ni

particulars [pərtíkjələːrz] *npl* (facts) 詳細 shōsai; (personal details) 経歴 keíreki

parting [pɑːrtiŋ] *n* (action) 分ける事 wakérù kotó; (farewell) 別れ wakáre;

(BRIT: hair) 分け目 wakéme

♦adj (words, gift etc) 別れの wakáre no

partisan [pɑːrˈtizən] adj (politics, views) 党派心の tōhashín no

♦n (supporter) 支援者 shiénsha; (fighter) パルチザン parúchizàn

partition [pɑːrˈtiʃən] n (wall, screen) 間仕切 majîkìri; (POL: of country) 分割 buńkatsu

partly [pɑːrtˈliː] adv (to some extent) 幾分か ikúbun ka

partner [pɑːrtˈnəːr] n (wife, husband) 配偶者 haígùsha; (girlfriend, boyfriend) 交際の相手 kōsai no aíte; (COMM) 共同経営者 kyódōkeieìsha; (SPORT) パートナー pátònà; (at dance) 相手 aíte

partnership [pɑːrtˈnəːrʃip] n (COMM) 共同経営事業 kyódōkeieijigyō; (POL) 協力 kyóryoku

partridge [pɑːrˈtridʒ] n ウズラ uzúra

part-time [pɑːrtˈtaim] adj (work, staff) 非常勤の hijōkin no, パートタイムの pátotaìmu no

♦adv (work, study) パートタイムで pátotaìmu de

part with vt fus (money, possessions) ...を手放す ...wo tebánasù

party [pɑːrˈtiː] n (POL) 政党 seftō; (celebration, social event) パーティ pátì; (group of people) 一行 ikkō, パーティ pátì; (LAW) 当事者 tōjìsha; (individual) 人 hitó

♦cpd (POL) 党の tō no

party dress n パーティドレス pátìdorèsu

party line n (TEL) 共同線 kyódōsen

pass [pæs] vt (spend: time) 過ごす sugósù; (hand over: salt, newspaper etc) 渡す watásù; (go past: place) 通り過ぎる tōrisugírù; (overtake: car, person etc) 追越す oíkosù; (exam) ...に合格する ...ni gōkaku suru; (approve: law, proposal) 可決する kakétsu suru

♦vi (go past, stand in line) 通る tōrù; (in exam) 合格する gōkaku suru, パスする pású suru

♦n (permit, identity: membership card) 会員証 kaíinshō; (in mountains) 峠 tōge; (SPORT) パス pású;

(SCOL: also: pass mark): **to get a pass in** ...で及第する ...de kyūdai suru, ...でパスする ...de pású suru

to pass something through something ...を...に通す ...wo ...ni tōsu

to make a pass at someone (inf) ...にモーションを掛ける ...ni mōshon wo kakérù

passable [pæsˈəbəl] adj (road) 通行できる tsūkō dekirù; (acceptable: work) まずまずの mázumazu no

passage [pæsˈidʒ] n (also: passageway: indoors) 廊下 rōka; (: outdoors) 通路 tsūro; (in book) 一節 issétsu; (ANAT): **the nasal passages** 鼻 こう bikō; (act of passing) 通過 tsūka; (journey: on boat) 船旅 funátabi

pass away vi (die) 死ぬ shinú

passbook [pæsˈbuk] n 銀行通帳 giñkōtsūchō

pass by vi (go past) ...のそばを通る ...no sóba wo tōru

♦vt (ignore) 無視する múshi suru

passenger [pæsˈindʒəːr] n (in car, boat, plane etc) 乗客 jōkyaku

passer-by [pæsˈəːrbaiˈ] n 通行人 tsūkōnin

pass for vt fus ...で通る ...de tōru

passing [pæsˈiŋ] adj (fleeting: moment, glimpse, thought etc) 束の間の tsuká no ma no

in passing (incidentally) ついでに tsufde ni

passing place n (AUT) 待避所 taíhijo

passion [pæsˈən] n (love: for person) 情欲 jōyoku; (fig: for cars, football, politics etc) 熱狂 nekkyō、マニア mánìa

passionate [pæsˈənit] adj (affair, embrace, person etc) 情熱的な jōnetsuteki na

passive [pæsˈiv] adj (person, resistance) 消極的な shōkyokuteki na; (LING) 受動態の judōtai no, 受け身の ukémi no

pass on vt (news, object) 伝える tsutáerù; (illness) 移す utsúsu

Passover [pæsˈouvəːr] n 過越し祭 sugíkoshisai

passport [pæsˈpɔːrt] n (official document) 旅券 ryokén, パスポート pasúpòto

passport control n 出入国管理所 shutsúnyūkoku kanrijo

pass up vt (decline) 逃す nogásù

password [pǽs'wə:rd] n (secret word, phrase) 合言葉 aíkotòba, パスワード pasúwàdo

past [pæst] prep (drive, walk, run: in front of) ...を通り過ぎて ...wo tōrisugìte; (: beyond: also in time: later than) ...を過ぎて ...wo sugíte
◆adj (previous: government, monarch etc) 過去の kákò no; (: week, month etc) この前の konó maè no, 先... saki...
◆n (period and events prior to the present: also of person) 過去 kákò
he's past forty (older than) 彼は40才を過ぎている kárè wa yonjússaí wo sugíte irù

ten/quarter past eight 8時10分 [15分] 過ぎ hachíji juppún [jūgòfun]sugí

for the past few/3 days この数日 [3日] の間 konó sùjitsu(mikka) no aída

pasta [pɑ:s'tə] n パスタ pásùta

paste [peist] n (wet mixture) 練り物 nerímòno; (glue) の り norí; (CULIN: fish, meat, tomato etc paste) ペースト pḗsuto
◆vt (stick: paper, label, poster etc) 張る harú

pastel [pæstel'] adj (color) パステルの pásùteru no

pasteurized [pæs'tʃəraizd] adj (milk, cream) 低温殺菌された teíonsakkìn sareta

pastille [pæsti:l'] n (sweet) ドロップ dóròppu

pastime [pæs'taim] n (hobby) 趣味 shúmì

pastoral [pæs'tərəl] adj (REL: duties, activities) 牧師としての bókùshi toshite no

pastry [peis'tri:] n (dough) 生地 kíjì; (cake) 洋菓子 yōgàshi, ケーキ kḗki

pasture [pæs'tʃər] n (grassland) 牧場 bokújò

pasty [n pæs'ti: adj peis'ti:] n (meat and vegetable pie) ミートパイ mítòpài
◆adj (complexion, face) 青ざめた aóza-

metá

pat [pæt] vt (with hand: dog, someone's back etc) 軽くたたく karúkù tatákù

patch [pætʃ] n (piece of material) 継ぎ tsugí; (also: **eye patch**) 眼帯 gańtai; (area: damp, bald, black etc) 一部 ichíbù; (repair: on tire etc) 継ぎはぎ tsugíhàgi
◆vt (clothes) ...に継ぎを当てる ...ni tsugí wo atérù

to go through a bad patch 不運の時期 に合う fúùn no jíkì ni áù

patch up vt (mend temporarily) 応急的に直す ōkyūteki ni naosú; (quarrel) ...をやめて仲直りする ...wo yamétè nakánaori surú

patchwork [pætʃ'wə:rk] n (SEWING) パッチワーク patchíwàku

patchy [pætʃ'i:] adj (uneven: color) むらの多い murá no ōi; (incomplete: information, knowledge etc) 不完全な fukánzen na

pâté [pɑːtei'] n パテ páté の肉, 魚などを香辛料とすり合せて蒸焼きにして冷ました物 niků, sakaná nadò wo koshíńryō to surÁwasete mushíyàki ni shité samáshita monò

patent [pæt'ənt] n (COMM) 特許 tókkyo
◆vt (COMM) ...の特許を取る ...no tókkyo wo tórù
◆adj (obvious) 明白な meíhaku na

patent leather n: **patent leather shoes** エナメル靴 enámerugùtsu

paternal [pətər'nəl] adj (love, duty) 父親の chichíoya no; (grandmother etc) 父方の chichígata no

paternity [pətər'niti:] n 父親である事 chichíoya de arù kotó

path [pæθ] n (trail, track) 小道 kómìchi; (concrete path, gravel path etc) 道 michí; (of planet, missile) 軌道 kidō

pathetic [pəθet'ik] adj (pitiful: sight, cries) 哀れな áware na; (very bad) 哀れな程悪い áware na hodò warui

pathological [pæθəlɑdʒ'ikəl] adj (liar, hatred) 病的な byóteki na; (of pathology: work) 病理の byōri no

pathology [pəθɑːl'ədʒi:] n (medical field) 病理学 byōrigàku

pathos [pei'θɔs] *n* 悲哀 híái

pathway [pæ'θwei] *n* (path) 歩道 hodô

patience [pei'ʃəns] *n* (personal quality)
忍耐 níñtai; (*BRIT*: CARDS) 一人トランプ
hitóritorañpu

patient [pei'ʃənt] *n* (MED) 患者 kañja
♦*adj* (person) 忍耐強い níñtaizuyoi

patio [pæt'i:ou] *n* テラス têrasu

patriot [pei'tri:ət] *n* 愛国者 aíkokusha

patriotic [peitri:ɑt'ik] *adj* (person) 愛国
心の強い aíkokushin no tsuyói; (song,
speech etc) 愛国の aíkoku no

patriotism [pei'tri:ətizəm] *n* 愛国心 aíkokushin

patrol [pətroul'] *n* (MIL, POLICE) 巡回
juñkai, パトロール patórōru
♦*vt* (MIL, POLICE: city, streets etc) 巡
回する juñkai suru, パトロールする patórōru suru

patrol car *n* (POLICE) パトカー patókā

patrolman [pətroul'mən] (*pl* **patrolmen**:
US) *n* (POLICE) 巡査 juñsa

patron [pei'trən] *n* (customer, client) 客
kyakú; (benefactor: of charity) 後援者 kō-
eñsha

patron of the arts 芸術のパトロン geí-
jùtsu no pátóron

patronage [pei'trənidʒ] *n* (of artist,
charity etc) 後援 kōen

patronize [pei'trənaiz] *vt* (*pej*: look
down on) 尊大にあしらう soñdai ni ashí-
raù; (artist, writer, musician) 後援する
kōen suru; (shop, club, firm) ひいきにす
る hiíki ni surù

patron saint *n* (REL) 守護聖人 shugó-
seijin

patter [pæt'ə:r] *n* (sound: of feet) ぱたぱ
たという音 pátapata to iú oto; (of rain)
パラパラという音 párápara to iú oto;
(sales talk) 売込み口上 uríkomikōjō
♦*vi* (footsteps) ぱたぱたと歩く pátapata
to arúkù; (rain) ぱらぱらと降る párápara to fúrù

pattern [pæt'ə:rn] *n* (design) 模様 moyō;
(SEWING) 型紙 katágami, パターン pa-
táñ

paunch [pɔːntʃ] *n* 太鼓腹 taíkobara

pauper [pɔː'pə:r] *n* 貧乏人 biñbōnin

pause [pɔːz] *n* (temporary halt) 休止 kyū́-
shi, ポーズ pōzu
♦*vi* (stop temporarily) 休止する kyūshi
suru; (: while speaking) 間を置く má wo
okú

pave [peiv] *vt* (street, yard etc) 舗装する
hosō suru

to pave the way for (*fig*) ...を可能にす
る ...wo kanō ni suru

pavement [peiv'mənt] *n* (*US*) 路面 romén;
(*BRIT*) 歩道 hodō

pavilion [pəvil'jən] *n* (*BRIT*: SPORT)
選手更衣所 señshukōijo

paving [pei'viŋ] *n* (material) 舗装材 ho-
sōzai

paving stone *n* 敷石 shikíishi

paw [pɔː] *n* (of animal) 足 ashí

pawn [pɔːn] *n* (CHESS) ポーン pōñ; (*fig*)
操り人形 ayátsurinñgyō
♦*vt* 質に入れる shichí ni irérù

pawnbroker [pɔːn'broukə:r] *n* 質屋 shí-
chíya

pawnshop [pɔːn'ʃɑp] *n* 質屋 shichíya

pay [pei] *n* (wage, salary etc) 給料 kyū́-
ryō
♦*vb* (*pt, pp* **paid**)
♦*vt* (sum of money, debt, bill, wage) 払
う haraú
♦*vi* (be profitable) 利益になる ríeki ni
nárù

to pay attention (to) (...に) 注意する
(...ni) chūi suru

to pay someone a visit ...を訪問する
...wo hōmon suru

to pay one's respects to someone ...に
あいさつをする ...ni áisatsu wo surú

payable [pei'əbəl] *adj* (sum of money) 支
払うべき支払warbeki

payable to bearer (check) 持参人払い
の jisánninbarai no

pay back *vt* (money) 返す kaésù; (person) ...に仕返しをする ...ni shikáeshi wo
suru

payday [pei'dei] *n* 給料日 kyūryōbi

payee [peii:'] *n* (of check, postal order)
受取人 ukétorinñ

pay envelope (*US*) *n* 給料袋 kyūryōbu-
kùro

pay for vt fus (purchases) ...の代金を払う...no daíkin wò haraú; (fig) 償う tsugunaú

pay in vt (money, check etc) 預け入れる azúkeirerú, 入金する nyúkin suru

payment [pei'mant] n (act) 支払い shiháraí; (amount of money) 支払い金額 shiháraikingaku

a monthly payment 月賦 géppu

pay off vt (debt) 返済する heńsai suru; (person: with bribe etc) 買収する baíshū suru

♦vi (scheme, decision) 成功する seíkō suru

pay packet (BRIT) n = **pay envelope**

pay phone n 公衆電話 kōshúdeñwa

payroll [pei'roul] n 従業員名簿 jūgyóiňmeibo

pay slip n 給料明細書 kyúryōmeísaisho

pay up vt 払う haraú

PC [pi:si:'] n abbr = **personal computer**; (BRIT: = *police constable*) 巡査 júňsa

p.c. abbr = **per cent**

pea [pi:] n エンドウマメ eňdōmame

peace [pi:s] n (not war) 平和 heíwa; (calm: of place, surroundings) 静けさ shizúkesà; (: personal) 心の平和 kokóro no heíwa

peaceful [pi:s'fəl] adj (calm: place, time) 静寂な seíjaku na; (: person) 穏和な owá na

peach [pi:tʃ] n モモ momó

peacock [pi:'kɑːk] n クジャク kujáku

peak [pi:k] n (of mountain: top) 頂上 chốjō; (of cap) つば tsúba; (fig: physical, intellectual etc) 頂点 chóten, ピーク píku

peak hours npl ピーク時 pfku-ji

peak period n ピーク時 píkuji

peal [pi:l] n (of bells) 響き híbïki

peal of laughter 大きな笑い声 ōkìna waráigòe

peanut [pi:'nʌt] n 落花生 rakkáseì, ピーナッツ pínattsù

peanut butter n ピーナッツバター pínattsubatā

pear [pe:r] n セイヨウナシ seíyōnashì

pearl [pɔːrl] n 真珠 shíñju, パール pāru

peasant [pez'ənt] n 百姓 hyakúshō, 農夫

nốfu

peat [pi:t] n 泥炭 deítan

pebble [peb'əl] n 小石 koíshi

peck [pek] vt (also: **peck at**: subj: bird) つつく tsutsúkú

♦n (of bird) つつき tsutsúkú kotó; (kiss) 軽いキス karúi kísù

pecking order [pek'iŋ-] n (fig: hierarchy) 序列 jorétsu

peckish [pek'iʃ] (BRIT: inf) adj (hungry): *to be peckish* おなかがすいた onáka ga suíta

peculiar [pikju:l'jɑːr] adj (strange: person, taste, shape etc) 変った kawátta; (belonging exclusively): *peculiar to* 独特な dokútoku na

peculiarity [pikju:li:ær'iti:] n (strange habit, characteristic) 癖 kusé; (distinctive feature: of person, place etc) 特徴 tokúchō

pedal [ped'əl] n (on bicycle, car, machine) ペダル pédàru

♦vi (on bicycle) こぐ kógù

pedantic [pədæn'tik] adj げん学的な geñgakuteki na

peddler [ped'lər] n (also: **drug peddler**) 麻薬の売人 mayáku nò baínin

pedestal [ped'istal] n 台座 daíza

pedestrian [pədes'tri:ən] n 歩行者 hokốshà

♦adj 歩行者の hokốshà no

pedestrian crossing (BRIT) n 横断歩道 ōdañhodō

pediatrics [pi:di:æt'riks] (BRIT **paediatrics**) n (hospital department) 小児科 shōnika; (subject) 小児科学 shōnikagaku

pedigree [ped'əgri:] n (of animal) 血統 kettō; (fig: background) 経歴 keíreki

♦cpd (animal) 純血の juńketsu no

pee [pi:] (inf) vi (urinate) ...する o-shíkkò suru

peek [pi:k] vi のぞく nozóku

peel [pi:l] n (of orange, apple, potato) 皮 kawá

♦vt (vegetables, fruit) ...の皮をむく ...no kawá wo muku

♦vi (paint, wallpaper) はげる hagérù; (skin) むける mukérù

peep [pi:p] n (look) のぞき見 nozōkimi; (sound) 囁き声 nakígoè
♦vi (look) のぞく nozóku

peephole [pi:p'houl] n のぞき穴 nozōkiàna

peep out vi (be visible) のぞく nozóku

peer [pi:r] vi: *to peer at* ...をじっと見る ...wo jittò mírù
♦n (noble) 貴族 kízoku; (equal) 同等の人 dōtō nò hitó; (contemporary) 同輩 dōhai

peerage [pi:r'id3] n (rank) 貴族の地位 kízoku no chíi

peeved [pi:vd] adj (annoyed) 怒った okóttà

peevish [pi:'viʃ] adj (bad-tempered) 機嫌の悪い kigén nò warúì

peg [peg] n (hook, knob: for coat etc) フック fúkkû; (BRIT: also: clothes peg) 洗濯ばさみ seńtakubasàmi

pejorative [pidʒɔr'ativ] adj (word, expression) 軽べつ的な keíbetsuteki na

Peking [pi:kiŋ'] n 北京 pékīn

Pekin(g)ese [pi:kəniz'] n (dog) ペキニーズ pekínīzu

pelican [pel'ikən] n (ZOOL) ペリカン períkàn

pelican crossing (BRIT) n (AUT) 押しボタン式信号 oshíbotanshìki shíngō

pellet [pel'it] n (of paper, mud etc) 丸めた球 marúmeta tamá; (also: shotgun pellet) 散弾銃の弾 sańdajū no tamá

pelt [pelt] vt: *to pelt someone with something* ...に...を浴びせ掛ける ...ni ...wo abísekakerù
♦vi (rain) 激しく降りしきる fúrù; (inf: run) 駆ける kakérù
♦n (animal hide) 毛皮 kegáwa

pelvis [pel'vis] n 骨盤 kotsúban

pen [pen] n (for writing: fountain pen, ballpoint pen) ペン péñ; (: felt-tip pen etc) サインペン saíñpen; (enclosure: for sheep, pigs etc) 囲い kakói

penal [pi:'nəl] adj (colony, institution) 刑罰の kefbatsu no; (system, code, reform) 刑法の keñhō no

penalize [pi:'nəlaiz] vt (punish) 罰する bassúrù; (: SPORT) ...にペナルティーを科する ...ni penárutī no kasúrù

penalty [pen'əlti:] n (punishment) 罰 bátsù; (fine) 罰金 bakkín; (SPORT) ペナルティー penáruti

penalty (kick) n (RUGBY, SOCCER) ペナルティーキック penárutī kikkù

penance [pen'əns] n 償い tsugúnai

pence [pens] pl of penny

pencil [pen'səl] n (for writing, drawing) 鉛筆 eñpitsu

pencil case n 筆入れ fudéìre

pencil sharpener n 鉛筆削り eñpitsukezúri, シャープナー shāpunā

pendant [pen'dənt] n ペンダント péñdanto

pending [pen'diŋ] prep ...を待つ間 ...wo mátsù aída
♦adj (business) 未決の míketsu no; (lawsuit) 審理中の shińrichū no; (exam) 差迫った sashísemattà

pendulum [pen'dʒələm] n (of clock) 振子 furíko

penetrate [pen'itreit] vt (subj: person: enemy territory) ...に侵入する ...ni shíñnyū suru; (forest etc) ...に入り込む ...ni hañrikomū; (: water etc) 染込む shimíkomū; (: light) 通る tōru

penetrating [pen'itreitiŋ] adj (sound, glance, mind, observation) 鋭い surúdoi

penetration [penitrei'ʃən] n (action) 入り込み事 hañrikomō kotó

penfriend [pen'frend] (BRIT) n = pen pal

penguin [peŋ'gwin] n ペンギン péñgin

penicillin [penisil'in] n ペニシリン peníshirin

peninsula [pənin'sələ] n 半島 hañtō

penis [pi:'nis] n 陰茎 íñkei, ペニス pénis

penitent [pen'itənt] adj (person: very sorry) 後悔している kōkai shite irú

penitentiary [peniten'tʃəri:] n (US) 刑務所 kefmushò

penknife [pen'naif] n ペンナイフ peñnafu

pen name n ペンネーム peñnēmu

penniless [pen'i:lis] adj (person) 一文無し ichímoñnashi no

penny [pen'i:] n (pl pennies or BRIT pence) n (US) ペニー péní, セント séñto

(BRIT: after 1971: = one hundredth of a pound) ペニ peni

pen pal n ペンパル péñparu, ペンフレンド peñfureñdo

pension [pen'tʃən] n (state benefit) 年金 neñkin; (company pension etc) 恩給 oñkyū

pensioner [pen'tʃənər] n (old-age pensioner) 年金で生活する老人 neñkin de sefkatsu surù rōjin, 年金暮らしの人 neñkingurashì no hitó

pension fund n 年金基金 neñkinkikiñ

pensive [pen'siv] adj (person, expression etc) 考え込んだ kañgaekoñda

pentagon [pen'təgɑn] n: **the Pentagon** (US: POL) 国防総省 kokúbōsōshō, ペンタゴン peñtàgon

Pentecost [pen'təkɔːst] n 聖霊降臨祭 seíreikōriñsai

penthouse [pen'haus] n (flat) 屋上階 okūjōkai

pent-up [pent'ʌp'] adj (feelings) たまった tamáttà

penultimate [pinʌl'təmit] adj 最後から2番目の sáigo kara nibáñme no

people [piː'pəl] npl (persons) 人々 hitóbìto; (inhabitants) 住民 júmin; (citizens) 市民 shímìn; (POL): **the people** 国民 kokúmin

◆n (nation) 国民 kokúmin; (race) 民族 míñzoku

several people came 数人来ました sūnin kimashìta

people say that ... だと言われている ...da to iwárète irū, ...だそうです ...da sō da

pep [pep] (inf) n (energy, vigor) 元気 geñki

pepper [pep'əːr] n (spice) こしょう koshō; (hot pepper) トウガラシ tōgàrashi; (sweet pepper) ピーマン pímàn

◆vt (fig): **to pepper with ...** を振掛ける ...wo furíkakerù

peppermint [pep'əːrmint] n (sweet) ハッカあめ hakkáàme

peptalk [pep'tɔːk] (inf) n (encouraging talk) 激励演説 gekíreieñsetsù

pep up vt (enliven) 活気付ける kakkízukerù

per [pəːr] prep (of amounts, prices etc: for each) ...につき ...ni tsukí

per day/person 1日(1人)につき ... ichíníchi(hitórì) ni tsukí...

per annum 1年につき ... ichínèn ni tsukí...

per capita [-kæp'itə] adj (income) 一人当りの hitórì atarì no

◆adv 一人当り hitórì atarì

perceive [pəːrsiːv'] vt (sound) 聞く kíkù; (light) 見る mírù; (difference) 認識する nifishiki suru; (notice) ...に気が付く ...ni ki ga tsukú; (realize, understand) 分かる wakáru

per cent n パーセント páseñto

percentage [pəːrsen'tidʒ] n (amount) 割合 waríai, 率 rítsù

perception [pəːrsep'ʃən] n (insight) 洞察力 dōsatsuryòku; (opinion, understanding) 理解 rikái; (faculty) 知覚 chikáku

perceptive [pəːrsep'tiv] adj (person) 洞察力のある dōsatsuryòku no árù, 鋭敏な efbin na; (analysis, assessment) 鋭い surúdoì

perch [pəːrtʃ] n (for bird) 止り木 tomárigì; (fish) パーチ pāchi ◇スズキに似た淡水魚 suzúkì ni nità tañsuigyò

◆vi: **to perch (on)** (bird) (...に) 止る (...ni) tomárù; (person) (...に) 腰掛ける (...ni) koshíkakerù

percolator [pəːr'kəleitəːr] n (also: **coffee percolator**) パーコレーター pākorètā

percussion [pəːrkʌʃ'ən] n 打楽器 dagákkì ◇総称 sōshō

peremptory [pəremp'təːri] (pej) adj (person) 横柄な ōhei na; (order, instruction) 断固たる dañkotarù

perennial [pəren'iːəl] adj (flower, plant) 多年生の tanéñsei no; (fig: problem, feature etc) ありがちな arígachi na

perfect [adj, n pəːr'fikt vb pəːrfekt'] adj (without fault: person, weather, behavior etc) 完璧な kañpeki na; (utter: nonsense, stranger etc) 全くの mattáku no

◆n (also: **perfect tense**) 完了形 kañryōkei

◆*vt* (technique) 仕上げる shiágerù

perfection [pərfék'ʃən] *n* (faultlessness) 完璧さ kańpekisa

perfectionist [pərfék'ʃənist] *n* 完璧主義者 kańpekishugìsha

perfectly [pər'fiktli] *adv* (emphatic) 全く mattáku; (faultlessly: perform, do etc) 完璧に kańpeki ni; (completely: understand etc) 完全に kańzen ni

perforate [pər'fəreit] *vt* ...に穴を開ける ...ni aná wo akérù

perforations [pərfərei'ʃənz] *npl* (series of small holes) ミシン目 mishíñme

perform [pərfɔːrm'] *vt* (carry out: task, operation, ceremony etc) 行う okónaù, する surú; (piece of music) 演奏する eñsō suru; (play) 上演する jóen suru

◆*vi* (well, badly) する surú, やる yarú

performance [pərfɔːr'məns] *n* (of actor) 演技 eñgi; (of dancer) 踊り odóri; (of musician) 演奏 eñsō; (of singer) 歌い方 utáikata; (of play, show) 上演 jóen; (of car, engine) 性能 seínō; (of athlete, company, economy) 成績 seíseki

performer [pərfɔːr'mər] *n* (actor, dancer, singer etc) 芸能人 geínōjiñ

perfume [pər'fjuːm] *n* (cologne, toilet water, essence) 香水 kōsui; (pleasant smell: of flowers etc) 香り kaóri

perfunctory [pərfʌŋk'təriː] *adj* (kiss, remark etc) いい加減な ifkagen na

perhaps [pərhæps'] *adv* (maybe) たぶん tábùn, だろう tábùn ...daró

peril [per'əl] *n* (great danger) 危険 kikén

perimeter [pərim'itər] *n* 周辺 shūhen

period [piːr'iːəd] *n* (length of time) 期間 kikán; (SCOL) 時限 jigén; (full stop) 終止符 shūshifu, ピリオド píriòdo; (MED) 月経 gekkéì, メンス méñsu, 生理 seíri

◆*adj* (costume, furniture etc) 時代の jidái no

periodic(al) [piːriːɑːd'ik(əl)] *adj* (event, occurrence) 周期的な shūkiteki na, 定期的な teíkiteki na

periodical [piːriːɑːd'ikəl] *n* (magazine) 雑誌 zasshī

periodically [piːriːɑːd'ikliː] *adv* 定期的に teíkiteki ni

peripheral [pərif'əːrəl] *adj* 二次的な níji-

teki na; (on the edge: *also* COMPUT) 周辺の shūhen no

◆*n* (COMPUT) 周辺機器 shūhenkikì

periphery [pərif'əːriː] *n* (edge) 周辺 shūhen

periscope [per'iskoup] *n* 潜望鏡 señbōkyō

perish [per'iʃ] *vi* (die) 死ぬ shinú; (die out) 滅びる horóbirù; (rubber, leather etc) 腐る kusárù

perishable [per'iʃəbəl] *adj* (food) いたみやすい itámiyasuì

perjury [pər'dʒəːriː] *n* (LAW) 偽証 gishō

perk [pəːrk] (*inf*) *n* (extra) 役得 yakútoku

perk up *vi* (cheer up) 元気を出す geñki wo dásù

perky [pəːr'kiː] *adj* (cheerful) 朗らかな hogáraka na

perm [pəːrm] *n* (for hair) パーマ pãma

permanent [pər'mənənt] *adj* 永久的な eíkyūteki na

permeate [pər'miːeit] *vi* (pass through) 浸透する shiñtō suru; (*fig*: spread) 広がる hirógarù

◆*vt* (subj: liquid) ...に染込む ...ni shimíkomù; (: idea) ...に広まる ...ni hirómarù

permissible [pərmis'əbəl] *adj* (action, behavior) 許される yurúsarerù

permission [pərmiʃ'ən] *n* (consent, authorization) 許可 kyóka

permissive [pərmis'iv] *adj* (person, behavior, society) 甘い amáì

permit [*n* pər'mit *vb* pəːrmit'] *n* (official authorization) 許可証 kyokáshō

◆*vt* (allow) 許可する kyóka suru; (make possible) 可能にする kanó ni surù

permutation [pəːrmjətei'ʃən] *n* 置換え o-kíkae

pernicious [pərniʃ'əs] *adj* (very harmful: attitude, influence etc) 有害な yūgai na; (MED) 悪性の akúsei no

perpendicular [pəːrpəndik'jələːr] *adj* (line, surface) 垂直の suíchoku no; (cliff, slope) 険しい kewáshiì

perpetrate [pər'pitreit] *vt* (commit: crime) おかす okásù

perpetual [pərpetʃ'uːəl] *adj* (constant:

motion, darkness) 永久の eʃkyu no; (: noise, questions) 年から年中の negfaraneñjū no

perpetuate [pərˈpetʃʊeit] vt (situation, custom, belief etc) 永続させる eʃzoku saserŭ

perplex [pərˈpleks'] vt (person) まごつかせる magótsukaserŭ

persecute [pərˈsəkjuːt] vt (harass, oppress: minorities etc) 迫害する hakŭgai suru

persecution [pərˈsəkjuːʃən] n (of minorities etc) 迫害 hakŭgai

perseverance [pərˈsəviˈrəns] n 根気 koñki

persevere [pərˈsəviːr'] vi 辛抱強く続ける shifñbōzuyokŭ tsuzŭkerŭ

Persian [pərˈʒən] adj ペルシアの pérŭshia no
♦n ペルシア人 pérŭshiajĭn
the (Persian) Gulf ペルシア湾 pérŭshiawan

persist [pərˈsist'] vi: to persist (in doing something) (…をし) 続ける (…wo shi]tsuzŭkerŭ

persistence [pərˈsistəns] n (determination) 根気強さ koñkizuyŏsa

persistent [pərˈsistənt] adj (noise, smell, cough etc) いつまでも続く ftsŭmademo tsuzŭkŭ; (person: determined) 根気強い koñkizuyoĭ

person [pərˈsən] n 人 hitó
in person (appear, sing, recite etc) 本人が hoñnin ga

personal [pərˈsənəl] adj (belongings, phone etc) 個人の kojĭn no; (opinion, life, habits etc) 個人的な kojĭntekĭ na; (in person: visit) 本人自身の hoñninjishĭn no

personal assistant n 秘書 hishŏ

personal call n (TEL) 私用の電話 shiyŏ no deñwa

personal column n 私信欄 shishĭnraň

personal computer n パーソナルコンピュータ pâsonarukoñpyûta, パソコン pasókon

personality [pərˈsənælˈitiˌ] n (character) 人格 jiñkaku; (famous person) 有名人 yūmeijĭn

personally [pərˈsənəliˌ] adv (for my etc part) 個人的には kojĭntekĭ ni wà; (in person) 本人が hoñnin ga
to take something personally …を個人攻撃と受止める …wo kojĭnkōgekĭ to ukétomerŭ

personal organizer n 予定帳 yotéichŏ

personify [pərˈsanˈəfaiˌ] vt (evil) …の権化である …no góñge de árŭ; (good) …の化身である …no késhĭn de árŭ

personnel [pərˈsənelʹ] n 職員 shokŭin ♦総称 sôshŏ

perspective [pərˈspekˈtiv] n (ARCHIT, ART) 遠近法 eñkinhŏ; (way of thinking) 見方 mikáta
to get something into perspective (fig) 事情を考えて…を見る jijŏ wŏ kañgaetè …wo mírŭ

Perspex [pərˈspeks] ® n アクリル ákŭriru

perspiration [pərˈspəreiʃən] n 汗 ásè

persuade [pərˈsweidʹ] vt: to persuade someone to do something …する様に…を説き伏せる …surŭ yŏ ni …wo tokífuserŭ

persuasion [pərˈsweiʒən] n (act) 説得 settŏku; (creed) 信条 shifñjŏ

persuasive [pərˈsweisivˈ] adj (person, argument) 説得力のある settŏkŭryoku no árŭ

pertaining [pərˈteinˈiŋ]: pertaining to prep (relating to) …に関する …ni kañ suru

pertinent [pərˈtənənt] adj (answer, remark) 適切な tekísetsŭ na

perturb [pərˈtəːrbʹ] vt (person) 不安にする fuán ni surŭ

Peru [pəruːʹ] n ペルー pérû

peruse [pəruːzʹ] vt (newspaper, documents etc) …に目を通す …ni mé wo tôsŭ

Peruvian [pəruːʹviˌən] adj ペルーの pérû no
♦n ペルー人 pérûjĭn

pervade [pərˈveidʹ] vt (subj: smell, feeling) …に充満する …ni jûman suru

perverse [pərˈvəːrsʹ] adj (contrary: behavior) 天のじゃくの amá no jàku no

perversion [pərˈvəːrʹʒən] n (sexual) 変態

heftai; (of truth) 曲解 kyokkái; (of justice) 悪用 akúyó

pervert [n pəːr'vəːrt vb pərvəːrt'] n (sexual pervert) 変態 heftai
♦vt (person, mind) 堕落させる daráku saseru; (truth, someone's words) 曲解する kyokkái suru

pessimism [pes'əmizəm] n 悲観主義 hikánshùgi, ペシミズム peshímizùmu

pessimist [pes'əmist] n 悲観主義者 hikánshugisha, ペシミスト peshímisùto

pessimistic [pesəmis'tik] adj (person) 悲観的な hikánteki na, ペシミスティックな peshímisutikkù na

pest [pest] n (insect) 害虫 gaíchū; (fig: nuisance) うるさいやつ urúsai yatsù

pester [pes'təːr] vt (bother) 悩ませる nayámaserù

pesticide [pes'tisaid] n 殺虫剤 satchúzai

pet [pet] n (domestic animal) 愛がん動物 aígandóbutsu, ペット péttò
♦cpd (theory, hate etc) 十八番の ohákò no
♦vt (stroke: person, animal) 愛ぶする aíbu suru
♦vi (inf: sexually) ペッティングする pettíngu suru

teacher's pet (favorite) 先生のお気に入り seńsei nò o-kí nì irí

petal [pet'əl] n 花びら hanábira

peter [piː'təːr] vi: **peter out** vi (road, stream etc) だんだんなくなる dańdan nakúnarù; (conversation, meeting) しりすぼまりに終る shirísubomarì ni owáru

petite [pətiːt'] adj (referring to woman: small) 小柄な kogára na

petition [pətiʃ'ən] n (signed document) 陳情書 chifjóshò; (LAW) 請願 seígan

petrified [pet'rəfaid] adj (fig: terrified) 恐怖に駆られた kyófu nì karárèta

petrol [pet'rəl] (BRIT) n (fuel) ガソリン gasórin

two/four-star petrol レギュラー(ハイオク)ガソリン regyùrà(haíoku)gasórin

petrol can n ガソリン缶 gasórinkàn

petroleum [pətrou'liːəm] n 石油 sekíyu

petrol pump (BRIT) n (in garage) ガソリンポンプ gasórinpoňpu

petrol station (BRIT) n ガソリンスタンド gasórinsutaňdo

petrol tank (BRIT) n ガソリンタンク gasórintaňku

petticoat [pet'iːkout] n (underskirt) ペチコート péchikòto

petty [pet'i] adj (small, unimportant) ささいな sásài na; (small-minded) 狭量な kyóryò na

petty cash n (in office) 小口現金 koguchigeňkin

petty officer n (in navy) 下士官 kashíkaň

petulant [petʃ'ələnt] adj せっかちな sekkáchi na

pew [pjuː] n (in church) 長いす nagáisu

pewter [pjuː'təːr] n 白鑞 shfrōme

phallic [fæl'ik] adj (object, symbol) 陰茎状の iňkeijō no

phantom [fæn'təm] n (ghost) お化け o-bákè

pharmaceutical [fɑːrməsuː'tikəl] adj 製薬の seíyaku no

pharmacist [fɑːr'məsist] n 薬剤師 yakúzaishi

pharmacy [fɑːr'məsi] n 薬局 yakkyòku

phase [feiz] n (stage) 段階 dańkai
♦vt: **to phase something in/out** ...を段階的に取入れる(なくす) ...wo dańkaiteki ni toríirerù (nakúsù)

Ph.D. [piː'eitʃ'diː'] abbr = Doctor of Philosophy

pheasant [fez'ənt] n キジ kijí

phenomena [finam'ənə] npl of phenomenon

phenomenal [finam'ənəl] adj 驚異的な kyóiteki na

phenomenon [finam'ənan] (pl phenomena) n 現象 geńshō

philanthropist [filæn'θrəpist] n 慈善家 jizéňka

Philippines [fil'ipiːnz] npl: the Philippines フィリピン fírìpin

philosopher [filas'əfəːr] n (scholar) 哲学者 tetsúgakushà

philosophical [filəsɑːf'ikəl] adj (ideas, conversation) 哲学的な tetsúgakuteki na; (fig: calm, resigned) 冷静な reísei na

写真複写機 shashínfukushakí, コピー機 kópíkí

philosophy [fɪlɑs'əfi:] *n* (SCOL) 哲学 tetsúgaku; (set of ideas: of philosopher) ...の哲学 ...no tetsúgaku; (theory: of any person) 考え方 kañgaekatá, 思想 shisō

◆*vt* (picture, document etc) ...のコピーを取る ...no kópí wo tórù

phlegm [flem] *n* (substance) たん tañ

photocopy [fou'təkɑ:pi:] *n* コピー kópí

phlegmatic [flegmæt'ik] *adj* (person) のろまな norôma na

photogenic [foutədʒen'ik] *adj* (person) 写真写りの良い shashín-utsurí no yóì

phobia [fou'bi:ə] *n* (irrational fear: of insects, flying, water etc) 恐怖症 kyốfushō

photograph [fou'təgræf] *n* 写真 shashín

◆*vt* (person, object, place etc) 撮影する satsúeí suru

phone [foun] *n* (system) 電話 deñwa; (apparatus) 電話器 deñwakí

photographer [fətɑːg'rəfəːr] *n* カメラマン kámeramañ

◆*vt* ...に電話を掛ける ...ni deñwa wo kakérù

photographic [foutəgræf'ik] *adj* (equipment etc) 写真の shashín no

to be on the phone (BRIT: possess a phone) 電話を持っている deñwa wo motté irù; (be calling) 電話中である deñwa-chū de árù

photography [fətɑg'rəfi:] *n* (art, subject) 写真撮影 shashíñsatsûei

phone back *vt* ...に電話を掛け直す ...ni deñwa wo kakénaosù

phrase [freiz] *n* (group of words, expression) 言葉 ifkatá; (LING) 句 ku

◆*vt* (express) 表現する hyôgeñ suru

◆*vt* 電話を掛け直す deñwa wo kakénaosù

phrase book *n* (foreign language aid) 表現集 hyôgeñshū

phone book *n* (directory) 電話帳 deñwachō

physical [fiz'ikəl] *adj* (of the body: needs, punishment, exercise etc) 肉体的の nikútaiteki ná; (geography, properties) 物理的な butsúriteki ná, (world, universe, object) 自然の shizén no; (sciences) 物理学の butsúrigaku no

phone booth *n* 電話ボックス deñwabokkûsu

phone box (BRIT) *n* 電話ボックス deñwabokkûsu

physical education *n* 体育 tafiku

phone call *n* 電話 deñwa

physically [fiz'ikli:] *adv* (fit, attractive) 肉体的に nikútaiteki ni

phone-in [foun'in] (BRIT) *n* (RADIO, TV) 視聴者が電話で参加する番組 shichōsha ga deñwa dè sañka suru bañgumî

physician [fiziʃ'ən] *n* (doctor) 医者 ishá

physicist [fiz'əsist] *n* 物理学者 butsúrigakushā

phonetics [fənet'iks] *n* 音声学 oñseigakú

physics [fiz'iks] *n* 物理学 butsúrigaku

phone up *vt* ...に電話を掛ける ...ni deñwa wo kakérù

physiology [fizi:ɑː'lədʒi:] *n* (science) 生理学 sefrigakú; (functioning: of animal, plant) 生理 sefri

◆*vi* 電話を掛ける deñwa wo kakérù

physiotherapy [fizi:ouθeːr'əpi:] *n* (MED) 物理療法 butsúriryōhō

phoney [fou'ni:] *adj* (false: address) 偽のいその nísò no; (: accent) 偽の nisé no; (: person) 信用できない shiñ-yō dekínaî

physique [fizik'] *n* (build: of person) 体格 tafkaku

phonograph [fou'nəgræf] (US) *n* 蓄音機 chíkúoñkí

pianist [pi:'ænist] *n* (MUS) ピアニスト piáni̇sutò

phosphorus [fɑs'fərəs] *n* りん fin

piano [pi:æn'ou] *n* (MUS) ピアノ piáno

photo [fou'tou] *n* (photograph) 写真 shashín

piccolo [pik'əlou] *n* (MUS) ピッコロ pikkóro

photocopier [fou'təkɑːpiːəːr] *n* (machine)

pick [pik] *n* (tool: also: **pick-axe**) つるはし tsurûhashì

♦vt (select) 選ぶ erábù; (gather: fruit, flowers) 摘むtsúmù; (remove, take) 取る tórù; (lock) こじ開けるkojíakerù

take your pick (choose) 選ぶ erábù

the pick of (best) ...からえり抜かれた物 ...kara erínukareta mónð

to pick one's nose/teeth 鼻[歯]をほじる hanå[há]wò hojírù

to pick a quarrel (with someone) (...に) けんかを売る (...ni) keñka wò urú

pick at vt fus (food) ちびちび食べる chíbichibi tabérù

picket [pik'it] n (in strike) ピケ píkè

♦vt (factory, workplace etc) ...にピケを張る ...ni píkè wò hárù

pickle [pik'əl] n (also: **pickles**: as condiment) ピクルス píkurusu; (fig: mess) 苦境 kukyṓ

♦vt (CULIN: in vinegar) 酢漬にするsu-zúke ni surú; (: in salt water) 塩漬にする shiōzuke ni surú

pick on vt fus (person: criticize) 非難する hínàn suru; (: treat badly) いじめる ijímerù

pick out vt (distinguish) 識別する shikíbetsu suru; (choose from a group) 選び出す erábidasù, ピックアップする píkkúappù suru

pickpocket [pik'pɑːkit] n すり súrì

pick up vi (improve: health, economy, trade) 良くなる yókù naru

♦vt (object: from floor) 拾う hirôu; (POLICE: arrest) 逮捕する taíhò suru; (collect: person, parcel etc) 引取る hikítorù; (AUT: passenger) 乗せる nosérù; (person: for sexual encounter) 引っ掛ける hikkákerù; (learn: language, skill etc) 覚える obóerù; (RADIO) 受信する jushín suru

to pick up speed 加速する kasóku suru

to pick oneself up (after falling etc) 起き上る okíagarù

pickup [pik'ʌp] n (small truck) ピックアップ píkkúappù

picnic [pik'nik] n (outdoor meal) ピクニック pikuníkku

picture [pik'tʃəːr] n (painting, drawing, print) 絵 é; (photograph) 写真 shashín;

(TV) 画像 gazṓ; (film) 映画 éìga; (fig: description) 描写 byṓsha; (: situation) 事態 jítài

♦vt (imagine) 想像する sṓzṓ suru

picture book n 絵本 ehóñ

pictures [pik'tʃəːz] (BRIT) npl: **the pictures** (cinema) 映画 éìga

picturesque [piktʃəresk'] adj (place, building) 風情のある fúzèi no árù

pie [pai] n (CULIN: vegetable, meat, fruit) パイ páì

piece [piːs] n (bit or part of larger thing) かけら kakéra; (portion of cake, chocolate, bread etc) 一切れ hitókìre; (length: of string, ribbon) 一本 íppòn; (item): **a piece of clothing/furniture/advice** 1つ hitótsú

♦vt: **to piece together** (information) 総合する sṓgō suru; (parts of a whole) 繋ぎ合せる tsugíawaserù

to take to pieces (dismantle) 分解する buńkai suru

piecemeal [piːs'miːl] adv (irregularly) 少しずつ sukóshizutsù

piecework [piːs'wəːrk] n (work) 出来高払いの仕事 dekídakabarài no shigóto

pie chart n 円形グラフ efikeiguráfu

pier [piːr] n 桟橋 sañbashi

pierce [piːrs] n (puncture: surface, material, skin etc) 貫通する kañtsū suru

piercing [piːrs'iŋ] adj (fig: cry) 甲高い kańdakaì; (: eyes, stare) 鋭い surúdoì; (: wind) 刺す様な sásù yō na

piety [pai'əti:] n (REL) 信心 shifjín

pig [pig] n (ZOOL) ブタ butá; (pej: unkind person) 畜生 chíkushō; (: greedy person) 欲張り目 yokúbarìme

pigeon [pidʒ'ən] n (bird) ハト hátò

pigeonhole [pidʒ'ənhoul] n (for letters, messages) 小仕切り kojíkìri

piggy bank [pig'iː-] n (money box) 貯金箱 chokífbako

pigheaded [pig'hedid] (pej) adj (stubborn) 頑固な gañko na

piglet [pig'lit] n 子ブタ kobúta

pigment [pig'mənt] n 色素 shíkìso

pigskin [pig'skin] n ブタのなめし革 butá no namèshigawa

pigsty [pig'stai] n (on farm) ブタ小屋 butágoya

pigtail [pig'teil] n (plait) お下げ o-ságe

pike [paik] n (fish) カワカマス kawákamàsu, パイク páiku

pilchard [pil'tʃərd] n (fish) イワシ iwáshi

pile [pail] n (heap, stack) 山 yamá; (of carpet, velvet) 毛足 keáshi, パイル páiru
♦vt (also: **pile up**) objects 積上げる tsumíageru
♦vi (also: **pile up**) objects 積重なる tsumíkasanaru; (problems, work) たまる tamáru

pile into vt fus (car) ...に乗込む ...ni noríkomù

piles [pailz] npl (MED) じ痔 jí

pile-up [pail'ʌp] n (AUT) 衝突事故 shốtotsujikò

pilfering [pil'fəriŋ] n (petty thieving) くすねる事 kusúneru kotó

pilgrim [pil'grim] n (REL) 巡礼者 juńreisha

pilgrimage [pil'grəmidʒ] n (REL) 巡礼 juńrei

pill [pil] n (MED: tablet) 錠剤 jốzai
the pill (contraceptive pill) 経口避妊薬 kefkôhinih-yaku, ピル pírù

pillage [pil'idʒ] vt (loot: house, town) 略奪する ryakúdatsu suru

pillar [pil'ər] n (ARCHIT) 柱 hashíra

pillar box (BRIT) n (MAIL) ポスト pósùto

pillion [pil'jən] n: **to ride pillion** (on motorcycle) 後ろに相乗りする ushíro ni aínori surù

pillory [pil'ɔːriː] vt (criticize strongly) 非難する hínan suru

pillow [pil'ou] n (cushion: for head) まくら makúra

pillowcase [pil'oukeis] n (cover: for pillow) 枕カバー makúrakabà, ピロケース pírōkèsu

pilot [pai'lət] n (AVIAT) 操縦士 sốjūshi, パイロット pốrotto
♦cpd (scheme, study etc) 試験的な shikénteki na
♦vt (aircraft) 操縦する sốjū suru

pilot light n (on cooker, boiler, fire) 口火 kuchíbi

pimp [pimp] n ポン引き pońbiki, ひも himó

pimple [pim'pəl] n にきび níkibi

pin [pin] n (metal: for attaching, fastening) ピン píñ
♦vt (fasten with pin) ピンで止める píñ de tomérù
pins and needles (in arms, legs etc) しびれが切れる事 shibíre gà kiréru kotó
to pin someone down (fig) ...に約束させる ...ni yakúsoku saserù, ...にくぎを刺す ...ni kugí wò sásù
to pin something on someone (fig) ...に...のぬれぎぬを着せる ...ni ...no nuréginù wo kiséru

pinafore [pin'əfɔːr] n (also: **pinafore dress**) エプロンドレス epúrondorèsu

pinball [pin'bɔːl] n (game) スマートボール sumátobòru; (machine) スマートボール機 sumátobòruki

pincers [pin'sərz] npl (TECH) やっとこ yattóko, ペンチ péńchi, (of crab, lobster etc) はさみ hasámi

pinch [pintʃ] n (small amount: of salt etc) 一つまみ hitótsumami
♦vt (person: with finger and thumb) つねる tsunérù; (inf: steal) くすねる kusúnerù
at a pinch 緊急の場合 kíñkyū no baái

pincushion [pin'kuʃən] n (SEWING) 針刺し harísashì

pine [pain] n (also: **pine tree**) マツ mátsù; (wood) マツ材 matsúzài
♦vi: **to pine for** (person, place) 思い焦がれる omóikogarerù

pineapple [pain'æpəl] n (fruit) パイナップル pańnappùru

pine away vi (gradually die) 衰弱して死ぬ sufjaku shite shinú

ping [piŋ] n (noise) ぴゅーんという音 pyúñ to iú otò

ping-pong [piŋ'pɔːŋ] ® n (sport) 卓球 takkyû, ピンポン píñpon

pink [piŋk] adj ピンク色の piñkuiro no
♦n (color) ピンク色 piñkuiro; (BOT) ナデシコ nadéshîko

pinnacle [pin'əkəl] n (of building, mountain) 天辺 teppén; (fig) 頂点 chōten

pinpoint [pin'point] vt (discover) 発見する hakkén suru; (explain) 説明する setsúmei suru; (position of something) 正確に示す seíkaku ni shimésů

pint [paint] n (US: = 473 cc; BRIT: = 568 cc) パイント paínto

a pint of beer, (BRIT:) *a pint* ビールパイント bíru ichípaínto

pin-up [pin'ʌp] n (picture) ピンナップ写真(絵) pínnappushashin(e)

pioneer [paiəniːr'] n (initiator: of scheme, science, method) 先駆者 seíkusha, パイオニア paíonia; (early settler) 開拓者 kaítakusha

pious [pai'əs] adj (person) 信心深い shínjinbukai

pip [pip] n (seed of fruit) 種 tané; (BRIT: time signal on radio) 時報 jihō

pipe [paip] n (gen, also for smoking) パイプ paípu; (also: water pipe) 水道管 suídōkan; (also: gas pipe) ガス管 gasúkan

♦vt (water, gas, oil) パイプで運ぶ paípu de hakóbu

pipes [paipz] npl also: **bagpipes**) バグパイプ bagúpaipu

pipe cleaner n パイプクリーナー paípukurīnā

pipe down (inf) vi (be quiet) 黙る damárù

pipe dream n (hope, plan) 夢想 musō

pipeline [paip'lain] n (for oil, gas) パイプライン paípuraìn

piper [pai'pər] n (bagpipe player) バグパイプ奏者 bagúpaipu sōsha

piping [pai'piŋ] adj: **piping hot** (water, food, coffee) うんと熱い ûnto atsúi

piquant [piː'kənt] adj (food: spicy) ぴりっとした pirîttó shitá; (fig: interesting, exciting) 興味深い kyōmibukai

pique [piːk] n 立腹 rippúku

pirate [pai'rit] n (sailor) 海賊 kaízoku

♦vt (book, video, tape, cassette etc) ...の海賊版を作る ...no kaízokuban wo tsukúrù

pirate radio (BRIT) n 海賊放送 kaízokuhōsō

pirouette [piruet'] n つま先旋回 tsumásakisenkai

Pisces [pai'siːz] n (ASTROLOGY) 魚座 uōza

piss [pis] (inf!) vi (urinate) おしっこする oshíkkò suru

pissed [pist] (inf!) adj (US) 怒った okóttà; (drunk) 酔っ払った yoppárattà

pistol [pis'təl] n けん銃 keñjū, ピストル písůtoru

piston [pis'tən] n ピストン písůton

pit [pit] n (hole in ground) 穴 aná; (in face of something) くぼみ kubómi; (also: **coal pit**) 炭坑 tañkō; (quarry) 採石場 saísekijō

♦vt: **to pit one's wits against someone** ...と知恵比べをする ...to chiékurabe wo suru

pitch [pitʃ] n (BRIT: SPORT: ground) グラウンド guráundo; (MUS) 調子 chōshi, ピッチ pitchí; (fig: level, degree) 度合 doái; (tar) ピッチ pítchí

♦vt (throw) 投げる nagérù

♦vi (fall forwards) つんのめる tsuńnomerù

to pitch a tent (erect) テントを張る téñto wo hárù

pitch-black [pitʃ'blæk'] adj (night, place) 真っ暗な makkúra na

pitched battle [pitʃt-] n (violent fight) 激戦 gekísen

pitchfork [pitʃ'fɔːrk] n ホーク hōku

piteous [pit'iːəs] adj (sight, sound etc) 悲惨な hisáñ na

pitfall [pit'fɔːl] n (difficulty, danger) 落し穴 otóshiana, 危険 kikén

pith [piθ] n (of orange, lemon etc) わた watá

pithy [piθ'iː] adj (comment, saying etc) 中身の濃い nakámi no kôi

pitiful [pit'ifəl] adj (sight) 哀れな awáre na

pitiless [pit'ilis] adj (person) 冷酷な reíkoku na

pits [pits] npl (AUT) ピット pítto

pittance [pit'əns] n (very small income) スズメの涙 suzúme no namída

pity [pit'i:] *n* (compassion) 哀れみ awáremì

♦*vt* 哀れむ awáremù

what a pity! (expressing disappointment) 残念だ zafînen da

pivot [piv'ət] *n* (TECH) 旋回軸 sefikaijîku, ピボット pfbôtto; (*fig*) 中心 chûshin

pizza [pit'sə] *n* ピッツァ pfttsà, ピザ pfzà

placard [plæk'ɑːrd] *n* (sign: in public place) 掲示板 keíjiban; (: in march etc) プラカード purákàdo

placate [plei'keit] *vt* (person, anger) をなだめる nadámerù

place [pleis] *n* (in general: point, building, area) 所 tokóro, 場所 bashó; (position: of object) 位置 fchî; (seat) 席 sékì; (job, post etc) 場所 shokú, ポスト pôsùto; (*in home*) *at/to his place* 彼の家で(へ) kárè no fè de(é); (role: in society, system etc) 役割 yakúwarì

♦*vt* (put: object) 置く okú; (identify: person) 思い出す omóidasù

to take place (happen) 起る okórù

out of place (not suitable) 場違いの bachígaì no

in the first place (first of all) まず第一に mázù daîchi nì

to change places with someone ...と交代する ...to kótai suru

to be placed (in race, exam) 入賞する nyúshō suru

place of birth 出生地 shusséichì

placenta [pləsen'tə] *n* 胎盤 taîban

placid [plæs'id] *adj* (person) 穏和な ofwa na

plagiarism [plei'dʒəːrizəm] *n* ひょう窃 hyósetsu, 盗作 tósaku

♦*vt* (*fig*: subj: problems, difficulties) 悩ます nayámasù

plaice [pleis] *n inv* (fish) カレイ kárèi

plaid [plæd] *n* (cloth) チェックの生地 chékkù no kĭjĭ

plain [plein] *adj* (unpatterned) 無地の mújî no; (simple: dress, food) 質素な shísùsò na; (clear, easily understood) 明白な mefhaku na; (not beautiful) 不器量な bukíryò na

♦*adv* (wrong, stupid etc) 全く mattáku

♦*n* (area of land) 平原 heígen

plain chocolate *n* ブラックチョコレート burákkù chokoréto

plain-clothes [plein'klouz] *adj* (police officer) 私服の shifúkù no

plainly [plein'li:] *adv* (obviously) 明白に mefhaku ni; (hear, see, smell: easily) はっきりと hakkfri to; (state: clearly) ざっくばらんに zákkúbaran ni

plaintiff [plein'tif] *n* (LAW) 原告 gefkoku

plaintive [plein'tiv] *adj* (cry, voice) 哀れっぽい awáreppoì

plait [plæt] *n* (of hair) お下げ o-ságe; (of rope, leather) 編みひも状の物 amíhimojò no monó

plan [plæn] *n* (scheme, project) 計画 kefkaku, プラン púràn; (drawing) 図面 zúmèn; (schedule) 予定表 yotéihyò

♦*vt* (work out in advance: crime, holiday, future etc) 計画する kefkaku suru

♦*vi* (think ahead) 計画する kefkaku suru

to plan to do ...しようと計画する ...shíyō tò kefkaku suru

plane [plein] *n* (AVIAT) 飛行機 hfkòki; (MATH) 面 mèn; (*fig*: level) 段階 dafkai; (tool) かんな kanná; (*also*: **plane tree**) スズカケの木 suzúkàke no ki, プラタナス purátanàsu

planet [plæn'it] *n* 惑星 wakúsei

plank [plæŋk] *n* (of wood) 板切れ ítà

planner [plæn'əːr] *n* (*gen*) 計画をする人 kefkaku wo suru hitò; (*also*: **town planner**) 都市計画担当者 toshíkeikaku tantòshà; (of TV program, project) 計画者 kefkakushà

planning [plæn'iŋ] *n* (of future, project, event etc) 計画 kefkaku; (*also*: **town planning**) 都市計画 toshíkeikaku

family planning 家族計画 kazőkukeìkaku

planning permission *n* 建築許可 kefchikukyòka

plant [plænt] *n* (BOT) 植物 shokúbùtsu,

(machinery) 設備 sétsubi; (factory) プラント púranto
♦vt (seed, plant, sapling) 植える uérù; (field, garden) ...に植える ...ni uérù; (secretly: microphone, bomb, incriminating evidence etc) 仕掛ける shikákerù

plantation [plæntéɪʃən] n (of tea, rubber, sugar etc) 農園 nóen; (area planted out with trees) 植林地 shokúrínchi

plaque [plæk] n (commemorative plaque: on building etc) 銘板 meíban; (on teeth) 歯苔 shíkō

plasma [plæz'mə] n 血漿 kesséi

plaster [plæs'tɑːr] n (for walls) しっくい shikkúい; (also: **plaster of Paris**) 石こう sekkō; (BRIT: also: **sticking plaster**) ばんそうこう shikárbánsō
♦vt (wall, ceiling) ...にしっくいを塗る ...ni shikkúい wo nurú; (cover: **to plaster with ...**) ...にべったり張る ...ni ...wo bettári hárù

plastered [plæs'tɑːrd] (inf) adj 酔っ払った yopparátta

plasterer [plæs'tɑːrər] n (of walls, ceilings) 左官屋 sakán-ya

plastic [plæs'tɪk] n 合成樹脂 gōseíjushí, プラスチック purásuchikkú
♦adj (made of plastic: bucket, chair, cup etc) プラスチック製の purásuchikkúsei no

plastic bag n ポリ袋 porfbukuro

Plasticine [plæs'tɪsɪn] ® n 合成粘土 gōseinéndo

plastic surgery n 整形手術 sefkeíshujútsu

plate [pleɪt] n (dish) 皿 sarà; (plateful: of food, biscuits etc) 一皿 hitósara; (in book: picture, photograph) 1ページ大の挿絵 ichípéjidai nō sashíé, プレート púréto; (dental plate) 入れ歯 iréba

gold/silver plate n 貴金属の食器類 kikínzoku no shokkírui

plateau [plætou'] (pl **plateaus** or **plateaux**) n (GEO) 高原 kōgen

plate glass n (for window, door) 板ガラス itágarasu

platform [plæt'fɔːrm] n (at meeting, for band) 演壇 eídan; (raised structure: for landing, loading etc) 台 dáí; (RAIL) ホーム hómu; (BRIT: of bus) 踏段 fumídan, ステップ sutéppù; (POL) 綱領 kōryō

platinum [plæt'ənəm] n 白金 hakkín, プラチナ puráchina

platitude [plæt'ətuːd] n 決り文句 kimárimóňku

platonic [plətɑːn'ɪk] adj 純粋に精神的な junsui nī sefshínteki na, プラトニックな púratoníkkū na

platoon [plətuːn'] n 小隊 shōtai

platter [plæt'ɑːr] n 盛皿 morízara

plausible [plɔː'zəbəl] adj (theory, excuse, statement) もっともらしい mottómorashíī; (person) 口先のうまい kuchísaki nō umáì

play [pleɪ] n (THEATER, RADIO, TV) 劇 gékì
♦vt (subj: children: game) ...して遊ぶ ...shíte asóbù; (football, tennis, chess) やる yarú; (compete against) ...と試合をする ...to shiáí wo súrù; (part, role: in play, film etc) 演ずる eňzurú, ...にふんする ...ni fúnsuru; (instrument, tune) 演奏する efsō suru; (listen to: tape, record) 聞く kíkù
♦vi (children: on beach, swings etc) 遊ぶ asóbù; (MUS: orchestra, band) 演奏する efsō suru; (: record, tape, radio) かかる kakáru

to play safe 大事を取る dafji wo tórù

playboy [pleɪ'bɔɪ] n プレーボーイ puréböi

play down vt 軽く扱う karúku atsukaù

player [pleɪ'ɑːr] n (SPORT) 選手 sēnshu, プレーヤー puréyà; (MUS) 奏者 sōsha; (THEATER) 俳優 haíyū, 役者 yakúsha

playful [pleɪ'fəl] adj (person, animal) 遊び好きの asóbizuki no

playground [pleɪ'graund] n (in park) 遊び場 asóbiba; (in school) 校庭 kōtei, 運動場 uňdōjō

playgroup [pleɪ'gruːp] (BRIT) n 保育園 hoíkuèn

playing card [pleɪ'ɪŋ-] n トランプ toráňpu

playing field n グラウンド gurâundo

playmate [pleɪ'meɪt] n 遊び友達 asóbitomòdachi

play-off [plei'ɔːf] *n* (SPORT) 優勝決定戦 yūshōkettēisen, プレーオフ purḗofu

playpen [plei'pen] *n* ベビーサークル bebīsākuru

plaything [plei'θiŋ] *n* おもちゃ omòcha

playtime [plei'taim] *n* (SCOL) 休み時間 yasūmijikàn

play up *vi* (cause trouble: machine) 調子が悪くなる chōshi gà wárūku naru; (: children) 行儀を悪くする gyōgi wò wárūku suru

playwright [plei'rait] *n* 劇作家 gekisakka

plc [piːelsiː] *abbr* (= *public limited company*) 有限株式会社 yūgen kabushikigaishà

plea [pliː] *n* (request) 懇願 kóñgan; (LAW) 申立て mōshitate

plead [pliːd] *vt* (LAW) 申立てる mōshitaterù; (give as excuse: ignorance, ill health etc) …だと言い訳する …dá iↄ iↄwake surù

♦*vi* (LAW) 申立てる mōshitaterù; (beg): **to plead with someone** …に懇願する …ni kóñgan suru

pleasant [plez'ənt] *adj* (agreeable, nice: weather, chat, smile etc) 気持の良い kimóchi no yoì; (agreeable: person) 愛想の良い aíso no yoì

pleasantries [plez'əntriːz] *npl*: **to exchange pleasantries** あいさつを交わす aísatsu wo kawásù

please [pliːz] *excl* (polite request) どうぞ dōzo, どうか dōka; (polite acceptance): **yes, please** ええ、有難う eè, arígatò; (to attract someone's attention) 済みません sumímaseñ

♦*vt* (give pleasure or satisfaction to) 喜ばす yorókobasù

♦*vi* (give pleasure, satisfaction) 人を喜ばす hitò wò yorókobasù; (think fit): **do as you please** お好きな様にして下さい o-súki na yò ni shité kudasaí

please yourself! (*inf*) ご勝手に go-kátte nì

pleased [pliːzd] *adj* (happy, satisfied): **pleased (with)** (…で) 満足している

(…de) mañzoku shite irù

pleased to meet you 初めまして hajímemashìte

pleasing [pliː'ziŋ] *adj* (remark etc) 愉快な yúkài na; (picture) 楽しい tanóshiì; (person) 愛敬のある aíkyò no arù

pleasure [pleʒ'əːr] *n* (happiness, satisfaction) 快楽 kářaku; (activity of enjoying oneself, enjoyable experience) 楽しみ tanóshimi

it's a pleasure どういたしまして dō iↄ táshimashìte

pleasure boat *n* 遊覧船 yūransen

pleat [pliːt] *n* ひだ hídà, プリーツ purītsu

pledge [pledʒ] *n* (promise) 約束 yakúsoku

♦*vt* (promise: money, support, help) 約束する yakúsoku suru

plentiful [plen'tifəl] *adj* (food, supply, amount) 豊富な hōfu na

plenty [plen'tiː] *n*: **plenty of** (much, many) 沢山の takúsan no; (sufficient) 十分な jūbun na

pleurisy [plur'isiː] *n* ろく膜炎 rokúmakueñ

pliable [plai'əbəl] *adj* (material) しなやかな shináyàka na; (fig: person) 素直な súnào na

pliant [plai'ənt] *adj* = **pliable**

pliers [plai'əːrz] *npl* ペンチ péñchi

plight [plait] *n* (of person, country) 苦境 kukyō

plimsolls [plim'səlz] (BRIT) *npl* 運動靴 uñdōgutsu, スニーカー suníkà

plinth [plinθ] *n* 台座 dáìza

plod [plɑːd] *vi* (walk) とぼとぼ歩く tóbòtobo arúkù; (fig) 何とかやる nán to ka yarù

plonk [plɑːŋk] (*inf*) *n* (BRIT: wine) 安ワイン yasúwaìn

♦*vt*: **to plonk something down** たたきつける様に…を置く tatákitsukeru yò ni …wo okú

plot [plɑːt] *n* (secret plan) 陰謀 íñbò; (of story, play, film) 筋 sújì, プロット puróttò; (of land) 区画 kukáku

♦*vt* (sb's downfall etc) たくらむ takúramŭ; (AVIAT, NAUT: position on chart) 地図 に 書き込む chízu ni kakíkomŭ; (MATH: point on graph) グラフ における gŭráfu ni eru

♦vi (conspire) 陰謀 を 企てる ínbō wo kuwádaterŭ

plotter [plɑt'əːr] n (instrument) 製図道具 sefzudōgu

plough [plau] (US also: **plow**) n (AGR) すき sukí

♦vt (earth) 耕す tagáyasŭ

to plough money into (company, project etc) ...に金をつぎ込む ...ni kané wo tsugíkomŭ

ploughman's lunch [plau'mænz-] (BRIT) n 軽食 kefshoku ◊パブのランチで、パン、チーズ、ピクルスからなる pábŭ no ránchi de, páñ, chízu, píkŭrusu kara nárŭ

plough through vt fus (crowd) ...を かき分けて歩く ...wo kakíwakete arúkŭ

plow [plau] (US) = **plough**

ploy [plɔi] n 策略 sakúryaku

pluck [plʌk] vt (fruit, flower, leaf) 摘む tsúmŭ; (musical instrument) つま弾く tsumábikŭ; (bird) ...の羽をむしる ...no hané wŏ mushírŭ; (remove hairs from: eyebrow) ...の毛を抜く ...no ké wŏ nukŭ

♦n (courage) 勇気 yŭki

to pluck up courage 勇気を出す yŭki wo dásŭ

plug [plʌg] n (ELEC) 差し込み sashíkomi, プラグ púràgu; (stopper: in sink, bath) 栓 séñ; (AUT: also: **spark(ing) plug**) スパークプラグ supákŭpŭrágu

♦vt (hole) ふさぐ fuságŭ; (inf: advertise) 宜伝する señden suru

plug in vt (ELEC) ...のプラグを差し込む ...no púràgu wo sashíkomŭ

plum [plʌm] n (fruit) プラム púràmu

♦cpd (inf): **plum job** 甘い汁を吸える職 amái shirŭ wo suérŭ shokŭ

plumage [plu:'midʒ] n 羽 hané ◊鳥の体を覆う羽の総称 torí no karáda wo ōŭ hané no sōshō

plumb [plʌm] vt: *to plumb the depths* (fig) (of unpleasant emotion) 辛酸をなめ尽す shifsan wŏ namétsukusŭ; (of un-

pleasant expression) ...を極端に表現する ...wo kyokútan ni hyṓgen suru

plumber [plʌm'əːr] n 配管工 hafkankō

plumbing [plʌm'iŋ] n (piping) 水道設備 sufdōsetsubì; (trade, work) 配管業 hafkangyō

plume [plu:m] n (of bird) 羽 hané; (on helmet, horse's head) 前立 maédate

plummet [plʌm'it] vi: *to plummet (down)* (bird, aircraft) 真っ直ぐに落下する massúgŭ ni rakká surŭ; (price, amount, rate) 暴落する bóràku suru

plump [plʌmp] adj (person) ぽっちゃりした potcháří shita

♦vi: *to plump for* (inf: choose) 選ぶ erábŭ

plump up vt (cushion, pillow) 膨らませる fukúramaserŭ

plunder [plʌn'dəːr] n (activity) 略奪 ryakúdatsu; (stolen things) 分捕り品 buñdorihiñ

♦vt (steal from: city, tomb) 略奪する ryakúdatsu suru

plunge [plʌndʒ] n (dive: of bird, person) 飛び込み tobíkomi; (fig: of prices, rates etc) 暴落 bóràku

♦vt (hand, knife) 突っ込む tsukkómŭ

♦vi (fall: person, thing) 落ちる ochírŭ; (dive: bird, person) 飛び込む tobíkomŭ; (fig: prices, rates etc) 暴落する bóràku suru

to take the plunge 冒険する bṓken suru

plunger [plʌn'dʒəːr] n (for sink) プランジャー puráñjà ◊吸い棒の付いたゴムカップ nagái bṓ no tsuità gomúkappŭ

plunging [plʌn'dʒiŋ] adj (neckline) 切込みの深い kirfkomi no fukái

pluperfect [plu:'pəːr'fikt] n 過去完了形 kakókanryōkei

plural [plur'əl] adj 複数の fukúsū no ♦n 複数形 fukúsūkei

plus [plʌs] n (also: **plus sign**) 加符号 kafúgō, プラス púràsu

♦prep (MATH) ...に ...を加算して ...ni ...wo kazàn shite, ...に ...を足して ...wo tashíte; (in addition to) ...に加えて ...ni kuwáete

2 plus 2 is 4 2足す2は4 ní tasú ní wá yón

ten/twenty plus (more than) 10(20)以上 jû(nijû)ijô

plush [plʌʃ] *adj* (car, hotel etc) 豪華な gốka na

plutonium [pluːˈtəʊniːəm] *n* プルトニウム púrutoníumu

ply [plaɪ] *vt* (a trade) 営む itónamù
♦*vi* (ship) 往復する ốfuku suru
♦*n* (of wool, rope) 太さ futósa
to ply someone with drink ...に強引に酒を勧める ...ni gốin ní sakế nó susúmerù

plywood [ˈplaɪwʊd] *n* ベニヤ板 beníyaità

P.M. [piːˈem] *abbr* = Prime Minister

p.m. [piːˈem] *adv abbr* (= *post meridiem*) 午後 gógo

pneumatic [nuːˈmætɪk] *adj* (air-filled) 空気で膨らませた kûki de fukúramasetà; (powered by air) 空気... kûki...

pneumatic drill *n* 空気ドリル kûkidoríru

pneumonia [nuːˈməʊnjə] *n* 肺炎 haíen

poach [pəʊtʃ] *vt* (steal: fish) 密漁する mitsúryo suru; (: animals, birds) 密猟する mitsúryo suru; (cook: egg) 落し卵にする otóshitamagð ni suru, ポーチエッグにする pốchìtoeggù ni suru; (: fish) 煮る nirú
♦*vi* (steal: fish) 密漁する mitsúryo suru; (: animals, birds) 密猟する mitsúryo suru

poached [pəʊtʃt] *adj*: *poached egg* 落し卵 otóshitamagð, ポーチエッグ pốchìtoeggù

poacher [ˈpəʊtʃəːr] *n* (of fish) 密漁者 mitsúryoshà; (of animals, birds) 密猟者 mitsúryoshà

P.O. Box [piːˈəʊ-] *n abbr* = Post Office Box

pocket [ˈpɒkɪt] *n* (on jacket, trousers, suitcase, car door etc) ポケット pokéttò; (fig: small area) 孤立地帯 korítsuchitài
♦*vt* (put in one's pocket) ポケットに入れる pokéttð ni irérù; (steal) くすねる kusúnerù
to be out of pocket (BRIT) 損する sốn suru

pocketbook [ˈpɒkɪtbʊk] (US) *n* (wallet) 財布 saífu; (handbag) ハンドバッグ hańdobaggù

pocket calculator *n* 電卓 deńtaku

pocket knife *n* ポケットナイフ pokéttonaìfu

pocket money *n* 小遣い kózukaì

pod [pɒd] *n* さや sáyà

podgy [ˈpɒdʒiː] *adj* 小太りの kobútorì no

podiatrist [pəˈdaɪətrɪst] (US) *n* 足治療医 ashíchiryoì

poem [ˈpəʊəm] *n* 詩 shi

poet [ˈpəʊɪt] *n* 詩人 shíjìn

poetic [pəʊˈetɪk] *adj* (relating to poetry) 詩の shi no; (like poetry) 詩的な shitéki na

poet laureate *n* 桂冠詩人 keikanshijin

poetry [ˈpəʊɪtrɪ] *n* (LITERATURE) 詩 shi; 詩歌 shíìka

poignant [ˈpɔɪnjənt] *adj* (emotion, pain, grief etc) 痛ましい itámashiì

point [pɔɪnt] *n* (gen): 点 teñ, ポイント poíñto; (sharp ợnd; of needle, knife etc) せん端 señtan; (purpose) 目的 mokútekì; (significant part) 要点 yốteñ; (detail, aspect, quality) 特徴 tokúchð; (particular place or position) 地点 chitéñ; (moment) 時点 jítèn; (stage in development) 段階 dańkaì; (score: in competition, game, sport) 得点 tokúteñ, 点数 teñsù; (BRIT: ELEC: socket) コンセント końseñto; (*also*: decimal point) 小数点 shốsùteñ; (in numbers): *2 point 3 (2.3)* 2点3 ní teñ sañ
♦*vt* (show, mark) 指す sásù; (gun etc) 向ける mukérù
to point something at someone ...に...を向ける ...ni ...wo mukérù
♦*vi*: *to point at* (with finger, stick etc) ...を指す ...wo sásù
to be on the point of doing something ...する所である ...wo suru tokórò de árù
to make a point of doing 努めて...する tsutómete ...surú
to get/miss the point 相手が言おうとする事が分かる(分からない) aíte ga iwáñ to surú kotò ga wakárù (wakáranaì)
to come to the point 要点を言う yốteñ wo iú

wǒ iú

there's no point (in doing) (...するのは) 無意味だ (...surú no wa) muími dà

point-blank [point'blæŋk'] *adv* (say, ask) ずばり zubárí; (refuse) あっさり assárí; (*also*: **at point-blank range**) 至近距離で shikínkyorí de

pointed [poin'tid] *adj* (stick, pencil, chin, nose etc) とがった togátta; (*fig*: remark) 辛らつな shirátsu na

pointedly [poin'tidli:] *adv* (reply etc) 意味深長に ímìshinchō ni

pointer [poin'tə:r] *n* (on chart, machine) 針 hárí; (*fig*: piece of information or advice) ヒント hínto

pointless [point'lis] *adj* (useless, senseless) 無意味な muími na

point of view *n* (opinion) 観点 kaṅten

point out *vt* (in debate etc) ...を指摘する ...wo shitéki suru

points [points] *npl* (AUT) ポイント poínto; (RAIL) 転てつ機 teṅtetsukī, ポイント poínto

point to *vt fus* (fig) ...を指摘する ...wo shitéki suru

poise [poiz] *n* (composure) 落ち着き ochítsuki

poison [poi'zən] *n* (harmful substance) 毒 dokú

♦*vt* (person, animal: kill with poison) 毒殺する dokúsatsu suru; (: give poison to) ...に毒を飲ませる ...ni dokú wo nomáserù

poisonous [poi'zənəs] *adj* 有毒な yúdoku na, 毒...dokú...

poke [pouk] *vt* (jab with finger, stick etc) つつく tsutsúkù; (put: **to poke something in(to)** ...の中へ...を突っ込む ...no nákà e ...wo tsukkómù

poke about *vi* (search) 物色する busshóku suru

poker [pou'kə:r] *n* (metal bar) 火かき棒 hikákibō; (CARDS) ポーカー pōkā

poky [pou'ki:] *adj* (room, house) 狭苦しい semákurushiī

Poland [pou'lənd] *n* ポーランド pōrando

polar [pou'lə:r] *adj* (GEO, ELEC) 極地の kyókuchi no

polar bear *n* 北極グマ hokkyókugūma

polarize [pou'lə:raiz] *vt* 分裂させる buṅretsu saserú

Pole [poul] *n* ポーランド人 pōrandojīn

pole [poul] *n* (post, stick) 棒 bō, さお sáò; (GEO, ELEC) 極 kyóku

flag pole 旗ざお hatázao

telegraph/ telephone pole 電柱 deńchū

pole bean *n* (US) *n* (runner bean) インゲン íngen

pole vault *n* 棒高飛び bōtakátobi

police [pəli:s'] *n* (organization) 警察 keísatsu; (members) 警官 keíkan

♦*vt* (street, area, town) ...の治安を維持する ...no chíàn wò jíji suru

police car *n* パトカー patőkà

policeman [pəli:s'mən] (*pl* **policemen**) *n* 警官 keíkan

police state *n* (POL) 警察国家 keísatsukokkà

police station *n* 警察署 keísatsusho

policewoman [pəli:s'wumən] (*pl* **policewomen**) *n* 婦人警官 fujínkeìkan, 婦警 fukéì

policy [pɑ:l'isi:] *n* (POL, ECON: set of ideas, plans) 政策 seísaku; (*also*: **insurance policy**) 保険証券 hokéńshōken

polio [pou'li:ou] *n* 小児麻ひ shōnímahī, ポリオ pőrìo

Polish [pou'liʃ] *adj* ポーランドの pōrando no; (LING) ポーランド語の pōrando go no

♦*n* (LING) ポーランド語 pōrandogo

polish [pɑ:l'iʃ] *n* (*also*: **shoe polish**) 靴墨 kutsúzumi; (for furniture, floors etc) 光沢剤 kōtakuzaì; (shine: on shoes, floors, furniture etc) 光沢 kōtaku; (*fig*: refinement) 洗練 seńren

♦*vt* (put polish on, make shiny) 磨く migákù

polished [pɑ:l'iʃt] *adj* (*fig*: person, style) 洗練された seńren sareta

polish off *vt* (work) 仕上げる shiágerù; (food) 平らげる taíragerù

polite [pəlait'] *adj* (person: well-mannered) 礼儀正しい reígitadashīì; (socially superior: company, society) 上流の jōryū no

politeness [pəlait'nis] n 礼儀正しさ ref-
gitadashisa

political [pəlit'ikəl] adj (relating to politics) 政治の sefji no; (person) 政治に関心
ある seiji ni kanshin arù

politically [pəlit'ikli:] adv 政治的に sefji-
teki ni

politician [pɑ:liti'ən] n 政治家 sefjika

politics [pɑ:l'itiks] n (activity) 政治 sefji;
(subject) 政治学 sefjigaku
♦npl (beliefs, opinions) 政治的思想 sefji-
tekishisô

poll [poul] n (also: **opinion poll**) 世論調査
yorónchòsa; (political election) 選挙 sénkyo
♦vt (in opinion poll) ...の意見を聞く ...no
íken wo kikú; (number of votes) 獲得する
kakútoku suru

pollen [pɑ:l'ən] n 花粉 kafún

polling day [pou'liŋ-] (BRIT) n 投票日
tôhyòbi

polling station (BRIT) n 投票所 tôhyò-
jo

pollute [pəlu:t'] vt (air, water, land) 汚染
する osén suru

pollution [pəlu:'ʃən] n (process) 汚染 osén;
(substances) 汚染物質 osénbusshitsu

polo [pou'lou] n (sport) ポロ pôrò

polo-necked [pou'lounekt] adj (sweater)
とっくりえりの tokkúrieri no

poltergeist [poul'tərgaist] n けん騒霊
kefsòrei, ポルターガイスト porútàgatsu-
to

polyester [pɑ:li:es'tər] n ポリエステル
porfésuteru

polyethylene [pɑ:li:eθ'əlin] (US) n ポリ
エチレン porféchirèn

polystyrene [pɑ:li:stai'ri:n] n ポリスチ
レン porísuchirèn

polytechnic [pɑ:li:tek'nik] n 科学技術専
門学校 kagákugijutsu senmongakkô ◇
英国では大学レベルの高等教育機関 ef-
koku de wà daígakurebèru no kôtôkyôi-
ku kìkañ

polythene [pɑ:l'əθi:n] (BRIT) n = polyethylene

pomegranate [pɑ:m'əgrænit] n ザクロ
zákùro

pomp [pɑ:mp] n 華やかさ hanáyàkasa

pompom [pɑ:m'pɑ:m] n ポンポン pôñpon

pompon [pɑ:m'pɑ:n] n = pompom

pompous [pɑ:m'pəs] (pej) adj (person,
piece of writing) もったい振った mottâi-
buttâ

pond [pɑ:nd] n (natural, artificial) 池 iké

ponder [pɑ:n'dəːr] vt 熟考する jukkô suru

ponderous [pɑ:n'dəːrəs] adj (large and
heavy) 大きくて重い ôkikute omôi;
(speech, writing) 重苦しい omôkurushîî

pong [pɔ:ŋ] (BRIT: inf) n 悪臭 akûshû

pontificate [pɑ:ntif'ikeit] vi (fig): **to
pontificate (about)** (...について) も
ったい振って話す (...ni tsûite) mottâibut-
tè hanâsû

pontoon [pɑ:ntu:n'] n (for building) ポンツ
ーン pôñtsùn; (for seaplane etc) フロート
fúròto

pony [pou'ni:] n ポニー pônî

ponytail [pou'ni:teil] n (person's hairstyle) ポニー テール ponîtèru

pony trekking [-trek'iŋ] (BRIT) n 乗馬
旅行 jôbaryokô

poodle [pu:'dəl] n プードル pûdoru

pool [pu:l] n (also: **pool of water**) 水たま
り mizútamari; (pond) 池 iké; (also:
swimming pool) プール pûru; (fig: of
light, liquid) たまり tamâri; (SPORT) 玉
突 tamâtsuki, ビリヤード biríyàdo
♦vt (money, knowledge, resources) 出し
合う dashíaù, プールする pûru suru

typing pool タイピストのプール taípisuto no pûru

pools [pu:lz] npl (football pools) トトカ
ルチョ totókarùcho

poor [puːr] adj (not rich: person, place,
country) 貧しい mazúshiî, 貧乏な bíñbo
na; (bad) 粗末な somâtsu na
♦npl: **the poor** 貧乏人 bíñbònin ◇総称
sôshô

poor in (resources etc) ...が不足してい
る ...ga fusôku shite irû

poorly [puːr'liː] adj (ill) 病気の byôki no
♦adv (badly: designed) 粗末に sômàtsu
ni; (paid, furnished) 不十分に fujûbûn ni

pop [pɑ:p] n (MUS) ポップス pôppùsu;

popcorn [pɑpˈkɔːrn] n ポップコーン poppúkôn

pope [poup] n 法王 hôô

pop in vi 立寄る tachíyorù

poplar [pɑpˈlər] n ポプラ pópùra

poplin [pɑpˈlɪn] n ポプリン popúrìn

pop out vi 飛出る tobíderù

popper [pɑpˈər] n (BRIT: for fastening) スナップ sunáppù

poppy [pɑpˈiː] n ケシ keshí

Popsicle [pɑpˈsɪkəl] ((R) US) n (ice lolly) アイスキャンデー aísukyañdê

pop star n ポップスター poppúsutâ

populace [pɑpˈjələs] n 大衆 taíshū

popular [pɑpˈjələr] adj (well-liked: person, place, thing) 人気のある niñki no arù; (of ordinary people: idea, belief) 一般の ippán no, 流行の ryúkô no; (nonacademic) 一般向けの ippáñmuke no; (POL) 国民の kokúmin no

popularity [pɑpjəlærˈɪtiː] n (of person, thing, activity) 人気 niñki

popularize [pɑpˈjələraiz] vt (sport, music, fashion) 普及させる fukyǔ saserù; (science, ideas) 分かりやすくする wakáriyasukù surù

populate [pɑpˈjəleiˈʃən] n (inhabitants: of country, area) 住民 jūmin; (number of inhabitants) 人口 jíñkô

populous [pɑpˈjələs] adj (country, city, area) 人口の多い jíñkô no ôi

pop up vi 現れる aráwarerù

porcelain [pɔːrˈsəlin] n 磁器 jíkì

porch [pɔːrtʃ] n (ARCHIT: entrance) 玄関 geñkan; (US) ベランダ beráñda

porcupine [pɔːrˈkjəpain] n ヤマアラシ yamáarashi

pore [pɔːr] n (ANAT) 毛穴 keána; (BOT) 気孔 kikô; (GEO) 小穴 koána
♦vi: **to pore over** (book, article etc) 熟読する jukúdoku surù

pork [pɔːrk] n 豚肉 butániku

pornographic [pɔːrnəgræfˈik] adj (film, book, magazine) わいせつな waísetsu na, ポルノの porúno no

pornography [pɔːrnɑgˈrəfiː] n (films, books, magazines) ポルノ pórùno

porous [pɔːrˈəs] adj (soil, rock, clay etc) 小穴の多い koána nô ôi

porpoise [pɔːrˈpəs] n イルカ irúka

porridge [pɔːrˈidʒ] n オートミール ôtomīru

port [pɔːrt] n (harbor) 港 mínàto; (NAUT: left side) 左げん sagén; (wine) ポートワイン pôtowaìn
port of call 寄港地 kikôchi

portable [pɔːrˈtəbəl] adj (television, typewriter, telephone etc) 携帯用の keítai yô no, ポータブルの pôtaburu no

porter [pɔːrˈtər] n (for luggage) 赤帽 akábô, ポーター pôtâ; (doorkeeper) 門番 moñban

portfolio [pɔːrtfouˈliːou] n (case) かばん kabán; (POL) 大臣の職 dáìjin no shokú; (FINANCE) ポートフォリオ pôtofòrio; (of artist) 代表作品集 daíhyôsakuhìnshû

porthole [pɔːrˈthoul] n (船の) 舷窓 geñsô

portion [pɔːrˈʃən] n (part) 部分 búbùn; (helping of food) 一人前 ichíninmaè

portly [pɔːrtˈliː] adj (man) 太った futóttà

portrait [pɔːrˈtrit] n (picture) 肖像 shôzô, ポートレート pôtorêto

portray [pɔːrtreiˈ] vt (subj: artist) 描く egákù; (: actor) 演じる eñjirù

portrayal [pɔːrtreiˈəl] n (artist's: also representation in book, film etc) 描写 byôsha; (actor's) 演技 eñgi

Portugal [pɔːrˈtʃəgəl] n ポルトガル porútogaru

Portuguese [pɔːrtʃəgiːzˈ] adj ポルトガルの porútogaru no; (LING) ポルトガル語の porútogarugô no
♦n inv 住人 porútogarujìn; (LING) ポルトガル語 porútogarugô

pose [pouz] n (posture) ポーズ pôzu
♦vi (pretend): **to pose as ...** を装う ...wo yosóoù, ...の名をかたる ...no nà wô katárù
♦vt (question) 持出す mochídasù; (prob-

lem, danger) ...である ...de árù

to pose for (painting etc) ...のためにポーズを取る ...no tamé ní pōzu wo tórù

posh [pɔʃ] (*inf*) *adj* (smart: hotel, restaurant etc) 高級な kōkyū na; (: person, behavior) 上流階級の jōryūkaíkyū no

position [pəzíʃ'ən] *n* (place: of house, thing, person) 位置 fchì; (of person's body) 姿勢 shiséi; (social status) 地位 chíi; (job) 職 shokú; (in race, competition) 第...位 daí ...i; (attitude) 態度 taído; (situation) 立場 tachîba
♦*vt* (person, thing) 置く okú

positive [pɑːz'ətiv] *adj* (certain) 確信している kakúshin shite irú; (hopeful, confident) 積極的な sekkyókuteki na; (definite: decision, action, quality) 明確な meíkaku na

posse [pɑːs'i:] (*US*) *n* 捜索隊 sōsakutai

possess [pəzes'] *vt* (have, own: car, watch, radio etc) 所有する shoyū suru, 保有する hoyū suru; (quality, ability) ...がある ...ga árù, ...を持っている ...wo móttè irú; (subj: feeling, belief) 支配する shíhai suru

possession [pəzeʃ'ən] *n* (state of possessing) 所有 shoyū

to take possession of 占領する señryō suru

possessions [pəzeʃ'ənz] *npl* (belongings) 持物 mochímòno

possessive [pəzes'iv] *adj* (of another person) ...の愛情を独占したがる ...no afjo wò dokúsen shitagarù; (of things) 他人に使いたがらない tanín ni tsukáwasetagaranai; (LING) 所有を表す choyū wò aráwasù

possibility [pɑːsəbil'əti:] *n* 可能性 kanōsei; (possible event) 可能な事 kanō na kotò

possible [pɑːs'əbəl] *adj* (which can be done) 可能な kanō na; (event, reaction) 有り得る aríérù; (candidate, successor) 成り得る naríurù

it's possible (may be true) そうかも知れない sō ká mò shirénaì

as fast as possible できるだけ早く de-

kírù dakè hayákù

possibly [pɑːs'əbli:] *adv* (perhaps) あるいは arùíwa; (expressing surprise, shock, puzzlement) ...が考えられない ...ga kañgaerarenai; (emphasizing someone's efforts) できる限り dekírù kagirí

I cannot possibly come どう言っても私は行かれません dōatté mo watákushi wà ikáremaseñ

post [poust] *n* (*BRIT*: service, system) 郵便 yūbin; (: letters) 郵便 yūbin (butsu); (delivery) 配達 haftatsu ◊1回分の配達郵便を指す ikkáibun no haftatsu-yūbin wo sásù; (pole) 柱 hashíra; (job, situation) 職 shokú; (MIL) 持場 mochîba
♦*vt* (*BRIT*: send by post) 郵送する yūsō suru; (: put in mailbox) 投かんする tōkan suru; (: appoint) 配属する haízoku suru
to post someone to ...を...へ配属する ...wo ...e haíchi suru

postage [pous'tidʒ] *n* (charge) 郵便料金 yūbin ryōkin

postage stamp *n* (郵便) 切手 (yūbin) kitté

postal [pous'təl] *adj* (charges, service, strike) 郵便の yūbin no

postal order *n* 郵便為替 yūbin kawàse

postbox [poust'bɑːks] (*BRIT*) *n* (郵便) ポスト (yūbin) pósùto

postcard [poust'kɑrd] *n* (郵便) 葉書 (yūbin) hagáki

postcode [poust'koud] (*BRIT*) *n* 郵便番号 yūbin bañgō

postdate [poust'deit] *vt* (check) ...に先の日付を付ける ...ni sakí nò hízùke wo tsukérù

poster [pous'tər] *n* ポスター pósùtā

poste restante [poust res'tɑnt] (*BRIT*) *n* 局留 kyokúdòme

posterity [pɑːster'iti:] *n* 後世 kōsei

postgraduate [poustgrædʒ'uit] *n* 大学院生 daígakuiñsei

posthumous [pɑːs'tʃəməs] *adj* (award, publication) 死後の shígò no

postman [poust'mən] (*pl* **postmen**) *n* 郵便屋 yūbin-ya

postmark [poust'mɑrk] *n* 消印 keshíin

post-mortem [poustmɔr'təm] *n* 司法解剖 shihōkaíbō, 検死解剖 keñshikaíbō

post office *n* (building) 郵便局 yúbìňkyoku; (organization): **the Post Office** 郵政省 yúselshō

Post Office Box *n* 私書箱 shishòbàko

postpone [poust'poun'] *vt* 延期する eńki suru

postscript [poust'skript] *n* 追伸 tsuíshin

posture [pɑːs'tʃəːr] *n* (position of body) 姿勢 shiséi; (*fig*) 態度 táìdo

posy [pou'ziː] *n* 花束 hanátaba ◇小さい花束を指す chíìsaì hanátaba wo sásù

pot [pɑt] *n* (for cooking) なべ nábè; (*also*: **teapot**) ティーポット típottò; (*also*: **coffeepot**) コーヒーポット kóhīpottò; (tea/coffee in pot) ティー[コーヒー]一杯 tíì[kóhī] ippaì; (bowl, container: for paint etc) つぼ tsubò; (flowerpot) 植木鉢 uékibàchi; (*inf*: marijuana) マリファナ marífàna

◆*vt* (plant) 鉢に植える hachí nì uérù

to go to pot (*inf*: work, performance) 駄目になる damé nì narú

potato [pəteí'tou] (*pl* **potatoes**) *n* ジャガイモ jagáìmo

potato peeler [-piːˈləːr] *n* 皮むき器 kawámukìkì

potent [pout'ənt] *adj* (powerful: weapon, argument, drink) 強力な kyóryoku na; (man) 性的能力のある seftekinóryoku no árù

potential [pəten'tʃəl] *adj* (candidate: also) 成り得る narúrù; (sales, success) 可能な kanó na; (danger etc) 潜在する seňzai suru

◆*n* (talents, abilities) 潜在能力 seňzaìnóryoku; (promise, possibilities) 将来性 shóraisei

potentially [pəten'tʃəliː] *adv* 潜在的に seňzaìteki ni

pothole [pɑt'houl] *n* (in road) 穴ぼこ anáboko; (*BRIT*: underground) 洞くつ dókutsu

potholing [pɑt'houliŋ] (*BRIT*) *n*: **to go potholing** 洞くつを探検する dókutsu wò tañken suru

potion [pou'ʃən] *n* (of medicine, poison etc) 水薬 mizúgusùri

potluck [pɑt'lʌk'] *n*: **to take potluck** 有り合せの物で間に合せる aríawase no monò de ma ní awaserù

potted [pɑt'id] *adj* (food) つぼ詰めの tsubózume no; (plant) 鉢植えの hachíue no; (abbreviated: account, biography etc) 要約した yóyaku shita

potter [pɑt'əːr] *n* (pottery maker) 陶芸家 tógeika

◆*vi*: **to potter around/about in the garden** (*BRIT*) ぶらぶらと庭いじりをする búràbura to niwáìjiri wo suru

pottery [pɑt'əːriː] *n* (pots, dishes etc) 陶器 tóki; (factory, workshop) 陶器製造所 tókiseizòjo

potty [pɑt'iː] *adj* (*inf*: mad) 狂ったkurúttà

◆*n* (for child) おまる o-máru

pouch [pautʃ] *n* (for tobacco, coins etc) 小袋 kobúkùro; (ZOOL) 袋 fukúro

poultry [poul'triː] *n* (live chickens, ducks etc) 家きん kakíñ; (meat from chickens etc) 鳥肉 torínìku

pounce [pauns] *vi*: **to pounce on** (animal, person) ...に襲い掛る ...ni osóìkakarù; (*fig*: mistake, idea etc) 攻撃する kógeki suru

pound [paund] *n* (unit of weight) ポンド póndo; (*BRIT*: unit of money) ポンド póndo

◆*vt* (beat: table, wall etc) 強くたたく tsúyòku tatákù; (crush: grain, spice etc) 砕く kudákù

◆*vi* (heart) どきどきする dókìdoki suru

pound sterling *n* ポンド póndo

pour [pɔːr] *vt* (tea, wine, cereal etc) つぐ tsugú

◆*vi* (water, blood, sweat etc) 流れ出る nagárederù

to pour someone a drink ...に酒をついでやる ...ni saké wò tsuíde yarù

pour away/off *vt* 流して捨てる nagáshite suterú

pour in *vi* (people) ぞろぞろと入って来る zóròzoro to haítte kurù; (information) 続々と入る zókùzoku to háìru

pouring [pɔːr'iŋ] *adj*: **pouring rain** 土砂

降りの雨 dosháburi no amè

pour out vi (people) ぞろぞろと出て来る zórðzoro to detè kúrù

◆vt (tea, wine etc) つぐ tsugú; (fig: thoughts, feelings, etc) 堰を切った様に吐き出す sékì wo kíttá yố ni hakídasù

pout [paut] vi 脹れっ面をする fukúrettsura wð suru

poverty [pɔ:'vərti:] n 貧乏 bínbô

poverty-stricken [pɔ:'vərti:strikən] adj (people, town, country) 非常に貧しい hijó nì mazúshiì

powder [pau'də:r] n (tiny particles of solid substance) 粉 konáʔ; (face powder) おしろい oshíroi, パウダー pấňdā

◆vt: **to powder one's face** 顔におしろいをつける kaó nì oshíroi wo tsukérù

powder compact n コンパクト kóňpakuto

powdered milk [pau'də:rd-] n 粉ミルク konámirùku

powder puff n パフ páfù

powder room n 化粧室 keshóshìtsu

power [pau'ə:r] n (control: over people, activities) 権力 kéñryoku; (ability, opportunity) 能力 nõryoku; (legal right) 権利 kéñri; (of explosion, engine) 威力 rýoku; (electricity) 電力 déňryoku

to be in power (POL etc) 権力を握っている kéñryoku wo nigétte irú

power cut (BRIT) n 停電 teíden

powered [pau'ə:rd] adj: **powered by** …で動く …de ugókù

power failure n 停電 teíden

powerful [pau'ə:rfəl] adj (person, organization) 有力な yűryoku na; (body) 力強い chikárazuyoi; (blow, kick etc) 強力な kyőryoku na; (engine) 馬力の強い bárìki no tsuyoì; (speech, piece of writing) 力強い chikárazuyoì

powerless [pau'ə:rlis] adj (without control or influence) 無力な múryòku na

powerless to do …する力がない …súrù chikára ga naì

power point (BRIT) n コンセント kóňsento

power station n 発電所 hatsúdensho

p.p. [pi:'pi:'] abbr (= per procurationem):

p.p. J. *Smith* J.Smithの代理として jě sumísu no dafri tðshitě, (= *pages*) ページ pějì

PR [pi:ɑ:r'] abbr = **public relations**

practicable [præk'tikabəl] adj (scheme, task, idea) 実用的な jitsúyōteki na

practical [præk'tikəl] adj (not theoretical: difficulties, experience etc) 実際の jissái no; (person: sensible) 現実的な geñjitsuteki na; (good with hands) 器用な kíyō na; (ideas, methods) 現実的な geñjitsuteki na; (clothes, things: sensible) 実用的な jitsúyōteki na

practicality [præktikæl'iti:] n (no pl) 現実主義 geñjitsushũgi; (of situation etc) 現実 geñjitsu

practical joke n 悪ふざけ warúfuzàke

practically [præk'tikli:] adv (almost) ほとんど hotőndo

practice [præk'tis] n (habit) 習慣 shūkan; (of profession) 業務 gyómu; (REL) おきてを守る事 okíte wo mamórù kotð; (exercise, training) 練習 reńshū; (MED, LAW: business) 開業 kaígyō

◆vt (train at: musical instrument, sport etc) 練習する reńshū suru; (carry out: custom, craft etc) 行う okónaů; (religion) …のおきてを守る …no okíte wo mamorů; (profession) …に従事する …ni júji suru

◆vi (train) 練習する reńshū suru; (lawyer, doctor etc) …の業務をする …no gyómu wo suru

in practice (in reality) 実際には jissái ni wà

out of practice 腕が鈍っている udé gà ni-búttě

practicing [præk'tisiŋ] (BRIT **practising**) adj (Christian etc) おきてを守っているおきてを mamótte irù; (doctor, lawyer) 業務をしている gyómu wo shité irù

practise [præk'tis] vt, vi (BRIT) = **practice**

practitioner [præktiʃ'ənə:r] n (MED): **medical practitioner** 医者 ishá

pragmatic [prægmæt'ik] adj (person, reason etc) 現実的な geñjitsuteki na

prairie [pre:r'i:] n 草原 sõgen

praise [preiz] n (expression of approval, admiration) 賞賛 shōsan
♦vt (express approval, admiration: of person, thing, action etc) ほめる homérù

praiseworthy [preiz'wə:rði] adj (person, act etc) ほめるべき homérùbeki

pram [præm] (BRIT) n 乳母車 ubáguruma

prance [præns] vi (gaily 誇って歩く ibátte arúkù; (horse) 躍る様に歩く odóru yō ni arúkù

prank [præŋk] n いたずら itázura

prawn [prɔːn] n エビ ébi

pray [prei] vi (REL) 祈る inórù; (fig) 祈る inórù, 願う negáù

prayer [preiər] n (REL: activity, words) 祈り inóri

preach [pri:tʃ] vi (REL) 説教する sékkyo suru; (pej: moralize) お説教する o-sékkyo suru
♦vt (peace, doctrine etc) 説く tókù
  to preach a sermon 説教する sékkyo suru

preacher [pri:'tʃər] n (REL) 説教者 sekkyóshà

preamble [pri:'æmbəl] n (to spoken words) 前置き maéoki; (to written words) 前書 maégaki

precarious [prikeə'riəs] adj (dangerous: position, situation) 不安定な fuántei na; (fig) 危険な kikén na

precaution [prikɔ:'ʃən] n 用心 yōjin

precede [prisi:d'] vt (event, period of time) ...の前に起る ...no máè ni okórù; (person) ...の前を歩く ...no máè wo arúkù; (sentence, paragraph, chapter) ...の前にある ...no máè ni árù

precedence [pres'idəns] n (priority) 優先 yūsen

precedent [pres'idənt] n (action, official decision) 判例 hańrei; (something that has happened before) 先例 señrei

preceding [prisi:'diŋ] adj (chapter, programme, day) 前の máè no

precept [pri:'sept] n 教訓 kyōkun

precinct [pri:'siŋkt] n (US: part of city) 管区 kańku
  pedestrian precinct (BRIT) 歩行者天

国 hokóshateńgoku
  shopping precinct (BRIT) ショッピングセンター shóppiŋgu séñtā ♢車が閉出される kuruma ga shimédasarerù

precincts [pri:'siŋkts] npl (of a large building) 構内 kōnai

precious [preʃ'əs] adj (commodity: valuable, useful) 貴重な kichō na; (object, material) 高価な kōka na

precious stone n 宝石 hōseki

precipice [pres'əpis] n 断崖 dañgai

precipitate [prisip'iteit] vt (hasten) 早める hayámerù

precise [prisais'] adj (exact: time, nature etc) 正確な sefkaku na; (detailed: instructions, plans etc) 細かい komákaI

precisely [prisais'li:] adv (accurately) 正確に sefkaku ni; (exactly) その通り sonó tōri

precision [prisiʒ'ən] n 正確さ sefkakusa

preclude [priklu:d'] vt (action, event) 不可能にする fukánō ni suru

precocious [prikou'ʃəs] adj (child, talent) 早熟な sōjuku na

preconceived [pri:kənsi:vd'] adj:
  preconceived idea 先入観 señnyūkan

precondition [pri:kəndiʃ'ən] n 前提条件 zeñteijōken

precursor [prikə:r'sər] n (person) 先駆者 señkushà; (thing) 前触れ maébure

predator [pred'ətər] n 捕食者 hoshókushà

predecessor [pred'isesər] n (person) 前任者 zeńnìnsha

predestination [pri:destinei'ʃən] n 予定説 yotéisetsu

predicament [pridik'əmənt] n 苦境 kukyō

predict [pridikt'] vt 予言する yogén suru

predictable [pridik'təbəl] adj (event, behavior etc) 予知できる yóchI dekírù

prediction [pridik'ʃən] n 予言 yogén

predominantly [pridɑːm'ənntli:] adv 圧倒的に attóteki ni

predominate [pridɑːm'əneit] vi (person, thing) ...が圧倒的に多い ...ga attóteki ni ...; (feature, quality) 目立つ medátsu

pre-eminent [pri:em'ənənt] adj (person,

thing) 優れた sugúreta

pre-empt [pri:émpt] *vt* (decision, action, statement) 先取りする sakídori suru

preen [pri:n] *vt*: *to preen itself* (bird) 羽繕いをする hazúkùroi wo suru

to preen oneself 得意げる tokúîgaru

prefab [pri:fǽb] *n* プレハブ住宅 puréhabujútaku

prefabricated [pri:fǽb'rikeitid] *adj* (buildings) プレハブの puréhabu no

preface [pref'is] *n* (in book) 前書 maégaki

prefect [pri:'fékt] *n* (BRIT) (in school) 監督生 kafítokusèi

prefer [prifar'] *vt* (like better: person, thing, activity) ...の方を好む ...no hő wo konómů

to prefer doing/ to do ...する方が好きである ...suru hő ga sukí de arů

preferable [pref'ərəbəl] *adj* ...が望ましい ...ga nozómashii

preferably [pref'ərəblì] *adv* できれば dekíreba

preference [pref'ərəns] *n* (liking) 好み konómi

to give preference to ...を優先的に扱う ...wo yűsenteki ni atsúkaù

preferential [prefərén'tʃəl] *adj*: *preferential treatment* 優先的な取扱い yűsenteki nà torfatsukaì

prefix [pri:'fiks] *n* 接頭辞 settőjî

pregnancy [preg'nənsì:] *n* (of woman, female animal) 妊娠 nińshin

pregnant [preg'nənt] *adj* (woman, female animal) 妊娠している nińshin shite irù

prehistoric [pri:histər'ik] *adj* (person, dwelling, monster etc) 有史以前の yűshiizên no

prejudice [predʒ'ədis] *n* (unreasonable dislike) 偏見 heńken; (bias in favor) ひいき hfíkí

prejudiced [predʒ'ədist] *adj* (person: prejudiced against) ...に対して偏見のある ...ni tāïshite heńken no arù; (: prejudiced in favor) ...をひいきにした ...wo hfíkí ni shitá

preliminary [prilím'əne:rì:] *adj* (action,

discussion) 予備的な yobíteki na

prelude [prel'u:d] *n* (preliminary event) 前兆 zeńchō; (MUS) 序曲 jőkyðku

premarital [pri:mær'itəl] *adj* 婚前の końzen no

premature [pri:mətʃur'] *adj* (earlier than expected: baby) 早産の sőzan no; (death, arrival) 早過ぎた hayásugita; (too early: action, event etc) 時期尚早の jíkîshōsō no

premature aging 早老 sőrō

premeditated [primed'əteitid] *adj* 計画的な keíkakuteki na

premier [primjir'] *adj* (best) 最良の saíryō no

♦*n* (POL) 総理大臣 sőridaijìn, 首相 shushō

première [primjir'] *n* (of film) 初公開 hatsúkōkai; (of play) 初演 shoén

premise [prem'is] *n* 前提 zeńtei

premises [prem'isiz] *npl* (of business, institution) 構内 kōnai

on the premises 構内で kōnai de

premium [pri:'mi:əm] *n* (COMM: extra sum of money) 割増金 warímashikìn, プレミアム purémìamu; (: sum paid for insurance) 掛金 kakékìn

to be at a premium (expensive) 高価である kőka de arù; (hard to get) 手に入りにくい té nì hafíriníkuì

premium bond (BRIT) *n* 割増金付き債券 warímashikintsukisaìken ◇抽選による賞金が付く chúsen nì yorù shőkin ga tsukù

premonition [premənìʃ'ən] *n* 予感 yokán

preoccupation [pria:kjəpeiʃ'ən] *n* (obsession) 専念する事 seńnen surú kotő; (worry) 気掛かり kigákarì na koto

preoccupied [pria:k'jəpaid] *adj* (person) ...の事になった omóitsuめた

prep [prep] *n* (SCOL: study) 勉強 beńkyō

prepaid [pri:peid'] *adj* (paid in advance) 支払い済みの shihấraizumi no

preparation [prepəreiʃ'ən] *n* (activity) 準備 júnbi; (food) 料理 ryőri; (medicine) 薬品 yakúhin; (cosmetic) 化粧品 keshőhin

preparations [prepərei'ʃənz] *npl* (arrangements) 準備 júnbi

preparatory [prɪpǽrʼətɔːri] *adj* (report) 予備の yóbì no; (training) 準備の júnbi no

preparatory school *n* (*US*) 予備校 yobíkō; (*BRIT*) 私立小学校 shirítsu shōgakkō

prepare [prɪpeːrʼ] *vt* (make ready: plan, speech, room etc) 準備する júnbi suru; (CULIN) 調理する chōri suru
♦*vi*: **to prepare for** (event, action) …の準備をする …no júnbi wo suru
prepared to (willing) …する用意がある …surú yòi ga árù
prepared for (ready) …の用意ができている …no yòi ga dékìte irú

preponderance [prɪpɑ́ːndərəns] *n* (of people, things) 大多数 daítasū

preposition [prepəzíʃʼən] *n* (LING) 前置詞 zeńchishi

preposterous [prɪpɑ́ːstərəs] *adj* (suggestion, idea, situation) 途方もない tohōmonaì

prep school *n* = **preparatory school**

prerequisite [prirékʼwizit] *n* 必要条件 hitsúyōjōken

prerogative [prɪrɑ́ːgʼətiv] *n* (of person, group) 特権 tokken

Presbyterian [prezbitíːrʼiːən] *adj* 長老派の chōrōha no
♦*n* 長老派の信者 chōrōha no shíñja

preschool [príːskuːlʼ] *adj* (age, child, education) 就学前の shūgakumae no

prescribe [priskráibʼ] *vt* (MED: medicine) 処方する shohō suru; (treatment) 命ずる meízuru

prescription [priskrípʼʃən] *n* (MED: slip of paper) 処方せん shohōsen; (: medicine) 処方薬 shohōyaku

presence [prezʼəns] *n* (state of being somewhere) …に居る事 …ni irú kotð; (*fig*: strong personal quality) 風采いfūsai; (spirit, invisible influence) spirit
in someone's presence …の居る前で …no irú mað de

presence of mind *n* 機転 kitén

present [*adj, n* prezʼənt *vb* prizent'] *adj* (current: person, thing) 現在の geńzai no; (in attendance) 出席している shusséki shite irú
♦*n* (actuality): **the present** 現在 geńzai; (gift) 贈り物 okúrimono, プレゼント purézeñto
♦*vt* (give: prize, award etc) 贈る okúrù; (cause, provide: difficulty, threat etc) …になる …ni nárù; (information) 知らせる atáerù; (describe: person, thing) 描写する byōsha suru; (RADIO, TV) 提供する teíkyō suru; (formally introduce: person) 紹介する shōkai suru
to give someone a present …にプレゼントを上げる …ni purézeñto wo agérù
at present 今の所 imá no tokoro

presentable [prizénʼtəbəl] *adj* (person) 人前に出られる hitómae nì derárerù

presentation [prezəntéiʼʃən] *n* (of plan, proposal, report etc) 提出 teíshutsu; (appearance) 体裁 teísai; (formal ceremony) 贈呈式 zōteíshìki

present-day [prezʼəntdeiʼ] *adj* 現代の geńdai no

presenter [prizénʼtər] *n* (RADIO, TV) 司会者 shikáìsha

presently [prezʼəntli] *adv* (soon) 間もなく mamónàku; (now) 現在 geńzai

preservation [prezərveiʼʃən] *n* (act of preserving) 保存 hozóń; (state of being preserved) 保存状態 hozóñjōtai

preservative [prizəːrʼvətiv] *n* (for food, wood, metal etc) 保存剤 hozóñzai

preserve [prizəːrʼv] *vt* (maintain: situation, condition) 維持する íjì suru; (: building, manuscript) 保存する hozóń suru; (food) 保存する hozóń suru
♦*n* (often *pl*: jam, marmalade) ジャム jámu

preside [prizáidʼ] *vi*: **to preside (over)** (meeting, event etc) (…の) 議長をする (…no) gichō wò suru

presidency [prezʼidənsi] *n* (POL: post) 大統領職 daítōryōshoku; (: time in office) 大統領の任期 daítōryō no níñki

president [prezʼidənt] *n* (POL) 大統領 daítōryō; (of organization) …長 …chō

presidential [prezidenʼtʃəl] *adj* 大統領の daítōryō no

press [pres] *n*: **the Press** (newspapers)

報道機関 hōdōkikan; (journalists) 報道陣 hōdōjin; (printing press) 印刷機 insatsuki; (of switch, button, bell) 押す事 osú kotó

◆vt (hold one thing against another) 押付ける oshítsukerù; (button, switch, bell etc) 押す osú; (iron: clothes) …にアイロンを掛ける …ni afron wo kakérù; (put pressure on: person) せき立てる sekítaterù; (insist): **to press something on someone** …に…を押付ける …ni …wo oshítsukerù

◆vi (squeeze) 押える osáerù; (pressurize): **to press for** (improvement, change etc) …のために …no tamé ni határakù; (forcibly) 強要する kyōyō suru
we are pressed for time/money 時間(金)が足りない jíkan[kané]ga tarínai

press agency n 通信社 tsúshinsha

press conference n 記者会見 kishákaiken

pressing [pres'iŋ] adj (engagement, decision etc) 緊急の kínkyū no

press on vi (despite problems etc) ひるまずに続ける hirúmazù ni tsuzúkerù

press stud (BRIT) n スナップ sunáppù

press-up [pres'ʌp] (BRIT) n 腕立て伏せ udétatefùse

pressure [preʃ'əːr] n (physical force: also fig) 圧力 atsúryòku; (also: **air pressure**) 気圧 kiátsu; (also: **water pressure**) 水圧 suíatsu; (also: **oil pressure**) 油圧 yuátsu; (stress) 圧迫 appáku, プレッシャー purésshà
to put pressure on someone (to do) (…する様に) …に圧力を掛ける (…surú yō ni) …ni atsúryòku wo kakérù

pressure cooker n 圧力ガマ atsúryokugàma

pressure gauge n 圧力計 atsúryokukei

pressure group n (POL) 圧力団体 atsúryokudañtai, プレッシャーグループ purésshàgurùpu

pressurized [preʃ'əraizd] adj (cabin, container, spacesuit) 気圧を一定に保った kiátsu wo ittéi ni tamóttà

prestige [presti:ʒ'] n 名声 meísei

prestigious [prestidʒ'əs] adj 著名な cho-

méi na

presumably [prizu:'məbli:] adv たぶん tábùn, おそらく osóraku

presume [prizu:m'] vt: **to presume (that)** (suppose) …(だと) 推定する (…dá tò) suítei suru

presumption [prizʌmp'ʃən] n (supposition) 推定 suítei

presumptuous [prizʌmp'tʃuːəs] adj せん越な señ-etsu na

presuppose [prisəpouz'] vt …を前提とする …wo zeñtei tó suru

pretence [pritens'] (US also: **pretense**) n (false appearance) 見せ掛け misékake
under false pretences うそを言って úsò wo itté

pretend [pritend'] vt (feign) …の振りをする …no furí wò surù
◆vi (feign) 見せ掛ける misékakerù
to pretend to do …する振りをする …suru furí wò suru

pretense [pritens'] (US) n = pretence

pretentious [priten'tʃəs] adj (claiming importance, significance: person, play, film etc) うぬぼれた unúboreta

pretext [pri:'tekst] n 口実 kójitsu

pretty [prit'i:] adj (person, thing) きれいな kírèi na
◆adv (quite) かなり kánàri

prevail [priveil'] vi (be current: custom, belief) はやる hayárù; (gain acceptance, influence: proposal, principle) 勝つ kátsù

prevailing [privei'liŋ] adj (wind) 卓越風 takúetsufù; (dominant: fashion, attitude etc) 一般の ippán no

prevalent [prev'ələnt] adj (common) 一般的な ippánteki na

prevent [privent'] vt: **to prevent someone from doing something** …が…をするのを妨げる …ga …wo suru no wo samátagerù
to prevent something from happening …が起るのを防ぐ …ga okórù no wo fuségù

preventative [priven'tətiv] adj = preventive

prevention [priven'tʃən] n 予防 yobó

preventive [priven'tiv] adj (measures, medicine) 予防の yobō no

preview [pri:'vju:] n (of film) 試写会 shishákài; (of exhibition etc) 招待展示内覧 shōtaitenínairan

previous [pri:'vi:əs] adj (earlier: event, thing, period of time) 前の máe no

previously [pri:'vi:əsli:] adv 前に máe ni

pre-war [pri:'wɔ:r'] adj 戦前の señzen no

prey [prei] n 獲物 emóno

♦vi: **to prey on** (animal: feed on) ...を捕食する ...wo hoshóku suru

it was preying on his mind 彼はそれを気にしていた kárè wa soré wò kí ni shite itá

price [prais] n (amount of money) 値段 nedán, (fig) 代償 daíshō

♦vt (goods) ...に値段を付ける ...ni nedán wò tsukérù

priceless [prais'lis] adj 非常に貴重な hijō ni kichō na

price list n 値段表 nedánhyò

prick [prik] n (short, sharp pain) ちくっとする痛み chikúttò suru itámí

♦vt (make hole in) 鋭い物で刺す surúdoì monó de sásù; (cause pain) ちくっと刺す chikúttò sásù

to prick up one's ears (listen eagerly) 耳を澄まして聞く mimí wo sumáshite kikù

prickle [prik'əl] n (of plant) とげ togé; (sensation) ちくちくする痛み chíkùchiku suru itámí

prickly [prik'li:] adj (plant) とげだらけの togédaràke no; (fabric) ちくちくする chíkùchiku suru

prickly heat n あせも asémo

pride [praid] n (satisfaction) 誇り hokóri; (dignity, self-respect) 自尊心 jisónshin, プライド puráido; (pej: feeling of superiority) 高慢 kōman

♦vt: **to pride oneself on** ...を誇りとする ...wo hokóri tò suru

priest [pri:st] n (Christian: Catholic, Anglican etc) 司祭 shísaì; (non-Christian) 僧侶 sòryo

priestess [pri:s'tis] n (non-Christian) みこ mfkò

priesthood [pri:st'hud] n (position) 司祭職 shisáishoku

prig [prig] n 気取り屋 kídoriya

prim [prim] adj (pej) 堅苦しい katákurushii; (easily shocked) 上品ぶった jōhiñbutta

primarily [praimer'ili:] adv (above all) 主に ómò ni

primary [prai'me:ri:] adj (first in importance) 主要な shuyō na

♦n (US: election) 予備選挙 yobísèñkyo

primary school n 小学校 shōgakkō

primate [prai'meit] n (ZOOL) 霊長類 refchōrui

prime [praim] adj (most important) 最も重要な mottómò jūyō na; (best quality) 最上の saijō no

♦vt (wood) ...に下塗りをする ...ni shitánuri wò suru; (fig: person) ...に教え込む ...ni oshíekomů

prime example (typical) 典型的な例 teñkeiteki nà reí

Prime Minister n 総理大臣 sōridaìjin, 首相 shushō

primeval [praimi:'vəl] adj (existing since long ago): *primeval forest* 原生林 geñseìrin; (feelings, tribe) 原始的な gefshiteki na

primitive [prim'ətiv] adj 原始的な geñshiteki na

primrose [prim'rouz] n ツキミソウ tsukímisō

primus (stove) [prai'məs-] (BRIT) n 石油こんろ sekíyukoñro

prince [prins] n (son of king etc) 王子 ōji; (son of Japanese emperor) 親王 shíñnō

princess [prin'sis] n (daughter of king etc) 王女 ōjo; (daughter of Japanese emperor) 内親王 naíshinnō

principal [prin'səpəl] adj (most important: reason, character, aim etc) 主要な shuyō na; (of school) 校長 kōchō; (of college) 学長 gakúchō

principle [prin'səpəl] n (moral belief) 信念 shiñnen; (general rule) 原則 geñsoku; (scientific law) 法則 hōsoku *in principle* (theoretically) 原則として gensoku tòshitè

on principle (morally) 主義として shugí tòshitè

print [print] *n* (letters and numbers on page) 印刷文字 insatsumojì; (ART) 版画 hañga; (PHOT) 陽画 yôga, プリント purínto; (footprint) 足跡 ashfatò; (fingerprint) 指紋 shimón

♦*vt* (produce: book, newspaper, leaflet) 印刷する insatsu suru; (publish: story, article etc) 記載する kisái suru; (cloth) ...になつ染める ..ni nassén suru; (write in capitals) 活字体で書く katsûjitai dè kákù

out of print 絶版で zeppán de

printed matter [prin'tid-] *n* 印刷物 insatsubûtsu

printer [prin'tə:r] *n* (person, firm) 印刷屋 insatsúya; (machine) 印刷機 insatsukî

printing [prin'tiŋ] *n* (act, art) 印刷 insatsu

printout [print'aut] *n* (COMPUT) プリントアウト purîntoaûto

prior [prai'ə:r] *adj* (previous: knowledge, warning, consent etc) 事前の jizén no; (more important: claim, duty) より重要な yorî jûyô na

prior to ...の前に ...no máè ni

priority [praiɔ:r'iti:] *n* (most urgent task) 優先課題 yûsenkadaì; (most important thing, task) 最重要課題 saíjûyôkadaì

to have priority (over) (...に) 優先する (...ni) yûsen suru

prise [praiz] *vt: to prise open* こじ開ける kojîakerû

prism [priz'əm] *n* プリズム purízumu

prison [priz'ən] *n* (building) 刑務所 kefmusho

♦*cpd* 刑務所の keímusho no

prisoner [priz'ənə:r] *n* (in prison) 囚人 shûjin; (captured person) 捕虜 hôryo

prisoner of war *n* 戦争捕虜 señsôhoryò

pristine [pris'ti:n] *adj* (condition: new) 真新しい maátarashiì; (: like new) 新品同様の shiñpindôyô no

privacy [prai'vəsi:] *n* プライバシー purâibashî

private [prai'vit] *adj* (not public: property, club etc) 私有の shiyû no, プライベートの purâibèto no; (not state-owned: industry, service) 民間の miñkan no; (discussion, sitting etc) 非公開の hikôkaì no; (personal: activities, belongings) 個人の kôjîn no; (: thoughts, plans) 心の中の kokôro no naka nò; (quiet: place) 奥まった okûmattà; (: person) 内気な uchíki na; (confidential) 内密の naímitsu no; (intimate) 部外者立入禁止の bugáishatachfirikinshi no

♦*n* (MIL) 兵卒 heísotsu

「*private*」(on envelope) 親展 shiñten; (on door) 部外者立入禁止 bugáishatachfirikinshi

in private 内密に naímitsu ni

private enterprise *n* (not state owned) 民間企業 miñkan kígyò; (owned by individuals) 個人企業 kôjin kígyò

private eye *n* 私立探偵 shiritsûtantei

private property *n* 私有地 shiyûchì

private school *n* (fee-paying) 私立学校 shiritsûgakkô

privatize [prai'vətaiz] *vt* (government-owned company etc) 民間に払い下げる miñkan ni haráì sagerû

privet [priv'it] *n* イボタノキ ibôtanoki

privilege [priv'əlidʒ] *n* (advantage) 特権 tokkén; (opportunity) 光栄な機会 kôei na kikaì

privileged [priv'əlidʒd] *adj* (having advantages) 特権のある tokkén no arù; (having special opportunity) 光栄な機会を得た kôei na kikaì wo etá

privy [priv'i:] *adj: to be privy to* 内々に関知している naínai ni kâñchi shité irú

prize [praiz] *n* (award) 賞 shô

♦*adj* (first class) 典型的な teñkeiteki na

♦*vt* 重宝する chôhô suru

prize-giving [praiz'givîŋ] *n* 表彰式 hyôshôshìkì

prizewinner [praiz'winə:r] *n* 受賞者 jushôshà

pro [prou] *n* (SPORT) 職業選手 shokûgyôseñshu, プロ púrô

◆prep (in favor of) ...に賛成して ...ni sańsei shite

the pros and cons 賛否両論 sáńpiryóron

probability [prɑːbəbil'əti:] *n* (likelihood): *probability of/that* ...の(...が起る)公算 ...no (...ga okórů) kósan

in all probability たいてい taítei

probable [prɑːb'əbəl] *adj* (likely to happen) 起りそうな okóriső na; (likely to be true) ありそうな aríső na

probably [prɑːb'əbli:] *adv* たぶん tábùn, おそらく osóràku

probation [probei'ʃən] *n*: *on probation* (LAW) 保護観察 hogókañsatsu de; (employee) 見習いで minárai de

probe [proub] *n* (MED) ゾンデ zóñde; (SPACE) 探査衛星 tañsaeiséi; (enquiry) 調査 chósa

◆vt (investigate) 調査する chósa suru; (poke) つついて探る tsutsúite sagúrů

problem [prɑːb'ləm] *n* 問題 mońdai

problematic(al) [prɑːbləmæt'ik(əl)] *adj* 問題になる mońdai ni narů

procedure [prəsiː'dʒəːr] *n* (way of doing something) やり方 yaríkata; (ADMIN, LAW) 手続 tetsúzuki

proceed [prəsiːd'] *vi* (do afterwards): *to proceed to do something* ...をし始める ...wo shihájimerů; (continue): *to proceed (with)* (...を) 続ける (...wo) tsuzúkerů; (activity, event, process: carry on) 続ける tsuzúkerů; (person: go) 行く ikú

proceedings [prəsiː'diŋz] *npl* (organized events) 行事 gyóji; (LAW) 訴訟手続 soshótetsuzúki

proceeds [prou'siːdz] *npl* 収益 shúeki

process [prɑːs'es] *n* (series of actions: *also* BIOL, CHEM) 過程 katéi, プロセス purósèsu

◆vt (raw materials, food) 加工する kakó suru; (information) 処理する shórí suru

processing [prɑːs'esiŋ] *n* (PHOT) 現像 geñzó

procession [prəseʃ'ən] *n* 行列 gyóretsu

proclaim [prəkleim'] *vt* (announce) 宣言する señgen suru

proclamation [prɑːkləmei'ʃən] *n* 宣言 señgen

procrastinate [prəkræs'təneit] *vi* 先に延ばす sakí ni nobásu

procreation [proukriːei'ʃən] *n* 生殖 seíshoku

procure [prəkjuːr'] *vt* 調達する chótatsu suru

prod [prɑːd] *vt* (push: with finger, stick, knife etc) つつく tsutsúkù

◆n (with finger, stick, knife etc) 一突き hitótsuki

prodigal [prɑːd'əgəl] *adj*: *prodigal son/daughter* 放とう息子(娘) hótómusúko (musúme)

prodigious [prədidʒ'əs] *adj* 巨大な kyódai na

prodigy [prɑːd'ədʒiː] *n* 天才 teñsai

produce [*n* prou'duːs *vb* prəduːs'] *n* (AGR) 農産物 nósanbutsu

◆vt (cause: effect, result etc) 起す okósu; (make, create: object) 作る tsukúrů; (BIOL: fruit, seeds) つける tsukérů, ...には...がなる ...ní wa ...ga narú; (: young) 産む umú; (CHEM) 作り出す tsukúridasů; (fig: evidence, argument) 示す shimésů; (: bring or take out) 取出す toridasů; (play, film, program) 製作する seísaku suru

producer [prəduːs'əːr] *n* (of film, play, program, record) 製作者 seísakushà, プロデューサー puródyùsà; (country: of food, material) 生産国 seísankôku; (company: of food, material) 生産会社 seísangaisha

product [prɑːd'əkt] *n* (thing) 産物 sañbutsu; (result) 結果 kekká

production [prədʌk'ʃən] *n* (process of manufacturing, growing) 生産 seísan; (amount of goods manufactured, grown) 生産高 seísandàka; (THEATER) 上演 jóen

electricity production 発電 hatsúden

production line *n* 工程ライン kóteiraìn, ラインライン ráìn

productive [prədʌk'tiv] *adj* (person, thing: *also fig*) 生産的な seísanteki na

productivity [proudʌktiv'əti:] *n* 生産能

力 sefsannōryoku

profane [prəfein'] *adj* (secular, lay) 世俗的な sezokuteki na; (language etc) 下品な gehín na

profess [prəfes'] *vt* (claim) 主張する shuchō suru; (express: feeling, opinion) 明言する mefgen suru

profession [prəfes'an] *n* (job requiring special training) 知的職業 chitékishokugyō; (people) 同業者仲間 dōgyōshanakama

professional [prəfes'anəl] *adj* (skill, organization, advice) 専門職の sefmōnshoku no; (not amateur: photographer, musician etc) プロの púrō no; (highly trained) 専門家の sefmonka no; (of a high standard) 本職らしい honshokurashī

♦*n* (doctor, lawyer, teacher etc) 知的職業者 chitékishokugyōshá; (SPORT) プロ púrō; (skilled person) 玄人 kúrōto

professor [prəfes'ar] *n* (US) 教師 kyōshi, 先生 sefsei; (BRIT) 教授 kyōju

proficiency [prəfiʃ'ənsi:] *n* 熟練 jukúren

proficient [prəfiʃ'ənt] *adj* 熟練した jukúren shita

profile [prou'fail] *n* (of person's face) 横顔 yokógaò; (fig: article) 経歴 kefreki

profit [praːf'it] *n* (COMM) 利益 rīeki

♦*vi*: **to profit by/from** (fig) ...がためになる ...ga tamé ní narū

profitability [praːfitəbil'əti:] *n* (ECON) 収益性 shūekísei

profitable [praːf'itəbəl] *adj* (ECON) 利益になる rīeki ni narū

profound [prəfaund'] *adj* (great: shock, effect) 強い tsuyóĩ; (intellectual: idea, work) 深遠な shin-én na

profusely [prəfjuːs'liː] *adv* (bleed) 多量に taryō ni; (thank) 丁重に kasánegasáne

profusion [prəfjuː'ʒən] *n* 大量 tairyō

prognoses [praːgnou'siːz] *npl of* **prognosis**

prognosis [praːgnou'səs] (*pl* **prognoses**) *n* (forecast) 予想 yosō; (of illness) 予後 yógò

program [prou'græm] (*BRIT* **programme**) *n* (of actions, events) 計画 kef-

kaku; (RADIO, TV) 番組 bañgumi; (leaflet) プログラム purógūramu; (COMPUT) プログラム purógūramu

♦*vt* (machine, system) ...にプログラムを入れる ...ni purógūramu wo irérū

programing [prou'græmiŋ] (*BRIT* **programming**) *n* (COMPUT) プログラム作成 purógūramu sakúsèi, プログラミング purógūramīngu

programmer [prou'græmər] *n* (COMPUT) プログラマー purógūramā

progress [*n* praːg'res *vb* prəgres'] *n* (process of getting nearer to objective) 前進 zefshin; (changes, advances in society) 進歩 shīnpo; (development) 発展 hatten

♦*vi* (become more advanced, skilled) 進歩する shīnpo suru; (become higher in rank) 昇進する shōshin suru; (continue) 続く tsuzúkū

in progress (meeting, battle, match) 進行中で shiñkōchū de

progression [prəgreʃ'ən] *n* (gradual development) 進展 shiñten; (series) 連続 refzoku

progressive [prəgres'iv] *adj* (person) 進歩的な shiñpoteki na; (change) 段階的な dańkaiteki na

prohibit [prouhib'it] *vt* (forbid, make illegal) 禁じる kiñjirū

prohibition [prouəbiʃ'ən] *n* (law, rule) 禁則 kiñsoku; (forbidding: of strikes, alcohol etc) 禁止 kiñshi; (US): *Prohibition* 禁酒法時代 kiñshuhōjidài

prohibitive [prouhib'ətiv] *adj* (price etc) 法外な hōgai na, 手が出ない様なté gà dénái yōna

project [*n* praːdʒ'ekt *vb* prədʒekt'] *n* (large-scale plan, scheme) 計画 kefkaku, プロジェクト purójèkùto; (SCOL) 研究テーマ kefkyūtèma

♦*vt* (plan) 計画する kefkaku suru; (estimate: figure, amount) 見積る mitsúmorù; (light) 投射する tōsha suru; (film, picture) 映写する efsha suru

♦*vi* (stick out) 突出る tsukéderù

projectile [prədʒek'təl] *n* 弾丸, dañgan

projection [prədʒek'ʃən] *n* (estimate) 見積り mitsúmori; (overhang) 突起 tokkí;

(CINEMA) 映写 efsha

projector [prədʒek'tər] n 映写機 efshaki

proletarian [proulitεə'ri:ən] adj 無産階級の musánkaikyū no, プロレタリアの purόretaria no

proletariat [proulitεə'ri:ət] n 無産階級 musánkaikyū, プロレタリア purόretaria

proliferate [prəlif'ə:reit] vi 急増する kyūzō suru

prolific [prəlif'ik] adj (artist, composer, writer) 多作の tasáku no

prologue [prou'lɔːg] n (of play) 序幕 jomáku, プロローグ purόrōgu; (of book) 序言 jogén

prolong [prəlɔ:ŋ'] vt (life, meeting, holiday) 引延ばす hikínobasu, 延長する enchō suru

prom [prɑm] n abbr = promenade; (US: ball) 学生舞踏会 gakúseibutōkai

promenade [prɑməneid'] n (by sea) 海岸の遊歩道 kaígan no yūhodō

promenade concert (BRIT) n 立見席のある音楽会 tachímiseki no árù ongakukai

prominence [prɑm'ənəns] n (importance) 重要性 jūyōsei

prominent [prɑm'ənənt] adj (important) 重要な jūyō na; (very noticeable) 目立つ medátsu

promiscuous [prəmis'kju:əs] adj (person) 相手構わずにセックスをする aíte kamawazu ni sékkùsu wo suru

promise [prɑm'is] n (vow) 約束 yakúsoku; (talent) 才能 saínō; (hope) 見込み mikómi
♦vi (vow) 約束する yakúsoku suru
♦vt: **to promise someone something, promise something to someone** ...に...を約束する ...ni ...wo yakúsoku suru
to promise (someone) to do something/that (...に) ...すると約束する (...ni) ...surú to yakúsoku suru

promising [prɑm'isiŋ] adj (person, thing) 有望な yūbō na

promote [prəmout'] vt (employee) 昇進させる shōshin saserù; (product, pop star) 宣伝する senden suru; (ideas) 促進

する sokúshin suru

promoter [prəmou'tər] n (of event) 興業主 kόgyōshù, プロモーター purόmōtā; (of cause, idea) 推進者 suíshinsha

promotion [prəmou'ʃən] n (at work) 昇進 shōshin; (of product, event, idea) 宣伝 senden

prompt [prɑmpt] adj (rapid: reaction, response etc) 迅速な jinsoku na
♦adv (exactly) 丁度 chōdo
♦n (COMPUT) プロンプト purόnputo
♦vt (cause) ...の原因となる ...no geń-in to narù; (when talking) ...に水を向ける ...ni mizu wo mukérù
to prompt someone to do something ...が...をするよう仕掛けとなる ...ga ...wo surú kikkáke to narù

promptly [prɑmpt'li:] adv (immediately) 直ちに tádàchi ni; (exactly) 丁度 chōdo

prone [proun] adj (lying face down) うつ伏せの utsúbuse no
prone to (inclined to) ...しがちな ...shigáchi na

prong [prɔŋ] n (of fork) 歯 há

pronoun [prou'naun] n 代名詞 daímeishi

pronounce [prənauns'] vt (word) 発音する hatsúon suru; (declare) 宣言する señgen suru; (give verdict, opinion) 言渡す iíwatasù

pronounced [prənaunst'] adj (marked) 著しい ichíjirushiì

pronunciation [prənansiːei'ʃən] n 発音 hatsúon

proof [pruːf] n (evidence) 証拠 shōko; (TYP) 校正刷り kōseizuri, ゲラ gerá
♦adj: **proof against** ...に耐えられる ...ni taérarerù

prop [prɑp] n (stick, support: also fig) 支え sasáe
♦vt (also: **prop up**) 支える sasáerù; (lean): **to prop something against** ...に立掛ける ...ni tatékakerù

propaganda [prɑpəgæn'də] n 宣伝 senden, プロパガンダ purόpagañda

propagate [prɑp'əgeit] vt (idea, information) 普及させる fukyū saserù

propel [prəpel'] vt (vehicle, boat,

machine) 推進する suíshin suru; (fig: person) 駆立てる karftaterù

propeller [prəpɛl'ər] n プロペラ purópepurä

propensity [prəpɛn'siti:] n 傾向 kefkō

proper [prɑ:p'ər] adj (real, authentic) ちゃんとした chấnto shita; (correct) 正しい tadáshìi; (suitable) 適当な tekítō na; (socially acceptable) 社会の通念にかなった shákái no tsūnen ni kanáttả; (referring to place): **the village proper** 村そのもの murá sono monò

properly [prɑ:p'ər:li:] adv (adequately): eat, study) 充分に jūbun ni; (decently: behave) 正しく tadáshìku

proper noun n 固有名詞 koyúmeìshi

property [prɑ:p'ərti:] n (possessions) 財産 zấisan; (building and its land) 物件 bukkèn; (land owned) 所有地 shoyúchi; (quality: of substance, material etc) 特性 tokúsei

property owner n 地主 jinúshi

prophecy [prɑ:f'isi:] n 予言 yogén

prophesy [prɑ:f'isai] vt (predict) 予言する yogén suru

prophet [prɑ:f'it] n (REL) 予言者 yogénsha

prophetic [prəfɛt'ik] adj (statement, words) 予言的な yogénteki na

proportion [prəpɔ:r'ʃən] n (part: of group, amount) 割合 wáríai; (number: of people, things) 数 kázů; (ratio) 率 rítsù

proportional [prəpɔ:r'ʃənəl] adj: **proportional (to)** (...に) 比例する (...ni) hiréi suru

proportional representation n 比例代表制 hiréidaihyōsei

proportionate [prəpɔ:r'ʃənit] adj: **proportionate (to)** (...に) 比例する (...ni) hiréi suru

proposal [prəpou'zəl] n (plan) 提案 tefan

a proposal (of marriage) 結婚の申込み kekkón nò mōshikomi, プロポーズ purópōzu

propose [prəpouz'] vt (plan, idea) 提案する tefan suru; (motion) 提案する tefshutsu suru; (toast) ...の音頭を取る ... no ōndo wo tórù

♦vi (offer marriage) 結婚を申込む kekkón wô mōshikomù, プロポーズする purópōzu suru

to propose to do ...するつもりでいる ...suru tsumóri de irù

proposition [prɑ:pəzíʃ'ən] n (statement) 主張 shuchō; (offer) 提案 tefan

proprietor [prəprai'ətər] n (of hotel, shop, newspaper etc) 持主 mochínushi, オーナー ōnā

propriety [prəprai'əti:] n (seemliness) 礼儀正しさ refgitadashìsa

pro rata [-rɑ:'tə] adv 比例して hiréi shite

prosaic [prouzei'ik] adj (person, piece of writing) 散文的な sañbunteki na

prose [prouz] n (not poetry) 散文 sañbun

prosecute [prɑ:s'əkju:t] vt (LAW) 起訴する sósō suru

prosecution [prɑ:səkju:'ʃən] n (action) 訴追 sótsūì; (accusing side) 検察側 keñsatsugawa

prosecutor [prɑ:s'əkju:tər] n (also: **public prosecutor**) 検察官 keñsatsukàn

prospect [prɑ:s'pekt] n (possibility) 可能性 kanôsei; (outlook) 見込み mikômi

♦vi: **to prospect (for)** (gold etc) (...を) 探鉱する tañkō suru

prospecting [prɑ:s'pektiŋ] n (for gold, oil etc) 探鉱 tañkō

prospective [prəspek'tiv] adj (son-in-law, customer, candidate etc) ...になろうとしている ...ni narô tô shité irú

prospects [prɑ:s'pekts] npl (for work etc) 見込み mikômi

prospectus [prəspek'təs] n (of college, school, company) 要綱 yōkō

prosper [prɑ:s'pər] vi (business, city etc) 繁栄する hañ-ei suru

prosperity [prɑ:spe:r'iti:] n 繁栄 hañ-ei

prosperous [prɑ:s'pərəs] adj (person, city etc) 裕福な yúfuku na; (business etc) 繁盛している hañjō shite irú

prostitute [prɑ:s'titut] n (female) 売春婦 baíshunfù; (male) 男娼 dañshō

prostrate [prɑ:s'treit] adj (face down) うつ伏せの utsúbuse no

protagonist [proutæg'ənist] n (supporter) 支援者 shiénsha; (leading participant: in event, movement) その…の人 rídakaku nò hitò; (THEATER) 主役 shuyáku; (in story etc) 主人公 shujínkô

protect [prətekt'] vt (person, thing) 守る mamórù, 保護する hógo suru

protection [prətek'ʃən] n 保護 hógo

protective [prətek'tiv] adj (clothing, layer, etc) 防護の bôgo no; (gesture) 防衛の bôei no; (person) 保護的な hogóteki na

protégé [prou'təʒei] n 偉い人のひいきを受ける人 erái hitó nò hiíki wò ukérù hitó

protein [prou'tin] n たんぱく質 tañpakushītsu

protest [n prou'test vb prətest'] n (strong expression of disapproval, opposition) 抗議 kôgi
◆vi: to protest about/against/at …に抗議する …ni kôgi suru
◆vt (insist): to protest (that) (…だと) 主張する (…dá tò) shuchô suru

Protestant [prɑt'istənt] adj 新教の shiñkyô no, プロテスタントの purótesùtanto no
◆n 新教徒 shiñkyôto, プロテスタント教徒 purótesùtanto kyôto

protester [prətes'tər] n 抗議者 kôgisha

protocol [prou'təkɑl] n 外交儀礼 gaíkôgirèi

prototype [prou'tətaip] n 原型 geñkei

protracted [proutræk'tid] adj (absence, meeting etc) 長い nagáì

protrude [proutruːd'] vi (rock, ledge, teeth etc) 突出る tsukíderù

proud [praud] adj (pleased): **proud of** …を誇りとする …wo hokóri tò suru; (dignified) プライドのある puráido no arù; (arrogant) 尊大な soñdai na

prove [pruːv] vt (verify) 立証する risshô suru
◆vi: to prove (to be) correct etc 結局…が正しいと判明する kekkyóku …ga tadáshiì to hañmei suru
to prove oneself 自分の才能を立証する jibún nò saínô wò risshô suru

proverb [prɑv'ərb] n ことわざ kotówaza

proverbial [prəvər'biːəl] adj ことわざの kotówaza no

provide [prəvaid'] vt (give) 与える atáerù; (make available) 供給する kyôkyû suru
to provide someone with something …に…を供給する …ni …wo kyôkyû suru

provided (that) [prəvai'did-] conj …という条件で …to iu jôken de

provide for vt fus (person) …の面倒を見る …no meñdô wò mírù
◆vt (future event) …に備える …ni sonáerù

Providence [prɑv'idəns] n 摂理 sétsùri

providing [prəvai'diŋ] conj: **providing (that)** …という条件で …to iu jôken de

province [prɑv'ins] n (of country) 県 kêñ; (fig) 管轄 kañkatsu

provincial [prəvin'tʃəl] adj (town, newspaper etc) 地方の chihô no; (pej) 田舎じみた inákajimìta

provision [prəviʒ'ən] n (supplying) 供給 kyôkyû; (of contract, agreement) 規定 kitéi

provisional [prəviʒ'ənəl] adj (government, agreement, arrangement etc) 暫定的な zañteiteki na

provisions [prəviʒ'ənz] npl (food) 食料 shokúryô

proviso [prəvai'zou] n 規定 kitéi

provocation [prɑvəkei'ʃən] n 挑発 chôhatsu

provocative [prəvɑk'ətiv] adj (remark, article, gesture) 挑発的な chôhatsuteki na; (sexually stimulating) 扇情的な señjôteki na

provoke [prəvouk'] vt (annoy: person) 怒らせる okóraserù; (cause: fight, argument etc) 引起こす hikíokosù

prow [prau] n へさき hesáki, 船首 señshu

prowess [prau'is] n (outstanding ability) 手腕 shúwan

prowl [praul] vi (also: **prowl about, prowl around**) うろつく urótsukù
◆n: on the prowl あさり歩いて asáriaruìte

prowler [prau'lər] n うろつく人 urótsukù hitò

proximity [prɔ:ksim'iti:] *n* 近さ chikása

proxy [prɔ:k'si:] *n*: **by proxy** 代理を通じて dáiri wò tsújite

prude [pru:d] *n* 上品ぶる人 jóhinburu hitó

prudence [pru:'dəns] *n* (care, sense) 慎重さ shifichōsa

prudent [pru:'dənt] *adj* (careful, sensible) 慎重な shifichō na

prune [pru:n] *n* 干しプラム hoshípuramu
◆*vt* (bush, plant, tree) せん定する sefítei suru

pry [prai] *vi*: **to pry (into)** (...を) せん索する (...wo) sefísaku suru

PS [pi:es'] *abbr* = *postscript*

psalm [sɑ:m] *n* 詩編 shihén

pseudo- [su:'dou] *prefix* 偽... nisé...

pseudonym [sai'ki:] *n* 筆名 hitsúmei, ペンネーム pefinēmu

psyche [sai'ki:] *n* 精神 sefshin

psychiatric [saiki:æt'rik] *adj* (hospital, problem, treatment) 精神科の sefshinka no

psychiatrist [sikai'ətrist] *n* 精神科医 sefshinka-ì

psychiatry [sikai'ətri:] *n* 精神医学 sefshin-igàku

psychic [sai'kik] *adj* (person: also: **psychical**) 霊媒の reíbai no; (of the mind) 精神の sefshin no

psychoanalysis [saikouænæl'isis] *n* 精神分析 sefshinbuñseki

psychoanalyst [saikouæn'əlist] *n* 精神分析医 sefshinbunseki-ì

psychoanalyze [saikouæn'əlaiz] *vt* ...の精神分析をする ...no sefshinbuñseki wo suru

psychological [saikəlɑːdʒ'ikəl] *adj* (related to the mind: difference, problem etc) 精神的な seíshinteki na; (related to psychology: test, treatment etc) 心理的な shifíriteki na

psychologist [saikɑːl'ədʒist] *n* 心理学者 shifírigakùsha

psychology [saikɑːl'ədʒi:] *n* (study) 心理学 shifírigakù; (mind) 心理 shifiri

psychopath [sai'kəpæθ] *n* 精神病質者 sefshinbyōshitsushà

psychosomatic [saikousoumæt'ik] *adj* 精神身体の sefshinshiñtai no

psychotic [saikɑ:t'ik] *adj* 精神病の sefshinbyō no

PTO [pi:ti:'ou'] *abbr* (= *please turn over*) 裏面に続く rímen ni tsuzukú

pub [pʌb] *n abbr* (= *public house*) 酒場 sakába, パブ pábù

puberty [pju:'bə:rti:] *n* 思春期 shishúnki

pubic [pju:'bik] *adj*: **pubic hair** 陰毛 iñmō

public [pʌb'lik] *adj* (of people: support, opinion, interest) 国民の kokúmin no; (for people: building, service) 公共の kōkyō no; (for people to see: statement, action etc) 公の ōyake no
◆*n*: **the public** (all people of country, community) 公衆 kōshū no; (particular set of people) ...層 ...sō; (fans, supporters) 支持者 shijíshà

in public 公に ōyake ni, 人前で hitómaè de
to make public 公表する kōyō suru

public address system *n* 場内放送 (装置) jónaihōsò(sōchi)

publican [pʌb'likən] *n* パブの亭主 pábù no teíshu

publication [pʌblikei'ʃən] *n* (act) 出版 shuppán; (book, magazine) 出版物 shuppáñbutsu

public company *n* 株式会社 kabúshikigaìsha

public convenience (*BRIT*) *n* 公衆便所 kōshūbeñjo

public holiday *n* 休日 kyújitsu

public house (*BRIT*) *n* 酒場 sakába, パブ pábù

publicity [pʌblis'əti:] *n* (information) 宣伝 señden; (attention) 広く知られる事 híròku shiraréru kotó

publicize [pʌb'ləsaiz] *vt* (fact, event) 報道する hōdō suru

publicly [pʌb'likli:] *adv* 公に ōyake ni, 人前で hitómaè de

public opinion *n* 世論 yórðn

public relations *n* 広報活動 kōhōkatsu-dō, ピーアール pīaru

public school *n* (*US*) 公立学校 kōritsugakkō (BRIT) 私立学校 shiritsugakkō

public-spirited [pʌblɪkspɪritɪd] *adj* 公共心のある kōkyōshin nō árù

public transport *n* 公共輸送機関 kōkyōyusōkikàn

publish [pʌblɪʃ] *n* (book, magazine) 出版する shuppan suru, 発行する hakkō suru; (letter etc: in newspaper) 記載する kisái suru; (subj: person: article, story) 発表する happyō suru

publisher [pʌblɪʃəɾ] *n* (person) 発行者 hakkōshà; (company) 出版社 shuppánsha

publishing [pʌblɪʃɪŋ] *n* (profession) 出版業 shuppangyō

puce [pjuːs] *adj* 暗褐色の añkasshoku no

pucker [pʌkəɾ] *vt* (part of face) ...をしかめる wo shikámerù; (fabric etc) ...にしわを寄せる ...ni shiwá wo yoserù

pudding [pudɪŋ] *n* (cooked sweet food) プディング púdiñgu; (BRIT: dessert) デザート dezātò

black pudding ブラッドソーセージ buráddosōsèji

puddle [pʌdl] *n* (also: **a puddle of water**) 水溜まり mizutamari; (of blood etc) 溜まり tamari

puff [pʌf] *n* (of cigarette, pipe) 一服 ippúku; (gasp) あえぎ áegi; (of air, smoke) 一吹き hitófukaì

◆*vt*: **to puff one's pipe** パイプをふかす páïpu wo fukásù

◆*vi* (breathe loudly) あえぐ áegù

puffed [pʌft] (*inf*) *adj* (out of breath) 息を切らせた iki wo kirásetà

puff out *vt* (fill with air: one's chest, cheeks) 膨らます fukúramasù

puff pastry *n* パイ皮 paÍkawa

puffy [pʌfi] *adj* (eye) はれぼったい harébottaì; (face) むくんだ mukúnda

pull [pul] *n* (tug): **to give something a pull** ...を引っ張る ...wo hippárù

◆*vt* (*gen*) 引く hikú; (tug: rope, hair etc) 引っ張る hippárù

◆*vi* (tug) 引く hikú, 引っ張る hippárù

to pull to pieces 引裂く hikísakù

to pull one's punches 手加減する tekáge-

gen suru

to pull one's weight 仲間同様に働く nakámadōyō ni határakù

to pull oneself together 落着きを取り戻す ochítsuki wò torímodosù

to pull someone's leg (*fig*) ...をからかう ...wo karákaù

pull apart *vt* (break) ばらばらにする barábara ni suru

pull down *vt* (building) 取壊す toríkowasù

pulley [puli] *n* 滑車 kasshá

pull in *vi* (AUT: at the curb) ...に停車する ...ni teísha suru; (RAIL) 到着する tōchaku suru

pull off *vt* (take off: clothes etc) 脱ぐ núgù; (*fig*: difficult thing) ...に成功する ...ni seíkō suru

pull out *vi* (AUT: from curb) 発進する hasshín suru; (RAIL) 出発する shuppátsu suru

◆*vt* (extract) 取出す torídasù

pull over *vi* (AUT) 道路わきに寄せて停車する dōrowaki ni yosete teísha suru

pullover [pulouvəɾ] *n* セーター sētā

pull through *vi* (MED) 治る naórù

pull up *vi* (AUT, RAIL: stop) 停車する teísha suru

◆*vt* (raise: object, clothing) 引上げる hikágerù; (uproot) 引抜く hikínukù

pulp [pʌlp] *n* (of fruit) 果肉 kaníku

pulpit [pulpit] *n* (REL) 説教壇 sekkyōdan

pulsate [pʌlseit] *vi* 脈動する myakúdō suru

pulse [pʌls] *n* (ANAT) 脈拍 myakúhaku; (rhythm) 鼓動 kodō; (BOT) 豆類 mamérùi

pulverize [pʌlvəraiz] *vt* (crush to a powder) 砕く kudákù; (*fig*: destroy) 破壊する hakái suru

puma [puːmə] *n* ピューマ pyūma

pummel [pʌml] *vt* 続け様にげんこつで打つ tsuzúkezama ni geñkotsu de utsu

pump [pʌmp] *n* (for water, air, petrol) ポンプ póñpu; (shoe) パンプス páñpusu

◆*vt* (force: in certain direction: liquid, gas) ポンプで送る póñpu de okúrù; (obtain supply of: oil, water, gas) ポンプ

で汲む pómpu de kúmù

pumpkin [pʌmp'kin] n カボチャ kabócha

pump up vt (inflate) ポンプで膨らます pónpu de fukúramàsu

pun [pʌn] n しゃれ sharé

punch [pʌntʃ] n (blow) げんこつで打つ事 geñkotsu dè útsú kotó, パンチ páñchi; (tool: for making holes) パンチ páñchi; (drink) ポンチ póñchi

♦vt (hit): **to punch someone/something** げんこつで…を打つ geñkotsu de …wo útsú

punchline [pʌntʃ'lain] n 落ち óchì

punch-up [pʌntʃ'ʌp] n (BRIT: inf) けんか keñka

punctual [pʌŋk'tʃuəl] adj 時間を厳守する jfkañ wo geñshu suru

punctuation [pʌŋktʃuei'ʃən] n 句読法 kutóhō

puncture [pʌŋk'tʃəːr] n パンク páñku

♦vt …に穴を開ける …ni anā wò akéru

pundit [pʌn'dit] n 物知り monóshiri

pungent [pʌn'dʒənt] adj (smell, taste) 刺激的な shigékiteki na

punish [pʌn'iʃ] vt (person, crime) 罰する bassúrù

punishment [pʌn'iʃmənt] n (act) 罰する事 bassúrù kotó; (way of punishing) 罰 bátsù

punk [pʌŋk] n (also: **punk rock**) パンクロック pañkurokkù; (also: **punk rocker**) パンクロッカー pañkurokkà; (US: inf: hoodlum) ちんぴら chíñpira

punt [pʌnt] n (boat) ポート bóto 〈底が平らでさおで川底を突いて進める物を指す sokó ga taíra dè sáò de kawázoko wo tsuíte susúmeru mono wò sásù〉

punter [pʌn'təːr] n (BRIT: gambler) ばくち打ち bakúchichì; (inf: client, customer) 客 kyakú

puny [pju:'ni:] adj (person, effort) ちっぽけな chippókè na

pup [pʌp] n (young dog) 子イヌ kofnu

pupil [pju:'pəl] n (SCOL) 生徒 sefto; (of eye) どう孔 dókō

puppet [pʌp'it] n (doll) 操り人形 ayátsuriniñgyō; (fig: person) かいらい kaírai

puppy [pʌp'i:] n 子イヌ kofnu

purchase [pəːr'tʃis] n (act of buying) 購入 kónyū; (item bought) 買い物 kaímono

♦vt (buy: house, book, car etc) 買う kaú

purchaser [pəːr'tʃisəːr] n 買い手 kaíte

pure [pjuːr] adj (not mixed with anything: silk, gold etc) 純粋な juñsui na; (clean, healthy: water, air etc) 清潔な sefketsu na; (fig: woman, girl) 純潔な juñketsu na; (complete, total: chance, bliss) 全くの mattáku no

purée [pjurei'] n (of tomatoes, potatoes, apples etc) ピューレ pyūre

purely [pjuːr'li:] adv 単に táñ ni

purgatory [pəːr'gətɔːri:] n (REL) れん獄 reñgoku; (fig) 地獄 jigóku

purge [pəːrdʒ] n (POL) 粛正 shukúsei, パージ páji

♦vt (organization) 粛正する shukúsei suru, パージする páji suru

purify [pjuːr'əfai] vt (air, water etc) 浄化する jōka suru

purist [pjuːr'ist] n 純正主義者 juñseishugìshā

puritan [pjuːr'itən] n 禁欲主義者 kíñ-yoku shugìshā

purity [pjuːr'iti:] n (of silk, gold etc) 純粋さ juñsuisa; (of water, air etc) 清潔さ sefketsu; (fig: of woman, girl) 純潔 juñketsu

purple [pəːr'pəl] adj 紫色の murásakiìro no

purport [pəːr'pɔːrt] vi: **to purport to be/do** …である〈…ができる〉と主張する …de árù〈…ga dekírù〉to shuchō suru

purpose [pəːr'pəs] n (reason) 目的 mokúteki; (objective: of person) 目標 mokúhyō

on purpose 意図的に itóteki ni, わざと wáza to

purposeful [pəːr'pəsfəl] adj (person, look, gesture) 果敢な kákàn na

purr [pəːr] vi (cat) ごろごろとのどを鳴らす górògoro to nódò wo narásù

purse [pəːrs] n (for money) 財布 sáīfu; (US: handbag) ハンドバッグ hañdobaggù

♦vt (lips) すぼめる subómerù

purser [pɑːr'sər] n (NAUT) 事務長 jimúchō, パーサー pāsā

pursue [pərsu:'] vt (follow: person, thing) 追跡する tsuíseki suru; (fig: activity, interest) 行う okonaú; (: plan) 実行する jikkō suru; (: aim, result) 追い求める oímotomerù

pursuer [pərsu:'ər] n 追跡者 tsuísekishà

pursuit [pərsu:t'] n (chase: of person, thing) 追跡 tsuíseki; (fig: of happiness, pleasure etc) 追求 tsuíkyū; (pastime) 趣味 shúmì

pus [pʌs] n うみ umí

push [puʃ] n 押す事 osú kotò
♦vt (press, shove) 押す osú; (promote) 宣伝する séñden suru
♦vi (press, shove) 押す osú; (fig: demand urgently): **to push for** 要求する yōkyū suru

push aside vt 押しのける oshínokerù

pushchair [puʃ'tʃe:r] (BRIT) n いす型ベビーカー isúgata bebíkā

pusher [puʃ'ər] n (drug pusher) 売人 baínin

push off (inf) vi: **push off!** 消えうせろ kiéuserò

push on vi (continue) 続ける tsuzúkerù

pushover [puʃ'ouvər] (inf) n: **it's a pushover** 朝飯前だ asámeshimaè da

push through vt (crowd etc) ...を押し分けて進む ...wo oshíwakete susumù
♦vt (measure, scheme etc) 押し通す oshítōsu

push up vt total, prices 押し上げる oshíagerù

push-up [puʃ'ʌp] (US) n (press-up) 腕立て伏せ udétatefùse

pushy [puʃ'i:] (pej) adj 押しの強い oshí no tsuyoì

puss [pus] (inf) n ネコちゃん nékochañ

pussy(cat) [pus'i:(kæt)] (inf) n ネコちゃん nékochañ

put [put] (pt, pp **put**) vt (place: thing) 置く okú; (: person in institution etc) 入れる irérù; (express: idea, remark etc) 表現する hyōgen suru; (present: case, view) 説明する setsúmei suru; (ask: question) する súru; (place: person in state, situa-

tion) 追込む oíkomù, 置く okú; (: estimate) 推定する suítei suru; (write, type: word, sentence etc) 書く kákù

put about/around vt (rumor) 広める hirómerù

put across vt (ideas etc) 分からせる wakáraserù

put away vt (store) 仕舞っておく shimátte okú

put back vt (replace) 戻す modósù; (postpone) 延期する eñki suru; (delay) 遅らせる okúraserù

put by vt (money, supplies etc) 蓄えておく takúwaete okú

put down vt (on floor, table) 下ろす orósù; (in writing) 書く kákù; (riot, rebellion) 鎮圧する chiñ-atsu suru; (kill: animal) 安楽死させる añrakushi saséru; (attribute): **to put something down to** ...を...のせいにする ...wo seí ni suru

put forward vt (ideas, proposal) 提案する teían suru

put in vt (application, complaint) 提出する teíshutsu suru; (time, effort) つぎ込む tsugíkomù

put off vt (delay) 延期する eñki suru; (discourage) いやにさせる iyá ni saserù

put on vt (shirt, blouse, dress etc) 着る kírù; (hat etc) かぶる kabúrù; (shoes, pants, skirt etc) はく hakú; (gloves etc) はめる hamérù; (make-up, ointment etc) つける tsukérù; (light etc) つける tsukérù; (play etc) 上演する jōen suru; (brake) かける kakérù; (record, tape, video) かける kakérù; (kettle, dinner etc) 火にかける hí ní kakérù; (assume: look, behavior etc) 装う yosóoù; (gain): **to put on weight** 太る futórù

put out vt (fire, candle, cigarette, light) 消す kesú; (take out: rubbish, cat etc) 出す dásù; (one's hand) 伸ばす nobásù; (inf: person) ...を怒らせる okótte irú

putrid [pju:'trid] adj 腐った kusáttà

putt [pʌt] n (GOLF) パット pátto

put through vt (TEL: person, call) つなぐ tsunágù; (plan, agreement) 成功させる seíkō saserù

putting green [pʌt'iŋ-] n (GOLF: smooth area around hole) グリーン gurīn; (: for practice) パット練習場 páttoreñshūjō

putty [pʌt'iː] n パテ páte

put up vt (build) 建てる tatérù; (raise: umbrella) 広げる hirógerù; (: tent) 張る hárù; (: hood) かぶる kabúrù; (poster, sign etc) 張る hárù; (increase: price, cost) 上げる agérù; (accommodate) 泊める tomérù

put-up [put'ʌp] n: **put-up job** (BRIT) n 八百長 yaóchō

put up with vt fus 我慢する gámàn suru

puzzle [pʌz'əl] n (question, game) なぞなぞ nazónazo; (toy) パズル pázùru; (mystery) なぞ nazó
♦vt 当惑させる tówaku saserù
♦vi: **to puzzle over something** ...を思案する ...wo shíàn suru

puzzling [pʌz'liŋ] adj (thing, action) 訳の分からない wákè no wakáranai

pyjamas [pədʒɑːm'əz] (BRIT) npl = **pajamas**

pylon [pai'lɑn] n (for electric cables) 鉄塔 tettō

pyramid [pir'əmid] n (ARCHIT) ピラミッド pirámiddò; (shape, object, pile) ピラミッド状の物 pirámiddòjō no monō

Pyrenees [pir'əniːz] npl: **the Pyrenees** ピレネー山脈 pírènē sáñmyaku

python [pai'θɑːn] n ニシキヘビ nishíkihebì

Q

quack [kwæk] n (of duck) がーがー gàːgàː; (pej: doctor) やぶ医者 yabúisha
quad [kwɑːd] abbr = **quadrangle; quadruplet**
quadrangle [kwɑːd'ræŋgəl] n (courtyard) 中庭 nakániwa
quadruple [kwɑːdruː'pəl] vt (increase fourfold) 4倍にする 4bai ni suru
♦vi 4倍になる yoñbai ni naru
quadruplets [kwɑːdrʌ'plits] npl 四つ子 yotsúgo

quagmire [kwæg'maiəːr] n (bog) 湿地 shitchī; (muddy place) ぬかるみ nukárumi

quail [kweil] n (bird) ウズラ uzúra
♦vi: **to quail at/before** (anger, prospect) ...の前でおじけづく ...no maè de ojíkezukù

quaint [kweint] adj (house, village) 古風で面白い kofū de omóshiroì; (ideas, customs) 奇妙な kimyō na

quake [kweik] vi (with fear) 震える furúrù
♦n abbr = **earthquake**

Quaker [kwei'kəːr] n クエーカー教徒 kuēkākyōto

qualification [kwɑːləfəkei'ʃən] n (often pl: training, degree, diploma) 資格 shikákù; (skill, quality) 能力 nōryokù; (reservation, modification) 限定 geñtei, 条件 jōken

qualified [kwɑːl'əfaid] adj (trained) 資格のある shikákù no aru; (fit, competent): **qualified to ...**する能力がある ...suru nōryokù ga aru; (limited) 条件付きの jōkentsukī no

qualify [kwɑːl'əfai] vt (make competent) ...に資格を与える ...ni shikákù wo ataérù; (modify) 限定する gentei suru
♦vi (pass examination(s)): **to qualify (as)** ...の資格を取る ...no shikákù wo torū; (be eligible): **to qualify (for)** (...の) 資格がある (...no) shikákù ga aru; (in competition): **to qualify (for)** (...に) 進む ...ni susūmu) shikákù wo erú

quality [kwɑːl'iti:] n (standard: of work, product) 品質 hiñshitsu; (characteristic: of person) 性質 seshitsu; (: of wood, stone etc) 特徴 tokúchō

qualm [kwɑːm] n (doubt) 疑問 gímon **qualms of conscience** 良心のか責 ryōshin nō kasháku

quandary [kwɑːn'dri:] n: **to be in a quandary** 途方に暮れる tohō ni kuréru

quantity [kwɑːn'titi:] n (amount: of uncountable thing) 量 ryō; (: of countable things) 数 kazū

quantity surveyor n 積算士 sekisanshi ◇工事などの費用を見積りで計算する人 kōji nadò no hfyō wo mitsúmori de keísan suru hitò

quarantine [kwɔr'əntiːn] n (isolation) 隔離 kakúri

quarrel [kwɔːr'əl] n (argument) けんか keńka
◆vi: **to quarrel (with)** (...と) けんかする (...to) keńka suru

quarrelsome [kwɔːr'əlsəm] adj けんかっ早い kénkappayaì

quarry [kwɔːr'iː] n (for stone) 石切り場 ishíkiriba, 採石場 saísekijō; (animal) 獲物 emóno

quart [kwɔːrt] n クォート kwōto

quarter [kwɔːr'təːr] n (fourth part) 4分の1 yońbun no ichì; (US: coin) 25セント玉 nijúgosentodamà; (of year) 四半期 shíhàki; (district) 地区 chikú
◆vt (divide by four) 4等分する yońtōbun suru; (MIL: lodge) 宿泊させる shukúhakuku saseru

a quarter of an hour 15分 júgófun

quarter final n 準々決勝 junjunkesshō

quarterly [kwɔːr'təːrliː] adj (meeting, payment) 年4回の nèn-yoñkai no
◆adv (meet, pay) 年4回に nèn-yoñkai ni

quarters [kwɔːr'təːrz] npl (barracks) 兵舎 heísha; (living quarters) 宿舎 shukúsha

quartet(te) [kwɔːrtet'] n (group: of instrumentalists) 四重奏団 shijúsōdan, カルテット karútetto; (: of singers) 四重唱団 shijúshōdan, カルテット karútetto; (piece of music) 四重奏曲 shijúsōkyokù

quartz [kwɔːrts] n 水晶 suíshō

quash [kwɑʃ] vt (verdict, judgement) 破棄する hakí suru

quasi- [kwei'zai] prefix 疑似... gíji...

quaver [kwei'vəːr] n (BRIT: MUS) 八分音符 hachíbun ofipu
◆vi (voice) 震える furúeru

quay [kiː] n (also: **quayside**) 岸壁 ganpeki

queasy [kwiː'ziː] adj (nauseous) 吐気がするhakíke ga suru

queen [kwiːn] n (monarch) 女王 joō; (king's wife) 王妃 ōhì; (ZOOL: also:

queen bee) 女王バチ joōbachi; (CARDS, CHESS) クイーン kuíñ

queen mother n 皇太后 kōtaigō

queer [kwiːr] adj (odd) 変な hèn na
◆n (inf: homosexual) ホモ homó

quell [kwel] vt (opposition) 鎮める shizúmeru; (unease, fears) なだめる nadámeru, 静める shizúmeru

quench [kwentʃ] vt: **to quench one's thirst** のどの乾きをいやす nodò no kawàkí wo iyásu

querulous [kwer'ələs] adj (person, voice) 愚痴っぽい guchíppoì

query [kwiːr'iː] n (question) 質問 shitsúmon
◆vt (question) ...に聞く ...ni kikú, ...に質問する ...ni shitsúmon suru

quest [kwest] n 探求 tañkyū

question [kwes'tʃən] n (query) 質問 shitsúmon; (doubt) 疑問 gimón; (issue) 問題 mońdai; (in test: problem) 問ó問
◆vt (ask) ...に聞く ...ni kikú, ...に質問する ...ni shitsúmon suru; (interrogate) 尋問する jifimon suru; (doubt) ...に疑問を投げ掛ける ...ni gimóñ wo nagékakeru

beyond question 疑いもなく utágai mo naku

out of the question 全く不可能で mattáku fúkanô de

questionable [kwes'tʃənəbəl] adj (doubtful) 疑わしい utágawashiì

question mark n 疑問符 gimóñfu

questionnaire [kwestʃəner'] n 調査票 chōsàhyō, アンケート añkētò

queue [kjuː] (BRIT) n 列 retsù
◆vi (also: **queue up**) 列を作る retsù wo tsukúru

quibble [kwib'əl] vi 詰まらない議論をする tsumáranaì giròn wo suru

quiche [kiːʃ] n キッシュ kisshù ◇パイの一種 paì no isshù

quick [kwik] adj (fast: person, movement, action etc) 早い hayáì; (agile) 素早い subáyaì; (: mind) 理解の早い rikái no hayáì; (brief: look, visit) 短い mijíkaì, ちょっとした chottó shità
◆n: **cut to the quick** (fig) ...の感情を害する ...no kañjō wo gaí suru

be quick! 急いで isóide

quicken [kwik'ən] vt (pace, step) 早める hayámeru

♦vi (pace, step) 早くなる hayáku naru

quickly [kwik'li:] adv 早く hayáku

quicksand [kwik'sænd] n 流土砂 ryūdosha, クイックサンド kuíkkûsando

quick-witted [kwik'wit'id] adj (alert) 機敏な kíbín na

quid [kwid] (BRIT: inf) n inv ポンド poñdo

quiet [kwai'ət] adj (not loud or noisy) 静かな shizúka na; (silent) 何も言わない naní mo iwánai; (peaceful place) 平和な heiwa na; (calm: person) もの静かな monóshizuka na; (without fuss etc: ceremony) 簡単な kañtan na

♦n (peacefulness) 静けさ shizúkesa; (silence) 静かにする事 shizúka ni suru koto

♦vi (US: also: quiet down) (grow calm) 落着く ochítsuku, (grow silent) 静かになる shizúka ni naru

♦vt (person, animal) 落着かせる ochítsukaserú

quieten [kwai'ətən] (BRIT) = quiet vi, vt

quietly [kwai'ətli:] adv (speak, play) 静かに shizúka ni; (silently) 黙って damátte

quietness [kwai'itnis] n (peacefulness) 静けさ shizúkesa; (silence) 静かにする事 shizúka ni suru koto

quilt [kwilt] n (covering) ベッドカバー beddókabā; (also: continental quilt) 掛布団 kakebuton, キルト kirúto

quin [kwin] n abbr = quintuplet

quinine [kwi'nain] n キニーネ kiníñe

quintet(te) [kwintet'] n (group) 五重奏団 gojūsōdan, クインテット kuíntetto; (piece of music) 五重奏曲 gojūsōkyoku

quintuplets [kwintʌ'plits] npl 五つ子 itsútsugo

quip [kwip] n 警句 keíku

quirk [kwəːrk] n (unusual characteristic) 癖 kusé; (accident of fate, nature) 気まぐれ kimágure

quit [kwit] (pt, pp quit or quitted) vt (smoking, grumbling) やめる yaméru;

(job) 辞める yaméru; (premises) ...から出ていく ...kara deté iku

♦vi (give up) やめる yaméru; (resign) 辞める yaméru

quite [kwait] adv (rather) かなり kanári; (entirely) 全く mattáku, 完全に kañzen ni; (following a negative: almost): that's not quite big enough それはちょっと小さい sorê wa chottó chiisai

I saw quite a few of them 私はそれらをかなり沢山見ました watákushi wa soréra wo kanári takúsan mimashíta

quite (so!) 全くその通り mattáku sonó tōri

quits [kwits] adj: quits (with) (...と) あいこである ...to) o-áiko de aru

let's call it quits (call it even) おあいこにしましょう o-aíko ni shimáshō; (stop working etc) やめましょう yamémashō

quiver [kwiv'əːr] vi (tremble) 震える furúerù

quiz [kwiz] n (game) クイズ kuízu; (US: short test) 小テスト shótesùto

♦vt (question) 尋問する jiñmon suru

quizzical [kwiz'ikəl] adj (look, smile) なぞめいた nazómeita

quorum [kwɔːr'əm] n (of members) 定足数 teísokusū

quota [kwou'tə] n 割当数(量) waríatesū (ryō)

quotation [kwoutei'ʃən] n (from book, play etc) 引用文 iñ-yōbuñ; (estimate) 見積り mitsúmori

quotation marks npl 引用符 iñyōfú

quote [kwout] n (from book, play etc) 引用文 iñyōbuñ; (estimate) 見積り mitsúmori

♦vt (sentence, proverb etc) 引用する iñyō suru; (figure, example) 引合いに出す hikírai ni dasù; (price) 見積もる mitsúmorù

♦vi: to quote from (book, play etc) ...から引用する ...kara iñ-yō suru

quotes [kwouts] npl (quotation marks) 引用符 iñ-yōfú

quotient [kwou'ʃənt] n (factor) 指数 shísū

R

rabbi [ræb'ai] n ラビ rábí ◊ユダヤ教の聖職者 yudáyakyō nò sefshokushà

rabbit [ræb'it] n ウサギ usági

rabbit hutch n ウサギ小屋 uságigoyà

rabble [ræb'əl] (pej) n 群衆 gufshū

rabies [rei'biz] n 恐犬病 kyōkenbyō

RAC [ɑreisi:'] (BRIT) n abbr (= Royal Automobile Club) 英国自動車連盟 efkoku jidōsha reńmei

raccoon [rækun'] n アライグマ aráigùma

race [reis] n (species) 人種 jińshu; (competition: for speed) 競走 kyōsō, レース rēsù; (: for power, control) 競争 kyōsō; (public gambling event: also: **horse race**) 競馬 kefba; (: also: **bicycle race**) 競輪 kefrin; (: also: **motorboat race**) 競艇 kyōtei
♦vt (horse) 競馬に出場させる kefba ni shutsújō saserū; (compete against: person) ...と競走する ...to kyōsō suru
♦vi (compete: for speed) 競走する kyōsō suru; (: for power, control) 競争する kyōsō suru; (hurry) 急いで行く isóide ikū; (pulse) どきどきする dókìdoki suru; (engine) 空回りする karámawarì suru

race car (US) n レーシングカー rēshinkguká

race car driver (US) n レーサー rēsà

racecourse [reis'kɔːrs] n 競馬場 keíbajō

racehorse [reis'hɔːrs] n 競走馬 kyōsōba

racetrack [reis'træk] n (for people) トラック torákkù; (for cars) サーキット sākitto

racial [rei'ʃəl] adj 人種の jińshu no, 人種 ...の jińshu...

racing [rei'siŋ] n (horses) 競馬 keíba; (bicycles) 競輪 kefrin; (motorboats) 競艇 kyōtei; (cars) 自動車レース jidōsharēsu; (motorcycles) オートレース ōtorēsu

racing car (BRIT) n = **race car**

racing driver (BRIT) n = **race car driver**

racism [rei'sizəm] n 人種差別 jińshusabétsu

racist [rei'sist] adj (statement, policy) 人種差別的な jińshusabetsuteki na
♦n 人種差別主義者 jińshusabetsushugìsha

rack [ræk] n (also: **luggage rack**) 網棚 amídana; (shelf) 棚 taná; (also: **roof rack**) ルーフラック rūfurakkù; (dish rack) 水切りかご mizúkirikago
♦vt: **racked by** (pain, anxiety) ...でもだ え苦しんで ...de modáekurushíndè to rack one's brains 知恵を絞る chié wò shibórù

racket [ræk'it] n (for tennis, squash etc) ラケット rakéttò; (noise) 騒音 sóon; (swindle) 詐欺 sági

racoon [rækun'] n = **raccoon**

racquet [ræk'it] n (for tennis, squash etc) ラケット rakéttò

racy [rei'si:] adj きびきびした kíbìkibi shita

radar [rei'dɑːr] n レーダー rēdà

radial [rei'diəl] adj (also: **radial-ply**) ラジアルの rájìaru no

radiance [rei'di:əns] n (glow) 光 hikári

radiant [rei'di:ənt] adj (happy, joyful) 輝く kagáyakù

radiate [rei'di:eit] vt (heat) 放射する hōsha suru; (emotion) ...で輝く ...de kagáyakù
♦vi (lines) 放射状に広がる hōshajō nì hirógarū

radiation [reidi:ei'ʃən] n (radioactive) 放射能 hōshanō; (from sun etc) 放射 hōsha

radiator [rei'di:eitəːr] n ラジエーター rajíētā

radical [ræd'ikəl] adj (change etc) 抜本的な bappónteki na; (person) 過激な kagéki na; (organization) 過激派の kagékiha no, 過激派... kagékiha...

radii [rei'di:ai] npl of **radius**

radio [rei'di:ou] n (broadcasting) ラジオ放送 rajíohōsō; (device: for receiving broadcasts) ラジオ rajío; (: for transmitting and receiving signals) 無線通信機 muséntsūshìnki
♦vt (person) ...と無線で通信する ...to musén de tsūshin suru
on the radio ラジオで rájìo de

radioactive [reidiːouæk'tiv] *adj* 放射性 の hōshasei no

radiography [reidiːɔːg'rəfiː] *n* レントゲン撮影 refitogensatsuèi

radiology [reidiːɔː'ədʒiː] *n* 放射線医学 hōshasen-igāku

radio station *n* ラジオ放送局 rajîo hōsōkyòku

radiotherapy [reidiːouθeːr'əpiː] *n* 放射線療法 hōshasenryōhō

radish [ræd'iʃ] *n* はつかだいこん hatsúkadaîkon

radius [rei'diːəs] (*pl* **radii**) *n* (of circle) 半径 hañkei; (from point) 半径内の範囲 hañkeinai nò hán-î

RAF [ɑːreief'] *n abbr* = **Royal Air Force**

raffle [ræf'əl] *n* 宝くじ takárakùji 〈当る と金ではなく賞品をもらえる物を指す a-tárù to kane de wa nakù shóhin wò moráerù monó wò sásù〉

raft [ræft] *n* (craft) いかだ ikáda, (*also*: **life raft**) 救命いかだ kyúmei ikáda

rafter [ræf'təːr] *n* はり harí

rag [ræg] *n* (piece of cloth) ぞうきん zôkin; (torn cloth) ぼろ bórò; (*pej*: newspaper) 三流紙 safiryûshi (BRIT: UNIVERSITY: for charity) 慈善募金運動 jizénbokin-undô

rag-and-bone man [ræɡənboun'-] (*BRIT*) *n* = **ragman**

rag doll *n* 縫いぐるみ人形 nuíguruminîngyô

rage [reidʒ] *n* (fury) 憤怒 fúndo
◆*vi* (person) 怒り狂う ikárikuruù; (storm) 荒れ狂う arékuruù; (debate) 荒れ る arérù
it's all the rage (very fashionable) 大流行している daíryûkô shite irù

ragged [ræɡ'id] *adj* (edge) ぎざぎざの gízàgiza no; (clothes) ぼろぼろの boróboro no; (appearance) ぼろぼろの fuzôrôi no

ragman [ræɡ'mæn] (*pl* **ragmen**) *n* くず屋 kuzúyà

rags [ræɡz] *npl* (torn clothes) ぼろぼろの衣服 boróboro no ifùku

raid [reid] *n* (MIL) 襲撃 shúgeki; (criminal) 不法侵入 fuhôshiñnyû; (by police) 手

入れ tefrè
◆*vt* (MIL) 襲撃する shúgeki suru; (criminally) ...に不法侵入する ...ni fuhôshiñnyû suru; (subj: police) 手入れする tefrè suru

rail [reil] *n* 手すり tesúri
by rail (by train) 列車で resshá de

railings [rei'liŋ(z)] *n(pl)* (fence) さく sakû

railroad [reil'roud] (*US*) *n* (track) 線路 séñro; (company) 鉄道 tetsúdô

railroader [reil'roudəːr] (*US*) *n* 鉄道員 tetsûdôiñ

railroad line (*US*) *n* 鉄道線 tetsúdôsen

railroad station (*US*) *n* 駅 ékì

rails [reilz] *npl* (for train) レール rêru

railway [reil'wei] (*BRIT*) *n* = **railroad etc**

railwayman [reil'weimən] (*BRIT*: *pl* **railwaymen**) *n* = **railroader**

rain [rein] *n* 雨 ámè
◆*vi* 雨が降る ámè ga fùrû
in the rain 雨の中で ámè no nàkà de
it's raining 雨が降っている ámè ga futté irù

rainbow [rein'bou] *n* にじ nijî

raincoat [rein'kout] *n* レーンコート rêñkôto

raindrop [rein'drɑːp] *n* 雨の一滴 ámè no ittéki

rainfall [rein'fɔːl] *n* 降雨量 kôuryô

rainy [rei'niː] *adj* 雨模様の amémoyô no

raise [reiz] *n* (*payrise*) 賃上げ chiñ-age
◆*vt* (lift) 持ち上げる mochíagerù; (increase: salary) 上げる agérù; (: production) 増やす fuyásù; (improve: morale) 高める takámerù; (: standards) 引上げる hikíagerù; (produce: doubts, question) 引起こす hikíokosù; (rear: cattle) 飼育する shíîku suru; (: family) 育てる sodáterù; (cultivate: crop) 栽培する saíbai suru; (get together: army, funds, loan) 集める atsúmerù
to raise one's voice 声を大きくする kôè wo ôkiku suru

raisin [rei'zin] *n* 干しぶどう hoshíbudò, レーズン rêzun

rake [reik] *n* (tool) レーキ rêki
◆*vt* (garden) レーキで...の土をならす rê-

ki de ...no tsuchí wò narásù; (leaves) か集める kakátsumerù; (with machine gun) 掃射する sósha suru

rally [ræl'i:] n (POL etc) 集会 shúkai; (AUT) ラリー rarì; (TENNIS etc) ラリー rárì
♦vt (support) 集める atsumérù
♦vi (sick person, Stock Exchange) 持直し mochínaosù

rally round vt fus (fig: give support to) ...の支援に駆け付ける ...no shién ni kákétsukerù

RAM [ræm] n abbr = (**random access memory**) ラム rámù

ram [ræm] n (ZOOL: AUT) 雄ヒツジ oshítsùji
♦vt (crash into) ...に激突する ...ni gekítotsu suru; (push: bolt, fist etc) 押込む oshíkomù

ramble [ræm'bəl] n (walk) ハイキング háikingu
♦vi (walk) ハイキングする háikingu suru; (talk: also: **ramble on**) だらだらしゃべる dáràdara shaberù

rambler [ræm'blə:r] n (walker) ハイカー háikà; (BOT) ツルバラ tsurúbara

rambling [ræm'bliŋ] adj (speech) 取留めのない torítome no naï; (house) だだっ広い dadáppiroì; (BOT) つる性の tsurúsei no

ramp [ræmp] n 傾斜路 kefsharo
on/off ramp (US: AUT) 入口(出口)ランプ iríguchi(degúchi)ráñpu

rampage [ræm'peidʒ] n: **to be on the rampage** 暴れ回っている abáremawatte irù
♦vi: **they went rampaging through the town** 彼らは町中暴れ回った kárèra wa machíjū abáremawattà

rampant [ræm'pənt] adj (crime) はびこる habíkorù; (disease) まん延する mañ-en suru

rampart [ræm'pɑːrt] n (fortification) 城壁 jóheki

ramshackle [ræm'ʃækəl] adj (house, car, table) がたがたの gatágata no

ran [ræn] pt of **run**

ranch [ræntʃ] n 牧場 bokújō

rancher [ræn'tʃə:r] n 牧場主 bokújōshu

rancid [ræn'sid] adj (butter, bacon etc) 悪くなった wárùku natta

rancor [ræŋ'kə:r] (BRIT **rancour**) n 恨み urámi

random [ræn'dəm] adj (arrangement, selection) 手当り次第の teátarishidái no; (COMPUT, MATH) 無作為の musákùi no
♦n: **at random** 手当り次第に teátarishidái ni

random access n (COMPUT) ランダムアクセス rañdamuakúsesu

randy [ræn'di:] (inf) adj セックスをしたがっている sékkùsu wo shitágatte irù

rang [ræŋ] pt of **ring**

range [reindʒ] n (also: **mountain range**) 山脈 safimyaku; (of missile) 射程距離 shatékikyorì; (of voice) 声域 seíiki; (series: of proposals, offers, products) 一連の... ichíren no ...; (MIL: also: **shooting range**) 射撃場 shagékijō; (also: **kitchen range**) レンジ réñji
♦vt (place) 歩き回る arúkimawarù; (arrange) 並べる naráberù
♦vi: **to range over** (extend) ...にわたる ...ni watárò
to range from ... to ... ...から...までにわたる ...kárà ...mádè ni watárò

ranger [rein'dʒə:r] n 森林警備隊員 shiñrinkeibitaiin, レンジャー réñjà

rank [ræŋk] n (row) 列 retsú; (MIL) 階級 kaíkyù; (status) 地位 chfi; (BRIT: also: **taxi rank**) タクシー乗場 takúshinorìba
♦vi: **to rank among** ...のうちに数えられる ...no uchí ní kazőrarerù
♦adj (stinking) 臭い kusáì
the rank and file (fig: ordinary members) 一般の人 ippáñ no hitő, 一般人 ippáñjìn

rankle [ræŋ'kəl] vi (insult) わだかまる wadákamarù

ransack [ræn'sæk] vt (search) 物色する busshőku suru; (plunder) 略奪する ryakúdatsu suru

ransom [ræn'səm] n (money) 身代金 minőshirokiñ
to hold to ransom (fig: nation, company, individual) ...に圧力を掛ける ...ni

atsúryòku wo kakérù

rant [rænt] *vi* (rave) わめく waméků

rap [ræp] *vt* (on door, table) たたく tatákù

rape [reip] *n* (of woman) 強かん gókan; (BOT) アブラナ abúranà

♦*vt* (woman) 強かんする gókan suru

rape(seed) oil [reip'(si:d)-] *n* ナタネ油 natáneaburà

rapid [ræp'id] *adj* (growth, development, change) 急速な kyúsoku na

rapidity [rəpid'iti:] *n* (speed) 速さ háyasa

rapidly [ræp'idli:] *adv* (grow, develop, change) 急速に kyúsoku ni

rapids [ræp'idz] *npl* (GEO) 早瀬 hayáse

rapist [rei'pist] *n* 強かん者 gókansha

rapport [ræpɔːr'] *n* 親和関係 shińwakańkei

rapture [ræp'tʃər] *n* (delight) 歓喜 kánki

rapturous [ræp'tʃərəs] *adj* (applause) 熱狂的な nekkyóteki na

rare [reːr] *adj* (uncommon) まれな maré na; (unusual) 珍しい mezúrashii; (CULIN: steak) レアの reá no

rarely [reːr'li:] *adv* (seldom) めったに…ない méttà ni …náì

raring [reːr'iŋ] *adj*: **raring to go** (*inf*: keen) 意気込んでいる íkigonde irù

rarity [reːr'iti:] *n* (exception) 希有なもの kéù na monó; (scarcity) 希少性 kishósei

rascal [ræs'kəl] *n* (rogue) ごろつき gorótsuki; (mischievous child) いたずら子 itázurakkò

rash [ræʃ] *adj* (person) 向こう見ずの mukómìzu no; (promise, act) 軽率な kefsotsu na

♦*n* (MED) 発しん hasshín; (spate: of events, robberies) 多発 tahátsu

rasher [ræʃ'əːr] *n* (of bacon) 一切れ hitókìre

raspberry [ræz'be:ri:] *n* キイチゴ kiíchigo

rasping [ræs'piŋ] *adj*: **a rasping noise** きしむ音 kishímū otó

rat [ræt] *n* ネズミ nezúmi

rate [reit] *n* (speed) 速度 sókùdo; (of change, inflation) 進行度 shińkodo; (ratio: *also* of interest) 率 rítsū; (price: at hotel etc) 料金 ryókìn

♦*vt* (value, estimate) 評価する hyóka suru

to rate someone/something as …を…と評価する …wo …to hyóka suru

rateable value [rei'təbəl-] (*BRIT*) *n* 課税評価額 kazéi hyókagàku

ratepayer [reit'peiəːr] (*BRIT*) *n* 納税者 nózeisha ◇固定資産税の納税者について言う kotéishisañzei no nózeisha ni tsuíte iú

rates [reits] *npl* (*BRIT*: property tax) 固定資産税 kotéishisañzei; (fees) 料金 ryókìn

rather [ræð'əːr] *adv* (quite, somewhat) かなり kánàri; (to some extent) 少し sukóshi; (more accurately) 正確に言えば sefkaku ni iébà

it's rather expensive (quite) かなり値段が高い nedán ga takáì; (too) 値段が高過ぎる nedán ga takásugirù

there's rather a lot かなり沢山ある kánàri takúsan arú

I would rather go どちらかというと行きたいと思う dóchìra ka to iú tò ikítaì to omóu

ratify [ræt'əfai] *vt* (agreement, treaty) 批准する hijún suru

rating [rei'tiŋ] *n* (assessment) 評価 hyóka; (score) 評点 hyóten; (NAUT: *BRIT*: sailor) 海軍兵卒 kaígunhetsotsu

ratings [rei'tiŋz] *npl* (RADIO, TV) 視聴率 shichóritsu

ratio [rei'ʃou] *n* 率 rítsū

in the ratio of 100 to 1 100に1つという割合で hyaku ni hitotsù to iu warfai de

ration [ræʃ'ən] *n* (allowance: of food, petrol etc) 配給分 hafkyúbun

♦*vt* (food, petrol etc) 配給する haíkyu suru

rational [ræʃ'ənəl] *adj* (solution, reasoning) 合理的な góriteki na; (person) 訳の分かる wáke no wakárù

rationale [ræʃənæl'] *n* 根拠 kónkyo

rationalize [ræʃ'ənəlaiz] *vt* (justify) 正当化する seftóka suru

rationally [ræʃ'ənəli:] *adv* (sensibly) 合理的に góriteki ni

rationing [ræʃ'əniŋ] *n* (of food, petrol etc) 配給 haikyū

rations [rei'ʃənz] *npl* (MIL) 兵糧 hyórō

rat race *n* 競争の世界 kyósō nò sékài

rattle [ræt'əl] *n* (of door, window) がたがたという音 gátagata to iú oto; (of train, car, engine etc) ごう音 gōn; (of coins) じゃらじゃらという音 járajara to iú oto; (of chain) がらがらという音 gárágara to iú oto; (object: for baby) がらがら garágarà

◆*vi* (small objects) がらがら鳴る gárágara narú; (car, bus): **to rattle along** がたがた走る hashírù

◆*vt* (unnerve) どぎまぎさせる dógimagi saséru

rattlesnake [ræt'əlsneik] *n* ガラガラヘビ garágarahebì

raucous [rɔː'kəs] *adj* しゃがれ声の shagáregoè no

ravage [ræv'idʒ] *vt* (damage) 荒す arásù

ravages [ræv'idʒiz] *npl* (of time, weather) 荒廃 kōhai

rave [reiv] *vi* (in anger) わめく wamékù; (with enthusiasm) をべたほめする ...wo betábòme suru; (MED) うわごとを言う uwágoto wò iú

raven [rei'vən] *n* ワタリガラス watárigaràsu

ravenous [ræv'ənəs] *adj* 猛烈におなかがすいた mōretsu nì onáka ga suíta

ravine [rəvin'] *n* 渓谷 kefkoku

raving [rei'viŋ] *adj*: **raving lunatic** 気違い dokíchigaì

ravishing [ræv'iʃiŋ] *adj* (beautiful) 悩殺する nósatsu suru

raw [rɔː] *adj* (uncooked) 生の námà no; (not processed: cotton, sugar etc) 原料のままの gefiryō no; (sore) 赤むけした akámuke shità; (inexperienced) 青二才の aónisai no; (weather, day) 肌寒い hadázamuì

raw deal (*inf*) *n* ひどい仕打 hidôi shíùchi

raw material *n* (coal, oil, gas etc) 原料 gefiryô

ray [rei] *n* (also: **ray of light**) 光線 kősen; (also: **ray of heat**) 熱線 nessén

the rays of the sun 太陽の光線 tályō no kősen

a ray of hope 希望のひらめき kibô nò hirámeki

rayon [rei'ɑːn] *n* レーヨン rèyon

raze [reiz] *vt* 根こそぎ破壊する nekósogi hakái suru

razor [rei'zər] *n* (open razor) かみそり kamísorì; (safety razor) 安全かみそり afzenkamisòri; (electric razor) 電気かみそり defkikamisòri

razor blade *n* かみそりの刃 kamísorì no há

Rd *n* *abbr* = **road**

re [rei] *prep* (with regard to) ...に関して ...ni kâñ shite

reach [riːtʃ] *n* (range: of arm) 手が届く範囲 té gà todôkù hâñ-i; (scope: of imagination) 範囲 hâñ-i; (stretch of river etc) 区域 kúiki

◆*vt* (arrive at: place) ...に到着する ...ni tôchaku suru; (: conclusion, agreement, decision, end) ...に達する ...ni tassûrù; (be able to touch) ...に手が届く ...ni té gà todôkù; (by telephone) ...に連絡する ...ni refraku suru

◆*vi* (stretch out one's arm) 手を伸ばす té wò nobású

within reach 手の届く所に té nò todôkù tokórò ni

out of reach 手の届かない所に té nò todôkanaì tokórò ni

within reach of the shops/station 商店街(駅)の近くに shôteñgai(ékì)no chikákù ni

「keep out of the reach of children」 子供の手が届かない所に保管して下さい kodómo no té gà todôkanaì tokórò ni hokán shite kudásaì

reach out *vt* (hand) 伸ばす nobásù

◆*vi* 手を伸ばす té wò nobású

to reach out for something ...を取ろうとして手を伸ばす ...wo torô tò shite té wò nobású

react [riækt'] *vi* (CHEM): **to react (with)** (...と) 反応する (...to) hañnō su-

ru; (MED): **to react (to)** (...に対して)
副作用が起る (...ni táishite) fukúsayŏ ga
okórù; (respond): **to react (to)** (...に)
反応する (...ni) hańnŏ suru; (rebel): **to
react (against)** (...に)反発する (...ni)
hańpatsu suru

reaction [ri:ǽk'ʃən] n (response): **reaction (to)** (...に対する)反応 (...ni taísu-
rù) hańnŏ; (rebellion): **reaction
(against)** (...に対する)反発 (...ni taí-
surù) hańpatsu; (belief in conservatism)
反動 hańdŏ; (CHEM) 反応 hańnŏ; (MED)
副作用 fukúsayŏ

reactionary [ri:ǽk'ʃəneri:] adj (forces,
attitude) 反動的な hańdŏteki na

reactions [ri:ǽk'ʃənz] npl (reflexes) 反
応 hańnŏ

reactor [ri:ǽk'tər] n (also: **nuclear
reactor**) 原子炉 gefshírŏ

read [ri:d] (pt, pp **read**) vi (person, child)
...を読む ...wo yómù; (piece of writing,
letter etc) ...を書いてある ...to kâite árù
♦vt (book, newspaper, music etc) 読む
yómù; (mood, thoughts) 読取る yomíto-
rù; (meter, thermometer etc) ...を読む;
(study: at university) 学ぶ manábù

readable [ri:'dəbəl] adj (writing) 読める
yomérù; (book, author etc) 読ませるよ
máserù

reader [ri:'dər] n (of book, newspaper
etc) 読者 dókùsha; (book) リーダー ridà;
(BRIT: at university) 助教授 jokyójù
an avid reader 読書家 dokúshòka

readership [ri:'dərʃip] n (of newspaper
etc) 読者 dókùsha 総称 sŏsho

readily [red'əli:] adv (willingly) 快く ko-
kóroyokù; (easily) たやすく tayásukù;
(quickly) 直ぐに súgù ni

readiness [red'ənis] n (preparedness) 用
意ができている事 yŏi ga dekite iru koto;
(willingness) ...する意志 ...suru ishi
in readiness (prepared) 用意ができて
yŏi ga dekite

reading [ri:'diŋ] n (books, newspapers
etc) 読書 dokusho; (in church, as entertainment) 朗読 rŏdoku; (on meter, thermometer etc) 記録 kiroku

readjust [ri:ədʒʌst'] vt (alter: position,

knob, mirror etc) 調節する chŏsetsu suru
♦vi (adapt): **to readjust (to)** (...に)な
れる (...ni) nareru

read out vt 朗読する rŏdoku suru

ready [red'i:] adj (prepared) 用意ができ
ている yŏi ga dekite iru; (willing): ...する
意志がある ...surú ishí ga árù; (available)
用意されている yŏi ni sarete iru
♦n: **at the ready** (MIL) 銃を構えて jû
wo kamáete
to get ready
♦vi 支度する shitáku suru
♦vt 準備する júnbi suru

ready-made [red'i:meid] adj 既製の kiséi no

ready money n 現金 gefkin

ready reckoner [-rek'ənər] n 計算表
kefsańhyŏ

ready-to-wear [ri:ətəwe:r'] adj 既製
の kiséi no

reaffirm [ri:əfəːrm'] vt 再び言明する futátabi gefmei suru

real [ri:l] adj (actual, true: reason, interest, result etc) 本当の hońtŏ no; (not artificial: leather, gold etc) 本物の hofmono
no; (not imaginary: life, feeling) 実際の
jissái no; (for emphasis): **a real idiot/
miracle** 正真正銘のばか(奇跡) shŏshin-
shŏmei no bâka (kiséki)
in real terms 実質は jíʃitsu wa

real estate n 不動産 fudósan

realism [ri:'əlizəm] n (practicality) 現実
主義 gefjitsushugí; (ART) リアリズム ri-
árizùmu

realist [ri:'əlist] n 現実的な人 gefjitsuteki nà hitó

realistic [ri:əlis'tik] adj (practical) 現実
の gefjitsuteki na; (true to life) 写実的
な shajitsuteki na

reality [ri:ǽl'iti:] n (actuality, truth) 事
実 jíʃitsu
in reality 事実は jíʃitsu wa

realization [ri:əlizei'ʃən] n (understanding: of situation) 実感 jikkán; (fulfilment: of dreams, hopes) 実現 jitsúgen;
(of asset) 現金化 gefkinka

realize [ri:'əlaiz] vt (understand) 実感す

る jikkan suru; (fulfil: a dream, hope, project etc) 実現する jitsúgen suru; (COMM: asset) 現金に替える genkiñ ni kaeru

really [riːˈɑli] *adv* (for emphasis) 実にjitsú ni, とても totémo; (actually): *what really happened* 実際に起った事は jissái ni okótta kotó wa

really? (indicating interest) そうですかsó desu ka; (expressing surprise) 本当ですか hoñtó desu ka

really! (indicating annoyance) うんもう! úñ mó!

realm [relm] *n* (of monarch) 王国 ókoku; (fig: area of activity or study) 分野 buń-ya

realtor [riːˈɑltəːr] (US) *n* 不動産業者 fudōsangyósha

reap [riːp] *vt* (crop) ...の刈り入れをする ...no karíire wò suru; (fig: benefits, rewards) 収穫する shūkaku suru

reappear [riːəpiːˈr] *vi* 再び現れる futátabi arawareru

rear [riːr] *adj* (back) 後ろの ushíro no
♦*n* (back) 後ろ ushíro
♦*vt* (cattle) 飼育する shíiku suru; (family) 育てる sodáteru
♦*vi* (also: **rear up**: animal) 後足で立ち上る atóashi de tachfagaru

rearguard [riːˈrgɑːrd] *n* (MIL) 後衛 kóei

rearmament [riːɑːrmˈəmɑnt] *n* 再軍備 safguñbi

rearrange [riːəreinˈdʒ] *vt* 並べ直す narábenaosu

rear-view mirror [riːrˈvjuː'-] *n* (AUT) バックミラー bakkúmirā

reason [riːˈzən] *n* (cause) 理由 riyū; (ability to think) 理性 riséi
♦*vi: to reason with someone* ...の説得に当る ...no settóku ni atáru
it stands to reason that ...という事は当然である ...to iú kotó wa tózen de arú

reasonable [riːˈzənəbəl] *adj* (sensible) 訳の分かる wakáru; (fair: number, amount) 程々の hodóhodo no; (: quality) まあまあの mámá no; (: price) 妥当な dató na

reasonably [riːˈzənəbliː] *adv* (sensibly)

常識的に jóshikiteki ni; (fairly) 程々に hodóhodo ni

reasoned [riːˈzənd] *adj* (argument) 筋の通った súji no tótta

reasoning [riːˈzəniŋ] *n* (process) 推理 sufri

reassurance [riːəʃuːrˈəns] *n* 安心 áñdo

reassure [riːəʃuːˈr] *vt* (comfort) 安心させる añshin saséru

to reassure someone of ...に...だと安心させる ...ni ...da tò añshin saséru

reassuring [riːəʃuːrˈiŋ] *adj* (smile, manner) 安心させる añshin saséru

rebate [riːˈbeit] *n* (on tax etc) リベート ríbēto

rebel [*n* rebˈəl *vb* ribelˈ] *n* (against political system) 反逆者 hañgyakushá; (against society, parents etc) 反抗分子 hañkōbuñshi
♦*vi* (against political system) 反乱を起す hañran wò okósu; (against society, parents etc) 反抗する hañkō suru

rebellion [ribelˈjən] *n* (against political system) 反乱 hañran; (against society, parents etc) 反抗 hañkō

rebellious [ribelˈjəs] *adj* (subject) 反逆者の hañgyakushá no; (child, behavior) 反抗的な hañkōteki na

rebirth [riːbəːrθ'] *n* 復活 fukkátsu

rebound [*vb* riːbaundˈ *n* riːˈbaund] *vi* (ball) 跳ね返る hanékaeru
♦*n: on the rebound* (ball) 跳ね返った所を hanékaettá tokóró wo; (fig: person) ...した反動で ...shíta hañdō de

rebuff [ribʌfˈ] *n* 拒絶 kyozétsu

rebuild [riːbildˈ] (*pt, pp* **rebuilt**) *vt* (town, building etc) 建直す taténaosu; (economy, confidence) 立直す taténaosu

rebuke [ribjukˈ] *vt* しかる shikáru

rebut [ribʌtˈ] *vt* しりぞける shírízokeru

recalcitrant [rikælˈsitrənt] *adj* (child, behavior) 反抗的な hañkōteki na

recall [rikɔːlˈ] *vt* (remember) 思い出す omóidasu; (parliament, ambassador etc) 呼戻す yobfmodosu
♦*n* (ability to remember) 記憶 kíóku; (of ambassador etc) 召還 shōkan

recant [rikænˈt] *vi* 自説を取消す jísetsu

wò torfkesù

recap [ri:'kæp] vt (summarize) 要約する yōyaku suru

♦vi ...を要約する ...wo yōyaku suru

recapitulate [ri:kəpɪtʃ'uleit] vt, vi = recap

recapture [ri:kæp'tʃə:r] vt (town, territory etc) 奪還する dakkán suru; (atmosphere, mood etc) 取戻す torfmodosù

rec'd abbr = received

recede [risi:d'] vi (tide) ひく hikù; (lights etc) 遠のく tōnokù; (memory) 薄らぐ usúragù; (hair) はげる hagérù

receding [risi:'diŋ] adj (hair) はげつつある hagétsutsu arù; (chin) 無いに等しい nái ni hitóshiñ

receipt [risi:t'] n (document) 領収書 ryōshūsho; (from cash register) レシート reshītò; (act of receiving) 受取る事 ukétorù kotò

receipts [risi:ts'] npl (COMM) 収入 shúnyū

receive [risi:v'] vt (get: money, letter etc) 受け取る ukétorù; (criticism, acclaim) 受ける ukérù; (visitor, guest) 迎える mukáerù

to receive an injury けがする kegá surù

receiver [risi:'və:r] n (TEL) 受話器 juwáki; (RADIO, TV) 受信機 jushíñki; (of stolen goods) 故買屋 kobáiya; (COMM) 管財人 kañzainiñ

recent [ri:'sənt] adj (event, times) 近ごろの chikágòro no

recently [ri:'səntli:] adv 近ごろ chikágòro

receptacle [risep'təkəl] n 容器 yōki

reception [risep'ʃən] n (in hotel, office, hospital etc) 受付 ukétsuke; (party) レセプション resépushoñ; (welcome) 歓迎 kañgei; (RADIO, TV) 受信 jushíñ

reception desk n 受付 ukétsuke, フロント furóñto

receptionist [risep'ʃənist] n 受付係 ukétsukegakari

receptive [risep'tiv] adj (person, attitude) 前向きの maémuki no

recess [ri:'ses] n (in room) 壁のくぼみ

kabé nò kubómi; (secret place) 奥深い所 okúfukaî tokórò; (POL etc: holiday) 休廷時間 kyūkeijikàn

recession [riseʃ'ən] n 景気後退 keíkikòtai

recharge [ri:tʃɑ:rdʒ'] vt (battery) 充電する jūden suru

recipe [res'əpi:] n (CULIN) 調理法 chōrihò; (fig: for success) 秘けつ hikétsu; (: for disaster) やり方 yarîkata

recipient [risip'i:ənt] n (of letter, payment etc) 受取人 ukétorinin

reciprocal [risip'rəkəl] adj (arrangement, agreement) 相互の sōgò no

recital [risait'əl] n (concert) リサイタル rísaîtaru

recite [risait'] vt (poem) 暗唱する añshō suru

reckless [rek'lis] adj (driving, driver) 無謀な mubō na; (spending) 無茶な múcha na

recklessly [rek'lisli:] adv (drive) 無謀に mubō ni; (spend) むやみに múyami ni

reckon [rek'ən] vt (calculate) 計算する kefsan suru; (think): I reckon that ...だと思う ...dá tò omóù

reckoning [rek'əniŋ] n (calculation) 計算 kefsan

reckon on vt fus (expect) 当てにする até ni suru

reclaim [rikleim'] vt (demand back) ...の返還を要求する ...no heñkan wò yōkyū suru; (land: by filling in) 埋め立てる umétaterù; (: by draining) 干拓する kañtaku suru; (waste materials) 再生する safsei suru

reclamation [rekləmei'ʃən] n (of land: by filling in) 埋め立て umétate; (: by draining) 干拓 kañtaku

recline [riklain'] vi (sit or lie back) もたれる motárerù

reclining [riklain'iŋ] adj: reclining seat リクライニングシート rikúrainiñgushìto

recluse [rek'lu:s] n 隠とん者 iñtoñsha

recognition [rekəgniʃ'ən] n (of person, place) 認識 niñshiki; (of problem, fact) 意識 fshîki; (of achievement) 認める事

mitómeru kotǒ
transformed beyond recognition 見分
けが付かない程変化した miwáke ga tsu-
kanǎi hodo héñka shita

recognizable [rekəgnai'zəbəl] *adj*: **recognizable (by)** (...で) 見分けが付く
(...de) miwáke ga tsukú

recognize [rek'əgnaiz] *vt* (person, place,
attitude, illness) ...だと分かる ...dǎ tǒ
wakárù; (problem, need) 意識する fǎshíki
suru; (qualification, achievement) 認め
る mitómerù; (government) 承認する
shónin suru
to recognize by/as ...で(として) 分かる
...de (tǒshítè) wakárù

recoil [rikoil'] *vi* (person): *to recoil
from doing something* ...するのをいや
がる ...surú no wǒ iyágarù
♦*n* (of gun) 反動 hañdǒ

recollect [rekəlekt'] *vt* (remember) 思い
出す omóidasù

recollection [rekəlek'ʃən] *n* (memory)
思い出 omóide; (remembering) 思い出す
事 omóidasu kotǒ

recommend [rekəmend'] *vt* (book, shop,
person) 推薦する suísen suru; (course of
action) 勧める susúmerù

recommendation [rekəmendei'ʃən] *n*
(of book, shop, person) 推薦 suísen; (of
course of action) 勧告 kañkoku

recompense [rek'əmpens] *n* (reward) 報
酬 hóshǔ

reconcile [rek'ənsail] *vt* (two people) 仲
直りさせる nakánaori saserù; (two
facts, beliefs) 調和させる chǒwa saserù
to reconcile oneself to something (unpleasant situation, misery etc) ...だとあ
きらめる ...dǎ tǒ akíramerù

reconciliation [rekənsiliei'ʃən] *n* (of
people etc) 和解 wakái; (of facts etc) 調
和 chǒwa

recondition [ri:kəndi'ʃən] *vt* (machine)
修理する shǔri suru

reconnaissance [rikɑːn'isəns] *n* (MIL)
偵察 tefsatsu

reconnoiter [ri:kənɔi'təːr] (*BRIT* **recon-
noitre**) *vt* (MIL: enemy territory) 偵察す
る tefsatsu suru

reconsider [ri:kənsid'əːr] *vt* (decision,
opinion etc) 考え直す kañgaenaosù

reconstruct [ri:kənstrakt'] *vt* (building)
立て直す taténaosù; (policy, system) 練り
直す nerínaosù; (event, crime) 再現する
saígen suru

reconstruction [ri:kənstrak'ʃən] *n* (of
building, country) 再建 saíken; (of
crime) 再現 saígen

record [*n* rek'əːrd *vb* rekɔːrd'] *n* (gen)
記録 kiróku; (MUS: disk) レコード rekǒ-
dǒ; (history: of person, company) 履歴
riréki; (also: **criminal record**) 前科 zéñ-
ka
♦*vt* (write down) 記録する kiróku suru;
(temperature, speed etc) 表示する hyóji
suru; (MUS: song etc) 録音する rokúon
suru
in record time 記録の速さで kirókute-
ki hayása de
off the record adj (remark) オフレコの
ofúreko no
♦*adv* (speak) オフレコで ofúreko de

record card *n* (in file) ファイルカード
faírukǎdo

recorded delivery [rikɔːr'did-] (*BRIT*)
n (MAIL) 簡易書留 kañ-i kakítome

recorder [rikɔːr'dəːr] *n* (MUS: instrument) リコーダー rikǒdǎ

record holder *n* (SPORT) 記録保持者
kiróku hojíshà

recording [rikɔːr'diŋ] *n* 録音 rokúon

record player *n* レコードプレーヤー re-
kǒdopurèyǎ

recount [rikaunt'] *vt* (story, event etc)
述べる nobérù

re-count [*n* ri:'kaunt *vb* ri:kaunt'] *n*
(POL: of votes) 数え直し kazóenaoshi
♦*vt* (votes etc) 数え直す kazóenaosù

recoup [riku:p'] *vt*: *to recoup one's
losses* 損失を取戻す sofshitsu wǒ torímodosù

recourse [ri:'kɔːrs] *n*: *to have recourse
to* ...を用いる ...wo mochíirù

recover [rikʌv'əːr] *vt* (get back: stolen
goods, lost items, financial loss) 取戻す
torímodosù
♦*vi*: *to recover (from)* (illness) (...が)

治る (...ga) naórù; (operation, shock, experience) (...から) 立ち直る (...kará) tachínaorú

recovery [rikʌvˈəri] n (from illness, operation: in economy etc) 回復 kaffuku; (of stolen, lost items) 取戻し torímodoshi

re-create [ri:kriˈeit] vt 再現する saígen suru

recreation [rekriːeiˈʃən] n (play, leisure activities) 娯楽 goráku

recreational [rekriːeiˈʃənəl] adj 娯楽の goráku no

recrimination [rikriməneiˈʃən] n 責合い seméai

recruit [rikrúːt] n (MIL) 新兵 shínpei; (in company, organization) 新入社(会)員 shínnyūsha(kai)in
♦vt 募集する boshū suru

recruitment [rikrúːtˈmənt] n 募集 boshū

rectangle [rekˈtæŋgəl] n 長方形 chôhōkei

rectangular [rektæŋˈgjələr] adj (shape, object etc) 長方形の chôhōkei no

rectify [rekˈtəfai] vt (correct) 正す tadásù

rector [rekˈtər] n (REL) 主任司祭 shunínshisai

rectory [rekˈtəri] n (house) 司祭館 shisáikan

recuperate [rikuːˈpəreit] vi (recover: from illness etc) 回復する kaffuku suru

recur [rikəːr] vi (error, event) 繰返される kurfkaesarerù; (illness, pain) 再発する saíhatsu suru

recurrence [rikəːrˈəns] n (of error, event) 繰返し kurfkaeshi; (of illness, pain) 再発 saíhatsu

recurrent [rikəːrˈənt] adj 頻繁に起る hínpan nǐ okórù

red [red] n (color) 赤 ákà; (pej: POL) 過激派 kagékiha
♦adj 赤い akáì

to be in the red (bank account, business) 赤字になっている akáji ni natté irù

red carpet treatment n 盛大な歓迎式 seídai na kangeishiki

Red Cross n 赤十字 sekíjūji

redcurrant [redˈkɑːrənt] n アカフサスグリ akáfusasugùri

redden [redˈən] vt (turn red) 赤くする a-kákù suru
♦vi (blush) 赤面する sekímen suru

reddish [redˈiʃ] adj 赤っぽい akáppòi

redeem [ridiːm] vt (fig: situation, reputation) 救う sukúù; (something in pawn, loan) 請出す ukédasù; (REL: rescue) 救う sukúù

redeeming [ridiːˈmiŋ] adj: *redeeming feature* 欠点を補う取柄 kettén wǒ ogínaù torfe

redeploy [riːdiploiˈ] vt (resources) 配置し直す haíchi shínaosù

red-haired [redˈheːrd] adj 赤毛の akáge no

red-handed [redˈhænˈdid] adj: *to be caught red-handed* 現行犯で捕まる geñkōhan de tsukámarù

redhead [redˈhed] n 赤毛の人 akáge no hitó

red herring n (fig) 本論から注意をそらす物 hoñron kará chūi wo sorásù monó

red-hot [redˈhaːt] adj (metal) 真っ赤に焼けた makká nǐ yaketá

redirect [riːdərektˈ] vt (mail) 転送する teñsō suru

red light n: *to go through a red light* (AUT) 信号無視をする shiñgōmushi wo suru

red-light district [redˈlait-] n 赤線地区 akásenchikù

redo [riːduːˈ] (pt redid pp redone) vt やり直す yarínaosù

redolent [redˈələnt] adj: *redolent of* (smell: also fig) ...臭い ...kusái

redouble [riːdʌbˈəl] vt: *to redouble one's efforts* 一層努力する issō doryòku suru

redress [ridresˈ] n (compensation) 賠償 baíshō
♦vt (wrong) 償う tsugúnaù

Red Sea n: *the Red Sea* 紅海 kōkai

redskin [redˈskin] n (pej) インディアン Indian

red tape n (fig) 形式的手続き keshshikiteki tetsuzúki

reduce [rídus'] *vt* (decrease: spending, numbers etc) 減らす herásu

to reduce someone to (begging, stealing) ...を余儀なくさせる ...wo yoginaku saserú

to reduce someone to tears 泣かせる nakáserú

to reduce someone to silence 黙らせる damáraserú

「*reduce speed now*」(AUT) 徐行 jokô

at a reduced price (goods) 割引で waríbiki de

reduction [ridʌk'ʃən] *n* (in price) 値下げ neságe; (in numbers etc) 減少 geñshō

redundancy [ridʌn'dənsi:] *n* (dismissal) 解雇 kaíko; (unemployment) 失業 shitsúgyō

redundant [ridʌn'dənt] *adj* (worker) 失業中の shitsúgyōchū no; (detail, object) 余計な yokéi na

to be made redundant 解雇される kaíko sarérū

reed [ri:d] *n* (BOT) アシ ashí; (MUS: of clarinet etc) リード rído

reef [ri:f] *n* (at sea) 暗礁 añshō

reek [ri:k] *vi*: *to reek (of)* (...の) におい がぷんぷんする (...no) niói ga púñpun suru

reel [ri:l] *n* (of thread, string) 巻 makí; (of film, tape: *also* on fishing-rod) リール ríru; (dance) リール ríru

♦*vi* (sway) よろめく yorómekú

reel in *vt* (fish, line) 手繰り寄せる tagúriyoserú

ref [ref] (*inf*) *n abbr* = referee

refectory [rifek'tə:ri:] *n* (in school, college etc) 食堂 shokúdō

refer [rifə:r'] *vt* (person, patient): *to refer someone to* ...を...に回す ...wo ...ni mawásu; (matter, problem): *to refer something to* ...を...に委託する ...wo ...ni itáku suru

♦*vi*: *to refer to* (allude to) ...に言及する ...ni geñkyū suru; (consult) ...を参照する ...wo sañshō suru

referee [refəri:'] *n* (SPORT) 審判員 shiñpan-in, レフェリー réferī; (BRIT: for job application) 身元保証人 mimótohoshōnìn

♦*vt* (football match etc) ...のレフェリーをやる ...no réferī wo yarú

reference [ref'ə:rəns] *n* (mention) 言及 geñkyū; (in book, paper) 引用文献 iñ-yō buñken; (for job application: letter) 推薦状 suñseñjō

with reference to (COMM: in letter) ...に関しては ...ni kañshite wa

reference book *n* 参考書 sañkōsho

reference number *n* 整理番号 sebríbañgō

referenda [refəren'də] *npl of* **referendum**

referendum [refəren'dəm] (*pl* **referenda**) *n* 住民投票 jūmiñtōhyō

refill [*vb* ri:fil' *n* ri:'fil] *vt* (glass etc) ...にもう一杯つぐ ...ni mố ippaí tsugú; (pen etc) ...に…を詰替える ...ni ...wo tsumékaerú

♦*n* (of drink etc) お代り o-káwari; (for pen etc) スペアー supéā

refine [rifain'] *vt* (sugar, oil) 精製する seísei suru; (theory, idea) 洗練する señren suru

refined [rifaind'] *adj* (person, taste) 洗練された señren sareta

refinement [rifain'mənt] *n* (of person) 優雅さ yūgasa; (of system) 精度 seído

reflect [riflekt'] *vt* (light, image) 反射する hañsha suru; (situation, attitude) 反映する hañ-ei suru

♦*vi* (think) じっくり考える jikkúrí kañgaerú

it reflects badly/well on him それは彼の悪い(いい)所となる sore wa kárè no warúì [íi] tokóro wo monógatatte irú

reflection [riflek'ʃən] *n* (of light, heat) 反射 hañsha; (image) 影 kágè; (of situation, attitude) 反映する物 hañ-ei suru monð; (criticism) 非難 hínàn; (thought) 熟考 jukkō

on reflection よく考えると yókù kañgaerù to

reflector [riflek'tə:r] *n* 反射器 hañshakì; (AUT) 反射板 hañshateki na

♦*n* (PHYSIOLOGY, PSYCH) 反射 hañsha

reflexive [riflek'siv] *adj* (LING) 再帰形の
safki no

reform [rifɔrm'] *vt* (sinner, character)
改心 kaíshin; (of law, system) 改革 kaíkaku

♦*vt* (sinner) 改心させる kaíshin saserù;
(law, system) 改革する kaíkaku suru

Reformation [refərmei'ʃən] *n*: **the
Reformation** 宗教改革 shúkyòkaíkaku

reformatory [rifɔr'mətɔ:ri:] *n* (*US*) 感
化院 kaíkaìn

refrain [rifrein'] *vi*: **to refrain from
doing** ...をしない様にする ...wo shinái
yò ni suru

♦*n* (of song) 繰返し kuríkaeshi, リフレイ
ン rifúreìn

refresh [rifreʃ'] *vt* (subj: sleep, drink) 元
気付ける geñkizukerù

to refresh someone's memory ...に思い
出させる ...ni omóidasaserù

refresher course [rifreʃ'ər-] (*BRIT*) *n*
研修会 keñshùkaì

refreshing [rifreʃ'iŋ] *adj* (drink) 冷たく
ておいしい tsumétakùte ofshiì; (sleep) 気
分をさわやかにする kìbùn wo sawáyàka
ni suru

refreshments [rifreʃ'mənts] *npl* (food
and drink) 軽食 keíshoku

refrigeration [rifridʒərei'ʃən] *n* (of
food) 冷蔵 refzò

refrigerator [rifridʒ'ə:reitər] *n* 冷蔵庫
refzòko

refuel [ri:fju:'əl] *vi* 燃料を補給する neñ-
ryò wo hokyù suru

refuge [ref'ju:dʒ] *n* (shelter) 避難場所 hí-
nánbasho

to take refuge in ...に避難する ...ni hínàn suru

refugee [refjudʒi:'] *n* 難民 nañmin

refund [*n* ri:'fʌnd *vb* rifʌnd'] *n* 払い戻し
haráimodoshi

♦*vt* (money) 払い戻す haráimodosù

refurbish [ri:fər'biʃ] *vt* (shop, theater)
改装する kaísò suru

refusal [rifju:'zəl] *n* 断り kotówari, 拒否
kyóhì

first refusal (option) オプション権 o-

púshoǹken

refuse [rifju:z'] *vt* (request, offer, gift)
断る kotówarù; (invitation) 辞退する jí-
tài suru; (permission, consent) 拒む kobámù

♦*vi* (say no) 断る kotówarù; (horse) 飛越
を拒否する hiétsu wò kyóhì suru

to refuse to do something ...するのを
拒む ...surú no wò kobámù

refuse² [ref'ju:s] *n* (rubbish) ごみ gomí

refuse collection *n* ごみ収集 gomíshù-
shù

refute [rifju:t'] *vt* (argument) 論破する
roñpa suru

regain [rigein'] *vt* (power, position) 取戻
す torímodosù

regal [ri:'gəl] *adj* 堂々とした dódò to shità

regalia [rigei'li:ə] *n* (costume) 正装 seísò

regard [rigɑ:rd'] *n* (gaze) 観察 shíseǹ;
(attention, concern) 関心 kañshin;
(esteem) 尊敬 soñkei

♦*vt* (consider) 見なす mínasù

to give one's regards to ...から...によろ
しく伝える ...kará ...ni yoróshìku tsutáerù

with kindest regards 敬具 kéìgu

**regarding, as regards, with regard
to** (with reference to, concerning) ...に関
して ...ni kañshitè

regardless [rigɑ:rd'lis] *adv* (carry on,
continue) 構わず構 kamáwazù ni

regardless of (danger, consequences)
...を顧みず ...wo kaérimizù

regatta [rigæt'ə] *n* ヨット(ボート)競技
会 yottó (bòto) kyógìkaì

regenerate [ridʒen'æreit] *vt* (inner
cities, arts) よみがえらせる yomígaerà-
serù

regent [ri:'dʒənt] *n* 摂政 sesshó

regime [reiʒi:m'] *n* (system of government) 政治体制 seíjìtaìsei

regiment [redʒ'əmənt] *n* (MIL) 連隊 reñtai

regimental [redʒəmen'təl] *adj* 連隊の
reñtai no

region [ri:'dʒən] *n* (area: of land) 地区
chíkù; (: of body) ...部 ...bù; (administra-

tive division of country) 行政区 gyõsei-ku

in the region of (*fig*: approximately) 約 yáku

regional [ri:'dʒənəl] *adj* (organization, wine, geography) 地元の jimóto no; (provincial) 地方の chihõ no

register [redʒ'istər] *n* (list: of births, marriages, deaths, voters) 登録簿 tõroku-bo; (SCOL: of attendance) 出席簿 shussékibõ; (MUS: of voice) 声域 sefiki; (: of instrument) 音域 oñ-iki
♦*vt* (birth, death, marriage) 届け出る todokéderu, 登録する tõroku suru; (car) 登録する tõroku suru; (MAIL: letter) 書留にする kakítome ni suru; (subj: meter, gauge) 示す shimésu
♦*vi* (at hotel) チェックインする chekkúñ suru; (for work) 名前を登録する namáe wo tõroku suru; (as student) 入学手続きをする nyūgakutetsuzuki wo suru; (make impression) ぴんと来る piñ tò kúrù

registered [redʒ'istərd] *adj* (MAIL: letter, parcel) 書留の kakítome no

registered trademark *n* 登録商標 tõrokushõhyõ

registrar [redʒ'istrɑːr] *n* (official) 戸籍係 kosékigakàri; (in college, university) 教務係 kyõmugakàri; (*BRIT*: in hospital) 医務吏員 imúriñ

registration [redʒistrei'ʃən] *n* (*gen*) 登録 tõroku; (of birth, death) 届出 todókede; (AUT: *also*: **registration number**) ナンバー náñba

registry [redʒ'istri] *n* 登記所 tõkisho

registry office (*BRIT*) *n* 戸籍登記所 kosékitõkisho

to get married in a registry office 戸籍登記所で結婚する kosékitõkisho dè kekkóñ suru

regret [rigret'] *n* (sorrow) 悔み kuyámi
♦*vt* (decision, action) 後悔する kõkai suru; (loss, death) 悔む kuyámů; (inability to do something) 残念に思う zañneñ ni omóů; (inconvenience) 済まないと思う sumánai to omóů

regretfully [rigret'fəli] *adv* (sadly) 残念ながら zañneñ nagàra

regrettable [rigret'əbəl] *adj* (unfortunate: mistake, incident) あいにくの aíniku no

regular [reg'jələr] *adj* (even: breathing, pulse etc) 規則的な kísokuteki na; (evenly-spaced: intervals, meetings etc) 定期的な teíkiteki na; (symmetrical: features, shape etc) 対称的な taíshõteki na; (frequent: raids, exercise etc) 頻繁な híñpan na; (usual: time, doctor, customer etc) 通常の tsújõ no; (soldier) 正規の sefki no; (LING) 規則変化の kísokuheñka no
♦*n* (client etc) 常連 jõren

regularity [regjəlær'iti:] *n* (frequency) 高頻度 kõhíñdo

regularly [reg'jələːrli:] *adv* (at evenly-spaced intervals) 規則的に kísokuteki ni; (symmetrically: shaped etc) 対称的に taíshõteki ni; (often) 頻繁に híñpan ni

regulate [reg'jəleit] *vt* (conduct, expenditure) 規制する kiséi suru; (traffic, speed) 調整する chõsei suru; (machine, oven) 調節する chõsetsu suru

regulation [regjəlei'ʃən] *n* (of conduct, expenditure) 規制 kiséi; (of traffic, speed) 調整 chõsei; (of machine, oven) 調節 chõsetsu; (rule) 規則 kísoku

rehabilitation [ri:həbilitei'ʃən] *n* (of criminal, addict) 社会復帰 shakáifukkì, リハビリテーション rihábiritèshon

rehearsal [rihər'səl] *n* リハーサル rihãsaru

rehearse [rihəːrs'] *vt* (play, dance, speech etc) …のリハーサルをする …no rihãsaru wo suru

reign [rein] *n* (of monarch) 治世 chiséi; (*fig*: of terror etc) 支配 shíhai
♦*vi* (monarch) 君臨する kuñriñ suru; (*fig*: violence, fear etc) はびこる habíkorů; (: peace, order etc) 行渡る ikíwataru

reimburse [ri:imbərs'] *vt* (pay back) …に弁償する …ni beñshõ suru

rein [rein] *n* (for horse) 手綱 tazúna

reincarnation [ri:inkɑːrnei'ʃən] *n* (belief) 輪廻 ríñne

reindeer [rein'di:r] *n inv* トナカイ tonákai

reinforce [ri:infɔ:rs'] *vt* (strengthen: object) 補強する hokyō suru; (: situation) 強化する kyōka suru; (support: idea, statement) 裏付けする urázukerū

reinforced concrete [ri:infɔ:rst'-] *n* 鉄筋コンクリート tekkín konkuríto

reinforcement [ri:infɔ:rs'mənt] *n* (strengthening) 補強 hokyō

reinforcements [ri:infɔ:rs'mənts] *npl* (MIL) 援軍 eñgun

reinstate [ri:insteit'] *vt* (worker) 復職させる fukúshoku saserū; (tax, law, text) 元通りにする motódōri ni suru

reiterate [ri:it'əreit] *vt* (repeat) 繰返す kuríkaesū

reject [n ri:'dʒekt *vb* ridʒekt'] *n* (COMM) 傷物 kizúmono

♦*vt* (plan, proposal etc) 退ける shirízokerū; (offer of help) 断る kotówarū; (belief, political system) 拒絶する kyozétsu suru; (candidate) 不採用にする fusáiyō ni suru; (coin) 受付けない ukétsukenai; (goods, fruit etc) 傷物として処分する kizúmono toshíte shóbun suru

rejection [ridʒek'ʃən] *n* (of plan, proposal, offer of help etc) 拒否 kyóhi; (of belief etc) 拒絶 kyozétsu; (of candidate) 不採用 fusáiyō

rejoice [ridʒois'] *vi*: **to rejoice at/over** ...を喜ぶ...wo yorókobū

rejuvenate [ridʒu:'vəneit] *vt* (person) 若返らせる wakágaeraserū

relapse [rilæps'] *n* (MED) 再発 saíhatsu

relate [rileit'] *vt* (tell) 話す hanásu; (connect) 結び付ける musúbitsukerū

♦*vi*: **to relate to** (person, subject, thing) ...に関係する...ni kaíkei ga arú

related [rilei'tid] *adj* (person) 血縁がある ketsúen ga arú; (animal, language) 近縁の kiñ-en no

related to ...に関係がある ...ni kaíkei ga arú

relating [rilei'tiŋ]: **relating to** *prep* ...に関する ...ni kañ suru

relation [rilei'ʃən] *n* (member of family) 親せき shiñseki; (connection) 関係 kaíkei

relations [rilei'ʃənz] *npl* (dealings) 関係

kaíkei; (relatives) 親せき shiñseki

relationship [rilei'ʃəŋʃip] *n* (between two people, countries, things) 関係 kaíkei; (also: **family relationship**) 親族関係 shiñzokukañkei

relative [rel'ətiv] *n* (member of family) 親類 shiñrui, 親せき shiñseki

♦*adj* (comparative) 相対的な sōtaiteki na; (connected): **relative to** ...に関する ...ni kañ suru

relatively [rel'ətivli] *adv* (comparatively) 比較的に hikákuteki

relax [rilæks'] *vi* (person: unwind) くつろぐ kutsúrogū; (muscle) 緩む yurúmū

♦*vt* (one's grip) 緩める yurúmerū; (mind, person) くつろがせる kutsúrogaserū; (rule, control etc) 緩める yurúmerū

relaxation [ri:lækseı'ʃən] *n* (rest) 休み yasúmi; (of muscle, grip) 緩み yurúmi; (of rule, control etc) 緩和 kañwa; (recreation) 娯楽 goráku

relaxed [rilækst'] *adj* (person) 落着いた ochítsuitā; (discussion, atmosphere) くつろいだ kutsúróida

relaxing [rilæks'iŋ] *adj* (holiday, afternoon) くつろげる kutsúrogérū

relay [ri:'lei] *n* (race) リレー rírē

♦*vt* (message, question) 伝える tsutáerū; (programme, signal) 中継する chúkei suru

release [rilis'] *n* (from prison) 釈放 shakúhō; (from obligation) 免除 méñjo; (of gas, water etc) 放出 hōshutsu; (of film) 封切り fúkiri; (of book, record) 発売 hatsúbai

♦*vt* (prisoner: from prison) 釈放する shakúhō suru; (: from captivity) 解放する kaíhō suru; (gas etc) 放出する hōshutsu suru; (free: from wreckage etc) 救出する kyúshutsu suru; (TECH: catch, spring etc) 外す hazúsu; (book, record) 発売する hatsúbai suru; (film) 公開する kōkai suru; (report, news) 公表する kōhyō suru

relegate [rel'əgeit] *vt* (downgrade) 格下げする kakúsage suru; (BRIT: SPORT): **to be relegated** 格下げされる kakúsage saserū

relent [rilent'] *vi* (give in) ...の態度が軟化

する ...no táido ga nañka suru

relentless [rilent'lis] adj (unceasing) 絶間ない taémanaì; (determined) 執念深い shúneñbukai

relevance [rel'əvəns] n (of remarks, information) 意義 ígì; (of question etc) 関連 kañren

relevant [rel'əvənt] adj (fact, information, question) 意義ある ígì árù
  relevant to (situation, problem etc) ...に 関連のある ...ni kañren no arù

reliability [rilaiəbil'əti:] n (of person, machine) 信頼性 shiñraisei; (of information) 信ぴょう性 shiñpyōsei

reliable [rilai'əbəl] adj (person, firm) 信頼できる shiñrai dekírù; (method, machine) 信頼性のある shiñraisei no arù; (news, information) 信用できる shiñyō dekírù

reliably [rilai'əbli:] adv: **to be reliably informed that ...** 確かな情報筋による と...táshìka na jōhōsùjì ni yorù to ...

reliance [rilai'əns] n: **reliance (on)** (...への) 依存 (...é ñō) izón

relic [rel'ik] n (REL) 聖遺物体 sefbùtsu; (of the past) 遺物 ibútsu

relief [rili:f'] n (from pain, anxiety etc) 緩和 kañwa; (help, supplies) 救援物資 kyūenbusshī; (ART) 浮彫 ukíbori, レリーフ refīfu; (GEO) 際立つ事 kiwádatsu kotō

relieve [rili:v'] vt (pain, fear, worry) 緩和する kañwa suru; (patient) 安心させる añshin saserù; (bring help to: victims, refugees etc) ...に救援物資を渡す ...ni kyūenbusshī wo todōkerù; (take over from: colleague, guard) ...と交替する ...to kōtai suru
  to relieve someone of something (load) ...を持って上げる ...no ...wo mōttē agérù; (duties, post) ...を解任する ...wo kañnin suru
  to relieve oneself 小便する shṓben suru

religion [rilidʒ'ən] n 宗教 shūkyō

religious [rilidʒ'əs] adj (activities, faith) 宗教の shūkyō no; (person) 信心深い shíñjinbukai

relinquish [riliŋ'kwiʃ] vt (authority) ...か ら手を引く ...kara té wo híkù; (plan, habit) やめる yamérù

relish [rel'iʃ] n (CULIN) レリッシュ re-rísshù; (enjoyment) 楽しみ tanóshimi
  ◆vt (enjoy: food, competition) 楽しむ ta-nóshimù
  to relish the thought/idea/prospect of something/doing something ...を ...するのを心待ちに持つ ...wo ...surù nō wo) kokóromachi ni mótsù

relocate [ri:lou'keit] vt 移動させる idṓ saserù
  ◆vi 移動する idṓ suru

reluctance [rilʌk'təns] n (unwillingness) 気が進まない事 kí gà susúmanai kotò

reluctant [rilʌk'tənt] adj (unwilling) 気が進まない kí gà susúmanaì

reluctantly [rilʌk'təntli:] adv (unwillingly) いやいやながら iyáiya nagàra

rely on [rilai'-] vt fus (be dependent on) ...に頼る ...ni tayórù; (trust) ...を当てにする ...wo shiñ-yō suru

remain [rimein'] vi (survive, be left) 残る nokórù; (continue to be) 相変らず...であ る afkawarazù ...de árù; (stay) とどまる todómarù

remainder [rimein'dər] n (rest) 残り no-kóri

remaining [rimei'niŋ] adj 残りの nokóri no

remains [rimeinz'] npl (of meal) 食べ残り tabénokori; (of building) 廃虚 hãikyo; (corpse) 遺体 itái

remand [rimænd'] n: **on remand** 拘置中 で kōchichū de
  ◆vt: **to be remanded in custody** 拘置 される kōchi saserù

remand home (BRIT) n 少年院 shōnen-ìn

remark [rimɑːrk'] n (comment) 発言 hatsúgen
  ◆vt (comment) 言う iú

remarkable [rimɑːr'kəbəl] adj (outstanding) 著しい ichíjirushiì

remarry [rimær'i:] vi 再婚する safkon suru

remedial [rimi:'di:əl] adj (tuition, classes) 補修の hoshū no; (exercise) 矯正の kyōsei no

remedy [rem'idi:] n (cure) 治療法 chiryṓhṓ

◆vt (correct) 直す naósù

remember [rimem'bəːr] vt (call back to mind) 思い出す omóidasù; (bear in mind) 忘れない様にする wasúrenai yṓ ni suru; (send greetings): **remember me to him** 彼によろしくお伝え下さい kárè ni yoróshikù o-tsútae kudasái

remembrance [rimem'brəns] n (memory: of dead person) 思い出 omóide; (souvenir: of place, event) 記念品 kinénhin

remind [rinaind'] vt: **to remind someone to do something** ...するのを忘れない様に...に注意する ...surú no wo wasúrenai yṓ ni ...ni chūɪ suru

to remind someone of something ...に...を思い出させる ...ni ...wo omóidasaserù

she reminds me of her mother 彼女を見ると彼女の母親を思い出す kánojo wo mírù to kánòjo no hahāoya wo omóidasù

reminder [rimaind'əːr] n (souvenir) 記念品 kinénhin; (letter) 覚書 obóegaki

reminisce [remənis'] vi (about the past) 追懐する tsuḯkai suru

reminiscent [remənis'ənt] adj: **to be reminiscent of something** ...を思い出させる ...wo omóidasaserù

remiss [rimis'] adj (careless) 不注意な fuchū na

it was remiss of him 彼は不注意だった kárè wa fuchūí dáttà

remission [rimij'ən] n (of debt) 免除 mén̄jo; (of prison sentence) 減刑 geńkei; (of illness) 緩解 kańkai; (REL: of sins) 許し yurúshi

remit [rimit'] vt (send: money) 送金する sṓkin suru

remittance [rimit'əns] n (payment) 送金 sṓkin

remnant [rem'nənt] n (small part remaining) 残り nokóri; (of cloth) 切れ端 kiréhashi

remnants [rem'nənts] npl (COMM) 端切れ hagfre

remorse [rimɔːrs'] n (guilt) 後悔 kṓkai

remorseful [rimɔːrs'fəl] adj (guilty) 後悔している kṓkai shite irù

remorseless [rimɔːrs'lis] adj (fig: noise, pain) 絶間ない taémanaí

remote [rimout'] adj (distant: place, time) 遠い tōi; (person) よそよそしい yosóyososhiǐ; (slight: possibility, chance) かすかな kásūka na

remote control n 遠隔操作 eńkakusṓsa, リモートコントロール rimṓtokontoróru

remotely [rimout'li:] adv (distantly) 遠くに tōku ni; (slightly) かすかに kásūka ni

remould [ri:'mould] (BRIT) n (tire) 再生タイヤ saíseitaiya

removable [rimu:'vəbəl] adj (detachable) 取外しのできる toríhazushi nō dekírù

removal [rimu:'vəl] n (taking away) 取除く事 torínozoku kotṓ; (of stain) 消し取る事 keshítoru kotṓ; (BRIT: from house) 引っ越し hikkóshi; (from office: dismissal) 免職 meńshoku; (MED) 切除 sétsujo

removal van (BRIT) n 引っ越しトラック hikkóshi torakkú

remove [rimu:v'] vt (gen) 取除く torínozokù; (clothing) 脱ぐ núgù; (bandage etc) 外す hazúsù; (stain) 消し取る keshítorù; (employee) 解雇する kaíko suru; (MED: lung, kidney, appendix etc) 切除する sétsujo suru

removers [rimu:'vəːrz] (BRIT) npl (company) 引っ越し屋 hikkóshiya

remuneration [rimjuːnəːrei'ʃən] n (payment) 報酬 hṓshū

Renaissance [ren'isɑːns] n: **the Renaissance** ルネッサンス runéssànsu

render [ren'dəːr] vt (give: thanks, service) する surú; (make) させる saséru

rendering [ren'dəːriŋ] n (MUS: instrumental) 演奏 eńsṓ; (: song) 歌い方 utáikatà

rendez-vous [rɑːn'deivuː] n (meeting) 待ち合せ machíawase; (place) 待ち合せの

場所 machíawase nò bàshó

renegade [ren'əgeid] *n* 裏切り者 urágirimono

renew [rinu:'] *vt* (resume) 再び始める futátabi hajimérù; (loan, contract etc) 更新する kóshin suru; (negotiations) 再開する saíkai suru; (acquaintance, relationship) よみがえらせる yomígaeraserù

renewal [rinu:'əl] *n* (resumption) 再開 saíkai; (of license, contract etc) 更新 kóshin

renounce [rinauns'] *vt* (belief, course of action) 捨てる sutérů; (claim, right, peerage) 放棄する hóki suru

renovate [ren'əveit] *vt* (building, machine) 改造する kaízó suru

renovation [renəvei'ʃən] *n* 改造 kaízó

renown [rinaun'] *n* (fame) 名声 meísei

renowned [rinaund'] *adj* (famous) 有名な yùmei na

rent [rent] *n* (for house) 家賃 yáchìn

◆*vt* (take for rent: house) 賃借する chíńshaku suru; (: television, car) レンタルで借りる réntaru de karírù; (*also*: **rent out**: house) 賃貸する chíńtai suru; (: television, car) 貸出す kashídasù

rental [ren'təl] *n* (for television, car) レンタル料 réntaru

renunciation [rinʌnsei:'ʃən] *n* 放棄 hóki

reorganize [ri:ɔːr'gənaiz] *vt* 再編成する saíhensei suru

rep [rep] *n* (COMM) = **representative**; (THEATER) = **repertory**

repair [riper'] *n* (of clothes, shoes) 修繕 shúzen; (of car, road, building etc) 修理 shúri

◆*vt* (clothes, shoes) 修繕する shúzen suru; (car, engine, road, building) 修理する shúri suru

in good/bad repair 整備が行届いている (いない) seíbi gà íkítodoite irú (ínàì)

repair kit *n* 修理キット shúrikittò

repatriate [ri:pei'trieit] *vt* (refugee, soldier) 送還する sókan suru

repay [ripei'] (*pt, pp* **repaid**) *vt* (money, debt, loan) 返済する heńsai suru; (person) ...に借金を返済する ...ni shakkíń wo

hefísaì suru; (sb's efforts) ...に答える ...ni kotáerù; (favour) ...の恩返しをする ...no ońgaeshi suru

repayment [ripei'mənt] *n* (amount of money) 返済金 heńsaikín; (of debt, loan etc) 返済 heńsai

repeal [ripi:l'] *n* (of law) 廃止する haíshi suru

◆*vt* (law) 廃止 haíshi

repeat [ripi:t'] *n* (RADIO, TV) 再放送 saíhósó

◆*vt* (say/do again) 繰返す kuríkaesù; (RADIO, TV) 再放送する saíhósó surù

◆*vi* 繰返す kuríkaesù

repeatedly [ripi:t'idli:] *adv* (again and again) 再三 saísan

repel [ripel'] *vt* (drive away: enemy, attack) 撃退する gekítai suru; (disgust: subj: appearance, smell) ...に不快な感じを...ni fukái na kañji wo atáerù

repellent [ripel'ənt] *adj* いやな iyá na

◆*n*: *insect repellent* 虫よけ mushíyoke

repent [ripent'] *vi*: *to repent (of)* (sin, mistake) ...を後悔する (...wo) kókai suru

repentance [ripen'təns] *n* 後悔 kókai

repercussions [ri:pərkʌʃ'ənz] *npl* 反響 hañkyó

repertoire [rep'ərtwar] *n* レパートリー repátorí

repertory [rep'ərtɔːri:] *n* (*also*: **repertory theater**) レパートリー演劇 repátoriéñgeki

repetition [repitiʃ'ən] *n* (repeat) 繰返し kuríkaeshi

repetitive [ripet'ətiv] *adj* (movement, work) 単純反復の tañjunhañpuku no; (speech) くどい kudóì; (noise) 反復される hañpuku sarerù

replace [ripleis'] *vt* (put back) 元に戻す mótò ni modósù; (take the place of) ...に代る ...ni kawárù

replacement [ripleis'mənt] *n* (substitution) 置き換え okíkae; (substitute) 代りの物 kawári no monò

replay [ripei'] *n* (of match) 再試合 saíshiai; (of tape, film) 再生 saísei

replenish [riplen'iʃ] *vt* (glass) ...にもう一

杯つぐ ...ni mố ippài tsugú; (stock etc) 補充する hojú suru

replete [riplíːt] *adj* (well-fed) 満腹の mańpuku no

replica [rep'ləkə] *n* (copy) 複製 fukúsei, レプリカ repúrīka

reply [riplaí'] *n* (answer) 答え kotáè
♦*vi* (to question, letter) 答える kotáerù

reply coupon 返信券 heńshinken ◇切手と交換できる券 kitté tò kōkan dekirú kéň

report [ripɔːrt'] *n* (account) 報告書 hốkokushò; (PRESS, TV etc) 報道 hốdō; (BRIT: also: **school report**) レポート repốto; (of gun) 銃声 jūsei
♦*vt* (give an account of: event, meeting) 報告する hốkoku suru; (PRESS, TV etc) 報道する hốdō suru; (theft, accident, death) 届け出る todókederù
♦*vi* (make a report) 報告する hốkoku suru; (present oneself): **to report (to someone)** ...に 出頭する (...ni) shuttố suru; (be responsible to); **to report to someone** ...が直属である ...ga chokúzoku nò jóshi de arù

report card (US, SCOTTISH) *n* 通知表 tsúchihyò

reportedly [ripɔːr'tidli] *adv* うわさによると uwása ni yorù tò

reporter [ripɔːr'tər] *n* (PRESS, TV etc) 記者 kishá

repose [ripouz'] *n*: **in repose** (face, mouth) 平常で heijō de

reprehensible [reprihen'səbəl] *adj* (behavior) 不届きな futódōki na

represent [reprizent'] *vt* (person, nation) 代表する daíhyō suru; (view, belief) ...の典型的な例である ...no teńkeiteki nà reí de arù; (symbolize: idea, emotion) ...のシンボルである ...no shíňboru de arù; (constitute) ...である ...de arù; (describe): **to represent something as** ...として描写する ...wo ...toshite byốsha suru; (COMM) ...のセールスマンである ...no sếrusumàn de arù

representation [reprizentei'ʃən] *n* (state of being represented) 代表を立てている事 daíhyō wò tátète irú kotò; (pic-

ture) 絵 é; (statue) 彫像 chốzō; (petition) 陳情 chińjō

representations [reprizentei'ʃənz] *npl* (protest) 抗議 kốgi

representative [reprizen'tativ] *n* (of person, nation) 代表者 daíhyōsha; (of view, belief) 典型 teńkei; (COMM) セールスマン sếrusumàn; (US: POL) 下院議員 kaíngiìn
♦*adj* (group, survey, cross-section) 代表的な daíhyōteki na

repress [ripres'] *vt* (people, revolt) 抑圧する yokúatsu suru; (feeling, impulse) 抑制する yokúsei suru

repression [ripreʃ'ən] *n* (of people, country) 抑圧 yokúatsu; (of feelings) 抑制 yokúsei

repressive [ipres'iv] *adj* (society, measures) 抑圧的な yokúatsuteki na

reprieve [ripriːv'] *n* (LAW) 執行延期 shikkốeñki ◇特に死刑について言う tókù ni shikéi ni tsuité iú; (fig: delay) 延期 eñki

reprimand [rep'rəmænd] *n* (official rebuke) 懲戒 chốkai

reprint [*n* riː'print *vb* riːprint'] *n* 復刻版 fukkốkuban
♦*vt* 復刻する fukkốku suru

reprisal [ripraí'zəl] *n* 報復 hốfuku

reprisals [ripraí'zəlz] *npl* (acts of revenge) 報復行為 hốfukukôi

reproach [riproutʃ'] *n* (rebuke) 非難 hínàn
♦*vt*: **to reproach someone for something** ...の...を非難する ...no ...wo hínàn suru

reproachful [riproutʃ'fəl] *adj* (look, remark) 非難めいた hinánmeìta

reproduce [riːprədus'] *vt* (copy: document etc) 複製する fukúsei suru; (sound) 再生する saísei suru
♦*vi* (mankind, animal, plant) 繁殖する hańshoku suru

reproduction [riːprədʌk'ʃən] *n* (copy: of document, report etc) 複写 fukúsha, 複製 fukúsei; (of sound) 再生 saísei; (of painting, furniture) 複製品 fukúseihìn; (of mankind, animal etc) 繁殖 hańshoku

reproductive [riːprədʌkˈtiv] *adj* (system, process) 繁殖の hańshoku no

reproof [ripruːfˈ] *n* しっ責 shisséki

reprove [ripruːvˈ] *vt: to reprove someone for something* ...の事で...をしっ責する ...no kotó de ...o shisséki suru

reptile [repˈtail] *n* は虫類 hachúˈrui

republic [ripʌbˈlik] *n* 共和国 kyówakoˈku

republican [ripʌbˈlikən] *adj* (system, government etc)共和国の kyówakoku no; (*US*: POL): *Republican* 共和党の kyówatoˈ no ♦*n: Republican* 共和党員 kyówatoˈ-iˈn

repudiate [ripjuːˈdiːeit] *vt* (accusation, violence) 否定する hitéi suru

repugnant [ripʌgˈnənt] *adj* 不愉快な fuyúkai na

repulse [ripʌlsˈ] *vt* (enemy, attack) 撃退する gekítai suru

repulsive [ripʌlˈsiv] *adj* (sight, idea) 不愉快な fuyúkai na

reputable [repˈjətəbəl] *adj* 評判の良い hyóban no yoˈi

reputation [repjəteiˈʃən] *n* 評判 hyóban

reputed [ripjuːˈtid] *adj* (supposed) ...とさ れる ...to saréru

reputedly [ripjuːˈtidli:] *adv* (supposedly) 人の言うには hitó no iˈu ni wa

request [rikwestˈ] *n* (polite demand) 願い negái; (formal demand) 要望 yóbo; (RADIO, TV) リクエスト rikúesto ♦*vt: to request something of/from someone* (politely) ...に...をお願いする ...ni ...o o-négai suru; (formally) ...に ...を要望する ...ni ...wo yóbo suru; (RADIO, TV) リクエストする rikúesuto suru

request stop (*BRIT*) *n* 随時停留所 zuˈjiteiryūjo ◇乗降客がいる時だけバスが留る停留所 jōkōkyaku ga iˈru toki dakè básu ga tomárù tefryūjo

requiem [rekˈwiːəm] *n* (REL) 死者のためのミサ shiňša seˈsha; (MUS) 鎮魂曲 chiňkoňkyoku, レクイエム rekúiˈemu

require [rikwaiəːrˈ] *vt* (need) ...が必要である ...ga hitsúyō de arù; (order): *to*

require someone to do something ...に ...する事を要求する ...ni ...surú kotð wo yōkyú suru

requirement [rikwaiəːrˈmənt] *n* (need) 必要条件 hitsúyōjōken; (want) 要求 yókyu

requisite [rekˈwizit] *n* (requirement) 必要条件 hitsúyōjōken ♦*adj* (required) 必要な hitsúyō na

requisition [rekwiziˈʃən] *n: requisition (for)* (demand) ...の請求 (...no) sefkyū ♦*vt* (MIL) 徴発する chōhatsu suru

resale [riːˈseil] *n* 転売 teńbai

rescind [resindˈ] *vt* (law) 廃止する hafshi suru; (contract, order etc) 破棄する hákì suru

rescue [resˈkjuː] *n* (help) 救援 kyúen; (from drowning, accident) 人命救助 jiňmeikyújo ♦*vt: to rescue (from)* (person, animal) (...から) 救う (...kara) sukúð; (company) 救済する kyūsai suru

rescue party *n* 救援隊 kyúentai, レスキュー隊 resúkyútai

rescuer [resˈkjuːəːr] *n* 救助者 kyūjoshà

research [risəːrtʃˈ] *n* 研究 keňkyū ♦*vt* (story, subject) 研究する keňkyū suru; (person) ...について情報を集める ...ni tsúite jốhō wo atsúmerù

researcher [risəːrtʃˈəːr] *n* 研究者 keňkyúsha

resemblance [rizemˈbləns] *n* (likeness) 似ている事 nité irù kotð

resemble [rizemˈbəl] *vt* ...に似ている ...ni nité irù

resent [rizentˈ] *vt* ...に対して腹を立てる ...ni táìshite harái wò tatérù

resentful [rizentˈfəl] *adj* 怒っている o-kótte irù

resentment [rizentˈmənt] *n* 恨み urámi

reservation [rezəːrveiˈʃən] *n* (booking) 予約 yoyáku; (doubt) 疑い utágai; (for tribe) 居留地 kyoryúchī

reserve [rizəːrvˈ] *n* (store) 備蓄 bichíku, 蓄え takúwae; (SPORT) 補欠 hokétsu; (game reserve) 保護区 hogóˈku; (restraint) 遠慮 efiryo

◆vt (keep) 取って置く tóttè oku; (seats, table etc) 予約する yoyáku suru

in reserve 蓄えてあって takúwaete attè

reserved [rizə:rvd'] adj (restrained) 遠慮深い efiryobûkai

reserves [rizə:rvz'] npl (MIL) 予備軍 yobígùn

reservoir [rez'ərvwɑːr] n (of water) 貯水池 chosûchì

reshuffle [riːʃʌf'əl] n: Cabinet reshuffle (POL) 内閣改造 naíkakukaizô

reside [rizaid'] vi (person: live) 住む sumú

residence [rez'idəns] n (formal: home) 住い sumái; (length of stay) 滞在 taízai

residence permit (BRIT) n 在留許可 zaíryûkyokà

resident [rez'idənt] n (of country, town) 住民 jûmin; (in hotel) 泊り客 tomárikyakù

◆adj (population) 現住の geñjù no; (doctor) レジデントの réjîdentò no

residential [rezidenˈtʃəl] adj (area) 住宅の jûtaku no; (course) 住込みの sumíkomi no; (college) 全寮制の zeńryôsei no

residue [rez'iduː] n (remaining part) 残留物 zańryûbutsu

resign [rizain'] vt (one's post) 辞任する jínin suru

◆vi (from post) 辞任する jínin suru

to resign oneself to (situation, fact) あきらめて...を認める akírametè ...wo mitómerù

resignation [rezignei'ʃən] n (post) 辞任 jínin; (state of mind) あきらめ akírame

resigned [rizaind'] adj (to situation etc) あきらめている akíramete irù

resilience [rizil'jəns] n (of material) 弾力 dañryoku; (of person) 回復力 kaífukuryòku

resilient [rizil'jənt] adj (material) 弾力のある dañryoku no arù; (person) 立直りの速い tachínaori nò hayáì

resin [rez'in] n 樹脂 júshì

resist [rizist'] vt 抵抗する tekő suru

resistance [rizis'təns] n (gen) 抵抗 teíkô; (to illness, infection) 抵抗力 teíkôryoku

resolute [rez'əluːt] adj (person) 意志の強

い íshì no tsuyóì; (refusal) 断固とした dáñko to shità

resolution [rezəluː'ʃən] n (decision) 決心 kesshíñ; (determination) 決意 kétsùi; (of problem, difficulty) 解決 kaíketsu

resolve [rizɑːlv'] n (determination) 決意 kétsùbi

◆vt (problem, difficulty) 解決する kaíketsu suru

◆vi: to resolve to do ...しようと決心する ...shiyó tò kesshíñ suru

resolved [rizɑːlvd'] adj (determined) 決心している kesshíñ shité irù

resonant [rez'ənənt] adj 朗朗たる rórô taru

resort [rizɔːrt'] n (town) リゾート rizótð; (recourse) 利用 riyó

◆vi: to resort to ...を利用する ...wo riyó suru

in the last resort 結局 kekkyókù

resound [rizaund'] vi: to resound (with) (...の音が...中に) 鳴り響く (...no óto ga ...jū ni) naríhibikù

resounding [rizaun'diŋ] adj (noise) 響き渡る hibíkiwatarù; (fig. success) 完全な kañzen na

resource [ri:'sɔːrs] n (raw material) 資源 shígèn

resourceful [risɔːrs'fəl] adj (quick-witted) やり手の yaríte no

resources [ri:'sɔːrsiz] npl (coal, iron, etc) 天然資源 teńnenshigèn; (money) 財産 zaísan

respect [rispekt'] n (consideration, esteem) 尊敬 sofikei

◆vt 尊敬する sofikei suru

with respect to ...に関して ...ni kañ shite

in this respect この点では konó ten de

respectability [rispektəbil'əti:] n 名声 meísei

respectable [rispek'təbəl] adj (morally correct) 道理にかなった dóri ni kanáttà; (large: amount) かなりの kánàri no; (passable) まあまあの mâmâ no

respectful [rispekt'fəl] adj (person, behavior) 礼儀正しい reígitadashiì

respective [rispek'tiv] *adj* (separate) それぞれの soréz̄ore no

respectively [rispek'tivli:] *adv* それぞれ soréz̄ore

respects [rispekts] *npl* (greetings) あいさつ áIsatsu

respiration [respərei'ʃən] *n see* **artificial respiration**

respite [res'pit] *n* (rest) 休息 kyúsoku

resplendent [risplen'dənt] *adj* 華やかな hanáyāka na

respond [rispɑ:nd'] *vi* (answer) 答える kotáerù; (react: to pressure, criticism) 反応する hafinó suru

response [rispɑ:ns'] *n* (answer) 答え kotáe; (reaction) 反応 hafinó

responsibility [rispɑ:nsəbil'əti:] *n* (liability) 責任 sekínin; (duty) 義務 gímù

responsible [rispɑ:n'səbəl] *adj* (liable): **responsible (for)** (...の) 責任手ある (...no) sekínin gà árù; (character, person) 責任感のある sekíninkan no aru; (job) 責任の重い sekínin nò omóI

responsive [rispɑ:n'siv] *adj* (child, gesture) 敏感な bínkan na; (to demand, treatment) よく応じる yókù ójirù

rest [rest] *n* (relaxation) 休み yasúmi; (pause) 休止 kyúshi; (remainder) 残り nokóri; (object: to support something) 台 daI; (MUS) 休止符 kyúshifù

♦*vi* (relax) 休む yasúmu; (stop) 休止する kyúshi suru: **to rest on** (idea) ...に基づく ...ni motózukù; (weight, object) ...に置かれている ...ni okárete irù

♦*vt* (head, eyes, machine) 休ませる yasúmaserù; (lean): **to rest something on/against** ... ...に置く (立て掛ける) ...wo ...ni okú (yoríkakerù)

the rest of them (people) 残りの人たち nokóri nò hitótachi; (objects) 残りの物 nokóri no monð

it rests with him to ... ...するのは彼の責任だ ...surú no wa kárè no sekínin dà

restaurant [res'tərənt] *n* レストラン rḗsùtoran

restaurant car (*BRIT*) *n* 食堂車 shokúdðsha

restful [rest'fəl] *adj* 心を落着かせる ko-

kórð wo ochítsukaserù

rest home *n* 養老院 yōrōin

restitution [restitu:'ʃən] *n*: **to make restitution to someone for something** (compensate) ...に対して...の弁償をする ...ni táIshite ...no befishó wo suru

restive [res'tiv] *adj* (person, crew) 反抗的な hańkóteki na; (horse) 言う事を聞かない 言う事を聞かない kikánaI

restless [rest'lis] *adj* (person, audience) 落着かない ochítsukanaI

restoration [restərei'ʃən] *n* (of building etc) 修復 shūfūku; (of law and order, faith, health) 回復 kaffuku; (of something stolen) 返還 henkan; (to power, former state) 復旧 fukkyū

restore [ristɔ:r'] *vt* (building) 修復する shūfūku suru; (law and order, faith, health) 回復する kaffuku suru; (something stolen) 返す káèsu; (to power, former state) 元に戻す mótð ni modósù

restrain [ristrein'] *vt* (feeling, growth, inflation) 抑制する yokúsei suru; (person: **to restrain (from doing)** (...しない様に) 抑える (...shináI yð ni) osáerù

restrained [ristreind'] *adj* (style, person) 控え目な hikáeme na

restraint [ristreint'] *n* (restriction) 抑制 yokúsei; (moderation) 程々 hodóhodo; (of style) 控え目な調子 hikáeme nà chóshi

restrict [ristrikt'] *vt* (limit: growth, numbers etc) 制限する sefigen suru; (: vision) 邪魔する jámà suru; (confine: people, animals) ...の動きを制限する ...no ugóki wò sefigen suru; (: activities, membership) 制限する sefigen suru

restriction [ristrik'ʃən] *n* (gen) 制限 sefigen; (of vision) 妨げ samátagè; (limitation): **restriction (on)** (...の) 制限 (...no) sefigen

restrictive [ristrik'tiv] *adj* (environment) 束縛的な sokúbakuteki na; (clothing) きつい kitsúI

restrictive practices *npl* (INDUSTRY) 制限的慣行 sefigentekikańkō

rest room (*US*) *n* お手洗い o-téaraI

restructure [ri:strʌk'tʃər] *vt* (business,

economy) 再編成する saíheñsei suru

result [rizʌlt'] n (of event, action) 結果 kekká; (of match) スコア sukóa; (of exam, competition) 成績 seíseki

♦vi: **to result in** ...に終る ...ni owáru; **as a result of** ...の結果 ...no kekká

resume [rizuːm'] vt (work, journey) 続ける tsuzúkerù

♦vi (start again) また始まる matá hájimaru

résumé [rez'uːmei] n (summary) 要約 yōyaku; (US: curriculum vitae) 履歴書 rirékishò

resumption [rizʌmp'ʃən] n (of work, activity) 再開 saíkai

resurgence [risər'dʒəns] n 復活 fukkátsu

resurrection [rezərek'ʃən] n (of hopes, fears) よみがえらせる事 yomígaeraserù kotó; (REL): **the Resurrection** キリストの復活 kirísuto no fukkátsu

resuscitate [risʌs'əteit] vt (MED) そ生させる soséi saserù

resuscitation [risʌsətei'ʃən] n そ生 soséi

retail [riː'teil] adj (trade, department, shop, goods) 小売の koúri no

♦adv 小売で koúri de

retailer [riː'teilər] n (trader) 小売業者 koúrigyòsha

retail price n 小売価格 koúrikakàku

retain [ritein'] vt (keep) 保つ tamótsu

retainer [ritei'nər] n (fee) 依頼料 iráiryō

retaliate [ritæl'ieit] vi: **to retaliate (against)** (attack, ill-treatment) (...に対して) 報復する (...ni táishite) hōfuku suru

retaliation [ritælieiʃən] n 報復 hōfuku

retarded [ritɑr'did] adj (child) 知恵遅れの chiéokùre no; (development, growth) 遅れた okúreta

retch [retʃ] vi むかつく mukátsukù

retentive [riten'tiv] adj (memory) 優れた sugúreta

reticent [ret'isənt] adj 無口な múkùchi na

retina [ret'ənə] n (ANAT) 網膜 mōmaku

retire [ritaiər'] vi (give up work: gen) 引

退する iñtai suru; (: at a certain age) 定年退職する teíneñtaìshoku suru; (withdraw) 引下がる hikísagarù; (go to bed) 寝る nérù

retired [ritaiərd'] adj (person: gen) 引退した iñtai shita; (: at certain age) 定年退職した teíneñtaìshoku shita

retirement [ritaiər'mənt] n (giving up work: gen) 引退 iñtai; (: at certain age) 定年退職 teíneñtaìshoku

retiring [ritaiər'iŋ] adj (leaving) 退職する taíshoku suru; (shy) 内気な uchíki na

retort [ritɔrt'] vi しっぺ返しをする shíppégaeshì wo suru

retrace [ritreis'] vt **to retrace one's steps** 来た道を戻る kitá michí wo modórù

retract [ritrækt'] vt (statement, offer) 撤回する tekkái suru; (claws, aerial etc) 引っ込める hikkómerù

retrain [ritrein'] vt 再訓練する saíkuñren suru

retraining [ritrei'niŋ] n 再訓練 saíkuñren

retread [riː'tred] n (tire) 再生タイヤ saíseitaìya

retreat [ritriːt'] n (place) 隠れ家 kakúregà; (withdrawal) 避難 hínàn; (MIL) 退却 taíkyaku

♦vi (from danger, enemy) 避難する hínàn suru; (MIL) 退却する taíkyaku suru

retribution [retrəbjuː'ʃən] n 天罰 teñbatsu

retrieval [ritriː'vəl] n (of object) 回収 kaíshū; (of situation) 繕う事 tsukúroru kotó; (of honor) ばん回 bañkai; (of error) 償い tsugúnaì; (loss) 取返し toríkaeshi

retrieve [ritriːv'] vt (object) 回収する kaíshū suru; (situation) 繕う tsukúroù; (honor) ばん回する bañkai suru; (error) 償う tsugúnaù; (loss) 取返す toríkaesù

retriever [ritriː'vər] n (dog) リトリーバ犬 rítoríbakèn

retrograde [ret'rəgreid] adj 後戻りの atómodòri no

retrospect [ret'rəspekt] n: **in retrospect** 振返ってみると furíkaette miru tò

retrospective [retrəspek'tiv] adj (exhi-

return [rɪtˈəːn] *n* (going or coming back) 帰り kaérì; (of something stolen, borrowed etc) 返還 heńkan; (FINANCE: from land, shares, investment) 利回り rimáwari

◆*cpd* (journey) 帰りの kaérì no; (BRIT: ticket) 往復の ōfuku no; (match) 雪辱の setsújoku no

◆*vi* (person etc: come or go back) 帰る kaérù; (feelings, symptoms etc) 戻る modórù; (regain): **to return to** (consciousness) ...を回復する ...wo kaífuku suru; (power) ...に返り咲く ...ni kaérizakû

◆*vt* (favor, love etc) 返す kaésù; (something borrowed, stolen etc) 返却する heńkyaku suru; (LAW: verdict) ...と答申する ...to tóshin suru; (POL: candidate) 選出する seńshutsu suru; (ball) 返す kaésù

in return (for) (...の) お返しに (...no) o-káeshi ni

by return of post 折返し郵便で oríkaeshiyūbin de

many happy returns (of the day)! お誕生日おめでとう o-táńjōbi omédetō

returns [rɪtˈəːnz] *npl* (COMM) 利益 ríèki

reunion [riːjuːnˈjən] *n* (of family) 集い tsudóì; (of school, class etc) 同窓会 dōsōkai; (of two people) 再会 saíkai

reunite [riːjuːnaɪtˈ] *vt* (bring or come together again) 元のさやに収めさせる mótð no sáya ni osámesaserù; (reconcile) 和解させる wakái saserù

rev [rev] *n abbr* (AUT: = *revolution*) 回転 kaíten

◆*vt* (also: **rev up**: engine) ふかす fukásù

revamp [riːvæmpˈ] *vt* (organization, company, system) 改革する kaíkaku suru

reveal [rɪviːlˈ] *vt* (make known) 明らかにする akíràka ni suru; (unveil) 現す aráwasù

revealing [rɪviːlˈɪŋ] *adj* (action, statement) 手の内を見せるような té nð uchí wð misérù; (dress) 肌をあらわにする hádà

wo arawá ni suru

reveille [revˈəl] *n* (MIL) 起床らっぱ ki-shō rappá

revel [revˈəl] *vi*: **to revel in something/ in doing something** (enjoy) ...を [...する] 楽しむ ...wo [...surú no wð] tanóshimù

revelation [revəleiˈʃən] *n* (fact, experience) 意外な事実 igái na shíñchishíki

revelry [revˈəlriː] *n* どんちゃん騒ぎ doñchan sawági

revenge [rɪvendʒˈ] *n* (for injury, insult) 復しゅう fukúshū

to take revenge on (enemy) ...に復しゅうする ...ni fukúshū suru

revenue [revˈənuː] *n* (income: of individual, company, government) 収入 shūnyū

reverberate [rɪvəːrˈbəreit] *vi* (sound, thunder etc: *also fig*) 響く hibíkù

reverberation [rɪvəːrbəreiˈʃən] *n* (of sound, etc: *also fig*) 響き hibíki

revere [rɪvirˈ] *vt* 敬愛する kefai suru

reverence [revˈərəns] *n* 敬愛 kefai

Reverend [revˈərənd] *adj* (in titles) ...師 ...shī ◆聖職者の名前に付ける敬称 sefshokusha no namáe ni tsukérù kefshō

reversal [rɪvəːrˈsəl] *n* (of order) 反転 hañten; (of direction) 逆戻り gyakúmodòri; (of decision, policy) 逆転 gyakúten; (of roles) 入れ代り irékawari

reverse [rɪvəːrsˈ] *n* (opposite) 反対 hañtai; (back) 裏 urá; (AUT: *also*: **reverse gear**) バック bákkù; (setback, defeat) 失敗 shippái

◆*adj* (opposite: order, direction, process) 反対の hañtai no, 逆の gyakú no; (: side) 裏の urá no

◆*vt* (order, position, direction) 逆にする gyakú ni surù; (process, policy, decision) 引っ繰り返す hikkúrikaèsu; (roles) 入れ替える irékaerù; (car) バックさせる bákkù saserù

◆*vi* (BRIT: AUT) バックする bákkù suru

reverse-charge call [rɪvəːrsˈtʃɑːrdʒ-] (BRIT) *n* 受信人払い電話 jushínninbarai deñwa

reversing lights [rɪvəːrˈsiŋ-] (BRIT)

npl (AUT) バックライト bakkúraìto

revert [rɪvəːrt'] *vi*: **to revert to** (former state) ...に 戻る ...ni modóru; (LAW: money, property) ...に帰属する ...ni kizóku surù

review [rɪvjuː'] *n* (magazine) 評論雑誌 hyóronzasshì; (MIL) 閲兵 eppéi; (of book, film etc) 批評 hihyó; (examination: of situation, policy etc) 再検討 saíkentò

◆*vt* (MIL) 閲兵する eppéi suru; (book, film etc) ...の批評を書く ...no hihyó wð kákù; (situation, policy etc) 再検討する saíkentò suru

reviewer [rɪvjuː'əːr] *n* (of book, film etc) 批評家 hihyóshà

revile [rɪvail'] *vt* (insult) 侮辱する bujóku surù

revise [rɪvaiz'] *vt* (manuscript) 修正する shúsei suru; (opinion, price, procedure) 変える kaérù

◆*vi* (BRIT: study) 試験勉強する shikénbènkyð suru

revision [rɪviʒ'ən] *n* (amendment) 修正 shúsei; (for exam) 試験勉強 shikénbènkyð

revitalize [riːvai'təlaiz] *vt* ...に 新しい活力を与える ...ni atárashiì katsúryòku wo atáerù

revival [rɪvai'vəl] *n* (recovery) 回復 kaífuku; (of interest, faith) 復活 fukkátsu; (THEATER) リバイバル ríbàibaru

revive [rɪvaiv'] *vt* (person) ...の 意識を回復させる ...no íshìki wo kaífuku saserù; (economy, industry) 復興させる fukkó saserù; (custom, hope, courage) 復活させる fukkátsu saserù; (play) 再上演する saíjòen suru

◆*vi* (person: from faint) 意識を取戻す íshìki wo torímodosù; (: from ill-health) 元気になる gênki ni nárù; (activity, economy etc) 回復する kaífuku suru; (faith, interest etc) 復活する fukkátsu suru

revoke [rɪvouk'] *vt* 取消す toríkesù

revolt [rɪvoult'] *n* (rebellion) 反逆 hañgyaku

◆*vi* (rebel) 反逆する hañgyaku suru

revolting [rɪvoul'tiŋ] *adj* (disgusting) むかつかせる mukátsukaserù

revolution [revəluː'ʃən] *n* (POL) 革命 kakúmei; (rotation: of wheel, earth etc: also AUT) 回転 kaíten

revolutionary [revəluː'ʃəneːriː] *adj* (method, idea) 革命的な kakúmeitekì na; (leader, army) 革命の kakúmei no

◆*n* (POL: person) 革命家 kakúmeika

revolutionize [revəluː'ʃənaiz] *vt* (industry, society etc) ...に大変革をもたらす ...ni daíhenkaku wð motárasù

revolve [rɪvɑːlv'] *vi* (turn: earth, wheel etc) 回転する kaíten suru; (life, discussion): **to revolve (a)round** ...を中心に展開する ...wo chúshin nì teñkai suru

revolver [rɪvɑːl'vəːr] *n* けん 銃 kefijú, リボルバー ríbòruba (回転式の物を指す kaíteñshiki no mono wð sásù)

revolving [rɪvɑːl'viŋ] *adj* (chair etc) 回転式の kaíteñshiki no

revolving door *n* 回転ドア kaíten doa

revue [rɪvjuː'] *n* (THEATER) レビュー rébyù

revulsion [rɪvʌl'ʃən] *n* (disgust) 嫌悪 kéñ-o

reward [rɪwɔːrd'] *n* (for service, merit, work) 褒美 hóbi; (money for capture of criminal, information etc) 賞金 shókin

◆*vt*: **to reward (for)** (effort) ...の (...のために) 褒美を与える (...no tamé ni) hóbi wð atáerù

rewarding [rɪwɔːr'diŋ] *adj* (fig: worthwhile) やりがいのある yarígai no arù

rewind [riːwaind'] (*pt, pp* **rewound**) *vt* (tape, cassette) 巻戻す makímodosù

rewire [riːwaiəːr'] *vt* (house) ...の 電気配線を直す ...no deñki haìsen wo shináosù

rewrite [riːrait'] (*pt* **rewrote**, *pp* **rewritten**) *vt* 書直す kakínaosù

rhapsody [ræp'sədiː] *n* (MUS) 狂詩曲 kyóshikyòku, ラプソディー rápùsodi

rhetorical [rɪtɔːr'ikəl] *adj* (question, speech) 修辞的な shújiteki na

rheumatic [ruːmæt'ik] *adj* リューマチの ryúmachi no

rheumatism [ruː'mətizəm] *n* リューマチ ryūmachi

Rhine [rain] *n: the Rhine* ライン川 ráingawa

rhinoceros [rainɑs'ərəs] *n* サイ sái

rhododendron [roudəden'drən] *n* シャクナゲ shakúnage

Rhone [roun] *n: the Rhone* ローヌ川 rônùgawa

rhubarb [ruː'bɑːrb] *n* ルバーブ rubábù

rhyme [raim] *n* (of two words) 韻 ín; (verse) 詩 shí; (technique) 韻を踏む事 íñ wò fumú kotò

rhythm [rið'əm] *n* リズム rízùmu

rhythmic(al) [rið'mik(əl)] *adj* リズミカルな rizúmikàru na

rib [rib] *n* (ANAT) ろっ骨 rokkótsu

ribbon [rib'ən] *n* リボン ríbòn

in ribbons (torn) ずたずたになって zutázuta ni nattè

rice [rais] *n* (grain) 米 komé; (cooked) 御飯 góhàn

rice pudding *n* ライスプディング raísu pudìngu ◇御飯にミルク, 卵, 砂糖などを加えたデザート góhàn ni mírùku, tamágo, satō nadò wo kuwáetà dezátò

rich [ritʃ] *adj* (person, country) 金持の kanémochi no; (clothes, jewels) 高価なkôka na; (soil) 肥えたkoétà, 肥よくなhiyóku na; (food, diet) 濃厚なnôkò na; (color, voice, life) 豊かなyútàka na; (abundant): *rich in* (minerals, resources etc) ...に富んだ ...ni tóñda

♦*npl: the rich* 金持 kanémochi ◇総称 sôshō

riches [ritʃ'iz] *npl* (wealth) 富 tómì

richly [ritʃ'liː] *adv* (dressed, decorated) 豪華に gôka ni; (rewarded, deserved, earned) 十分に júbùñ ni

rickets [rik'its] *n* くる病 kurúbyō

rickety [rik'ətiː] *adj* (shaky) がたがたの gatágata no

rickshaw [rik'ʃɔː] *n* 人力車 jíñrikishà

ricochet [rikəʃei'] *vi* (bullet, stone) 跳ね飛ぶ hanétobù

rid [rid] (*pt, pp* **rid**) *vt: to rid someone of something* ...の...を取除く ...no ...wo torínozokù

to get rid of (something no longer required) 捨てる sutérù; (something unpleasant or annoying) ...を取除く ...wo torínozokù

ridden [rid'ən] *pp* of **ride**

riddle [rid'əl] *n* (conundrum) なぞなぞ nazónazo; (mystery) なぞ nazó

♦*vt: to be riddled with* ...だらけである ...dáràke de árù

ride [raid] *n* (in car, on bicycle, horse) 乗る事 norú kotò; (distance covered) 道のり michínorì

♦*vb* (*pt* **rode**, *pp* **ridden**)

♦*vi* (as sport) 乗馬をする jôba wo suru; (go somewhere: on horse, bicycle, bus) 乗って行く itté ikù

♦*vt* (a horse, bicycle, motorcycle) ...に乗る ...ni nórù; (distance) 行く ikú

to take someone for a ride (*fig*: deceive) べてんに掛ける petéñ nì kakérù

to ride a bicycle 自転車に乗る jitéñsha ni norú

to ride at anchor (NAUT) 停泊する teíhaku suru

rider [raid'əːr] *n* (on horse) 乗り手 norítè; (on bicycle, motorcycle) 乗る人 norú hitò, ライダー ráidā

ridge [ridʒ] *n* (of hill) 尾根 ónè; (of roof) 天辺 teppéñ; (wrinkle) うね uné

ridicule [rid'əkjuːl] *n* あざけり azákerì

♦*vt* あざける azákerù

ridiculous [ridik'jələs] *adj* (foolish) ばかな bakágeta

riding [rai'diŋ] *n* (sport, activity) 乗馬 jôba

riding school *n* 乗馬学校 jôbagakkō

rife [raif] *adj: to be rife* (bribery, corruption, superstition) はびこる habíkoru

to be rife with (rumors, fears) ...がはびこっている ...ga habíkotte irù

riffraff [rif'ræf] *n* (rabble) ろくでなしの連中 rokúdenashi nò reñchū

rifle [rai'fəl] *n* (gun) ライフル ráìfuru

♦*vt* (steal from: wallet, pocket etc) ...の中身を盗む ...no nakámi wò nusúmù

rifle range *n* (for sport) 射撃場 shagékijō; (at fair) 的 matéki shatéki

rifle through vt fus (papers) ...をかき回して捜す ...wo kakímawashite sagásù

rift [rift] n (split: in ground) 亀裂 kirétsu; (: in clouds) 切れ目 kíreme; (fig: disagreement) 仲たがい nakátagaÌ

rig [rig] n (also: **oil rig**) 油井掘削装置 yuséi kussaku sốchi
♦vt (election, game etc) 不正操作する fuséisŌsa suru

rigging [rig'iŋ] n (NAUT) 素具 sakúgù

right [rait] adj (correct: answer, solution, size etc) 正しい tadáshiȎ; (suitable: person, clothes, time) 適当な tekitŌ na; (: decision etc) 適切な tekísetsu na; (morally good) 正当な seitŌ na; (fair, just) 公正な kŌsei na; (not left) 右の migŌ no
♦n (what is morally right) 正義 seṻgi; (entitlement) 権利 kéṻri; (not left) 右 migÌ
♦adv (correctly: answer etc) 正しく tadáshiȽku; (properly, fairly: treat etc.) 公正に kŌsei ni; (not on the left) 右に migÌ ni; (directly, exactly): **right now** 今すぐ ímà súgù
♦vt (put right way up: ship, car etc) 起す okósù; (correct: fault, situation, wrong) 正す tadásù
♦excl では da wá

to be right (person) ...の言う事が合っている ...no iú kotŌ ga atté irú; (answer) 正解である seṻkai de arú; (clock, reading etc) 合っている atté irú

by rights 当然 tŌzen

on the right 右に migÌ ni

to be in the right ...の方が正しい ...no hŌ gá tadáshiȎ

right away すぐに súgù ni

right in the middle 丁度真ん中に chŌdo mañnaka ni

right angle n (MATH) 直角 chokkáku

righteous [rait'ʃəs] adj (person) 有徳な yútoku na; (anger) 当然な tŌzen na

rightful [rait'fəl] adj (heir, owner) 合法の gŌhŌ no; (place, share) 正当な seitŌ na

right-handed [rait'hændid] adj (person) 右利きの migÌkiki no

right-hand man [rait'hænd'-] n 右腕 migÌfude

right-hand side n 右側 migÌgawa

rightly [rait'li:] adv (with reason) 当然 tŌzen

right of way n (on path etc) 通行権 tsúkoken; (AUT) 先行権 seňkōken

right-wing [rait'wiŋ] adj (POL) 右翼の úyōku no

rigid [ridʒ'id] adj (structure, back etc) 曲らない magárenaÌ; (attitude, views etc) 厳格な geňkaku na; (principle, control etc) 厳しい kibíshiȎ

rigmarole [rig'mæroul] n (procedure) 手続 tetsúzuki

rigor [rig'ɔːr] (BRIT **rigour**) n (strictness) 厳格さ geňkakusa; (severity): **rigors of life/winter** 生活/冬の厳しさ seṻkatsu/fuyú no kibíshisa

rigorous [rig'ɔːrəs] adj (control, test) 厳密な geňmitsu na; (training) 厳しい kibíshiȎ

rig out (BRIT) vt: **to rig out as** ...の仮装をする ...no kasŌ wŌ suru

to rig out in ...を着る ...wo kírù

rig up vt 取り上げる tsukúriagerú

rile [rail] vt (annoy) ...を怒らせる ...wo okóraserú

rim [rim] n (of glass, dish) 緑 fuchí; (of spectacles) フレーム furémù; (of wheel) リム rímù

rind [raind] n (of bacon, fruit, cheese) 皮 kawá

ring [riŋ] n (of metal, light, smoke) 輪 wá; (for finger) 指輪 yubíwa; (of spies, drug-dealers etc) 組織 sŌshiki; (for boxing, of circus) リング ríňgu; (bullring) 闘牛場 tŌgyŪjŌ; (sound of bell) ベルの音 berú no otŌ
♦vb (pt **rang**, pp **rung**)
♦vi (person: by telephone) 電話を掛ける deñwa wŌ kakérù; (telephone, bell, doorbell) 鳴る narú; (also: **ring out**: voice, words) 響く naríhibikù
♦vt (BRIT: TEL) ...に電話を掛ける ...ni deñwa wŌ kakérù; (bell etc) 鳴らす narásù

a ring of people 車座になった人々 kurúmaza ni nattá hitŌbìto

a ring of stones 環状に並んだ石 kañjŌ

ni naranða ishí

to give someone a ring (BRIT: TEL)
...ni denwa wo kakerú

my ears are ringing 耳鳴りがする mimínari ga surú

ring back (BRIT) vt (TEL) ...に電話を
掛け直す ...ni denwa wo kakénaosù

♦vi (TEL) 電話を掛け直す denwa wo kakénaosù

ringing [riŋ'iŋ] n (of telephone, bell) 鳴
る音 narú otò; (in ears) 耳鳴り mimínari

ringing tone n (TEL) ダイヤルトーン
daíyarutòn

ringleader [riŋ'li:də:r] n (of gang) 主犯
shúhàn

ringlets [riŋ'lits] npl (of hair) 巻き毛 makíge

ring off (BRIT) vi (TEL) 電話を切る
denwa wo kírù

ring road n (BRIT) 環状線 kanjōsen

ring up (BRIT) vt (TEL) ...に電話を掛け
る ...ni denwa wo kakerú

rink [riŋk] n (also: **ice rink**) スケートリ
ンク sukétorìnku

rinse [rins] n (of dishes, hands) すすぎ
susúgì; (of hair) リンスする事 ríñsu suru
kotð; (dye: for hair) リンス ríñsu

♦vt (dishes, hands etc) すすぐ susúgù;
(hair etc) リンスする ríñsu suru;

rinse out clothes すすぐ susúgù;
(: mouth) ゆすぐ yusúgù

riot [rai'ət] n (disturbance) 騒動 sódò

♦vi (crowd, protestors etc) 暴動を起こ
す bódò wo okósù

a riot of colors 色取り取り iródoridòri

to run riot (children, football fans etc)
大暴れをする ósawàgi wo suru

riotous [rai'əs] adj (mob, assembly
etc) 暴動的な bódòteki na; (behavior, living) 遊とうざんまいの yútòzañmai no;
(party) どんちゃん騒ぎの doñchan sawàgi no

rip [rip] n (tear) 破れ目 yabúremè

♦vt (paper, cloth) 破る yabúrù

♦vi (paper, cloth) 破れる yabúrerù

ripcord [rip'kɔ:rd] n (on parachute) 引き
綱 hikízðna

ripe [raip] adj (fruit, grain, cheese) 熟し
た jukú shità

ripen [rai'pən] vt (subj: sun) 熟させる jukú saserú

♦vi (fruit, crop) 熟する jukú suru

ripple [rip'əl] n (wave) さざ波 sazánami;
(of laughter, applause) ざわめき zawá-
meki

♦vi (water) さざ波が立つ sazánami ga
tátsù

rise [raiz] n (slope) 上り坂 nobórizaka;
(hill) 丘 oká; (increase: in wages: BRIT)
賃上げ chíñ-age; (: in temperature, temperature) 上昇 jóshò; (fig: to power etc) 出世
shusse

♦vi (pt **rose**, pp **risen**) (prices, numbers)
上がる agárù; (waters) 水かさが増す mi-
zúkasa gà masú; (sun, moon) 昇る nobórù; (person: from bed etc) 起きる okírù;
(sound, voice) 大きくなる ókiku nárù;
(also: **rise up**: tower, building) そびえる
sobíerù; (: rebel) 立ち上がる tachíagarù;
(in rank) 昇進する shóshin suru

to give rise to ...を起す ...wo okósù

to rise to the occasion 腕前を見せる
udémaè wo misérù

risen [riz'ən] pp of **rise**

rising [rai'ziŋ] adj (increasing: number,
prices) 上がる agárù; (tide) 満ちる michírù; (sun, moon) 昇る noború

risk [risk] n (danger) 危険 kikén;
(INSURANCE) リスク rísùku

♦vt (endanger) 危険にさらす kikén nì sarásù; (chance) ...の危険を冒す ...no kíkèn
wo okósù

to take/run the risk of doing ...する
危険を冒す ...surú kikén wo okósù

at risk 危険にさらされている kikén nì sarasá-
sáreté

at one's own risk 自分の責任で jibún no
sekínin de

risky [ris'ki:] adj (dangerous) 危険な kikén na

risqué [riskei'] adj (joke) わいせつがかっ
た waísetsugakattà

rissole [ris'əl] n (of meat, fish etc) メン
チカツ meñchikatsu

rite [rait] n 儀式 gíshìki

last rites (REL) 終油の秘蹟 shúyu nð
hiséki

ritual [rɪtʃʊəl] *adj* (law, dance) 儀式的な gishíkiteki na
♦*n* 儀式 gíshìki

rival [rai'vəl] *n* ライバル ráibaru
♦*adj* ライバルの ráibaru no
♦*vt* (match) ...に匹敵する ...ni hittéki suru

rivalry [rai'vəlri:] *n* (competition) 競争 kyósō

river [riv'ər] *n* 川 kawá
♦*cpd* (port, traffic) 川の kawá no
up/down river 川上[下]へ kawákami [shimo] e

riverbank [riv'ərbæŋk] *n* 川岸 kawágishi

riverbed [riv'ərbed] *n* 河原 kawára

rivet [riv'it] *n* (bolt) リベット ribéttò
♦*vt* (fig): *to rivet one's eyes/attention on* ...に注目する ...ni chúmoku suru

Riviera [riviær'ə] *n: the (French) Riviera* リビエラ ribiéra
the Italian Riviera イタリアのリビエ ラ itária nò ribiéra

road [roud] *n* (gen) 道 michí, 道路 dōro
♦*cpd* (accident, sense) 交通の kótsū no
major/minor road 優先(非優先)道路 yúsen(hiyúsen)dōro

roadblock [roud'blɑk] *n* 検問所 kenmonjo

roadhog [roud'hɔg] *n* マナーの悪いドラ イバー mánā no warúi doráibā

road map *n* 道路地図 dōrochízù

road safety *n* 交通安全 kōtsū ánzen

roadside [roud'said] *n* 道路脇 dōrowaki

roadsign [roud'sain] *n* 道路標識 dōro-hyōshiki

road user *n* ドライバー doráibā

roadway [roud'wei] *n* 車道 shadō

roadworks [roud'wərks] *npl* 道路工事 dōrokōji

roadworthy [roud'wərði:] *adj* (car) 整 備状態のいい seíbijōtai no íi

roam [roum] *vi* (wander) さまよう samáyoù

roar [rɔːr] *n* (of animal) ほえ声 hoégoè; (of crowd) どよめき doyómeki; (of vehicle, storm) とどろき todóroki
♦*vi* (animal) ほえる hoérù; (person) どな

る donárù; (crowd) どよめく doyómekù; (engine, wind etc) とどろく todórokù
a roar of laughter 大笑い ōwarai
to roar with laughter 大笑いする ō-warai suru
to do a roaring trade 商売が繁盛 する ...no shōbai ga hanjō suru

roast [roust] *n* (of meat) ロースト rōsuto
♦*vt* (meat, potatoes) オーブンで焼く ō-bun de yakú; (coffee) いる frù

roast beef *n* ローストビーフ rōsutobiïfu

rob [rɑb] *vt* (person, house, bank) ...から 盗む ...kara nusúmu
to rob someone of something ...から ...を 盗む ...karà ...wo nusúmu; (*fig*: deprive) 奪う ubáù

robber [rɑb'ər] *n* 泥棒 dorőbō

robbery [rɑb'əri:] *n* (theft) 盗み nusúmi

robe [roub] *n* (for ceremony etc) ローブ rōbu; (also: **bath robe**) バスローブ basú-rōbu; (*US*) ひざ掛け hizákake

robin [rɑb'in] *n* コマドリ komádori

robot [rou'bɑt] *n* ロボット robóttò

robust [roubʌs'] *adj* (person) たくましい takúmashiì; (economy) 健全な kenzen na; (appetite) おう盛な ōsei na

rock [rɑk] *n* (substance) 岩石 gansēki; (boulder) 岩 iwá; (*US*: small stone, pebble) 小石 koíshi; (*BRIT*: sweet) 水あめ 糖 kōrizatō
♦*vt* (swing gently: cradle) 優しく揺する yasáshiku yusurú; (: child) あやす ayásù; (shake: subj: explosion, waves etc) 激し く揺すぶる hagéshiku yusuburù
♦*vi* (object) 揺れる yurérù; (person) 震え る furérù
on the rocks (drink) オンザロックで oñ-zarokkù de; (marriage etc) 危ぶまれて ayábumarete

rock and roll *n* ロックンロール rokkún-rōru

rock-bottom [rɑk'bɑt'əm] *adj* (*fig*: lowest point) 最低の saftei no

rockery [rɑk'əri:] *n* (in garden) 庭石 niwá-ishi 〈総称〉sōshō

rocket [rɑk'it] *n* (space rocket) ロケッ ト rokéttò; (missile) ロケット弾 rokétto-dañ; (firework) ロケット花火 rokétto hanàbi

rocking chair n 揺りいす yu-rîsu

rocking horse n 揺り木馬 yurîmokùba

rocky [rɒk'iː] adj (covered with rocks) 岩だらけの iwádaràke no; (unsteady: table) 不安定な fuántei na; (unstable: business, marriage) 危ぶまれている ayábumarete irù

rod [rɒd] n (pole) さお saò; (also: **fishing rod**) 釣ざお tsurízao

rode [roud] pt of **ride**

rodent [rou'dənt] n げっ歯類 gesshîrùi

rodeo [rou'diou] n ロデオ ródèo

roe [rou] n (species: also: **roe deer**) ノロ ジカ norójìka; (of fish) 卵 tamágò
    hard roe 腹子 harákò
    soft roe 白子 shîrákò

rogue [roug] n 野郎 yaró

role [roul] n 役 yakù

roll [roul] n (of paper, cloth etc) 巻き makí; (of banknotes) 札束 satsútabà; (also: **bread roll**) ロールパン rôrupañ; (register, list) 名簿 meíbo; (of drums etc) とどろき todóroki
    ♦vt (ball, stone etc) 転がす korógasù; (also: **roll up**: string) 巻く makú; (: sleeves) まくる makúrù; (cigarette) 巻く makú; (eyes) 白黒させる shîrókuro sasérù; (also: **roll out**: pastry) 延ばす nobású; (flatten: lawn, road, surface) ならす narásù
    ♦vi (ball, stone etc) 転がる korógarù; (drum) 鳴り響く narhibikù; (vehicle: also: **roll along**) 走る hashírù; (ship) 揺れる yurérù

roll about/around vi 転がる korógarù

roll by vi (time) 過ぎる sugírù

roll call n 点呼 téñko

roller [rou'lər] n (gen) ローラー rôra; (for hair) カーラー kárà

roller coaster n [-kous'tər] ジェットコースター jettókòsutà

roller skates npl ローラースケート rôrasukèto

roll in vi (mail, cash) 大量に入る taíryò ni hafrù

rolling [rou'liŋ] adj (landscape) うねりの

多い unéri no ồi

rolling pin n めん棒 méñbo

rolling stock n (RAIL) 車両 sharyô ◊総称 sôshô

roll over vi 寝返りを打つ negáeri wò útsù

roll up vi (inf: arrive) やって来る yatté kurù
    ♦vt (carpet, newspaper, umbrella etc) 巻く makú

ROM [rɑm] n abbr (COMPUT: = read only memory) ロム rômù

Roman [rou'mən] adj ローマの rôma no

Roman Catholic adj ローマカトリックの rômakatorikkù no
    ♦n ローマカトリック信者 rômakatorikku shiñja

romance [roumæns'] n (love affair) 恋愛 reñ-ai; (charm) ロマンス rômàñsu; (novel) 恋愛小説 reñ-ai shôsetsu

Romania [roumei'niːə] n = **Rumania**

Roman numeral n ローマ数字 rômasûji

romantic [roumæn'tik] adj ロマンチックな rômánchikkù na

Rome [roum] n ローマ rôma

romp [rɑmp] n 騒々しい遊び sôzòshiì asóbi
    ♦vi (also: **romp about**: children, dogs etc) はしゃぎ回る hashágimawarù

rompers [rɑm'pərz] npl ロンパース roñpàsu

roof [ruːf] (pl **roofs**) n 屋根 yánè, ルーフ rûfu
    ♦vt (house, building etc) 屋根を付ける yánè wo tsukérù
    the roof of one's mouth 口がい kôgai

roofing [ruː'fiŋ] n 屋根ふき材 yanéfukizài

roof rack n (AUT) ルーフラック rûfurakkù

rook [ruk] n (bird) ミヤマガラス miyámagaràsu; (CHESS) ルック rúkkù

room [ruːm] n (in house, hotel etc) 部屋 heyá; (space) 空間 kûkan, 場所 bashó; (scope: for improvement, change etc) 余地 yóchi

「**rooms for rent**」, 「**rooms to let**」貸間

あり kashíma arí

single/double room シングル〔ダブル〕部屋 shíŋguru(dabúru)beyà

rooming house [ˈruːmɪŋ-] n (US) n 下宿屋 geshúkuya

roommate [ˈruːmmeit] n ルームメート rūmumèto ◇寄宿舎などで同室に泊まる人 kishúkusha nádo de dóshitsu ni tomárù hitó

rooms [ruːmz] npl (lodging) 下宿 geshúku

room service n (in hotel) ルームサービス rūmusābisu

roomy [ˈruːmi] adj (building, car) 広々とした hiróbíro to shitá; (garment) ゆったりした yuttári shitá

roost [ruːst] vi (birds) ねぐらにつく negúra ni tsukú

rooster [ˈruːstər] n オンドリ ońdóri

root [ruːt] n (BOT) 根 né, (MATH) 根 kóñ; (of problem, belief) 根源 koñgen
♦vi (plant) 根を下ろす né wò orósù; (belief) 定着する teíchaku suru
   the root of a hair 毛根 mókoñ
   the root of a tooth 歯根 shikóñ

root about vi (fig: search) かき回す kakímawasù

root for vt fus (support) ...を応援する ...wo óeñ surù

root out vt (find) 捜し出す sagáshidasù

roots [ruːts] npl (family origins) ルーツ rūtsu

rope [roup] n (thick string) ロープ rōpu, (NAUT) 綱 tsuná; (for climbing) ザイル záiru
♦vt (tie) 縛る shibárù; (climbers: also: **rope together**) ザイルでつなぐ záiru de tsunágù; (an area: also: **rope off**) 綱で仕切る縄を張る nawá dè shikírù
   to know the ropes (fig: know how to do something) こつが分かっている kotsú gà wakátte irù

rope in vt (fig: person) 誘い込む sasóikomù

rope ladder n 縄ばしご nawábashigo

rosary [ˈrouzəri] n ロザリオ rozárìo

rose [rouz] pt of **rise**
♦n (single flower) バラ bará; (shrub) バ

ラの木 bará nò kí; (on watering can) は口 hasókuchi

rosé [rouzei] n ロゼワイン rozéwaìn

rosebud [ˈrouzˈbʌd] n バラのつぼみ bará nò tsubómi

rosebush [ˈrouzˈbuʃ] n バラの木 bará no ki

rosemary [ˈrouzˈmeːri] n ローズマリー rózumarì

rosette [rouzet] n ロゼット rozéttò

roster [ˈrɑːstər] n: **duty roster** 勤務当番表 kiñmutóbañhyo

rostrum [ˈrɑːstrəm] n 演壇 eñdan

rosy [ˈrouzi] adj (color) バラ色の bará-ì-ro no; (face, cheeks) 血色のよい kesshóku no ì; (situation) 明るい akáruì
   a rosy future 明るい見通し akáruì mitóshi

rot [rɑːt] n (decay) 腐敗 fuhái; (fig: pej: rubbish) でたらめ detárame
♦vt (cause to decay: teeth, wood, fruit etc) 腐らす kusárasù
♦vi (decay: teeth, wood, fruit etc) 腐る kusárù

rota [ˈroutə] n (BRIT) n 勤務当番表 kiñmutóbañhyo

rotary [ˈroutəri] adj 回転式の kaíteñshiki no

rotate [ˈrouteit] vt (revolve) 回転させる kaíteñ saserù; (change round: jobs) 交替でやる kótai de yarù
♦vi (revolve) 回転する kaíteñ suru

rotating [ˈrouteitiŋ] adj (movement) 回転する kaíteñ suru

rotation [routeiʃən] n (revolving) 回転 kaíteñ; (changing round: jobs) 交替 kótai; (of crops) 輪作り rińsaku

rote [rout] n: **by rote** 暗記で ańki de

rotor [ˈroutər] n (also: **rotor blade**) 翼 kaíteñyoku, ローター rótà

rotten [ˈrɑːtən] adj (decayed: fruit, meat, wood, eggs etc) 腐った kusátta; (fig: person, situation) いやな iyá nà; (inf: bad) ひどい hidóì
   a rotten tooth 虫歯 mushíba
   to feel rotten (ill) 気分が悪い kíbùn ga warúì

rotund [routʌnd] adj (person) 丸々と太

った marúmarù to futóttā

rouble [ruːbəl] n = **ruble**

rouge [ruːʒ] n お紅 hóbeni

rough [rʌf] adj (skin, surface, cloth) 粗い aráî; (terrain, road) 凸凹の dekóboko no; (voice) しゃがれた shagáretà; (person, manner: violent) 荒っぽい aráppoi; (: brusque) ぶっきらぼうな bukkírabò na; (treatment) 荒い aráî; (weather, sea) 荒れた aréta; (town, area) 治安の悪い chiánno warúî; (plan, sketch) 大まかな ōmaka na; (guess) 大よその óyoso no

♦n (GOLF): **in the rough** ラフに aráfu ni

to rough it 原始的な生活をする genfshiteki na séikatsu wo suru

to sleep rough (BRIT) 野宿する nójùku suru

roughage [rʌfidʒ] n 繊維 sén-i

rough-and-ready [rʌfˈənrediː] adj 原始的な genfshiteki na

roughcast [rʌfˈkæst] n (for wall) 小石を混ぜたしっくい kóishi wò mazéta shikkúî

rough copy n 下書き shitágaki

rough draft n 案案 soán

roughly [rʌfˈliː] adv (handle) 荒っぽく aráppokù; (make) 大まかに ōmaka ni; (speak) ぶっきらぼうに bukkírabò ni; (approximately) 大よそ óyoso

roughness [rʌfˈnis] n (of surface) 荒さ aràsa; (of character) がさつさ gasátsusa

roulette [ruːlet] n ルーレット rúretto

Roumania [ruːˈmeɪniːə] n = **Rumania**

round [raund] adj 丸い marúî; (figures, sum) 概数の gaisū no

♦n (BRIT: of toast) 一切 hitókire; (of policeman, milkman, doctor) 巡回 junkai; (game of cards) 一勝負 hitóshōbu; (: in competition) 一回 íkkai, 一回戦 kaísen; (of ammunition) 一発 íppatsu; (BOXING) ラウンド ráundo; (also: round of golf) ラウンド ráundo; (of talks) 一連 ichíren

♦vt (corner) 回る mawáru

♦prep (surround): **round his neck/ the table** 首[家]の回りに kubí[ié]no mawári ni; (in a circular movement): **to move round the room** 部屋の中を一回りする heyá no nakà wo hitómawari

suru: to sail round the world 世界一周の航海をする sékàishū nò kōkai wo suru; (in various directions): **to move round a room/house** 部屋[家]の中を動き回る heyá [ié]no nakà wo ugókimawarù; (approximately): **round about 300** 大よそ300 óyoso sañbyaku

♦adv: **all round** 回りに mawári ni

a round of golf ゴルフのワンラウンド górùfu no wañraundo

the long way round 遠回り tōmawari

all the year round 一年中 ichínenjū

it's just round the corner (fig) 直ぐそこまで来ている súgù sokó madè kité irù

round the clock 24時間 nijū-yo jíkàn

to go round to someone's (house) …のうちに行く …no uchí ni ikú

to go round the back 裏に回る urá nì mawáru

to go round a house ある家を訪ねる árù ié wò tazúnerù

enough to go round みんなに足りる程 mfnna ni tarírù hodò

a round of applause 拍手 hákùshu

a round of drinks/sandwiches みんなに一通りの飲み物[サンドウイッチ]をおごる事 mfnna ni hitótòri no nomímòno [sañdòuicchī]wo ogórù kotó

roundabout [raundˈəbaut] (BRIT) n (AUT) ロータリー rótàrī; (at fair) メリーゴーラウンド meríg̀òraundo

♦adj (route) 遠回りの tōmawari no; (means) 遠回しの tōmawashi no

rounders [raunˈdərz] npl (game) ラウンダーズ raúndàzu ◊野球に似た英国のゲーム yakyū ni nità efkoku no gēmu

roundly [raundˈliː] adv (fig: criticize) 厳しく kibíshikù

round off vt (speech etc) 終える oérù

round-shouldered [raundˈjouldərd] adj ねこ背の nekóbè no

round trip n 往復旅行 ōfukuryokō

round up vt (cattle, people) 駆集める karfatsumerù; (price, figure) 概数にする gaisū ni suru

roundup [raundˈʌp] n (of news, information) まとめ matóme; (of animals) 駆集め karfatsume; (of criminals) 一斉逮捕

isséitalho

rouse [rauz] vt (wake up) 起こす okósù; (stir up) 引起す hikíokosù

rousing [rau'ziŋ] adj (cheer, welcome) 熱狂的な nekkyōteki na

rout [raut] n (MIL) 敗走 haísō
♦vt (defeat) 敗走させる haísō saserù

route [ruːt] n (way) ルート rūto; (of bus, train) 路線 rosén; (of shipping) 航路 kōro; (of procession) 通り道 tōrimichi

route map (BRIT) n (for journey) 道路地図 dōrochizu

routine [ruːtiːn'] adj (work) 日常の nichíjō no; (procedure) お決りの o-kímari no
♦n (habits) 習慣 shūkan; (drudgery) 反復作業 hañpukusagyō; (THEATER) お決りの演技 o-kímari nò éngi

rove [rouv] vt (area, streets) はいかいす る haíkai suru

row[1] [rou] n (line of people, things) 列 rétsù; (KNITTING) 段 dáñ; (in boat) こぐ事 kogú kotò
♦vi (in boat) こぐ kogú
♦vt (boat) こぐ kogú
in a row (fig) 一列に ichíretsu ni

row[2] [rau] n (racket) 騒ぎ sáwàgi; (noisy quarrel) 口論 kōron; (dispute) 論争 roñsō; (BRIT inf: scolding): **to give someone a row** …に大目玉を食らわす …ni ōmédama wo kuráwasù
♦vi (argue) 口論する kōron suru

rowboat [rou'bout] (US) n ボート bōto

rowdy [rau'diː] adj (person: noisy) 乱暴な rañbō na; (occasion) 騒々しい sōzōshiī

rowing [rou'iŋ] n (sport) ボートレース bōtorèsu

rowing boat (BRIT) n = **rowboat**

royal [rɔi'əl] adj 国王(女王)の kokúō(jṓō) no

Royal Air Force (BRIT) n 英国空軍 eíkokukũgun

royalty [rɔi'əltiː] n (royal persons) 王族 ṓzoku; (payment to author) 印税 iñzei

rpm [ɑːrpiːem'] n abbr (= revolutions per minute) 毎分回転数 maffunkaíteñsū

RSVP [ɑːresviːpiː'] abbr (= répondez s'il vous plaît) 御返事を請うgo-héñji wò kṓ

Rt Hon. (BRIT) abbr (= Right Hon-

ourable) 閣下 kákkà

rub [rʌb] vt こする kosúrù
♦n: **to give something a rub** こする kosúrù
to rub one's hands (together) もみ手をする momíde wò suru
to rub someone the wrong way (US) **or to rub someone up the wrong way** (BRIT) 怒らせる okóraserù

rubber [rʌb'əːr] n (substance) ゴム gómù; (BRIT: eraser) 消しゴム keshígomu

rubber band n 輪ゴム wagómu

rubber plant n ゴムの木 gómù no ki

rubbery [rʌb'əːriː] adj (material, substance) ゴムの様な gómù no yō na; (meat, food) 固い katáì

rubbish [rʌb'iʃ] n (waste material) ごみ gomí; (junk) 廃品 haíhin; (fig: pej: nonsense) ナンセンス náñsensu

rubbish bin (BRIT) n ごみ箱 gomíbako

rubbish dump n ごみ捨て場 gomísuteba

rubble [rʌb'əl] n (debris) がれき garéki; (CONSTR) バラス barásu

ruble [ruː'bəl] (BRIT **rouble**) n (currency) ルーブル rūburu

rub off vi (paint) こすり取る kosúritorù

rub off on vt fus …に移る …ni utsúrù

rub out vt (erase) 消す kesú

ruby [ruː'biː] n ルビー rūbī

rucksack [rʌk'sæk] n リュックサック ryukkúsakkù

rudder [rʌd'əːr] n (of ship) かじ kajî; (of plane) 方向かじ hṓkōda

ruddy [rʌd'iː] adj (face, complexion) 血色の良い kesshőku no yoì; (BRIT: inf: damned) くそったれの kusóttare no

rude [ruːd] adj (impolite: person, manners, word) 無礼な búrèi na; (shocking: word, behavior) 下品な gehín na

rudeness [ruːd'nis] n (impoliteness) 無礼 búrèi

rudimentary [ruːdəmen'təːriː] adj (equipment, knowledge) 原始的な geñshiteki na

rudiments [ruː'dəmənts] npl (basics) 基本 kihón

rueful [ruː'fəl] adj 悲しい kanáshiì

ruffian [rʌfˈiːən] n ごろつき gorótsuki

ruffle [rʌfˈəl] vt (hair) 乱す midásù; (clothes) しわくちゃにする shiwákucha ni surù; (fig: person) 怒らせる okóraserù
(BRIT: blanket) ひざ掛け hizákake

rug [rʌg] n (on floor) じゅうたん jūtan;
(BRIT: blanket) ひざ掛け hizákake

rugby [rʌgˈbiː] n (also: rugby football)
ラグビー rágùbi

rugged [rʌgˈid] adj (landscape) 岩だらけ
の iwádarake no; (features) ごつい go-
tsuí; (character) 無愛想な buáiso na

rugger [rʌgˈəːr] (BRIT: inf) n ラグビー
rágùbi

ruin [ruːˈin] n (destruction: of building)
破壊 hakái; (: of hopes, plans) ざ折 za-
tsu; (downfall) 失墜 shittsú; (: bankruptcy) 破産 hasán; (remains: of building) 廃墟 haíkyo
♦vt (destroy: building) 破壊する hakái
suru; (: hopes, plans, health) 損なう kowá-
nu; (: future) 台無しにする daínashi ni
surù; (: person) 失墜させる shittsú saserù; (: financially) 破産に追込む hasán ni
oíkomù

ruinous [ruːˈinəs] adj (expense, interest)
破滅的な hamétsuteki na

ruins [ruːˈinz] npl (of building, castle etc)
廃墟 haíkyo

rule [ruːl] n (norm, regulation) 規則 kisóku; (government) 君臨 kuńrin; (ruler) 物
差し monósashi
♦vt (country, person) 支配する shíhai suru
♦vi (leader, monarch etc) 君臨する kuńrin suru; (LAW) 裁定する saítei suru
as a rule 普通は futsū wà

ruled [ruːld] adj (paper) けい紙 keíshi

rule out vt (idea, possibility etc) 除外す
る jogái suru

ruler [ruːˈləːr] n (sovereign) 元首 geńshu;
(for measuring) 物差し monósashi

ruling [ruːˈliŋ] adj (party) 支配する shíhai suru
♦n (LAW) 決定 kettéi
ruling party 与党 yótō
ruling class 支配階級 shiháikaíkyū

rum [rʌm] n ラム酒 ramúshu

Rumania [ruːmeiˈniːə] n ルーマニア rú-
mania

Rumanian [ruːmeiˈniːən] adj ルーマニア
の rūmania no; (LING) ルーマニア語の
rūmaniagǒ no
♦n (person) ルーマニア人 rūmaniajín;
(LING) ルーマニア語 rūmaniagǒ

rumble [rʌmˈbəl] n ごう音 gōon, とどろ
き todóroki
♦vi (make rumbling noise: heavy truck)
ごう音を響かせて走る gōon wò hibíkase-
te hashírù; (: stomach) 鳴る narú; (:
pipes) ゴボゴボいう gobógobo íu; (:
thunder) とどろく todórokù

rummage [rʌmˈidʒ] vi (search) 引っかき
回して探す hikkákimawashite sagásù

rumor [ruːˈməːr] (BRIT **rumour**) n うわ
さ uwása
♦vt: *it is rumored that ...* ...だとうわ
さされている ...dà tò uwása sarete irú

rump [rʌmp] n (of animal) しり shirí; (of
group, political party) 残党 zaítō

rump steak n ランプステーキ rańpusu-
tēki

rumpus [rʌmˈpəs] n 騒ぎ sawági

run [rʌn] n (fast pace, exercise) 駆け足
kakéàshi; (for exercise) ジョギング jogíñgu; (in
car) ドライブ doráibu; (distance traveled) 行程 kótei; (journey) 区間 kukán;
(series) 連続 rénzoku; (SKI) ゲレンデ ge-
réñde; (CRICKET, BASEBALL) 得点
tokúten; (THEATER) 上演期間 jóenkikan; (in tights, stockings) ほころび ho-
kórobi
♦vb (pt **ran**, pp **run**)
♦vt (race, distance) 走る hashírù; (operate: business, hotel) 経営する keíei suru;
(: competition, course) する okónaù;
(: house) ...の切盛りをする ...no kirímori
serù; (pass: hand) 通す tōsu; (water) 出す
dásù; (bath) ...に水をはる ...ni mizú wò
hárù; (PRESS: feature) 載せる nosérù
♦vi (move quickly: animal) 走る hashírù; (flee)
逃げる nigérù; (work: machine) 作動する
sadó suru; (bus, train: operate) 動く ugókù; (: travel) 運行する uñkō suru; (continue:
play) 上演される jóen sarerù; (: contract)
継続する kefzoku suru; (flow: river, liquid) 流れる nagárerù; (colors) 落ちる o-

chírù; (washing) 色落ちする iróochi suru; (in election) 立候補する rikkóho suru; (nose) 鼻水が出る hanámizu ga dérù

there was a run on ... (meat, tickets) ...を買いに殺到した hitóbito wa ...wo kaí ni sattó shità

in the long run 結局 (は) yúku-yuku (wà)

on the run 逃亡中で tóbochū de

I'll run you to the station 駅まで車で送ろう ékì made kurúma de okúrō

to run a risk 危険を冒す kiken wò okásù

run about/around *vi* (children) はしゃぎ回る hashágimawarù

run across *vt fus* (find) 偶然に見付ける gúzen ni mitsúkerù

run away *vi* (from home, situation) 逃げる nigérù

runaway [rʌ́nəwei] *adj* (horse, truck) 暴走の bōsō no; (person) 逃走中の tósochū no

run down *vt* (production, factory) ...の規模を縮小する ...no kíbò wo shukúshō suru; (AUT: person) ひく hikú; (criticize) けなす kenásù

to be run down (person: tired) へとへとになっている hetóheto nì natté irù

rung [rʌŋ] *pp of* **ring**

♦*n* (of ladder) 一段 ichídàn

run in (BRIT) *vt* (car) ...のならし運転をする ...no naráshiuñten wo suru

run into *vt fus* (meet: person, trouble) ...に出会う ...ni deáù; (collide with) ...にぶつかる ...ni butsúkarù

runner [rʌ́nər] *n* (in race: person) 競走の選手 kyósō no sefíshu, ランナー ráñnā; (: horse) 競走馬 kyósōba; (on sledge) 滑り木 subérigi, ランナー ráñnā; (for drawer etc) レール rēru

runner bean (BRIT) *n* サヤインゲン sayáiñgeñ

runner-up [rʌnərʌ́p] *n* 第2位入賞者 daíni-i nyúshòsha

running [rʌ́niŋ] *n* (sport) ジョギング jógìngu; (of business, organization) 経営 keíei

♦*adj* (water) 水道の suídō no

to be in/out of the running for something ...の候補者である (でなくなっている) ...no kóhòsha de árù (de nakúnatte irù)

6 days running 連続6日間 reñzoku muikákan

running commentary *n* 生中継 namáchūkei

running costs *npl* (of car, machine etc) 維持費 ijíhi

runny [rʌ́ni] *adj* (honey, egg) 緩い yurúi; (nose) 垂れる tarérù; (eyes) 目やにの出る meyáni no dérù

run off *vt* (water) ...から流れ落ちる ...kara nagáreochirù; (copies) 印刷する iñsatsu suru

♦*vi* (person, animal) 逃げる nigérù

run-of-the-mill [rʌnʌvðəmíl] *adj* (ordinary) ご普通の gokú futsú no

run out *vi* (person) 走って出る hashítte derù; (liquid) 流れ出る nagárederù; (lease, passport) 切れる kirérù; (money) なくなる nakúnarù

run out of *vt fus* (money, time, ideas) ...がなくなる ...ga nakúnarù

run over *vt* (AUT) ひく hikú

♦*vt fus* (revise) おさらいする o-sárai suru

runt [rʌnt] *n* (animal) 末熟児 mijúkuji; (pej: person) どちび dochíbi

run through *vt fus* (instructions) ...に目を通す ...ni mé wo tōsu; (rehearse, practice: play) ...を練習する hitótōri reñshū suru

run up *vt* (debt) ...がかさむ ...ga kasámù

to run up against (difficulties) ...にぶつかる ...ni butsúkarù

run-up [rʌ́nʌp] *n* (BRIT): **run-up to** (election etc) ...への準備期間 ...é nò juñbikikan

runway [rʌ́nwei] *n* (AVIAT) 滑走路 kassóro

rupee [ruːpíː] *n* (currency) ルピー rúpì

rupture [rʌ́ptʃər] *n* (MED) ヘルニア herúnia

rural [rúːrəl] *adj* (area) 田舎の ináka no; (economy) 地方の chíhō no

ruse [ruːz] *n* 策略 sakúryaku

rush

rush [rʌʃ] n (hurry) 大急ぎ ōisogi;
(COMM: sudden demand) 急激な需要
kyūgeki nà juyō; (of water, current) 奔
流 hōryū; (of feeling, emotion) 高まり
takámari; (BOT) イグサ igúsa
♦vt (hurry) 急がせる isógaserú
♦vi (person) 急ぐ isógu; (air, water) 速く
流れる háyaku nagárerú

rush hour n ラッシュアワー rasshúawā

rusk [rʌsk] n (biscuit) ラスク rásùku

Russia [rʌʃə] n ロシア róshìa

Russian [rʌʃən] adj ロシアの róshìa no;
(LING) ロシア語の roshígago no
♦n (person) ロシア人 roshíajìn; (LING)
ロシア語 roshígago

rust [rʌst] n さび sabí
♦vi (iron, machine etc) さびる sabírù

rustic [rʌs'tik] adj (style, furniture) 田舎
風の ínākafū no

rustle [rʌs'əl] vi (leaves) さかさかいう
kásàkasa iú
♦vt (paper) かさかさ動かす kásàkasa u-
gókasù; (US: cattle) 盗む nusúmù

rustproof [rʌst'pruːf] adj (car, machine)
さびない sabínaì

rusty [rʌs'tiː] adj (car) さびた sábìta;
(fig: skill) の勘が鈍くなった...no kań
gà níbùku natta

rut [rʌt] n (groove) わだち wadáchi;
(ZOOL: season) 発情期 hatsújōki
to be in a rut 型にはまっている katá ní
hamátte irù

ruthless [ruːθ'lis] adj (person) 血も涙も
ない chí mo namída mò náì; (action) 残
酷な zańkoku na

rye [rai] n (cereal) ライ麦 raímugì

rye bread n ライパン raípaǹ

S

Sabbath [sæb'əθ] n (Jewish) 土曜日 do-
yōbì; (Christian) 日曜日 nichíyòbi

sabbatical [səbæt'ikəl] n (also: **sabbatical year**) 一年休暇 ichínen kyūka ◊7年置
きに大学教授などに与えられる1年の長期
有給休暇 nanánen okí ní daígakukyōju
nádò ni atáeraretù ichínen no chōkyū-

kyúkyūka

sabotage [sæb'ətɑːʒ] n 破壊工作 hakái-
kōsaku
♦vt (machine, building) 破壊する hakái
suru; (plan, meeting) 妨害する bōgai suru

saccharin(e) [sæk'əːrin] n サッカリン
sakkárìn

sachet [sæʃei'] n (of shampoo, sugar, etc)
小袋 kobúkùro ◊一回分ずつのシャンプ
ー、砂糖などを入れた小さな包 ikkáíbun
zutsu no sháñpū, satō nádò wo iréta
chìlsana tsutsúmi

sack [sæk] n (bag: for flour, coal, grain,
etc) 袋 fukúro
♦vt (dismiss) 首にする kubí ni surù;
(plunder) 略奪する ryakúdatsu suru
to get the sack 首になる kubí ni narù

sacking [sæk'iŋ] n (dismissal) 解雇 káiko; (material) ズック zúkkù

sacrament [sæk'rəmənt] n (ceremony:
Protestant) 聖礼典 seíreìten; (: Catholic)
秘跡 hiséki

sacred [sei'krid] adj (of religion: music,
history, writings) 宗教の shúkyò no;
(holy: animal, building, memory) 神聖な
shíñsei na

sacrifice [sæk'rəfais] n (offering of
someone/something) 犠牲 giséi; (thing/
person offered) いけにえ ikénie
♦vt (animal, deity) を犠牲 ni surù; (fig:
human lives, health, career) 犠牲にする giséi ni
surù

sacrilege [sæk'rəlidʒ] n 冒とく bōtoku

sacrosanct [sæk'rousæŋkt] adj (also
fig) 神聖な shíñsei na

sad [sæd] adj (unhappy: person, day,
story, news) 悲しい kanáshiì; (: look) 悲
しそうな kanáshisò na; (deplorable:
state of affairs) 嘆かわしい nagékawa-
shiì

saddle [sæd'əl] n (for horse) くら kurá;
(of bicycle) サドル sadoru
♦vt (horse) に...くらを付ける ...ni kurá
wò tsukérù
to be saddled with (inf) ...の重荷を負
わされる ...no omóni wò owásarerù

saddlebag [sæd'əlbæg] n (on bicycle)

ドルバッグ sadórubaggù

sadism [sei'dizəm] *n* サディズム sadízumu

sadistic [sədis'tik] *adj* サディスティック na sadísutikkù na

sadly [sæd'li:] *adv* (unhappily) 悲しそう に kanáshisō ni; (unfortunately) 残念なが ら zańneńnagara; (seriously: mistaken, neglected) ひどく hídòku
 sadly lacking (in) 残念ながら (...が) ない zańneńnagara (...ga) náì

sadness [sæd'nis] *n* 悲しみ kanáshimi

sae [eseii:'] *abbr* (= *stamped addressed envelope*) 返信用封筒 heńshiń-yō fūtó〜(住 所を書き、切手を張った物を相手に差し 出して)、宛先を書き、切手を張った物を相 手に asáki wò káki, kitté wò hattá mono wò sású

safari [səfɑ:'ri:] *n* サファリ sáfàri

safe [seif] *adj* (out of danger) 安全な場所 にいる(ある afízen na bashó nì irú (árù); (not dangerous, sure: place) 安全な afízen na; (unharmed: return, journey) 無事な bují na; (without risk: bet, subject, appointment) 安全な afízen na; できる安心 dekírù (: seat in parliament) 落選する恐れのない rakúsen suru osore no náì
 n (for valuables, money) 金庫 kíñko
 safe from (attack) ...される心配のない 場所にいる(ある ...saréru shiphaí no náì bashó nì irú (árù)
 safe and sound (return, sleep, etc) 無事 で bují de
 (just) to be on the safe side 念のため に neí no tame ni

safe-conduct [seif'kɑn'dʌkt] *n* (right to pass) 通行許可証 tsūkōkyokashō

safe-deposit [seif'dipɑ:zit] *n* (vault) 貸 金庫室 kashíkìñkoshitsu; (*also*: **safe deposit box**) 貸金庫 kashíkìñko

safeguard [seif'gɑrd] *n* 保護手段 hógoshudan
 vt 保護する hógo surù

safekeeping [seifki:'piŋ] *n* 保管 hokán

safely [seif'li:] *adv* (without risk: assume, say) 安心して afíshin shite; (without mishap: drive) 安全に afízen ni; (arrive) 無事に bují ni

safety [seif'ti:] *n* 安全 afízen

safety belt *n* 安全ベルト afízenberùto, シートベルト shītoberùto

safety pin *n* 安全ピン afízenpìn

safety valve *n* 安全弁 afízenben

saffron [sæf'rən] *n* (powder) サフラン sáfùran

sag [sæg] *vi* (breasts, hem) 垂れ下がる tarésagarù; (roof) 凹む kubómu

saga [sæg'ə] *n* (long story, *also fig*) 長編 物語 chōheñmonogátàri

sage [seidʒ] *n* (herb) セージ sēji; (wise man) 賢人 keńjìn

Sagittarius [sædʒiter'i:əs] *n* (sign of Zodiac) 射手座 itéza

Sahara [səher:ə] *n*: **the Sahara (Desert)** サハラ砂漠 sáhàra sabàku

said [sed] *pt, pp* of **say**

sail [seil] *n* (on boat) 帆 hó; (trip): *to go for a sail* ヨットに乗る yóttò ni norú
 vt (boat) 操縦する sōjū surù
 vi (travel: ship) 航海する kókai surù; (SPORT) ヨットに乗る yóttò ni norú; (begin voyage: ship) 出航する shukkō surù; (: passenger) 船で出発する fúnè de shuppátsu suru
 they sailed into Copenhagen 彼らはコ ペンハーゲンに入港した kárèra wa ko-péñhàgen ni nyúkō shità

sailboat [seil'bout] (*US*) *n* ヨット yóttò

sailing [sei'liŋ] *n* (SPORT) ヨット遊び yottóasobi
 to go sailing ヨットに乗る yóttò ni no-rú, ヨット遊びをする yottóasòbi wo suru

sailing boat *n* ヨット yóttò

sailing ship *n* 帆船 hañsen

sailor [sei'lər] *n* (seaman) 船乗り funá-nòri

sail through *vt fus* (*fig*: exams, interview etc) ...に楽々と合格する ...ni rakú-rakù to gōkaku suru

saint [seint] *n* (*also fig*) 聖人 seíjin

saintly [seint'li:] *adj* (person, life, expression) 聖人の様な seíjin no yō nà

sake [seik] *n*: *for the sake of some-one/something* ...のために ...no tamé ni

salad [sæl'əd] *n* サラダ sáràda

salad bowl *n* サラダボール sarádabòru

salad cream (BRIT) n マヨネーズ mayónèzu

salad dressing n サラダドレッシング sarádadoresshìngu

salami [səlɑ:ˈmi:] n サラミ sārámi

salary [ˈsæləri] n 給料 kyūryō

sale [seil] n (act of selling: commercial goods etc) 販売 hañbai; (: house, land etc) 売却 baíkyaku; (at reduced prices) 安売り yasúuri, セール séru; (auction) 競売 kyóbai
「**for sale**」売物 urímono
on sale 発売中 hatsúbaichū
on sale or return (goods) 委託販売で itákuhañbai de

saleroom [ˈseilru:m] BRIT n = salesroom

sales [seilz] npl (total amount sold) 売上 uríage

sales clerk (BRIT **sales assistant**) n 店員 teñ-in

salesman [ˈseilzmən] (pl **salesmen**) n (in shop) 男子店員 dañshiteñ-in; (representative) セールスマン sérusumàn

salesroom [ˈseilzru:m] (US) n 競売場 kyóbaijō

saleswoman [ˈseilzˌwumən] (pl **saleswomen**) n 女子店員 joshíteñ-in

salient [ˈseiliːənt] adj (features, points) 重要な jūyō na

saliva [səˈlaivə] n だ液 daéki

sallow [ˈsælou] adj (complexion) 血色の悪い kesshóku no warúi

salmon [ˈsæmən] n inv サケ sákè

salon [səˈlɑ:n] n (hairdressing salon, beauty salon) 美容院 biyóìn

saloon [səˈlu:n] n (US: bar) 酒場 sakába; (BRIT: AUT) セダン sédàn; (ship's lounge) 広間 híròma

salt [sɔ:lt] n 塩 shió
♦vt (preserve: fish, beef, etc) 塩漬にする shiózuke ni suru; (put salt on) ...に塩を掛ける ...ni shió wo kakérù

salt cellar n 塩入れ shió-ire

saltwater [ˈsɔ:ltˌwɔ:tər] adj (fish, plant) 海水の kaísui no

salty [ˈsɔ:lti:] adj しょっぱい shoppái

salutary [ˈsæljəteri:] adj (lesson,

reminder) ためになる tamé ni narù

salute [səˈlu:t] n (MIL) 敬礼 kéfrei; (with guns) 礼砲 reíhō; (gen: greeting) あいさつ áìsatsu
♦vt (MIL) ...に敬礼する ...ni keírei suru; (fig) ...に敬意を現す ...ni kéìi wo aráwasù

salvage [ˈsælvidʒ] n (action: gen) 救助作業 kyūjo sagyō; (: of shipwreck) 海難救助作業 kaínan kyūjo sagyō; (things saved) サルベージ sarúbèji, 救助された物 kyūjo sareta monó
♦vt 救助する kyūjo suru; (fig: situation etc) 収拾する shūshū suru

salvation [sælveiˈʃən] n (REL) 霊魂の救い reíkon no sukúì; (economic etc) 救済 kyūsai

Salvation Army n 救世軍 kyūseigùn

salvo [ˈsælvou] n (in battle) 一斉射撃 isséishagèki; (ceremonial) 一斉祝砲 isséishukùhō

same [seim] adj 同じ onáji
♦pron: **the same** 同じ物 onáji monò
the same book as ...と同じ本 ...to onáji hoñ
at the same time (at the same moment) 同時に dóji ni; (yet) とはいえ tó wa ie
all/just the same それにしても soré ni shite mò
to do the same (as someone) (...と) 同じ事をする (...to) onáji koto wò suru
the same to you! お前もだ omáe mo dà 〈悔辱を返す時に言う bujóku wò kaésu toki nî iñ

sample [ˈsæmpəl] n (MED: blood/urine sample) 検体 keñtai, サンプル sáñpuru; (of work, merchandise) 見本 mihóñ, サンプル sáñpuru
♦vt (food) 試食する shishóku suru; (drink) 試飲する shíiñ suru

sanatoria [sænətˈɔ:riːə] npl of **sanatorium**

sanatorium [sænəˈtɔ:riːəm] (pl **sanatoria**) n = **sanitarium**

sanctify [ˈsæŋktəfai] vt 神聖にする shíñsei ni surú

sanctimonious [sæŋktəˈmouniːəs] adj

(person, remarks) 宗教心を装う shúkyoshìn wo yosóoú

sanction [sæŋkʃən] n (approval) お墨付き osúmìtsukì, 認可 nínka
♦vt (give approval to) 認可する nínka suru

sanctions [sæŋkʃənz] npl (severe measures) 制裁処置 sefsaishochì

sanctity [sæŋktiti] n 神聖さ shínseisa

sanctuary [sæŋktʃuerì] n (also: **bird sanctuary**) 鳥類保護区 chōruihogokù, サンクチュアリ sańkuchùari; (place of refuge) 避難所 hinánjo; (REL: in church) 内陣 naíjin

sand [cænd] n (material, fine grains) 砂 suná; (beach: also: **sands**) 砂浜 sunáhama
♦vt (piece of furniture: also: **sand down**) 紙やすりで磨く kamfyasùri de migáku

sandal [sændəl] n (shoe) サンダル sándaru

sandbox [sændbaks] US n (for children) 砂場 sunába

sandcastle [sændkæsəl] n 砂の城 suná no shíro

sand dune n 砂丘 sakyū

sandpaper [sændpeipər] n 紙やすり kamfyasùri, サンドペーパー sańdopèpā

sandpit [sændpit] (BRIT) n = **sandbox**

sandstone [sændstoun] n 砂岩 ságan

sandwich [sændwitʃ] n サンドイッチ sańdoitchì
♦vt: **sandwiched between** ...の間に挟まれて ...no aída ni hasámarete
cheese/ham sandwich チーズ（ハム）サンドイッチ chízu (hámu) sańdoitchì

sandwich course (BRIT) n サンドイッチコース sańdoitchikòsu ○勉強と現場実習を交互に行う課程 beńkyō tò geńbajisshū wo kōgò ni okónaù katéi

sandy [sændi] adj (beach) 砂の suná no; (color) 砂色の suná-iro no

sane [sein] adj (person) 正気の shōki no; (sensible: action, system) 合理的な gōrìteki na

sang [sæŋ] pt of **sing**

sanitarium [sæniterì:əm] (US) n 療養所 ryōyōjo, サナトリウム sanátoriùmu

sanitary [sæniterì] adj (system, arrangements, inspector) 衛生の efsei no; (clean) 衛生的な efseiteki na

sanitary napkin (BRIT **sanitary towel**) n 生理用ナプキン sefriyō napùkin

sanitation [sænitéiʃən] n (in house) 衛生設備 efseisetsùbi; (in town) 衛生設備 gesúidōsetsùbi

sanitation department [US n 清掃局 sefsōkyòku

sanity [sæniti] n (quality of being sane: of person) 正気 shōki; (common sense: of suggestion etc) 合理性 gōrisei

sank [sæŋk] pt of **sink**

Santa Claus [sæntə klɔːz] n サンタクロース sańtakuròsu

sap [sæp] n (of plants) 樹液 juéki
♦vt (strength, confidence) 失わせていく ushínawasete ikú

sapling [sæplíŋ] n 苗木 naégi

sapphire [sæfaiər] n サファイア safáia

sarcasm [sɑːrkæzəm] n 皮肉 hínìku

sarcastic [sɑːrkæstik] adj (person) いやみ さを iyámizùki na; (remark, smile) 皮肉な hínìku na

sardine [sɑːrdíːn] n イワシ iwáshi

Sardinia [sɑːrdíniə] n サルディニア島 sardíniatō

sardonic [sɑːrdɑːnik] adj (smile) あざける様な azákeru yō na

sari [sɑːríː] n サリー sárī

sash [sæʃ] n (Western) サッシュ sásshù; (Japanese) 帯 óbi

sat [sæt] pt, pp of **sit**

Satan [sei'tən] n 大魔王 daímaō, サタン sátàn

satchel [sætʃəl] n (child's) かばん kabán

satellite [sætəlait] n (body in space) 衛星 efsei; (communications satellite) 通信衛星 tsūshin-eìsei

satellite dish n パラボラアンテナ parábora ańtena

satin [sæt'ən] n サテン sátèn
♦adj サテンの sátèn no

satire [sæt'aiər] n (form of humor) 風刺 fūshi; (novel) 風刺小説 fūshishōsètsu; (play) 風刺劇 fūshigekì

satirical [sətírikəl] adj (remarks, draw-

satisfaction [sætisfækʃən] *n* (pleasure) 満足 mánzoku; (refund, apology etc) 謝罪 shazái

satisfactory [sætisfæktəri] *adj* (patient's condition) 良い yói; (results, progress) 満足できる mánzoku dekiru

satisfy [sætisfai] *vt* (please) 満足させる mánzoku saserú; (meet: needs, demand) ...に応じる ...ni ōjirú; (convince) 納得させる nattóku saserú

satisfying [sætisfaiiŋ] *adj* (meal, job, feeling) 満足な mánzoku na

saturate [sætʃəreit] *vt*: **to saturate (with)** (also *fig*) (...で)一杯にする (...de) ippái ni surú

saturation [sætʃəreiʃən] *n* (also *fig*) 飽和状態 hōwájōtai

Saturday [sætərdei] *n* 土曜日 doyōbí

sauce [sɔːs] *n* (sweet, savory) ソース sōsu

saucepan [sɔːspæn] *n* ソースパン sōsupan

saucer [sɔːsər] *n* 受皿 ukézāra, ソーサー sōsa

saucy [sɔːsiː] *adj* (cheeky) ずうずうしい zūzūshíi

Saudi [saudiː]: **Saudi Arabia** *n* サウジアラビア saújiarabia

Saudi (Arabian) *adj* サウジアラビアの saújiarabia no

sauna [sɔːnə] *n* サウナ sáuna

saunter [sɔːntər] *vi* のんびりと歩く nonbíri to árúku

sausage [sɔːsidʒ] *n* ソーセージ sōséji

sausage roll *n* ソーセージパン sōséji pan

sauté [sɔːtei] *adj*: **sauté potatoes** フライポテト furáipoteto

savage [sævidʒ] *adj* (cruel, fierce: dog) どうもうな dōmō na; (: attack) 残忍な zanínin na; (: primitive: tribe) 未開な mikái na

♦*n* 野蛮人 yabánjin

savagery [sævidʒriː] *n* 残忍さ zannínsa

save [seiv] *vt* (rescue: someone, someone's life, marriage) 救う sukúu; (economize on: money, time) 節約する setsúyaku suru; (put by: receipts etc) 取って置く tótte oku; (: money) 蓄える takúwaeru;

(COMPUT) 格納する kakúnō suru, セーブする sébu suru; (avoid: work, trouble) 省く habúku; (keep: seat) 確保する kakúho suru; (SPORT: shot, ball) セーブする sébu suru

♦*vi* (also: **save up**) 貯金する chokín suru

♦*n* (SPORT) セーブ sébu

♦*prep* (except) (...を)除いて (...wo) nozóite

saving [seiviŋ] *n* (on price etc) 節約 setsúyaku

♦*adj*: **the saving grace of something** ...の唯一の長所 ...no yúitsu no chōsho

savings [seiviŋz] *npl* (money) 貯金 chokín

savings account *n* 普通預金口座 futsúyokinkōza

savings bank *n* 普通銀行 futsúginkō

savior [seivjər] (*BRIT* **saviour**) *n* (gen) 救い主 sukúinushi; (REL) 救世主 kyúseishu

savor [seivər] (*BRIT* **savour**) *vt* (food, drink, experience) 味わう ajíwaú

savory [seivəriː] (*BRIT* **savoury**) *adj* (dish: not sweet: spicy) ぴりっとした pirítto shita; (: salt-flavored) 塩味の shióaji no

saw [sɔː] *n* (tool) のこぎり nokógiri

♦*vt* (*pt* **sawed**, *pp* **sawed** *or* **sawn**) のこぎりで切る nokógiri de kírù

♦*pt of* **see**

sawdust [sɔːdʌst] *n* のこくず nokókuzù

sawed-off [sɔːdˈɔːf] (*US*): **sawed-off shotgun** 短身散弾銃 tanshin sandanjū ◇のこぎりで銃身を短く切った散弾銃 nokógiri de júshin wo mijíkaku kittá sandanjū

sawmill [sɔːmil] *n* 製材所 seźaisho

sawn-off [sɔːnˈɔːf] *adj* (*BRIT*) = **sawed-off**

saxophone [sæksəfoun] *n* サキソホーン sakísohōn

say [sei] *n*: **to have one's say** 意見を言う íken wo iú

♦*vt* (*pt, pp* **said**) 言う iú

to have a/some say in something ...について ある程度の発言権がある ...ni tsúite áru teídō no hatsúgenken ga árù

to say yes/no 承知する〔しない〕shōchi suru (shinai)

could you say that again? もう一度言ってくれませんか mō ichidò itté kuremasèn ka

that is to say つまり tsúmari

that goes without saying それは言うまでもない soré wà iú made mo naì

saying [sei'iŋ] n (proverb) ことわざ kotówaza; (words of wisdom) 格言 kakúgen; (often repeated phrase) 愛用の言葉 aíyō no kotoba

scab [skæb] n (on wound) かさぶた kasábuta; (pej: strike-breaker) スト破り sutóyaburi

scaffold [skæf'əld] n (for execution) 死刑台 shikéidai; (for building etc) = **scaffolding**

scaffolding [skæf'əldiŋ] n 足場 ashíba

scald [skɔːld] n やけど yakédo (熱湯や蒸気などによるやけどを指す nettō ya jōkí nado ni yórù yakédo wò sásù)

♦vt (burn: skin) やけどさせる yakédo saserù

scale [skeil] n (gen: set of numbers) 目盛 memórì; (of salaries, fees etc) 段階 dañkai; (of fish) うろこ urókò; (MUS) 音階 oñkai; (of map, model) 縮小率 shukúshōritsu; (size, extent) 規模 kíbò

♦vt (mountain, tree) 登る nobórù

on a large scale 大規模で daíkibò de

scale of charges 料金表 ryōkínhyò

scale down vt 縮小する shukúshō suru

scales [skeilz] npl (for weighing) 量り hakárì

scallop [skɑl'əp] n (ZOOL) ホタテガイ hotátegài; (SEWING) スカラップ sukárappù

scalp [skælp] n 頭の皮膚 atáma no hifù, 頭皮 tōhi

♦vt ...の頭皮をはぐ ...no tōhì wo hágù

scalpel [skæl'pəl] n メス mésù

scamper [skæm'pəːr] vi: **to scamper away/off** (child, animal) ばたばた走って行く pátapata hashítte ikù

scampi [skæm'pi:] npl エビフライ ebífurài

scan [skæn] vt (examine: horizon) 見渡す miwátasu; (glance at quickly: newspaper) ...にさっと目を通す ...ni sáttò mé wò tōsù; (TV, RADAR) 走査する sōsa suru

♦n (MED) スキャン sukyán

scandal [skæn'dəl] n (shocking event) 醜聞スキャンダル shūbun, sukyándaru; (defamatory: reports, rumors) 陰口 kagéguchi; (gossip) うわさ uwása; (fig: disgrace) 恥ずべき事 hazúbeki kotò

scandalize [skæn'dəlaiz] vt 憤慨させる fuñgai saserù

scandalous [skæn'dələs] adj (disgraceful, shocking: behavior etc) 破廉恥な harénchi na

Scandinavian [skændənei'viːən] adj スカンディナビアの sukándinabìa no

scant [skænt] adj (attention) 不十分な fujūbùn na

scanty [skæn'ti:] adj (meal) ささやかな sasáyàka na; (underwear) 極めて小さい kiwámète chífsal

scapegoat [skeip'gout] n 身代り migáwari

scar [skɑːr] n (on skin: also fig) 傷跡 kizúato

♦vt (also fig) 傷跡を残す kizúato wò nokósù

scarce [skeːrs] adj (rare, not plentiful) 少ない sukúnaì

to make oneself scarce (inf) 消えうせる kiéuserù

scarcely [skeːrs'liː] adv (hardly) ほとんど...ない hotóñdo ...naì; (with numbers: barely) わずかに わずかに wázùka ni

scarcity [skeːr'sitiː] n (shortage) 不足 fusóku

scare [skeːr] n (fright) 恐怖 kyōfu; (public fear) 恐慌 kyōkō

♦vt (frighten) 怖がらせる kowágaraserù

bomb scare 爆弾騒ぎ bakúdan sawàgi

to scare someone stiff ...に怖い思いをさせる ...ni kowái omoì wo saserù

scarecrow [skeːr'krou] n かかし kakáshi

scared [skeːrd] adj: **to be scared** 怖がる kowágarù

scare off/away vt おどかして追払う o-

scarf [skɑːrf] (pl **scarfs** or **scarves**) n (long) マフラー máfurā; (square) スカーフ sukáfū

scarlet [skɑːrˈlit] adj (color) ひ色 híiro

scarlet fever n しょう紅熱 shōkōnetsu

scarves [skɑːrvz] npl of **scarf**

scary [skeːrˈiː] (inf) adj 怖い kowáī

scathing [skeiˈðiŋ] adj (comments, attack) 辛らつな shirfratsu na

scatter [skætˈəːr] vt (spread: seeds, papers) まき散らす makíchirasū; (put to flight: flock of birds, crowd of people) 追散らす ofchirasū

◆vi (crowd) 散る chírū

scatterbrained [skætˈəːrbreind] (inf) adj (forgetful) おつむの弱い o-tsúmū no yowáī

scavenger [skævˈindʒəːr] n (person) くず拾い kuzúhiroi

scenario [sineːrˈiːou] n (THEATER, CINEMA) 脚本 kyákuhon, シナリオ shinárīo; (fig) 筋書 suʃígaki

scene [siːn] n (THEATER, fig) 場 ba, シーン shīn; (of crime, accident) 現場 génba; (sight, view) 景色 késhiki; (fuss) 騒ぎ sáwāgi

scenery [siːˈnəːriː] n (THEATER) 大道具 ōdōgu; (landscape) 景色 késhiki

scenic [siːˈnik] adj (picturesque) 景色の美しい késhiki no utsúkushiī

scent [sent] n (pleasant smell) 香り kaóri; (track) 通った後のにおい tōtta áto no niói; (fig) 手がかり tegákari; (liquid perfume) 香水 kōsui

scepter [sepˈtəːr] (BRIT **sceptre**) n しゃく shaku

sceptic [skepˈtik] (BRIT) n = **skeptic** etc

schedule [skedʒˈuːl] n (of trains, buses) 時間割 jikánwari; (list of events and times) 時刻表 jikókuhyō; (list of prices, details etc) 表 hyō

◆vt (timetable, visit) 予定する yotéi suru

on schedule (trains, buses) 定刻通りに tefkokudōri ni; (project etc) 予定通りに yotéidōri ni

to be ahead of schedule 予定時間より

早い yotéijikàn yórī hayáī

to be behind schedule 予定時間に遅れる yotéijikàn ni okúrerù

scheduled flight [skedʒˈuːld-] n 定期便 tefkibin

schematic [skiːmætˈik] adj (diagram etc) 模式的な moshíkiteki na

scheme [skiːm] n (personal plan, idea) もくろみ mokúromi; (dishonest plan, plot) 陰謀 ínbō; (formal plan: pension plan etc) 計画 kefkaku, 案 áň; (arrangement) 配置 háīchi

◆vi (intrigue) たくらむ takúramū

◆vt たくらむ事 takúramū kotó

scheming [skiːmˈiŋ] adj 腹黒い haráguroī

n たくらみ takúrami

schism [skizˈəm] n 分裂 bunfretsu

schizophrenic [skitsəfrenˈik] adj 精神分裂症の sefshinbunretsushō no

scholar [skɑːlˈəːr] n (pupil) 学者 gakúshūsha; (learned person) 学者 gakúsha

scholarly [skɑːlˈəːrliː] adj (text, approach) 学問的な gakúmonteki na; (person) 博学的な hakúgakuteki na

scholarship [skɑːlˈəːrʃip] n (academic knowledge) 学問 gakúmon; (grant) 奨学金 shōgakukiň

school [skuːl] n (place where children learn: gen) 学校 gakkō; (also: **elementary school**) 小学校 shōgakkō; (also: **secondary school**: lower) 中学校 chúgakkō; (: higher) 高(校 kō(tōgakkō; (US: university) 大学 dafgaku

◆cpd 学校の gakkō no

school age n 学齢 gakúrei

schoolbook [skuːlˈbuk] n 教科書 kyóka-shò

schoolboy [skuːlˈbɔi] n 男子生徒 dañshiseìto

schoolchildren [skuːlˈtʃildrən] npl 生徒 seìto

schooldays [skuːlˈdeiz] npl 学校時代 gakkōjidài

schoolgirl [skuːlˈgəːrl] n 女子生徒 joshíseìto

schooling [skuːlˈiŋ] n (education at school) 学校教育 gakkōkyōiku

schoolmaster [skuːlˈmæstəːr] n 教師

kyōshi, 教員 kyōin, 先生 sensei ◇男子教員 danshikyōin

schoolmistress [skuːlˈmistris] *n* 教師 kyōshi, 教員 kyōin, 先生 sensei ◇女子教員 joshíkyōin

schoolteacher [skuːlˈtiːtʃər] *n* 教師 kyōshi, 教員 kyōin, 先生 sensei ◇男女を問わず使う dánjo wo tówazu tsukáū

schooner [skuːˈnəːr] *n* (ship) 帆船 hańsen

sciatica [saiˈætikə] *n* 座骨神経痛 zakótsushinkeītsū

science [saiˈəns] *n* (study of natural things) 科学 kágaku; (branch of such knowledge) ...学 ...gaku

science fiction *n* 空想科学物語 kūsōkagakumonogatári, SF esuefu

scientific [saiəntifˈik] *adj* (research, instruments) 科学の kágaku no

scientist [saiˈəntist] *n* 科学者 kagákushā

scintillating [sintˈəleitiŋ] *adj* (fig: conversation, wit, smile) 輝く様な kagáyakū yō na

scissors [sizˈəːrz] *npl* (*also*: **a pair of scissors**) はさみ hasámi

scoff [skaːf] *vt* (BRIT: *inf*: eat) がつがつ食う gátsūgatsu kúū
♦*vi*: **to scoff (at)** (mock) ...をあざける ...wo azākerū

scold [skould] *vt* しかる shikárū

scone [skoun] *n* スコーン sukóon ◇小さなホットケーキの一種 chísa na hottókēki no ísshū

scoop [skuːp] *n* (measuring scoop: for flour etc) スクープ sukúppu; (for ice cream) サーバー sāba; (PRESS) スクープ sukúppu

scoop out *vt* すくい出す sukúidasū

scoop up *vt* すくい上げる sukúiagerū

scooter [skuːˈtəːr] *n* (*also*: **motor scooter**) スクーター sukúta; (toy) スクーター sukúta ◇片足を乗せて走る遊び道具 katáashi wo nosete hashírū asóbidōgu

scope [skoup] *n* (opportunity) 機会 kikái; (range: of plan, undertaking) 範囲 hán-i; (: of person) 能力 nōryoku

scorch [skɔːrtʃ] *vt* (clothes) 焦がす kogásū; (earth, grass) 枯らす karásū

score [skɔːr] *n* (total number of points etc) 得点 tokúten, スコア sukóa; (MUS) 楽譜 gakúfu; (twenty) 20 níjū
♦*vt* (goal, point, mark) 取る tórū; (achieve: success) 収める osámerū
♦*vi* (in game) 得点する tokúten suru; (FOOTBALL etc) トライする torái suru; (keep score) 得点を記録する tokúten wo kiróku suru

scores of (very many) 多数の tasú no

on that score その点に関して sonó teń ni kańshite

to score 6 out of 10 10回中6回成功する jukkáichū rokkái sefkō suru

scoreboard [skɔːrˈbɔːrd] *n* スコアボード sukóabōdo

score out *vt* 線を引いて消す séń wo hítte kesú

scorn [skɔːrn] *n* 軽べつ kefbetsu
♦*vt* 軽べつする kefbetsu suru

scornful [skɔːrnˈfəl] *adj* (laugh, disregard) 軽べつ的な kefbetsuteki na

Scorpio [skɔːrˈpiːou] *n* (sign of Zodiac) さそり座 sasóriza

scorpion [skɔːrˈpiən] *n* サソリ sasori

Scot [skaːt] *n* スコットランド人 sukóttorandojìn

Scotch [skaːtʃ] *n* (whisky) スコッチ sukótchī

scotch [skaːtʃ] *vt* (end: rumor) 消し止める keshítomerù; (plan, idea) 没にする bótsu ni suru

scot-free [skaːtˈfriːʔ] *adv*: **to get off scot-free** (unpunished) 何の罰も受けないまま no bátsu mo ukénai

Scotland [skaːtˈlənd] *n* スコットランド sukóttorando

Scots [skaːts] *adj* (accent, people) スコットランドの sukóttorando no

Scotsman [skaːtsˈmən] (*pl* **Scotsmen**) *n* スコットランドの男性 sukóttorando no dansei

Scotswoman [skaːtsˈwumən] (*pl* **Scotswomen**) *n* スコットランドの女性 sukóttorando no joséi

Scottish [skaːtˈiʃ] *adj* (history, clans, people) スコットランドの sukóttorando no

scoundrel [skaun'drəl] n 悪党 akútò

scour [skaur] vt (search: countryside etc) くまなく捜し回る kumánàku sagáshimawarù

scourge [skə:rdʒ] n (cause of trouble: also fig) 悩みの種 nayámi no tanè

scout [skaut] n (MIL) 斥候 sekkő; (also: **boy scout**) ボーイスカウト bőisukauto; **girl scout** (US) ガールスカウト gárusukaùto

scout around vi 捜し回る sagáshimawarù

scowl [skaul] vi 顔をしかめる káð wo shikámerù
to scowl at someone しかめっつらをして...をにらむ shikámettsura wò shité ...wo nirámù

scrabble [skræb'əl] vi (claw): **to scrabble (at)** (...を)引っかく (...wo) hikkákù; (also: **scrabble around**: search) 手探りで探す teságuri de sagásù
♦n: **Scrabble** ® スクラブル sukúraburu ◇単語作りゲーム tańgozukurigēmu

scraggy [skræg'i:] adj (animal, body, neck etc) やせこけた yasékoketà

scram [skræm] (inf) vi (get away fast) うせる usérù

scramble [skræm'bəl] n (difficult climb) よじ上り yojínobori; (struggle, rush) 奪い合い ubáiai
♦vi: **to scramble out/through** 慌てて出る〔通る〕awátete derù 〔tőru〕
to scramble for ...の奪い合いをする ...no ubáiai wo surù

scrambled eggs [skræm'bəld -] npl いり卵 iritamagő, スクランブルエッグ sukúranburu eggù

scrap [skræp] n (bit of paper, material etc) 切れ端 kiréhashi; (: of information) 少し sukőshi; (: of truth) 少し sukőshi; (fight) けんか keñka; (also: **scrap iron**) くず鉄 kuzútetsu
♦vt (discard: machines etc) くず鉄にする kuzútetsu ni surù; (: plans etc) 捨てる sutérù
♦vi けんかする keñka suru

scrapbook [skræp'buk] n スクラップブック sukúrappubukkù

scrap dealer n くず鉄屋 kuzútetsuyà

scrape [skreip] n (fig: difficult situation) 窮地 kyűchi
♦vt (scrape off: potato skin etc) むく mukú; (scrape against: hand, car) こする kosúrù
♦vi: **to scrape through** (exam etc) ...をどうにか切抜ける ...wo dő ni ka kirínukerù

scrape together vt (money) かき集める kakfatsumerù

scrap heap n (fig): **on the scrap heap** 捨てられて sutérarete

scrap merchant n (BRIT) = **scrap dealer**

scrap paper n 古い紙 furúi kamí, 古紙 kőshi, ほご紙 hőgō

scrappy [skræp'i:] adj (piece of work) 雑な zatsú na

scraps [skræps] npl (leftovers: food, material etc) くず kúzu

scratch [skrætʃ] n (cut: on body, furniture: also from claw) かき傷 kakíkizu
♦cpd: **scratch team** 寄集めチーム yoséatsumechīmu
♦vt (rub: one's nose etc) かく kákù; (damage: paint, car) 傷付ける kizútsukerù; (with claw, nail) ひっかく hikkákù
♦vi (rub one's body) ...をかく ...wo kákù
to start from scratch 何もない所から始める naní mo naì tokőro karà hajfmerù
to be up to scratch いい線をいている íi sén wo itté irù

scrawl [skrɔ:l] n なぐり書き nagúrigaki
♦vi なぐり書きする nagúrigaki suru

scrawny [skrɔ:'ni:] adj (person, neck) やせこけた yasékoketà

scream [skri:m] n 悲鳴 himéi
♦vi 悲鳴を上げる himéi wo agerù

scree [skri:] n 岩くず iwákuzu ◇崩れ落ちてたい積した岩くずを指す kuzúreochité taíseki shità iwákuzu no sasù

screech [skri:tʃ] vi (person) 金切り声を出す kanákirigoè wo dásù; (bird) きーきー声で鳴く kíkī goè de nákù; (tires, brakes) きーきーと鳴る kíkī to nárù

screen [skri:n] n (CINEMA) スクリーン

sukúrīn; (TV, COMPUT) ブラウン管 buráunkan; (movable barrier) ついたて tsuítate; (fig: cover) 幕 makú

◆vt (protect, conceal) 覆い隠す ōíkakusù; (from the wind etc) ...のよけになる ...no...yoké ni narù; (film) 映写する eísha suru; (television program) 放映する hōéi suru; (candidates etc) 審査する shíñsa suru

screening [skriː'niŋ] n (MED) 健康診断 keñkōshíñdan

screenplay [skriːn'plei] n 映画脚本 eígakyakúhon

screw [skruː] n (for fixing something) ねじ néjī

◆vt (fasten) ねじで留める neji de tomérù

screwdriver [skruː'draivəːr] n ねじ回し nejímawashī

screw up vt (paper etc) くしゃくしゃにする kushákūsha ni suru

to screw up one's eyes 目を細める mé wò hosómerù

scribble [skrib'əl] n 走り書き hashírigakī

◆vt (write carelessly: note etc) 走り書きする hashírigakī suru

◆vi (make meaningless marks) 落書きする rakúgakī suru

script [skript] n (CINEMA etc) 脚本 kyakúhon, スクリプト sukúrīputo; (system of writing) 文字 mójì

scripture(s) [skrip'tʃəːr(z)] n(pl) (holy writing(s) of a religion) 聖典 seíten

scroll [skroul] n (official paper) 巻物 makímono

scrounge [skraundʒ] vt (inf): *to scrounge something off/from someone* ...に...をねだる ...ni...wo nedárù

◆n: *on the scrounge* たかって takátte

scrub [skrʌb] n (land) 低木地帯 teíbokuchitāi

◆vt (rub hard: floor, hands, pan, washing) ごしごし洗う góshìgoshi aráù; (inf: reject: idea) 取り止める toríyamerù

scruff [skrʌf] n: *by the scruff of the neck* 首筋をつかんで kubísuji wò tsukáñde

scruffy [skrʌf'iː] adj (person, object,

appearance) 薄汚い usúgitanaì

scrum(mage) [skrʌm'(idʒ)] n (RUGBY) スクラム sukúrāmu

scruple [skruː'pəl] n (gen pl) 良心のとがめ ryōshīn no togáme

scrupulous [skruː'pjələs] adj (painstaking: care, attention) 細心の saíshìn no; (fair-minded: honesty) 公正な kōseí na

scrutinize [skruː'tənaiz] vt (examine closely) 詳しく調べる kuwáshikù shíráberù

scrutiny [skruː'təni] n (close examination) 吟味 gíñmi

to keep someone under scrutiny ...を監視する ...wo kañshi suru

scuff [skʌf] vt (shoes, floor) すり減らす suríherasù

scuffle [skʌf'əl] n (fight) 乱闘 rañtō

sculptor [skʌlp'təːr] n 彫刻家 chōkokuka

sculpture [skʌlp'tʃəːr] n 彫刻 chōkoku

scum [skʌm] n (on liquid) 汚い泡 kitánai awâ; (pej: people) 人間のくず niñgen nò kúzù

scupper [skʌp'əːr] (BRIT: inf) vt (plan, idea) 邪魔して失敗させる jamá shite shippaí saserù

scurrilous [skəːr'ələs] adj 口汚い kuchígitanaì

scurry [skəːr'iː] vi ちょこちょこ走る chókòchoko hashírù

scurry off vi ちょこちょこ走って行く chókòchoko hashítte ikù

scuttle [skʌt'əl] n (also: **coal scuttle**) 石炭入れ sekítan-ire

◆vt (ship) 沈没させる chíñbotsu saserù

◆vi (scamper): *to scuttle away/off* ちょこちょこ走っていく chókòchoko hashítte ikù

scythe [saið] n 大がま ōgama ◇柄も刃も長いかまと mò hā mò nagáī kámā

sea [siː] n 海 úmì; (fig: very many) 多数 tasū; (: very much) 多量 taryō

◆cpd (breeze, bird, air etc) 海の úmì no

by sea (travel) 海路で kaíro de

on the sea (boat) 海上で kaíjō de; (town) 海辺の umíbe no

out to/at sea 沖に okí ni

to be all at sea (fig) 頭が混乱している atáma gà kofíran shite irú

a sea of faces (fig) 無数の海 kaō nò úmi

seaboard [si:bɔːrd] n 海岸 kaígan

seafood [si:fuːd] n 魚介類 gyokáirùi, シーフード shífūdo ◇料理に使う魚介類を指す ryōrí ni tsukáù gyokáirùi wo sásù

seafront [si:frʌnt] n 海岸 kaígan ◇海辺の町などの海沿いの部分を指す umíbe nò machí nadò no umízoi no bubún wo sásù

sea-going [si:gouiŋ] adj (ship) 遠洋航海用の eñ-yōkókaiyō no

seagull [si:gʌl] n カモメ kamóme

seal [si:l] n (animal) アザラシ azárashi ◇セイウチを除いて全てのひれ足類を含む sefuchí wo nozóïte súbète no hiréashirùi wo fúkumù; (official stamp) 印章 ifishō; (closure) 封印 fúïn
◆vt (close: envelope) の封をする ...no fū wò suru; (: opening) 封じる fūjirù

sea level n 海抜 kaíbatsu

sea lion n トド tódò

seal off vt (place) 封鎖する fúsa suru

seam [si:m] n (line of stitches) 縫い目 nuíme; (where edges meet) 縫目 tsugíme, 合せ目 awáseme; (of coal etc) 薄層 hakúsō

seaman [si:mən] (pl seamen) n 船乗り funánori

seamy [si:mi:] adj: **the seamy side of** ...の汚い裏面 ...no kitánaï rímèn, ...の恥部 ...no chíbu

seance [sei'ɑːns] n 降霊会 kōreíkaì

seaplane [si:plein] n 水上飛行機 suíjōhikōki

seaport [si:pɔːrt] n 港町 mínatomàchi

search [sɔːrtʃ] n (hunt: for person, thing) 捜索 sōsaku; (COMPUT) 探索 tañsaku, 検索 keñsaku; (inspection: of someone's home) 家宅捜査 katákusòsa
◆vt (look in: place) の中を捜す ...no nakà wo sagásù; (examine: memory) 捜す sagásù; (person) の身体検査をする ...no shintaikeñsa wo suru
◆vi: **to search for** を捜す ...wo sagásù

in search of ...を求めて ...wo motómetè

searching [sɔːr'tʃiŋ] adj (question, look) 鋭い surúdoi

searchlight [sɔːrtʃ'lait] n サーチライト sāchiraìto

search party n 捜索隊 sōsakutai

search through vt fus ...の中をくまなく捜す ...no nakà wo kumánàku sagásù

search warrant n 捜査令状 sōsareìjō

seashore [si:ʃɔːr] n 海岸 kaígan

seasick [si:sik] adj 船酔いになった funáyoì ni nátta

seaside [si:said] n 海辺 umíbe

seaside resort n 海辺の行楽地 umíbe nò kōrakuchì

season [si:zən] n (of year) 季節 kisétsù; (time of year for something: football season etc) シーズン shízun; (series: of films etc) シリーズ shírīzu
◆vt (food) ...に味を付ける ...ni ajì wò tsukérù

in season (fruit, vegetables) しゅんで shún de

out of season (fruit, vegetables) 季節外れで kisétsuhàzure de

seasonal [si:zənəl] adj (work) 季節的な kisétsuteki na

seasoned [si:zənd] adj (fig: traveler) 経験豊かな keíkèn yútàka na

seasoning [si:zəniŋ] n 調味料 chōmiryō, 薬味 yakúmi

season ticket n (RAIL) 定期券 teíkiken; (THEATER) シーズン入場券 shízun nyūjōken

seat [si:t] n (chair) いす isú; (in vehicle, theater: place) 席 sékì; (PARLIAMENT) 議席 giséki; (buttocks: also of trousers) しり shirí
◆vt (place: guests etc) 座らせる suwáraserù; (subj: table, theater: have room for) ...人分の席がある ...nifíbun no sékì ga árù

to be seated 座る suwárù

seat belt n シートベルト shítoberùto

sea water n 海水 kaísui

seaweed [si:wiːd] n 海草 kaísō

seaworthy [si:wəːrði:] adj (ship) 航海に耐えられる航海に taérarerù ni taérarerù

sec. abbr = **second(s)**

secluded [siklu:'did] adj (place) 人里離れた hitózato hanaretà; (life) 隠とんの iñton no

seclusion [sɪkluːʒən] n 隔離 kákùri

second [sekʹənd] adj (after first) 第二 (の) dái nî (no)
◆adv (come, be placed: in race etc) 二番 に níbàn ni; (when listing) 第二に dái nî (no)
◆n (unit of time) 秒 byǒ; (AUT: also: **second gear**) セカンド sekándo; (COMM: imperfect) 二流品 niryūhǐn; (BRIT: SCOL: degree) 2級優等卒業学位 nǐkyū yūtō sotsugyō gakǔi ¶ see also **first**
◆vt (motion) ...に支持を表明する ...ni shíjì wo hyómei suru; (BRIT: worker) 派遣 する haken suru

secondary [sekʹəndeːriː] adj (less important) 二次的な nijíteki na

secondary school n 中等高等学校 chútōkōtōgakkō

second-class [sekʹəndklæs] adj (hotel, novel, work) 2等の níryū no; (tickets, transport) 2等の nítō no
◆adv (travel) 2等で nítō de

secondhand [sekʹəndhænd] adj (clothing, car) 中古の chūko no

second hand n (on clock) 秒針 byǒshìn

secondly [sekʹəndli] adv 2番目に níban me ni

secondment [sekʹəndmənt] (BRIT) n 派遣 haken

second-rate [sekʹəndreit] adj (film etc) 二流の niryū no

second thoughts npl ためらい tamérai
on second thought (US) or **thoughts** (BRIT) 気が変って ki ga kawattě

secrecy [siːʹkrisiː] n: **to swear someone to secrecy** ...に秘密を誓わせる ...ni hímftsu wŏ chikáwaseru

secret [siːʹkrit] adj (plan, passage, agent) 秘密の hímftsu no; (admirer, drinker) ひそかな hisóka na
◆n 秘密 hímftsu
in secret 内密に naímitsu ni

secretarial [sekriteːʹriːəl] adj (work, course, staff, studies) 秘書の hishó no

secretariat [sekriteːʹriːət] n 事務局 jímúkyòku

secretary [sekʹriteːriː] n (COMM) 秘書 hishó; (of club) 書記 shokí
Secretary of State (for) (BRIT: POL) (...)大臣 (...)dáījin

secretion [sikriːʹʃən] n (substance) 分泌 物 buńpitsubùtsu

secretive [siːʹkritiv] adj 秘密主義 の hímftsushùgi no

secretly [siːʹkritli] adv (tell, marry) 内密に naímitsu ni

sect [sekt] n 宗派 shūha

sectarian [sekteːʹriːən] adj (riots etc) 宗派間の shūhakàn no

section [sekʹʃən] n (part) 部分 búbùn; (department) ...部...bù; (of document) 章 shō; (of opinion) ...部 ...bù; (cross-section) 断面図 dańmenzù

sector [sekʹtəːr] n (part) 部門 búmòn; (MIL) 戦闘地区 seńtōchìku

secular [sekʹjələːr] adj (music, society etc) 世俗の sezóku no; (priest) 教区の kyōku no

secure [sikjuːʹr] adj (safe: person) 安全な 場所にいる añzen na bashò ni irú; (: money) 安全な場所にある añzen na bashò ni árù; (: building) 防犯対策完備の bōhántaisakukañbi no; (firmly fixed, strong: rope, shelf) 固定された kotéi saréta
◆vt (fix: rope, shelf etc) 固定する kotéi suru; (get: job, contract etc) 確保する kákùho suru

security [sikjuːʹritiː] n (protection) 警備 kéïbi; (for one's future) 保証 hoshó; (FINANCE) 担保 táñpo

sedan [sidænʹ] (US) n (AUT) セダン sédàn

sedate [sideitʹ] adj (person, pace) 落着いた ochítsuità
◆vt (MED: with injection) ...に鎮静剤を 注射する ...ni chíñseizài wo chūsha suru; (: with pills) ...に鎮静剤を飲ませる ...ni chíñseizài wo nomáserù

sedation [sideiʹʃən] n (MED): **under sedation** 薬で鎮静されて kusúri dè chíñsei saretè

sedative [sedʹətiv] n 鎮静剤 chíñseizài

sedentary [sedʹənteːriː] adj (occupation,

work) 座ってする suwátte surú

sediment [sed'əmənt] *n* (in bottle) おり orf; (in lake etc) 底の沈積物 sokó nò tafsekibútsu

seduce [sidus'] *vt* (entice: gen) 魅了する miryô suru; (: sexually) 誘惑する yūwaku suru, たらし込む taráshikomu

seduction [sidʌk'ʃən] *n* (attraction) 魅惑 miwáku; (act of seducing) 誘惑 yūwaku

seductive [sidʌk'tiv] *adj* (look, voice, *also fig* offer) 誘惑的な yūwakutekí na

see [si:] (*pt* **saw**, *pp* **seen**) *vt* (gen) 見る mírû; (accompany): **to see someone to the door** ...を戸口まで送る ...wo tógùchi máde okúrù; (understand) 分かる wakárù
   ◆*vi* (gen) 見える miérù; (find out) 調べる shiráberù
   ◆*n* (REL) 教区 kyōkù
   to see that someone does something ...が...する様に気を付ける ...ga...surú yō ni kí wo tsukérù
   see you soon! またね matá ne

see about *vt fus* ...の問題を調べて片付ける ...no mońdai wò shirábete katazùkeru

seed [si:d] *n* (of plant, fruit) 種 tánè; (sperm) 精液 sefeki; (*fig*: gen pl) 種 tánè; (TENNIS) シード shído
   to go to seed (plant) 種ができる tánè ga dekfrù; (*fig*) 衰える otóroerù

seedling [si:d'liŋ] *n* 苗 náè

seedy [si:'di:] *adj* (shabby: person, place) 見すぼらしい misúborashìi

seeing [si:'iŋ] *conj*: **seeing (that)** ...だから ...dákara

seek [si:k] (*pt*, *pp* **sought**) *vt* (truth, shelter, advice, post) 求める motómerù

seem [si:m] *vi* ...に見える ...ni miérù
   there seems to be ....がある様です ...ga árù yô desù

seemingly [si:'miŋli:] *adv* ...らしく ...rashîkù

seen [si:n] *pp* of **see**

see off *vt* ...を見送る ...wo miókurù

seep [si:p] *vi* (liquid, gas) 染み透る shimítòru

seesaw [si:'sɔ:] *n* シーソー shísò

seethe [si:ð] *vi* (place: with people/things) 騒然としている sōzen to shite irú
   to seethe with anger 怒りで煮え繰り返る ikari dè níekurikaerù

see through *vt fus* 見かけで見やり通す sáigo made yarítòsu
   ◆*vt fus* 見抜く minúkù

see-through [si:'θru:] *adj* (blouse etc) すけすけルックの sukésukerukkù no

see to *vt fus* ...の世話をする ...no sewá wò suru

segment [seg'mənt] *n* (part: gen) 一部 ichíbù; (of orange) ふさ fusá

segregate [seg'rəgeit] *vt* 分け隔てる wakérù

seismic [saiz'mik] *adj* (activity) 地震の jishín no

seize [si:z] *vt* (grasp) つかむ tsukámù; (take possession of: power, control, territory) 奪う ubáù; (: hostage) 捕まえる tsukámaerù; (opportunity) 捕える toráerù

seize up *vi* (TECH: engine) 焼け付ける yakétsukù

seize (up)on *vt fus* ...に飛びつく ...ni tobftsukù

seizure [si:'ʒər] *n* (MED) 発作 hossá; (LAW) 没収 bosshū; (: of power) 強奪 gōdatsu

seldom [sel'dəm] *adv* めったに...ない méttà ni...náì

select [silekt'] *adj* (school, group, area) 一流の ichíryū no
   ◆*vt* (choose) 選ぶ erábù

selection [silek'ʃən] *n* (being chosen) 選ばれる事 erábareru kotò; (COMM: range available) 選択 sefitaku

selective [silek'tiv] *adj* (careful in choosing) 選択的な sefitakutekí na; (not general: strike etc) 限られた範囲の kagfrareta háñ-i no

self [self] (*pl* **selves**) *n*: **the self** 自我 jígà
   ◆*prefix* 自分で(の)... jibún de (no) ...

self-assured [self'əʃʊrd'] *adj* 自信のある jishín no arù

self-catering [self'kei'tərɪŋ] *adj* (BRIT: holiday, apartment) 自炊の jisúi no

self-centered [self'sen'tərd] (BRIT **self-centred**) *adj* 自己中心な jikóchūshinno

self-colored [self'kʌl'ərd] (BRIT **self-coloured**) adj (of one color) 単色の tañshoku no

self-confidence [self'kɑːn'fidəns] n 自信 jishîn

self-conscious [self'kɑːn'tʃəs] adj (nervous) 照れる terêru

self-contained [self'kənteind'] (BRIT) adj (flat) 設備完備の setsūbikañbi no

self-control [self'kəntroul'] n 自制 jiséi

self-defense [self'difens'] (BRIT **self-defence**) n 自己防衛 jikóbōei
in self-defense 自己防衛で jikôbōei de

self-discipline [self'dis'əplin] n 気力 kíryòku

self-employed [self'implɔid'] adj 自営業の jiéigyō no

self-evident [self'ev'idənt] adj 自明の jiméi no

self-governing [self'gʌv'ərniŋ] adj 独立の dokúritsu no

self-indulgent [self'indʌl'dʒənt] adj 勝手気ままな kattékimama na

self-interest [self'in'trist] n 自己利益 jikôrièki

selfish [sel'fiʃ] adj 身勝手な migátte na

selfishness [sel'fiʃnis] n 利己主義 rikôshūgi

selfless [self'lis] adj 献身的な keñshinteki na

self-made [self'meid'] adj: *self-made man* 自力でたたき上げた人 jiríki dè tatákiageta hitð

self-pity [self'pit'i:] n 自己れんびん jikôreñbin

self-portrait [self'pɔːr'trit] n 自画像 jigázò

self-possessed [self'pəzest'] adj 落着いた ochîtsuità

self-preservation [self'prezərvei'ʃən] n 本能的自己保存 hoñnótekijikó

self-respect [self'rispekt'] n 自尊心 jisôñshin

self-righteous [self'rai'tʃəs] adj 独善的な dokúzenteki na

self-sacrifice [self'sæk'rəfais] n 献身 keñshin

self-satisfied [self'sæt'isfaid] adj 自己満足の jikómañzoku no

self-service [self'sər'vis] adj (shop, restaurant, service station) セルフサービスの serúfusābisu no

self-sufficient [self'səfiʃ'ənt] adj (farm, country) 自給自足の jikýūjisòku no; (person) 独立独歩の dokúritsudoppò no

self-taught [self'tɔːt'] adj 独学の dokúgaku no

sell [sel] (pt, pp **sold**) vt (gen) 売る urú; (fig: idea) 売込む urîkomù
♦vi (goods) 売れる urérù
to sell at/for $10 値段は10ドルである nedán wà 10 dòru de árù

sell-by date [sel'bai-] (BRIT) n 賞味期限 shōmikigèn

seller [sel'ər] n 売手 urîte

selling price [sel'iŋ-] n 値段 nedán

sell off vt 売払う urîharaù

sell out vi (use up stock): *to sell out (of something)* (...が)売切れる (...ga) urîkirerù
the tickets are sold out 切符は売切れだ kippú wà urîkire da

sellotape [sel'əteip] ® (BRIT) n セロテープ serótèpu

selves [selvz] pl of **self**

semaphore [sem'əfɔːr] n 手旗 tebáta

semblance [sem'bləns] n 外観 gaîkan

semen [siː'mən] n 精液 seîeki

semester [simes'tər] (US) n 学期 gakkî

semi... [sem'i:] prefix 半分の... hañbûn no

semicircle [sem'i:sərkəl] n 半円形 hañeñkei

semicolon [sem'i:koulən] n セミコロン semíkoròn

semiconductor [semi:kəndʌk'tər] n 半導体 hañdōtai

semidetached (house) [semi:ditætʃt'] (BRIT) n 二戸建て住宅 nikôdate jūtaku

semifinal [semi:fai'nəl] n 準決勝 juñkesshō

seminar [sem'ənɑːr] n セミナー sémìnā

seminary [sem'əneːriː] n (REL) 神学校 shiñgakkō

semiskilled [semi:skild'] adj (work,

worker) 半熟練の hañjukúren no

senate [sen'it] *n* 上院 jōín

senator [sen'ətər] *n* 上院議員 jōíngíìn

send [send] *(pt, pp* **sent)** *vt* (dispatch) 送る okúrù; (transmit: signal) 送信する sōshin suru

send away *vt* (letter, goods) 送る okúrù; (unwelcome visitor) 追払う oíharaú

send away for *vt fus* 郵便で注文する yūbín dè chūmon suru

send back *vt* 送り返す okúrikaesù

send for *vt fus* (thing) 取寄せる toríyoseru; (person) 呼寄せる yobíyoserù

send off *vt* (goods) 送る okúrù; *(BRIT: SPORT*: player) 退場させる taíjō saserù

send-off [send'ɔ:f] *n*: *a good send-off* 華麗らしい送別 subáráshíì sōbetsu

send out *vt* (invitation) 送る okúrù; (signal) 発信する hasshín suru

send up *vt* (price, blood pressure) 上昇させる jōshō saserù; (astronaut) 打上げる uchíagerù; *(BRIT*: parody) 風刺する fūshi suru

senile [si:'nail] *adj* 老いぼれた oíboretà, ぼけた bóketà; *(MED)* 老人性の rōjinsei no

senior [si:n'jə:r] *adj* (older) 年上の toshíue no; (on staff: position, officer) 幹部の kánbu no; (of higher rank: partner) 親分の oyábun no

senior citizen *n* 老人 rōjin, 高齢者 kōreisha

seniority [si:njɔ:r'iti:] *n* (in service) 年功 nenkō

sensation [sensei'ʃən] *n* (feeling) 感覚 kañkaku, (great success) 大成功 daíseikō

sensational [sensei'ʃənəl] *adj* (wonderful) 素晴らしい subárashíì; (causing much interest: headlines) 扇情的な señjōteki na; (: result) センセーショナルな señsēshōnaru na

sense [sens] *n* (physical) 感覚 kañkaku; (feeling: of guilt, shame etc) 感じ kanjí; (good sense) 常識 jōshiki; (meaning: of word, phrase etc) 意味 ímì

◆*vt* (become aware of) 感じる kañjirù

it makes sense (can be understood) 意味が分かる ími ga wakárù; (is sensible) 賢明だ keñmei dà

sense of humor ユーモアを解する心 yúmòa wo kaí surú kokóro, ユーモアの センス yúmòa no séñsu

senseless [sens'lis] *adj* (pointless: murder) 無意味な mumi na; (unconscious) 気絶した kizétsu shita

sensible [sen'səbəl] *adj* (person) 利口な rikō na; (reasonable: price, advice) 合理的な gōriteki na; (: decision, suggestion) 賢明な keñmei na

sensitive [sen'sətiv] *adj* (understanding) 理解のある rikai no árù; (nerve, skin) 敏感な biñkan na; (instrument) 高感度の kōkandō no; *(fig*: touchy) 怒りっぽい okórippòi; (: issue) 微妙な kiwádòi

sensitivity [sensitiv'əti:] *n* (understanding) 理解 rikai; (responsiveness: to touch etc) 敏感さ biñkansa; (: of instrument) 感度 kándo; (touchiness: of person) 怒りっぽさ okórippòsa; (delicate nature: of issue etc) 微妙さ kiwádòsa

sensual [sen'ʃuəl] *adj* (of the senses: rhythm etc) 官能的な kañnōteki na; (relating to sexual pleasures) 肉感的な nikkánteki na

sensuous [sen'ʃuəs] *adj* (lips, material etc) 官能的な kañnōteki na

sent [sent] *pt, pp of* **send**

sentence [sen'təns] *n (LING)* 文 búñ, *(LAW)* 宣告 señkoku

◆*vt: to sentence someone to death/to 5 years in prison* ...に死刑/懲役5年の判決を言渡す ...ni shikéi (chōeki gonèn) nò hañketsu wò íwatasū

sentiment [sen'təmənt] *n* (tender feelings) 感情 kañjō; (opinion, *also* pl) 意見 íkèn

sentimental [sentəmen'təl] *adj* (song) 感傷的な kañshōteki na, センチメンタルな señchiméñtaru na; (person) 情にもろい ...jō nì morói

sentry [sen'tri:] *n* 番兵 bañpei

separate *[adj* sep'rit *vb* sep'areit] *adj* (distinct: piles, occasions, ways, rooms) 別々の betsúbetsu no

♦*vt* (split up: people, things) 分ける wakérù; (make a distinction between:
twins) 見分ける miwākérù; (: ideas etc)
区別する kubétsu suru
♦*vi* (split up, move apart) 分かれる wakárerù

separately [sep'ritli:] *adv* 別々に betsúbetsu ni

separates [sep'rits] *npl* (clothes) セパレ
ーツ sepárètsu

separation [seporei'∫ən] *n* (being apart)
分離 bunri; (time spent apart) 別れ別れ
になっている期間 wakárewakāre ni natté irù kikàn; (LAW) 別居 bekkyó

September [septem'bə:r] *n* 9月 kúgàtsu

septic [sep'tik] *adj* (wound, finger etc) 感
染した kańsen shita

septic tank *n* 浄化槽 jōkasō

sequel [si:'kwəl] *n* (follow-up) 後日談 go-
jítsùdàn; (of film, story) 続編 zokúhen

sequence [si:'kwins] *n* (ordered chain) 連
続 reńzoku; (also: **dance sequence, film
sequence**) 一場面 ichíbamèn, シークエン
ス shíkueñsu

sequin [si:'kwin] *n* シークイン shíkuìn,
スパンコール supánkòru

serene [səri:n'] *adj* (smile, expression
etc) 穏やかな odáyàka na

serenity [səren'iti:] *n* 穏やかさ odáyàka-
sa

sergeant [sɑːr'dʒənt] *n* (MIL etc) 軍曹
gúnsò; (POLICE) 巡査部長 juńsabùchō

serial [si:'ri:əl] *n* 連載物 reńzokumòno

serialize [si:'ri:əlaiz] *vt* (in newspaper,
magazine) 連載する reńsai suru; (on
radio, TV) 連続物として放送する refízo-
kumono toshìte hōsō suru

serial number *n* 製造番号 sefzóbañgō

series [si:'ri:z] *n inv* (group) 一連 ichíren;
(of books, TV programs) シリーズ shirí-
zù

serious [si:'ri:əs] *adj* (person, manner) 真
剣な shiñken na; (important: matter) 大
事な daíjì na; (grave: illness, condition)
重い omóì

seriously [si:'ri:əsli:] *adv* (talk, take) 真
剣に shiñken ni; (hurt) ひどく hídðku

seriousness [si:'ri:əsnis] *n* (of person,

manner) 真剣さ shiñkensa; (importance)
重大さ júdaisa; (gravity) 重さ omósa

sermon [səːr'mən] *n* (also *fig*) 説教 sek-
kyó

serrated [sə:rei'tid] *adj* (edge, knife) 刃
のこぎり状の nokógirijō no

serum [si:r'əm] *n* 血清 kessei

servant [səːr'vənt] *n* (gen) 召使い meshí-
tsukài; (*fig*) 人に仕える物 hitó ni tsukáerù monó

serve [səːrv] *vt* (gen: company, country)
仕える tsukáerù; (in shop: goods) 売る
urú; (: customer) ...の用をうかがう ...no
yõ wo ukágaù; (subj: train) ...の足になる
...no ashí ni narù; (apprenticeship) 務め
る tsutómerù
♦*vi* (at table) 給仕する kyúji suru; (TEN-
NIS) サーブする sábu suru; (be useful):
to serve as/for ...として役に立つ ...to-
shité irù kikàn; (be enough):
to serve to do ...をするのに役に立つ
...wo súru n̄ yakú ni tatsú
it serves him right 自業自得だ jigójì-
tòku da
to serve a prison term 服役する fukúe-
ki suru

serve out/up *vt* (food) 出す dásù

service [səːr'vis] *n* (gen: help) 役に立つ事
yakú ni tatsú koto; (in hotel) サービス
sábisu; (REL) 式 shikí; (AUT) 整備 seíbi;
(TENNIS) サーブ sábu; (plates, dishes
etc) 一そろい hitósorði; (: **train service**) 鉄道 (の便 tetsúdò nð bèñ; (also:
plane service) 空の便 sórà no bèñ
♦*vt* (car, washing machine) 整備する seíbi suru
military/national service 兵役 heíeki
to be of service to someone ...に役に立つ
...ni yakú ni tatsú

serviceable [səːr'visəbəl] *adj* 役に立つ
yakú ni tatsú

service area *n* (on motorway) サービス
エリア sábisu erìa

service charge (BRIT) *n* サービス料
sábisuryō

serviceman [səːr'vismæn] (*pl* **service-
men**) *n* (MIL) 軍人 guñjin

Services [sər'visiz] *npl: the Services* (army, navy etc) 軍隊 gúntai

service station *n* ガソリンスタンド gasōrinsutaňdo; (*BRIT: on motorway*) サービスエリア sābisu erīa

serviette [sər'viet'] (*BRIT*) *n* 紙ナプキン kamínapùkin

servile [sər'vail] *adj* (person, obedience) おもねる様な omónerù yō na

session [seʃ'ən] *n* (period of activity: recording/drinking session) ...する為に集まる事 ...surú tamè nì atsúmarù kotò

to be in session (court) 開廷中である kaíteichū de arù; (Parliament etc) 開会中である kaíkaichū de arù

set [set] *n* (collection of things) 一そろい hitósorði, 一式 hitóshìki, セット séttò; (radio set) ラジオ rájìo; (TV set) テレビ térèbi; (TENNIS) セット séttð; (group of people) 連中 reñchū; (MATH) セット séttð; (CINEMA, THEATER) 舞台装置 butáisòchi, セット séttð; (HAIRDRESSING) セット séttð

♦*adj* (fixed: rules, routine) 決りの kimári no; (ready) 用意ができた yói ga dekità

♦*vb* (*pt, pp* set)

♦*vt* (place) 置く ókù; (fix, establish: time, price, rules etc) 決める kiméru; (: record) 作る tsukúru; (adjust: alarm, watch) セットする séttð suru; (impose: task) 命ずる meízurù; (: exam) 作る tsukúru

♦*vi* (sun) 沈む shizúmù; (jam, jelly, concrete) 固まる katámarù; (broken bone) 治る náorù

to set the table 食卓の用意をする shokútaku no yōi wo suru

to be set on doing something どうしても...をしようと決めている dōshite mo ...wo surū tò kiméte irù

to set to music ...に曲を付ける ...ni kyokú wò tsukérù

to set on fire ...に火を付ける ...ni hí wò tsukérù

to set free ...を解放する hañkáhe yarù, 自由にする jiyú ni surù

to set something going ...を始めさせる

...wo hajímesaserù

to set sail 出帆する shukkő suru

set about *vt fus* (task) 始める hajímerù

set aside *vt* (money etc) 取って置く ...tò tè okù; (time) 空けておく akéte okù

set back *vt* (cost): *to set someone back $5* 5ドル払わなければならない yo dōrù haráwànakereba naránaì; (in time): *to set someone back (by)* ...を遅らせる ...wo (...) okúraserù

setback [set'bæk] *n* (hitch) 苦難 kúnaň

set menu *n* 定食メニュー teíshokumenyū

set off *vi* 出発する shuppátsu suru

♦*vt* (bomb) 爆発させる bakúhatsu saserù; (alarm) 鳴らす narásù; (chain of events) ...の引金となる ...no hikígane to narù; (show up well: jewels) 引立たせる hikítataserù

set out *vi* (depart) 出発する shuppátsu suru

♦*vt* (arrange: goods etc) 並べて置く narábete okù; (state: arguments) 述べる nobérù

to set out to do something ...をするつもりである ...wo surú tsumorì de arù

settee [seti:'] *n* ソファー sốfā

setting [set'iŋ] *n* (background) 背景 haíkei; (position: of controls) セット séttð; (of jewel) はめ込み台 hamékomídai

the setting of the sun 日没 nichíbotsu

settle [set'əl] *vt* (argument, matter) ...に決着を付ける ...ni ketcháku wò tsukérù; (accounts) 清算する seísan suru; (MED: calm: person) 落着かせる ochítsukaserù

♦*vi* (*also: settle down*) 一ヵ所に落着く ikkásho ni ochítsukù; (bird) 降りる orírù; (dust etc) つもる tsukú; (calm down: children) 静まる shizúmarù

to settle for something ...で我慢する ...de gámaň suru

to settle on something ...に決める ...ni kimérù

settle in *vi* 新しい所に落着く atárashii tokórò ni ochítsukù

settle up *vi: to settle up with someone* ...に借金を返す ...ni shakkíñ wo káèsu

settlement [setˈəlmənt] *n* (payment) 清算 seisan; (agreement) 和解 wakái; (village etc) 集落 shúraku

settler [setˈlər] *n* 入植者 nyūshokushá

set up *vt* (organization) 設立する setsúritsu suru

setup [setˈʌp] *n* (organization) 機構 kikṓ; (situation) 様子 yṓsu, 状況 jōkyō

seven [sevˈən] *num* 七(の) nána (no), 七つ(の) nanátsu (no)

seventeen [sevˈəntiːn] *num* 十七 (の) jūnana (no)

seventh [sevˈənθ] *num* 第七(の) dái nanā (no)

seventy [sevˈəntiː] *num* 七十 (の) nanájū (no)

sever [sevˈər] *vt* (artery, pipe) 切断する setsúdan suru; (relations) 切る kírù, 断つ tátsù

several [sevˈərəl] *adj* (things) 幾つかの-kútsu ka no; (people) 幾人かの íkunin ka no

♦*pron* 幾つか íkutsu ka

several of us 私たちの中から幾人か watákushitàchi no náka kara íkunin ka

severance [sevˈərəns] *n* (of relations) 断交 dankṓ

severance pay *n* 退職金 taíshokukìn

severe [sivˈiːr] *adj* (serious: pain) 激しい hageshíì; (: damage) 大きな ṓki na; (: shortage) 深刻な shíñkoku na; (: hard: winter, climate) 厳しい kibíshiì; (stern) 厳格な geñkaku na; (plain: dress) 簡素な kańso na

severity [sevˈiːriti] *n* (seriousness: of pain) 激しさ hageshísa; (: of damage) 大きさ ṓkisa; (: of shortage) 深刻さ shíñkoku sa; (bitterness: of winter, climate) 厳しさ kibíshiṣa; (sternness) 厳格さ geñkakusa; (plainness: of dress) 簡素さ kańsosa

sew [sou] (*pt* **sewed**, *pp* **sewn**) *vt* 縫う nuú

sewage [suːˈidʒ] *n* (waste) 汚水 osúi

sewer [suːˈər] *n* 下水道 gesúidō

sewing [souˈiŋ] *n* (activity) 裁縫 saíhō; (items being sewn) 縫物 nuímono

sewing machine *n* ミシン míshìn

sewn [soun] *pp of* **sew**

sew up *vt* (item of clothing) 縫い合せる nuíawaserù

sex [seks] *n* (gender) 性別 seíbetsu; (lovemaking) セックス sékkùsu

to have sex with someone ...とセックスをする ...to sékkùsu wo suru

sexist [seksˈist] *adj* 性差別の seísabetsu no

sextet [seksˈtet] *n* (group) セクステット sekúsutettò

sexual [sekˈʃuəl] *adj* (of the sexes: reproduction) 有性の yúsei no; (: equality) 男女の dáñjo no; (of sex: attraction) 性的な seíteki na; (: relationship) 肉体の nikútai no

sexy [sekˈsiː] *adj* (pictures, underwear etc) セクシーな sékùshī na

shabby [ʃæbˈiː] *adj* (person, clothes) 見すぼらしい misúborashiì; (trick, treatment) 卑劣な hirétsu na

shack [ʃæk] *n* バラック barákkù

shackles [ʃækˈəlz] *npl* (on foot) 足かせ ashíkasè; (on hands) 手かせ tékàse; (*fig*) 束縛 sokúbaku

shade [ʃeid] *n* (shelter) 日陰 hikáge; (*also:* **lampshade**) ランプのかさ ráñpu no kása; (of colour) 色合 iróaì; (small quantity): *a shade too large* ちょっと大き過ぎる chottó ōkisugirù

♦*vt* (shelter) ...の日よけになる ...no hiyóke ni narù; (eyes) ...に手をかざす ...ni te wð kazásù

in the shade 日陰に hikáge ni

a shade more もうちょっと mō chottó

shadow [ʃædˈou] *n* 影 kágè

♦*vt* (follow) 尾行する bikṓ suru

shadow cabinet (*BRIT*) *n* (POL) 影の内閣 kágè no naíkaku

shadowy [ʃædˈoui] *adj* (in shadow) 影の多い kágè no ōi; (dim: figure, shape) 影の様な kágè no yṓ na

shady [ʃeiˈdiː] *adj* (place) 日陰の ある hikáge no arù; (trees) 日よけになる hiyóke ni narù; (*fig*: dishonest: person, deal) いかがわしい ikágawashìì

shaft [ʃæft] *n* (of arrow) 矢柄 yagára; (of spear) 柄 e; (AUT, TECH) 回転軸 kaíteñjiku, シャフト sháfùto; (of mine) 縦坑 ta-

tékō, (of elevator) 通路 tsúrō
a shaft of light 一条の光 ichíjō no hikarí

shaggy [ʃæg'iː] adj (appearance, beard, dog) ぼさぼさの bosábosa na

shake [ʃeik] (pt **shook**, pp **shaken**) vt (gen) 揺すぶる yusúburù; (bottle) 振る furù; (cocktail) シェイクする shefkù suru; (building) 揺るがす yurúgasù; (weaken: beliefs, resolve) ぐらつかせる gurátsukaserù; (upset, surprise) ...にショックを与える ...ni shókkù wo atáerù
♦vi (tremble) 震える furúerù

to shake one's head (in refusal, dismay) 頭を振る atáma wò fúrù

to shake hands with someone ...と握手をする ...to ákushu wo suru

shaken [ʃei'kən] pp of **shake**

shake off vt (lit) 振り落す furíotosù; (fig: pursuer) まく makù

shake up vt (lit: ingredients) よく振る yókù furu; (fig: organization) 一新する isshìn suru

shaky [ʃei'kiː] adj (hand, voice) 震える furúerù; (table, building) ぐらぐらする gúragura suru

shall [ʃæl] aux vb: *I shall go* 行きます ikímasù

shall I open the door? ドアを開けましょうか dóà wo akémashò ka

I'll get some, shall I? 少し取ってきましょうか sukóshi totté kimashò ka

shallow [ʃæl'ou] adj (water, box, breathing) 浅い asáì; (fig: ideas etc) 浅薄な seńpaku na

sham [ʃæm] n いんちき ińchiki
♦vt ...の振りをする ...no furí wo suru

shambles [ʃæm'bəlz] n 大混乱, daíkoñran

shame [ʃeim] n (embarrassment) 恥 hajf; (disgrace) 不面目 fuméñboku
♦vt 辱める hazúkashimerù

it is a shame that ... ...であるのは残念だ ...de árù no wa zańneñ da

it is a shame to do ... ...するのはもったいない ...surú no wa mottáinaì

what a shame! 残念だ zańneñ da

shamefaced [ʃeim'feist] adj 恥ずかしそうな hazúkashisō na

shameful [ʃeim'fəl] adj (disgraceful) 恥ずべき hazúbekì

shameless [ʃeim'lis] adj (liar, deception) 恥知らずの hajíshirazù no

shampoo [ʃæmpuː'] n シャンプー shańpū
♦vt シャンプーする shańpū suru

shampoo and set シャンプーとセット shańpū to séttò

shamrock [ʃæm'rɑːk] n ツメクサ tsumékusa, クローバー kurōbā

shandy [ʃæn'diː] n シャンディー shańdī ◇ビールをレモネードで割った飲物 bíru wo remónědo de wátta nomímonó

shan't [ʃænt] = **shall not**

shanty town [ʃæn'tiː-] n バラック集落 barákkushūraku

shape [ʃeip] n (form, outline) 形 katáchi
♦vt (fashion, form) 形作る katáchizukurù; (someone's ideas, life) 方向付ける hōkōzukerù

to take shape (painting) 段々格好がすっく dańdañ kakkō ga tsukù; (plan) 具体化してくる gutáika shite kurù

-**shaped** [ʃeipt] suffix: *heart-shaped* ハート形の hátògata no

shapeless [ʃeip'lis] adj 不格好な bukákkō na

shapely [ʃeip'liː] adj (woman, legs) 美しい utsúkushiì

shape up vi (events) 具体化してくる gutáika shite kurù; (person) 期待通りに進歩する kitáidōri ni shiňpo suru

share [ʃeːr] n (part received) 分け前 wakémaè; (part contributed) 分担分 mochíbun, 負担分 futáňbun; (COMM) 株 kabú
♦vt (books, toys, room) 共有する kyōyū suru; (cost) 分担する buńtan suru; (one's lunch) 分けてやる wakéte yarù; (have in common: features, qualities etc) ...の点で似ている ...no téň de nité irù

shareholder [ʃeːr'houldəːr] n 株主 kabúnùshi

share out vi 分配する buńpai suru

shark [ʃɑːrk] n サメ samé

sharp [ʃɑːrp] adj (razor, knife) よく切れる yókù kirérù; (point, teeth) 鋭い surúdoì; (nose, chin) とがった togáttta; (outline) くっきりした kukkíri shitá; (sud-

鋭い surúdoi; (cold) 身を切る様な mí wò kírù yō na; (taste) 舌を刺す様な shitá wò sásù yō na; (MUS) ピッチが高過ぎる píttchī ga takásugirū; (contrast) 強い tsuyōī; (increase) 急な kyū na; (voice) 甲高い kandakaī; (person: quick-witted) 抜け目のない nukéme no naī; (dishonest: practice etc) 不正な fuséi na

♦*n* (MUS) えい音記号 efonkigō, シャープ shápù

♦*adv: at 2 o'clock sharp* 2 時きっかりに níji kikkárî ni

sharpen [ʃɑ:ʳpən] *vt* (stick etc) とがらせる togáraserù; (pencil) 削る kezúrù; (fig: appetite) そそる sosórù

sharpener [ʃɑ:ʳpənəʳ] *n* (*also*: **pencil sharpener**) 鉛筆削り efpitsukezórì

sharp-eyed [ʃɑ:ʳpˈaid] *adj* 目の鋭い mé nò surudói

sharply [ʃɑ:ʳplì] *adv* (turn, stop) 急に kyū ni; (stand out) くっきりと kukkírî to; (contrast) 強く tsuyóků; (criticize, retort) 辛らつに shifíratsu ni

shatter [ʃætəʳ] *vt* (break) 割る warú, 木っ端みじんにする kóppàmijin ni surú; (fig: ruin) 台無しにする dafnashí ni surù; (: upset) がっくりさせる gakkúrî saserù

♦*vi* (break) 割れる warérù

shave [ʃeiv] *vt* (person, face, legs etc) そる sórù

♦*vi* ひげをそる higé wò sórù

♦*n: to have a shave* (at barber's) ひげをそってもらう higé wò sóttè moráù; (oneself) ひげをそる higé wò sórù

shaver [ʃeivəʳ] *n* (*also*: **electric shaver**) 電気かみそり defikikamísorì

shaving [ʃeivɪŋ] *n* (action) ひげをそる事 higé wò sórù kotó

shaving brush *n* シェービングブラシ shēbìnguburàshi

shaving cream, shaving foam *n* シェービングクリーム shēbìngukurīmu

shavings [ʃeivɪŋz] *npl* (of wood etc) かんなくず kafinakuzú

shawl [ʃɔ:l] *n* 肩掛 katákàke, ショール shốrù

she [ʃi:] *pron* 彼女は(が) kánòjo wa (ga)

sheaf [ʃi:f] *n* (*npl* **sheaves**) *n* (of corn, papers)

束 tábà

shear [ʃi:əʳ] (*pt* **sheared**, *pp* **shorn**) *vt* (sheep)...の毛を刈る ...no ké wò karú

shear off *vi* 折れる orérù

shears [ʃi:əʳz] *npl* (for hedge) はさみ hasámi

sheath [ʃi:θ] *n* (of knife) さや sáyà; (contraceptive) コンドーム kofidómu, スキン sukíñ

sheaves [ʃi:vz] *npl of* **sheaf**

she-cat [ʃi:ˈkæt] *n* 雌ネコ mesúnèko

shed [ʃed] *n* 小屋 koyá

♦*vt* (*pt, pp* **shed**) (leaves, fur, hair etc) 落す otósù; (skin) 脱皮する dappí surù; (tears) 流す nagású

to shed blood 人を殺す hitó wò korósù

to shed a load (subj: truck etc) 荷崩れを起す nikúzure wò okósù

she'd [ʃi:d] = **she had; she would**

sheen [ʃi:n] *n* つやつや tsuyátsuya

sheep [ʃi:p] *n inv* ヒツジ hitsújî

sheepdog [ʃi:pdɔ:g] *n* 牧用犬 bokúyòken

sheepish [ʃi:piʃ] *adj* 恥ずかしそうな hazúkashisō na

sheepskin [ʃi:pskin] *n* ヒツジの毛皮 hitsújî no kegáwa, シープスキン shípusukìñ

sheer [ʃi:əʳ] *adj* (utter) 全くの mattáku no; (steep) 垂直の suíchoku na; (almost transparent) ごく薄手の gokú usúde no

♦*adv* (straight up: rise) 垂直に suíchoku ni

sheet [ʃi:t] *n* (on bed) シーツ shītsù; (of paper, glass, metal) 一枚 ichímaì

a sheet of ice アイスバーン aísubàn

sheik(h) [ʃi:k] *n* 首長 shuchō

shelf [ʃelf] (*pl* **shelves**) *n* 棚 taná

shell [ʃel] *n* (on beach) 貝殻 kaígarà; (of egg, nut etc) 殻 kará; (explosive) 弾丸 dañgan; (of building) 骨組み honégumì

♦*vt* (peas) むく múků; (MIL: fire on) 砲撃する hógeki surù

she'll [ʃi:l] = **she will; she shall**

shellfish [ʃelˈfiʃ] *n inv* (crab) カニ kanî; (prawn, shrimp etc) エビ ebí; (lobster) ロブスター robúsùtā; (scallop, clam etc) 貝 kaî 小料理用語として魚および水生の生物を指す ryōrìyōgo toshite kará no arù chimé no seíbutsu wo sásù

shelter [ʃel'tər] n (building) シェルター
shérútā; (protection: for hiding) 隠れ場
所 kakúrebashò; (: from rain) 雨宿りの
場所 amáyàdori no bashò
♦vt (protect) 守る mamórù; (give lodging to: homeless, refugees) ...に避難の場
所を提供する ...ni hínàn no bashò wò
teíkyō suru; (: wanted man) かくまう
kakúmaù
♦vi (from rain etc) 雨宿りをする amáyàdori wo suru; (from danger) 避難する
hínàn suru; (: hide) 隠れる kakúrerù

sheltered [ʃel'tərd] adj (life) 世間の荒波
から守られた sékèn no arānami karà
mamóraretà; (spot) 雨風を避けられるよ
まcかぜ
mèkaze wo sakérarerù
sheltered housing 老人・身障者用住宅
rójīn, shínshōshayō jūtaku

shelve [ʃelv] vt (fig: plan) 棚上げにする
taná-age ni surù

shelves [ʃelvz] npl of **shelf**

shepherd [ʃep'ərd] n ヒツジ飼い hitsúji-
kāi
♦vt (guide) 案内する aſnai suru

shepherd's pie (BRIT) n シェパードパ
イ shepādopai ◇ひき肉にマッシュポテト
を乗せて焼いた料理 hikíniku ni masshū-
potèto wo nosète yaítà ryōrì

sheriff [ʃer'if] (US) n 保安官 hoánkan

sherry [ʃer'iː] n シェリー酒 sheríshū

she's [ʃiːz] = **she is**; **she has**

Shetland [ʃet'land] n (also: **the Shet-
lands, the Shetland Isles**) シェットラン
ド諸島 shettórandò shotō

shield [ʃiːld] n (MIL) 盾 táté; (SPORT:
trophy) 盾型トロフィー tatégata toróñ;
(protection) ...よけ ...yóke
♦vt: **to shield (from)** ...の(...)よけにな
る ...no (...) yóke ni narù

shift [ʃift] n (change) 変更 heñkō; (work-
period) 交替 kōtai; (group of workers) 交
替組 kōtaigùmi
♦vt (move) ...の位置を変える ...no ichí
wo kaérù; (remove: stain) 抜く nukú
♦vi (move: wind, person) 変る kawárù

shiftless [ʃift'lis] adj (person) ろくでなし
の rokúdenashi no

shift work n 交替でする作業 kōtai de
suru sagyō

shifty [ʃif'tiː] adj (person, eyes) うさん臭
い usánkusaì

shilling [ʃil'iŋ] (BRIT) n シリング shírìn-
gu ◇かつての英国の硬貨でポンドの1/20
katsúte no efkoku no kōka de póñdo no
nijūbun no ichí

shilly-shally [ʃil'iːʃæliː] vi ぐずぐずする
gúzùguzu suru

shimmer [ʃim'ər] vi ちらちら光る chíra-
chira hikárù

shin [ʃin] n 向こうずね mukōzune

shine [ʃain] n つや tsuyá
♦vb (pt, pp **shone**)
♦vi (sun) 照る térù; (torch, light, eyes) 光
る hikárù; (fig: person) 優れる sugúrerù
♦vt (glasses) ふく fukú; (shoes) 磨く migákù
to shine a torch on something ...を懐
中電燈で照す ...wo kaíchūdentō de terásù

shingle [ʃiŋ'gəl] n (on beach) 砂利 jarí

shingles [ʃiŋ'gəlz] n (MED) 帯状ヘルペス
taíjōherupèsu

shiny [ʃai'niː] adj (coin) ぴかぴかの piká-
pika no; (shoes, hair, lipstick) つやつや
の tsuyátsuya no

ship [ʃip] n 船 fúnè
♦vt (transport by ship) 船で運ぶ fúnè de
hakóbù; (send: goods) 輸送する yusō suru

shipbuilding [ʃip'bildiŋ] n 造船 zōsen

shipment [ʃip'mənt] n (goods) 輸送貨物
yusōkamòtsu

shipper [ʃip'ər] n 送り主 okúrinùshi

shipping [ʃip'iŋ] n (transport of cargo)
運送 uñsō; (ships collectively) 船舶 séñ-
paku

shipshape [ʃip'ʃeip] adj きちんとした kichíñ to shita

shipwreck [ʃip'rek] n (event) 難破 nañpa;
(ship) 難破船 nañpasen
♦vt: **to be shipwrecked** 難破する nañpa
suru

shipyard [ʃip'jaːrd] n 造船所 zōsenjo

shire [ʃaiər] (BRIT) n 郡 gúñ

shirk [ʃəːrk] vt (work, obligations) 怠る

okótarù

shirt [ʃəːt] *n* (man's) ワイシャツ waíshatsu; (woman's) シャツブラウス shatsúburaùsu

in (one's) shirt sleeves 上着を脱いで uwági wò núlde

shit [ʃit] (*inf!*) *excl* くそっ kusót

shiver [ʃívʼəːr] *n* (act of shivering) 身震い mibúruì

◆*vi* 震える furúerù

shoal [ʃoul] *n* (of fish) 群れ muré; (*fig: also*: **shoals**) 大勢 ōzeí

shock [ʃɑk] *n* (start, impact) 衝撃 shōgeki; (ELEC) 感電 kańden; (emotional) 打撃 dagéki, ショック shókkù; (MED) ショック shókkù

◆*vt* (upset, offend) ...にショックを与える ...ni shókkù wo atáerù

shock absorber *n* 緩衝器 kańshōkì

shocking [ʃɑkʼiŋ] *adj* (awful: standards, accident) ひどい hidóì; (outrageous: play, book) 衝撃的な shōgekiteki na

shod [ʃɑd] *pt, pp of* **shoe**

shoddy [ʃɑdʼiː] *adj* (goods, workmanship) 粗雑な sozátsu na

shoe [ʃuː] *n* (for person) 靴 kutsú; (for horse's hoof) てい鉄 teítetsu

◆*vt* (*pt, pp* **shod**) (horse) ...にてい鉄を付ける ...ni teítetsu wò tsukérù

shoebrush [ʃuːʼbrʌʃ] *n* 靴ブラシ kutsúburàshi

shoelace [ʃuːʼleis] *n* 靴ひも kutsúhìmo

shoe polish *n* 靴磨き kutsúmigàki

shoeshop [ʃuːʼʃɑp] *n* 靴屋 kutsúya

shoestring [ʃuːʼstriŋ] *n* (*fig*): *on a shoestring* わずかの金で wázùka no kané de

shone [ʃoun] *pt, pp of* **shine**

shoo [ʃuː] *excl* しっ shít 《動物を追払う時に言う言葉 dōbutsu wò oíharaù toki ni iú kotoba

shook [ʃuk] *pt of* **shake**

shoot [ʃuːt] *n* (on branch, seedling) 若枝 wakáeda

◆*vb* (*pt, pp* **shot**)

◆*vt* (gun) 撃つ útsù; (arrow) 射る írù; (kill: bird, robber etc) 撃ち殺す uchíkorosù; (wound) 撃する sogéki suru; (execute) 銃殺する jūsatsu suru; (film) 撮

影する satsúei suru; *to shoot (at)* (...を目掛けて)撃つ(射る)(...wo megákete) útsù 〔írù〕; (SOCCER) シュートする shūto suru

shoot down *vt* (plane) 撃ち落とす uchíotosù

shoot in/out *vi* (rush) 飛込む〔飛出す〕 tobíkomù 〔tobídasù〕

shooting [ʃuːʼtiŋ] *n* (shots) 発砲事件 happójìken; (HUNTING) 狩猟 shuryō

shooting star *n* 流れ星 nagáreboshi

shoot up *vi* (*fig*) 急上昇する kyújōshō suru

shop [ʃɑp] *n* (selling goods) 店 misé; (*also*: **workshop**) 作業場 sagyōba

◆*vi* (*also*: **go shopping**) 買物する kaímono suru

shop assistant (*BRIT*) *n* 店員 teń-in

shop floor (*BRIT*) *n* 労働側 rōdōgawa

shopkeeper [ʃɑpʼkiːpəːr] *n* 店主 teńshu

shoplifting [ʃɑpʼliftiŋ] *n* 万引 mańbìki

shopper [ʃɑpʼəːr] *n* (person) 買物客 kaímonokyàku

shopping [ʃɑpʼiŋ] *n* (goods) 買物 kaímono

shopping bag *n* ショッピングバッグ shoppíngubaggù

shopping center (*BRIT* **shopping centre**) *n* ショッピングセンター shoppíngusentā

shop-soiled [ʃɑpʼsɔild] *adj* (goods) 棚ざらしの tanázarashi no

shop steward (*BRIT*) *n* (INDUSTRY) 職場代表 shokúbadaihyō

shop window *n* ショーウインドー shōuindo

shore [ʃɔːr] *n* 岸 kishí

◆*vt*: *to shore up* 補強する hokyō suru

on shore 陸に riku ní

shorn [ʃɔːrn] *pp of* **shear**

short [ʃɔːrt] *adj* (not long) 短い mijíkaì; (person: not tall) 背の低い sé nò hikúì; (curt) ぶっきらぼうな bukkírabō na; (insufficient) 不足している fusóku shite irù

to be short of something ...が不足している ...ga fusóku shite irù

in short 要するに yō surù ni

short of doing ...をしなければ ...wo shinákereba

it is short for それは...の短縮形です sorё wâ ... no tañshukukei desu

to cut short (speech, visit) 予定より短くする yotéi yorī mijíkakū suru

everything short of ...を除いて何でも ...wo nozökte nán de mo

to fall short of ...に達しない ...ni tasshinál

to run short of ...が足りなくなる ...ga tarínakunarū

to stop short (while walking etc) 急に立止まる kyū ni tachidomarū; (while doing something) 急にやめる kyū ni yamerū

to stop short of ...まではしない ...mádě wa shinál

shortage [ʃɔːrtidʒ] *n*: *a shortage of* ...不足 ...busóku

shortbread [ʃɔːrtˈbred] *n* ショートブレッド shōtoburedddō (小麦粉、バター、砂糖で作った菓子 komúgiko, bátā, satō de tsukúttá kashī

short-change [ʃɔːrtˈtʃeindʒ] *vt* ...に約銭を少なく渡す ...ni tsurísen wŏ sukúnakū watásŭ

short-circuit [ʃɔːrtsɑːrkit] *n* (ELEC) ショート shōto

shortcoming [ʃɔːrtˈkʌmiŋ] *n* 欠点 ketten

short(crust) pastry [ʃɔːrtˈkrʌst]-(BRIT) *n* パイ生地 páikijī

shortcut [ʃɔːrtˈkʌt] *n* 近道 chikámichi

shorten [ʃɔːrtən] *vt* (clothes, visit) 短くする mijíkakū suru

shortfall [ʃɔːrtˈfɔːl] *n* 不足 fusóku

shorthand [ʃɔːrtˈhænd] *n* (speed) 速記 sokkí

shorthand typist (BRIT) *n* 速記もできるタイピスト sokkí mo dekírū taípisuto

shortlist [ʃɔːrtˈlist] (BRIT) *n* (for job) 予備審査の合格者リスト yobíshiñsa no gókakushā risúto

short-lived [ʃɔːrtˈlivd] *adj* つかの間のtsuká no ma no

shortly [ʃɔːrtˈliː] *adv* 間もなく ma mŏ nákŭ

shorts [ʃɔːrts] *npl*: *(a pair of) shorts* (short trousers) 半ズボン hañzúbon

(men's underwear) パンツ páñtsu

short-sighted [ʃɔːrtˈsaiˈtid] (BRIT) *adj* 近視の kiñgan no; (fig) 先見の明のないseñken no mei no nai

short-staffed [ʃɔːrtˈstæft] *adj*: *to be short-staffed* 人手不足である hitódebū-soku de aru

short story *n* 短編小説 tañpenshōsetsu

short-tempered [ʃɔːrtˈtempərd] *adj* 短気な tánki na

short-term [ʃɔːrtˈtəːrm] *adj* (effect, borrowing) 短期の tánki no

shortwave [ʃɔːrtˈweiv] *n* (RADIO) 短波 tañpa

shot [ʃɑt] *pt, pp* of **shoot**

♦*n* (of gun) 発砲 happō; (try, *also* SOCCER etc) シュート shúto; (injection) 注射 chūsha; (PHOT) ショット shóttō

a good/poor shot (person) 射撃のうまい(下手な)人 shagéki no umaí (hetá na) hitó

like a shot (without any delay) 鉄砲玉の様に teppődama no yô ni

shotgun [ʃɑtˈgʌn] *n* 散弾銃 sañdañjū

should [ʃud] *aux vb*: *I should go now* もう行かとましなくして も mŏ o-ttoma shina-kute wa

he should be there now 彼は今あそこにいるはずです kárě wa fmá asóko ni irú hazū desu

I should go if I were you 私だったら、行きますよ watákushi dattára, ikímasû yô

I should like to ...をしたいと思いますが ...wo shitái tō omóimasū ga

shoulder [ʃoulˈdər] *n* (ANAT) 肩 kátá

♦*vt* (fig: responsibility, blame) 負う óu

shoulder bag *n* ショルダーバッグ shorúdābaggu

shoulder blade *n* 肩甲骨 keñkōkotsu

shoulder strap *n* ショルダーストラップ shorúdāsutorappū

shouldn't [ʃudˈənt] = **should not**

shout [ʃaut] *n* 叫び声 sakébigoe

♦*vt* 大声で言う ógoě de iú

♦*vi* (*also*: shout out) 叫ぶ sakébu

shout down *vt* (speaker) どなって黙らせる donátte damáraserū

shouting [ʃaut'iŋ] n 叫び声 sakêbigoè

shove [ʃʌv] vt 押す osú; (inf: put): **to shove something in ...を...に押し込む** ...wo...ni oshîkomû

shovel [ʃʌv'əl] n (gen) スコップ sukóppù, シャベル shábèru; (mechanical) パワーシャベル pawáshabèru
♦vt (snow) かく kákû; (coal, earth) すくう sukúû

shove off vi: **shove off!** (inf) うせろ usêro

show [ʃou] n (demonstration: of emotion) 表現 hyôgen; (semblance) 見せ掛け misêkake; (exhibition: flower show etc) 展示会 tenjîkai, ショー shô; (THEATER, TV) ショー shô
♦vb (pt showed, pp shown)
♦vt (indicate) 示す shimésù, 見せる misêru; (exhibit) 展示する tenji suru; (courage etc) 示す shimésù; (illustrate, depict) 描写する byôsha suru; (film: in movie theater) 上映する jôei suru; (program, film: on television) 放送する hôsō suru
♦vi (be evident) 見える miêrù; (appear) 現れる aráwarerù

for show 格好だけの kakkô dake no
on show (exhibits etc) 展示中 tenjîchū

show business n 芸能界 geînōkai

showdown [ʃou'daun] n 対決 taîketsu

shower [ʃau'əːr] n (of rain) にわか雨 niwákaamè; (of stones etc) ...の雨 ...no ámè; (for bathing in) シャワー shâwā
♦vi 浴びてくる futté kurù
♦vt: **to shower someone with** ...の上に...を降らす ...no ué ni...wo furásù
to have a shower シャワーを浴びる shâwā wo abírù

showerproof [ʃau'əːrpruːf] adj 防水の bôsui no にわか雨程度なら耐えられるが強い雨にはぬれてしまうコートなどについて言う niwákaamè tēido nara taérarerù ga tsuyóì amè ni wa nuréteshimaù kôto nado ni tsûite iû

show in vt (person) 中へ案内する nákà e annâi suru

showing [ʃou'iŋ] n (of film) 上映 jôei

show jumping [-dʒʌmp'iŋ] n (of horses) 障害飛越 shôgaihìetsu

shown [ʃoun] pp of show

show off vi (pej) 気取る kidôru
♦vt (display) 見せびらかす misêbirakasù

show-off [ʃou'ɔːf] (inf) n (person) 自慢屋 jimân-ya

show out vt (person) 出口へ案内する dêguchi e annâi suru

showpiece [ʃou'piːs] n (of exhibition etc) 立派な見本 rippá nà mihôn

showroom [ʃou'ruːm] n ショールーム shôrūmu

show up vi (stand out) 目立つ medâtsù; (inf: turn up) 現れる aráwarerù
♦vt (uncover: imperfections etc) 暴露する bákùro suru

shrank [ʃræŋk] pt of shrink

shrapnel [ʃræp'nəl] n 弾丸の破片 dangan no hahén

shred [ʃred] n (gen pl) 切れ端 kiréhashi
♦vt (gen) ずたずたにする zutázuta ni suru; (CULIN) 刻む kizámu

shredder [ʃred'əːr] n (vegetable shredder) 削り器 kezûriki; (document shredder) シュレッダー shúrèddā

shrewd [ʃruːd] adj (businessman) 抜け目のない nukême no naî; (assessment) 賢明な keîmei na

shriek [ʃriːk] n 金切り声 kanákirigoè
♦vi 金切り声を出す kanákirigoè wo dásù

shrill [ʃril] adj (cry, voice) 甲高い kandákai

shrimp [ʃrimp] n (shellfish) えび ebî

shrine [ʃrain] n (place of worship) 礼拝堂 reîhaidō; (for relics) 聖遺物容器 seîbutsuyōki; (fig: building) 殿堂 dendô; (: place) 聖地 seîchi

shrink [ʃriŋk] (pt shrank, pp shrunk) vi (cloth) 縮む chijîmù; (be reduced: profits, audiences) 減る herú; (move: also: **shrink away**) 縮まって逃げる chijîkomattè nigérù
♦vt (cloth) 縮める chijîmerù
♦n (inf: pej: psychiatrist) 精神科医 seíshinka-i
to shrink from (doing) something ...を(するのを)いやがる ...wo (surú no wò) iyágarù

shrinkage [ʃrɪŋ'kɪdʒ] n 縮まる分 chijímarù búñ

shrinkwrap [ʃrɪŋk'ræp] n ラップで包む ráppù de tsutsúmù

shrivel [ʃrɪv'əl] (also: **shrivel up**) vt しおれさせる shióreserù
♦vi しおれる shiórerù

shroud [ʃraud] n 覆い ōi
♦vt: **shrouded in mystery** なぞに包まれて nazó ni tsutsúmarete

Shrove Tuesday n 謝肉祭の火曜日 shaníkusài no kayōbi

shrub [ʃrʌb] n 低木 teíboku

shrubbery [ʃrʌb'əːri] n 植込み uémoki

shrug [ʃrʌg] n 肩をすくめる事 kátà wo sukúmerù kotó
♦vt, vi: **to shrug (one's shoulders)** 肩をすくめる kátà wo sukúmerù
♦**shrug off** vt (criticism) 受流す ukénagasù; (illness) 無視する múshi suru

shrunk [ʃrʌŋk] pp of **shrink**

shudder [ʃʌd'əːr] n 身震い mibúrùi
♦vi (person: with fear, revulsion) 身震いする mibúrùi suru

shuffle [ʃʌf'əl] vt (cards) 混ぜる mazérù
♦vi (walk) 足を引きずって歩く ashí wò hikízutte arukú
to shuffle (one's feet) (while standing, sitting) 足をもぞもぞ動かす ashí wò mózòmozo ugókasù

shun [ʃʌn] vt (publicity, neighbors etc) 避ける sakérù

shunt [ʃʌnt] vt (train) 分岐線に入れる buñkisen ni irerù; (object) 動かす ugókasù

shut [ʃʌt] (pt, pp **shut**) vt (door) 閉める shimérù; (shop) しまう shimáù; (mouth, eyes) 閉じる tojírù
♦vi (door, eyes, shop) 閉る shimárù
♦**shut down** vt (for a time) 休業させる kyūgyō saserù; (forever) 閉鎖する heísa suru
♦vi (for a time) 休業する kyūgyō surù; (forever) 閉鎖になる heísa ni narù
♦**shut off** vt (supply etc) 遮断する shadán suru

shutter [ʃʌt'əːr] n (on window: also PHOT) シャッター sháttà

shuttle [ʃʌt'əl] n (plane etc) シャトル

shátoru; (also: **space shuttle**) スペースシャトル supésushatòru; (also: **shuttle service**) 折り返し運転 oríkaeshi uñten

shuttlecock [ʃʌt'əlkɑːk] n シャトルコック shattórukokkù

shut up vi (inf: keep quiet) 黙る damárù
♦vt (close) しまう shimaù; (silence) 黙らせる damáraserù

shy [ʃai] adj (timid: animal) 臆病な okúbyō na; (reserved) 内気な uchíki na

shyness [ʃai'nis] n (timidity: of animal) 臆病 okúbyō; (reservedness) 内気 uchíki

Siamese [saiamíːz] adj: **Siamese cat** シャムネコ shamúneko

Siberia [saibíːriːə] n シベリア shibéria

sibling [sib'liŋ] n 兄弟 kyōdai ◇男兄弟にも女兄弟 (姉妹) にも使う otókokyōdai (shímài) ní mo tsukáù

Sicily [sis'liː] n シチリア shichíria

sick [sik] adj (ill) 病気の byōki no; (nauseated) むかついた mukátsuita; (humor) 病的な byōteki na; (vomiting): **to be sick** 吐く hákù
to feel sick むかつく mukátsukù
to be sick of (fig) ...にうんざりしている ...ni uñzari shite irù

sick bay n (on ship) 医務室 imúshitsu

sicken [sik'ən] vt むかつかせる mukátsukaserù

sickening [sik'əniŋ] adj (fig) 不快な fukái na

sickle [sik'əl] n かま káma

sickly [sik'liː] adj (child, plant) 病気がちな byóikigachi na; (causing nausea: smell) むかつかせる mukátsukaserù

sickness [sik'nis] n (illness) 病気 byōki; (vomiting) おう吐 ōto

sick pay n 病気手当 byōkiteàte

side [said] n (of object) 側面 yokó; (of body) 脇腹 wakíbara; (of lake) 岸 kishí; (aspect) 側面 sokúmen; (team) side部 bú
♦adj (door, entrance) 横の yokó no
♦vi: **to side with someone** ...の肩を持つ ...no kátà wo mótsù
the side of the road 路肩 rokáta
the side of a hill 山腹 sañpuku
by the side of ...の横に ...no yokó ni

side by side 横に並んで yokó ni naránde

from side to side 左右に sáyū ni

from all sides 四方八方から shihóhappō kara

to take sides (with) (...に)味方する (...ni) mikáta suru

sideboard [said'bɔːrd] *n* 食器戸棚 shokkítodāna, サイドボード saídobòdo

sideboards [said'bɔːrdz] (*BRIT*) *npl* = **sideburns**

sideburns [said'bəːrnz] *npl* もみあげ momíage

side drum *n* (MUS) 小太鼓 kodáíko

side effect *n* (MED, *fig*) 副作用 fukúsayō

sidelight [said'lait] *n* (AUT) 車幅灯 shafúkutō

sideline [said'lain] *n* (SPORT) サイドライン saídorain; (*fig*: supplementary job) 副業 fukúgyō

sidelong [said'lɔːŋ] *adj*: **to give someone/something a sidelong glance** ...を横目で見る ...wo yokóme de mírù

sidesaddle [said'sædəl] *adv*: **to ride sidesaddle** 馬に横乗りする umá ni yokónori surù

side show *n* (stall at fair, circus) 見世物屋台 misémonoyatái

sidestep [said'step] *vt* (*fig*) 避けて通る sakétetōru

side street *n* わき道 wakímíchi

sidetrack [said'træk] *vt* (*fig*): ...の話を脱線させる ...no hanáshi wo dassén saserù

sidewalk [said'wɔːk] (*US*) *n* 歩道 hodō

sideways [said'weiz] *adv* (go in) 横向きに yokómuki ni; (lean) 横へ yokó e

siding [sai'diŋ] *n* (RAIL) 側線 sokúsen

sidle [sai'dəl] *vi*: **to sidle up (to)** (...に) こっそり近寄る (...ni) kossóri chikáyorù

siege [siːdʒ] *n* (gen, MIL) 包囲 hóī

siesta [siːes'tə] *n* 昼寝 hirúne

sieve [siv] *n* ふるい furúi

♦*vt* ふるう furúu

sift [sift] *vt* (*fig*: also: **sift through**: information) ふるい分ける furúiwakerù; (sieve) ふるう furúu

sigh [sai] *n* ため息 taméíki

♦*vi* ため息をつく taméíki wo tsukú

sight [sait] *n* (faculty) 視覚 shikáku; (spectacle) 光景 kókei; (on gun) 照準器 shójunki

in sight 見掛ける mikákerù

in sight 見える所に míerù tokóro ni

on sight (shoot) 見付け次第 mitsúkeshídai

out of sight 見えない所に míenaí tokóro ni

sightseeing [sait'siːiŋ] *n* 名所見物 meíshokenbutsu

to go sightseeing 名所見物に行く meíshokenbutsu ni ikú

sign [sain] *n* (with hand) 合図 áízu; (indication: of present condition) しるし shírūshi; (: of future condition) 兆し kizáshi; (notice) 看板 kanban; (written) 張紙 harígami

♦*vt* (document) ...に署名(サイン)する ...ni shómei (sáīn) suru; (player) 雇う yatóù

to sign something over to someone ...を...に譲渡する ...wo...ni jótò suru

signal [sig'nəl] *n* (gen) 信号 shíngō; (equipment on highway, railway) 信号機 shíngōki

♦*vi* (make signs: also AUT) 合図をする áízu wo suru

♦*vt* (person) ...に合図をする ...ni áízu wo suru; (message) ...する様に合図をする ...suru yó ni aízu wo suru

signalman [sig'nəlmən] (*pl* **signalmen**) *n* (RAIL) 信号手 shíngōshu

signature [sig'nətʃəːr] *n* 署名 shómei, サイン sáīn

signature tune *n* テーマ音楽 têmaongaku

signet ring [sig'nit-] *n* 印章指輪 ínshóyubiwa

significance [signif'əkəns] *n* (importance) 重要性 jūyósei

significant [signif'ikənt] *adj* (full of meaning: look, smile) 意味深い imbukái; (important: amount, discovery) 重要な jūyó na

signify [sig'nəfai] *vt* 意味する ímì suru

sign language *n* 手話 shúwà

sign on vi (MIL) 入隊する nyútai surū; (BRIT: as unemployed) 失業手当を請求する shitsugyōteàte wo seīkyū suru; (for course) 受講手続きをする jukōtetsuzúki wo suru

♦vt (MIL: recruits) 入隊させる nyútai saserū; (employee) 雇う yatoú

signpost [sain'poust] n 案内標識 afinaihyōshiki

sign up vi (MIL) 入隊する nyútai suru; (for course) 受講手続きをする jukōtetsuzúki wo suru

silence [sai'ləns] n (of person) 沈黙 chínmoku; (of place) 静けさ shizúkesà

♦vt (person, opposition) 黙らせる damáraserū

silencer [sai'lənsə:r] n (on gun) 消音器 shōónki, サイレンサー safrenhsà; (BRIT: AUT) 消音器 shōónki, マフラー máfūrā

silent [sai'lənt] adj (person) 黙っている damátte irū; (place) しんとした shíñto shitá; (machine) 音のない otó no naì; (film) 無声の muséi no

to remain silent 黙っている damátte irū

silent prayer 黙とう mokútō

silent partner n (COMM) 出資者 shusshíshà ◇資本金の一部を出すが、業務に直接関与しない社員 shíhoñkin no ichíbù wo dásù ga, gyōmù ni chokúsetsu kañyo shináì sha-ín ni tsuite iú

silhouette [siluet'] n シルエット shírúetto

silicon chip [sil'ikən-] n シリコンチップ shírikonchíppù

silk [silk] n 絹 kínú

♦adj (scarf, shirt) 絹の kínù no

silky [sil'ki:] adj (material, skin) 絹の様な kínù no yō na

silly [sil'i:] adj (person, idea) ばかな bákà na

silo [sai'lou] n (on farm, for missile) サイロ sáîro

silt [silt] n (in harbor, river etc) 沈泥 chíndei

silver [sil'və:r] n (metal) 銀 gíñ; (coins) 硬貨 kōkà; (items made of silver) 銀製品

gifiseíhin

♦adj (color) 銀色の gíñ-iro no; (made of silver) 銀の gíñ no

silver paper (BRIT) n 銀紙 gíñgami

silver-plated [sil'və:rplei'tid] adj 銀めっきの gifimekkí no

silversmith [sil'və:rsmiθ] n 銀細工師 gíñzaikúshì

silvery [sil'və:ri] adj (like silver) 銀の様な gíñ no yō na

similar [sim'ələ:r] adj: **similar (to)** (...に)似た (...ni) nitá

similarity [siməlær'iti:] n 似ている事 nité irū kotó

similarly [sim'ələ:rli:] adv 同じ様に onáji yō ni

simile [sim'əli:] n 例え tatóé

simmer [sim'ə:r] vi (CULIN) ぐつぐつ煮える gútsùgutsu niérù

simpering [sim'pə:riŋ] adj (person) ばかみたいな作り笑いをする bákàmitai na tsukūriwarāi wo surū

a simpering smile ばかみたいな作り笑いbákàmitai na tsukūriwarāi

simple [sim'pəl] adj (easy) 簡単な kañtan na; (plain: dress, life) 素朴な sobôku na, シンプルな shíñpuru na; (foolish) ばかな bákà na; (COMM: interest) 単純な tañjun na

simplicity [simplis'əti:] n (ease) 簡単さ kañtansa; (plainness) 素朴さ sobôkusa; (foolishness) 白痴 hakuchi

simplify [sim'pləfai] vt 簡単にする kañtan ni surú

simply [sim'pli:] adv (in a simple way: live) 素朴に sobôku ni; (talk) 平易に héii ni; (just, merely) 単に tañ ni

simulate [sim'jəleit] vt (enthusiasm, innocence) 装う yosóoù

simulated [sim'jəleitid] adj (hair, fur) 偽の nisé no, 人工の jíñkō no; (nuclear explosion) 模擬の mógi no

simultaneous [saiməltei'ni:əs] adj (translation, broadcast) 同時の dōji no

simultaneously [saiməltei'ni:əsli:] adv 同時に dōji ni

sin [sin] n 罪 tsúmi

♦vi 罪を犯す tsúmi wo okásù

since [sins] adv それ以来 soré irái
♦prep ...以来 ...irái
♦conj (time) ...して以来 ...shité irái;
(because) ...ので ...nóde
since then, ever since それ以来 soré
irái

sincere [sinsí:r'] adj 誠実な seíjitsu na

sincerely [sinsí:r'li:] adv: **yours sincerely** (in letters) 敬具 kéígu

sincerity [sinser'iti:] n 誠実さ seíjitsusa

sinew [sin'ju:] n (of person, animal) けん
kéń, 筋 sújì

sinful [sin'fəl] adj (thought, person) 罪深
い tsumībukaí

sing [siŋ] (pt sang, pp sung) vt 歌う utaú
♦vi (gen) 歌う utaú; (bird) 鳴く nakú

Singapore [siŋ'gəpɔ:r] n シンガポール
shíñgapōru

singe [sinʤ] vt 焦がす kogásu

singer [siŋ'ər] n 歌手 kāshù

singing [siŋ'iŋ] n (noise: of people) 歌声
utágoè; (: of birds) 鳴声 nakígoè, (art) 声
楽 seígaku

single [siŋ'gəl] adj (individual) 一つ一つ
の hítòtsuhitotsu no; (unmarried) 独身の
dokúshin no; (not double) 一つだけの hitótsu dake nò
♦n (BRIT: also: **single ticket**) 片道乗車
券 katámichijōshakèn; (record) シングル
盤 shíñguruban

single-breasted [siŋ'gəlbres'tid] adj
(jacket, suit) シングルの shíñguru no

single file n: **in single file** 一列縦隊で
ichíretsujūtai de

single-handed [siŋ'gəlhæn'did] adv
(sail, shoulder something) 一人で hitórì de

single-minded [siŋ'gəlmain'did] adj 一
つだけの目的を追う hitótsu dake nò mokúteki wò oú

single out vt (choose) 選び出す erábidasù; (distinguish) 区別する kúbetsu suru

single room n シングル部屋 shíñguru-
beya

singles [siŋ'gəlz] n (TENNIS) シングル
ス shíñgurusu

singly [siŋ'gli:] adv (alone, one by one:
people) 一人ずつ hitóri zutsu; (: things)
一つずつ hitótsu zutsu

singular [siŋ'gjəlæ:r] adj (odd: occurrence) 変った kawátta; (outstanding:
beauty) まれに ichíjirushíī; (LING) 単数
の tańsū no
♦n (LING) 単数 tańsū

sinister [sin'istæ:r] adj 怪しげな ayáshige na

sink [siŋk] n 流し nagáshi
♦vb (pt sank, pp sunk)
♦vt (ship) 沈没させる chiñbotsu saserù;
(well, foundations) 掘る hórù
♦vi (ship) 沈没する chiñbotsu suru;
(heart, spirits) しょげる shogérù, がっか
りする gakkárì suru; (ground) 沈下する
chiñka suru; (also: **sink back, sink
down**: into chair) 身を沈める身に身に沈
zúmerù; (: to one's knees etc) しゃがみ込
む shágamikomù; (: head etc) うなだれる
unádarerù

to sink something into (teeth, claws
etc) ...に...を食込ませる ...ni...wo kufíko-
maserù

sink in vi (fig: words) 理解される理解
sarérù, 身に染みる mi ni shimírù

sinner [sin'æ:r] n 罪人 tsumíbìto

sinus [sai'nəs] n (ANAT) 副鼻こう fukú-
bikō

sip [sip] n 一口 hitókùchi
♦vt ちびりちびり飲む chibírichibiri nō-
mù

siphon [sai'fən] n サイホン sáíhon

siphon off vt (liquid) サイホンで汲み出
す sáíhon de kumídasù; (money etc) ほか
へ回す hoká è mawásù

sir [sə:r] n (to man) ...に対する丁寧な呼び
掛け.日本語では表現しない dañsei ni tai
surú teínei na yobíkake. nihóñgo de wa
hyōgen shinaí
 Sir John Smith ジョン・スミス卿 jóñ
sumísukyō
 yes sir はい háî

siren [sai'rən] n サイレン sáíren

sirloin [sə:r'lɔin] n (also: **sirloin steak**)
サーロインステーキ sắroinsutềki

sissy [sis'i:] (inf) n 弱虫 yowámùshi

sister [sis'tə:r] n (relation: gen) 女きょう
だい oñnakyòdai, 姉妹 shímaì; (also:
older sister) 姉 ané, 姉さん nếsan; (also:

younger sister) 妹 imóto; (nun) 修道女 shúdōjo; (BRIT: nurse) 看護婦 kańgòfu

sister-in-law [sis'tərinlɔ:'] (pl **sisters-in-law**) n (older) 義理の姉 girí nò ané; (younger) 義理の妹 girí nò imóto

sit [sit] (pt, pp sat) vi (sit down) 座る suwárù, 腰掛ける koshíkakerù; (be sitting) 座っている suwátte irù, 腰掛けている koshíkakete irù; (assembly) 開会である kaíkaíchū de arù; (for painter) モデルになる módèru ni nárù

◆vt (exam) 受ける ukérù

sitcom [sit'kɑm] n abbr (= situation comedy) 連続放送コメディー refízoku hósókomèdī

sit down vi 座る suwárù, 腰掛ける koshíkakerù

site [sait] n (place) 場所 bashó; (also: **building site**) 用地 yóchì

◆vt (factory, cruise missiles) 置く ókù

sit-in [sit'in] n (demonstration) 座り込み suwárikomi

sit in on vt fus (meeting) 傍聴する bóchō suru

sitting [sit'iŋ] n (of assembly etc) 開会 kaíkai; (in canteen) 食事の時間 shokúji no jíkan

we have two sittings for lunch 昼食は2交代で出されます chūshoku wà nikódai de dasáremasù

sitting room n 居間 imá

situated [sitʃ'ueitid] adj ...にある ...ni árù

situation [sitʃuei'ʃən] n (state) 状況 jókyō; (job) 職 shokú; (location) 立地条件 ritchíjōken

「**situations vacant**」 (BRIT) 求人欄 kyújin ◇新聞などの求人欄のタイトル shínbun nadò no kyújinran no táìtoru

sit up vi (after lying) 上体を起す jótai wò okósù; (straight) きちんと座る kichíñto suwárù; (not go to bed) 起きている ókìte irù

six [siks] num 六 (の) rokú (no), 六つ (の) múttsù (no)

sixteen [siks'ti:n'] num 十六 (の) júroku (no)

sixth [siksθ] num 第六 (の) dáì roku (no)

sixty [siks'ti:] num 六十 (の) rokújù (no)

size [saiz] n (gen) 大きさ ókisa; (extent: of project etc) 規模 kfbò; (of clothing, shoes) サイズ sáìzu; (glue) サイズ sáìzu ◇紙のにじみ止め kamí nò nijímidome

sizeable [sai'zəbəl] adj (crowd, income etc) かなり大きい kánàri ókiì

size up vt (person, situation) 判断する hańdan suru

sizzle [siz'əl] vi (sausages etc) じゅうじゅうと音を立てる jújù to otó wò tatérù

skate [skeit] n (ice skate) スケート sukétò; (roller skate) ローラースケート rórāsukétò; (fish) エイ éì

◆vi スケートをする sukétò wo suru

skateboard [skeit'bɔ:rd] n スケートボード sukétobōdo

skater [skei'tər] n スケートをする人 sukétò wo suru hitò, スケーター sukétā

skating [skei'tiŋ] n (SPORT) スケート sukétò

skating rink n スケートリンク sukétorìñku

skeleton [skel'itən] n (bones) がい骨 gáìkotsu; (TECH: framework) 骨組 honégumì; (outline) 骨子 kósshì

skeleton staff n 最小限度の人員 saíshōgeñdo no jiń-in

skeptic [skep'tik] (US) n 疑い深い人 utágaibukaì hitó

skeptical [skep'tikəl] (US) adj 疑っている utagátte irù, 信用しない shiń-yō shinaì

skepticism [skep'tisizəm] (US) n 疑問 gimón

sketch [sketʃ] n (drawing) スケッチ sukétchì; (outline) 骨子 kósshì; (THEATER, TV) 寸劇 sufígeki, スキット sukíttò

◆vt スケッチする sukétchì suru; (also: **sketch out**: ideas) ...のあらましを言う ...no arámashi wò iú

sketchbook [sketʃ'buk] n スケッチブック sukétchibukkù

sketchy [sketʃ'i:] adj (coverage, notes etc) 大雑把な ózappà na

skewer [skju:'ər] n くし kushí

ski [ski:] *n* スキー sukī
♦*vi* スキーをする sukī wo surù
ski boot *n* スキー靴 sukīgùtsu
skid [skid] *n* (AUT) スリップ surìppù
♦*vi* (*gen*, AUT) スリップする surìppù suru
skier [ski:'ə:r] *n* スキーヤー sukīyà
skiing [ski:'iŋ] *n* スキー sukī
ski jump *n* スキージャンプ sukījañpu
skilful [skil'fəl] (*BRIT*) *adj* = **skillful**
ski lift *n* スキーリフト sukīrifùto
skill [skil] *n* (ability, dexterity) 熟練 jukúren; (work requiring training: computer skill etc) 技術 gíjùtsu
skilled [skild] *adj* (able) 上手な jōzu na; (worker) 熟練の jukúren no
skillful [skil'fəl] (*BRIT*: **skilful**) *adj* 上手な jōzu na
skim [skim] *vt* (milk) ...の上澄みをすくい取る ...no uwázumi wò sukúitorù; (glide over) ...すれすれに飛ぶ ...surésure nì tobú
♦*vi*: *to skim through* (book) ...をざっと読む ...wo záttò yómù
skimmed milk [skimd-] *n* 脱脂乳 dasshínyù
skimp [skimp] *vt* (*also*: **skimp on**: work) いいかげんにする iíkagen nì suru; (: cloth etc) けちる kechírù
skimpy [skim'pi:] *adj* (meager: meal) 少な過ぎる sukúnasugirù; (too small: skirt) 短過ぎる mijíkasugirù
skin [skin] *n* (*gen*: of person, animal) 皮膚 hífù; (: of fruit) 皮 kawá; (complexion) 顔の肌 kaó nò hádà
♦*vt* (fruit etc) ...の皮をむく ...no kawá wò múkù; (animal) ...の皮を剝ぐ ...no kawá wò hágù
skin-deep [skin'di:p'] *adj* (superficial) 表面だけの hyṓmeñ daké no
skin-diving [skin'daiviŋ] *n* スキンダイビング sukíndaìbingu
skinny [skin'i:] *adj* (person) やせた yaséta
skintight [skin'tait] *adj* (jeans etc) 体にぴったりの karáda nì pittárì no
skip [skip] *n* (movement) スキップ sukíppù; (*BRIT*: container) ごみ箱 gomíbàko
♦*vi* (jump) スキップする sukíppù suru; (with rope) 縄跳びする nawátobì suru
♦*vt* (pass over: boring parts) とばす tobásù; (miss: lunch) 抜く nukú; (: lecture) すっぽかす suppókasù
ski pants *npl* スキーズボン sukīzubòn
ski pole *n* スキーストック sukīsutokkù
skipper [skip'ə:r] *n* (NAUT) 船長 señchō; (SPORT) 主将 shushō, キャプテン kyápùten
skipping rope [skip'iŋ-] (*BRIT*) *n* 縄跳の縄 nawátobi nò nawá
skirmish [skə:r'miʃ] *n* (*also* MIL) こぜりあい kozérìai
skirt [skə:rt] *n* スカート sukā́tò
♦*vt* (*fig*: go round) 避けて通る sákète tṓrù
skirting board [skə:r'tiŋ-] (*BRIT*) *n* 幅木 habáki
ski slope *n* ゲレンデ gerénde
ski suit *n* スキー服 sukīfùku
skit [skit] *n* スキット sukíttò
skittle [skit'əl] *n* スキットルのピン sukíttòru no píñ
skittles [skit'əlz] *n* (game) スキットル sukíttòru ◊9本のピンを木のボールで倒すボーリングに似た遊び kyū́hòn no píñ wo kí no bṑru de taosu bōringu ni nita asobì
skive [skaiv] (*BRIT*: *inf*) *vi* サボる sabórù
skulk [skʌlk] *vi* うろつく urótsukù
skull [skʌl] *n* (ANAT) 頭がい骨 zugáìkotsu
skunk [skʌŋk] *n* (animal) スカンク sukáñku
sky [skai] *n* 空 sórà
skylight [skai'lait] *n* 天窓 teñmado
skyscraper [skai'skreipə:r] *n* 摩天楼 maténrō
slab [slæb] *n* (stone) 石板 sekíban; (of cake, cheese) 厚い一切れ atsúi hitokìre
slack [slæk] *adj* (loose: rope, trousers etc) たるんでいる tarúnde irù; (slow: period) 忙しくない isógashikunaì; (careless: security, discipline) いい加減な iíkagen na
slacken [slæk'ən] (*also*: **slacken off**) *vi*

(demand) 減る herú; (speed) 落ちる ochírù

◆vt (trousers) 緩める yurúmerù; (speed) 緩める yurúmerù, 落とす otósù

slacks [slæks] npl ズボン zubóñ, スラックス surákkùsu

slag heap [slæg-] n ぼた山 botáyama

slag off (BRIT: inf) vt (criticize) …の悪口を言う …no warúgùchi wo iú

slain [slein] pp of slay

slalom [slɑː'ləm] n 回転競技 kaíteñkyō-gi, スラローム surárōmu

slam [slæm] vt (door) ばたんと閉める batáñ to shimérù; (throw) 投げつける nagétsukerù; (criticize) 非難する hínàn suru

◆vi (door) ばたんと閉まる batáñ to shimárù

slander [slæn'dər] n 中傷 chūshō

slang [slæŋ] n (informal language) 俗語 zokûgo, スラング suráñgu; (jargon: prison slang etc) 符丁 fuchō

slant [slænt] n (sloping: position) 傾斜 keísha; (fig: approach) 見方 mikáta

slanted [slæn'tid] adj (roof) 傾斜のある keísha no arú; (eyes) つり上った tsurfa-gattà

slanting [slæn'tiŋ] adj = slanted

slap [slæp] n (hit) 平手打ち hiráteuchi, びんた bíñta

◆vt (child, face) ぴしゃりと打つ pishárì to útsù

◆adv (directly) まともに matómo ní

to slap something on something (paint etc) …を…にいい加減に塗り付ける …wo …ni ifkagen ní nurítsukerù

slapdash [slæp'dæʃ] adj (person, work) いい加減な ifkagen na

slapstick [slæp'stik] n (comedy) どたばた喜劇 dotábata kigèki

slap-up [slæp'ʌp] adj: *a slap-up meal* (BRIT) 御馳走 gochísō

slash [slæʃ] vt (cut: upholstery, wrists etc) 切る kírù (特に長くて深い切傷を付けるという意味を含う tōkú ni nagákute fukáì kiríkìzu wo tsukérù to iú imì de tsukáù); (fig: prices) 下げる sagérù

slat [slæt] n (of wood, plastic) 板片 ↔百葉箱に使われる様な薄くて細い板を指す

hyakúyōbàko ni tsukáwareru yō na usúkùte hosói ità wo sásù

slate [sleit] n (material) 粘板岩 neñbangan; (piece: for roof) スレート surēto

◆vt (fig: criticize) けなす keñású

slaughter [slɔː'tər] n (of animals) と殺 tosátsu; (of people) 虐殺 gyakúsatsu

◆vt (animals) と殺する tosátsu suru; (people) 虐殺する gyakúsatsu suru

slaughterhouse [slɔː'tərhaus] n と殺場 tosátsujō

Slav [slɑːv] adj スラブ民族の surábumiñzoku no

slave [sleiv] n 奴隷 doréi

◆vi (also: **slave away**) あくせく働く ákùseku határakù

slavery [slei'vəːri] n (system) 奴隷制度 doréiseìdo; (condition) 奴隷の身分 doréi no míbùn

slavish [slei'viʃ] adj (obedience) 卑屈な hikútsu na; (copy) 盲目的な mōmokuteki na

slay [slei] (pt slew, pp slain) vt 殺す korósù

sleazy [sliː'ziː] adj (place) 薄汚い usúgitanal

sledge [sledʒ] n そり sórì

sledgehammer [sledʒ'hæmər] n 大づち ōzúchì

sleek [sliːk] adj (shiny, smooth: hair, fur etc) つやつやの tsuyátsuyà no; (car, boat etc) 優雅な yūga na

sleep [sliːp] n 睡眠 suímiñ

◆vi (pt, pp **slept**) (gen) 眠る nemúrù, 寝る nerú; (spend night) 泊る tomárù

to go to sleep (person) 眠る nemúrù, 寝る nerú

sleep around vi 色々な人とセックスをする iróiro na hito tò sékkùsu wo suru

sleeper [sliː'pəːr] (BRIT) n (RAIL: on track) まくら木 makúragi; (: train) 寝台列車 shiñdaíressha

sleep in vi (oversleep) 寝坊する nebō suru

sleeping bag [sliː'piŋ-] n 寝袋 nebúkùro

sleeping car n (RAIL) 寝台車 shiñdaíshà

sleeping partner (BRIT) n (COMM)

= silent partner

sleeping pill n 睡眠薬 suímiñ-yaku

sleepless [sliːpˈlis] adj: *a sleepless night* 眠れない夜 nemúrenai yorù

sleepwalker [sliːpˈwɔːkər] n 夢遊病者 muyúbyōshá

sleepy [sliːˈpiː] adj (person) 眠い nemúi; (fig: village etc) ひっそりとした hissórì to shita

sleet [sliːt] n みぞれ mizóre

sleeve [sliːv] n (of jacket etc) そで sodé; (of record) ジャケット jákètto

sleeveless [sliːvˈlis] adj (garment) そでなしの sodénashì no, スリーブレスの suríburèsu no

sleigh [slei] n そり sórì

sleight [slait] n: *sleight of hand* 奇術 kíjùtsu

slender [slenˈdəːr] adj (slim: figure) ほっそりした hossórì shita, スリムな suríumuliu, (waall: means, majority) わずかな wázùka na

slept [slept] pt, pp of **sleep**

slew [sluː] vi (BRIT) = **slue**
  ♦pt of **slay**

slice [slais] n (of meat, bread, lemon) スライス surálsu; (utensil: fish slice) フライ返し furáigaèshi; (: cake slice) ケーキサーバー kékìsābā
  ♦vt (bread, meat etc) スライスする surálsu suru

slick [slik] adj (skillful: performance) 鮮やかな azáyàka na; (clever: salesman, answer) 抜け目のない nukéme no naì
  ♦n (also: **oil slick**) 油膜 yumáku

slid [slid] pt, pp of **slide**

slide [slaid] n (downward movement) 下落 geráku; (in playground) 滑り台 subéridài; (PHOT) スライド suráido; (BRIT: also: **hair slide**) 髪留 kamídòme, ヘアクリップ heákurìppu
  ♦vb (pt, pp **slid**)
  ♦vt 滑らせる subéraserù
  ♦vi (slip) 滑る subérù; (glide) 滑る様に動く subéru yō ni ugókù

slide rule n 計算尺 kefsanjaku

sliding [slaiˈdiŋ] adj: *sliding door* 引戸 hikídò

sliding scale n スライド制 suráidosei

slight [slait] adj (slim: figure) やせ型の yaségata no; (frail) か弱い kayówaì; (small: increase, difference) わずかな wázùka na; (error, accent, pain etc) ちょっとした chóttò shita; (trivial) ささいな sásài na
  ♦n (insult) 侮辱 bujóku

not in the slightest 少しも...ない sukóshì mo ...naì

slightly [slaitˈliː] adv (a bit, rather) 少し sukóshì

slim [slim] adj (person, figure) ほっそりした hossórì shita; (chance) わずかな wázùka na
  ♦vi (lose weight) やせる yasérù

slime [slaim] n ぬるぬるした物 núrùnuru shita monó

slimming [slimˈiŋ] n (losing weight) そう身 sóshin

slimy [slaiˈmiː] adj (pond) ぬるぬるした物に覆われた núrùnuru shita monó nì úwareta

sling [sliŋ] n (MED) 三角きん aǹkákùkin, (for baby) 子守り帯 komóriobì; (weapon) 石投げ器 ishínagekì
  ♦vt (pt, pp **slung**) (throw) 投げる nagérù

slip [slip] n (while walking) 踏外し fumíhazushi; (of vehicle) スリップ suríppù; (mistake) 過ち ayámachì; (underskirt) スリップ suríppù; (also: **slip of paper**) 一枚の紙 ichímaì no kamí 0 通常メモ用紙, 伝票などの様な小さい紙を指す通常 memóyòshi, defpyó nadò no yō nì chfsáì kamí wò sásù
  ♦vt (slide) こっそり...を...にやる kossórì ...wo ...ni yarú
  ♦vi (slide) 滑る subérù; (lose balance) 踏外す fumíhazusù; (decline) 悪くなる wárùku nárù; (move smoothly): *to slip into/out of* (room etc) そっと...を(出て行く) sottó háirù (détè iku)

to give someone the slip をまく ...wo mákù

a slip of the tongue うっかり言ってしまう事 ukkárì itté shimaù kotó

to slip something on/off さっと...を脱ぐ[着る] sáttò ...wo kírù (nugu)

slip away vi (go) そっと立ち去る sóttò tachísaru

slip in vt (put) こっそり入れる kossórī irérù
♦vi (errors) いつの間にか入ってしまう ítsu no ma ni kà haítte shimaù

slip out vi (go out) そっと出て行く sóttò détè ikù

slipped disc [slipt-] n つい間板ヘルニア tsuíkànbanherunìa

slipper [slip'ər] n (carpet slipper) スリッパ suríppà

slippery [slip'ə:ri:] adj (road) 滑りやすい subériyasuî; (fish etc) つかみにくい tsukámīnikuî

slip road (BRIT) n (on motorway: access road) 入路 nyúro; (: exit road) 出口 deguchi

slipshod [slip'ʃɑd] adj いい加減な ifkagen na

slip up vi (make mistake) 間違いをする machígai wo surù

slip-up [slip'ʌp] n (error) 間違い machígaì

slipway [slip'wei] n 造船台 zósendaì

slit [slit] n (cut) スリット surítto; (opening) すき間 sukíma
♦vt (pt, pp slit) 切り開く kiríhiraku

slither [sliθ'ə:r] vi (person) 足を取られながら歩く ashí wò torárenagara arukù; (snake etc) はう háù

sliver [sliv'ə:r] n (of glass, wood) 破片 hahén; (of cheese etc) 一切れ hitókìre

slob [slɑb] (inf) n (man) だらしない野郎 daráshinaì yaró; (woman) だらしないあま daráshinaì áma

slog [slɑg] (BRIT) vi (work hard) あくせく働く ákùseku határakù
♦n: it was a hard slog 苦労した kuró shita

slogan [slou'gən] n スローガン surógan

slop [slɑp] vi (also: **slop over**) こぼれる kobóreru
♦vt こぼす kobósù

slope [sloup] n (gentle hill) 坂道 sakámichi; (side of mountain) 山腹 sańpuku; (ski slope) ゲレンデ gerénde; (slant) 傾斜 keísha

♦vi: to slope down 下り坂になる kudárizaka ni narù

slope up vi 上り坂になる nobórizaka ni narù

sloping [slou'piŋ] adj (ground, roof) 傾斜になっている keísha ni natte irù; (handwriting) 斜めの naname no

sloppy [slɑp'i:] adj (work, appearance) だらしない daráshinaì

slot [slɑt] n (in machine) 投入口 tónyuguchi, スロット suróttò
♦vt: to slot something into ... (のスロットなど) に ... を入れる ... no suróttò nado) ni ... wo irérù

sloth [slɔːθ] n (laziness) 怠惰 táìda

slot machine n (BRIT: vending machine) 自動販売機 jidóhanbaìkì; (for gambling) スロットマシーン suróttomashìn

slouch [slautʃ] vi: to slouch (person) だらしない姿勢で...する daráshinaì shiséi dè ... surù

slovenly [slʌv'ənli:] adj (dirty: habits, conditions) 汚い kitánaì; (careless: piece of work) だらしない daráshinaì

slow [slou] adj (music, journey) ゆっくりした yukkúrī shita; (service: 遅い osóì, のろい noróì; (person: not clever) 物覚えの悪い monóobòe no warúì; (watch, clock): to be slow 遅れている okúrete irù
♦adv ゆっくりと yukkúrī to, 遅く osókù
♦adv (also: **slow down**, **slow up**: vehicle) ...no supído wo otósù; (: business etc) 低速させる teímei saserù
♦vt (also: **slow down**, **slow up**: vehicle) スピードを落す supído wo otósù; (: business etc) 下火になる shitábi nī narù
「slow」(road sign) 徐行 jokó

slowly [slou'li:] adv ゆっくりと yukkúrī to, 遅く osókù

slow motion n: in slow motion スローモーションで surómoshon de

sludge [slʌdʒ] n (mud) ヘドロ hedóro

slue [slu:] (US veer) vi スリップする suríppů suru

slug [slʌg] n (creature) なめくじ namékujì; (bullet) 弾丸 dangan, 鉄砲玉 teppódama

sluggish [slʌg'iʃ] *adj* (stream, engine, person) 緩慢な kañman na; (COMM: trading) 不活発な fukáppatsu na

sluice [slu:s] *n* (*also*: **sluicegate**) 水門 suímon; (channel) 水路 súìro

slum [slʌm] *n* (house) 汚い家 kitánaì ié; (area) 貧民街 hiñmiñgai, スラム súràmu

slump [slʌmp] *n* (economic) 不景気 fukéìki; (COMM) スランプ suráñpu

♦*vi* (fall: person) 崩れ落ちる kuzúreochirù; (: prices) 暴落する bṓraku suru

slung [slʌŋ] *pt, pp of* **sling**

slur [slə:r] *n* (*fig*): ***slur (on)*** (...の)悪口 (...no) warúkùchi

♦*vt* (words) 口ごもって言う kuchígomottè iú

slush [slʌʃ] *n* (melted snow) 溶けかかった雪 tokékakattà yukí

slush fund *n* 裏金用資金 uráganeyōshikiñ

slut [slʌt] (*inf!*) *n* ばいた baítà

sly [slai] *adj* (smile, expression, remark) 意味ありげな imíarige na; (person: clever, wily) ずるい zurúì

smack [smæk] *n* (slap) 平手打ち hiráteuchi; (on face) びんた bíñta

♦*vt* (hit: *gen*) 平手で打つ hiráte dè útsù; (: child) ぶつ bútsù; (: on face) ...にびんたを食らわす ...ni bíñta wo kurawásù

♦*vi*: ***to smack of*** (smell of) ...くさい ...kusáì; (remind one of) ...を思わせる ...wo omówaserù

small [smɔ:l] *adj* (person, object) 小さい chiísaì; (child: young) 幼い osánaì; (quantity, amount) 少しの sukóshì no

small ads (*BRIT*) *npl* 分類広告 buñruikṑkoku

small change *n* 小銭 kozéni

small fry *npl* (unimportant people) 下っ端 shitáppa

smallholder [smɔ:l'houldə:r] (*BRIT*) *n* 小自作農 shṓjisakunṑ

small hours *npl*: ***in the small hours*** 深夜に shíñya ni

smallpox [smɔ:l'pɑ:ks] *n* 天然痘 teñneñtō

small talk *n* 世間話 sekéñbanàshi

smart [smɑ:rt] *adj* (neat, tidy) きちんとした kichíñ to shitá; (fashionable: clothes etc) しゃれた sharéta, いきな ikí na, スマートな sumā̀tò na; (: house, restaurant) しゃれた shareta, 高級な kṓkyū na; (clever) 頭がいい atáma ga iì; (quick) 早い hayáì

♦*vi* しみる shimírù; (*fig*) 悔しがる kuyáshigarù

smarten up [smɑ:r'tən-] *vi* 身なりを直す mínàri wo naósù

♦*vt* きれいにする kírèi ni suru

smash [smæʃ] *n* (collision: *also*: **smash-up**) 衝突 shṓtotsu; (smash hit) 大ヒット daíhittò

♦*vt* (break) めちゃめちゃに壊す mechámecha nì kowásù; (car etc) 衝突してめちゃめちゃにする shṓtotsu shitè mechámecha ni surù; (SPORT: record) 破る yabúrù

♦*vi* (break) めちゃめちゃに壊れる mechámecha nì kowárerù; (against wall etc) 激突する gekítotsu suru

smashing [smæʃ'iŋ] (*inf*) *adj* 素晴らしい subárashiì

smattering [smæt'ə:riŋ] *n*: ***a smattering of*** ...をほんの少し ...wo hoñno sukoshì

smear [smi:'ə:r] *n* (trace) 染み shimí; (MED) スミア sumíà

♦*vt* (spread) 塗る nurú; (make dirty) 汚す yogósù

smear campaign *n* 中傷作戦 chū́shōsakuseñ

smell [smel] *n* (odor) におい nióì; (sense) 臭覚 kyū́kaku

♦*vb* (*pt, pp* **smelt** *or* **smelled**)

♦*vt* (become aware of odor) ...のにおいがする ...no nioi ga suru; (sniff) かぐ kagú

♦*vi* (*pej*) におう nióù, 臭い kusáì; (food etc) ...においがする ...nióì ga suru

to smell of ...のにおいがする ...no nióì ga suru

smelly [smel'i:] *adj* (cheese, socks) 臭い kusáì

smile [smail] *n* ほほえみ hohóemi

♦*vi* ほほえむ hohóemù

smirk [smə:rk] *n* にやにや笑い niyániya warái

smithy [smíθi:] *n* 鍛冶屋の仕事場 kajíya no shigótoba

smock [smɑːk] *n* (gen) 上っ張り uwáppari; (children's) スモック sumókkù; (US: overall) 作業着 sagyógi

smog [smɑːg] *n* スモッグ sumóggù

smoke [smouk] *n* 煙 kemúri
♦*vi* (person) タバコを吸う tabáko wò súù; (chimney) 煙を出す kemúri wò dásù
♦*vt* (cigarettes) 吸う súù

smoked [smoukt] *adj* (bacon etc) 燻製の kuńsei no; (glass) いぶした ibúshita

smoker [smou'kɑ:r] *n* (person) タバコを吸う人 tabáko wò súù hitò, 喫煙者 kitsúeñsha; (RAIL) 喫煙車 kitsúeñsha

smokescreen [smouk'skri:n] *n* (also fig) 煙幕 eñmaku

smoking [smou'kiŋ] *n* (act) 喫煙 kitsúen
「no smoking」 (sign) 禁煙 kiń-en

smoky [smou'ki:] *adj* (atmosphere, room) 煙い kemúi; (taste) 燻製の（様な） kuńsei no (yô na)

smolder [smoul'dɑːr] (US) *vi* (fire: also fig: anger, hatred) くすぶる kusúburù

smooth [smuːð] *adj* (gen) 滑らかな namérāka na; (sauce) つぶつぶのない tsubútsubu no nai; (flat: sea) 穏やかな odáyāka na; (flavor, whisky) まろやかな maróyāka na; (movement) 滑らかな namérāka na; (pej: person) 口先のうまい kuchísaki nò umái
♦*vt* (also: **smooth out**: skirt, piece of paper etc) ...のしわを伸ばす ...no shiwá wò nobásù; (: creases) 伸ばす nobásù; (: difficulties) 取除く torínozokù

smother [smʌð'ɑːr] *vt* (fire) ...を...をかぶせて消す ...ni ...wo kabúsete kesù; (suffocate: person) 窒息させる chissóku saserù; (repress: emotions) 抑える osáerù

smoulder [smoul'dɑːr] (BRIT) *vi* = **smolder**

smudge [smʌdʒ] *n* 汚れ yogóre
♦*vt* 汚す yogósù

smug [smʌg] *adj* 独り善がりの hitóriyogàri no

smuggle [smʌg'əl] *vt* (diamonds etc) 密

輸する mitsúyu suru; (refugees) 密入国させる mitsúnyūkoku saserù

smuggler [smʌg'lɑːr] *n* 密輸者 mitsúyu-sha

smuggling [smʌg'liŋ] *n* (traffic) 密輸 mitsúyu

smutty [smʌt'i:] *adj* (fig: joke, book) わいせつな wafsetsu na

snack [snæk] *n* (light meal) 軽食 kefshoku; (food) スナック sunákkù

snack bar *n* スナックバー sunákkubà, スナック sunákkù

snag [snæg] *n* 障害 shôgai

snail [sneil] *n* カタツムリ katátsumùri ◇ 一般に水生の貝類を一般に ippán nì suísei nò makígai wo mo sásù

snake [sneik] *n* (gen) ヘビ hébì

snap [snæp] *n* (sound) ぱちっという音 pachítto iú oto; (photograph) 写真 shashín
♦*adj* (decision etc) 衝動的な shôdôteki na
♦*vt* (break) 折る órù; (fingers) 鳴らす narásù
♦*vi* (break) 折れる orérù; (fig: person: speak sharply) 辛らつな事を言う shifrātsu na kotò wo iú
to snap shut (trap, jaws etc) がちゃっと閉まる gacháttò shimárù

snap at *vt fus* (subj: dog) かみつこうとする kamítsukð to suru

snap off *vt* (break) 折れる orérù ◇折れ て取れる場合に使う órète torérù baái nì tsukáð

snappy [snæp'i:] (inf) *adj* (answer, slogan) 威勢のいい iséi no ìì
make it snappy (hurry up) 早くしなさい háyàku shinásaì

snapshot [snæp'ʃɑːt] *n* 写真 shashín

snap up *vt* (bargains) すばやく買う súgù káù

snare [sneːr] *n* わな wánà

snarl [snɑːrl] *vi* (animal) うなる unárù; (person) どなる donárù

snatch [snætʃ] *n* (small piece of conversation, song etc) 断片 dañpeñ
♦*vt* (snatch away: handbag, child etc) ひったくる hittákurù; (fig: opportunity) 利用する riyô suru; (: look, some sleep etc)

急いでやる isóide yarú

sneak [sniːk] (pt, pp **sneaked** also US **snuck**) vi: **to sneak in/out** こっそり入る(出る) kossóri háiru (deru)

♦n (inf) 告げ口するひと tsugéguchi suru hitó

to sneak up on someone ...に忍び寄る ...ni shinóbiyorù

sneakers [sniː'kɔːrz] npl 運動靴 uñdōgutsu, スニーカー suníkā

sneer [sniːr] vi (laugh nastily) 冷笑する reíshō suru; (mock): **to sneer at** ...をあざわらう ...wo azáwarau

sneeze [sniːz] n くしゃみ kushámi

♦vi くしゃみをする kushámi wo suru

sniff [snif] n (sound) 鼻をくんくん鳴らす音 haná wo kúñkun narásù otó; (smell: by dog, person) くんくんかぐ鼻の... kagú kotó

♦vi (person: when crying etc) 鼻をくんくん鳴らす haná wo kúñkun narásù

♦vt (gen) かぐ kagú; (glue, drugs) 鼻で吸う haná de súù

snigger [snig'ɔːr] vi くすくす笑う kúsùkusu waráū

snip [snip] n (cut) はさみで切る事 hasámi de kírù kotó; (BRIT: inf: bargain) 掘出し物 horídashimonó

♦vt (cut) はさみで切る hasámi de kírù

sniper [snai'pɔːr] n 狙撃兵 sogékihèi

snippet [snip'it] n (of information, news) 断片 dañpen

snivelling [sniv'əliŋ] adj (whimpering) めそめそ泣く mésòmeso nakú

snob [snɑːb] n 俗物 zokúbutsu

snobbery [snɑːb'əːriː] n 俗物根性 zokúbutsukoñjō

snobbish [snɑːb'iʃ] adj 俗物的な zokúbutsuteki na

snooker [snuk'ɔːr] n ビリヤード birīyādo

snoop [snuːp] vi: **to snoop about** こそこそのぞき回る kosósorì nozókimawarù

snooty [snuː'tiː] adj (person, letter, reply) 横柄な ōhèi na

snooze [snuːz] n 昼寝 hirúne

♦vi 昼寝する hirúne suru

snore [snɔːr] vi いびき ibíki

♦vi いびきをかく ibíki wo kákù

snorkel [snɔːr'kəl] n (for swimming) シュノーケル shunókèru

snort [snɔːrt] n 鼻を鳴らす事 haná wo narásù koto

♦vi (animal, person) 鼻を鳴らす haná wo narásù

snout [snaut] n ふん fúñ

snow [snou] n 雪 yukí

♦vi 雪が降る yukí gà fúrù

snowball [snou'bɔːl] n 雪のつぶて yukí nò tsubúte

♦vi (fig: problem, campaign) どんどん大きくなる dóñdon ōkìku nárù

snowbound [snou'baund] adj (people) 雪に閉じ込められた yukí ni tojfkomerarèta; (vehicles) 雪で立ち往生した yukí dè tachíōjō shita

snowdrift [snou'drift] n 雪の吹きだまり yukí nò fukídamarì

snowdrop [snou'drɑːp] n 雪の花 yukí no haná

snowfall [snou'fɔːl] n (amount) 降雪量 kōsetsuryō; (a fall of snow) 降雪 kōsetsu

snowflake [snou'fleik] n 雪のひとひら yukí nò hitóhira

snowman [snou'mæn] (pl **snowmen**) n 雪だるま yukídaruma

snowplow [snou'plau] (BRIT **snowplough**) n 除雪車 josétsushà

snowshoe [snou'ʃuː] n かんじき kañjiki

snowstorm [snou'stɔːrm] n 吹雪 fúbùki

snub [snʌb] vt (person) 鼻であしらう haná dè ashíraù

♦n 侮辱 bujóku

snub-nosed [snʌb'nouzd] adj 鼻先の反った hanásaki nò sottá

snuck [snʌk] (US) pt, pp of **sneak**

snuff [snʌf] n かぎタバコ kagítabàko

snug [snʌg] adj (sheltered: person, place) こじんまりした kojfnmari shita; (person) 心地好い kokóchiyoi; (well-fitting) ぴったりした pittárì shita

snuggle [snʌg'əl] vi: **to snuggle up to someone** ...に体を擦り付ける ...ni karáda wo surítsukerù

KEYWORD

so [sou] *adv* **1** (thus, likewise) そう số, そ
の通り sonó tồri

so saying he walked away そう言って
彼は歩き去った số itté kárè wa arúki-
sattà

*while she was so doing, he ... 彼女が
それをやっている間彼は... kánòjo ga sa-
ré wò yatté irú aìda kárè wa...

if so だとすれば dá tò sureba

*do you enjoy soccer? if so, come to
the game* フットボールは好きですか、
だったら試合を見に来て下さい futtbố-
ru ga sukí desu ká, dáttara shiái wò mi
ní kìtc kudnsaï

I didn't do it - you did so! やったの
は私じゃない、お前だ yatta no wa
watákushi ja naì —iyá, omáe dá

so do I, so am I etc 私もそうです watakushi mô sô desu

I like swimming - so do I 私は水泳が
好きです-私もそうです watákushi wà
sufei ga sukí desu -watákushi mô sô
desu

I'm still at school - so am I 私はまだ
学生です-私もそうです watákushi wà
máda gakúsei desu -watákushi mô sô
desu

I've got work to do - so has Paul 私
には仕事がありますが—ポールもそうで
すよ watákushi ni wà shigoto ga arímasu karà –pôru mo sô desù yô

it's 5'o'clock - so it is! 5時です—あっ、
そうですね gójì desu –ât, sô desu né

I hope so そう希望します số kibô shi-
masu

I think so そうだと思います sô da tò
omóimasū

so far これまで koré made

how do you like the book so far? こ
れまでの本はどうでしたか koré made
sonô hon wa dô deshita ka

so far I haven't had any problems
ここまでは問題はありません kokó made
wa mofidai wà arimaseñ

2 (in comparisons etc: to such a degree)
そんなに sofina nì

so quickly (that) (...がある程) 素早
く (...ga áru hodo) subáyàku, とても素早
く (...したので...) totémo subáyàku
(...shitá no dè ...)

so big (that) (...がある程) 大きな
(...ga árù hodo) ôkina, とても大きい (の
で...) totémo ôkii (nó dè ...)

she's not so clever as her brother 彼
女は兄さん程利口ではない kánòjo wa
nífsañ hodo rîkô de wa naï

we were so worried 私たちはとても心
配していましたよ watákushitàchi wa totémo shiñpai shite imashìta yô

I wish you weren't so clumsy あなた
の不器用さはどうにかなりませんか a-
nátà no bukíyôsà wa dố ni ka narímasen
kå né

I'm so glad to see you あなたを見てほ
っとしました anátà wo mîtè hôttô shimashìta

3: so much *adv* そんなに沢山で sofina nì
takúsan de

♦*adj* そんなに沢山の sofina nì takúsan
de

I've got so much work 私は仕事が山程
あります watákushi wà shigóto ga yamá
hodô arímasu

I love you so much あなたを心から愛
しています anátà wo kokórô kara âï
shite imasu

there are so many things to do する
事が山程あります surú kotò ga yamá
hodô arímasu

there are so many people to meet 私
が会うべき人は余りにも大勢です
watákushi gà ôubeki hitótàchi wa amári ni mô ôzei desù (phrases): *10 or so*
10個ぐらい jùkkô gurai

so long! (*inf*: goodbye) じゃね jã nè, ま
たね matã nè

♦*conj* **1** (expressing purpose): *so as to
do* ...する様(ため)に ...surú yồ(tamê)ni

we hurried so as not to be late 遅れ
ない様に急いで行きました okúrenai yố
ni isôtde ikímashìta

so (that) ...する様(ため)に...surú yồ

〔tamé〕ni

I brought it so (that) you could see it あなたに見せるために持ってきましたんだので見えるように kárè ga kónakatta nó de watákushi wà kaérimashíta

2 (expressing result) ...であるから...... de árù kara ..., ...のので ...のnó de ...

he didn't arrive so I left 彼が来なかったので私は帰りました kárè ga kónakatta nó de watákushi wà kaérimashíta

so I was right after all 結局私の言った通りでした kekkyókù watákushi nò ittá tòri deshita

so you see, I could have gone ですからね、行こうと思えば行けたんです kara né, ikô tò omóèba ikétaん desù

---

soak [souk] *vt* (drench) ずぶぬれにする zubúnure ni suru; (steep in water) 水に漬ける mízú ni tsukéru
◆*vi* (dirty washing, dishes) 漬かる tsukárù

soak in *vi* (be absorbed) 染み込む shimíkomù

soak up *vt* (absorb) 吸収する kyúshú ni suru

soap [soup] *n* 石けん sekkén

soapflakes [soup'fleiks] *npl* フレーク石けん furékùsekkén ◇洗濯用の固形石けんをフレークにした物を指す sefitakuyô no kokéisekkén wo furékù ni shitá monò wo sásù

soap opera *n* メロドラマ meródorama ◇テレビやラジオの連続物を指す térèbi ya rájìo no reñzokumonò wo sásù

soap powder *n* 粉石けん konásekkén

soapy [sou'pi:] *adj* (hands etc) 石けんのついた sekkén no tsuità
soapy water 石けん水 sekkénsui

soar [sɔːr] *vi* (on wings) 舞い上がる maíagarù; (rocket) 空中に上がる kúchú ni agárù; (price, production, temperature) 急上昇する kyú{jó}shó suru; (building etc) そびえ立つ sobíetatsù

sob [sɑːb] *n* しゃくり泣き shakúrinaki
◆*vi* 泣きじゃくる nakíjakurù

sober [sou'bə:r] *adj* (serious) まじめな majímè na; (dull: color, style) 地味な ji-

mí na; (not drunk) しらふの shírafu no

sober up *vt* ...の酔いを覚ます ...no yoí wò samásù
◆*vi* 酔いが覚める yoí ga samérù

so-called [sou'kɔːld'] *adj* (friend, expert) いわゆる iwáyurù ◇多くの場合不信や軽べつなどを表す ôkù no baái fushín yà kefbetsu nadò wo aráwasù

soccer [sɑːk'əːr] *n* サッカー sákkà

sociable [sou'ʃəbəl] *adj* 愛想の良い aísò no yoí

social [sou'ʃəl] *adj* (gen: history, structure, background) 社会の shakái no; (leisure: event, life) 社交的な shakóteki na; (sociable: animal) 社会性のある shakáisei no arú
◆*n* (party) 懇親会 koñshinkai

social club *n* 社交クラブ shakókurabu

socialism [sou'ʃəlizəm] *n* 社会主義 shakáishugí

socialist [sou'ʃəlist] *adj* 社会主義の shakáishugí no
◆*n* 社会主義者 shakáishugisha

socialize [sou'ʃəlaiz] *vi*: *to socialize (with)* (...と) 交際する (...to) kôsai suru

socially [sou'ʃəli:] *adv* (visit) 社交的に shakóteki ni; (acceptable) 社会的に shakáiteki ni

social security (*BRIT*) *n* 社会保障 shakáihoshō

social work *n* ソーシャルワーク sôsharuwàku

social worker *n* ソーシャルワーカー sôsharuwàkà

society [səsai'əti:] *n* (people, their lifestyle) 社会 shakái; (club) 会 káì; (*also*: *high society*) 上流社会 jôryúshakai

sociologist [sousi:ɑːl'ədʒist] *n* 社会学者 shakáigakùsha

sociology [sousi:ɑːl'ədʒi:] *n* 社会学 shakáigaku

sock [sɑːk] *n* 靴下 kutsúshita

socket [sɑːk'it] *n* (gen: cavity) 受け口 ukéguchi; (ANAT: of eye) 眼か gáñka; (ELEC: for light bulb) ソケット sokéttò; (*BRIT*: ELEC: wall socket) コンセント kóñsento

sod [sɔːd] n (of earth) 草の生えた土 kusá nò háeta tsuchí; (BRIT: inf!) くそ kusó

soda [sou'də] n (CHEM) ナトリウム化合物 natóriùmu kagōbutsu の一般にか性ソーダ, 重曹などを指す ippán nì kaséisōda, jūsō nadò wo sásù; (also: **soda water**) ソーダ水 sốdàsui; (US: also: **soda pop**) 清涼飲料 seíryoīnryō

sodden [sɔːd'ən] adj びしょぬれのbishó-nure no

sodium [sou'di:əm] n ナトリウム natóriùmu

sofa [sou'fə] n ソファー sófà

soft [sɔːft] adj (not hard) 柔らかい yawárakaì; (gentle, not loud: voice, music) 静かな shízuka na; (not bright: light, color) 柔らかな yawáraka na; (kind: heart, approach) 優しい yasáshiì

soft drink n 清涼飲料水 seíryoīnryōsui

soften [sɔːf'ən] vt (gen: make soft) 柔らかくする yawárakaku suru; (effect, blow, expression) 和らげる yawáragerù
♦vi (gen: become soft) 柔らかくなる yawárakaku narù; (voice, expression) 優しくなる yasáshiku narù

softly [sɔːft'li:] adv (gently) 優しく yasáshiku; (quietly) 静かに shízùka ni

softness [sɔːft'nis] n (gen) 柔らかさ yawárakasa; (gentleness) 優しさ yasáshisa

soft spot n: **to have a soft spot for someone** ...が大好きである ...ga dáisuki de árù

software [sɔːft'we:r] n (COMPUT) ソフトウエア sofútouèà

soggy [sɑːg'i:] adj (ground, sandwiches etc) ぐちゃぐちゃの guchágucha no

soil [sɔil] n (earth) 土壌 dójò; (territory) 土地 tochí
♦vt 汚す yogósù

solace [sɑːl'is] n 慰め nagúsame

solar [sou'lə:r] adj (eclipse, power etc) 太陽の táiyō nò

sold [sould] pt, pp of **sell**

solder [sɑːd'ə:r] vt はんだ付けにする hañdazuke nì suru
♦n はんだ hañda

soldier [soul'dʒə:r] n (in army) 兵隊 heítai; (not a civilian) 軍人 guñjin

sold out adj (COMM: goods, tickets, concert etc) 売切れの uríkire de

sole [soul] n (of foot) 足の裏 ashí nò urá; (of shoe) 靴の底 kutsú nò sokó; (fish: pl inv) シタビラメ shitábiràme
♦adj (unique) 唯一の yuítsu no

solely [soul'li:] adv ...だけ ...dáke

solemn [sɑːl'əm] adj (person) 厳厳な kíñgen na; (music) 荘重な sốchō na; (promise) 真剣な shíñken na

sole trader n (COMM) 自営業者 jiéigyōsha

solicit [səlis'it] vt (request) 求める motómerù
♦vi (prostitute) 客引きする kyakúbiki suru

solicitor [səlis'itə:r] (BRIT) n (for wills etc, in court) 弁護士 beñgoshi

solid [sɑːl'id] adj (not hollow) 中空でない chūkū de naì; (not liquid) 固形の kokéi no; (reliable: person, foundations etc) しっかりした shikkárì shita; (entire) まる... marú...; (pure: gold etc) 純粋の juñsui no
♦n (solid object) 固体 kotái

solidarity [sɑːlidær'it:i] n 団結 dañketsu

solidify [səlid'əfai] vi (fat etc) 固まる katámarù

solids [sɑːl'idz] npl (food) 固形食 kokéishòku

solitaire [sɑːl'iter] n (gem) 一つはめの石玉 hitótsuhame nò hōseki; (game) 一人遊び hitóriasobì

solitary [sɑːl'iteri] adj (person, animal, life) 単独の tañdoku no; (alone: walk) 一人だけする hitórì dake de suru; (isolated) 人気のない hitóke no naì; (single: person) 一人だけの hitórì dake no; (: animal, object) 一つだけの hitótsu dake no

solitary confinement n 独房監禁 dokúbō kañkin

solitude [sɑːl'ətud] n 人里を離れている事 hitózato wò hanárete iru kotò

solo [sou'lou] n (piece of music, performance) 独奏 dokúsō
♦adv (fly) 単独で tañdoku de

soloist [sou'louist] n 独奏者 dokúsōshà

soluble [sɑːl'jəbəl] adj (aspirin etc) 溶ける tokérù

solution [səluː'ʃən] *n* (of puzzle, problem, mystery: answer) 解決 kaíketsu; (liquid) 溶液 yóeki

solve [saːlv] *vt* (puzzle, problem, mystery) 解決する kaíketsu suru

solvent [saːl'vənt] *adj* (COMM) 支払い能力のある shiháraínōryoku no aru
♦*n* (CHEM) 溶剤 yózai

somber [saːm'baːr] (*BRIT* **sombre**) *adj* (dark: color, place) 暗い kuráì; (serious: person, view) 陰気な fiṅki na

---

KEYWORD

---

some [sʌm] *adj* 1 (a certain amount or number of) 幾らかの ikúraka no, 幾つかの fkútsuka no, 少しの sukóshi no

some tea/water/biscuits お茶〔水, ビスケット〕o-chá〔mizú, bisúkettò〕○この用法では日本語で表現しない場合が多い konó yōhō de wa nihóngo de hyógen shinaí baái ga óì

some children came 何人かの子供が来た nánninka no kodómo gà kitá

there's some milk in the fridge 冷蔵庫にミルクがあります reízōko ni mírùku ga arímasu

he asked me some questions 彼は色々な事を聞きました kárè wa iróiro na kotò wo kikímashita

there were some people outside 数人の人が外に立っていた súnìn no hitó gà sótò ni tatté ità

I've got some money, but not much 金はあるにはありますが、少しだけです kané wa árù ni wa arímasu gà, sukóshi dake désù

2 (certain: in contrasts) ある árù

some people say that .... と言っている人がいます ...tò itté irù hitó ga imasù

some people hate fish, while others love it 魚の嫌いな人もいれば大好きな人もいます sakána no kiráì na hitó mo iréba daísuki na hitò mo imásù

some films were excellent, but most were mediocre 中には優れた映画もあったが、大部分は平凡な物だった nákà ni wa sugúreta eìga mo attá gà, taíhan wa heíbon na monò dáttà

3 (unspecified) 何かの nánika no, だれかの dáreka no

some woman was asking for you だれか女の人があなたを訪ねていましたよ dáreka ofna no hitò ga anátà wo tazúnete imashīta yő

he was asking for some book (or other) 彼は何かの本を捜していました kárè wa nánika no hòn wo sagáshite imashīta

some day いつか ítsùka, そのうち uchí

we'll meet again some day そのうちまた会うチャンスがあるでしょう sonó uchī matá aú chánsu ga árù deshō

shall we meet some day next week? 来週のいつかに会いましょうか raíshū nó ítsùka ni aímashō ká

♦*pron* 1 (a certain number) 幾つか fkútsuka

I've got some (books etc) 私は幾つか持っています watákushi wà fkútsuka móttè imasù

some (of them) have been sold 幾つかは売れてしまいました súkò wa urète shimaimashīta

some went for a taxi and some walked 何人かはタクシーを拾いに行ったが、残りの人は歩きました nánninka wa tákùshī wo hiróì ni itta gà, nokórì no hitó wa arúìta

2 (a certain amount) 幾分か ikúbun ká

I've got some (money, milk) 私は幾分か持っています watákushi wà ikúbun ká móttè imasù

some was left 少し残っていた sukóshi nokótte ità

could I have some of that cheese? そのチーズを少しもらっていいかしら sonó chīzù wo sukóshi morátte iì kashìra

I've read some of the book その本の一部を読みました sonó hoñ no ichíbù wo yomímashīta

♦*adv:* *some 10 people* 10人ぐらい júnìn gurai

somebody [sʌm'baːdi] *pron* = **someone**

somehow [sʌm'hau] *adv* (in some way)

何とかして nán to ka shite; (for some reason) どういう訳か dô iu wáke ka

KEYWORD

someone [sʌm'wʌn] *pron* だれか dáreka, 人 hitó

there's someone coming 人が来ます hitó gä kimásü

I saw someone in the garden だれか 庭にいました dáreka niwá nî imáshita

someplace [sʌm'pleis] (*US*) *adv* = somewhere

somersault [sʌm'ərsɔːlt] *n* とんぼ返り toñbogaéri

♦*vi* (person, vehicle) とんぼ返りする toñbogaéri suru

KEYWORD

something [sʌm'θiŋ] *pron* 何か nánika

something nice 何かいい物 nánika shi mono

something to do 何かする事 nánika su-ru kotô

there's something wrong 何かおかし い nánika okáshiî

would you like something to eat/ drink? 何か食べませんか(飲みませんか) nánika tabémaseñ(nomímaseñ)ka

sometime [sʌm'taim] *adv* (in future) い つか ftsüka; (in past): *sometime last month* 先月のいつか señgetsu no ftsüka

sometimes [sʌm'taimz] *adv* 時々 tokído-ki

somewhat [sʌm'wʌt] *adv* 少し sukóshi

KEYWORD

somewhere [sʌm'weːr] *adv* (be) どこか に(で) dókoka ni(de); (go) どこかへ dó-koka e

I must have lost it somewhere どこか に落した様です dókoka ni otóshita yô desu

it's somewhere or other in Scotland スコットランドのどこかにあります su-kóttorañdo no dókoka ni arímasü

somewhere else (be) どこか外の所に

(で) dókoka hoká no tokoró ni(de); (go) どこか外の所へ dókoka hoká no tokoró e

son [sʌn] *n* 息子 musúko

sonar [sou'nɑːr] *n* ソナー sónā

song [sɔːŋ] *n* (MUS) 歌 utá; (of bird) さえ ずり saézurí

sonic [sɑn'ik] *adj*: *sonic boom* ソニック ブーム soñíkkubûmu

son-in-law [sʌn'inlɔː] (*pl* sons-in-law) *n* 義理の息子 girí no musuko

sonnet [sɑn'it] *n* ソネット sonétto

sonny [sʌn'iː] (*inf*) *n* 坊や bôya

soon [suːn] *adv* (in a short time) もうすぐ mô sugû, (a short time after) 間もなく mamónaku; (early) 早く hayákü

soon afterwards それから間もなく so-ré karà mamónaku ↑*see also* as

sooner [suː'nɑːr] *adv* (time) もっと早く móttő hayákü; (preference): *I would sooner do that* 私はむしろあれをやりたい watákushi wà múshíro aré wô yarítaî

sooner or later 遅かれ早かれ osókare hayakâre

soot [sut] *n* すす súsü

soothe [suːð] *vt* (calm: person, animal) 落 着かせる ochítsukaserû; (reduce: pain) 和らげる yawáragerû

sophisticated [səfis'tikeitid] *adj* (woman, lifestyle, audience) 世慣れた yonáreta; (machinery) 精巧な seíkô na; (arguments) 洗練された señren saréta

sophomore [sɑf'əmɔːr] (*US*) *n* 2年生 ni-néñsei

soporific [sɑpərif'ik] *adj* (speech) 眠気 を催させる nemúke wò moyóosaserû; (drug) 睡眠の suímin no

sopping [sɑp'iŋ] *adj*: *sopping (wet)* (hair, clothes etc) びしょぬれの bishónu-re no

soppy [sɑp'iː] (*pej*) *adj* (sentimental) セ ンチな señchi na

soprano [səpræn'ou] *n* (singer) ソプラノ sopúrano

sorcerer [sɔːr'sərər] *n* 魔法使い mahô-tsukâi

sordid [sɔːr'did] *adj* (dirty: bed-sit etc) 汚らしい kitánarashii; (wretched: story etc) 浅ましい asámashiì, えげつない egétsunaì

sore [sɔːr] *adj* (painful) 痛い itáì
♦*n* (shallow) ただれ tadáre; (deep) かいよう kaíyò

sorely [sɔːr'liː] *adv*: **I am sorely tempted to** …をほど…しようと思っている yohódo …shiyò to omótte irù

sorrow [sɔːr'ou] *n* (regret) 悲しみ kanáshimi

sorrowful [sɔːr'oufal] *adj* (day, smile etc) 悲しい kanáshiì

sorrows [sɔːr'ouz] *npl* (causes of grief) 不幸 fukō

sorry [sɔːr'iː] *adj* (regretful) 残念な zañneñ na; (condition, excuse) 情けない nasákenaì

sorry! (apology) 済みません sumímaseñ

sorry? (pardon) はい? hãi? ◇相手の言葉を聞取れなかった時に言う aíte no kotóba wo kikítorenakatta tokí ni iú

to feel sorry for someone …に同情する …ni dōjò suru

sort [sɔːrt] *n* (type) 種類 shúrùi
♦*vt* (also: **sort out**: papers, mail, belongings) より分ける yoríwakerù; (: problems) 解決する kaíketsu suru

sorting office [sɔːr'tiŋ-] *n* 郵便物振分け場 yūbinbutsufuriwakejō

SOS [esoues] *n* エスオーエス esú ō esú

so-so [sou'sou'] *adv* (average) まあまあ maámaa

soufflé [sufleɪ'] *n* スフレ sûfùre

sought [sɔːt] *pt, pp of* **seek**

soul [soul] *n* (spirit etc) 魂 támashiì; (person) 人 hitó

soul-destroying [soul'distrɔiŋ] *adj* (work) ぼけさせる様な bokésaseru yō na

soulful [soul'fal] *adj* (eyes, music) 表情豊かな hyōjō yútàka na

sound [saund] *adj* (healthy) 健康な keñkō na; (safe, not damaged) 無傷の mukízu no; (secure: investment) 安全な añzen na; (reliable, thorough) 信頼できる shiñrai dekírù; (sensible) 堅実な keñjitsu na

♦*adv*: **sound asleep** ぐっすり眠って gussúrì nemútte

♦*n* (noise) 音 otó; (volume on TV etc) 音声 ôñsei; (GEO) 海峡 kaíkyo

♦*vt* (alarm, horn) 鳴らす narásù

♦*vi* (alarm, horn) 鳴る narù; (*fig*: seem) …の様である …no yò de árù

to sound like …の様に聞える …no yò ni kikóerù

sound barrier *n* 音速障害 oñsokushṓgai

sound effects *npl* 音響効果 oñkyōkōka

soundly [saund'liː] *adv* (sleep) ぐっすり gussúrì; (beat) 手ひどく tehídokù

sound out *vt* (person, opinion) 打診する dashīn suru

soundproof [saund'pruːf] *adj* (room etc) 防音の bōon no

soundtrack [saund'træk] *n* (of film) サウンドトラック saúndotorakkù

soup [suːp] *n* スープ sûpu

in the soup (*fig*) 困って komátte

soup plate *n* スープ皿 sûpuzarà

soupspoon [suːp'spuːn] *n* スープスプーン sûpusupùn

sour [sau'ər] *adj* (bitter) 酸っぱい suppáī; (milk) 酸っぱくなった suppáku nátta; (*fig*: bad-tempered) 機嫌の悪い kigén no warùī

it's sour grapes (*fig*) 負け惜しみだ makéoshimi da

source [sɔːrs] *n* (also *fig*) 源 mínàmoto

south [sauθ] *n* 南 mínàmi
♦*adj* 南の mínàmi no
♦*adv* (movement) 南へ mínàmi e; (position) 南に mínàmi ni

South Africa *n* 南アフリカ mínàmi afúrìka

South African *adj* 南アフリカの mínàmi afúrìka no
♦*n* 南アフリカ人 mínàmi afúrìkajìn

South America *n* 南米 nañbei

South American *adj* 南米の nañbei nò
♦*n* 南米人 nañbeijìn

south-east [sauθiːst'] *n* 南東 nañtō

southerly [sʌð'əːrliː] *adj* (to/towards the south: aspect) 南への mínàmi e nò; (from the south wind) 南からの mínàmi kara nð

southern [sʌðˈəːn] *adj* (in or from the south of region) 南の minámi no; (to/towards the south) 南向きの minámimuki no

the southern hemisphere 南半球 minámihankyū

South Pole n 南極 nańkyoku

southward(s) [sauθˈwəd(z)] *adv* 南へ minámi e

south-west [sauθwest̩ˈ] n 南西 nańsei

souvenir [suːvənɪəʳ] n (memento) 記念品 kinéhhin

sovereign [sɑːvˈrɪn] n (ruler) 君主 kúnshu

sovereignty [sɑːvˈrənti] n 主権 shukéñ

soviet [souˈviːit] *adj* ソビエトの sobíetð no

the Soviet Union ソ連 sóren

sow[1] [sau] n (pig) 牝豚 mesúbuta

sow[2] [sou] (pt sowed, pp sown) vt (gen: seeds) まく mákù; (fig: spread: suspicion etc) 広める hirómerù

soy [sɔi] (BRIT **soya**) n: **soy bean** 大豆 dáīzu

soy sauce しょう油 shóyù

spa [spɑː] n (also: **spa town**) 鉱泉町 kósentimachi; (US: also: **health spa**) ヘルスセンター herúsuseñtā

space [speis] n (gap) すき間 sukíma, ギャップ gyáppù; (place: empty) 空所 kúsho, 余白 yoháku; (room) 空間 kúkan; (beyond Earth) 宇宙 空間 uchúkukan, スペース supésu; (interval, period) 間 ma

♦*cpd* 宇宙... úchū...

♦*vt* (also: **space out**: text, visits, payments) 間隔を置く kańkaku wò okú

spacecraft [speis̩kræft] n 宇宙 船 uchúsen

spaceman [speis̩mæn] (pl **spacemen**) n 宇宙飛行士 uchúhikōshi

spaceship [speis̩ʃip] n = **spacecraft**

spacewoman [speis̩wumən] (pl **spacewomen**) n 女性宇宙飛行士 joséi uchúhikōshi

spacing [speisˈiŋ] n (between words) スペース supésu

spacious [speiˈʃəs] *adj* (car, room etc) 広

い hirói

spade [speid] n (tool) スコップ sukóppù; (child's) おもちゃのスコップ omóchà no sukóppù

spades [speidz] npl (CARDS: suit) スペード supédo

spaghetti [spəgetˈiː] n スパゲッティ supágettì

Spain [spein] n スペイン supéň

span [spæn] n (of bird, plane) 翼長 yokúchō; (of arch) スパン supán; (in time) 期間 kikán

♦*vt* (river) ...に またがる ...ni matágarù; (fig: time) ...に渡る ...ni watárù

Spaniard [spænˈjəːd] n スペイン人 supéinjìn

spaniel [spænˈjəl] n スパニエル supánièru

Spanish [spænˈiʃ] *adj* スペインの supéň no; (LING) スペイン語の supéingo no

♦n (LING) スペイン語 supéingo

♦npl: **the Spanish** スペイン人 supéinjìn ◊総称 sóshō

spank [spæŋk] vt (someone, someone's bottom) ...のしりをたたく ...no shírì wò tatákù

spanner [spænˈəːr] (BRIT) n スパナ supánà

spar [spɑːr] n (pole) マスト másùto

♦*vi* (BOXING) スパーリングする supáringu suru

spare [speər] *adj* (free) 空きの akí no; (surplus) 余った amátta

♦n = **spare part**

♦*vt* (do without: trouble etc) ...なしで済ます ...náshì de sumásù; (make available) 与える atáerù; (refrain from hurting: person, city etc) 助けてやる tasúkete yarù

to spare (surplus: time, money) 余った amátta

spare part n 交換用部品 kókan-yóbuhin

spare time n 余暇 yóka

spare wheel n (AUT) スペアタイア supéataià

sparing [speərˈiŋ] *adj*: **to be sparing with** ...を倹約する ...wo keñ-yaku suru

sparingly [speərˈiŋliː] *adv* (use) 控え目に

hikáeme ni

spark [spɑːrk] *n* 火花 híbàna, スパーク supáků; (*fig*: of wit etc) ひらめき hirámekī

spark(ing) plug [spɑːrk'(iŋ)-] *n* スパークプラグ supákupurāgu

sparkle [spɑːr'kəl] *n* きらめき kirámekī
♦*vi* (shine: diamonds, water) きらめく kirámekù

sparkling [spɑːr'kliŋ] *adj* (wine) 泡立つ awádatsù; (conversation, performance) きらめく様な kirámeku yō na

sparrow [spær'ou] *n* スズメ suzúme

sparse [spɑːrs] *adj* (rainfall, hair, population) 少ない sukúnaì

spartan [spɑːr'tən] *adj* (*fig*) 簡素な kánso na

spasm [spæz'əm] *n* (MED) けいれん kefren

spasmodic [spæzmɑːd'ik] *adj* (*fig*: not continuous, irregular) 不規則な fukísoku na

spastic [spæs'tik] *n* 脳性麻痺患者 nōseimáhikaṇja

spat [spæt] *pt, pp* of **spit**

spate [speit] *n* (*fig*): **a spate of** (letters, protests etc) 沢山の takúsan no

spatter [spæt'əːr] *vt* (liquid, surface) …を…にはねかす …wo …ni hanékasù

spatula [spætʃ'ələ] *n* (CULIN, MED) へら hérà

spawn [spɔːn] *vi* (fish etc) 産卵する sañran suru
♦*n* (frog spawn etc) 卵 tamágò

speak [spiːk] (*pt* **spoke**, *pp* **spoken**) *vt* (language) 話す hanásù; (truth) 言う iú
♦*vi* (use voice) 話す hanásù; (make a speech) 演説する eñzetsu suru
to speak to someone …に話し掛ける …ni hanáshikakerù
to speak to someone of/about something …に…のことを話す …ni …no kotó wò hanásù
speak up! もっと大きな声で話しなさい móttò ōkìna kóè de hanáshi nasaì

speaker [spiː'kəːr] *n* (in public) 演説者 eñzetsushà; (*also*: **loudspeaker**) スピーカー supíkà; (POL): **the Speaker** (US,

BRIT) 下院議長 ka-íngichō

spear [spiːr] *n* (weapon) やり yarí
♦*vt* 刺す sásù

spearhead [spiːr'hed] *vt* (attack etc) …の先頭に立つ …no seftō nī tátsù

spec [spek] (*inf*) *n*: **on spec** 山をかけて yamá wo kakète

special [speʃ'əl] *adj* 特別な tokúbetsu na
special delivery 速達 sokútatsu
special school (BRIT) 特殊学校 tokúshugakkō
special adviser 特別顧問 tokúbetsukomòn
special permission 特別許可 tokúbetsukyokà

specialist [speʃ'əlist] *n* (gen) 専門家 señmonka; (MED) 専門医 señmoñ-i

speciality [speʃiːæl'əti] *n* = **specialty**

specialize [speʃ'əlaiz] *vi*: **to specialize (in)** (…を) 専門にやる (…wo) señmonteki ni yarú

specially [speʃ'əliː] *adv* (especially) 特に tókù ni; (on purpose) 特別に tokúbetsu ni

specialty [speʃ'əltiː] *n* (dish) 名物 mefbutsu; (study) 専門 señmon

species [spiː'iːz] *n inv* 種 shú

specific [spisif'ik] *adj* (fixed) 特定の tokútei no; (exact) 正確な seftkaku na

specifically [spisif'ikliː] *adv* (especially) 特に tókù ni; (exactly) 明確に mefkaku ni

specification [spesəfəkei'ʃən] *n* (TECH) 仕様 shiyō; (requirement) 条件 jōken

specifications [spesəfəkei'ʃənz] *npl* (TECH) 仕様 shiyō

specify [spes'əfai] *vt* (time, place, color etc) 指定する shitéi suru

specimen [spes'əmən] *n* (single example) 見本 mihòn; (sample for testing, *also* MED) 標本 hyóhon

speck [spek] *n* (of dirt, dust etc) 粒 tsúbò

speckled [spek'əld] *adj* (hen, eggs) 点々と teñteñhyoṇō no

specs [speks] (*inf*) *npl* 眼鏡 mégàne

spectacle [spek'təkal] *n* (scene) 光景 kốkei; (grand event) スペクタクル supékutakuru

spectacles [spek'təkəlz] *npl* 眼鏡 mégane

spectacular [spektæk'jələ:r] *adj* (dramatic) 劇的な gekîteki na; (success) 目覚しい mezámashiî

spectator [spek'teitəːr] *n* 観客 kańkyaku

specter [spek'təːr] (*US*) *n* (ghost) 幽霊 yûrei

spectra [spek'trə] *npl of* **spectrum**

spectre [spek'təːr] (*BRIT*) *n* = **specter**

spectrum [spek'trəm] (*pl* **spectra**) *n* (color/radio wave spectrum) スペクトル supékutoru

speculate [spek'jəleit] *vi* (FINANCE) 投機をする tôki wo suru, (try to guess); to **speculate about** ...についてあれこれと憶測する ...ni tsúîte arékòre to okúsoku suru

speculation [spekjəlei'ʃən] *n* (FINANCE) 投機 tôki; (guesswork) 憶測 okúsoku

speech [spi:tʃ] *n* (faculty) 話す能力 hanásu nôryoku; (spoken language) 話し言葉 hanáshikotòba; (formal talk) 演説 eñzetsu, スピーチ supíchi; (THEATER) せりふ serîfu

speechless [spi:tʃ'lis] *adj* (be, remain etc) 声も出ない kôè mo deñaî

speed [spi:d] *n* (rate, fast travel) 速度 sókùdo, スピード supîdò; (haste) 急ぎ isógi; (promptness) 素早さ subáyasà
  at full/top speed 全速力で zeñsokuryòku de

speed boat *n* モーターボート môtàboto

speedily [spi:d'ili:] *adv* 素早く subáyaku

speeding [spi:'diŋ] *n* (AUT) スピード違反 supîdo-ìhan

speed limit *n* 速度制限 sokúdoseìgen

speedometer [spi:dɑːm'itəːr] *n* 速度計 sokúdokeì

speed up *vi* (*also fig*) 速度を増す sókùdo wo masú
  ♦*vt* (*also fig*) ...の速度を増す ...no sókùdo wo masú, 速める hayámerù

speedway [spi:d'wei] *n* (sport) オートレース ôtorēsu

speedy [spi:'di:] *adj* (fast: car) スピードの出る supîdò no dérù; (prompt: reply,

recovery, settlement) 速い hayáì

spell [spel] *n* (*also*: **magic spell**) 魔法 mahô; (period of time) 期間 kikàn
  ♦*vt* (*pt, pp* **spelled** *or* (*Brit*) **spelt**) (*also*: **spell out**) ...のつづりを言う ...no tsuzúrì wo iú; (*fig*: advantages, difficulties) ...の兆しである ...no kizáshì de arù
  to cast a spell on someone ...に魔法を掛ける ...ni mahô wò kakérù
  he can't spell 彼はスペルが苦手だ kárè wa supérù ga nigáte dà

spellbound [spel'baund] *adj* (audience etc) 魅せられた miséraretà

spelling [spel'iŋ] *n* つづり tsuzúri, スペリング supérìngu

spend [spend] (*pt, pp* **spent**) *vt* (money) 使う tsukáû; (time, life) 過す sugósù

spendthrift [spend'θrift] *n* 浪費家 rôhìka

spent [spent] *pt, pp of* **spend**

sperm [spəːrm] *n* 精子 seîshi

spew [spju:] *vt* 吐き出す hakídasù

sphere [sfiːr] *n* (round object) 球 kyû; (area) 範囲 hañ-i

spherical [sfer'ikəl] *adj* (round) 丸い marûî

sphinx [sfiŋks] *n* スフィンクス suffíňkusu

spice [spais] *n* 香辛料 kôshiñryò, スパイス supáìsu
  ♦*vt* (food) ...にスパイスを入れる ...ni supáìsu wo irérù

spick-and-span [spik'ənspæn'] *adj* きちんときれいな kichíñ to kírèi na

spicy [spai'si:] *adj* (food) スパイスの利いた supáìsu no kiîtà

spider [spai'dəːr] *n* クモ kúmò

spike [spaik] *n* (point) くい kuî; (BOT) 穂 hô

spill [spil] (*pt, pp* **spilt** *or* **spilled**) *vt* (liquid) こぼす kobósù
  ♦*vi* (liquid) こぼれる kobórerù

spill over *vi* (liquid: *also fig*) あふれる afúrerù

spin [spin] *n* (trip in car) ドライブ doráìbu; (AVIAT) きりもみ kirímomi; (on ball) スピン supìn
  ♦*vb* (*pt, pp* **spun**)

♦*vt* (wool etc) 紡ぐ tsumúgù; (ball, coin) 回転させる kaíten saserù
♦*vi* (make thread) 紡ぐ tsumúgù; (person, head) 目が回る mé gà mawárù

spinach [spin'itʃ] *n* (plant, food) ホウレンソウ hōrènsō

spinal [spai'nəl] *adj* (injury etc) 背骨の sebóne no

spinal cord *n* せき髄 sekízùi

spindly [spind'li:] *adj* (legs, trees etc) か細い kabósoī

spin-dryer [spindrai'əːr] *n* (BRIT) 脱水機 dassúikī

spine [spain] *n* (ANAT) 背骨 sebóne; (thorn: of plant, hedgehog etc) とげ togé

spineless [spain'lis] *adj* (*fig*) 意気地なし の ikújinàshi no

spinning [spin'iŋ] *n* (art) 紡績 bóseki

spinning top *n* こま kómà

spinning wheel *n* 糸車 tsumúgigurùma

spin-off [spin'ɔːf] *n* (*fig*: by-product) 副産物 fukúsañbutsu

spin out *vt* (talk, job, money, holiday) 引延ばす hikínobasù

spinster [spin'stəːr] *n* オールドミス őrudomìsu

spiral [spai'rəl] *n* 螺形 rasénkei
♦*vi* (*fig*: prices etc) うなぎ登りに上るu-náginobòri ni noboru

spiral staircase *n* 螺旋階段 rasénkaidàn

spire [spai'əːr] *n* せん塔 seńtō

spirit [spir'it] *n* (soul) 魂 támàshii; (ghost: demon) 幽霊 yūrei; (energy) 元気 géñki; (courage) 勇気 yūki; (frame of mind) 気分 kíbùn; (sense) 精神 seíshin

in good spirits 気分上々で kíbùn jốjō de

spirited [spir'itid] *adj* (performance, retort, defense) 精力的な seíryokuteki na

spirit level *n* 水準器 suíjuñki

spirits [spir'its] *npl* (drink) 蒸留酒 jōryūshu

spiritual [spir'itʃuəl] *adj* (of the spirit: home, welfare, needs) 精神的な seíshinteki na; (religious: affairs) 霊的な reíteki na

na

n (*also*: **Negro spiritual**) 黒人霊歌 kokújinreìka

spit [spit] *n* (for roasting) 焼きぐし yakígushi; (saliva) つばき tsubáki
♦*vi* (*pt, pp* **spat**) (throw out saliva) つばを吐く tsúbà wo hákù; (sound: fire, cooking) じゅうじゅういう jữjū iu; (rain) ばらっと parátsukù

spite [spait] *n* 恨み urámi
♦*vt* (person) ...に意地悪をする ...ni ijíwarù wo suru

in spite of ...にもかかわらず ...ní mò kakáwarazù

spiteful [spait'fəl] *adj* (child, words etc) 意地悪な ijíwarù na

spittle [spit'əl] *n* つばき tsubáki

splash [splæʃ] *n* (sound) ざぶん zabúñ to iú otò; (of color) 派手なはん点 hadé nà hañteñ
♦*vt* はね掛ける hanékakerù
♦*vi* (*also*: **splash about**) ぴちゃぴちゃ水をはねる pichápicha mizú wò hanérù

spleen [spliːn] *n* (ANAT) ひ臓 hízò

splendid [splen'did] *adj* (excellent: idea, recovery) 素晴らしい subárashiì; (impressive: architecture, affair) 立派な ríppà na

splendor [splen'dəːr] (BRIT **splendour**) *n* (impressiveness) 輝き kagáyakì

splendors [splen'dəːrz] *npl* (features) 特色 tokúshoku

splint [splint] *n* 副木 fukúboku

splinter [splin'təːr] *n* (of wood, glass) 破片 hahèn; (in finger) とげ togé
♦*vi* (bone, wood, glass etc) 砕ける kudákerù

split [split] *n* (crack) 割れ目 waréme; (tear) 裂け目 sakéme; (*fig*: division) 分裂 buñretsu; (: difference) 差異 sá-ì
♦*vb* (*pt, pp* **split**)
♦*vt* (divide) 割る wárù, 裂く sákù; (party) 分裂させる buñretsu saserù; (share equally: work) 手分けしてやる te-wáke shite yarù; (: profits) 山分けする yamáwake suru
♦*vi* (divide) 割れる warérù

split up *vi* (couple) 別れる wakárerù

(group, meeting) 解散する kaísan suru

splutter [splʌt'əːr] n (engine etc) ぱちぱち音を立てる páchìpachi otò wò tatérù; (person) どもる domórù

spoil [spoil] (pt, pp **spoilt** or **spoiled**) vt (damage, mar) 台無しにする daínashi ni surù; (child) 甘やかす amáyakasù

spoils [spoilz] npl (loot: also fig) 分捕り品 bufídorìhǐn

spoilsport [spoil'spɔːrt] n 座を白けさせる人 zá wò shirákesaserù hitó

spoke [spouk] pt of **speak**

◆n (of wheel) スポーク supókù

spoken [spou'kən] pp of **speak**

spokesman [spouks'mən] (pl **spokesmen**) n スポークスマン supókusumàn

spokeswoman [spouks'wumən] (pl **spokeswomen**) n 女性報道官 joséi hōdōkan, 女性スポークスマン joséi supòkusumàn

sponge [spʌndʒ] n (for washing with) スポンジ supónjì; (also: **sponge cake**) スポンジケーキ supónjikèki

◆vt (wash) スポンジで洗う supónji de aráù

◆vi: **to sponge off/on someone** ...にたかる ...ni takárù

sponge bag (BRIT) n 洗面バッグ seímenbagû ○洗面道具を入れて携帯するバッグ seímendògu wo irète keitai surù bággù

sponsor [spɑn'səːr] n (of player, event, club, program) スポンサー supónsā; (of charitable event etc) 協賛者 kyósañsha, (for application) 保証人 hoshóniñ; (for bill in parliament etc) 提出者 teíshutsushà

◆vt (player, event, club, program etc) ...のスポンサーになる ...no supóñsā ni nárù; (charitable event etc) ...の協賛者になる ...no kyósañsha ni nárù; (applicant) ...の保証人になる ...no hoshóniñ ni nárù; (proposal, bill etc) 提出する teíshutsu suru

sponsorship [spɑn'səːrʃip] n (financial support) 金銭的援助 kiñsentékieñjo

spontaneous [spɑntei'niəs] adj (unplanned: gesture) 自発的な jihátsuteki

na

spooky [spuː'kiː] (inf) adj (place, atmosphere) お化けが出そうな o-bàke gà desó nà

spool [spuːl] n (for thread) 糸巻 itómàki; (for film, tape etc) リール rīru

spoon [spuːn] n スプーン supúñ

spoon-feed [spuːn'fiːd] vt (baby, patient) スプーンで食べさせる supúñ de tabésaserù; (fig: students etc) ...に一方的に教え込む ...ni ippôteki ni oshíekomù

spoonful [spuːn'ful] n スプーン一杯分 supúñ ippáìbun

sporadic [spɔːræd'ik] adj (glimpses, attacks etc) 散発的な sañpatsuteki na

sport [spɔːrt] n (game) スポーツ supótsu; (person) 気さくな人 kísàku nà hitó

◆vt (wear) これみよがしに身に付ける korémiyogàshi ni mi ni tsukérù

sporting [spɔːr'tiŋ] adj (event etc) スポーツの supótsu no; (generous) 気前がいい kimáe ga íì

to give someone a sporting chance ...にちゃんとしたチャンスを与える ...ni chañtô shita cháñsu wo atáerù

sport jacket (US) n スポーツジャケット supótsujakètto

sports car [spɔːrts-] n スポーツカー supótsukā

sports jacket (BRIT) n = **sport jacket**

sportsman [spɔːrts'mən] (pl **sportsmen**) n スポーツマン supótsumàn

sportsmanship [spɔːrts'mənʃip] n スポーツマンシップ supótsumanshìppù

sportswear [spɔːrts'weər] n スポーツウエア supótsuuèa

sportswoman [spɔːrts'wumən] (pl **sportswomen**) n スポーツウーマン supótsuùman

sporty [spɔːr'tiː] adj (good at sports) スポーツ好きの supótsuzuki no

spot [spɑt] n (mark) 染み shimí; (on pattern, skin etc) はん点 hañteñ; (place: also fig) 場所 bashò; (RADIO, TV) コーナー kōnä; (small amount): **a spot of** 少しの sukóshì no

◆vt (notice: person, mistake etc) ...に気

が付く ...ni kí gà tsúkù

on the spot (in that place) 現場に genba ni; (immediately) その場で sonó ba de, 即座に sókùza ni; (in difficulty) 困って komáttè

spot check n 抜取り検査 nukítorikeñsa

spotless [spɑːtˈlis] adj (shirt, kitchen etc) 清潔な sefketsu na

spotlight [spɑːtˈlait] n スポットライト supóttoraitò

spotted [spɑːtˈid] adj (pattern) はん点模様の hafíténmoyó no

spotty [spɑːtˈiː] adj (face, youth: with freckles) そばかすだらけの sobákusudaráke no; (: with pimples) にきびだらけの nikíbidaráke no

spouse [spaus] n (male/female) 配偶者 haígúsha

spout [spaut] n (of jug) つぎ口 tsugígúchì; (of pipe) 排水口 haísuíkò

sprain [sprein] n ねんざ neñza

♦vt: **to sprain one's ankle/wrist** 足首 [手首]をねんざする ashíkùbi(tèkùbi)wo neñza suru

sprang [spræŋ] pt of **spring**

sprawl [sprɔːl] vi (person: lie) 寝そべる nesóberù; (: sit) だらしない格好で座る daráshinai kakkô de suwárù; (place) 無秩序に広がる muchítsujò ni hirógarù

spray [sprei] n (small drops) 水煙 mizúkemùri; (sea spray) しぶき shíbùki; (container: hair spray etc) スプレー supúrè; (garden spray) 噴霧器 fufímukì; (of flowers) 小枝 koéda

♦vt (sprinkle) 噴霧器で...に...を掛ける fufímukì de ...ni ...wo kakérù; (crops) 消毒す る shódoku suru

spread [spred] n (range, distribution) 広がり hirógari; (CULIN: for bread) スプレッド supúreddò; (inf: food) ごちそう gochísoù

♦vb (pt, pp **spread**)

♦vt (lay out) 並べる naráberù; (butter) 塗る nurù; (wings, arms, sails) 広げる hirógerù; (workload, wealth) 分配する buñpai suru; (scatter) ...を撒く ...wo mákù

♦vi (disease, news) 広がる hirógarù

(also: **spread out**: stain) 広がる hirógarù

spread-eagled [spredˈiːgəld] adj 大の字に寝た daí no jí ni netá

spread out vi (move apart) 散らばる chirábarù

spreadsheet [spredˈʃiːt] n (COMPUT) ス プレッドシート supúreddoshiìto

spree [spriː] n: **to go on a spree** ...にふけ る ...ni fukérù

sprightly [spraitˈliː] adj (old person) か くしゃくとした kakúshaku to shitá

spring [spriŋ] n (leap) 跳躍 chôyaku; (coiled metal) ばね báně; (season) 春 hárù; (of water) 泉 izúmi

♦vi (pt **sprang**, pp **sprung**) (leap) 跳ぶ tobu

in spring (season) 春に hárù ni

springboard [spriŋˈbɔːrd] n スプリング ボード supúringubòdo

spring-cleaning [spriŋˈkliːˈniŋ] n 大掃 除 ôsôji ◆春とは関係なく言う hárù to wa kañkeinakù iú

springtime [spriŋˈtaim] n 春 hárù

spring up vi (thing: appear) 現れる ará-warerù

sprinkle [spriŋˈkəl] vt (scatter: liquid) ま く mákù; (: salt, sugar) 振り掛ける furí-kakerù

to sprinkle water on, sprinkle with water ...に水をまく ...ni mizú wo mákù

sprinkler [spriŋˈklər] n (for lawn, to put out fire) スプリンクラー supúrinku-rà

sprint [sprint] n (race) 短距離競走 tañ-kyorikyòsò, スプリント supúriñto

♦vi (gen: run fast) 速く走る háyaku ha-shírù; (SPORT) スプリントる supúriñto suru

sprinter [sprintˈər] n スプリンター su-púriñtà

sprout [spraut] vi (plant, vegetable) 発芽 する hatsúga suru

sprouts [sprauts] npl (also: **Brussels sprouts**) 芽キャベツ mekyábètsu

spruce [spruːs] n inv (BOT) トウヒ tôhì

♦adj (neat, smart) スマートな sumâto na

sprung [sprʌŋ] pp of **spring**

spry [sprai] adj (old person) かくしゃく

とした kakúshaku to shitá

spun [spʌn] pt, pp of **spin**

spur [spəːr] n 拍車 hakúsha; (fig) 刺激 shigéki

♦vt (also: **spur on**) 激励する gekírei suru

on the spur of the moment とっさに tossá ni

spurious [spjur'iːəs] adj (false: attraction) 見せ掛けの misékake no; (: argument) 間違った machígattá

spurn [spəːrn] vt (reject) はねつける hanétsukerù

spurt [spəːrt] n (of blood etc) 噴出 fuńshutsu; (of energy) 奮発 fuńpatsu

♦vi (blood, flame) 噴出す fukídasù

spy [spai] n スパイ supái

♦vi: **to spy on** こっそり見張る kossőri miháru

♦vt (see) 見付ける mitsúkerù

spying [spai'iŋ] n スパイ行為 supáikòi

sq. abbr = **square**

squabble [skwɑːb'əl] vi 口げんかする kuchígeñka suru

squad [skwɑːd] n (MIL, POLICE) 班 háń; (SPORT) チーム chīmu

squadron [skwɑːd'rən] n (MIL) 大隊 dáitai

squalid [skwɑːl'id] adj (dirty, unpleasant: conditions) 汚い kitánaráshii; (sordid: story etc) えげつない egétsunaí

squall [skwɔːl] n (stormy wind) スコール sukőru

squalor [skwɑːl'əːr] n 汚い環境 kitánai kańkyờ

squander [skwɑːn'dəːr] vt (money) 浪費する rōhi suru; (chances) 逃す nogásù

square [skweːr] n (shape) 正方形 sefhőkei; (in town) 広場 hírőba; (inf: person) 堅物 katábutsu

♦adj (in shape) 正方形の sefhőkei no; (inf: ideas, tastes) 古臭い furúkusaí

♦vt (arrange) ...を...に一致させる ...wo ...ni itchí saserù; (MATH) 2乗する nijő suru; (reconcile) ...と調和させる ...wo ...to chőwa saserù

all square 貸し借りなし kashíkàri náshi

a square meal 十分な食事 júbùn na

shokúji

2 meters square 2メーター平方 ni mếtầ heíhò

2 square meters 2平方メーター ni heíhò mếtầ

squarely [skweːr'liː] adv (directly: fall, land etc) まともに matőmo ni; (fully: confront) きっぱりと kippárì to

squash [skwɑːʃ] n (US: marrow etc) カボチャ kabőcha; (BRIT: drink): **lemon/ orange squash** レモン〔オレンジ〕スカッシュ remőn (oréñji) sukasshù; (SPORT) スカッシュ sukásshù

♦vt つぶす tsubúsu

squat [skwɑːt] adj ずんぐりした zuńgurí shita

♦vi (also: **squat down**) しゃがむ shagámù

squatter [skwɑːt'əːr] n 不法居住者 fuhőkyojúsha

squawk [skwɔːk] vi (bird) ぎゃーぎゃー鳴く gyágyà nakú

squeak [skwiːk] vi (door etc) きしむ kishímù; (mouse) ちゅーちゅー鳴く chūchū nakú

squeal [skwiːl] vi (children) きゃーきゃー言う kyákyà iú; (brakes etc) キーキー言う kīkī iú

squeamish [skwiː'miʃ] adj やたら...に弱い yatára ...ni yowáì

squeeze [skwiːz] n (gen: of hand) 握り締める事 nigírishimerù kotő; (ECON) 金融引締め kiń-yúhikishime

♦vt (gen) 絞る shibőrù; (hand, arm) 握り締める nigírishimerù

squeeze out vt (juice etc) 絞り出す shibórídasù

squelch [skweltʃ] vi ぐちゃぐちゃ音を立てる gúchàgucha otő wő tatérù

squid [skwid] n イカ iká

squiggle [skwig'əl] n のたくった線 notákuttà séñ

squint [skwint] vi (have a squint) 斜視である shashí de árù

♦n (MED) 斜視 shashí

squire [skwai'əːr] n (BRIT) 大地主 őjínùshi

squirm [skwəːrm] vi 身もだえする mimódðæ suru

squirrel [skwəɪrˈəl] *n* リス rísù

squirt [skwəɪrt] *vi* 噴出す fukídasù

♦*vt* 噴掛ける fukíkakerù

Sr *abbr* = senior

St *abbr* = saint; street

stab [stæb] *n* (with knife etc) ひと刺し hitóðashì; (*inf*: try): **to have a stab at (doing) something** ...をやってみる ...wo yatté mirù

♦*vt* (person, body) 刺す sásù

a stab of pain 刺す様な痛み sásù yō na itámi

stability [stəbilˈətiː] *n* 安定 antéi

stabilize [steiˈbəlaiz] *vt* (prices) 安定させる antéi saserù

♦*vi* (prices, one's weight) 安定する antéi suru

stable [steiˈbəl] *adj* (prices, patient's condition) 安定した antéi shita; (marriage) 揺るぎない yurúgì naì

♦*n* (for horse) 馬小屋 umágoya

staccato [stəkɑːˈtou] *adv* スタッカート sutákkāto

stack [stæk] *n* (pile) ...の山 ...no yamá

♦*vt* (pile) 積む tsumú

stadium [steiˈdiːəm] *n* 競技場 kyōgijō, スタジアム sutájiamu

staff [stæf] *n* (work force) 職員 shokúin; (*BRIT*: SCOL) 教職員 kyōshokúin

♦*vt* ...の職員として働く ...no shokúin to-shite határakù

stag [stæg] *n* 雄ジカ ójìka

stage [steidʒ] *n* (in theater etc) 舞台 bútài; (platform) 台 dái; (profession): **the stage** 俳優業 haíyūgyō; (point, period) 段階 dañkai

♦*vt* (play) 上演する jóen suru; (demonstration) 行う okónaù

in stages 少しずつ sukóshi zutsù

stagecoach [steidʒˈkoutʃ] *n* 駅馬車 ekíbashà

stage manager *n* 舞台監督 butáikàntoku

stagger [stægˈər] *vi* よろめく yorómekù

♦*vt* (amaze) 仰天させる gyóten saserù; (hours, holidays) ずらす zurásù

staggering [stægˈəriŋ] *adj* (amazing) 仰天させる gyóten saserù

stagnant [stægˈnənt] *adj* (water) よどんだ yodóñda; (economy etc) 停滞した teítai shita

stagnate [stægˈneit] *vi* (economy, business, person) 停滞する teítai suru; (person) だれる darérù

stag party *n* スタッグパーティ sutággupàti

staid [steid] *adj* (person, attitudes) 古めかしい furúmekashìi

stain [stein] *n* (mark) 染み shimí; (coloring) 着色剤 chakúshokuzaì, ステイン sutéin

♦*vt* (mark) 汚す yogósù; (wood) ...にステインを塗る ...ni sutéin wo nùrú

stained glass window [steind-] *n* ステンドグラスの窓 suténdogùrasu no mádò

stainless steel [stein'lis-] *n* ステンレス sutéñresu

stain remover [-riːmuːˈvəːr] *n* 染み抜き shímìnukì

stair [steːr] *n* (step) 段 dáñ, ステップ sutéppù

staircase [steːrˈkeis] *n* 階段 kaídan

stairs [steːrz] *npl* (flight of steps) 階段 kaídan

stairway [steːrˈwei] *n* = staircase

stake [steik] *n* (post) くい kúî; (COMM: interest) 利害関係 rigáikañkei; (BETTING: *gen pl*) 賞金 shōkin

♦*vt* (money, life, reputation) かける kakérù

to stake a claim to ...に対する所有権を主張する ...ni taí surù shoyúken wo shuchō suru

to be at stake 危ぶまれる ayábumarerù

stalactite [stəlækˈtait] *n* しょう乳石 shōnyūseki

stalagmite [stəlægˈmait] *n* 石じゅん sekíjun

stale [steil] *adj* (bread) 固くなった katákù nattà; (food, air) 古くなった fúrùku nattà; (air) よどんだ yodóñda; (smell) が臭い kabíkusaì; (beer) 気の抜けた kì nò nukétà

stalemate [steil'meit] n (CHESS) ステールメート sutérumèto; (fig) 行き詰り ikízumari

stalk [stɔːk] n (of flower, fruit) 茎 kukí
♦vt (person, animal) ...に忍び寄る ...ni shinóbiyorù

stalk off vi 威張って行く ibátte ikú

stall [stɔːl] n (in market) 屋台 yátai; (in stable) 馬房 babő
♦vt (AUT: engine, car) エンストを起す efūsuto wò okósù; (fig: delay: person) 引止める hikítomerù; (: decision etc) 引延ばす hikínobasù
♦vi (AUT: engine, car) エンストを起す efūsuto wò okósù; (fig: person) 時間稼ぎをする jikánkasegì wo osú

stallion [stæl'jən] n 種ウマ tanéùma

stalls [stɔːlz] npl (in cinema, theater) 特別席 tokúbetsusèki

stalwart [stɔːl'wərt] adj (worker, supporter, party member) 不動の fudő no

stamina [stæm'inə] n スタミナ sutámina

stammer [stæm'ər] n どもり dómori
♦vi どもる domórù

stamp [stæmp] n (postage stamp) 切手 kitté; (rubber stamp) スタンプ sutánpu; (mark, also fig) 特徴 tokúchō
♦vi (also: stamp one's foot) 足を踏み鳴らす ashŭ wò fumínarasù
♦vt (letter) ...に切手を張る ...ni kitté wò harú; (mark) 特徴付ける tokúchōzukerù; (with rubber stamp) ...にスタンプを押す ...ni sutánpu wo osú

stamp album n 切手帳 kittéchō

stamp collecting [-kəlek'tiŋ] n 切手収集 kittéshùshū

stampede [stæmpiːd'] n (of animal herd) 暴走 bōsō; (fig: of people) 殺到 sattō

stance [stæns] n (way of standing) 立っている姿勢 tatté irú shìsèi; (fig) 姿勢 shísèi

stand [stænd] n (position) 構え kámae; (for taxis) 乗場 norība; (hall, music stand) 台 dái; (SPORT) スタンド sutándo; (stall) 屋台 yátai
♦vb (pt, pt stood)
♦vi (be: person, unemployment etc) ...になっている ...ni natté irù; (be on foot) 立

つ tátsù; (rise) 立ち上る tachǎgarù; (remain: decision, offer) 有効である yūkō de arù; (in election etc) 立候補する rikkōho suru
♦vt (place: object) 立てる tatérù; (tolerate, withstand: person, thing) ...に耐える ...ni taérù; (treat, invite to) ...におごる ogórù
to make a stand (fig) 立場を執る tachība wò tórù
to stand for parliament (BRIT) 議員選挙に出馬する giínsenkyo ni shutsúba suru

standard [stæn'dərd] n (level) 水準 sufjun; (norm, criterion) 基準 kijún; (flag) 旗 hatá
♦adj (normal: size etc) 標準的な hyōjunteki na; (text) 権威のある kén'i no arù

standardize [stæn'dərdaiz] vt 規格化する kikákuka suru

standard lamp (BRIT) n フロアスタンド furóasutandò

standard of living n 生活水準 sefkatsusuijūn

standards [stæn'dərdz] npl (morals) 道徳基準 dōtoku kijún

stand by vi (be ready) 待機する táiki suru
♦vt fus (opinion, decision) 守る mamórù; (person) ...の力になる ...no chikára ni narú

stand-by [stænd'bai] n (reserve) 非常用の物 hijōyō no monó
to be on stand-by 待機している táiki shité irù

stand-by ticket n (AVIAT) キャンセル待ちの切符 kyánseru machi no kippú

stand down vi (withdraw) 引下がる hikfsagarù

stand for vt fus (signify) 意味する fmì suru; (represent) 代表する daíhyō suru; (tolerate) 容認する yōnin suru

stand-in [stænd'in] n 代行 daíkō

stand in for vt fus (replace) ...の代役を務める ...no daíyaku wò tsutómerù

standing [stæn'diŋ] adj (on feet: ovation) 立ち上っている tachǎgatte irù; (permanent: invitation) 持続の jizóku no, 継続の keízoku no

♦*n* (status) 地位 chíi

of many years' standing 数年前から続いている sū́nen maè kara tsuzúite irú

standing joke *n* お決りの冗談 o-kímari nò jṓdaǹ

standing order (*BRIT*) *n* (at bank) 自動振替 jidṓfurīkae ◇支払額が定額である場合に使う shiháraḷgaku ga teḯgaku de arú báaǐ ni tsukáú

standing room *n* 立見席 tachímiseki

stand-offish [stændɔ'fi∫] *adj* 無愛想な buáǐso na

stand out *vi* (be prominent) 目立つ medátsū

standpoint [stænd'point] *n* 観点 kaǹteǹ

standstill [stænd'stil] *n: at a standstill* (*also fig*) 止って todókōtte

to come to a standstill 止ってしまう tomátte shimaú

stand up *vi* (rise) 立ち上る tachíagarū

stand up for *vt fus* (defend) 守る mamórū

stand up to *vt fus* (withstand: *also fig*) …に立向かう ...ni tachímukaú

stank [stæŋk] *pt of* **stink**

staple [stei'pəl] *n* (for papers) ホチキスの針 hóchīkisu no hárì

♦*adj* (food etc) 主要の shuyṓ no

♦*vt* (fasten) ホチキスで留める hóchīkisu de tomérú

stapler [stei'plər] *n* ホチキス hóchīkisu

star [stɑːr] *n* (in sky) 星 hoshí; (celebrity) スター sutā́

♦*vi: to star in ...* で主演する ...de shuén suru

♦*vt* (THEATER, CINEMA) 主役とする shuyéku to surú

starboard [stɑːr'bɔːrd] *n* 右げん úgeǹ

starch [stɑːrt∫] *n* (for shirts etc) のり noríi; (CULIN) でんぷん deńpun

stardom [stɑːr'dəm] *n* スターの身分 sutā́ no mibún

stare [steːr] *n* じろじろ見る事 jírójiro mírú koto

♦*vi: to stare at* じろじろ見る jírójiro mírú

starfish [stɑːr'fi∫] *n* ヒトデ hitode

stark [stɑːrk] *adj* (bleak) 殺風景な sap-

pū́kei na

♦*adv: stark naked* 素っ裸の suppádaka no

starling [stɑːr'liŋ] *n* ムクドリ mukúdori

starry [stɑːr'iː] *adj* (night, sky) 星がよく見える hoshí gà yókù míérù

starry-eyed [stɑːr'iːaid] *adj* (innocent) 天真らん漫な teńshinranman na

stars [stɑːrz] *npl: the stars* (horoscope) 星占い hoshíuranáǐ

start [stɑːrt] *n* (beginning) 初め hajíme; (departure) 出発 shuppátsu; (sudden movement) ぎくっとする事 gíkúttó suru kotó; (advantage) リード rḯdo

♦*vt* (begin) 始める hajímerū; (cause) 引起こす hikíokosù; (found: business etc) 創立する sṓritsu suru; (engine) かける kakérù

♦*vi* (begin) 始まる hajímarū; (with fright) ぎくっとする gíkúttó suru; (train etc) 出発する shuppátsu suru

to start doing/to do something ... を し始める ...wo shihájimerū

starter [stɑːr'tər] *n* (AUT) スターター sutā́tā; (SPORT: official) スターター sutā́tā; (*BRIT*: CULIN) 最初の料理 saísho no ryṓri

starting point [stɑːr'tiŋ-] *n* 出発点 shuppátsuteǹ

startle [stɑːr'təl] *vt* 驚かす odórokasù

startling [stɑːr'tliŋ] *adj* (news etc) 驚く様な odóroku yṓ na

start off *vi* (begin) 始める hajímerū; (begin moving) 出発する shuppátsu suru

start up *vi* (business etc) 開業する kaígyō suru; (engine) かかる kakárù; (car) 走り出す hashíridasù

♦*vt* (business etc) 創立する sṓritsu suru; (engine) かける kakérù; (car) 走らせる hashíraserù

starvation [stɑːrvei'∫ən] *n* 飢餓 kígà

starve [stɑːrv] *vi* (*inf*: be very hungry) おなかがぺこぺこである onáka ga pekópeko de árù; (*also*: **starve to death**) 餓死する gáshī suru

♦*vt* (person, animal: not give food to) 飢えさせる uésaserù; (: to death) 餓死させる gáshī saserù

state [steit] n (condition) 状態 jōtai; (government) 国 kuní

♦vt (say, declare) 明言する meĩgen suru

to be in a state 取乱している torímidashite irū

stately [steit'li:] adj (home, walk etc) 優雅な yūga na

statement [steit'mənt] n (declaration) 陳述 chínjutsu

States [steits] npl: **the States** 米国 beñkoku

statesman [steits'mən] (pl **statesmen**) n リーダー格の政治家 rídā-kaku no seijìka

static [stæt'ik] n (RADIO, TV) 雑音 zatsúon

♦adj (not moving) 静的な seĩteki na

static electricity n 静電気 seídeñki

station [stei'ʃən] n (RAIL) 駅 ékí; (police station etc) 署 shó; (RADIO) 放送局 hōsōkyoku

♦vt (position: guards etc) 配置する háíchi suru

stationary [stei'ʃəneri:] adj (vehicle) 動いていない ugóite inaí

stationer [stei'ʃənər] n 文房具屋 buñbōguya

stationer's (shop) [stei'ʃənərz-] n 文房具店 buñbōguteñ

stationery [stei'ʃəneri:] n 文房具 buñbōgu

stationmaster [stei'ʃənmæstər] n (RAIL) 駅長 ekíchō

station wagon (US) n ワゴン車 wagóñsha

statistic [stətis'tik] n 統計値 tōkeichì

statistical [stətis'tikəl] adj (evidence, techniques) 統計学的な tōkeigakuteki na

statistics [stətis'tiks] n (science) 統計学 tōkeigaku

statue [stætʃ'u:] n 像 zō

stature [stætʃ'ur] n 身長 shíñchō

status [stei'təs] n (position) 身分 mĩbun; (official classification) 資格 shikàku; (importance) 地位 chíi

the status quo 現状 geñjō

status symbol n ステータスシンボル sutétasushiñboru

statute [stætʃ'u:t] n 法律 hōritsu

statutory [stætʃ'u:tɔ:ri:] adj (powers, rights etc) 法定の hōtei no

staunch [stɔ:ntʃ] adj (ally) 忠実な chūjitsu na

stave off [steiv-] vt (attack, threat) 防ぐ fuségù

stay [stei] n (period of time) 滞在期間 taízaikikan

♦vi (remain) 居残る inókorù; (with someone, as guest) 泊る tomárù; (in place: spend some time) とどまる todómarù

to stay put とどまる todómarù

to stay the night 泊る tomárù

stay behind vi 居残る inókorù

stay in vi (at home) 家にいる ié ní irū

staying power [stei'iŋ-] n 根気 koñki

stay on vi 残る nokórù

stay out vi (of house) 家に戻らない ié ní modóranaĩ

stay up vi (at night) 起きている ókìte irū

stead [sted] n: **in someone's stead** ...の代りに ...no kawàri ni

to stand someone in good stead ...の役に立つ ...no yakú ni tatsù

steadfast [sted'fæst] adj 不動の fudō no

steadily [sted'ili:] adv (firmly) 着実に chakújitsu ni; (constantly) ずっと zuttó; (fixedly) じっと jittó; (walk) しっかりと shikkári to

steady [sted'i:] adj (constant: job, boyfriend, speed) 決った kimáttà, 変らない kawáranaĩ; (regular: rise in prices) 着実な chakújitsu na; (person, character) 堅実な keñjitsu na; (firm: hand etc) 震えない furénaĩ; (calm: look, voice) 落着いた ochítsuita

♦vt (stabilize) 安定させる afitei saserū; (nerves) 静める shizúmerù

steak [steik] n (also: **beefsteak**) ビーフステーキ bífusutēki; (beef, fish, pork etc) ステーキ sutēki

steal [sti:l] (pt **stole**, pp **stolen**) vt 盗む nusúmù

♦vi (thieve) 盗む nusúmù; (move secretly) こっそりと行く kossóri to ikú

stealth [stelθ] *n*: **by stealth** こっそりと kossórì

stealthy [stel'θi:] *adj* (movements, actions) ひそかな hisókà na

steam [sti:m] *n* (mist) 水蒸気 suíjòki; (on window) 曇り kumóri
♦*vt* (CULIN) 蒸す músù
♦*vi* (give off steam) 水蒸気を立てる suíjòki wo tatérù

steam engine *n* 蒸気機関 jòkikìkàn

steamer [sti:'mə:r] *n* 汽船 kisén

steamroller [sti:m'roulə:r] *n* ロードローラー rôdorôrà

steamship [sti:m'ʃip] *n* = **steamer**

steamy [sti:'mi:] *adj* (room) 湯気でもうもうした yúgè de mômò no; (window) 湯気で曇った yúgè de kumóttà; (heat, atmosphere) 蒸暑い mushíatsuì

steel [sti:l] *n* 鋼鉄 kôtetsu
♦*adj* 鋼鉄の kôtetsu no

steelworks [sti:l'wə:rks] *n* 製鋼所 sefkòjo

steep [sti:p] *adj* (stair, slope) 険しい kewáshiì; (increase) 大幅な ôhaba na; (price) 高い takáì
♦*vt* (fig: soak) 浸す hitásù

steeple [sti:'pəl] *n* せん塔 sefitò

steeplechase [sti:'pəltʃeis] *n* 障害レース shôgairèsu

steer [sti:r] *vt* (vehicle) 運転する ufiten suru; (person) 導く michíbikù
♦*vi* (maneuver) 車を操る kurúma wò ayátsurù

steering [sti:r'iŋ] *n* (AUT) ステアリング sutéaringù

steering wheel *n* ハンドル hafídoru

stem [stem] *n* (of plant) 茎 kukí; (of glass) 足 ashí
♦*vt* (stop: blood, flow, advance) 止める tomérù

stem from *vt fus* (subj: condition, problem) ...に由来する ...ni yurái suru

stench [stentʃ] *n* 悪臭 akúshuu

stencil [sten'səl] *n* (lettering) ステンシルで書いた文字 sutéñshiru de kálta mójì; (pattern used) ステンシル sutéñshiru
♦*vt* (letters, designs etc) ステンシルで書く sutéñshiru de kákù

stenographer [stənɔ:g'rəfə:r] (US) *n* 速記者 sokkíshà

step [step] *n* (footstep, also *fig*) 一歩 íppò; (sound) 足音 ashíoto; (of stairs) 段 dáñ, ステップ sutéppù
♦*vi*: **to step forward** 前に出る máe ni dérù **to step back** 後ろに下がる ushíro nì sagárù

in/out of step (with) (...と) 歩調が合って[ずれて] (...to) hochó ga attè [zurête]

stepbrother [step'brʌðə:r] *n* 異父〔母〕兄弟 ífù〔bò〕kyôdài

stepdaughter [step'dɔ:tə:r] *n* まま娘 mamámusùme

step down *vi* (*fig*: resign) 辞任する jinín suru

stepfather [step'fɑːðə:r] *n* まま父 mamáchichi

stepladder [step'lædə:r] *n* 脚立 kyatátsu

stepmother [step'mʌðə:r] *n* まま母 mamáhaha

step on *vt fus* (something: walk on) 踏む fumú

stepping stone *n* 飛石 tobíishi

steps [steps] (*BRIT*) *npl* = **stepladder**

stepsister [step'sistə:r] *n* 異父〔母〕姉妹 ífù〔bò〕shímài

stepson [step'sʌn] *n* まま息子 mamámusùko

step up *vt* (increase: efforts, pace etc) 増す masú

stereo [ster'i:ou] *n* (system) ステレオ sutéreo; (record player) レコードプレーヤー rekôdopurèyà
♦*adj* (also: **stereophonic**) ステレオの sutéreo no

stereotype [ster'i:ətaip] *n* 固定概念 kotéigaìnen

sterile [ster'əl] *adj* (free from germs: bandage etc) 殺菌した sakkín shita; (barren: woman, female animal) 子供の生めない umènai; (: man, male animal) 子供を作れない kodómò wo tsukúrenaì; (land) 不毛の fumô no

sterilize [ster'əlaiz] *vt* (thing, place) 殺菌する sakkín suru; (woman) ...に避妊手術をする ...ni hiníñshujùtsu wo suru

sterling [stəːˈlɪŋ] adj (silver) 純銀の juñgin no

◆n (ECON) 英国通貨 eñkokutsúka

one pound sterling 英貨1ポンド éika ichf poñdo

stern [stəːrn] adj (father, warning etc) 厳しい kibíshiì

◆n (of boat) 船尾 séñbi

stethoscope [steθˈəskoup] n 聴診器 chōshíñki

stew [stuː] n シチュー shichúu

◆vt (meat, vegetables) 煮込む nikómù; (fruit) 煮る nirú

steward [stuːˈəːrd] n (on ship, plane, train) スチュワード suchúwàdo

stewardess [stuːˈəːrdis] n (especially on plane) スチュワーデス suchúwàdesu

stick [stik] n (gen: of wood) 棒 bō; (as weapon) こん棒 koñbō; (walking stick) つえ tsúè

◆vb (pt, pp **stuck**)

◆vt (with glue etc) 張る harú; (inf: place) 置く okú; (: tolerate) …の最後まで我慢する …no sáigo made gámàn surú; (thrust): *to stick something into* …の中へ…を突っ込む …no nákà e …wo tsukkómù

◆vi (become attached) くっつく kuttsúkù; (be immovable) 引っ掛る hikkákàrù; (in mind etc) 焼付く yakítsukù

a stick of dynamite ダイナマイト1本 dainamáito ippoñ

sticker [stikˈəːr] n ステッカー sutékkà

sticking plaster [stikˈiŋ-] n ばんそうこう bañsōkō

stickler [stikˈləːr] n: *to be a stickler for* …に関してやかましい …ni káñ shite yakámashiì

stick out vi (ears etc) 突出る tsukíderù

stick up vi (hair etc) 立つ tátsù

stick-up [stikˈʌp] (inf) n ピストル強盗 pisútoru gōtō

stick up for vt fus (person) …の肩をもつ …no kátà wo mótsù; (principle) 守る mamórù

sticky [stikˈiː] adj (messy: hands etc) べたべたしている bétàbeta shité irù; (label) 粘着の neñchaku no; (fig: situation) 厄介な yákkai na

stiff [stif] adj (hard, firm: brush) 堅い katáì; (hard: paste, egg-white) 固まった katámattà; (moving with difficulty: arms, legs, back) こわばった kowábattà; (: door, zip etc) 堅い katáì; (formal: manner, smile) 堅苦しい katágurushiì; (difficult, severe: competition, sentence) 厳しい kibíshiì; (strong: drink, breeze) 強い tsuyóì; (high: price) 高い takáì

◆adv (bored, worried, scared) ひどく hídòku

stiffen [stifˈən] vi (body, muscles, joints) こわばる kowábarù

stiff neck n 首が回らない事 kubí gà mawáranaì kotó

stifle [staiˈfəl] vt (cry, yawn) 抑える osáerù; (opposition) 抑圧する yokúatsu suru

stifling [staiˈfliŋ] adj (heat) 息苦しい ikígurushiì

stigma [stigˈmə] n (fig: of divorce, failure, defeat etc) 汚名 ómèi

stile [stail] n 踏段 fumídan ◇牧場のさくの両側に設けられ、人間が越えられるが家畜が出られない様になった bokújō nò sakú nò ryógawa nì mōkérarè, niñgen gà koérarerù ga kachíku gà derárenaì yō ni shíta monð

stiletto [stiletˈou] (BRIT) n (also: **stiletto heel**) ハイヒール haíhīru

still [stil] adj (person, water, air) 動かない ugókanaì; (place) 静寂な sefjaku na

◆adv (up to this time, yet) まだ mádà; (even) 更に sárà ni; (nonetheless) それにしても soré ni shite mò

stillborn [stilˈbɔːrn] adj 死産の shízan no

still life n 静物画 seíbutsuga

stilt [stilt] n (pile) 脚柱 kyakúchū; (for walking on) 竹馬 takéuma

stilted [stilˈtid] adj (behavior, conversation) 堅苦しい katágurushiì

stimulant [stimˈjələnt] n 興奮剤 kakúseizai

stimulate [stimˈjəleit] vt (person, demand) 刺激する shigéki suru

stimulating [stimˈjəleitiŋ] adj (conversation, person, experience) 刺激的な shigékiteki na

stimuli [stim'jəlai] *npl of* **stimulus**

stimulus [stim'jələs] *n (pl stimuli)* *n* (encouragement, *also* MED) 刺激 shigéki

sting [stiŋ] *n* (wound) 虫刺され mushísasaré; (pain) 刺す様な痛み sásù yō na itámi; (organ) 針 hárì
♦*vb (pt, pp stung)*
♦*vt* (insect, plant etc) 刺す sásù; (fig) 傷付ける kizútsukerù
♦*vi* (insect, plant etc) 刺す sásù; (eyes, ointment etc) しみる shimírù

stingy [stin'dʒi:] *adj* けちな kéchī na

stink [stiŋk] *n* (smell) 悪臭 akúshū
♦*vi (pt stank, pp stunk)* (smell) におう nióù

stinking [stiŋ'kiŋ] *(inf) adj* くそったれの kusóttàre no

stint [stint] *n* 仕事の期間 shigóto no kikàn
♦*vi*: **to stint on** (work, ingredients etc) ...をけちる ...wo kechírù

stipulate [stip'jəleit] *vt* ...の条件を付ける ...no jōken wo tsukérù

stir [stə:r] *n (fig:* agitation) 騒ぎ sáwàgi
♦*vt* (tea etc) かき混ぜる kakímazerù; (fig: emotions) 刺激する shigéki suru
♦*vi* (move slightly) ちょっと動く chóttò ugókù

stirrup [stə:r'əp] *n* あぶみ abúmi

stir up *vt* (trouble) 引起こす hikíokosù

stitch [stitʃ] *n* (SEWING, MED) 一針 hitóhàri; (KNITTING) ステッチ sutétchì; (pain) わき腹のけいれん wakíbara no keíren
♦*vt* (sew: gen, MED) 縫う núù

stoat [stout] *n* てん tén

stock [stɑːk] *n* (supply) 資源 shígèn; (COMM) 在庫品 zaíkohìn; (AGR) 家畜 kachíku; (CULIN) 煮出し汁 nidáshìjiru, ストック sutőkkū; (descent) 血統 kettő; (FINANCE: government stock etc) 株式 kabúshìki
♦*adj (fig:* reply, excuse etc) お決りの o-kímari no
♦*vt* (have in stock) 常備する jőbì suru
stocks and shares 債券 saíken
in/out of stock 在庫ある[ない] zaíko gà árù (nai)

to take stock of *(fig)* 検討する kentő suru

stockbroker [stɑk'broukəːr] *n* 株式仲買人 kabúshikinakagainin

stock cube *(BRIT) n* 固形スープの素 kokéi sūpu no moto

stock exchange *n* 株式取引所 kabúshikitoríhikijo

stocking [stɑk'iŋ] *n* ストッキング sutőkkìngu

stockist [stɑk'ist] *(BRIT) n* 特約店 tokúyakuten

stock market *n* 株式市場 kabúshikishijō

stock phrase *n* 決り文句 kimárimonku

stockpile [stɑk'pail] *n* 備蓄 bichíku
♦*vt* 貯蔵する chozó suru

stocktaking [stɑk'teikiŋ] *(BRIT) n* (COMM) 棚卸し tanáoroshi

stock up with *vt* ...を仕入れる ...wo shiírerù

stocky [stɑ.k'i:] *adj* (strong, short) がっしりした gasshírì shita; (short, stout) ずんぐりした zungurí shita

stodgy [stɑdʒ'i:] *adj* (food) こってりした kottérì shita

stoical [stou'ikəl] *adj* 平然とした heízen tō shita

stoke [stouk] *vt* (fire, furnace, boiler) ...に燃料をくべる ...ni nefíryō wo kubérù

stole [stoul] *pt of* **steal**
♦*n* ストール sutőrù

stolen [stou'lən] *pp of* **steal**

stolid [stɑl'id] *adj* (person, behavior) 表情の乏しい hyőjō no tobóshiì

stomach [stʌm'ək] *n* (ANAT) 胃 i; (belly) おなか onáka
♦*vt* (fig) 耐える taérù

stomachache [stʌm'əkeik] *n* 腹痛 fukútsū

stone [stoun] *n* (rock) 石 ishí; (pebble) 小石 koíshi; (gem) 宝石 hōseki; (in fruit) 種 tánè; (MED) 結石 kessékì; (BRIT: weight) ストーン sutőn〈体重の単位, 約 6.3 kg tajū no tañ-i, yákù 6.3 kg〉
♦*adj* (pottery) ストーンウエアの sutőn-ueà no

♦vt (person) ...に石を投げつける ...ni ishi wo nagetsukerù; (fruit) ...の種を取る ...no tánè wo tórù

stone-cold [stoun'kould'] *adj* 冷え切った hiékíttà

stone-deaf [stoun'def'] *adj* かなつんぼの kanátsuǹbo no

stonework [stoun'wə:rk] *n* (stones) 石造りの物 ishízukúrí no monó

stony [stou'ni:] *adj* (ground) 石だらけの ishídaràke no; (*fig*: glance, silence etc) 冷淡な reftan na

stood [stud] *pt, pp* of **stand**

stool [stu:l] *n* スツール sutsúru

stoop [stu:p] *vi* (*also*: **stoop down**: bend) 腰をかがめる koshí wo kagámerù; (*also*: **have a stoop**) 腰が曲っている koshí gà magátte irú

stop [sta:p] *n* (halt) 停止 tefshi; (short stay) 立寄り tachíyori; (in punctuation: *also*: **full stop**) ピリオド pírìodo; (bus stop etc) 停留所 teíryūjo

♦vt (break off) 止める tomérù; (block: pay, check) ...の支払を停止させる ...no shíharai wo tefshi saserù; (prevent: *also*: **put a stop to**) やめさせる yamésaserù

♦vi (halt: motion) 立ち止る tachídomarù; (: watch, clock) 止る tomárù; (end: rain, noise etc) やむ yamú

to stop doing something ...するのをやめる ...surú no wo yaméru

stop dead *vi* 急に止る kyū̀ ni tomárù

stopgap [sta:p'gæp] *n* (person/thing) 間に合せの人[物] ma nì awase nò hitő [monő]

stop off *vi* 立寄る tachíyorù

stopover [sta:p'ouvə:r] *n* (gen) 立寄って泊る事 tachíyotte tomárù kotŏ; (AVIAT) 給油着陸 kyū̀yuchakúriku

stoppage [sta:p'idʒ] *n* (strike) ストライキ sutőraìki; (blockage) 停止 tefshi

stopper [sta:p'ə:r] *n* 栓 seň

stop press *n* 最新ニュース safshinnyū̀su

stop up *vt* (hole) ふさぐ fuságù

stopwatch [sta:p'wa:tʃ] *n* ストップウォッチ sutőppuuotch̀

storage [stɔ:r'idʒ] *n* 保管 hokáñ

storage heater *n* 蓄熱ヒーター chikú-

netsuhítà ◇深夜など電気需要の少ない時に熱を作って蓄える. 昼間それを放射するヒーター shíň-ya nádò deńkijuyō no sukúnai tokî ni netsû wo tsukutté takúwaè, hiruma soré wo hōsha suru hítà

store [stɔ:r] *n* (stock) 蓄え takúwaè; (depot) 倉庫 sōko; (*BRIT*: large shop) デパート depátò; (*US*) 店 misé; (reserve) 備蓄 bichíku

♦vt (provisions, information etc) 蓄える takúwaerù

in store 未来に待構えて mírài ni machíkamaetè

storeroom [stɔ:r'ru:m] *n* 倉庫 sōko

stores [stɔ:rz] *npl* (provisions) 物資 bússhi

store up *vt* (nuts, sugar, memories) 蓄える takúwaerù

storey [stɔ:r'i:] (*BRIT*: floor) *n* = **story**

stork [stɔ:rk] *n* コウノトリ kōnotòri

storm [stɔ:rm] *n* (bad weather) 嵐 áràshi; (*fig*: of criticism, applause etc) 爆発 bakúhatsu

♦vi (*fig*: speak angrily) どなる donárù

♦vt (attack: place) 攻撃する kōgeki suru

stormy [stɔ:r'mi:] *adj* (weather) 荒れ模様の arémoyō no; (*fig*: debate, relations) 激しい hagéshî

story [stɔ:r'i:] *n* (gen: *also*: **history**) 物語 monőgatàri; (lie) うそ úsò; (*US*) 階 kái

storybook [stɔ:r'i:buk] *n* 童話の本 dōwa no hoň

stout [staut] *adj* (strong: branch etc) 丈夫な jōbu na; (fat) 太った futőttà; (resolute: friend, supporter) 不動の fudő no

♦n (beer) スタウト sutátto

stove [stouv] *n* (for cooking) レンジ reňji; (for heating) ストーブ sutő̀bu

stow [stou] *vt* (*also*: **stow away**) しまう shimáù

stowaway [stou'əwei] *n* 密航者 mikkő̀sha

straddle [stræd'əl] *vt* (chair, fence etc: *also fig*) ...にまたがる ...ni matágarù

straggle [stræg'əl] *vi* (houses etc) 散在する sañzai suru; (people etc) 落こする rakúgo suru

straggly [stræg'li:] *adj* (hair) ぼさぼさし

た bósabosa shita

straight [streit] *adj* (line, road, back, hair) 真っ直ぐの massúgu no; (honest: answer) 正直な shójiki na; (simple: choice, fight) 簡潔な kañketsu na
♦*adv* (directly) 真っ直ぐに massúgu ni; (drink) ストレートで sutóreēto de

to put/get something straight (make clear) 明らかにする akfräka ni suru
straight away, straight off (at once) 直ちに tádachi ni

straighten [strei'tən] *vt* (skirt, bed etc) 整える totónoerù

straighten out *vt* (fig: problem, situation) 解決する kañketsu suru

straight-faced [streit'feist] *adj* まじめな顔をした majíme nà kaó wo shitá

straightforward [streitfɔːr'wərd] *adj* (simple) 簡単な kañtan na; (honest) 正直な shójiki na

strain [strein] *n* (pressure) 負担 fután; (TECH) ひずみ hizúmi; (MED: tension) 緊張 kiñchō; (breed) 血統 kettő
♦*vt* (back etc) 痛める itámerù; (stretch: resources) ...に負担をかける ...ni fután wò kakérù; (CULIN: food) こす kosú

back strain (MED) ぎっくり腰 gikkúrigòshi

strained [streind] *adj* (back, muscle) 痛めた itámetà; (relations) 緊迫した kiñpaku shità

a strained laugh 作り笑い tsukúriwaräi

strainer [strei'nər] *n* (CULIN) こし器 koshíkì

strains [streinz] *npl* (MUS) 旋律 seńritsu

strait [streit] *n* (GEO) 海峡 kaíkyō

strait-jacket [streit'dʒækit] *n* 拘束衣 kósokuī

strait-laced [streit'leist] *adj* しかつめらしい shikátsumerashiì

straits [streits] *npl: to be in dire straits* (fig) 困り果てている komárihatete irù

strand [strænd] *n* (of thread, hair, rope) 一本 íppon

stranded [stræn'did] *adj* (holiday-makers) 足留めされた ashídome saretà

strange [streindʒ] *adj* (not known) 未知の míchi no; (odd) 変な hén na

strangely [streindʒ'liː] *adv* (act, speak) 変った風に kawátta fū ni ¶ *see also* **enough**

stranger [strein'dʒər] *n* (unknown person) 知らない人 shiránai hitő; (from another area) よそ者 yosómono

strangle [stræŋ'gəl] *vt* (victim) 絞め殺す shiměkorosù; (fig: economy) 圧迫する appáku suru

stranglehold [stræŋ'gəlhould] *n* (fig) 圧力 yokúatsu

strap [stræp] *n* 肩ひも katáhimo, ストラップ sutórappù

strapping [stræp'iŋ] *adj* たくましい takúmashiì

strata [stræt'ə] *npl of* **stratum**

stratagem [stræt'ədʒəm] *n* 策略 sakúryàku

strategic [strəti:'dʒik] *adj* (positions, withdrawal, weapons etc) 戦略的な señryakuteki na

strategy [stræt'idʒiː] *n* (plan, *also* MIL) 作戦 sakúsen

stratum [strei'təm] *(pl* **strata***)* *n* (gen) 層 só; (in earth's surface) 地層 chisō; (in society) 階層 kaísō

straw [strɔː] *n* (dried stalks) わら wárà; (drinking straw) ストロー sutórō

that's the last straw! もう我慢できないも我慢 dekínai

strawberry [strɔː'beriː] *n* イチゴ ichígo

stray [strei] *adj* (animal) のら... norá...; (bullet) 流れ... nagáre...; (scattered) 点在する teñzai suru
♦*vi* (children, animals) はぐれる hagúrerù; (thoughts) 横道にそれる yokómichi nì sorérù

streak [strik] *n* (stripe: *gen*) 筋 sújì
♦*vt* ...に筋を付ける ...ni sújì wo tsukérù
♦*vi: to streak past* スピードで通り過ぎる hmáoyùpìde tōrisúgirù

stream [strim] *n* (small river) 小川 ogáwa; (of people, vehicles, smoke) 流れ nagáre; (of questions, insults etc) 連続 reńzoku

◆vt (SCOL: students) 能力別に分ける nóryokubètsu ni wakérù
◆vi (water, oil, blood) 流れる nagárerù
to stream in/out (people) 流れ込む(出る) nagárekomù(derù)

streamer [stri:'mə:r] n 紙テープ kamítēpu

streamlined [stri:m'laind] adj 流線形の ryūsenkei no

street [stri:t] n 道 michí

streetcar [stri:t'ka:r] (US) n 路面電車 roméndeñsha

street lamp n 街灯 gaítō

street plan n 市街地図 shigáichizù

streetwise [stri:t'waiz] (inf) adj 街中の悪知恵を持っている urámachī no warújì e wò motté irù

strength [streŋkθ] n (physical) 体力 táíryoku; (of girder, knot etc) 強さ tsúyòsa; (fig: power, number) 勢力 seíryoku

strengthen [streŋk'θən] vt (building, machine) 補強する hokyō surù; (fig: group, argument, relationship) 強くする tsúyòku surù

strenuous [stren'ju:əs] adj (energetic: exercise) 激しい hageshíì; (determined: efforts) 精力的な seíryokuteki na

stress [stres] n (force, pressure, also TECH) 圧力 atsúryòku; (mental strain) ストレス sutórèsu; (emphasis) 強調 kyóchō
◆vt (point, importance etc) 強調する kyóchō surù; (syllable) ...にアクセントを置く ...ni ákùsento wo okú

stretch [stretʃ] n (area: of sand, water etc) 一帯 ittái
◆vi (person, animal) 背伸びする sénòbi surù; (extend): **to stretch to/as far as** ...まで続く ...máde tsuzúkù
◆vt (pull) 伸ばす nobásù; (subj: job, task: make demands of) ...に努力を要求する ...ni dóryòku wo yōkyū surù

stretcher [stretʃ'ə:r] n 担架 táñka

stretch out vi 体を伸ばす karáda wo nobásù
◆vt (arm etc) 伸ばす nobásù; (spread) 広げる hirógerù

strewn [stru:n] adj: **strewn with** ...が散

らばっている ...ga chirábatte irù

stricken [strik'ən] adj (person) 打ちひしがれた uchíhishìgareta; (city, industry etc) 災いに見舞われた wazáwai nì mimáwareta
stricken with (arthritis, disease) ...にかかっている ...ni kákàtte irù

strict [strikt] adj (severe, firm: person, rule) 厳しい kibíshiì; (precise: meaning) 厳密な geñmitsu na

strictly [strikt'li:] adv (severely) 厳しく kibíshikù; (exactly) 厳密に geñmitsu ni

stridden [strid'ən] pp of **stride**

stride [straid] n (step) 大また の一歩 ōmàta no íppò
◆vi (pt **strode**, pp **stridden**) 大またに歩く ōmàta ni arúkù

strident [straid'ənt] adj (voice, sound) 甲高い kañdakai

strife [straif] n 反目 hañmoku

strike [straik] n (of workers) ストライキ sutóraìki; (of mineral oil) 発見 hakkén; (MIL: attack) 攻撃 kōgeki
◆vb (pt, pp **struck**)
◆vt (hit: person, thing) 打つ útsù; (fig: subj: idea, thought) ...の心に浮ぶ ...no kókòro ni ukábù; (oil etc) 発見する hakkén surù; (bargain, deal) 決める kimérù
◆vi (go on strike) ストライキに入る sutóraìki ni háìru; (attack: soldiers) 攻撃する kōgeki surù; (: illness) 襲う osóù; (: disaster) 見舞う mimáù; (clock) 鳴る narú

on strike (workers) ストライキ中で sutóraikichū de
to strike a match マッチを付ける mátchì wo tsukérù

strike down vt (kill) 殺す korósù; (harm) 襲う osóù

striker [strai'kə:r] n (person on strike) ストライキ参加者 sutóraikisankasha; (SPORT) 攻撃選手 kōgekiseñshu

strike up (MUS) 演奏し始める eñsō shihajimerù; (conversation) 始める hajmerù; (friendship) 結ぶ musúbù

striking [strai'kiŋ] adj (noticeable) 目立つ medátsù; (attractive) 魅力的な miryókuteki na

string [striŋ] n (thin rope) ひも himo; (row: of beads etc) 数珠つなぎの物 juzútsunági no monó; (: of disasters etc) 一連 ichíren; (MUS) 弦 gén

♦vt (pt, pp strung): to string together つなぐ tsunágù

a string of islands 列島 rettō

to pull strings (fig) コネを利用する kóně wo riyó suru

to string out 一列に並べる ichíretsu ni naráberù

string bean n さや豆 sayámame

string(ed) instrument [striŋ(d)-] n (MUS) 弦楽器 gefigakkī

stringent [strin'dʒənt] adj (rules, measures) 厳しい kibíshiī

strings [striŋz] npl: *the strings* (MUS: section of orchestra) 弦楽器 gefigakkī

strip [strip] n (gen) 細長い切れ hosónagaī kiré; (of land, water) 細長い一帯 hosónagaī ittái

♦vt (undress) 裸にする hadáka ni surú; (paint) はがす hagásù; (also: **strip down**: machine) 分解する buŋkai suru

♦vi (undress) 裸になる hadáka ni narú

strip cartoon n 四こま漫画 yofikoma mañga

stripe [straip] n (gen) しま shima; (MIL, POLICE) そで章 sodéshō

striped [straipt] adj しま模様の shimámoyō no

strip lighting n 蛍光灯 keíkōtō

stripper [strip'ər] n ストリッパー sutórippā

striptease [strip'ti:z] n ストリップショー sutórippushō

strive [straiv] (pt **strove**, pp **striven**) vi: *to strive for something/to do something* ...しようと努力する ...shiyó to dóryòku suru

striven [striv'ən] pp of **strive**

strode [stroud] pt of **stride**

stroke [strouk] n (blow) 一撃 ichígeki; (SWIMMING) ストローク sutórōku; (MED) 脳卒中 nósotchū; (of paintbrush) 筆の運び fudé no hakóbi

♦vt (caress) なでる nadérù

at a stroke 一気に íkkī ni

stroll [stroul] n 散歩 safipo

♦vi 散歩する safipo suru

stroller [strou'lər] (US) n (pushchair) いす型ベビーカー isúgata bebíkā

strong [strɔːŋ] adj (person, arms, grasp) 強い tsuyóì; (stick) 丈夫な jóbu na; (wind) 強い tsuyóì; (imagination) 想像力のある sōzóryoku no árù; (personality) 気性の激しい kishó no hagéshiì; (influence) 強い tsuyóì; (nerves) 頑丈な gafijó na; (smell) 強烈な kyóretsu na; (coffee) 濃い koì; (taste) 際立った kiwádattà

they are 50 strong 50人いる gojúnin iru

stronghold [strɔːŋ'hould] n とりで toríde; (fig) 根城 nejíro

strongly [strɔːŋ'liː] adv (solidly: construct) 頑丈に gafijó ni; (with force: push, defend) 激しく hageshikù; (deeply: feel, believe) 強く tsuyóku

strongroom [strɔːŋ'ruːm] n 金庫室 kiñkoshītsu

strove [strouv] pt of **strive**

struck [strʌk] pt, pp of **strike**

structural [strʌk'tʃərəl] adj (damage, defect) 構造的な kózoteki na

structure [strʌk'tʃər] n (organization) 組織 sóshíki; (building) 構造物 kózobùtsu

struggle [strʌg'əl] n 闘争 tósō

♦vi (try hard) 努力する dóryòku suru; (fight) 戦う tatákaù

strum [strʌm] vt (guitar) つま弾く tsumábikù

strung [strʌŋ] pt, pp of **string**

strut [strʌt] n (wood, metal) 支柱 shíchū

♦vi 威張って歩く ibátte arukú

stub [stʌb] n (of check, ticket etc) 控え hikáe; (of cigarette) 吸殻 suígara

♦vt: *to stub one's toe* つま先をぶつける tsumásaki wo butsúkerù

stubble [stʌb'əl] n (AGR) 切り株 kiríkàbu; (on chin) 不精ひげ bushóhige

stubborn [stʌb'ərn] adj (child, determination) 頑固な gáñko na

stub out vt (cigarette) もみ消す momíkesù

stuck [stʌk] pt, pp of **stick**

♦adj (jammed) 引っ掛かっている hikkákatte irú

stuck-up [stʌkʹʌpʹ] (inf) adj 天ぐになっている teñgu nì natté irū

stud [stʌd] n (on clothing etc) 飾りボタン kazáribotàn; (earring) 丸玉 marúdamà (on sole of boot) スパイク supáiku; (also: **stud farm**) 馬の繁殖牧場 umá nò hańshokubokujō; (also: **stud horse**) 種馬 tanéuma

♦vt (fig: **studded with** ...をちりばめた ...wo chiríbametà

student [stuʹdənt] n (at university) 学生 gakúseì; (at lower schools) 生徒 seíto

♦adj (nurse, life, union) 学生の gakúseì no

student driver (US) n 仮免許運転者 karímeñkyo unteñsha

studies [stʌdʹiːz] npl (subjects studied) 勉強の科目 beñkyō nò kamőku

studio [stuʹdiːou] n (TV etc) スタジオ sutájìo; (sculptor's etc) アトリエ atórìè

studio apartment (BRIT **studio flat**) n ワンルームマンション wañrùmu máñshon

studious [stuʹdiːəs] adj (person) 勉強家の beñkyōka no; (careful: attention) 注意深い chúibukaì

studiously [stuʹdiːəslì] adv (carefully) 注意深く chúibukakù

study [stʌdʹiː] n (activity) 勉強 beñkyō; (room) 書斎 shosái

♦vt (learn about: subjects) 勉強する beñkyō suru; (examine: face, evidence) 調べる shiráberù

♦vi 勉強する beñkyō suru

stuff [stʌf] n (thing(s)) 物 monő, 事 kotő; (substance) 素質 soshítsu

♦vt (soft toy: also CULIN) ...に詰める ...ni tsumérù; (dead animals etc) ...を製にする hakúsei ni surù; (inf: push: object) 差込む sashíkomù

stuffing [stʌfʹiŋ] n (gen, CULIN) 詰め物 tsumémòno

stuffy [stʌfʹiː] adj (room) 空気の悪い kúki nò warúì; (person, ideas) 古臭い furúkusaì

stumble [stʌmʹbəl] vi つまずく tsumázukù

to **stumble across/on** (fig) ...に出くわす ...ni dekúwasù

stumbling block [stʌmʹbliŋ-] n 障害 shőgai

stump [stʌmp] n (of tree) 切株 kiríkàbu; (of limb) 断端 dañtan

♦vt: to be **stumped** まごつく magótsukù

stun [stʌn] vt (subj: news) あ然とさせる azen to saserú; (: blow on head) 気絶させる kizetsu saserú

stung [stʌŋ] pt, pp of **sting**

stunk [stʌŋk] pp of **stink**

stunning [stʌnʹiŋ] adj (fig: news, event) 仰天させる gyōten saserú; (: girl, dress) 美しい utsúkushiì

stunt [stʌnt] n (in film) スタント sutánto; (also: **publicity stunt**) 宣伝用のトリック señden-yō no toríkkù

stunted [stʌnʹtid] adj (trees, growth etc) 成長を阻害された seíchō wò sogái saretà

stuntman [stʌntʹmæn] (pl **stuntmen**) n スタントマン sutántoman

stupefy [stuʹpəfai] vt ぼう然とさせる bōzen to saserú

stupendous [stupenʹdəs] adj 途方もない tohőmonaì

stupid [stuʹpid] adj (person, question) ばかな bákà na

stupidity [stupidʹitiː] n 愚かさ orőkasà

stupor [stuʹpər] n 前後不覚 zeñgofukakù

sturdy [stəːrʹdiː] adj (person, thing) がっちりした gatchírì shita

stutter [stʌtʹəːr] n どもり dőmòri

♦vi どもる domőru

sty [stai] n (also: **pigsty**) 豚小屋 butágoya

stye [stai] n (MED) ものもらい monómoraì

style [stail] n (way, attitude) やり方 yaríkata; (elegance) 優雅さ yūgàsa; (design) スタイル sutáiru

stylish [staiʹliʃ] adj 優雅な yūgà na

stylus [staiʹləs] n (of record player) 針 harí

suave [swɑːv] adj 物柔らかな monōgoshi no teinei na

subconscious [sʌbkɔnˈtʃəs] adj (desire etc) 潜在意識の seńzaiishīki no

subcontract [sʌbkɑntrækt´] vt 下請に出す shitáuke nî dásù

subdivide [sʌbdivaid´] vt 小分けする kowáke suru

subdue [səbduː´] vt (rebels etc) 征服する seffuku suru; (passions) 抑制する yokúsei suru

subdued [səbduːd´] adj (light) 柔らかな yawárakà na; (person) 落込んだ ochíkoñda

subject [n sʌbˈdʒikt vb səbjekt´] n (matter) 話 題 wadái; (SCOL) 学科 gakká; (of kingdom) 臣 民 shíminñ; (GRAMMAR) 主語 shúgò

◆vt: **to subject someone to something** ...を...にさらす ...wo ...ni sarásù

to be subject to (law) ...に服従しなければならない ...ni fukújū shinakerèba naránaî; (heart attacks) ...が起りやすい ...ga okóriyasuî

to be subject to tax 課税される kazéi sarerù

subjective [səbdʒek´tiv] adj 主観的な shukánteki na

subject matter n (content) 内容 naíyo

subjugate [sʌbˈdʒəgeit] vt (people) 征服する seffuku suru

subjunctive [səbdʒʌŋk´tiv] n 仮定法 katéihō

sublet [sʌb´let] vt また貸しする matágashi suru

sublime [səblaim´] adj 素晴らしい subárashi

submachine gun [sʌbməʃin´-] n 軽機関銃 kefkikañjū

submarine [sʌbˈməriːn] n 潜水艦 seńsuikan

submerge [səbmərˈdʒ] vt 水中に沈める suíchū nî shizúmerù

◆vi (submarine, sea creature) 潜る mogúrù

submission [səbmiʃ´ən] n (state) 服従 fukújū; (claim) 申請書 shiñseisho; (of plan) 提出 teíshutsu

submissive [səbmis´iv] adj 従順な jújun na

submit [səbmit´] vt (proposal, application etc) 提出する teíshutsu suru

◆vi: **to submit to something** ...に従う ...ni shitágaù

subnormal [sʌbnɔːr´məl] adj (below average: temperatures) 通常以下の tsújōikā no

subordinate [səbɔːr´dənit] adj 二次的な nijīteki na

◆n 部下 búkà

subpoena [səpiː´nə] n (LAW) 召喚状 shōkañjō

subscribe [səbskraib´] vi: **to subscribe to** (opinion) ...に同意する ...ni dōī suru; (fund) ...に寄付する ...ni kifú suru; (magazine etc) ...を購読する ...wo kōdoku suru

subscriber [səbskraib´əːr] n (to periodical, telephone) 購読者 kōdokushā; (to telephone) 加入者 kanyūshā

subscription [səbskrip´ʃən] n (to magazine etc) 購読契約 kōdokukeíyàku

subsequent [sʌb´səkwənt] adj (following) その後の sonó atò no; (resulting) その結果として起る sonó kekkà toshite okórù

subsequently [sʌb´səkwəntli] adv その後 sonó atò

subside [səbsaid´] vi (feeling) 収る osámarù; (flood) ひく hikú; (wind) やむ yamú

subsidence [səbsaid´əns] n (in road etc) 陥没 kañbotsu

subsidiary [səbsid´iːriː] adj (question, details) 二次的な nijīteki na

◆n (also: **subsidiary company**) 子会社 kogáisha

subsidize [sʌb´sidaiz] vt (education, industry etc) ...に補助金を与える ...ni hojókiň wo atáerù

subsidy [sʌb´sidiː] n 補助金 hojókiň

subsistence [səbsis´təns] n (ability to live) 最低限度の生活水準 saíteigeñdo no seíkatsusuijùn

subsistence allowance (BRIT) n (advance payment) 支度金 shitákukiň (for expenses etc) 特別手当 tokúbetsu teâte

substance [sʌb'stəns] n (product, material) 物質 busshítsu

substantial [səbstæn'tʃəl] adj (solid) 頑丈な gafijô na; (fig: reward, meal) 多い ôi

substantially [səbstæn'tʃəli] adv (by a large amount) 大いに ôi ni; (in essence) 本質的に honshitsuteki ni

substantiate [səbstæn'tʃieit] vt 裏付けする urázukerû

substitute [sʌb'stitut] n (person) 代人 dafnin; (thing) 代用品 dafyôhin
◆vt: **to substitute A for B** B の代りにA を置く B no kawári nǐ A wò okú

substitution [sʌbstitu:'ʃən] n (act of substituting) 置換え okíkae; (SOCCER) 選手交代 seńshukôtai

subterfuge [sʌb'tə:rfjuːdʒ] n 策略 sakúryàku

subterranean [sʌbtərei'ni:ən] adj 地下の chiká no

subtitle [sʌb'taitəl] n 字幕スーパー jimákusûpā

subtle [sʌt'əl] adj (slight: change) 微妙な bimyô na; (indirect: person) 腹芸のうまい harágeì no umáì

subtlety [sʌt'əlti:] n (small detail) 微妙な所 bimyô na tokórò; (art of being subtle) 腹芸 harágeì

subtotal [sʌbtou'təl] n 小計 shôkei

subtract [səbtrækt'] vt ...から...を引く ...kárà ...wò hikú

subtraction [səbtræk'ʃən] n 引算 hikízan

suburb [sʌb'əːrb] n 都市周辺の自治体 toshíshûhen no jichítaì

suburban [səbəːr'bən] adj (train, lifestyle etc) 郊外の kôgai no

suburbia [səbəːr'bia] n 郊外 kôgai

suburbs [sʌb'əːrbz] npl: **the suburbs** (area) 郊外 kôgai

subversive [səbvəːr'siv] adj (activities, literature) 破壊的な hakáiteki na

subway [sʌb'wei] n (US: underground railway) 地下鉄 chikátetsu; (BRIT: underpass) 地下道 chikádô

succeed [səksiːd'] vi (plan etc) 成功する

sefkô suru; (person: in career etc) 出世する shusshô suru
◆vt (in job) ...の後任になる ...no kônin ni narú; (in order) ...の後に続く ...no átò ni tsuzúkù

to succeed in doing ...する事に成功する ...surú kotð ni sefkô suru

succeeding [səksiː'diŋ] adj (following) その後の sonó go no

success [səkses'] n (achievement) 成功 sefkô; (hit, also person) 大ヒット dafhittð

successful [səkses'fəl] adj (venture) 成功した sefkô shita; (writer) 出世した shusshô shita

to be successful 成功する sefkô suru

to be successful in doing ...する事に成功する ...surú kotð ni sefkô suru

successfully [səkses'fəli:] adv (complete, do) うまく úmàku

succession [səkseʃ'ən] n (series) 連続 reñzoku; (to throne etc) 継承 keíshô

in succession 立続けに tatétsuzuke ni

successive [səkses'iv] adj 連続の refizoku no

successor [səkses'əːr] n 後任 kônin

succinct [səksiŋkt'] adj 簡潔な kañketsu na

succulent [sʌk'jələnt] adj 汁が多くておいしい shírù ga ôkùte oíshiì

succumb [səkʌm'] vi (to temptation) 負ける makérù; (to illness: become very ill) ...で倒れる ...de taórerù; (: die) ...で死ぬ ...de shinú

such [sʌtʃ] adj (emphasizing similarity) この(その, あの)様な konó (sonó, anó) yô na; (of that kind): **such a book** ...の ような本 sofina hoñ; (so much): **such courage** そんな勇気 sofina yûki
◆adv この(そんな, あんな)に kofina (sofina, afina)hiñ

such books そんな本 sofina hoñ

such a long trip あんなに長い旅行 afína ni nagái ryokô

such a lot of そんなに沢山の sofina nǐ takúsan no

such as (like) ...の様な ...no yô na

as such その物 sonó monô

such-and-such [sʌtʃ'ənsʌtʃ] *adj* しかじかの shikájìka no

suck [sʌk] *vt (gen:* ice-lolly *etc)* なめる namérù; *(bottle, breast)* 吸う súù

sucker [sʌk'əːr] *n* (ZOOL) 吸盤 kyúban; *(inf:* easily cheated person*)* かも kámò

suction [sʌk'ʃən] *n* 吸引 kyúin

Sudan [suːdæn'] *n* スーダン sûdan

sudden [sʌd'ən] *adj* (unexpected, rapid: increase, shower, change) 突然の totsúzen no

all of a sudden (unexpectedly) 突然 totsúzen

suddenly [sʌd'ənliː] *adv* (unexpectedly) 突然 totsúzen

suds [sʌdz] *npl* 石けんの泡 sekkén no awâ

sue [suː] *vt* ...を相手取って訴訟を起す ...wo aftedottè soshổ wò okôsù

suede [sweid] *n* スエード suédò

suet [suː'it] *n* 脂肪 shibô ◇料理に使うシャモジウジの脂肪を指す ryôri ni tsukáù ushf yà hitợjì nồ katái shibô wò sásù

Suez [suː'ez] *n: the Suez Canal* スエズ運河 suézu ùñga

suffer [sʌf'əːr] *vt* (undergo: hardship etc) 経験する kefken suru; (bear: pain, rudeness) 我慢する gámàn suru

♦*vi* (be harmed: person, results etc) 苦しむ kurúshìmu; (results etc) 悪くなる wárùku nárù

to suffer from (illness etc) ...の病気にかかっている ...no byổki ni kakátte irù

sufferer [sʌf'əːrəːr] *n* (MED) 患者 kañja

suffering [sʌf'əːriŋ] *n* (hardship) 苦しみ kurúshìmi

suffice [səfais'] *vi* 足りる tarírù

sufficient [səfiʃ'ənt] *adj* 十分な júbùn na

sufficiently [səfiʃ'əntliː] *adv* 十分に júbùn ni

suffix [sʌf'iks] *n* 接尾辞 setsúbìjì

suffocate [sʌf'əkeit] *vi* 窒息する chissóku suru

suffocation [sʌfəkei'ʃən] *n* 窒息 chissóku

suffrage [sʌf'ridʒ] *n* (right to vote) 参政権 sañseiken

suffused [səfjuːzd'] *adj: suffused with* (light, color, tears) ...で満たされた ...de mitásaretà

sugar [ʃug'əːr] *n* 砂糖 satô

♦*vt* (tea etc) ...に砂糖を入れる ...ni satô wò irérù

sugar beet *n* サトウダイコン satôdàikon

sugar cane *n* サトウキビ satôkìbi

suggest [səgdʒest'] *vt* (propose) 提案する teían suru; (indicate) 示唆する shísà suru

suggestion [səgdʒes'tʃən] *n* (proposal) 提案 teían; (indication) 示唆 shísà

suggestive [səgdʒes'tiv] *(pej) adj* (remarks, looks) 卑わいな hiwáì na

suicide [suː'isaid] *n* (death, *also fig*) 自殺 jisátsu; (person) 自殺者 jisátsushà ¶ *see also* **commit**

suit [suːt] *n* (man's) 背広 sebfro; (woman's) スーツ sûtsu; (LAW) 訴訟 soshổ; (CARDS) 組札 kumffúdà

♦*vt (gen:* be convenient, appropriate) ...に都合がいい ...nì tsugô ga iì; (color, clothes) ...に似合う ...ni niáù; (adapt): *to suit something to* ...を...に合せる ...wo ...ni awáserù

well suited (well matched: couple) お似合いの o-niáì no

suitable [suː'təbəl] *adj* (convenient: time, moment) 都合のいい tsugô no iì; (appropriate: person, clothes etc) 適当な tekftô na

suitably [suː'təbliː] *adv* (dressed) 適当に tekftô ni; (impressed) 期待通りに kitái-dồri ni

suitcase [suːt'keis] *n* スーツケース sûtsukèsu

suite [swiːt] *n* (of rooms) スイートルーム suítorùmu; (MUS) 組曲 kumfkyòku; (furniture): *bedroom / dining room suite* 寝室(食堂)用の一そろい shiñshitsu(shokûdồ)yồ kágù no hitósoròi

suitor [suː'təːr] *n* 求婚者 kyúkoñsha

sulfur [sʌl'fəːr] *(US) n* 硫黄 iô

sulk [sʌlk] *vi* すねる sunérù

sulky [sʌl'kiː] *adj* (child, silence) すねた sunéta

sullen [sʌl'ən] *adj* (person, silence) すねた sunéta

sulphur [sʌlˈfər] n = sulfur

sultan [sʌlˈtən] n サルタン sárũtan ◊ イスラム教国の君主 isúramukyókoku no kúnshu

sultana [sʌltænˈə] n (fruit) 白いレーズン shirói résun

sultry [sʌlˈtriː] adj (weather) 蒸暑い mushfatsuï

sum [sʌm] n (calculation) 計算 kefsan; (amount) 金額 kíngaku; (total) 合計 gókei

summarize [sʌmˈəːraiz] vt 要約する yóyaku suru

summary [sʌmˈəːriː] n 要約 yóyaku

summer [sʌmˈəːr] n 夏 natsú
◆adj (dress, school) 夏の natsú no
in summer 夏に natsú ni

summer holidays npl 夏休み natsúyasûmi

summerhouse [sʌmˈəːrhaus] n (in garden) 東屋 azúmayà

summertime [sʌmˈəːrtaim] n (season) 夏 natsú

summer time n (by clock) サマータイム samátaïmu

summer vacation (US) n 夏休み natsúyasûmi

summit [sʌmˈit] n (of mountain) 頂上 chójò; (also: summit conference/meeting) 首脳会議 shunókaïgi, サミット sámíttò

summon [sʌmˈən] vt (person, police, help) 呼び寄せる yobíyoseru, (to a meeting) 召集する shóshu suru; (LAW: witness) 召喚する shókan suru

summons [sʌmˈənz] n (LAW) 召喚書 shókanjhó, (fig) 呼出し yobídashi
◆vt (JUR) 召喚する shókan suru

summon up vt (strength, energy, courage) 奮い起す furúiokosù

sump [sʌmp] (BRIT) n (AUT) オイルパン ofrupan

sumptuous [sʌmpˈtʃuːəs] adj 豪華な gókà na

sum up vt (describe) 要約する yóyaku suru
◆vi (summarize) 要約する yóyaku suru

sun [sʌn] n (star) 太陽 taíyò; (sunshine) 日光 nfkkò

sunbathe [sʌnˈbeið] vi 日光浴する nikkóyoku suru

sunburn [sʌnˈbəːrn] n (painful) 日焼け hiyáke

sunburnt [sʌnˈbəːrnt] adj (tanned) 日に焼けた hi nf yaketà; (painfully) ひどく日焼けした hídòku hiyáke shita

Sunday [sʌnˈdei] n 日曜日 nichfyóbi

Sunday school n 日曜学校 nichfyógakkó

sundial [sʌnˈdail] n 日時計 hidókèi

sundown [sʌnˈdaun] n 日没 nichíbotsu

sundries [sʌnˈdriːz] npl (miscellaneous items) その他 sonó tà

sundry [sʌnˈdriː] adj (various) 色々な iró-iro na
all and sundry だれもかも dáre mo kámò

sunflower [sʌnˈflauər] n ヒマワリ himáwàri

sung [sʌŋ] pp of sing

sunglasses [sʌnˈglæsiz] npl サングラス sangúrasu

sunk [sʌŋk] pp of sink

sunlight [sʌnˈlait] n 日光 nfkkò

sunlit [sʌnˈlit] adj 日に照らされた hi nf terasaretà

sunny [sʌnˈiː] adj (weather, day) 晴れた háretà; (place) 日当りの良い hiátari no yoï

sunrise [sʌnˈraiz] n 日の出 hi nó de

sun roof n (AUT) サンルーフ sánrüfu

sunset [sʌnˈset] n 日没 nichíbotsu

sunshade [sʌnˈʃeid] n (over table) パラソル párãsoru

sunshine [sʌnˈʃain] n 日光 nfkkò

sunstroke [sʌnˈstrouk] n 日射病 nisshábyò

suntan [sʌnˈtæn] n 日焼け hiyáke

suntan lotion n 日焼け止めローション hiyákedome róshon

suntan oil n サンタンオイル safitan oírù

super [suːˈpəːr] (inf) adj 最高の saíkò no

superannuation [suːpəːrænjuːeiˈʃən] n 年金の掛金 nefkin no kákékìn

superb [suːpəːrˈb] adj 素晴らしい subárashiï

supercilious [suːpərˈsilʲiːəs] adj (disdainful, haughty) 横柄な ōhei na

superficial [suːpərˈfiʃʲəl] adj (wound) 浅い asái; (knowledge) 表面的な hyṓmenteki na; (shallow: person) 浅はかな asáhaka na

superfluous [suːpərˈfluːəs] adj 余計な yokéi na

superhuman [suːpərˈhjuːˈmən] adj 超人的な chōjinteki na

superimpose [suːpərˈimpouʒ] vt 重ね合せる kasáneawaserú

superintendent [suːpərˈintendənt] n (of place, activity) ...長 ...chō; (POLICE) 警視 keíshi

superior [səpiːrʲiːər] adj (better) (より) すぐれた (yorʸ) sugúretá; (more senior) 上位の jṓi no; (smug) 偉ぶった erábuttá
♦*n* 上司 jṓshi

superiority [səpiːrʲiːˈɔːlʲitʲiː] n 優位性 yū́isei

superlative [səpərˈlətʲiv] n (LING) 最上級 saíjōkyū

superman [suːˈpərmæn] (pl **supermen**) n 超人 chōjin

supermarket [suːˈpərmɑːrkit] n スーパー sū́pā

supernatural [suːpərˈnætʃʲɔrəl] adj (creature, force etc) 超自然の chōshizen no
♦*n: the supernatural* 超自然の現象 chōshizen no geńshō

superpower [suːˈpərpauˈər] n (POL) 超大国 chṓtaikoku

supersede [suːpərˈsiːd] vt ...に取って代る ...ni tótté kawárù

supersonic [suːpərˈsɑːnik] adj (flight, aircraft) 超音速の chōonsoku no

superstar [suːˈpərstɑːr] n (CINEMA, SPORT etc) スーパースター sū́pāsutā

superstition [suːpərˈstiʃʲən] n 迷信 meíshin

superstitious [suːpərˈstiʃʲəs] adj (person) 迷信深い meíshinbukáì; (practices) 迷信的な meíshinteki na

supertanker [suːˈpərtæŋkər] n スーパータンカー sū́pātaṅkā

supervise [suːˈpərvaiz] vt (person, activity) 監督する kańtoku suru

supervision [suːpərˈviʒʲən] n 監督 kańtoku

supervisor [suːˈpərvaizər] n (of workers, students) 監督者 kańtokusha

supine [suːˈpain] adj 仰向きの aṓmuki no

supper [sapˈər] n (early evening) 夕食 yū́shoku; (late evening) 夜食 yashóku

supplant [sapˈlænt] vt (person, thing) ...に取って代る ...ni tótté kawárù

supple [sapˈəl] adj (person, body, leather etc) しなやかな shináyaka na

supplement [n sapˈləmənt vb sapˈləment] n (additional amount, e.g. vitamin supplement) 補給品 hokyū́hin; (of book) 補遺 hoí; (of newspaper, magazine) 付録 furóku
♦*vt* 補足する hosóku suru

supplementary [sapləmənˈtəriː] adj (question) 補足的な hosókuteki na

supplementary benefit (BRIT) n 生活保護 seíkatsuhogó

supplier [səplaiˈər] n (COMM: person, firm) 供給業者 kyṓkyūgyōsha

supplies [səplaizˈ] npl (food) 食料 shokúryō; (MIL) 軍需品 guńjuhin

supply [səplaiˈ] vt (provide) 供給する kyōkyū suru; (equip): *to supply (with)* (...を) 支給する (...wo) shikyū suru
♦*n* (stock) 在庫品 zaíkohin; (supplying) 供給 kyōkyū

supply teacher (BRIT) n 代行教師 daíkōkyōshi

support [səpɔːrtˈ] n (moral, financial etc) 支援 shíen; (TECH) 支柱 shíchū
♦*vt* (morally: football team etc) 支援する shíen suru; (financially: family etc) 養う yashínaú; (TECH: hold up) 支える sasáerù; (sustain: theory etc) 裏付けする urázukerù

supporter [səpɔːrtˈər] n (POL etc) 支援者 shíensha; (SPORT) ファン fań

suppose [səpouzˈ] vt (think likely) ...だと思う ...dá tò omoú; (imagine) 想像する sṓzō suru; (duty): *to be supposed to do something* ...する事になっている ...surú kotó ni natté irú

supposedly [səpouˈzidliː] adv ...だとされ

て …dá tò sarétè

supposing [səpəuˈziŋ] *conj* もし … môshi...

suppress [səˈpres'] *vt* (revolt) 鎮圧する chín-atsu suru; (information) 隠す kakúsū; (feelings, yawn) 抑える osáerū

suppression [səˈpreʃən] *n* (of revolt) 鎮圧 chín-atsu; (of information) 隠ぺい inpei; (of feelings etc) 抑制 yokúsei

supremacy [səˈpreməsi] *n* 優越 yúetsu

supreme [səˈpriːm'] *adj* (in titles: court etc) 最高の saíkō no; (effort, achievement) 最上の saíjō no

surcharge [səɪrˈʧɑːrʤ] *n* (extra cost) 追加料金 tsufkaryōkin

sure [ʃuɹ] *adj* (definite, convinced) 確信している kakúshin shite irū; (aim, remedy) 確実な kakújitsu na; (friend) 頼りになる táyòri ni nárū

to make sure of something …を確かめる …wo tashíkamerú

to make sure that …だと確かめる …dá tò tashíkamerú

sure! (of course) いいとも íi to mo

sure enough 案の定 añ no jō

sure-footed [ʃuɹˈfutˈid] *adj* 足のしっかりした ashí nò shikkárì shita

surely [ʃuɹˈliː] *adv* (certainly; US: also: *sure*) 確かに táshìka ni

surety [ʃuɹˈətiː] *n* (money) 担保 táñpo

surf [səɪrf] *n* 打ち寄せる波 uchíyoseru namī

♦*vi* サーフィンをする sáfìn wo suru

surface [səɪrˈfis] *n* (of object) 表面 hyómen; (of lake, pond) 水面 suímen

♦*vt* (road) 舗装する hosố suru

♦*vi* (fish, person in water: also *fig*) 浮上する fujố suru

surface mail *n* 普通郵便 futsúyūbin

surfboard [səɪrfˈbɔːrd] *n* サーフボード sáfubōdo

surfeit [səɪrˈfit] *n*: *a surfeit of* …の過剰 …no kajố

surfing [səɪrˈfiŋ] *n* サーフィン sáfìn

surge [səɪrʤ] *n* (increase: also *fig*) 高まり takámarī

♦*vi* (water) 波打つ namfutsū; (people, vehicles) 突進する tosshín suru; (emotion) 高まる takámarū

surgeon [səɪrˈʤən] *n* 外科医 gekấ-ì

surgery [səɪrˈʤəːriː] *n* (treatment) 手術 shújutsu; (*BRIT*: room) 診察室 shíñsatsushītsu; (*BRIT*: *also*: *surgery hours*) 診療時間 shíñryō jikan

surgical [səɪrˈʤikəl] *adj* (instrument, mask etc) 外科用の gekáyò no; (treatment) 外科の gekấ no

surgical spirit (*BRIT*) *n* 消毒用アルコール shôdokuyố arúkōru

surly [səɪrˈliː] *adj* 無愛想な buấisō na

surmount [səɪrˈmaunt'] *vt* (*fig*: problem, difficulty) 乗越える noríkoerū

surname [səɪrˈneim] *n* 名字 myôji

surpass [səɪrˈpæs'] *vt* (person, thing) しのぐ shinôgù

surplus [səɪrˈpləs] *n* (extra, *also* COMM, ECON) 余剰分 yojóbùn

♦*adj* (stock, grain etc) 余剰の yojố no

surprise [səɪrˈpraiz'] *n* (unexpected) 思い掛け無い物 omóigakenai monố; (astonishment) 驚き odórokì

♦*vt* (astonish) 驚かす odórokasū; (catch unawares: army, thief) …の不意を突く …no fuí wò tsukú

surprising [səɪrˈpraiziŋ] *adj* 驚くべき odórokubèki

surprisingly [səɪrˈpraiziŋliː] *adv* (easy, helpful) 驚く程 odóroku hodò

surrealist [səːriˈəlist] *adj* (paintings etc) 超現実主義の chôgenjitsushūgi no

surrender [sərenˈdəɪr] *n* 降伏 kốfuku

♦*vi* (army, hijackers etc) 降伏する kốfuku suru

surreptitious [səɪrəptiˈʃəs] *adj* ひそかな hisôka na

surrogate [səɪrˈəgit] *n* 代理の dafri no

surrogate mother *n* 代理母 dafrihahà

surround [səraundˈ] *vt* (subj: walls, hedge etc) 囲む kakômù; (MIL, POLICE etc) 包囲する hối suru

surrounding [səraunˈdiŋ] *adj* (countryside) 周囲の shûi no

surroundings [səraunˈdiŋz] *npl* 周辺 shûhen

surveillance [səɪrveiˈləns] *n* 監視 kañshi

survey [*n* səɪrˈvei *vb* səɪrveiˈ] *n* (examination: of land, house) 測量 sokúryō;

(investigation: of habits etc) 調査 chōsa
♦vt (land, house etc) 測量する sokúryō suru; (look at: scene, work etc) 見渡す miwátasù

surveyor [sərvei'ər] n (of land, house) 測量技師 sokúryōgishi

survival [sərvai'vəl] n (continuation of life) 生存 sefzon; (relic) 遺物 ibútsu

survive [sərvaiv'] vi (person, thing) 助かる tasúkarù; (custom etc) 残る nokórù
♦vt (outlive: person) ...より長生きする ...yórì nagáikì suru

survivor [sərvai'vər] n (of illness, accident) 生存者 sefzonsha

susceptible [səsep'təbəl] adj: **susceptible (to)** (affected by: heat, injury) (...に) 弱い (...ni) yowáì; (influenced by: flattery, pressure) (...に) 影響されやすい (...ni) efkyō sareyasuì

suspect [adj, n sʌs'pekt vb səspekt'] adj 怪しい ayáshiì
♦n 容疑者 yōgisha
♦vt (person) ...が怪しいと思う ...ga ayáshiì to omóù; (think) ...ではないかと思う ...dé wà naì ka to omóù

suspend [səspend'] vt (hang) つるす tsurúsù; (delay, stop) 中止する chūshì suru; (from employment) 停職処分にする tefshokushobùn ni suru

suspended sentence [səspen'did-] n (LAW) 執行猶予付きの判決 shikkóyùyotsuki no hañketsu

suspender belt [səspen'dər-] n ガーターベルト gātàberùto

suspenders [səspen'dərz] npl (US) ズボンつり zubóftsuri; (BRIT) ガーターベルトのストッキング留め gātàberùto no sutókkingudòme

suspense [səspens'] n (uncertainty) 気掛り kigákari; (in film etc) サスペンス sásùpensu

to keep someone in suspense はらはらさせる hárahara saserù

suspension [səspen'ʃən] n (from job, team) 停職 tefshoku; (AUT) サスペンション sasúpenshòn; (of driver's license, payment) 停止 tefshi

suspension bridge n つり橋 tsurfbàshi

suspicion [səspiʃ'ən] n (distrust) 疑い utágai; ((bad) feeling) 漠然とした感じ bakúzen to shita kañji

suspicious [səspiʃ'əs] adj (suspecting: look) 疑い深い utágaibukaì; (causing suspicion: circumstances) 怪しげな ayáshige na

sustain [səstein'] vt (continue: interest etc) 維持する ijí suru; (subj: food, drink) ...に力を付ける ...ni chikára wò tsukérù; (suffer: injury) 受ける ukérù

sustained [səsteind'] adj (effort, attack) 絶間ない taémanaì

sustenance [sʌs'tənəns] n 食物 shokúmòtsu

swab [swɑːb] n (MED) 綿球 meñkyù

swagger [swæg'ər] vi 威張って歩く ibátte arukú

swallow [swɑːl'ou] n (bird) ツバメ tsubáme
♦vt (food, pills etc) 飲込む nomíkomù; (fig: story) 信じ込む shiñjìkomù; (: insult) ...に黙って耐える ...ni dámàtte taérù; (one's pride, one's words) 抑える osáerù

swallow up vt (savings etc) 飲込む nomíkomù

swam [swæm] pt of swim

swamp [swɑːmp] n 沼地 numáchi
♦vt (with water etc) 水没させる suíbotsu saserù; (fig: person) 圧倒する attō suru

swan [swɑːn] n ハクチョウ hakúchō

swap [swɑːp] n 交換 kōkan
♦vt: **to swap (for)** (exchange (for)) (...) と交換する (...to) kōkan suru; (replace (with)) (...と) 取替える (...to) toríkaerù

swarm [swɔːrm] n (of bees) 群れ muré; (of people) 群衆 gufshù
♦vi (bees) 群れて巣別れする muré dè sukáwakare suru; (people) 群がる murágarù; (place): **to be swarming with** ... うじゃうじゃいる ...ni ...ga újàujà irú

swarthy [swɔːr'ðiː] adj 浅黒い aságuroì

swastika [swɑːs'tikə] n かぎ十字 kagíjùji

swat [swɑːt] vt (insect) たたく tatákù

sway [swei] vi (person, tree) 揺れる yurérù

♦vt (influence) 揺さぶる yusáburù

swear [swe'ər] (pt **swore**, pp **sworn**) vi (curse) 悪態をつく ákutai wò tsukú

♦vt (promise) 誓う chikáù

swearword [swer'wərd] n 悪態 ákutai

sweat [swet] n 汗 ásè

♦vi 汗をかく ásè wo kákù

sweater [swet'ər] n セーター sḗtā

sweatshirt [swet'ʃərt] n トレーナー torḗnā

sweaty [swet'i:] adj (clothes, hands) 汗ばんだ asébaǹda

Swede [swi:d] n スウェーデン人 suéden-jìn

swede [swi:d] (BRIT) n スウェーデンカブ suédeǹkabu

Sweden [swi:d'ən] n スウェーデン suéden

Swedish [swi:'diʃ] adj スウェーデンの suéden no; (LING) スウェーデン語の suédeǹgo no

♦n (LING) スウェーデン語 suédeǹgo

sweep [swi:p] n (act of sweeping) 掃く事 háku kotó; (also: **chimney sweep**) 煙突掃除夫 eńtotsusṓjifù

♦vb (pt, pp **swept**)

♦vt (brush) 掃く hákù; (with arm) 払う haráù; (subj: current) 流す nagásù

♦vi (hand, arm) 振る furú; (wind) 吹きまくる fukímakurù

sweep away vt 除去する torínozokù

sweeping [swi:'piŋ] adj (gesture) 大振りな ōburi na; (generalized: statement) 十把一からげの jíppahitókàrage no

sweep past vi (at great speed) 猛スピードで通り過ぎる mṓsupìdo de tōrisugírù; (majestically) 堂々と通り過ぎる dṓdò tò tōrisuguru

sweep up vi 掃き取る hakítorù

sweet [swi:t] n (candy) あめ amé; (BRIT: pudding) デザート dezáto

♦adj (not savory: taste) 甘い amáì; (fig: air, water, smell, sound) 快い kokóroyoì; (: kind) 親切な shíñsetsu na; (attractive: baby, kitten) かわいい kawáìi

sweetcorn [swi:t'kɔːrn] n トウモロコシ tōmórokoshi

sweeten [swi:'tən] vt (add sugar to) 甘くする amáku surù; (soften: temper) なだめる nadámerù

sweetheart [swi:t'hɑːrt] n (boyfriend/girlfriend) 恋人 koíbito

sweetness [swi:t'nis] n (amount of sugar) 甘さ amása; (of air, water, smell, sound) 快さ kokóroyosà; (kindness) 親切 shíñsetsu; (attractiveness: of baby, kitten) かわいさ kawáìsa

sweetpea [swi:t'pi:] n スイートピー suítopī

swell [swel] n (of sea) うねり unéri

♦adj (US: inf: excellent) 素晴らしい subárashiì

♦vi (pt **swelled**, pp **swollen** or **swelled**) (increase: numbers) 増える fuérù; (get stronger: sound, feeling) 増す masú; (also: **swell up**: face, ankle etc) はれる harérù

swelling [swel'iŋ] n (MED) はれ haré

sweltering [swel'təriŋ] adj (heat, weather, day) うだる様な udáru yō na

swept [swept] pt, pp of **sweep**

swerve [swəːrv] vi (person, animal, vehicle) それる sorérù

swift [swift] n (bird) アマツバメ amátsubāme

♦adj (happening quickly: recovery) じん速な jíñsoku na; (moving quickly: stream, glance) 早い hayáì

swiftly [swift'li:] adv (move, react, reply) 早く háyàku

swig [swig] (inf) n (drink) がぶ飲み gabúnomi

swill [swil] vt (also: **swill out**, **swill down**) がぶがぶ飲む gábùgabu nómù

swim [swim] n: **to go for a swim** 泳ぎに行く oyógi ni ikú

♦vb (pt **swam**, pp **swum**)

♦vi (person, animal) 泳ぐ oyógù; (head, room) 回る mawárù

♦vt (the Channel, a length) 泳いで渡る oyóide watárù

swimmer [swim'ər] n 泳ぐ人 oyógù hitó

swimming [swim'iŋ] n 水泳 suíei

swimming cap n 水泳用の帽子 suíeiyō no bṓshi

swimming costume (*BRIT*) *n* 水着 mizúgi

swimming pool *n* 水泳プール suíeipûru

swimming trunks *npl* 水泳パンツ suíeipañtsu

swimsuit [swim'su:t] *n* 水着 mizúgi

swindle [swin'dəl] *n* 詐欺 sági

♦*vt* ぺてんにかける peten ni kakérù

swine [swain] (*inf!*) *n* 畜生 me chikushō-me

swing [swiŋ] *n* (in playground) ぶらんこ búranko; (movement) 揺れ yuré; (change: in opinions etc) 変動 heñdō; (MUS: also rhythm) スイング suíñgu

♦*vb* (*pt, pp* **swung**)

♦*vt* (arms, head etc) 振る furú; (*also*: **swing round**: vehicle etc) 回す mawásù

♦*vi* (pendulum) 揺れる yurérù; (on a swing) ぶらんこに乗る búranko ni norú; (*also*: **swing round**: person, animal) 振向く furímukù; (: vehicle) 向きを変える múkì wo kaérù

to be in full swing (party etc) たけなわである takénawa de arú

swing bridge *n* 旋回橋 señkaikyō

swingeing [swin'dʒiŋ] (*BRIT*) *adj* (blow, attack) 激しい hagéshiì; (cuts) 法外な hôgai na

swinging door [swiŋ'iŋ-] (*BRIT* **swing door**) *n* 自在ドア jizáidôa

swipe [swaip] *vt* (hit) たたく tatákù; (*inf*: steal) かっ払う kappáraù

swirl [swəːrl] *vi* (water, smoke, leaves) 渦巻く uzúmakù

swish [swiʃ] *vt* (tail etc) 音を立てて振る otó wo tátète furú

♦*vi* (clothes) 衣ずれの音を立てる kinúzure nò otó wo tatérù

Swiss [swis] *adj* スイスの suísu no

♦*n inv* スイス人 suísujîn

switch [switʃ] *n* (for light, radio etc) スイッチ suítchì; (change) 取替え toríkae

♦*vt* (change) 取替える toríkaerù

switchboard [switʃ'bɔːrd] *n* (TEL) 交換台 kôkandai

switch off *vt* (light, radio) 消す kesú; (engine, machine) 止める tomérù

switch on *vt* (light, machine) つ

ける tsukérù; (engine) かける kakérù

Switzerland [swit'sərlənd] *n* スイス suílsu

swivel [swiv'əl] *vi* (*also*: **swivel round**) 回る mawárù

swollen [swou'lən] *pp* of **swell**

swoon [swu:n] *vi* 気絶する kizétsu suru

swoop [swu:p] *n* (by police etc) 手入れ te-íre

♦*vi* (*also*: **swoop down**: bird, plane) 舞降りる mafórirù

swop [swɑ:p] = **swap**

sword [sɔːrd] *n* 刀 katána

swordfish [sɔːrd'fiʃ] *n* メカジキ mekáji-ki

swore [swɔːr] *pt* of **swear**

sworn [swɔːrn] *pp* of **swear**

♦*adj* (statement, evidence) 宣誓付きの señseitsuki no; (enemy) 年来の neñrai no

swot [swɑ:t] *vi* がり勉する garíben suru

swum [swʌm] *pp* of **swim**

swung [swʌŋ] *pt, pp* of **swing**

sycamore [sik'əmɔːr] *n* カエデ kaéde

syllable [sil'əbəl] *n* 音節 oñsetsu

syllabus [sil'əbəs] *n* 講義概要 kôgigaiyō

symbol [sim'bəl] *n* (sign, *also* MATH) 記号 kigō; (representation) 象徴 shôchō

symbolic(al) [simbɑl'ik(əl)] *adj* 象徴的な shôchōteki na

symbolism [sim'bəlizəm] *n* 象徴の意味 shôchōteki imí

symbolize [sim'bəlaiz] *vt* 象徴する shôchō suru

symmetrical [simet'rikəl] *adj* 対称的な taíshōteki na

symmetry [sim'itri:] *n* 対称 taíshō

sympathetic [simpəθet'ik] *adj* (showing understanding) 同情的な dôjōteki na; (likeable: character) 人好きのする hitózuki no surú; (showing support): *sympathetic to(wards)* ...に好意的である ...ni kôiteki de arú

sympathies [sim'pəθi:z] *npl* (support, tendencies) 支援 shíeñ

sympathize [sim'pəθaiz] *vi*: *to sympathize with* (person) ...に同情する ...ni dôjō suru; (feelings, cause) ...に共感する ...ni kyôkan suru

sympathizer [simˈpəθaizəʳ] n (POL) 支援者 shiénsha

sympathy [simˈpəθi] n (pity) 同情 dōjō
with our deepest sympathy 心からお悔みを申上げます kokórō kara o-kúyami wò mōshiagemasù
in sympathy (workers: come out) 同情して dōjō shite

symphony [simˈfəni] n 交響曲 kōkyōkyoku

symposia [simpouˈziːə] npl of **symposium**

symposium [simpouˈziːəm] (pl **symposiums** or **symposia**) n シンポジウム shinpojiùmu

symptom [simpˈtəm] n (indicator: MED) 症状 shōjō; (: gen) しるし shirúshi

synagogue [sinˈəgɑːg] n ユダヤ教会堂 yudáyakyōkaidō

synchronize [sinˈkrənaiz] vt (watches, sound) 合せる awáserù

syncopated [sinˈkəpeitid] adj (rhythm, beat) シンコペートした shifíkopèto shita

syndicate [sinˈdəkit] n (of people, businesses, newspapers) シンジケート shifíjikèto

syndrome [sinˈdroum] n (also: MED) 症侯群 shōkōgun

synonym [sinˈənim] n 同意語 dōigo

synopses [sinɑːpˈsiːz] npl of **synopsis**

synopsis [sinɑːpˈsis] (pl **synopses**) n 概要 gaíyō

syntax [sinˈtæks] n (LING) 統語法 tōgohō, シンタックス shifítakkùsu

syntheses [sinˈθəsiːz] npl of **synthesis**

synthesis [sinˈθəsis] (pl **syntheses**) n (of ideas, styles) 総合する sōgō suru

synthetic [sinθetˈik] adj (man-made: materials) 合成の gōsei no

syphilis [sifˈəlis] n 梅毒 baídoku

syphon [saiˈfən] = **siphon**

Syria [siːrˈiːə] n シリア shírìa

Syrian [siːrˈiːən] adj シリアの shírìa no ♦n シリア人 shiríajin

syringe [sərindʒˈ] n 注射器 chūshakì

syrup [sirˈəp] n シロップ shiróppù

system [sisˈtəm] n (organization) 組織 sóshìki; (POL): *the system* 体制 taísei;

(method) やり方 yaríkata; (the body) 身体 shifítai
the digestive system (MED) 消化器系 shōkakikèi
the nervous system (MED) 神経系 shifíkeikèi

systematic [sistəmæˈtik] adj (methodical) 組織的な soshíkiteki na

system disk n (COMPUT) システムディスク shisútemu disûku

systems analyst [sisˈtəmz-] n システムアナリスト shisútemu anarisùto

T

ta [tɑː] (BRIT: inf) excl (thanks) どうも dōmo

tab [tæb] n (on file etc) 耳 mimí; (on drinks can etc) ブルタブ purútabù, ブルトップ purútoppù; (label: name tab) 名札 nafúda
to keep tabs on (fig) 監視する kafíshi suru

tabby [tæbˈiː] n (also: **tabby cat**) とら毛のネコ torâge nò nékò

table [teiˈbəl] n (piece of furniture) テーブル tēburu; (MATH, CHEM etc) 表 hyṓ
♦vt (BRIT: motion etc) 上程する jōtei suru; (US: put off: proposal etc) 棚上げにする tanâ-age ni suru
to lay/set the table 食卓に皿を並べる shokútaku nì sarà wò naráberù

tablecloth [teiˈbəlklɔːθ] n テーブルクロス tēburukurosù

table d'hôte [tæˈbl dout] adj (menu, meal) 定食の teíshoku no

table lamp n 電気スタンド defíki sutándo

tablemat [teiˈbəlmæt] n (for plate) テーブルマット tēburumattò; (for hot dish) なべ敷 nabéshikì

table of contents n 目次 mokúji

tablespoon [teiˈbəlspuːn] n (type of spoon) テーブルスプーン tēburusupūn; (also: **tablespoonful**: as measurement) 大さじ一杯 ōsaji ippái

tablet [tæbˈlit] n (MED) 錠剤 jōzai

a stone tablet 石板 sekíban

table tennis n 卓球 takkyū

table wine n テーブルワイン tḗburuwaìn

tabloid [tӕb'lɔid] n (newspaper) タブロイド新聞 tabúroido shínbun

taboo [təbuːʔ] n (religious, social) タブー tabū
♦*adj* (subject, place, name etc) タブーの tabū no

tabulate [tӕb'jəleit] *vt* (data, figures) 表にする hyō ni surú

tacit [tӕs'it] *adj* (agreement, approval etc) 暗黙の ánmoku no

taciturn [tӕs'itə:rn] *adj* (person) 無口な múkùchi na

tack [tӕk] n (nail) びょう byō, (fig) やり方 yaríkata
♦*vt* (nail) びょうで留める byō de tomérù; (stitch) 仮縫する karínui suru
♦*vi* (NAUT) 間切る magírù

tackle [tӕk'əl] n (gear: fishing tackle etc) 道具 dōgù; (for lifting) ろくろ rókùro, 滑車 kássha; (FOOTBALL, RUGBY) タックル tákkùru
♦*vt* (deal with difficulty) ...と取組む ...to toríkumù; (challenge: person) ...に掛合う ...ni kakéaù; (grapple with: person, animal) ...と取組む ...to toríkumù; (FOOTBALL, RUGBY) タックルする tákkùru suru

tacky [tӕk'iː] *adj* (sticky) べたべたする bétàbeta suru; (pej: of poor quality) 安っぽい yasúppoì

tact [tӕkt] n 如才なさ josáinasà

tactful [tӕkt'fəl] *adj* 如才ない josáinaì

tactical [tӕk'tikəl] *adj* (move, withdrawal, voting) 戦術的な seńjutsuteki na

tactics [tӕk'tiks] n 用兵学 yōheìgaku
♦*npl* 駆引き kakéhìki

tactless [tӕkt'lis] *adj* 気転の利かない kitén no kikanaì

tadpole [tӕd'poul] n オタマジャクシ otámajakùshi

taffy [tӕf'iː] n (US) (toffee) タフィー táfì つあめの一種 amé nò ísshū

tag [tӕg] n (label) 札 fudá

tag along *vi* ついて行く tsúite ikú

tail [teil] n (of animal) しっ尾 shíppò; (of plane) 尾部 bíbù; (of shirt, coat) すそ susó
♦*vt* (follow: person, vehicle) 尾行する bikō suru

tail away/off *vi* (in size, detail etc) 次 に減る shídài ni herú

tailback [teil'bӕk] n (BRIT) (AUT) 交通渋滞 kōtsūjūtai

tail end n 末端 mattán

tailgate [teil'geit] n (AUT: of hatchback) 後尾ドア kóbìdòa

tailor [teil'əːr] n 仕立屋 shitáteya

tailoring [teil'əːriŋ] n (cut) 仕立て方 shitáteka ta; (craft) 仕立て shitáteshòku

tailor-made [teil'əːrmeid'] *adj* (suit) あつらえの atsúrae no; (fig: part in play, person for job) おあつらえ向きの o-átsuraemuki no

tails [teilz] *npl* (formal suit) えん尾服 eńbifùku

tailwind [teil'wind] n 追風 oíkaze

tainted [teint'id] *adj* (food, water, air) 汚染された osén saretá; (fig: profits, reputation etc) 汚れた yogóretà

Taiwan [tai'wɑːn'] n 台湾 taíwañ

take [teik] (*pt* **took**, *pp* **taken**) *vt* (photo, notes, holiday etc) とる tórù; (shower, walk, decision etc) する surú; (grab: someone's arm etc) 取る tórù; (gain: prize) 得る érù; (require: effort, courage, time) ...が必要である ...ga hitsúyò de arú; (tolerate: pain etc) 耐える taérù; (hold: passengers etc) 収容する shūyō suru; (accompany, bring, carry: person) 連れて行く tsuréte ikú; (: thing) 持って行く motté ikú; (exam, test) 受ける ukérù
to take something from (drawer etc) ...を...から取出す ...wo ...kárà toridásù; (steal from: person) ...を...から盗む ...wo ...kárà nusúmù

I take it that ... ...だと思っていいです ね ...dá tò omótte iì desu né

take after *vt fus* (resemble) ...に似ている ...ni nité irù

take apart *vt* 分解する búñkai suru

take away *vt* (remove) 下げる sagérù; (carry off) 持って行く motté ikú; (MATH) 引く hikú

takeaway [teiˈkəwei] (BRIT) n = **takeout**

take back vt (return) 返す kaésù; (one's words) 取消す toríkesù

take down vt (dismantle: building) 解体する kaítai suru; (write down: letter etc) 書き取る kakítorù

take in vt (deceive) だます damásù; (understand) 理解する rikái suru; (include) 含む fukúmù; (lodger) 泊める tomérù

take off vi (AVIAT) 離陸する rírìku suru; (go away) 行ってしまう itté shimaù
♦vt (remove) 外す hazúsù

takeoff [teikˈɔːf] n (AVIAT) 離陸 rírìku

take on vt (work) 引受ける híkìfukerù, (employee) 雇う yatóð; (opponent) …と戦う …to tatákaù

take out vt (invite) 外食に連れて行く gaíshoku nī tsurétè ikù; (remove) 取出す torídasù

takeout [teikˈaut] n (US) n (shop, restaurant) 持帰り料理店 mochíkaeriryōritèn; (food) 持帰り料理 mochíkaeriryòri

take over vt (business, country) 乗っ取る nottórù
♦vi: **to take over from someone** …と交替する …to kōtai suru

takeover [teikˈouvər] n (COMM) 乗っ取り nottóri

take to vt fus (person, thing, activity) 気に入る ki nī irù, 好きになる sukí ni narù; (engage in: hobby etc) やり出す yarídasù

take up vt (a dress) 短くする mijíkaku suru; (occupy: post, time, space) …について …ni tsukú); (: time) …がかかる …ga kakárù; (engage in: hobby etc) やり出す yarídasù

to take someone up on something (offer, suggestion) …に応じる …ni ōjirù

takings [teiˈkiŋz] npl (COMM) 売上 uríage

talc [tælk] n (also: **talcum powder**) タルカムパウダー tarúkamupaùda

tale [teil] n (story, account) 物語 monógatàri

to tell tales (fig: to teacher, parents etc) 告げ口する tsugéguchi suru

talent [tælˈənt] n 才能 saínō

talented [tælˈəntid] adj 才能 ある saínō arù

talk [tɔːk] n (a prepared speech) 演説 eñzetsu; (conversation) 話 hanáshi; (gossip) うわさ uwása
♦vi (speak) 話す hanásù; (give information) しゃべる shabérù

to talk about …について話す …ni tsúìte hanásù

to talk someone into doing something …する様に…を説得する …surú yō ni …wo settóku suru

to talk someone out of doing something …しない様に…を説得する …shinái yō ni …wo settóku suru

to talk shop 仕事の話をする shigóto nò hanáshi wo suru

talkative [tɔːˈkətiv] adj おしゃべりな o-shábèri na

talk over vt (problem etc) 話し合う hanáshiaù

talks [tɔːks] npl (POL etc) 会談 kaídan

talk show n おしゃべり番組 o-shábèri bañgumi

tall [tɔːl] adj (person) 背が高い sé ga takáì; (object) 高い takáì

to be 6 feet tall (person) 身長が6フィートである shíñchō gà 6 fíto de arù

tall story n ほら話 horábanàshi

tally [tælˈiː] n (of marks, amounts of money etc) 記録 kiróku
♦vi: **to tally (with)** (subj: figures, stories etc) …と合う …to) aù

talon [tælˈən] n かぎづめ kagízume

tambourine [tæmˈbəriːn] n タンバリン táñbarin

tame [teim] adj (animal, bird) なれた nárèta; (fig: story, style) 平凡な heíbon na

tamper [tæmˈpəːr] vi: **to tamper with something** …をいじる …wo ijírù

tampon [tæmˈpɑːn] n タンポン táñpon

tan [tæn] n (also: **suntan**) 日焼け hiyáke
♦vi (person, skin) 日に焼ける hi ní yakerù
♦adj (color) 黄かっ色の ókasshòku no

tandem [tæmˈdəm] n: **in tandem** (together) 2人で futári de

tang [tæŋ] *n* (smell) 鼻をつくにおい haná wò tsukú nìòi; (taste) ぴりっとした味 pírttò shita ají

tangent [tǽndʒənt] *n* (MATH) 接線 sessén

to go off at a tangent (fig) わき道へそれる wakímichi e sorérù

tangerine [tændʒərin] *n* ミカン míkàn

tangible [tǽndʒəbəl] *adj* (proof, benefits) 具体的な gutáiteki na

tangle [tǽŋgəl] *n* もつれ motsúre

to get in(to) a tangle (also fig) もつれる motsúrerù

tank [tæŋk] *n* (also: water tank) 貯水タンク chosúitañku; (for fish) 水槽 suísō; (MIL) 戦車 sénsha

tanker [tǽŋkʼəːr] *n* (ship) タンカー táñkà; (truck) タンクローリー tañkúrōrī

tanned [tænd] *adj* (skin) 日に焼けた hi ní yaketà

tantalizing [tǽntəlaizɪŋ] *adj* (smell, possibility) 興味をそそる kyómi wò sosórû

tantamount [tǽntəmaunt] *adj*: *tantamount to* ...と同然である ...to dózen de arû

tantrum [tǽntrəm] *n* かんしゃく kañshaku

tap [tæp] *n* (on sink etc) 蛇口 jagúchi; (also: gas tap) ガスの元栓 gásù no motósen; (gentle blow) 軽くたたく事 karúku tataků kotó

♦*vt* (hit gently) 軽くたたく karúku tataků; (resources) 利用する riyó suru; (telephone) 盗聴する tóchō suru

on tap (fig: resources) いつでも利用できる ítsùdemo riyó dekirù

tap-dancing [tǽpdænsiŋ] *n* タップダンス tappúdañsu

tape [teip] *n* (also: magnetic tape) 磁気テープ jikítèpu; (cassette) カセットテープ kasséttotèpu; (sticky tape) 粘着テープ neñchakutèpu; (for tying) ひも himó

♦*vt* (record: sound) 録音する rokúon suru; (: image) 録画する rokúga suru; (stick with tape) テープで張る tèpu de harú

tape deck *n* テープデッキ tèpudekkì

tape measure *n* メジャー mèjā

taper [teipʼəːr] *n* (candle) 細いろうそく hosóì rōsókù

♦*vi* (narrow) 細くなる hósoku narú

tape recorder *n* テープレコーダー tèpurekōdà

tapestry [tǽpʼistri] *n* (object) タペストリー tapésutòrī; (art) ししゅう shishū

tar [tɑːr] *n* コールタール kōrútàru

tarantula [tərǽntʃələ] *n* タランチュラ táràñchura

target [tɑːrgit] *n* (thing aimed at, *also* fig) 的 matô

tariff [tǽrif] *n* (tax on goods) 関税 kañzei; (BRIT: in hotels, restaurants) 料金表 ryókinhyō

tarmac [tɑːrmæk] *n* (BRIT: on road) アスファルト asúfarùto; (AVIAT) エプロン épùron

tarnish [tɑːrniʃ] *vt* (metal) さびさせる sabfsaserù; (fig: reputation etc) 汚す yogósù

tarpaulin [tɑːrpɔːlin] *n* シート shito

tarragon [tǽrəgən] *n* タラゴン táràgon ◇香辛料の一種 kōshíñryō no isshū

tart [tɑːrt] *n* (CULIN) タルト tárùto ◇菓子の一種 kāshí no isshū; (BRIT: inf: prostitute) ぱいた bàita

♦*adj* (flavor) 酸っぱい suppáì

tartan [tɑːrtʼən] *n* (cloth) タータンチェック tātánchekkù

♦*adj* (rug, scarf etc) タータンチェックの tátanchekkù no

tartar [tɑːrtʼəːr] *n* (on teeth) 歯石 shiséki

tartar(e) sauce [tɑːrtʼəːr-] *n* タルタルソース tarútarusòsu

tart up (BRIT) *vt* (inf: object) 派手にする hadé ni surú

to tart oneself up おめかしをする o-mékashì wò suru

task [tæsk] *n* 仕事 shigóto

to take to task ...の責任を問う ...no sekínin wò tóù

task force *n* (MIL, POLICE) 機動部隊 kidóbùtai

Tasmania [tæzmeiʼniə] *n* タスマニア tasúmania

tassel [tǽsʼəl] *n* 房 fusá

taste [teist] n (also: **sense of taste**) 味覚 mikáku; (flavor: also: **aftertaste**) 味 ajî; (sample) 一口 hitókùchi; (fig: glimpse, idea) 味わい ajîwaì

♦vt (get flavor of) 味わう ajîwaù; (test) 試食する shishóku suru

♦vi: **to taste of/like** (fish etc) …の味がする …no ajî ga surù

you can taste the garlic (in it) (含まれている) ニンニクの味がする (fukúmarete irù) nínniku nð ajî ga surù

in good/bad taste 趣味の良い(悪い) shúmi ga íi(warúì)

tasteful [teist'fəl] adj (furnishings) 趣味の良い shúmi no yðì

tasteless [teist'lis] adj (food) 味がない…ajî ga naì; (remark, joke, furnishings) 趣味の悪い shúmi no warúì

tasty [teis'ti:] adj (food) おいしい oishíì

tatters [tæt'ərz] npl: **in tatters** (clothes, papers etc) ずたずたになって zutázuta ni nattè

tattoo [tætu:'] n (on skin) 入れ墨 irézumi; (spectacle) パレード parédò

♦vt (name, design) …の入れ墨をする …no irézumi wò suru

tatty [tæt'i:] adj (BRIT: inf) 薄汚い usúgitanaì

taught [tɔ:t] pt, pp of **teach**

taunt [tɔ:nt] n あざける azákerì

♦vt あざける azákerì

Taurus [tɔ:r'əs] n 牡牛座 oúshìza

taut [tɔ:t] adj ぴんと張った pín tð hattà

tavern [tæv'ərn] n (old) 酒場 sakába

tax [tæks] n 税金 zeîkin

♦vt (earnings, goods etc) …に税金をかける …ni zeîkin wo kakérù; (fig: test: memory) 最大限に使う saîdaîgen ni tsukáù; (patience) 試練にかける shírèn ni kakérù

taxable [tæk'səbəl] adj (income) 課税される kazéi sarerù

taxation [tæksei'ʃən] n (system) 課税 kazéi; (money paid) 税金 zeîkin

tax avoidance [-əvɔi'dəns] n 節税 setsúzei

tax disc (BRIT) n (AUT) 納税ステッカ ー nózeishisutekkà

tax evasion n 脱税 datsúzei

tax-free [tæks'fri:'] adj (goods, services) 免税の mefizei no

taxi [tæk'si:] n タクシー tákùshī

♦vi (AVIAT: plane) 滑走する kassô suru

taxi driver n タクシーの運転手 tákùshī no ufitefishu

taxi rank (BRIT) n = **taxi stand**

taxi stand n タクシー乗場 takúshīnorìba

tax payer [-pei'ər] n 納税者 nózeisha

tax relief n 減税 gefizei

tax return n 確定申告書 kakúteishinkokushò

TB [ti:bi:'] n abbr = **tuberculosis**

tea [ti:] n (drink: Japanese) お茶 o-chá; (: English) 紅茶 kôcha; (BRIT: meal) お やつ o-yátsù

high tea (BRIT) n 夕食 yúshoku◇夕方早目に食べる食事 yúgata hayáme nì tabérù shokúji

tea bag n ティーバッグ tíbaggù

tea break (BRIT) n 休憩 kyúkei

teach [ti:tʃ] (pt, pp **taught**) vt (gen) 教える oshférù; (be a teacher of) …(の)教師をする …(の)kyóshi wò suru

♦vi (be a teacher: in school etc) 教師をする kyóshi wò suru

teacher [ti:'tʃər] n 教師 kyóshi, 先生 sefisei

teaching [ti:'tʃiŋ] n (work of teacher) 教 職 kyóshòku

tea cosy n お茶帽子 o-chábòshi

tea cup n (Western) ティーカップ tíkappù; (Japanese) 湯飲み茶碗 yunómijawàn, 湯飲み yunómi

teak [ti:k] n チーク chíku

tea leaves npl 茶殻 chagára

team [ti:m] n (group: gen, SPORT) チーム chímu; (of animals) 一組 hitókumi

teamwork [ti:m'wərk] n チームワーク chímuwàku

teapot [ti:'pɑt] n きゅうす kyúsu

tear¹ [ter] n (hole) 裂け目 sakéme

♦vb (pt **tore**, pp **torn**)

♦vt (rip) 破る yabúrù

♦vi (become torn) 破れる yabúrerù

tear² [ti:r] n (in eye) 涙 námìda

in tears 泣いている nafte irù

tear along vi (rush) 猛スピードで走って
行く mōsupīdð de hashītte ikú

tearful [tiəˈfəl] adj (family, face) 涙ぐん
だ namídagundà

tear gas n 催涙ガス safruigasū

tearoom [tiːˈruːm] n 喫茶店 kissáteñ

tear up vt (sheet of paper etc) ずたずた
に破る zutázuta nī yabúrù

tease [tiːz] vt からかう karákaoû

tea set n 茶器セット chakfsettô

teaspoon [tiːˈspuːn] n (type of spoon) ティ
ースプーン tísupûn; (also: **teaspoon-
ful**: as measurement) 小さじ一杯 kosáji
ippái

teat [tiːt] n (ANAT) 乳首 chikúbì; (also:
bottle teat) 乳首状の乳首 honyúbìn no
chikúbì

teatime [tiːˈtaim] n おやつの時間 o-yátsu no jikán

tea towel n ふきん fukíñ

technical [tekˈnikəl] adj (terms,
advances) 技術の gǐjútsu no

technical college (BRIT) n 高等専門学
校 kótōsenmongakkô

technicality [teknikælˈiti] n (point of
law) 法律の専門的細目 hóritsu nð sef-
monteki saimòku; (detail) 細かい事 komákaì kotó

technically [tekˈnikli] adv (strictly
speaking) 正確に言えば sefkaku nī iébà;
(regarding technique) 技術的に gǐjútsuteki ni

technician [tekˈniʃən] n 技術者 gijútsu-
shà

technique [tekˈniːk] n 技術 gǐjútsu

technological [teknəlɑdʒˈikəl] adj 技術
的な gǐjútsuteki na

technology [tekˈnɑlədʒi:] n 科学技術
kagákugijùtsu

teddy (bear) [tedˈi:-] n クマのぬいぐる
み kumá no nufgùrumi

tedious [tiːˈdiːəs] adj (work, discussions
etc) 退屈な tafkutsu na

tee [tiː] n (GOLF) ティー tí

teem [tiːm] vi: **to teem with** (visitors,
tourists etc) ぞろぞろ来ている ...ga
zórôzoro kité irù

it is teeming (with rain) 雨が激しく
降っている áme ga hageshikù fútte irù

teenage [tiːnˈeidʒ] adj (children, fashions
etc) ティーンエージャーの tín-ejà no

teenager [tiːnˈeidʒər] n ティーンエージ
ャー tín-ejà

teens [tiːnz] npl: **to be in one's teens** 年
齢は10代である nefrei wa jûdài de árù

tee-shirt [tiːˈʃəːrt] n = **T-shirt**

teeter [tiːˈtər] vi (also: fig) ぐらつく gu-
rátsukû

teeth [tiːθ] npl of **tooth**

teethe [tiːð] vi (baby) 歯が生える há gà
haérù

teething ring [tiːˈðiŋ-] n おしゃぶり
o-shábùri ◊リング状の物を指す rífigujô
no monó wò sásù

teething troubles npl (fig) 初期の困難
shôkì no nâñnan

teetotal [tiːtoutˈəl] adj (person) 酒を飲ま
ない saké wò nománaî

telecommunications [teləkəmju-
nikeiˈʃənz] npl 電気通信 defkitsûshin

telegram [telˈəgræm] n 電報 defipô

telegraph [telˈəgræf] n (system) 電信
defishiñ

telegraph pole n 電柱 defchû

telepathic [teləpæθˈik] adj テレパシー
の terépàshì no

telepathy [təlepˈəθi:] n テレパシー terépàshì

telephone [telˈəfoun] n 電話 defiwa
◆vt (person) ...に電話をかける ...ni defiwa wò kakérû; (message) 電話で伝える
defiwa de tsutáerù

on the telephone (talking) 電話中で defi-
wachû de; (possessing phone) 電話を持っ
ている defiwa wò mótte irù

telephone booth n 電話ボックス defi-
wabokkûsu

telephone box (BRIT) n = **telephone
booth**

telephone call n 電話 defiwa

telephone directory n 電話帳 defiwa-
chô

telephone number n 電話番号 defiwa-
bañgô

telephonist [teləˈfounist] (BRIT) n 電話
交換手 defiwakōkañshu

telescope [tel'əskoup] n 望遠鏡 bōenkyō

telescopic [teliskəp'ik] adj (lens) 望遠の bōen no; (collapsible: tripod, aerial) 入れ子式の irékoshiki no

television [tel'əviʒən] n (all senses) テレビ térebi

on television テレビで térebi de

television set n テレビ受像機 terébi juzōki

telex [tel'eks] n テレックス terékkùsu
♦vt (company) ...にテレックスを送る ...ni terékkùsu wo okúrù; (message) テレックスで送る terékkùsu de okúrù

tell [tel] (pt, pp **told**) vt (say) ...に言う ...ni iú; (relate: story) 述べる nobérù; (distinguish): **to tell something from** ...から...を区別する ...kará ...wò kúbetsu suru
♦vi (talk): **to tell (of)** ...について語る ...ni tsúite hanásù; (have an effect) 効果的である kōkateki de arù
to tell someone to do something ...に...する様に言う ...ni ...surú yō ni iú

teller [tel'ər] n (in bank) 出納係 suitōgakàri

telling [tel'iŋ] adj (remark, detail) 意味深い imíbukài

tell off vt: **to tell someone off** しかる shikárù

telltale [tel'teil] adj (sign) 証拠の shōko no

telly [tel'i:] (BRIT: inf) n abbr = **television**

temerity [təmer'iti:] n ずうずうしさ zúzúshisa

temp [temp] n abbr (= **temporary**) 臨時職員 rínjishokuin

temper [tem'pər] n (nature) 性質 seíshitsu; (mood) 機嫌 kigén; (fit of anger) かんしゃく kańshaku
♦vt (moderate) 和らげる yawáragerù
to be in a temper 怒っている okótte irú
to lose one's temper 怒る okórù

temperament [tem'pərəmənt] n (nature) 性質 seíshitsu

temperamental [tempərəmen'təl] adj (person, fig: car) 気まぐれな kimágùre na

temperate [tem'pərit] adj (climate, country) 温暖な ońdan na

temperate zone n 温帯 ońtai

temperature [tem'pərətʃər] n (of person, place) 温度 ōndo
to have/run a temperature 熱がある netsú ga arù

tempest [tem'pist] n 嵐 árashi

tempi [tem'pi:] npl of **tempo**

temple [tem'pəl] n (building) 神殿 shiñden; (ANAT) こめかみ kómekami

tempo [tem'pou] (pl **tempos** or **tempi**) n (MUS) テンポ téňpo; (fig: of life etc) ペース pḕsu

temporarily [tempərer'ili:] adv 一時的に ichíjiteki ni

temporary [tem'pərer:i:] adj (passing) 一時的な ichíjiteki na; (worker, job) 臨時の rínji no

tempt [tempt] vt (attract) を誘惑する yūwàku suru
to tempt someone into doing something ...する様に...を誘惑する ...surú yō ni ...wo yūwàku suru

temptation [temptei'ʃən] n 誘惑 yūwàku

tempting [temp'tiŋ] adj (offer) 魅惑的な miwákuteki na; (food) おいしそうな ofshisō na

ten [ten] num 十 (の) jū (no)

tenacity [tənæs'iti:] n (of person, animal) 根気強さ koñkizùyosa

tenancy [ten'ənsi:] n (possession of room, land etc) 賃借 chíňshaku; (period of possession) 賃借期間 chíňshakukikàn

tenant [ten'ənt] n (rent-payer) 店子 tanáko, テナント tenáňto

tend [tend] vt (crops, sick person) ...の世話をする ...no sewá wò suru
♦vi: **to tend to do something** ...しがちである ...shigáchi de arù

tendency [ten'dənsi:] n (of person, thing) 傾向 keíkō

tender [ten'dər] adj (person, heart, care) 優しい yasáshiì; (sore) 触ると痛いさわると itái; (meat) 柔らかい yawárakaì; (age) 幼い osánaì
♦n (COMM: offer) 見積り mitsúmori; (money): **legal tender** 通貨 tsūka

◆vt (offer, resignation) 提出する tefshutsu suru

to tender an apology 陳謝する chínsha suru

tenderness [ten'dərnis] n (affection) 優しき yasáshìsà; (of meat) 柔らかさ yawárakasà

tendon [ten'dən] n けん kéñ

tenement [ten'əmənt] n 安アパート yasúapàto

tenet [ten'it] n 信条 shíñjō

tennis [ten'is] n テニス téñisu

tennis ball n テニスボール tenísubòru

tennis court n テニスコート tenísukòto

tennis player n テニス選手 tenísuseñshu

tennis racket n テニスラケット tenísurakettò

tennis shoes npl テニスシューズ tenísushùzu

tenor [ten'ər] n (MUS) テノール tenórù

tenpin bowling [ten'pin-] n ボウリング bóriñgu

tense [tens] adj (person, smile, muscle) 緊張した kíñchō shita; (period) 緊迫した kíñpaku shita

◆n (LING) 時制 jiséi

tension [ten'ʃən] n (nervousness) 緊張 kíñchō; (between ropes etc) 張力 chóryoku

tent [tent] n テント téñto

tentacle [ten'təkəl] n (of octopus etc) あし ashí

tentative [ten'tətiv] adj (step, smile) 自信のない jishíñ no naí; (conclusion, plans) 差し当っての sashíatattè no

tenterhooks [ten'tərhuks] n: *on tenterhooks* はらはらして hárahara shite

tenth [tenθ] num 第十 (の) dáijū (no)

tent peg n テントのくい téñto no kuí

tent pole n テントの支柱 téñto no shíchū

tenuous [ten'juːəs] adj (hold, links, connection etc) 弱い yowáî

tenure [ten'jəːr] n (of land, buildings etc) 保有権 hoyúkeñ; (of office) 在職期間 zaíshokukìkaň

tepid [tep'id] adj (tea, pool etc) ぬるい nurúî

term [təːrm] n (word, expression) 用語 yṓgo; (period in power etc) 期間 kíkàñ; (SCOL) 学期 gakkí

◆vt (call) ...と言う to iú

in the short/long term 短(長)期間で tañ(chō)kíkàn de

terminal [təːr'mənəl] adj (disease, cancer, patient) 末期の mákkì no

◆n (ELEC) 端子 táñshi; (COMPUT) 端末機 tañmatsukì; (also: **air terminal**) ターミナルビル tāminarubìru; (also: **coach terminal**) バスターミナル basútāminaru

terminate [təːr'məneit] vt (discussion, contract, pregnancy) 終らせる owáraserù, 終える oérù; (contract) 破棄する hákì suru; (pregnancy) 中絶する chúzetsu suru

termini [təːr'mənai] npl of **terminus**

terminology [təːrmənɑːl'ədʒiː] n 用語 yṓgo ◇総称 sṓshō

terminus [təːr'mənəs] n (pl -mini) n (for buses, trains) ターミナル táminaru

terms [təːrmz] npl (conditions: also COMM) 条件 jōkeñ

to be on good terms with someone ...と仲がいい ...to nákà ga íi

to come to terms with (problem) ...と折合いがつく ...to oríaî ga tsukú

terrace [ter'əs] n (BRIT: row of houses) 長屋 nagáyà; (patio) テラス térasu; (AGR) 段々畑 dañdañbatake

terraced [ter'əst] adj (house) 長屋の nagáyà no; (garden) ひな壇式の hinádañshikì no

terraces [ter'əsiz] (BRIT) npl (SPORT): *the terraces* 立見席 tachímisèki

terracotta [terəkɑːt'ə] n テラコッタ terácottà

terrain [tərein'] n 地面 jímèn

terrible [ter'əbəl] adj ひどい hídòi

terribly [ter'əbliː] adv (very) とても totémo; (very badly) ひどく hídòku

terrier [ter'iːr] n テリア téria

terrific [tərifik'] adj (very great: thunderstorm, speed) 大変な taíheñ na; (wonderful: time, party) 素晴らしい subárashī̀

terrify [terˈəfai] vt おびえさせる obîesaserù

territorial [territɔːˈriːəl] adj (waters, boundaries, dispute) 領土の ryôdò no

territory [terˈitɔːriː] n (gen) 領土 ryôdò; (fig) 縄張 nawábarī

terror [terˈər] n (great fear) 恐怖 kyôfu

terrorism [terˈərizəm] n テロ terò

terrorist [terˈərist] n テロリスト teròrisùto

terrorize [terˈəraiz] vt おびえさせる obîesaserù

terse [təːrs] adj (style) 簡潔な kañketsu na; (reply) そっけない sokkénaì ◊言葉数が少なく簡潔な返事などについて言う kotóbakazù ga sukúnakù buâlsoì na heñji nadò ni tsûîte iû

Terylene [terˈəliːn] Ⓡ n テリレン térĭren ◊人工繊維の一種 jiñkósen̄-i no fsshū

test [test] n (trial, check: also MED, CHEM) テスト tésùto; (of courage etc) 試験 shíren; (SCOL) テスト tésùto; (also: **driving test**) 運転免許の試験 uñtenmêñkyo no shíken
◊vt (gen) テストする tésùto suru

testament [tesˈtəmənt] n 証明 shômei
the **Old/New Testament** 旧(新)約聖書 kyū(shin̄)yaku seishò

testicle [tesˈtikəl] n 睾丸 kôgan

testify [tesˈtəfai] vi (LAW) 証言する shôgen suru
to **testify to something** …だと証言する …ga …dá to shôgen suru

testimony [tesˈtəmouniː] n (LAW: statement) 証言 shôgen; (clear proof) 証拠 shôko

test match n (CRICKET, RUGBY) 国際戦 kokúsaisen, 国際試合 kokúsaijiaì

test pilot n テストパイロット tesútopairòtto

test tube n 試験管 shikénkaǹ

tetanus [tetˈənəs] n 破傷風 hashôfū

tether [tetˈər] vt (animal) つなぐ tsunágù
◊n: **at the end of one's tether** 行き詰って ikízumattè

text [tekst] n 文書 bûǹsho

textbook [tekstˈbuk] n 教科書 kyôkashò

textiles [teksˈtailz] npl (fabrics) 織物 orímòno; (textile industry) 織物業界 orímonogyôkaì

texture [teksˈtʃər] n (of cloth, skin, soil, silk) 手触り tezáwàri

Thailand [taiˈlænd] n タイ国

Thames [temz] n: **the Thames** テムズ川 témùzugawa

KEYWORD

than [ðæn] conj (in comparisons) ...より(も) ...yórĭ(mo)

you have more than 10 あなたは10個以上持っています anátā wa júkkò ĩjō móttē ĩmasu

I have more than you/Paul 私はあなた(ポール)より沢山持っています watákushi wa anátā(pôru)yori takúsaǹ móttē ĩmasu

I have more pens than pencils 私は鉛筆よりペンを沢山持っています watákushi wa eñpitsu yorí péǹ wo takúsaǹ móttē ĩmasu

she is older than you think 彼女はあなたが思っているより年ですよ kánòjo wa anátā ga omóttē irū yórĭ toshí desù yó

more than once 数回 sūkaì

---

thank [θæŋk] vt (person) ...に感謝する ...ni káǹsha suru

thank you (very much) (大変) 有難うございました(taîhen) arígatō gozáĩmashìtā

thank God! ああ良かった ã yôkatta

thankful [θæŋkˈfəl] adj: **thankful (for)** (...を) 有難く思っている(...wo) arígatakù omóttè irū

thankless [θæŋkˈlis] adj (task) 割の悪い warî no warúî

thanks [θæŋks] npl 感謝 káǹsha
◊excl (also: **many thanks, thanks a lot**) 有難う arígatō

Thanksgiving (Day) [θæŋksgivˈiŋ-] n 感謝祭 kañshasaì

thanks to prep ...のおかげで ...no o-kâge dè

KEYWORD

that [ðæt] (demonstrative adj, pron: *pl*
those) adj (demonstrative) その sonó、あ
の anó

that man/woman/book その(あの)男
性(女性、本) sonó (anó) dañsei (jósei,
hoñ)

leave those books on the table その本
をテーブルの上に置いていって下さい so-
nó hoñ wo tēburu no ué nì ōite itté
kudásaì

that one それ sorē、あれ aré

that one over there あそこにある物
asóko nì árù monó

I want this one, not that one 欲しい
のはこれで、あれは要りません hoshíi
no wà koré desù, aré wà irímaseñ

◆pron 1 (demonstrative) それ sorē、あれ
aré

who's/what's that? あれはだれですか
(何ですか) aré wà dáre desu ká(náñ
desu ká)

is that you? あなたですか anátā desu
ká

I prefer this to that あれよりこちらの
方が良いです aré yorí kochíra no hō gà
sukí desù

will you eat all that? あれを全部食
べるつもりですか aré wò zēñbu tabéru
tsumórì desù ká

that's my house 私の家はあれです watákushì no ié wà aré desù

that's what he said 彼はそう言いまし
たよ kárè wa sō iimashìta yó

what happened after that? それから
どうなりましたか soré kará dō narima-
shìta ká

that is (to say) つまり tsūmàri、すなわ
ち sunáwàchi

2 (relative): *the book (that) I read* 私
の読んだ本 watákushì no yóñda hóñ

the books that are in the library 図
書館にある本 toshókàn ni árù hóñ

the man (that) I saw 私の見た男 watákushì no mītá otóko

all (that) I have 私が持っているだけ
watákushì gà móttè irú dàke

the box (that) I put it in それを入れ
た箱 soré wò ireta hakó

the people (that) I spoke to 私が声を
掛けた人々 watákushì gà kóè wo kákè-
ta hitóbìto

3 (relative: of time): *the day (that) he
came* 彼が来た日 kárè ga kitá hì

*the evening/winter (that) he came
to see us* 彼が私たちの家に来た夜(冬)
kárè ga watákushitàchi no ié ni kitá
yorù(fuyù)

◆conj ...だと ...dá tò

he thought that I was ill 私が病気だ
と彼は思っていました watákushì gà
byōkì dá tò kárè wa omótte imashìta

she suggested that I phone you あな
たに電話する様にと彼女は私に勧めまし
た anátā ni deñwa suru yō ni to káñojo
wa watákushì ni susúmemashìta

◆adv (demonstrative) それ程 soré hodo、
あれ程 aré hodo、そんなに sofina nì、あん
なに afina nì

I can't work that much あんなに働け
ません afina nì határakemaseñ

I didn't realize it was that bad 事態
があれ程悪くなっているとは思っていま
せんでした jítaì ga aré hodò wárùku
nátté irù to wa omótte imaseñ deshìta

that high/big あれ位高い aré kuraí
takái

*the wall's about that high and that
thick* 塀はこれ位高くてこれ位厚い heí
wà koré guraì tákàkute koré guraì
atsúì

thatched [θætʃt] adj (roof, cottage) わら
ぶきの warábuki no

thaw [θɔ:] n 雪解けの陽気 yukídokè no
yṓkì

◆vi (ice) 溶ける tokéru; (food) 解凍さ
れる kaítō sarerú

◆vt (food: *also*: **thaw out**) 解凍する
kaítō suru

KEYWORD

the [ðə] def art 1 (gen) その sonó ◇ 通常
日本語では表現しない tsújō nihóngo de
wà hyṓgeñ shinaí

the history of France フランスの歴史
Furáñsu no rekíshì

furánsu nò rekíshi
the books/children are in the library 本(子供たち)は図書館にあります(います) hôn(kodómotáchi)wa toshókàn ni arímasù(imásù)

she put it on the table/gave it to the postman 彼女はテーブルに置きました(郵便屋さんにあげました) kánojo wa têburu ni okímashìta(yûbin-yasan nì agémashìta)

he took it from the drawer 彼は引出しから取り出しました kárè wa hikídashi kara torídashimashìta

I haven't got the time/money 私にはそれだけの時間(金)がありません watákushì ni wa soré dake no jikán(kanè)gà arímasèn

to play the piano/violin ピアノ(バイオリン)をひく píáno(baíorin)wo hikú

the age of the computer コンピュータの時代 kónpyùta no jídái

I'm going to the butcher's/the cinema 肉屋に(映画を見に)行って来ます nikúyà ni (eíga wò mí nì)ítté kimasù

2 (+ adjective to form noun)

the rich and the poor 金持と貧乏人 kanémochì to bínbònin

the wounded were taken to the hospital 負傷者は病院に運ばれた fushôshà wa byôìn ni hákóbareta

to attempt the impossible 不可能な事をやろうとする fukánò na kotô wo yaró to surù

3 (in titles): *Elizabeth the First* エリザベス1世 erízabesu ísséi

Peter the Great ピョートル大帝 pyôtòru taítei

4 (in comparisons): *the more he works the more he earns* 彼は働けば働く程もうかる kárè wa határakèba határaku hodò môkarù

the more I love it the less I like it 見れば見る程いやになります mírèba mírù hodo iyá ni narimasù

theater [θí:ətər] (*BRIT* **theatre**) *n* (building with stage) 劇場 gekíjò; (art form) 演劇 engékì; (*also*: **lecture theater**) 講義室 kôgishìtsu; (MED: *also*: **operating theater**) 手術室 shujútsushìtsu

theater-goer [θí:ətərgouər,] *n* 芝居好き shibáizùki

theatrical [θíæt'rikəl] *adj* (event, production) 演劇の engékì no; (gestures) 芝居染みた shibáijimìta

theft [θeft] *n* 窃盗 settô

their [ðeːr] *adj* 彼らの kárèra no ¶ *see also* **my**

theirs [ðeːrz] *pron* 彼らの物 kárèra no monó ¶ *see also* **mine**

them [ðem] *pron* (direct) 彼らを kárèra wo; (indirect) 彼らに kárèra ni; (stressed, after prep) 彼ら kárèra ¶ *see also* **me**

theme [θi:m] *n* (main subject) 主題 shudái, テーマ têma; (MUS) テーマ têma

theme park *n* テーマ遊園地 têmayûénchi

theme song *n* 主題歌 shídáika

themselves [ðəmselvz'] *pl pron* (reflexive) 彼ら自身を kárèra jishín wo; (after prep) 彼ら自身 kárèra jishín ¶ *see also* **oneself**

then [ðen] *adv* (at that time) その時(に) sonó tokì (ni); (next, later, and also) それから soré kara
♦*conj* (therefore) だから dá kàra
♦*adj*: **the then president** 当時の大統領 tôjì no daítòryo
by then (past) その時迄には sonó tokì made ni wa; (future) その時になったら sonó tokì ni nattára
from then on その時から sonó tokì kara

theology [θi:ɑl'ədʒi:] *n* 神学 shíngaku

theorem [θíɪr'əm] *n* 定理 teíri

theoretical [θiːəret'ikəl] *adj* (biology, possibility) 理論的な riróntekìna

theorize [θí:əraiz] *vi* 学説を立てる gakúsetsu wò tatérù

theory [θiːər'iː] *n* (all senses) 理論 rírònn
in theory 理論的には riróntekì ni wa

therapeutic(al) [θeːrəpju:'tik(əl)] *adj* 治療の chiryô no

therapist [θeːr'əpist] *n* セラピスト serápisùto

therapy [θeər'əpi:] n 治療 chiryō

KEYWORD

there [ðɛər] adv 1: *there is, there are* …がある(いる) …ga árū[irú]

there are 3 of them (things) 3つありま す mìttsu arímasù; (people) 3人います saníniñ imásù

there is no one here 誰もいません dáre mo imáseñ

there is no bread left パンがなくなり ました pán ga nakúnarimashìta

there has been an accident 事故があ りました jíkò ga arímashìta

there will be a meeting tomorrow 明 日会議があります asú kaígi ga arímasù 2 (referring to place) そこに(で、へ) sokó nì[dè, e], あそこに(で、へ) asókó nì [dè, e]

where is the book? - it's there 本はど こにありますかーあそこにあります hóñ wa dókò ni arímasù ká - asóko nì arímasù

put it down there そこに置いて下さい sokó nì oíte kudasaì

he went there on Friday 彼は金曜日 に行きました kárè wa kiñ-yóbi ni ikímashìta

I want that book there そこの本が欲 しい sokó nò hóñ ga hoshíì

there he is! いました imáshìta 3: *there, there* (especially to child) よし よし yóshì yóshì

there, there, it's not your fault/ don't cry よしよし、お前のせいじゃな いから(泣かないで) yóshì yóshì, omáe nò seí ja naì kara(nakánaìde)

thereabouts [ðeər'əbauts] adv (place) そ こら辺 sokórahèn; (amount) それぐらい soré gurai

thereafter [ðeər'æf'tər] adv それ以来 so- ré iraì

thereby [ðeərbai'] adv それによって soré ni yotté

therefore [ðeər'fɔːr] adv だから dá kàra

there's [ðeərz] = there is; there has

thermal [θəər'məl] adj (underwear) 防寒

用の bókan-yō no; (paper) 感熱の kañnetsu no; (printer) 熱式の netsúshìki no

thermal spring n 温泉 oñsen

thermometer [θəərmɑːm'itər] n (for room/body temperature) 温度計 oñdokēi

Thermos [θəər'məs]Ⓡ n (also: **Thermos flask**) 魔法瓶 mahóbìñ

thermostat [θəər'məstæt] n サーモスタ ット sámosutàtto

thesaurus [θisɔːr'əs] n シソーラス shisórāsu

these [ðiːz] pl adj これらの korérā no ◆pl pron これらは[を] korérā wa(wo)

theses [θiː'siːz] npl of thesis

thesis [θiː'sis] (pl **theses**) n (for doctor- ate etc) 論文 roñbuñ

they [ðei] pl pron 彼らは[が] kárèra wa (ga)

they say that … (it is said that) …と言 われている …to iwárete irú

they'd [ðeid] = they had; they would

they'll [ðeil] = they shall, they will

they're [ðeər] = they are

they've [ðeiv] = they have

thick [θik] adj (in shape: slice, jersey etc) 厚い atsúi; (line, hair) 太い futói; (in consistency: sauce, mud, fog etc) 濃い kói; (: forest) 深い fukái; (stupid) 鈍い nibúi

in the thick of the battle 戦いのさなかに tatákai nò sánàka ni

it's 20 cm thick 厚さは20センチだ atsúsa wa nijússeñchi da

thicken [θik'ən] vi (fog etc) 濃くなる kó-kù naru; (plot) 込入ってくる komíitte kurù ◆vt (sauce etc) 濃くする kókù suru

thickness [θik'nis] n 厚み atsúmi

thicket [θik'set] n (person, body) がっちりした gatchíri shita

thickskinned [θik'skind] adj (fig: person) 無神経な mushíñkei na

thief [θiːf] (pl **thieves**) n 泥棒 doróbō

thieves [θiːvz] npl of thief

thigh [θai] n 太もも futómomo

thimble [θim'bəl] n 指抜き yubínuki

thin [θin] adj (gen) 薄い usúi; (line) 細い hosói; (person, animal) やせた yaséta (crowd) まばらな mabára na

♦vt: **to thin (down)** (sauce, paint) 薄め
る usúmerù

thing [θiŋ] n (gen) 物事 monógòto; (physical object) 物 monó; (matter) 事 kotó
to have a thing about someone/
something ...が大嫌いか …ga dáìkirai de árù; (fascination) ...が大
好きである …ga dáìsukì de árù
poor thing かわいそうに kawáisò ni
the best thing would be to ....する
のが一番いいだろう ...surú no ga ichíbaň
iĭ darô
how are things? どうですか dô desu
ká

things [θiŋz] npl (belongings) 持物 mochímòno

think [θiŋk] (pt, pp **thought**) vi (reflect)
考える kańgaerù; (believe) 思う omóù

♦vt (imagine) ...と思う ...dá tó omóù
what did you think of them? 彼らの
事をどう思いましたか kárèra no kotó
wo dô omóimashìta ka
to think about something/someone
...について考える ...ni tsúìte kańgaerù
I'll think about it 考えておくね ka-
ńgaete okù ne
to think of doing something ...しよう
と思う ...shiyô to omóù
I think so/not そうだ(違う)と思う sô
dà (chigáù) to omóù
to think well of someone ...に対して
好感を持つ ...ni táìshite kôkaň wò mótsù
think over vt (offer, suggestion) よく考
える yókù kańgaerù

think tank n シンクタンク shiňkutaň-
ku

think up vt (plan, scheme, excuse) 考え
出す kańgaedasù

thinly [θin'li:] adv (cut, spread) 薄く usú-
kù

third [θə:rd] num 第三 (の) dái san (no)

♦n (fraction) 3分の1 sańbun no ichi;
(AUT: also: **third gear**) サードギヤ sā-
dogìya; (BRIT: SCOL: degree) 3級優等
卒業学位 sańkyū yūtō sotsugyō gakùi
¶ see also **first**

thirdly [θə:rd'li:] adv 第三に dái san ni

third party insurance (BRIT) n 損害
保険 sońgaibaishòhokeň

third-rate [θə:rd'reit'] adj 三流の sańryū no

Third World n: **the Third World** 第
三世界 dái san sékài

thirst [θə:rst] n 渇き kawáki

thirsty [θə:rs'ti:] adj (person, animal) の
どが渇いた nódò ga kawáità; (work) の
どが渇くような nódò ga kawáku yō na
to be thirsty (person, animal) のどが渇
いている nódò ga kawáìte irù

thirteen [θə:r'ti:n'] num 十三 (の) jū́-
san (no)

thirty [θə:r'ti:] num 三十 (の) sáñju
(no)

<hr>

KEYWORD

this [ðis] (pl **these**) adj (demonstrative)
この konó
this man/woman/book この男性〔女性,
本〕 konó dansei〔josei, hon〕
these people/children/records この人
たち〔子供たち, レコード〕 konó hitótà-
chi〔kodomotàchi, rekôdo〕
this one これ koré
it's not that picture but this one
that I like 私が好きなのはあの絵では
なくて, この絵です watákushi ga sukí
na no wà anó e de wa nakùte, konó e de
desù

♦pron (demonstrative) これ koré
what is this? これは何ですか koré wa
nań desu ká
who is this? この方はどなたですか konó katà wa dónàta desu ká
I prefer this to that 私はあれよりこの
方が好きです watákushi wà aré yorí
konó hō ga sukí desù
this is where I live 私の住いはここで
す watákushi no sumài wa kokó desù
this is what he said 彼はこう言いまし
た kárè wa kô iimashìta
this is Mr Brown (in introductions/
photo) こちらはブラウンさんです kochí-
ra wà buráùnsan desu; (on telephone) こ
ちらはブラウンですが kochíra wà burá-

ùn desu ka

◆*adv* (demonstrative): **this high/long** 高さ[長さ]はこれぐらいで tákasa(nágasa)wa koré gurái de

it was about this big 大きさはこれぐらいでした ókìsa wa korégurái deshita

the car is this long 車の長さはこれぐらいです kuruma no nagása wa koré gurái desu

we can't stop now we've gone this far ここまで来たらやめられません kokó madè kitára yameraremasén

thistle [θís'əl] *n* アザミ azámi

thong [θɔːŋ] *n* バンド bándo

thorn [θɔːrn] *n* とげ togé

thorny [θɔːr'niː] *adj* (plant, tree) とげの多い togé no ói; (problem) 厄介な yákkai na

thorough [θɜ'rou] *adj* (search, wash) 徹底的な tettéiteki na; (knowledge, research) 深い fukái; (person: methodical) きちようめんな kichómen na

thoroughbred [θɜ'roubred] *adj* (horse) サラブレッド saráburéddò

thoroughfare [θɜː'roufeːr] *n* 目抜き通り menúkidòri

「**no thoroughfare**」通行禁止 tsūkókinshi

thoroughly [θɜː'rouliː] *adv* (examine, study, wash, search) 徹底的に tettéiteki ni; (very) とても totémo

those [ðouz] *pl adj* それらの sorérà no, あれらの arérà no

◆*pl pron* それらを sorérà wo, あれらを arérà wo

though [ðou] *conj* ...にもかかわらず...ní mô kakáwarazù

◆*adv* しかし shikáshì

thought [θɔːt] *pt, pp of* think

◆*n* (idea, reflection) 考え kañgaè; (opinion) 意見 íkèn

thoughtful [θɔːt'fəl] *adj* (person: deep in thought) 考えこんでいる kañgaekonde irû; (: serious) 真剣な shiñkèn na; (considerate: person) 思いやりのある omóiyari no arù

thoughtless [θɔːt'lis] *adj* (inconsiderate:

behavior, words, person) 心ない kokóronaì

thousand [θau'zənd] *num* 千 (の) séñ (no)

two thousand 二千 (の) niséñ (no)

thousands of 何千もの... nañzeñ mo no ...

thousandth [θau'zəndθ] *num* 第 千 (の) dái señ (no)

thrash [θræʃ] *vt* (beat) たたく tatákù; (defeat) ...に快勝する ...ni kaíshō suru

thrash about/around [θræʃ-] *vi* のたうつ notáutsù

thrash out *vt* (problem) 討議する tógi suru

thread [θred] *n* (yarn) 糸 ítò; (of screw) ねじ山 nejíyama

◆*vt* (needle) ...に糸を通す ...ni ítò wo tósù

threadbare [θred'beːr] *adj* (clothes, carpet) 擦切れた suríkireta

threat [θret] *n* (*also fig*) 脅し odóshi; (*fig*) 危険 kikén

threaten [θret'ən] *vi* (storm, danger) 迫る semárù

◆*vt*: **to threaten someone with/to do** ...で[...すると言って]...を脅す ...de [...surú tò itté]...wò odósù

three [θriː] *num* 三 (の) sáñ (no)

three-dimensional [θriː'dimen'tʃənəl] *adj* 立体の rittái no

three-piece suit [θriː'piːs-] *n* 三つそろい mitsúzoròi

three-piece suite *n* 応接三点セットせつ santensettò

three-ply [θriː'plai] *adj* (wool) 三重織りの safíjùori no

thresh [θreʃ] *vt* (AGR) 脱穀する dakkóku suru

threshold [θreʃ'ould] *n* 敷居 shikíi

threw [θruː] *pt of* throw

thrift [θrift] *n* 節約 setsúyaku

thrifty [θrif'tiː] *adj* 節約家の setsúyakuka no

thrill [θril] *n* (excitement) スリル súrìru; (shudder) ぞっとする事 zottó suru kotò

◆*vt* (person, audience) わくわくさせる wákùwaku sasérù

to be thrilled (with gift etc) 大喜びである ōyorōkobi de árū

thriller [θríl'ær] n (novel, play, film) スリラー surfrā

thrilling [θríl'iŋ] adj (ride, performance, news etc) わくわくさせる wákuwaku sasérù

thrive [θraiv] (pt **throve**, pp **thrived** or **thriven**) vi (grow: plant) 生茂る ofshigerù; (: person, animal) よく育つ yókù sodátsù; (: business) 盛んになる sakán ni narù; (do well): **to thrive on something** …で栄える …de sakáerù

thriven [θríven] pp of **thrive**

thriving [θraiv'iŋ] adj (business, community) 繁盛している hánjō shité irù

throat [θrout] n のど nódò

to have a sore throat のどが痛い nódò ga itái

throb [θrɑb] n (of heart) 鼓動 kodō; (of wound) うずき uzúki; (of engine) 振動 shifidō

♦vi (heart) どきどきする dókìdoki suru; (head, arm: with pain) ずきずきする zúkìzuki suru; (machine: vibrate) 振動する shifidō suru

throes [θrouz] npl: **in the throes of** (war, moving house etc) …と取組んでいるさなかに …to torfkunde irú sánàka ni

thrombosis [θrɑmbou'sis] n 血栓症 kesséfishō

throne [θroun] n 王座 ōza

throng [θrɔŋ] n 群衆 gufishū

♦vt (streets etc) …に殺到する …ni sattó suru

throttle [θrɑt'əl] n (AUT) スロットル suróttoru

♦vt (strangle) …ののどを絞める …no nódò wo shimérù

through [θru] prep (space) …を通って …wo tōttě; (time) …の間中 …no áida jū; (by means of) …を使って …wo tsukáttě; (owing to) …の原因で …ga gefí-in dě

♦adj (ticket, train) 直通の chokútsū no

♦adv 通して tōshíte

to put someone through to someone (TEL) …を…につなぐ …wo …ni tsunágu

to be through (TEL) つながれる tsuná-

garerù; (relationship: finished) 終る owárù

「**no through road**」(BRIT) 行き止り ikídomari

throughout [θruːaut'] prep (place) …の至る所に …no itárù tokoro ni; (time) …の間中 …no áida jū

♦adv 至る所に itárù tokoro ni

throve [θrouv] pt of **thrive**

throw [θrou] n (gen) 投げる事 nagérù kotó

♦vt (pt **threw**, pp **thrown**) (object) 投げる nagérù; (rider) 振り落す furótosò; (fig: person: confuse) 迷わせる mayówaserù

to throw a party パーティをやる pátì wo yárù

throw away vt (rubbish) 捨てる sutérù; (money) 浪費する rōhi suru

throwaway [θrou'əwei] adj (toothbrush) 使い捨ての tsukáisute no; (remark) 捨てぜりふ染みた sutézerifujimìta

throw-in [θrou'in] n (SPORT) スローイン surōìn

throw off vt (get rid of: burden, habit) かなぐり捨てる kanágurisutérù; (cold) …が治る …ga naórù

throw out vt (rubbish, idea) 捨てる sutérù; (person) ほうり出す hōridasù

throw up vi (vomit) 吐く hákù

thru [θru] (US) = **through**

thrush [θrʌʃ] n (bird) つぐみ tsugúmi

thrust [θrʌst] n (TECH) 推進力 sufishíñryoku

♦vt (pt, pp **thrust**) (person, object) 強く押す tsúyòku osú

thud [θʌd] n ばたんという音 batán to iú otò

thug [θʌg] n (pej) ちんぴら chífipira; (criminal) 犯罪者 hafizaìsha

thumb [θʌm] n (ANAT) 親指 oyáyubi

♦vt: **to thumb a lift** ヒッチハイクする hitchíhaiku suru

thumbtack [θʌm'tæk] (US) n 画びょう gabyō

thumb through vt fus (book) 拾い読みする hiróiyomi suru

thump [θʌmp] n (blow) 一撃 ichígeki; (sound) どしんという音 doshín to iú otò
♦vt (person, object) たたく tatákū
♦vi (heart etc) どきどきする dókidoki suru

thunder [θʌn'dər] n 雷 kamínari
♦vi 雷が鳴る kamínari ga narú; (fig: train etc): **to thunder past** ごう音を立てて通り過ぎる gōon wò tátète tōrisugírù

thunderbolt [θʌn'dərboult] n 落雷 rakúrai

thunderclap [θʌn'dərklæp] n 雷鳴 raímei

thunderstorm [θʌn'dərstɔːrm] n 雷雨 raíu

thundery [θʌn'dəriː] adj (weather) 雷が鳴る kamínari ga narú

Thursday [θəːrz'deī] n 木曜日 mokúyòbi

thus [ðʌs] adv (in this way) こうして kō shìte; (consequently) 従って shitágattè

thwart [θwɔːrt] vt (person, plans) 邪魔する jamá suru

thyme [taim] n タイム táimu

thyroid [θai'rɔid] n (also: **thyroid gland**) 甲状腺 kōjōsen

tiara [tiːær'ə] n ティアラ tîara

Tibet [tibet'] n チベット chibéttò

tic [tik] n チック chíkku

tick [tik] n (sound of clock) かちかち kachíkachi; (mark) 印 shirúshi; (ZOOL) だに danî; (BRIT: inf): **in a tick** もうすぐ mō sugù
♦vi (clock, watch) かちかちいう kachíkachi iú
♦vt (item on list) ...に印を付ける ...ni shirúshi wò tsukérù

ticket [tik'it] n (for public transport, theater etc) 切符 kippú; (in shop: on goods) 値札 nefúda; (for raffle, library etc) チケット chikéttò; (also: **parking ticket**) 駐車違反のチケット chūsha-ihàn no chikéttò

ticket collector n 改札係 kaísatsugakàri

ticket office n (RAIL, theater etc) 切符売場 kippú urîba

tickle [tik'əl] vt (person, dog) くすぐる

kusúguru
♦vi (feather etc) くすぐったい kusúguttai

ticklish [tik'liʃ] adj (person) くすぐったがる kusúguttagàru; (problem) 厄介な yákkaì na

tick off vt (item on list) ...に印を付ける ...ni shirúshi wò tsukérù; (person) しかる shikárù

tick over vi (engine) アイドリングする aídoringu suru; (fig: business) 低迷する teímei suru

tidal [taid'əl] adj (force) 潮の shió no; (estuary) 干満のある kañman no arù

tidal wave n 津波 tsunámi

tidbit [tid'bit] (US) n (food) うまいもの 一口 umái monò hitőkuchi; (news) 好奇心をあおり立てるうわさ話 kōkìshìn wo aòritatérù uwásabanàshì

tiddlywinks [tid'liːwiŋks] n おはじき ohájìki

tide [taid] n (in sea) 潮 shió; (fig: of events, fashion, opinion) 動向 dōkō
high/low tide 満(干)潮 mañ(kañ)chō

tide over vt (help out) ...の一時的な助けになる ...no ichíjiteki nà tasúke ni narú

tidy [tai'diː] adj (room, dress, desk, work) きちんとした kichíñ to shita; (person) きれい好きな kiréizuki na
♦vt (also: **tidy up**: room, house etc) 片付ける katázukerù

tie [tai] n (string etc) ひも himő; (BRIT: necktie) ネクタイ nékùtai; (fig: link) 縁 éñ; (SPORT: even score) 同点 dōten
♦vt (fasten: parcel) 縛る shibárù; (: shoelaces, ribbon) 結ぶ musúbu
♦vi (SPORT) 同点になる dōten nì narú
to tie in a bow ちょう結びにする chōmusùbi ni suru
to tie a knot in something ...に結び目を作る ...ni musúbime wò tsukúrù

tie down vt (fig: person: restrict) 束縛する sokúbaku suru; (: to date, price etc) 縛り付ける shibáritsukerù

tier [tiːr] n (of stadium etc) 列 rétsù; (of cake) 層 sō

tie up vt (parcel) ...にひもを掛ける ...ni himó wò kakérù; (dog, boat) つなぐ tsunágù; (prisoner) 縛る shibárù; (arrangements) 整える totónoerù

to be tied up (busy) 忙しい isógashiì

tiger [tai'gəːr] n トラ torá

tight [tait] adj (firm: rope) ぴんと張った pín tò hattá; (scarce: money) 少ない sukúnaì; (narrow: shoes, clothes) きつい kitsúi; (bend) 急な kyú na; (strict: security, budget, schedule) 厳しい kibíshiì; (inf: drunk) 酔っ払った yoppárattá
♦adv (hold, squeeze, shut) 堅く katáku

tighten [tait'ən] vt (rope, screw) 締める shimérù; (grip) 固くする katáku suru; (security) 厳しくする kibíshikù suru
♦vi (grip) 固くなる katáku narù; (rope) 締る shimárù

tightfisted [tait'fis'tid] adj けちな kéchi na

tightly [tait'liː] adv (grasp) 固く katáku

tightrope [tait'roup] n 綱渡りの綱 tsunáwatàri no tsuná

tights [taits] npl タイツ táitsu

tile [tail] n (on roof) かわら kawára; (on floor, wall) タイル táiru

tiled [taild] adj (roof) かわらぶきの kawárabuki no; (floor, wall) タイル張りの taírubari no

till [til] n (in shop etc) レジの引出し réjì no hikídashi
♦vt (land: cultivate) 耕す tagáyasù
♦prep, conj = **until**

tiller [til'əːr] n (NAUT) だ柄 dahéi, チラー chírā

tilt [tilt] vt 傾ける katámukerù
♦vi 傾く katámukù

timber [tim'bəːr] n (material) 材木 zaímoku; (trees) 材木用の木 zaímokuyò no kí

time [taim] n (gen) 時間 jíkàn; (epoch: often pl) 時代 jidái; (by clock) 時刻 jíkòku; (moment) 瞬間 shuñkan; (occasion) 回 kái; (MUS) テンポ téñpo
♦vt (measure time of: race, boiling an egg etc) ...の時間を計る ...no jíkàn wo hakárù; (fix moment for: visit etc) ...の時期を選ぶ ...no jíkì wo erábù; (remark

etc) ...のタイミングを合せる ...no taímingu wo awáserù

a long time 長い間 nagái aidà

for the time being 取りあえず toríaezú

4 at a time 4つずつ yóttsu zútsu

from time to time 時々 tokídòki

at times 時には tokí ni wà

in time (soon enough) 間に合って ma ní attè; (after some time) やがて yagáte; (MUS) ...のリズムに合せて ... no rízùmu ni awáserù

in a week's time 1週間で isshúkan de

in no time 直ぐに súgù ni

any time いつでも ítsù de mo

on time 時間に合って ma ní attè

5 times 5 5かける5 gó kakerù gó

what time is it? 何時ですか náñji desu ká

to have a good time 楽しむ tanóshimù

time bomb n 時限爆弾 jigénbakùdan

time lag n 遅れ okúre

timeless [taim'lis] adj 普遍的な fuhénteki na

time limit n 期限 kígèn

timely [taim'liː] adj (arrival, reminder) 時宜を得た jígì wo étà, 丁度いい時の chōdo ii tokì no, タイムリーな taímurī na

time off n 休暇 kyúka

timer [tai'məːr] n (time switch) タイムスイッチ taímusuitchì; (in cooking) タイマー táimā

time scale (BRIT) n 期間 kíkan

time-share [taim'ʃeːr] n リゾート施設の共同使用権 rizótoshisètsu no kyódōshiyōken

time switch n タイムスイッチ taímusuitchì, タイマー taimā

timetable [taim'teibəl] n (RAIL etc) 時刻表 jikókuhyò; (SCOL etc) 時間割 jikánwari

time zone n 時間帯 jikántai

timid [tim'id] adj (shy) 気が小さい ki gá chísaì; (easily frightened) 臆病な okúbyò na

timing [tai'miŋ] n (SPORT) タイミング taímingu

the timing of his resignation 彼の辞

退のタイミング kárè no jítai no taímingu

timpani [tim'pəni] *npl* ティンパニー tînpanî

tin [tin] *n* (material) すず súzù; (*also:* **tin plate**) ブリキ burîkí; (container: biscuit tin etc) 箱 hakó; (: *BRIT:* can) 缶 kán

tinfoil [tin'foil] *n* ホイル hóìru

tinge [tindʒ] *n* (of color) 薄い色合 usúì íròaí; (of feeling) 気味 kimí

♦*vt:* **tinged with** (color) ...の色合を帯びた ...no íròaí wo óbìta; (feeling) ...の気味を帯びた ...no kimí wo óbìta

tingle [tin'gəl] *vi* (person, arms etc) ぴりぴりする bíríbìri suru

tinker [tiŋk'əːr] : **to tinker with** *vt fus* いじくる ijíkurů

tinned [tind] (*BRIT*) *adj* (food, salmon, peas) 缶詰の kañzumè no

tin opener [-ou'pənəːr] (*BRIT*) *n* 缶切り kañkírì

tinsel [tin'səl] *n* ティンセル tîñseru

tint [tint] *n* (color) 色合い íròaí; (for hair) 染毛剤 sefímozai

tinted [tin'tid] *adj* (hair) 染めた sóméta; (spectacles, glass) 色付きの íròtsuki no

tiny [tai'ni:] *adj* 小さな chíìsa na

tip [tip] *n* (end: of paintbrush etc) 先端 señtan; (gratuity) チップ chíppù; (*BRIT:* for rubbish) ごみ捨て場 gomí suteba; (advice) 助言 jogén

♦*vt* (waiter) ...にチップをあげる ...ni chíppù wo agéru; (tilt) 傾ける katámukerù; (overturn: *also:* **tip over**) 引っ繰り返す hikkúrikaesù; (empty: *also:* **tip out**) 空ける akéru

tip-off [tip'ɔːf] *n* (hint) 内報 naîhō

tipped [tipt] (*BRIT*) *adj* (cigarette) フィルター付きの fírútàtsuki no

Tipp-Ex [tip'eks] (®) *BRIT* *n* 修正ペン shúseipeñ (*白い修正液の出るフェルトペン shiróì shúseièki no derú ferútopeñ

tipsy [tip'si:] (*inf*) *adj* 酔っ払った yoppárattá

tiptoe [tip'tou] *n*: **on tiptoe** つま先立って tsumásakidàtte

tiptop [tip'tɑːp] *adj*: **in tiptop condition** 状態が最高で jótai ga saîkō dè

tire [taiəːr] *n* (*BRIT* **tyre**) タイヤ tâìya

♦*vt* (make tired) 疲れさせる tsukáresaserù

♦*vi* (become tired) 疲れる tsukárerù; (become wearied) うんざりする uñzari suru

tired [taiərd] *adj* (person, voice) 疲れた tsukárèta

to be tired of something ...にうんざりしている ...ni uñzari shité irù

tireless [taiər'lis] *adj* (worker) 疲れを知らない tsukáre wò shiránaì; (efforts) たゆまない tayúmanaì

tire pressure *n* タイヤの空気圧 tâìya no kúkiatsù

tiresome [taiər'səm] *adj* (person, thing) うんざりさせる uñzarí saserù

tiring [taiər'iŋ] *adj* 疲れさせる tsukáresaserù

tissue [tiʃ'u:] *n* (ANAT, BIO) 組織 sóshìki; (paper handkerchief) ティッシュ tîsshù

tissue paper *n* ティッシュペーパー tisshúpèpā

tit [tit] *n* (bird) シジュウカラ shijúkàra

to give tit for tat しっぺ返しする shippégaèshi suru

titbit [tit'bit] = **tidbit**

titillate [tit'əleit] *vt* 刺激する shigékì suru (特に性的描写などについて言う tókù ni seîteki byòsha nádò ni tsuîte iú

title [tait'əl] *n* (of book, play etc) 題 dái; (personal rank etc) 肩書 katágaki; (BOXING etc) タイトル tâìtoru

title deed *n* (LAW) 権利証書 keñrishòsho

title role *n* 主役 shuyáku

titter [tit'əːr] *vi* くすくす笑う kusúkusu waráù

TM [ti:'em'] *abbr* = **trademark**

to [tu:] *prep* **1** (direction) ...へ ...e

to go to France/London/school/the station フランス(ロンドン, 学校, 駅)へ行く furánsu(róndon, gakkō, ékì)e ikù

to go to Claude's/the doctor's クロー

ドの家[医者]へ行く kuródð no ié(ishá)e
ikú

the road to Edinburgh エジンバラへ
の道 ejiŋbara é nò michí

to the left/right 左(右)へ hidári(migí)e

2 (as far as) ...まで ...máde

from here to London ここからロンド
ンまで kokó karà róndon made

to count to 10 10まで数える jū made
kazóerù

from 40 to 50 people 40ないし50人の
人 yónjū nàishi gojūnìn no hitó

3 (with expressions of time): **a quarter
to 5** 5時15分前 gójì júgofùn máè

it's twenty to 3 3時20分前です sánji
nijúppùn máè desu

4 (for, of) ...の ...no

the key to the front door 玄関のかぎ
génkan no kagí

she is secretary to the director 彼女
は所長の秘書です kánòjo wa shochó nò
hishó desù

a letter to his wife 妻への手紙 tsúma
e no tegámi

5 (expressing indirect object) ...に ...ni

to give something to someone ...に...を
与える ...ni ...wò atáerù

to talk to someone ...に話す ...ni hanà-
sù

I sold it to a friend 友達にそれを売り
ました tomódachi nì soré wò urímashīta

to cause damage to something ...に損
害を与える ...ni sòŋgai wò atáerù

**to be a danger to someone/some-
thing** ...を危険にさらす ...wò kìken nī
sarásù

to carry out repairs to something
...を修理する ...wò shūrì suru

you've done something to your hair
あなたは髪型を変えましたね anátà wa
kamígata wo kaémashīta né

6 (in relation to) ...に対して ...ni táīshte
A is to B as C is to D A対Dの関係は
C対Dの関係に等しい A táī B no kaŋkei
wā C táī D no kaŋkei ni hìtóshī

3 goals to 2 スコア3対2 sukóà wa
sañ táī nì

---

30 miles to the gallon ガソリン1ガロ
ンで30マイル走れる gasórin ichígarðn de
sañjimaĩru hashírerù

7 (purpose, result): **to come to someone's aid** ...を助けに来る ...wò tasúke nì
kúrù

to sentence someone to death ...に死刑
の宣告を下す ...ni shikéi nð señkoku wð
kudásù

to my surprise 驚いた事に odóroita
kotò ni

♦**with vb 1** (simple infinitive): **to go/eat**
行く(食べる)事 ikú(tabérù)kotð

2 (following another verb): **to want to
do** ...したい ...shitáì

to try to do ...をしようとする ...wò shiyó tò suru

to start to do ...を...し始める ...wò shihā-
jimerù

3 (with vb omitted): **I don't want to** そ
れをしたくない soré wð shitákùnai

you ought to あなたはそうすべきです
anátà wa sô sùbeki desu

4 (purpose, result): ...するために ...surú
tamè ni, ...する様に ...surú yô ni, ...にし
...shí nī

I did it to help you あなたを助け様と
思ってあれをした anátà wo tasúke-
yô to omóttè soré wð shimàshīta

he came to see you 彼はあなたに会い
に来ました kárè wa anátà nì áì nì kimā-
shīta

I went there to meet him 彼に会おう
としてあそこへ行きました kárè ni áð tò
shite asóko e ikimashīta

5 (equivalent to relative clause): **I have
things to do** 私はする事ある有ります
iróiro ð suru kotð ga arímasù

he has a lot to lose if... ...が起れば、
彼は大損をするだろう ...gà okórebà, kárè
wa ôzón wo suru darð

the main thing is to try 一番大切なの
は努力する事 ichíban tāīsetsu nà no wā
dóryðku suru

6 (after adjective etc): **ready to go** 行く
準備ができた ikú juñbi ga dékīta

too old/young to ... ...するので年を取
り過ぎている[若過ぎる] ...surú no nì tī-

shî wŏ torîsugite irú(wákásugirú)
it's too heavy to lift 重くて持上げられません omôkute mochîageraremaseñ

♦*adv: push/pull the door to* ドアを閉める dôabo shimerú(ぴったり閉めない場合に使う pittári shiménai baái nî tsukáũ

---

toad [toud] *n* ヒキガエル hikígaeru

toadstool [toud'stu:l] *n* キノコ kínòko

toast [toust] *n* (CULIN) トースト tôsuto; (drink, speech) 乾杯 kañpai
♦*vt* (CULIN: bread etc) 焼く yákû; (drink to) ...のために乾杯する ...no tamé nî kañpai suru

toaster [tous'tə:r] *n* トースター tôsutā

tobacco [təbæk'ou] *n* タバコ tabáko

tobacconist [təbæk'ənist] *n* タバコ売り tabákòuri

tobacconist's (shop) [təbæk'ənists-] *n* タバコ屋 tabákoya

toboggan [təbɑg'ən] *n* (*also* child's) トボガン tobógañ

today [tədei'] *adv* (*also* 今日 (は) kyô (ua))
♦*n* 今日 kyô; (fig) 現在 geñzai

toddler [tɑd'lə:r] *n* 幼児 yôji

to-do [tədu:'] *n* (fuss) 騒ぎ sáwàgi

toe [tou] *n* (of foot) 足指 ashîyùbi; (of shoe, sock) つま先 tsumásaki
♦*vt*: *to toe the line* (fig) 服従する fukújù suru

toenail [tou'neil] *n* 足のつめ ashî no tsumé

toffee [tɔːfi:] *n* = *taffy*

toffee apple (BRIT) *n* タフィー衣のりんご tafîgoromo no riñgo

toga [tou'gə] *n* トーガ tôga

together [təgeð'əːr] *adv* (with each other) 一緒に ísshò ni; (at same time) 同時に dôji ni

together with ...と一緒に ...to ísshò ni

toil [tɔil] *n* 労苦 rôkù
♦*vi* あくせく働く ákùseku határakù

toilet [tɔi'lit] *n* (apparatus) 便器 béňki, (room with this apparatus) 便所 beñjo, お手洗い o-teárài, トイレ tôìre

---

toilet bag (for woman) 化粧バッグ keshôbaggù; (for man) 洗面バッグ señmeñbaggù

toilet paper *n* トイレットペーパー tofrettopêpā

toiletries [tɔi'litriːz] *npl* 化粧品 keshôhiñ

toilet roll *n* トイレットペーパーのロール tofrettopêpā no rôru

toilet soap *n* 化粧せっけん keshôsekkèn

toilet water *n* 化粧水 keshôshi

token [tou'kən] *n* (sign, souvenir) 印 shirúshi; (substitute coin) コイン kôìn
♦*adj* (strike, payment etc) 名目の mefmoku no

book/record/gift token (BRIT) 商品券 shôhiñkeñ

Tokyo [tou'ki:ou] *n* 東京 tôkyò

told [tould] *pt*, *pp of* tell

tolerable [tɑl'əːrəbəl] *adj* (bearable) 我慢できる gámàn dekírù; (fairly good) まあまあの mâmâ no

tolerance [tɑl'əːrəns] *n* (patience) 寛容 kañ-yō (TECH) 耐入力 tafryūryòku

tolerant [tɑl'əːrənt] *adj*: *tolerant (of)* (...に) 耐えられる (...ni) taérarerù

tolerate [tɑl'əːreit] *vt* (pain, noise, injustice) 我慢する gámàn suru

toll [toul] *n* (of casualties, deaths) 数 kázù; (tax, charge) 料金 ryôkin
♦*vi* (bell) 鳴る narú

tomato [təmei'tou] (*pl* **tomatoes**) *n* トマト tómàto

tomb [tuːm] *n* 墓 haká

tomboy [tɑm'bɔi] *n* お転婆 o-téñba

tombstone [tuːm'stoun] *n* 墓石 hakâ-ishi

tomcat [tɑm'kæt] *n* 雄ネコ osûneko

tomorrow [təmɔːr'ou] *adv* (*also* fig) 明日 asú, あした ashíta
♦*n* 明日 asú, あした ashíta

the day after tomorrow あさって a-sáttè

tomorrow morning あしたの朝 ashíta nò ása

ton [tʌn] *n* トン tóñ ◊BRIT = 1016 kg; US = 907 kg

tons of (inf) ものすごく沢山の monósugòku takúsan no

tone [toun] *n* (of voice) 調子 chôshi; (of

instrument) 音色 ne-íro; (of color) 色調 shikíchō

♦vi (colors: also: **tone in**) 合う áu

tone-deaf [toun'def] adj 音痴の ónchi no

tone down vt (color, criticism, demands) 和らげる yawáragerù; (sound) 小さくする chíísaku suru

tone up vt (muscles) 強くする tsúyoku suru

tongs [tɔːŋz] npl (also: **coal tongs**) 炭ばさみ sumíbasàmi; (curling tongs) 髪ごて kamígote

tongue [tʌŋ] n (ANAT) 舌 shitá; (CULIN) タン tañ; (language) 言語 géñgo

tongue in cheek (speak, say) からかって karákattè

tongue-tied [tʌŋ'taid] adj (fig) ものも言えない monó mò iénaì

tongue-twister [tʌŋ'twistər] n 早口言葉 hayákuchi kotobà

tonic [tɑːn'ik] n (MED, also fig) 強壮剤 kyōsōzai; (also: **tonic water**) トニックウオーター toníkkuuōtà

tonight [tənait'] adv (this evening) 今日の夕方 kyō no yūgata; (this night) 今夜 kóñ-ya

♦n (this evening) 今日の夕方 kyō no yūgata; (this night) 今夜 kóñ-ya

tonnage [tʌn'idʒ] n (NAUT) トン数 toñsū

tonsil [tɑːn'səl] n へんとうせん heñtōsen

tonsillitis [tɑːnsəlai'tis] n へんとうせん炎 heñtōsen-èn

too [tuː] adv (excessively) あまりに...過ぎる amári ni ...sugíru; (also) ... も（また）...mo (matá)

too much adv あまり沢山の amári takusañ de

♦adj あまり沢山の amári takusañ no

too many adv あまり沢山の amári takusañ no

♦pron あまり沢山 amári takusañ

took [tuk] pt of **take**

tool [tuːl] n 道具 dōgu

tool box n 道具箱 dōgubako

toot [tuːt] n (of horn) ぶーぶー pūpū; (of whistle) ぴーぴー pīpī

♦vi (with car-horn) クラクションを鳴らす kurákùshon wo narásù

tooth [tuːθ] (pl **teeth**) n (ANAT, TECH) 歯 há

toothache [tuːθ'eik] n 歯の痛み há nò itámi, 歯痛 shitsū

toothbrush [tuːθ'brʌʃ] n 歯ブラシ habúràshi

toothpaste [tuːθ'peist] n 歯磨き hamigaki

toothpick [tuːθ'pik] n つまようじ tsumáyōji

top [tɑːp] n (of mountain, tree, head, ladder) 天辺 teppéñ; (page) 頭 atáma; (of cupboard, table, box) ...の上 ...no ué; (of list etc) 筆頭 hittō; (lid: of box, jar, bottle) ふた futá; (blouse etc) トップ tóppù; (toy) こま kómà

♦adj (highest: shelf, step) 一番上の ichíban ue no; (: marks) 最高の saíkō no; (in rank: salesman etc) ぴかーの piká-ichí no

♦vt (be first in: poll, vote, list) ...の首位に立つ ...no shū́i ni tátsù; (exceed: estimate etc) 越える koérù

on top of (above) ...の上に ...no ué ni; (in addition to) ...に加えて ...ni kuwáetè

from top to bottom 上から下まで ué kara shitá madè

top floor n 最上階 saíjōkai

top hat n シルクハット shirúkuhattò

top-heavy [tɑːp'hevi:] adj (object) 不安定な fuáñtei na; (administration) 幹部の多過ぎる káñbu no ōsugírù

topic [tɑːp'ik] n 話題 wadái

topical [tɑːp'ikəl] adj 時事問題の jijímoñdai no

topless [tɑːp'lis] adj (bather, waitress, swimsuit) トップレスの tóppùresu no

top-level [tɑːp'lev'əl] adj (talks, decision) 首脳の shunō no

topmost [tɑːp'moust] adj (branch etc) 一番上の ichíban ue no

top off (US) vt = **top up**

topple [tɑːp'əl] vt (government, leader) 倒す taósù

♦vi (person, object) 倒れる taórerù

top-secret [tɑːp'si:'krit] adj 極秘の gokǔhi no

topsy-turvy [tɑːpˈsiːtəˈvɪ] *adj* (world) はちゃめちゃの háchāmecha no

♦*adv* (fall, land etc) 逆様に sakásama ni

top up *vt* (bottle etc) 一杯にする ippái ni suru

torch [tɔːrtʃ] *n* (with flame) たいまつ táimatsu; (BRIT: electric) 懐中電とう kaíchūdentō

tore [tɔːr] *pt of* tear

torment [*n* tɔːrˈment *vb* tɔːrˈment] *n* 苦しみ kurúshimī

♦*vt* (subj: feelings, guilt etc) 苦しませる kurúshimaserū; 悩ませる nayámaserū; (fig: annoy: subj: person) いじめる ijímerū

torn [tɔːrn] *pp of* tear

tornado [tɔːrˈneiˈdou] (*pl* tornadoes) *n* 竜巻 tatsúmaki

torpedo [tɔːrˈpiːˈdou] (*pl* torpedoes) *n* 魚雷 gyorái

torrent [tɔːrˈənt] *n* (flood) 急流 kyūryū; (fig) 奔流 hoñryū

torrential [tɔːrˈenʃəl] *adj* (rain) 土砂降りの doshábuuri no

torrid [tɔːrˈid] *adj* (sun) しゃく熱の shakúnetsu no; (love affair) 情熱的な jōnetsuteki na

torso [tɔːrˈsou] *n* 胴 dō

tortoise [tɔːrˈtəs] *n* カメ kámè

tortoiseshell [tɔːrˈtəsʃel] *adj* べっ甲の bekkō no

tortuous [tɔːrˈtʃuːəs] *adj* (path) 曲りくねった magárikunettà; (argument) 回りくどい mawárikudoì; (mind) 邪悪な jaáku na

torture [tɔːrˈtʃər] *n* (also fig) 拷問 gōmon

♦*vt* (also fig) 拷問にかける gōmon ni kakérū

Tory [tɔːrˈiː] (BRIT) *adj* 保守党の hoshútō no

♦*n* 保守党員 hoshútōin

toss [tɔːs] *vt* (throw) 投げる nagérū; (one's head) 振る furú

to toss a coin コインをトスする kóin wo tósū surú

to toss up for something コインをトスして...を決める kóin wo tósū shité ...wo

kimérū

to toss and turn (in bed) ころげ回る korógemawarū

tot [tɑːt] *n* (BRIT: drink) おちょこ一杯 ochóko íppaì; (child) 小さい子供 chiísaì kodómo

total [touˈtəl] *adj* (complete: number, workforce etc) 全体の zeńtai no; (: failure, wreck etc) 完全な kañzen na

♦*n* 合計 gōkei

♦*vt* (add up: numbers, objects) 合計する gōkei suru; (add up to: X dollars/pounds) 合計は...になる gōkei wā ...ni nárū

totalitarian [toutælitəˈriːən] *adj* 全体主義の zeńtaishūgi no

totally [touˈtəliː] *adv* (agree, write off, unprepared) 全く mattáku

totter [tɑːtˈər] *vi* (person) よろめく yorómekū

touch [tʌtʃ] *n* (sense of touch) 触覚 shokkáku; (contact) 触る事 sawáru kotó

♦*vt* (with hand, foot) ...に触る ...ni sawárū; (tamper with) ...にいじる ijíru; (make contact with) ...に接触する ...ni sesshóku suru; (emotionally) 感動させる kañdō saserū

a touch of (fig: frost etc) 少しばかり sukóshi bakári

to get in touch with someone ...に連絡する ...ni refraku suru

to lose touch (friends) ...との連絡が途絶える ...tó no refraku ga tódaerū

touch-and-go [tʌtʃˈəngouˈ] *adj* 危ない abúnai

touchdown [tʌtʃˈdaun] *n* (of rocket, plane: on land) 着陸 chakúriku; (: on water) 着水 chakúsui; (US FOOTBALL) タッチダウン tatchídaùn

touched [tʌtʃt] *adj* (moved) 感動した kañdō shita

touching [tʌtʃˈiŋ] *adj* 感動的な kañdōteki na

touchline [tʌtʃˈlain] *n* (SPORT) サイドライン saídoraìn

touch on *vt fus* (topic) ...に触れる ...ni furérū

touch up *vt* (paint) 修正する shúsei suru

touchy [tʌtʃ'i:] *adj* (person) 気難しいki-mūzukashíi

tough [tʌf] *adj* (strong, hard-wearing: material) 丈夫な jōbu na; (meat) 固いka-táι; (person: physically) 頑丈な ganjō na; (: mentally) 神経が太い shíñkei gà futói; (difficult: task, problem, way of life) 難しいmuzukashíi; (firm: stance, negotiations, policies) 譲らない yuzúranai

toughen [tʌf'ən] *vt* (someone's character) 強くする tsúyoku suru; (glass etc) 強化する kyōka suru

toupee [tupei'] *n* かつら katsúra ◊男性のはげを隠す小さな物を指す dañsei no hagè wo kakúsù chíisa na monò wo sásù

tour [tur] *n* (journey) 旅行 ryokō; (also: **package tour**) ツアー tsúā; (of town, factory, museum) 見学 keñgaku; (by pop group etc) 巡業 juñgyō

◆*vt* (country, city, factory etc) 観光旅行する kañkōryokō suru; (city) 見物するkeñbutsu suru; (factory etc) 見学するkeñgaku suru

tourism [tur'izəm] *n* (business) 観光 kañkō

tourist [tur'ist] *n* 観光客 kañkōkyaku
◆*cpd* (attractions etc) 観光の kañkō no

tourist class *n* (on plane, ship) ツーリストクラス tsúrisutokurāsu

tourist office *n* 観光案内所 kañkōan-naisho

tournament [tur'nəmənt] *n* トーナメント tōnamento

tousled [tau'zəld] *adj* (hair) 乱れた midáreta

tout [taut] *vi*: **to tout for business** (business) 御用聞きする goyōkiki suru
◆*n* (also: **ticket tout**) だふ屋 dafúya

tow [tou] *vt* (vehicle, caravan, trailer) 引く hikú, けん引する keñ-in suru
「**in** (US) **or** (BRIT) **on tow**」 (AUT) けん引中 keñ-iñchū

toward(s) [tɔːrd(z)] *prep* (direction) ...の方へ...no hō e; (attitude) ...に対して ...ni táishite; (purpose) ...に向かって ...ni mukátte; (in time) ...のちょっと前に ...no chóttò maè ni

towel [tau'əl] *n* (hand/bath towel) タオル táoru

towelling [tau'əliŋ] *n* (fabric) タオル地 taórujì

tower rack (BRIT: **towel rail**) *n* タオル掛け taórukàke

tower [tau'ər] *n* 塔 tō

tower block (BRIT) *n* 高層ビル kōsōbirù

towering [tau'əriŋ] *adj* (buildings, trees, cliffs) 高くそびえる tákàku sobíerù; (figure) 体の大きな karáda nò ōkìi na

town [taun] *n* 町 machí
to go to town 町に出掛ける machí ni dekákerù; (*fig*: on something) 思い切りやる omóikiri yarù, 派手にやる hadé ni yarú

town center *n* 町の中心部 machí nò chūshìnbu

town council *n* 町議会 chōgikaì

town hall *n* 町役場 machíyakùba

town plan *n* 町の道路地図 machí nò dōrochizú

town planning *n* 開発計画 kaíhatsukeìkaku

towrope [tou'roup] *n* けん引用ロープ keñ-iñ-yō rōpù

tow truck (US) *n* (breakdown lorry) レッカー車 rekkásha

toxic [tɑk'sik] *adj* (fumes, waste etc) 有毒の yūdòku no

toy [tɔi] *n* おもちゃ omóchà

toyshop [tɔi'ʃɑp] *n* おもちゃ屋 omóchà-ya

toy with *vt fus* (object, food) いじくり回す ijíkurimawasù; (idea) ...しようかなと考えてみる ...shiyō kà na to kañgaete mirù

trace [treis] *n* (sign) 跡 átò; (small amount) 微量 biryō
◆*vt* (draw) トレースする torésù suru; (follow) 追跡する tsuíseki suru; (locate) 見付ける mitsúkerù

tracing paper [treis'iŋ-] *n* トレーシングペーパー torḗshingupēpā

track [træk] *n* (mark) 跡 átò; (path: *gen*) 道 michí; (: of bullet etc) 弾道 dañdō; (: of suspect, animal) 足跡 ashíatò; (RAIL) 線路 séñro; (on tape, record: *also* SPORT)

トラック torákkù

♦vt (follow: animal, person) 追跡する tsufséki suru

*to keep track of ...*を監視する ...wo kafíshi suru

track down vt (prey) 追詰める tsuitsúmerù; (something lost) 見付ける mitsúkerù

tracksuit [træk'su:t] n トレーニングウエア toréningu ueà

tract [trækt] n (GEO) 地帯 chitái; (pamphlet) 論文 rónbun

traction [træk'ʃən] n (power) けん引力 keñ-iñryoku; (MED): *in traction* けん引療法中 keñ-iñryōhōchū

tractor [træk'tər] n トラクター torákutà

trade [treid] n (activity) 貿易 bōeki; (skill) 技術 gíjùtsu; (job) 職業 shokúgyō

♦vi (do business) 商売する shōbai suru

♦vt (exchange): *to trade something (for something)* (...と) ...を交換する (...to) ...wō kōkan suru

trade fair n トレードフェアー toredo feà

trade in vt (old car etc) 下取りに出す shitádori ni dásù

trademark [treid'mɑːrk] n 商標 shōhyō

trade name n 商品名 shōhiñmei

trader [trei'dər] n 貿易業者 bōekigyōsha

tradesman [treidz'mən] (pl **tradesmen**) n 商人 shōnin

trade union n 労働組合 rōdōkumìai

trade unionist [-jun'jənist] n 労働組合員 rōdōkumiaiìn

tradition [trədiʃ'ən] n 伝統 deñtō

traditional [trədiʃ'ənəl] adj (dress, costume, meal) 伝統的な deñtōteki na

traffic [træf'ik] n (movement: of people, vehicles) 往来 ōrai; (: of drugs etc) 売買 báibai; (air traffic, road traffic etc) 交通 kōtsū

♦vi: *to traffic in* (liquor, drugs) 売買する báibai suru

traffic circle (US) n ロータリー rōtarī

traffic jam n 交通渋滞 kōtsūjūtai

traffic lights npl 信号(機) shiñgō(kì)

traffic warden n 違反駐車取締官 ihán-

chūsha toríshimarikàn

tragedy [trædʒ'idi:] n 悲劇 higéki

tragic [trædʒ'ik] adj (death, consequences) 悲劇的な higékiteki na; (play, novel etc) 悲劇の higéki no

trail [treil] n (path) 小道 komìchi; (track) 跡路 ashíato; (of smoke, dust) 尾 ó

♦vt (drag) 後ろに引く úshiro ni hikú; (follow: person, animal) 追跡する tsuiséki suru

♦vi (hang loosely) 後ろに垂れる ushíro ni tarérù; (in game) 負けている makéte irù

trail behind vi (lag) 遅れる okúrerù

trailer [trei'lər] n (AUT) トレーラー toréra; (: caravan) キャンピングカー kyañpingukà; (CINEMA) 予告編 yokókuheñ

trailer truck (US) n トレーラートラック torératorakkù

train [trein] n (RAIL) 列車 resshá; (underground train) 地下鉄 chikátetsu; (of dress) トレイン toréiñ

♦vt (educate: mind) 教育する kyōiku suru; (teach skills to: apprentice, doctor, dog etc) 訓練する kuñren suru; (athlete) 鍛える kitáerù; (point: camera, hose, gun etc): *to train on* 向ける mukérù

♦vi (learn a skill) 訓練を受ける kuñren wò ukérù; (SPORT) トレーニングする toréniñgu suru

one's train of thought 考えの流れ kañgaé no nagáre

trained [treind] adj (worker, teacher) 技術が確かな gíjùtsu ga táshika na; (animal) 訓練された kuñren saretà

trainee [treini:'] n (apprentice: hairdresser etc) 見習 minárai; (teacher etc) 実習生 jisshūsei

trainer [trei'nər] n (SPORT: coach) コーチ kōchi; (: shoe) スニーカー suníkà; (of animals) 訓練師 kuñreñshi

training [trei'niŋ] n (for occupation) 訓練 kuñren; (SPORT) トレーニング toréniñgu

in training トレーニング中 toréningu-chū

training college n (gen) 職業大学 shokúgyōdaigàku; (for teachers) 教育大学

kyōikudaigaku

training shoes *npl* スニーカー suníkā

traipse [treips] *vi* 足を棒にして歩き回る ashí wò bō ni shité arúkimawarù

trait [treit] *n* 特徴 tokúchō

traitor [trei'tər] *n* 裏切者 urágirimóno

tram [træm] (*BRIT*) *n* (*also*: **tramcar**) 路面電車 roméndeñsha

tramp [træmp] *n* (person) ルンペン rúñpen; (*inf*: *pej*: woman) 浮気女 uwákioñna
  ♦*vi* どしんどしん歩く doshíñdoshin arúkù

trample [træm'pəl] *vt*: **to trample (underfoot)** 踏み付ける fumítsukerù

trampoline [træmpəlin'] *n* トランポリン toráñporin

trance [træns] *n* (*gen*) こん睡状態 koñsuijōtai; (*fig*) ぼう然とした状態 bōzen to shitá jōtai

tranquil [træŋ'kwil] *adj* (place, old age) 平穏な heíon na; (sleep) 静かな shízùka na

tranquillity [træŋkwil'iti:] *n* 平静さ heíseisa

tranquillizer [træŋ'kwəlaizər] *n* (*MED*) 鎮静剤 chiñseizai

transact [trænsækt'] *vt*: **to transact business** 取引する torîhìki suru

transaction [trænsæk'ʃən] *n* (piece of business) 取引 torîhìki

transatlantic [trænsətlæn'tik] *adj* (trade, phone-call etc) 英米間の eíbeikàn no

transcend [trænsend'] *vt* 越える koérù

transcript [træn'skript] *n* (of tape recording etc) 記録文書 kiróku buñsho

transfer [træns'fər] *n* (moving: of employees etc) 異動 idō; (: of money) 振替 furíkae; (POL: of power) 引継ぎ hikítsugi; (SPORT) トレード torédo; (picture, design) 写し絵 utsúshiè
  ♦*vt* (move: employees) 転任させる teńnin saserù; (: money) 振替える furíkaerù; (: power) 譲る yuzúrù

to transfer the charges (*BRIT*: *TEL*) コレクトコールにする korékutokòru ni suru

transform [træns'fɔːrm] *vt* 変化させる

héñka saserù

transformation [trænsfərmei'ʃən] *n* 変化 héñka

transfusion [trænsfju:'ʒən] *n* (*also*: **blood transfusion**) 輸血 yukétsu

transient [træn'ʃənt] *adj* 一時的な ichíjiteki na

transistor [trænzis'tər] *n* (*ELEC*) トランジスタ toráñjisùta; (*also*: **transistor radio**) トランジスタラジオ toráñjisuta rajìo

transit [træn'sit] *n*: **in transit** (people, things) 通過中の tsūkachū no

transition [trænziʃ'ən] *n* 移行 ikō

transitional [trænziʃ'ənəl] *adj* (period, stage) 移行の ikō no

transitive [træn'sətiv] *adj* (*LING*): **transitive verb** 他動詞 tadōshi

transit lounge *n* (at airport etc) トランジットラウンジ toráñjitto raùñji

transitory [træn'sitɔːri:] *adj* つかの間の tsuká no ma nò

translate [trænz'leit] *vt* (word, book etc) 翻訳する hoñ-yaku suru

translation [trænzlei'ʃən] *n* (act/result of translating) 訳 yákù

translator [trænslei'tər] *n* 訳者 yákùsha

transmission [trænsmiʃ'ən] *n* (of information, disease) 伝達 deñtatsu; (TV: broadcasting, program broadcast) 放送 hōsō; (AUT) トランスミッション toráñsumisshòn

transmit [trænsmit'] *vt* (message, signal, disease) 伝達する deñtatsu suru

transmitter [trænsmit'ər] *n* (piece of equipment) トランスミッタ toráñsumittà

transparency [trænspær'ənsi:] *n* (of glass etc) 透明度 tōmeìdo; (*PHOT*: slide) スライド suráìdo

transparent [trænspær'ənt] *adj* (see-through) 透明の tōmei no

transpire [trænspaiər'] *vi* (turn out) 明らかになる akíràka ni nárù; (happen) 起る okórù

transplant [*vb* trænzplænt' *n* trænz'-plænt] *vt* (seedlings: *also*: MED: organ)

移植する ishóku suru
♦n (MED) 移植 ishóku

transport [n træns'pɔːrt vb træns-pɔːrt'] n (moving people, goods) 輸送 yusō; (also: **road/rail transport** etc) 輸送機関 yusōkikàn; (car) 車 kurúma
♦vt (carry) 輸送する yusō suru

transportation [trænspɔːrteiʃən] n (transport) 輸送 yusō; (means of transport) 輸送機関 yusōkikàn

transport café (BRIT) n トラック運転手向きのレストラン torákkuunteñshu mukí no resútoraǹ

transvestite [trænsvestait] n 女装趣味の男性 josōshùmi no dañsei

trap [træp] n (snare, trick) わな wánà; (carriage) 軽馬車 keíbashà
♦vt (animal) わなで捕える wánà de toráerù; (person: trick) わなにかける wánà ni kakérù; (: confine: in bad marriage, burning building): **to be trapped** 逃げられなくなっている nigérarenakù natté irù

trap door n 落し戸 otóshidò

trapeze [træpiːz'] n 空中ぶらんこ kūchúburankò

trappings [træp'iŋz] npl 飾り kazári

trash [træʃ] n (rubbish: also pej) ごみ gomí; (: nonsense) でたらめ detárame

trash can (US) n ごみ入れ gomíirè

trauma [trɔː'mə] n 衝撃 shōgeki, ショック shókkù

traumatic [trɔːmæt'ik] adj 衝撃的な shōgekiteki na

travel [træv'əl] n (traveling) 旅行 ryokō
♦vi (person) 旅行する ryokō suru; (news, sound) 伝わる tsutáwarù; (wine etc): **to travel well/badly** 運搬に耐えられる(耐えられない) uñpan ni taérarerù (taérarenaì)
♦vt (distance) 旅行する ryokō suru

travel agency n 旅行代理店 ryokódairitèn

travel agent n 旅行業者 ryokógyòsha

traveler [træv'ələr] n (BRIT **traveller**) n 旅行者 ryokōshà

traveler's check [træv'ələrz-] (BRIT **traveller's cheque**) n トラベラーズチェ

ック toráberàzuchekkù

traveling [træv'əliŋ] (BRIT **travelling**) n 旅行 ryokō

travels [træv'əlz] npl (journeys) 旅行 ryokō

travel sickness n 乗物酔い norímono-yoì

travesty [træv'isti] n パロディー párodì

trawler [trɔː'lər] n トロール漁船 torōrugyòsen

tray [trei] n (for carrying) お盆 o-bón; (on desk) デスクトレー desúkutorè

treacherous [tretʃ'ərəs] adj (person, look) 裏切りの urágirimòno no; (ground, tide) 危険な kikén na

treachery [tretʃ'əriː] n 裏切り urágirì

treacle [triː'kəl] n 糖みつ tōmitsu

tread [tred] n (step) 歩調 hochō; (sound) 足音 ashíotò; (of stair) 踏面 fumízùra; (of tire) トレッド toréddò
♦vi (pt **trod**, pp **trodden**) 歩く arúkù

tread on vt fus 踏む fumú

treason [triː'zən] n 反逆罪 hañgyakuzài

treasure [treʒ'ər] n (gold, jewels etc) 宝物 takáramono; (person) 重宝な人 chōhō nà hitó
♦vt (value: object) 重宝する chōhō suru; (: friendship) 大事にしている daíji nì shité irù; (: memory, thought) 心に銘記する kokórò ni méki suru

treasurer [treʒ'ərər] n 会計 kaíkei

treasures [treʒ'ərz] npl (art treasures etc) 貴重品 kichōhìn

treasury [treʒ'əriː] n: (US) **the Treasury Department**, (BRIT) **the Treasury** 大蔵省 ōkurashō

treat [triːt] n (present) 贈物 okúrimono
♦vt (handle, regard: person, object) 扱う atsúkaù; (MED: patient, illness) 治療する chiryō suru; (TECH: coat) 処理する shórì suru

to treat someone to something ...に...をおごる ...ni ...wo ogórù

treatment [triːt'mənt] n (attention, handling) 扱い方 atsúkaikata; (MED) 治療 chiryō

treaty [triː'tiː] n 協定 kyōtei

treble [treb'əl] adj 3倍の sañbai no;

(MUS) 高音部の kōonbu no
♦*vt* 3倍にする sanbai ni suru
♦*vi* 3倍になる sanbai ni narū

treble clef *n* (MUS) 高音部記号 kōonbu-kigō

tree [triː] *n* 木 kí

tree trunk *n* 木の幹 kí nò míkí

trek [trek] *n* (long difficult journey: on foot) 徒歩旅行 tohóryokō; (: by car) 自動車旅行 jidósharyokō; (tiring walk) 苦し い道のり kurúshiī michínori

trellis [trel'is] *n* (for climbing plants) 棚 tanā

tremble [trem'bəl] *vi* (voice, body, trees: with fear, cold etc) 震える furúerù; (ground) 揺れる yurérù

tremendous [trimen'dəs] *adj* (enormous amount etc) ばく大な bakúdai na; (excellent: success, holiday, view etc) 素 晴らしい subárashiī

tremor [trem'ɔːr] *n* (trembling: of excitement, fear: in voice) 震え furúe; (*also*: **earth tremor**) 地震 jishín

trench [trentʃ] *n* (channel) 溝 mizó; (for defense) ざんごう zafigō

trend [trend] *n* (tendency) 傾向 kefkō; (of events) 動向 dōkō; (fashion) トレンド torḗndo

trendy [tren'diː] *adj* (idea, person, clothes) トレンディな torḗndi na

trepidation [trepidei'ʃən] *n* (apprehension) 不安 fuán

trespass [tres'pæs] *vi*: **to trespass on** (private property) ...に不法侵入する ...ni fuhóshinnyū suru

「**no trespassing**」立入禁止 tachfirikinshi

trestle [tres'əl] *n* (support for table etc) うま umá

trial [trail] *n* (LAW) 裁判 sáiban; (test: of machine etc) テスト tésuto

on trial (LAW) 裁判に掛けられて sáiban ni kákérarete
by trial and error 試行錯誤で shikósakùgo de

trial period *n* テスト期間 tésuto kikàn

trials [trailz] *npl* (unpleasant experiences) 試練 shíren

triangle [trai'æŋgəl] *n* (MATH) 三角 sáñkaku; (MUS) トライアングル toráiañguru

triangular [traiæŋ'gjələr] *adj* 三角形の sañkakkéi no

tribal [trai'bəl] *adj* (warrior, warfare, dance) 種族の shúzòku no

tribe [traib] *n* 種族 shúzòku

tribesman [traibz'mən] (*pl* **tribesmen**) *n* 種族の男性 shúzòku no dañsei

tribulations [tribjəlei'ənz] *npl* 苦労 kúrò, 苦難 kúnàn

tribunal [traibju:'nəl] *n* 審判委員会 shiñpan ííňkai

tributary [trib'jəteːri] *n* 支流 shiryú

tribute [trib'juːt] *n* (compliment) ほめの言葉 homé no kotobà
to pay tribute to ...をほめる ...wò homérù

trice [trais] *n*: **in a trice** あっという間に áttó iú ma ni

trick [trik] *n* (magic trick) 手品 tejína; (prank, joke) いたずら itázura; (skill, knack) こつ kotsú; (CARDS) トリック toríkkù
♦*vt* (deceive) だます damásù
to play a trick on someone ...にいたず らをする ...ni itázura wò suru
that should do the trick これでいい はずだ koré de iī hazú dà

trickery [trik'ɔːri] *n* 詐欺 kefryaku

trickle [trik'əl] *n* (of water etc) 滴り shitátari
♦*vi* (water, rain etc) 滴る shitátarù

tricky [trik'iː] *adj* (job, problem, business) 厄介な yákkài na

tricycle [trai'sikəl] *n* 三輪車 sañríshà

trifle [trai'fəl] *n* (small detail) ささいな事 sásài na kotó; (CULIN) トライフル toráifuru ◇カステラにゼリー、フルーツ、プリンなどをのせたデザート kasútera ni zérī, furútsù, púriñ nádò wo nosétà dezátò
♦*adv*: **a trifle long** ちょっと長い chóttò nagái

trifling [traif'liŋ] *adj* (detail, matter) さ さいな sásài na

trigger [trig'ɔːr] *n* (of gun) 引金 hikígane

trigger off vt (reaction, riot) ...の引き金となる ...no hikígane tò narú

trigonometry [trigənɔm'ətri:] n 三角法 sañkakuhō

trill [tril] vi (birds) さえずる saézurù

trim [trim] adj (house, garden) 手入れの行届いた teíre no ikítodoità; (figure) すらっとした suráttò shitá

♦n (haircut etc) 刈る事 karú kotò; (on car) 飾り kazári

♦vt (cut: hair, beard) 刈る karú; (decorate): **to trim (with)** (...で) 飾る (...de) kazárù; (NAUT: a sail) 調節する chōsetsu suru

trimmings [trim'iŋz] npl (CULIN) お決りの付け合せ o-kímarì no tsukéawase

trinket [triŋ'kit] n (ornament) 安い飾り yasúi kokímono; (piece of jewellery) 安い装身具 yasúi sōshiñgu

trio [tri:'ou] n (gen) 三つ組 mitsúgumi; (MUS) トリオ tórìo

trip [trip] n (journey) 旅行 ryokṓ; (outing) 遠足 eñsoku; (stumble) つまずき tsumázukì

♦vi (stumble) つまずく tsumázukù; (go lightly) 軽快に歩く keíkai ni arúkù

on a trip 旅行中で ryokṓchū de

tripe [traip] n (CULIN) トライプ torắipu ◇ウシ、ブタなどの胃の料理 ushf, butá nadò no í no ryṓri; (pej: rubbish)下らない物 kudáranai monò ◇特に人の発言や文書について言う tốkū ni hitó no hatsúgen yà bûñsho ni tsúîte iú

triple [trip'əl] adj (ice cream, somersault etc) トリプルの torípùru no

triplets [trip'lits] npl 三つ子 mitsúgo

triplicate [trip'ləkit] n: **in triplicate** 三通で sañtsū de

tripod [trai'pɑd] n 三脚 sañkyaku

trip up vi (stumble) つまずく tsumázukù

♦vt (person) つまずかせる tsumázukaserù

trite [trait] adj 陳腐な chíñpu na

triumph [trai'əmf] n (satisfaction) 大満足 daímañzoku; (great achievement) 輝かしい勝利 kagáyakashiî shṓri

♦vi: **to triumph (over)** (...に) 打勝つ (...ni) uchíkatsù

triumphant [traiʌm'fənt] adj (team, wave, return) 意気揚々とした íkiyōyō to shitá

trivia [triv'i:ə] npl 詰まらない事 tsumáranai kotò

trivial [triv'i:əl] adj (unimportant) 詰まらない tsumáranaî; (commonplace) 平凡な heíbon na

trod [trɑd] pt of **tread**

trodden [trɑd'ən] pp of **tread**

trolley [trɑl'i:] n (for luggage, shopping, also in supermarkets) 手車 tegúruma; (table on wheels) ワゴン wágòn; (also: **trolley bus**) トロリーバス toróríbàsu

trombone [trɑmboun'] n トロンボーン toróñbòn

troop [tru:p] n (of people, monkeys etc) 群れ muré

troop in/out vi ぞろぞろと入って来る〔出て行く〕 zórozuro to haffru kuff [déte ikú]

trooping the color [tru:p'iŋ-] (BRIT) (ceremony) 軍旗敬礼の分列行進 kuñkikeírei no bunfretsu kōshin

troops [tru:ps] npl (MIL) 兵隊 heítai

trophy [trou'fi:] n トロフィー tóròfī

tropic [trɑp'ik] n 回帰線 kaíkisen

the tropics 熱帯地方 nettái chihō

tropical [trɑp'ikəl] adj (rain forest etc) 熱帯 (地方) の nettái(chihō) no

trot [trɑt] n (fast pace) 小走り kobáshìri; (of horse) 速足 hayáashi, トロット toróttò

♦vi (horse) トロットで駆ける toróttò de kakérù; (person) 小走りで行く kobáshìri de ikú

on the trot (BRIT: fig) 立続けに taté tsuzuke ni

trouble [trʌb'əl] n (difficulty) 困難 koñnan; (worry) 心配 shíñpai; (bother, effort) 苦労 kúrō; (unrest) トラブル torábùru; (MED): **heart etc trouble** ...病 ...byō

♦vt (worry) ...に心配を掛ける ...ni shíñpai wò kakérù; (person: disturb) 面倒をかける mefidō wo kakérù

◆vi: to trouble to do something わざわざ...する wázáwaza ...suru

to be in trouble (gen) 困っている komátte irú; (ship, climber etc) 危険にあっている kiken ni atte irú

it's no trouble! 迷惑ではありませんから mélwaku de wa arfmásen kará

what's the trouble? (with broken television etc) どうなっていますかご os natté imasú ká; (doctor to patient) いかがですか ikága desù ká

troubled [trʌb'əld] adj (person, country, life, era) 不安な fuán na

troublemaker [trʌb'əlmeikər] n トラブルを起す常習犯 toráburu wo okósù jóshūhan; (child) 問題児 mofidáiji

troubles [trʌb'əlz] npl (personal, POL etc) 問題 mofidai

troubleshooter [trʌb'əlʃuːtər] n (in conflict) 調停人 chōteinin

troublesome [trʌb'əlsəm] adj (child, cough etc) 厄介な yákkai na

trough [trɔːf] n (also: **drinking trough**) 水入れ mizúire; (feeding trough) えさ入れ esá-ire; (depression) 谷間 tanima

troupe [truːp] n (of actors, singers, dancers) 団 dán

trousers [trau'zərz] npl ズボン zubón

short trousers 半ズボン hańzubón

trousseau [truː'sou] (pl **trousseaux** or **trousseaus**) n 嫁入り道具 yomé-iri dōgu

trout [traut] n inv マス masu

trowel [trau'əl] n (garden tool) 移植ごて ishókugòte; (builder's tool) こて koté

truant [truː'ənt] (BRIT) n: **to play truant** 学校をサボる gakkō wo sabórù

truce [truːs] n 休戦 kyūsen

truck [trʌk] n (US) トラック torákkù; (RAIL) 台車 dafshà

truck driver n トラック運転手 torákkù untehshu

truck farm (US) n 野菜農園 yasáinoen

trudge [trʌdʒ] vi (also: **trudge along**) とぼとぼと歩く tóbotobo arúkù

true [truː] adj (real: motive) 本当の hofitō no; (accurate: likeness) 正確な sefkaku na; (genuine: love) 本物の hofimono no; (faithful: friend) 忠実な chújitsu na

to come true (dreams, predictions) 実現される jitsúgen sarerù

truffle [trʌf'əl] n (fungus) トリュフ tóryùfu; (sweet) トラッフル toráffùru ◇菓子の一種 káshì no fsshū

truly [truː'liː] adv (really) 本当に hofitō ni; (truthfully) 真実に shfijitsu ni; (faithfully) **yours truly** (in letter) 敬具 kéigu

trump [trʌmp] n (also: **trump card**: also fig) 切札 kirffúda

trumped-up [trʌmpt'ʌp'] adj (charge, pretext) でっち上げた detchfagetà

trumpet [trʌm'pit] n トランペット torámpetto

truncheon [trʌn'tʃən] n 警棒 kefbō

trundle [trʌn'dəl] vt (push chair etc) ごろごろ動かす górògoro ugókasù

◆vi: to trundle along (vehicle) 重そうに動く omósō ni ugókù; (person) ゆっくり行く yukkúrì ikú

trunk [trʌŋk] n (of tree, person) 幹 mfkì; (of person) 胴 dō; (of elephant) 鼻 haná; (case) トランク toráňku; (US: AUT) トランク toráňku

trunks [trʌŋks] npl (also: **swimming trunks**) 水泳パンツ suíei pañtsu

truss [trʌs] n (MED) ヘルニアバンド herúnia bañdo

truss (up) vt (CULIN) 縛る shibárù

trust [trʌst] n (faith) 信用 shfň-yō; (responsibility) 責任 sekfnin; (LAW) 信託 shíñtaku

◆vt (rely on, have faith in) 信用する shfň-yō suru; (hope) きっと...だろうね kittó ...dárō nè; (entrust): **to trust something to someone** を...に任せる ...wo ...ni makáserù

to take something on trust (advice, information) 証拠なしで...を信じる shō-ko nashì de ...wo shińjirù

trusted [trʌs'tid] adj (friend, servant) 信用された shfň-yō saretà

trustee [trʌsti:'] n (LAW) 受託者 jutákushà; (of school etc) 理事 rfjî

trustful/trusting [trʌst'fəl/trʌs'tiŋ] adj (person, nature, smile) 信用する shfň-yō suru

trustworthy [trʌst'wəːrði:] adj (person,

report) 信用できる shiń-yō dekirú;

truth [truːθ] n (true fact) 真実 shińjitsu; (universal principle) 真理 shíńri

truthful [truːθ'fəl] adj (person, answer) 正直な shōjíki na

try [trai] n (attempt) 努力 dóryòku; (RUGBY) トライ torái
♦vt (attempt) やってみる yatté mirú; (test: something new: also: **try out**) 試す tamésù; (LAW: person) 裁判にかける saíban ni kakérù; (strain: patience) ぎりぎりまで追込む girígiri madè oíkomù
♦vi (make effort, attempt) 努力する dóryòku suru

to have a try やってみる yatté mirú
to try to do something (seek、しようとする...wo shiyô to suru

trying [trai'iŋ] adj (person) 気難しい kimúzukashiì; (experience) 苦しい kurúshiì

try on vt (dress, hat, shoes) 試着する shicháku suru

tsar [zɑːr] n ロシア皇帝 roshía kótei

T-shirt [tiː'ʃəːrt] n Tシャツ tíshàtsu

T-square [tiː'skwɛːr] n T定規 tíjògi

tub [tʌb] n (container: shallow) たらい taráì; (: deeper) おけ ókè; (bath) 湯舟 yúbùne

tuba [tuː'bə] n チューバ chúbà

tubby [tʌb'iː] adj 太った futótta

tube [tuːb] n (pipe) 管 kúdà; (container, in tire) チューブ chúbù; (BRIT: underground) 地下鉄 chikátetsu

tuberculosis [tuːbəːrkjəlou'sis] n 結核 kekkáku

tube station (BRIT) n 地下鉄の駅 chikátetsu no ékì

tubular [tuː'bjələːr] adj (furniture, metal) 管状の kańjō no; (furniture) パイプ製の paípusei no

TUC [tiːjuːsiː'] n abbr (BRIT: = Trades Union Congress) 英国労働組合会議 efkoku ródōkumiai kaìgi

tuck [tʌk] n (sewing) ひだ hídà
♦vt (put) 押込む oshíkomù

tuck away vt (money) 仕舞い込む shimáikomù; (building): **to be tucked away** 隠れている kakúrete irù

tuck in vt (clothing) 押込む oshíkomù;

(child) 毛布にくるんで寝かせる mōfú ni kurúnde nekáserù
♦vi (eat) かぶりつく kabúritsukú

tuck shop (BRIT) n 売店 baíten ◇学校内でお菓子などを売る売店を指す gakkónai de o-káshi nadò wo urú baíten wò sásù

tuck up vt (invalid, child) 毛布にくるんで寝かせる mōfú ni kurúnde nekáserù

Tuesday [tuːz'dei] n 火曜日 kayóbì

tuft [tʌft] n (of hair, grass etc) 一房 hitófùsa

tug [tʌg] n (ship) タグボート tagúbòto
♦vt 引っ張る hippárù

tug-of-war [tʌg'əvwɔːr] n (SPORT) 綱引き tsunáhikì; (fig) 競り合い serfaì ◇二者間の競り合いを指す nishákan no serfaì wo sásù

tuition [tuːiʃ'ən] n (BRIT) 教授 kyójù; (: private tuition) 個人教授 kojíñkyòju; (US: school fees) 授業料 jugyóryò

tulip [tuː'lip] n チューリップ chúrìnpu

tumble [tʌm'bəl] n (fall) 転倒 teńtō
♦vi (fall: person) 転ぶ koróbù; (water) 落ちる ochírù

to tumble to something (inf) ...に気が付く ...ni ki gá tsukù

tumbledown [tʌm'bəldaun] adj (building) 荒れ果てた aréhatetà

tumble dryer (BRIT) n 乾燥機 kańsóki

tumbler [tʌm'bləːr] n (glass) コップ koppú

tummy [tʌm'iː] (inf) n (belly, stomach) おなか onáka

tumor [tuː'məːr] (BRIT **tumour**) n しゅよう shúyō

tumult [tuː'məlt] n 大騒ぎ ōsawàgi

tumultuous [tuːməlʲtʃuːəs] adj (welcome, applause etc) にぎやかな nigíyaka na

tuna [tuː'nə] n inv (also: **tuna fish**) マグロ maguro; (in can, sandwich) ツナ tsúnà

tune [tuːn] n (melody) 旋律 señritsu
♦vt (MUS) 調律する chóritsu suru; (RADIO, TV) ...に合せる awáserù; (AUT) チューンアップする chúñ-appù suru

to be in/out of tune (instrument, singer)

調子が合って〔外れて〕いる chōshi gà atte (hazúrete)irù

to be in/out of tune with (fig) …と気が合っている(いない) …to ki gà atte iru (inái)

tuneful [tuːnfəl] *adj* (music) 旋律のきれいな seńritsu nò kírèi na

tuner [tuːnər] *n*: *piano tuner* 調律師 chóritsushì

tune in *vi* (RADIO, TV): *to tune in (to)* (…に) 聞く (…wo) kikú

tune up *vi* (musician, orchestra) 調子を合せる chóshi wò awáserù

tunic [tuːnik] *n* チュニック chuníkkù

Tunisia [tuːniːʒə] *n* チュニジア chuníjia

tunnel [tʌnəl] *n* (passage) トンネル tońneru; (in mine) 坑道 kōdō

♦*vi* トンネルを掘る tonńeru wo hórù

turban [təːrbən] *n* ターバン tābàn

turbine [təːrbain] *n* タービン tābìn

turbulence [təːrbjələns] *n* (AVIAT) 乱気流 rańkiryū

turbulent [təːrbjələnt] *adj* (water) 荒れ狂う aríkuruù; (fig: career) 起伏の多い kifúku no ōi

tureen [təriːn] *n* スープ鉢 sūpubàchi, チューリン chūrìn

turf [təːrf] *n* (grass) 芝生 shibáfu; (clod) 芝土 shibátsuchi

♦*vt* (area) 芝生を敷く shibáfu wò shikú

turgid [təːrdʒid] *adj* (speech) 仰々しい gyōgyōshìi

Turk [təːrk] *n* トルコ人 torúkojìn

Turkey [təːrki] *n* トルコ torúko

turkey [təːrki] *n* (bird, meat) 七面鳥 shichímenchō, ターキー tākī

Turkish [təːrkiʃ] *adj* トルコの torúko no; (LING) トルコ語の torúkogo no

♦*n* (LING) トルコ語 torúkogo

Turkish bath *n* トルコ風呂 torúkoburò

turmoil [təːrmɔil] *n* 混乱 końran

in turmoil 混乱して końran shitè

turn [təːrn] *n* (change) 変化 hénka; (in road) カーブ kābu; (tendency: of mind, events) 傾向 keíkō; (performance) 出し物 dashímòno; (chance) 番 báñ; (MED) 発作 hossá

♦*vt* (handle, key) 回す mawásù; (collar, page) めくる mekúrù; (steak) 裏返す urágaesù; (change): *to turn something into* …に変える …wo …ni kaérù

♦*vi* (object) 回る mawárù; (person: look back) 振り向く furímukú; (reverse direction: in car) Uターンする yútān suru; (: wind) 向きが変る mukí gà kawárù; (milk) 悪くなる warúku narù; (become) なる narù

a good turn 親切 shińsetsu

it gave me quite a turn ああ、怖かった ā, kowákatta

「*no left turn*」(AUT) 左折禁止 sasétsukiñshi

it's your turn あなたの番です anáta nò báñ desu

in turn 次々と tsugítsugi tò

to take turns (at) 交替で (…を) する kōtai dè (…wo) suru

turn away *vi* 顔をそむける kaó wò somúkerù

♦*vt* (applicants) 門前払いする mońzenbarài suru

turn back *vi* 引返す hikíkaesù

♦*vt* (person, vehicle) 引返させる hikíkaesaserù; (clock) 遅らせる okúraserù

turn down *vt* (refuse: request) 断る kotówarù; (reduce: heating) 下げる yowáku suru; (fold: bedclothes) 折返す oríkaesù

turn in *vi* (inf: go to bed) 寝る nerú

♦*vt* (fold) 折込む oríkomù

turning [təːrniŋ] *n* (in road) 曲り角 magárikadò

turning point *n* (fig) 変り目 kawárimè

turnip [təːrnip] *n* カブ kábù

turn off *vi* (from road) 横道に入る yokómichi ni hàiru

♦*vt* (light, radio etc) 消す kesú; (tap) …の水を止める …no mizú wò tomérù; (engine) 止める tomérù

turn on *vt* (light, radio etc) つける tsukérù; (tap) 水を出す …no mizú wò dàsu; (engine) かける kakérù

turn out *vt* (light, gas) 消す kesú; (produce) 作る tsukúrù

♦*vi* (voters) 出る dérù

to turn out to be (prove to be) 結局、で あると分かる kekkyóku ...de áru to wakáru

turnout [tǝːrn'aut] n (of voters etc) 人出 hitóde

turn over vi (person) 寝返りを打つ negáeri wò utsú
♦vt (object) 引っ繰り返す hikkúrikaesu; (page) をめくる wo mekúru

turnover [tǝːrn'ouvǝr] n (COMM: amount of money) 売上高 uríagedàka; (: of goods) 回転率 kaítenrìtsu; (: of staff) 異動率 idóritsu

turnpike [tǝːrn'paik] (US) n 有料道路 yúryōdórō

turn round vi (person) 振向く furímukū; (vehicle) Uターンする yútàn suru; (rotate) 回転する kaíten suru

turnstile [tǝːrn'stail] n ターンスタイル tánsutàiru

turntable [tǝːrn'teibǝl] n (on record player) ターンテーブル tántèburu

turn up vi (person) 現れる aráwareru; (lost object etc) 見付かる mitsúkaru
♦vt (collar) 立てる tatérù; (radio, stereo etc) ...のボリュームを上げる ...no boryúmu wò agérù; (heater) 強くする tsúyoku suru

turn-up [tǝːrn'ʌp] (BRIT) n (on trousers) 折返し orīkaeshi

turpentine [tǝːr'pǝntain] n (also: **turps**) テレビン油 terébìn-yu

turquoise [tǝːr'kɔiz] n (stone) トルコ石 torúkoìshi
♦adj (color) 青みどりの aómidòri no

turret [tǝːr'it] n (on building) 小塔 shótō; (on tank) 旋回砲塔 seńkaihōtō

turtle [tǝːr'tǝl] n カメ kámè

turtleneck (sweater) [tǝːr'tǝlnek-] n タートルネック tátorunekkù

tusk [tʌsk] n きば kíbà

tussle [tʌs'ǝl] n (fight, scuffle) 取っ組み 合い tokkúmiài

tutor [tuː'tǝr] n (SCOL) チューター chútā; (private tutor) 家庭教師 katéikyōshi

tutorial [tuːtɔːr'iːǝl] n (SCOL) 討論授業 tóronjugyō

tuxedo [tʌksiː'dou] (US) n タキシード ta-

kíshìdo

TV [tiːviː] n abbr = **television**

twang [twæŋ] n (of instrument) ぴゅん という音 byún to iú otò; (of voice) 鼻声 hanágoe

tweed [twiːd] n ツイード tsuídò

tweezers [twiːzǝrz] npl ピンセット píñsetto

twelfth [twelfθ] num 第十二の dái júni no

twelve [twelv] num 十二 (の) júni (no)
at twelve (o'clock) (midday) 正午に shōgo ni; (midnight) 真夜中に reíji ni

twentieth [twen'tiːθ] num 第二十の dái nìjū no

twenty [twen'tiː] num 二十 (の) nìjū (no)

twice [twais] adv 2回 níkài
twice as much ...の二倍 ...no nibái

twiddle [twid'ǝl] vt いじくる ijíkùru
♦vi: *to twiddle (with) something* ...を いじくる ...wo ijíkùru
to twiddle one's thumbs (fig) する事がなくてぼん やりしている surú koto gà nakute boñyari shite iru

twig [twig] n 小枝 koéda
♦vi (inf: realize) 気が付く ki gá tsukú

twilight [twai'lait] n 夕暮れ yúgure

twin [twin] adj (sister, brother) 双子の futágo no; (towers, beds etc) 対の tsuí no, ツインの tsuíñ no
♦n 双子の一人 futágo nò hitórì
♦vt (towns etc) 姉妹都市にする shímàitoshì ni suru

twin-bedded room [twin'bedid-] n ツイ ンルーム tsuíñrūmu

twine [twain] n ひも himó
♦vi (plant) 巻付く makítsukù

twinge [twindʒ] n (of pain) うずき uzúkì; (of conscience) かしゃく kasháku; (of regret) 苦しみ kurúshimì

twinkle [twiŋ'kǝl] vi (star, light, eyes) き らめく kirámekù

twirl [twǝːrl] vt くるくる回す kúrùkuru mawásù
♦vi くるくる回る kúrùkuru mawárù

twist [twist] n (action) ひねり hinéri; (in road, coil, flex) 曲り magári; (in story) ひねり hinéri

♦vt (turn) ひねる hinérù; (injure: ankle etc) ねんざする nénza suru; (weave) より合さる yoríawasarù; (roll around) 巻付ける makítsukerù; (fig: meaning, words) 曲げる magérù

♦vi (road, river) 曲りくねる magárikunerù

twit [twit] (inf) n ばか bákà

twitch [twitʃ] n (pull) ぐいと引く事 guítò hikú kotò; (nervous) 引きつり hikítsuri

♦vi (muscle, body) 引きつる hikítsurù

two [tu:] num □ (の) nf (no), 二つ (の) futátsù (no)

to put two and two together (fig) あれこれを総合してなぞを解く arékòre wo sōgō shité nazò wo tókù

two-door [tu:'dɔ:r] adj (AUT) ツードアの tsúdoà no

two-faced [tu:'feist] adj (pej: person) 二枚舌の nimáijìta no

twofold [tu:'fould] adv: *to increase twofold* 倍になる bai ni narù

two-piece (suit) [tu:'pi:s-] n ツーピースの服 tsúpìsu no fuku

two-piece (swimsuit) [tu:'pi:s-] n ツーピースの水着 tsúpìsu no mizúgi

twosome [tu:'səm] n (people) 二人組 futárigùmi

two-way [tu:'wei'] adj: *two-way traffic* 両方向交通 ryóhōkōkōtsū

tycoon [taikun'] n: *(business) tycoon* 大物実業家 ómonojitsugyóka

type [taip] n (category, model, example) 種類 shúrui; (TYP) 活字 katsúji

♦vt (letter etc) タイプする táipu suru

type-cast [taip'kæst] adj (actor) はまり役の hamáriyaku no

typeface [taip'feis] n 書体 shotái

typescript [taip'skript] n タイプライターで打った原稿 tafpuraìtā de útta génkò

typewriter [taip'raitər] n タイプライター tafpuraìtā

typewritten [taip'ritən] adj タイプライターで打った tafpuraìtā de útta

typhoid [tai'fɔid] n 腸チフス chóchifùsu

typhoon [taifun'] n 台風 taffū

typical [tip'ikəl] adj 典型的な teñkeiteki na

na

typify [tip'əfai] vt ...の典型的な例である ...no teñkeiteki nà reí de arù

typing [taip'iŋ] n タイプライターを打つ事 tafpuraìtā wo útsù kotó

typist [taip'ist] n タイピスト tafpisùto

tyranny [tir'əni:] n 暴政 bōsei

tyrant [tai'rənt] n 暴君 bōkun

tyre [taiər] (BRIT) n = **tire**

tzar [zɑːr] n = **tsar**

U

U-bend [ju:'bend] n (in pipe) トラップトラップ toráppu

ubiquitous [ju:bik'witəs] adj いたる所にある itáru tokoro nì aru

udder [ʌd'əːr] n 乳房 chibúsa (ウシ、ヤギなどについて言う ushí, yagí nado ni tsuite iú

UFO [ju:efou'] n abbr (= *unidentified flying object*) 未確認飛行物体 mikákunin hikóbuttai, ユーフォー yūfò

Uganda [ju:gæn'də] n ウガンダ ugáñda

ugh [ʌ] excl おえっ oé

ugliness [ʌg'li:nis] n 醜さ miníkusà

ugly [ʌg'li:] adj (person, dress etc) 醜い miníkuì; (dangerous: situation) 物騒な bússō na

UK [ju:'kei'] n abbr = **United Kingdom**

ulcer [ʌl'səːr] n かいよう kafyō

Ulster [ʌl'stəːr] n アルスター arúsutā

ulterior [ʌltiːr'iːəːr] adj: *ulterior motive* 下心 shitágokòro

ultimate [ʌl'təmit] adj (final: aim, destination, result) 最後の saîgo no; (greatest: insult, deterrent, authority) 最大の saídai no

ultimately [ʌl'təmitli:] adv (in the end) やがて yagáte; (basically) 根本的に koñponteki ni

ultimatum [ʌltimei'təm] n 最後通ちょう saígotsūchō

ultrasound [ʌl'trəsaund] n (MED) 超音波 chōōnpa

ultraviolet [ʌltrəvai'əlit] adj (rays, light) 紫外線の shigáisen no

umbilical cord [ʌmbil'ikəl-] n へその緒 hesó no o

umbrella [ʌmbrel'ə] n (for rain) 傘 kasá, 雨傘 amágasà; (for sun) 日傘 higása, パラソル parásoru

umpire [ʌm'paiər] n (TENNIS, CRICKET) 審判 shinpan, アンパイア aṇpaia

♦vt (game) ...のアンパイアをする ...no aṇpaia wo suru

umpteen [ʌmp'tin'] adj うんと沢山の uṇto takusan no

umpteenth [ʌmp'tinθ'] adj: **for the umpteenth time** 何回目か分からないが naṇkaime ka wakáranai ga

UN [ju:'en'] n abbr = **United Nations**

unable [ʌnei'bəl] adj: **to be unable to do something** ...する事ができない ...suru koto gà dekínai

unaccompanied [ʌnəkʌm'pənid] adj (child, woman) 同伴者のいない dóhànsha no inai; (luggage) 別送の bessó no; (song) 無伴奏の mubáñsō no

unaccountably [ʌnəkaunt'əbli] adv 妙に myó ni

unaccustomed [ʌnəkʌs'təmd] adj: **to be unaccustomed to** (public speaking, Western clothes etc) ...になれていない ...ni naréte inai

unanimous [ju:næn'əməs] adj (vote) 満場一致の maṇjōitchi no; (people) 全員同意の zeṇ-indói no

unanimously [ju:næn'əməsli] adv (vote) 満場一致で maṇjōitchi de

unarmed [ʌnɑːrmd'] adj 武器を持たない búkì wo motánai, 丸腰の marúgoshi no **unarmed combat** 武器を使わない武術 búkì wo tsukáwanai bújùtsu

unashamed [ʌnəʃeimd'] adj (greed) 恥知らずの hajíshirazu no; (pleasure) 人目をはばからない hitóme wo habákaranài

unassuming [ʌnəsu:'miŋ] adj (person, manner) 気取らない kidóranai

unattached [ʌnətætʃt'] adj (person) 独身の dokúshin no; (part etc) 遊んでいる asónde iru

unattended [ʌnəten'did] adj (car, luggage, child) ほったらかしの hottáraka-

shi no

unattractive [ʌnətræk'tiv] adj (person, character) いやな iyá na; (building, appearance, idea) 魅力のない miryóku no nai

unauthorized [ʌnɔːθ'əraizd] adj (visit, use, version) 無許可の mukyóka no

unavoidable [ʌnəvɔi'dəbəl] adj (delay) 避けられない sakérarenài

unaware [ʌnəweːr'] adj: **to be unaware of** ...に気が付いていない ...ni ki gá tsúite inai

unawares [ʌnəweːrz'] adv (catch, take) 不意に fuí ni

unbalanced [ʌnbæl'ənst] adj (report) 偏った katáyottà; (mentally) 狂った kurúttà

unbearable [ʌnbeːr'əbəl] adj (heat, pain) 耐えられない taérarenai; (person) 我慢できない程いやな gamán dekínai hodo iyá na

unbeatable [ʌnbi:'təbəl] adj (team) 無敵の mutéki nò; (quality) 最高の saíkō no

unbeknown(st) [ʌnbinoun'(st)] adj: **unbeknown(st) to me/Peter** 私(ピーター)に気付かれずに watákushi (pītā) ni kizúkarezù ni

unbelievable [ʌnbili:'vəbəl] adj 信じられない shíñjirarenai

unbend [ʌnbend'] (pt, pp **bent**) vi (relax) くつろぐ kutsúrogù

♦vt (wire) 真っ直ぐにする massúgù ni suru

unbiased [ʌnbai'əst] adj (person, report) 公正な kốsei na

unborn [ʌnbɔ:rn'] adj (child, young) おなかの中のonáka no nakā no

unbreakable [ʌnbrei'kəbəl] adj (glassware, crockery etc) 割れない waréna; (other objects) 壊れない kowárenai

unbroken [ʌnbrou'kən] adj (seal) 開けてない akéte nai; (silence, series) 続く tsuzúku; (record) 破られていない yabúraretè inai; (spirit) くじけない kujíkenai

unbutton [ʌnbʌt'ən] vt ...のボタンを外す ...no botán wo hazúsu

uncalled-for [ʌnkɔ:ld'fɔːr] adj (remark)

余計な yokéi na; (rudeness etc) いわれの ない iware no nai

uncanny [ʌnˈkænɪ] *adj* (silence, resemblance, knack) 不気味な bukími na

unceasing [ʌnˈsiːsɪŋ] *adj* 引っ切り無しの hikkírinashī no

unceremonious [ʌnserəˈmoʊnɪəs] *adj* (abrupt, rude) ぶしつけな bushítsuke na

uncertain [ʌnˈsɜːtən] *adj* (hesitant: voice, steps) 自信のない jishín no nai; (unsure) 不確実な fukákújitsu na

uncertainty [ʌnˈsɜːtɪ] *n* (not knowing) 不確実さ fukákújitsusa; (*also pl*: doubts) 疑問 gimón

unchanged [ʌnˈtʃeɪndʒd] *adj* (condition) 変っていない kawátte inai

unchecked [ʌnˈtʃekt] *adv* (grow, continue) 無制限に musélgen ni

uncivilized [ʌnˈsɪvɪlaɪzd] *adj* (gen: country, people) 未開の mikái no; (*fig*: behavior, hour etc) 野蛮な yában na

uncle [ʌŋˈkəl] *n* おじ ojí

uncomfortable [ʌnˈkʌmftəbəl] *adj* (physically, *also* furniture) 使い心地の悪い tsukáigokochi no warúi; (uneasy) 不安な fuán na; (unpleasant: situation, fact) 厄介な yakkái na

uncommon [ʌnˈkɒmən] *adj* (rare, unusual) 珍しい mezúrashii

uncompromising [ʌnˈkɒmprəmaɪzɪŋ] *adj* (person, belief) 融通の利かない yúzū no kikánai

unconcerned [ʌnkənˈsɜːnd] *adj* (indifferent) 関心がない kańshin ga nai; (not worried) 平気な heíki na

unconditional [ʌnkənˈdɪʃənəl] *adj* 無条件の mujókèn no

unconscious [ʌnˈkɒntʃəs] *adj* (in faint, *also* MED) 意識不明の ishíkifumeí no; (unaware): **unconscious of...** に気が付かない ...ni kí ga tsukanaí

♦*n*: **the unconscious** 潜在意識 seńzaiíshìki

unconsciously [ʌnˈkɒntʃəslɪ] *adv* (unawares) 無意識に mufushíki ni

uncontrollable [ʌnkəntroʊˈləbəl] *adj* (child, animal) 手に負えない te ni oénai; (temper) 抑制のきかない yokúsei no ki-

kánai; (laughter) やめられない yamérarenaí

unconventional [ʌnkənˈventʃənəl] *adj* 型破りの katáyabùri no

uncouth [ʌnkuːθ] *adj* 無様な buzáma na

uncover [ʌnˈkʌvər] *vt* (take lid, veil etc off) ...の覆いを取る ...no ōí wo torū; (plot, secret) 発見する hakkén suru

undecided [ʌndɪˈsaɪdɪd] *adj* (person) 決定していない kettéi shite inai; (question) 未決定の mikettéi no

undeniable [ʌndɪˈnaɪəbəl] *adj* (fact, evidence) 否定できない hitéi dekínai

under [ʌndər] *prep* (beneath) ...の下に ...no shitá ni; (in age, price: less than) ...以下で ...ikà ni; (according to: law, agreement etc) ...によって ...ni yotté; (someone's leadership) ...のもとに ...no motò ni

♦*adv* (go, fly etc) ...の下に[で] ...no shitá ni[de]

under there あそこの下に[で] asóko no shitá ni[de]

under repair 修理中 shūríchū

under... *prefix* 下の... shitá no...

under-age [ʌndəreɪdʒ] *adj* (person, drinking) 未成年の miséinen no

undercarriage [ʌndəkærɪdʒ] (*BRIT*) *n* (AVIAT) 着陸装置 chakúrikusōchi

undercharge [ʌndərtʃɑːrdʒ] *vt* ...から正当な料金を取らない ...kara séitō na ryōkìn wo tóranái

underclothes [ʌndərklouz] *npl* 下着 shitági

undercoat [ʌndərkout] *n* (paint) 下塗り shitánuri

undercover [ʌndərkʌvər] *adj* (work, agent) 秘密の himítsu no

undercurrent [ʌndərkʌrənt] *n* (*fig*: of feeling) 底流 teíryū

undercut [ʌndərkʌt] (*pt, pp* **undercut**) *vt* (person, prices) ...より低い値段で物を売る ...yorí hikúì nedán de monó wo urū

underdog [ʌndərdɔg] *n* 弱者 jakúsha

underdone [ʌndərdʌn] *adj* (CULIN) 生焼けの namáyake no

underestimate [ʌndərestəmeit] *vt* (person, thing) 見くびる mikúbiru

underexposed [ʌndərɪkspouzd'] *adj*
(PHOT) 露出不足の roshútsubusoku no

underfed [ʌndərfed'] *adj* (person, animal) 栄養不足の eíyōbusoku no

underfoot [ʌndərfut'] *adv* (crush, trample) 脚の下に(で) ashí no shitá ni(de)

undergo [ʌndərgou'] (*pt* **underwent** *pp* **undergone**) *vt* (test, operation, treatment) 受ける ukérù
to undergo change 変る kawáru

undergraduate [ʌndərgrædʒ'uːit] *n* 学部の学生 gakúbu no gakúsei

underground [ʌndərgraund] *n* (BRIT: railway) 地下鉄 chikátetsu; (POL) 地下組織 chikásoshiki
♦*adj* (car park) 地下の chiká no; (newspaper, activities) 潜りの mogúri no
♦*adv* (work) 潜りで mogúri de; (fig): *to go underground* 地下に潜る chiká ni mogúrù

undergrowth [ʌndərgrouθ] *n* 下生え shitábae

underhand [ʌndərhænd] *adj* (fig) ずるい zurúi

underhanded [ʌndərhæn'did] *adj* = **underhand**

underlie [ʌndərlai'] (*pt* **underlay** *pp* **underlain**) *vt* (fig: be basis of) ...の根底になっている ...no kofítei ni natté irù

underline [ʌndərlain'] *vt* 下線をひく kasén wo hikú, ...にアンダーラインを引く ...ni afidáraìn wo hikú; (fig) 強調する kyóchō suru

underling [ʌndərliŋ] (*pej*) *n* 手下 teshíta

undermine [ʌndərmain] *vt* (confidence) 失わせる ushínawaserù; (authority) 弱める yowámerù

underneath [ʌndərniːθ'] *adv* 下に(で) shitá ni(de)
♦*prep* ...の下に(で) ...no shitá ni(de)

underpaid [ʌndərpeid'] *adj* 安給料の yasúkyūryō no

underpants [ʌndərpænts] *npl* パンツ pańtsu

underpass [ʌndərpæs] (BRIT) *n* 地下道 chikádō

underprivileged [ʌndərpriv'əlidʒd] *adj*

(country, race, family) 恵まれない megúmarenai

underrate [ʌndəreit'] *vt* (person, power etc) 見くびる mikúbirù; (size) 見誤る miáyamarù

undershirt [ʌn'dərʃərt] (US) *n* アンダーシャツ afidáshatsù

undershorts [ʌn'dərʃɔːrts] (US) *npl* パンツ pańtsu

underside [ʌn'dərsaid] *n* (of object) 下側 shitágawa; (of animal) おなか onáka

underskirt [ʌn'dərskɔːrt] (BRIT) *n* アンダースカート afidásukātò

understand [ʌndərstænd'] (*pt*, *pp* **understood**) *vt* 分かる wakárù, 理解する rikái suru
♦*vi* (believe): *I understand that* ...だそうですね ...da sódesù ne, ...だと聞いていますが ...da tò kíite imasu ga
♦*vt* (think, believe) ...だと理解する ...da tò rikái suru

understandable [ʌndərstæn'dəbəl] *adj* (behavior, reaction, mistake) 理解できる rikái dekíru

understanding [ʌndərstæn'diŋ] *adj* (kind) 思いやりのある omóiyari no áru
♦*n* (gen) 理解 rikái; (agreement) 合意 gói

understatement [ʌn'dərsteit'mənt] *n* (of quality) 控え目な表現 hikáeme na hyógen
that's an understatement! それは控え目過ぎるよ sore wa hikáemesugírù yo

understood [ʌndərstud'] *pt*, *pp of* **understand**
♦*adj* (agreed) 合意された gói sareta; (implied) 暗黙の afimoku no

understudy [ʌn'dərstʌdiː] *n* (actor, actress) 代役 daíyaku

undertake [ʌndərteik'] (*pt* **undertook** *pp* **undertaken**) *vt* (task) 引受ける hikíukerù
to undertake to do something ...する事を約束する ...surú koto wo yakúsoku suru

undertaker [ʌn'dərteikəːr] *n* 葬儀屋 sógiyà

undertaking [ʌn'dərteikiŋ] *n* (job) 事業 jigyó; (promise) 約束 yakúsoku

undertone [ʌn'dərtoun] *n*: *in an undertone* 小声 kogóe

underwater [ʌndəːwɔːtəːr] adv (use) 水中に[で] suíchū ni(de); (swim) 水中に潜って suíchū ni mogútte
◆adj (exploration) 水中の suíchū no; (camera etc) 潜水用の sénsuiyō no

underwear [ʌndəːwɛːr] n 下着 shítagi

underworld [ʌndəːwəːrld] n (of crime) 暗黒街 afikokugai

underwriter [ʌndəːraitəːr] n (INSURANCE) 保険業者 hokéngyōsha

undesirable [ʌndizaiəːrəbəl] adj (person, thing) 好ましくない konómashikunai

undies [ʌndiːz] (inf) npl 下着 shítagi ◇女性用を指す joséiyō wo sasú

undisputed [ʌndispjuːtid] adj (fact) 否定できない hitéi dekinái; (champion etc) 断トツの dafítotsu no

undo [ʌnduː] (pt **undid** pp **undone**) vt (unfasten) 外す hazúsu; (spoil) 台無しにする dafnashi ni suru

undoing [ʌnduːiŋ] n 破滅 hamétsu

undoubted [ʌndautid] adj 疑う余地のない utágau yochí no nai

undoubtedly [ʌndautidliː] adv 疑う余地なく utágau yochí naku

undress [ʌndrɛs] vi 服を脱ぐ fukú wo nugú

undue [ʌnduː] adj (excessive) 余分な yobún na

undulating [ʌndʒəleitiŋ] adj (countryside, hills) 起伏の多い kifúku no ōi

unduly [ʌnduːliː] adv (excessively) 余分に yobún ni

unearth [ʌnəːrθ] vt (skeleton etc) 発掘する hakkútsu suru; (fig: secrets etc) 発見する hakkén suru

unearthly [ʌnəːrθliː] adj (hour) とんでもない tofide mo nai

uneasy [ʌniːziː] adj (person: not comfortable) 窮屈な kyúkutsu na; (: worried: also feeling) 不安な fuáñ na; (peace, truce) 不安定な fuáñtei na

uneconomic(al) [ʌniːkɔnəmˈik(əl)] adj 不経済な fukéizai na

uneducated [ʌnedʒˈukeitid] adj (person) 教育のない kyóiku no nai

unemployed [ʌnemplɔid] adj (worker)

失業中の shitsúgyōchū no
◆npl: **the unemployed** 失業者 shitsúgyōsha ◇総称 sóshō

unemployment [ʌnemplɔiˈmənt] n 失業 shitsúgyō

unending [ʌnendiŋ] adj 果てし無い hatéshi nai

unerring [ʌnəːriŋ] adj (instinct etc) 確実な kakújitsu na

uneven [ʌniːvən] adj (not regular: teeth) 不ぞろいの fuzórōi no; (performance etc) むらのある murá no aru; (road etc) 凸凹の dekóboko na

unexpected [ʌnikspekˈtid] adj (arrival) 不意の fuí no; (success etc) 思い掛けない omóigakenai, 意外な igái na

unexpectedly [ʌnikspekˈtidliː] adv (arrive) 不意に fuí ni; (succeed) 意外に igái ni

unfailing [ʌnfeiˈliŋ] adj (support, energy) 尽きる事のない tsukíru koto to nai

unfair [ʌnfɛːr] adj: **unfair (to)** (...に対して) 不当な (...ni taishite) futó na

unfaithful [ʌnfeiˈθful] adj (lover, spouse) 浮気な uwáki na

unfamiliar [ʌnfəmiˈljəːr] adj (place, person, subject) 知らない shiránai
to be unfamiliar with ... を知らない ...wo shiránai

unfashionable [ʌnfæʃˈənəbəl] adj (clothes, ideas, place) はやらない hayáranai

unfasten [ʌnfæsˈən] vt (undo) 外す hazúsu; (open) 開ける akéru

unfavorable [ʌnfeiˈvəːrəbəl] (BRIT **unfavourable**) adj (circumstances, weather) 良くない yokúnai; (opinion, report) 批判的な hihánteki na

unfeeling [ʌnfiːˈliŋ] adj 冷たい tsumétai, 冷酷な reíkoku na

unfinished [ʌnfiˈniʃt] adj (incomplete) 未完成の mikáñsei no

unfit [ʌnfiˈt] adj (physically) 運動不足の uñdōbusoku no; (incompetent): **unfit (for)** (...に) 不向きな (...ni) fumúki na
to be unfit for work 仕事に不向きな shigóto ni fumúki de aru

unfold [ʌnfould'] *vt* (sheets, map) 広げる hirógeru

♦*vi* (situation) 展開する teñkai suru

unforeseen [ʌnfɔːrsiːn'] *adj* (circumstances etc) 予期しなかった yokî shinákatta, 思い掛けない omóigakenaí

unforgettable [ʌnfərget'əbəl] *adj* 忘れられない wasûrerarenaí

unforgivable [ʌnfərgiv'əbəl] *adj* 許せない yurúsenaí

unfortunate [ʌnfɔːr'tʃənət] *adj* (poor) 哀れな awáre na; (event) 不幸な fukô na; (remark) まずい mazûi

unfortunately [ʌnfɔːr'tʃənitli] *adv* 残念ながら zañneñnagara

unfounded [ʌnfaun'did] *adj* (criticism, fears) 根拠のない koñkyo no naí

unfriendly [ʌnfrend'liː] *adj* (person, behavior, remark) 不親切な fushíñsetsu na

ungainly [ʌngein'liː] *adj* ぎこちない gikôchinaí

ungodly [ʌngɑːd'liː] *adj* (hour) とんでもない toñdemonaí

ungrateful [ʌngreit'fəl] *adj* (person) 恩知らずの ofishírazu no

unhappiness [ʌnhæp'iːnis] *n* 不幸せ fushíáwase, 不幸 fukô

unhappy [ʌnhæp'iː] *adj* (sad) 悲しい kanáshii; (unfortunate) 不幸な fukô na; (childhood) 恵まれない megúmarenaí; (dissatisfied): **unhappy about/with** (arrangements etc) ...に不満がある ...ni fumán ga aru

unharmed [ʌnhɑːrmd'] *adj* 無事な bují na

unhealthy [ʌnhel'θiː] *adj* (person) 病弱な byôjaku na; (place) 健康に悪い keñkô ni warûi; (fig: interest) 不健全な fukéñzen na

unheard-of [ʌnhəːrd'əv] *adj* (shocking) 前代未聞の zeñdaimímon no; (unknown) 知られていない shirárete inaí

unhurt [ʌnhəːrt'] *adj* 無事な bují na

unidentified [ʌnaiden'təfaid] *adj* 未確定の mikákûtei no ¶*see also* **UFO**

uniform [juː'nəfɔːrm] *n* 制服 seifuku, ユニフォーム yunífômu

♦*adj* (length, width etc) 一定の ittéi no

uniformity [juːnəfɔːr'miti:] *n* 均一性 kiñitsusei

unify [juː'nəfai] *vt* 統一する tôîtsu suru

unilateral [juːnəlæt'ərəl] *adj* (disarmament etc) 一方的な ippôteki na

uninhabited [ʌninhæb'itid] *adj* (island etc) 無人の mujín no; (house) 空き家になっている akíya ni natté iru

unintentional [ʌninten'tʃənəl] *adj* 意図的でない ítôteki de naí

union [juːn'jən] *n* (joining) 合併 gappéi; (grouping) 連合 reñgô; (*also*: **trade union**) 組合 kumíai

♦*cpd* (activities, leader etc) 組合の kumíai no

Union Jack *n* 英国国旗 efkokukôkki, ユニオンジャック yunîoñjakkû

unique [juːniːk'] *adj* 独特な dokûtoku na, ユニークな yuníkû na

unisex [juː'niseks] *adj* (clothes, hairdresser etc) ユニセックスの yunísekkusu no

unison [juː'nisən] *n*: **in unison** (*say*) 一斉に ichîdô ni; (sing) 同音で dôon de, ユニゾンで yunízon de

unit [juː'nit] *n* (single whole, *also* measurement) 単位 tañ-i; (section: of furniture etc) ユニット yunítto; (team, squad) 班 hán

kitchen unit 台所用ユニット daídokoroyô yunítto

unite [juːnait'] *vt* (join: gen) 一緒にする isshô ni suru, 一つにする hitôtsu ni suru; (: country, party) 結束させる kessoku saseru

♦*vi* 一緒になる isshô ni naru, 一つになる hitôtsu ni naru

united [juːnai'tid] *adj* (gen) 一緒になった isshô ni natta, 一つになった hitôtsu ni natta; (effort) 団結した dañketsu shita

United Kingdom *n* 英国 efkoku

United Nations (Organization) *n* 国連 kokûren

United States (of America) *n* (アメリカ) 合衆国 (amérika)gasshûkoku

unit trust (*BRIT*) *n* ユニット型投資信託 yunítttogata tôshishiñtaku

unity [ju:'niti:] *n* 一致 itchí

universal [ju:nəvəːr'səl] *adj* 普遍的な fuhénteki na

universe [ju:'nəvəːrs] *n* 宇宙 uchū

university [ju:nəvəːr'siti:] *n* 大学 daígaku

unjust [ʌndʒʌst'] *adj* 不当な futō na

unkempt [ʌnkempt'] *adj* (appearance) だらしのない daráshi no nai; (hair, beard) もじゃもじゃの mojámoja no

unkind [ʌnkaind'] *adj* (person, behavior, comment etc) 不親切な fushfnsetsu na

unknown [ʌnnoun'] *adj* 知られていない shirárete inái

unlawful [ʌnlɔ:'fəl] *adj* (act, activity) 非合法な higóhō na

unleash [ʌnli:ʃ'] *vt* (fig: feeling, forces etc) 爆発させる bakúhatsu saseru

unless [ʌnles'] *conj* ...しなければ(でなければ) ...shínakereba (denákereba)
unless he comes 彼が来なければ karè ga kônákereba

unlike [ʌnlaik'] *adj* (not alike) 似ていない nité inai; (not like) 違う chigáta
◆*prep* (different from) ...と違って ...to chígatte

unlikely [ʌnlaik'li:] *adj* (not likely) ありそうもない arísō mo nai; (unexpected: combination etc) 驚くべき odórokubeki

unlimited [ʌnlim'itid] *adj* (travel, wine etc) 無制限の muséîgen no

unlisted [ʌnlis'tid] (*BRIT* **ex-directory**) *adj* (ex-directory) 電話帳に載っていない deñwachō ni notté inaì

unload [ʌnloud'] *vt* (box, car etc) ...の積荷を降ろす ...no tsumíni wo orósù

unlock [ʌnlɑk'] *vt* ...のかぎを開ける ...no kagî wo akéru

unlucky [ʌnlʌk'i:] *adj* (person) 運の悪いun̄ no warúì; (object, number) 縁起の悪い eñgi no warúì
to be unlucky (person) 運が悪い uñ ga warúì

unmarried [ʌnmærid] *adj* (person) 独身の dokúshin no; (mother) 未婚の mikón no

unmask [ʌnmæsk'] *vt* (reveal: thief etc) ...の正体を暴く ...no shōtaí wo abákù

unmistakable [ʌnmistei'kəbəl] *adj* (voice, sound, person) 間違いのない machígaeyō no nai

unmitigated [ʌnmit'əgeitid] *adj* (disaster etc) 紛れもない magíre mò nai

unnatural [ʌnnætʃ'əral] *adj* 不自然な fushízen na

unnecessary [ʌnnes'isəːri:] *adj* 不必要な fuhítsuyō na

unnoticed [ʌnnou'tist] *adj:* (*to go/pass*) *unnoticed* 気付かれない kizúkarenai

UNO [u:'nou] *n abbr* = **United Nations Organization**

unobtainable [ʌnəbtei'nəbəl] *adj* (item) 手に入らない te nì haíranaì; (TEL): *this number is unobtainable* この電話番号は現在使用されていません koňō deńwabangō wa geňzai shiyō sarete imáseñ

unobtrusive [ʌnəbtru:'siv] *adj* (person) 遠慮がちな eñryogachi na; (thing) 目立たない medátanaì

unofficial [ʌnəfiʃ'əl] *adj* (news) 公表されていない kōhyō sarete inaì; (strike) 公認されていない kōnin sarete inaì

unorthodox [ʌnɔ:r'θədɑks] *adj* (treatment) 通常でない tsújō de nai; (REL) 正統でない seítō de nai

unpack [ʌnpæk'] *vi* 荷物の中身を出して片付ける nimótsu no nakámi wo dashíte katázukerù
◆*vt* (suitcase etc) ...の中身を出して片付ける ...no nakámi wo dashíte katázukerù

unpalatable [ʌnpæl'ətəbəl] *adj* (meal) まずい mazúì; (truth) 不愉快な fuyúkai na

unparalleled [ʌnpær'əleld] *adj* (unequalled) 前代未聞の zeñdaimimon na

unpleasant [ʌnplez'ənt] *adj* (disagreeable: thing) いやな iyá na; (: person, manner) 不愉快な fuyúkai na

unplug [ʌnplʌg'] *vt* (iron, TV etc) ...のプラグを抜く ...no puràgu wo nukú

unpopular [ʌnpɑp'jələːr] *adj* (person, decision etc) 不評の fuhyō no

unprecedented [ʌnpres'identid] *adj* 前代未聞の zeñdaimimon na

unpredictable [ʌnpridik'təbəl] *adj*

(weather, reaction) 予測できない yosóku dekínal; (person): **he is unpredictable** 彼のする事は予測できない karè no suru koto wa yosóku dekínai

unprofessional [ʌnprəfeʃ'ənəl] *adj* (attitude, conduct) 職業倫理に反する shokúgyórihri ni hañ suru

unqualified [ʌnkwɑːl'əfaid] *adj* (teacher, nurse etc) 資格のない shikáku no nal; (complete: disaster) 全くの mattáku no, 大...dal...; (: success) 完全な kañzen na, 大...dal...

unquestionably [ʌnkwes'tʃənəbli] *adv* 疑いもなく utágai mò naku

unravel [ʌnræv'əl] *vt* (ball of string) ほぐす hogúsù; (mystery) 解明する kaímei suru

unreal [ʌnriːl'] *adj* (not real) 偽の nisé no; (extraordinary) うその様な usó no yó na

unrealistic [ʌnriːəlis'tik] *adj* (person, project) 非現実的な higénjitsuteki na

unreasonable [ʌnriː'zənəbəl] *adj* (person, attitude) 不合理な fugóri na; (demand) 不当な futó na; (length of time) 非常識な hijóshìki na

unrelated [ʌnrilei'tid] *adj* (incident) 関係のない kañkei no nal, 無関係な mukáñkei na; (family) 親族でない shińzoku de nal

unrelenting [ʌnrilen'tiŋ] *adj* 執念深い shūnenbukai

unreliable [ʌnrilai'əbəl] *adj* (person, firm) 信頼できない shiñrai dekínal; (machine, watch, method) 当てにならない até ni naranal

unremitting [ʌnrimit'iŋ] *adj* (efforts, attempts) 絶間ない taéma nal

unreservedly [ʌnrizər'vidli] *adv* 心から kokórò kara

unrest [ʌnrest'] *n* (social, political, industrial etc) 不安 fuáñ

unroll [ʌnroul'] *vt* 広げる hirógeru

unruly [ʌnruː'li] *adj* (child, behavior) 素直でない sunáo de nai, 手に負えない te ní oénai; (hair) もじゃもじゃの mojámojà no

unsafe [ʌnseif'] *adj* (in danger) 危険にさ

らされた kinkén ni sarásareta; (journey, machine, bridge etc) 危険な kikén na, 危ない abúnai

unsaid [ʌnsed'] *adj*: **to leave something unsaid** ...を言わないでおく ...wo iwánaide okù

unsatisfactory [ʌnsætisfæk'tɑːri] *adj* (progress, work, results) 不満足な fumáñzoku na

unsavory [ʌnsei'vɑːri] (*BRIT* **unsavoury**) *adj* (*fig*: person, place) いかがわしい ikágawashìl

unscathed [ʌnskeiðd'] *adj* 無傷の mukízu no

unscrew [ʌnskruː'] *vt* (bottletop etc) ねじって開ける nejítte akéru; (sign, mirror etc) ...のねじを抜く ...no nejî wo nukú

unscrupulous [ʌnskruː'pjələs] *adj* (person, behavior) 悪徳... akútoku...

unsettled [ʌnset'əld] *adj* (person) 落付かない ochítsukanaì; (weather) 変りやすい kawáriyasuì

unshaven [ʌnʃei'vən] *adj* 不精ひげの bushóhìge no

unsightly [ʌnsait'li] *adj* (mark, building etc) 醜い miníkuì, 目障りな mezáwàri na

unskilled [ʌnskild'] *adj* (work, worker) 未熟練の mijúkuren no

unspeakable [ʌnspiː'kəbəl] *adj* (indescribable) 言語に絶するgeñgo ni zéssuru, 想像を絶する sózó wo zéssurù; (awful) ひどい hidóì

unstable [ʌnstei'bəl] *adj* (piece of furniture) ぐらぐらする gurágura suru; (government) 不安定な fuáñtei na; (mentally) 情緒不安定な jóchofuáñtei na

unsteady [ʌnsted'iː] *adj* (step, legs) ふらふらする furáfura suru; (hands, voice) 震える furúeru; (ladder) ぐらぐらするgurágura suru

unstuck [ʌnstʌk'] *adj*: **to come unstuck** (label etc) 取れてしまう toréte shimaù; (*fig*: plan, idea etc) 失敗する shippái suru

unsuccessful [ʌnsəkses'fəl] *adj* (attempt) 失敗した shippái shita; (writer) 成功しない seíkó shinaì, 売れない urénaì; (proposal) 採用されなかった saíyó sarénakatta *to be unsuccessful* (in attempting something) 失敗する shippai suru; (application) 採用されない saiyō sarénai

unsuccessfully [ʌnsəksés'fəli:] *adv* (try) 成功せずに seíkō sezu ni

unsuitable [ʌnsu:'təbəl] *adj* (inconvenient: time, moment) 不適当な futékitō na; (inappropriate: clothes) 場違いの bachígai no; (: person) 不適当な futékitō na

unsure [ʌnʃu:r'] *adj* (uncertain) 不確実な fukákujitsu na

unsure about ...について確信できない ...ni tsuíte kakúshin dekínai

to be unsure of oneself 自信がない jishín ga nai

unsuspecting [ʌnsəspek'tiŋ] *adj* 気付いていない kizúite inai

unsympathetic [ʌnsimpəθet'ik] *adj* (showing little understanding) 同情しない dójō shinai; (unlikeable) いやな iyá na

untapped [ʌntæpt'] *adj* (resources) 未開発の mikáihatsu no

unthinkable [ʌnθiŋk'əbəl] *adj* 考えられない kañgaerarénai

untidy [ʌntai'di:] *adj* (room) 散らかった chírakatta; (person, appearance) だらしない daráshii na

untie [ʌntai'] *vt* (knot, parcel, ribbon) ほどく hodóku; (prisoner) ...の繩をほどく ...no nawá wo hodóku; (parcel, dog) ...のひもをほどく ...no himó wo hodóku

until [ʌntil'] *prep* ...まで madé

◆*conj* ...するまで ...suru madé

until he comes 彼が来るまで karé ga kurú made

until now 今まで imámade

until then その時まで sonó toki madé

untimely [ʌntaim'li:] *adj* (inopportune: moment, arrival) 時機の悪い jikí no warúi

an untimely death 早死に hayájini, 若死に wakájini

untold [ʌntould'] *adj* (story) 明かされていない akásarete inái; (joy, suffering, wealth) 想像を絶する sózō wo zessúru

untoward [ʌntɔ:rd'] *adj* 困った komátta

unused [ʌnju:zd'] *adj* (not used: clothes, portion etc) 未使用の mishíyō no

unusual [ʌnju:'ʒuːəl] *adj* (strange) 変った kawátta; (rare) 珍しい mezúrashii; (exceptional, distinctive) 並外れた namíhazureta

unveil [ʌnveil'] *vt* (statue) ...の除幕式を行う ...no jomákushíkishi wo okónau

unwanted [ʌnwɔn'tid] *adj* (clothing etc) 不要の fuyō no; (child, pregnancy) 望まなかった nozómarenakatta

unwavering [ʌnwei'vəriŋ] *adj* (faith) 揺るぎ無い yurúginaí; (gaze) じっとした jittó shita

unwelcome [ʌnwel'kəm] *adj* (guest) 歓迎されない kañgeisarénai; (news) 悪い warúi

unwell [ʌnwel'] *adj*: *to feel unwell* 気分が悪い kibún ga warúi

to be unwell 病気である byóki de aru

unwieldy [ʌnwi:l'di:] *adj* (object, system) 大きくて扱いにくい ōkíkute atsúkainikuí

unwilling [ʌnwil'iŋ] *adj*: *to be unwilling to do something* ...するのをいやがっている ...surú no wo iyagátte iru

unwillingly [ʌnwil'iŋli:] *adv* いやがって iyágatte

unwind [ʌnwaind'] (*pt*, *pp* **unwound**) *vt* (undo) ほどく hodóku

◆*vi* (relax) くつろぐ kutsúrogu

unwise [ʌnwaiz'] *adj* (person) 思慮の足りない shiryó no tarínai; (decision) 浅はかな asáhaka na

unwitting [ʌnwit'iŋ] *adj* (victim, accomplice) 気付かない kizúkanai

unworkable [ʌnwə:r'kəbəl] *adj* (plan) 実行不可能な jikkófukanō na

unworthy [ʌnwə:r'ði:] *adj* ...の値打がない ...no neúchi ga naí

unwrap [ʌnræp'] *vt* 開ける akéru

unwritten [ʌnrit'ən] *adj* (law) 慣習の kañshū no; (agreement) 口頭での kótō de no

KEYWORD

up [ʌp] *prep*: *to go up something* ...を登る ...wo nobóru

to be up something ...の上に（登って）いる ...no ué ni nobotte iru

he went up the stairs/the hill 彼は階段(坂)を登った かれ wa かĭだん(さか) wo のぼった

the cat was up a tree ネコは木の上にいた ねこ wa きの うえ に いた

we walked/climbed up the hill 私たちは丘を登った わたくしたち wa おか wo のぼった

they live further up the street 彼らはこの道をもう少し行った所に住んでいます すれ かれら wa この みち wo もう すこし いった ところ に すんで います

go up that road and turn left この道を交差点まで行って左に曲って下さい この みち wo こうさてん まで いって ひだり に まがって ください

◆*adv* 1 (upwards, higher) 上に〔で、へ〕うえ に(de, e)

up in the sky/the mountains 空(山の上)に そら(やま の うえ)に

put it a bit higher up もう少し高い所に置いて下さい もう すこし たかい ところ に おいて ください

up there あの上に あの うえ に

what's the cat doing up there? ネコは何であそこの上にいるのかしら ねこ wa なんで あそこ の うえ に いる の かしら

up above 上の方に〔で〕うえ の ほう に(de, on)

there's a village and above, on the hill, a monastery 村があって、その上の丘に修道院があるむら が あって、そのうえ の おか に しゅうどういん が ある

2: *to be up* (out of bed) 起きている okite iru; (prices, level) 上がっている agǎtte iru; (building) 建ててある tatete aru; (tent) 張ってある hatte aru

3: *up to* (as far as) ...まで ...made

I've read up to p. 60 私は60ページまで読みました わたくし wa ろくじゅうぺーじ まで よみました

the water came up to his knees 水深は彼のひざまでだった すいしん wa かれ の ひざ まで だった

up to now 今(これ)まで いま(これ)まで

I can spend up to $10 10ドルまで使えます じゅうどる まで つかえます

4: *to be up to* (depending on) ...の責任である ...no せきにん de aru, ...次第である ...shidǎi de aru

it's up to you あなた次第です あなた しだい desu

it's not up to me to decide 決めるのは私の責任ではない きめる no wa わたくし no せきにん de wa naǐ

5: *to be up to* (equal to) ...に合う ...ni au

he's not up to it (job, task etc) 彼にはその仕事は無理です かれ ni wa そのしごと wa むりĭ desu

his work is not up to the required standard 彼の仕事は基準に合いません かれ no しごと wa kijǔn ni aǐmasen

6: *to be up to* (inf: be doing) やっているyatté iru

what is he up to? (showing disapproval, suspicion) あいつは何をやらかしているんだろうね aǐtsu wa nanǐ wo yarǎkashite irǔn darǒ ne

◆*n*: *ups and downs* (in life, career) 浮き沈み ukǐshizumi

we all have our ups and downs だれだっていい時と悪い時がありますよ darě datte iǐ toki to warǔǐ toki ga arǐmasu yo

his life had its ups and downs, but he died happy 彼の人生には浮き沈みが多かったが、死ぬ時は幸せだった かれ no jǐnsei ni wa ukǐshizumi ga ǒkatta ga, shinǔ toki wa shiǎwase datta

upbringing [ʌpˈbriŋiŋ] *n* 養育 yǒiku

update [ʌpdeit'] *vt* (records, information) 更新する kǒshin suru

upgrade [ʌpˈgreid'] *vt* (improve: house) 改装する kaǐchiku suru; (job) 格上げする kakǔage suru; (employee) 昇格させる shǒkaku saseru

upheaval [ʌphi:'vəl] *n* 変動 héndǒ

uphill [*adj* ʌpˈhil *adv* ʌpˈhil'] *adj* (climb) 上りの nobǒri no; (*fig*: task) 困難な konʾnan na

◆*adv*: *to go uphill* 坂を上る sakā wo nobǒru

uphold [ʌphould'] (*pt, pp* upheld) *vt* (law, principle, decision) 守る mamǒrū

upholstery [ʌphoul'stəri:] *n* いすに張っ

た生地 isú ni hattá kijí

upkeep [ʌp'kiːp] n (maintenance) 維持 ijí

upon [əpɑn'] prep ...の上に(で) ...no ué ni (de)

upper [ʌp'əːr] adj 上の方の ué no hō nò
♦n (of shoe) 甲皮 kôhi

upper-class [ʌp'əːrklæs'] adj (families, accent) 上流の jôryū no

upper hand n: to have the upper hand 優勢である yūsei de aru

uppermost [ʌp'əːrmoust'] adj 一番上の ichíbañ ué no
what was uppermost in my mind 私が真っ先に考えたのは watákushi ga massákñ ni kañgaeta no wa

upright [ʌp'rait] adj (straight) 直立の chokúritsu no; (vertical) 垂直の suíchokuku no; (fig: honest) 正直な shôjiki na

uprising [ʌp'raizìŋ] n 反乱 hañran

uproar [ʌp'rɔːr] n (protests, shouts) 大騒ぎ ōsawàgi

uproot [ʌpruːt'] vt (tree) 根こそぎにする nekósogi ni suru; (fig: family) 故郷から追出す kokyō kara oídasù

upset [n ʌp'set vb ʌpset'] (pt, pp upset) n (to plan etc) 乱す midásu
♦vt (knock over: glass etc) 倒す taósù; (routine, plan) 台無しにする daínashi ni suru; (person: offend, make unhappy) 動転させる dôten saseru
♦adj (unhappy) 動転した dôten shita
to have an upset stomach 胃の具合が悪い i nò gúai ga warúì

upshot [ʌp'ʃɑt] n 結果 kekká

upside down [ʌp'said-] adv (hang, hold) 逆様に(で) sakásama ni(de)
to turn a place upside down (fig) 家中を引っかき回す iejū wo híkkakīmawasu

upstairs [ʌp'steːrz] adv (be) (で) 2階に(で) nikái ni(de); (go) 2階へ nikái e
♦adj (window, room) 2階の nikái no
♦n 2階 nikái

upstart [ʌp'stɑːrt] n 横柄な奴 ōhei na yatsù

upstream [ʌp'striːm] adv 川上に(で, へ) kawākami ni(de, e), 上流に(で, へ) jôryū ni(de, e)

uptake [ʌp'teik] n: to be quick/slow on

the uptake 物分かりがいい(悪い) mono-nőwakàri ga íi(warúì)

uptight [ʌp'tait'] adj ぴりぴりした piri-piri shita

up-to-date [ʌp'tədeit'] adj (most recent: information) 最新の safshin no; (person) 最新の情報に通じている safshin no jôhō ni tsūjíte irù

upturn [ʌp'təːrn] n (in luck) 好転 kôten; (COMM: in market) 上向き uwámuki

upward [ʌp'wəːrd] adj (movement, glance) 上への ué no

upwards [ʌp'wəːrdz] adv (move, glance) 上の方へ ué no hō è; (more than): upward(s) of ...以上の ...íjō no

uranium [jurei'niːəm] n ウラン uràn, ウラニウム uránìumū

urban [əːr'bən] adj 都会の tokái no

urbane [əːrbein'] adj 上品な jôhin na

urchin [əːr'tʃin] n (child) がき gakí; (waif) 浮浪児 furôjì

urge [əːrdʒ] n (need, desire) 衝動 shôdō
♦vt: to urge someone to do something ...する様に...を説得する ...surú yō ni ...wo settóku suru

urgency [əːr'dʒənsiː] n (importance) 緊急性 kíñkyūseī; (of tone) 緊迫した調子 kíñpaku shita chôshi

urgent [əːr'dʒənt] adj (need, message) 緊急な kíñkyū na; (voice) 切迫した seppáku shita

urinal [juːr'ənəl] n 小便器 shôbeñki

urinate [juːr'əneit] vi 小便をする shôbeñ wo suru

urine [juːr'in] n 尿 nyô, 小便 shôbeñ

urn [əːrn] n (container) 骨つぼ kotsútsubo; (also: coffee/tea urn) 大型コーヒー(紅茶)メーカー daígata kôhī(kôcha)mèkā

Uruguay [juːr'əgwei] n ウルグアイ urúguai

us [ʌs] pron 私たちを(に) watákushitachi wo(ni) ¶ see also me

US(A) [juːˈes(ei')] n abbr = United States of America

usage [juːˈsidʒ] n (LING) 慣用 kañyō

use [n juːs vb juːz] n (using) 使用 shiyō; (usefulness, purpose) 役に立つ事 yakú ni tatsu koto 利益 ríeki

♦vt (object, tool, phrase etc) 使う tsuka-u, 用いる mochíírù, 使用する shíyō suru

in use 使用中 shíyōchū

out of use 廃れて sutáretè

to be of use 役に立つ yakú ni tatsu

it's no use (not useful) 使えません tsu-káemasen; (pointless) 役に立ちません yakú ni tachimasen, 無意味です muímí desu

she used to do it 前は彼女はそれをする習慣でした maè wa kanòjo wa soré wo suru shúkan deshita

to be used to ...に慣れている ...ni naréte iru

used [juːzd] adj (object) 使われた tsuká-wareta; (car) 中古の chūko no

useful [juːsʹfəl] adj 役に立つ yakú ni tatsu, 有益な yūēki na, 便利な beñri na

usefulness [juːsʹfəlnis] n 実用性 jitsúyō-sei

useless [juːsʹlis] adj (unusable) 使えない tsukáenai, 役に立たない yakú ni tatanai; (pointless) 無意味な muímí na, 無駄な mudá na; (person: hopeless) 能無しの nō-nashi no, 役に立たない yakú ni tatanai

user [juːʹzəːr] n 使用者 shíyōsha

user-friendly [juːʹzəːrfrendʹliː] adj (computer) 使いやすい tsukáiyasui, ユーザーフレンドリーな yúzāfuréndorì na

use up vt 全部使ってしまう zeñbu tsu-kátte shimaú, 使い尽す tsukáitsukusú

usher [ʌʹʃəːr] n (at wedding) 案内係 afína-igakàri

usherette [ʌʃəretʹ] n (in cinema) 女性案内係 joséi afínaigakàri

USSR [juːeseseːrʹ] n: the USSR ソ連 sorèn

usual [juːʹʒuːəl] adj (time, place etc) いつもの itsúmo no

as usual いつもの様に itsúmo no yō ni

usually [juːʹʒuːəliː] adv 普通は futsū wa

usurp [juːsəːrpʹ] vt (of title, position) 強奪する gódatsu suru

utensil [juːtenʹsəl] n 用具 yōgu

kitchen utensils 台所用具 daídokoro yōgu

uterus [juːʹtəːrəs] n 子宮 shíkyū

utility [juːtilʹiti:] n (usefulness) 有用性

yúyōsei, 実用性 jitsúyōsei; (also: public utility) 公益事業 kōekijigyō

utility room n 洗濯部屋 señtakubeya

utilize [juːʹtəlaiz] vt (object) 利用する ri-yō suru, 使う tsukáu

utmost [ʌtʹmoust] adj 最大の saídai no

♦n: to do one's utmost 全力を尽す zeñ-ryoku wo tsukusù

utter [ʌtʹəːr] adj (total: amazement, fool, waste, rubbish) 全くの mattáku no

♦vt (sounds) 出す dásù, 発する hassúru; (words) 口に出す kuchí ni dasù, 言う iù

utterance [ʌtʹəːrəns] n 発言 hatsúgen, 言葉 kotóba

utterly [ʌtʹəːrliː] adv 全く mattáku

U-turn [juːʹtəːrn] n Uターン yútàn

V

v. abbr = verse; versus; volt; (= vide) ...を見よ ...wo mìyo

vacancy [veiʹkənsiː] n (BRIT: job) 欠員 ketsúin; (room) 空き部屋 akíbeya

vacant [veiʹkənt] adj (room, seat, toilet) 空いている aíte iru; (look, expression) うつろの utsúro no

vacant lot (US) n 空き地 akíchi

vacate [veiʹkeit] vt (house, one's seat) 空ける akéru; (job) 辞める yaméru

vacation [veikeiʹʃən] n (esp US: holiday) 休暇 kyūka; (SCOL) 夏休み natsúyasùmi

vaccinate [vækʹsəneit] vt: to vaccinate someone (against something) ...に (...の...の) 予防注射をする ...ni (...no) yobó-chūsha wo suru

vaccine [vækʹsiːn] n ワクチン wakúchin

vacuum [vækʹjuːm] n (empty space) 真空 shíñkū

vacuum cleaner n (真空) 掃除機 (shíñ-kū)sójikì

vacuum-packed [vækʹjuːmpækt] adj 真空パックの shíñkūpakkù no

vagabond [vægʹəbɑnd] n 浮浪者 furō-shā, ルンペン ruñpen

vagina [vədʒaiʹnə] n ちつ chítsù

vagrant [veiʹgrənt] n 浮浪者 furōshà, ルンペン ruñpen

vague [veig] *adj* (blurred: memory, outline) ぼんやりとした boñ-yarî to shita; (uncertain: look, idea, instructions) 漠然とした bakûzen to shita; (person: not precise) 不正確な fuseîkaku na; (: evasive) 煮え切らない niékiranái

vaguely [veig'li:] *adv* (not clearly) ぼんやりとして boñ-yarî to shite; (without certainty) 漠然と bakûzen to, 不正確に fuseîkaku ni; (evasively) あいまいに af-mai ni

vain [vein] *adj* (conceited) うぬぼれた unûboreta; (useless: attempt, action) 無駄な mudá na

in vain 何のかいもなく nañ no kaî no nakû

valentine [væl'əntain] *n* (*also*: **valentine card**) バレンタインカード baréntaiñkâdo; (person) バレンタインデーの恋人 baréntaiñdê no koîbito

valet [væl'ei] *n* 召使い meshîtsukái

valiant [væl'jənt] *adj* (attempt, effort) 勇敢な yûkan na

valid [væl'id] *adj* (ticket, document) 有効な yûkô na; (argument, reason) 妥当な datô na

validity [vəlid'iti:] *n* (of ticket, document) 有効性 yûkôsê; (of argument, reason) 妥当性 datôsê

valley [væl'i:] *n* 谷(間) tanî(ma)

valor [væl'ə:r] (*BRIT* **valour**) *n* 勇ましさ isámashisà

valuable [væl'ju:əbəl] *adj* (jewel etc) 高価な kôka na; (time, help, advice) 貴重な kichô na

valuables [væl'ju:əbəlz] *npl* (jewellery etc) 貴重品 kichôhin

valuation [vælju:ei'ʃən] *n* (worth: of house etc) 評価額 hyôka kachî; (judgment of quality) 評価 hyôka

value [væl'ju:] *n* (financial worth) 価値 kachî, 価格 kakáku; (importance, usefulness) 価値 kachî

♦*vt* (fix price or worth of) ...に値を付ける ...ni ne wô tsukérû; (appreciate) 大切にする taîsetsu ni suru, 重宝する chôhô suru

values [væl'ju:z] *npl* (principles, beliefs)

価値観 kachíkañ

value added tax [-æd'id-] (*BRIT*) *n* 付加価値税 fukâkachízeî

valued [væl'ju:d] *adj* (appreciated: customer, advice) 大切な taîsetsu na

valve [vælv] *n* 弁 beñ, バルブ barûbu

vampire [væm'paiə:r] *n* 吸血鬼 kyûketsûki

van [væn] (*AUT*) *n* バン bañ

vandal [væn'dəl] *n* 心無い破壊者 kokôronaî hakáishà

vandalism [væn'dəlizəm] *n* 破壊行動 hakáikôdô

vandalize [væn'dəlaiz] *vt* 破壊する hakái suru

vanguard [væn'gɑ:rd] *n* (*fig*): *in the vanguard of* ...の先端に立って ...no señtan nî tattê

vanilla [vənil'ə] *n* バニラ banîra

vanilla ice cream *n* バニラアイスクリーム banîra aîsukurîmu

vanish [væn'iʃ] *vi* (disappear suddenly) 見えなくなる miénàku narû, 消える kiéru

vanity [væn'iti:] *n* (of person: unreasonable pride) 虚栄心 kyoéishin

vantage point [væn'tidʒ-] *n* (lookout place) 観察点 kañsatsuten; (viewpoint) 有利な立場 yûri na tachîba

vapor [vei'pə:r] (*BRIT* **vapour**) *n* (gas) 気体 kitái; (mist, steam) 蒸気 jôki

variable [ver'i:əbəl] *adj* (likely to change: mood, quality, weather) 変りやすい kawáriyasû; (able to be changed: temperature, height, speed) 調節できる chôsetsu dekírû

variance [ver'i:əns] *n*: *to be at variance (with)* (people) (...と) 仲たがいしている (...to) nakátagaì shité iru; (facts) (...と) 矛盾している (...to) mujúñshitê iru

variation [veri:ei'ʃən] *n* (change in level, amount, quantity) 変化 heñka, 変動 heñdô; (different form: of plot, musical theme etc) 変形 heñkei

varicose [ver'ikous] *adj*: *varicose veins* 拡張蛇行静脈 kakúchôdakôjômyaku

varied [veː'riːd] *adj* (diverse: opinions, reasons) 様々な sámàzama na; (full of changes: career) 多彩な tasái na

variety [vərai'ətiː] *n* (degree of choice, diversity) 変化 heñka, バラエティー baráeti; (varied collection, quantity) 様々な 物 sámàzama na mono; (type) 種類 shurúi

variety show *n* バラエティーショー baráetishò

various [veː'riːəs] *adj* 色々な iróiro na

varnish [vɑːr'niʃ] *n* (product applied to surface) ニス nísù

♦*vt* (apply varnish to: wood, piece of furniture etc) ...にニスを塗る ...ni nísù wo nurú; (: nails) ...にマニキュアをする ...ni maníkyùa wo suru

nail varnish マニキュア maníkyua

vary [veː'riː] *vt* (make changes to: routine, diet) 変える kaéru

♦*vi* (be different: sizes, colors) ...が色々ある ...ga iróiro aru; (become different): **to vary with** (weather, season etc) ...によって変る ...ni yótte kawáru

vase [veis] *n* 花瓶 kabín

Vaseline [væs'əliːn]® *n* ワセリン wasérin

vast [væst] *adj* (wide: area, knowledge) 広い hirói; (enormous: expense etc) ばく大な bakúdai na

VAT [væt] *n abbr* = **value added tax**

vat [væt] *n* 大おけ ókè

Vatican [væt'ikən] *n*: **the Vatican** (palace) バチカン宮殿 bachíkan kyúdeñ; (authority) ローマ法王庁 rōma hōōchō

vault [vɔːlt] *n* (of roof) 丸天井 marúteñjò; (tomb) 地下納骨堂 chiká nōkotsudō; (in bank) 金庫室 kiñkoshitsú

♦*vt* (also: **vault over**) 飛越える tobíkoerù

vaunted [vɔːn'tid] *adj*: **much-vaunted** ご自慢の go-jímàn no

VCR [viːsiːɑːr'] *n abbr* = **video cassette recorder**

VD [viːdiː'] *n abbr* = **venereal disease**

VDU [viːdiːjuː'] *n abbr* = **visual display unit**

veal [viːl] *n* 子ウシ肉 koúshiniku

veer [viːr] *vi* (vehicle, wind) 急に向きを変える kyū ni mukí wo kaéru

vegetable [vedʒ'təbəl] *n* (BOT) 植物 shokúbùtsu; (edible plant) 野菜 yasái

♦*adj* (oil etc) 植物性の shokúbutsusei no

vegetarian [vedʒite'riːən] *n* 菜食主義者 saíshokushugìsha

♦*adj* (diet etc) 菜食主義の saíshokushugì no

vegetate [vedʒ'iteit] *vi* 無為に暮す muí ni kurásu

vegetation [vedʒite'ʃən] *n* (plants) 植物 shokúbutsu ◇総称 sōshō

vehement [viː'əmənt] *adj* (strong: attack, passions, denial) 猛烈な mōretsu na

vehicle [viː'ikəl] *n* (machine) 車 kurúma; (fig: means of expressing) 手段 shudáň

veil [veil] *n* ベール bèru

veiled [veild] *adj* (fig: threat) 隠された kakúsareta

vein [vein] *n* (ANAT) 静脈 jōmyàku; (of ore etc) 脈 myakú

vein of a leaf 葉脈 yōmyaku

velocity [vəlɑs'itiː] *n* 速度 sokúdo

velvet [vel'vit] *n* ビロード biródo, ベルベット berúbetto

♦*adj* ビロードの biródo no, ベルベットの berúbetto no

vendetta [vendet'ə] *n* 復しゅう fukúshū

vending machine [ven'diŋ-] *n* 自動販売機 jidōhanbaiki

vendor [ven'dɑːr] *n* (of house, land) 売手 urítè; (of cigarettes, beer etc) 売子 uríko

veneer [vəniːr'] *n* (on furniture) 化粧板 keshōban; (fig: of person, place) 虚飾 kyoshóku

venereal [vəniː'riːəl] *adj*: **venereal disease** 性病 seíbyò

Venetian blind [vəniː'ʃən-] *n* ベネシャンブラインド benéshanburaindò

Venezuela [venizwei'lə] *n* ベネズエラ benézuèra

vengeance [ven'dʒəns] *n* (revenge) 復しゅう fukúshū

with a vengeance (fig: to a greater extent) 驚く程 odórokù hodo

venison [ven'isən] *n* シカ肉 shikániku

venom [ven'əm] *n* (of snake, insect) 毒 dokú; (bitterness, anger) 悪意 ákui

venomous [ven'əməs] *adj* (poisonous: snake, insect) 毒...dokú...; (full of bitterness: look, stare) 敵意に満ちた tekí no michīta

vent [vent] *n* (also: **air vent**) 通気孔 tsūkikō; (in jacket) ベンツ beńtsu
◆*vt* (fig: feelings, anger) ぶちまける buchímakeru

ventilate [ven'təleit] *vt* (room, building) 換気する kaṅki suru

ventilation [ventəlei'ʃən] *n* 換気 kaṅki

ventilator [ven'təleitər] *n* (TECH) 換気装置 kaṅkisōchi, ベンチレーター beńchirētā; (MED) 人工呼吸器 jiṅkōkokyūki, レスピレタ resúpiretā

ventriloquist [ventril'əkwist] *n* 腹話術師 fukúwajutsushi

venture [ven'tʃər] *n* (risky undertaking) 冒険 bōken
◆*vt* (opinion) おずおず言う ozúozu iú
◆*vi* (dare to go) おずおず行く ozúozu ikú
business venture 投機 tōki

venue [ven'ju:] *n* (place fixed for something) 開催地 kaísaichi

veranda(h) [vərænda] *n* ベランダ beránda

verb [və:rb] *n* 動詞 dōshi

verbal [və:r'bəl] *adj* (spoken: skills etc) 言葉の kotóba no; (: translation etc) 口頭の kótō no; (of a verb) 動詞の dōshi no

verbatim [və:rbei'tim] *adj* 言葉通りの kotóbadōri no
◆*adv* 言葉通りに kotóbadōri ni

verbose [və:rbous'] *adj* (person) 口数の多い kuchíkazu no ōi; (speech, report etc) 冗長な jōchō na

verdict [və:r'dikt] *n* (LAW) 判決 haṅketsu; (fig: opinion) 判断 haṅdan

verge [və:rdʒ] *n* (BRIT: of road) 路肩 rokáta
「**soft verges**」(BRIT: AUT) 路肩軟弱 rokáta nañjaku
to be on the verge of doing something ...する所である ...surú tokoro dè arū

verge on *vt fus* ...同然である ...dōzen de arū

verify [ver'əfai] *vt* (confirm, check) 確認する kakúnin suru

veritable [ver'itəbəl] *adj* (reinforcer: = real) 全くの mattáku no

vermin [və:r'min] *npl* (animals) 害獣 gaíjū; (insects etc) 害虫 gaíchū

vermouth [vərmu:θ'] *n* ベルモット berúmottò

vernacular [vərnæk'jələr] *n* (language) その土地の言葉 sonó tochi no kotóba

versatile [və:r'sətəl] *adj* (person) 多才の tasái no; (substance, machine, tool etc) 用途の多い tsukáimichi no ōi

verse [və:rs] *n* (poetry) 詩 shi; (one part of a poem: also in bible) 節 setsú

versed [və:rst] *adj*: *(well-)versed in* ...に詳しい ...ni kuwáshii

version [və:r'ʒən] *n* (form: of design, production) 型 katá; (: of book, play etc) ...版 ...ban; (account: of events, accident etc) 説明 setsúmei

versus [və:r'səs] *prep* ...対... ...tai ...

vertebra [və:r'təbrə] *n (pl* **vertebrae**) 脊椎 sekítsui

vertebrae [və:r'təbrei] *npl of* **vertebra**

vertebrate [və:r'təbrit] *n* せきつい動物 sekítsuidōbutsu

vertical [və:r'tikəl] *adj* 垂直の suíchoku no

vertigo [və:r'təgou] *n* めまい memái

verve [və:rv] *n* (vivacity) 気迫 kiháku

very [ver'i:] *adv* (+ adjective, adverb) とても totémo, 大変 taíhen, 非常に hijō ni
◆*adj: it's the very book he'd told me about* 彼が話していたのは正にこの本だ karé ga hanáshite ita no wà masá ni sonó hon da
the very last 正に最後の masá ni saígo no
at the very least 少なくとも sukúnakutomo
very much 大変 taíhen

vessel [ves'əl] *n* (NAUT) 船 fune; (container) 容器 yōki *see* **blood**

vest [vest] *n* (US: waistcoat) チョッキ chókki; (BRIT) アンダーシャツ añdāshatsu shatsù

vested interests [ves'tid-] *npl* 自分の利益 jibún no rièki, 私利 shirì

vestige [ves'tidʒ] *n* 残り nokóri

vet [vet] (*BRIT*) *n abbr* = **veterinary surgeon**

♦*vt* (examine: candidate) 調べる shiráberù

veteran [vet'ərən] *n* (of war) …戦争で戦った人…seńsō de tatákatta hito; (former soldier) 退役軍人 tafékigunjìn; (old hand) ベテラン betéran

veterinarian [vetərənær'i:ən] (*US*) *n* 獣医 jūi

veterinary [vet'ə:rəne:ri:] *adj* (practice, care etc) 獣医の jūi no

veterinary surgeon (*BRIT*) *n* = **veterinarian**

veto [vi:'tou] (*pl* **vetoes**) *n* (right to forbid) 拒否権 kyohíken; (act of forbidding) 拒否権の行使 kyohíken no kōshì

♦*vt* …に拒否権を行使する …ni kyohíken wo kōshì suru

vex [veks] *vt* (irritate, upset) 怒らせる o-kóraserù

vexed [vekst] *adj* (question) 厄介な yakkái na

via [vai'ə] *prep* (through, by way of) …を経て …wo hetè, …経由 …kéiyu

viable [vai'əbəl] *adj* (project) 実行可能な jikkōkanō na; (company) 存立できる soñritsu dekirù

viaduct [vai'ədʌkt] *n* 陸橋 rikkyō

vibrant [vai'brənt] *adj* (lively) 力強い chikárazuyoi; (bright) 生き生きした ikíiki shita; (full of emotion: voice) 感情のこもった kañjō no komótta

vibrate [vai'breit] *vi* (house, machine etc) 振動する shiñdō suru

vibration [vaibrei'ʃən] *n* 振動 shiñdō

vicar [vik'ə:r] *n* 主任司祭 shuníntshisai

vicarage [vik'ə:ridʒ] *n* 司祭館 shisáikañ

vicarious [vaikær'i:əs] *adj* (pleasure) 他人の身に感じる他人 ni mi ni nat té kañjirù

vice [vais] *n* (moral fault) 悪癖 akútoku; (TECH) 万力 mañriki

vice- [vais] *prefix* 副… fukù…

vice-president [vais'prez'idənt] *n* (*US* POL) 副大統領 fukúdaitōryō

vice squad *n* 風俗犯罪取締班 fūzokuhañzai toríshimarihañ

vice versa [vais'vəːr'sə] *adv* 逆の場合も同じ gyakú no bāi mo onáji

vicinity [visin'əti:] *n* (area): **in the vicinity (of)** (…の) 近所に (…no) kiñjo ni

vicious [viʃ'əs] *adj* (violent: attack, blow) 猛烈な mōretsu na; (cruel: words, look) 残酷な zañkoku na; (horse, dog) どう猛な dōmō na

vicious circle *n* 悪循環 akújuñkan

victim [vik'tim] *n* (person, animal, business) 犠牲者 giséisha

victimize [vik'təmaiz] *vt* (strikers etc) 食い物にする kuímono nî suru

victor [vik'tə:r] *n* 勝利者 shōrísha

Victorian [viktɔːr'iən] *adj* ヴィクトリア朝の bikútoriachō no

victorious [viktɔːr'i:əs] *adj* (triumphant: team, shout) 勝ち誇る kachíhokoru

victory [vik'tə:ri:] *n* 勝利 shōrì

video [vid'i:ou] *cpd* ビデオの bideo no

♦*n* (video film) ビデオ映画 bideo eiga; (*also*: **video cassette**) ビデオカセット bidéokasettō; (*also*: **video cassette recorder**) ビデオテープレコーダー bidéo tēpurekōdā, VTR buitiārù

video tape *n* ビデオテープ bidéotēpù

vie [vai] *vi*: **to vie (with someone)(for something)** (…のために) (…と) 競り合う (…no tamé ni) (…to) seríaù

Vienna [vi:en'ə] *n* ウィーン uīñ

Vietnam [vi:etnɑm'] *n* ベトナム betónamu

Vietnamese [vi:etnɑmi:z'] *adj* ベトナムの betónamu no; (LING) ベトナム語の betónamugò no

♦*n inv* (person) ベトナム人 betónamujîn; (LING) ベトナム語 betónamugò

view [vju:] *n* (sight) 景色 keshìki; (outlook) 見方 mikáta; (opinion) 意見 ikèn

♦*vt* (look at: *also fig*) 見る mirù

on view (in museum etc) 展示中で teñjichū de

in full view (of) (…の) 見ている前で (…no) mitè iru maè de

in view of the weather こういう天気
だから kō fu teñki da kara

in view of the fact that …だという事
を考えて …da tó iu koto wo kañgaeté

in my view 私の考えでは watákushi no
kañgae de wa

viewer [vju:ər] n (person) 見る人 mirú
hito

viewfinder [vju:faindər] n ファインダ
ー faīndā

viewpoint [vju:pɔint] n (attitude) 考え
方 kañgaekata, 見地 keñchi; (place) 観察
する地点 kañsatsu suru chitéñ

vigil [vidʒil] n 不寝番 fushíñbañ

vigilance [vidʒiləns] n 用心 yōjiñ

vigilant [vidʒələnt] adj 用心する yōjiñ
suru

vigor [vigər] (BRIT **vigour**) n (energy:
of person, campaign) 力強さ chikárazu-
yosá

vigorous [vigərəs] adj (full of energy:
person) 元気のいい geñki no iì; (: action,
campaign) 強力な kyōryoku na; (: plant)
よく茂った yokú shigéttá

vile [vail] adj (evil: action) 下劣な geré-
tsu na; (: language) 下品な gehíñ na; (unpleasant: smell, weather, food, temper)
ひどい hidoì

villa [vil'ə] n (country house) 別荘 bessō;
(suburban house) 郊外の屋敷 kōgai no
yashikí

village [vilidʒ] n 村 murá

villager [vilidʒər] n 村民 soñmiñ

villain [vil'in] n (scoundrel) 悪党 akútō;
(in novel) 悪役 akúyaku; (BRIT: criminal) 犯人 hañniñ

vindicate [vindikeit] vt (person: free
from blame) …の正しさを立証する …no
tadashisá wo risshōsuru; (action: justify)
…が正当である事を立証する …ga seftō
de arú koto wo risshō suru

vindictive [vindik'tiv] adj (person) 執念
深い shūneñbukaí; (action etc) 復しゅう
心による fukúshūshiñ ni yoru

vine [vain] n (climbing plant) ツル tsurú;
(grapevine) ブドウの木 budó no ki

vinegar [vin'əgər] n 酢 su

vineyard [vin'jərd] n ブドウ園 budóeñ

vintage [vin'tidʒ] n (year) ブドウ収穫年
budó shūkakuneñ

◆cpd (classic: comedy, performance etc)
典型的な teñkeiteki na

vintage car n クラシックカー kura-
shíkka à

vintage wine n 当り年のワイン atári-
doshi no waíñ

vinyl [vai'nil] n ビニール biníru

viola [viːou'lə] n (MUS) ビオラ bìòra

violate [vai'əleit] vt (agreement, peace)
破る yaburù; (graveyard) 汚す kegasù

violation [vai'əlei'ʃən] n (of agreement
etc) 違反 iháñ

violence [vai'ələns] n (brutality) 暴力 bō-
ryòku; (strength) 乱暴 rañbō

violent [vai'ələnt] adj (brutal: behavior)
暴力の bōryoku no, 乱暴な rañbō na;
(intense: debate, criticism) 猛烈な mōrè-
tsu na

a violent death 変死 heñshi

violet [vai'əlit] adj 紫色の murásakiiro
no
◆n (color) 紫 murasàki; (plant) スミレ
sumíre

violin [vaiəlin'] n バイオリン baíoriñ

violinist [vaiəlin'ist] n バイオリン奏者
baíoriñshà, バイオリニスト baíoriniisu-
to

VIP [viːaipiː] n abbr (= very important
person) 要人 yōjiñ, 貴賓 kihíñ, ブイアイ
ピー bufaipī, ビップ bíppù

viper [vai'pər] n クサリヘビ kusárihebì

virgin [vər'dʒin] n (person) 処女 shojò,
バージン bājiñ
◆adj (snow, forest etc) 処女... shojò...

virginity [vərdʒin'əti:] n (of person) 処
女 shojò

Virgo [vər'gou] n (sign) 乙女座 otómeza

virile [vir'əl] adj 男らしい otókorashiì

virility [viril'iti:] n (sexual power) 性的
能力 seíteki nōryoku; (fig: masculine
qualities) 男らしさ otókorashisà

virtually [vər'tʃuːəliː] adv (almost) 事実
上 jijítsujō

virtue [vər'tʃuː] n (moral correctness) 徳
toku, 徳行 tokkō; (good quality) 美徳 bi-
tòku; (advantage) 利点 ritéñ, 長所 chō-

shô
by virtue of ...である事で ... de arù koto de

virtuosi [vɑːtjuːˈoːzi:] *npl of* virtuoso

virtuoso [vɑːtjuːˈoːzou] (*pl* virtuosos *or* virtuosi) *n* 名人 meíjin

virtuous [ˈvɑːtʃuəs] *adj* (displaying virtue) 良心的な ryôshinteki na, 高潔な kôketsu na, 敬けんな kefken na

virulent [ˈvirjələnt] *adj* (disease) 悪性の akúsei no 危険な kiken na; (actions, feelings) 憎悪に満ちた zôô ni michîta

virus [ˈvaiˈrəs] *n* ウイルス uírusu

visa [ˈviːzə] *n* 査証 sashô, ビザ bíza

vis-à-vis [ˌviːzɑːˈviː] *prep* (compared to) ...と比べて ...to kurábete; (in regard to) ...に関して ...ni kañ shite

viscose [ˈviskouz] *n* ビスコース人絹 bisúkoosujiñkeñ, ビスコースレーヨン bisúkoosúréeyoñ

viscous [ˈviskəs] *adj* ねばねばした neba shita

visibility [ˌvizəbilˈiti:] *n* 視界 shikái

visible [ˈvizəbəl] *adj* (able to be seen or recognized: *also fig*) 目に見える me ni mierû

vision [ˈviʒən] *n* (sight: ability) 視力 shiryóku; (: sense) 視覚 shikáku; (foresight) ビジョン bíjoñ; (in dream) 幻影 geñei

visit [ˈvizˈit] *n* (to person, place) 訪問 hômon
◆*vt* (person: *US also*: visit with) 訪問する hómon suru, 訪ねる tazúnerû, ...へ遊びに行く ...no tokóro e asóbi ni ikú; (place) 訪問する hômon suru, 訪れる tazúneru

visiting hours [ˈvizˈitiŋ-] *npl* (in hospital etc) 面会時間 meñkaijìkan

visitor [ˈvizˈitəːr] *n* (person visiting, invited) 客 kyakú; (tourist) 観光客 kañkôkyàku

visor [ˈvaiˈzəːr] *n* (of helmet etc) 面 meñ; (of cap etc) ひさし hisáshi; (AUT: *also*: sun visor) 日よけ hiyóke

vista [ˈvistə] *n* (view) 景色 keshíki

visual [ˈviʒuːəl] *adj* (arts etc) 視覚の shikáku no

visual aid *n* 視覚教材 shikákukyòzai

visual display unit *n* モニター monítà, ディスプレー disúpuree

visualize [ˈviʒuːəlaiz] *vt* (picture, imagine) 想像する sôzô suru

vital [ˈvaitˈəl] *adj* (essential, important, crucial) 重要な jûyô na; (full of life: person) 活発な kappátsu na; (necessary for life: organ) 生命に必要な seímei ni hitsúyô na

vitality [vaitælˈiti:] *n* (liveliness) 元気 géñki

vitally [ˈvaitəli:] *adv*: **vitally important** 極めて重要な kiwámète jûyô na

vital statistics *npl* (of population) 人口動態統計 jiñkôdôtakèi; (*inf*: woman's measurements) スリーサイズ surísaizù

vitamin [ˈvaitəmin] *n* ビタミン bitámin

vivacious [viveiˈʃəs] *adj* にぎやかな nigíyàka na

vivid [ˈvivˈid] *adj* (clear: description, memory) 鮮明な seímei na; (bright: color, light) 鮮やかな azáyàka na; (imagination) はつらつとした hatsúràtsu to shitá

vividly [ˈvivˈidli:] *adv* (describe) 目に見える様に me ni mierû yô ni; (remember) はっきりと hakkírì to

vivisection [viviˈsekˈʃən] *n* 生体解剖 seítaikaibô

V-neck [ˈviˈnek] *n* (*also*: **V-neck jumper/pullover**) Vネックセーター buínekkusètà

vocabulary [voukæbˈjəlæˈriː] *n* (words known) 語い goí

vocal [ˈvouˈkəl] *adj* (of the voice) 声のkóe no; (articulate) はっきり物を言う hakkírì monó wo iû

vocal c(h)ords *npl* 声帯 seítai

vocation [voukeiˈʃən] *n* (calling) 使命感 shiméìkan; (chosen career) 職業 shokúgyô

vocational [voukeiˈʃənəl] *adj* (training etc) 職業の shokúgyô no

vociferous [vousifˈəːrəs] *adj* (protesters, demands) やかましい yakámashii, しつこい shitsúkoì

vodka [ˈvodˈkə] *n* ウオッカ uókkà

vogue [voug] *n* 流行 ryúkô

in vogue 流行して ryūkō shite

voice [vɔis] *n* (of person) 声 koè
♦*vt* (opinion) 表明する hyōmei suru

void [vɔid] *n* (emptiness) 空虚 kūkyò;
(hole) 穴 aná, 空間 kūkan
♦*adj* (invalid) 無効の mukō no; (empty):
void of ...が全くない ...ga mattàku naí

volatile [vɑːlǝtəl] *adj* (liable to change:
situation) 不安定な fuántei na; (: person)
気まぐれな kimágure na; (: liquid) 揮発
性の kihátsusei no

volcanic [vɑːkǽnik] *adj* (eruption) 火山
の kazàn no; (rock etc) 火山性の kazàn-
sei no

volcano [vɑːkéinou] *n* (pl **volcanoes**) 火
山 kazán

volition [voulíʃǝn] *n: of one's own
volition* 自発的に jihátsuteki ni, 自由意
志で jiyúishì de

volley [vɑːli] *n* (of stones etc) 一斉に投
げられる... issèi ni nagérareru ...; (of
questions etc) 連発 refpatsu; (TENNIS
etc) ボレー borè
a volley of gunfire 一斉射撃 isséishagèki

volleyball [vɑːlibɔːl] *n* バレーボール ba-
rébōrù

volt [voult] *n* ボルト borúto

voltage [voultidʒ] *n* 電圧 deñ-atsu

voluble [vɑːljǝbǝl] *adj* (person) 口達者な
kuchídasshà na; (speech etc) 流ちょうな
ryūchō na

volume [vɑːljum] *n* (space) 容積 yōsèki;
(amount) 容量 yōryō; (book) 本 hoñ;
(sound level) 音量 ofiryō, ボリューム bo-
ryūmu
Volume 2 第2巻 daínikan

voluminous [vǝlúːminǝs] *adj* (clothes)
だぶだぶの dabúdabu no; (correspon-
dence, notes) 大量の taíryō no, 多数のた
sū no

voluntarily [vɑːlǝntǝrˈili] *adv* (willingly) 自発的に jihátsuteki ni, 自由意志で jiyúishì de

voluntary [vɑːlǝnteri] *adj* (willing,
done willingly): exile, redundancy) 自発
的な jihátsuteki na, 自由意志による jiyū-
ishi ni yoru; (unpaid: work, worker) 奉仕

の hōshi no

volunteer [vɑːlǝntiːrʰ] *n* (unpaid helper)
奉仕者 hōshìsha, ボランティア borántia;
(to army etc) 志願者 shigáñsha
♦*vt* (information) 自発的に言う jihátsuteki ni iú, 提供する teñkyō suru
♦*vi* (for army etc): ...への入隊を志願する
...e no nyūtai wo shigàn suru
to volunteer to do ...しようと申出る
...shiyótto mōshíderu

voluptuous [vǝlʌ́ptʃuǝs] *adj* (movement, body, feeling) 官能的な kaññotèki
na, 色っぽい iróppoi

vomit [vɑːmit] *n* 吐いた物 haìta monó,
反吐 hedò
♦*vt* 吐く hakú
♦*vi* 吐く hakú

vote [vout] *n* (method of choosing) 票決
hyōketsu; (indication of opinion) 投票 tōhyō; (votes cast) 投票数 tōhyōsū;
(also: **right to vote**) 投票権 tōhyōkèn
♦*vt* (elect): *to be voted chairman etc*
座長に選出される zachō ni señshutsu sa-
rèru; (propose): *to vote that* ...という事
を提案する ...to iú koto wo teñan suru
♦*vi* (in election etc) 投票する tōhyō suru
vote of thanks 感謝決議 kañshaketsu-
gi

voter [vouttǝːr] *n* (person voting) 投票者
tōhyōsha; (person with right to vote) 有
権者 yūkeñsha

voting [vouttiŋ] *n* 投票 tōhyō

vouch for [vautʃ-] *vt fus* (person, quality etc) 保証する hoshō suru

voucher [vauttʃǝːr] *n* (for meal: also:
luncheon voucher) 食券 shokkèn; (with
petrol, cigarettes etc) クーポン kūpon;
(also: **gift voucher**) ギフト券 gifútokèn

vow [vau] *n* 誓い chikái
♦*vt: to vow to do/that* ...する事(...だと
いう事)を誓う ...surú koto(...da to iú
koto)wo chikáu

vowel [vauǝl] *n* 母音 boín

voyage [vɔiidʒ] *n* (journey: by ship,
spacecraft) 旅 tabí, 旅行 ryokō

V-sign [viːˈsain] (BRIT) *n* Vサイン buì-
sain ♦手の甲を相手に向けると軽べつの
サイン; 手のひらを向けると勝利のサイ

ン té no kō wo afte ni mukéru to kefbetsu no saĺn; te nō hirā wo mukéru to shōrí no saĺn

vulgar [vʌlˈgəːr] *adj* (rude: remarks, gestures, graffiti) 下品な gehín na; (in bad taste: decor, ostentation) 野暮な yabó na

vulgarity [vʌlgærˈiti:] *n* (rudeness) 下品な言葉 gehín na kotóba; (ostentation) 野暮った い事 yabótta kotó

vulnerable [vʌlˈnəːrəbəl] *adj* (person, position) やられやすい yaráreyasuí, 無防備な mubóbì na

vulture [vʌlˈtʃəːr] *n* ハゲタカ hagétaka

W

wad [wɑːd] *n* (of cotton wool, paper) 塊 katámari; (of bańknótes etc) 束 tabá

waddle [wɑːdˈəl] *vi* (duck, baby) よちよ ち歩く yochíyochi arúkù; (fat person) よ たよた歩く yotáyota arúkù

wade [weid] *vi*: *to wade through* (water) …の中を歩いて通る …no nakà wo arúite tōrù; (*fig*: a book) 苦労して読む kú kurō shité yomù

wafer [weiˈfəːr] *n* (biscuit) ウエハース u éhāsu

waffle [wɑːfˈəl] *n* (CULIN) ワッフル waffúru; (empty talk) 下らない話 kudáranai hanáshi

♦*vi* (in speech, writing) 下らない話をす る kudáranai hanáshi wo suru

waft [wæft] *vt* (sound, scent) 漂わせる tadáyowaserù

♦*vi* (sound, scent) 漂う tadáyou

wag [wæg] *vt* (tail, finger) 振る furú

♦*vi*: *the dog's tail was wagging* イヌ はしっぽを振っていた inú wà shippō wo futté ità

wage [weidʒ] *n* (*also*: **wages**) 賃金 chíngin, 給料 kyúryō

♦*vt*: *to wage war* 戦争をする señsō wo suru

wage earner [-əːrˈnəːr] *n* 賃金労働者 chínginrōdōsha

wage packet *n* 給料袋 kyúryōbukùro

wager [weiˈdʒəːr] *n* かけ kaké

waggle [wægˈəl] *vt* (hips) 振る furú; (eyebrows etc) ぴくぴくさせる pikúpiku saséru

wag(g)on [wægˈən] *n* (*also*: **horsedrawn wag(g)on**) 荷馬車 nibásha; (BRIT: RAIL) 貨車 kashá

wail [weil] *n* (of person) 泣き声 nakígoè; (of siren etc) うなり unári

♦*vi* (person) 泣き声をあげる nakígoè wo agérù; (siren) うなる unarú

waist [weist] *n* (ANAT, *also* of clothing) ウエスト uésuto

waistcoat [weistˈkout] (BRIT) *n* チョッ キ chókki, ベスト besúto

waistline [weistˈlain] *n* (of body) 胴回り dōmawàri, ウエスト uésuto; (of garment) ウエストライン uésutoraìn

wait [weit] *n* (interval) 待ち時間 machí jikan

♦*vi* 待つ matsú

to lie in wait for …を待伏せする …wo machíbuse suru

I can't wait to (*fig*) 早く…したい hayáku …shítaí

to wait for someone/something …を 待つ …wo matsú

wait behind *vi* 居残って待つ inokotte matsú

waiter [weiˈtəːr] *n* (in restaurant etc) 給 仕 kyúji, ウエーター uétā, ボーイ bôi

waiting [weiˈtiŋ] *n*: *no waiting* (BRIT: AUT) 停車禁止 teísha kiíshi

waiting list *n* 順番待ちの名簿 juñbanmachi no meíbo

waiting room *n* (in surgery, railway station) 待合室 machíaishitsu

wait on *vt fus* (people in restaurant) …に給仕する …ni kyúji suru

waitress [weiˈtris] *n* ウエートレス uétôresu

waive [weiv] *vt* (rule) 適用するのをやめ る tekíyō suru no wò yamérù; (rights etc) 放棄する hókì suru

wake [weik] (*pt* **woke** *or* **waked**, *pp* **woken** *or* **waked**) (*also*: **wake up**) 起 t okósù

♦*vi* (*also*: **wake up**) 目が覚める me gà samérù

◆*n* (for dead person) 通夜 tsuyá, tsūya; (NAUT) 航跡 kōséki

waken [wei'kən] *vt, vi* = wake

Wales [weilz] *n* ウェールズ uērūzu
the Prince of Wales プリンスオブウェールズ purínsu obu uēruzu

walk [wɔːk] *n* (hike) ハイキング haíkingu; (shorter) 散歩 sanpo; (gait) 歩調 hochō; (in park, along coast etc) 散歩道 sanpomichi, 遊歩道 yūhodō
◆*vi* (go on foot) 歩く arúku; (for pleasure, exercise) 散歩する sanpo suru
◆*vt* (distance) 歩く arúkū; (dog) 散歩に連れて行く sanpo ni tsurète ikú
10 minutes' walk from here ここから徒歩で10分の所に kokó karà tohò dò juppùn no tokórò ni
people from all walks of life あらゆる身分の人々 aráyurù mibùn no hitóbìto

walker [wɔːk'əːr] *n* (person) ハイカー haíkā

walkie-talkie [wɔːˈkiːtɔːˈkiː] *n* トランシーバー toránshìbā

walking [wɔːˈkiŋ] *n* ハイキング haíkingu

walking shoes *npl* 散歩靴 sanpogutsu

walking stick *n* 杖 sutékkì

walk out *vi* (audience) 出て行く detè ikú; (workers) ストライキをする sutóraìki wo suru

walkout [wɔːkˈaut] *n* (of workers) ストライキ sutóraìki

walk out on (inf) *vt fus* (family etc) 見捨てる misúterù

walkover [wɔːˈkouvəːr] (inf) *n* (competition, exam etc) 朝飯前 asámeshimaè

walkway [wɔːˈkwei] *n* 連絡通路 refrakutsùrô

wall [wɔːl] *n* (gen) 壁 kabé; (city wall etc) 城壁 jōheki

walled [wɔːld] *adj* (city) 城壁に囲まれた jōheki ni kakómareta; (garden) 塀をめぐらした塀 wo megúrashita

wallet [wɑːl'it] *n* 札入れ satsúire, 財布 saffu

wallflower [wɔːlˈflauəːr] *n* ニオイアラセイトウ nióiaraseitô
to be a wallflower (fig) だれもダンスの相手になってくれない daré mo dañsu

no aíte ni nattè kurénai, 壁の花である kabé no hana de arù

wallop [wɑːl'əp] (inf) *vt* ぶん殴る buñnaguru

wallow [wɑːl'ou] *vi* (animal: in mud, water) ころげ回る korógemawarù; (person: in sentiment, guilt) ふける fukérù

wallpaper [wɔːlˈpeipəːr] *n* 壁紙 kabégami
◆*vt* (room) ...に壁紙を張る ...ni kabégami wo harú

wally [wei'liː] (BRIT: inf) *n* ばか bakà

walnut [wɔːl'nət] *n* (nut) クルミ kurúmi; (also: walnut tree) クルミの木 kurúmi no ki; (wood) クルミ材 kurúmizaí

walrus [wɔːl'rəs] (*pl* walrus *or* walruses) *n* セイウチ sefuchi

waltz [wɔːlts] *n* (dance, MUS) 円舞曲 efbukyòku, ワルツ warùtsu
◆*vi* (dancers) ワルツを踊る warùtsu wo odóru

wan [wɑːn] *adj* (person, complexion) 青白い aójiroì; (smile) 悲しげな kanáshige nà

wand [wɑːnd] *n* (also: magic wand) 魔法の棒 mahō no bō

wander [wɑːn'dəːr] *vi* (person) ぶらぶら歩く burábura arúkù; (attention) 散漫になる safmañ ni narù; (mind, thoughts: here and there) さまよう samáyoù; (: to specific topic) 漂う tadáyoù
◆*vt* (the streets, the hills etc) ...をぶらぶら歩く ...wo burábura arúkù

wane [wein] *vi* (moon) 欠ける kakérù; (enthusiasm, influence etc) 減る herú

wangle [wæŋ'gəl] (inf) *vt* うまい具合に獲得する umái guaì ni kakútoku suru

want [wɑːnt] *vt* (wish for) 望む nozómu, ...が欲しい ...ga hoshíì; (need, require) ...が必要である ...ga hitsúyò de arù
◆*n: for want of* ...がないので ...ga naì no de
to want to do ...したい ...shitái
to want someone to do something ...に...してもらいたい ...ni ...shité moraìtaì

wanted [wɑːnt'id] *adj* (criminal etc) 指名手配中の shiméitehàichū no

「*wanted*」 (in advertisements) 求む mo-
tómū

wanting [wɑːntiŋ] *adj*: **to be found
wanting** 期待を裏切る kitái wo urágirù

wanton [wɑːntən] *adj* (gratuitous) 理由
のない riyū no nai; (promiscuous) 浮気な
uwáki na

wants [wɑːnts] *npl* (needs) 必要とする物
hitsúyō to suru monó, ニーズ nízù

war [wɔːr] *n* 戦争 señsō
to make war (on) (*also fig*) ...と戦う
...to tatákau

ward [wɔːrd] *n* (in hospital) 病棟 byótō;
(POL) 区 ku; (LAW: child: *also*: **ward of
court**) 被後見人 hikôkennin

warden [wɔːrdən] *n* (of park, game
reserve, youth hostel) 管理人 kañrinin;
(of prison etc) 所長 shochō; (BRIT: *also*:
traffic warden) 交通監視官 kōtsūkan-
shikaň

warder [wɔːrdər] *n* (BRIT) 看守 kañ-
shu

ward off *vt* (attack, enemy) 食止める
kuftomeru; (danger, illness) 防ぐ fuségù

wardrobe [wɔːrdroub] *n* (for clothes) 洋
服だんす yōfukudañsu; (collection of
clothes) 衣装 ishō; (CINEMA, THEA-
TER) 衣装部屋 ishōbeya

warehouse [wɛːrhaus] *n* 倉庫 sōkó

wares [wɛːrz] *npl* 商品 shōhin, 売物 urímono

warfare [wɔːrfɛːr] *n* 戦争 señsō

warhead [wɔːrhed] *n* 弾頭 dañtō

warily [wɛːrili] *adv* 用心深く yōjínbuka-
kakù

warlike [wɔːrlaik] *adj* (nation) 好戦的な
kōsenteki na; (appearance) 武装した bu-
sōshita

warm [wɔːrm] *adj* (meal, soup, day,
clothes etc) 暖かい atátakaì; (thanks) 心
からの kokóro kara no; (applause, welcome) 熱烈な netsúretsu na; (person,
heart) 優しい yasáshiì, 温情のある oñjō
no arù

it's warm (just right) 暖かい atátakaì;
(too warm) 暑い atsúì

I'm warm 暑い atsúì

warm water ぬるま湯 murúmayù

warm-hearted [wɔːrm'hɑːrtid] *adj* 心
の優しい kokóro no yasáshiì

warmly [wɔːrmli] *adv* (applaud, welcome) 熱烈に netsúretsu ni

to dress warmly 厚着する atsúgi suru

warmth [wɔːrmθ] *n* (heat) 暖かさ atáta-
kasa; (friendliness) 温かみ atátakami

warm up *vi* (person, room, soup, etc) 暖
まる atátamarù; (weather) 暖かくなる a-
tátakaku narù; (athlete) 準備運動をする
juñbiuñdō wo suru, ウォーミングアップ
する uómínguappù suru

♦*vt* (food etc) 暖める atátamerù;
(engine) 暖気運転する dañkiuñten suru

warn [wɔːrn] *vt* (advise): **to warn someone of/that** ...に...があると [...だと]
警告する ...ni ...ga arù to [...da to] keíkoku
suru

to warn someone not to do ...に...しな
いよう警告する ...ni ...shinái yo keíkoku
suru

warning [wɔːrniŋ] *n* 警告 keíkoku

warning light *n* 警告灯 keíkokutō

warning triangle *n* (AUT) 停止表示板
teíshihyōjibaǹ

warp [wɔːrp] *vi* (wood etc) ゆがむ yugámu

♦*vt* (fig: character) ゆがめる yugámeru

warrant [wɔːrənt] *n* (voucher) 証明書
shōmeísho; (LAW: for arrest) 逮捕状 taí-
hojō; (: search warrant) 捜索令状 sōsa-
kureíjō

warranty [wɔːrənti] *n* (guarantee) 保証
hoshō

warren [wɔːrən] *n* (*also*: **rabbit warren**)
ウサギ小屋 uságigoya; (*fig*: of passages,
streets) 迷路 meíro

warrior [wɔːrjər] *n* 戦士 señshi

Warsaw [wɔːrsɔː] *n* ワルシャワ warú-
shawa

warship [wɔːrʃip] *n* 軍艦 guñkan

wart [wɔːrt] *n* いぼ ibó

wartime [wɔːrtaim] *n*: **in wartime** 戦
時中 señjichū

wary [wɛːri] *adj* 用心深い yōjínbukaì

was [wʌz] *pt of* **be**

wash [wɔːʃ] *vt* (gen) 洗う aráu; (clothes
etc) 洗濯する señtaku suru

◆*vi* (person) 手を洗う te wŏ aráu; (sea etc): *to wash over/against something* ...に打寄せる ...ni uchíyoseru, ...を洗う ...wo aráu

◆*n* (clothes etc) 洗濯物 señtakumono; (washing program) 洗い aráí; (of ship) 航跡の波 kŏsekí no namí

to have a wash 手を洗う te wŏ aráu

to give something a wash ...を洗う ...wo aráu

washable [wɔːʃəbəl] *adj* 洗濯できる señtaku dekírù

wash away *vt* (stain) 洗い落す araíotosu; (subj: flood, river etc) 流す nagasu

washbasin [wɔːʃbeisin] (*US also*: **washbowl**) *n* 洗面器 señmeñki

washcloth [wɔːʃklɔːθ] (*US*) *n* (face cloth) フェースタオル fēsutaoru

washer [wɔːʃəːr] *n* (TECH: metal) 座金 zagáne, ワッシャー wasshā; (machine) 洗濯機 señtakuki

washing [wɔːʃiŋ] *n* (dirty, clean) 洗濯物 señtakumono

washing machine *n* 洗濯機 señtakuki

washing powder (*BRIT*) *n* 洗剤 señzai

washing-up [wɔːʃiŋʌp] *n* (action) 皿洗い sarāarai; (dirty dishes) 汚れた皿 yogóretà sarā

washing-up liquid (*BRIT*) *n* 台所用洗剤 daídokoroyō señzai

wash off *vi* 洗い落される araíotosareru

wash-out [wɔːʃaut] (*inf*) *n* (failed event) 失敗 shippai

washroom [wɔːʃruːm] (*US*) *n* お手洗い o-téaraí

wash up *vi* (*US*) 手を洗う te wŏ aráu; (*BRIT*) 皿洗いをする saráarai wo suru

wasn't [wʌzʼənt] = **was not**

wasp [wɔsp] *n* アシナガバチ ashínagabàchi (スズメバチなど肉食昆虫のハチの総称 suzúmebachi nado nikúshokusei no hachi no sōshō

wastage [weistidʒ] *n* (amount wasted, loss) 浪費 rōhi

natural wastage 自然消耗 shizénshōmō

waste [weist] *n* (act of wasting: life, money, energy, time) 浪費 rōhi; (rubbish)

廃棄物 haíkibutsu; (*also*: **household waste**) ごみ gomí

◆*adj* (material) 廃棄の haíki no; (left over) 残りの nokórimono no ōt; (land) 荒れ荒れた aréta

to lay waste (destroy: area, town) 破壊する hakái suru

waste away *vi* 衰弱する suíjaku suru

waste disposal unit (*BRIT*) *n* ディスポーザー disúpōzā

wasteful [weistfəl] *adj* (person) 無駄使いの多い mudázūkai no ōt; (process) 不経済な fukéizai na

waste ground (*BRIT*) *n* 空き地 akíchi

wastepaper basket [weistpeipəːr-] *n* くずかご kuzúkàgo

waste pipe *n* 排水管 haísuikan

wastes [weists] *npl* (area of land) 荒れ野 aréno

watch [wɔːtʃ] *n* (*also*: **wristwatch**) 腕時計 udédokèi; (act of watching) 見張り mihári; (vigilance) 警戒 keíkai; (group of guards: MIL, NAUT) 番兵 bañpei; (NAUT: spell of duty) 当直 tŏchoku, ワッチ watchī

◆*vt* (look at: people, objects, TV etc) 見る mírù; (spy on, guard) 見張る miháru; (be careful of) ...に気を付ける ...ni ki wŏ tsukerù

◆*vi* (look) 見る mírù; (keep guard) 見張る miháru

watchdog [wɔːtʃdɔːg] *n* (dog) 番犬 bañken; (*fig*) 監視者 kañshisha, お目付け役 o-métsukeyaku

watchful [wɔːtʃfəl] *adj* 注意深い chūibukaì

watchmaker [wɔːtʃmeikəːr] *n* 時計屋 tokéiya

watchman [wɔːtʃmən] (*pl* **watchmen**) *n* *see* **night**

watch out *vi* 気を付ける ki wŏ tsukerù, 注意する chūì suru

watch out! 危ない! abúnai!

watch strap *n* 腕時計のバンド udédokèi no bañdo

water [wɔ:'tər] n (cold) 水 mizú; (hot)
(お) 湯 (o)yú

♦vt (plant) ...に水をやる ...ni mizú wo
yarú

♦vi (eyes) 涙が出る namída ga derú;
(mouth) よだれが出る yodáre ga derú

in British waters 英国領海に[で] efko-
kuryōkai ni[de]

water cannon n 放水砲 hōsuihō

water closet (BRIT) n トイレ tóɪre

watercolor [wɔ:'tərkʌlər] n (picture)
水彩画 suisaiga

watercress [wɔ:'tərkres] n クレソン ku-
réson

water down vt (milk etc) 水で薄める
mizú de usúmeru; (fig: story) 和らげる
yawáragerū

♦waterfall [wɔ:'tərfɔːl] n 滝 takí

water heater n 湯沸器 yuwákashikì

watering can [wɔ:'təriŋ-] n じょうろ
jōró

water level n 水位 suíi

water lily n スイレン suíren

waterline [wɔ:'tərlain] n (NAUT) 喫水
線 kissúisen

waterlogged [wɔ:'tərlɔːgd] adj (ground)
水浸しの mizúbitashi no

water main n 水道本管 suídōhonkàn

watermelon [wɔ:'tərmelən] n スイカ
suíka

waterproof [wɔ:'tərpruːf] adj (trousers,
jacket etc) 防水の bōsui no

watershed [wɔ:'tərʃed] n (GEO: natural
boundary) 分水界 buísuikaì; (: high
ridge) 分水嶺 buísuirei; (fig) 分岐点 buñ-
kitén

water-skiing [wɔ:'tərskiːiŋ] n 水上スキ
ー suíjōsukī

watertight [wɔ:'tərtait] adj (seal) 水密
の suímitsu no

waterway [wɔ:'tərwei] n 水路 suíro

waterworks [wɔ:'tərwərks] n (building) 浄水場 jōsuijō

watery [wɔ:'təriː] adj (coffee) 水っぽい
mizúppoì; (eyes) 涙ぐんだ namídagundà

watt [wɑːt] n ワット wattò

wave [weiv] n (of hand) 一振り hitófuri;
(on water) 波 namí; (RADIO) 電波 deñ-

pa; (in hair) ウェーブ uébù; (fig: surge) 高
まり takámarì, 急増 kyūzō

♦vt (signal) 手を振る te wo furú;
(branches, grass) 揺れる yuréru; (flag)
なびく nabíkù

♦vt (hand, flag, handkerchief) 振る furù;
(gun, stick) 振回し振回す furímawasū

wavelength [weiv'leŋkθ] n (RADIO) 波
長 hachō

on the same wavelength (fig) 気が合っ
て ki gá attè

waver [wei'vər] n (voice) 震える furúeru; (love) 揺らぐ yurágu; (person) 動揺す
る dōyō suru

his gaze did not waver 彼は目を反ら
さなかった kárè wa mé wò sorásanakat-
tà

wavy [wei'viː] adj (line) くねくねした ku-
nékune shita; (hair) ウェーブのある uébù
no aru

wax [wæks] n (polish, for skis) ワックス
wakkúsu; (also: earwax) 耳あか mimíá-
kà

♦vt (floor, car, skis) ...にワックスを掛け
る ...ni wakkúsu wo kakéru

♦vi (moon) 満ちる michírù

waxworks [wæks'wərks] npl (models)
ろう人形 rōniñgyō

♦n (place) ろう人形館 rōniñgyōkan

way [wei] n (route) ...へ行く道 ...e ikú
michí; (path) 道 michí; (access) 出入口
degúchi; (distance) 距離 kyóri; (direction) 方向 hōkō; (manner, method) 方法
hōhō; (habit) 習慣 shúkan

which way? - this way? こちらへ？-こ
ちらへ dochíra e？ -kochíra e

on the way (en route) 途中で tochū de

to be on one's way 今向かっている imá
mukátte irù, 今途中である imá tochū de
arù

to be in the way (also fig) 邪魔である
jamá de arù

*to go out of one's way to do some-
thing* わざわざ...する wazáwaza ...suru

under way (project etc) 進行中で shiñkōchū de

to lose one's way 道に迷う michí ni
mayóù

in a way ある意味では arù imĭ de wa
in some ways ある面では arù men de wa

no way! (*inf*) 絶対に駄目だ zettái ni damé dà

by the way ... ところで tokóro dè

「*way in*」(*BRIT*) 入口 iríguchi

「*way out*」(*BRIT*) 出口 degùchi

the way back 帰路 kíro

「*give way*」(*BRIT*: AUT) 進路譲れ shínro yuzúre

waylay [weilei'] (*pt, pp* **waylaid**) *vt* 待伏 せする machíbuse suru

wayward [wei'wərd] *adj* (behavior, child) わがままな wagámáma na

W.C. [dʌb'əlju:si:'] (*BRIT*) トイレ toĭre

we [wi:] *pl pron* 私たちは[が] watákushitáchi wa[gà]

weak [wi:k] *adj* (*gen*) 弱い yowái; (dollar, pound) 安い yasúî; (excuse) 下手な hetá nà; (argument) 説得力のない settőkuryoku no naĭ; (tea) 薄い usúî

weaken [wi:'kən] *vi* (person, resolve) 弱 る yowárù; (health) 衰える otóroerù; (influence, power) 劣る otórù

◆*vt* (person, government) 弱くする yo-wákù suru

weakling [wik'liŋ] *n* (physically) 虚弱児 kyojákujì; (morally) 骨無し honénashi

weakness [wik'nis] *n* (frailty) 弱さ yo-wàsa; (fault) 弱点 jakúten

to have a weakness for ...に目がない ...ni me gà naĭ

wealth [welθ] *n* (money, resources) 富 tomĭ, 財産 zaĭsan; (of details, knowledge etc) 豊富な hőfu na

wealthy [wel'θi:] *adj* (person, family, country) 裕福な yűfuku na

wean [wi:n] *vt* (baby) 離乳させる rínyǔ saséru

weapon [wep'ən] *n* 武器 bukĭ

wear [we:r] *n* (*use*) 使用 shiyő; (damage: through use) 消耗 shőmō; (clothing): *sportswear* スポーツウェア supőtsùuea

◆*vb* (*pt* **wore**, *pp* **worn**)

◆*vt* (shirt, blouse, dress etc) 着る kirú; (hat etc) かぶる kabúrù; (shoes, pants, skirt etc) はく hakú; (gloves etc) はめる

hamĕru; (make-up) つける tsukérù; (damage: through use) すり減らす suríf urusú

◆*vi* (last) 使用に耐える shiyő ni taérù; (rub through etc: carpet, shoes, jeans) す り減る suríherù

babywear 幼児ウェア yőjíuea

evening wear イブニングウェア ibúninguèa

wear and tear *n* 消耗 shőmō

wear away *vt* すり減らす suríherasu

◆*vi* (inscription etc) すり減って消える suríhette kíeru

wear down *vt* (heels) すり減らす suríf herasu; (person, strength) 弱くする yowá-kù suru, 弱らせる yowáraserù

wear off *vi* (pain etc) なくなる nakúnaru

wear out *vt* (shoes, clothing) 使い古す tsukáifurusù; (person) すっかり疲れさせ る sukkárĭ tsukáresaserù; (strength) なく す nakúsu

weary [wi:r'i:] *adj* (tired) 疲れ果てた tsu-kárehatetà; (dispirited) がっかりした gakkárĭ shita

◆*vi: to weary of* ...に飽きる ...ni akírù

weasel [wi:'zəl] *n* イタチ itáchi

weather [weð'ə:r] *n* 天気 teńki, 天候 teń-kō

◆*vt* (storm, crisis) 乗切る noríkirù

under the weather (*fig*: ill) 気分が悪い kíbun ga warúî

weather-beaten [weð'ərbi:tən] *adj* (face, skin, building, stone) 風雪に鍛えら れた fűsetsu ni kitáeraretà

weathercock [weð'ərkɑːk] *n* 風見鶏 ka-zámídorî

weather forecast *n* 天気予報 teńkiyohő

weatherman [weð'ə:rmæn] (*pl* **weath-ermen**) *n* 天気予報係 teńkiyohōgakarî

weather vane [-vein] *n* = **weather-cock**

weave [wi:v] (*pt* **wove**, *pp* **woven**) *vt* (cloth) 織る orú; (basket) 編む amú

weaver [wi:'və:r] *n* 機織職人 hatáorishokunin

weaving [wi:'viŋ] *n* (craft) 機織 hatáori

web [web] *n* (*also:* **spiderweb**) クモの巣 kumð no su; (on duck's foot) 水かき mi-zúkaki; (network, *also fig*) 網 amí

we'd [wi:d] = **we had; we would**

wed [wed] (*pt, pp* **wedded**) *vt* (marry) ...と結婚する ...to kekkón suru
♦*vi* 結婚する kekkón suru

wedding [wed'iŋ] *n* 結婚式 kekkónshiki

silver/golden wedding (anniversary) 銀(金)婚式 gin(kíñ)kónshiki

wedding day *n* (day of the wedding) 結婚の日 kekkón no hí; (*US*: anniversary) 結婚記念日 kekkón kinénbi

wedding dress *n* 花嫁衣装 hanáyome i-shò, ウエディングドレス uédiñgudorèsu

wedding present *n* 結婚祝い kekkón i-wai

wedding ring *n* 結婚指輪 kekkón yubíwa

wedge [wedʒ] *n* (*of wood etc*) くさび ku-sábi; (of cake) 一切れ hitókire
♦*vt* (jam with a wedge) くさびで留める kusábi dè toméru; (pack tightly: of people, animals) 押込む oshíkomù

Wednesday [wenz'dei] *n* 水曜日 sufyóbi

wee [wi:] (*SCOTTISH*) *adj* (little) 小さい chíisaì

weed [wi:d] *n* 雑草 zassó
♦*vt* (garden) ...の草むしりをする ...no ku-sámushirì wo suru

weedkiller [wi:d'kilər] *n* 除草剤 josózaì

weedy [wi:'di:] *adj* (man) 柔そうな yawá-sō na

week [wi:k] *n* 週間 shúkan

a week today/on Friday 来週の今日 (金曜日) raíshū no kyó(kíñyòbi)

weekday [wi:k'dei] *n* (*gen*, COMM) 平日 heíjitsu, ウイークデー uíkudè

weekend [wi:k'end] *n* 週末 shúmatsu, ウイークエンド uíkuèndo

weekly [wi:k'li:] *adv* (deliver etc) 毎週 maíshū
♦*adj* (newspaper) 週刊の shúkan no; (payment) 週払いの shúbarai no; (visit etc) 毎週の maíshū no
♦*n* (magazine) 週刊誌 shúkanshì; (newspaper) 週刊新聞 shúkanshìnbun

weep [wi:p] (*pt, pp* **wept**) *vi* (person) 泣く

naku

weeping willow [wi:'piŋ-] *n* シダレヤナギ shídáreyanàgi

weigh [wei] *vt* ...の重さを計る ...no omó-sa wo hakárù
♦*vi* ...の重さは...である ...no omósa wa ...de arù

to weigh anchor いかりを揚げる ikári wo agérù

weigh down *vt* (person, pack animal etc) ...の動きを遅くする ...no ugóki ga osóku narù; (*fig*: with worry): **to be weighed down** ...で沈み込む ...de shizúmikòmu

weight [weit] *n* (metal object) 重り omó-ri; (heaviness) 重さ omósa

to lose/put on weight 体重が減る(増える) taíjū ga herú(fuerù)

weighting [wei'tiŋ] (*BRIT*) *n* (allowance) 地域手当 chíikiteatè

weightlifter [weit'liftər] *n* 重量挙げ選手 júryàge seńshu

weighty [wei'ti:] *adj* (*heavy*) 重い omói; (important: matters) 重大な júdai na

weigh up *vt* (person, offer, risk) 評価する hyóka suru

weir [wi:r] *n* せき sekí

weird [wi:rd] *adj* 奇妙な kimyó na

welcome [wel'kəm] *adj* (visitor, suggestion, change) 歓迎すべき kangeísubeki; (news) うれしい ureshíi
♦*n* 歓迎 kańgei
♦*vt* (visitor, delegation, suggestion, change) 歓迎する kańgei suru; (be glad of: news) うれしく思う uréshìku omóu

thank you - you're welcome! どうも有難う-どういたしまして dómo arígàto-dō itáshimashìte

weld [weld] *n* 溶接 yósetsu
♦*vt* 溶接する yósetsu suru

welfare [wel'fer] *n* (well-being) 幸福 kó-fuku, 福祉 fukúshì; (social aid) 生活保護 sefkatsuhogò

welfare state *n* 福祉国家 fukúshikokkà

welfare work *n* 福祉事業 fukúshijigyò

well [wel] *n* (for water) 井戸 idð; (*also:* **oil well**) 油井 yuséi

♦adv (to a high standard, thoroughly):
also for emphasis with adv, adj or prep
phrase) よく yokū

♦adj: **to be well** (person: in good health)
元気である génki de árù

♦excl そう、ねえ sō, né

as well (in addition) も mo

as well as (in addition to) ...の外に ...no
hoká ni

well done! よくやった yokū yattá

get well soon! 早く治ります様に hayáku naórimasu yō nī, お大事に o-dáiji ni

to do well (person) 順調である junchō
de árù; (business) 繁盛する hanjō suru

we'll [wiːl] = **we will; we shall**

well-behaved [welbiheivd'] adj (child,
dog) 行儀の良い gyōgi no yoí

well-being [wel'biː'iŋ] n 幸福 kōfuku, 福
祉 fukúshi

well-built [wel'bilt'] adj (person) 体格の
良い taíkaku no yoí

well-deserved [wel'dizə:rvd'] adj (success, prize) 努力相応の doryōkusōō no

well-dressed [wel'drest'] adj 身なりの良
い minári no yoí

well-heeled [wel'hiːld'] (inf) adj
(wealthy) 金持の kanémochí no

wellingtons [wel'iŋtənz] npl (also: **wel-
lington boots**) ゴム長靴 gomúnagagutsu

well-known [wel'noun'] adj (famous:
person, place) 有名な yūmei na

well-mannered [wel'mænərd] adj 礼儀
正しい reígitádashíi

well-meaning [wel'miː'niŋ] adj (person)
善意の zeń-i no; (offer etc) 善意に基づく
zeń-i ni motózukú

well-off [wel'ɔːf'] adj (rich) 金持の kanémochi no

well-read [wel'red'] adj 博学の hakúgaku no

well-to-do [wel'tədu:'] adj 金持の kanémochí no

well up vi (tears) こみ上げる komfageru

well-wisher [wel'wiʃər] n (friends,
admirers) 支持者 shijīsha, ファン faň

Welsh [welʃ] adj ウェールズの uéruzu no;
(LING) ウェールズ語の uéruzugo no

♦n (LING) ウェールズ語 uéruzugo

Welsh npl: **the Welsh** ウェールズ人 uéruzujin

Welshman/woman [welʃ'mən/wumən]
(pl **Welshmen/women**) n ウェールズ人
の男性(女性) uéruzujin no daňsei(joséi)

Welsh rarebit [-reːr'bit] n チーズトー
スト chīzūtōsūto

went [went] pt of **go**

wept [wept] pt, pp of **weep**

we're [wiːr] = **we are**

weren't [wəːr'ənt] = **were not**

west [west] n (direction) 西 nishf; (part
of country) 西部 seíbu

♦adj (wing, coast, side) 西の nishf no, 西
側の nishígawa no

♦adv (to/towards the west) 西へ nishf e

west wind 西風 nishfkaze

West n: **the West** (POL: US plus western Europe) 西洋 seíyō

West Country: **the West Country**
(BRIT) n 西部地方 seíbuchíhō

westerly [wes'tərli:] adj (point) 西寄り
の nishfyori no; (wind) 西からの nishf kara no

western [wes'tə:rn] adj (of the west) 西
の nishf no; (POL: of the West) 西洋の
seíyō no

♦n (CINEMA) 西部劇 seíbugeki

West Germany n 西ドイツ nishídoitsu

West Indian adj 西インド諸島の nishfindoshotō no

♦n 西インド諸島の人 nishfindoshotō no
hitó

West Indies [-in'diːz] npl 西インド諸島
nishfindoshotō

westward(s) [west'wərd(z)] adv 西へ nishf e

wet [wet] adj (damp) ぬれた nuréta;
(wet through) ぬれた nuréta; (rainy:
weather, day) 雨模様の amémoyō no

♦n (BRIT: POL) 穏健派の人 oňkéṅha no
hitó

to get wet (person, hair, clothes) ぬれる
nuréru

「**wet paint**」ペンキ塗立て peňki nurftate

to be a wet blanket (fig) 座を白けさせ

る za wo shirákesaseru

wet suit n ウェットスーツ uéttōsútsu

we've [wiːv] = **we have**

whack [wæk] vt たたく tatákù

whale [weil] n (ZOOL) クジラ kujíra

wharf [wɔːrf] (pl **wharves**) n 岸壁 ganpeki

wharves [wɔːrvz] npl of **wharf**

KEYWORD

---

what [wɑt] adj 1 (in direct/indirect questions) 何の náñ no, 何... náñì...

what size is it? サイズは幾つですか sáìzu wa íkùtsu desu ká

what color is it? 何色ですか nánì iro desu ká

what shape is it? 形はどうっています か katáchi wà dō nattè imásù ká

what books do you need? どんな本が いりますか dóñna hoñ ga irímasù ká

he asked me what books I needed 私 にはどんな本がいるかと彼は聞いていま した watákushi nì wà dóñna hoñ ga irú ka to kárè wa kíîtè imáshìta

2 (in exclamations) 何て... náñte...

what a mess! 何て有様だ náñte arísama dà

what a fool I am! 私は何てばかだ watákushi wà nàñte bákà da

♦pron 1 (interrogative) 何 náñì, 何 náñ

what are you doing? 何をしています か nánì wo shité imasù ká

what is happening? どうなっています か dō nattè imásù ká

what's in there? その中に何が入って いますか sonó nakà ni nánì ga háittè imasu ká

what is it? - it's a tool 何ですか-道 具です náñ desu ká - dōgu desu

what are you talking about? 何の話 ですか náñ no hanáshì desu ká

what is it called? これは何と言います か kórè wa náñ to iîmasù ká

what about me? 私はどうすればいいん ですか watákushi wà dō surèba íîñ desu ká

what about doing ...? ...しませんか ...shímaseñ ká

2 (relative): *is that what happened?* 事件は今話した通りですか jíken wa ímà hanáshita tòri desu ká

I saw what you did/was on the table あなたのした事/テーブルにあった 物を見ました anátà no shítà kotò[tébùru ni attá monò]wo mimáshìta

he asked me what she had said 彼は 彼女の言った事を私に尋ねた kárè wa kánòjo no ittá kotò wo watákushi nì tazúnetà

tell me what you're thinking about 今何を考えているよと下さい今 nánì wo kañgaete irù kà oshíete kudasai

what you say is wrong あなたの言っ ている事は間違っています anátà no ittè irù kotò wa machígattè imásù

♦excl (disbelieving) 何!

what, no coffee! 何、コーヒーがない んだって？ nánì, kóhì ga náñ datté?

I've crashed the car - what! 車をぶ つけてしまった-何？kurúma wò butsúkete shimattà - nánì?

---

whatever [wɑtev'ər] adj: *whatever book* どんな本でも dóñna hoñ de mo

♦pron: *do whatever is necessary/you want* 何でも必要(好き)な事をしなさい nañ de mo hitsúyō[sukí]na koto wo shínàsai

whatever happens 何が起っても nanì ga okòtte mo

no reason whatever/whatsoever 全く 理由がない mattáku ríyū ga nai

nothing whatever 全く何もない mattáku nanì mo nai

whatsoever [wɑtsouev'ər] adj = **whatever**

wheat [wiːt] n 小麦 komúgi

wheedle [wid'əl] vt: *to wheedle someone into doing something* ...を口車に 乗せて...させる ...wo kuchíguruma ni noséte ...saséru

to wheedle something out of someone 口車に乗せて...を...からだまし取る kuchíguruma ni noséte ...wo ...karà damáshitorù

wheel [wiːl] n (of vehicle etc) 車 kurúma,

車輪 sharín, ホイール hoīru; (also: **steer-ing wheel**) ハンドル hańdoru; (NAUT) だ輪 darín

♦vt (pram etc) 押す osú

♦vi (birds) 旋回する sefíkai suru; (also: **wheel round**: person) 急に向き直る kyū ní mukínaorú

wheelbarrow [wiːlˈbærou] n 一輪車 i-chírínsha, ネコ車 nekóguruma

wheelchair [wiːlˈtʃeːr] n 車いす kurúmaisù

wheel clamp n (AUT) ◇違反駐車の自動車車輪に付けて走れなくする金具 iháňchūsha no jidóshasharìn ni tsukéte hashíranaku surù kanágu

wheeze [wiz] vi (person) ぜいぜい言う zeízei iú

KEYWORD

when [wen] adv いつ ítsù

when did it happen? いつ起ったですか ítsù okóttan desu ká

I know when it happened いつ起ったのかは私と分かっています ítsù okótta kà wa chánto wakátte imasù

are you going to Italy? イタリアには いつ行きますか itárìa ni wa ítsù ikímasù ká

when will you be back? いつ帰って来ますか ítsù kaétte kimasù ká

♦conj 1 (at, during, after the time that) ...する時 ...surú tokī, ...すると ...surú tò, ...したら ...shítarà, ...してから ...shíté karà

she was reading when I came in 私が部屋に入った時彼女は本を読んでいました watákushi gà heyá ni háitta tokī kánòjo wa hón wo yóňde imáshìta

when you've read it, tell me what you think これを読んだらご意見を聞かせて下さい kórè wo yóňdara go-íkèn wo kikásete kudasaí

be careful when you cross the road 道路を横断する時は気を付けて下さい dōro wo ōdan surú tokī ni wa kí wo tsukéte ně

that was when I needed you あなたにいて欲しかったのはその時ですよ aná-

tā ni íte hoshíkatta no wa sonó tokí desu yó

2: (on, at which): **on the day when I met him** 彼に会った日は kárè ni átta hí wa

one day when I was raining 雨が降っていたある日 ámè ga fútté itá árù hí

3 (whereas): **you said I was wrong when in fact I was right** あなたは私が間違っていると言いましたが、事実は間違っていませんでした anátā wa watákushi gà machígatte irú to ifmashita gà, jíjitsu wa machígatte imásen deshīta

why did you buy that when you can't afford it? 金の余裕がないのになぜあれを買ったんですか kané nō yoyū gà náì no ni náze arě wò kattáň desu ká

whenever [wenevˈəːr] adv いつか ítsù ka
♦conj (any time) ...するというでも ...surú to itsúmo...; (every time that) ...する度に ...surú tabí ni

where [weːr] adv (place, direction) どこ に(で) dokō (ni, de)
♦conj ...の所に(で) ...no tokōro ni(de)
this is where ... これは...する所です kórè wa ... surú tokoro desu

whereabouts [weːrˈəbauts] adv どの辺に donō heň ni
♦n: **nobody knows his whereabouts** 彼の居場所は誰も...だれ bo ibásho wa fuméi da

whereas [weːrˈæz] conj ...であるのに対して ...de árù no ni taîshite

whereby [weːrˈbai] pron それによってそれ ni yottê

whereupon [weːrˈəpən] conj すると surú to

wherever [weːrˈevˈəːr] conj (no matter where) どこに(で)しても dokō ni(de) ...shite mo; (not knowing where) どこにか知らないが dokō ni ...kà shiranai ga
♦adv (interrogative: surprise) 一体全体どこに(で) ittái zentai dokō ní

wherewithal [weːrˈwiθɔːl] n 金 kané

whet [wet] vt (appetite) そそる sosóru

whether [weðˈəːr] conj ...かどうか ...ka dō ká

I don't know whether to accept or not 引き受けるべきかどうかは分からない hikfukerubeki kā dō kā wa wakāranaī

whether you go or not 行くにしても行かないにしても ikú nī shité mō ikánai nī shité mō

it's doubtful whether he will come 彼はたぶん来ないだろう kárě wa tabūn konái daró

KEYWORD

which [wɪtʃ] *adj* 1 (interrogative: direct, indirect) どの dónð, どちらの dóchīra no
which picture do you want? どちらの絵がいいんですか dóchīra no é ga iñ desu ká

which books are yours? あなたの本はどれとどれですか anátá no hóñ wa dóre tô dóre lu dóře desu ká

tell me which picture/books you want どの絵本が欲しいか言って下さい dóně é[hóñ]gā hoshíi kā itté kudasaí

which one? どれ dóre

which one do you want? どれが欲しいんですか dóre ga hoshíī desu ká

which one of you did it? あなたたちのだれがやったんですか anáta tachi no dáre ga yattáñ desu ká

2: *in which case* その場合 sonó baaí
the train may be late, in which case don't wait up 列車が遅れるかもしれないが、その場合先に寝て下さい réssha ga okúreru ka mð shirénai ga, sonó baaí sakí ni neté kudasaí

by which time その時 sonó tokī
we got there at 8 pm, by which time the cinema was full 映画館に着いたのは夜の8時でしたが、もう満席になっていました efgakan ni tsúlta no wa yórùno hachíji deshita ga, mô mañseki ni natté imashìta

♦*pron* 1 (interrogative) どれ dóre
which (of these) are yours? どれとどれがあなたのですか dóre tô dóre ga anátá no monð desú ká

which of you are coming? あなたたちのだれとだれが一緒に来てくれますか anátátachi no dáre tô dáre ga fsshò ni

kité kuremasù ká

here are the books/files - tell me which you want 本(ファイル)はこれだけありますよ どれとどれが欲しいんですか hóñ(faīru)wa koré dake árímasu ga, dóre to dóre ga hoshíiñ desu ká

I don't mind which どれでもいいんですよ dóre de mo iíñ desu yó

2 (relative): *the apple which you ate/which is on the table* あなたの食べた〔テーブルにある〕りんご anátá no tábeta (tēburu ni árú)ríngo

the meeting which we attended 私、が出席した会議 watákushītachi ga shusséki shitá kái̇gi

the chair on which you are sitting あなたが座っ ていいいす anátá ga suwátte irú ísú

the book of which you spoke あなたが話していた本 anátá ga hanáshite itá hóñ

he said he knew, which is true/I feared 彼は知っていると言ったが、その通りでした〔私の心配していた通りでした〕 kárě wa shitté irū to ittá gã, sonó tòri deshita(watákushi nð shíñpai shite ita tòri deshita)

after which その後 sonó atò

whichever [wɪtʃev'ər] *adj*: *take whichever book you prefer* どれでもいいから好きな本を取って下さい dóre de mo ií kara sukí na hoñ wo totté kudasaí

whichever book you take あなたがどの本を取っても anátá ga dóð hoñ wo totté mo

whiff [wɪf] *n* (of perfume, gasoline, smoke) ちょっと...のにおいがすること chottó ...no nìoī ga suru koto

while [waɪl] *n* (period of time) 間 aída
♦*conj* (at the same time as) ...する間 ...surú aida; (as long as) ...する限りは ...surú kagírì wa; (although) ...にもかかわらず ...surú nī mo kakáwaràzu

for a while しばらくの間 shibáràku no aída

while away *vt* (time) つぶす tsubúsu

whim [wɪm] *n* 気まぐれ kimágure

whimper [wim'pər] n (cry, moan) 哀れ
っぽい泣き声 awáreppoi nakígoè
◆vi (child, animal) 哀れっぽい声を
出す awáreppoi kóè wo dasù

whimsical [wim'zikəl] adj (person) 気ま
ぐれな kimágure na; (poem) 奇抜な kibátsu na; (look, smile) 変な heñ na

whine [wain] n (of pain) 哀れっぽいなき
声 awáreppoi nakígoè; (of engine, siren)
うなり unári
◆vi (person, animal) 哀れっぽい声を
出す awáreppoi nakígoè wo dasù;
(engine, siren) うなる unárù; (fig: complain) 愚痴をこぼす guchí wo kobósù

whip [wip] n (lash, riding whip) むち mu
chí; (POL) 院内幹事 ifinaikañji
◆vt (person, animal) むち打つ muchfu-
tsù; (cream, eggs) 泡立てる awádaterù,
ホイップする hoíppù suru; (move quickly): **to whip something out/off** ...を素早
く取出す[はずす, 脱ぐ] sattò torídasu
(hazúsu, nugú]

whipped cream [wipt-] n ホイップクリ
ーム hoíppùkurímù

whip-round [wip'raund] (BRIT) n 募金
bokín

whirl [wəːrl] vt (arms, sword etc) 振回す
furímawasù
◆vi (dancers) ぐるぐる回る gurúguru
mawárù; (leaves, water etc) 渦巻く uzúmakù

whirlpool [wəːrl'puːl] n 渦巻 uzúmàki

whirlwind [wəːrl'wind] n 竜巻 tatsúmà-
ki

whir(r) [wəːr] vi (motor etc) うなり unári

whisk [wisk] n (CULIN) 泡立て器 awá-
datekì
◆vt (cream, eggs) 泡立てる awádaterù
to whisk someone away/off ...を素早
く連去る ...wo subáyakù tsurésarù

whiskers [wis'kəːrz] npl (of animal,
man) ひげ higé

whiskey [wis'kiː] (BRIT **whisky**) n ウィ
スキー ufsukî

whisper [wis'pəːr] n (low voice) ささや
き sasáyakì
◆vi ささやく sasáyakù

◆vt ささやく sasáyakù

whist [wist] (BRIT) n ホイスト hofsuto

whistle [wis'əl] n (sound) 口笛 kuchíbue;
(object) 笛 fué
◆vi (person) 口笛を吹く kuchíbue wo fukù; (bird) ぴーぴーさえずる pípì saézurù;
(bullet) ひゅーとうなる hyú to unárù;
(kettle) ぴゅーと鳴る pyú to narú

white [wait] adj (color) 白い shirói; (pale:
person, face) 青白い aójirõi; (with fear)
青ざめた aózameta
◆n (color) 白 shirô; (person) 白人 hakújin;
(of egg) 白身 shiromì

white coffee (BRIT) n ミルク入りコー
ヒー mirúkuirikôhì

white-collar worker [wait'kɑːl'əːr-] n
サラリーマン sarárìmàn, ホワイトカラー
howáitòkarâ

white elephant n (fig) 無用の長物 mu-
yô no chòbutsu

white lie n 方便のうそ hôben no usó

white paper n (POL) 白書 hakúsho

whitewash [wait'wɑʃ] n (paint) のろ
のろ石灰, 白亜, のりを水に混ぜた塗料
sekkái, hakúà, norí wo mizú ni mazèta
toryô
◆vt (building) ...にのろを塗る ...ni norô
wo nurû; (fig: happening, career, reputation) ...の表面を繕う ...no hyômeñ wo
tsukúroù

whiting [wai'tiŋ] n inv (fish) タラ tará

Whitsun [wit'sən] n 聖霊降臨節 seíreì-
kôriñsetsu

whittle [wit'əl] vt: **to whittle away,
whittle down** (costs: reduce) 減らす herásu

whiz(z) [wiz] vi: **to whizz past/by** (person, vehicle etc) ぴゅーんと通り過ぎる
byûn to tôrisugirù

whiz(z) kid (inf) n 天才 teñsai

KEYWORD

who [huː] pron 1 (interrogative) だれ dárè, どなた dónàta
who is it?, who's there? だれですか
dárè desu ka
who are you looking for? だれを捜し
ているんですか dárè wo sagáshite irûñ

desu ká
I told her who I was 彼女に名乗りました kánojo ni nanórimashíta
I told her who was coming to the party パーティの出席予定者を彼女に知らせました pátī no shussékiyoteísha no kánojo ni shirásemashíta
who did you see? だれを見ましたか dáre wo mimáshíta ká
2 (relative): *my cousin who lives in New York* ニューヨークに住んでいるいとこ nyúyòku ni súnde iru itókŏ
the man/woman who spoke to me 私に話しかけた男性(女性) watákushi ni hanáshikaketá dansei(josei)
those who can swim 泳げる人たち oyógerù hitótтachi

whodunit [hu:dʌn'it] (*inf*) *n* 探偵小説 taíteishósetsu

whole [houl] *adj* (entire) 全体の zeńtái no; (not broken) 無傷の mukízu no
♦*n* (entire unit) 全体 zeńtái no; (all): *the whole of* 全体の zeńtái no
the whole of the town 町全体 machízeńtai
on the whole, as a whole 全体として zeńtai toshite

whole food(s) [houl'fu:d(z)] *n(pl)* 無加工の食べ物 mukákō no tabémonò

wholehearted [houl'hɑːr'tid] *adj* (agreement etc) 心からの kokóro kàra no

wholemeal [houl'miːl] *adj* (bread, flour) 全粒の zeńryů no, 全麦の zeńbaku no

wholesale [houl'seil] *n* (business) 卸 oróshi, 卸売 oróshiúri
♦*adj* (price) 卸の oróshi nò; (destruction) 大規模の daskíbò no
♦*adv* (buy, sell) 卸で oróshi de

wholesaler [houl'seilɑːr] *n* 問屋 toń-ya

wholesome [houl'sʌm] *adj* (food, climate) 健康に良い keńkō ni yoì; (person) 健全な keńzen na

wholewheat [houl'wiːt] *adj* = **wholemeal**

wholly [houl'liː] *adv* (completely) 完全に kańzen ni

whom [huːm] *pron* **1** (interrogative) だれを dáre wo, どなたを dónàta wo
whom did you see? だれを見ましたか dáre wo mimáshíta ká
to whom did you give it? だれに渡しましたか dáre ni watáshimashíta ká
tell me from whom you received it だれに[から]それをもらったかを教えて下さい dáre ni[kára] soré wò morátta kà wo oshéte kudasaí
2 (relative): *the man whom I saw/to whom I spoke* 私が見た[話し掛けた]男性 watákushi ga mítă(hanáshikaketá) dansei
the lady with whom I am talking 私と話している女性 watákushi tò hanáshite itá josei

whooping cough [wuː'piŋ-] *n* 百日ぜき hyákúnichizékî

whore [hɔːr] (*inf: pej*) *n* 兇女 baíta

whose [huːz] *adj* **1** (possessive: interrogative) だれの dáre no, どなたの dónàta no
whose book is this?, whose is this book? これはだれの本ですか koré wà dáre no hóñ desu ká
whose pencil have you taken? だれの鉛筆を持って来たんですか dáre no eñpitsu wò motté kitáñ desu ká
whose daughter are you? あなたはどなたの娘さんですか anátà wa dónàta no musúme-sañ desu ká
I don't know whose it is だれの物か私には分かりません dáre no monó kà watákushi ni wà wakárimaseñ
2 (possessive: relative): *the man whose son you rescued* あなたが助けた子供の父親 anátà ga tasúketa kodomo no chichíoya
the girl whose sister you were speaking to あなたと話していた女性の妹 anátà to hanáshite itá josei no imôto
the woman whose car was stolen 車を盗まれた女性 kurúma wò nusúmareta

joséi

◆*pron* だれの物 dáre no monő, どなたの物 dónàta no monő

whose is this? これはだれのですか kórè wa dáre no desu ká

I know whose it is だれの物か知っています dáre no monő ka shitté imasù

whose are these? これらはだれの物ですか korérà wa dáre no monő desù ká

```
KEYWORD
```

why [wai] *adv* なぜ názè, どうして dőshìte

why is he always late? どうして彼はいつも遅刻するのですか dőshìte kárè wa ítsùmo chikőku suru nő desu ká

why don't you come too? あなたも来ませんか anáta mo kimásèn ká

I'm not coming - why not? 私は行きません-どうしてですか watákushi wa kímasèn - dőshìte desu ká

fancy a drink? - why not? 一杯やろうかね-いいね íppai yarő kà - íi ne

why not do it now? 今すぐやりませんか ímà súgù yarímasèn ka

◆*conj* なぜ názè, どうして dőshìte

I wonder why he said that どうしてそんな事を言ったのかしら dőshìte sofina kotő wo ittá nő kashira

the reason why 理由 riyű

that's not (the reason) why I'm here 私が来たのはそのためじゃありません watákushi gà kitá no wa sonő tamè ja arímasèn

◆*excl* (expressing surprise, shock, annoyance etc) ◇日本語では表現しない場合が多い nihőngo de wa hyőgen shinaí baai ga ői

why, it's you! おや、あなたでしたか oyá, anáta deshita ká

why, that's impossible/quite unacceptable! そんな事はできません(認められません) sofina kotő wa dekímaseñ (mitőmeraremaseñ)

I don't understand, why it's obvious! 訳が分かりません-ばかでも分かる事だよ wákè ga wakárimaseñ - báka de

mo wakárù kotő dà yő

whyever [waiev'ə:r] *adv* 一体 なぜ ittai názè

wicked [wik'id] *adj* (crime, man, witch) 極悪の gokúaku no; (smile) 意地悪そうな ijíwaruső na

wickerwork [wik'ə:rwə:rk] *n* (basket, chair etc) 藤編みの tőami no, 籐編み細工品 tőamizaikuhin, 枝編み細工品 edáami no edáamizaikuhin

◆*n* (objects) 藤編み細工品 tőamizaikuhin, 枝編み細工品 edáamizaikuhin

wicket [wik'it] *n* (CRICKET: stumps) 三柱門 sańchűmòn, ウイケット ufkètto; (: grass area) ピッチ pítchî

◇2つのウイケット間のグランド futátsu nő ufkettokàn no gurándò

wide [waid] *adj* (gen) 広い hirői; (grin) 楽しげな tanőshigè na

◆*adv: to open wide* (window etc) 広く開ける hirőku akéru

to shoot wide ねらいを外す nerái wo hazűsu

wide-angle lens [waid'æŋ'gəl-] *n* 広角レンズ kőkaku reñzu

wide-awake [waid'əweik'] *adj* すっかり目が覚めた sukkárî me gà samèta

widely [waid'li:] *adv* (gen) 広く hirőku; (differing) 甚だしく hanáhadashikù

widen [waid'ən] *vt* (road, river, experience) 広くする hirőku suru, 広げる hirőgeru

◆*vi* (road, river, gap) 広くなる hirőku narű, 広がる hirőgaru

wide open [waid'] *adj* (window, eyes, mouth) 大きく開けた őkìku akéta

widespread [waidspred'] *adj* (belief etc) はびこった habíkottà

widow [wid'ou] *n* 未亡人 mibőjìn, 後家 goké

widowed [wid'oud] *adj* (mother, father) やもめになった yamőme ni nattá

widower [wid'ou:r] *n* 男やもめ otőko-yamőme

width [widθ] *n* (distance) 広さ hirősa; (of cloth) 幅 habá

wield [wi:ld] *vt* (sword, power) 振るう furűu

wife [waif] (*pl* **wives**) *n* (*gen*) 妻 tsumá;
(one's own) 家内 kánài; (someone else's)
奥さん okūsan

wig [wig] *n* かつら katsúra

wiggle [wig'əl] *vt* (hips) くねらす kunérasù; (ears etc) ぴくぴく動かす pikúpiku
ugókasù

wild [waild] *adj* (animal, plant) 野生の
yaséi no; (rough: land) 荒れ果てた aréhateta; (: weather, sea) 荒れ狂う arékuruù;
(person, behavior, applause) 興奮した
kōfun shita; (idea) 突飛な toppí na;
(guess) 当てずっぽうの atézuppò no

wilderness [wil'dərnis] *n* 荒野 kóyà, 原
野 genya, 未開地 mikáichì

wild-goose chase [waild'gus'-] *n* (*fig*)
無駄な捜索 mudá na sōsaku

wildlife [waild'laif] *n* (animals) 野生動物
yaséidòbutsu

wildly [waild'li:] *adv* (behave) 狂った様
に kurútta yō ni; (applaud) 熱狂的に nek-
kyṓteki ni, 無性に mushṓ ni; (: happen)
めっぽうに meppṓ ni; (guess) 当てずっぽう
に atézuppò ni; (happy) 最高に saíkō ni

wilds [waildz] *npl* 荒野 kóyà, 原野 genya, 未開地 mikáichì

wilful [wil'fəl] (*US also*: **willful**) *adj*
(obstinate: child, character) わがままな
wagámamà na; (deliberate: action, disregard etc) 故意の koì no

KEYWORD

will [wil] *vt*: *pt, pp* **willed** *aux vb* 1 (forming future tense): *I will finish it
tomorrow* 明日終ります ashíta owárimasù

I will have finished it by tomorrow
明日にでもなれば終るでしょう asú ni dé-
mo náreba owárù deshō

*will you do it? - yes I will/no I
won't* やりますか - はい, やります[いい
え, やりません] yarímasù ká - hái, yarímasù (iíè, yarímaseñ)

when will you finish it? いつ終りま
すか ítsù owárimasù ká

2 (in conjectures, predictions): *he will/
he'll be there by now* 彼はもう着いて
いるでしょう kárè wa mō tsúite irú de-

shō

that will be the postman 郵便屋さん
でしょう yūbinya-san deshō

this medicine will help you この薬な
ら効くでしょう konó kusuri narà kikú
deshō

this medicine won't help you この薬
は何の役にも立ちません konó kusuri wà
nañ no yakú ni mò tachímaseñ

3 (in commands, requests, offers): *will
you be quiet!* 黙りなさい damárinasaī

will you come? 来てくれますか kíte
kuremasù ká

will you help me? 手伝ってくれますか
tetsúdattè kurémasù ká

will you have a cup of tea? お茶を
いかがですか o-chá wò ikága desù ká

I won't put up with it! 我慢できませ
ん gámàn dekímaseñ

♦*vt*: *to will someone to do something*
意志の力で...に...をさせようとする íshì
no chikára dè ...ni ...wò saséyò tò suru

he willed himself to go on 彼は精神力
だけで続けようとした kárè wa seíshinryòku dake dè tsuzúkeyò tò shita

♦*n* (volition) 意志 íshì; (testament) 遺言
yuígon

---

willful [wil'fəl] (*US*) *adj* = **wilful**

willing [wil'iŋ] *adj* (with goodwill) 進ん
で...する susúnde ...surù; (enthusiastic) 熱
心な nesshín na

he's willing to do it 彼はそれを引き受
けてくれるそうです kárè wa soré wò
hikíukète kureru sō desu

willingly [wil'iŋli:] *adv* 進んで susúnde

willingness [wil'iŋnis] *n* 好意 kōī

willow [wil'ou] *n* ヤナギ yanági

willpower [wil'pauər] *n* 精神力 seíshinryòku

willy-nilly [wil'i:nil'i:] *adv* 否応なしに i-
yāō nashī ni

wilt [wilt] *vi* (flower, plant) 枯れる karéru

wily [wai'li:] *adj* (fox, move, person) ずる
賢い zurúgashikoī

win [win] *n* (in sports etc) 勝利 shōrī, 勝
ち kachí

♦vb (pt, pp won)

♦vt (game, competition) ...で 勝つ ...de katsù; (election) ...で当選する ...de tōsen suru; (obtain: prize, medal) もらう moráu, 受ける ukérù; (money) 当てる atérù; (support, popularity) 獲得する kakútoku suru

♦vi 勝つ katsù

wince [wins] vi 顔がこわばる kaó ga kowábaru

winch [wintʃ] n ウインチ uńchi

wind¹ [wind] n (air) 風 kazé; (MED) 呼吸 kokyū; (breath) 息 ikí

♦vt (take breath away from) ...の息を切らせる ...no ikí wo kiráserù

wind² [waind] (pt, pp wound) vt (roll: thread, rope) 巻く makú; (wrap: bandage) 巻付ける makítsukerù; (clock, toy) ...のぜんまいを巻く ...no zeńmai wo makú

♦vi (road, river) 曲りくねる magárikunerù

windfall [wind'fɔ:l] n (money) 棚ぼた tanábota

winding [wain'diŋ] adj (road) 曲りくねった magárikunettà; (staircase) らせん状の rasénjō no

wind instrument n (MUS) 管楽器 kañgakki

windmill [wind'mil] n 風車 kazáguruma

window [win'dou] n 窓 madò

window box n ウインドーボックス uńdōbokkùsu

window cleaner n (person) 窓ふき職人 madófukishokùnin

window envelope n 窓付き封筒 madótsukifūtò

window ledge n 窓下枠 madóshitawàku

window pane n 窓ガラス madógarasu

window-shopping [win'douʃɑpiŋ] n ウインドーショッピング uńdōshoppìngu

windowsill [win'dousil] n 窓下枠 madóshitawàku

windpipe [wind'paip] n 気管 kikán

windscreen [wind'skri:n] (BRIT) n = windshield

windshield [wind'ʃi:ld] (US) n フロント

ガラス furóntogaràsu, ウインドシールド uńdoshīrùdo

windshield washer n ウインドシールドワシャー uńdoshīrùdowashā

windshield wiper [-waip'ər] n ワイパー waìpā

windswept [wind'swept] adj (place) 吹きさらしの fukísarashi no; (person) 風で髪が乱れた kazé de kamí ga midárèta

wind up vt (clock, toy) ...のぜんまいを巻く ...no makú; (debate) 終りにする owári ni suru

windy [win'di:] adj (weather, day) 風の強い kazé no tsuyói

it's windy 風が強い kazé ga tsuyói

wine [wain] n ブドウ酒 bedóshu, ワイン waìn

wine bar n ワインバー waìnbā

wine cellar n ワインの地下貯蔵庫 waìn no chikáchozòko

wine glass n ワイングラス waìngurasu

wine list n ワインリスト waìnrisuto

wine merchant n ワイン商 waìnshō

wine waiter n ソムリエ somúrie

wing [wiŋ] n (of bird, insect, plane) 羽根 hané, 翼 tsubása; (of building) 翼 yokú; (BRIT: AUT) フェンダー feńdā

winger [wiŋ'ər] n (SPORT) ウインガー uńgā

wings [wiŋz] npl (THEATER) そで sodé

wink [wiŋk] n (of eye) ウインク uńku

♦vi (with eye) ウインクする uńku suru; (light etc) 瞬く matátakù

winner [win'ər] n (of prize, race, competition) 勝者 shōsha

winning [win'iŋ] adj (team, competitor, entry) 勝った kattà; (shot, goal) 決勝の kesshō no; (smile) 愛敬たっぷりの aíkyō tappùri no

winnings [win'iŋz] npl 賞金 shōkin

win over vt (person: persuade) 味方にする mikáta ni suru

win round (BRIT) vt = win over

winter [win'tər] n (season) 冬 fuyú

in winter 冬には fuyú ni wa

winter sports npl ウインタースポーツ uńtāsupōtsù

wintry [win'tri:] adj (weather, day) 冬っ

しい fuyúrashìi

wipe [waip] *n: to give something a wipe* …をふく …wo fukú

♦*vt* (rub) ふく fukú; (erase: tape) 消す kesú

wipe off *vt* (remove) ふき取る fukítorù

wipe out *vt* (debt) 完済する kańsai suru; (memory) 忘れる wasúreru; (destroy: city, population) 壊滅する kaímetsu suru

wipe up *vt* (mess) ふき取る fukítorù

wire [wai'əːr] *n* (metal etc) 針金 harígane; (ELEC) 電線 defisen; (telegram) 電報 defipō

♦*vt* (house) …の配線工事をする …no hafsenkōjī wo suru; (also: **wire up**: electrical fitting) 取付ける torítsukerù; (person: telegram) …に電報を打つ …ni defipō wo utsù

wireless [wai'əːrlis] (BRIT) *n* ラジオ rajìo

wiring [wai'əːriŋ] *n* (ELEC) 配線 haísen

wiry [wai'əːri] *adj* (person) やせて筋張った yasête no kyōjin na; (hair) こわい kowái

wisdom [wiz'dəm] *n* (of person) 知恵 chié; (of action, remark) 適切さ tekísetsusa

wisdom tooth *n* 親知らず oyáshirazu

wise [waiz] *adj* (person, action, remark) 賢い kashíkoi, 賢明な keímei na

...wise *suffix: timewise/moneywise etc* 時間[金銭]的に jikán(kifsen)teki ni

wisecrack [waiz'kræk] *n* 皮肉な冗談 hiníku na jōdan

wish [wiʃ] *n* (desire) 望み nozómi, 希望 kibō; (specific) 望みの物 nozómi no mono

♦*vt* (want) 望む nozómù, 希望する kibō suru

best wishes (for birthday, etc) おめでとう omédetō

with best wishes (in letter) お体を大事に o-kárada wo o-dáiji ni

to wish someone goodbye …に別れのあいさつを言う …ni wakáre no aísatsu wo iu, …にさよならを言う …ni sayónara wo iu

he wished me well 彼は「成功を祈る」と言っthem karè wa 「seíkō wo inorù」to iímashìta

to wish to do …したいと思う …shitái to omóu

to wish someone to do something …に …してもらいたいと思う …ni …shité moraitái to omóu

to wish for …が欲しいと思う …ga hoshíi to omóu

wishful [wiʃ'fəl] *adj: it's wishful thinking* その考えは甘い sonó kangaè wa amái, それは有り得ない事だ soré wa aríenai kotó da

wishy-washy [wiʃ'i:waʃi:] (*inf*) *adj* (color) 薄い usúi; (ideas, person) 迫力のない hakúryoku no naì

wisp [wisp] *n* (of grass, hair) 小さな束 chíisana tabà; (of smoke) 一筋 hitósùji

wistful [wist'fəl] *adj* (look, smile) 残念そうな zańnensō na

wit [wit] *n* (wittiness) ユーモア yumóa, ウイット uíttò; (intelligence: *also*: **wits**) 知恵 chié; (person) ウイットのある人 uíttò no aru hitò

KEYWORD

with [wiθ] *prep* **1** (accompanying, in the company of) …と …to, …と一緒に …to ísshò ni

I was with him 私は彼と一緒にいました watákushì wa karè to ísshò ni imáshìta

we stayed with friends 私たちは友達の家に泊りました watákushìtachi wa tomódachi no iè ni tomárimashìta

we'll take the children with us 子供たちを一緒に連れて行きます kodómotachi wo ísshò ni tsuréte ikimasu

mix the sugar with the eggs 砂糖を卵に混ぜて下さい satō wò tamágo ni mázète kudásaì

I'll be with you in a minute 直ぐ行きますからお待ち下さい súgù ikímasu karà o-máchi kudásaì

I'm with you (I understand) 分かります wakárimasù

to be with it (*inf*: up-to-date) 現代的である geñdaiteki de arù; (: alert) 抜け目がない nukéme ga nâī

2 (descriptive): *a room with a view* 見晴らしのいい部屋 mihárashi nò íi heyá
the man with the grey hat/blue eyes 灰色の帽子をかぶった(青い目の)男 haíro nò bōshi wò kabútta(aôī mé nò)otôko

3 (indicating manner, means, cause):
with tears in her eyes 目に涙を浮かべながら mé nî námìda wo ukábènagara
to walk with a stick つえをついて歩く tsûe wo tsufte arûku
red with anger 怒りで顔を真っ赤にして ikári dè kaô wò makká ni shitè
to shake with fear 恐怖に震える kyófu de furúerù
to fill something with water を水で一杯にする ...wò mizú dè íppái nî surù
you can open the door with this key このかぎでドアを開けられます konô kagî dè dôa wo akéraremasù

---

withdraw [wiðdrɔ́ː] (*pt* **withdrew** *pp* **withdrawn**) *vt* (object) 取出す torídasu; (offer, remark) 取消す torîkesu, 撤回する tekkái suru
♦*vi* (troops) 撤退する tettái suru; (person) 下がる sagárù
to withdraw money (from the bank) 金を引出す kané wo hikídasù

withdrawal [wiðdrɔ́əl] *n* (of offer, remark) 撤回 tekkái; (of troops) 撤退 tettái; (of services) 停止 tefshi; (of participation) 取りやめる事 toríyameru koto; (of money) 引出し hikídashi

withdrawal symptoms *n* (MED) 禁断症状 kiñdanshöjô

withdrawn [wiðdrɔ́ːn] *adj* (person) 引っ込みがちな hikkómigachi na

wither [wíðˈəːr] *vi* (plant) 枯れる karéru

withhold [wiðhóuld] (*pt, pp* **withheld**) *vt* (tax etc) 源泉徴収する geñsenchöshú suru; (permission) 拒む kobámù; (information) 隠す kakúsù

within [wiðín] *prep* (inside: referring to place, time, distance) ...以内に(で) ...inái

ni(de)
♦*adv* (inside) 中の nakâ no
within reach (of) (...に) 手が届く所に(で) ...ni tê gà todôkù tokoro ni(de)
within sight (of) (...が) 見える所に(で) ...ga miérù tokoro ni(de)
within the week 今週中に koñshúchū ni
within a mile of ...の1マイル以内に ...no ichîmairu inái ni

without [wiðáut] *prep* ...なしで ...nashî de
without a coat コートなしで kôtô nashî de
without speaking 何も言わないで naní mo iwanaîde
to go without something ...なしで済ます ...nashî de sumásu

withstand [wiðstǽnd] (*pt, pp* **withstood**) *vt* (winds, attack, pressure) ...に耐える ...ni taérù

witness [wít'nis] *n* (person who sees) 目撃者 mokûgekishâ; (person who countersigns document: *also* LAW) 証人 shônin
♦*vt* (event) 見る mírù, 目撃する mokûgeki suru; (document) 保証人として...にサインする hoshônin toshite ...ni saîn suru
to bear witness to (*fig*: offer proof of) ...を証明する ...wo shômei suru

witness stand (BRIT **witness box**) *n* 証人席 shônînseki

witticism [wít'sizəm] *n* (remark) 冗談 jôdan

witty [wít'i] *adj* (person) ウイットのある uîttô no arù; (remark etc) おどけた odôketa

wives [waivz] *npl of* **wife**

wizard [wiz'əːrd] *n* 魔法使い mahôtsukai

wk *abbr* = **week**

wobble [wɑːb'əl] *vi* (legs) よろめく yorómekù; (chair) ぐらぐらする guràgura suru; (jelly) ぷるぷるする purùpuru suru

woe [wou] *n* 悲しみ kanáshimi

woke [wouk] *pt of* **wake**

woken [wou'kən] *pp of* **wake**

wolf [wulf] (*pl* **wolves**) *n* オオカミ ôkami

wolves [wulvz] *npl of* **wolf**

woman [wum'ən] (pl **women**) n 女 ofina, 女性 joséi

woman doctor n 女医 joi

womanly [wum'ənli:] adj (virtues etc) 女性らしい joséirashii

womb [wum] n (ANAT) 子宮 shikyū

women [wim'ən] pl of **woman**

women's lib [wim'ənzlib'] (inf) n ウーマンリブ ūmanríbu

won [wʌn] pt, pp of **win**

wonder [wʌn'dəːr] n (miracle) 不思議 fushígi; (feeling) 驚異 kyōi
♦vi: **to wonder whether/why** ...かしら [なぜ...かしら]と思う ...ka shira (nazé ...ka shira)'to omóu
to wonder at (marvel at) ...に驚く ...ni odórokú
to wonder about ...の事を考える ...no kotó wo kangáeru
it's no wonder (that) ... (という事)は不思議ではない ... (to iú koto) wà fushígi de wà naí

wonderful [wʌn'dəːrfəl] adj (excellent) 素晴らしい subárashii; (miraculous) 不思議な fushígi na

wonderfully [wʌn'dəːrfəli:] adv (excellently) 素晴らしく subárashikù; (miraculously) 不思議に fushígi ni

won't [wount] = **will not**

woo [wu:] vt (woman) ...に言い寄る ...ni iyorú; (audience etc) ...に...を媚びる ...ni kobíru

wood [wud] n (timber) 木材 mokúzai, 木ki; (forest) 森 morí, 林 hayáshi, 木立 kodáchi

wood carving n (act, object) 木彫 kibóri

wooded [wud'id] adj (slopes, area) 木の茂った kí nò shigéttà

wooden [wud'ən] adj (object) 木でできたkí de dekita, 木製の mokúsei no; (house) 木造の mokúzō no; (fig: performance, actor) でくの坊の様な dekúnobō no yō nā

woodpecker [wud'pekəːr] n キツツキ kitsútsukî

woodwind [wud'wind] npl (MUS) 木管楽器 mokkángakkì

woodwork [wud'wəːrk] n (skill) 木材工芸 mokúzaikōgeì

woodworm [wud'wəːrm] n キクイムシ kikúimùshi

wool [wul] n (material, yarn) 毛糸 keíto, ウール ūrù
to pull the wool over someone's eyes (fig) ...をだます ...wo damásu

woolen [wul'ən] (BRIT **woollen**) adj (socks, ties etc) 毛糸の keíto no, ウールの ūrù no
the woolen industry 羊毛加工業界 yōmōkakōgyōkaì

woolens [wul'ənz] npl 毛糸衣服 keítoirhì

wooly [wul'i:] (BRIT **woolly**) adj (socks, hat etc) 毛糸の keíto no, ウールの ūrù no; (fig: ideas) 取留めのない torítome no naì; (person) 考え方のはっきりしない kafígaekatà no hakkírì shinái

word [wəːrd] n (unit of language: written, spoken) 語 go, 単語 tańgo, 言葉 kotóba; (promise) 約束 yakúsokú; (news) 知らせ shiráse, ニュース nyūsù
♦vt (letter, message) ...の言回しを書く ...no iímawashì wo erábù
in other words 言換えると iíkaerù to
to break/keep one's word 約束を破る (守る) yakúsoku wo yabúrú (mamórù)
to have words with someone ...と口げんかをする ...to kuchígeñka wo suru

wording [wəːr'diŋ] n (of message, contract etc) 言回し iímawashì

word processing n ワードプロセシング wādopuroseshìngu

word processor [-prɑ:'sesəːr] n ワープロ wāpuro

wore [wɔːr] pt of **wear**

work [wəːrk] n (gen) 仕事 shigóto; (job) 職 shokú; (ART, LITERATURE) 作品 sakúhin
♦vi (person: labor) 働く határaku; (mechanism) 動く ugókù; (be successful: medicine etc) 効く kikú
♦vt (clay, wood etc) 加工する kakō suru; (land) 耕す tagáyasù; (mine) 採掘する sakútsu suru; (machine) 動かす ugókasù; (cause: effect) もたらす motárasù; (: miracle) 行う okónau

to be out of work 失業中である shitsúgyōchū de aru

to work loose (part) 緩む yurúmù; (knot) 解ける tokérù

workable [wəːrkəbəl] adj (solution) 実行可能な jikkṓkanō na

workaholic [wəːrkəhɑːlik] n 仕事中毒の人 shigótochūdoku no hito, ワーカホリック wākahorίkkù

worker [wəːrkəːr] n 労働者 rōdōshá

workforce [wəːrkfɔːrs] n 労働人口 rōdōjinkō

working class [wəːrkiŋ-] n 労働者階級 rōdōshakaίkyū

working-class [wəːrkiŋklæs] adj 労働者階級の rōdōshakaίkyū no

working order n: **in working order** ちゃんと動く状態で chanto ugokú jōtai de

workman [wəːrkmən] (pl **workmen**) n 作業員 sagyṓin

workmanship [wəːrkmənʃip] n (skill) 腕前 udémae

work on vt fus (task) ...に取組む ...ni toríkumu; (person: influence) 説得する settóku suru; (principle) ...に基づく ...ni motózukù

work out vi (plans etc) うまくいく umáku iku
♦vt (problem) 解決する kaíketsu suru; (plan) 作る tsukúrù
it works out at $100 100ドルになる hyakúdòru ni narú

works [wəːrks] n (BRIT: factory) 工場 kōjō
♦npl (of clock, machine) 機構 kikṓ

worksheet [wəːrkʃiːt] n ワークシート wākushītò

workshop [wəːrkʃɑːp] n (at home, in factory) 作業場 sagyṓjò; (practical session) ワークショップ wākushoppù

work station n ワークステーション wākusutēshòn

work-to-rule [wəːrktɔːruːl] (BRIT) n 順法闘争 junpṓtōsò

work up vt: **to get worked up** 怒る okórù

world [wəːrld] n 世界 sekái

♦cpd (champion) 世界...sekái...; (power, war) 国際的... kokúsaiteki..., 国際... kokúsai...

to think the world of someone (fig: admire) ...を高く評価する ...wo takáku hyōka suru; (: love) ...が大好きである ...ga daísuki de aru

worldly [wəːrldliː] adj (not spiritual) 世俗的な sezókuteki na; (knowledgeable) 世才にたけた sesái ni takéta

worldwide [wəːrldwaíd] adj 世界的な sekáiteki na

worm [wəːrm] n (also: **earthworm**) ミミズ mimízu

worn [wɔːrn] pp of **wear**
♦adj (carpet) 使い古した tsukáifurushità; (shoe) 履き古した hakífurushità

worn-out [wɔːrnaut] adj (object) 使い古した tsukáifurushità; (person) へとへとに疲れた hetóheto ni tsukárèta

worried [wəːriːd] adj (anxious) 心配している shifpai shite irú

worry [wəːriː] n (anxiety) 心配 shifpai
♦vt (person) 心配させる shifpai saserù
♦vi (person) 心配する shifpai suru

worrying [wəːriːiŋ] adj 心配な shifpai na

worse [wəːrs] adj さらに悪い sarà ni wárùi
♦adv 更に悪く sarà ni warúku
♦n 更に悪い事 sarà ni warúì koto
a change for the worse 悪化 akká

worsen [wəːrsən] vt 悪くする warúku suru
♦vi 悪くなる warúku naru

worse off adj (financially) 収入が減った shúnyū ga hettá; (fig): **you'll be worse off this way** そんな事は損後でではない sofina koto wa tokúsaku de wa naì

worship [wəːrʃip] n (act) 礼拝 reíhai
♦vt (god) 礼拝する reíhai suru; (person, thing) 崇拝する sūhái suru
Your Worship (BRIT: to mayor, judge) 閣下 kakká

worst [wəːrst] adj 最悪の saíaku no
♦adv もひどく mottṓmo hidóku
♦n 最悪 saíaku
at worst 最悪の場合 saíaku no baái

worth [wəːrθ] n (value) 価値 kachí

♦*adj*: **to be worth $100** 価格は100ドルである kakáku wa hyakúdoru de arú

it's worth it やる価値がある yarú kachí ga aru

to be worth one's while (to do) (...する事は) ...のためになる (...surú koto wa) ...no tamé ni naru

worthless [wə:rθˈlis] *adj* (person, thing) 価値のない kachí no nai

worthwhile [wə:rθˈwail'] *adj* (activity, cause) ためになる tamé ni naru

worthy [wə:rˈði:] *adj* (person) 尊敬すべき sofíkeisubeki; (motive) 良い yoi

worthy of ...にふさわしい ...ni fusáwashii

KEYWORD

would [wud] *aux vb* 1 (conditional tense): **if you asked him he would do it** 彼にお願いすればやってくれるでしょう kárè ni o-négai ourèba yatté kureru deshô

if you had asked him he would have done it 彼に頼めばやってくれた事でしょう kárè ni tanómeba yatté kuretá kotó deshô

2 (in offers, invitations, requests): **would you like a biscuit?** ビスケットはいかがですか bisúkettò wa ikágà desu ká

would you ask him to come in? 彼に入ってもらって下さい kárè ni háitte morátte kudasai

would you open the window please? 窓を開けてくれませんか mádò wo akéte kuremasù ká

3 (in indirect speech): **I said I would do it** 私はやってあげると約束しました watákushi wà yatté agerù to yakúsoku shimashita

he asked me if I would go with him 一緒に行ってくれると彼に頼まれました isshó ní itté kurè ni kárè ni tanómaremashita

4 (emphatic): **it WOULD have to snow today!** 今日に限って雪が降るなんてなあ kyô ní kagittè yukí gà fúrù nánte ná

you WOULD say that, wouldn't you! あんたの言いそうな事だ áñta no iísô na kotó dà

5 (insistence): **she wouldn't behave** あの子はどうしても言う事を聞いてくれない anó kò wa dô shite mò iú kotó wo kíkte kurenaí

6 (conjecture): **it would have been midnight** だとすれば夜中の12時という事になりますdà tò súrèba yonáka nò júnijì to iú kotó ni narímasù

it would seem so そうらしいね sô rashíì né

7 (indicating habit): **he would go there on Mondays** 彼は毎週月曜日にそこへ行く事にしていました kárè wa máshū getsúyòbi ni sokó è ikú kotó ni shité imashìta

he would spend every day on the beach 彼は毎日浜辺でごろごろしていました kárè wa máìnichi hamá dè gorògoro shite imáshìta

---

would-be [wud'bi:'] *(pej) adj* ...志望の ...shibô no

wouldn't [wud'ant] = would not

wound[1] [waund] *pt, pp* of wind

wound[2] [wu:nd] *n* 傷 kizú

♦*vt* ...に傷を負わせる ...ni kizú wo owáseru, 負傷させる fushô saséru

wove [wouv] *pt* of weave

woven [wou'vən] *pp* of weave

wrangle [ræŋˈgəl] *n* 口論 kôron

wrap [ræp] *n* (stole) 肩掛 katakake, ストール sutórù; (cape) マント mañto, ケープ kêpù

♦*vt* (cover) 包む tsutsúmù; (pack: *also*: **wrap up**) こん包する kofípô suru; (wind: tape etc) 巻付ける makítsukerù

wrapper [ræp'ər] *n* (on chocolate) 包み tsutsúmi; (BRIT: of book) カバー kabâ

wrapping paper [ræp'iŋ-] *n* (brown) クラフト紙 kuráfùtoshi; (fancy) 包み紙 tsutsúmigami

wrath [ræθ] *n* 怒り ikári

wreak [ri:k] *vt* (havoc) もたらす motárasu

to wreak vengeance on ...に復讐しゅうす

る ...ni fukúshū suru

wreath [ri:θ] n (funeral wreath) 花輪 ha-náwa

wreck [rek] n (vehicle) 残がい zaígai; (ship) 難破船 nanpasen; (pej: person) 変り果てた人 kawárihatetà hitó
♦vt (car etc) めちゃめちゃに壊す mechá-mecha ni kowásù; (fig: chances) 台無しにする daínashi ni suru

wreckage [rek'idʒ] n (of car, plane, ship, building) 残がい zaígai

wren [ren] n (ZOOL) ミソサザイ misósazai

wrench [rentʃ] n (TECH: adjustable) スパナ supánà; (: fixed size) レンチ reńchi; (tug) ひねり hinéri; (fig) 心痛 shíntsū
♦vt (twist) ひねる hinérù
to wrench something from someone
...から ...をねじり取る ...kara ...wo nejíritorù

wrestle [res'əl] vi: *to wrestle (with someone)* (fight) (...と) 格闘する (...to) kakútō suru; (for sport) (...と) レスリングする (...to) resúringu suru
to wrestle with (fig) ...と取組む ...to toríkumu, ...と戦う ...to tatákau

wrestler [res'lər] n レスラー resúrā

wrestling [res'liŋ] n レスリング resúringu

wretched [retʃ'id] adj (poor, unhappy) 不幸な fukó na; (inf: very bad) どうしようもない dò shiyó mo nai

wriggle [rig'əl] vi (also: wriggle about: person, fish, snake etc) うねうねする u-néune suru

wring [riŋ] (pt, pp wrung) vt (wet clothes) 絞る shibórù; (hands) もむ mómù; (bird's neck) ひねる hinérù; (fig): *to wring something out of someone* (...を) 強いる ...ni ...wo hákaserù

wrinkle [riŋ'kəl] n (on skin, paper etc) しわ shiwá
♦vt (nose, forehead etc) ...にしわを寄せる ...ni shiwá wo yoserù
♦vi (skin, paint etc) しわになる shiwá ni naru

wrist [rist] n 手首 tekúbi

wristwatch [rist'wɑːtʃ] n 腕時計 udédo-kèi

writ [rit] n 令状 reíjō

write [rait] (pt wrote, pp written) vt 書く kakù
♦vi 書く kakù
to write to someone ...に手紙を書く ...ni tegámi wo kakù

write down vt 書く kakù, 書留める ka-kítomeru

write off vt (debt) 帳消しにする chōke-shi ni suru; (plan, project) 取りやめる to-ríyameru

write-off [rait'ɔːf] n 修理不可能な物 shūrífukánō na mono

writer [rait'ər] n (author) 著者 choshá; (professional) 作家 sakká; (person who writes) 書手 kakíte

write up vt (report, minutes etc) 詳しく書く kuwáshikù kakù

writhe [raið] vi 身もだえする mimódàe suru

writing [rait'iŋ] n (words written) 文字 moji, 文章 buńshō; (handwriting) 筆跡 hisséki; (of author) 作品 sakúhin, 作風 sakúfū; (activity) 書物で shōmén de
in writing 書面で shōmén de

writing paper n 便せん bifsen

written [rit'ən] pp of **write**

wrong [rɔːŋ] adj (bad) 良くない yokúnai; (incorrect: number, address etc) 間違った machígattà; (not suitable) 不適当な futékitō na; (reverse: side of material) 裏側の urágawa no; (unfair) 不正な fuséi na
♦adv 間違って machígatte, 誤って ayá-matte
♦n (injustice) 不正 fuséi
♦vt (treat unfairly) ...に悪い事をする ...ni warúi koto wo surù
you are wrong to do it それは不正な事です sore wa fuséi na koto desù
you are wrong about that, you've got it wrong それは違います sorè wa chigáimasù
to be in the wrong 間違っている machígattè iru
what's wrong? どうしましたか dò shi-máshita ká

to go wrong (person) 間違う machígaù; (plan) 失敗する shippái suru; (machine) 狂う kurúù

wrongful [rɔːŋ'fəl] *adj* (imprisonment, dismissal) 不当な futō na

wrongly [rɔːŋ'li:] *adv* 間違って machígatte

wrote [rout] *pt* of write

wrought [rɔːt] *adj*: *wrought iron* 錬鉄 refítetsu

wrung [rʌŋ] *pt, pp* of wring

wry [rai] *adj* (smile, humor, expression) 皮肉っぽい hiníkuppoì

wt. *abbr* = weight

X

Xmas [eks'mis] *n abbr* = Christmas

X-ray [eks'rei] *n* (ray) エックス線 ekkúsusen, (photo) レントゲン写真 reńtogenshashin

◆*vt* …のレントゲンを撮る …no reńtogen wo torù

xylophone [zai'ləfoun] *n* 木琴 mokkín

Y

yacht [jɑːt] *n* ヨット yottò

yachting [jɑːt'iŋ] *n* ヨット遊び yottóasobi

yachtsman [jɑːts'mən] (*pl* **yachtsmen**) *n* ヨット乗り yottónori

Yank [jæŋk] (*pej*) *n* ヤンキー yańkī

Yankee [jæŋk'i:] (*pej*) *n* = Yank

yap [jæp] *vi* (dog) きゃんきゃんほえる kyańkyan hoérù

yard [jɑːrd] *n* (of house etc) 庭 niwá; (measure) ヤード yādò

yardstick [jɑːrd'stik] *n* (*fig*) 尺度 shakúdò

yarn [jɑːrn] *n* (thread) 毛糸 keíto; (tale) ほら話 horábanashi

yawn [jɔːn] *n* あくび akúbi

◆*vi* あくびする akúbi suru

yawning [jɔːn'iŋ] *adj* (gap) 大きなお*kína*

yd. *abbr* = yard(s)

yeah [je] (*inf*) *adv* はい haì

to be 8 years old 8才である hassái de aru

an eight-year-old child 8才の子供 hassái no kodómo

yearly [jiːr'li:] *adj* 毎年の maínen no, maítoshi no

◆*adv* 毎年 maínen, maítoshi

yearn [jəːrn] *vi: to yearn for something* …を切に望む …wo setsú ni nozómu

to yearn to do…をしたいと切に望む …wo shitáì to setsú ni nozómu

yeast [jiːst] *n* 酵母 kōbò, イースト īsùto

yell [jel] *n* 叫び sakébi

◆*vi* 叫ぶ sakébù

yellow [jel'ou] *adj* 黄色い kiíroi

yelp [jelp] *n* (of animal) キャンと鳴く事 kyáñ to nakú koto; (of person) 悲鳴 himéi

◆*vi* (animal) きゃんと鳴く kyaǹ to nakú; (person) 悲鳴を上げる himéi wò agérù

yeoman [jou'mən] (*pl* **yeomen**) *n*: *yeoman of the guard* 国王の親衛隊員 kokúō no shiń-eitaìin

yes [jes] *adv* はい haì

◆*n* はいという返事 haì to iú henji

to say/answer yes 承諾する shōdaku suru

yesterday [jes'tə:rdei] *adv* 昨日 kinő, sakújitsu

◆*n* 昨日 kinő, sakújitsu

yesterday morning/evening 昨日の朝 (夕方) kinő no asá (yūgata)

all day yesterday 昨日一日 kinő ichí-nichi

yet [jet] *adv* まだ madà; (already) もう mố

◆*conj* がしかし ga shikáshì

it is not finished yet まだできていない mada dekíte inái

the best yet これまでの物で最も良い物 koré madè no mono dè mottómo yoi mono

as yet まだ madà

yew [juː] *n* (tree) イチイ ichíi

Yiddish [jid'iʃ] *n* イディッシュ語 idísshugo

yield [jiːld] n (AGR) 収穫 shūkaku; (COMM) 収益 shūeki
♦vt (surrender: control, responsibility) 譲る yuzúru; (produce: results, profit) もたらす motárasù
♦vi (surrender) 譲る yuzúru; (US: AUT) 道を譲る michí wo yuzúru

YMCA [waiemsiːeiʹ] n abbr (= Young Men's Christian Association) キリスト教青年会 kírísutokyōseínènkai, ワイエムスエー wafemushíè

yog(h)ourt [jouʹgərt] n ヨーグルト yōgúrùto

yog(h)urt [jouʹgərt] n ヨーグルト yōgúrùto

yoke [jouk] n (of oxen) くびき kubíkì; (fig) 重荷 omóni

yolk [jouk] n 卵黄 rań-ō, 黄身 kimí

KEYWORD

you [juː] pron 1 (subj: sing) あなたは(が) anátá wa(ga); (: pl) あなたたちは(が) anátátachi wa (ga)
you are very kind あなたはとても親切ですね anátá wa totémo shínsetsu desu ne, ご親切に有難うございます go-shínsetsu ni arígátō gozáimasù
you Japanese enjoy your food あなたたち日本人は食べるのが好きですね anátátachi nihónjìn wa tabéru no ga sukí desù né
you and I will go あなたと私が行く事になっています anátá to watákushi gà ikú kotò ni natté imasù
2 (obj: direct, indirect: sing) あなたを (に) anátá wo(ni); (: pl) あなたたちを (に) anátátachi wo(ni)
I know you 私はあなたを知っています watákushi wà anátá wo shitté imasù
I gave it to you 私はそれをあなたに渡しました watákushi wà soré wò anátá ni watáshimashita
3 (stressed): **I told YOU to do it** それをしなさいと言ったのはあなたです yatté iú no wà anátá ni ittán desu yó
4 (after prep, in comparisons)
it's for you あなたのためです anátá no tamé desù

can I come with you? 一緒に行っていいですか isshō nī itté ǐ desu ká
she's younger than you 彼女はあなたより若いです kánojo wa anátá yori wakái desu
5 (impersonal: one)
fresh air does you good 新鮮な空気は健康にいい shínsen nà kūki wa keńkō ni ǐ
you never know どうなるか分かりませんね dō narú ka wakárimaseñ né
you can't do that! それはいけません soré wà ikémaseñ

you'd [juːd] = **you had; you would**

you'll [juːl] = **you will; you shall**

young [jʌŋ] adj (person, animal, plant) 若い wakái
♦npl (of animal) 子 ko; (people): **the young** 若者 wakámono

younger [jʌŋʹgəːr] adj (brother etc) 年下の toshíshita no

youngster [jʌŋʹstəːr] n 子供 kodómo

your [juːr] adj (singular) あなたの anátá no; (plural) あなたたちの anátátachi no
¶ see also **my**

you're [juːr] = **you are**

yours [juːrz] pron (singular) あなたの物 anátá no mono; (plural) あなたたちの物 anátátachi no mono ¶ see also **mine**; **faithfully**; **sincerely**

yourself [juːrselfʹ] pron あなた自身 anátá jishín ¶ see also **oneself**

yourselves [juːrselvzʹ] pl pron あなたたち自身 anátátachi jishín ¶ see also **oneself**

youth [juːθ] n (young days) 若い時分 wakái jibun; (young man: pl **youths**) 少年 shōnen

youth club n 青少年クラブ seíshōnen kurábu

youthful [juːθʹfəl] adj (person) 若い wakái; (looks) 若々しい wakáwakashíi; (air, enthusiasm) 若者独特の wakámono-dokútoku no

youth hostel n ユースホステル yūsúhosùteru

Youth Training (BRIT) 職業訓練 sho-

kúgyōkunreñ ◊失業青少年のためのもの
shitsūgyōseishōnen no tamé no monð

you've [juːv] = **you have**

Yugoslav [juːˈɡouslɑːv] adj ユーゴスラビアの yúgòsurabìa no
♦ n ユーゴスラビア人 yúgòsurabìajin

Yugoslavia [juːˈɡouslɑːˈviːə] n ユーゴスラビア yúgòsurabìa

yuppie [ˈjʌpˈiː] n (inf) ヤッピー yappī
♦ adj ヤッピーの yappī no

YWCA [waidʌbəljusíeiʔ] n abbr (= Young Women's Christian Association) キリスト教女子青年会 kirísutokyōjoshìsefnenkai, ワイダブリューシーエー wafdaburyūshīē

Z

Zambia [ˈzæmˈbiːə] n ザンビア zañbia

zany [ˈzeiˈniː] adj (ideas, sense of humor) ばかげた bakágeta

zap [zæp] vt (COMPUT: delete) 削除する sakūjo suru

zeal [ziːl] n (enthusiasm) 熱情 nelsuljō; (also: religious zeal) 壮信 kyōshiñ

zealous [ˈzeləs] adj 熱狂的な nekkyōteki na

zebra [ˈziːbrə] n シマウマ shimáuma

zebra crossing (BRIT) n 横断歩道 ōdañhodō

zenith [ˈziːˈniθ] n 頂点 chōtèn

zero [ˈziːrou] n 零点 reiteñ, ゼロ zerð

zest [zest] n (for life) 熱意 netsùi; (of orange) 皮 kawá

zigzag [ˈzigˈzæg] n ジグザグ jigûzagu
♦ vi ジグザグに動く jigûzagu ni ugókù

Zimbabwe [zimˈbɑːˈbwei] n ジンバブウエ jiñbabùbue

zinc [ziŋk] n 亜鉛 àeñ

zip [zip] n (also: zip fastener) = zipper
♦ vt (also: zip up) = zipper

zip code (US) n 郵便番号 yūbiñbañgō

zipper [ˈzipˈɑːr] (US) n チャック chakkû, ジッパー jippà, ファスナー fasûnā
♦ vt (also: zipper up) ...のチャックを締める ...no chakkû wo shimérù

zodiac [ˈzouˈdiːæk] n 十二宮図 jūnikyūzu

zombie [ˈzɑmˈbiː] n (fig: like a zombie) ロボットの様に（な）robóttð no yǒ ni (na)

zone [zoun] n (area, also MIL) 地帯 chitái

zoo [zuː] n 動物園 dòbutsùen

zoologist [zouˈɑːˈlɑdʒist] n 動物学者 dôbutsugakûsha

zoology [zouˈɑːlˈədʒi] n 動物学 dòbutsugàku

zoom [zuːm] vi: to zoom past 猛スピードで通り過ぎる mòsupîdo de tôrîsugiru

zoom lens n ズームレンズ zúmureñzu

zucchini [zuːkiːˈniː] (US) n inv ズッキーニ zukkīnî